ADVANCE PRAISE FOR INTRODUCTION TO OPERATIONS RESEARCH, SEVENTH EDITION

Reviewers seem to agree that this is clearly the best edition yet. Here is a sampling of comments:

"The new edition seems to contain the most current information available."

"The new edition of Hillier/Lieberman is very well done and greatly enhances this classic text."

"The authors have done an admirable job of rewriting and reorganizing to reflect modern management practices and the latest software developments."

"It is a complete package."

"Hillier/Lieberman has recaptured any advantage it may have lost (to other competitors) in the past."

"The changes in this new edition make Hillier/Lieberman the preeminent book for operations research and I would highly recommend it."

INTRODUCTION TO
OPERATIONS RESEARCH

McGraw-Hill Series in Industrial Engineering and Management Science

CONSULTING EDITORS

Kenneth E. Case, *Department of Industrial Engineering and Management, Oklahoma State University*
Philip M. Wolfe, *Department of Industrial and Management Systems Engineering, Arizona State University*

Barnes
Statistical Analysis for Engineers and Scientists: A Computer-Based Approach
Bedworth, Henderson, and Wolfe
Computer-Integrated Design and Manufacturing
Blank and Tarquin
Engineering Economy
Ebeling
Reliability and Maintainability Engineering
Grant and Leavenworth
Statistical Quality Control
Harrell, Ghosh, and Bowden
Simulation Using PROMODEL
Hillier and Lieberman
Introduction to Operations Research
Gryna
Quality Planning and Analysis: From Product Development through Use
Kelton, Sadowski, and Sadowski
Simulation with ARENA
Khalil
Management of Technology
Kolarik
Creating Quality: Concepts, Systems, Strategies, and Tools
Creating Quality: Process Design for Results
Law and Kelton
Simulation Modeling and Analysis
Nash and Sofer
Linear and Nonlinear Programming
Nelson
Stochastic Modeling: Analysis and Simulation
Niebel and Freivalds
Methods, Standards, and Work Design
Pegden
Introduction to Simulation Using SIMAN
Riggs, Bedworth, and Randhawa
Engineering Economics
Sipper and Bulfin
Production: Planning, Control, and Integration
Steiner
Engineering Economics Principles

INTRODUCTION TO OPERATIONS RESEARCH

Seventh Edition

FREDERICK S. HILLIER,
Stanford University

GERALD J. LIEBERMAN,
Late of Stanford University

Cases developed by Karl Schmedders and Molly Stephens

Tutorial software developed by Mark Hillier and Michael O'Sullivan

Boston   Burr Ridge, IL   Dubuque, IA   Madison, WI   New York
San Francisco   St. Louis   Bangkok   Bogotá   Caracas   Lisbon   London
Madrid   Mexico City   Milan   New Delhi   Seoul   Singapore   Sydney
Taipei   Toronto

McGraw-Hill Higher Education

*A Division of The **McGraw-Hill** Companies*

INTRODUCTION TO OPERATIONS RESEARCH

Published by McGraw-Hill, an imprint of The McGraw-Hill Companies, Inc., 1221 Avenue of the Americas, New York, NY, 10020. Copyright © 2001, 1995, 1990, 1986, 1980, 1974, 1967, by The McGraw-Hill Companies, Inc. All rights reserved. No part of this publication may be reproduced or distributed in any form or by any means, or stored in a database or retrieval system, without the prior written consent of The McGraw-Hill Companies, Inc., including, but not limited to, in any network or other electronic storage or transmission, or broadcast for distance learning.

Some ancillaries, including electronic and print components, may not be available to customers outside the United States.

This book is printed on acid-free paper.

2 3 4 5 6 7 8 9 0   DOC/DOC   0 9 8 7 6 5 4 3 2 1 0

ISBN   0-07-246121-7

Vice president/Editor-in-chief: *Kevin Kane*
Publisher: *Thomas Casson*
Executive editor: *Eric M. Munson*
Developmental editor: *Maja Lorkovic*
Marketing manager: *John Wannemacher*
Project manager: *Christine A. Vaughan*
Manager, new book production: *Melonie Salvati*
Coordinator, freelance design: *Gino Cieslik*
Supplement coordinator: *Cathy Tepper*
Media technology producer: *Judi David*
Cover design: *Gino Cieslik*
Cover Illustration: *Paul Turnbaugh*
Compositor: *York Graphic Services, Inc.*
Typeface: *10/12 Times*
Printer: *R. R. Donnelley & Sons Company*

Library of Congress Cataloging-in-Publication Data

Hillier, Frederick S.
    Introduction to operations research/Frederick S. Hillier, Gerald J. Lieberman; cases
developed by Karl Schmedders and Molly Stephens; tutorial software developed by
Mark Hillier and Michael O'Sullivan.—7th ed.
      p. cm.
  ISBN 0-07-246121-7
    1. Operations research. I. Lieberman, Gerald J. II. Title.
T57.6. H53 2001
658.4′034—dc21   00-025683

www.mhhe.com

ABOUT THE AUTHORS

Frederick S. Hillier was born and raised in Aberdeen, Washington, where he was an award winner in statewide high school contests in essay writing, mathematics, debate, and music. As an undergraduate at Stanford University he ranked first in his engineering class of over 300 students. He also won the McKinsey Prize for technical writing, won the Outstanding Sophomore Debater award, played in the Stanford Woodwind Quintet, and won the Hamilton Award for combining excellence in engineering with notable achievements in the humanities and social sciences. Upon his graduation with a B.S. degree in Industrial Engineering, he was awarded three national fellowships (National Science Foundation, Tau Beta Pi, and Danforth) for graduate study at Stanford with specialization in operations research. After receiving his Ph.D. degree, he joined the faculty of Stanford University, and also received visiting appointments at Cornell University, Carnegie-Mellon University, the Technical University of Denmark, the University of Canterbury (New Zealand), and the University of Cambridge (England). After 35 years on the Stanford faculty, he took early retirement from his faculty responsibilities in 1996 in order to focus full time on textbook writing, and so now is Professor Emeritus of Operations Research at Stanford.

Dr. Hillier's research has extended into a variety of areas, including integer programming, queueing theory and its application, statistical quality control, and the application of operations research to the design of production systems and to capital budgeting. He has published widely, and his seminal papers have been selected for republication in books of selected readings at least ten times. He was the first-prize winner of a research contest on "Capital Budgeting of Interrelated Projects" sponsored by The Institute of Management Sciences (TIMS) and the U.S. Office of Naval Research. He and Dr. Lieberman also received the honorable mention award for the 1995 Lanchester Prize (best English-language publication of any kind in the field of operations research), which was awarded by the Institute of Operations Research and the Management Sciences (INFORMS) for the 6th edition of this book.

Dr. Hillier has held many leadership positions with the professional societies in his field. For example, he has served as Treasurer of the Operations Research Society of America (ORSA), Vice President for Meetings of TIMS, Co-General Chairman of the 1989 TIMS International Meeting in Osaka, Japan, Chair of the TIMS Publications Committee, Chair of the ORSA Search Committee for Editor of *Operations Research*, Chair of the ORSA Resources Planning Committee, Chair of the ORSA/TIMS Combined Meetings Committee, and Chair of the John von Neumann Theory Prize Selection Committee for INFORMS.

He currently is serving as the Series Editor for the International Series in Operations Research and Management Science being published by Kluwer Academic Publishers.

In addition to *Introduction to Operations Research* and the two companion volumes, *Introduction to Mathematical Programming* and *Introduction to Stochastic Models in Operations Research*, his books are *The Evaluation of Risky Interrelated Investments* (North-Holland, 1969), *Queueing Tables and Graphs* (Elsevier North-Holland, 1981, co-authored by O. S. Yu, with D. M. Avis, L. D. Fossett, F. D. Lo, and M. I. Reiman), and *Introduction to Management Science: A Modeling and Case Studies Approach with Spreadsheets* (Irwin/McGraw-Hill, co-authored by M. S. Hillier and G. J. Lieberman).

The late **Gerald J. Lieberman** sadly passed away shortly before the completion of this edition. He had been Professor Emeritus of Operations Research and Statistics at Stanford University, where he was the founding chair of the Department of Operations Research. He was both an engineer (having received an undergraduate degree in mechanical engineering from Cooper Union) and an operations research statistician (with an A.M. from Columbia University in mathematical statistics, and a Ph.D. from Stanford University in statistics).

Dr. Lieberman was one of Stanford's most eminent leaders in recent decades. After chairing the Department of Operations Research, he served as Associate Dean of the School of Humanities and Sciences, Vice Provost and Dean of Research, Vice Provost and Dean of Graduate Studies, Chair of the Faculty Senate, member of the University Advisory Board, and Chair of the Centennial Celebration Committee. He also served as Provost or Acting Provost under three different Stanford presidents.

Throughout these years of university leadership, he also remained active professionally. His research was in the stochastic areas of operations research, often at the interface of applied probability and statistics. He published extensively in the areas of reliability and quality control, and in the modeling of complex systems, including their optimal design, when resources are limited.

Highly respected as a senior statesman of the field of operations research, Dr. Lieberman served in numerous leadership roles, including as the elected President of The Institute of Management Sciences. His professional honors included being elected to the National Academy of Engineering, receiving the Shewhart Medal of the American Society for Quality Control, receiving the Cuthbertson Award for exceptional service to Stanford University, and serving as a fellow at the Center for Advanced Study in the Behavioral Sciences. In addition, the Institute of Operations Research and the Management Sciences (INFORMS) awarded him and Dr. Hillier the honorable mention award for the 1995 Lanchester Prize for the 6th edition of this book. In 1996, INFORMS also awarded him the prestigious Kimball Medal for his exceptional contributions to the field of operations research and management science.

In addition to *Introduction to Operations Research* and the two companion volumes, *Introduction to Mathematical Programming* and *Introduction to Stochastic Models in Operations Research*, his books are *Handbook of Industrial Statistics* (Prentice-Hall, 1955, co-authored by A. H. Bowker), *Tables of the Non-Central t-Distribution* (Stanford University Press, 1957, co-authored by G. J. Resnikoff), *Tables of the Hypergeometric Probability Distribution* (Stanford University Press, 1961, co-authored by D. Owen), *Engineering Statistics*, Second Edition (Prentice-Hall, 1972, co-authored by A. H. Bowker), and *Introduction to Management Science: A Modeling and Case Studies Approach with Spreadsheets* (Irwin/McGraw-Hill, 2000, co-authored by F. S. Hillier and M. S. Hillier).

ABOUT THE CASE WRITERS

Karl Schmedders is assistant professor in the Department of Managerial Economics and Decision Sciences at the Kellogg Graduate School of Management (Northwestern University), where he teaches quantitative methods for managerial decision making. His research interests include applications of operations research in economic theory, general equilibrium theory with incomplete markets, asset pricing, and computational economics. Dr. Schmedders received his doctorate in operations research from Stanford University, where he taught both undergraduate and graduate classes in operations research. Among the classes taught was a case studies course in operations research, and he subsequently was invited to speak at a conference sponsored by the Institute of Operations Research and the Management Sciences (INFORMS) about his successful experience with this course. He received several teaching awards at Stanford, including the university's prestigious Walter J. Gores Teaching Award.

Molly Stephens is currently pursuing a J.D. degree with a concentration in technology and law. She graduated from Stanford University with a B.S. in Industrial Engineering and an M.S. in Operations Research. A champion debater in both high school and college, and president of the Stanford Debating Society, Ms. Stephens taught public speaking in Stanford's School of Engineering and served as a teaching assistant for a case studies course in operations research. As a teaching assistant, she analyzed operations research problems encountered in the real world and the transformation of these problems into classroom case studies. Her research was rewarded when she won an undergraduate research grant from Stanford to continue her work and was invited to speak at an INFORMS conference to present her conclusions regarding successful classroom case studies. Following graduation, Ms. Stephens worked at Andersen Consulting as a systems integrator, experiencing real cases from the inside, before resuming her graduate studies.

DEDICATION

To the memory of our parents

and

To the memory of one of the true
giants of our field, Jerry Lieberman,
whose recent passing prevented him
from seeing the publication
of this edition

TABLE OF CONTENTS

CHAPTER 16
Markov Chains   802

CHAPTER 17
Queueing Theory   834

CHAPTER 18
The Application of Queueing Theory   907

SUPPLEMENTS ON THE BOOK'S WEBSITE, WWW.MHHE.COM/HILLIER

Some of these supplements are password protected, but are available to all instructors who adopt this textbook.

SUPPLEMENT TO APPENDIX 3.1
More about LINGO

SUPPLEMENT TO CHAPTER 8
An Algorithm for the Assignment Problem

SUPPLEMENT TO CHAPTER 18
The Evaluation of Travel Time

PREFACE

It now is 33 years since the first edition of this book was published in 1967. We have been humbled by having had both the privilege and the responsibility of introducing so many students around the world to our field over such a long span of time. With each new edition, we have worked toward the goal of meeting the changing needs of new generations of students by helping to define the modern approach to teaching the current status of operations research effectively at the introductory level. Over 33 years, much has changed in both the field and the pedagogical needs of the students being introduced to the field. These changes have been reflected in the substantial revisions of successive editions of this book. We believe that this is true for the current 7th edition as well.

The enthusiastic response to our first six editions has been most gratifying. It was a particular pleasure to have the 6th edition receive honorable mention for the 1995 INFORMS Lanchester Prize (the prize awarded for the year's most outstanding English-language publication of any kind in the field of operations research), including receiving the following citation. "This is the latest edition of the textbook that has introduced approximately one-half million students to the methods and models of Operations Research. While adding material on a variety of new topics, the sixth edition maintains the high standard of clarity and expositional excellence for which the authors have long been known. In honoring this work, the prize committee noted the enormous cumulative impact that the Hillier-Lieberman text has had on the development of our field, not only in the United States but also around the world through its many foreign-language editions."

As we enter a new millennium, the particular challenge for this new edition was to revise a book with deep roots in the 20th century so thoroughly that it would become fully suited for the 21st century. We made a special effort to meet this challenge, especially in regard to the software and pedagogy in the book.

A WEALTH OF SOFTWARE OPTIONS

The new CD-ROM that accompanies the book provides an exciting array of software options that reflect current practice.

One option is to use the increasingly popular spreadsheet approach with Excel and its Solver. Using spreadsheets as a key medium of instruction clearly is one new wave in the teaching of operations research. The new Sec. 3.6 describes and illustrates how to use Excel and its Solver to formulate and solve linear programming models on a spreadsheet. Similar discussions and examples also are included in several subsequent chapters for other kinds of models. In addition, the CD-ROM provides an Excel file for many of the chapters that displays the spreadsheet formulation and solution for the relevant examples in the chapter. Several of the Excel files also include a number of Excel templates for solving the models in the chapter. Another key resource is a collection of Excel add-ins on the CD-ROM (Premium Solver, TreePlan, SensIt, and RiskSim) that are integrated into the corresponding chapters. In addition, Sec. 22.6 describes how some simulations can be performed efficiently on spreadsheets by using another popular Excel add-in (@RISK) that can be downloaded temporarily from a website.

Practitioners of operations research now usually use a modeling language to formulate and manage models of the very large size commonly encountered in practice. A modeling language system also will support one or more sophisticated software packages that can be called to solve a model once it has been formulated appropriately. The new Sec. 3.7 discusses the application of modeling languages and illustrates it with one modeling language (MPL) that is relatively amenable to student use. The student version of MPL is provided on the CD-ROM, along with an extensive MPL tutorial. Accompanying MPL as its primary solver is the student version of the renowned state-of-the-art software package, CPLEX. The student version of CONOPT also is provided as the solver for nonlinear programming. We are extremely pleased to be able to provide such powerful and popular software to students using this book. To further assist students, many of the chapters include an MPL/CPLEX file (or MPL/CPLEX/CONOPT file in the case of the nonlinear programming chapter) on the CD-ROM that shows how MPL and CPLEX would formulate and solve the relevant examples in the chapter. These files also illustrate how MPL and CPLEX can be integrated with spreadsheets.

As described in the appendix to Chaps. 3 and 4, a third attractive option is to employ the student version of the popular and student-friendly software package LINDO and its modeling language companion LINGO. Both packages can be downloaded free from the LINDO Systems website. Associated tutorial material is included on the CD-ROM, along with a LINDO/LINGO file for many of the chapters showing how LINDO and LINGO would formulate and solve the relevant examples in the chapter. Once again, integration with spreadsheets also is illustrated.

Complementing all these options on the CD-ROM is an updated version of the tutorial software that many instructors have found so useful for their students with the 5th and 6th editions. A program called OR Tutor provides 16 demonstration examples from the 6th edition, but now with an attractive new design based on JavaScript. These demos vividly demonstrate the evolution of an algorithm in ways that cannot be duplicated on the printed page. Most of the interactive routines from the 6th edition also are included on the CD-ROM, but again with an attractive new design. This design features a spreadsheet format based on VisualBasic. Each of the interactive routines enables the student to interactively execute one of the algorithms of operations research, making the needed decision at each step while the computer does the needed arithmetic. By enabling the student to focus on concepts rather than mindless number crunching when doing homework to learn an algorithm, we have found that these interactive routines make the learning process *far* more efficient and effective as well as more stimulating. In addition to these routines, the CD-ROM includes a few of the automatic routines from the 6th edition (again redesigned with VisualBasic) for those cases that are not covered by the software options described above. We were very fortunate to have the services of Michael O'Sullivan, a talented programmer and an advanced Ph.D. student in operations research at Stanford, to do all this updating of the software that had been developed by Mark S. Hillier for the 5th and 6th editions.

Microsoft Project is introduced in Chap. 10 as a useful tool for project management. This software package also is included on the CD-ROM.

NEW EMPHASES

Today's students in introductory operations research courses tend to be very interested in learning more about the relevance of the material being covered, including how it is actually being used in practice. Therefore, without diluting any of the features of the 6th edition, the focus of the revision for this edition has been on increasing the motivation and excitement of the students by making the book considerably more "real world" oriented and accessible. The new emphasis on the kinds of software that practitioners use is one thrust in this direction. Other major new features are outlined below.

Twenty-five elaborate new cases, embedded in a realistic setting and employing a stimulating storytelling approach, have been added at the end of the problem sections. All but one of these cases were developed jointly by two talented case writers, Karl Schmedders (a faculty member at the Kellogg Graduate School of Management at Northwestern University) and Molly Stephens (recently an operations research consultant with Andersen Consulting). We also have further fleshed out six cases that were in the 6th edition. The cases generally require relatively challenging and comprehensive analyses with substantial use of the computer. Therefore, they are suitable for student projects, working either individually or in teams, and can then lead to class discussion of the analysis.

A complementary new feature is that many new problems embedded in a realistic setting have been added to the problem section of many chapters. Some of the current problems also have been fleshed out in a more interesting way.

This edition also places much more emphasis on providing perspective in terms of what is actually happening in the practice of operations research. What kinds of applications are occurring? What sizes of problems are being solved? Which models and techniques are being used most widely? What are their shortcomings and what new developments are beginning to address these shortcomings? These kinds of questions are being addressed to convey the relevance of the techniques under discussion. Eight new sections (Secs. 10.7, 12.2, 15.6, 18.5, 19.8, 20.1, 20.10, and 22.2) are fully devoted to discussing the practice of operations research in such ways, along with briefer mentions elsewhere.

The new emphases described above benefited greatly from our work in developing our recent new textbook with Mark S. Hillier (*Introduction to Management Science: A Modeling and Case Studies Approach with Spreadsheets,* Irwin/McGraw-Hill, 2000). That book has a very different orientation from this one. It is aimed directly at business students rather than students who may be in engineering and the mathematical sciences, and it provides almost no coverage of the mathematics and algorithms of operations research. Nevertheless, its applied orientation enabled us to adapt some excellent material developed for that book to provide a more well-rounded coverage in this edition.

OTHER FEATURES

In addition to all the new software and new emphases just described, this edition received a considerable number of other enhancements as well.

The previous section on project planning and control with PERT/CPM has been replaced by a complete new chapter (Chap. 10) with an applied orientation. Using the activity-on-node (AON) convention, this chapter provides an extensive modern treatment of the topic in a very accessible way.

Other new topics not yet mentioned include the SOB mnemonic device for determining the form of constraints in the dual problem (in Sec. 6.4), 100 percent rules for simultaneous changes when conducting sensitivity analysis (in Sec. 6.7), sensitivity analysis with Bayes' decision rule (in Sec. 15.2), a probability tree diagram for calculating posterior probabilities (in Sec. 15.3), a single-server variation of the nonpreemptive priorities model where the service for different priority classes of customers now have different mean service rates (in Sec. 17.8), a new simpler analysis of a stochastic continuous-review inventory model (Sec. 19.5), the mean absolute deviation as a measure of performance for forecasting methods (in Sec. 20.7), and the elements of a major simulation study (Sec. 22.5).

We also have added much supplementary text material on the book's new website, www.mhhe.com/hillier. Some of these supplements are password protected, but are available to all instructors who adopt this textbook. For the most part, this material appeared in previous editions of this book and then was subsequently deleted (for space reasons), to the disappointment of some instructors. Some also appeared in our *Introduction to Mathematical Programming* textbook. As delineated in the table of contents, this supplementary material includes a chapter on additional special types of linear programming problems, a review or primer chapter on probability theory, and a chapter on reliability, along with supplements to a few chapters in the book.

In addition to providing this supplementary text material, the website will give updates about the book, including an errata, as the need arises.

We made two changes in the order of the chapters. The decision analysis chapter has been moved forward to Chap. 15 in front of the stochastic chapters. The game theory chapter has been moved backward to Chap. 14 to place it next to the related decision analysis chapter. We believe that these changes provide a better transition from topics that are mainly deterministic to those that are mainly stochastic.

Every chapter has received significant revision and updating, ranging from modest refining to extensive rewriting. Chapters receiving a particularly major revision and reorganization included Chaps. 15 (Decision Analysis), 19 (Inventory Theory), 20 (Forecasting), and 22 (Simulation). Many sections in the linear programming and mathematical programming chapters also received major revisions and updating.

The overall thrust of all the revision efforts has been to build upon the strengths of previous editions while thoroughly updating and clarifying the material in a contemporary setting to fully meet the needs of today's students.

We think that the net effect has been to make this edition even more of a "student's book"—clear, interesting, and well-organized with lots of helpful examples and illustrations, good motivation and perspective, easy-to-find important material, and enjoyable homework, without too much notation, terminology, and dense mathematics. We believe and trust that the numerous instructors who have used previous editions will agree that this is the best edition yet. This feeling has been reinforced by the generally enthusiastic reviews of drafts of this edition.

The prerequisites for a course using this book can be relatively modest. As with previous editions, the mathematics has been kept at a relatively elementary level. Most of Chaps. 1 to 14 (introduction, linear programming, and mathematical programming) require no mathematics beyond high school algebra. Calculus is used only in Chaps. 13 (Nonlinear Programming) and in one example in Chap. 11 (Dynamic Programming). Matrix notation is used in Chap. 5 (The Theory of the Simplex Method), Chap. 6 (Duality Theory and Sensitivity Analysis), Sec. 7.4 (An Interior-Point Algorithm), and Chap. 13, but the only background needed for this is presented in Appendix 4. For Chaps. 15 to 22 (probabilistic models), a previous introduction to probability theory is assumed, and calculus is used in a few places. In general terms, the mathematical maturity that a student achieves through taking an elementary calculus course is useful throughout Chaps. 15 to 22 and for the more advanced material in the preceding chapters.

The content of the book is aimed largely at the upper-division undergraduate level (including well-prepared sophomores) and at first-year (master's level) graduate students. Because of the book's great flexibility, there are many ways to package the material into a course. Chapters 1 and 2 give an introduction to the subject of operations research. Chapters 3 to 14 (on linear programming and on mathematical programming) may essentially be covered independently of Chaps. 15 to 22 (on probabilistic models), and vice versa. Furthermore, the individual chapters among Chaps. 3 to 14 are almost independent, except that they all use basic material presented in Chap. 3 and perhaps in Chap. 4. Chapter 6 and Sec. 7.2 also draw upon Chap. 5. Sections 7.1 and 7.2 use parts of Chap. 6. Section 9.6 assumes an acquaintance with the problem formulations in Secs. 8.1 and 8.3, while prior exposure to Secs. 7.3 and 8.2 is helpful (but not essential) in Sec. 9.7. Within Chaps. 15 to 22, there is considerable flexibility of coverage, although some integration of the material is available.

An elementary survey course covering linear programming, mathematical programming, and some probabilistic models can be presented in a quarter (40 hours) or semester by selectively drawing from material throughout the book. For example, a good survey of the field can be obtained from Chaps. 1, 2, 3, 4, 15, 17, 19, 20, and 22, along with parts of Chaps. 9, 11, 12, and 13. A more extensive elementary survey course can be completed in two quarters (60 to 80 hours) by excluding just a few chapters, for example, Chaps. 7, 14, and 21. Chapters 1 to 8 (and perhaps part of Chap. 9) form an excellent basis for a (one-quarter) course in linear programming. The material in Chaps. 9 to 14 covers topics for another (one-quarter) course in other deterministic models. Finally, the material in Chaps. 15 to 22 covers the probabilistic (stochastic) models of operations research suitable for presentation in a (one-quarter) course. In fact, these latter three courses (the material in the entire text) can be viewed as a basic one-year sequence in the techniques of operations research, forming the core of a master's degree program. Each course outlined has been presented at either the undergraduate or the graduate level at Stanford University, and this text has been used in the manner suggested.

To assist the instructor who will be covering only a portion of the chapters and who prefers a slimmer book containing only those chapters, all the material (including the supplementary text material on the book's website) has been placed in McGraw-Hill's PRIMIS system. This system enables an instructor to pick and choose precisely which material to include in a self-designed book, and then to order copies for the students at an economical price. For example, this enables instructors who previously used our *Introduction to Mathematical Programming* or *Introduction to Stochastic Models in Operations Research* textbooks to obtain updated versions of the same material from the PRIMIS system. For this reason, we will not be publishing new separate editions of these other books.

Again, as in previous editions, we thank our wives, Ann and Helen, for their encouragement and support during the long process of preparing this 7th edition. Our children, David, John, and Mark Hillier, Janet Lieberman Argyres, and Joanne, Michael, and Diana Lieberman, have literally grown up with the book and our periodic hibernations to prepare a new edition. Now, most of them have used the book as a text in their own college courses, given considerable advice, and even (in the case of Mark Hillier) become a software collaborator. It is a joy to see them and (we trust) the book reach maturity together.

And now I must add a very sad note. My close friend and co-author, Jerry Lieberman, passed away on May 18, 1999, while this edition was in preparation, so I am writing this preface on behalf of both of us. Jerry was one of the great leaders of our field and he had a profound influence on my life. More than a third of a century ago, we embarked on a mission together to attempt to develop a path-breaking book for teaching operations research at the introductory level. Ever since, we have striven to meet and extend the same high standards for each new edition. Having worked so closely with Jerry for so many years, I believe I understand well how he would want the book to evolve to meet the needs of each new generation of students. As the substantially younger co-author, I am grateful that I am able to carry on our joint mission to continue to update and improve the book, both with this edition and with future editions as well. It is the least I can do to honor Jerry.

I welcome your comments, suggestions, and errata to help me improve the book in the future.

ACKNOWLEDGMENTS

We are indebted to an excellent group of reviewers who provided sage advice throughout the revision process. This group included Jeffery Cochran, Arizona State University; Yahya Fathi, North Carolina State University; Yasser Hosni and Charles Reilly, University of Central Florida; Cerry Klein, University of Missouri—Columbia; Robert Lipset, Ohio University; Mark Parker, United States Air Force Academy; Christopher Rump, State University of New York at Buffalo; and Ahmad Seifoddini, California Polytechnic State University—San Luis Obispo. We also received helpful advice from Judith Liebman, Siegfried Schaible, David Sloan, and Arthur F. Veinott, Jr., as well as many instructors who sent us letters or e-mail messages. In addition, we also thank many dozens of Stanford students and many students at other universities who gave us helpful written suggestions.

This edition was very much of a team effort. Our case writers, Karl Schmedders and Molly Stephens (both graduates of our department), made a vital contribution. One of our department's current Ph.D. students, Roberto Szechtman, did an excellent job in preparing the solutions manual. Another Ph.D. student, Michael O'Sullivan, was very skillful in updating the software that Mark Hillier had developed for the 5th and 6th editions. Mark (who was born the same year as the first edition and now is a tenured faculty member in the Management Science Department at the University of Washington) helped to oversee this updating and also provided both the spreadsheets and the Excel files (including many Excel templates) for this edition. Linus Schrage of the University of Chicago and LINDO Systems (and who took an introductory operations research course from me 37 years ago) supervised the development of LINGO/LINDO files for the various chapters as well as providing tutorial material for the CD-ROM. Another long-time friend, Bjarni Kristjansson (who heads Maximal Software), did the same thing for the MPL/CPLEX files and MPL tutorial material, as well as arranging to provide student versions of MPL, CPLEX, CONOPT, and OptiMax 2000 for the CD-ROM. One of our department's Ph.D. graduates, Irv Lustig, was the ILOG project manager for providing CPLEX. Linus, Bjarni, and Irv all were helpful in checking material going into this edition regarding their software. Ann Hillier devoted numerous long days and nights to sitting with a Macintosh, doing word processing and constructing many figures and tables, in addition to endless cutting and pasting, photocopying, and FedExing of material. Helen Lieberman also carried a heavy burden in supporting Jerry. They all were vital members of the team.

The inside back cover lists the various companies and individuals who have provided software for the CD-ROM. We greatly appreciate their key contributions.

It was a real pleasure working with McGraw-Hill's thoroughly professional editorial and production staff, including Eric Munson (executive editor), Maja Lorkovic (developmental editor), and Christine Vaughan (project manager).

Frederick S. Hillier
Stanford University (fhillier@Leland.Stanford.edu)   **January 2000**

+30 +10 -D Wood

1
Introduction

1.1 THE ORIGINS OF OPERATIONS RESEARCH

Since the advent of the industrial revolution, the world has seen a remarkable growth in the size and complexity of organizations. The artisans' small shops of an earlier era have evolved into the billion-dollar corporations of today. An integral part of this revolutionary change has been a tremendous increase in the division of labor and segmentation of management responsibilities in these organizations. The results have been spectacular. However, along with its blessings, this increasing specialization has created new problems, problems that are still occurring in many organizations. One problem is a tendency for the many components of an organization to grow into relatively autonomous empires with their own goals and value systems, thereby losing sight of how their activities and objectives mesh with those of the overall organization. What is best for one component frequently is detrimental to another, so the components may end up working at cross purposes. A related problem is that as the complexity and specialization in an organization increase, it becomes more and more difficult to allocate the available resources to the various activities in a way that is most effective for the organization as a whole. These kinds of problems and the need to find a better way to solve them provided the environment for the emergence of **operations research** (commonly referred to as **OR**).

The roots of OR can be traced back many decades, when early attempts were made to use a scientific approach in the management of organizations. However, the beginning of the activity called *operations research* has generally been attributed to the military services early in World War II. Because of the war effort, there was an urgent need to allocate scarce resources to the various military operations and to the activities within each operation in an effective manner. Therefore, the British and then the U.S. military management called upon a large number of scientists to apply a scientific approach to dealing with this and other strategic and tactical problems. In effect, they were asked to do *research on* (military) *operations.* These teams of scientists were the first OR teams. By developing effective methods of using the new tool of radar, these teams were instrumental in winning the Air Battle of Britain. Through their research on how to better manage convoy and antisubmarine operations, they also played a major role in winning the Battle of the North Atlantic. Similar efforts assisted the Island Campaign in the Pacific.

When the war ended, the success of OR in the war effort spurred interest in applying OR outside the military as well. As the industrial boom following the war was running its course, the problems caused by the increasing complexity and specialization in organizations were again coming to the forefront. It was becoming apparent to a growing number of people, including business consultants who had served on or with the OR teams during the war, that these were basically the same problems that had been faced by the military but in a different context. By the early 1950s, these individuals had introduced the use of OR to a variety of organizations in business, industry, and government. The rapid spread of OR soon followed.

At least two other factors that played a key role in the rapid growth of OR during this period can be identified. One was the substantial progress that was made early in improving the techniques of OR. After the war, many of the scientists who had participated on OR teams or who had heard about this work were motivated to pursue research relevant to the field; important advancements in the state of the art resulted. A prime example is the *simplex method* for solving linear programming problems, developed by George Dantzig in 1947. Many of the standard tools of OR, such as linear programming, dynamic programming, queueing theory, and inventory theory, were relatively well developed before the end of the 1950s.

A second factor that gave great impetus to the growth of the field was the onslaught of the *computer revolution.* A large amount of computation is usually required to deal most effectively with the complex problems typically considered by OR. Doing this by hand would often be out of the question. Therefore, the development of electronic digital computers, with their ability to perform arithmetic calculations thousands or even millions of times faster than a human being can, was a tremendous boon to OR. A further boost came in the 1980s with the development of increasingly powerful personal computers accompanied by good software packages for doing OR. This brought the use of OR within the easy reach of much larger numbers of people. Today, literally millions of individuals have ready access to OR software. Consequently, a whole range of computers from mainframes to laptops now are being routinely used to solve OR problems.

1.2 THE NATURE OF OPERATIONS RESEARCH

As its name implies, operations research involves "research on operations." Thus, operations research is applied to problems that concern how to conduct and coordinate the *operations* (i.e., the *activities*) within an organization. The nature of the organization is essentially immaterial, and, in fact, OR has been applied extensively in such diverse areas as manufacturing, transportation, construction, telecommunications, financial planning, health care, the military, and public services, to name just a few. Therefore, the breadth of application is unusually wide.

The *research* part of the name means that operations research uses an approach that resembles the way research is conducted in established scientific fields. To a considerable extent, the *scientific method* is used to investigate the problem of concern. (In fact, the term *management science* sometimes is used as a synonym for operations research.) In particular, the process begins by carefully observing and formulating the problem, including gathering all relevant data. The next step is to construct a scientific (typically mathematical) model that attempts to abstract the essence of the real problem. It is then hypothesized that this model is a sufficiently precise representation of the essential features of the situation that the conclusions (solutions) obtained from the model are also valid for the real problem. Next, suitable experiments are conducted to test this hypothesis, modify it as needed, and eventually verify some form of the hypothesis. (This step is frequently referred to as *model validation.*) Thus, in a certain sense, operations research involves creative scientific research into the fundamental properties of operations. However, there is more to it than this. Specifically, OR is also concerned with the practical management of the organization. Therefore, to be successful, OR must also provide positive, understandable conclusions to the decision maker(s) when they are needed.

Still another characteristic of OR is its broad viewpoint. As implied in the preceding section, OR adopts an organizational point of view. Thus, it attempts to resolve the conflicts of interest among the components of the organization in a way that is best for the organization as a whole. This does not imply that the study of each problem must give explicit consideration to all aspects of the organization; rather, the objectives being sought must be consistent with those of the overall organization.

An additional characteristic is that OR frequently attempts to find a *best* solution (referred to as an *optimal* solution) for the problem under consideration. (We say *a* best instead of *the* best solution because there may be multiple solutions tied as best.) Rather than simply improving the status quo, the goal is to identify a best possible course of action. Although it must be interpreted carefully in terms of the practical needs of management, this "search for optimality" is an important theme in OR.

All these characteristics lead quite naturally to still another one. It is evident that no single individual should be expected to be an expert on all the many aspects of OR work or the problems typically considered; this would require a group of individuals having diverse backgrounds and skills. Therefore, when a full-fledged OR study of a new problem is undertaken, it is usually necessary to use a *team approach.* Such an OR team typically needs to include individuals who collectively are highly trained in mathematics, statistics and probability theory, economics, business administration, computer science, engineering and the physical sciences, the behavioral sciences, and the special techniques of OR. The team also needs to have the necessary experience and variety of skills to give appropriate consideration to the many ramifications of the problem throughout the organization.

1.3 THE IMPACT OF OPERATIONS RESEARCH

Operations research has had an impressive impact on improving the efficiency of numerous organizations around the world. In the process, OR has made a significant contribution to increasing the productivity of the economies of various countries. There now are a few dozen member countries in the International Federation of Operational Research Societies (IFORS), with each country having a national OR society. Both Europe and Asia have federations of OR societies to coordinate holding international conferences and publishing international journals in those continents.

It appears that the impact of OR will continue to grow. For example, according to the U.S. Bureau of Labor Statistics, OR currently is one of the fastest-growing career areas for U.S. college graduates.

To give you a better notion of the wide applicability of OR, we list some actual award-winning applications in Table 1.1. Note the diversity of organizations and applications in the first two columns. The curious reader can find a complete article describing each application in the January–February issue of *Interfaces* for the year cited in the third col-

TABLE 1.1 Some applications of operations research

Organization	Nature of Application	Year of Publication*	Related Chapters†	Annual Savings
The Netherlands Rijkswaterstaat	Develop national water management policy, including mix of new facilities, operating procedures, and pricing.	1985	2–8, 13, 22	$15 million
Monsanto Corp.	Optimize production operations in chemical plants to meet production targets with minimum cost.	1985	2, 12	$2 million
United Airlines	Schedule shift work at reservation offices and airports to meet customer needs with minimum cost.	1986	2–9, 12, 17, 18, 20	$6 million
Citgo Petroleum Corp.	Optimize refinery operations and the supply, distribution, and marketing of products.	1987	2–9, 20	$70 million
San Francisco Police Department	Optimally schedule and deploy police patrol officers with a computerized system.	1989	2–4, 12, 20	$11 million
Texaco, Inc.	Optimally blend available ingredients into gasoline products to meet quality and sales requirements.	1989	2, 13	$30 million
IBM	Integrate a national network of spare parts inventories to improve service support.	1990	2, 19, 22	$20 million +$250 million less inventory
Yellow Freight System, Inc.	Optimize the design of a national trucking network and the routing of shipments.	1992	2, 9, 13, 20, 22	$17.3 million
New Haven Health Department	Design an effective needle exchange program to combat the spread of HIV/AIDS.	1993	2	33% less HIV/AIDS
AT&T	Develop a PC-based system to guide business customers in designing their call centers.	1993	17, 18, 22	$750 million
Delta Airlines	Maximize the profit from assigning airplane types to over 2500 domestic flights.	1994	12	$100 million
Digital Equipment Corp.	Restructure the global supply chain of suppliers, plants, distribution centers, potential sites, and market areas.	1995	12	$800 million
China	Optimally select and schedule massive projects for meeting the country's future energy needs.	1995	12	$425 million
South African defense force	Optimally redesign the size and shape of the defense force and its weapons systems.	1997	12	$1.1 billion
Proctor and Gamble	Redesign the North American production and distribution system to reduce costs and improve speed to market.	1997	8	$200 million
Taco Bell	Optimally schedule employees to provide desired customer service at a minimum cost.	1998	12, 20, 22	$13 million
Hewlett-Packard	Redesign the sizes and locations of buffers in a printer production line to meet production goals.	1998	17, 18	$280 million more revenue

*Pertains to a January–February issue of *Interfaces* in which a complete article can be found describing the application.
†Refers to chapters in this book that describe the kinds of OR techniques used in the application.

umn of the table. The fourth column lists the chapters in *this* book that describe the kinds of OR techniques that were used in the application. (Note that many of the applications combine a variety of techniques.) The last column indicates that these applications typically resulted in annual savings in the millions (or even tens of millions) of dollars. Furthermore, additional benefits not recorded in the table (e.g., improved service to customers and better managerial control) sometimes were considered to be even more important than these financial benefits. (You will have an opportunity to investigate these less tangible benefits further in Probs. 1.3-1 and 1.3-2.)

Although most routine OR studies provide considerably more modest benefits than these award-winning applications, the figures in the rightmost column of Table 1.1 do accurately reflect the dramatic impact that large, well-designed OR studies occasionally can have.

We will briefly describe some of these applications in the next chapter, and then we present two in greater detail as case studies in Sec. 3.5.

1.4 ALGORITHMS AND OR COURSEWARE

An important part of this book is the presentation of the major **algorithms** (systematic solution procedures) of OR for solving certain types of problems. Some of these algorithms are amazingly efficient and are routinely used on problems involving hundreds or thousands of variables. You will be introduced to how these algorithms work and what makes them so efficient. You then will use these algorithms to solve a variety of problems on a computer. The CD-ROM called **OR Courseware** that accompanies the book will be a key tool for doing all this.

One special feature in your OR Courseware is a program called **OR Tutor.** This program is intended to be your personal tutor to help you learn the algorithms. It consists of many *demonstration examples* that display and explain the algorithms in action. These "demos" supplement the examples in the book.

In addition, your OR Courseware includes many *interactive routines* for executing the algorithms interactively in a convenient spreadsheet format. The computer does all the routine calculations while you focus on learning and executing the logic of the algorithm. You should find these interactive routines a very efficient and enlightening way of doing many of your homework problems.

In practice, the algorithms normally are executed by commercial software packages. We feel that it is important to acquaint students with the nature of these packages that they will be using after graduation. Therefore, your OR Courseware includes a wealth of material to introduce you to three particularly popular software packages described below. Together, these packages will enable you to solve nearly all the OR models encountered in this book very efficiently. We have added our own *automatic routines* to the OR Courseware only in a few cases where these packages are not applicable.

A very popular approach now is to use today's premier spreadsheet package, *Microsoft Excel,* to formulate small OR models in a spreadsheet format. The **Excel Solver** then is used to solve the models. Your OR Courseware includes a separate Excel file for nearly every chapter in this book. Each time a chapter presents an example that can be solved using Excel, the complete spreadsheet formulation and solution is given in that chapter's Excel file. For many of the models in the book, an *Excel template* also is provided that already includes all the equations necessary to solve the model. Some *Excel add-ins* also are included on the CD-ROM.

After many years, **LINDO** (and its companion modeling language **LINGO**) continues to be a dominant OR software package. Student versions of LINDO and LINGO now can be downloaded free from the Web. As for Excel, each time an example can be solved with this package, all the details are given in a LINGO/LINDO file for that chapter in your OR Courseware.

CPLEX is an elite state-of-the-art software package that is widely used for solving large and challenging OR problems. When dealing with such problems, it is common to also use a *modeling system* to efficiently formulate the mathematical model and enter it into the computer. **MPL** is a user-friendly modeling system that uses CPLEX as its main solver. A student version of MPL and CPLEX is available free by downloading it from the Web. For your convenience, we also have included this student version in your OR Courseware. Once again, all the examples that can be solved with this package are detailed in MPL/CPLEX files for the corresponding chapters in your OR Courseware.

We will further describe these three software packages and how to use them later (especially near the end of Chaps. 3 and 4). Appendix 1 also provides documentation for the OR Courseware, including OR Tutor.

To alert you to relevant material in OR Courseware, the end of each chapter from Chap. 3 onward has a list entitled *Learning Aids for This Chapter in Your OR Courseware*. As explained at the beginning of the problem section for each of these chapters, symbols also are placed to the left of each problem number or part where any of this material (including demonstration examples and interactive routines) can be helpful.

PROBLEMS

1.3-1. Select one of the applications of operations research listed in Table 1.1. Read the article describing the application in the January–February issue of *Interfaces* for the year indicated in the third column. Write a two-page summary of the application and the benefits (including nonfinancial benefits) it provided.

1.3-2. Select three of the applications of operations research listed in Table 1.1. Read the articles describing the applications in the January–February issue of *Interfaces* for the years indicated in the third column. For each one, write a one-page summary of the application and the benefits (including nonfinancial benefits) it provided.

2

Overview of the Operations Research Modeling Approach

The bulk of this book is devoted to the mathematical methods of operations research (OR). This is quite appropriate because these quantitative techniques form the main part of what is known about OR. However, it does not imply that practical OR studies are primarily mathematical exercises. As a matter of fact, the mathematical analysis often represents only a relatively small part of the total effort required. The purpose of this chapter is to place things into better perspective by describing all the major phases of a typical OR study.

One way of summarizing the usual (overlapping) phases of an OR study is the following:

1. Define the problem of interest and gather relevant data.
2. Formulate a mathematical model to represent the problem.
3. Develop a computer-based procedure for deriving solutions to the problem from the model.
4. Test the model and refine it as needed.
5. Prepare for the ongoing application of the model as prescribed by management.
6. Implement.

Each of these phases will be discussed in turn in the following sections.

Most of the award-winning OR studies introduced in Table 1.1 provide excellent examples of how to execute these phases well. We will intersperse snippets from these examples throughout the chapter, with references to invite your further reading.

2.1 DEFINING THE PROBLEM AND GATHERING DATA

In contrast to textbook examples, most practical problems encountered by OR teams are initially described to them in a vague, imprecise way. Therefore, the first order of business is to study the relevant system and develop a well-defined statement of the problem to be considered. This includes determining such things as the appropriate objectives, constraints on what can be done, interrelationships between the area to be studied and other areas of the organization, possible alternative courses of action, time limits for making a decision, and so on. This process of problem definition is a crucial one because it greatly affects how relevant the conclusions of the study will be. It is difficult to extract a "right" answer from the "wrong" problem!

The first thing to recognize is that an OR team is normally working in an *advisory capacity.* The team members are not just given a problem and told to solve it however they see fit. Instead, they are advising management (often one key decision maker). The team performs a detailed technical analysis of the problem and then presents recommendations to management. Frequently, the report to management will identify a number of alternatives that are particularly attractive under different assumptions or over a different range of values of some policy parameter that can be evaluated only by management (e.g., the trade-off between *cost* and *benefits*). Management evaluates the study and its recommendations, takes into account a variety of intangible factors, and makes the final decision based on its best judgment. Consequently, it is vital for the OR team to get on the same wavelength as management, including identifying the "right" problem from management's viewpoint, and to build the support of management for the course that the study is taking.

Ascertaining the *appropriate objectives* is a very important aspect of problem definition. To do this, it is necessary first to identify the member (or members) of management who actually will be making the decisions concerning the system under study and then to probe into this individual's thinking regarding the pertinent objectives. (Involving the decision maker from the outset also is essential to build her or his support for the implementation of the study.)

By its nature, OR is concerned with the welfare of the *entire organization* rather than that of only certain of its components. An OR study seeks solutions that are optimal for the overall organization rather than suboptimal solutions that are best for only one component. Therefore, the objectives that are formulated ideally should be those of the entire organization. However, this is not always convenient. Many problems primarily concern only a portion of the organization, so the analysis would become unwieldy if the stated objectives were too general and if explicit consideration were given to all side effects on the rest of the organization. Instead, the objectives used in the study should be as specific as they can be while still encompassing the main goals of the decision maker and maintaining a reasonable degree of consistency with the higher-level objectives of the organization.

For profit-making organizations, one possible approach to circumventing the problem of suboptimization is to use *long-run profit maximization* (considering the time value of money) as the sole objective. The adjective *long-run* indicates that this objective provides the flexibility to consider activities that do not translate into profits *immediately* (e.g., research and development projects) but need to do so *eventually* in order to be worthwhile. This approach has considerable merit. This objective is specific enough to be used conveniently, and yet it seems to be broad enough to encompass the basic goal of profit-making organizations. In fact, some people believe that all other legitimate objectives can be translated into this one.

However, in actual practice, many profit-making organizations do not use this approach. A number of studies of U.S. corporations have found that management tends to adopt the goal of *satisfactory profits,* combined with *other objectives,* instead of focusing on long-run profit maximization. Typically, some of these *other* objectives might be to maintain stable profits, increase (or maintain) one's share of the market, provide for product diversification, maintain stable prices, improve worker morale, maintain family control of the business, and increase company prestige. Fulfilling these objectives might achieve long-run profit maximization, but the relationship may be sufficiently obscure that it may not be convenient to incorporate them all into this one objective.

Furthermore, there are additional considerations involving social responsibilities that are distinct from the profit motive. The five parties generally affected by a business firm located in a single country are (1) the *owners* (stockholders, etc.), who desire profits (dividends, stock appreciation, and so on); (2) the *employees,* who desire steady employment at reasonable wages; (3) the *customers,* who desire a reliable product at a reasonable price; (4) the *suppliers,* who desire integrity and a reasonable selling price for their goods; and (5) the *government* and hence the *nation,* which desire payment of fair taxes and consideration of the national interest. All five parties make essential contributions to the firm, and the firm should not be viewed as the exclusive servant of any one party for the exploitation of others. By the same token, international corporations acquire additional obligations to follow socially responsible practices. Therefore, while granting that management's prime responsibility is to make profits (which ultimately benefits all five parties), we note that its broader social responsibilities also must be recognized.

OR teams typically spend a surprisingly large amount of time *gathering relevant data* about the problem. Much data usually are needed both to gain an accurate understanding of the problem and to provide the needed input for the mathematical model being formulated in the next phase of study. Frequently, much of the needed data will not be available when the study begins, either because the information never has been kept or because what was kept is outdated or in the wrong form. Therefore, it often is necessary to install a new computer-based *management information system* to collect the necessary data on an ongoing basis and in the needed form. The OR team normally needs to enlist the assistance of various other key individuals in the organization to track down all the vital data. Even with this effort, much of the data may be quite "soft," i.e., rough estimates based only on educated guesses. Typically, an OR team will spend considerable time trying to improve the precision of the data and then will make do with the best that can be obtained.

Examples. An OR study done for the **San Francisco Police Department**[1] resulted in the development of a computerized system for optimally scheduling and deploying police patrol officers. The new system provided annual savings of $11 million, an annual $3 million increase in traffic citation revenues, and a 20 percent improvement in response times. In assessing the *appropriate objectives* for this study, three fundamental objectives were identified:

1. Maintain a high level of citizen safety.
2. Maintain a high level of officer morale.
3. Minimize the cost of operations.

To satisfy the first objective, the police department and city government jointly established a desired level of protection. The mathematical model then imposed the requirement that this level of protection be achieved. Similarly, the model imposed the requirement of balancing the workload equitably among officers in order to work toward the second objective. Finally, the third objective was incorporated by adopting the long-term goal of minimizing the number of officers needed to meet the first two objectives.

---

[1]P. E. Taylor and S. J. Huxley, "A Break from Tradition for the San Francisco Police: Patrol Officer Scheduling Using an Optimization-Based Decision Support System," *Interfaces,* **19**(1): 4–24, Jan.–Feb. 1989. See especially pp. 4–11.

The **Health Department of New Haven, Connecticut** used an OR team[1] to design an effective needle exchange program to combat the spread of the virus that causes AIDS (HIV), and succeeded in reducing the HIV infection rate among program clients by 33 percent. The key part of this study was an innovative *data collection program* to obtain the needed input for mathematical models of HIV transmission. This program involved complete tracking of *each* needle (and syringe), including the identity, location, and date for each person receiving the needle and each person returning the needle during an exchange, as well as testing whether the returned needle was HIV-positive or HIV-negative.

An OR study done for the **Citgo Petroleum Corporation**[2] optimized both refinery operations and the supply, distribution, and marketing of its products, thereby achieving a profit improvement of approximately $70 million per year. *Data collection* also played a key role in this study. The OR team held data requirement meetings with top Citgo management to ensure the eventual and continual quality of data. A state-of-the-art management database system was developed and installed on a mainframe computer. In cases where needed data did not exist, LOTUS 1-2-3 screens were created to help operations personnel input the data, and then the data from the personal computers (PCs) were uploaded to the mainframe computer. Before data was inputted to the mathematical model, a preloader program was used to check for data errors and inconsistencies. Initially, the preloader generated a paper log of error messages 1 inch thick! Eventually, the number of error and warning messages (indicating bad or questionable numbers) was reduced to less than 10 for each new run.

We will describe the overall Citgo study in much more detail in Sec. 3.5.

2.2 FORMULATING A MATHEMATICAL MODEL

After the decision maker's problem is defined, the next phase is to reformulate this problem in a form that is convenient for analysis. The conventional OR approach for doing this is to construct a mathematical model that represents the essence of the problem. Before discussing how to formulate such a model, we first explore the nature of models in general and of mathematical models in particular.

Models, or idealized representations, are an integral part of everyday life. Common examples include model airplanes, portraits, globes, and so on. Similarly, models play an important role in science and business, as illustrated by models of the atom, models of genetic structure, mathematical equations describing physical laws of motion or chemical reactions, graphs, organizational charts, and industrial accounting systems. Such models are invaluable for abstracting the essence of the subject of inquiry, showing interrelationships, and facilitating analysis.

[1]E. H. Kaplan and E. O'Keefe, "Let the Needles Do the Talking! Evaluating the New Haven Needle Exchange," *Interfaces,* **23**(1): 7–26, Jan.–Feb. 1993. See especially pp. 12–14.

[2]D. Klingman, N. Phillips, D. Steiger, R. Wirth, and W. Young, "The Challenges and Success Factors in Implementing an Integrated Products Planning System for Citgo," *Interfaces,* **16**(3): 1–19, May–June 1986. See especially pp. 11–14. Also see D. Klingman, N. Phillips, D. Steiger, and W. Young, "The Successful Deployment of Management Science throughout Citgo Petroleum Corporation," *Interfaces,* **17**(1): 4–25, Jan.–Feb. 1987. See especially pp. 13–15. This application will be described further in Sec. 3.5.

Mathematical models are also idealized representations, but they are expressed in terms of mathematical symbols and expressions. Such laws of physics as $F = ma$ and $E = mc^2$ are familiar examples. Similarly, the mathematical model of a business problem is the system of equations and related mathematical expressions that describe the essence of the problem. Thus, if there are n related quantifiable decisions to be made, they are represented as **decision variables** (say, $x_1, x_2, \ldots, x_n$) whose respective values are to be determined. The appropriate measure of performance (e.g., profit) is then expressed as a mathematical function of these decision variables (for example, $P = 3x_1 + 2x_2 + \cdots + 5x_n$). This function is called the **objective function.** Any restrictions on the values that can be assigned to these decision variables are also expressed mathematically, typically by means of inequalities or equations (for example, $x_1 + 3x_1x_2 + 2x_2 \leq 10$). Such mathematical expressions for the restrictions often are called **constraints.** The constants (namely, the coefficients and right-hand sides) in the constraints and the objective function are called the **parameters** of the model. The mathematical model might then say that the problem is to choose the values of the decision variables so as to maximize the objective function, subject to the specified constraints. Such a model, and minor variations of it, typifies the models used in OR.

Determining the appropriate values to assign to the parameters of the model (one value per parameter) is both a critical and a challenging part of the model-building process. In contrast to textbook problems where the numbers are given to you, determining parameter values for real problems requires *gathering relevant data.* As discussed in the preceding section, gathering accurate data frequently is difficult. Therefore, the value assigned to a parameter often is, of necessity, only a rough estimate. Because of the uncertainty about the true value of the parameter, it is important to analyze how the solution derived from the model would change (if at all) if the value assigned to the parameter were changed to other plausible values. This process is referred to as **sensitivity analysis,** as discussed further in the next section (and much of Chap. 6).

Although we refer to "the" mathematical model of a business problem, real problems normally don't have just a single "right" model. Section 2.4 will describe how the process of testing a model typically leads to a succession of models that provide better and better representations of the problem. It is even possible that two or more completely different types of models may be developed to help analyze the same problem.

You will see numerous examples of mathematical models throughout the remainder of this book. One particularly important type that is studied in the next several chapters is the **linear programming model,** where the mathematical functions appearing in both the objective function and the constraints are all linear functions. In the next chapter, specific linear programming models are constructed to fit such diverse problems as determining (1) the mix of products that maximizes profit, (2) the design of radiation therapy that effectively attacks a tumor while minimizing the damage to nearby healthy tissue, (3) the allocation of acreage to crops that maximizes total net return, and (4) the combination of pollution abatement methods that achieves air quality standards at minimum cost.

Mathematical models have many advantages over a verbal description of the problem. One advantage is that a mathematical model describes a problem much more concisely. This tends to make the overall structure of the problem more comprehensible, and it helps to reveal important cause-and-effect relationships. In this way, it indicates more clearly what additional data are relevant to the analysis. It also facilitates dealing with the problem in its entirety and considering all its interrelationships simultaneously. Finally, a mathematical model forms a bridge to the use of high-powered mathematical techniques and computers to analyze the problem. Indeed, packaged software for both personal computers and mainframe computers has become widely available for solving many mathematical models.

However, there are pitfalls to be avoided when you use mathematical models. Such a model is necessarily an abstract idealization of the problem, so approximations and simplifying assumptions generally are required if the model is to be *tractable* (capable of being solved). Therefore, care must be taken to ensure that the model remains a valid representation of the problem. The proper criterion for judging the validity of a model is whether the model predicts the relative effects of the alternative courses of action with sufficient accuracy to permit a sound decision. Consequently, it is not necessary to include unimportant details or factors that have approximately the same effect for all the alternative courses of action considered. It is not even necessary that the absolute magnitude of the measure of performance be approximately correct for the various alternatives, provided that their relative values (i.e., the differences between their values) are sufficiently precise. Thus, all that is required is that there be a high *correlation* between the prediction by the model and what would actually happen in the real world. To ascertain whether this requirement is satisfied, it is important to do considerable *testing* and consequent modifying of the model, which will be the subject of Sec. 2.4. Although this testing phase is placed later in the chapter, much of this *model validation* work actually is conducted during the model-building phase of the study to help guide the construction of the mathematical model.

In developing the model, a good approach is to begin with a very simple version and then move in evolutionary fashion toward more elaborate models that more nearly reflect the complexity of the real problem. This process of *model enrichment* continues only as long as the model remains tractable. The basic trade-off under constant consideration is between the *precision* and the *tractability* of the model. (See Selected Reference 6 for a detailed description of this process.)

A crucial step in formulating an OR model is the construction of the objective function. This requires developing a quantitative measure of performance relative to each of the decision maker's ultimate objectives that were identified while the problem was being defined. If there are multiple objectives, their respective measures commonly are then transformed and combined into a composite measure, called the **overall measure of performance.** This overall measure might be something tangible (e.g., profit) corresponding to a higher goal of the organization, or it might be abstract (e.g., utility). In the latter case, the task of developing this measure tends to be a complex one requiring a careful comparison of the objectives and their relative importance. After the overall measure of performance is developed, the objective function is then obtained by expressing this measure as a mathematical function of the decision variables. Alternatively, there also are methods for explicitly considering multiple objectives simultaneously, and one of these (goal programming) is discussed in Chap. 7.

Examples.   An OR study done for **Monsanto Corp.**[1] was concerned with optimizing production operations in Monsanto's chemical plants to minimize the cost of meeting the target for the amount of a certain chemical product (maleic anhydride) to be produced in a given

---

[1]R. F. Boykin, "Optimizing Chemical Production at Monsanto," *Interfaces,* **15**(1): 88–95, Jan.–Feb. 1985. See especially pp. 92–93.

month. The decisions to be made are the dial setting for each of the catalytic reactors used to produce this product, where the setting determines both the amount produced and the cost of operating the reactor. The form of the resulting mathematical model is as follows:

Choose the values of the *decision variables* R_{ij}
$(i = 1, 2, \ldots, r; j = 1, 2, \ldots, s)$
so as to

$$\text{Minimize} \quad \sum_{i=1}^{r} \sum_{j=1}^{s} c_{ij} R_{ij},$$

subject to

$$\sum_{i=1}^{r} \sum_{j=1}^{s} p_{ij} R_{ij} \geq T$$

$$\sum_{j=1}^{s} R_{ij} = 1, \quad \text{for } i = 1, 2, \ldots, r$$

$$R_{ij} = 0 \text{ or } 1,$$

where $R_{ij} = \begin{cases} 1 & \text{if reactor } i \text{ is operated at setting } j \\ 0 & \text{otherwise} \end{cases}$

c_{ij} = cost for reactor i at setting j
p_{ij} = production of reactor i at setting j
T = production target
r = number of reactors
s = number of settings (including off position)

The *objective function* for this model is $\sum \sum c_{ij} R_{ij}$. The *constraints* are given in the three lines below the objective function. The *parameters* are c_{ij}, p_{ij}, and T. For Monsanto's application, this model has over 1,000 *decision variables* R_{ij} (that is, $rs > 1,000$). Its use led to annual savings of approximately $2 million.

The Netherlands government agency responsible for water control and public works, the **Rijkswaterstaat,** commissioned a major OR study[1] to guide the development of a new national water management policy. The new policy saved hundreds of millions of dollars in investment expenditures and reduced agricultural damage by about $15 million per year, while decreasing thermal and algae pollution. Rather than formulating *one* mathematical model, this OR study developed a comprehensive, integrated system of 50 models! Furthermore, for some of the models, both simple and complex versions were developed. The simple version was used to gain basic insights, including trade-off analyses. The complex version then was used in the final rounds of the analysis or whenever greater accuracy or more detailed outputs were desired. The overall OR study directly involved over 125 person-years of effort (more than one-third in data gathering), created several dozen computer programs, and structured an enormous amount of data.

---

[1]B. F. Goeller and the PAWN team: "Planning the Netherlands' Water Resources," *Interfaces,* **15**(1): 3–33, Jan.–Feb. 1985. See especially pp. 7–18.

2.3 DERIVING SOLUTIONS FROM THE MODEL

After a mathematical model is formulated for the problem under consideration, the next phase in an OR study is to develop a procedure (usually a computer-based procedure) for deriving solutions to the problem from this model. You might think that this must be the major part of the study, but actually it is not in most cases. Sometimes, in fact, it is a relatively simple step, in which one of the standard **algorithms** (systematic solution procedures) of OR is applied on a computer by using one of a number of readily available software packages. For experienced OR practitioners, finding a solution is the fun part, whereas the real work comes in the preceding and following steps, including the *postoptimality analysis* discussed later in this section.

Since much of this book is devoted to the subject of how to obtain solutions for various important types of mathematical models, little needs to be said about it here. However, we do need to discuss the nature of such solutions.

A common theme in OR is the search for an **optimal,** or best, **solution.** Indeed, many procedures have been developed, and are presented in this book, for finding such solutions for certain kinds of problems. However, it needs to be recognized that these solutions are optimal only with respect to the model being used. Since the model necessarily is an idealized rather than an exact representation of the real problem, there cannot be any utopian guarantee that the optimal solution for the model will prove to be the best possible solution that could have been implemented for the real problem. There just are too many imponderables and uncertainties associated with real problems. However, if the model is well formulated and tested, the resulting solution should tend to be a good approximation to an ideal course of action for the real problem. Therefore, rather than be deluded into demanding the impossible, you should make the test of the practical success of an OR study hinge on whether it provides a better guide for action than can be obtained by other means.

Eminent management scientist and Nobel Laureate in economics Herbert Simon points out that **satisficing** is much more prevalent than optimizing in actual practice. In coining the term *satisficing* as a combination of the words *satisfactory* and *optimizing,* Simon is describing the tendency of managers to seek a solution that is "good enough" for the problem at hand. Rather than trying to develop an overall measure of performance to optimally reconcile conflicts between various desirable objectives (including well-established criteria for judging the performance of different segments of the organization), a more pragmatic approach may be used. Goals may be set to establish minimum satisfactory levels of performance in various areas, based perhaps on past levels of performance or on what the competition is achieving. If a solution is found that enables all these goals to be met, it is likely to be adopted without further ado. Such is the nature of satisficing.

The distinction between optimizing and satisficing reflects the difference between theory and the realities frequently faced in trying to implement that theory in practice. In the words of one of England's OR leaders, Samuel Eilon, "Optimizing is the science of the ultimate; satisficing is the art of the feasible."[1]

OR teams attempt to bring as much of the "science of the ultimate" as possible to the decision-making process. However, the successful team does so in full recognition of the

---

[1]S. Eilon, "Goals and Constraints in Decision-making," *Operational Research Quarterly,* **23:** 3–15, 1972—address given at the 1971 annual conference of the Canadian Operational Research Society.

overriding need of the decision maker to obtain a satisfactory guide for action in a reasonable period of time. Therefore, the goal of an OR study should be to conduct the study in an optimal manner, regardless of whether this involves finding an optimal solution for the model. Thus, in addition to pursuing the science of the ultimate, the team should also consider the cost of the study and the disadvantages of delaying its completion, and then attempt to maximize the net benefits resulting from the study. In recognition of this concept, OR teams occasionally use only **heuristic procedures** (i.e., intuitively designed procedures that do not guarantee an optimal solution) to find a good **suboptimal solution.** This is most often the case when the time or cost required to find an optimal solution for an adequate model of the problem would be very large. In recent years, great progress has been made in developing efficient and effective heuristic procedures (including so-called metaheuristics), so their use is continuing to grow.

The discussion thus far has implied that an OR study seeks to find only one solution, which may or may not be required to be optimal. In fact, this usually is not the case. An optimal solution for the original model may be far from ideal for the real problem, so additional analysis is needed. Therefore, **postoptimality analysis** (analysis done after finding an optimal solution) is a very important part of most OR studies. This analysis also is sometimes referred to as **what-if analysis** because it involves addressing some questions about *what* would happen to the optimal solution *if* different assumptions are made about future conditions. These questions often are raised by the managers who will be making the ultimate decisions rather than by the OR team.

The advent of powerful spreadsheet software now has frequently given spreadsheets a central role in conducting postoptimality analysis. One of the great strengths of a spreadsheet is the ease with which it can be used interactively by anyone, including managers, to see what happens to the optimal solution when changes are made to the model. This process of experimenting with changes in the model also can be very helpful in providing understanding of the behavior of the model and increasing confidence in its validity.

In part, postoptimality analysis involves conducting **sensitivity analysis** to determine which parameters of the model are most critical (the "sensitive parameters") in determining the solution. A common definition of *sensitive parameter* (used throughout this book) is the following.

> For a mathematical model with specified values for all its parameters, the model's **sensitive parameters** are the parameters whose value cannot be changed without changing the optimal solution.

Identifying the sensitive parameters is important, because this identifies the parameters whose value must be assigned with special care to avoid distorting the output of the model.

The value assigned to a parameter commonly is just an *estimate* of some quantity (e.g., unit profit) whose exact value will become known only after the solution has been implemented. Therefore, after the sensitive parameters are identified, special attention is given to estimating each one more closely, or at least its range of likely values. One then seeks a solution that remains a particularly good one for all the various combinations of likely values of the sensitive parameters.

If the solution is implemented on an ongoing basis, any later change in the value of a sensitive parameter immediately signals a need to change the solution.

In some cases, certain parameters of the model represent policy decisions (e.g., resource allocations). If so, there frequently is some flexibility in the values assigned to these parameters. Perhaps some can be increased by decreasing others. Postoptimality analysis includes the investigation of such trade-offs.

In conjunction with the study phase discussed in the next section (testing the model), postoptimality analysis also involves obtaining a sequence of solutions that comprises a series of improving approximations to the ideal course of action. Thus, the apparent weaknesses in the initial solution are used to suggest improvements in the model, its input data, and perhaps the solution procedure. A new solution is then obtained, and the cycle is repeated. This process continues until the improvements in the succeeding solutions become too small to warrant continuation. Even then, a number of alternative solutions (perhaps solutions that are optimal for one of several plausible versions of the model and its input data) may be presented to management for the final selection. As suggested in Sec. 2.1, this presentation of alternative solutions would normally be done whenever the final choice among these alternatives should be based on considerations that are best left to the judgment of management.

Example. Consider again the **Rijkswaterstaat** OR study of national water management policy for the Netherlands, introduced at the end of the preceding section. This study did not conclude by recommending just a single solution. Instead, a number of attractive alternatives were identified, analyzed, and compared. The final choice was left to the Dutch political process, culminating with approval by Parliament. *Sensitivity analysis* played a major role in this study. For example, certain parameters of the models represented environmental standards. Sensitivity analysis included assessing the impact on water management problems if the values of these parameters were changed from the current environmental standards to other reasonable values. Sensitivity analysis also was used to assess the impact of changing the assumptions of the models, e.g., the assumption on the effect of future international treaties on the amount of pollution entering the Netherlands. A variety of *scenarios* (e.g., an extremely dry year and an extremely wet year) also were analyzed, with appropriate probabilities assigned.

2.4 TESTING THE MODEL

Developing a large mathematical model is analogous in some ways to developing a large computer program. When the first version of the computer program is completed, it inevitably contains many bugs. The program must be thoroughly tested to try to find and correct as many bugs as possible. Eventually, after a long succession of improved programs, the programmer (or programming team) concludes that the current program now is generally giving reasonably valid results. Although some minor bugs undoubtedly remain hidden in the program (and may never be detected), the major bugs have been sufficiently eliminated that the program now can be reliably used.

Similarly, the first version of a large mathematical model inevitably contains many flaws. Some relevant factors or interrelationships undoubtedly have not been incorporated into the model, and some parameters undoubtedly have not been estimated correctly. This is inevitable, given the difficulty of communicating and understanding all the aspects and subtleties of a complex operational problem as well as the difficulty of collecting reliable data. Therefore, before you use the model, it must be thoroughly tested to try to identify and correct as many flaws as possible. Eventually, after a long succession of improved models, the OR team concludes that the current model now is giving reasonably valid results. Although some minor flaws undoubtedly remain hidden in the model (and may never be detected), the major flaws have been sufficiently eliminated that the model now can be reliably used.

This process of testing and improving a model to increase its validity is commonly referred to as **model validation.**

It is difficult to describe how model validation is done, because the process depends greatly on the nature of the problem being considered and the model being used. However, we make a few general comments, and then we give some examples. (See Selected Reference 2 for a detailed discussion.)

Since the OR team may spend months developing all the detailed pieces of the model, it is easy to "lose the forest for the trees." Therefore, after the details ("the trees") of the initial version of the model are completed, a good way to begin model validation is to take a fresh look at the overall model ("the forest") to check for obvious errors or oversights. The group doing this review preferably should include at least one individual who did not participate in the formulation of the model. Reexamining the definition of the problem and comparing it with the model may help to reveal mistakes. It is also useful to make sure that all the mathematical expressions are *dimensionally consistent* in the units used. Additional insight into the validity of the model can sometimes be obtained by varying the values of the parameters and/or the decision variables and checking to see whether the output from the model behaves in a plausible manner. This is often especially revealing when the parameters or variables are assigned extreme values near their maxima or minima.

A more systematic approach to testing the model is to use a **retrospective test.** When it is applicable, this test involves using historical data to reconstruct the past and then determining how well the model and the resulting solution would have performed if they had been used. Comparing the effectiveness of this hypothetical performance with what actually happened then indicates whether using this model tends to yield a significant improvement over current practice. It may also indicate areas where the model has shortcomings and requires modifications. Furthermore, by using alternative solutions from the model and estimating their hypothetical historical performances, considerable evidence can be gathered regarding how well the model predicts the relative effects of alternative courses of actions.

On the other hand, a disadvantage of retrospective testing is that it uses the same data that guided the formulation of the model. The crucial question is whether the past is truly representative of the future. If it is not, then the model might perform quite differently in the future than it would have in the past.

To circumvent this disadvantage of retrospective testing, it is sometimes useful to continue the status quo temporarily. This provides new data that were not available when the model was constructed. These data are then used in the same ways as those described here to evaluate the model.

Documenting the process used for model validation is important. This helps to increase confidence in the model for subsequent users. Furthermore, if concerns arise in the future about the model, this documentation will be helpful in diagnosing where problems may lie.

Examples.   Consider once again the **Rijkswaterstaat** OR study of national water management policy for the Netherlands, discussed at the end of Secs. 2.2 and 2.3. The process of model validation in this case had three main parts. First, the OR team checked the general behavior of the models by checking whether the results from each model moved in reasonable ways when changes were made in the values of the model parameters. Second, retrospective testing was done. Third, a careful technical review of the models, methodology, and results was conducted by individuals unaffiliated with the project, including Dutch experts. This process led to a number of important new insights and improvements in the models.

Many new insights also were gleaned during the model validation phase of the OR study for the **Citgo Petroleum Corp.,** discussed at the end of Sec. 2.1. In this case, the model of refinery operations was tested by collecting the actual inputs and outputs of the refinery for a series of months, using these inputs to fix the model inputs, and then comparing the model outputs with the actual refinery outputs. The process of properly calibrating and recalibrating the model was a lengthy one, but ultimately led to routine use of the model to provide critical decision information. As already mentioned in Sec. 2.1, the validation and correction of input data for the models also played an important role in this study.

Our next example concerns an OR study done for **IBM**[1] to integrate its national network of spare-parts inventories to improve service support for IBM's customers. This study resulted in a new inventory system that improved customer service while reducing the value of IBM's inventories by over $250 million and saving an additional $20 million per year through improved operational efficiency. A particularly interesting aspect of the model validation phase of this study was the way that *future users* of the inventory system were incorporated into the testing process. Because these future users (IBM managers in functional areas responsible for implementation of the inventory system) were skeptical about the system being developed, representatives were appointed to a *user team* to serve as advisers to the OR team. After a preliminary version of the new system had been developed (based on a multiechelon inventory model), a *preimplementation test* of the system was conducted. Extensive feedback from the user team led to major improvements in the proposed system.

2.5 PREPARING TO APPLY THE MODEL

What happens after the testing phase has been completed and an acceptable model has been developed? If the model is to be used repeatedly, the next step is to install a well-documented *system* for applying the model as prescribed by management. This system will include the model, solution procedure (including postoptimality analysis), and oper-

---

[1]M. Cohen, P. V. Kamesam, P. Kleindorfer, H. Lee, and A. Tekerian, "Optimizer: IBM's Multi-Echelon Inventory System for Managing Service Logistics," *Interfaces,* **20**(1): 65–82, Jan.–Feb. 1990. See especially pp. 73–76. This application will be described further in Sec. 19.8.

ating procedures for implementation. Then, even as personnel changes, the system can be called on at regular intervals to provide a specific numerical solution.

This system usually is *computer-based.* In fact, a considerable number of computer programs often need to be used and integrated. *Databases* and *management information systems* may provide up-to-date input for the model each time it is used, in which case interface programs are needed. After a solution procedure (another program) is applied to the model, additional computer programs may trigger the implementation of the results automatically. In other cases, an *interactive* computer-based system called a **decision support system** is installed to help managers use data and models to support (rather than replace) their decision making as needed. Another program may generate *managerial reports* (in the language of management) that interpret the output of the model and its implications for application.

In major OR studies, several months (or longer) may be required to develop, test, and install this computer system. Part of this effort involves developing and implementing a process for maintaining the system throughout its future use. As conditions change over time, this process should modify the computer system (including the model) accordingly.

Examples. The **IBM** OR study introduced at the end of Sec. 2.4 provides a good example of a particularly large computer system for applying a model. The system developed, called *Optimizer,* provides optimal control of service levels and spare-parts inventories throughout IBM's U.S. parts distribution network, which includes two central automated warehouses, dozens of field distribution centers and parts stations, and many thousands of outside locations. The parts inventory maintained in this network is valued in the billions of dollars. Optimizer consists of four major modules. A forecasting system module contains a few programs for estimating the failure rates of individual types of parts. A data delivery system module consists of approximately 100 programs that process over 15 gigabytes of data to provide the input for the model. A decision system module then solves the model on a weekly basis to optimize control of the inventories. The fourth module includes six programs that integrate Optimizer into IBM's Parts Inventory Management System (PIMS). PIMS is a sophisticated information and control system that contains millions of lines of code.

Our next example also involves a large computer system for applying a model to control operations over a national network. This system, called *SYSNET,* was developed as the result of an OR study done for **Yellow Freight System, Inc.**[1] Yellow Freight annually handles over 15 million shipments by motor carrier over a network of 630 terminals throughout the United States. SYSNET is used to optimize both the routing of shipments and the design of the network. Because SYSNET requires extensive information about freight flows and forecasts, transportation and handling costs, and so on, a major part of the OR study involved integrating SYSNET into the corporate management information system. This integration enabled periodic updating of all the input for the model. The implementation of SYSNET resulted in annual savings of approximately $17.3 million as well as improved service to customers.

---

[1] J. W. Braklow, W. W. Graham, S. M. Hassler, K. E. Peck, and W. B. Powell, "Interactive Optimization Improves Service and Performance for Yellow Freight System," *Interfaces,* **22**(1): 147–172, Jan.–Feb. 1992. See especially p. 163.

Our next example illustrates a *decision support system.* A system of this type was developed for **Texaco**[1] to help plan and schedule its blending operations at its various refineries. Called *OMEGA* (Optimization Method for the Estimation of Gasoline Attributes), it is an *interactive* system based on a nonlinear optimization model that is implemented on both personal computers and larger computers. Input data can be entered either manually or by interfacing with refinery databases. The user has considerable flexibility in choosing an objective function and constraints to fit the current situation as well as in asking a series of *what-if questions* (i.e., questions about *what* would happen *if* the assumed conditions change). OMEGA is maintained centrally by Texaco's information technology department, which enables constant updating to reflect new government regulations, other business changes, and changes in refinery operations. The implementation of OMEGA is credited with annual savings of more than $30 million as well as improved planning, quality control, and marketing information.

2.6 IMPLEMENTATION

After a system is developed for applying the model, the last phase of an OR study is to implement this system as prescribed by management. This phase is a critical one because it is here, and only here, that the benefits of the study are reaped. Therefore, it is important for the OR team to participate in launching this phase, both to make sure that model solutions are accurately translated to an operating procedure and to rectify any flaws in the solutions that are then uncovered.

The success of the implementation phase depends a great deal upon the support of both top management and operating management. The OR team is much more likely to gain this support if it has kept management well informed and encouraged management's active guidance throughout the course of the study. Good communications help to ensure that the study accomplishes what management wanted and so deserves implementation. They also give management a greater sense of ownership of the study, which encourages their support for implementation.

The implementation phase involves several steps. First, the OR team gives operating management a careful explanation of the new system to be adopted and how it relates to operating realities. Next, these two parties share the responsibility for developing the procedures required to put this system into operation. Operating management then sees that a detailed indoctrination is given to the personnel involved, and the new course of action is initiated. If successful, the new system may be used for years to come. With this in mind, the OR team monitors the initial experience with the course of action taken and seeks to identify any modifications that should be made in the future.

Throughout the entire period during which the new system is being used, it is important to continue to obtain feedback on how well the system is working and whether the assumptions of the model continue to be satisfied. When significant deviations from the original assumptions occur, the model should be revisited to determine if any modifications should be made in the system. The postoptimality analysis done earlier (as described in Sec. 2.3) can be helpful in guiding this review process.

[1]C. W. DeWitt, L. S. Lasdon, A. D. Waren, D. A. Brenner, and S. A. Melhem, "OMEGA: An Improved Gasoline Blending System for Texaco," *Interfaces,* **19**(1): 85–101, Jan.–Feb. 1989. See especially pp. 93–95.

Upon culmination of a study, it is appropriate for the OR team to *document* its methodology clearly and accurately enough so that the work is *reproducible. Replicability* should be part of the professional ethical code of the operations researcher. This condition is especially crucial when controversial public policy issues are being studied.

Examples. This last point about *documenting* an OR study is illustrated by the Rijkswaterstaat study of national water management policy for the Netherlands discussed at the end of Secs. 2.2, 2.3, and 2.4. Management wanted unusually thorough and extensive documentation, both to support the new policy and to use in training new analysts or in performing new studies. Requiring several years to complete, this documentation aggregated 4000 single-spaced pages and 21 volumes!

Our next example concerns the **IBM** OR study discussed at the end of Secs. 2.4 and 2.5. Careful planning was required to implement the complex Optimizer system for controlling IBM's national network of spare-parts inventories. Three factors proved to be especially important in achieving a successful implementation. As discussed in Sec. 2.4, the first was the inclusion of a *user team* (consisting of operational managers) as advisers to the OR team throughout the study. By the time of the implementation phase, these operational managers had a strong sense of ownership and so had become ardent supporters for installing Optimizer in their functional areas. A second success factor was a very extensive *user acceptance test* whereby users could identify problem areas that needed rectifying prior to full implementation. The third key was that the new system was *phased in gradually,* with careful testing at each phase, so the major bugs could be eliminated before the system went live nationally.

Our final example concerns **Yellow Freight's** SYSNET system for routing shipments over a national network, as described at the end of the preceding section. In this case, there were four key elements to the implementation process. The first was selling the concept to upper management. This was successfully done through validating the accuracy of the cost model and then holding *interactive sessions* for upper management that demonstrated the effectiveness of the system. The second element was the development of an implementation strategy for gradually phasing in the new system while identifying and eliminating its flaws. The third involved working closely with operational managers to install the system properly, provide the needed support tools, train the personnel who will use the system, and convince them of the usefulness of the system. The final key element was the provision of management incentives and enforcement for the effective implementation of the system.

2.7 CONCLUSIONS

Although the remainder of this book focuses primarily on *constructing* and *solving* mathematical models, in this chapter we have tried to emphasize that this constitutes only a portion of the overall process involved in conducting a typical OR study. The other phases described here also are very important to the success of the study. Try to keep in perspective the role of the model and the solution procedure in the overall process as you move through the subsequent chapters. Then, after gaining a deeper understanding of mathematical models, we suggest that you plan to return to review this chapter again in order to further sharpen this perspective.

OR is closely intertwined with the use of computers. In the early years, these generally were mainframe computers, but now personal computers and workstations are being widely used to solve OR models.

In concluding this discussion of the major phases of an OR study, it should be emphasized that there are many exceptions to the "rules" prescribed in this chapter. By its very nature, OR requires considerable ingenuity and innovation, so it is impossible to write down any standard procedure that should always be followed by OR teams. Rather, the preceding description may be viewed as a model that roughly represents how successful OR studies are conducted.

SELECTED REFERENCES

1. Fortuin, L., P. van Beek, and L. van Wassenhove (eds.): *OR at wORk: Practical Experiences of Operational Research,* Taylor & Francis, Bristol, PA, 1996.
2. Gass, S. I.: "Decision-Aiding Models: Validation, Assessment, and Related Issues for Policy Analysis," *Operations Research,* **31**: 603–631, 1983.
3. Gass, S. I.: "Model World: Danger, Beware the User as Modeler," *Interfaces,* **20**(3): 60–64, May–June 1990.
4. Hall, R. W.: "What's So Scientific about MS/OR?" *Interfaces,* **15**(2): 40–45, March–April 1985.
5. Miser, H. J.: "The Easy Chair: Observation and Experimentation," *Interfaces,* **19**(5): 23–30, Sept.–Oct. 1989.
6. Morris, W. T.: "On the Art of Modeling," *Management Science,* **13**: B707–717, 1967.
7. Murthy, D. N. P., N. W. Page, and E. Y. Rodin: *Mathematical Modeling: A Tool for Problem Solving in Engineering, Physical, Biological and Social Sciences,* Pergamon Press, Oxford, England, 1990.
8. Simon, H. A.: "Prediction and Prescription in Systems Modeling," *Operations Research,* **38**: 7–14, 1990.
9. Tilanus, C. B., O. B. DeGans, and J. K. Lenstra (eds.): *Quantitative Methods in Management: Case Studies of Failures and Successes,* Wiley, New York, 1986.
10. Williams, H. P.: *Model Building in Mathematical Programming,* 3d ed., Wiley, New York, 1990.

PROBLEMS

2.1-1. Read the article footnoted in Sec. 2.1 that describes an OR study done for the San Francisco Police Department.
(a) Summarize the background that led to undertaking this study.
(b) Define part of the problem being addressed by identifying the six directives for the scheduling system to be developed.
(c) Describe how the needed data were gathered.
(d) List the various tangible and intangible benefits that resulted from the study.

2.1-2. Read the article footnoted in Sec. 2.1 that describes an OR study done for the Health Department of New Haven, Connecticut.
(a) Summarize the background that led to undertaking this study.

(b) Outline the system developed to track and test each needle and syringe in order to gather the needed data.
(c) Summarize the initial results from this tracking and testing system.
(d) Describe the impact and potential impact of this study on public policy.

2.2-1. Read the article footnoted in Sec. 2.2 that describes an OR study done for the Rijkswaterstaat of the Netherlands. (Focus especially on pp. 3–20 and 30–32.)
(a) Summarize the background that led to undertaking this study.
(b) Summarize the purpose of each of the five mathematical models described on pp. 10–18.

(c) Summarize the "impact measures" (measures of performance) for comparing policies that are described on pp. 6–7 of this article.

(d) List the various tangible and intangible benefits that resulted from the study.

2.2-2. Read Selected Reference 4.

(a) Identify the author's example of a model in the natural sciences and of a model in OR.

(b) Describe the author's viewpoint about how basic precepts of using models to do research in the natural sciences can also be used to guide *research on operations* (OR).

2.3-1. Refer to Selected Reference 4.

(a) Describe the author's viewpoint about whether the sole goal in using a model should be to find its optimal solution.

(b) Summarize the author's viewpoint about the complementary roles of modeling, evaluating information from the model, and then applying the decision maker's judgment when deciding on a course of action.

2.4-1. Refer to pp. 18–20 of the article footnoted in Sec. 2.2 that describes an OR study done for the Rijkswaterstaat of the Netherlands. Describe an important lesson that was gained from model validation in this study.

2.4-2. Read Selected Reference 5. Summarize the author's viewpoint about the roles of observation and experimentation in the model validation process.

2.4-3. Read pp. 603–617 of Selected Reference 2.

(a) What does the author say about whether a model can be completely validated?

(b) Summarize the distinctions made between *model validity, data validity, logical/mathematical validity, predictive validity, operational validity,* and *dynamic validity.*

(c) Describe the role of *sensitivity analysis* in testing the *operational validity* of a model.

(d) What does the author say about whether there is a validation methodology that is appropriate for all models?

(e) Cite the page in the article that lists basic validation steps.

2.5-1. Read the article footnoted in Sec. 2.5 that describes an OR study done for Texaco.

(a) Summarize the background that led to undertaking this study.

(b) Briefly describe the user interface with the decision support system OMEGA that was developed as a result of this study.

(c) OMEGA is constantly being updated and extended to reflect changes in the operating environment. Briefly describe the various kinds of changes involved.

(d) Summarize how OMEGA is used.

(e) List the various tangible and intangible benefits that resulted from the study.

2.5-2. Refer to the article footnoted in Sec. 2.5 that describes an OR study done for Yellow Freight System, Inc.

(a) Referring to pp. 147–149 of this article, summarize the background that led to undertaking this study.

(b) Referring to p. 150, briefly describe the computer system SYSNET that was developed as a result of this study. Also summarize the applications of SYSNET.

(c) Referring to pp. 162–163, describe why the *interactive* aspects of SYSNET proved important.

(d) Referring to p. 163, summarize the outputs from SYSNET.

(e) Referring to pp. 168–172, summarize the various benefits that have resulted from using SYSNET.

2.6-1. Refer to pp. 163–167 of the article footnoted in Sec. 2.5 that describes an OR study done for Yellow Freight System, Inc., and the resulting computer system SYSNET.

(a) Briefly describe how the OR team gained the support of upper management for implementing SYSNET.

(b) Briefly describe the implementation strategy that was developed.

(c) Briefly describe the field implementation.

(d) Briefly describe how management incentives and enforcement were used in implementing SYSNET.

2.6-2. Read the article footnoted in Sec. 2.4 that describes an OR study done for IBM and the resulting computer system Optimizer.

(a) Summarize the background that led to undertaking this study.

(b) List the complicating factors that the OR team members faced when they started developing a model and a solution algorithm.

(c) Briefly describe the preimplementation test of Optimizer.

(d) Briefly describe the field implementation test.

(e) Briefly describe national implementation.

(f) List the various tangible and intangible benefits that resulted from the study.

2.7-1. Read Selected Reference 3. The author describes 13 detailed phases of any OR study that develops and applies a computer-based model, whereas this chapter describes six broader phases. For each of these broader phases, list the detailed phases that fall partially or primarily within the broader phase.

3

Introduction to Linear Programming

The development of linear programming has been ranked among the most important scientific advances of the mid-20th century, and we must agree with this assessment. Its impact since just 1950 has been extraordinary. Today it is a standard tool that has saved many thousands or millions of dollars for most companies or businesses of even moderate size in the various industrialized countries of the world; and its use in other sectors of society has been spreading rapidly. A major proportion of all scientific computation on computers is devoted to the use of linear programming. Dozens of textbooks have been written about linear programming, and *published* articles describing important applications now number in the hundreds.

What is the nature of this remarkable tool, and what kinds of problems does it address? You will gain insight into this topic as you work through subsequent examples. However, a verbal summary may help provide perspective. Briefly, the most common type of application involves the general problem of allocating *limited resources* among *competing activities* in a best possible (i.e., *optimal*) way. More precisely, this problem involves selecting the level of certain activities that compete for scarce resources that are necessary to perform those activities. The choice of activity levels then dictates how much of each resource will be consumed by each activity. The variety of situations to which this description applies is diverse, indeed, ranging from the allocation of production facilities to products to the allocation of national resources to domestic needs, from portfolio selection to the selection of shipping patterns, from agricultural planning to the design of radiation therapy, and so on. However, the one common ingredient in each of these situations is the necessity for allocating resources to activities by choosing the levels of those activities.

Linear programming uses a mathematical model to describe the problem of concern. The adjective *linear* means that all the mathematical functions in this model are required to be *linear functions*. The word *programming* does not refer here to computer programming; rather, it is essentially a synonym for *planning*. Thus, linear programming involves the *planning of activities* to obtain an optimal result, i.e., a result that reaches the specified goal best (according to the mathematical model) among all feasible alternatives.

Although allocating resources to activities is the most common type of application, linear programming has numerous other important applications as well. In fact, *any* problem whose mathematical model fits the very general format for the linear programming model is a linear programming problem. Furthermore, a remarkably efficient solution procedure, called the **simplex method,** is available for solving linear programming problems of even enormous size. These are some of the reasons for the tremendous impact of linear programming in recent decades.

Because of its great importance, we devote this and the next six chapters specifically to linear programming. After this chapter introduces the general features of linear programming, Chaps. 4 and 5 focus on the simplex method. Chapter 6 discusses the further analysis of linear programming problems *after* the simplex method has been initially applied. Chapter 7 presents several widely used extensions of the simplex method and introduces an *interior-point algorithm* that sometimes can be used to solve even larger linear programming problems than the simplex method can handle. Chapters 8 and 9 consider some special types of linear programming problems whose importance warrants individual study.

You also can look forward to seeing applications of linear programming to other areas of operations research (OR) in several later chapters.

We begin this chapter by developing a miniature prototype example of a linear programming problem. This example is small enough to be solved graphically in a straightforward way. The following two sections present the general *linear programming model* and its basic assumptions. Sections 3.4 and 3.5 give some additional examples of linear programming applications, including three case studies. Section 3.6 describes how linear programming models of modest size can be conveniently displayed and solved on a spreadsheet. However, some linear programming problems encountered in practice require truly *massive* models. Section 3.7 illustrates how a massive model can arise and how it can still be formulated successfully with the help of a special modeling language such as MPL (described in this section) or LINGO (described in the appendix to this chapter).

3.1 PROTOTYPE EXAMPLE

The WYNDOR GLASS CO. produces high-quality glass products, including windows and glass doors. It has three plants. Aluminum frames and hardware are made in Plant 1, wood frames are made in Plant 2, and Plant 3 produces the glass and assembles the products.

Because of declining earnings, top management has decided to revamp the company's product line. Unprofitable products are being discontinued, releasing production capacity to launch two new products having large sales potential:

Product 1: An 8-foot glass door with aluminum framing
Product 2: A 4 $\times$ 6 foot double-hung wood-framed window

Product 1 requires some of the production capacity in Plants 1 and 3, but none in Plant 2. Product 2 needs only Plants 2 and 3. The marketing division has concluded that the company could sell as much of either product as could be produced by these plants. However, because both products would be competing for the same production capacity in Plant 3, it is not clear which *mix* of the two products would be *most profitable.* Therefore, an OR team has been formed to study this question.

The OR team began by having discussions with upper management to identify management's objectives for the study. These discussions led to developing the following definition of the problem:

Determine what the *production rates* should be for the two products in order to *maximize their total profit,* subject to the restrictions imposed by the limited production capacities available in the three plants. (Each product will be produced in batches of 20, so the *production rate* is defined as the number of batches produced per week.) *Any* combination of production rates that satisfies these restrictions is permitted, including producing none of one product and as much as possible of the other.

The OR team also identified the data that needed to be gathered:

1. Number of hours of production time available per week in each plant for these new products. (Most of the time in these plants already is committed to current products, so the available capacity for the new products is quite limited.)
2. Number of hours of production time used in each plant for each batch produced of each new product.
3. Profit per batch produced of each new product. (*Profit per batch produced* was chosen as an appropriate measure after the team concluded that the incremental profit from each additional batch produced would be roughly *constant* regardless of the total number of batches produced. Because no substantial costs will be incurred to initiate the production and marketing of these new products, the total profit from each one is approximately this *profit per batch produced* times *the number of batches produced.*)

Obtaining reasonable estimates of these quantities required enlisting the help of key personnel in various units of the company. Staff in the manufacturing division provided the data in the first category above. Developing estimates for the second category of data required some analysis by the manufacturing engineers involved in designing the production processes for the new products. By analyzing cost data from these same engineers and the marketing division, along with a pricing decision from the marketing division, the accounting department developed estimates for the third category.

Table 3.1 summarizes the data gathered.

The OR team immediately recognized that this was a linear programming problem of the classic **product mix** type, and the team next undertook the formulation of the corresponding mathematical model.

Formulation as a Linear Programming Problem

To formulate the mathematical (linear programming) model for this problem, let

x_1 = number of batches of product 1 produced per week

x_2 = number of batches of product 2 produced per week

Z = total profit per week (in thousands of dollars) from producing these two products

Thus, x_1 and x_2 are the *decision variables* for the model. Using the bottom row of Table 3.1, we obtain

$Z = 3x_1 + 5x_2.$

The objective is to choose the values of x_1 and x_2 so as to *maximize* $Z = 3x_1 + 5x_2$, subject to the restrictions imposed on their values by the limited production capacities available in the three plants. Table 3.1 indicates that each batch of product 1 produced per week uses 1 hour of production time per week in Plant 1, whereas only 4 hours per week are available. This restriction is expressed mathematically by the inequality $x_1 \leq 4$. Similarly, Plant 2 imposes the restriction that $2x_2 \leq 12$. The number of hours of production

TABLE 3.1 Data for the Wyndor Glass Co. problem

Plant	Production Time per Batch, Hours Product 1	Production Time per Batch, Hours Product 2	Production Time Available per Week, Hours
1	1	0	4
2	0	2	12
3	3	2	18
Profit per batch	$3,000	$5,000	

time used per week in Plant 3 by choosing x_1 and x_2 as the new products' production rates would be $3x_1 + 2x_2$. Therefore, the mathematical statement of the Plant 3 restriction is $3x_1 + 2x_2 \leq 18$. Finally, since production rates cannot be negative, it is necessary to restrict the decision variables to be nonnegative: $x_1 \geq 0$ and $x_2 \geq 0$.

To summarize, in the mathematical language of linear programming, the problem is to choose values of x_1 and x_2 so as to

$$\text{Maximize} \quad Z = 3x_1 + 5x_2,$$

subject to the restrictions

$$x_1 \leq 4$$
$$2x_2 \leq 12$$
$$3x_1 + 2x_2 \leq 18$$

and

$$x_1 \geq 0, \quad x_2 \geq 0.$$

(Notice how the layout of the coefficients of x_1 and x_2 in this linear programming model essentially duplicates the information summarized in Table 3.1.)

Graphical Solution

This very small problem has only two decision variables and therefore only two dimensions, so a graphical procedure can be used to solve it. This procedure involves constructing a two-dimensional graph with x_1 and x_2 as the axes. The first step is to identify the values of (x_1, x_2) that are permitted by the restrictions. This is done by drawing each line that borders the range of permissible values for one restriction. To begin, note that the nonnegativity restrictions $x_1 \geq 0$ and $x_2 \geq 0$ require (x_1, x_2) to lie on the *positive* side of the axes (including actually *on* either axis), i.e., in the first quadrant. Next, observe that the restriction $x_1 \leq 4$ means that (x_1, x_2) cannot lie to the right of the line $x_1 = 4$. These results are shown in Fig. 3.1, where the shaded area contains the only values of (x_1, x_2) that are still allowed.

In a similar fashion, the restriction $2x_2 \leq 12$ (or, equivalently, $x_2 \leq 6$) implies that the line $2x_2 = 12$ should be added to the boundary of the permissible region. The final restriction, $3x_1 + 2x_2 \leq 18$, requires plotting the points (x_1, x_2) such that $3x_1 + 2x_2 = 18$

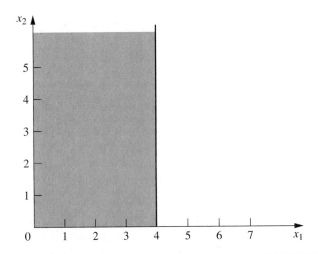

FIGURE 3.1
Shaded area shows values of
(x_1, x_2) allowed by $x_1 \geq 0$,
$x_2 \geq 0$, $x_1 \leq 4$.

(another line) to complete the boundary. (Note that the points such that $3x_1 + 2x_2 \leq 18$ are those that lie either underneath or on the line $3x_1 + 2x_2 = 18$, so this is the limiting line above which points do not satisfy the inequality.) The resulting region of permissible values of (x_1, x_2), called the **feasible region,** is shown in Fig. 3.2. (The demo called *Graphical Method* in your OR Tutor provides a more detailed example of constructing a feasible region.)

FIGURE 3.2
Shaded area shows the set of
permissible values of (x_1, x_2),
called the feasible region.

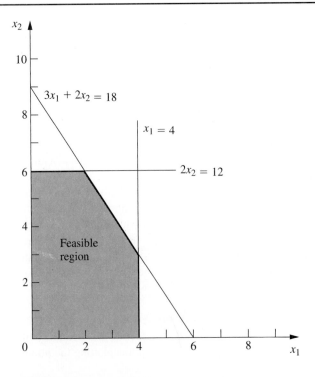

The final step is to pick out the point in this feasible region that maximizes the value of $Z = 3x_1 + 5x_2$. To discover how to perform this step efficiently, begin by trial and error. Try, for example, $Z = 10 = 3x_1 + 5x_2$ to see if there are in the permissible region any values of (x_1, x_2) that yield a value of Z as large as 10. By drawing the line $3x_1 + 5x_2 = 10$ (see Fig. 3.3), you can see that there are many points on this line that lie within the region. Having gained perspective by trying this arbitrarily chosen value of $Z = 10$, you should next try a larger arbitrary value of Z, say, $Z = 20 = 3x_1 + 5x_2$. Again, Fig. 3.3 reveals that a segment of the line $3x_1 + 5x_2 = 20$ lies within the region, so that the maximum permissible value of Z must be at least 20.

Now notice in Fig. 3.3 that the two lines just constructed are parallel. This is no coincidence, since *any* line constructed in this way has the form $Z = 3x_1 + 5x_2$ for the chosen value of Z, which implies that $5x_2 = -3x_1 + Z$ or, equivalently,

$$x_2 = -\frac{3}{5}x_1 + \frac{1}{5}Z$$

This last equation, called the **slope-intercept form** of the objective function, demonstrates that the *slope* of the line is $-\frac{3}{5}$ (since each unit increase in x_1 changes x_2 by $-\frac{3}{5}$), whereas the *intercept* of the line with the x_2 axis is $\frac{1}{5}Z$ (since $x_2 = \frac{1}{5}Z$ when $x_1 = 0$). The fact that the slope is fixed at $-\frac{3}{5}$ means that *all* lines constructed in this way are parallel.

Again, comparing the $10 = 3x_1 + 5x_2$ and $20 = 3x_1 + 5x_2$ lines in Fig. 3.3, we note that the line giving a larger value of Z ($Z = 20$) is farther up and away from the origin than the other line ($Z = 10$). This fact also is implied by the slope-intercept form of the objective function, which indicates that the intercept with the x_1 axis ($\frac{1}{5}Z$) increases when the value chosen for Z is increased.

FIGURE 3.3
The value of (x_1, x_2) that maximizes $3x_1 + 5x_2$ is (2, 6).

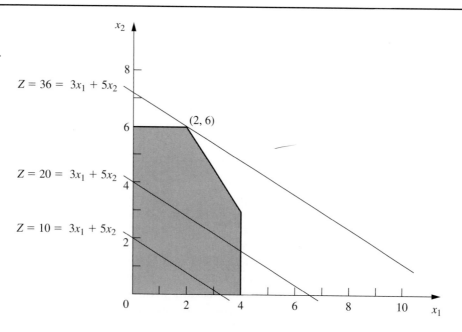

These observations imply that our trial-and-error procedure for constructing lines in Fig. 3.3 involves nothing more than drawing a family of parallel lines containing at least one point in the feasible region and selecting the line that corresponds to the largest value of Z. Figure 3.3 shows that this line passes through the point $(2, 6)$, indicating that the **optimal solution** is $x_1 = 2$ and $x_2 = 6$. The equation of this line is $3x_1 + 5x_2 = 3(2) + 5(6) = 36 = Z$, indicating that the optimal value of Z is $Z = 36$. The point $(2, 6)$ lies at the intersection of the two lines $2x_2 = 12$ and $3x_1 + 2x_2 = 18$, shown in Fig. 3.2, so that this point can be calculated algebraically as the simultaneous solution of these two equations.

Having seen the trial-and-error procedure for finding the optimal point $(2, 6)$, you now can streamline this approach for other problems. Rather than draw several parallel lines, it is sufficient to form a single line with a ruler to establish the slope. Then move the ruler with fixed slope through the feasible region in the direction of improving Z. (When the objective is to *minimize Z,* move the ruler in the direction that *decreases Z.*) Stop moving the ruler at the last instant that it still passes through a point in this region. This point is the desired *optimal solution.*

This procedure often is referred to as the **graphical method** for linear programming. It can be used to solve any linear programming problem with two decision variables. With considerable difficulty, it is possible to extend the method to three decision variables but not more than three. (The next chapter will focus on the *simplex method* for solving larger problems.)

Conclusions

The OR team used this approach to find that the optimal solution is $x_1 = 2$, $x_2 = 6$, with $Z = 36$. This solution indicates that the Wyndor Glass Co. should produce products 1 and 2 at the rate of 2 batches per week and 6 batches per week, respectively, with a resulting total profit of $36,000 per week. No other mix of the two products would be so profitable—*according to the model.*

However, we emphasized in Chap. 2 that well-conducted OR studies do not simply find *one* solution for the *initial* model formulated and then stop. All six phases described in Chap. 2 are important, including thorough testing of the model (see Sec. 2.4) and postoptimality analysis (see Sec. 2.3).

In full recognition of these practical realities, the OR team now is ready to evaluate the validity of the model more critically (to be continued in Sec. 3.3) and to perform sensitivity analysis on the effect of the estimates in Table 3.1 being different because of inaccurate estimation, changes of circumstances, etc. (to be continued in Sec. 6.7).

Continuing the Learning Process with Your OR Courseware

This is the first of many points in the book where you may find it helpful to use your *OR Courseware* in the CD-ROM that accompanies this book. A key part of this courseware is a program called OR Tutor. This program includes a complete demonstration example of the *graphical method* introduced in this section. Like the many other demonstration examples accompanying other sections of the book, this computer demonstration highlights concepts that are difficult to convey on the printed page. You may refer to Appendix 1 for documentation of the software.

When you formulate a linear programming model with more than two decision variables (so the graphical method cannot be used), the *simplex method* described in Chap. 4

enables you to still find an optimal solution immediately. Doing so also is helpful for *model validation,* since finding a *nonsensical* optimal solution signals that you have made a mistake in formulating the model.

We mentioned in Sec. 1.4 that your OR Courseware introduces you to three particularly popular commercial software packages—the Excel Solver, LINGO/LINDO, and MPL/CPLEX—for solving a variety of OR models. All three packages include the simplex method for solving linear programming models. Section 3.6 describes how to use Excel to formulate and solve linear programming models in a spreadsheet format. Descriptions of the other packages are provided in Sec. 3.7 (MPL and LINGO), Appendix 3.1 (LINGO), Sec. 4.8 (CPLEX and LINDO), and Appendix 4.1 (LINDO). In addition, your OR Courseware includes a file for each of the three packages showing how it can be used to solve each of the examples in this chapter.

3.2 THE LINEAR PROGRAMMING MODEL

The Wyndor Glass Co. problem is intended to illustrate a typical linear programming problem (miniature version). However, linear programming is too versatile to be completely characterized by a single example. In this section we discuss the general characteristics of linear programming problems, including the various legitimate forms of the mathematical model for linear programming.

Let us begin with some basic terminology and notation. The first column of Table 3.2 summarizes the components of the Wyndor Glass Co. problem. The second column then introduces more general terms for these same components that will fit many linear programming problems. The key terms are *resources* and *activities,* where m denotes the number of different kinds of resources that can be used and n denotes the number of activities being considered. Some typical resources are money and particular kinds of machines, equipment, vehicles, and personnel. Examples of activities include investing in particular projects, advertising in particular media, and shipping goods from a particular source to a particular destination. In any application of linear programming, all the activities may be of one general kind (such as any one of these three examples), and then the individual activities would be particular alternatives within this general category.

As described in the introduction to this chapter, the most common type of application of linear programming involves allocating resources to activities. The amount available of each resource is limited, so a careful allocation of resources to activities must be made. Determining this allocation involves choosing the *levels* of the activities that achieve the best possible value of the *overall measure of performance.*

TABLE 3.2 Common terminology for linear programming

Prototype Example	General Problem
Production capacities of plants 3 plants	Resources m resources
Production of products 2 products Production rate of product j, x_j	Activities n activities Level of activity j, x_j
Profit Z	Overall measure of performance Z

Certain symbols are commonly used to denote the various components of a linear programming model. These symbols are listed below, along with their interpretation for the general problem of allocating resources to activities.

Z = value of overall measure of performance.

x_j = level of activity j (for $j = 1, 2, \ldots , n$).

c_j = increase in Z that would result from each unit increase in level of activity j.

b_i = amount of resource i that is available for allocation to activities (for $i = 1, 2, \ldots , m$).

a_{ij} = amount of resource i consumed by each unit of activity j.

The model poses the problem in terms of making decisions about the levels of the activities, so $x_1, x_2, \ldots , x_n$ are called the **decision variables.** As summarized in Table 3.3, the values of c_j, b_i, and a_{ij} (for $i = 1, 2, \ldots , m$ and $j = 1, 2, \ldots , n$) are the *input constants* for the model. The c_j, b_i, and a_{ij} are also referred to as the **parameters** of the model.

Notice the correspondence between Table 3.3 and Table 3.1.

A Standard Form of the Model

Proceeding as for the Wyndor Glass Co. problem, we can now formulate the mathematical model for this general problem of allocating resources to activities. In particular, this model is to select the values for $x_1, x_2, \ldots , x_n$ so as to

$$\text{Maximize} \quad Z = c_1 x_1 + c_2 x_2 + \cdots + c_n x_n,$$

subject to the restrictions

$$a_{11} x_1 + a_{12} x_2 + \cdots + a_{1n} x_n \leq b_1$$
$$a_{21} x_1 + a_{22} x_2 + \cdots + a_{2n} x_n \leq b_2$$
$$\vdots$$
$$a_{m1} x_1 + a_{m2} x_2 + \cdots + a_{mn} x_n \leq b_m,$$

TABLE 3.3 Data needed for a linear programming model involving the allocation of resources to activities

Resource	Resource Usage per Unit of Activity				Amount of Resource Available
	Activity				
	1	2	. . .	n	
1	a_{11}	a_{12}	. . .	a_{1n}	b_1
2	a_{21}	a_{22}	. . .	a_{2n}	b_2
.					.
.	. . .	. . .	. . .	. . .	.
.					.
m	a_{m1}	a_{m2}	. . .	a_{mn}	b_m
Contribution to Z per unit of activity	c_1	c_2	. . .	c_n	

and

$$x_1 \geq 0, \qquad x_2 \geq 0, \qquad \ldots, \qquad x_n \geq 0.$$

We call this *our standard form*[1] for the linear programming problem. Any situation whose mathematical formulation fits this model is a linear programming problem.

Notice that the model for the Wyndor Glass Co. problem fits our standard form, with $m = 3$ and $n = 2$.

Common terminology for the linear programming model can now be summarized. The function being maximized, $c_1x_1 + c_2x_2 + \cdots + c_nx_n$, is called the **objective function.** The restrictions normally are referred to as **constraints.** The first m constraints (those with a *function* of all the variables $a_{i1}x_1 + a_{i2}x_2 + \cdots + a_{in}x_n$ on the left-hand side) are sometimes called **functional constraints** (or *structural constraints*). Similarly, the $x_j \geq 0$ restrictions are called **nonnegativity constraints** (or *nonnegativity conditions*).

Other Forms

We now hasten to add that the preceding model does not actually fit the natural form of some linear programming problems. The other *legitimate forms* are the following:

1. Minimizing rather than maximizing the objective function:

   Minimize $Z = c_1x_1 + c_2x_2 + \cdots + c_nx_n.$

2. Some functional constraints with a greater-than-or-equal-to inequality:

   $a_{i1}x_1 + a_{i2}x_2 + \cdots + a_{in}x_n \geq b_i$ for some values of i.

3. Some functional constraints in equation form:

   $a_{i1}x_1 + a_{i2}x_2 + \cdots + a_{in}x_n = b_i$ for some values of i.

4. Deleting the nonnegativity constraints for some decision variables:

   x_j unrestricted in sign   for some values of j.

Any problem that mixes some of or all these forms with the remaining parts of the preceding model is still a linear programming problem. Our interpretation of the words *allocating limited resources among competing activities* may no longer apply very well, if at all; but regardless of the interpretation or context, all that is required is that the mathematical statement of the problem fit the allowable forms.

Terminology for Solutions of the Model

You may be used to having the term *solution* mean the final answer to a problem, but the convention in linear programming (and its extensions) is quite different. Here, *any* specification of values for the decision variables $(x_1, x_2, \ldots, x_n)$ is called a **solution,** regardless of whether it is a desirable or even an allowable choice. Different types of solutions are then identified by using an appropriate adjective.

---

[1]This is called *our* standard form rather than *the* standard form because some textbooks adopt other forms.

A **feasible solution** is a solution for which *all* the constraints are *satisfied.*

An **infeasible solution** is a solution for which *at least one* constraint is *violated.*

In the example, the points (2, 3) and (4, 1) in Fig. 3.2 are *feasible solutions,* while the points (−1, 3) and (4, 4) are *infeasible solutions.*

The **feasible region** is the collection of all feasible solutions.

The feasible region in the example is the entire shaded area in Fig. 3.2.

It is possible for a problem to have **no feasible solutions.** This would have happened in the example if the new products had been required to return a net profit of at least $50,000 per week to justify discontinuing part of the current product line. The corresponding constraint, $3x_1 + 5x_2 \geq 50$, would eliminate the entire feasible region, so no mix of new products would be superior to the status quo. This case is illustrated in Fig. 3.4.

Given that there are feasible solutions, the goal of linear programming is to find a best feasible solution, as measured by the value of the objective function in the model.

An **optimal solution** is a feasible solution that has the *most favorable value* of the objective function.

The **most favorable value** is the *largest value* if the objective function is to be *maximized,* whereas it is the *smallest value* if the objective function is to be *minimized.*

Most problems will have just one optimal solution. However, it is possible to have more than one. This would occur in the example if the *profit per batch produced* of product 2 were changed to $2,000. This changes the objective function to $Z = 3x_1 + 2x_2$, so that all the points

FIGURE 3.4
The Wyndor Glass Co. problem would have no feasible solutions if the constraint $3x_1 + 5x_2 \geq 50$ were added to the problem.

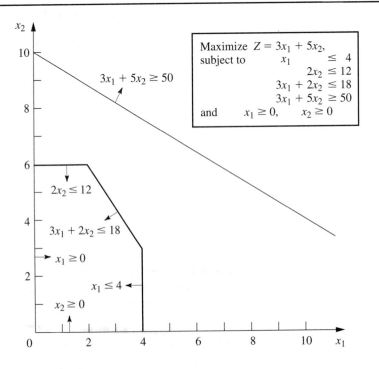

Maximize $Z = 3x_1 + 5x_2,$
subject to $x_1 \qquad \leq 4$
                    $2x_2 \leq 12$
           $3x_1 + 2x_2 \leq 18$
           $3x_1 + 5x_2 \geq 50$
and $x_1 \geq 0, \qquad x_2 \geq 0$

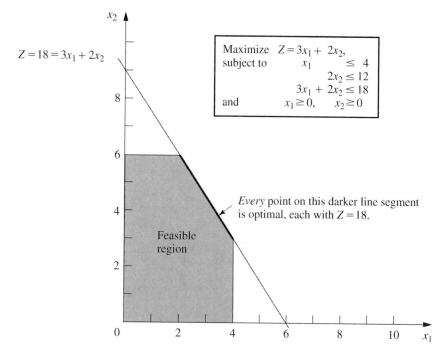

FIGURE 3.5
The Wyndor Glass Co. problem would have multiple optimal solutions if the objective function were changed to $Z = 3x_1 + 2x_2$.

on the line segment connecting (2, 6) and (4, 3) would be optimal. This case is illustrated in Fig. 3.5. As in this case, *any* problem having **multiple optimal solutions** will have an *infinite* number of them, each with the same optimal value of the objective function.

Another possibility is that a problem has **no optimal solutions.** This occurs only if (1) it has no feasible solutions or (2) the constraints do not prevent improving the value of the objective function (Z) indefinitely in the favorable direction (positive or negative). The latter case is referred to as having an **unbounded Z.** To illustrate, this case would result if the last two functional constraints were mistakenly deleted in the example, as illustrated in Fig. 3.6.

We next introduce a special type of feasible solution that plays the key role when the simplex method searches for an optimal solution.

> A **corner-point feasible (CPF) solution** is a solution that lies at a corner of the feasible region.

Figure 3.7 highlights the five CPF solutions for the example.

Sections 4.1 and 5.1 will delve into the various useful properties of CPF solutions for problems of any size, including the following relationship with optimal solutions.

> **Relationship between optimal solutions and CPF solutions:** Consider any linear programming problem with feasible solutions and a bounded feasible region. The problem must possess CPF solutions and at least one optimal solution. Furthermore, the best CPF solution *must* be an optimal solution. Thus, if a problem has exactly one optimal solution, it *must* be a CPF solution. If the problem has multiple optimal solutions, at least two *must* be CPF solutions.

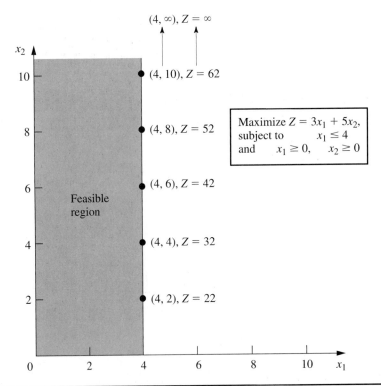

$(4, \infty), Z = \infty$

x_2

$(4, 10), Z = 62$

$(4, 8), Z = 52$

Maximize $Z = 3x_1 + 5x_2$,
subject to $\quad x_1 \leq 4$
and $\quad x_1 \geq 0, \quad x_2 \geq 0$

$(4, 6), Z = 42$

Feasible
region

$(4, 4), Z = 32$

$(4, 2), Z = 22$

FIGURE 3.6
The Wyndor Glass Co.
problem would have no
optimal solutions if the only
functional constraint were
$x_1 \leq 4$, because x_2 then
could be increased
indefinitely in the feasible
region without ever reaching
the maximum value of
$Z = 3x_1 + 5x_2$.

The example has exactly one optimal solution, $(x_1, x_2) = (2, 6)$, which is a CPF so-lution. (Think about how the graphical method leads to the one optimal solution being a CPF solution.) When the example is modified to yield multiple optimal solutions, as shown in Fig. 3.5, two of these optimal solutions—(2, 6) and (4, 3)—are CPF solutions.

3.3 ASSUMPTIONS OF LINEAR PROGRAMMING

All the assumptions of linear programming actually are implicit in the model formulation given in Sec. 3.2. However, it is good to highlight these assumptions so you can more easily evaluate how well linear programming applies to any given problem. Furthermore, we still need to see why the OR team for the Wyndor Glass Co. concluded that a linear programming formulation provided a satisfactory representation of the problem.

Proportionality

Proportionality is an assumption about both the objective function and the functional con-straints, as summarized below.

> **Proportionality assumption:** The contribution of each activity to the *value of the objective function Z* is *proportional* to the *level of the activity* x_j, as repre-sented by the $c_j x_j$ term in the objective function. Similarly, the contribution of each activity to the *left-hand side of each functional constraint* is *proportional* to the *level of the activity* x_j, as represented by the $a_{ij} x_j$ term in the constraint.

FIGURE 3.7
The five dots are the five CPF solutions for the Wyndor Glass Co. problem.

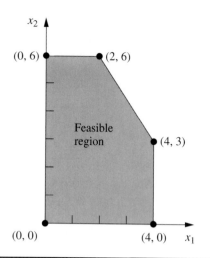

Consequently, this assumption rules out any exponent other than 1 for any variable in any term of any function (whether the objective function or the function on the left-hand side of a functional constraint) in a linear programming model.[1]

To illustrate this assumption, consider the first term $(3x_1)$ in the objective function $(Z = 3x_1 + 5x_2)$ for the Wyndor Glass Co. problem. This term represents the profit generated per week (in thousands of dollars) by producing product 1 at the rate of x_1 batches per week. The *proportionality satisfied* column of Table 3.4 shows the case that was assumed in Sec. 3.1, namely, that this profit is indeed proportional to x_1 so that $3x_1$ is the appropriate term for the objective function. By contrast, the next three columns show different hypothetical cases where the proportionality assumption would be violated.

Refer first to the *Case 1* column in Table 3.4. This case would arise if there were *start-up costs* associated with initiating the production of product 1. For example, there

[1]When the function includes any *cross-product terms,* proportionality should be interpreted to mean that *changes* in the function value are proportional to *changes* in each variable (x_j) individually, given any fixed values for all the other variables. Therefore, a cross-product term satisfies proportionality as long as each variable in the term has an exponent of 1. (However, any cross-product term violates the *additivity assumption,* discussed next.)

TABLE 3.4 Examples of satisfying or violating proportionality

	Profit from Product 1 ($000 per Week)			
	Proportionality Satisfied	Proportionality Violated		
x_1		Case 1	Case 2	Case 3
0	0	0	0	0
1	3	2	3	3
2	6	5	7	5
3	9	8	12	6
4	12	11	18	6

might be costs involved with setting up the production facilities. There might also be costs associated with arranging the distribution of the new product. Because these are one-time costs, they would need to be amortized on a per-week basis to be commensurable with Z (profit in thousands of dollars per week). Suppose that this amortization were done and that the total start-up cost amounted to reducing Z by 1, but that the profit without considering the start-up cost would be $3x_1$. This would mean that the contribution from product 1 to Z should be $3x_1 - 1$ for $x_1 > 0$, whereas the contribution would be $3x_1 = 0$ when $x_1 = 0$ (no start-up cost). This profit function,[1] which is given by the solid curve in Fig. 3.8, certainly is *not* proportional to x_1.

   At first glance, it might appear that *Case 2* in Table 3.4 is quite similar to Case 1. However, Case 2 actually arises in a very different way. There no longer is a start-up cost, and the profit from the first unit of product 1 per week is indeed 3, as originally assumed. However, there now is an *increasing marginal return;* i.e., the *slope* of the *profit function* for product 1 (see the solid curve in Fig. 3.9) keeps increasing as x_1 is increased. This violation of proportionality might occur because of economies of scale that can sometimes be achieved at higher levels of production, e.g., through the use of more efficient high-volume machinery, longer production runs, quantity discounts for large purchases of raw materials, and the learning-curve effect whereby workers become more efficient as they gain experience with a particular mode of production. As the incremental cost goes down, the incremental profit will go up (assuming constant marginal revenue).

---

[1]If the contribution from product 1 to Z were $3x_1 - 1$ for *all* $x_1 \geq 0$, including $x_1 = 0$, then the fixed constant, -1, could be deleted from the objective function without changing the optimal solution and proportionality would be restored. However, this "fix" does not work here because the -1 constant does not apply when $x_1 = 0$.

FIGURE 3.8
The solid curve violates the proportionality assumption because of the start-up cost that is incurred when x_1 is increased from 0. The values at the dots are given by the Case 1 column of Table 3.4.

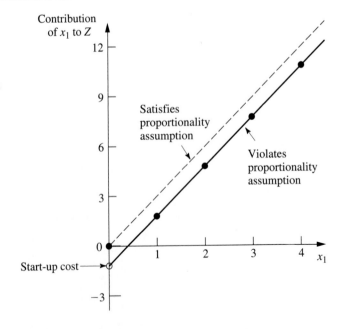

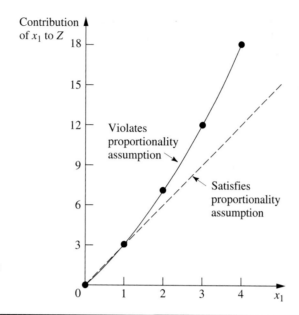

FIGURE 3.9
The solid curve violates the proportionality assumption because its slope (the *marginal return* from product 1) keeps increasing as x_1 is increased. The values at the dots are given by the Case 2 column of Table 3.4.

Referring again to Table 3.4, the reverse of Case 2 is *Case 3,* where there is a *decreasing marginal return.* In this case, the *slope* of the *profit function* for product 1 (given by the solid curve in Fig. 3.10) keeps decreasing as x_1 is increased. This violation of proportionality might occur because the *marketing costs* need to go up more than proportionally to attain increases in the level of sales. For example, it might be possible to sell product 1 at the rate of 1 per week ($x_1 = 1$) with no advertising, whereas attaining sales to sustain a production rate of $x_1 = 2$ might require a moderate amount of advertising, $x_1 = 3$ might necessitate an extensive advertising campaign, and $x_1 = 4$ might require also lowering the price.

All three cases are hypothetical examples of ways in which the proportionality assumption could be violated. What is the actual situation? The actual profit from produc-

FIGURE 3.10
The solid curve violates the proportionality assumption because its slope (the *marginal return* from product 1) keeps decreasing as x_1 is increased. The values at the dots are given by the Case 3 column in Table 3.4.

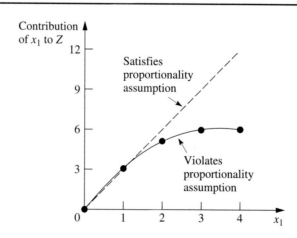

ing product 1 (or any other product) is derived from the sales revenue minus various direct and indirect costs. Inevitably, some of these cost components are not strictly proportional to the production rate, perhaps for one of the reasons illustrated above. However, the real question is whether, after all the components of profit have been accumulated, proportionality is a reasonable approximation for practical modeling purposes. For the Wyndor Glass Co. problem, the OR team checked both the objective function and the functional constraints. The conclusion was that proportionality could indeed be assumed without serious distortion.

For other problems, what happens when the proportionality assumption does not hold even as a reasonable approximation? In most cases, this means you must use *nonlinear programming* instead (presented in Chap. 13). However, we do point out in Sec. 13.8 that a certain important kind of nonproportionality can still be handled by linear programming by reformulating the problem appropriately. Furthermore, if the assumption is violated only because of start-up costs, there is an extension of linear programming (*mixed integer programming*) that can be used, as discussed in Sec. 12.3 (the fixed-charge problem).

Additivity

Although the proportionality assumption rules out exponents other than 1, it does not prohibit *cross-product terms* (terms involving the product of two or more variables). The additivity assumption does rule out this latter possibility, as summarized below.

> **Additivity assumption:** *Every* function in a linear programming model (whether the objective function or the function on the left-hand side of a functional constraint) is the *sum* of the *individual contributions* of the respective activities.

To make this definition more concrete and clarify why we need to worry about this assumption, let us look at some examples. Table 3.5 shows some possible cases for the objective function for the Wyndor Glass Co. problem. In each case, the *individual contributions* from the products are just as assumed in Sec. 3.1, namely, $3x_1$ for product 1 and $5x_2$ for product 2. The difference lies in the last row, which gives the *function value* for Z when the two products are produced jointly. The *additivity satisfied* column shows the case where this *function value* is obtained simply by adding the first two rows ($3 + 5 = 8$), so that $Z = 3x_1 + 5x_2$ as previously assumed. By contrast, the next two columns show hypothetical cases where the additivity assumption would be violated (but not the proportionality assumption).

TABLE 3.5 Examples of satisfying or violating additivity for the objective function

| | | Value of Z | |
| | | Additivity Violated | |
(x_1, x_2)	Additivity Satisfied	Case 1	Case 2
(1, 0)	3	3	3
(0, 1)	5	5	5
(1, 1)	8	9	7

Referring to the *Case 1* column of Table 3.5, this case corresponds to an objective function of $Z = 3x_1 + 5x_2 + x_1x_2$, so that $Z = 3 + 5 + 1 = 9$ for $(x_1, x_2) = (1, 1)$, thereby violating the additivity assumption that $Z = 3 + 5$. (The proportionality assumption still is satisfied since after the value of one variable is fixed, the increment in Z from the other variable is proportional to the value of that variable.) This case would arise if the two products were *complementary* in some way that *increases* profit. For example, suppose that a major advertising campaign would be required to market either new product produced by itself, but that the same single campaign can effectively promote both products if the decision is made to produce both. Because a major cost is saved for the second product, their joint profit is somewhat more than the *sum* of their individual profits when each is produced by itself.

Case 2 in Table 3.5 also violates the additivity assumption because of the extra term in the corresponding objective function, $Z = 3x_1 + 5x_2 - x_1x_2$, so that $Z = 3 + 5 - 1 = 7$ for $(x_1, x_2) = (1, 1)$. As the reverse of the first case, Case 2 would arise if the two products were *competitive* in some way that *decreased* their joint profit. For example, suppose that both products need to use the same machinery and equipment. If either product were produced by itself, this machinery and equipment would be dedicated to this one use. However, producing both products would require switching the production processes back and forth, with substantial time and cost involved in temporarily shutting down the production of one product and setting up for the other. Because of this major extra cost, their joint profit is somewhat less than the *sum* of their individual profits when each is produced by itself.

The same kinds of interaction between activities can affect the additivity of the constraint functions. For example, consider the third functional constraint of the Wyndor Glass Co. problem: $3x_1 + 2x_2 \leq 18$. (This is the only constraint involving both products.) This constraint concerns the production capacity of Plant 3, where 18 hours of production time per week is available for the two new products, and the function on the left-hand side $(3x_1 + 2x_2)$ represents the number of hours of production time per week that would be used by these products. The *additivity satisfied* column of Table 3.6 shows this case as is, whereas the next two columns display cases where the function has an extra cross-product term that violates additivity. For all three columns, the *individual contributions* from the products toward using the capacity of Plant 3 are just as assumed previously, namely, $3x_1$ for product 1 and $2x_2$ for product 2, or $3(2) = 6$ for $x_1 = 2$ and $2(3) = 6$ for

TABLE 3.6 Examples of satisfying or violating additivity for a functional constraint

| | | Amount of Resource Used | |
| | | | Additivity Violated |
(x_1, x_2)	Additivity Satisfied	Case 3	Case 4
(2, 0)	6	6	6
(0, 3)	6	6	6
(2, 3)	12	15	10.8

$x_2 = 3$. As was true for Table 3.5, the difference lies in the last row, which now gives the *total function value* for production time used when the two products are produced jointly.

For Case 3 (see Table 3.6), the production time used by the two products is given by the function $3x_1 + 2x_2 + 0.5x_1x_2$, so the *total function value* is $6 + 6 + 3 = 15$ when $(x_1, x_2) = (2, 3)$, which violates the additivity assumption that the value is just $6 + 6 = 12$. This case can arise in exactly the same way as described for Case 2 in Table 3.5; namely, extra time is wasted switching the production processes back and forth between the two products. The extra cross-product term $(0.5x_1x_2)$ would give the production time wasted in this way. (Note that wasting time switching between products leads to a positive cross-product term here, where the total function is measuring production time used, whereas it led to a negative cross-product term for Case 2 because the total function there measures profit.)

For Case 4 in Table 3.6, the function for production time used is $3x_1 + 2x_2 - 0.1x_1^2x_2$, so the *function value* for $(x_1, x_2) = (2, 3)$ is $6 + 6 - 1.2 = 10.8$. This case could arise in the following way. As in Case 3, suppose that the two products require the same type of machinery and equipment. But suppose now that the time required to switch from one product to the other would be relatively small. Because each product goes through a sequence of production operations, individual production facilities normally dedicated to that product would incur occasional idle periods. During these otherwise idle periods, these facilities can be used by the other product. Consequently, the total production time used (including idle periods) when the two products are produced jointly would be less than the *sum* of the production times used by the individual products when each is produced by itself.

After analyzing the possible kinds of interaction between the two products illustrated by these four cases, the OR team concluded that none played a major role in the actual Wyndor Glass Co. problem. Therefore, the additivity assumption was adopted as a reasonable approximation.

For other problems, if additivity is not a reasonable assumption, so that some of or all the mathematical functions of the model need to be *nonlinear* (because of the cross-product terms), you definitely enter the realm of nonlinear programming (Chap. 13).

Divisibility

Our next assumption concerns the values allowed for the decision variables.

> **Divisibility assumption:** Decision variables in a linear programming model are allowed to have *any* values, including *noninteger* values, that satisfy the functional and nonnegativity constraints. Thus, these variables are *not* restricted to just integer values. Since each decision variable represents the level of some activity, it is being assumed that the activities can be run at *fractional levels*.

For the Wyndor Glass Co. problem, the decision variables represent production rates (the number of batches of a product produced per week). Since these production rates can have *any* fractional values within the feasible region, the divisibility assumption does hold.

In certain situations, the divisibility assumption does not hold because some of or all the decision variables must be restricted to *integer values*. Mathematical models with this restriction are called *integer programming* models, and they are discussed in Chap. 12.

Certainty

Our last assumption concerns the *parameters* of the model, namely, the coefficients in the objective function c_j, the coefficients in the functional constraints a_{ij}, and the right-hand sides of the functional constraints b_i.

> **Certainty assumption:** The value assigned to each parameter of a linear programming model is assumed to be a *known constant*.

In real applications, the certainty assumption is seldom satisfied precisely. Linear programming models usually are formulated to select some future course of action. Therefore, the parameter values used would be based on a prediction of future conditions, which inevitably introduces some degree of uncertainty.

For this reason it is usually important to conduct **sensitivity analysis** after a solution is found that is optimal under the assumed parameter values. As discussed in Sec. 2.3, one purpose is to identify the *sensitive* parameters (those whose value cannot be changed without changing the optimal solution), since any later change in the value of a sensitive parameter immediately signals a need to change the solution being used.

Sensitivity analysis plays an important role in the analysis of the Wyndor Glass Co. problem, as you will see in Sec. 6.7. However, it is necessary to acquire some more background before we finish that story.

Occasionally, the degree of uncertainty in the parameters is too great to be amenable to sensitivity analysis. In this case, it is necessary to treat the parameters explicitly as *random variables*. Formulations of this kind have been developed, as discussed in Secs. 23.6 and 23.7 on the book's web site, www.mhhe.com/hillier.

The Assumptions in Perspective

We emphasized in Sec. 2.2 that a mathematical model is intended to be only an idealized representation of the real problem. Approximations and simplifying assumptions generally are required in order for the model to be tractable. Adding too much detail and precision can make the model too unwieldy for useful analysis of the problem. All that is really needed is that there be a reasonably high correlation between the prediction of the model and what would actually happen in the real problem.

This advice certainly is applicable to linear programming. It is very common in real applications of linear programming that almost *none* of the four assumptions hold completely. Except perhaps for the *divisibility assumption,* minor disparities are to be expected. This is especially true for the *certainty assumption,* so sensitivity analysis normally is a must to compensate for the violation of this assumption.

However, it is important for the OR team to examine the four assumptions for the problem under study and to analyze just how large the disparities are. If any of the assumptions are violated in a major way, then a number of useful alternative models are available, as presented in later chapters of the book. A disadvantage of these other models is that the algorithms available for solving them are not nearly as powerful as those for linear programming, but this gap has been closing in some cases. For some applications, the powerful linear programming approach is used for the initial analysis, and then a more complicated model is used to refine this analysis.

As you work through the examples in the next section, you will find it good practice to analyze how well each of the four assumptions of linear programming applies.

3.4 ADDITIONAL EXAMPLES

The Wyndor Glass Co. problem is a prototype example of linear programming in several respects: It involves allocating limited resources among competing activities, its model fits our standard form, and its context is the traditional one of improved business planning. However, the applicability of linear programming is much wider. In this section we begin broadening our horizons. As you study the following examples, note that it is their underlying mathematical model rather than their context that characterizes them as linear programming problems. Then give some thought to how the same mathematical model could arise in many other contexts by merely changing the names of the activities and so forth.

These examples are scaled-down versions of actual applications (including two that are included in the case studies presented in the next section).

Design of Radiation Therapy

MARY has just been diagnosed as having a cancer at a fairly advanced stage. Specifically, she has a large malignant tumor in the bladder area (a "whole bladder lesion").

Mary is to receive the most advanced medical care available to give her every possible chance for survival. This care will include extensive *radiation therapy*.

Radiation therapy involves using an external beam treatment machine to pass ionizing radiation through the patient's body, damaging both cancerous and healthy tissues. Normally, several beams are precisely administered from different angles in a two-dimensional plane. Due to attenuation, each beam delivers more radiation to the tissue near the entry point than to the tissue near the exit point. Scatter also causes some delivery of radiation to tissue outside the direct path of the beam. Because tumor cells are typically microscopically interspersed among healthy cells, the radiation dosage throughout the tumor region must be large enough to kill the malignant cells, which are slightly more radiosensitive, yet small enough to spare the healthy cells. At the same time, the aggregate dose to critical tissues must not exceed established tolerance levels, in order to prevent complications that can be more serious than the disease itself. For the same reason, the total dose to the entire healthy anatomy must be minimized.

Because of the need to carefully balance all these factors, the design of radiation therapy is a very delicate process. The goal of the design is to select the combination of beams to be used, and the intensity of each one, to generate the best possible dose distribution. (The dose strength at any point in the body is measured in units called *kilorads*.) Once the treatment design has been developed, it is administered in many installments, spread over several weeks.

In Mary's case, the size and location of her tumor make the design of her treatment an even more delicate process than usual. Figure 3.11 shows a diagram of a cross section of the tumor viewed from above, as well as nearby critical tissues to avoid. These tissues include critical organs (e.g., the rectum) as well as bony structures (e.g., the femurs and pelvis) that will attenuate the radiation. Also shown are the entry point and direction for the only two beams that can be used with any modicum of safety in this case. (Actually,

FIGURE 3.11
Cross section of Mary's tumor (viewed from above), nearby critical tissues, and the radiation beams being used.

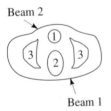

Beam 2

Beam 1

1. Bladder and tumor
2. Rectum, coccyx, etc.
3. Femur, part of pelvis, etc.

we are simplifying the example at this point, because normally dozens of possible beams must be considered.)

For any proposed beam of given intensity, the analysis of what the resulting radiation absorption by various parts of the body would be requires a complicated process. In brief, based on careful anatomical analysis, the energy distribution within the two-dimensional cross section of the tissue can be plotted on an isodose map, where the contour lines represent the dose strength as a percentage of the dose strength at the entry point. A fine grid then is placed over the isodose map. By summing the radiation absorbed in the squares containing each type of tissue, the average dose that is absorbed by the tumor, healthy anatomy, and critical tissues can be calculated. With more than one beam (administered sequentially), the radiation absorption is additive.

After thorough analysis of this type, the medical team has carefully estimated the data needed to design Mary's treatment, as summarized in Table 3.7. The first column lists the areas of the body that must be considered, and then the next two columns give the fraction of the radiation dose at the entry point for each beam that is absorbed by the respective areas on average. For example, if the dose level at the entry point for beam 1 is 1 kilorad, then an average of 0.4 kilorad will be absorbed by the entire healthy anatomy in the two-dimensional plane, an average of 0.3 kilorad will be absorbed by nearby critical tissues, an average of 0.5 kilorad will be absorbed by the various parts of the tumor, and 0.6 kilorad will be absorbed by the center of the tumor. The last column gives the restrictions on the total dosage from both beams that is absorbed on average by the respective areas of the body. In particular, the average dosage absorption for the healthy anatomy must be *as small as possible,* the critical tissues must *not exceed* 2.7 kilorads, the average over the entire tumor must *equal* 6 kilorads, and the center of the tumor must be *at least* 6 kilorads.

Formulation as a Linear Programming Problem. The two decision variables x_1 and x_2 represent the dose (in kilorads) at the entry point for beam 1 and beam 2, respectively. Because the total dosage reaching the healthy anatomy is to be minimized, let Z denote this quantity. The data from Table 3.7 can then be used directly to formulate the following linear programming model.[1]

---

[1]Actually, Table 3.7 simplifies the real situation, so the real model would be somewhat more complicated than this one and would have dozens of variables and constraints. For details about the general situation, see D. Sonderman and P. G. Abrahamson, "Radiotherapy Treatment Design Using Mathematical Programming Models," *Operations Research,* **33:**705–725, 1985, and its ref. 1.

TABLE 3.7 Data for the design of Mary's radiation therapy

Area	Fraction of Entry Dose Absorbed by Area (Average)		Restriction on Total Average Dosage, Kilorads
	Beam 1	Beam 2	
Healthy anatomy	0.4	0.5	Minimize
Critical tissues	0.3	0.1	≤ 2.7
Tumor region	0.5	0.5	= 6
Center of tumor	0.6	0.4	≥ 6

$$\text{Minimize} \qquad Z = 0.4x_1 + 0.5x_2,$$

subject to

$$0.3x_1 + 0.1x_2 \leq 2.7$$
$$0.5x_1 + 0.5x_2 = 6$$
$$0.6x_1 + 0.4x_2 \geq 6$$

and

$$x_1 \geq 0, \qquad x_2 \geq 0.$$

Notice the differences between this model and the one in Sec. 3.1 for the Wyndor Glass Co. problem. The latter model involved *maximizing Z,* and all the functional constraints were in $\leq$ form. This new model does not fit this same standard form, but it does incorporate three other *legitimate* forms described in Sec. 3.2, namely, *minimizing Z,* functional constraints in $=$ form, and functional constraints in $\geq$ form.

However, both models have only two variables, so this new problem also can be solved by the *graphical method* illustrated in Sec. 3.1. Figure 3.12 shows the graphical solution. The *feasible region* consists of just the dark line segment between (6, 6) and (7.5, 4.5), because the points on this segment are the only ones that simultaneously satisfy all the constraints. (Note that the equality constraint limits the feasible region to the line containing this line segment, and then the other two functional constraints determine the two endpoints of the line segment.) The dashed line is the objective function line that passes through the optimal solution $(x_1, x_2) = (7.5, 4.5)$ with $Z = 5.25$. This solution is optimal rather than the point (6, 6) because *decreasing Z* (for positive values of Z) pushes the objective function line toward the origin (where $Z = 0$). And $Z = 5.25$ for (7.5, 4.5) is less than $Z = 5.4$ for (6, 6).

Thus, the optimal design is to use a total dose at the entry point of 7.5 kilorads for beam 1 and 4.5 kilorads for beam 2.

Regional Planning

The SOUTHERN CONFEDERATION OF KIBBUTZIM is a group of three kibbutzim (communal farming communities) in Israel. Overall planning for this group is done in its Coordinating Technical Office. This office currently is planning agricultural production for the coming year.

The agricultural output of each kibbutz is limited by both the amount of available irrigable land and the quantity of water allocated for irrigation by the Water Commissioner (a national government official). These data are given in Table 3.8.

TABLE 3.8 Resource data for the Southern Confederation of Kibbutzim

Kibbutz	Usable Land (Acres)	Water Allocation (Acre Feet)
1	400	600
2	600	800
3	300	375

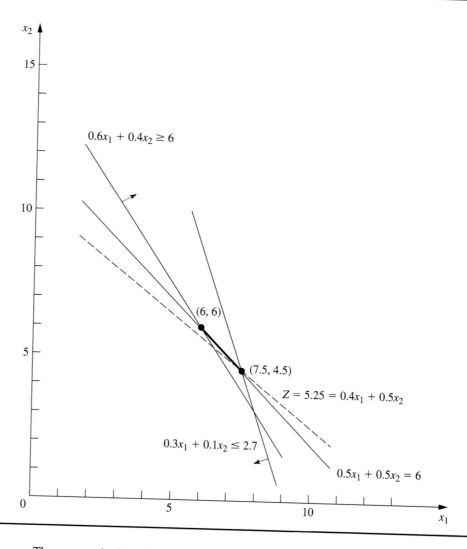

FIGURE 3.12
Graphical solution for the design of Mary's radiation therapy.

The crops suited for this region include sugar beets, cotton, and sorghum, and these are the three being considered for the upcoming season. These crops differ primarily in their expected net return per acre and their consumption of water. In addition, the Ministry of Agriculture has set a maximum quota for the total acreage that can be devoted to each of these crops by the Southern Confederation of Kibbutzim, as shown in Table 3.9.

TABLE 3.9 Crop data for the Southern Confederation of Kibbutzim

Crop	Maximum Quota (Acres)	Water Consumption (Acre Feet/Acre)	Net Return ($/Acre)
Sugar beets	600	3	1,000
Cotton	500	2	750
Sorghum	325	1	250

Because of the limited water available for irrigation, the Southern Confederation of Kibbutzim will not be able to use all its irrigable land for planting crops in the upcoming season. To ensure equity between the three kibbutzim, it has been agreed that every kibbutz will plant the same proportion of its available irrigable land. For example, if kibbutz 1 plants 200 of its available 400 acres, then kibbutz 2 must plant 300 of its 600 acres, while kibbutz 3 plants 150 acres of its 300 acres. However, any combination of the crops may be grown at any of the kibbutzim. The job facing the Coordinating Technical Office is to plan how many acres to devote to each crop at the respective kibbutzim while satisfying the given restrictions. The objective is to maximize the total net return to the Southern Confederation of Kibbutzim as a whole.

Formulation as a Linear Programming Problem.   The quantities to be decided upon are the number of acres to devote to each of the three crops at each of the three kibbutzim. The decision variables x_j ($j = 1, 2, \ldots, 9$) represent these nine quantities, as shown in Table 3.10.

Since the measure of effectiveness Z is the total net return, the resulting linear programming model for this problem is

$$\text{Maximize} \quad Z = 1{,}000(x_1 + x_2 + x_3) + 750(x_4 + x_5 + x_6) + 250(x_7 + x_8 + x_9),$$

subject to the following constraints:

1. Usable land for each kibbutz:

$$x_1 + x_4 + x_7 \leq 400$$
$$x_2 + x_5 + x_8 \leq 600$$
$$x_3 + x_6 + x_9 \leq 300$$

2. Water allocation for each kibbutz:

$$3x_1 + 2x_4 + x_7 \leq 600$$
$$3x_2 + 2x_5 + x_8 \leq 800$$
$$3x_3 + 2x_6 + x_9 \leq 375$$

3. Total acreage for each crop:

$$x_1 + x_2 + x_3 \leq 600$$
$$x_4 + x_5 + x_6 \leq 500$$
$$x_7 + x_8 + x_9 \leq 325$$

TABLE 3.10 Decision variables for the Southern Confederation of Kibbutzim problem

	Allocation (Acres)		
	Kibbutz		
Crop	1	2	3
Sugar beets	x_1	x_2	x_3
Cotton	x_4	x_5	x_6
Sorghum	x_7	x_8	x_9

4. Equal proportion of land planted:

$$\frac{x_1 + x_4 + x_7}{400} = \frac{x_2 + x_5 + x_8}{600}$$

$$\frac{x_2 + x_5 + x_8}{600} = \frac{x_3 + x_6 + x_9}{300}$$

$$\frac{x_3 + x_6 + x_9}{300} = \frac{x_1 + x_4 + x_7}{400}$$

5. Nonnegativity:

$$x_j \geq 0, \qquad \text{for } j = 1, 2, \ldots, 9.$$

This completes the model, except that the equality constraints are not yet in an appropriate form for a linear programming model because some of the variables are on the right-hand side. Hence, their final form[1] is

$$3(x_1 + x_4 + x_7) - 2(x_2 + x_5 + x_8) = 0$$
$$(x_2 + x_5 + x_8) - 2(x_3 + x_6 + x_9) = 0$$
$$4(x_3 + x_6 + x_9) - 3(x_1 + x_4 + x_7) = 0$$

The Coordinating Technical Office formulated this model and then applied the simplex method (developed in the next chapter) to find an optimal solution

$$(x_1, x_2, x_3, x_4, x_5, x_6, x_7, x_8, x_9) = \left(133\frac{1}{3}, 100, 25, 100, 250, 150, 0, 0, 0\right),$$

as shown in Table 3.11. The resulting optimal value of the objective function is $Z = 633,333\frac{1}{3}$, that is, a total net return of $633,333.33.

---

[1]Actually, any one of these equations is redundant and can be deleted if desired. Also, because of these equations, any two of the usable land constraints also could be deleted because they automatically would be satisfied when both the remaining usable land constraint and these equations are satisfied. However, no harm is done (except a little more computational effort) by including unnecessary constraints, so you don't need to worry about identifying and deleting them in models you formulate.

TABLE 3.11 Optimal solution for the Southern Confederation of Kibbutzim problem

| | Best Allocation (Acres) | | |
| | Kibbutz | | |
Crop	1	2	3
Sugar beets	$133\frac{1}{3}$	100	25
Cotton	100	250	150
Sorghum	0	0	0

Controlling Air Pollution

The NORI & LEETS CO., one of the major producers of steel in its part of the world, is located in the city of Steeltown and is the only large employer there. Steeltown has grown and prospered along with the company, which now employs nearly 50,000 residents. Therefore, the attitude of the townspeople always has been, "What's good for Nori & Leets is good for the town." However, this attitude is now changing; uncontrolled air pollution from the company's furnaces is ruining the appearance of the city and endangering the health of its residents.

A recent stockholders' revolt resulted in the election of a new enlightened board of directors for the company. These directors are determined to follow socially responsible policies, and they have been discussing with Steeltown city officials and citizens' groups what to do about the air pollution problem. Together they have worked out stringent air quality standards for the Steeltown airshed.

The three main types of pollutants in this airshed are particulate matter, sulfur oxides, and hydrocarbons. The new standards require that the company reduce its annual emission of these pollutants by the amounts shown in Table 3.12. The board of directors has instructed management to have the engineering staff determine how to achieve these reductions in the most economical way.

The steelworks has two primary sources of pollution, namely, the blast furnaces for making pig iron and the open-hearth furnaces for changing iron into steel. In both cases the engineers have decided that the most effective types of abatement methods are (1) increasing the height of the smokestacks,[1] (2) using filter devices (including gas traps) in the smokestacks, and (3) including cleaner, high-grade materials among the fuels for the furnaces. Each of these methods has a technological limit on how heavily it can be used (e.g., a maximum feasible increase in the height of the smokestacks), but there also is considerable flexibility for using the method at a fraction of its technological limit.

Table 3.13 shows how much emission (in millions of pounds per year) can be eliminated from each type of furnace by fully using any abatement method to its technological limit. For purposes of analysis, it is assumed that each method also can be used less fully to achieve any fraction of the emission-rate reductions shown in this table. Furthermore, the fractions can be different for blast furnaces and for open-hearth furnaces. For either type of furnace, the emission reduction achieved by each method is not substantially affected by whether the other methods also are used.

---

[1]Subsequent to this study, this particular abatement method has become a controversial one. Because its effect is to reduce ground-level pollution by spreading emissions over a greater distance, environmental groups contend that this creates more acid rain by keeping sulfur oxides in the air longer. Consequently, the U.S. Environmental Protection Agency adopted new rules in 1985 to remove incentives for using tall smokestacks.

TABLE 3.12 Clean air standards for the Nori & Leets Co.

Pollutant	Required Reduction in Annual Emission Rate (Million Pounds)
Particulates	60
Sulfur oxides	150
Hydrocarbons	125

TABLE 3.13 Reduction in emission rate (in millions of pounds per year) from the maximum feasible use of an abatement method for Nori & Leets Co.

Pollutant	Taller Smokestacks		Filters		Better Fuels	
	Blast Furnaces	Open-Hearth Furnaces	Blast Furnaces	Open-Hearth Furnaces	Blast Furnaces	Open-Hearth Furnaces
Particulates	12	9	25	20	17	13
Sulfur oxides	35	42	18	31	56	49
Hydrocarbons	37	53	28	24	29	20

After these data were developed, it became clear that no single method by itself could achieve all the required reductions. On the other hand, combining all three methods at full capacity on both types of furnaces (which would be prohibitively expensive if the company's products are to remain competitively priced) is much more than adequate. Therefore, the engineers concluded that they would have to use some combination of the methods, perhaps with fractional capacities, based upon the relative costs. Furthermore, because of the differences between the blast and the open-hearth furnaces, the two types probably should not use the same combination.

An analysis was conducted to estimate the total annual cost that would be incurred by each abatement method. A method's annual cost includes increased operating and maintenance expenses as well as reduced revenue due to any loss in the efficiency of the production process caused by using the method. The other major cost is the *start-up cost* (the initial capital outlay) required to install the method. To make this one-time cost commensurable with the ongoing annual costs, the time value of money was used to calculate the annual expenditure (over the expected life of the method) that would be equivalent in value to this start-up cost.

This analysis led to the total annual cost estimates (in millions of dollars) given in Table 3.14 for using the methods at their full abatement capacities. It also was determined that the cost of a method being used at a lower level is roughly proportional to the fraction of the abatement capacity given in Table 3.13 that is achieved. Thus, for any given fraction achieved, the total annual cost would be roughly that fraction of the corresponding quantity in Table 3.14.

The stage now was set to develop the general framework of the company's plan for pollution abatement. This plan specifies which types of abatement methods will be used and at what fractions of their abatement capacities for (1) the blast furnaces and (2) the open-hearth furnaces. Because of the combinatorial nature of the problem of finding a

TABLE 3.14 Total annual cost from the maximum feasible use of an abatement method for Nori & Leets Co. ($ millions)

Abatement Method	Blast Furnaces	Open-Hearth Furnaces
Taller smokestacks	8	10
Filters	7	6
Better fuels	11	9

plan that satisfies the requirements with the smallest possible cost, an OR team was formed to solve the problem. The team adopted a linear programming approach, formulating the model summarized next.

Formulation as a Linear Programming Problem.   This problem has six decision variables x_j, $j = 1, 2, \ldots, 6$, each representing the use of one of the three abatement methods for one of the two types of furnaces, expressed as a *fraction of the abatement capacity* (so x_j cannot exceed 1). The ordering of these variables is shown in Table 3.15. Because the objective is to minimize total cost while satisfying the emission reduction requirements, the data in Tables 3.12, 3.13, and 3.14 yield the following model:

$$\text{Minimize} \quad Z = 8x_1 + 10x_2 + 7x_3 + 6x_4 + 11x_5 + 9x_6,$$

subject to the following constraints:

1. Emission reduction:

$$
\begin{aligned}
12x_1 + 9x_2 + 25x_3 + 20x_4 + 17x_5 + 13x_6 &\geq 60 \\
35x_1 + 42x_2 + 18x_3 + 31x_4 + 56x_5 + 49x_6 &\geq 150 \\
37x_1 + 53x_2 + 28x_3 + 24x_4 + 29x_5 + 20x_6 &\geq 125
\end{aligned}
$$

2. Technological limit:

$$x_j \leq 1, \quad \text{for } j = 1, 2, \ldots, 6$$

3. Nonnegativity:

$$x_j \geq 0, \quad \text{for } j = 1, 2, \ldots, 6.$$

The OR team used this model[1] to find a minimum-cost plan

$$(x_1, x_2, x_3, x_4, x_5, x_6) = (1, 0.623, 0.343, 1, 0.048, 1),$$

with $Z = 32.16$ (total annual cost of \$32.16 million). Sensitivity analysis then was conducted to explore the effect of making possible adjustments in the air standards given in Table 3.12, as well as to check on the effect of any inaccuracies in the cost data given in Table 3.14. (This story is continued in Case 6.1 at the end of Chap. 6.) Next came detailed planning and managerial review. Soon after, this program for controlling air pollution was fully implemented by the company, and the citizens of Steeltown breathed deep (cleaner) sighs of relief.

---

[1] An equivalent formulation can express each decision variable in natural units for its abatement method; for example, x_1 and x_2 could represent the number of *feet* that the heights of the smokestacks are increased.

TABLE 3.15 Decision variables (fraction of the maximum feasible use of an abatement method) for Nori & Leets Co.

Abatement Method	Blast Furnaces	Open-Hearth Furnaces
Taller smokestacks	x_1	x_2
Filters	x_3	x_4
Better fuels	x_5	x_6

Reclaiming Solid Wastes

The SAVE-IT COMPANY operates a reclamation center that collects four types of solid waste materials and treats them so that they can be amalgamated into a salable product. (Treating and amalgamating are separate processes.) Three different grades of this product can be made (see the first column of Table 3.16), depending upon the mix of the materials used. Although there is some flexibility in the mix for each grade, quality standards may specify the minimum or maximum amount allowed for the proportion of a material in the product grade. (This proportion is the weight of the material expressed as a percentage of the total weight for the product grade.) For each of the two higher grades, a fixed percentage is specified for one of the materials. These specifications are given in Table 3.16 along with the cost of amalgamation and the selling price for each grade.

The reclamation center collects its solid waste materials from regular sources and so is normally able to maintain a steady rate for treating them. Table 3.17 gives the quantities available for collection and treatment each week, as well as the cost of treatment, for each type of material.

The Save-It Co. is solely owned by Green Earth, an organization devoted to dealing with environmental issues, so Save-It's profits are used to help support Green Earth's activities. Green Earth has raised contributions and grants, amounting to $30,000 per week, to be used exclusively to cover the entire treatment cost for the solid waste materials. The board of directors of Green Earth has instructed the management of Save-It to divide this money among the materials in such a way that *at least half* of the amount available of each material is actually collected and treated. These additional restrictions are listed in Table 3.17.

Within the restrictions specified in Tables 3.16 and 3.17, management wants to determine the *amount* of each product grade to produce *and* the exact *mix* of materials to be used for each grade. The objective is to maximize the net weekly profit (total sales income *minus* total amalgamation cost), exclusive of the fixed treatment cost of $30,000 per week that is being covered by gifts and grants.

Formulation as a Linear Programming Problem. Before attempting to construct a linear programming model, we must give careful consideration to the proper definition of the decision variables. Although this definition is often obvious, it sometimes becomes

TABLE 3.16 Product data for Save-It Co.

Grade	Specification	Amalgamation Cost per Pound ($)	Selling Price per Pound ($)
A	Material 1: Not more than 30% of total Material 2: Not less than 40% of total Material 3: Not more than 50% of total Material 4: Exactly 20% of total	3.00	8.50
B	Material 1: Not more than 50% of total Material 2: Not less than 10% of total Material 4: Exactly 10% of total	2.50	7.00
C	Material 1: Not more than 70% of total	2.00	5.50

TABLE 3.17 Solid waste materials data for the Save-It Co.

Material	Pounds per Week Available	Treatment Cost per Pound ($)	Additional Restrictions
1	3,000	3.00	1. For each material, at least half of the
2	2,000	6.00	pounds per week available should be
3	4,000	4.00	collected and treated.
4	1,000	5.00	2. $30,000 per week should be used to
			treat these materials.

the crux of the entire formulation. After clearly identifying what information is really desired and the most convenient form for conveying this information by means of decision variables, we can develop the objective function and the constraints on the values of these decision variables.

In this particular problem, the decisions to be made are well defined, but the appropriate means of conveying this information may require some thought. (Try it and see if you first obtain the following *inappropriate* choice of decision variables.)

Because one set of decisions is the *amount* of each product grade to produce, it would seem natural to define one set of decision variables accordingly. Proceeding tentatively along this line, we define

y_i = number of pounds of product grade i produced per week   ($i = A, B, C$).

The other set of decisions is the *mix* of materials for each product grade. This mix is identified by the proportion of each material in the product grade, which would suggest defining the other set of decision variables as

z_{ij} = proportion of material j in product grade i ($i = A, B, C; j = 1, 2, 3, 4$).

However, Table 3.17 gives both the treatment cost and the availability of the materials by *quantity* (pounds) rather than *proportion,* so it is this *quantity* information that needs to be recorded in some of the constraints. For material j ($j = 1, 2, 3, 4$),

Number of pounds of material j used per week = $z_{Aj}y_A + z_{Bj}y_B + z_{Cj}y_C$.

For example, since Table 3.17 indicates that 3,000 pounds of material 1 is available per week, one constraint in the model would be

$z_{A1}y_A + z_{B1}y_B + z_{C1}y_C \leq 3,000.$

Unfortunately, this is not a legitimate linear programming constraint. The expression on the left-hand side is *not* a linear function because it involves products of variables. Therefore, a linear programming model cannot be constructed with these decision variables.

Fortunately, there is another way of defining the decision variables that will fit the linear programming format. (Do you see how to do it?) It is accomplished by merely replacing each *product* of the old decision variables by a single variable! In other words, define

$x_{ij} = z_{ij}y_i$ (for $i = A, B, C; j = 1, 2, 3, 4$)
      = number of pounds of material j allocated to product grade i per week,

and then we let the x_{ij} be the decision variables. Combining the x_{ij} in different ways yields the following quantities needed in the model (for $i = A,\ B,\ C;\ j = 1,\ 2,\ 3,\ 4$).

$$x_{i1} + x_{i2} + x_{i3} + x_{i4} = \text{number of pounds of product grade } i \text{ produced per week.}$$
$$x_{Aj} + x_{Bj} + x_{Cj} = \text{number of pounds of material } j \text{ used per week.}$$

$$\frac{x_{ij}}{x_{i1} + x_{i2} + x_{i3} + x_{i4}} = \text{proportion of material } j \text{ in product grade } i.$$

The fact that this last expression is a *nonlinear* function does not cause a complication. For example, consider the first specification for product grade A in Table 3.16 (the proportion of material 1 should not exceed 30 percent). This restriction gives the nonlinear constraint

$$\frac{x_{A1}}{x_{A1} + x_{A2} + x_{A3} + x_{A4}} \le 0.3.$$

However, multiplying through both sides of this inequality by the denominator yields an *equivalent* constraint

$$x_{A1} \le 0.3(x_{A1} + x_{A2} + x_{A3} + x_{A4}),$$

so

$$0.7x_{A1} - 0.3x_{A2} - 0.3x_{A3} - 0.3x_{A4} \le 0,$$

which is a legitimate linear programming constraint.

With this adjustment, the three quantities given above lead directly to all the functional constraints of the model. The objective function is based on management's objective of maximizing net weekly profit (total sales income *minus* total amalgamation cost) from the three product grades. Thus, for each product grade, the profit per pound is obtained by subtracting the amalgamation cost given in the third column of Table 3.16 from the selling price in the fourth column. These *differences* provide the coefficients for the objective function.

Therefore, the complete linear programming model is

$$\text{Maximize} \quad Z = 5.5(x_{A1} + x_{A2} + x_{A3} + x_{A4}) + 4.5(x_{B1} + x_{B2} + x_{B3} + x_{B4})$$
$$+ 3.5(x_{C1} + x_{C2} + x_{C3} + x_{C4}),$$

subject to the following constraints:

1. Mixture specifications (second column of Table 3.16):

$$x_{A1} \le 0.3(x_{A1} + x_{A2} + x_{A3} + x_{A4}) \qquad \text{(grade } A, \text{ material 1)}$$
$$x_{A2} \ge 0.4(x_{A1} + x_{A2} + x_{A3} + x_{A4}) \qquad \text{(grade } A, \text{ material 2)}$$
$$x_{A3} \le 0.5(x_{A1} + x_{A2} + x_{A3} + x_{A4}) \qquad \text{(grade } A, \text{ material 3)}$$
$$x_{A4} = 0.2(x_{A1} + x_{A2} + x_{A3} + x_{A4}) \qquad \text{(grade } A, \text{ material 4).}$$

$$x_{B1} \le 0.5(x_{B1} + x_{B2} + x_{B3} + x_{B4}) \qquad \text{(grade } B, \text{ material 1)}$$
$$x_{B2} \ge 0.1(x_{B1} + x_{B2} + x_{B3} + x_{B4}) \qquad \text{(grade } B, \text{ material 2)}$$
$$x_{B4} = 0.1(x_{B1} + x_{B2} + x_{B3} + x_{B4}) \qquad \text{(grade } B, \text{ material 4).}$$

$$x_{C1} \le 0.7(x_{C1} + x_{C2} + x_{C3} + x_{C4}) \qquad \text{(grade } C, \text{ material 1).}$$

2. Availability of materials (second column of Table 3.17):

$$x_{A1} + x_{B1} + x_{C1} \leq 3{,}000 \quad \text{(material 1)}$$
$$x_{A2} + x_{B2} + x_{C2} \leq 2{,}000 \quad \text{(material 2)}$$
$$x_{A3} + x_{B3} + x_{C3} \leq 4{,}000 \quad \text{(material 3)}$$
$$x_{A4} + x_{B4} + x_{C4} \leq 1{,}000 \quad \text{(material 4)}.$$

3. Restrictions on amounts treated (right side of Table 3.17):

$$x_{A1} + x_{B1} + x_{C1} \geq 1{,}500 \quad \text{(material 1)}$$
$$x_{A2} + x_{B2} + x_{C2} \geq 1{,}000 \quad \text{(material 2)}$$
$$x_{A3} + x_{B3} + x_{C3} \geq 2{,}000 \quad \text{(material 3)}$$
$$x_{A4} + x_{B4} + x_{C4} \geq 500 \quad \text{(material 4)}.$$

4. Restriction on treatment cost (right side of Table 3.17):

$$3(x_{A1} + x_{B1} + x_{C1}) + 6(x_{A2} + x_{B2} + x_{C2}) + 4(x_{A3} + x_{B3} + x_{C3})$$
$$+ 5(x_{A4} + x_{B4} + x_{C4}) = 30{,}000.$$

5. Nonnegativity constraints:

$$x_{A1} \geq 0, \quad x_{A2} \geq 0, \quad \ldots, \quad x_{C4} \geq 0.$$

This formulation completes the model, except that the constraints for the mixture specifications need to be rewritten in the proper form for a linear programming model by bringing all variables to the left-hand side and combining terms, as follows:

Mixture specifications:

$$0.7x_{A1} - 0.3x_{A2} - 0.3x_{A3} - 0.3x_{A4} \leq 0 \quad \text{(grade } A, \text{ material 1)}$$
$$-0.4x_{A1} + 0.6x_{A2} - 0.4x_{A3} - 0.4x_{A4} \geq 0 \quad \text{(grade } A, \text{ material 2)}$$
$$-0.5x_{A1} - 0.5x_{A2} + 0.5x_{A3} - 0.5x_{A4} \leq 0 \quad \text{(grade } A, \text{ material 3)}$$
$$-0.2x_{A1} - 0.2x_{A2} - 0.2x_{A3} + 0.8x_{A4} = 0 \quad \text{(grade } A, \text{ material 4)}.$$

$$0.5x_{B1} - 0.5x_{B2} - 0.5x_{B3} - 0.5x_{B4} \leq 0 \quad \text{(grade } B, \text{ material 1)}$$
$$-0.1x_{B1} + 0.9x_{B2} - 0.1x_{B3} - 0.1x_{B4} \geq 0 \quad \text{(grade } B, \text{ material 2)}$$
$$-0.1x_{B1} - 0.1x_{B2} - 0.1x_{B3} + 0.9x_{B4} = 0 \quad \text{(grade } B, \text{ material 4)}.$$

$$0.3x_{C1} - 0.7x_{C2} - 0.7x_{C3} - 0.7x_{C4} \leq 0 \quad \text{(grade } C, \text{ material 1)}.$$

An optimal solution for this model is shown in Table 3.18, and then these x_{ij} values are used to calculate the other quantities of interest given in the table. The resulting optimal value of the objective function is $Z = 35{,}108.90$ (a total weekly profit of \$35,108.90).

The Save-It Co. problem is an example of a **blending problem.** The objective for a blending problem is to find the best blend of ingredients into final products to meet certain specifications. Some of the earliest applications of linear programming were for *gasoline blending,* where petroleum ingredients were blended to obtain various grades of gasoline. The award-winning OR study at Texaco discussed at the end of

TABLE 3.18 Optimal solution for the Save-It Co. problem

	Pounds Used per Week				Number of Pounds Produced per Week
	Material				
Grade	1	2	3	4	
A	412.3 (19.2%)	859.6 (40%)	447.4 (20.8%)	429.8 (20%)	2149
B	2587.7 (50%)	517.5 (10%)	1552.6 (30%)	517.5 (10%)	5175
C	0	0	0	0	0
Total	3000	1377	2000	947	

Sec. 2.5 dealt with gasoline blending (although Texaco used a *nonlinear* programming model). Other blending problems involve such final products as steel, fertilizer, and animal feed.

Personnel Scheduling

UNION AIRWAYS is adding more flights to and from its hub airport, and so it needs to hire additional customer service agents. However, it is not clear just how many more should be hired. Management recognizes the need for cost control while also consistently providing a satisfactory level of service to customers. Therefore, an OR team is studying how to schedule the agents to provide satisfactory service with the smallest personnel cost.

Based on the new schedule of flights, an analysis has been made of the *minimum* number of customer service agents that need to be on duty at different times of the day to provide a satisfactory level of service. The rightmost column of Table 3.19 shows the number of agents needed for the time periods given in the first column. The other entries

TABLE 3.19 Data for the Union Airways personnel scheduling problem

	Time Periods Covered					Minimum Number of Agents Needed
	Shift					
Time Period	1	2	3	4	5	
6:00 A.M. to 8:00 A.M.	✔					48
8:00 A.M. to 10:00 A.M.	✔	✔				79
10:00 A.M. to noon	✔	✔				65
Noon to 2:00 P.M.	✔	✔	✔			87
2:00 P.M. to 4:00 P.M.		✔	✔			64
4:00 P.M. to 6:00 P.M.			✔	✔		73
6:00 P.M. to 8:00 P.M.			✔	✔		82
8:00 P.M. to 10:00 P.M.				✔		43
10:00 P.M. to midnight				✔	✔	52
Midnight to 6:00 A.M.					✔	15
Daily cost per agent	$170	$160	$175	$180	$195	

in this table reflect one of the provisions in the company's current contract with the union that represents the customer service agents. The provision is that each agent work an 8-hour shift 5 days per week, and the authorized shifts are

Shift 1:   6:00 A.M. to 2:00 P.M.
Shift 2:   8:00 A.M. to 4:00 P.M.
Shift 3:   Noon to 8:00 P.M.
Shift 4:   4:00 P.M. to midnight
Shift 5:   10:00 P.M. to 6:00 A.M.

Checkmarks in the main body of Table 3.19 show the hours covered by the respective shifts. Because some shifts are less desirable than others, the wages specified in the contract differ by shift. For each shift, the daily compensation (including benefits) for each agent is shown in the bottom row. The problem is to determine how many agents should be assigned to the respective shifts each day to minimize the *total* personnel cost for agents, based on this bottom row, while meeting (or surpassing) the service requirements given in the rightmost column.

Formulation as a Linear Programming Problem.   Linear programming problems always involve finding the best *mix of activity levels.* The key to formulating this particular problem is to recognize the nature of the activities.

Activities correspond to shifts, where the *level* of each activity is the number of agents assigned to that shift. Thus, this problem involves finding the *best mix of shift sizes.* Since the decision variables always are the levels of the activities, the five decision variables here are

x_j = number of agents assigned to shift j,   for j = 1, 2, 3, 4, 5.

The main restrictions on the values of these decision variables are that the number of agents working during each time period must satisfy the minimum requirement given in the rightmost column of Table 3.19. For example, for 2:00 P.M. to 4:00 P.M., the total number of agents assigned to the shifts that cover this time period (shifts 2 and 3) must be at least 64, so

$$x_2 + x_3 \geq 64$$

is the functional constraint for this time period.

Because the objective is to minimize the total cost of the agents assigned to the five shifts, the coefficients in the objective function are given by the last row of Table 3.19.

Therefore, the complete linear programming model is

$$\text{Minimize} \quad Z = 170x_1 + 160x_2 + 175x_3 + 180x_4 + 195x_5,$$

subject to

x_1	≥ 48	(6–8 A.M.)
$x_1 + x_2$	≥ 79	(8–10 A.M.)
$x_1 + x_2$	≥ 65	(10 A.M. to noon)
$x_1 + x_2 + x_3$	≥ 87	(Noon–2 P.M.)
$x_2 + x_3$	≥ 64	(2–4 P.M.)
$x_3 + x_4$	≥ 73	(4–6 P.M.)

$$
\begin{aligned}
x_3 + x_4 && \geq 82 && \text{(6–8 P.M.)} \\
x_4 && \geq 43 && \text{(8–10 P.M.)} \\
x_4 + x_5 && \geq 52 && \text{(10 P.M.–midnight)} \\
x_5 && \geq 15 && \text{(Midnight–6 A.M.)}
\end{aligned}
$$

and

$$x_j \geq 0, \qquad \text{for } j = 1, 2, 3, 4, 5.$$

With a keen eye, you might have noticed that the third constraint, $x_1 + x_2 \geq 65$, actually is not necessary because the second constraint, $x_1 + x_2 \geq 79$, ensures that $x_1 + x_2$ will be larger than 65. Thus, $x_1 + x_2 \geq 65$ is a *redundant* constraint that can be deleted. Similarly, the sixth constraint, $x_3 + x_4 \geq 73$, also is a *redundant* constraint because the seventh constraint is $x_3 + x_4 \geq 82$. (In fact, three of the nonnegativity constraints—$x_1 \geq 0$, $x_4 \geq 0$, $x_5 \geq 0$—also are redundant constraints because of the first, eighth, and tenth functional constraints: $x_1 \geq 48$, $x_4 \geq 43$, and $x_5 \geq 15$. However, no computational advantage is gained by deleting these three nonnegativity constraints.)

The optimal solution for this model is $(x_1, x_2, x_3, x_4, x_5) = (48, 31, 39, 43, 15)$. This yields $Z = 30,610$, that is, a total daily personnel cost of \$30,610.

This problem is an example where the divisibility assumption of linear programming actually is not satisfied. The number of agents assigned to each shift needs to be an integer. Strictly speaking, the model should have an additional constraint for each decision variable specifying that the variable must have an integer value. Adding these constraints would convert the linear programming model to an integer programming model (the topic of Chap. 12).

Without these constraints, the optimal solution given above turned out to have integer values anyway, so no harm was done by not including the constraints. (The form of the functional constraints made this outcome a likely one.) If some of the variables had turned out to be noninteger, the easiest approach would have been to *round up* to integer values. (Rounding up is feasible for this example because all the functional constraints are in $\geq$ form with nonnegative coefficients.) Rounding up does not ensure obtaining an optimal solution for the integer programming model, but the error introduced by rounding up such large numbers would be negligible for most practical situations. Alternatively, integer programming techniques described in Chap. 12 could be used to solve exactly for an optimal solution with integer values.

Section 3.5 includes a case study of how United Airlines used linear programming to develop a personnel scheduling system on a vastly larger scale than this example.

Distributing Goods through a Distribution Network

The Problem. The DISTRIBUTION UNLIMITED CO. will be producing the same new product at two different factories, and then the product must be shipped to two warehouses, where either factory can supply either warehouse. The distribution network available for shipping this product is shown in Fig. 3.13, where F1 and F2 are the two factories, W1 and W2 are the two warehouses, and DC is a distribution center. The amounts to be shipped from F1 and F2 are shown to their left, and the amounts to be received at W1 and W2 are shown to their right. Each arrow represents a feasible shipping lane. Thus, F1 can ship directly to W1 and has three possible routes (F1 $\rightarrow$ DC $\rightarrow$ W2, F1 $\rightarrow$ F2 $\rightarrow$

DC → W2, and F1 → W1 → W2) for shipping to W2. Factory F2 has just one route to W2 (F2 → DC → W2) and one to W1 (F2 → DC → W2 → W1). The cost per unit shipped through each shipping lane is shown next to the arrow. Also shown next to F1 → F2 and DC → W2 are the maximum amounts that can be shipped through these lanes. The other lanes have sufficient shipping capacity to handle everything these factories can send.

The decision to be made concerns how much to ship through each shipping lane. The objective is to minimize the total shipping cost.

Formulation as a Linear Programming Problem.   With seven shipping lanes, we need seven decision variables ($x_{F1\text{-}F2}$, $x_{F1\text{-}DC}$, $x_{F1\text{-}W1}$, $x_{F2\text{-}DC}$, $x_{DC\text{-}W2}$, $x_{W1\text{-}W2}$, $x_{W2\text{-}W1}$) to represent the amounts shipped through the respective lanes.

There are several restrictions on the values of these variables. In addition to the usual nonnegativity constraints, there are two *upper-bound constraints*, $x_{F1\text{-}F2} \leq 10$ and $x_{DC\text{-}W2} \leq 80$, imposed by the limited shipping capacities for the two lanes, F1 → F2 and DC → W2. All the other restrictions arise from five *net flow constraints*, one for each of the five locations. These constraints have the following form.

Net flow constraint for each location:

Amount shipped out − amount shipped in = required amount.

As indicated in Fig. 3.13, these required amounts are 50 for F1, 40 for F2, −30 for W1, and −60 for W2.

FIGURE 3.13
The distribution network for Distribution Unlimited Co.

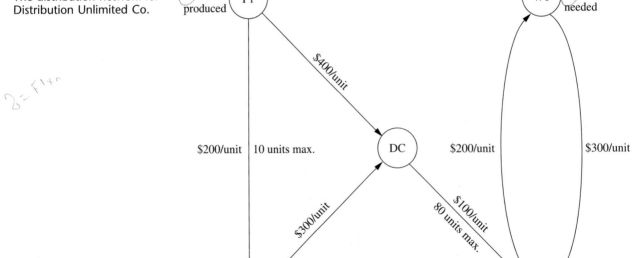

What is the required amount for DC? All the units produced at the factories are ultimately needed at the warehouses, so any units shipped from the factories to the distribution center should be forwarded to the warehouses. Therefore, the total amount shipped from the distribution center to the warehouses should *equal* the total amount shipped from the factories to the distribution center. In other words, the *difference* of these two shipping amounts (the required amount for the net flow constraint) should be *zero*.

Since the objective is to minimize the total shipping cost, the coefficients for the objective function come directly from the unit shipping costs given in Fig. 3.13. Therefore, by using money units of hundreds of dollars in this objective function, the complete linear programming model is

$$\text{Minimize} \quad Z = 2x_{F1\text{-}F2} + 4x_{F1\text{-}DC} + 9x_{F1\text{-}W1} + 3x_{F2\text{-}DC} + x_{DC\text{-}W2}$$
$$+ 3x_{W1\text{-}W2} + 2x_{W2\text{-}W1},$$

subject to the following constraints:

1. Net flow constraints:

$$x_{F1\text{-}F2} + x_{F1\text{-}DC} + x_{F1\text{-}W1} \qquad\qquad\qquad \leq\; = 50 \text{ (factory 1)}$$
$$-x_{F1\text{-}F2} \qquad\qquad\qquad + x_{F2\text{-}DC} \qquad\qquad\qquad \leq\; = 40 \text{ (factory 2)}$$
$$- x_{F1\text{-}DC} \qquad\quad - x_{F2\text{-}DC} + x_{DC\text{-}W2} \qquad\qquad = 0 \text{ (distribution center)}$$
$$- x_{F1\text{-}W1} \qquad\qquad\qquad\quad + x_{W1\text{-}W2} - x_{W2\text{-}W1} = -30 \text{ (warehouse 1)}$$
$$- x_{DC\text{-}W2} - x_{W1\text{-}W2} + x_{W2\text{-}W1} = -60 \text{ (warehouse 2)}$$

2. Upper-bound constraints:

$$x_{F1\text{-}F2} \leq 10, \qquad x_{DC\text{-}W2} \leq 80$$

3. Nonnegativity constraints:

$$x_{F1\text{-}F2} \geq 0, \qquad x_{F1\text{-}DC} \geq 0, \qquad x_{F1\text{-}W1} \geq 0, \qquad x_{F2\text{-}DC} \geq 0, \qquad x_{DC\text{-}W2} \geq 0,$$
$$x_{W1\text{-}W2} \geq 0, \qquad x_{W2\text{-}W1} \geq 0.$$

You will see this problem again in Sec. 9.6, where we focus on linear programming problems of this type (called the *minimum cost flow problem*). In Sec. 9.7, we will solve for its optimal solution:

$$x_{F1\text{-}F2} = 0, \qquad x_{F1\text{-}DC} = 40, \qquad x_{F1\text{-}W1} = 10, \qquad x_{F2\text{-}DC} = 40, \qquad x_{DC\text{-}W2} = 80,$$
$$x_{W1\text{-}W2} = 0, \qquad x_{W2\text{-}W1} = 20.$$

The resulting total shipping cost is $49,000.

You also will see a case study involving a *much* larger problem of this same type at the end of the next section.

3.5 SOME CASE STUDIES

To give you a better perspective about the great impact linear programming can have, we now present three case studies of *real* applications. Each of these is a *classic* application, initiated in the early 1980s, that has come to be regarded as a standard of excellence for future applications of linear programming. The first one will bear some strong similarities to the Wyndor Glass Co. problem, but on a realistic scale. Similarly, the second and third are realistic versions of the last two examples presented in the preceding section (the Union Airways and Distribution Unlimited examples).

Choosing the Product Mix at Ponderosa Industrial[1]

Until its sale in 1988, PONDEROSA INDUSTRIAL was a plywood manufacturer based in Anhuac, Chihuahua, that supplied 25 percent of the plywood in Mexico. Like any plywood manufacturer, Ponderosa's many products were differentiated by thickness and by the quality of the wood. The plywood market in Mexico is competitive, so the market establishes the prices of the products. The prices can fluctuate considerably from month to month, and there may be great differences between the products in their price movements from even one month to the next. As a result, each product's contribution to Ponderosa's total profit was continually varying, and in different ways for different products.

Because of its pronounced effect on profits, a critical issue facing management was the choice of *product mix*—how much to produce of each product—on a monthly basis. This choice was a very complex one, since it had to take into account the current amounts available of various resources needed to produce the products. The most important resources were logs in four quality categories and production capacities for both the pressing operation and the polishing operation.

Beginning in 1980, linear programming was used on a monthly basis to guide the product-mix decision. The linear programming model had an objective of maximizing the total profit from all products. The model's constraints included the various resource constraints as well as other relevant restrictions such as the minimum amount of a product that must be provided to regular customers and the maximum amount that can be sold. (To aid planning for the procurement of raw materials, the model also considered the impact of the product-mix decision for the upcoming month on production in the following month.) The model had 90 decision variables and 45 functional constraints.

This model was used each month to find the product mix for the upcoming month that would be optimal if the estimated values of the various parameters of the model prove to be accurate. However, since some of the parameter values could change quickly (e.g., the unit profits of the products), *sensitivity analysis* was done to determine the effect if the estimated values turned out to be inaccurate. The results indicated when adjustments in the product mix should be made (if time permitted) as unanticipated market changes occurred that affected the price (and so the unit profit) of certain products.

One key decision each month concerned the number of logs in each of the four quality categories to purchase. The amounts available for the upcoming month's production actually were parameters of the model. Therefore, after the purchase decision was made and then the corresponding optimal product mix was determined, *postoptimality analysis* was conducted to investigate the effect of adjusting the purchase decision. For example, it is very easy with linear programming to check what the impact on total profit would be if a quick purchase were to be made of additional logs in a certain quality category to enable increasing production for the upcoming month.

Ponderosa's linear programming system was *interactive,* so management received an immediate response to its "what-if questions" about the impact of encountering parame-

[1]A. Roy, E. E. DeFalomir, and L. Lasdon: "An Optimization-Based Decision Support System for a Product Mix Problem," *Interfaces,* **12**(2):26–33, April 1982.

ter values that differ from those in the original model. What if a quick purchase of logs of a certain kind were made? What if product prices were to fluctuate in a certain way? A variety of such scenarios can be investigated. Management effectively used this power to reach better decisions than the "optimal" product mix from the original model.

The impact of linear programming at Ponderosa was reported to be "tremendous." It led to a dramatic shift in the types of plywood products emphasized by the company. The improved product-mix decisions were credited with increasing the overall profitability of the company by 20 percent. Other contributions of linear programming included better utilization of raw material, capital equipment, and personnel.

Two factors helped make this application of linear programming so successful. One factor is that a *natural language* financial planning system was interfaced with the codes for finding an optimal solution for the linear programming model. Using natural language rather than mathematical symbols to display the components of the linear programming model and its output made the process understandable and meaningful for the managers making the product-mix decisions. Reporting to management in the language of managers is necessary for the successful application of linear programming.

The other factor was that the linear programming system used was *interactive*. As mentioned earlier, after an optimal solution was obtained for one version of the model, this feature enabled managers to ask a variety of "what-if" questions and receive immediate responses. Better decisions frequently were reached by exploring other plausible scenarios, and this process also gave managers more confidence that their decision would perform well under most foreseeable circumstances.

In any application, this ability to respond quickly to management's needs and queries through postoptimality analysis (whether interactive or not) is a vital part of a linear programming study.

Personnel Scheduling at United Airlines[1]

Despite unprecedented industry competition in 1983 and 1984, UNITED AIRLINES managed to achieve substantial growth with service to 48 new airports. In 1984, it became the only airline with service to cities in all 50 states. Its 1984 operating profit reached $564 million, with revenues of $6.2 billion, an increase of 6 percent over 1983, while costs grew by less than 2 percent.

Cost control is essential to competing successfully in the airline industry. In 1982, upper management of United Airlines initiated an OR study of its personnel scheduling as part of the cost control measures associated with the airline's 1983–1984 expansion. The goal was to schedule personnel at the airline's reservations offices and airports so as to minimize the cost of providing the necessary service to customers.

At the time, United Airlines employed over 4,000 reservations sales representatives and support personnel at its 11 reservations offices and about 1,000 customer service agents at its 10 largest airports. Some were part-time, working shifts from 2 to 8 hours; most were full-time, working 8- or 10-hour-shifts. Shifts start at several different times. Each reservations office was open (by telephone) 24 hours a day, as was each of the major airports. However, the number of employees needed at each location to provide the re-

[1]T. J. Holloran and J. E. Bryn, "United Airlines Station Manpower Planning System," *Interfaces,* **16**(1): 39–50, Jan.–Feb. 1986.

quired level of service varied greatly during the 24-hour day, and might fluctuate considerably from one half-hour to the next.

Trying to design the work schedules for all the employees at a given location to meet these service requirements most efficiently is a nightmare of combinatorial considerations. Once an employee begins working, he or she will be there continuously for the entire shift (2 to 10 hours, depending on the employee), *except* for either a meal break or short rest breaks every 2 hours. Given the *minimum* number of employees needed on duty for *each* half-hour interval over a 24-hour day (where these requirements change from day to day over a 7-day week), *how many* employees of *each shift length* should begin work at *what start time* over *each* 24-hour day of a 7-day week? Fortunately, linear programming thrives on such combinatorial nightmares.

Actually, several OR techniques described in this book were used in the computerized planning system developed to attack this problem. Both *forecasting* (Chap. 20) and *queuing theory* (Chaps. 17 and 18) were used to determine the minimum number of employees needed on duty for each half-hour interval. *Integer programming* (Chap. 12) was used to determine the times of day at which shifts would be allowed to start. However, the core of the planning system was *linear programming,* which did all the actual scheduling to provide the needed service with the smallest possible labor cost. A complete work schedule was developed for the first full week of a month, and then it was reused for the remainder of the month. This process was repeated each month to reflect changing conditions.

Although the details about the linear programming model have not been published, it is clear that the basic approach used is the one illustrated by the Union Airways example of personnel scheduling in Sec. 3.4. The objective function being minimized represents the total personnel cost for the location being scheduled. The main functional constraints require that the number of employees on duty during each time period will not fall below minimum acceptable levels.

However, the Union Airways example has only five decision variables. By contrast, the United Airlines model for some locations has over 20,000 decision variables! The difference is that a real application must consider myriad important details that can be ignored in a textbook example. For example, the United Airlines model takes into account such things as the meal and break assignment times for each employee scheduled, differences in shift lengths for different employees, and days off over a weekly schedule, among other scheduling details.

This application of linear programming was reported to have had "an overwhelming impact not only on United management and members of the manpower planning group, but also for many who had never before heard of management science (OR) or mathematical modeling." It earned rave reviews from upper management, operating managers, and affected employees alike. For example, one manager described the scheduling system as

> Magical, . . . just as the [customer] lines begin to build, someone shows up for work, and just as you begin to think you're overstaffed, people start going home.[1]

In more tangible terms, this application was credited with saving United Airlines more than $6 million *annually* in just direct salary and benefit costs. Other benefits included improved customer service and reduced need for support staff.

[1]Holloran and Bryn, "United Airlines Station Manpower Planning System," p. 49.

After some updating in the early 1990s, the system is providing similar benefits today.

One factor that helped make this application of linear programming so successful was "the support of operational managers and their staffs." This was a lesson learned by experience, because the OR team initially failed to establish a good line of communication with the operating managers, who then resisted the team's initial recommendations. The team leaders described their mistake as follows:

> The cardinal rule for earning the trust and respect of operating managers and support staffs—"getting them involved in the development process"—had been violated.[1]

The team then worked much more closely with the operating managers—with outstanding results.

Planning Supply, Distribution, and Marketing at Citgo Petroleum Corporation[2]

CITGO PETROLEUM CORPORATION specializes in refining and marketing petroleum. In the mid-1980s, it had annual sales of several billion dollars, ranking it among the 150 largest industrial companies in the United States.

After several years of financial losses, Citgo was acquired in 1983 by Southland Corporation, the owner of the 7-Eleven convenience store chain (whose sales include 2 billion gallons of quality motor fuels annually). To turn Citgo's financial losses around, Southland created a task force composed of Southland personnel, Citgo personnel, and outside consultants. An eminent OR consultant was appointed director of the task force to report directly to both the president of Citgo and the chairman of the board of Southland.

During 1984 and 1985, this task force applied various OR techniques (as well as information systems technologies) throughout the corporation. It was reported that these OR applications "have changed the way Citgo does business and resulted in approximately $70 million per year profit improvement."[3]

The two most important applications were both *linear programming systems* that provided management with powerful planning support. One, called the *refinery LP system,* led to great improvements in refinery yield, substantial reductions in the cost of labor, and other important cost savings. This system contributed approximately $50 million to profit improvement in 1985. (See the end of Sec. 2.4 for discussion of the key role that *model validation* played in the development of this system.)

However, we will focus here on the other linear programming system, called the supply, distribution, and marketing modeling system (or just the *SDM system*), that Citgo is continuing to use. The SDM system is particularly interesting because it is based on a special kind of linear programming model that uses *networks,* just like the model for the Distribution Unlimited example presented at the end of Sec. 3.4. The model for the SDM system provides a representation of Citgo's entire marketing and distribution network.

At the time the task force conducted its OR study, Citgo owned or leased 36 product storage terminals which were supplied through five distribution center terminals via a dis-

---

[1]Ibid, p. 47.

[2]See the references cited in footnote 2 on p. 10.

[3]See p. 4 of the second reference cited in footnote 2 on p. 10.

tribution network of pipelines, tankers, and barges. Citgo also sold product from over 350 exchange terminals that were shared with other petroleum marketers. To supply its customers, product might be acquired by Citgo from its refinery in Lake Charles, LA, or from spot purchases on one of five major spot markets, product exchanges, and trades with other industry refiners. These product acquisition decisions were made daily. However, the time from such a decision until the product reached the intended customers could be as long as 11 weeks. Therefore, the linear programming model used an 11-week planning horizon.

The SDM system is used to coordinate the supply, distribution, and marketing of each of Citgo's major products (originally four grades of motor fuel and No. 2 fuel oil) throughout the United States. Management uses the system to make decisions such as where to sell, what price to charge, where to buy or trade, how much to buy or trade, how much to hold in inventory, and how much to ship by each mode of transportation. Linear programming guides these decisions and when to implement them so as to minimize total cost or maximize total profit. The SDM system also is used in "what-if" sessions, where management asks what-if questions about scenarios that differ from those assumed in the original model.

The linear programming model in the SDM system has the same form as the model for the Distribution Unlimited example presented at the end of Sec. 3.4. In fact, both models fit an important special kind of linear programming problem, called the *minimum cost flow problem,* that will be discussed in Sec. 9.6. The main functional constraints for such models are *equality constraints,* where each one prescribes what the net flow of goods out of a specific location must be.

The Distribution Unlimited model has just seven decision variables and five equality constraints. By contrast, the Citgo model for each major product has about 15,000 decision variables and 3,000 equality constraints!

At the end of Sec. 2.1, we described the important role that *data collection* and *data verification* played in developing the Citgo models. With such huge models, a massive amount of data must be gathered to determine all the parameter values. A state-of-the-art management database system was developed for this purpose. Before using the data, a preloader program was used to check for data errors and inconsistencies. The importance of doing so was brought forcefully home to the task force when, as mentioned in Sec. 2.1, the initial run of the preloader program generated a paper log of error messages an inch thick! It was clear that the data collection process needed to be thoroughly debugged to help ensure the validity of the models.

The SDM linear programming system has greatly improved the efficiency of Citgo's supply, distribution, and marketing operations, enabling a huge reduction in product inventory with no drop in service levels. During its first year, the value of petroleum products held in inventory was reduced by $116.5 million. This huge reduction in capital tied up in carrying inventory resulted in saving about $14 million annually in interest expenses for borrowed capital, adding $14 million to Citgo's annual profits. Improvements in coordination, pricing, and purchasing decisions have been estimated to add at least another $2.5 million to annual profits. Many *indirect* benefits also are attributed to this application of linear programming, including improved data, better pricing strategies, and elimination of unnecessary product terminals, as well as improved communication and coordination between supply, distribution, marketing, and refinery groups.

Some of the factors that contributed to the success of this OR study are the same as for the two preceding case studies. Like Ponderosa Industrial, one factor was developing output reports in the language of managers to really meet their needs. These output reports are designed to be easy for managers to understand and use, and they address the issues that are important to management. Also like Ponderosa, another factor was enabling management to respond quickly to the dynamics of the industry by using the linear programming system extensively in "what-if" sessions. As in so many applications of linear programming, *postoptimality* analysis proved more important than the initial optimal solution obtained for one version of the model.

Much as in the United Airlines application, another factor was the enthusiastic support of operational managers during the development and implementation of this linear programming system.

However, the most important factor was the unlimited support provided to the task force by top management, ranging right up to the chief executive officer and the chairman of the board of Citgo's parent company, Southland Corporation. As mentioned earlier, the director of the task force (an eminent OR consultant) reported directly to both the president of Citgo and the chairman of the board of Southland. This backing by top management included strong organizational and financial support.

The organizational support took a variety of forms. One example was the creation and staffing of the position of senior vice-president of operations coordination to evaluate and coordinate recommendations based on the models which spanned organizational boundaries.

When discussing both this linear programming system and other OR applications implemented by the task force, team members described the financial support of top management as follows:

> The total cost of the systems implemented, $20 million to $30 million, was the greatest obstacle to this project. However, because of the information explosion in the petroleum industry, top management realized that numerous information systems were essential to gather, store, and analyze data. The incremental cost of adding management science (OR) technologies to these computers and systems was small, in fact very small in light of the enormous benefits they provided.[1]

3.6 DISPLAYING AND SOLVING LINEAR PROGRAMMING MODELS ON A SPREADSHEET

Spreadsheet software, such as Excel, is a popular tool for analyzing and solving small linear programming problems. The main features of a linear programming model, including all its parameters, can be easily entered onto a spreadsheet. However, spreadsheet software can do much more than just display data. If we include some additional information, the spreadsheet can be used to quickly analyze potential solutions. For example, a potential solution can be checked to see if it is feasible and what Z value (profit or cost) it achieves. Much of the power of the spreadsheet lies in its ability to immediately see the results of any changes made in the solution.

In addition, the Excel Solver can quickly apply the simplex method to find an optimal solution for the model.

[1]Ibid, p. 21.

To illustrate this process, we now return to the Wyndor example introduced in Sec. 3.1.

Displaying the Model on a Spreadsheet

After expressing profits in units of thousands of dollars, Table 3.1 in Sec. 3.1 gives all the parameters of the model for the Wyndor problem. Figure 3.14 shows the necessary additions to this table for an Excel spreadsheet. In particular, a row is added (row 9, labeled "Solution") to store the values of the decision variables. Next, a column is added (column E, labeled "Totals"). For each functional constraint, the number in column E is the numerical value of the left-hand side of that constraint. Recall that the left-hand side represents the actual amount of the resource used, given the values of the decision variables in row 9. For example, for the Plant 3 constraint in row 7, the amount of this resource used (in hours of production time per week) is

Production time used in Plant 3 $= 3x_1 + 2x_2$.

In the language of Excel, the equivalent equation for the number in cell E7 is

E7 = C7*C9 + D7*D9.

Notice that this equation involves the sum of two products. There is a function in Excel, called SUMPRODUCT, that will sum up the product of each of the individual terms in two different ranges of cells. For instance, SUMPRODUCT(C7:D7,C9:D9) takes each of the individual terms in the range C7:D7, multiplies them by the corresponding term in the range C9:D9, and then sums up these individual products, just as shown in the above equation. Although optional with such short equations, this function is especially handy as a shortcut for entering longer linear programming equations.

Next, $\leq$ signs are entered in cells F5, F6, and F7 to indicate the form of the functional constraints. (When using a trial-and-error approach, the spreadsheet still will allow you to enter infeasible trial solutions that violate the $\leq$ signs, but these signs serve as a reminder to reject such trial solutions if no changes are made in the numbers in column G.)

FIGURE 3.14
The spreadsheet for the Wyndor problem before using the Excel Solver, so the values of the decision variables and the objective function are just entered as zeros.

	A	B	C	D	E	F	G
1		Wyndor Glass Co. Product-Mix Problem					
2							
3			Hours Used per Unit Produced				Hours
4			Doors	Windows	Totals		Available
5		Plant 1	1	0	0	$\leq$	4
6		Plant 2	0	2	0	$\leq$	12
7		Plant 3	3	2	0	$\leq$	18
8		Unit Profit ($thousands)	3	5	0		
9		Solution	0	0			

	E
5	=SUMPRODUCT(C5:D5,C9:D9)
6	=SUMPRODUCT(C6:D6,C9:D9)
7	=SUMPRODUCT(C7:D7,C9:D9)
8	=SUMPRODUCT(C8:D8,C9:D9)

Finally, the value of the objective function is entered in cell E8. Much like the other values in column E, it is the sum of products. The equation for cell E8 is =SUMPRODUCT(C8:D8,C9:D9). The lower right-hand side of Fig. 3.14 shows all the formulas that need to be entered in the "Totals" column (column E) for the Wyndor problem.

Once the model is entered in this spreadsheet format, it is easy to analyze any potential solution. When values for the decision variables are entered in the spreadsheet, the "Totals" column immediately calculates the total amount of each resource used, as well as the total profit. Hence, by comparing column E with column G, it can be seen immediately whether the potential solution is feasible. If so, cell E8 shows how much profit it would generate. One approach to trying to solve a linear programming model would be trial and error, using the spreadsheet to analyze a variety of solutions. However, you will see next how Excel also can be used to quickly find an *optimal solution.*

Using the Excel Solver to Solve the Model

Excel includes a tool called Solver that uses the simplex method to find an optimal solution. (A more powerful version of Solver, called *Premium Solver,* also is available in your OR Courseware.) Before using Solver, all the following components of the model need to be included on the spreadsheet:

1. Each decision variable
2. The objective function and its value
3. Each functional constraint

The spreadsheet layout shown in Fig. 3.14 includes all these components. The parameters for the functional constraints are in rows 5, 6, and 7, and the coefficients for the objective function are in row 8. The values of the decision variables are in cells C9 and D9, and the value of the objective function is in cell E8. Since we don't know what the values of the decision variables should be, they are just entered as zeros. The Solver will then change these to the optimal values after solving the problem.

The Solver can be started by choosing "Solver" in the Tools menu. The Solver dialogue box is shown in Fig. 3.15. The "Target Cell" is the cell containing the value of the objective function, while the "Changing Cells" are the cells containing the values of the decision variables.

Before the Solver can apply the simplex method, it needs to know exactly where each component of the model is located on the spreadsheet. You can either type in the cell addresses or click on them. Since the target cell is cell E8 and the changing cells are in the range C9:D9, these addresses are entered into the Solver dialogue box as shown in Fig. 3.15. (Excel then automatically enters the dollar signs shown in the figure to fix these addresses.) Since the goal is to maximize the objective function, "Max" also has been selected.

Next, the addresses for the functional constraints need to be added. This is done by clicking on the "Add . . ." button on the Solver dialogue box. This brings up the "Add Constraint" dialogue box shown in Fig. 3.16. The location of the values of the left-hand sides and the right-hand sides of the functional constraints are specified in this dialogue box. The cells E5 through E7 all need to be less than or equal to the corresponding cells in G5 through G7. There also is a menu to choose between <=, =, or >=, so <= has been chosen for these constraints. (This choice is needed even though ≤ signs were pre-

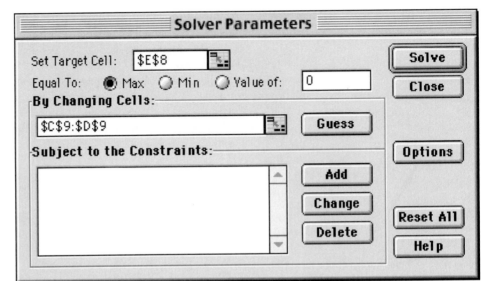

FIGURE 3.15
The Solver dialogue box after specifying which cells in Fig. 3.14 contain the values of the objective function and the decision variables, plus indicating that the objective function is to be maximized.

viously entered in column F of the spreadsheet because Solver uses only the functional constraints that are specified with the Add Constraint dialogue box.)

If there were more functional constraints to add, you would click on Add to bring up a new Add Constraint dialogue box. However, since there are no more in this example, the next step is to click on OK to go back to the Solver dialogue box.

The Solver dialogue box now summarizes the complete model (see Fig. 3.17) in terms of the spreadsheet in Fig. 3.14. However, before asking Solver to solve the model, one more step should be taken. Clicking on the Options . . . button brings up the dialogue box shown in Fig. 3.18. This box allows you to specify a number of options about how the problem will be solved. The most important of these are the Assume Linear Model option and the Assume Non-Negative option. Be sure that both options are checked as shown in the figure. This tells Solver that the problem is a *linear* programming problem with nonnegativity constraints for all the decision variables, and that the simplex method

FIGURE 3.16
The Add Constraint dialogue box after specifying that cells E5, E6, and E7 in Fig. 3.14 are required to be less than or equal to cells G5, G6, and G7, respectively.

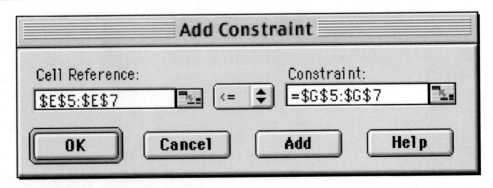

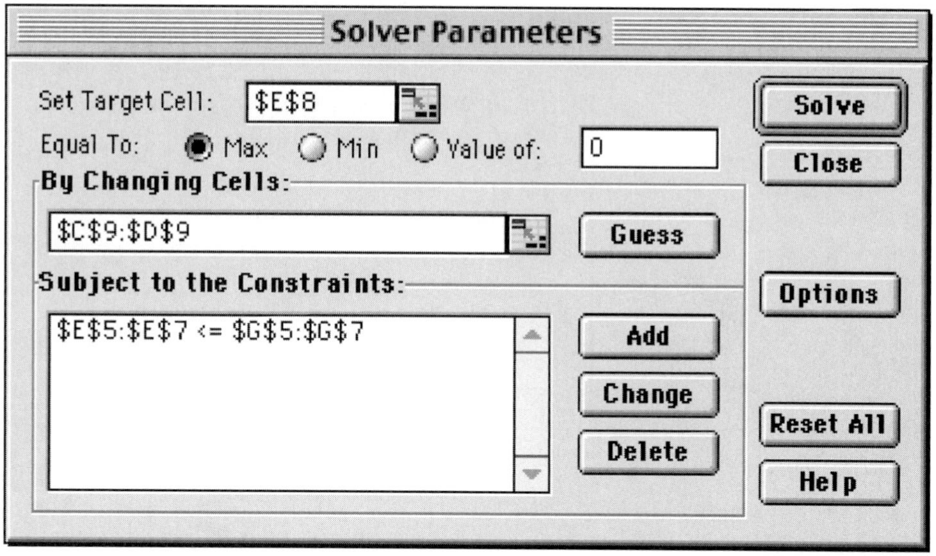

FIGURE 3.17
The Solver dialogue box after specifying the entire model in terms of the spreadsheet.

FIGURE 3.18
The Solver Options dialogue box after checking the Assume Linear Model and Assume Non-Negative options to indicate that we are dealing with a linear programming model with nonnegativity constraints that needs to be solved by the simplex method.

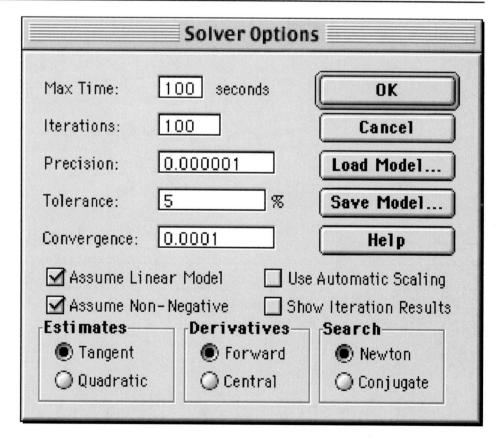

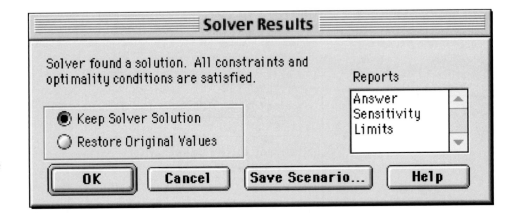

FIGURE 3.19
The Solver Results dialogue box that indicates that an optimal solution has been found.

should be used to solve the problem.[1] Regarding the other options, accepting the default values shown in the figure usually is fine for small problems. Clicking on the OK button then returns you to the Solver dialogue box.

Now you are ready to click on Solve in the Solver dialogue box, which will cause the Solver to execute the simplex method in the background. After a few seconds (for a small problem), Solver will then indicate the results. Typically, it will indicate that it has found an optimal solution, as specified in the Solver Results dialogue box shown in Fig. 3.19. If the model has no feasible solutions or no optimal solution, the dialogue box will indicate that instead by stating that "Solver could not find a feasible solution" or that "the Set Cell values do not converge." The dialogue box also presents the option of generating various reports. One of these (the Sensitivity Report) will be discussed in detail in Sec. 4.7.

After solving the model, the Solver replaces the original value of the decision variables in the spreadsheet with the optimal values, as shown in Fig. 3.20. The spreadsheet also indicates the value of the objective function, as well as the amount of each resource that is being used.

---

[1]In older versions of Excel prior to Excel 97, the Assume Non-Negative option is not available, so nonnegativity constraints have to be added with the Add Constraint dialogue box.

FIGURE 3.20
The spreadsheet obtained after solving the Wyndor problem.

	A	B	C	D	E	F	G
1		Wyndor Glass Co. Product-Mix Problem					
2							
3			Hours Used per Unit Produced				Hours
4			Doors	Windows	Totals		Available
5		Plant 1	1	0	2	≤	4
6		Plant 2	0	2	12	≤	12
7		Plant 3	3	2	18	≤	18
8		Unit Profit ($thousands)	3	5	36		
9		Solution	2	6			

3.7 FORMULATING VERY LARGE LINEAR PROGRAMMING MODELS

Linear programming models come in many different sizes. For the examples in Secs. 3.1 and 3.4, the model sizes range from three functional constraints and two decision variables (for the Wyndor and radiation therapy problems) up to 17 functional constraints and 12 decision variables (for the Save-It Company problem). The latter case may seem like a rather large model. After all, it does take a substantial amount of time just to write down a model of this size. However, by contrast, the models for the classic case studies presented in Sec. 3.5 are much, much larger. For example, the models in the Citgo case study typically have about 3,000 functional constraints and 15,000 decision variables.

The Citgo model sizes are not at all unusual. Linear programming models in practice commonly have hundreds or thousands of functional constraints. In fact, there have been some recently reported cases of a few hundred thousand constraints. The number of decision variables frequently is even larger than the number of functional constraints, and occasionally will range into the millions.

Formulating such monstrously large models can be a daunting task. Even a "medium-sized" model with a thousand functional constraints and a thousand decision variables has over a million parameters (including the million coefficients in these constraints). It simply is not practical to write out the algebraic formulation, or even to fill in the parameters on a spreadsheet, for such a model.

So how are these very large models formulated in practice? It requires the use of a *modeling language.*

Modeling Languages

A mathematical programming modeling language is software that has been specifically designed for efficiently formulating large linear programming models (and related models). Even with thousands of functional constraints, they typically are of a relatively few types where the constraints of the same type follow the same pattern. Similarly, the decision variables will fall into a small number of categories. Therefore, using large blocks of data in databases, a modeling language will simultaneously formulate all the constraints of the same type by simultaneously dealing with the variables of each type. We will illustrate this process soon.

In addition to efficiently formulating large models, a modeling language will expedite a number of model management tasks, including accessing data, transforming data into model parameters, modifying the model whenever desired, and analyzing solutions from the model. It also may produce summary reports in the vernacular of the decision makers, as well as document the model's contents.

Several excellent modeling languages have been developed over the last couple of decades. These include AMPL, MPL, GAMS, and LINGO.

The student version of one of these, MPL (short for mathematical programming language), is provided for you on the CD-ROM along with extensive tutorial material. The latest student version also can be downloaded from the website, maximal-usa.com. MPL is a product of Maximal Software, Inc. A new feature is extensive support for Excel in MPL. This includes both importing and exporting Excel ranges from MPL. Full support also is provided for the Excel VBA macro language through OptiMax 2000. (The student version of OptiMax 2000 is on the CD-ROM as well.) This product allows the user to fully integrate MPL models into Excel and solve with any of the powerful solvers that MPL supports, including **CPLEX** (described in Sec. 4.8).

LINGO is a product of LINDO Systems, Inc. The latest student version of LINGO is available by downloading it from the website, www.lindo.com. LINDO Systems also provides a completely spreadsheet-oriented optimizer called What'sBest, also available on this website.

The CD-ROM includes MPL, LINGO, and What'sBest formulations for essentially every example in this book to which these modeling languages can be applied.

Now let us look at a simplified example that illustrates how a very large linear programming model can arise.

An Example of a Problem with a Huge Model

Management of the WORLDWIDE CORPORATION needs to address a *product-mix problem,* but one that is vastly more complex than the Wyndor product-mix problem introduced in Sec. 3.1. This corporation has 10 plants in various parts of the world. Each of these plants produces the same 10 products and then sells them within its region. The *demand* (sales potential) for each of these products from each plant is known for each of the next 10 months. Although the amount of a product sold by a plant in a given month cannot exceed the demand, the amount produced can be larger, where the excess amount would be stored in inventory (at some unit cost per month) for sale in a later month. Each unit of each product takes the same amount of space in inventory, and each plant has some upper limit on the total number of units that can be stored (the *inventory capacity*).

Each plant has the same 10 production processes (we'll refer to them as *machines*), each of which can be used to produce any of the 10 products. Both the production cost per unit of a product and the production rate of the product (number of units produced per day devoted to that product) depend on the combination of plant and machine involved (but not the month). The number of working days (*production days available*) varies somewhat from month to month.

Since some plants and machines can produce a particular product either less expensively or at a faster rate than other plants and machines, it is sometimes worthwhile to ship some units of the product from one plant to another for sale by the latter plant. For each combination of a plant being shipped from (the *fromplant*) and a plant being shipped to (the *toplant*), there is a certain cost per unit shipped of any product, where this unit shipping cost is the same for all the products.

Management now needs to determine how much of each product should be produced by each machine in each plant during each month, as well as how much each plant should sell of each product in each month and how much each plant should ship of each product in each month to each of the other plants. Considering the worldwide price for each product, the objective is to find the feasible plan that maximizes the total profit (total sales revenue *minus* the sum of the total production costs, inventory costs, and shipping costs).

The Structure of the Resulting Model

Because of the inventory costs and the limited inventory capacities, it is necessary to keep track of the amount of each product kept in inventory in each plant during each month. Consequently, the linear programming model has four types of decision variables: production quantities, inventory quantities, sales quantities, and shipping quantities. With 10 plants, 10 machines, 10 products, and 10 months, this gives a total of 21,000 decision variables, as outlined below.

Decision Variables.

10,000 production variables: one for each combination of a plant, machine, product, and month

1,000 inventory variables: one for each combination of a plant, product, and month

1,000 sales variables: one for each combination of a plant, product, and month

9,000 shipping variables: one for each combination of a product, month, plant (the fromplant), and another plant (the toplant)

Multiplying each of these decision variables by the corresponding unit cost or unit revenue, and then summing over each type, the following objective function can be calculated:

Objective Function.

Maximize   profit = total sales revenue − total cost,

where

Total cost = total production cost + total inventory cost + total shipping cost.

When maximizing this objective function, the 21,000 decision variables need to satisfy nonnegativity constraints as well as four types of functional constraints—production capacity constraints, plant balance constraints (equality constraints that provide appropriate values to the inventory variables), maximum inventory constraints, and maximum sales constraints. As enumerated below, there are a total of 3,100 functional constraints, but all the constraints of each type follow the same pattern.

Functional Constraints.

1,000 production capacity constraints (one for each combination of a plant, machine, and month):

Production days used ≤ production days available,

where the left-hand side is the sum of 10 fractions, one for each product, where each fraction is that product's production quantity (a decision variable) *divided* by the product's production rate (a given constant).

1,000 plant balance constraints (one for each combination of a plant, product, and month):

Amount produced + inventory last month + amount shipped in = sales + current inventory + amount shipped out,

where the *amount produced* is the sum of the decision variables representing the production quantities at the machines, the *amount shipped in* is the sum of the decision variables representing the shipping quantities in from the other plants, and the *amount shipped out* is the sum of the decision variables representing the shipping quantities out to the other plants.

100 maximum inventory constraints (one for each combination of a plant and month):

Total inventory ≤ inventory capacity,

where the left-hand side is the sum of the decision variables representing the inventory quantities for the individual products.

1,000 maximum sales constraints (one for each combination of a plant, product, and month):

Sales ≤ demand.

Now let us see how the MPL modeling language, a product of Maximal Software, Inc., can formulate this huge model very compactly.

Formulation of the Model in MPL

The modeler begins by assigning a title to the model and listing an *index* for each of the entities of the problem, as illustrated below.

```
TITLE
    Production_Planning;

INDEX
    product    : = (A1, A2, A3, A4, A5, A6, A7, A8, A9, A10);
    month      : = (Jan, Feb, Mar, Apr, May, Jun, Jul, Aug, Sep, Oct);
    plant      : = (p1, p2, p3, p4, p5, p6, p7, p8, p9, p10);
    fromplant  : = plant;
    toplant    : = plant;
    machine    : = (m1, m2, m3, m4, m5, m6, m7, m8, m9, m10);
```

Except for the months, the entries on the right-hand side are arbitrary labels for the respective products, plants, and machines, where these same labels are used in the data files. Note that a colon is placed after the name of each entry and a semicolon is placed at the end of each statement (but a statement is allowed to extend over more than one line).

A big job with any large model is collecting and organizing the various types of data into data files. In this case, eight data files are needed to hold the product prices, demands, production costs, production rates, production days available, inventory costs, inventory capacities, and shipping costs. Numbering these data files as 1, 2, 3, . . . , 8, the next step is to give a brief suggestive name to each one and to identify (inside square brackets) the index or indexes over which the data in the file run, as shown below.

```
DATA
    Price [product]                        : = DATAFILE 1;
    Demand [plant, product, month]         : = DATAFILE 2;
    ProdCost [plant, machine, product]     : = DATAFILE 3;
    ProdRate [plant, machine, product]     : = DATAFILE 4;
    ProdDaysAvail [month]                  : = DATAFILE 5;
    InvtCost [product]                     : = DATAFILE 6;
    InvtCapacity [plant]                   : = DATAFILE 7;
    ShipCost [fromplant, toplant]          : = DATAFILE 8;
```

Next, the modeler gives a short name to each type of decision variable. Following the name, inside square brackets, is the index or indexes over which the subscripts run.

```
VARIABLES
   Produce [plant, machine, product, month]      → Prod;
   Inventory [plant, product, month]             → Invt;
   Sales [plant, product, month]                 → Sale;
   Ship [product, month, fromplant, toplant]
      WHERE (fromplant <> toplant);
```

In the case of the decision variables with names longer than four letters, the arrows on the right point to four-letter abbreviations to fit the size limitations of many solvers. The last line indicates that the fromplant subscript and toplant subscript are not allowed to have the same value.

There is one more step before writing down the model. To make the model easier to read, it is useful first to introduce *macros* to represent the summations in the objective function.

```
MACROS
   Total Revenue   : = SUM (plant, product, month: Price*Sales);
   TotalProdCost   : = SUM (plant, machine, product, month:
                           ProdCost*Produce);
   TotalInvtCost   : = SUM (plant, product, month:
                           InvtCost*Inventory);
   TotalShipCost   : = SUM (product, month, fromplant, toplant:
                           ShipCost*Ship);
   TotalCost       : = TotalProdCost + TotalInvtCost + TotalShipCost;
```

The first four macros use the MPL keyword SUM to execute the summation involved. Following each SUM keyword (inside the parentheses) is, first, the index or indexes over which the summation runs. Next (after the colon) is the vector product of a data vector (one of the data files) times a variable vector (one of the four types of decision variables).

Now this model with 3,100 functional constraints and 21,000 decision variables can be written down in the following compact form.

```
MODEL

   MAX Profit = TotalRevenue − TotalCost;

SUBJECT TO
   ProdCapacity [plant, machine, month]  → PCap;
      SUM (product: Produce/ProdRate) ≤ ProdDaysAvail;

   PlantBal [plant, product, month]  → PBal;
         SUM (machine: Produce) + Inventory [month − 1]
       + SUM (fromplant: Ship[fromplant, toplant: = plant])
     =
         Sales + Inventory
       + SUM (toplant: Ship[from plant: = plant, toplant]);

   MaxInventory [plant, month]  → MaxI;
      SUM (product: Inventory) ≤ InvtCapacity;

BOUNDS
   Sales ≤ Demand;

END
```

For each of the four types of constraints, the first line gives the name for this type. There is one constraint of this type for each combination of values for the indexes inside the square brackets following the name. To the right of the brackets, the arrow points to a four-letter abbreviation of the name that a solver can use. Below the first line, the general form of constraints of this type is shown by using the SUM operator.

For each production capacity constraint, each term in the summation consists of a decision variable (the production quantity of that product on that machine in that plant during that month) divided by the corresponding production rate, which gives the number of production days being used. Summing over the products then gives the total number of production days being used on that machine in that plant during that month, so this number must not exceed the number of production days available.

The purpose of the plant balance constraint for each plant, product, and month is to give the correct value to the current inventory variable, given the values of all the other decision variables including the inventory level for the preceding month. Each of the SUM operators in these constraints involves simply a sum of decision variables rather than a vector product. This is the case also for the SUM operator in the maximum inventory constraints. By contrast, the left-hand side of the maximum sales constraints is just a single decision variable for each of the 1,000 combinations of a plant, product, and month. (Separating these upper-bound constraints on individual variables from the regular functional constraints is advantageous because of the computational efficiencies that can be obtained by using the *upper bound technique* described in Sec. 7.3.) No lower-bound constraints are shown here because MPL automatically assumes that all 21,000 decision variables have nonnegativity constraints unless nonzero lower bounds are specified. For each of the 3,100 functional constraints, note that the left-hand side is a linear function of the decision variables and the right-hand side is a constant taken from the appropriate data file. Since the objective function also is a linear function of the decision variables, this model is a legitimate linear programming model.

To solve the model, MPL supports various leading **solvers** (software packages for solving linear programming models and related models) that can be installed into MPL. As discussed in Sec. 4.8, **CPLEX** is a particularly prominent and powerful solver. The version of MPL in your OR Courseware already has installed the student version of CPLEX, which uses the simplex method to solve linear programming models. Therefore, to solve such a model formulated with MPL, all you have to do is choose *Solve CPLEX* from the *Run* menu or press the *Run Solve* button in the *Toolbar.* You then can display the solution file in a view window by pressing the *View* button at the bottom of the *Status Window.*

This brief introduction to MPL illustrates the ease with which modelers can use modeling languages to formulate huge linear programming models in a clear, concise way. To assist you in using MPL, an MPL Tutorial is included on the CD-ROM. This tutorial goes through all the details of formulating smaller versions of the production planning example considered here. You also can see elsewhere on the CD-ROM how all the other linear programming examples in this chapter and subsequent chapters would be formulated with MPL and solved by CPLEX.

The LINGO Modeling Language

LINGO is another popular modeling language that is featured in this book. The company that produces LINGO, LINDO Systems, also produces a widely used solver called **LINDO** as well as a spreadsheet solver, What'sBest. All three share a common set of solvers based on the simplex method and, in more advanced versions, on the kind of algorithmic techniques introduced in Secs. 4.9 and 7.4 as well. (We will discuss LINDO further in Sec. 4.8 and Appendix 4.1.) As mentioned earlier, the student version of LINGO is available to you through downloading from the website, www.lindo.com.

Like MPL, LINGO enables a modeler to efficiently formulate a huge linear programming model in a clear, concise way. It also can be used for a wide variety of other models.

LINGO uses *sets* as its fundamental building block. For example, in the Worldwide Corp. production planning problem, the sets of interest include the collections of products, plants, machines, and months. Each member of a set may have one or more *attributes* associated with it, such as the price of a product, the inventory capacity of a plant, the production rate of a machine, and the number of production days available in a month. These attributes provide data for the model. Some set attributes, such as production quantities and shipping quantities, can be decision variables for the model. As with MPL, the SUM operator is commonly used to write the objective function and each constraint type in a compact form. After completing the formulation, the model can be solved by selecting the *Solve* command from the LINGO menu or pressing the *Solve* button on the toolbar.

An appendix to this chapter describes LINGO further and illustrates its use on a couple of small examples. A supplement on the CD-ROM shows how LINGO can be used to formulate the model for the Worldwide Corp. production planning example. A LINGO tutorial on the CD-ROM provides the details needed for doing basic modeling with this modeling language. The LINGO formulations and solutions for the various examples in both this chapter and many other chapters also are included on the CD-ROM.

3.8   CONCLUSIONS

Linear programming is a powerful technique for dealing with the problem of allocating limited resources among competing activities as well as other problems having a similar mathematical formulation. It has become a standard tool of great importance for numerous business and industrial organizations. Furthermore, almost any social organization is concerned with allocating resources in some context, and there is a growing recognition of the extremely wide applicability of this technique.

However, not all problems of allocating limited resources can be formulated to fit a linear programming model, even as a reasonable approximation. When one or more of the assumptions of linear programming is violated seriously, it may then be possible to apply another mathematical programming model instead, e.g., the models of integer programming (Chap. 12) or nonlinear programming (Chap. 13).

APPENDIX 3.1   THE LINGO MODELING LANGUAGE

LINGO is a mathematical modeling language designed particularly for formulating and solving a wide variety of optimization problems, including linear programming, integer programming (Chap. 12), and nonlinear programming (Chap. 13) problems. Extensive details and a downloadable student version can be found at www.lindo.com.

Simple problems are entered into LINGO in a fairly natural fashion. To illustrate, consider the following linear programming problem.

Maximize $Z = 20x + 31y,$

subject to

$$2x + 5y \leq 16$$
$$4x - 3y = 6$$

FIGURE A3.1
Screen shots showing the LINGO formulation and the LINGO solution report for a simple linear programming problem.

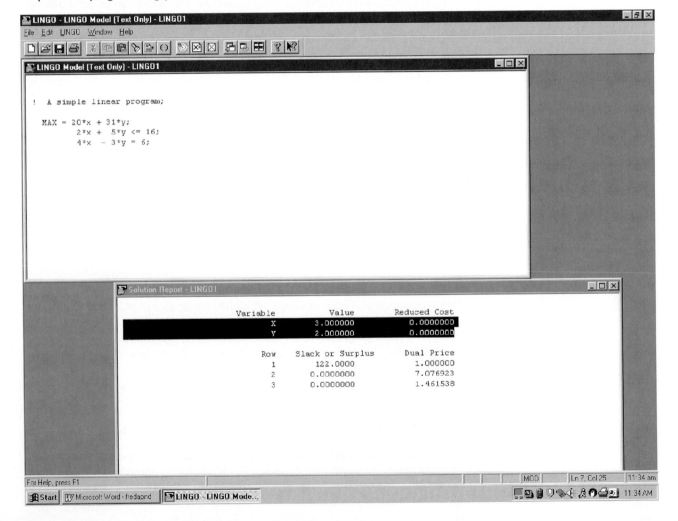

and

$$x \geq 0, \qquad y \geq 0.$$

The screen shot in the top half of Fig. A3.1 shows how this problem would be formulated with LINGO.

The first line of this formulation is just a comment describing the model. Note that the comment is preceded by an exclamation point and ended by a semicolon. This is a requirement for all comments in a LINGO formulation. The second line gives the objective function (without bothering to include the Z variable) and indicates that it is to be maximized. Note that each multiplication needs to be indicated by an asterisk. The objective function is ended by a semicolon, as is each of the functional constraints on the next two lines. The nonnegativity constraints are not shown in this formulation because these constraints are automatically assumed by LINGO. (If some variable x did *not* have a nonnegativity constraint, you would need to add @FREE(x); at the end of the formulation.)

Variables can be shown as either lowercase or uppercase, since LINGO is case-insensitive. For example, a variable x_1 can be typed in as either $x1$ or $X1$. Similarly, words can be either lowercase or uppercase (or a combination). For clarity, we will use uppercase for all reserved words that have a predefined meaning in LINGO.

Notice the menu bar at the top of the LINGO window in Fig. A3.1. The 'File' and 'Edit' menu items behave in a standard Windows fashion. To solve a model once it has been entered, click on the 'bullseye' icon. (If you are using a platform other than a Windows-based PC, instead type the GO command at the colon prompt and press the enter key.) Before attempting to solve the model, LINGO will first check whether your model has any syntax errors and, if so, will indicate where they occur. Assuming no such errors, a *solver* will begin solving the problem, during which time a *solver status* window will appear on the screen. (For linear programming models, the solver used is LINDO, which will be described in some detail in the appendix to the next chapter.) When the solver finishes, a *Solution Report* will appear on the screen.

The bottom half of Fig. A3.1 shows the solution report for our example. The *Value* column gives the optimal values of the decision variables. The first entry in the *Slack or Surplus* column shows the corresponding value of the objective function. The next two entries indicate the difference between the two sides of the respective constraints. The *Reduced Cost* and *Dual Price* columns provide some sensitivity analysis information for the problem. After discussing postoptimality analysis (including sensitivity analysis) in Sec. 4.7, we will explain what reduced costs and dual prices are while describing LINDO in Appendix 4.1. These quantities provide only a portion of the useful sensitivity analysis information. To generate a full sensitivity analysis report (such as shown in Appendix 4.1 for LINDO), the *Range* command in the LINGO menu would need to be chosen next.

Just as was illustrated with MPL in Sec. 3.7, LINGO is designed mainly for efficiently formulating very large models by simultaneously dealing with all constraints or variables of the same type. We soon will use the following example to illustrate how LINGO does this.

Example.   Consider a *production-mix problem* where we are concerned with what mix of four products we should produce during the upcoming week. For each product, each unit produced requires a known amount of production time on each of three machines. Each machine has a certain number of hours of production time available per week. Each product provides a certain profit per unit produced.

Table A3.1 shows three types of data: machine-related data, product-related data, and data related to combinations of a machine and product. The objective is to determine how much to produce of each product so that total profit is maximized while not exceeding the limited production capacity of each machine.

TABLE A3.1 Data needed for the product-mix example

| | Production Time per Unit, Hours | | | | |
| | Product | | | | Production Time |
Machine	P01	P02	P03	P04	Available per Week, Hours
Roll	1.7	2.1	1.4	2.4	28
Cut	1.1	2.5	1.7	2.6	34
Weld	1.6	1.3	1.6	0.8	21
Profit per unit	26	35	25	37	

In standard algebraic form, the structure of the linear programming model for this problem is to choose the nonnegative production levels (number of units produced during the upcoming week) for the four products so as to

Maximize $\sum_{j=1}^{4} c_j x_j,$

subject to

$$\sum_{j=1}^{4} a_{ij} x_j \leq b_j \qquad \text{for } i = 1, 2, 3;$$

where

x_j = production level for product P0j

c_j = unit profit for product P0j

a_{ij} = production time on machine i per unit of product P0j

b_i = production time available per week on machine i.

This model is small enough, with just 4 decision variables and 3 functional constraints, that it could be written out completely, term by term, but it would be tedious. In some similar applications, there might instead be hundreds of decision variables and functional constraints, so writing out a term-by-term version of this model each week would not be practical. LINGO provides a much more efficient and compact formulation, comparable to the above summary of the model, as we will see next.

Formulation of the Model in LINGO

This model has a repetitive nature. All the decision variables are of the same type and all the functional constraints are of the same type. LINGO uses *sets* to describe this repetitive nature.[1] The simple sets of interest in this case are

1. The set of machines, {*Roll, Cut, Weld*}.
2. The set of products, {P01, P02, P03, P04}.

[1]Order is implied in LINGO sets so, strictly speaking, they are not truly sets in the usual mathematical sense.

The attributes of interest for the members of these sets are

1. Attribute for each machine: Number of hours of production time available per week.
2. Attributes for each product: Profit per unit produced; Number of units produced per week.

Thus, the first two types of attributes are input data that will become parameters of the model, whereas the last type (number of units produced per week of the respective products) provides the decision variables for the model. Let us abbreviate these attributes as follows.

machine: ProdHoursAvail
product: Profit, Produce.

One other key type of information is the number of hours of production time that each unit of each product would use on each of the machines. This number can be viewed as an *attribute* for the members of the *set* of all combinations of a product and a machine. Since this set is derived from the two simple sets, it is referred to as a *derived set*. Let us abbreviate the attribute for members of this set as follows.

MaPr (machine, product): ProdHoursUsed

A LINGO formulation typically has three sections.

1. A SETS section that specifies the sets and their attributes. You can think of it as describing the structure of the data.
2. A DATA section that either provides the data to be used or indicates where it is to be obtained.
3. A section that provides the mathematical model itself.

We begin by showing the first two sections for the example below.

```
! LINGO3h;
! Product mix example;
! Notice: the SETS section says nothing about the number or names of
    the machines or products. That information is determined
    completely by supplied data;
SETS:
! The simple sets;
Machine: ProdHoursAvail;
Product: Profit, Produce;
! A derived set;
MaPr (Machine, Product): ProdHoursUsed;
ENDSETS
DATA:
! Get the names of the machines;
    Machine = Roll Cut Weld;
! Hours available on each machine;
ProdHoursAvail = 28  34  21;

! Get the names of the products;
  Product = P01  P02  P03  P04;
! Profit contribution per unit;
  Profit =   26   35   25    37;

! Hours needed per unit of product;
ProdHoursUsed = 1.7  2.1  1.4  2.4  ! Roll;
                1.1  2.5  1.7  2.6  ! Cut;
                1.6  1.3  1.6  0.8; ! Weld;
ENDDATA
```

Before presenting the mathematical model itself, we need to introduce two key *set looping functions* that enable applying an operation to all members of a set by using a single statement. One is the @SUM function, which computes the sum of an expression over all members of a set. The general form of @SUM is @SUM(set: expression). For every member of the set, the expression is computed, and then they are all added up. For example,

    @SUM(Product(j): Profit(j)*Produce(j))

sums the expression following the colon—the unit profit of a product *times* the production rate of the product—over all members of the set preceding the colon. In particular, since this set is the set of products {Product(j) for $j = 1, 2, 3, 4$}, the sum is over the index j. Therefore, this specific @SUM function provides the objective function,

$$\sum_{j=1}^{4} c_j x_j,$$

given earlier for the model.

The second key set looping function is the @FOR function. This function is used to generate constraints over members of a set. The general form is @FOR(set: constraint). For example,

    @FOR(Machine(i):
       @SUM(Product(i): ProdHoursUsed(i, j)*Produce (j))
                         <= ProdHoursAvail (i, j);
          );

says to generate the constraint following the colon for each member of the set preceding the colon. (The "less than or equal to" symbol, $\leq$, is not on the standard keyboard, so LINGO treats the standard keyboard symbols <= as equivalent to $\leq$.) This set is the set of machines {Machine (i) for $i = 1, 2, 3$}, so this function loops over the index i. For each i, the constraint following the colon was expressed algebraically earlier as

$$\sum_{j=1}^{4} a_{ij} x_j \leq b_j.$$

Therefore, after the third section of the LINGO formulation (the mathematical model itself) is added, we obtain the complete formulation shown below:

    ! LINGO3h;
    ! Product mix example;
    SETS:
    !The simple sets;
       Machine: ProdHoursAvail;
       Product: Profit, Produce;
    !A derived set;
       MaPr(Machine, Product): ProdHoursUsed;
    ENDSETS
    DATA:
    !Get the names of the machines;
        Machine = Roll Cut Weld;
    ! Hours available on each machine;
    ProdHoursAvail = 28 34 21;

```
! Get the names of the products;
    Product = P01  P02  P03  P04;
! Profit contribution per unit;
    Profit =   26   35   25   37;

! Hours needed per unit of product;
ProdHoursUsed = 1.7  2.1  1.4  2.4    ! Roll;
                1.1  2.5  1.7  2.6    ! Cut;
                1.6  1.3  1.6  0.8;   ! Weld;
ENDDATA
! Maximize total profit contribution;
MAX = @SUM( Product(i): Profit(i) * Produce(i));

! For each machine i;
  @FOR( Machine( i):
! Hours used must be <= hours available;
  @SUM( Product( j): ProdHoursUsed( i, j) * Produce( j))
            <= ProdHoursAvail;
      );
```

The model is solved by pressing the 'bullseye' button on the LINGO command bar. Pressing the 'x =' button on the command bar produces a report that looks in part as follows:

Variable	Value	Reduced Cost
PRODUCE(P01)	0.0000000	3.577921
PRODUCE(P02)	10.00000	0.0000000
PRODUCE(P03)	5.000000	0.0000000
PRODUCE(P04)	0.0000000	1.441558

Row	Slack or Surplus	Dual Price
1	475.0000	1.000000
2	0.0000000	15.25974
3	0.5000000	0.0000000
4	0.0000000	2.272727

Thus, we should produce 10 units of product P02 and 5 units of product P03, where Row 1 gives the resulting total profit of 475. Notice that this solution exactly uses the available capacity on the first and third machines (since Rows 2 and 4 give a Slack or Surplus of 0) and leaves the second machine with 0.5 hour of idleness. (We will discuss reduced costs and dual prices in Appendix 4.1 in conjunction with LINDO.)

The rows section of this report is slightly ambiguous in that you need to remember that Row 1 in the model concerns the objective function and the subsequent rows involve the constraints on machine capacities. This association can be made more clear in the report by giving names to each constraint in the model. This is done by enclosing the name in [ ], placed just in front of the constraint. See the following modified fragment of the model.

```
[Totprof] MAX = @SUM( Product: Profit * Produce);

! For each machine i;
  @FOR( Machine( i):
! Hours used must be <= hours available;
  [Capc] @SUM( Product( j): ProdHoursUsed( i, j) * Produce( j))
            <= ProdHoursAvail;
      );
```

The solution report now contains these row names.

Row	Slack or Surplus	Dual Price
TOTPROF	475.0000	1.000000
CAPC(ROLL)	0.0000000	15.25974
CAPC(CUT)	0.5000000	0.0000000
CAPC(WELD)	0.0000000	2.272727

An important feature of a LINGO model like this one is that it is completely "scalable" in products and machines. In other words, if you wanted to solve another version of this product-mix problem with a different number of machines and products, you would only have to enter the new data in the DATA section. You would not need to change the SETS section or any of the equations. This conversion could be done by clerical personnel without any understanding of the model equations.

Importing and Exporting Spreadsheet Data with LINGO

The above example was completely self-contained in the sense that all the data were directly incorporated into the LINGO formulation. In some other applications, a large body of data will be stored in some source and will need to be entered into the model from that source. One popular place for storing data is spreadsheets.

LINGO has a simple function, @OLE(), for retrieving and placing data from and into spreadsheets. To illustrate, let us suppose the data for our product-mix problem were originally entered into a spreadsheet as shown in Fig. A3.2. For the moment we are interested only in the shaded cells

FIGURE A3.2
Screen shot showing data for the product-mix example entered in a spreadsheet.

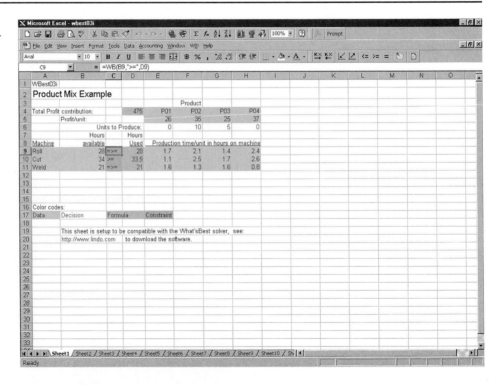

in columns A-B and E-H. The data in these cells completely describe our little product-mix example. We want to avoid retyping these data into our LINGO model. Suppose that this spreadsheet is stored in the file d:\dirfred7\wbest03i.xls. The only part of the LINGO model that needs to be changed is the DATA section as shown below.

```
DATA:
! Get the names of the machines;
    Machine = @OLE( 'd:\dirfred7\wbest03i.xls');
! Hours available on each machine;
  ProdHoursAvail = @OLE( 'd:\dirfred7\wbest03i.xls');

! Get the names of the products;
    Product = @OLE( 'd:\dirfred7\wbest03i.xls');
! Profit contribution per unit;
    Profit = @OLE( 'd:\dirfred7\wbest03i.xls');

! Hours needed per unit of product;
  ProdHoursUsed = @OLE( 'd:\dirfred7\wbest03i.xls');

! Send the solution values back;
  @OLE( 'd:\dirfred7\wbest03i.xls') = Produce;
ENDDATA
```

The @OLE() function acts as your "plumbing contractor." It lets the data flow from the spreadsheet to LINGO and back to the spreadsheet. So-called Object Linking and Embedding (OLE) is a feature of the Windows operating system. LINGO exploits this feature to make a link between the LINGO model and a spreadsheet. The first five uses of @OLE() above illustrate that this function can be used on the right of an assignment statement to retrieve data from a spreadsheet. The last use above illustrates that this function can be placed on the left of an assignment statement to place solution results into the spreadsheet instead. Notice from Fig. A3.2 that the optimal solution has been placed back into the spreadsheet in cells E6:H6. One simple but hidden step that had to be done beforehand in the spreadsheet was to define range names for the various collections of cells containing the data. Range names can be defined in Excel by using the mouse and the *Insert, Name, Define* menu item. For example, the set of cells A9:A11 was given the range name of Machine. Similarly, the set of cells E4:H4 was given the range name Product.

Importing and Exporting from a Database with LINGO

Another common repository for data in a large firm is in a database. In a manner similar to @OLE(), LINGO has a connection function, @ODBC(), for transferring data from and to a database. This function is based around the Open DataBase Connectivity (ODBC) standard for communicating with SQL (Structured Query Language) databases. Most popular databases, such as Oracle, Paradox, DB/2, MS Access, and SQL Server, support the ODBC convention.

Let us illustrate the ODBC connection for our little product-mix example. Suppose that all the data describing our problem are stored in a database called acces03j. The modification required in the LINGO model is almost trivial. Only the DATA section needs to be changed, as illustrated in the following fragment from the LINGO model.

```
DATA:
! Get the names of the machines and available hours;
  Machine, ProdHoursAvail = @ODBC( 'acces03j');

! Get the names of the products and profits;
  Product, Profit = @ODBC( 'acces03j');
```

```
! Hours needed per unit of product;
  ProdHoursUsed  = @ODBC( 'acces03j');

! Send the solution values back;
  @ODBC( 'acces03j') = Produce;
ENDDATA
```

Notice that, similar to the spreadsheet-based model, the size of the model in terms of the number of variables and constraints is determined completely by what is found in the database. The LINGO model automatically adjusts to what is found in the database.

Now let us show what is in the database considered above. It contains three related tables. We give these tables names to match those in the LINGO model, namely, 'Machine,' to hold machine-related data, 'Product,' to hold product-related data, and 'MaPr,' to hold data related to combinations of machines and products. Here is what the tables look like on the screen:

Machine

Machine	ProdHoursAvail
Roll	28
Cut	34
Weld	21

Product

Product	Profit	Produce
P01	26	
P02	35	
P03	25	
P04	37	

MaPr

Machine	Product	ProdHoursUsed
Roll	P01	1.7
Roll	P02	2.1
Roll	P03	1.4
Roll	P04	2.4
Cut	P01	1.1
Cut	P02	2.5
Cut	P03	1.7
Cut	P04	2.6
Weld	P01	1.6
Weld	P02	1.3
Weld	P03	1.6
Weld	P04	0.8

Notice that the 'Produce' column has been left blank in the Product table. Once we solve the model, the 'Produce' amounts get inserted into the database and the Product table looks as follows:

Product

Product	Profit	Produce
P01	26	0
P02	35	10
P03	25	5
P04	37	0

There is one complication in using ODBC in Windows 95. The user must "register" the database with the Windows ODBC administrator. One does this by accessing (with mouse clicks) the My Computer/Control Panel/ODBC32 window. Once there, the user must give a name to the database (which may differ from the actual name of the file in which the data tables reside) and specify the directory in which the database file resides. It is this registered name that should be used in the LINGO model. Because the database has been registered, you did not see a directory specification in the @ODBC('acces03j') in the LINGO model. The ODBC manager knows the location of the database just from its name.

More about LINGO

Only some of the capabilities of LINGO have been illustrated in this appendix. More details can be found in the documentation that accompanies LINGO when it is downloaded. LINGO is available in a variety of sizes. The smallest version is the *demo* version that can be downloaded from www.lindo.com. It is designed for textbook-sized problems (currently a maximum of 150 functional constraints and 300 decision variables). However, the largest version (called the *extended* version) is limited only by the storage space available. Tens of thousands of functional constraints and hundreds of thousands of decision variables are not unusual.

If you would like to see how LINGO can formulate a huge model like the production planning example introduced in Sec. 3.7, a supplement to this appendix on the book's website, www.mhhe.com/hillier, shows the LINGO formulation of this example. By reducing the number of products, plants, machines, and months, the supplement also introduces actual data into the formulation and then shows the complete solution. The supplement goes on to discuss and illustrate the debugging and verification of this large model. The supplement also describes further how to retrieve data from external files (including spreadsheets) and how to insert results in existing files.

In addition to this supplement, the CD-ROM includes both a LINGO tutorial and LINGO/LINDO files with numerous examples of LINGO formulations.

SELECTED REFERENCES

1. Anderson, D. R., D. J. Sweeney, and T. A. Williams: *An Introduction to Management Science,* 9th ed., West, St. Paul, MN, 2000, chaps. 2, 4.
2. Gass, S.: *An Illustrated Guide to Linear Programming,* Dover Publications, New York, 1990.
3. Hillier, F. S., M. S. Hillier, and G. J. Lieberman: *Introduction to Management Science: A Modeling and Case Studies Approach with Spreadsheets,* Irwin/McGraw-Hill, Burr Ridge, IL, 2000, chaps. 2, 3.

4. *LINGO User's Guide,* LINDO Systems, Inc., Chicago, IL, e-mail: info@lindo.com, 1999.

5. *MPL Modeling System* (*Release* 4.0) manual, Maximal Software, Inc., Arlington, VA, e-mail: info@maximal-usa.com, 1998.

6. Williams, H. P.: *Model Building in Mathematical Programming,* 3d ed., Wiley, New York, 1990.

LEARNING AIDS FOR THIS CHAPTER IN YOUR OR COURSEWARE

A Demonstration Example in OR Tutor:

Graphical Method

An Excel Add-In:

Premium Solver

"Ch. 3—Intro to LP" Files for Solving the Examples:

Excel File
LINGO/LINDO File
MPL/CPLEX File

Supplement to Appendix 3.1:

More about LINGO (appears on the book's website, www.mhhe.com/hillier).

See Appendix 1 for documentation of the software.

PROBLEMS

The symbols to the left of some of the problems (or their parts) have the following meaning:

D: The demonstration example listed above may be helpful.

C: Use the computer to solve the problem by applying the simplex method. The available software options for doing this include the Excel Solver or Premium Solver (Sec. 3.6), MPL/CPLEX (Sec. 3.7), LINGO (Appendix 3.1), and LINDO (Appendix 4.1), but follow any instructions given by your instructor regarding the option to use.

An asterisk on the problem number indicates that at least a partial answer is given in the back of the book.

D **3.1-1.*** For each of the following constraints, draw a separate graph to show the nonnegative solutions that satisfy this constraint.
(a) $x_1 + 3x_2 \leq 6$
(b) $4x_1 + 3x_2 \leq 12$
(c) $4x_1 + x_2 \leq 8$

(d) Now combine these constraints into a single graph to show the feasible region for the entire set of functional constraints plus nonnegativity constraints.

D **3.1-2.** Consider the following objective function for a linear programming model:

Maximize $Z = 2x_1 + 3x_2$

(a) Draw a graph that shows the corresponding objective function lines for $Z = 6$, $Z = 12$, and $Z = 18$.
(b) Find the slope-intercept form of the equation for each of these three objective function lines. Compare the slope for these three lines. Also compare the intercept with the x_2 axis.

3.1-3. Consider the following equation of a line:

$20x_1 + 40x_2 = 400$

(a) Find the slope-intercept form of this equation.

(b) Use this form to identify the slope and the intercept with the x_2 axis for this line.

(c) Use the information from part (b) to draw a graph of this line.

D **3.1-4.*** Use the graphical method to solve the problem:

Maximize $Z = 2x_1 + x_2,$

subject to

$$
\begin{aligned}
x_2 &\le 10 \\
2x_1 + 5x_2 &\le 60 \\
x_1 + x_2 &\le 18 \\
3x_1 + x_2 &\le 44
\end{aligned}
$$

and

$$ x_1 \ge 0, \qquad x_2 \ge 0. $$

D **3.1-5.** Use the graphical method to solve the problem:

Maximize $Z = 10x_1 + 20x_2,$

subject to

$$
\begin{aligned}
-x_1 + 2x_2 &\le 15 \\
x_1 + x_2 &\le 12 \\
5x_1 + 3x_2 &\le 45
\end{aligned}
$$

and

$$ x_1 \ge 0, \qquad x_2 \ge 0. $$

3.1-6. The Whitt Window Company is a company with only three employees which makes two different kinds of hand-crafted windows: a wood-framed and an aluminum-framed window. They earn $60 profit for each wood-framed window and $30 profit for each aluminum-framed window. Doug makes the wood frames, and can make 6 per day. Linda makes the aluminum frames, and can make 4 per day. Bob forms and cuts the glass, and can make 48 square feet of glass per day. Each wood-framed window uses 6 square feet of glass and each aluminum-framed window uses 8 square feet of glass.

The company wishes to determine how many windows of each type to produce per day to maximize total profit.

(a) Describe the analogy between this problem and the Wyndor Glass Co. problem discussed in Sec. 3.1. Then construct and fill in a table like Table 3.1 for this problem, identifying both the activities and the resources.

(b) Formulate a linear programming model for this problem.

D **(c)** Use the graphical model to solve this model.

(d) A new competitor in town has started making wood-framed windows as well. This may force the company to lower the price they charge and so lower the profit made for each wood-framed window. How would the optimal solution change (if at all) if the profit per wood-framed window decreases from $60 to $40? From $60 to $20?

(e) Doug is considering lowering his working hours, which would decrease the number of wood frames he makes per day. How would the optimal solution change if he makes only 5 wood frames per day?

3.1-7. The Apex Television Company has to decide on the number of 27- and 20-inch sets to be produced at one of its factories. Market research indicates that at most 40 of the 27-inch sets and 10 of the 20-inch sets can be sold per month. The maximum number of work-hours available is 500 per month. A 27-inch set requires 20 work-hours and a 20-inch set requires 10 work-hours. Each 27-inch set sold produces a profit of $120 and each 20-inch set produces a profit of $80. A wholesaler has agreed to purchase all the television sets produced if the numbers do not exceed the maxima indicated by the market research.

(a) Formulate a linear programming model for this problem.

D **(b)** Use the graphical method to solve this model.

3.1-8. The WorldLight Company produces two light fixtures (products 1 and 2) that require both metal frame parts and electrical components. Management wants to determine how many units of each product to produce so as to maximize profit. For each unit of product 1, 1 unit of frame parts and 2 units of electrical components are required. For each unit of product 2, 3 units of frame parts and 2 units of electrical components are required. The company has 200 units of frame parts and 300 units of electrical components. Each unit of product 1 gives a profit of $1, and each unit of product 2, up to 60 units, gives a profit of $2. Any excess over 60 units of product 2 brings no profit, so such an excess has been ruled out.

(a) Formulate a linear programming model for this problem.

D **(b)** Use the graphical method to solve this model. What is the resulting total profit?

3.1-9. The Primo Insurance Company is introducing two new product lines: special risk insurance and mortgages. The expected profit is $5 per unit on special risk insurance and $2 per unit on mortgages.

Management wishes to establish sales quotas for the new product lines to maximize total expected profit. The work requirements are as follows:

Department	Work-Hours per Unit		Work-Hours Available
	Special Risk	**Mortgage**	
Underwriting	3	2	2400
Administration	0	1	800
Claims	2	0	1200

(a) Formulate a linear programming model for this problem.

D **(b)** Use the graphical method to solve this model.

(c) Verify the exact value of your optimal solution from part (b) by solving algebraically for the simultaneous solution of the relevant two equations.

3.1-10. Weenies and Buns is a food processing plant which manufactures hot dogs and hot dog buns. They grind their own flour for the hot dog buns at a maximum rate of 200 pounds per week. Each hot dog bun requires 0.1 pound of flour. They currently have a contract with Pigland, Inc., which specifies that a delivery of 800 pounds of pork product is delivered every Monday. Each hot dog requires $\frac{1}{4}$ pound of pork product. All the other ingredients in the hot dogs and hot dog buns are in plentiful supply. Finally, the labor force at Weenies and Buns consists of 5 employees working full time (40 hours per week each). Each hot dog requires 3 minutes of labor, and each hot dog bun requires 2 minutes of labor. Each hot dog yields a profit of $0.20, and each bun yields a profit of $0.10.

Weenies and Buns would like to know how many hot dogs and how many hot dog buns they should produce each week so as to achieve the highest possible profit.

(a) Formulate a linear programming model for this problem.

D **(b)** Use the graphical method to solve this model.

3.1-11.* The Omega Manufacturing Company has discontinued the production of a certain unprofitable product line. This act created considerable excess production capacity. Management is considering devoting this excess capacity to one or more of three products; call them products 1, 2, and 3. The available capacity on the machines that might limit output is summarized in the following table:

Machine Type	Available Time (Machine Hours per Week)
Milling machine	500
Lathe	350
Grinder	150

The number of machine hours required for each unit of the respective products is

Productivity coefficient (in machine hours per unit)

Machine Type	Product 1	Product 2	Product 3
Milling machine	9	3	5
Lathe	5	4	0
Grinder	3	0	2

The sales department indicates that the sales potential for products 1 and 2 exceeds the maximum production rate and that the sales potential for product 3 is 20 units per week. The unit profit would be $50, $20, and $25, respectively, on products 1, 2, and 3. The objective is to determine how much of each product Omega should produce to maximize profit.

(a) Formulate a linear programming model for this problem.

C **(b)** Use a computer to solve this model by the simplex method.

D **3.1-12.** Consider the following problem, where the value of c_1 has not yet been ascertained.

$$\text{Maximize} \quad Z = c_1 x_1 + x_2,$$

subject to

$$x_1 + x_2 \leq 6$$
$$x_1 + 2x_2 \leq 10$$

and

$$x_1 \geq 0, \qquad x_2 \geq 0.$$

Use graphical analysis to determine the optimal solution(s) for (x_1, x_2) for the various possible values of $c_1(-\infty < c_1 < \infty)$.

D **3.1-13.** Consider the following problem, where the value of k has not yet been ascertained.

$$\text{Maximize} \quad Z = x_1 + 2x_2,$$

subject to

$$-x_1 + x_2 \leq 2$$
$$x_2 \leq 3$$
$$kx_1 + x_2 \leq 2k + 3, \qquad \text{where } k \geq 0$$

and

$$x_1 \geq 0, \qquad x_2 \geq 0.$$

The solution currently being used is $x_1 = 2, x_2 = 3$. Use graphical analysis to determine the values of k such that this solution actually is optimal.

D **3.1-14.** Consider the following problem, where the values of c_1 and c_2 have not yet been ascertained.

$$\text{Maximize} \quad Z = c_1 x_1 + c_2 x_2,$$

subject to

$$2x_1 + x_2 \leq 11$$
$$-x_1 + 2x_2 \leq 2$$

and

$$x_1 \geq 0, \qquad x_2 \geq 0.$$

Use graphical analysis to determine the optimal solution(s) for (x_1, x_2) for the various possible values of c_1 and c_2. (*Hint:* Separate the cases where $c_2 = 0$, $c_2 > 0$, and $c_2 < 0$. For the latter two cases, focus on the ratio of c_1 to c_2.)

3.2-1. The following table summarizes the key facts about two products, A and B, and the resources, Q, R, and S, required to produce them.

Resource	Resource Usage per Unit Produced		Amount of Resource Available
	Product A	Product B	
Q	2	1	2
R	1	2	2
S	3	3	4
Profit per unit	3	2	

All the assumptions of linear programming hold.
(a) Formulate a linear programming model for this problem.
D **(b)** Solve this model graphically.
(c) Verify the exact value of your optimal solution from part (*b*) by solving algebraically for the simultaneous solution of the relevant two equations.

3.2-2. The shaded area in the following graph represents the feasible region of a linear programming problem whose objective function is to be maximized.

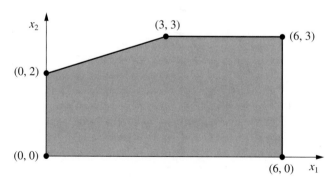

Label each of the following statements as True or False, and then justify your answer based on the graphical method. In each case, give an example of an objective function that illustrates your answer.
(a) If (3, 3) produces a larger value of the objective function than (0, 2) and (6, 3), then (3, 3) must be an optimal solution.
(b) If (3, 3) is an optimal solution and multiple optimal solutions exist, then either (0, 2) or (6, 3) must also be an optimal solution.
(c) The point (0, 0) cannot be an optimal solution.

3.2-3.* This is your lucky day. You have just won a $10,000 prize. You are setting aside $4,000 for taxes and partying expenses, but you have decided to invest the other $6,000. Upon hearing this news, two different friends have offered you an opportunity to become a partner in two different entrepreneurial ventures, one planned by each friend. In both cases, this investment would involve expending some of your time next summer as well as putting up cash. Becoming a *full* partner in the first friend's venture would require an investment of $5,000 and 400 hours, and your estimated profit (ignoring the value of your time) would be $4,500. The corresponding figures for the second friend's venture are $4,000 and 500 hours, with an estimated profit to you of $4,500. However, both friends are flexible and would allow you to come in at any *fraction* of a full partnership you would like. If you choose a fraction of a full partnership, all the above figures given for a full partnership (money investment, time investment, and your profit) would be multiplied by this same fraction.

Because you were looking for an interesting summer job anyway (maximum of 600 hours), you have decided to participate in one or both friends' ventures in whichever combination would maximize your total estimated profit. You now need to solve the problem of finding the best combination.
(a) Describe the analogy between this problem and the Wyndor Glass Co. problem discussed in Sec. 3.1. Then construct and fill in a table like Table 3.1 for this problem, identifying both the activities and the resources.
(b) Formulate a linear programming model for this problem.
D **(c)** Use the graphical method to solve this model. What is your total estimated profit?

D **3.2-4.** Use the graphical method to find all optimal solutions for the following model:

$$\text{Maximize} \quad Z = 500x_1 + 300x_2,$$

subject to

$$15x_1 + 5x_2 \leq 300$$
$$10x_1 + 6x_2 \leq 240$$
$$8x_1 + 12x_2 \leq 450$$

and

$$x_1 \geq 0, \qquad x_2 \geq 0.$$

D **3.2-5.** Use the graphical method to demonstrate that the following model has no feasible solutions.

$$\text{Maximize} \quad Z = 5x_1 + 7x_2,$$

subject to

$$2x_1 - x_2 \leq -1$$
$$-x_1 + 2x_2 \leq -1$$

and

$$x_1 \geq 0, \qquad x_2 \geq 0.$$

D **3.2-6.** Suppose that the following constraints have been provided for a linear programming model.

$$-x_1 + 3x_2 \leq 30$$
$$-3x_1 + x_2 \leq 30$$

and

$$x_1 \geq 0, \qquad x_2 \geq 0.$$

(a) Demonstrate that the feasible region is unbounded.
(b) If the objective is to maximize $Z = -x_1 + x_2$, does the model have an optimal solution? If so, find it. If not, explain why not.
(c) Repeat part (b) when the objective is to maximize $Z = x_1 - x_2$.
(d) For objective functions where this model has no optimal solution, does this mean that there are no good solutions according to the model? Explain. What probably went wrong when formulating the model?

3.3-1. Reconsider Prob. 3.2-3. Indicate why each of the four assumptions of linear programming (Sec. 3.3) appears to be reasonably satisfied for this problem. Is one assumption more doubtful than the others? If so, what should be done to take this into account?

3.3-2. Consider a problem with two decision variables, x_1 and x_2, which represent the levels of activities 1 and 2, respectively. For each variable, the permissible values are 0, 1, and 2, where the feasible combinations of these values for the two variables are determined from a variety of constraints. The objective is to maximize a certain measure of performance denoted by Z. The values of Z for the possibly feasible values of (x_1, x_2) are estimated to be those given in the following table:

x_1	x_2		
	0	**1**	**2**
0	0	4	8
1	3	8	13
2	6	12	18

Based on this information, indicate whether this problem completely satisfies each of the four assumptions of linear programming. Justify your answers.

3.4-1.* For each of the four assumptions of linear programming discussed in Sec. 3.3, write a one-paragraph analysis of how well you feel it applies to each of the following examples given in Sec. 3.4:

(a) Design of radiation therapy (Mary).
(b) Regional planning (Southern Confederation of Kibbutzim).
(c) Controlling air pollution (Nori & Leets Co.).

3.4-2. For each of the four assumptions of linear programming discussed in Sec. 3.3, write a one-paragraph analysis of how well it applies to each of the following examples given in Sec. 3.4.
(a) Reclaiming solid wastes (Save-It Co.).
(b) Personnel scheduling (Union Airways).
(c) Distributing goods through a distribution network (Distribution Unlimited Co.).

D **3.4-3.** Use the graphical method to solve this problem:

Maximize $\qquad Z = 15x_1 + 20x_2,$

subject to

$$x_1 + 2x_2 \geq 10$$
$$2x_1 - 3x_2 \leq 6$$
$$x_1 + x_2 \geq 6$$

and

$$x_1 \geq 0, \qquad x_2 \geq 0.$$

D **3.4-4.** Use the graphical method to solve this problem:

Minimize $\qquad Z = 3x_1 + 2x_2,$

subject to

$$x_1 + 2x_2 \leq 12$$
$$2x_1 + 3x_2 = 12$$
$$2x_1 + x_2 \geq 8$$

and

$$x_1 \geq 0, \qquad x_2 \geq 0.$$

D **3.4-5.** Consider the following problem, where the value of c_1 has not yet been ascertained.

Maximize $\qquad Z = c_1 x_1 + 2x_2,$

subject to

$$4x_1 + x_2 \leq 12$$
$$x_1 - x_2 \geq 2$$

and

$$x_1 \geq 0, \qquad x_2 \geq 0.$$

Use graphical analysis to determine the optimal solution(s) for (x_1, x_2) for the various possible values of c_1.

D **3.4-6.** Consider the following model:

Minimize $\qquad Z = 40x_1 + 50x_2,$

subject to

$$2x_1 + 3x_2 \geq 30$$
$$x_1 + x_2 \geq 12$$
$$2x_1 + x_2 \geq 20$$

and

$$x_1 \geq 0, \qquad x_2 \geq 0.$$

(a) Use the graphical method to solve this model.
(b) How does the optimal solution change if the objective function is changed to $Z = 40x_1 + 70x_2$?
(c) How does the optimal solution change if the third functional constraint is changed to $2x_1 + x_2 \geq 15$?

3.4-7. Ralph Edmund loves steaks and potatoes. Therefore, he has decided to go on a steady diet of only these two foods (plus some liquids and vitamin supplements) for all his meals. Ralph realizes that this isn't the healthiest diet, so he wants to make sure that he eats the right quantities of the two foods to satisfy some key nutritional requirements. He has obtained the following nutritional and cost information:

Ingredient	Grams of Ingredient per Serving Steak	Grams of Ingredient per Serving Potatoes	Daily Requirement (Grams)
Carbohydrates	5	15	≥ 50
Protein	20	5	≥ 40
Fat	15	2	≤ 60
Cost per serving	$4	$2	

Ralph wishes to determine the number of daily servings (may be fractional) of steak and potatoes that will meet these requirements at a minimum cost.
(a) Formulate a linear programming model for this problem.
D (b) Use the graphical method to solve this model.
C (c) Use a computer to solve this model by the simplex method.

3.4-8. Dwight is an elementary school teacher who also raises pigs for supplemental income. He is trying to decide what to feed his pigs. He is considering using a combination of pig feeds available from local suppliers. He would like to feed the pigs at minimum cost while also making sure each pig receives an adequate supply of calories and vitamins. The cost, calorie content, and vitamin content of each feed is given in the table below.

Contents	Feed Type A	Feed Type B
Calories (per pound)	800	1,000
Vitamins (per pound)	140 units	70 units
Cost (per pound)	$0.40	$0.80

Each pig requires at least 8,000 calories per day and at least 700 units of vitamins. A further constraint is that no more than one-third of the diet (by weight) can consist of Feed Type A, since it contains an ingredient which is toxic if consumed in too large a quantity.
(a) Formulate a linear programming model for this problem.
D (b) Use the graphical method to solve this model. What is the resulting daily cost per pig?

3.4-9. Web Mercantile sells many household products through an on-line catalog. The company needs substantial warehouse space for storing its goods. Plans now are being made for leasing warehouse storage space over the next 5 months. Just how much space will be required in each of these months is known. However, since these space requirements are quite different, it may be most economical to lease only the amount needed each month on a month-by-month basis. On the other hand, the additional cost for leasing space for additional months is much less than for the first month, so it may be less expensive to lease the maximum amount needed for the entire 5 months. Another option is the intermediate approach of changing the total amount of space leased (by adding a new lease and/or having an old lease expire) at least once but not every month.

The space requirement and the leasing costs for the various leasing periods are as follows:

Month	Required Space (Sq. Ft.)	Leasing Period (Months)	Cost per Sq. Ft. Leased
1	30,000	1	$ 65
2	20,000	2	$100
3	40,000	3	$135
4	10,000	4	$160
5	50,000	5	$190

The objective is to minimize the total leasing cost for meeting the space requirements.
(a) Formulate a linear programming model for this problem.
C (b) Solve this model by the simplex method.

3.4-10. Larry Edison is the director of the Computer Center for Buckly College. He now needs to schedule the staffing of the center. It is open from 8 A.M. until midnight. Larry has monitored the usage of the center at various times of the day, and determined that the following number of computer consultants are required:

Time of Day	Minimum Number of Consultants Required to Be on Duty
8 A.M.–noon	4
Noon–4 P.M.	8
4 P.M.–8 P.M.	10
8 P.M.–midnight	6

Two types of computer consultants can be hired: full-time and part-time. The full-time consultants work for 8 consecutive hours in any of the following shifts: morning (8 A.M.–4 P.M.), afternoon (noon–8 P.M.), and evening (4 P.M.–midnight). Full-time consultants are paid $14 per hour.

Part-time consultants can be hired to work any of the four shifts listed in the above table. Part-time consultants are paid $12 per hour.

An additional requirement is that during every time period, there must be at least 2 full-time consultants on duty for every part-time consultant on duty.

Larry would like to determine how many full-time and how many part-time workers should work each shift to meet the above requirements at the minimum possible cost.
(a) Formulate a linear programming model for this problem.
C (b) Solve this model by the simplex method.

3.4-11.* The Medequip Company produces precision medical diagnostic equipment at two factories. Three medical centers have placed orders for this month's production output. The table to the right shows what the cost would be for shipping each unit from each factory to each of these customers. Also shown are the number of units that will be produced at each factory and the number of units ordered by each customer. (Go to the next column.)

From \ To	Unit Shipping Cost			Output
	Customer 1	Customer 2	Customer 3	
Factory 1	$600	$800	$700	400 units
Factory 2	$400	$900	$600	500 units
Order size	300 units	200 units	400 units	

A decision now needs to be made about the shipping plan for how many units to ship from each factory to each customer.
(a) Formulate a linear programming model for this problem.
C (b) Solve this model by the simplex method.

3.4-12. The Fagersta Steelworks currently is working two mines to obtain its iron ore. This iron ore is shipped to either of two storage facilities. When needed, it then is shipped on to the company's steel plant. The diagram below depicts this distribution network, where M1 and M2 are the two mines, S1 and S2 are the two storage facilities, and P is the steel plant. The diagram also shows the monthly amounts produced at the mines and needed at the plant, as well as the shipping cost and the maximum amount that can be shipped per month through each shipping lane. (Go to the left column below the diagram.)

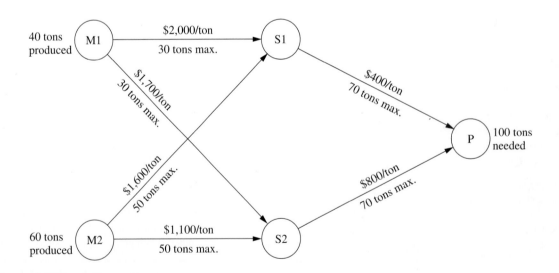

Management now wants to determine the most economical plan for shipping the iron ore from the mines through the distribution network to the steel plant.
(a) Formulate a linear programming model for this problem.
C (b) Solve this model by the simplex method.

3.4-13.* Al Ferris has $60,000 that he wishes to invest now in order to use the accumulation for purchasing a retirement annuity in 5 years. After consulting with his financial adviser, he has been offered four types of fixed-income investments, which we will label as investments A, B, C, D.

Investments A and B are available at the beginning of each of the next 5 years (call them years 1 to 5). Each dollar invested in A at the beginning of a year returns $1.40 (a profit of $0.40) 2 years later (in time for immediate reinvestment). Each dollar invested in B at the beginning of a year returns $1.70 three years later.

Investments C and D will each be available at one time in the future. Each dollar invested in C at the beginning of year 2 returns $1.90 at the end of year 5. Each dollar invested in D at the beginning of year 5 returns $1.30 at the end of year 5.

Al wishes to know which investment plan maximizes the amount of money that can be accumulated by the beginning of year 6.

(a) All the functional constraints for this problem can be expressed as equality constraints. To do this, let A_t, B_t, C_t, and D_t be the amount invested in investment A, B, C, and D, respectively, at the beginning of year t for each t where the investment is available and will mature by the end of year 5. Also let R_t be the number of available dollars *not* invested at the beginning of year t (and so available for investment in a later year). Thus, the amount invested at the beginning of year t *plus* R_t must equal the number of dollars available for investment at that time. Write such an equation in terms of the relevant variables above for the beginning of each of the 5 years to obtain the five functional constraints for this problem.

(b) Formulate a complete linear programming model for this problem.

c (c) Solve this model by the simplex model.

3.4-14. The Metalco Company desires to blend a new alloy of 40 percent tin, 35 percent zinc, and 25 percent lead from several available alloys having the following properties:

Property	Alloy				
	1	2	3	4	5
Percentage of tin	60	25	45	20	50
Percentage of zinc	10	15	45	50	40
Percentage of lead	30	60	10	30	10
Cost ($/lb)	22	20	25	24	27

The objective is to determine the proportions of these alloys that should be blended to produce the new alloy at a minimum cost.

(a) Formulate a linear programming model for this problem.

c (b) Solve this model by the simplex method.

3.4-15. The Weigelt Corporation has three branch plants with excess production capacity. Fortunately, the corporation has a new product ready to begin production, and all three plants have this capability, so some of the excess capacity can be used in this way. This product can be made in three sizes—large, medium, and small—that yield a net unit profit of $420, $360, and $300, respectively. Plants 1, 2, and 3 have the excess capacity to produce 750, 900, and 450 units per day of this product, respectively, regardless of the size or combination of sizes involved.

The amount of available in-process storage space also imposes a limitation on the production rates of the new product. Plants 1, 2, and 3 have 13,000, 12,000, and 5,000 square feet, respectively, of in-process storage space available for a day's production of this product. Each unit of the large, medium, and small sizes produced per day requires 20, 15, and 12 square feet, respectively.

Sales forecasts indicate that if available, 900, 1,200, and 750 units of the large, medium, and small sizes, respectively, would be sold per day.

At each plant, some employees will need to be laid off unless most of the plant's excess production capacity can be used to produce the new product. To avoid layoffs if possible, management has decided that the plants should use the same percentage of their excess capacity to produce the new product.

Management wishes to know how much of each of the sizes should be produced by each of the plants to maximize profit.

(a) Formulate a linear programming model for this problem.

c (b) Solve this model by the simplex method.

3.4-16* A cargo plane has three compartments for storing cargo: front, center, and back. These compartments have capacity limits on both *weight* and *space*, as summarized below:

Compartment	Weight Capacity (Tons)	Space Capacity (Cubic Feet)
Front	12	7,000
Center	18	9,000
Back	10	5,000

Furthermore, the weight of the cargo in the respective compartments must be the same proportion of that compartment's weight capacity to maintain the balance of the airplane.

The following four cargoes have been offered for shipment on an upcoming flight as space is available:

Cargo	Weight (Tons)	Volume (Cubic Feet/Ton)	Profit ($/Ton)
1	20	500	320
2	16	700	400
3	25	600	360
4	13	400	290

Any portion of these cargoes can be accepted. The objective is to determine how much (if any) of each cargo should be accepted and how to distribute each among the compartments to maximize the total profit for the flight.

(a) Formulate a linear programming model for this problem.

c **(b)** Solve this model by the simplex method to find one of its multiple optimal solutions.

3.4-17. Comfortable Hands is a company which features a product line of winter gloves for the entire family—men, women, and children. They are trying to decide what mix of these three types of gloves to produce.

Comfortable Hands' manufacturing labor force is unionized. Each full-time employee works a 40-hour week. In addition, by union contract, the number of full-time employees can never drop below 20. Nonunion part-time workers can also be hired with the following union-imposed restrictions: (1) each part-time worker works 20 hours per week, and (2) there must be at least 2 full-time employees for each part-time employee.

All three types of gloves are made out of the same 100 percent genuine cowhide leather. Comfortable Hands has a long-term contract with a supplier of the leather, and receives a 5,000 square feet shipment of the material each week. The material requirements and labor requirements, along with the *gross profit* per glove sold (not considering labor costs) is given in the following table.

Glove	Material Required (Square Feet)	Labor Required (Minutes)	Gross Profit (per Pair)
Men's	2	30	$8
Women's	1.5	45	$10
Children's	1	40	$6

Each full-time employee earns $13 per hour, while each part-time employee earns $10 per hour. Management wishes to know what mix of each of the three types of gloves to produce per week, as well as how many full-time and how many part-time workers to employ. They would like to maximize their *net profit*—their gross profit from sales minus their labor costs.

(a) Formulate a linear programming model for this problem.

c **(b)** Solve this model by the simplex method.

3.4-18. Oxbridge University maintains a powerful mainframe computer for research use by its faculty, Ph.D. students, and research associates. During all working hours, an operator must be available to operate and maintain the computer, as well as to perform some programming services. Beryl Ingram, the director of the computer facility, oversees the operation.

It is now the beginning of the fall semester, and Beryl is confronted with the problem of assigning different working hours to her operators. Because all the operators are currently enrolled in the university, they are available to work only a limited number of hours each day, as shown in the following table.

		Maximum Hours of Availability				
Operators	Wage Rate	Mon.	Tue.	Wed.	Thurs.	Fri.
K. C.	$10.00/hour	6	0	6	0	6
D. H.	$10.10/hour	0	6	0	6	0
H. B.	$ 9.90/hour	4	8	4	0	4
S. C.	$ 9.80/hour	5	5	5	0	5
K. S.	$10.80/hour	3	0	3	8	0
N. K.	$11.30/hour	0	0	0	6	2

There are six operators (four undergraduate students and two graduate students). They all have different wage rates because of differences in their experience with computers and in their programming ability. The above table shows their wage rates, along with the maximum number of hours that each can work each day.

Each operator is guaranteed a certain minimum number of hours per week that will maintain an adequate knowledge of the operation. This level is set arbitrarily at 8 hours per week for the undergraduate students (K. C., D. H., H. B., and S. C.) and 7 hours per week for the graduate students (K. S. and N. K.).

The computer facility is to be open for operation from 8 A.M. to 10 P.M. Monday through Friday with exactly one operator on duty during these hours. On Saturdays and Sundays, the computer is to be operated by other staff.

Because of a tight budget, Beryl has to minimize cost. She wishes to determine the number of hours she should assign to each operator on each day.

(a) Formulate a linear programming model for this problem.

c **(b)** Solve this model by the simplex method.

3.4-19. Slim-Down Manufacturing makes a line of nutritionally complete, weight-reduction beverages. One of their products is a strawberry shake which is designed to be a complete meal. The strawberry shake consists of several ingredients. Some information about each of these ingredients is given below.

Ingredient	Calories from Fat (per tbsp)	Total Calories (per tbsp)	Vitamin Content (mg/ tbsp)	Thickeners (mg/ tbsp)	Cost (¢/ tbsp)
Strawberry flavoring	1	50	20	3	10
Cream	75	100	0	8	8
Vitamin supplement	0	0	50	1	25
Artificial sweetener	0	120	0	2	15
Thickening agent	30	80	2	25	6

The nutritional requirements are as follows. The beverage must total between 380 and 420 calories (inclusive). No more than 20 percent of the total calories should come from fat. There must be at least 50 milligrams (mg) of vitamin content. For taste reasons, there must be at least 2 tablespoons (tbsp) of strawberry flavoring for each tablespoon of artificial sweetener. Finally, to maintain proper thickness, there must be exactly 15 mg of thickeners in the beverage.

Management would like to select the quantity of each ingredient for the beverage which would minimize cost while meeting the above requirements.

(a) Formulate a linear programming model for this problem.

C (b) Solve this model by the simplex method.

3.4-20. Joyce and Marvin run a day care for preschoolers. They are trying to decide what to feed the children for lunches. They would like to keep their costs down, but also need to meet the nutritional requirements of the children. They have already decided to go with peanut butter and jelly sandwiches, and some combination of graham crackers, milk, and orange juice. The nutritional content of each food choice and its cost are given in the table below.

Food Item	Calories from Fat	Total Calories	Vitamin C (mg)	Protein (g)	Cost (¢)
Bread (1 slice)	10	70	0	3	5
Peanut butter (1 tbsp)	75	100	0	4	4
Strawberry jelly (1 tbsp)	0	50	3	0	7
Graham cracker (1 cracker)	20	60	0	1	8
Milk (1 cup)	70	150	2	8	15
Juice (1 cup)	0	100	120	1	35

The nutritional requirements are as follows. Each child should receive between 400 and 600 calories. No more than 30 percent of the total calories should come from fat. Each child should consume at least 60 milligrams (mg) of vitamin C and 12 grams (g) of protein. Furthermore, for practical reasons, each child needs exactly 2 slices of bread (to make the sandwich), at least twice as much peanut butter as jelly, and at least 1 cup of liquid (milk and/or juice).

Joyce and Marvin would like to select the food choices for each child which minimize cost while meeting the above requirements.

(a) Formulate a linear programming model for this problem.

C (b) Solve this model by the simplex method.

3.5-1. Read the article footnoted in Sec. 3.5 that describes the first case study presented in that section: "Choosing the Product Mix at Ponderosa Industrial."

(a) Describe the two factors which, according to the article, often hinder the use of optimization models by managers.

(b) Section 3.5 indicates without elaboration that using linear programming at Ponderosa "led to a dramatic shift in the types of plywood products emphasized by the company." Identify this shift.

(c) With the success of this application, management then was eager to use optimization for other problems as well. Identify these other problems.

(d) Photocopy the two pages of appendixes that give the mathematical formulation of the problem and the structure of the linear programming model.

3.5-2. Read the article footnoted in Sec. 3.5 that describes the second case study presented in that section: "Personnel Scheduling at United Airlines."

(a) Describe how United Airlines prepared shift schedules at airports and reservations offices prior to this OR study.

(b) When this study began, the *problem definition phase* defined five specific project requirements. Identify these project requirements.

(c) At the end of the presentation of the corresponding example in Sec. 3.4 (personnel scheduling at Union Airways), we pointed out that the divisibility assumption does not hold for this kind of application. An integer solution is needed, but linear programming may provide an optimal solution that is non-integer. How does United Airlines deal with this problem?

(d) Describe the flexibility built into the scheduling system to satisfy the group culture at each office. Why was this flexibility needed?

(e) Briefly describe the tangible and intangible benefits that resulted from the study.

3.5-3. Read the 1986 article footnoted in Sec. 2.1 that describes the third case study presented in Sec. 3.5: "Planning Supply, Distribution, and Marketing at Citgo Petroleum Corporation."

(a) What happened during the years preceding this OR study that made it vastly more important to control the amount of capital tied up in inventory?

(b) What geographical area is spanned by Citgo's distribution network of pipelines, tankers, and barges? Where do they market their products?

(c) What time periods are included in the model?

(d) Which computer did Citgo use to solve the model? What were typical run times?

(e) Who are the four types of model users? How does each one use the model?

(f) List the major types of reports generated by the SDM system.

(g) What were the major implementation challenges for this study?

(h) List the direct and indirect benefits that were realized from this study.

3.6-1.* You are given the following data for a linear programming problem where the objective is to maximize the profit from allocating three resources to two nonnegative activities.

Resource	Resource Usage per Unit of Each Activity		Amount of Resource Available
	Activity 1	**Activity 2**	
1	2	1	10
2	3	3	20
3	2	4	20
Contribution per unit	$20	$30	

Contribution per unit = profit per unit of the activity.

(a) Formulate a linear programming model for this problem.
D **(b)** Use the graphical method to solve this model.
(c) Display the model on an Excel spreadsheet.
(d) Use the spreadsheet to check the following solutions: $(x_1, x_2) = (2, 2), (3, 3), (2, 4), (4, 2), (3, 4), (4, 3)$. Which of these solutions are feasible? Which of these feasible solutions has the best value of the objective function?
C **(e)** Use the Excel Solver to solve the model by the simplex method.

3.6-2. Ed Butler is the production manager for the Bilco Corporation, which produces three types of spare parts for automobiles. The manufacture of each part requires processing on each of two machines, with the following processing times (in hours):

Machine	Part		
	A	**B**	**C**
1	0.02	0.03	0.05
2	0.05	0.02	0.04

Each machine is available 40 hours per month. Each part manufactured will yield a unit profit as follows:

	Part		
	A	**B**	**C**
Profit	$50	$40	$30

Ed wants to determine the mix of spare parts to produce in order to maximize total profit.
(a) Formulate a linear programming model for this problem.
(b) Display the model on an Excel spreadsheet.

(c) Make three guesses of your own choosing for the optimal solution. Use the spreadsheet to check each one for feasibility and, if feasible, to find the value of the objective function. Which feasible guess has the best objective function value?
(d) Use the Excel Solver to solve the model by the simplex method.

3.6-3. You are given the following data for a linear programming problem where the objective is to minimize the cost of conducting two nonnegative activities so as to achieve three benefits that do not fall below their minimum levels.

Benefit	Benefit Contribution per Unit of Each Activity		Minimum Acceptable Level
	Activity 1	**Activity 2**	
1	5	3	60
2	2	2	30
3	7	9	126
Unit cost	$60	$50	

(a) Formulate a linear programming model for this problem.
D **(b)** Use the graphical method to solve this model.
(c) Display the model on an Excel spreadsheet.
(d) Use the spreadsheet to check the following solutions: $(x_1, x_2) = (7, 7), (7, 8), (8, 7), (8, 8), (8, 9), (9, 8)$. Which of these solutions are feasible? Which of these feasible solutions has the best value of the objective function?
C **(e)** Use the Excel Solver to solve this model by the simplex method.

3.6-4.* Fred Jonasson manages a family-owned farm. To supplement several food products grown on the farm, Fred also raises pigs for market. He now wishes to determine the quantities of the available types of feed (corn, tankage, and alfalfa) that should be given to each pig. Since pigs will eat any mix of these feed types, the objective is to determine which mix will meet certain nutritional requirements at a *minimum cost*. The number of units of each type of basic nutritional ingredient contained within a kilogram of each feed type is given in the following table, along with the daily nutritional requirements and feed costs:

Nutritional Ingredient	Kilogram of Corn	Kilogram of Tankage	Kilogram of Alfalfa	Minimum Daily Requirement
Carbohydrates	90	20	40	200
Protein	30	80	60	180
Vitamins	10	20	60	150
Cost (¢)	84	72	60	

(a) Formulate a linear programming model for this problem.
(b) Display the model on an Excel spreadsheet.
(c) Use the spreadsheet to check if $(x_1, x_2, x_3) = (1, 2, 2)$ is a feasible solution and, if so, what the daily cost would be for this diet. How many units of each nutritional ingredient would this diet provide daily?
(d) Take a few minutes to use a trial-and-error approach with the spreadsheet to develop your best guess for the optimal solution. What is the daily cost for your solution?
c **(e)** Use the Excel Solver to solve the model by the simplex method.

3.6-5. Maureen Laird is the chief financial officer for the Alva Electric Co., a major public utility in the midwest. The company has scheduled the construction of new hydroelectric plants 5, 10, and 20 years from now to meet the needs of the growing population in the region served by the company. To cover at least the construction costs, Maureen needs to invest some of the company's money now to meet these future cash-flow needs. Maureen may purchase only three kinds of financial assets, each of which costs $1 million per unit. Fractional units may be purchased. The assets produce income 5, 10, and 20 years from now, and that income is needed to cover at least minimum cash-flow requirements in those years. (Any excess income above the minimum requirement for each time period will be used to increase dividend payments to shareholders rather than saving it to help meet the minimum cash-flow requirement in the next time period.) The following table shows both the amount of income generated by each unit of each asset and the minimum amount of income needed for each of the future time periods when a new hydroelectric plant will be constructed.

	Income per Unit of Asset			Minimum Cash Flow Required
Year	Asset 1	Asset 2	Asset 3	
5	$2 million	$1 million	$0.5 million	$400 million
10	$0.5 million	$0.5 million	$1 million	$100 million
20	0	$1.5 million	$2 million	$300 million

Maureen wishes to determine the mix of investments in these assets that will cover the cash-flow requirements while minimizing the total amount invested.
(a) Formulate a linear programming model for this problem.
(b) Display the model on a spreadsheet.
(c) Use the spreadsheet to check the possibility of purchasing 100 units of Asset 1, 100 units of Asset 2, and 200 units of Asset 3. How much cash flow would this mix of investments generate 5, 10, and 20 years from now? What would be the total amount invested?

(d) Take a few minutes to use a trial-and-error approach with the spreadsheet to develop your best guess for the optimal solution. What is the total amount invested for your solution?
c **(e)** Use the Excel Solver to solve the model by the simplex method.

3.7-1. The Philbrick Company has two plants on opposite sides of the United States. Each of these plants produces the same two products and then sells them to wholesalers within its half of the country. The orders from wholesalers have already been received for the next 2 months (February and March), where the number of units requested are shown below. (The company is not obligated to completely fill these orders but will do so if it can without decreasing its profits.)

	Plant 1		Plant 2	
Product	February	March	February	March
1	3,600	6,300	4,900	4,200
2	4,500	5,400	5,100	6,000

Each plant has 20 production days available in February and 23 production days available in March to produce and ship these products. Inventories are depleted at the end of January, but each plant has enough inventory capacity to hold 1,000 units total of the two products if an excess amount is produced in February for sale in March. In either plant, the cost of holding inventory in this way is $3 per unit of product 1 and $4 per unit of product 2.

Each plant has the same two production processes, each of which can be used to produce either of the two products. The production cost per unit produced of each product is shown below for each process in each plant.

	Plant 1		Plant 2	
Product	Process 1	Process 2	Process 1	Process 2
1	$62	$59	$61	$65
2	$78	$85	$89	$86

The production rate for each product (number of units produced per day devoted to that product) also is given below for each process in each plant.

	Plant 1		Plant 2	
Product	Process 1	Process 2	Process 1	Process 2
1	100	140	130	110
2	120	150	160	130

The net sales revenue (selling price minus normal shipping costs) the company receives when a plant sells the products to its own customers (the wholesalers in its half of the country) is $83 per unit of product 1 and $112 per unit of product 2. However, it also is possible (and occasionally desirable) for a plant to make a shipment to the other half of the country to help fill the sales of the other plant. When this happens, an extra shipping cost of $9 per unit of product 1 and $7 per unit of product 2 is incurred.

Management now needs to determine how much of each product should be produced by each production process in each plant during each month, as well as how much each plant should sell of each product in each month and how much each plant should ship of each product in each month to the other plant's customers. The objective is to determine which feasible plan would maximize the total profit (total net sales revenue minus the sum of the production costs, inventory costs, and extra shipping costs).

(a) Formulate a complete linear programming model in algebraic form that shows the individual constraints and decision variables for this problem.

c (b) Formulate this same model on an Excel spreadsheet instead. Then use the Excel Solver to solve the model.

c (c) Use MPL to formulate this model in a compact form. Then use the MPL solver CPLEX to solve the model.

c (d) Use LINGO to formulate this model in a compact form. Then use the LINGO solver to solve the model.

c **3.7-2.** Reconsider Prob. 3.1-11.
(a) Use MPL/CPLEX to formulate and solve the model for this problem.
(b) Use LINGO to formulate and solve this model.

c **3.7-3.** Reconsider Prob. 3.4-11.
(a) Use MPL/CPLEX to formulate and solve the model for this problem.
(b) Use LINGO to formulate and solve this model.

c **3.7-4.** Reconsider Prob. 3.4-15.
(a) Use MPL/CPLEX to formulate and solve the model for this problem.
(b) Use LINGO to formulate and solve this model.

c **3.7-5.** Reconsider Prob. 3.4-18.
(a) Use MPL/CPLEX to formulate and solve the model for this problem.
(b) Use LINGO to formulate and solve this model.

c **3.7-6.** Reconsider Prob. 3.6-4.
(a) Use MPL/CPLEX to formulate and solve the model for this problem.
(b) Use LINGO to formulate and solve this model.

c **3.7-7.** Reconsider Prob. 3.6-5.
(a) Use MPL/CPLEX to formulate and solve the model for this problem.
(b) Use LINGO to formulate and solve this model.

3.7-8. A large paper manufacturing company, the Quality Paper Corporation, has 10 paper mills from which it needs to supply 1,000 customers. It uses three alternative types of machines and four types of raw materials to make five different types of paper. Therefore, the company needs to develop a detailed production distribution plan on a monthly basis, with an objective of minimizing the total cost of producing and distributing the paper during the month. Specifically, it is necessary to determine jointly the amount of each type of paper to be made at each paper mill on each type of machine *and* the amount of each type of paper to be shipped from each paper mill to each customer.

The relevant data can be expressed symbolically as follows:

D_{jk} = number of units of paper type k demanded by customer j,

r_{klm} = number of units of raw material m needed to produce 1 unit of paper type k on machine type l,

R_{im} = number of units of raw material m available at paper mill i,

c_{kl} = number of capacity units of machine type l that will produce 1 unit of paper type k,

C_{il} = number of capacity units of machine type l available at paper mill i,

P_{ikl} = production cost for each unit of paper type k produced on machine type l at paper mill i,

T_{ijk} = transportation cost for each unit of paper type k shipped from paper mill i to customer j.

(a) Using these symbols, formulate a linear programming model for this problem by hand.
(b) How many functional constraints and decision variables does this model have?
c (c) Use MPL to formulate this problem.
c (d) Use LINGO to formulate this problem.

CASE 3.1   AUTO ASSEMBLY

Automobile Alliance, a large automobile manufacturing company, organizes the vehicles it manufactures into three families: a family of trucks, a family of small cars, and a family of midsized and luxury cars. One plant outside Detroit, MI, assembles two models from the family of midsized and luxury cars. The first model, the Family Thrillseeker, is a four-door sedan with vinyl seats, plastic interior, standard features, and excellent gas mileage. It is marketed as a smart buy for middle-class families with tight budgets, and each Family Thrillseeker sold generates a modest profit of $3,600 for the company. The second model, the Classy Cruiser, is a two-door luxury sedan with leather seats, wooden interior, custom features, and navigational capabilities. It is marketed as a privilege of affluence for upper-middle-class families, and each Classy Cruiser sold generates a healthy profit of $5,400 for the company.

Rachel Rosencrantz, the manager of the assembly plant, is currently deciding the production schedule for the next month. Specifically, she must decide how many Family Thrillseekers and how many Classy Cruisers to assemble in the plant to maximize profit for the company. She knows that the plant possesses a capacity of 48,000 labor-hours during the month. She also knows that it takes 6 labor-hours to assemble one Family Thrillseeker and 10.5 labor-hours to assemble one Classy Cruiser.

Because the plant is simply an assembly plant, the parts required to assemble the two models are not produced at the plant. They are instead shipped from other plants around the Michigan area to the assembly plant. For example, tires, steering wheels, windows, seats, and doors all arrive from various supplier plants. For the next month, Rachel knows that she will be able to obtain only 20,000 doors (10,000 left-hand doors and 10,000 right-hand doors) from the door supplier. A recent labor strike forced the shutdown of that particular supplier plant for several days, and that plant will not be able to meet its production schedule for the next month. Both the Family Thrillseeker and the Classy Cruiser use the same door part.

In addition, a recent company forecast of the monthly demands for different automobile models suggests that the demand for the Classy Cruiser is limited to 3,500 cars. There is no limit on the demand for the Family Thrillseeker within the capacity limits of the assembly plant.

(a) Formulate and solve a linear programming problem to determine the number of Family Thrillseekers and the number of Classy Cruisers that should be assembled.

Before she makes her final production decisions, Rachel plans to explore the following questions independently except where otherwise indicated.

(b) The marketing department knows that it can pursue a targeted $500,000 advertising campaign that will raise the demand for the Classy Cruiser next month by 20 percent. Should the campaign be undertaken?

(c) Rachel knows that she can increase next month's plant capacity by using overtime labor. She can increase the plant's labor-hour capacity by 25 percent. With the new assembly plant capacity, how many Family Thrillseekers and how many Classy Cruisers should be assembled?

(d) Rachel knows that overtime labor does not come without an extra cost. What is the maximum amount she should be willing to pay for all overtime labor beyond the cost of this labor at regular time rates? Express your answer as a lump sum.

(e) Rachel explores the option of using both the targeted advertising campaign and the overtime labor-hours. The advertising campaign raises the demand for the Classy Cruiser by 20 percent, and the overtime labor increases the plant's labor-hour capacity by 25 percent. How many Family Thrillseekers and how many Classy Cruisers should be assembled using the advertising campaign and overtime labor-hours if the profit from each Classy Cruiser sold continues to be 50 percent more than for each Family Thrillseeker sold?

(f) Knowing that the advertising campaign costs $500,000 and the maximum usage of overtime labor-hours costs $1,600,000 beyond regular time rates, is the solution found in part (e) a wise decision compared to the solution found in part (a)?

(g) Automobile Alliance has determined that dealerships are actually heavily discounting the price of the Family Thrillseekers to move them off the lot. Because of a profit-sharing agreement with its dealers, the company is therefore not making a profit of $3,600 on the Family Thrillseeker but is instead making a profit of $2,800. Determine the number of Family Thrillseekers and the number of Classy Cruisers that should be assembled given this new discounted price.

(h) The company has discovered quality problems with the Family Thrillseeker by randomly testing Thrillseekers at the end of the assembly line. Inspectors have discovered that in over 60 percent of the cases, two of the four doors on a Thrillseeker do not seal properly. Because the percentage of defective Thrillseekers determined by the random testing is so high, the floor supervisor has decided to perform quality control tests on every Thrillseeker at the end of the line. Because of the added tests, the time it takes to assemble one Family Thrillseeker has increased from 6 to 7.5 hours. Determine the number of units of each model that should be assembled given the new assembly time for the Family Thrillseeker.

(i) The board of directors of Automobile Alliance wishes to capture a larger share of the luxury sedan market and therefore would like to meet the full demand for Classy Cruisers. They ask Rachel to determine by how much the profit of her assembly plant would decrease as compared to the profit found in part (a). They then ask her to meet the full demand for Classy Cruisers if the decrease in profit is not more than $2,000,000.

(j) Rachel now makes her final decision by combining all the new considerations described in parts (f), (g), and (h). What are her final decisions on whether to undertake the advertising campaign, whether to use overtime labor, the number of Family Thrillseekers to assemble, and the number of Classy Cruisers to assemble?

CASE 3.2   CUTTING CAFETERIA COSTS

A cafeteria at All-State University has one special dish it serves like clockwork every Thursday at noon. This supposedly tasty dish is a casserole that contains sautéed onions, boiled sliced potatoes, green beans, and cream of mushroom soup. Unfortunately, students fail to see the special quality of this dish, and they loathingly refer to it as the Killer Casserole. The students reluctantly eat the casserole, however, because the cafeteria provides only a limited selection of dishes for Thursday's lunch (namely, the casserole).

Maria Gonzalez, the cafeteria manager, is looking to cut costs for the coming year, and she believes that one sure way to cut costs is to buy less expensive and perhaps lower-quality ingredients. Because the casserole is a weekly staple of the cafeteria menu, she concludes that if she can cut costs on the ingredients purchased for the casserole, she can significantly reduce overall cafeteria operating costs. She therefore decides to invest time in determining how to minimize the costs of the casserole while maintaining nutritional and taste requirements.

Maria focuses on reducing the costs of the two main ingredients in the casserole, the potatoes and green beans. These two ingredients are responsible for the greatest costs, nutritional content, and taste of the dish.

Maria buys the potatoes and green beans from a wholesaler each week. Potatoes cost $0.40 per pound, and green beans cost $1.00 per pound.

All-State University has established nutritional requirements that each main dish of the cafeteria must meet. Specifically, the total amount of the dish prepared for all the students for one meal must contain 180 grams (g) of protein, 80 milligrams (mg) of iron, and 1,050 mg of vitamin C. (There are 453.6 g in 1 lb and 1,000 mg in 1 g.) For simplicity when planning, Maria assumes that only the potatoes and green beans contribute to the nutritional content of the casserole.

Because Maria works at a cutting-edge technological university, she has been exposed to the numerous resources on the World Wide Web. She decides to surf the Web to find the nutritional content of potatoes and green beans. Her research yields the following nutritional information about the two ingredients:

	Potatoes	Green Beans
Protein	1.5 g per 100 g	5.67 g per 10 ounces
Iron	0.3 mg per 100 g	3.402 mg per 10 ounces
Vitamin C	12 mg per 100 g	28.35 mg per 10 ounces

(There are 28.35 g in 1 ounce.)

Edson Branner, the cafeteria cook who is surprisingly concerned about taste, informs Maria that an edible casserole must contain at least a six to five ratio in the weight of potatoes to green beans.

Given the number of students who eat in the cafeteria, Maria knows that she must purchase enough potatoes and green beans to prepare a minimum of 10 kilograms (kg) of casserole each week. (There are 1,000 g in 1 kg.) Again for simplicity in planning, she assumes that only the potatoes and green beans determine the amount of casserole that can be prepared. Maria does not establish an upper limit on the amount of casserole to prepare, since she knows all leftovers can be served for many days thereafter or can be used creatively in preparing other dishes.

(a) Determine the amount of potatoes and green beans Maria should purchase each week for the casserole to minimize the ingredient costs while meeting nutritional, taste, and demand requirements.

Before she makes her final decision, Maria plans to explore the following questions independently except where otherwise indicated.

(b) Maria is not very concerned about the taste of the casserole; she is only concerned about meeting nutritional requirements and cutting costs. She therefore forces Edson to change the recipe to allow for only at least a one to two ratio in the weight of potatoes to green beans. Given the new recipe, determine the amount of potatoes and green beans Maria should purchase each week.

(c) Maria decides to lower the iron requirement to 65 mg since she determines that the other ingredients, such as the onions and cream of mushroom soup, also provide iron. Determine the amount of potatoes and green beans Maria should purchase each week given this new iron requirement.

(d) Maria learns that the wholesaler has a surplus of green beans and is therefore selling the green beans for a lower price of $0.50 per lb. Using the same iron requirement from part (c) and the new price of green beans, determine the amount of potatoes and green beans Maria should purchase each week.

(e) Maria decides that she wants to purchase lima beans instead of green beans since lima beans are less expensive and provide a greater amount of protein and iron than green beans. Maria again wields her absolute power and forces Edson to change the recipe to include lima beans instead of green beans. Maria knows she can purchase lima beans for $0.60 per lb from the wholesaler. She also knows that lima beans contain 22.68 g of protein per 10 ounces of lima beans, 6.804 mg of iron per 10 ounces of lima beans, and no vitamin C. Using the new cost and nutritional content of lima beans, determine the amount of potatoes and lima beans Maria should purchase each week to minimize the ingredient costs while meeting nutritional, taste, and demand requirements. The nutritional requirements include the reduced iron requirement from part (c).

(f) Will Edson be happy with the solution in part (e)? Why or why not?

(g) An All-State student task force meets during Body Awareness Week and determines that All-State University's nutritional requirements for iron are too lax and that those for vitamin C are too stringent. The task force urges the university to adopt a policy that requires each serving of an entrée to contain at least 120 mg of iron and at least 500 mg of vitamin C. Using potatoes and lima beans as the ingredients for the dish and using the new nutritional requirements, determine the amount of potatoes and lima beans Maria should purchase each week.

CASE 3.3   STAFFING A CALL CENTER[1]

California Children's Hospital has been receiving numerous customer complaints because of its confusing, decentralized appointment and registration process. When customers want to make appointments or register child patients, they must contact the clinic or department they plan to visit. Several problems exist with this current strategy. Parents do not always know the most appropriate clinic or department they must visit to address their children's ailments. They therefore spend a significant amount of time on the phone being transferred from clinic to clinic until they reach the most appropriate clinic for their needs. The hospital also does not publish the phone numbers of all clinic and departments, and parents must therefore invest a large amount of time in detective work to track down the correct phone number. Finally, the various clinics and departments do not communicate with each other. For example, when a doctor schedules a referral with a colleague located in another department or clinic, that department or clinic almost never receives word of the referral. The parent must contact the correct department or clinic and provide the needed referral information.

[1]This case is based on an actual project completed by a team of master's students in the Department of Engineering-Economic Systems and Operations Research at Stanford University.

In efforts to reengineer and improve its appointment and registration process, the children's hospital has decided to centralize the process by establishing one call center devoted exclusively to appointments and registration. The hospital is currently in the middle of the planning stages for the call center. Lenny Davis, the hospital manager, plans to operate the call center from 7 A.M. to 9 P.M. during the weekdays.

Several months ago, the hospital hired an ambitious management consulting firm, Creative Chaos Consultants, to forecast the number of calls the call center would receive each hour of the day. Since all appointment and registration-related calls would be received by the call center, the consultants decided that they could forecast the calls at the call center by totaling the number of appointment and registration-related calls received by all clinics and departments. The team members visited all the clinics and departments, where they diligently recorded every call relating to appointments and registration. They then totaled these calls and altered the totals to account for calls missed during data collection. They also altered totals to account for repeat calls that occurred when the same parent called the hospital many times because of the confusion surrounding the decentralized process. Creative Chaos Consultants determined the average number of calls the call center should expect during each hour of a weekday. The following table provides the forecasts.

Work Shift	Average Number of Calls
7 A.M.–9 A.M.	40 calls per hour
9 A.M.–11 A.M.	85 calls per hour
11 A.M.–1 P.M.	70 calls per hour
1 P.M.–3 P.M.	95 calls per hour
3 P.M.–5 P.M.	80 calls per hour
5 P.M.–7 P.M.	35 calls per hour
7 P.M.–9 P.M.	10 calls per hour

After the consultants submitted these forecasts, Lenny became interested in the percentage of calls from Spanish speakers since the hospital services many Spanish patients. Lenny knows that he has to hire some operators who speak Spanish to handle these calls. The consultants performed further data collection and determined that on average, 20 percent of the calls were from Spanish speakers.

Given these call forecasts, Lenny must now decide how to staff the call center during each 2 hour shift of a weekday. During the forecasting project, Creative Chaos Consultants closely observed the operators working at the individual clinics and departments and determined the number of calls operators process per hour. The consultants informed Lenny that an operator is able to process an average of six calls per hour. Lenny also knows that he has both full-time and part-time workers available to staff the call center. A full-time employee works 8 hours per day, but because of paperwork that must also be completed, the employee spends only 4 hours per day on the phone. To balance the schedule, the employee alternates the 2-hour shifts between answering phones and completing paperwork. Full-time employees can start their day either by answering phones or by completing paperwork on the first shift. The full-time employees speak either Spanish or English, but none of them are bilingual. Both Spanish-speaking and English-speaking employees are paid $10 per hour for work before 5 P.M. and $12 per hour for work after 5 P.M. The full-time employees can begin work at the beginning of the 7 A.M. to 9 A.M. shift, 9 A.M. to 11 A.M. shift, 11 A.M. to 1 P.M. shift, or 1 P.M. to 3 P.M. shift. The part-time employees work for 4 hours, only answer calls, and only speak English. They can start work at the beginning of the 3 P.M. to 5 P.M. shift or the 5 P.M. to 7 P.M. shift, and like the full-time employees, they are paid $10 per hour for work before 5 P.M. and $12 per hour for work after 5 P.M.

For the following analysis consider only the labor cost for the time employees spend answering phones. The cost for paperwork time is charged to other cost centers.

(a) How many Spanish-speaking operators and how many English-speaking operators does the hospital need to staff the call center during each 2-hour shift of the day in order to answer all calls? Please provide an integer number since half a human operator makes no sense.

(b) Lenny needs to determine how many full-time employees who speak Spanish, full-time employees who speak English, and part-time employees he should hire to begin on each shift. Creative Chaos Consultants advise him that linear programming can be used to do this in such a way as to minimize operating costs while answering all calls. Formulate a linear programming model of this problem.

(c) Obtain an optimal solution for the linear programming model formulated in part (b) to guide Lenny's decision.

(d) Because many full-time workers do not want to work late into the evening, Lenny can find only one qualified English-speaking operator willing to begin work at 1 P.M. Given this new constraint, how many full-time English-speaking operators, full-time Spanish-speaking operators, and part-time operators should Lenny hire for each shift to minimize operating costs while answering all calls?

(e) Lenny now has decided to investigate the option of hiring bilingual operators instead of monolingual operators. If all the operators are bilingual, how many operators should be working during each 2-hour shift to answer all phone calls? As in part (a), please provide an integer answer.

(f) If all employees are bilingual, how many full-time and part-time employees should Lenny hire to begin on each shift to minimize operating costs while answering all calls? As in part (b), formulate a linear programming model to guide Lenny's decision.

(g) What is the maximum percentage increase in the hourly wage rate that Lenny can pay bilingual employees over monolingual employees without increasing the total operating costs?

(h) What other features of the call center should Lenny explore to improve service or minimize operating costs?

4

Solving Linear Programming Problems: The Simplex Method

We now are ready to begin studying the *simplex method,* a general procedure for solving linear programming problems. Developed by George Dantzig in 1947, it has proved to be a remarkably efficient method that is used routinely to solve huge problems on today's computers. Except for its use on tiny problems, this method is always executed on a computer, and sophisticated software packages are widely available. Extensions and variations of the simplex method also are used to perform *postoptimality analysis* (including sensitivity analysis) on the model.

This chapter describes and illustrates the main features of the simplex method. The first section introduces its general nature, including its geometric interpretation. The following three sections then develop the procedure for solving any linear programming model that is in our standard form (maximization, all functional constraints in $\leq$ form, and nonnegativity constraints on all variables) and has only *nonnegative* right-hand sides b_i in the functional constraints. Certain details on resolving ties are deferred to Sec. 4.5, and Sec. 4.6 describes how to adapt the simplex method to other model forms. Next we discuss postoptimality analysis (Sec. 4.7), and describe the computer implementation of the simplex method (Sec. 4.8). Section 4.9 then introduces an alternative to the simplex method (the interior-point approach) for solving large linear programming problems.

4.1 THE ESSENCE OF THE SIMPLEX METHOD

The simplex method is an *algebraic* procedure. However, its underlying concepts are *geometric.* Understanding these geometric concepts provides a strong intuitive feeling for how the simplex method operates and what makes it so efficient. Therefore, before delving into algebraic details, we focus in this section on the big picture from a geometric viewpoint.

To illustrate the general geometric concepts, we shall use the Wyndor Glass Co. example presented in Sec. 3.1. (Sections 4.2 and 4.3 use the *algebra* of the simplex method to solve this same example.) Section 5.1 will elaborate further on these geometric concepts for larger problems.

To refresh your memory, the model and graph for this example are repeated in Fig. 4.1. The five constraint boundaries and their points of intersection are highlighted in this figure because they are the keys to the analysis. Here, each **constraint boundary** is a line that forms the boundary of what is permitted by the corresponding constraint. The points

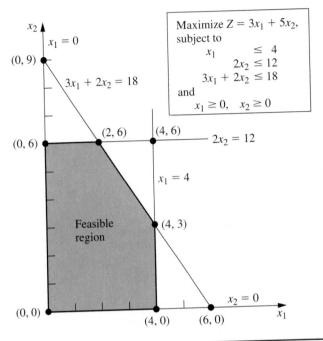

FIGURE 4.1
Constraint boundaries and
corner-point solutions for the
Wyndor Glass Co. problem.

of intersection are the **corner-point solutions** of the problem. The five that lie on the corners of the *feasible region*—(0, 0), (0, 6), (2, 6), (4, 3), and (4, 0)—are the *corner-point feasible solutions* (**CPF solutions**). [The other three—(0, 9), (4, 6), and (6, 0)—are called *corner-point infeasible solutions.*]

In this example, each corner-point solution lies at the intersection of *two* constraint boundaries. (For a linear programming problem with n decision variables, each of its corner-point solutions lies at the intersection of n constraint boundaries.[1]) Certain pairs of the CPF solutions in Fig. 4.1 share a constraint boundary, and other pairs do not. It will be important to distinguish between these cases by using the following general definitions.

> For any linear programming problem with n decision variables, two CPF solutions are **adjacent** to each other if they share $n - 1$ constraint boundaries. The two adjacent CPF solutions are connected by a line segment that lies on these same shared constraint boundaries. Such a line segment is referred to as an **edge** of the feasible region.

Since $n = 2$ in the example, two of its CPF solutions are adjacent if they share *one* constraint boundary; for example, (0, 0) and (0, 6) are adjacent because they share the $x_1 = 0$ constraint boundary. The feasible region in Fig. 4.1 has five edges, consisting of the five line segments forming the boundary of this region. Note that two edges emanate from each CPF solution. Thus, each CPF solution has two adjacent CPF solutions (each lying at the other end of one of the two edges), as enumerated in Table 4.1. (In each row

---

[1] Although a corner-point solution is defined in terms of n constraint boundaries whose intersection gives this solution, it also is possible that one or more *additional* constraint boundaries pass through this same point.

TABLE 4.1 Adjacent CPF solutions for each CPF solution of the Wyndor Glass Co. problem

CPF Solution	Its Adjacent CPF Solutions
(0, 0)	(0, 6) and (4, 0)
(0, 6)	(2, 6) and (0, 0)
(2, 6)	(4, 3) and (0, 6)
(4, 3)	(4, 0) and (2, 6)
(4, 0)	(0, 0) and (4, 3)

of this table, the CPF solution in the first column is adjacent to each of the two CPF solutions in the second column, but the two CPF solutions in the second column are *not* adjacent to each other.)

One reason for our interest in adjacent CPF solutions is the following general property about such solutions, which provides a very useful way of checking whether a CPF solution is an optimal solution.

> **Optimality test:** Consider any linear programming problem that possesses at least one optimal solution. If a CPF solution has no *adjacent* CPF solutions that are *better* (as measured by Z), then it *must* be an *optimal* solution.

Thus, for the example, (2, 6) must be optimal simply because its $Z = 36$ is larger than $Z = 30$ for (0, 6) and $Z = 27$ for (4, 3). (We will delve further into why this property holds in Sec. 5.1.) This optimality test is the one used by the simplex method for determining when an optimal solution has been reached.

Now we are ready to apply the simplex method to the example.

Solving the Example

Here is an outline of what the simplex method does (from a geometric viewpoint) to solve the Wyndor Glass Co. problem. At each step, first the conclusion is stated and then the reason is given in parentheses. (Refer to Fig. 4.1 for a visualization.)

Initialization: Choose (0, 0) as the *initial* CPF solution to examine. (This is a convenient choice because no calculations are required to identify this CPF solution.)

Optimality Test: Conclude that (0, 0) is *not* an optimal solution. (Adjacent CPF solutions are better.)

Iteration 1: Move to a better *adjacent* CPF solution, (0, 6), by performing the following three steps.

1. Considering the two edges of the feasible region that emanate from (0, 0), choose to move along the edge that leads up the x_2 axis. (With an objective function of $Z = 3x_1 + 5x_2$, moving up the x_2 axis increases Z at a faster rate than moving along the x_1 axis.)
2. Stop at the first new constraint boundary: $2x_2 = 12$. [Moving farther in the direction selected in step 1 leaves the feasible region; e.g., moving to the second new constraint boundary hit when moving in that direction gives (0, 9), which is a corner-point *infeasible* solution.]

3. Solve for the intersection of the new set of constraint boundaries: (0, 6). (The equations for these constraint boundaries, $x_1 = 0$ and $2x_2 = 12$, immediately yield this solution.)

Optimality Test: Conclude that (0, 6) is *not* an optimal solution. (An adjacent CPF solution is better.)

Iteration 2: Move to a better adjacent CPF solution, (2, 6), by performing the following three steps.

1. Considering the two edges of the feasible region that emanate from (0, 6), choose to move along the edge that leads to the right. (Moving along this edge increases Z, whereas backtracking to move back down the x_2 axis decreases Z.)
2. Stop at the first new constraint boundary encountered when moving in that direction: $3x_1 + 2x_2 = 12$. (Moving farther in the direction selected in step 1 leaves the feasible region.)
3. Solve for the intersection of the new set of constraint boundaries: (2, 6). (The equations for these constraint boundaries, $3x_1 + 2x_2 = 18$ and $2x_2 = 12$, immediately yield this solution.)

Optimality Test: Conclude that (2, 6) *is* an optimal solution, so stop. (None of the adjacent CPF solutions are better.)

This sequence of CPF solutions examined is shown in Fig. 4.2, where each circled number identifies which iteration obtained that solution.

Now let us look at the six key solution concepts of the simplex method that provide the rationale behind the above steps. (Keep in mind that these concepts also apply for solving problems with more than two decision variables where a graph like Fig. 4.2 is not available to help quickly find an optimal solution.)

The Key Solution Concepts

The first solution concept is based directly on the relationship between optimal solutions and CPF solutions given at the end of Sec. 3.2.

FIGURE 4.2
This graph shows the sequence of CPF solutions (⓪, ①, ②) examined by the simplex method for the Wyndor Glass Co. problem. The optimal solution (2, 6) is found after just three solutions are examined.

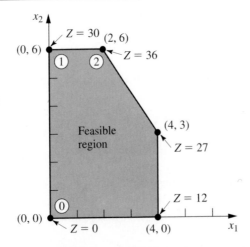

Solution concept 1: The simplex method focuses solely on CPF solutions. For any problem with at least one optimal solution, finding one requires only finding a best CPF solution.[1]

Since the number of feasible solutions generally is infinite, reducing the number of solutions that need to be examined to a small finite number (just three in Fig. 4.2) is a tremendous simplification.

The next solution concept defines the flow of the simplex method.

Solution concept 2: The simplex method is an *iterative algorithm* (a systematic solution procedure that keeps repeating a fixed series of steps, called an *iteration,* until a desired result has been obtained) with the following structure.

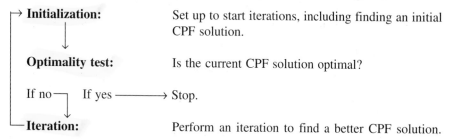

Initialization:	Set up to start iterations, including finding an initial CPF solution.
Optimality test:	Is the current CPF solution optimal?
If no ─┐ If yes ──→ Stop.	
Iteration:	Perform an iteration to find a better CPF solution.

When the example was solved, note how this flow diagram was followed through two iterations until an optimal solution was found.

We next focus on how to get started.

Solution concept 3: Whenever possible, the initialization of the simplex method chooses the *origin* (all decision variables equal to zero) to be the initial CPF solution. When there are too many decision variables to find an initial CPF solution graphically, this choice eliminates the need to use algebraic procedures to find and solve for an initial CPF solution.

Choosing the origin commonly is possible when all the decision variables have nonnegativity constraints, because the intersection of these constraint boundaries yields the origin as a corner-point solution. This solution then is a CPF solution *unless* it is *infeasible* because it violates one or more of the functional constraints. If it is infeasible, special procedures described in Sec. 4.6 are needed to find the initial CPF solution.

The next solution concept concerns the choice of a better CPF solution at each iteration.

Solution concept 4: Given a CPF solution, it is much quicker computationally to gather information about its *adjacent* CPF solutions than about other CPF solutions. Therefore, each time the simplex method performs an iteration to move from the current CPF solution to a better one, it *always* chooses a CPF solution that is *adjacent* to the current one. No other CPF solutions are considered. Consequently, the entire path followed to eventually reach an optimal solution is along the *edges* of the feasible region.

---

[1]The only restriction is that the problem must possess CPF solutions. This is ensured if the feasible region is bounded.

The next focus is on which adjacent CPF solution to choose at each iteration.

Solution concept 5: After the current CPF solution is identified, the simplex method examines each of the edges of the feasible region that emanate from this CPF solution. Each of these edges leads to an *adjacent* CPF solution at the other end, but the simplex method does not even take the time to solve for the adjacent CPF solution. Instead, it simply identifies the *rate of improvement in Z* that would be obtained by moving along the edge. Among the edges with a *positive* rate of improvement in Z, it then chooses to move along the one with the *largest* rate of improvement in Z. The iteration is completed by first solving for the adjacent CPF solution at the other end of this one edge and then relabeling this adjacent CPF solution as the *current* CPF solution for the optimality test and (if needed) the next iteration.

At the first iteration of the example, moving from $(0, 0)$ along the edge on the x_1 axis would give a rate of improvement in Z of 3 (Z increases by 3 per unit increase in x_1), whereas moving along the edge on the x_2 axis would give a rate of improvement in Z of 5 (Z increases by 5 per unit increase in x_2), so the decision is made to move along the latter edge. At the second iteration, the only edge emanating from $(0, 6)$ that would yield a *positive* rate of improvement in Z is the edge leading to $(2, 6)$, so the decision is made to move next along this edge.

The final solution concept clarifies how the optimality test is performed efficiently.

Solution concept 6: Solution concept 5 describes how the simplex method examines each of the edges of the feasible region that emanate from the current CPF solution. This examination of an edge leads to quickly identifying the rate of improvement in Z that would be obtained by moving along the edge toward the adjacent CPF solution at the other end. A *positive* rate of improvement in Z implies that the adjacent CPF solution is *better* than the current CPF solution, whereas a *negative* rate of improvement in Z implies that the adjacent CPF solution is *worse*. Therefore, the optimality test consists simply of checking whether *any* of the edges give a *positive* rate of improvement in Z. If *none* do, then the current CPF solution is optimal.

In the example, moving along *either* edge from $(2, 6)$ decreases Z. Since we want to maximize Z, this fact immediately gives the conclusion that $(2, 6)$ is optimal.

4.2   SETTING UP THE SIMPLEX METHOD

The preceding section stressed the geometric concepts that underlie the simplex method. However, this algorithm normally is run on a computer, which can follow only algebraic instructions. Therefore, it is necessary to translate the conceptually geometric procedure just described into a usable algebraic procedure. In this section, we introduce the *algebraic language* of the simplex method and relate it to the concepts of the preceding section.

The algebraic procedure is based on solving systems of equations. Therefore, the first step in setting up the simplex method is to convert the functional *inequality constraints* to equivalent *equality constraints*. (The nonnegativity constraints are left as inequalities because they are treated separately.) This conversion is accomplished by introducing **slack**

variables. To illustrate, consider the first functional constraint in the Wyndor Glass Co. example of Sec. 3.1

$$x_1 \leq 4.$$

The slack variable for this constraint is defined to be

$$x_3 = 4 - x_1,$$

which is the amount of slack in the left-hand side of the inequality. Thus,

$$x_1 + x_3 = 4.$$

Given this equation, $x_1 \leq 4$ if and only if $4 - x_1 = x_3 \geq 0$. Therefore, the original constraint $x_1 \leq 4$ is entirely *equivalent* to the pair of constraints

$$x_1 + x_3 = 4 \qquad \text{and} \qquad x_3 \geq 0.$$

Upon the introduction of slack variables for the other functional constraints, the original linear programming model for the example (shown below on the left) can now be replaced by the equivalent model (called the *augmented form* of the model) shown below on the right:

Original Form of the Model
Maximize $\quad Z = 3x_1 + 5x_2,$
subject to
$\qquad x_1 \qquad\quad \leq 4$
$\qquad\qquad 2x_2 \leq 12$
$\qquad 3x_1 + 2x_2 \leq 18$
and
$\qquad x_1 \geq 0, \qquad x_2 \geq 0.$

Augmented Form of the Model[1]
Maximize $\quad Z = 3x_1 + 5x_2,$
subject to
$(1) \qquad x_1 \qquad\quad + x_3 \qquad\qquad = 4$
$(2) \qquad\qquad 2x_2 \qquad + x_4 \qquad = 12$
$(3) \qquad 3x_1 + 2x_2 \qquad\qquad + x_5 = 18$
and
$\qquad x_j \geq 0, \qquad \text{for } j = 1, 2, 3, 4, 5.$

Although both forms of the model represent exactly the same problem, the new form is much more convenient for algebraic manipulation and for identification of CPF solutions. We call this the **augmented form** of the problem because the original form has been *augmented* by some supplementary variables needed to apply the simplex method.

If a slack variable equals 0 in the current solution, then this solution lies on the constraint boundary for the corresponding functional constraint. A value greater than 0 means that the solution lies on the *feasible* side of this constraint boundary, whereas a value less than 0 means that the solution lies on the *infeasible* side of this constraint boundary. A demonstration of these properties is provided by the demonstration example in your OR Tutor entitled *Interpretation of the Slack Variables.*

The terminology used in the preceding section (corner-point solutions, etc.) applies to the original form of the problem. We now introduce the corresponding terminology for the augmented form.

> An **augmented solution** is a solution for the original variables (the *decision variables*) that has been augmented by the corresponding values of the *slack variables.*

---

[1]The slack variables are not shown in the objective function because the coefficients there are 0.

For example, augmenting the solution (3, 2) in the example yields the augmented solution (3, 2, 1, 8, 5) because the corresponding values of the slack variables are $x_3 = 1$, $x_4 = 8$, and $x_5 = 5$.

A **basic solution** is an *augmented* corner-point solution.

To illustrate, consider the corner-point infeasible solution (4, 6) in Fig. 4.1. Augmenting it with the resulting values of the slack variables $x_3 = 0$, $x_4 = 0$, and $x_5 = -6$ yields the corresponding basic solution (4, 6, 0, 0, -6).

The fact that corner-point solutions (and so basic solutions) can be either feasible or infeasible implies the following definition:

A **basic feasible (BF) solution** is an *augmented* CPF solution.

Thus, the CPF solution (0, 6) in the example is equivalent to the BF solution (0, 6, 4, 0, 6) for the problem in augmented form.

The only difference between basic solutions and corner-point solutions (or between BF solutions and CPF solutions) is whether the values of the slack variables are included. For any basic solution, the corresponding corner-point solution is obtained simply by deleting the slack variables. Therefore, the geometric and algebraic relationships between these two solutions are very close, as described in Sec. 5.1.

Because the terms *basic solution* and *basic feasible solution* are very important parts of the standard vocabulary of linear programming, we now need to clarify their algebraic properties. For the augmented form of the example, notice that the system of functional constraints has 5 variables and 3 equations, so

Number of variables − number of equations = 5 − 3 = 2.

This fact gives us 2 *degrees of freedom* in solving the system, since any two variables can be chosen to be set equal to any arbitrary value in order to solve the three equations in terms of the remaining three variables.[1] The simplex method uses zero for this arbitrary value. Thus, two of the variables (called the *nonbasic variables*) are set equal to zero, and then the simultaneous solution of the three equations for the other three variables (called the *basic variables*) is a *basic solution*. These properties are described in the following general definitions.

A **basic solution** has the following properties:

1. Each variable is designated as either a nonbasic variable or a basic variable.
2. The *number of basic variables* equals the number of functional constraints (now equations). Therefore, the *number of nonbasic variables* equals the total number of variables *minus* the number of functional constraints.
3. The **nonbasic variables** are set equal to zero.
4. The values of the **basic variables** are obtained as the simultaneous solution of the system of equations (functional constraints in augmented form). (The set of basic variables is often referred to as **the basis.**)
5. If the basic variables satisfy the *nonnegativity constraints,* the basic solution is a **BF solution.**

---

[1]This method of determining the number of degrees of freedom for a system of equations is valid as long as the system does not include any redundant equations. This condition always holds for the system of equations formed from the functional constraints in the augmented form of a linear programming model.

To illustrate these definitions, consider again the BF solution (0, 6, 4, 0, 6). This solution was obtained before by augmenting the CPF solution (0, 6). However, another way to obtain this same solution is to choose x_1 and x_4 to be the two nonbasic variables, and so the two variables are set equal to zero. The three equations then yield, respectively, $x_3 = 4$, $x_2 = 6$, and $x_5 = 6$ as the solution for the three basic variables, as shown below (with the basic variables in bold type):

$$x_1 = 0 \text{ and } x_4 = 0 \text{ so}$$

(1)	x_1 $\quad + \mathbf{x_3}$	$= 4$	$\mathbf{x_3} = 4$
(2)	$2\mathbf{x_2} \quad + x_4$	$= 12$	$\mathbf{x_2} = 6$
(3)	$3x_1 + 2\mathbf{x_2} \quad + \mathbf{x_5}$	$= 18$	$\mathbf{x_5} = 6$

Because all three of these basic variables are nonnegative, this *basic solution* (0, 6, 4, 0, 6) is indeed a *BF solution*.

Just as certain pairs of CPF solutions are *adjacent*, the corresponding pairs of BF solutions also are said to be adjacent. Here is an easy way to tell when two BF solutions are adjacent.

> Two BF solutions are **adjacent** if *all but one* of their *nonbasic variables* are the same. This implies that *all but one* of their *basic variables* also are the same, although perhaps with different numerical values.

Consequently, moving from the current BF solution to an adjacent one involves switching one variable from nonbasic to basic and vice versa for one other variable (and then adjusting the values of the basic variables to continue satisfying the system of equations).

To illustrate *adjacent BF solutions*, consider one pair of adjacent CPF solutions in Fig. 4.1: (0, 0) and (0, 6). Their augmented solutions, (0, 0, 4, 12, 18) and (0, 6, 4, 0, 6), automatically are adjacent BF solutions. However, you do not need to look at Fig. 4.1 to draw this conclusion. Another signpost is that their nonbasic variables, (x_1, x_2) and (x_1, x_4), are the same with just the one exception—x_2 has been replaced by x_4. Consequently, moving from (0, 0, 4, 12, 18) to (0, 6, 4, 0, 6) involves switching x_2 from nonbasic to basic and vice versa for x_4.

When we deal with the problem in augmented form, it is convenient to consider and manipulate the objective function equation at the same time as the new constraint equations. Therefore, before we start the simplex method, the problem needs to be rewritten once again in an equivalent way:

Maximize $\quad Z$,

subject to

(0)	$Z - 3x_1 - 5x_2$	$= 0$
(1)	$x_1 \quad + x_3$	$= 4$
(2)	$2x_2 \quad + x_4$	$= 12$
(3)	$3x_1 + 2x_2 \quad + x_5$	$= 18$

and

$$x_j \geq 0, \quad \text{for } j = 1, 2, \ldots, 5.$$

It is just as if Eq. (0) actually were one of the original constraints; but because it already is in equality form, no slack variable is needed. While adding one more equation, we also have added one more unknown (Z) to the system of equations. Therefore, when using Eqs. (1) to (3) to obtain a basic solution as described above, we use Eq. (0) to solve for Z at the same time.

Somewhat fortuitously, the model for the Wyndor Glass Co. problem fits *our standard form,* and all its functional constraints have nonnegative right-hand sides b_i. If this had not been the case, then additional adjustments would have been needed at this point before the simplex method was applied. These details are deferred to Sec. 4.6, and we now focus on the simplex method itself.

4.3 THE ALGEBRA OF THE SIMPLEX METHOD

We continue to use the prototype example of Sec. 3.1, as rewritten at the end of Sec. 4.2, for illustrative purposes. To start connecting the geometric and algebraic concepts of the simplex method, we begin by outlining side by side in Table 4.2 how the simplex method solves this example from both a geometric and an algebraic viewpoint. The geometric viewpoint (first presented in Sec. 4.1) is based on the *original form* of the model (no slack variables), so again refer to Fig. 4.1 for a visualization when you examine the second column of the table. Refer to the *augmented form* of the model presented at the end of Sec. 4.2 when you examine the third column of the table.

We now fill in the details for each step of the third column of Table 4.2.

Initialization

The choice of x_1 and x_2 to be the *nonbasic* variables (the variables set equal to zero) for the initial BF solution is based on solution concept 3 in Sec. 4.1. This choice eliminates the work required to solve for the *basic variables* (x_3, x_4, x_5) from the following system of equations (where the basic variables are shown in bold type):

$$x_1 = 0 \text{ and } x_2 = 0 \text{ so}$$

$$
\begin{array}{lllll}
(1) & x_1 & + \boldsymbol{x_3} & = 4 & \boldsymbol{x_3} = 4 \\
(2) & 2x_2 & + \boldsymbol{x_4} & = 12 & \boldsymbol{x_4} = 12 \\
(3) & 3x_1 + 2x_2 & + \boldsymbol{x_5} = 18 & & \boldsymbol{x_5} = 18
\end{array}
$$

Thus, the **initial BF solution** is (0, 0, 4, 12, 18).

Notice that this solution can be read immediately because each equation has just one basic variable, which has a coefficient of 1, and this basic variable does not appear in any other equation. You will soon see that when the set of basic variables changes, the simplex method uses an algebraic procedure (Gaussian elimination) to convert the equations to this same convenient form for reading every subsequent BF solution as well. This form is called **proper form from Gaussian elimination.**

Optimality Test

The objective function is

$$Z = 3x_1 + 5x_2,$$

TABLE 4.2 Geometric and algebraic interpretations of how the simplex method solves the Wyndor Glass Co. problem

Method Sequence	Geometric Interpretation	Algebraic Interpretation
Initialization	Choose (0, 0) to be the initial CPF solution.	Choose x_1 and x_2 to be the nonbasic variables (= 0) for the initial BF solution: (0, 0, 4, 12, 18).
Optimality test	Not optimal, because moving along either edge from (0, 0) increases Z.	Not optimal, because increasing either nonbasic variable (x_1 or x_2) increases Z.
Iteration 1		
Step 1	Move up the edge lying on the x_2 axis.	Increase x_2 while adjusting other variable values to satisfy the system of equations.
Step 2	Stop when the first new constraint boundary ($2x_2 = 12$) is reached.	Stop when the first basic variable (x_3, x_4, or x_5) drops to zero (x_4).
Step 3	Find the intersection of the new pair of constraint boundaries: (0, 6) is the new CPF solution.	With x_2 now a basic variable and x_4 now a nonbasic variable, solve the system of equations: (0, 6, 4, 0, 6) is the new BF solution.
Optimality test	Not optimal, because moving along the edge from (0, 6) to the right increases Z.	Not optimal, because increasing one nonbasic variable (x_1) increases Z.
Iteration 2		
Step 1	Move along this edge to the right.	Increase x_1 while adjusting other variable values to satisfy the system of equations.
Step 2	Stop when the first new constraint boundary ($3x_1 + 2x_2 = 18$) is reached.	Stop when the first basic variable (x_2, x_3, or x_5) drops to zero (x_5).
Step 3	Find the intersection of the new pair of constraint boundaries: (2, 6) is the new CPF solution.	With x_1 now a basic variable and x_5 now a nonbasic variable, solve the system of equations: (2, 6, 2, 0, 0) is the new BF solution.
Optimality test	(2, 6) is optimal, because moving along either edge from (2, 6) decreases Z.	(2, 6, 2, 0, 0) is optimal, because increasing either nonbasic variable (x_4 or x_5) decreases Z.

so $Z = 0$ for the initial BF solution. Because none of the basic variables (x_3, x_4, x_5) have a *nonzero* coefficient in this objective function, the coefficient of each nonbasic variable (x_1, x_2) gives the rate of improvement in Z if that variable were to be increased from zero (while the values of the basic variables are adjusted to continue satisfying the system of equations).[1] These rates of improvement (3 and 5) are *positive*. Therefore, based on solution concept 6 in Sec. 4.1, we conclude that (0, 0, 4, 12, 18) is not optimal.

For each BF solution examined after subsequent iterations, at least one basic variable has a nonzero coefficient in the objective function. Therefore, the optimality test then will use the new Eq. (0) to rewrite the objective function in terms of just the nonbasic variables, as you will see later.

---

[1] Note that this interpretation of the coefficients of the x_j variables is based on these variables being on the right-hand side, $Z = 3x_1 + 5x_2$. When these variables are brought to the left-hand side for Eq. (0), $Z - 3x_1 - 5x_2 = 0$, the nonzero coefficients change their signs.

Determining the Direction of Movement (Step 1 of an Iteration)

Increasing one nonbasic variable from zero (while adjusting the values of the basic variables to continue satisfying the system of equations) corresponds to moving along one edge emanating from the current CPF solution. Based on solution concepts 4 and 5 in Sec. 4.1, the choice of which nonbasic variable to increase is made as follows:

$$Z = 3x_1 + 5x_2$$

Increase x_1?   Rate of improvement in $Z = 3$.
Increase x_2?   Rate of improvement in $Z = 5$.
$5 > 3$, so choose x_2 to increase.

As indicated next, we call x_2 the *entering basic variable* for iteration 1.

> At any iteration of the simplex method, the purpose of step 1 is to choose one *nonbasic variable* to increase from zero (while the values of the basic variables are adjusted to continue satisfying the system of equations). Increasing this nonbasic variable from zero will convert it to a *basic variable* for the next BF solution. Therefore, this variable is called the **entering basic variable** for the current iteration (because it is entering the basis).

Determining Where to Stop (Step 2 of an Iteration)

Step 2 addresses the question of how far to increase the entering basic variable x_2 before stopping. Increasing x_2 increases Z, so we want to go as far as possible without leaving the feasible region. The requirement to satisfy the functional constraints in augmented form (shown below) means that increasing x_2 (while keeping the nonbasic variable $x_1 = 0$) changes the values of some of the basic variables as shown on the right.

$$
\begin{array}{lll}
 & & x_1 = \quad 0, \qquad \text{so} \\
(1) \quad x_1 \qquad + x_3 \qquad\qquad = 4 & & x_3 = \quad 4 \\
(2) \qquad\quad 2x_2 \quad + x_4 \qquad = 12 & & x_4 = 12 - 2x_2 \\
(3) \quad 3x_1 + 2x_2 \qquad\quad + x_5 = 18 & & x_5 = 18 - 2x_2.
\end{array}
$$

The other requirement for feasibility is that all the variables be *nonnegative*. The nonbasic variables (including the entering basic variable) are nonnegative, but we need to check how far x_2 can be increased without violating the nonnegativity constraints for the basic variables.

$$x_3 = 4 \geq 0 \qquad\qquad \Rightarrow \text{ no upper bound on } x_2.$$

$$x_4 = 12 - 2x_2 \geq 0 \Rightarrow x_2 \leq \frac{12}{2} = 6 \quad \leftarrow \text{minimum.}$$

$$x_5 = 18 - 2x_2 \geq 0 \Rightarrow x_2 \leq \frac{18}{2} = 9.$$

Thus, x_2 can be increased just to 6, at which point x_4 has dropped to 0. Increasing x_2 beyond 6 would cause x_4 to become negative, which would violate feasibility.

These calculations are referred to as the **minimum ratio test.** The objective of this test is to determine which basic variable drops to zero first as the entering basic variable is increased. We can immediately rule out the basic variable in any equation where the coefficient of the entering basic variable is zero or negative, since such a basic variable would not decrease as the entering basic variable is increased. [This is what happened with x_3 in Eq. (1) of the example.] However, for each equation where the coefficient of the entering basic variable is *strictly positive* (> 0), this test calculates the *ratio* of the right-hand side to the coefficient of the entering basic variable. The basic variable in the equation with the *minimum ratio* is the one that drops to zero first as the entering basic variable is increased.

> At any iteration of the simplex method, step 2 uses the *minimum ratio test* to determine which basic variable drops to zero first as the entering basic variable is increased. Decreasing this basic variable to zero will convert it to a *nonbasic variable* for the next BF solution. Therefore, this variable is called the **leaving basic variable** for the current iteration (because it is leaving the basis).

Thus, x_4 is the leaving basic variable for iteration 1 of the example.

Solving for the New BF Solution (Step 3 of an Iteration)

Increasing $x_2 = 0$ to $x_2 = 6$ moves us from the *initial* BF solution on the left to the *new* BF solution on the right.

	Initial BF solution	New BF solution
Nonbasic variables:	$x_1 = 0, \quad x_2 = 0$	$x_1 = 0, \quad x_4 = 0$
Basic variables:	$x_3 = 4, \quad x_4 = 12, \quad x_5 = 18$	$x_3 = ?, \quad x_2 = 6, \quad x_5 = ?$

The purpose of step 3 is to convert the system of equations to a more convenient form (proper form from Gaussian elimination) for conducting the optimality test and (if needed) the next iteration with this new BF solution. In the process, this form also will identify the values of x_3 and x_5 for the new solution.

Here again is the complete original system of equations, where the *new* basic variables are shown in bold type (with Z playing the role of the basic variable in the objective function equation):

$$
\begin{array}{lll}
(0) & \mathbf{Z} - 3x_1 - 5\mathbf{x_2} & = 0 \\
(1) & x_1 \qquad\; + \mathbf{x_3} & = 4 \\
(2) & \qquad 2\mathbf{x_2} \quad + x_4 & = 12 \\
(3) & 3x_1 + 2\mathbf{x_2} \qquad + \mathbf{x_5} & = 18.
\end{array}
$$

Thus, x_2 has replaced x_4 as the basic variable in Eq. (2). To solve this system of equations for Z, x_2, x_3, and x_5, we need to perform some **elementary algebraic operations** to reproduce the current pattern of coefficients of x_4 (0, 0, 1, 0) as the new coefficients of x_2. We can use either of two types of elementary algebraic operations:

1. Multiply (or divide) an equation by a nonzero constant.
2. Add (or subtract) a multiple of one equation to (or from) another equation.

To prepare for performing these operations, note that the coefficients of x_2 in the above system of equations are -5, 0, 2, and 3, respectively, whereas we want these coefficients to become 0, 0, 1, and 0, respectively. To turn the coefficient of 2 in Eq. (2) into 1, we use the first type of elementary algebraic operation by dividing Eq. (2) by 2 to obtain

$$
(2) \qquad x_2 + \frac{1}{2}x_4 = 6.
$$

To turn the coefficients of -5 and 3 into zeros, we need to use the second type of elementary algebraic operation. In particular, we add 5 times this new Eq. (2) to Eq. (0), and subtract 2 times this new Eq. (2) from Eq. (3). The resulting complete new system of equations is

$$
\begin{aligned}
(0) \quad & Z - 3x_1 && + \tfrac{5}{2}x_4 && = 30 \\
(1) \quad & x_1 && + x_3 && = 4 \\
(2) \quad & x_2 && + \tfrac{1}{2}x_4 && = 6 \\
(3) \quad & 3x_1 && - x_4 + x_5 && = 6.
\end{aligned}
$$

Since $x_1 = 0$ and $x_4 = 0$, the equations in this form immediately yield the new BF solution, $(x_1, x_2, x_3, x_4, x_5) = (0, 6, 4, 0, 6)$, which yields $Z = 30$.

This procedure for obtaining the simultaneous solution of a system of linear equations is called the *Gauss-Jordan method of elimination,* or **Gaussian elimination** for short.[1] The key concept for this method is the use of elementary algebraic operations to reduce the original system of equations to proper form from Gaussian elimination, where each basic variable has been eliminated from all but one equation (*its* equation) and has a coefficient of $+1$ in that equation.

Optimality Test for the New BF Solution

The current Eq. (0) gives the value of the objective function in terms of just the current nonbasic variables

$$
Z = 30 + 3x_1 - \frac{5}{2}x_4.
$$

Increasing either of these nonbasic variables from zero (while adjusting the values of the basic variables to continue satisfying the system of equations) would result in moving toward one of the two *adjacent* BF solutions. Because x_1 has a *positive* coefficient, increasing x_1 would lead to an adjacent BF solution that is better than the current BF solution, so the current solution is not optimal.

Iteration 2 and the Resulting Optimal Solution

Since $Z = 30 + 3x_1 - \frac{5}{2}x_4$, Z can be increased by increasing x_1, but not x_4. Therefore, step 1 chooses x_1 to be the entering basic variable.

For step 2, the current system of equations yields the following conclusions about how far x_1 can be increased (with $x_4 = 0$):

$$
x_3 = 4 - x_1 \geq 0 \;\Rightarrow\; x_1 \leq \frac{4}{1} = 4.
$$

$$
x_2 = 6 \geq 0 \qquad\qquad \Rightarrow \text{no upper bound on } x_1.
$$

$$
x_5 = 6 - 3x_1 \geq 0 \Rightarrow x_1 \leq \frac{6}{3} = 2 \quad \leftarrow \text{minimum.}
$$

Therefore, the minimum ratio test indicates that x_5 is the leaving basic variable.

[1]Actually, there are some technical differences between the Gauss-Jordan method of elimination and Gaussian elimination, but we shall not make this distinction.

For step 3, with x_1 replacing x_5 as a basic variable, we perform elementary algebraic operations on the current system of equations to reproduce the current pattern of coefficients of x_5 (0, 0, 0, 1) as the new coefficients of x_1. This yields the following new system of equations:

$$(0) \quad Z \qquad\qquad\qquad + \frac{3}{2}x_4 + \quad x_5 = 36$$

$$(1) \qquad\qquad\qquad x_3 + \frac{1}{3}x_4 - \frac{1}{3}x_5 = \ 2$$

$$(2) \qquad\quad x_2 \quad + \frac{1}{2}x_4 \qquad\qquad = \ 6$$

$$(3) \qquad x_1 \qquad\quad - \frac{1}{3}x_4 + \frac{1}{3}x_5 = \ 2.$$

Therefore, the next BF solution is $(x_1, x_2, x_3, x_4, x_5) = (2, 6, 2, 0, 0)$, yielding $Z = 36$. To apply the *optimality test* to this new BF solution, we use the current Eq. (0) to express Z in terms of just the current nonbasic variables,

$$Z = 36 - \frac{3}{2}x_4 - x_5.$$

Increasing either x_4 or x_5 would *decrease Z,* so neither adjacent BF solution is as good as the current one. Therefore, based on solution concept 6 in Sec. 4.1, the current BF solution must be optimal.

In terms of the original form of the problem (no slack variables), the optimal solution is $x_1 = 2$, $x_2 = 6$, which yields $Z = 3x_1 + 5x_2 = 36$.

To see another example of applying the simplex method, we recommend that you now view the demonstration entitled *Simplex Method—Algebraic Form* in your OR Tutor. This vivid demonstration simultaneously displays both the algebra and the geometry of the simplex method as it dynamically evolves step by step. Like the many other demonstration examples accompanying other sections of the book (including the next section), this computer demonstration highlights concepts that are difficult to convey on the printed page.

To further help you learn the simplex method efficiently, your OR Courseware includes a procedure entitled *Solve Interactively by the Simplex Method.* This routine performs nearly all the calculations while you make the decisions step by step, thereby enabling you to focus on concepts rather than get bogged down in a lot of number crunching. Therefore, you probably will want to use this routine for your homework on this section. The software will help you get started by letting you know whenever you make a mistake on the first iteration of a problem.

The next section includes a summary of the simplex method for a more convenient tabular form.

4.4 THE SIMPLEX METHOD IN TABULAR FORM

The algebraic form of the simplex method presented in Sec. 4.3 may be the best one for learning the underlying logic of the algorithm. However, it is not the most convenient form for performing the required calculations. When you need to solve a problem by hand (or interactively with your OR Courseware), we recommend the *tabular form* described in this section.[1]

The tabular form of the simplex method records only the essential information, namely, (1) the coefficients of the variables, (2) the constants on the right-hand sides of the equations, and (3) the basic variable appearing in each equation. This saves writing the symbols for the variables in each of the equations, but what is even more important is the fact that it permits highlighting the numbers involved in arithmetic calculations and recording the computations compactly.

Table 4.3 compares the initial system of equations for the Wyndor Glass Co. problem in algebraic form (on the left) and in tabular form (on the right), where the table on the right is called a *simplex tableau.* The basic variable for each equation is shown in bold type on the left and in the first column of the simplex tableau on the right. [Although only the x_j variables are basic or nonbasic, Z plays the role of the basic variable for Eq. (0).] All variables *not* listed in this *basic variable* column (x_1, x_2) automatically are *nonbasic variables.* After we set $x_1 = 0$, $x_2 = 0$, the *right side* column gives the resulting solution for the basic variables, so that the initial BF solution is (x_1, x_2, x_3, x_4, x_5) = (0, 0, 4, 12, 18) which yields $Z = 0$.

> The *tabular form* of the simplex method uses a **simplex tableau** to compactly display the system of equations yielding the current BF solution. For this solution, each variable in the leftmost column equals the corresponding number in the rightmost column (and variables not listed equal zero). When the optimality test or an iteration is performed, the only relevant numbers are those to the right of the Z column. The term **row** refers to just a row of numbers to the right of the Z column (including the *right side* number), where row *i* corresponds to Eq. (*i*).

We summarize the tabular form of the simplex method below and, at the same time, briefly describe its application to the Wyndor Glass Co. problem. Keep in mind that the logic is identical to that for the algebraic form presented in the preceding section. Only the form for displaying both the current system of equations and the subsequent iteration has changed (plus we shall no longer bother to bring variables to the right-hand side of an equation before drawing our conclusions in the optimality test or in steps 1 and 2 of an iteration).

[1]A form more convenient for automatic execution on a computer is presented in Sec. 5.2.

TABLE 4.3 Initial system of equations for the Wyndor Glass Co. problem

(a) Algebraic Form	Basic Variable	Eq.	Z	x_1	x_2	x_3	x_4	x_5	Right Side
(0) **Z** $- 3x_1 - 5x_2 = 0$	Z	(0)	1	−3	−5	0	0	0	0
(1) $x_1 + \mathbf{x}_3 = 4$	x_3	(1)	0	1	0	1	0	0	4
(2) $2x_2 + \mathbf{x}_4 = 12$	x_4	(2)	0	0	2	0	1	0	12
(3) $3x_1 + 2x_2 + \mathbf{x}_5 = 18$	x_5	(3)	0	3	2	0	0	1	18

Summary of the Simplex Method (and Iteration 1 for the Example)

Initialization.   Introduce slack variables. Select the *decision variables* to be the *initial nonbasic variables* (set equal to zero) and the *slack variables* to be the *initial basic variables*. (See Sec. 4.6 for the necessary adjustments if the model is not in our standard form—maximization, only $\leq$ functional constraints, and all nonnegativity constraints—or if any b_i values are negative.)

For the Example: This selection yields the initial simplex tableau shown in Table 4.3b, so the initial BF solution is (0, 0, 4, 12, 18).

Optimality Test.   The current BF solution is optimal if and only if *every* coefficient in row 0 is nonnegative (≥ 0). If it is, stop; otherwise, go to an iteration to obtain the next BF solution, which involves changing one nonbasic variable to a basic variable (step 1) and vice versa (step 2) and then solving for the new solution (step 3).

For the Example: Just as $Z = 3x_1 + 5x_2$ indicates that increasing either x_1 or x_2 will increase Z, so the current BF solution is not optimal, the same conclusion is drawn from the equation $Z - 3x_1 - 5x_2 = 0$. These coefficients of -3 and -5 are shown in row 0 of Table 4.3b.

Iteration.   *Step 1:* Determine the *entering basic variable* by selecting the variable (automatically a nonbasic variable) with the *negative coefficient* having the largest absolute value (i.e., the "most negative" coefficient) in Eq. (0). Put a box around the column below this coefficient, and call this the **pivot column.**

For the Example: The most negative coefficient is -5 for x_2 ($5 > 3$), so x_2 is to be changed to a basic variable. (This change is indicated in Table 4.4 by the box around the x_2 column below -5.)

Step 2: Determine the *leaving basic variable* by applying the minimum ratio test.
Minimum Ratio Test

1. Pick out each coefficient in the pivot column that is strictly positive (> 0).
2. Divide each of these coefficients into the *right side* entry for the same row.
3. Identify the row that has the *smallest* of these ratios.
4. The basic variable for that row is the leaving basic variable, so replace that variable by the entering basic variable in the basic variable column of the next simplex tableau.

TABLE 4.4 Applying the minimum ratio test to determine the first leaving basic variable for the Wyndor Glass Co. problem

Basic Variable	Eq.	Z	Coefficient of: x_1	x_2	x_3	x_4	x_5	Right Side	Ratio
Z	(0)	1	-3	-5	0	0	0	0	
x_3	(1)	0	1	0	1	0	0	4	
x_4	(2)	0	0	2	0	1	0	$12 \rightarrow \dfrac{12}{2} = 6 \leftarrow$ minimum	
x_5	(3)	0	3	2	0	0	1	$18 \rightarrow \dfrac{18}{2} = 9$	

Put a box around this row and call it the **pivot row.** Also call the number that is in *both* boxes the **pivot number.**

For the Example: The calculations for the minimum ratio test are shown to the right of Table 4.4. Thus, row 2 is the pivot row (see the box around this row in the first simplex tableau of Table 4.5), and x_4 is the leaving basic variable. In the next simplex tableau (see the bottom of Table 4.5), x_2 replaces x_4 as the basic variable for row 2.

Step 3: Solve for the *new BF solution* by using **elementary row operations** (multiply or divide a row by a nonzero constant; add or subtract a multiple of one row to another row) to construct a new simplex tableau in proper form from Gaussian elimination below the current one, and then return to the optimality test. The specific elementary row operations that need to be performed are listed below.

1. Divide the pivot row by the pivot number. Use this *new* pivot row in steps 2 and 3.
2. For each other row (including row 0) that has a *negative* coefficient in the pivot column, *add* to this row the *product* of the absolute value of this coefficient and the new pivot row.
3. For each other row that has a *positive* coefficient in the pivot column, *subtract* from this row the *product* of this coefficient and the new pivot row.

For the Example: Since x_2 is replacing x_4 as a basic variable, we need to reproduce the first tableau's pattern of coefficients in the column of x_4 (0, 0, 1, 0) in the second tableau's column of x_2. To start, divide the pivot row (row 2) by the pivot number (2), which gives the new row 2 shown in Table 4.5. Next, we add to row 0 the product, 5 times the new row 2. Then we subtract from row 3 the product, 2 times the new row 2 (or equivalently, subtract from row 3 the *old* row 2). These calculations yield the new tableau shown in Table 4.6 for iteration 1. Thus, the new BF solution is (0, 6, 4, 0, 6), with $Z = 30$. We next return to the optimality test to check if the new BF solution is optimal. Since the new row 0 still has a negative coefficient (-3 for x_1), the solution is not optimal, and so at least one more iteration is needed.

TABLE 4.5 Simplex tableaux for the Wyndor Glass Co. problem after the first pivot row is divided by the first pivot number

Iteration	Basic Variable	Eq.	Z	x_1	x_2	x_3	x_4	x_5	Right Side
					Coefficient of:				
0	Z	(0)	1	-3	-5	0	0	0	0
	x_3	(1)	0	1	0	1	0	0	4
	x_4	(2)	0	0	2	0	1	0	12
	x_5	(3)	0	3	2	0	0	1	18
1	Z	(0)	1						
	x_3	(1)	0						
	x_2	(2)	0	0	1	0	$\frac{1}{2}$	0	6
	x_5	(3)	0						

TABLE 4.6 First two simplex tableaux for the Wyndor Glass Co. problem

Iteration	Basic Variable	Eq.	Z	Coefficient of:					Right Side
				x_1	x_2	x_3	x_4	x_5	
0	Z	(0)	1	-3	-5	0	0	0	0
	x_3	(1)	0	1	0	1	0	0	4
	x_4	(2)	0	0	2	0	1	0	12
	x_5	(3)	0	3	2	0	0	1	18
1	Z	(0)	1	-3	0	0	$\frac{5}{2}$	0	30
	x_3	(1)	0	1	0	1	0	0	4
	x_2	(2)	0	0	1	0	$\frac{1}{2}$	0	6
	x_5	(3)	0	3	0	0	-1	1	6

Iteration 2 for the Example and the Resulting Optimal Solution

The second iteration starts anew from the second tableau of Table 4.6 to find the next BF solution. Following the instructions for steps 1 and 2, we find x_1 as the entering basic variable and x_5 as the leaving basic variable, as shown in Table 4.7.

For step 3, we start by dividing the pivot row (row 3) in Table 4.7 by the pivot number (3). Next, we add to row 0 the product, 3 times the new row 3. Then we subtract the new row 3 from row 1.

We now have the set of tableaux shown in Table 4.8. Therefore, the new BF solution is (2, 6, 2, 0, 0), with $Z = 36$. Going to the optimality test, we find that this solution is *optimal* because none of the coefficients in row 0 is negative, so the algorithm is finished. Consequently, the optimal solution for the Wyndor Glass Co. problem (before slack variables are introduced) is $x_1 = 2$, $x_2 = 6$.

Now compare Table 4.8 with the work done in Sec. 4.3 to verify that these two forms of the simplex method really are *equivalent*. Then note how the algebraic form is superior for learning the logic behind the simplex method, but the tabular form organizes the

TABLE 4.7 Steps 1 and 2 of iteration 2 for the Wyndor Glass Co. problem

Iteration	Basic Variable	Eq.	Z	Coefficient of:					Right Side	Ratio
				x_1	x_2	x_3	x_4	x_5		
1	Z	(0)	1	-3	0	0	$\frac{5}{2}$	0	30	
	x_3	(1)	0	1	0	1	0	0	4	$\frac{4}{1} = 4$
	x_2	(2)	0	0	1	0	$\frac{1}{2}$	0	6	
	x_5	(3)	0	3	0	0	-1	1	6	$\frac{6}{3} = 2 \leftarrow$ minimum

TABLE 4.8 Complete set of simplex tableaux for the Wyndor Glass Co. problem

Iteration	Basic Variable	Eq.	Coefficient of:							Right Side
			Z	x_1	x_2	x_3	x_4	x_5		
0	Z	(0)	1	-3	-5	0	0	0		0
	x_3	(1)	0	1	0	1	0	0		4
	x_4	(2)	0	0	2	0	1	0		12
	x_5	(3)	0	3	2	0	0	1		18
1	Z	(0)	1	-3	0	0	$\frac{5}{2}$	0		30
	x_3	(1)	0	1	0	1	0	0		4
	x_2	(2)	0	0	1	0	$\frac{1}{2}$	0		6
	x_5	(3)	0	3	0	0	-1	1		6
2	Z	(0)	1	0	0	0	$\frac{3}{2}$	1		36
	x_3	(1)	0	0	0	1	$\frac{1}{3}$	$-\frac{1}{3}$		2
	x_2	(2)	0	0	1	0	$\frac{1}{2}$	0		6
	x_1	(3)	0	1	0	0	$-\frac{1}{3}$	$\frac{1}{3}$		2

work being done in a considerably more convenient and compact form. We generally use the tabular form from now on.

An additional example of applying the simplex method in tabular form is available to you in the OR Tutor. See the demonstration entitled *Simplex Method—Tabular Form.*

4.5 TIE BREAKING IN THE SIMPLEX METHOD

You may have noticed in the preceding two sections that we never said what to do if the various choice rules of the simplex method do not lead to a clear-cut decision, because of either ties or other similar ambiguities. We discuss these details now.

Tie for the Entering Basic Variable

Step 1 of each iteration chooses the nonbasic variable having the *negative* coefficient with the *largest absolute value* in the current Eq. (0) as the entering basic variable. Now suppose that two or more nonbasic variables are tied for having the largest negative coefficient (in absolute terms). For example, this would occur in the first iteration for the Wyndor Glass Co. problem if its objective function were changed to $Z = 3x_1 + 3x_2$, so that the initial Eq. (0) became $Z - 3x_1 - 3x_2 = 0$. How should this tie be broken?

The answer is that the selection between these contenders may be made *arbitrarily.* The optimal solution will be reached eventually, regardless of the tied variable chosen, and there is no convenient method for predicting in advance which choice will lead there sooner. In this example, the simplex method happens to reach the optimal solution (2, 6) in three iterations with x_1 as the initial entering basic variable, versus two iterations if x_2 is chosen.

Tie for the Leaving Basic Variable—Degeneracy

Now suppose that two or more basic variables tie for being the leaving basic variable in step 2 of an iteration. Does it matter which one is chosen? Theoretically it does, and in a very critical way, because of the following sequence of events that could occur. First, all the tied basic variables reach zero simultaneously as the entering basic variable is increased. Therefore, the one or ones *not* chosen to be the leaving basic variable also will have a value of zero in the new BF solution. (Note that basic variables with a value of *zero* are called **degenerate**, and the same term is applied to the corresponding BF solution.) Second, if one of these degenerate basic variables retains its value of zero until it is chosen at a subsequent iteration to be a leaving basic variable, the corresponding entering basic variable also must remain zero (since it cannot be increased without making the leaving basic variable negative), so the value of Z must remain unchanged. Third, if Z may remain the same rather than increase at each iteration, the simplex method may then go around in a loop, repeating the same sequence of solutions periodically rather than eventually increasing Z toward an optimal solution. In fact, examples have been artificially constructed so that they do become entrapped in just such a perpetual loop.

Fortunately, although a perpetual loop is theoretically possible, it has rarely been known to occur in practical problems. If a loop were to occur, one could always get out of it by changing the choice of the leaving basic variable. Furthermore, special rules[1] have been constructed for breaking ties so that such loops are always avoided. However, these rules frequently are ignored in actual application, and they will not be repeated here. For your purposes, just break this kind of tie arbitrarily and proceed without worrying about the degenerate basic variables that result.

No Leaving Basic Variable—Unbounded Z

In step 2 of an iteration, there is one other possible outcome that we have not yet discussed, namely, that *no* variable qualifies to be the leaving basic variable.[2] This outcome would occur if the entering basic variable could be increased *indefinitely* without giving negative values to *any* of the current basic variables. In tabular form, this means that *every* coefficient in the pivot column (excluding row 0) is either negative or zero.

As illustrated in Table 4.9, this situation arises in the example displayed in Fig. 3.6 on p. 36. In this example, the last two functional constraints of the Wyndor Glass Co. problem have been overlooked and so are not included in the model. Note in Fig. 3.6 how x_2 can be increased indefinitely (thereby increasing Z indefinitely) without ever leaving the feasible region. Then note in Table 4.9 that x_2 is the entering basic variable but the

---

[1]See R. Bland, "New Finite Pivoting Rules for the Simplex Method," *Mathematics of Operations Research,* **2:** 103–107, 1977.

[2]Note that the analogous case (no *entering* basic variable) cannot occur in step 1 of an iteration, because the optimality test would stop the algorithm first by indicating that an optimal solution had been reached.

TABLE 4.9 Initial simplex tableau for the Wyndor Glass Co. problem without the last two functional constraints

Basic Variable	Eq.	Coefficient of:					Right Side	Ratio
		Z	x_1	x_2	x_3			
Z	(0)	1	-3	-5	0		0	
x_3	(1)	0	1	$\boxed{0}$	1		4	None

With $x_1 = 0$ and x_2 increasing, $x_3 = 4 - 1x_1 - 0x_2 = 4 > 0$.

only coefficient in the pivot column is zero. Because the minimum ratio test uses only coefficients that are greater than zero, there is no ratio to provide a leaving basic variable.

The interpretation of a tableau like the one shown in Table 4.9 is that the constraints do not prevent the value of the objective function Z increasing indefinitely, so the simplex method would stop with the message that Z is *unbounded*. Because even linear programming has not discovered a way of making infinite profits, the real message for practical problems is that a mistake has been made! The model probably has been misformulated, either by omitting relevant constraints or by stating them incorrectly. Alternatively, a computational mistake may have occurred.

Multiple Optimal Solutions

We mentioned in Sec. 3.2 (under the definition of **optimal solution**) that a problem can have more than one optimal solution. This fact was illustrated in Fig. 3.5 by changing the objective function in the Wyndor Glass Co. problem to $Z = 3x_1 + 2x_2$, so that every point on the line segment between (2, 6) and (4, 3) is optimal. Thus, all optimal solutions are a *weighted average* of these two optimal CPF solutions

$$(x_1, x_2) = w_1(2, 6) + w_2(4, 3),$$

where the weights w_1 and w_2 are numbers that satisfy the relationships

$$w_1 + w_2 = 1 \quad \text{and} \quad w_1 \geq 0, \quad w_2 \geq 0.$$

For example, $w_1 = \frac{1}{3}$ and $w_2 = \frac{2}{3}$ give

$$(x_1, x_2) = \frac{1}{3}(2, 6) + \frac{2}{3}(4, 3) = \left(\frac{2}{3} + \frac{8}{3}, \frac{6}{3} + \frac{6}{3}\right) = \left(\frac{10}{3}, \ 4\right)$$

as one optimal solution.

In general, any weighted average of two or more solutions (vectors) where the weights are nonnegative and sum to 1 is called a **convex combination** of these solutions. Thus, every optimal solution in the example is a convex combination of (2, 6) and (4, 3).

This example is typical of problems with multiple optimal solutions.

As indicated at the end of Sec. 3.2, *any* linear programming problem with multiple optimal solutions (and a bounded feasible region) has at least two CPF solutions that are optimal. *Every* optimal solution is a convex combination of these optimal CPF solutions. Consequently, in augmented form, every optimal solution is a convex combination of the optimal BF solutions.

(Problems 4.5-5 and 4.5-6 guide you through the reasoning behind this conclusion.)

The simplex method automatically stops after *one* optimal BF solution is found. However, for many applications of linear programming, there are intangible factors not incorporated into the model that can be used to make meaningful choices between alternative optimal solutions. In such cases, these other optimal solutions should be identified as well. As indicated above, this requires finding all the other optimal BF solutions, and then every optimal solution is a convex combination of the optimal BF solutions.

After the simplex method finds one optimal BF solution, you can detect if there are any others and, if so, find them as follows:

> Whenever a problem has more than one optimal BF solution, at least one of the nonbasic variables has a coefficient of zero in the final row 0, so increasing any such variable will not change the value of Z. Therefore, these other optimal BF solutions can be identified (if desired) by performing additional iterations of the simplex method, each time choosing a nonbasic variable with a zero coefficient as the entering basic variable.[1]

To illustrate, consider again the case just mentioned, where the objective function in the Wyndor Glass Co. problem is changed to $Z = 3x_1 + 2x_2$. The simplex method obtains the first three tableaux shown in Table 4.10 and stops with an optimal BF solution. How-

[1]If such an iteration has no *leaving* basic variable, this indicates that the feasible region is unbounded and the entering basic variable can be increased indefinitely without changing the value of Z.

TABLE 4.10 Complete set of simplex tableaux to obtain all optimal BF solutions for the Wyndor Glass Co. problem with $c_2 = 2$

Iteration	Basic Variable	Eq.	Z	x_1	x_2	x_3	x_4	x_5	Right Side	Solution Optimal?
0	Z	(0)	1	−3	−2	0	0	0	0	No
	x_3	(1)	0	1	0	1	0	0	4	
	x_4	(2)	0	0	2	0	1	0	12	
	x_5	(3)	0	3	2	0	0	1	18	
1	Z	(0)	1	0	−2	3	0	0	12	No
	x_1	(1)	0	1	0	1	0	0	4	
	x_4	(2)	0	0	2	0	1	0	12	
	x_5	(3)	0	0	2	−3	0	1	6	
2	Z	(0)	1	0	0	**0**	0	1	18	Yes
	x_1	(1)	0	1	0	1	0	0	4	
	x_4	(2)	0	0	0	3	1	−1	6	
	x_2	(3)	0	0	1	$-\dfrac{3}{2}$	0	$\dfrac{1}{2}$	3	
Extra	Z	(0)	1	0	0	0	**0**	1	18	Yes
	x_1	(1)	0	1	0	0	$-\dfrac{1}{3}$	$\dfrac{1}{3}$	2	
	x_3	(2)	0	0	0	1	$\dfrac{1}{3}$	$-\dfrac{1}{3}$	2	
	x_2	(3)	0	0	1	0	$\dfrac{1}{2}$	0	6	

ever, because a nonbasic variable (x_3) then has a zero coefficient in row 0, we perform one more iteration in Table 4.10 to identify the other optimal BF solution. Thus, the two optimal BF solutions are (4, 3, 0, 6, 0) and (2, 6, 2, 0, 0), each yielding $Z = 18$. Notice that the last tableau also has a *nonbasic* variable (x_4) with a zero coefficient in row 0. This situation is inevitable because the extra iteration does not change row 0, so this leaving basic variable necessarily retains its zero coefficient. Making x_4 an entering basic variable now would only lead back to the third tableau. (Check this.) Therefore, these two are the only BF solutions that are optimal, and all *other* optimal solutions are a convex combination of these two.

$$(x_1, x_2, x_3, x_4, x_5) = w_1(2, 6, 2, 0, 0) + w_2(4, 3, 0, 6, 0),$$
$$w_1 + w_2 = 1, \qquad w_1 \geq 0, \qquad w_2 \geq 0.$$

4.6 ADAPTING TO OTHER MODEL FORMS

Thus far we have presented the details of the simplex method under the assumptions that the problem is in our standard form (maximize Z subject to functional constraints in $\leq$ form and nonnegativity constraints on all variables) and that $b_i \geq 0$ for all $i = 1, 2, \ldots, m$. In this section we point out how to make the adjustments required for other legitimate forms of the linear programming model. You will see that all these adjustments can be made during the initialization, so the rest of the simplex method can then be applied just as you have learned it already.

The only serious problem introduced by the other forms for functional constraints (the $=$ or $\geq$ forms, or having a negative right-hand side) lies in identifying an *initial BF solution*. Before, this initial solution was found very conveniently by letting the slack variables be the initial basic variables, so that each one just equals the *nonnegative* right-hand side of its equation. Now, something else must be done. The standard approach that is used for all these cases is the **artificial-variable technique.** This technique constructs a more convenient *artificial problem* by introducing a dummy variable (called an *artificial variable*) into each constraint that needs one. This new variable is introduced just for the purpose of being the initial basic variable for that equation. The usual nonnegativity constraints are placed on these variables, and the objective function also is modified to impose an exorbitant penalty on their having values larger than zero. The iterations of the simplex method then automatically force the artificial variables to disappear (become zero), one at a time, until they are all gone, after which the *real* problem is solved.

To illustrate the artificial-variable technique, first we consider the case where the only nonstandard form in the problem is the presence of one or more equality constraints.

Equality Constraints

Any equality constraint

$$a_{i1}x_1 + a_{i2}x_2 + \cdots + a_{in}x_n = b_i$$

actually is equivalent to a pair of inequality constraints:

$$a_{i1}x_1 + a_{i2}x_2 + \cdots + a_{in}x_n \leq b_i$$
$$a_{i1}x_1 + a_{i2}x_2 + \cdots + a_{in}x_n \geq b_i.$$

However, rather than making this substitution and thereby increasing the number of constraints, it is more convenient to use the artificial-variable technique. We shall illustrate this technique with the following example.

Example. Suppose that the Wyndor Glass Co. problem in Sec. 3.1 is modified to *require* that Plant 3 be used at full capacity. The only resulting change in the linear programming model is that the third constraint, $3x_1 + 2x_2 \leq 18$, instead becomes an equality constraint

$$3x_1 + 2x_2 = 18,$$

so that the complete model becomes the one shown in the upper right-hand corner of Fig. 4.3. This figure also shows in darker ink the feasible region which now consists of *just* the line segment connecting $(2, 6)$ and $(4, 3)$.

After the slack variables still needed for the inequality constraints are introduced, the system of equations for the augmented form of the problem becomes

$$
\begin{aligned}
(0) \quad & Z - 3x_1 - 5x_2 && = 0 \\
(1) \quad & x_1 + x_3 && = 4 \\
(2) \quad & 2x_2 + x_4 && = 12 \\
(3) \quad & 3x_1 + 2x_2 && = 18.
\end{aligned}
$$

Unfortunately, these equations do not have an obvious initial BF solution because there is no longer a slack variable to use as the initial basic variable for Eq. (3). It is necessary to find an initial BF solution to start the simplex method.

This difficulty can be circumvented in the following way.

FIGURE 4.3
When the third functional constraint becomes an equality constraint, the feasible region for the Wyndor Glass Co. problem becomes the line segment between $(2, 6)$ and $(4, 3)$.

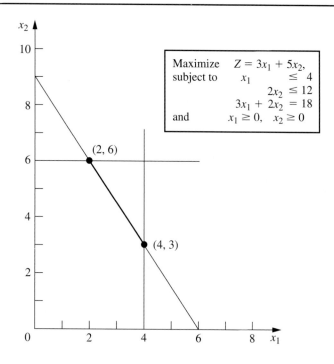

Maximize $Z = 3x_1 + 5x_2$,
subject to $x_1 \leq 4$
$2x_2 \leq 12$
$3x_1 + 2x_2 = 18$
and $x_1 \geq 0, \quad x_2 \geq 0$

Obtaining an Initial BF Solution.   The procedure is to construct an **artificial problem** that has the same optimal solution as the real problem by making two modifications of the real problem.

1. Apply the **artificial-variable technique** by introducing a *nonnegative* **artificial variable** (call it $\bar{x}_5$)[1] into Eq. (3), just as if it were a slack variable

    (3) $3x_1 + 2x_2 + \bar{x}_5 = 18.$

2. Assign an *overwhelming penalty* to having $\bar{x}_5 > 0$ by changing the objective function $Z = 3x_1 + 5x_2$ to

    $Z = 3x_1 + 5x_2 - M\bar{x}_5,$

    where M symbolically represents a *huge* positive number. (This method of forcing $\bar{x}_5$ to be $\bar{x}_5 = 0$ in the optimal solution is called the **Big M method**.)

Now find the optimal solution for the real problem by applying the simplex method to the artificial problem, starting with the following initial BF solution:

Initial BF Solution
Nonbasic variables: $x_1 = 0,$ $x_2 = 0$
Basic variables: $x_3 = 4,$ $x_4 = 12,$ $\bar{x}_5 = 18.$

Because $\bar{x}_5$ plays the role of the slack variable for the third constraint in the artificial problem, this constraint is equivalent to $3x_1 + 2x_2 \le 18$ (just as for the original Wyndor Glass Co. problem in Sec. 3.1). We show below the resulting artificial problem (before augmenting) next to the real problem.

The Real Problem	*The Artificial Problem*
	Define $\bar{x}_5 = 18 - 3x_1 - 2x_2.$
Maximize $Z = 3x_1 + 5x_2,$	Maximize $Z = 3x_1 + 5x_2 - M\bar{x}_5,$
subject to	subject to
$x_1 \qquad\qquad \le 4$	$x_1 \qquad\qquad \le 4$
$\qquad 2x_2 \le 12$	$\qquad 2x_2 \qquad \le 12$
$3x_1 + 2x_2 = 18$	$3x_1 + 2x_2 \qquad \le 18$
and	(so $3x_1 + 2x_2 + \bar{x}_5 = 18$)
$x_1 \ge 0, \qquad x_2 \ge 0.$	and
	$x_1 \ge 0, \qquad x_2 \ge 0, \qquad \bar{x}_5 \ge 0.$

Therefore, just as in Sec. 3.1, the feasible region for (x_1, x_2) for the artificial problem is the one shown in Fig. 4.4. The only portion of this feasible region that coincides with the feasible region for the real problem is where $\bar{x}_5 = 0$ (so $3x_1 + 2x_2 = 18$).

Figure 4.4 also shows the order in which the simplex method examines the CPF solutions (or BF solutions after augmenting), where each circled number identifies which iteration obtained that solution. Note that the simplex method moves counterclockwise here

---

[1] We shall always label the artificial variables by putting a bar over them.

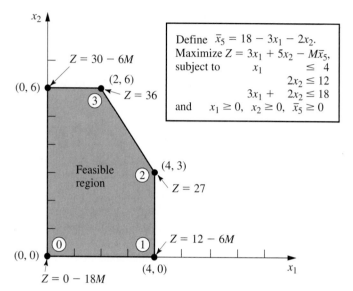

FIGURE 4.4
This graph shows the feasible region and the sequence of CPF solutions (⓪, ①, ②, ③) examined by the simplex method for the artificial problem that corresponds to the real problem of Fig. 4.3.

whereas it moved clockwise for the original Wyndor Glass Co. problem (see Fig. 4.2). The reason for this difference is the extra term $-M\bar{x}_5$ in the objective function for the artificial problem.

Before applying the simplex method and demonstrating that it follows the path shown in Fig. 4.4, the following preparatory step is needed.

Converting Equation (0) to Proper Form. The system of equations after the artificial problem is augmented is

$$
\begin{aligned}
(0) \quad & Z - 3x_1 - 5x_2 && + M\bar{x}_5 = 0 \\
(1) \quad & x_1 && + x_3 && = 4 \\
(2) \quad & 2x_2 && + x_4 && = 12 \\
(3) \quad & 3x_1 + 2x_2 && + \bar{x}_5 = 18
\end{aligned}
$$

where the initial basic variables $(x_3, x_4, \bar{x}_5)$ are shown in bold type. However, this system is not yet in proper form from Gaussian elimination because a basic variable $\bar{x}_5$ has a nonzero coefficient in Eq. (0). Recall that all basic variables must be algebraically eliminated from Eq. (0) before the simplex method can either apply the optimality test or find the entering basic variable. This elimination is necessary so that the negative of the coefficient of each nonbasic variable will give the rate at which Z would increase if that nonbasic variable were to be increased from 0 while adjusting the values of the basic variables accordingly.

To algebraically eliminate $\bar{x}_5$ from Eq. (0), we need to subtract from Eq. (0) the product, M times Eq. (3).

$$
\begin{array}{l}
Z - 3x_1 - 5x_2 + M\bar{x}_5 = 0 \\
\underline{-M(3x_1 + 2x_2 + \bar{x}_5 = 18)} \\
\text{New (0)} \quad Z - (3M + 3)x_1 - (2M + 5)x_2 = -18M.
\end{array}
$$

Application of the Simplex Method.   This new Eq. (0) gives Z in terms of *just* the nonbasic variables (x_1, x_2),

$$Z = -18M + (3M + 3)x_1 + (2M + 5)x_2.$$

Since $3M + 3 > 2M + 5$ (remember that M represents a huge number), increasing x_1 increases Z at a faster rate than increasing x_2 does, so x_1 is chosen as the entering basic variable. This leads to the move from $(0, 0)$ to $(4, 0)$ at iteration 1, shown in Fig. 4.4, thereby increasing Z by $4(3M + 3)$.

The quantities involving M never appear in the system of equations except for Eq. (0), so they need to be taken into account only in the optimality test and when an entering basic variable is determined. One way of dealing with these quantities is to assign some particular (huge) numerical value to M and use the resulting coefficients in Eq. (0) in the usual way. However, this approach may result in significant rounding errors that invalidate the optimality test. Therefore, it is better to do what we have just shown, namely, to express each coefficient in Eq. (0) as a linear function $aM + b$ of the *symbolic* quantity M by separately recording and updating the current numerical value of (1) the *multiplicative* factor a and (2) the *additive* term b. Because M is assumed to be so large that b always is negligible compared with M when $a \neq 0$, the decisions in the optimality test and the choice of the entering basic variable are made by using just the *multiplicative* factors in the usual way, except for breaking ties with the *additive* factors.

Using this approach on the example yields the simplex tableaux shown in Table 4.11. Note that the artificial variable $\bar{x}_5$ is a *basic variable* ($\bar{x}_5 > 0$) in the first two tableaux and a *nonbasic variable* ($\bar{x}_5 = 0$) in the last two. Therefore, the first two BF solutions for this artificial problem are *infeasible* for the real problem whereas the last two also are BF solutions for the real problem.

This example involved only one equality constraint. If a linear programming model has more than one, each is handled in just the same way. (If the right-hand side is negative, multiply through both sides by -1 first.)

Negative Right-Hand Sides

The technique mentioned in the preceding sentence for dealing with an equality constraint with a negative right-hand side (namely, multiply through both sides by -1) also works for any inequality constraint with a negative right-hand side. Multiplying through both sides of an inequality by -1 also reverses the direction of the inequality; i.e., $\leq$ changes to $\geq$ or vice versa. For example, doing this to the constraint

$$x_1 - x_2 \leq -1 \qquad \text{(that is, } x_1 \leq x_2 - 1)$$

gives the equivalent constraint

$$-x_1 + x_2 \geq 1 \qquad \text{(that is, } x_2 - 1 \geq x_1)$$

but now the right-hand side is positive. Having nonnegative right-hand sides for all the functional constraints enables the simplex method to begin, because (after augmenting) these right-hand sides become the respective values of the *initial basic variables,* which must satisfy nonnegativity constraints.

TABLE 4.11 Complete set of simplex tableaux for the problem shown in Fig. 4.4

Iteration	Basic Variable	Eq.	Z	x_1	x_2	x_3	x_4	$\bar{x}_5$	Right Side
0	Z	(0)	1	$-3M-3$	$-2M-5$	0	0	0	$-18M$
	x_3	(1)	0	1	0	1	0	0	4
	x_4	(2)	0	0	2	0	1	0	12
	$\bar{x}_5$	(3)	0	3	2	0	0	1	18
1	Z	(0)	1	0	$-2M-5$	$3M+3$	0	0	$-6M+12$
	x_1	(1)	0	1	0	1	0	0	4
	x_4	(2)	0	0	2	0	1	0	12
	$\bar{x}_5$	(3)	0	0	2	-3	0	1	6
2	Z	(0)	1	0	0	$-\dfrac{9}{2}$	0	$M+\dfrac{5}{2}$	27
	x_1	(1)	0	1	0	1	0	0	4
	x_4	(2)	0	0	0	3	1	-1	6
	x_2	(3)	0	0	1	$-\dfrac{3}{2}$	0	$\dfrac{1}{2}$	3
Extra	Z	(0)	1	0	0	0	$\dfrac{3}{2}$	$M+1$	36
	x_1	(1)	0	1	0	0	$-\dfrac{1}{3}$	$\dfrac{1}{3}$	2
	x_3	(2)	0	0	0	1	$\dfrac{1}{3}$	$-\dfrac{1}{3}$	2
	x_2	(3)	0	0	1	0	$\dfrac{1}{2}$	0	6

We next focus on how to augment $\geq$ constraints, such as $-x_1 + x_2 \geq 1$, with the help of the artificial-variable technique.

Functional Constraints in $\geq$ Form

To illustrate how the artificial-variable technique deals with functional constraints in $\geq$ form, we will use the model for designing Mary's radiation therapy, as presented in Sec. 3.4. For your convenience, this model is repeated below, where we have placed a box around the constraint of special interest here.

Radiation Therapy Example

Minimize $Z = 0.4x_1 + 0.5x_2,$

subject to

$$0.3x_1 + 0.1x_2 \leq 2.7$$

$$0.5x_1 + 0.5x_2 = 6$$

$$\boxed{0.6x_1 + 0.4x_2 \geq 6}$$

and

$$x_1 \geq 0, \qquad x_2 \geq 0.$$

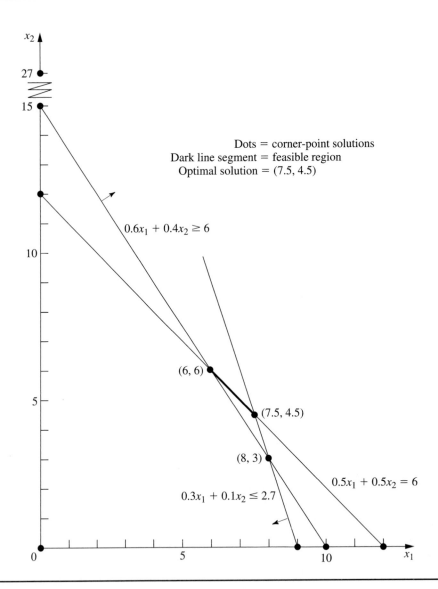

FIGURE 4.5
Graphical display of the radiation therapy example and its corner-point solutions.

The graphical solution for this example (originally presented in Fig. 3.12) is repeated here in a slightly different form in Fig. 4.5. The three lines in the figure, along with the two axes, constitute the five constraint boundaries of the problem. The dots lying at the intersection of a pair of constraint boundaries are the *corner-point solutions*. The only two corner-point *feasible* solutions are (6, 6) and (7.5, 4.5), and the feasible region is the line segment connecting these two points. The optimal solution is $(x_1, x_2) = (7.5, 4.5)$, with $Z = 5.25$.

We soon will show how the simplex method solves this problem by directly solving the corresponding artificial problem. However, first we must describe how to deal with the third constraint.

Our approach involves introducing *both* a surplus variable x_5 (defined as $x_5 = 0.6x_1 + 0.4x_2 - 6$) and an artificial variable $\bar{x}_6$, as shown next.

$$
\begin{array}{lll}
& 0.6x_1 + 0.4x_2 & \geq 6 \\
\rightarrow & 0.6x_1 + 0.4x_2 - x_5 & = 6 & (x_5 \geq 0) \\
\rightarrow & 0.6x_1 + 0.4x_2 - x_5 + \bar{x}_6 = 6 & & (x_5 \geq 0, \bar{x}_6 \geq 0).
\end{array}
$$

Here x_5 is called a **surplus variable** because it subtracts the surplus of the left-hand side over the right-hand side to convert the inequality constraint to an equivalent equality constraint. Once this conversion is accomplished, the artificial variable is introduced just as for any equality constraint.

After a slack variable x_3 is introduced into the first constraint, an artificial variable $\bar{x}_4$ is introduced into the second constraint, and the Big *M* method is applied, so the complete artificial problem (in augmented form) is

$$
\begin{array}{ll}
\text{Minimize} & Z = 0.4x_1 + 0.5x_2 + M\bar{x}_4 + M\bar{x}_6, \\
\text{subject to} & 0.3x_1 + 0.1x_2 + x_3 = 2.7 \\
& 0.5x_1 + 0.5x_2 \quad\quad + \bar{x}_4 = 6 \\
& 0.6x_1 + 0.4x_2 \quad\quad\quad\quad - x_5 + \bar{x}_6 = 6
\end{array}
$$

and $x_1 \geq 0, \quad x_2 \geq 0, \quad x_3 \geq 0, \quad \bar{x}_4 \geq 0, \quad x_5 \geq 0, \quad \bar{x}_6 \geq 0.$

Note that the coefficients of the artificial variables in the objective function are $+M$, instead of $-M$, because we now are minimizing Z. Thus, even though $\bar{x}_4 > 0$ and/or $\bar{x}_6 > 0$ is possible for a feasible solution for the artificial problem, the huge unit penalty of $+M$ prevents this from occurring in an optimal solution.

As usual, introducing artificial variables enlarges the feasible region. Compare below the original constraints for the real problem with the corresponding constraints on (x_1, x_2) for the artificial problem.

Constraints on (x_1, x_2) *for the Real Problem*	*Constraints on* (x_1, x_2) *for the Artificial Problem*
$0.3x_1 + 0.1x_2 \leq 2.7$	$0.3x_1 + 0.1x_2 \leq 2.7$
$0.5x_1 + 0.5x_2 = 6$	$0.5x_1 + 0.5x_2 \leq 6$ (= holds when $\bar{x}_4 = 0$)
$0.6x_1 + 0.4x_2 \geq 6$	No such constraint (except when $\bar{x}_6 = 0$)
$x_1 \geq 0, \quad x_2 \geq 0$	$x_1 \geq 0, \quad x_2 \geq 0$

Introducing the artificial variable $\bar{x}_4$ to play the role of a slack variable in the second constraint allows values of (x_1, x_2) *below* the $0.5x_1 + 0.5x_2 = 6$ line in Fig. 4.5. Introducing x_5 and $\bar{x}_6$ into the third constraint of the real problem (and moving these variables to the right-hand side) yields the equation

$$0.6x_1 + 0.4x_2 = 6 + x_5 - \bar{x}_6.$$

Because both x_5 and $\bar{x}_6$ are constrained only to be nonnegative, their difference $x_5 - \bar{x}_6$ can be any positive or negative number. Therefore, $0.6x_1 + 0.4x_2$ can have any value, which has the effect of eliminating the third constraint from the artificial problem and allowing points on either side of the $0.6x_1 + 0.4x_2 = 6$ line in Fig. 4.5. (We keep the third constraint in the system of equations only because it will become relevant again later, after the Big *M* method forces $\bar{x}_6$ to be zero.) Consequently, the feasible region for the artificial problem is the entire polyhedron in Fig. 4.5 whose vertices are $(0, 0)$, $(9, 0)$, $(7.5, 4.5)$, and $(0, 12)$.

Since the origin now is feasible for the artificial problem, the simplex method starts with $(0, 0)$ as the initial CPF solution, i.e., with $(x_1, x_2, x_3, \bar{x}_4, x_5, \bar{x}_6) = (0, 0, 2.7, 6, 0, 6)$ as the initial BF solution. (Making the origin feasible as a convenient starting point for the simplex method is the whole point of creating the artificial problem.) We soon will trace the entire path followed by the simplex method from the origin to the optimal solution for both the artificial and real problems. But, first, how does the simplex method handle *minimization?*

Minimization

One straightforward way of minimizing Z with the simplex method is to exchange the roles of the positive and negative coefficients in row 0 for both the optimality test and step 1 of an iteration. However, rather than changing our instructions for the simplex method for this case, we present the following simple way of converting any minimization problem to an equivalent maximization problem:

$$\textit{Minimizing} \qquad Z = \sum_{j=1}^{n} c_j x_j$$

is equivalent to

$$\textit{maximizing} \qquad -Z = \sum_{j=1}^{n} (-c_j) x_j;$$

i.e., the two formulations yield the same optimal solution(s).

The two formulations are equivalent because the smaller Z is, the larger $-Z$ is, so the solution that gives the *smallest* value of Z in the entire feasible region must also give the *largest* value of $-Z$ in this region.

Therefore, in the radiation therapy example, we make the following change in the formulation:

$$\begin{aligned} &\text{Minimize} & Z &= 0.4x_1 + 0.5x_2 \\ \rightarrow \quad &\text{Maximize} & -Z &= -0.4x_1 - 0.5x_2. \end{aligned}$$

After artificial variables $\bar{x}_4$ and $\bar{x}_6$ are introduced and then the Big M method is applied, the corresponding conversion is

$$\begin{aligned} &\text{Minimize} & Z &= 0.4x_1 + 0.5x_2 + M\bar{x}_4 + M\bar{x}_6 \\ \rightarrow \quad &\text{Maximize} & -Z &= -0.4x_1 - 0.5x_2 - M\bar{x}_4 - M\bar{x}_6. \end{aligned}$$

Solving the Radiation Therapy Example

We now are nearly ready to apply the simplex method to the radiation therapy example. By using the maximization form just obtained, the entire system of equations is now

$$\begin{aligned} (0) \quad & -Z + 0.4x_1 + 0.5x_2 + M\bar{x}_4 + M\bar{x}_6 = 0 \\ (1) \quad & 0.3x_1 + 0.1x_2 + x_3 \phantom{+ M\bar{x}_4 + M\bar{x}_6} = 2.7 \end{aligned}$$

(2) $\qquad 0.5x_1 + 0.5x_2 \quad + \quad \bar{x}_4 \qquad\qquad = 6$
(3) $\qquad 0.6x_1 + 0.4x_2 \qquad\qquad - x_5 + \quad \bar{x}_6 = 6.$

The basic variables $(x_3, \bar{x}_4, \bar{x}_6)$ for the initial BF solution (for this artificial problem) are shown in bold type.

Note that this system of equations is not yet in proper form from Gaussian elimination, as required by the simplex method, since the basic variables $\bar{x}_4$ and $\bar{x}_6$ still need to be algebraically eliminated from Eq. (0). Because $\bar{x}_4$ and $\bar{x}_6$ both have a coefficient of M, Eq. (0) needs to have subtracted from it *both* M times Eq. (2) *and* M times Eq. (3). The calculations for all the coefficients (and the right-hand sides) are summarized below, where the vectors are the relevant rows of the simplex tableau corresponding to the above system of equations.

Row 0:

$$
\begin{array}{rrrrrrr}
[0.4, & 0.5, & 0, & M, & 0, & M, & 0] \\
-M[0.5, & 0.5, & 0, & 1, & 0, & 0, & 6] \\
-M[0.6, & 0.4, & 0, & 0, & -1, & 1, & 6] \\
\hline
\text{New row } 0 = [-1.1M + 0.4, & -0.9M + 0.5, & 0, & 0, & M, & 0, & -12M]
\end{array}
$$

The resulting initial simplex tableau, ready to begin the simplex method, is shown at the top of Table 4.12. Applying the simplex method in just the usual way then yields the sequence of simplex tableaux shown in the rest of Table 4.12. For the optimality test and the selection of the entering basic variable at each iteration, the quantities involving M are treated just as discussed in connection with Table 4.11. Specifically, whenever M is present, only its multiplicative factor is used, unless there is a tie, in which case the tie is broken by using the corresponding additive terms. Just such a tie occurs in the last selection of an entering basic variable (see the next-to-last tableau), where the coefficients of x_3 and x_5 in row 0 both have the same multiplicative factor of $-\frac{5}{3}$. Comparing the additive terms, $\frac{11}{6} < \frac{7}{3}$ leads to choosing x_5 as the entering basic variable.

Note in Table 4.12 the progression of values of the artificial variables $\bar{x}_4$ and $\bar{x}_6$ and of Z. We start with large values, $\bar{x}_4 = 6$ and $\bar{x}_6 = 6$, with $Z = 12M$ $(-Z = -12M)$. The first iteration greatly reduces these values. The Big M method succeeds in driving $\bar{x}_6$ to zero (as a new nonbasic variable) at the second iteration and then in doing the same to $\bar{x}_4$ at the next iteration. With both $\bar{x}_4 = 0$ and $\bar{x}_6 = 0$, the basic solution given in the last tableau is guaranteed to be feasible for the real problem. Since it passes the optimality test, it also is optimal.

Now see what the Big M method has done graphically in Fig. 4.6. The feasible region for the artificial problem initially has four CPF solutions—(0, 0), (9, 0), (0, 12), and (7.5, 4.5)—and then replaces the first three with two new CPF solutions—(8, 3), (6, 6)—after $\bar{x}_6$ decreases to $\bar{x}_6 = 0$ so that $0.6x_1 + 0.4x_2 \geq 6$ becomes an additional constraint. (Note that the three replaced CPF solutions—(0, 0), (9, 0), and (0, 12)—actually were corner-point *infeasible* solutions for the real problem shown in Fig. 4.5.) Starting with the origin as the convenient initial CPF solution for the artificial problem, we move around the boundary to three other CPF solutions—(9, 0), (8, 3), and (7.5, 4.5). The last of these is the first one that also is feasible for the real problem. Fortuitously, this first feasible solution also is optimal, so no additional iterations are needed.

TABLE 4.12 The Big M method for the radiation therapy example

Iteration	Basic Variable	Eq.	Z	x_1	x_2	x_3	$\bar{x}_4$	x_5	$\bar{x}_6$	Right Side
0	Z	(0)	-1	$-1.1M + 0.4$	$-0.9M + 0.5$	0	0	M	0	$-12M$
	x_3	(1)	0	0.3	0.1	1	0	0	0	2.7
	$\bar{x}_4$	(2)	0	0.5	0.5	0	1	0	0	6
	$\bar{x}_6$	(3)	0	0.6	0.4	0	0	-1	1	6
1	Z	(0)	-1	0	$-\frac{16}{30}M + \frac{11}{30}$	$\frac{11}{3}M - \frac{4}{3}$	0	M	0	$-2.1M - 3.6$
	x_1	(1)	0	1	$\frac{1}{3}$	$\frac{10}{3}$	0	0	0	9
	$\bar{x}_4$	(2)	0	0	$\frac{1}{3}$	$-\frac{5}{3}$	1	0	0	1.5
	$\bar{x}_6$	(3)	0	0	0.2	-2	0	-1	1	0.6
2	Z	(0)	-1	0	0	$-\frac{5}{3}M + \frac{7}{3}$	0	$-\frac{5}{3}M + \frac{11}{6}$	$\frac{8}{3}M - \frac{11}{6}$	$-0.5M - 4.7$
	x_1	(1)	0	1	0	$\frac{20}{3}$	0	$\frac{5}{3}$	$-\frac{5}{3}$	8
	$\bar{x}_4$	(2)	0	0	0	$\frac{5}{3}$	1	$\frac{5}{3}$	$-\frac{5}{3}$	0.5
	x_2	(3)	0	0	1	-10	0	-5	5	3
3	Z	(0)	-1	0	0	0.5	$M - 1.1$	0	M	-5.25
	x_1	(1)	0	1	0	5	-1	0	0	7.5
	x_5	(2)	0	0	0	1	0.6	1	-1	0.3
	x_2	(3)	0	0	1	-5	3	0	0	4.5

For other problems with artificial variables, it may be necessary to perform additional iterations to reach an optimal solution after the first feasible solution is obtained for the real problem. (This was the case for the example solved in Table 4.11.) Thus, the Big M method can be thought of as having two phases. In the *first phase,* all the artificial variables are driven to zero (because of the penalty of M per unit for being greater than zero) in order to reach an initial BF solution for the *real* problem. In the *second phase,* all the artificial variables are kept at zero (because of this same penalty) while the simplex method generates a sequence of BF solutions for the real problem that leads to an optimal solution. The *two-phase method* described next is a streamlined procedure for performing these two phases directly, without even introducing M explicitly.

The Two-Phase Method

For the radiation therapy example just solved in Table 4.12, recall its real objective function

Real problem: Minimize $Z = 0.4x_1 + 0.5x_2$.

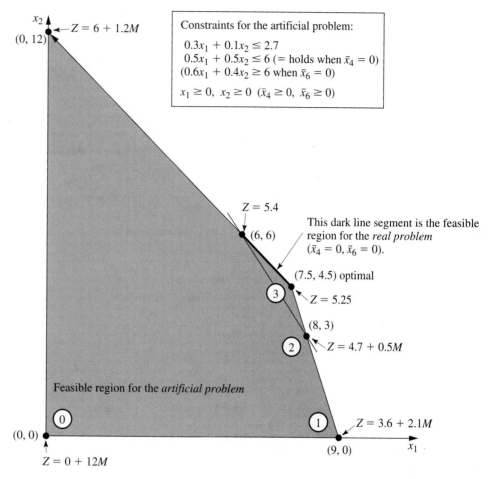

Constraints for the artificial problem:

$$0.3x_1 + 0.1x_2 \leq 2.7$$
$$0.5x_1 + 0.5x_2 \leq 6 \ (= \text{holds when } \bar{x}_4 = 0)$$
$$(0.6x_1 + 0.4x_2 \geq 6 \text{ when } \bar{x}_6 = 0)$$

$$x_1 \geq 0, \ x_2 \geq 0 \ (\bar{x}_4 \geq 0, \ \bar{x}_6 \geq 0)$$

x_2

$Z = 6 + 1.2M$

$(0, 12)$

$Z = 5.4$

$(6, 6)$

This dark line segment is the feasible region for the *real problem* $(\bar{x}_4 = 0, \bar{x}_6 = 0)$.

$(7.5, 4.5)$ optimal

③

$Z = 5.25$

$(8, 3)$

②

$Z = 4.7 + 0.5M$

Feasible region for the *artificial problem*

⓪

$(0, 0)$

$Z = 0 + 12M$

①

$Z = 3.6 + 2.1M$

$(9, 0)$

x_1

FIGURE 4.6
This graph shows the feasible region and the sequence of CPF solutions (⓪, ①, ②, ③) examined by the simplex method (with the Big M method) for the artificial problem that corresponds to the real problem of Fig. 4.5.

However, the Big M method uses the following objective function (or its equivalent in maximization form) throughout the entire procedure:

Big M method: Minimize $Z = 0.4x_1 + 0.5x_2 + M\bar{x}_4 + M\bar{x}_6.$

Since the first two coefficients are negligible compared to M, the two-phase method is able to drop M by using the following two objective functions with completely different definitions of Z in turn.

Two-phase method:

Phase 1:   Minimize $Z = \bar{x}_4 + \bar{x}_6$ (until $\bar{x}_4 = 0, \bar{x}_6 = 0$).
Phase 2:   Minimize $Z = 0.4x_1 + 0.5x_2$ (with $\bar{x}_4 = 0, \bar{x}_6 = 0$).

The phase 1 objective function is obtained by dividing the Big M method objective function by M and then dropping the negligible terms. Since phase 1 concludes by obtaining a BF solution for the real problem (one where $\bar{x}_4 = 0$ and $\bar{x}_6 = 0$), this solution is then used as the *initial* BF solution for applying the simplex method to the real problem (with its real objective function) in phase 2.

Before solving the example in this way, we summarize the general method.

Summary of the Two-Phase Method.   *Initialization:* Revise the constraints of the original problem by introducing artificial variables as needed to obtain an obvious initial BF solution for the *artificial problem.*

Phase 1: The objective for this phase is to find a BF solution for the *real problem.* To do this,

Minimize $Z = \Sigma$ artificial variables, subject to revised constraints.

The optimal solution obtained for this problem (with $Z = 0$) will be a BF solution for the real problem.

Phase 2: The objective for this phase is to find an *optimal solution* for the real problem. Since the artificial variables are not part of the real problem, these variables can now be dropped (they are all zero now anyway).[1] Starting from the BF solution obtained at the end of phase 1, use the simplex method to solve the real problem.

For the example, the problems to be solved by the simplex method in the respective phases are summarized below.

Phase 1 Problem (Radiation Therapy Example):

Minimize $Z = \bar{x}_4 + \bar{x}_6,$

subject to

$$
\begin{aligned}
0.3x_1 + 0.1x_2 + x_3 && &= 2.7 \\
0.5x_1 + 0.5x_2 && + \bar{x}_4 &= 6 \\
0.6x_1 + 0.4x_2 && - x_5 + \bar{x}_6 &= 6
\end{aligned}
$$

and

$$ x_1 \geq 0, \quad x_2 \geq 0, \quad x_3 \geq 0, \quad \bar{x}_4 \geq 0, \quad x_5 \geq 0, \quad \bar{x}_6 \geq 0. $$

Phase 2 Problem (Radiation Therapy Example):

Minimize $Z = 0.4x_1 + 0.5x_2,$

subject to

$$
\begin{aligned}
0.3x_1 + 0.1x_2 + x_3 &= 2.7 \\
0.5x_1 + 0.5x_2 &= 6 \\
0.6x_1 + 0.4x_2 - x_5 &= 6
\end{aligned}
$$

and

$$ x_1 \geq 0, \quad x_2 \geq 0, \quad x_3 \geq 0, \quad x_5 \geq 0. $$

---

[1] We are skipping over three other possibilities here: (1) artificial variables > 0 (discussed in the next subsection), (2) artificial variables that are degenerate basic variables, and (3) retaining the artificial variables as non-basic variables in phase 2 (and not allowing them to become basic) as an aid to subsequent postoptimality analysis. Your OR Courseware allows you to explore these possibilities.

The only differences between these two problems are in the objective function and in the inclusion (phase 1) or exclusion (phase 2) of the artificial variables $\bar{x}_4$ and $\bar{x}_6$. Without the artificial variables, the phase 2 problem does not have an obvious *initial BF solution*. The sole purpose of solving the phase 1 problem is to obtain a BF solution with $\bar{x}_4 = 0$ and $\bar{x}_6 = 0$ so that this solution (without the artificial variables) can be used as the initial BF solution for phase 2.

Table 4.13 shows the result of applying the simplex method to this phase 1 problem. [Row 0 in the initial tableau is obtained by converting Minimize $Z = \bar{x}_4 + \bar{x}_6$ to Maximize $(-Z) = -\bar{x}_4 - \bar{x}_6$ and then using *elementary row operations* to eliminate the basic variables $\bar{x}_4$ and $\bar{x}_6$ from $-Z + \bar{x}_4 + \bar{x}_6 = 0$.] In the next-to-last tableau, there is a tie for the *entering basic variable* between x_3 and x_5, which is broken arbitrarily in favor of x_3. The solution obtained at the end of phase 1, then, is $(x_1, x_2, x_3, \bar{x}_4, x_5, \bar{x}_6) = (6, 6, 0.3, 0, 0, 0)$ or, after $\bar{x}_4$ and $\bar{x}_6$ are dropped, $(x_1, x_2, x_3, x_5) = (6, 6, 0.3, 0)$.

As claimed in the summary, this solution from phase 1 is indeed a BF solution for the *real* problem (the phase 2 problem) because it is the solution (after you set $x_5 = 0$) to the system of equations consisting of the three functional constraints for the phase 2 problem. In fact, after deleting the $\bar{x}_4$ and $\bar{x}_6$ columns as well as row 0 for each iteration, Table

TABLE 4.13 Phase 1 of the two-phase method for the radiation therapy example

Iteration	Basic Variable	Eq.	Z	x_1	x_2	x_3	$\bar{x}_4$	x_5	$\bar{x}_6$	Right Side
0	Z	(0)	−1	−1.1	−0.9	0	0	1	0	−12
	x_3	(1)	0	0.3	0.1	1	0	0	0	2.7
	$\bar{x}_4$	(2)	0	0.5	0.5	0	1	0	0	6
	$\bar{x}_6$	(3)	0	0.6	0.4	0	0	−1	1	6
1	Z	(0)	−1	0	$-\frac{16}{30}$	$\frac{11}{3}$	0	1	0	−2.1
	x_1	(1)	0	1	$\frac{1}{3}$	$\frac{10}{3}$	0	0	0	9
	$\bar{x}_4$	(2)	0	0	$\frac{1}{3}$	$-\frac{5}{3}$	1	0	0	1.5
	$\bar{x}_6$	(3)	0	0	0.2	−2	0	−1	1	0.6
2	Z	(0)	−1	0	0	$-\frac{5}{3}$	0	$-\frac{5}{3}$	$\frac{8}{3}$	−0.5
	x_1	(1)	0	1	0	$\frac{20}{3}$	0	$\frac{5}{3}$	$-\frac{5}{3}$	8
	$\bar{x}_4$	(2)	0	0	0	$\frac{5}{3}$	1	$\frac{5}{3}$	$-\frac{5}{3}$	0.5
	x_2	(3)	0	0	1	−10	0	−5	5	3
3	Z	(0)	−1	0	0	0	1	0	1	0
	x_1	(1)	0	1	0	0	−4	−5	5	6
	x_3	(2)	0	0	0	1	$\frac{3}{5}$	1	−1	0.3
	x_2	(3)	0	0	1	0	6	5	−5	6

4.13 shows one way of using Gaussian elimination to solve this system of equations by reducing the system to the form displayed in the final tableau.

Table 4.14 shows the preparations for beginning phase 2 after phase 1 is completed. Starting from the final tableau in Table 4.13, we drop the artificial variables ($\bar{x}_4$ and $\bar{x}_6$), substitute the phase 2 objective function ($-Z = -0.4x_1 - 0.5x_2$ in maximization form) into row 0, and then restore the proper form from Gaussian elimination (by algebraically eliminating the basic variables x_1 and x_2 from row 0). Thus, row 0 in the last tableau is obtained by performing the following *elementary row operations* in the next-to-last tableau: from row 0 subtract both the product, 0.4 times row 1, and the product, 0.5 times row 3. Except for the deletion of the two columns, note that rows 1 to 3 never change. The only adjustments occur in row 0 in order to replace the phase 1 objective function by the phase 2 objective function.

The last tableau in Table 4.14 is the initial tableau for applying the simplex method to the phase 2 problem, as shown at the top of Table 4.15. Just one iteration then leads to the optimal solution shown in the second tableau: $(x_1, x_2, x_3, x_5) = (7.5, 4.5, 0, 0.3)$. This solution is the desired optimal solution for the real problem of interest rather than the artificial problem constructed for phase 1.

Now we see what the two-phase method has done graphically in Fig. 4.7. Starting at the origin, phase 1 examines a total of four CPF solutions for the artificial problem. The first three actually were corner-point infeasible solutions for the real problem shown in Fig. 4.5. The fourth CPF solution, at $(6, 6)$, is the first one that also is feasible for the real

TABLE 4.14 Preparing to begin phase 2 for the radiation therapy example

	Basic Variable	Eq.	Z	\(x_1\)	\(x_2\)	\(x_3\)	\(\bar{x}_4\)	\(x_5\)	\(\bar{x}_6\)	Right Side
						Coefficient of:				
Final Phase 1 tableau	Z	(0)	-1	0	0	0	1	0	1	0
	x_1	(1)	0	1	0	0	-4	-5	5	6
	x_3	(2)	0	0	0	1	$\frac{3}{5}$	1	-1	0.3
	x_2	(3)	0	0	1	0	6	5	-5	6
Drop $\bar{x}_4$ and $\bar{x}_6$	Z	(0)	-1	0	0	0		0		0
	x_1	(1)	0	1	0	0		-5		6
	x_3	(2)	0	0	0	1		1		0.3
	x_2	(3)	0	0	1	0		5		6
Substitute phase 2 objective function	Z	(0)	-1	0.4	0.5	0		0		0
	x_1	(1)	0	1	0	0		-5		6
	x_3	(2)	0	0	0	1		1		0.3
	x_2	(3)	0	0	1	0		5		6
Restore proper form from Gaussian elimination	Z	(0)	-1	0	0	0		-0.5		-5.4
	x_1	(1)	0	1	0	0		-5		6
	x_3	(2)	0	0	0	1		1		0.3
	x_2	(3)	0	0	1	0		5		6

TABLE 4.15 Phase 2 of the two-phase method for the radiation therapy example

Iteration	Basic Variable	Eq.	Coefficient of:					Right Side
			Z	x_1	x_2	x_3	x_5	
0	Z	(0)	−1	0	0	0	−0.5	−5.4
	x_1	(1)	0	1	0	0	−5	6
	x_3	(2)	0	0	0	1	1	0.3
	x_2	(3)	0	0	1	0	5	6
1	Z	(0)	−1	0	0	0.5	0	−5.25
	x_1	(1)	0	1	0	5	0	7.5
	x_5	(2)	0	0	0	1	1	0.3
	x_2	(3)	0	0	1	−5	0	4.5

FIGURE 4.7
This graph shows the sequence of CPF solutions for phase 1 (⓪, ①, ②, ③) and then for phase 2 (⓪, ①) when the two-phase method is applied to the radiation therapy example.

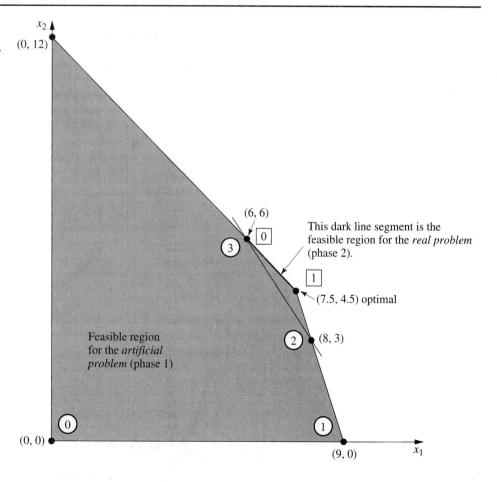

problem, so it becomes the initial CPF solution for phase 2. One iteration in phase 2 leads to the optimal CPF solution at (7.5, 4.5).

If the tie for the entering basic variable in the next-to-last tableau of Table 4.13 had been broken in the other way, then phase 1 would have gone directly from (8, 3) to (7.5, 4.5). After (7.5, 4.5) was used to set up the initial simplex tableau for phase 2, the *optimality test* would have revealed that this solution was optimal, so no iterations would be done.

It is interesting to compare the Big M and two-phase methods. Begin with their objective functions.

Big M Method:

Minimize $Z = 0.4x_1 + 0.5x_2 + M\bar{x}_4 + M\bar{x}_6.$

Two-Phase Method:

Phase 1:   Minimize $Z = \bar{x}_4 + \bar{x}_6.$
Phase 2:   Minimize $Z = 0.4x_1 + 0.5x_2.$

Because the $M\bar{x}_4$ and $M\bar{x}_6$ terms dominate the $0.4x_1$ and $0.5x_2$ terms in the objective function for the Big M method, this objective function is essentially equivalent to the phase 1 objective function as long as $\bar{x}_4$ and/or $\bar{x}_6$ is greater than zero. Then, when both $\bar{x}_4 = 0$ and $\bar{x}_6 = 0$, the objective function for the Big M method becomes completely equivalent to the phase 2 objective function.

Because of these virtual equivalencies in objective functions, the Big M and two-phase methods generally have the same sequence of BF solutions. The one possible exception occurs when there is a tie for the entering basic variable in phase 1 of the two-phase method, as happened in the third tableau of Table 4.13. Notice that the first three tableaux of Tables 4.12 and 4.13 are almost identical, with the only difference being that the multiplicative factors of M in Table 4.12 become the sole quantities in the corresponding spots in Table 4.13. Consequently, the additive terms that broke the tie for the entering basic variable in the third tableau of Table 4.12 were not present to break this same tie in Table 4.13. The result for this example was an extra iteration for the two-phase method. Generally, however, the advantage of having the additive factors is minimal.

The two-phase method streamlines the Big M method by using only the multiplicative factors in phase 1 and by dropping the artificial variables in phase 2. (The Big M method could combine the multiplicative and additive factors by assigning an actual huge number to M, but this might create numerical instability problems.) For these reasons, the two-phase method is commonly used in computer codes.

No Feasible Solutions

So far in this section we have been concerned primarily with the fundamental problem of identifying an initial BF solution when an obvious one is not available. You have seen how the artificial-variable technique can be used to construct an artificial problem and obtain an initial BF solution for this artificial problem instead. Use of either the Big M method or the two-phase method then enables the simplex method to begin its pilgrimage toward the BF solutions, and ultimately toward the optimal solution, for the *real* problem.

However, you should be wary of a certain pitfall with this approach. There may be no obvious choice for the initial BF solution for the very good reason that there are no feasible solutions at all! Nevertheless, by constructing an artificial feasible solution, there is nothing to prevent the simplex method from proceeding as usual and ultimately reporting a supposedly optimal solution.

Fortunately, the artificial-variable technique provides the following signpost to indicate when this has happened:

> If the original problem has *no feasible solutions,* then either the Big M method or phase 1 of the two-phase method yields a final solution that has at least one artificial variable *greater* than zero. Otherwise, they *all* equal zero.

To illustrate, let us change the first constraint in the radiation therapy example (see Fig. 4.5) as follows:

$$0.3x_1 + 0.1x_2 \le 2.7 \quad \rightarrow \quad 0.3x_1 + 0.1x_2 \le 1.8,$$

so that the problem no longer has any feasible solutions. Applying the Big M method just as before (see Table 4.12) yields the tableaux shown in Table 4.16. (Phase 1 of the two-phase method yields the same tableaux except that each expression involving M is replaced by just the multiplicative factor.) Hence, the Big M method normally would be indicating that the optimal solution is $(3, 9, 0, 0, 0, 0.6)$. However, since an artificial variable $\bar{x}_6 = 0.6 > 0$, the real message here is that the problem has no feasible solutions.

TABLE 4.16 The Big M method for the revision of the radiation therapy example that has no feasible solutions

Iteration	Basic Variable	Eq.	Z	x_1	x_2	x_3	$\bar{x}_4$	x_5	$\bar{x}_6$	Right Side
0	Z	(0)	-1	$-1.1M + 0.4$	$-0.9M + 0.5$	0	0	M	0	$-12M$
	x_3	(1)	0	0.3	0.1	1	0	0	0	1.8
	$\bar{x}_4$	(2)	0	0.5	0.5	0	1	0	0	6
	$\bar{x}_6$	(3)	0	0.6	0.4	0	0	-1	1	6
1	Z	(0)	-1	0	$-\frac{16}{30}M + \frac{11}{30}$	$\frac{11}{3}M - \frac{4}{3}$	0	M	0	$-5.4M - 2.4$
	x_1	(1)	0	1	$\frac{1}{3}$	$\frac{10}{3}$	0	0	0	6
	$\bar{x}_4$	(2)	0	0	$\frac{1}{3}$	$-\frac{5}{3}$	1	0	0	3
	$\bar{x}_6$	(3)	0	0	0.2	-2	0	-1	1	2.4
2	Z	(0)	-1	0	0	$M + 0.5$	$1.6M - 1.1$	M	0	$-0.6M - 5.7$
	x_1	(1)	0	1	0	5	-1	0	0	3
	x_2	(2)	0	0	1	-5	3	0	0	9
	$\bar{x}_6$	(3)	0	0	0	-1	-0.6	-1	1	0.6

Variables Allowed to Be Negative

In most practical problems, negative values for the decision variables would have no physical meaning, so it is necessary to include nonnegativity constraints in the formulations of their linear programming models. However, this is not always the case. To illustrate, suppose that the Wyndor Glass Co. problem is changed so that product 1 already is in production, and the first decision variable x_1 represents the *increase* in its production rate. Therefore, a negative value of x_1 would indicate that product 1 is to be cut back by that amount. Such reductions might be desirable to allow a larger production rate for the new, more profitable product 2, so negative values should be allowed for x_1 in the model.

Since the procedure for determining the *leaving basic variable* requires that all the variables have nonnegativity constraints, any problem containing variables allowed to be negative must be converted to an *equivalent* problem involving only nonnegative variables before the simplex method is applied. Fortunately, this conversion can be done. The modification required for each variable depends upon whether it has a (negative) lower bound on the values allowed. Each of these two cases is now discussed.

Variables with a Bound on the Negative Values Allowed.   Consider any decision variable x_j that is allowed to have negative values which satisfy a constraint of the form

$$x_j \geq L_j,$$

where L_j is some negative constant. This constraint can be converted to a nonnegativity constraint by making the change of variables

$$x_j' = x_j - L_j, \qquad \text{so} \qquad x_j' \geq 0.$$

Thus, $x_j' + L_j$ would be substituted for x_j throughout the model, so that the redefined decision variable x_j' cannot be negative. (This same technique can be used when L_j is *positive* to convert a functional constraint $x_j \geq L_j$ to a nonnegativity constraint $x_j' \geq 0$.)

To illustrate, suppose that the current production rate for product 1 in the Wyndor Glass Co. problem is 10. With the definition of x_1 just given, the complete model at this point is the same as that given in Sec. 3.1 except that the nonnegativity constraint $x_1 \geq 0$ is replaced by

$$x_1 \geq -10.$$

To obtain the equivalent model needed for the simplex method, this decision variable would be redefined as the *total* production rate of product 1

$$x_j' = x_1 + 10,$$

which yields the changes in the objective function and constraints as shown:

$Z = 3x_1 + 5x_2$	$Z = 3(x_1' - 10) + 5x_2$	$Z = -30 + 3x_1' + 5x_2$
$x_1 \leq 4$	$x_1' - 10 \leq 4$	$x_1' \leq 14$
$2x_2 \leq 12$	$2x_2 \leq 12$	$2x_2 \leq 12$
$3x_1 + 2x_2 \leq 18$	$3(x_1' - 10) + 2x_2 \leq 18$	$3x_1' + 2x_2 \leq 48$
$x_1 \geq -10, \quad x_2 \geq 0$	$x_1' - 10 \geq -10, \quad x_2 \geq 0$	$x_1' \geq 0, \quad x_2 \geq 0$

Variables with No Bound on the Negative Values Allowed. In the case where x_j does *not* have a lower-bound constraint in the model formulated, another approach is required: x_j is replaced throughout the model by the *difference* of two new *nonnegative* variables

$$x_j = x_j^+ - x_j^-, \qquad \text{where } x_j^+ \geq 0, \ x_j^- \geq 0.$$

Since x_j^+ and x_j^- can have any nonnegative values, this difference $x_j^+ - x_j^-$ can have *any* value (positive or negative), so it is a legitimate substitute for x_j in the model. But after such substitutions, the simplex method can proceed with just nonnegative variables.

The new variables x_j^+ and x_j^- have a simple interpretation. As explained in the next paragraph, each BF solution for the new form of the model necessarily has the property that *either* $x_j^+ = 0$ or $x_j^- = 0$ (or both). Therefore, at the optimal solution obtained by the simplex method (a BF solution),

$$x_j^+ = \begin{cases} x_j & \text{if } x_j \geq 0, \\ 0 & \text{otherwise;} \end{cases}$$

$$x_j^- = \begin{cases} |x_j| & \text{if } x_j \leq 0, \\ 0 & \text{otherwise;} \end{cases}$$

so that x_j^+ represents the positive part of the decision variable x_j and x_j^- its negative part (as suggested by the superscripts).

For example, if $x_j = 10$, the above expressions give $x_j^+ = 10$ and $x_j^- = 0$. This same value of $x_j = x_j^+ - x_j^- = 10$ also would occur with larger values of x_j^+ and x_j^- such that $x_j^+ = x_j^- + 10$. Plotting these values of x_j^+ and x_j^- on a two-dimensional graph gives a line with an endpoint at $x_j^+ = 10$, $x_j^- = 0$ to avoid violating the nonnegativity constraints. This endpoint is the only corner-point solution on the line. Therefore, only this endpoint can be part of an overall CPF solution or BF solution involving all the variables of the model. This illustrates why each BF solution necessarily has either $x_j^+ = 0$ or $x_j^- = 0$ (or both).

To illustrate the use of the x_j^+ and x_j^-, let us return to the example on the preceding page where x_1 is redefined as the increase over the current production rate of 10 for product 1 in the Wyndor Glass Co. problem.

However, now suppose that the $x_1 \geq -10$ constraint was not included in the original model because it clearly would not change the optimal solution. (In some problems, certain variables do not need explicit lower-bound constraints because the functional constraints already prevent lower values.) Therefore, before the simplex method is applied, x_1 would be replaced by the difference

$$x_1 = x_1^+ - x_1^-, \qquad \text{where } x_1^+ \geq 0, \ x_1^- \geq 0,$$

as shown:

$$
\begin{array}{ll}
\text{Maximize} & Z = 3x_1 + 5x_2, \\
\text{subject to} & x_1 \qquad\qquad \leq 4 \\
& \qquad\quad 2x_2 \leq 12 \\
& 3x_1 + 2x_2 \leq 18 \\
& \qquad\quad x_2 \geq 0 \text{ (only)}
\end{array}
\qquad \rightarrow \qquad
\begin{array}{ll}
\text{Maximize} & Z = 3x_1^+ - 3x_1^- + 5x_2, \\
\text{subject to} & x_1^+ - x_1^- \qquad\qquad \leq 4 \\
& \qquad\qquad\quad 2x_2 \leq 12 \\
& 3x_1^+ - 3x_1^- + 2x_2 \leq 18 \\
& x_1^+ \geq 0, \quad x_1^- \geq 0, \quad x_2 \geq 0
\end{array}
$$

From a computational viewpoint, this approach has the disadvantage that the new equivalent model to be used has more variables than the original model. In fact, if *all* the original variables lack lower-bound constraints, the new model will have *twice* as many variables. Fortunately, the approach can be modified slightly so that the number of variables is increased by only one, regardless of how many original variables need to be replaced. This modification is done by replacing each such variable x_j by

$$x_j = x_j' - x'', \qquad \text{where } x_j' \geq 0, \, x'' \geq 0,$$

instead, where x'' is the *same* variable for all relevant j. The interpretation of x'' in this case is that $-x''$ is the current value of the *largest* (in absolute terms) negative original variable, so that x_j' is the amount by which x_j exceeds this value. Thus, the simplex method now can make some of the x_j' variables larger than zero even when $x'' > 0$.

4.7 POSTOPTIMALITY ANALYSIS

We stressed in Secs. 2.3, 2.4, and 2.5 that *postoptimality analysis*—the analysis done *after* an optimal solution is obtained for the initial version of the model—constitutes a very major and very important part of most operations research studies. The fact that postoptimality analysis is very important is particularly true for typical linear programming applications. In this section, we focus on the role of the simplex method in performing this analysis.

Table 4.17 summarizes the typical steps in postoptimality analysis for linear programming studies. The rightmost column identifies some algorithmic techniques that involve the simplex method. These techniques are introduced briefly here with the technical details deferred to later chapters.

Reoptimization

As discussed in Sec. 3.7, linear programming models that arise in practice commonly are very large, with hundreds or thousands of functional constraints and decision variables. In such cases, many variations of the basic model may be of interest for considering different scenarios. Therefore, after having found an optimal solution for one version of a linear programming model, we frequently must solve again (often many times) for the so-

TABLE 4.17 Postoptimality analysis for linear programming

Task	Purpose	Technique
Model debugging	Find errors and weaknesses in model	Reoptimization
Model validation	Demonstrate validity of final model	See Sec. 2.4
Final managerial decisions on resource allocations (the b_i values)	Make appropriate division of organizational resources between activities under study and other important activities	Shadow prices
Evaluate estimates of model parameters	Determine crucial estimates that may affect optimal solution for further study	Sensitivity analysis
Evaluate trade-offs between model parameters	Determine best trade-off	Parametric linear programming

lution of a slightly different version of the model. We nearly always have to solve again several times during the model debugging stage (described in Secs. 2.3 and 2.4), and we usually have to do so a large number of times during the later stages of postoptimality analysis as well.

One approach is simply to reapply the simplex method from scratch for each new version of the model, even though each run may require hundreds or even thousands of iterations for large problems. However, a *much more efficient* approach is to *reoptimize*. Reoptimization involves deducing how changes in the model get carried along to the *final* simplex tableau (as described in Secs. 5.3 and 6.6). This revised tableau and the optimal solution for the prior model are then used as the *initial tableau* and the *initial basic solution* for solving the new model. If this solution is feasible for the new model, then the simplex method is applied in the usual way, starting from this initial BF solution. If the solution is not feasible, a related algorithm called the *dual simplex method* (described in Sec. 7.1) probably can be applied to find the new optimal solution,[1] starting from this initial basic solution.

The big advantage of this **reoptimization technique** over re-solving from scratch is that an optimal solution for the revised model probably is going to be *much* closer to the prior optimal solution than to an initial BF solution constructed in the usual way for the simplex method. Therefore, assuming that the model revisions were modest, only a few iterations should be required to reoptimize instead of the hundreds or thousands that may be required when you start from scratch. In fact, the optimal solutions for the prior and revised models are frequently the same, in which case the reoptimization technique requires only one application of the optimality test and *no* iterations.

Shadow Prices

Recall that linear programming problems often can be interpreted as allocating resources to activities. In particular, when the functional constraints are in $\leq$ form, we interpreted the b_i (the right-hand sides) as the amounts of the respective resources being made available for the activities under consideration. In many cases, there may be some latitude in the amounts that will be made available. If so, the b_i values used in the initial (validated) model actually may represent management's *tentative initial decision* on how much of the organization's resources will be provided to the activities considered in the model instead of to other important activities under the purview of management. From this broader perspective, some of the b_i values can be increased in a revised model, but only if a sufficiently strong case can be made to management that this revision would be beneficial.

Consequently, information on the economic contribution of the resources to the measure of performance (Z) for the current study often would be extremely useful. The simplex method provides this information in the form of *shadow prices* for the respective resources.

The **shadow price** for resource i (denoted by y_i^*) measures the *marginal value* of this resource, i.e., the rate at which Z could be increased by (slightly) increasing the amount of

---

[1]The one requirement for using the dual simplex method here is that the *optimality test* is still passed when applied to row 0 of the *revised* final tableau. If not, then still another algorithm called the *primal-dual method* can be used instead.

this resource (b_i) being made available.[1,2] The simplex method identifies this shadow price by $y_i^* =$ coefficient of the ith slack variable in row 0 of the final simplex tableau.

To illustrate, for the Wyndor Glass Co. problem,

Resource $i =$ production capacity of Plant i ($i = 1, 2, 3$) being made available to the two new products under consideration,

$b_i =$ hours of production time per week being made available in Plant i for these new products.

Providing a substantial amount of production time for the new products would require adjusting production times for the current products, so choosing the b_i value is a difficult managerial decision. The tentative initial decision has been

$$b_1 = 4, \qquad b_2 = 12, \qquad b_3 = 18,$$

as reflected in the basic model considered in Sec. 3.1 and in this chapter. However, management now wishes to evaluate the effect of changing any of the b_i values.

The shadow prices for these three resources provide just the information that management needs. The final tableau in Table 4.8 (see p. 128) yields

$$y_1^* = 0 = \text{shadow price for resource 1,}$$

$$y_2^* = \frac{3}{2} = \text{shadow price for resource 2,}$$

$$y_3^* = 1 = \text{shadow price for resource 3.}$$

With just two decision variables, these numbers can be verified by checking graphically that individually increasing any b_i by 1 indeed would increase the optimal value of Z by y_i^*. For example, Fig. 4.8 demonstrates this increase for resource 2 by reapplying the graphical method presented in Sec. 3.1. The optimal solution, (2, 6) with $Z = 36$, changes to $(\frac{5}{3}, \frac{13}{2})$ with $Z = 37\frac{1}{2}$ when b_2 is increased by 1 (from 12 to 13), so that

$$y_2^* = \Delta Z = 37\frac{1}{2} - 36 = \frac{3}{2}.$$

Since Z is expressed in thousands of dollars of profit per week, $y_2^* = \frac{3}{2}$ indicates that adding 1 more hour of production time per week in Plant 2 for these two new products would increase their total profit by $1,500 per week. Should this actually be done? It depends on the marginal profitability of other products currently using this production time. If there is a current product that contributes less than $1,500 of weekly profit per hour of weekly production time in Plant 2, then some shift of production time to the new products would be worthwhile.

We shall continue this story in Sec. 6.7, where the Wyndor OR team uses shadow prices as part of its *sensitivity analysis* of the model.

---

[1]The increase in b_i must be sufficiently small that the current set of basic variables remains optimal since this rate (marginal value) changes if the set of basic variables changes.

[2]In the case of a functional constraint in $\geq$ or $=$ form, its shadow price is again defined as the rate at which Z could be increased by (slightly) increasing the value of b_i, although the interpretation of b_i now would normally be something other than the amount of a resource being made available.

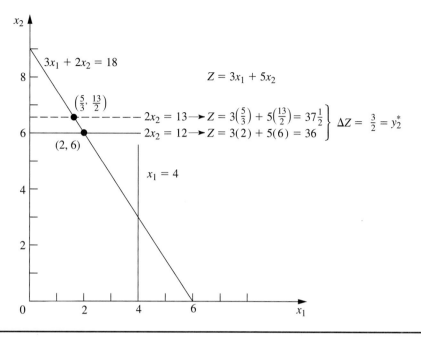

FIGURE 4.8
This graph shows that the shadow price is $y_2^* = \frac{3}{2}$ for resource 2 for the Wyndor Glass Co. problem. The two dots are the optimal solutions for $b_2 = 12$ or $b_2 = 13$, and plugging these solutions into the objective function reveals that increasing b_2 by 1 increases Z by $y_2^* = \frac{3}{2}$.

Figure 4.8 demonstrates that $y_2^* = \frac{3}{2}$ is the rate at which Z could be increased by increasing b_2 slightly. However, it also demonstrates the common phenomenon that this interpretation holds only for a small increase in b_2. Once b_2 is increased beyond 18, the optimal solution stays at $(0, 9)$ with no further increase in Z. (At that point, the set of basic variables in the optimal solution has changed, so a new final simplex tableau will be obtained with new shadow prices, including $y_2^* = 0$.)

Now note in Fig. 4.8 why $y_1^* = 0$. Because the constraint on resource 1, $x_1 \leq 4$, is *not binding* on the optimal solution $(2, 6)$, there is a *surplus* of this resource. Therefore, increasing b_1 beyond 4 cannot yield a new optimal solution with a larger value of Z.

By contrast, the constraints on resources 2 and 3, $2x_2 \leq 12$ and $3x_1 + 2x_2 \leq 18$, are **binding constraints** (constraints that hold with equality at the optimal solution). Because the limited supply of these resources ($b_2 = 12$, $b_3 = 18$) *binds* Z from being increased further, they have *positive* shadow prices. Economists refer to such resources as *scarce goods*, whereas resources available in surplus (such as resource 1) are *free goods* (resources with a zero shadow price).

The kind of information provided by shadow prices clearly is valuable to management when it considers reallocations of resources within the organization. It also is very helpful when an increase in b_i can be achieved only by going outside the organization to purchase more of the resource in the marketplace. For example, suppose that Z represents *profit* and that the unit profits of the activities (the c_j values) include the costs (at regular prices) of all the resources consumed. Then a *positive* shadow price of y_i^* for resource i means that the total profit Z can be increased by y_i^* by purchasing 1 more unit of this resource at its regular price. Alternatively, if a *premium* price must be paid for the resource in the marketplace, then y_i^* represents the *maximum* premium (excess over the regular price) that would be worth paying.[1]

The theoretical foundation for shadow prices is provided by the duality theory described in Chap. 6.

Sensitivity Analysis

When discussing the *certainty assumption* for linear programming at the end of Sec. 3.3, we pointed out that the values used for the model parameters (the a_{ij}, b_i, and c_j identified in Table 3.3) generally are just *estimates* of quantities whose true values will not become known until the linear programming study is implemented at some time in the future. A main purpose of sensitivity analysis is to identify the **sensitive parameters** (i.e., those that cannot be changed without changing the optimal solution). The sensitive parameters are the parameters that need to be estimated with special care to minimize the risk of obtaining an erroneous optimal solution. They also will need to be monitored particularly closely as the study is implemented. If it is discovered that the true value of a sensitive parameter differs from its estimated value in the model, this immediately signals a need to change the solution.

How are the sensitive parameters identified? In the case of the b_i, you have just seen that this information is given by the shadow prices provided by the simplex method. In particular, if $y_i^* > 0$, then the optimal solution changes if b_i is changed, so b_i is a sensitive parameter. However, $y_i^* = 0$ implies that the optimal solution is not sensitive to at least small changes in b_i. Consequently, if the value used for b_i is an estimate of the amount of the resource that will be available (rather than a managerial decision), then the b_i values that need to be monitored more closely are those with *positive* shadow prices—especially those with *large* shadow prices.

When there are just two variables, the sensitivity of the various parameters can be analyzed graphically. For example, in Fig. 4.9, $c_1 = 3$ can be changed to any other value from 0 to 7.5 without the optimal solution changing from (2, 6). (The reason is that any value of c_1 within this range keeps the slope of $Z = c_1 x_1 + 5x_2$ between the slopes of the lines $2x_2 = 12$ and $3x_1 + 2x_2 = 18$.) Similarly, if $c_2 = 5$ is the only parameter changed, it can have any value greater than 2 without affecting the optimal solution. Hence, neither c_1 nor c_2 is a sensitive parameter.

The easiest way to analyze the sensitivity of each of the a_{ij} parameters graphically is to check whether the corresponding constraint is *binding* at the optimal solution. Because $x_1 \leq 4$ is *not* a binding constraint, any sufficiently small change in its coefficients ($a_{11} = 1$, $a_{12} = 0$) is not going to change the optimal solution, so these are *not* sensitive parameters. On the other hand, both $2x_2 \leq 12$ and $3x_1 + 2x_2 \leq 18$ are *binding constraints,* so changing *any* one of their coefficients ($a_{21} = 0$, $a_{22} = 2$, $a_{31} = 3$, $a_{32} = 2$) is going to change the optimal solution, and therefore these are sensitive parameters.

Typically, greater attention is given to performing sensitivity analysis on the b_i and c_j parameters than on the a_{ij} parameters. On real problems with hundreds or thousands of constraints and variables, the effect of changing one a_{ij} value is usually negligible, but

---

[1]If the unit profits do *not* include the costs of the resources consumed, then y_i^* represents the maximum *total* unit price that would be worth paying to increase b_i.

FIGURE 4.9
This graph demonstrates the sensitivity analysis of c_1 and c_2 for the Wyndor Glass Co. problem. Starting with the original objective function line [where $c_1 = 3$, $c_2 = 5$, and the optimal solution is (2, 6)], the other two lines show the extremes of how much the slope of the objective function line can change and still retain (2, 6) as an optimal solution. Thus, with $c_2 = 5$, the allowable range for c_1 is $0 \leq c_1 \leq 7.5$. With $c_1 = 3$, the allowable range for c_2 is $c_2 \geq 2$.

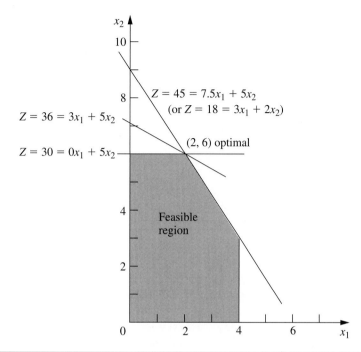

changing one b_i or c_j value can have real impact. Furthermore, in many cases, the a_{ij} values are determined by the technology being used (the a_{ij} values are sometimes called *technological coefficients*), so there may be relatively little (or no) uncertainty about their final values. This is fortunate, because there are far more a_{ij} parameters than b_i and c_j parameters for large problems.

For problems with more than two (or possibly three) decision variables, you cannot analyze the sensitivity of the parameters graphically as was just done for the Wyndor Glass Co. problem. However, you can extract the same kind of information from the simplex method. Getting this information requires using the *fundamental insight* described in Sec. 5.3 to deduce the changes that get carried along to the final simplex tableau as a result of changing the value of a parameter in the original model. The rest of the procedure is described and illustrated in Secs. 6.6 and 6.7.

Using Excel to Generate Sensitivity Analysis Information

Sensitivity analysis normally is incorporated into software packages based on the simplex method. For example, the Excel Solver will generate sensitivity analysis information upon request. As was shown in Fig. 3.19 (see page 72), when the Solver gives the message that it has found a solution, it also gives on the right a list of three reports that can be provided. By selecting the second one (labeled "Sensitivity") after solving the Wyndor Glass Co. problem, you will obtain the *sensitivity report* shown in Fig. 4.10. The upper table in this report provides sensitivity analysis information about the decision variables and their coefficients in the objective function. The lower table does the same for the functional constraints and their right-hand sides.

Adjustable Cells

Cell	Name	Final Value	Reduced Cost	Objective Coefficient	Allowable Increase	Allowable Decrease
$C$9	Solution Doors	2	0	3	4.5	3
$D$9	Solution Windows	6	0	5	1E+30	3

Constraints

Cell	Name	Final Value	Shadow Price	Constraint R.H. Side	Allowable Increase	Allowable Decrease
$E$5	Plant 1 Totals	2	0	4	1E+30	2
$E$6	Plant 2 Totals	12	1.5	12	6	6
$E$7	Plant 3 Totals	18	1	18	6	6

FIGURE 4.10
The sensitivity report provided by the Excel Solver for the Wyndor Glass Co. problem.

Look first at the upper table in this figure. The "Final Value" column indicates the optimal solution. The next column gives the *reduced costs*. (We will not discuss these reduced costs now because the information they provide can also be gleaned from the rest of the upper table.) The next three columns provide the information needed to identify the *allowable range to stay optimal* for each coefficient c_j in the objective function.

> For any c_j, its **allowable range to stay optimal** is the range of values for this coefficient over which the current optimal solution remains optimal, assuming no change in the other coefficients.

The "Objective Coefficient" column gives the current value of each coefficient, and then the next two columns give the *allowable increase* and the *allowable decrease* from this value to remain within the allowable range. Therefore,

$$3 - 3 \le c_1 \le 3 + 4.5, \quad \text{so} \quad 0 \le c_1 \le 7.5$$

is the allowable range for c_1 over which the current optimal solution will stay optimal (assuming $c_2 = 5$), just as was found graphically in Fig. 4.9. Similarly, since Excel uses $1E + 30$ (10^{30}) to represent infinity,

$$5 - 3 \le c_2 \le 5 + \infty, \quad \text{so} \quad 2 \le c_2$$

is the allowable range to stay optimal for c_2.

The fact that both the allowable increase and the allowable decrease are greater than zero for the coefficient of both decision variables provides another useful piece of information, as described below.

> When the upper table in the sensitivity report generated by the Excel Solver indicates that both the allowable increase and the allowable decrease are greater than zero for every objective coefficient, this is a signpost that the optimal solution in the "Final Value" column is the only optimal solution. Conversely, having any allowable increase or allowable decrease equal to zero is a signpost that there are multiple optimal solutions. Changing the corresponding coefficient a tiny amount beyond the zero allowed and re-solving provides another optimal CPF solution for the original model.

Now consider the lower table in Fig. 4.10 that focuses on sensitivity analysis for the three functional constraints. The "Final Value" column gives the value of each constraint's left-hand side for the optimal solution. The next two columns give the shadow price and the current value of the right-hand side (b_i) for each constraint. When just one b_i value is then changed, the last two columns give the *allowable increase* or *allowable decrease* in order to remain within its *allowable range to stay feasible.*

> For any b_i, its **allowable range to stay feasible** is the range of values for this right-hand side over which the current optimal BF solution (with adjusted values[1] for the basic variables) remains feasible, assuming no change in the other right-hand sides.

Thus, using the lower table in Fig. 4.10, combining the last two columns with the current values of the right-hand sides gives the following allowable ranges to stay feasible:

$$2 \leq b_1$$
$$6 \leq b_2 \leq 18$$
$$12 \leq b_3 \leq 24.$$

This sensitivity report generated by the Excel Solver is typical of the sensitivity analysis information provided by linear programming software packages. You will see in Appendix 4.1 that LINDO provides essentially the same report. MPL/CPLEX does also when it is requested with the Solution File dialogue box. Once again, this information obtained algebraically also can be derived from graphical analysis for this two-variable problem. (See Prob. 4.7-1.) For example, when b_2 is increased from 12 in Fig. 4.8, the originally optimal CPF solution at the intersection of two constraint boundaries $2x_2 = b_2$ and $3x_1 + 2x_2 = 18$ will remain feasible (including $x_1 \geq 0$) only for $b_2 \leq 18$.

The latter part of Chap. 6 will delve into this type of analysis more deeply.

Parametric Linear Programming

Sensitivity analysis involves changing one parameter at a time in the original model to check its effect on the optimal solution. By contrast, **parametric linear programming** (or **parametric programming** for short) involves the systematic study of how the optimal solution changes as *many* of the parameters change *simultaneously* over some range. This study can provide a very useful extension of sensitivity analysis, e.g., to check the effect of "correlated" parameters that change together due to exogenous factors such as the state of the economy. However, a more important application is the investigation of *trade-offs* in parameter values. For example, if the c_j values represent the unit profits of the respective activities, it may be possible to increase some of the c_j values at the expense of decreasing others by an appropriate shifting of personnel and equipment among activities. Similarly, if the b_i values represent the amounts of the respective resources being made available, it may be possible to increase some of the b_i values by agreeing to accept decreases in some of the others. The analysis of such possibilities is discussed and illustrated at the end of Sec. 6.7.

---

[1]Since the values of the basic variables are obtained as the simultaneous solution of a system of equations (the functional constraints in augmented form), at least some of these values change if one of the right-hand sides changes. However, the adjusted values of the current set of basic variables still will satisfy the nonnegativity constraints, and so still will be feasible, as long as the new value of this right-hand side remains within its allowable range to stay feasible. If the adjusted basic solution is still feasible, it also will still be optimal. We shall elaborate further in Sec. 6.7.

In some applications, the main purpose of the study is to determine the most appropriate trade-off between two basic factors, such as *costs* and *benefits*. The usual approach is to express one of these factors in the objective function (e.g., minimize total cost) and incorporate the other into the constraints (e.g., benefits ≥ minimum acceptable level), as was done for the Nori & Leets Co. air pollution problem in Sec. 3.4. Parametric linear programming then enables systematic investigation of what happens when the initial tentative decision on the trade-off (e.g., the minimum acceptable level for the benefits) is changed by improving one factor at the expense of the other.

The algorithmic technique for parametric linear programming is a natural extension of that for sensitivity analysis, so it, too, is based on the simplex method. The procedure is described in Sec. 7.2.

4.8 COMPUTER IMPLEMENTATION

If the electronic computer had never been invented, undoubtedly you would have never heard of linear programming and the simplex method. Even though it is possible to apply the simplex method by hand to solve tiny linear programming problems, the calculations involved are just too tedious to do this on a routine basis. However, the simplex method is ideally suited for execution on a computer. It is the computer revolution that has made possible the widespread application of linear programming in recent decades.

Implementation of the Simplex Method

Computer codes for the simplex method now are widely available for essentially all modern computer systems. These codes commonly are part of a sophisticated software package for mathematical programming that includes many of the procedures described in subsequent chapters (including those used for postoptimality analysis).

These production computer codes do not closely follow either the algebraic form or the tabular form of the simplex method presented in Secs. 4.3 and 4.4. These forms can be streamlined considerably for computer implementation. Therefore, the codes use instead a *matrix form* (usually called the *revised simplex method*) that is especially well suited for the computer. This form accomplishes exactly the same things as the algebraic or tabular form, but it does this while computing and storing only the numbers that are actually needed for the current iteration; and then it carries along the essential data in a more compact form. The revised simplex method is described in Sec. 5.2.

The simplex method is used routinely to solve surprisingly large linear programming problems. For example, powerful desktop computers (especially workstations) commonly are used to solve problems with *many thousand* functional constraints and a larger number of decision variables. We now are beginning to hear reports of successfully solved problems ranging into the hundreds of thousands of functional constraints and millions of decision variables.[1] For certain *special types* of linear programming problems (such as the

---

[1] Do not try this at home. Attacking such a massive problem requires an especially sophisticated linear programming system that uses the latest techniques for exploiting sparcity in the coefficient matrix as well as other special techniques (e.g., *crashing techniques* for quickly finding an advanced initial BF solution). When problems are re-solved periodically after minor updating of the data, much time often is saved by using (or modifying) the last optimal solution to provide the initial BF solution for the new run.

transportation, assignment, and minimum cost flow problems to be described later in the book), even larger problems now can be solved by *specialized* versions of the simplex method.

Several factors affect how long it will take to solve a linear programming problem by the general simplex method. The most important one is the *number of ordinary functional constraints*. In fact, computation time tends to be roughly proportional to the cube of this number, so that doubling this number may multiply the computation time by a factor of approximately 8. By contrast, the number of variables is a relatively minor factor.[1] Thus, doubling the number of variables probably will not even double the computation time. A third factor of some importance is the *density* of the table of constraint coefficients (i.e., the *proportion* of the coefficients that are *not* zero), because this affects the computation time *per iteration*. (For large problems encountered in practice, it is common for the density to be under 5 percent, or even under 1 percent, and this much "sparcity" tends to greatly accelerate the simplex method.) One common rule of thumb for the *number of iterations* is that it tends to be roughly twice the number of functional constraints.

With large linear programming problems, it is inevitable that some mistakes and faulty decisions will be made initially in formulating the model and inputting it into the computer. Therefore, as discussed in Sec. 2.4, a thorough process of testing and refining the model (*model validation*) is needed. The usual end product is not a single static model that is solved once by the simplex method. Instead, the OR team and management typically consider a long series of variations on a basic model (sometimes even thousands of variations) to examine different scenarios as part of postoptimality analysis. This entire process is greatly accelerated when it can be carried out *interactively* on a *desktop computer*. And, with the help of both mathematical programming modeling languages and improving computer technology, this now is becoming common practice.

Until the mid-1980s, linear programming problems were solved almost exclusively on *mainframe computers*. Since then, there has been an explosion in the capability of doing linear programming on desktop computers, including personal computers as well as workstations. Workstations, including some with parallel processing capabilities, now are commonly used instead of mainframe computers to solve massive linear programming models. The fastest personal computers are not lagging far behind, although solving huge models usually requires additional memory.

Linear Programming Software Featured in This Book

A considerable number of excellent software packages for linear programming and its extensions now are available to fill a variety of needs. One that is widely regarded to be a particularly powerful package for solving massive problems is **CPLEX,** a product of ILOG, Inc., located in Silicon Valley. For more than a decade, CPLEX has helped to lead the way in solving larger and larger linear programming problems. An extensive research and development effort has enabled a series of upgrades with dramatic increases in efficiency. CPLEX 6.5 released in March 1999 provided another order-of-magnitude improvement. This software package has successfully solved real linear programming problems arising in industry with as many as 2 million functional constraints and a comparable number of

---

[1]This statement assumes that the revised simplex method described in Sec. 5.2 is being used.

decision variables! CPLEX 6.5 often uses the simplex method and its variants (such as the dual simplex method presented in Sec. 7.1) to solve these massive problems. In addition to the simplex method, CPLEX 6.5 also features some other powerful weapons for attacking linear programming problems. One is a lightning-fast algorithm that uses the *interior-point approach* introduced in the next section. This algorithm can solve some huge general linear programming problems that the simplex method cannot (and vice versa). Another feature is the *network simplex method* (described in Sec. 9.7) that can solve even larger special types of linear programming problems. CPLEX 6.5 also extends beyond linear programming by including state-of-the-art algorithms for *integer programming* (Chap. 12) and *quadratic programming* (Sec. 13.7).

Because it often is used to solve really large problems, CPLEX normally is used in conjunction with a mathematical programming *modeling language.* As described in Sec. 3.7, modeling languages are designed for efficiently formulating large linear programming models (and related models) in a compact way, after which a solver is called upon to solve the model. Several of the prominent modeling languages support CPLEX as a solver. ILOG also has recently introduced its own modeling language, called *OPL Studio,* that can be used with CPLEX. (A trial version of OPL Studio is available at ILOG's website, www.ilog.com.)

As we mentioned in Sec. 3.7, the student version of CPLEX is included in your OR Courseware as the solver for the MPL modeling language. This version features the simplex method for solving linear programming problems.

LINDO (short for *Linear, INteractive, and Discrete Optimizer*) is another prominent software package for linear programming and its extensions. A product of LINDO Systems based in Chicago, LINDO has an even longer history than CPLEX. Although not as powerful as CPLEX, the largest version of LINDO has solved problems with tens of thousands of functional constraints and hundreds of thousands of decision variables. Its long-time popularity is partially due to its ease of use. For relatively small (textbook-sized) problems, the model can be entered and solved in an intuitive straightforward manner, so LINDO provides a convenient tool for students to use. However, LINDO lacks some of the capabilities of modeling languages for dealing with large linear programming problems. For such problems, it may be more efficient to use the LINGO modeling language to formulate the model and then to call the solver it shares with LINDO to solve the model.

You can download the student version of LINDO from the website, www.lindo.com. Appendix 4.1 provides an introduction to how to use LINDO. The CD-ROM also includes a LINDO tutorial, as well as LINDO formulations for all the examples in this book to which it can be applied.

Spreadsheet-based solvers are becoming increasingly popular for linear programming and its extensions. Leading the way are the solvers produced by Frontline Systems for Microsoft Excel, Lotus 1-2-3, and Corel Quattro Pro. In addition to the basic solver shipped with these packages, two more powerful upgrades—*Premium Solver* and *Premium Solver Plus*—also are available. Because of the widespread use of spreadsheet packages such as Microsoft Excel today, these solvers are introducing large numbers of people to the potential of linear programming for the first time. For textbook-sized linear programming problems (and considerably larger problems as well), spreadsheets provide a convenient way to formulate and solve the model, as described in Sec. 3.6. The more powerful spreadsheet solvers can solve fairly large models with many thousand decision variables. However, when the spreadsheet grows to an unwieldy size, a good modeling language and its solver may provide a more efficient approach to formulating and solving the model.

Spreadsheets provide an excellent communication tool, especially when dealing with typical managers who are very comfortable with this format but not with the algebraic formulations of OR models. Therefore, optimization software packages and modeling languages now can commonly import and export data and results in a spreadsheet format. For example, the MPL modeling language now includes an enhancement (called the *OptiMax 2000 Component Library*) that enables the modeler to create the feel of a spreadsheet model for the user of the model while still using MPL to formulate the model very efficiently. (The student version of OptiMax 2000 is included in your OR Courseware.)

Premium Solver is one of the Excel add-ins included on the CD-ROM. You can install this add-in to obtain a much better performance than with the standard Excel Solver.

Consequently, all the software, tutorials, and examples packed on the CD-ROM are providing you with several attractive software options for linear programming.

Available Software Options for Linear Programming.

1. Demonstration examples (in OR Tutor) and interactive routines for efficiently learning the simplex method.
2. Excel and its Premium Solver for formulating and solving linear programming models in a spreadsheet format.
3. MPL/CPLEX for efficiently formulating and solving large linear programming models.
4. LINGO and its solver (shared with LINDO) for an alternative way of efficiently formulating and solving large linear programming models.
5. LINDO for formulating and solving linear programming models in a straightforward way.

Your instructor may specify which software to use. Whatever the choice, you will be gaining experience with the kind of state-of-the-art software that is used by OR professionals.

4.9   THE INTERIOR-POINT APPROACH TO SOLVING LINEAR PROGRAMMING PROBLEMS

The most dramatic new development in operations research during the 1980s was the discovery of the interior-point approach to solving linear programming problems. This discovery was made in 1984 by a young mathematician at AT&T Bell Laboratories, Narendra Karmarkar, when he successfully developed a new algorithm for linear programming with this kind of approach. Although this particular algorithm experienced only mixed success in competing with the simplex method, the key solution concept described below appeared to have great potential for solving *huge* linear programming problems beyond the reach of the simplex method. Many top researchers subsequently worked on modifying Karmarkar's algorithm to fully tap this potential. Much progress has been made (and continues to be made), and a number of powerful algorithms using the interior-point approach have been developed. Today, the more powerful software packages that are designed for solving really large linear programming problems (such as CPLEX) include at least one algorithm using the interior-point approach along with the simplex method. As research continues on these algorithms, their computer implementations continue to improve. This has spurred renewed research on the simplex method, and its computer implementations continue to improve as well (recall the dramatic advance by CPLEX 6.5

cited in the preceding section). The competition between the two approaches for supremacy in solving huge problems is continuing.

Now let us look at the key idea behind Karmarkar's algorithm and its subsequent variants that use the interior-point approach.

The Key Solution Concept

Although radically different from the simplex method, Karmarkar's algorithm does share a few of the same characteristics. It is an *iterative* algorithm. It gets started by identifying a feasible *trial solution*. At each iteration, it moves from the current trial solution to a better trial solution in the feasible region. It then continues this process until it reaches a trial solution that is (essentially) optimal.

The big difference lies in the nature of these trial solutions. For the simplex method, the trial solutions are *CPF solutions* (or BF solutions after augmenting), so all movement is along edges on the *boundary* of the feasible region. For Karmarkar's algorithm, the trial solutions are **interior points,** i.e., points *inside* the boundary of the feasible region. For this reason, Karmarkar's algorithm and its variants are referred to as **interior-point algorithms.**

To illustrate, Fig. 4.11 shows the path followed by the interior-point algorithm in your OR Courseware when it is applied to the Wyndor Glass Co. problem, starting from the

FIGURE 4.11
The curve from (1, 2) to (2, 6) shows a typical path followed by an interior-point algorithm, right through the *interior* of the feasible region for the Wyndor Glass Co. problem.

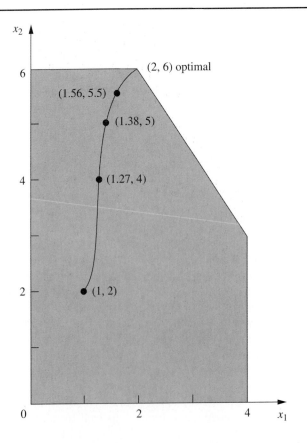

TABLE 4.18 Output of interior-point algorithm in OR Courseware
for Wyndor Glass Co. problem

Iteration	x_1	x_2	z
0	1	2	13
1	1.27298	4	23.8189
2	1.37744	5	29.1323
3	1.56291	5.5	32.1887
4	1.80268	5.71816	33.9989
5	1.92134	5.82908	34.9094
6	1.96639	5.90595	35.429
7	1.98385	5.95199	35.7115
8	1.99197	5.97594	35.8556
9	1.99599	5.98796	35.9278
10	1.99799	5.99398	35.9639
11	1.999	5.99699	35.9819
12	1.9995	5.9985	35.991
13	1.99975	5.99925	35.9955
14	1.99987	5.99962	35.9977
15	1.99994	5.99981	35.9989

initial trial solution (1, 2). Note how all the trial solutions (dots) shown on this path are inside the boundary of the feasible region as the path approaches the optimal solution (2, 6). (All the subsequent trial solutions not shown also are inside the boundary of the feasible region.) Contrast this path with the path followed by the simplex method around the boundary of the feasible region from (0, 0) to (0, 6) to (2, 6).

Table 4.18 shows the actual output from your OR Courseware for this problem.[1] (Try it yourself.) Note how the successive trial solutions keep getting closer and closer to the optimal solution, but never literally get there. However, the deviation becomes so infinitesimally small that the final trial solution can be taken to be the optimal solution for all practical purposes.

Section 7.4 presents the details of the specific interior-point algorithm that is implemented in your OR Courseware.

Comparison with the Simplex Method

One meaningful way of comparing interior-point algorithms with the simplex method is to examine their theoretical properties regarding computational complexity. Karmarkar has proved that the original version of his algorithm is a **polynomial time algorithm**; i.e., the time required to solve *any* linear programming problem can be bounded above by a polynomial function of the size of the problem. Pathological counterexamples have been constructed to demonstrate that the simplex method does not possess this property, so it is an **exponential time algorithm** (i.e., the required time can be bounded above only by an exponential function of the problem size). This difference in *worst-case performance*

---

[1]The routine is called *Solve Automatically by the Interior-Point Algorithm*. The option menu provides two choices for a certain parameter of the algorithm α (defined in Sec. 7.4). The choice used here is the default value of $\alpha = 0.5$.

is noteworthy. However, it tells us nothing about their comparison in average performance on real problems, which is the more crucial issue.

The two basic factors that determine the performance of an algorithm on a real problem are the *average computer time per iteration* and the *number of iterations*. Our next comparisons concern these factors.

Interior-point algorithms are far more complicated than the simplex method. Considerably more extensive computations are required for each iteration to find the next trial solution. Therefore, the computer time per iteration for an interior-point algorithm is many times longer than that for the simplex method.

For fairly small problems, the numbers of iterations needed by an interior-point algorithm and by the simplex method tend to be somewhat comparable. For example, on a problem with 10 functional constraints, roughly 20 iterations would be typical for either kind of algorithm. Consequently, on problems of similar size, the total computer time for an interior-point algorithm will tend to be many times longer than that for the simplex method.

On the other hand, a key advantage of interior-point algorithms is that large problems do not require many more iterations than small problems. For example, a problem with 10,000 functional constraints probably will require well under 100 iterations. Even considering the very substantial computer time per iteration needed for a problem of this size, such a small number of iterations makes the problem quite tractable. By contrast, the simplex method might need 20,000 iterations and so might not finish within a reasonable amount of computer time. Therefore, interior-point algorithms often are faster than the simplex method for such huge problems.

The reason for this very large difference in the number of iterations on huge problems is the difference in the paths followed. At each iteration, the simplex method moves from the current CPF solution to an adjacent CPF solution along an edge on the boundary of the feasible region. Huge problems have an astronomical number of CPF solutions. The path from the initial CPF solution to an optimal solution may be a very circuitous one around the boundary, taking only a small step each time to the next adjacent CPF solution, so a huge number of steps may be required to reach an optimal solution. By contrast, an interior-point algorithm bypasses all this by shooting through the interior of the feasible region toward an optimal solution. Adding more functional constraints adds more constraint boundaries to the feasible region, but has little effect on the number of trial solutions needed on this path through the interior. This makes it possible for interior-point algorithms to solve problems with a huge number of functional constraints.

A final key comparison concerns the ability to perform the various kinds of postoptimality analysis described in Sec. 4.7. The simplex method and its extensions are very well suited to and are widely used for this kind of analysis. Unfortunately, the interior-point approach currently has limited capability in this area.[1] Given the great importance of postoptimality analysis, this is a crucial drawback of interior-point algorithms. However, we point out next how the simplex method can be combined with the interior-point approach to overcome this drawback.

---

[1]However, research aimed at increasing this capability continues to make progress. For example, see H. J. Greenberg, "Matrix Sensitivity Analysis from an Interior Solution of a Linear Program," *INFORMS Journal on Computing,* **11**: 316–327, 1999, and its references.

The Complementary Roles of the Simplex Method and the Interior-Point Approach

Ongoing research is continuing to provide substantial improvements in computer implementations of both the simplex method (including its variants) and interior-point algorithms. Therefore, any predictions about their future roles are risky. However, we do summarize below our current assessment of their complementary roles.

The simplex method (and its variants) continues to be the standard algorithm for the routine use of linear programming. It continues to be the most efficient algorithm for problems with less than a few hundred functional constraints. It also is the most efficient for some (but not all) problems with up to several thousand functional constraints and nearly an unlimited number of decision variables, so most users are continuing to use the simplex method for such problems. However, as the number of functional constraints increases even further, it becomes increasingly likely that an interior-point approach will be the most efficient, so it often is now used instead. As the size grows into the tens of thousands of functional constraints, the interior-point approach may be the only one capable of solving the problem. However, this certainly is not always the case. As mentioned in the preceding section, the latest state-of-the-art software (CPLEX 6.5) is successfully using the simplex method and its variants to solve some truly massive problems with hundreds of thousands, or even millions of functional constraints and decision variables.

These generalizations about how the interior-point approach and the simplex method should compare for various problem sizes will not hold across the board. The specific software packages and computer equipment being used have a major impact. The comparison also is affected considerably by the *specific type* of linear programming problem being solved. As time goes on, we should learn much more about how to identify specific types which are better suited for one kind of algorithm.

One of the by-products of the emergence of the interior-point approach has been a major renewal of efforts to improve the efficiency of computer implementations of the simplex method. As we indicated, impressive progress has been made in recent years, and more lies ahead. At the same time, ongoing research and development of the interior-point approach will further increase its power, and perhaps at a faster rate than for the simplex method.

Improving computer technology, such as massive parallel processing (a huge number of computer units operating in parallel on different parts of the same problem), also will substantially increase the size of problem that either kind of algorithm can solve. However, it now appears that the interior-point approach has much greater potential to take advantage of parallel processing than the simplex method does.

As discussed earlier, a key disadvantage of the interior-point approach is its limited capability for performing postoptimality analysis. To overcome this drawback, researchers have been developing procedures for switching over to the simplex method after an interior-point algorithm has finished. Recall that the trial solutions obtained by an interior-point algorithm keep getting closer and closer to an optimal solution (the best CPF solution), but never quite get there. Therefore, a switching procedure requires identifying a CPF solution (or BF solution after augmenting) that is very close to the final trial solution.

For example, by looking at Fig. 4.11, it is easy to see that the final trial solution in Table 4.18 is very near the CPF solution (2, 6). Unfortunately, on problems with thousands of decision variables (so no graph is available), identifying a nearby CPF (or BF) solution is a very challenging and time-consuming task. However, good progress has been made in developing procedures to do this.

Once this nearby BF solution has been found, the optimality test for the simplex method is applied to check whether this actually is the optimal BF solution. If it is not optimal, some iterations of the simplex method are conducted to move from this BF solution to an optimal solution. Generally, only a very few iterations (perhaps one) are needed because the interior-point algorithm has brought us so close to an optimal solution. Therefore, these iterations should be done quite quickly, even on problems that are too huge to be solved from scratch. After an optimal solution is actually reached, the simplex method and its variants are applied to help perform postoptimality analysis.

Because of the difficulties involved in applying a switching procedure (including the extra computer time), some practitioners prefer to just use the simplex method from the outset. This makes good sense when you only occasionally encounter problems that are large enough for an interior-point algorithm to be modestly faster (before switching) than the simplex method. This modest speed-up would not justify both the extra computer time for a switching procedure and the high cost of acquiring (and learning to use) a software package based on the interior-point approach. However, for organizations which frequently must deal with extremely large linear programming problems, acquiring a state-of-the-art software package of this kind (including a switching procedure) probably is worthwhile. For sufficiently huge problems, the only available way of solving them may be with such a package.

Applications of huge linear programming models sometimes lead to savings of millions of dollars. Just one such application can pay many times over for a state-of-the-art software package based on the interior-point approach plus switching over to the simplex method at the end.

4.10   CONCLUSIONS

The simplex method is an efficient and reliable algorithm for solving linear programming problems. It also provides the basis for performing the various parts of postoptimality analysis very efficiently.

Although it has a useful geometric interpretation, the simplex method is an algebraic procedure. At each iteration, it moves from the current BF solution to a better, adjacent BF solution by choosing both an entering basic variable and a leaving basic variable and then using Gaussian elimination to solve a system of linear equations. When the current solution has no adjacent BF solution that is better, the current solution is optimal and the algorithm stops.

We presented the full algebraic form of the simplex method to convey its logic, and then we streamlined the method to a more convenient tabular form. To set up for starting the simplex method, it is sometimes necessary to use artificial variables to obtain an initial BF solution for an artificial problem. If so, either the Big M method or the two-phase method is used to ensure that the simplex method obtains an optimal solution for the real problem.

Computer implementations of the simplex method and its variants have become so powerful that they now are frequently used to solve linear programming problems with many thousand functional constraints and decision variables, and occasionally vastly larger problems. Interior-point algorithms also provide a powerful tool for solving very large problems.

APPENDIX 4.1   AN INTRODUCTION TO USING LINDO

The LINDO software is designed to be easy to learn and to use, especially for small problems of the size you will encounter in this book. In addition to linear programming, it also can be used to solve both integer programming problems (Chap. 12) and quadratic programming problems (Sec. 13.7). Our focus in this appendix is on its use for linear programming.

LINDO allows you to enter a model in a straightforward algebraic way. For example, here is a nice way of entering the LINDO model for the Wyndor Glass Co. example introduced in Sec. 3.1.

! Wyndor Glass Co. Problem. LINDO model
! X1 = batches of product 1 per week
! X2 = batches of product 2 per week

! Profit, in 1000 of dollars

MAX Profit) 3 X1 + 5 X2

Subject to

! Production time
Plant1) X1 <= 4
Plant2) 2 X2 <= 12
Plant3) 3 X1 + 2 X2 <= 18
END

In addition to the basic model, this formulation includes several clarifying comments, where each comment is indicated by starting with an exclamation point. Thus, the first three lines give the title and the definitions of the decision variables. The decision variables can be either lowercase or uppercase, but uppercase usually is used so the variables won't be dwarfed by the following "subscripts." Another option is to use a suggestive word (or abbreviation of a word), such as the name of the product being produced, to represent the decision variable throughout the model, provided the word does not exceed eight letters.

The fifth line of the LINDO formulation indicates that the objective of the model is to maximize the objective function, $3x_1 + 5x_2$. The word Profit followed by a parenthesis clarifies that this quantity being maximized is profit. The comment on the fourth line further clarifies that the objective function is expressed in units of thousands of dollars. The number 1000 in this comment does not have the usual comma in front of the last three digits because LINDO does not accept commas. (It also does not accept parentheses in algebraic expressions.)

The comment on the seventh line points out that the following constraints are on the production times being used. The next three lines start by giving a name (followed by a parenthesis) for each of the functional constraints. These constraints are written in the usual way except for the inequality signs. Because many keyboards do not include ≤ and ≥ signs, LINDO interprets either < or <= as ≤ and either > or >= as ≥. (On systems that include ≤ and ≥ signs, LINDO will not recognize them.)

The end of the constraints is signified by the word END. No nonnegativity constraints are stated because LINDO automatically assumes that all the variables have these constraints. If, say, x_1 had not had a nonnegativity constraint, this would have to be indicated by typing FREE X1 on the next line below END.

To solve this model in the Windows version of LINDO, either select the Solve command from the Solve menu or press the Solve button on the toolbar. On a platform other than Windows, simply type GO followed by a return at the colon prompt. Figure A4.1 shows the resulting solution report delivered by LINDO.

Both the top line and bottom line in this figure indicate that an optimal solution was found at iteration 2 of the simplex method. Next comes the value of the objective function for this solution. Below this, we have the values of x_1 and x_2 for the optimal solution.

The column to the right of these values gives the **reduced costs.** We have not discussed reduced costs in this chapter because the information they provide can also be gleaned from the *allowable range to stay optimal* for the coefficients in the objective function, and these allowable ranges also are readily available (as you will see in the next figure). When the variable is a *basic variable* in the optimal solution (as for both variables in the Wyndor problem), its reduced cost automatically is 0. When the variable is a *nonbasic variable,* its reduced cost provides some interesting information. This variable is 0 because its coefficient in the objective function is too small (when maximizing the objective function) or too large (when minimizing) to justify undertaking the activity represented by the variable. The reduced cost indicates how much this coefficient can be *increased* (when maximizing) or *decreased* (when minimizing) before the optimal solution would change and this variable would become a *basic variable.* However, recall that this same information already is available from the allowable range to stay optimal for the coefficient of this variable in the objective function. The reduced cost (for a nonbasic variable) is just the *allowable increase* (when maximizing) from the current value of this coefficient to remain within its allowable range to stay optimal or the *allowable decrease* (when minimizing).

Below the variable values and reduced costs in Fig. A4.1, we next have information about the three functional constraints. The *Slack or Surplus* column gives the difference between the two sides of each constraint. The *Dual Prices* column gives, by another name, the *shadow prices* discussed in Sec. 4.7 for these constraints.[1] (This alternate name comes from the fact found in Sec. 6.1 that these shadow prices are just the optimal values of the *dual* variables introduced in Chap. 6.)

When LINDO provides you with this solution report, it also asks you whether you want to do range (sensitivity) analysis. Answering yes (by pressing the Y key) provides you with the additional *range report* shown in Fig. A4.2. This report is identical to the last three columns of the

---

[1]However, beware that LINDO uses a different sign convention from the common one adopted here (see the second footnote for the definition of shadow price in Sec. 4.7), so that for minimization problems, its shadow prices (dual prices) are the negative of ours.

FIGURE A4.1
The solution report provided by LINDO for the Wyndor Glass Co. problem.

```
LP OPTIMUM FOUND AT STEP 2

   OBJECTIVE FUNCTION VALUE

   Profit)   36.00000

VARIABLE        VALUE        REDUCED COST
    X1        2.000000          .000000
    X2        6.000000          .000000

    ROW     SLACK OR SURPLUS      DUAL PRICES
 Plant1)        2.000000           .000000
 Plant2)         .000000          1.500000
 Plant3)         .000000          1.000000

NO. ITERATIONS= 2
```

```
RANGES  IN  WHICH  THE  BASIS  IS  UNCHANGED:

                    OBJ  COEFFICIENT  RANGES
     VARIABLE       CURRENT      ALLOWABLE      ALLOWABLE
                     COEF        INCREASE       DECREASE
         X1        3.000000      4.500000       3.000000
         X2        5.000000      INFINITY       3.000000

                    RIGHTHAND  SIDE  RANGES
       ROW         CURRENT      ALLOWABLE      ALLOWABLE
                     RHS        INCREASE       DECREASE
     Plant1        4.000000     INFINITY       2.000000
     Plant2       12.000000     6.000000       6.000000
     Plant3       18.000000     6.000000       6.000000
```

FIGURE A4.2
The range report provided by LINDO for the Wyndor Glass Co. problem.

tables in the *sensitivity report* generated by the Excel Solver, as shown earlier in Fig. 4.10. Thus, as already discussed in Sec. 4.7, the first two rows of this range report indicate that the *allowable range to stay optimal* for each coefficient in the objective function (assuming no other change in the model) is

$$0 \leq c_1 \leq 7.5$$
$$2 \leq c_2$$

Similarly, the last three rows indicate that the *allowable range to stay feasible* for each right-hand side (assuming no other change in the model) is

$$2 \leq b_1$$
$$6 \leq b_2 \leq 18$$
$$12 \leq b_3 \leq 24$$

To print your results with the Windows version of LINDO, you simply need to use the Print command to send the contents of the active window to the printer. If you are running LINDO on a platform other than Windows, you can use the DIVERT command (followed by the file name) to send screen output to a file, which can then print from either the operating system or a word processing package.

These are the basics for getting started with LINDO. The LINDO tutorial on the CD-ROM also provides some additional details. The LINGO/LINDO files on the CD-ROM for various chapters show the LINDO formulations for numerous examples. In addition, LINDO includes a Help menu to provide guidance. These resources should enable you to apply LINDO to any linear programming problem you will encounter in this book. (We will discuss applications to other problem types in Chaps. 12 and 13.) For more advanced applications, the LINDO *User's Manual* (Selected Reference 4 for this chapter) might be needed.

SELECTED REFERENCES

1. Bazaraa, M. S., J. J. Jarvis, and H. D. Sherali: *Linear Programming and Network Flows,* 2d ed., Wiley, New York, 1990.
2. Calvert, J. E., and W. L. Voxman: *Linear Programming,* Harcourt Brace Jovanovich, Orlando, FL, 1989.

3. Dantzig, G.B., and M.N. Thapa: *Linear Programming 1: Introduction,* Springer, New York, 1997.
4. *LINDO User's Manual,* LINDO Systems, Inc., Chicago, IL, e-mail: info@lindo.com, 1999.
5. Vanderbei, R. J.: *Linear Programming: Foundations and Extensions,* Kluwer Academic Publishers, Boston, MA, 1996.

LEARNING AIDS FOR THIS CHAPTER IN YOUR OR COURSEWARE

Demonstration Examples in OR Tutor:

Interpretation of the Slack Variables
Simplex Method—Algebraic Form
Simplex Method—Tabular Form

Interactive Routines:

Enter or Revise a General Linear Programming Model
Set Up for the Simplex Method—Interactive Only
Solve Interactively by the Simplex Method

An Automatic Routine:

Solve Automatically by the Interior-Point Algorithm

An Excel Add-In:

Premium Solver

Files (Chapter 3) for Solving the Wyndor and Radiation Therapy Examples:

Excel File
LINGO/LINDO File
MPL/CPLEX File

See Appendix 1 for documentation of the software.

PROBLEMS

The symbols to the left of some of the problems (or their parts) have the following meaning:

D: The corresponding demonstration example listed above may be helpful.
I: We suggest that you use the corresponding interactive routine listed above (the printout records your work).
C: Use the computer with any of the software options available to you (or as instructed by your instructor) to solve the problem automatically. (See Sec. 4.8 for a listing of the options featured in this book and on the CD-ROM.)

An asterisk on the problem number indicates that at least a partial answer is given in the back of the book.

4.1-1. Consider the following problem.

Maximize $Z = x_1 + 2x_2,$

subject to

$$x_1 \leq 2$$
$$x_2 \leq 2$$
$$x_1 + x_2 \leq 3$$

and

$$x_1 \geq 0, \qquad x_2 \geq 0.$$

(a) Plot the feasible region and circle all the CPF solutions.

(b) For each CPF solution, identify the pair of constraint boundary equations that it satisfies.

(c) For each CPF solution, use this pair of constraint boundary equations to solve algebraically for the values of x_1 and x_2 at the corner point.

(d) For each CPF solution, identify its adjacent CPF solutions.

(e) For each pair of adjacent CPF solutions, identify the constraint boundary they share by giving its equation.

4.1-2. Consider the following problem.

$$\text{Maximize} \quad Z = 3x_1 + 2x_2,$$

subject to

$$2x_1 + x_2 \le 6$$
$$x_1 + 2x_2 \le 6$$

and

$$x_1 \ge 0, \quad x_2 \ge 0.$$

(a) Use the graphical method to solve this problem. Circle all the corner points on the graph.

(b) For each CPF solution, identify the pair of constraint boundary equations it satisfies.

(c) For each CPF solution, identify its adjacent CPF solutions.

(d) Calculate Z for each CPF solution. Use this information to identify an optimal solution.

(e) Describe graphically what the simplex method does step by step to solve the problem.

4.1-3. A certain linear programming model involving two activities has the feasible region shown below.

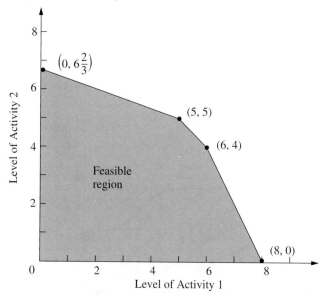

The objective is to maximize the total profit from the two activities. The unit profit for activity 1 is \$1,000 and the unit profit for activity 2 is \$2,000.

(a) Calculate the total profit for each CPF solution. Use this information to find an optimal solution.

(b) Use the solution concepts of the simplex method given in Sec. 4.1 to identify the sequence of CPF solutions that would be examined by the simplex method to reach an optimal solution.

4.1-4.* Consider the linear programming model (given in the back of the book) that was formulated for Prob. 3.2-3.

(a) Use graphical analysis to identify all the *corner-point solutions* for this model. Label each as either feasible or infeasible.

(b) Calculate the value of the objective function for each of the CPF solutions. Use this information to identify an optimal solution.

(c) Use the solution concepts of the simplex method given in Sec. 4.1 to identify which sequence of CPF solutions might be examined by the simplex method to reach an optimal solution. (*Hint:* There are *two* alternative sequences to be identified for this particular model.)

4.1-5. Repeat Prob. 4.1-4 for the following problem.

$$\text{Maximize} \quad Z = x_1 + 2x_2,$$

subject to

$$x_1 + 3x_2 \le 8$$
$$x_1 + x_2 \le 4$$

and

$$x_1 \ge 0, \quad x_2 \ge 0.$$

4.1-6. Repeat Prob. 4.1-4 for the following problem.

$$\text{Maximize} \quad Z = 3x_1 + 2x_2,$$

subject to

$$x_1 \le 4$$
$$x_1 + 3x_2 \le 15$$
$$2x_1 + x_2 \le 10$$

and

$$x_1 \ge 0, \quad x_2 \ge 0.$$

4.1-7. Describe graphically what the simplex method does step by step to solve the following problem.

$$\text{Maximize} \quad Z = 2x_1 + 3x_2,$$

subject to

$$-3x_1 + x_2 \le 1$$
$$4x_1 + 2x_2 \le 20$$

$$4x_1 - x_2 \leq 10$$
$$-x_1 + 2x_2 \leq 5$$

and

$$x_1 \geq 0, \qquad x_2 \geq 0.$$

4.1-8. Describe graphically what the simplex method does step by step to solve the following problem.

Minimize $\quad Z = 5x_1 + 7x_2,$

subject to

$$2x_1 + 3x_2 \geq 42$$
$$3x_1 + 4x_2 \geq 60$$
$$x_1 + x_2 \geq 18$$

and

$$x_1 \geq 0, \qquad x_2 \geq 0.$$

4.1-9. Label each of the following statements about linear programming problems as true or false, and then justify your answer.
(a) For minimization problems, if the objective function evaluated at a CPF solution is no larger than its value at every adjacent CPF solution, then that solution is optimal.
(b) Only CPF solutions can be optimal, so the number of optimal solutions cannot exceed the number of CPF solutions.
(c) If multiple optimal solutions exist, then an optimal CPF solution may have an adjacent CPF solution that also is optimal (the same value of Z).

4.1-10. The following statements give inaccurate paraphrases of the six solution concepts presented in Sec. 4.1. In each case, explain what is wrong with the statement.
(a) The best CPF solution always is an optimal solution.
(b) An iteration of the simplex method checks whether the current CPF solution is optimal and, if not, moves to a new CPF solution.
(c) Although any CPF solution can be chosen to be the initial CPF solution, the simplex method always chooses the origin.
(d) When the simplex method is ready to choose a new CPF solution to move to from the current CPF solution, it only considers adjacent CPF solutions because one of them is likely to be an optimal solution.
(e) To choose the new CPF solution to move to from the current CPF solution, the simplex method identifies all the adjacent CPF solutions and determines which one gives the largest rate of improvement in the value of the objective function.

4.2-1. Reconsider the model in Prob. 4.1-4.
(a) Introduce slack variables in order to write the functional constraints in augmented form.

(b) For each CPF solution, identify the corresponding BF solution by calculating the values of the slack variables. For each BF solution, use the values of the variables to identify the nonbasic variables and the basic variables.
(c) For each BF solution, demonstrate (by plugging in the solution) that, after the nonbasic variables are set equal to zero, this BF solution also is the simultaneous solution of the system of equations obtained in part (a).

4.2-2. Reconsider the model in Prob. 4.1-5. Follow the instructions of Prob. 4.2-1 for parts (a), (b), and (c).
(d) Repeat part (b) for the corner-point infeasible solutions and the corresponding basic infeasible solutions.
(e) Repeat part (c) for the basic infeasible solutions.

4.2-3. Follow the instructions of Prob. 4.2-1 for the model in Prob. 4.1-6.

D,I **4.3-1.** Work through the simplex method (in algebraic form) step by step to solve the model in Prob. 4.1-4.

4.3-2. Reconsider the model in Prob. 4.1-5.
(a) Work through the simplex method (in algebraic form) *by hand* to solve this model.
D,I **(b)** Repeat part (a) with the corresponding interactive routine in your OR Tutor.
C **(c)** Verify the optimal solution you obtained by using a software package based on the simplex method.

4.3-3. Follow the instructions of Prob. 4.3-2 for the model in Prob. 4.1-6.

D,I **4.3-4.*** Work through the simplex method (in algebraic form) step by step to solve the following problem.

Maximize $\quad Z = 4x_1 + 3x_2 + 6x_3,$

subject to

$$3x_1 + x_2 + 3x_3 \leq 30$$
$$2x_1 + 2x_2 + 3x_3 \leq 40$$

and

$$x_1 \geq 0, \qquad x_2 \geq 0, \qquad x_3 \geq 0.$$

D,I **4.3-5.** Work through the simplex method (in algebraic form) step by step to solve the following problem.

Maximize $\quad Z = x_1 + 2x_2 + 4x_3,$

subject to

$$3x_1 + x_2 + 5x_3 \leq 10$$
$$x_1 + 4x_2 + x_3 \leq 8$$
$$2x_1 + 2x_3 \leq 7$$

and

$$x_1 \geq 0, \qquad x_2 \geq 0, \qquad x_3 \geq 0.$$

D,I **4.3-6.** Work through the simplex method (in algebraic form) step by step to solve the following problem.

Maximize $\quad Z = x_1 + 2x_2 + 2x_3,$

subject to

$$5x_1 + 2x_2 + 3x_3 \leq 15$$
$$x_1 + 4x_2 + 2x_3 \leq 12$$
$$2x_1 \quad + \quad x_3 \leq 8$$

and

$$x_1 \geq 0, \qquad x_2 \geq 0, \qquad x_3 \geq 0.$$

4.3-7. Consider the following problem.

Maximize $\quad Z = 5x_1 + 3x_2 + 4x_3,$

subject to

$$2x_1 + x_2 + x_3 \leq 20$$
$$3x_1 + x_2 + 2x_3 \leq 30$$

and

$$x_1 \geq 0, \qquad x_2 \geq 0, \qquad x_3 \geq 0.$$

You are given the information that the *nonzero* variables in the optimal solution are x_2 and x_3.
(a) Describe how you can use this information to adapt the simplex method to solve this problem in the minimum possible number of iterations (when you start from the usual initial BF solution). Do *not* actually perform any iterations.
(b) Use the procedure developed in part (a) to solve this problem by hand. (Do *not* use your OR Courseware.)

4.3-8. Consider the following problem.

Maximize $\quad Z = 2x_1 + 4x_2 + 3x_3,$

subject to

$$x_1 + 3x_2 + 2x_3 \leq 30$$
$$x_1 + x_2 + x_3 \leq 24$$
$$3x_1 + 5x_2 + 3x_3 \leq 60$$

and

$$x_1 \geq 0, \qquad x_2 \geq 0, \qquad x_3 \geq 0.$$

You are given the information that $x_1 > 0$, $x_2 = 0$, and $x_3 > 0$ in the optimal solution.
(a) Describe how you can use this information to adapt the simplex method to solve this problem in the minimum possible number of iterations (when you start from the usual initial BF solution). Do *not* actually perform any iterations.

(b) Use the procedure developed in part (a) to solve this problem by hand. (Do *not* use your OR Courseware.)

4.3-9. Label each of the following statements as true or false, and then justify your answer by referring to specific statements (with page citations) in the chapter.
(a) The simplex method's rule for choosing the entering basic variable is used because it always leads to the *best* adjacent BF solution (largest Z).
(b) The simplex method's minimum ratio rule for choosing the leaving basic variable is used because making another choice with a larger ratio would yield a basic solution that is not feasible.
(c) When the simplex method solves for the next BF solution, elementary algebraic operations are used to eliminate each nonbasic variable from all but one equation (*its* equation) and to give it a coefficient of $+1$ in that one equation.

D,I **4.4-1.** Repeat Prob. 4.3-1, using the tabular form of the simplex method.

D,I,C **4.4-2.** Repeat Prob. 4.3-2, using the tabular form of the simplex method.

D,I,C **4.4-3.** Repeat Prob. 4.3-3, using the tabular form of the simplex method.

4.4-4. Consider the following problem.

Maximize $\quad Z = 2x_1 + x_2,$

subject to

$$x_1 + x_2 \leq 40$$
$$4x_1 + x_2 \leq 100$$

and

$$x_1 \geq 0, \qquad x_2 \geq 0.$$

(a) Solve this problem graphically in a freehand manner. Also identify all the CPF solutions.
(b) Now repeat part (a) when using a ruler to draw the graph carefully.
D (c) Use hand calculations to solve this problem by the simplex method in algebraic form.
D,I (d) Now use your OR Courseware to solve this problem interactively by the simplex method in algebraic form.
D (e) Use hand calculations to solve this problem by the simplex method in tabular form.
D,I (f) Now use your OR Courseware to solve this problem interactively by the simplex method in tabular form.
C (g) Use a software package based on the simplex method to solve the problem.

4.4-5. Repeat Prob. 4.4-4 for the following problem.

Maximize $Z = 2x_1 + 3x_2,$

subject to

$$x_1 + 2x_2 \le 30$$
$$x_1 + x_2 \le 20$$

and

$$x_1 \ge 0, \qquad x_2 \ge 0.$$

4.4-6. Consider the following problem.

Maximize $Z = 2x_1 + 4x_2 + 3x_3,$

subject to

$$3x_1 + 4x_2 + 2x_3 \le 60$$
$$2x_1 + x_2 + 2x_3 \le 40$$
$$x_1 + 3x_2 + 2x_3 \le 80$$

and

$$x_1 \ge 0, \qquad x_2 \ge 0, \qquad x_3 \ge 0.$$

D,I **(a)** Work through the simplex method step by step in algebraic form.

D,I **(b)** Work through the simplex method step by step in tabular form.

C **(c)** Use a software package based on the simplex method to solve the problem.

4.4-7. Consider the following problem.

Maximize $Z = 3x_1 + 5x_2 + 6x_3,$

subject to

$$2x_1 + x_2 + x_3 \le 4$$
$$x_1 + 2x_2 + x_3 \le 4$$
$$x_1 + x_2 + 2x_3 \le 4$$
$$x_1 + x_2 + x_3 \le 3$$

and

$$x_1 \ge 0, \qquad x_2 \ge 0, \qquad x_3 \ge 0.$$

D,I **(a)** Work through the simplex method step by step in algebraic form.

D,I **(b)** Work through the simplex method in tabular form.

C **(c)** Use a computer package based on the simplex method to solve the problem.

4.4-8. Consider the following problem.

Maximize $Z = 2x_1 - x_2 + x_3,$

subject to

$$x_1 - x_2 + 3x_3 \le 4$$
$$2x_1 + x_2 \le 10$$
$$x_1 - x_2 - x_3 \le 7$$

and

$$x_1 \ge 0, \qquad x_2 \ge 0, \qquad x_3 \ge 0.$$

D,I **(a)** Work through the simplex method step by step in algebraic form to solve this problem.

D,I **(b)** Work through the simplex method step by step in tabular form to solve the problem.

C **(c)** Use a computer package based on the simplex method to solve the problem.

D,I **4.4-9.** Work through the simplex method step by step (in tabular form) to solve the following problem.

Maximize $Z = 2x_1 - x_2 + x_3,$

subject to

$$3x_1 + x_2 + x_3 \le 6$$
$$x_1 - x_2 + 2x_3 \le 1$$
$$x_1 + x_2 - x_3 \le 2$$

and

$$x_1 \ge 0, \qquad x_2 \ge 0, \qquad x_3 \ge 0.$$

D,I **4.4-10.** Work through the simplex method step by step to solve the following problem.

Maximize $Z = -x_1 + x_2 + 2x_3,$

subject to

$$x_1 + 2x_2 - x_3 \le 20$$
$$-2x_1 + 4x_2 + 2x_3 \le 60$$
$$2x_1 + 3x_2 + x_3 \le 50$$

and

$$x_1 \ge 0, \qquad x_2 \ge 0, \qquad x_3 \ge 0.$$

4.5-1. Consider the following statements about linear programming and the simplex method. Label each statement as true or false, and then justify your answer.
(a) In a particular iteration of the simplex method, if there is a tie for which variable should be the leaving basic variable, then the next BF solution must have at least one basic variable equal to zero.
(b) If there is no leaving basic variable at some iteration, then the problem has no feasible solutions.
(c) If at least one of the basic variables has a coefficient of zero in row 0 of the final tableau, then the problem has multiple optimal solutions.
(d) If the problem has multiple optimal solutions, then the problem must have a bounded feasible region.

4.5-2. Suppose that the following constraints have been provided for a linear programming model with decision variables x_1 and x_2.

$$-x_1 + 3x_2 \leq 30$$
$$-3x_1 + x_2 \leq 30$$

and

$$x_1 \geq 0, \qquad x_2 \geq 0.$$

(a) Demonstrate graphically that the feasible region is unbounded.
(b) If the objective is to maximize $Z = -x_1 + x_2$, does the model have an optimal solution? If so, find it. If not, explain why not.
(c) Repeat part (b) when the objective is to maximize $Z = x_1 - x_2$.
(d) For objective functions where this model has no optimal solution, does this mean that there are no good solutions according to the model? Explain. What probably went wrong when formulating the model?
D,I (e) Select an objective function for which this model has no optimal solution. Then work through the simplex method step by step to demonstrate that Z is unbounded.
C (f) For the objective function selected in part (e), use a software package based on the simplex method to determine that Z is unbounded.

4.5-3. Follow the instructions of Prob. 4.5-2 when the constraints are the following:

$$2x_1 - x_2 \leq 20$$
$$x_1 - 2x_2 \leq 20$$

and

$$x_1 \geq 0, \qquad x_2 \geq 0.$$

D,I **4.5-4.** Consider the following problem.

Maximize $\qquad Z = 5x_1 + x_2 + 3x_3 + 4x_4,$

subject to

$$x_1 - 2x_2 + 4x_3 + 3x_4 \leq 20$$
$$-4x_1 + 6x_2 + 5x_3 - 4x_4 \leq 40$$
$$2x_1 - 3x_2 + 3x_3 + 8x_4 \leq 50$$

and

$$x_1 \geq 0, \qquad x_2 \geq 0, \qquad x_3 \geq 0, \qquad x_4 \geq 0.$$

Work through the simplex method step by step to demonstrate that Z is unbounded.

4.5-5. A basic property of any linear programming problem with a bounded feasible region is that every feasible solution can be expressed as a convex combination of the CPF solutions (perhaps in more than one way). Similarly, for the augmented form of the problem, every feasible solution can be expressed as a convex combination of the BF solutions.

(a) Show that *any* convex combination of *any* set of feasible solutions must be a feasible solution (so that any convex combination of CPF solutions must be feasible).
(b) Use the result quoted in part (a) to show that any convex combination of BF solutions must be a feasible solution.

4.5-6. Using the facts given in Prob. 4.5-5, show that the following statements must be true for any linear programming problem that has a bounded feasible region and multiple optimal solutions:
(a) Every convex combination of the optimal BF solutions must be optimal.
(b) No other feasible solution can be optimal.

4.5-7. Consider a two-variable linear programming problem whose CPF solutions are $(0, 0)$, $(6, 0)$, $(6, 3)$, $(3, 3)$, and $(0, 2)$. (See Prob. 3.2-2 for a graph of the feasible region.)
(a) Use the graph of the feasible region to identify all the constraints for the model.
(b) For each pair of adjacent CPF solutions, give an example of an objective function such that all the points on the line segment between these two corner points are multiple optimal solutions.
(c) Now suppose that the objective function is $Z = -x_1 + 2x_2$. Use the graphical method to find all the optimal solutions.
D,I (d) For the objective function in part (c), work through the simplex method step by step to find all the optimal BF solutions. Then write an algebraic expression that identifies all the optimal solutions.

D,I **4.5-8.** Consider the following problem.

Maximize $\qquad Z = x_1 + x_2 + x_3 + x_4,$

subject to

$$x_1 + x_2 \leq 3$$
$$x_3 + x_4 \leq 2$$

and

$$x_j \geq 0, \qquad \text{for } j = 1, 2, 3, 4.$$

Work through the simplex method step by step to find all the optimal BF solutions.

4.6-1.* Consider the following problem.

Maximize $\qquad Z = 2x_1 + 3x_2,$

subject to

$$x_1 + 2x_2 \leq 4$$
$$x_1 + x_2 = 3$$

and

$$x_1 \geq 0, \qquad x_2 \geq 0.$$

(a) Solve this problem graphically.
(b) Using the Big *M* method, construct the complete first simplex tableau for the simplex method and identify the corresponding initial (artificial) BF solution. Also identify the initial entering basic variable and the leaving basic variable.
I (c) Continue from part (b) to work through the simplex method step by step to solve the problem.

4.6-2. Consider the following problem.

   Maximize $Z = 4x_1 + 2x_2 + 3x_3 + 5x_4$,

subject to

   $2x_1 + 3x_2 + 4x_3 + 2x_4 = 300$
   $8x_1 + x_2 + x_3 + 5x_4 = 300$

and

   $x_j \geq 0$,   for $j = 1, 2, 3, 4$.

(a) Using the Big *M* method, construct the complete first simplex tableau for the simplex method and identify the corresponding initial (artificial) BF solution. Also identify the initial entering basic variable and the leaving basic variable.
I (b) Work through the simplex method step by step to solve the problem.
(c) Using the two-phase method, construct the complete first simplex tableau for phase 1 and identify the corresponding initial (artificial) BF solution. Also identify the initial entering basic variable and the leaving basic variable.
I (d) Work through phase 1 step by step.
(e) Construct the complete first simplex tableau for phase 2.
I (f) Work through phase 2 step by step to solve the problem.
(g) Compare the sequence of BF solutions obtained in part (b) with that in parts (d) and (f). Which of these solutions are feasible only for the artificial problem obtained by introducing artificial variables and which are actually feasible for the real problem?
C (h) Use a software package based on the simplex method to solve the problem.

4.6-3. Consider the following problem.

   Minimize $Z = 3x_1 + 2x_2$,

subject to

   $2x_1 + x_2 \geq 10$
   $-3x_1 + 2x_2 \leq 6$
   $x_1 + x_2 \geq 6$

and

   $x_1 \geq 0$, $x_2 \geq 0$.

(a) Solve this problem graphically.
(b) Using the Big *M* method, construct the complete first simplex tableau for the simplex method and identify the corresponding

initial (artificial) BF solution. Also identify the initial entering basic variable and the leaving basic variable.
I (c) Work through the simplex method step by step to solve the problem.

4.6-4.* Consider the following problem.

   Minimize $Z = 2x_1 + 3x_2 + x_3$,

subject to

   $x_1 + 4x_2 + 2x_3 \geq 8$
   $3x_1 + 2x_2 \geq 6$

and

   $x_1 \geq 0$, $x_2 \geq 0$, $x_3 \geq 0$.

(a) Reformulate this problem to fit our standard form for a linear programming model presented in Sec. 3.2.
I (b) Using the Big *M* method, work through the simplex method step by step to solve the problem.
I (c) Using the two-phase method, work through the simplex method step by step to solve the problem.
(d) Compare the sequence of BF solutions obtained in parts (b) and (c). Which of these solutions are feasible only for the artificial problem obtained by introducing artificial variables and which are actually feasible for the real problem?
C (e) Use a software package based on the simplex method to solve the problem.

4.6-5. For the Big *M* method, explain why the simplex method never would choose an artificial variable to be an entering basic variable once all the artificial variables are nonbasic.

4.6-6. Consider the following problem.

   Maximize $Z = 90x_1 + 70x_2$,

subject to

   $2x_1 + x_2 \leq 2$
   $x_1 - x_2 \geq 2$

and

   $x_1 \geq 0$, $x_2 \geq 0$.

(a) Demonstrate graphically that this problem has no feasible solutions.
C (b) Use a computer package based on the simplex method to determine that the problem has no feasible solutions.
I (c) Using the Big *M* method, work through the simplex method step by step to demonstrate that the problem has no feasible solutions.
I (d) Repeat part (c) when using phase 1 of the two-phase method.

4.6-7. Follow the instructions of Prob. 4.6-6 for the following problem.

$$\text{Minimize} \quad Z = 5{,}000x_1 + 7{,}000x_2,$$

subject to

$$-2x_1 + x_2 \geq 1$$
$$x_1 - 2x_2 \geq 1$$

and

$$x_1 \geq 0, \qquad x_2 \geq 0.$$

4.6-8. Consider the following problem.

$$\text{Maximize} \quad Z = 2x_1 + 5x_2 + 3x_3,$$

subject to

$$x_1 - 2x_2 + x_3 \geq 20$$
$$2x_1 + 4x_2 + x_3 = 50$$

and

$$x_1 \geq 0, \qquad x_2 \geq 0, \qquad x_3 \geq 0.$$

(a) Using the Big M method, construct the complete first simplex tableau for the simplex method and identify the corresponding initial (artificial) BF solution. Also identify the initial entering basic variable and the leaving basic variable.

I **(b)** Work through the simplex method step by step to solve the problem.

I **(c)** Using the two-phase method, construct the complete first simplex tableau for phase 1 and identify the corresponding initial (artificial) BF solution. Also identify the initial entering basic variable and the leaving basic variable.

I **(d)** Work through phase 1 step by step.

(e) Construct the complete first simplex tableau for phase 2.

I **(f)** Work through phase 2 step by step to solve the problem.

(g) Compare the sequence of BF solutions obtained in part (b) with that in parts (d) and (f). Which of these solutions are feasible only for the artificial problem obtained by introducing artificial variables and which are actually feasible for the real problem?

C **(h)** Use a software package based on the simplex method to solve the problem.

4.6-9. Consider the following problem.

$$\text{Minimize} \quad Z = 2x_1 + x_2 + 3x_3,$$

subject to

$$5x_1 + 2x_2 + 7x_3 = 420$$
$$3x_1 + 2x_2 + 5x_3 \geq 280$$

and

$$x_1 \geq 0, \qquad x_2 \geq 0, \qquad x_3 \geq 0.$$

I **(a)** Using the two-phase method, work through phase 1 step by step.

C **(b)** Use a software package based on the simplex method to formulate and solve the phase 1 problem.

I **(c)** Work through phase 2 step by step to solve the original problem.

C **(d)** Use a computer code based on the simplex method to solve the original problem.

4.6-10.* Consider the following problem.

$$\text{Minimize} \quad Z = 3x_1 + 2x_2 + 4x_3,$$

subject to

$$2x_1 + x_2 + 3x_3 = 60$$
$$3x_1 + 3x_2 + 5x_3 \geq 120$$

and

$$x_1 \geq 0, \qquad x_2 \geq 0, \qquad x_3 \geq 0.$$

I **(a)** Using the Big M method, work through the simplex method step by step to solve the problem.

I **(b)** Using the two-phase method, work through the simplex method step by step to solve the problem.

(c) Compare the sequence of BF solutions obtained in parts (a) and (b). Which of these solutions are feasible only for the artificial problem obtained by introducing artificial variables and which are actually feasible for the real problem?

C **(d)** Use a software package based on the simplex method to solve the problem.

4.6-11. Follow the instructions of Prob. 4.6-10 for the following problem.

$$\text{Minimize} \quad Z = 3x_1 + 2x_2 + 7x_3,$$

subject to

$$-x_1 + x_2 = 10$$
$$2x_1 - x_2 + x_3 \geq 10$$

and

$$x_1 \geq 0, \qquad x_2 \geq 0, \qquad x_3 \geq 0.$$

4.6-12. Follow the instructions of Prob. 4.6-10 for the following problem.

$$\text{Minimize} \quad Z = 3x_1 + 2x_2 + x_3,$$

subject to

$$x_1 + x_2 = 7$$
$$3x_1 + x_2 + x_3 \geq 10$$

and

$$x_1 \geq 0, \qquad x_2 \geq 0, \qquad x_3 \geq 0.$$

4.6-13. Label each of the following statements as true or false, and then justify your answer.

(a) When a linear programming model has an equality constraint, an artificial variable is introduced into this constraint in order to start the simplex method with an obvious initial basic solution that is feasible for the original model.

(b) When an artificial problem is created by introducing artificial variables and using the Big M method, if all artificial variables in an optimal solution for the artificial problem are equal to zero, then the real problem has no feasible solutions.

(c) The two-phase method is commonly used in practice because it usually requires fewer iterations to reach an optimal solution than the Big M method does.

4.6-14. Consider the following problem.

Maximize $Z = x_1 + 4x_2 + 2x_3,$

subject to

$$4x_1 - x_2 + x_3 \leq 5$$
$$-x_1 - x_2 + 2x_3 \leq 10$$

and

$$x_2 \geq 0, \qquad x_3 \geq 0$$

(no nonnegativity constraint for x_1).

(a) Reformulate this problem so all variables have nonnegativity constraints.

D,I (b) Work through the simplex method step by step to solve the problem.

C (c) Use a software package based on the simplex method to solve the problem.

4.6-15.* Consider the following problem.

Maximize $Z = -x_1 + 4x_2,$

subject to

$$-3x_1 + x_2 \leq 6$$
$$x_1 + 2x_2 \leq 4$$
$$x_2 \geq -3$$

(no lower bound constraint for x_1).

(a) Solve this problem graphically.

(b) Reformulate this problem so that it has only two functional constraints and all variables have nonnegativity constraints.

D,I (c) Work through the simplex method step by step to solve the problem.

4.6-16. Consider the following problem.

Maximize $Z = -x_1 + 2x_2 + x_3,$

subject to

$$3x_2 + x_3 \leq 120$$
$$x_1 - x_2 - 4x_3 \leq 80$$
$$-3x_1 + x_2 + 2x_3 \leq 100$$

(no nonnegativity constraints).

(a) Reformulate this problem so that all variables have nonnegativity constraints.

D,I (b) Work through the simplex method step by step to solve the problem.

C (c) Use a computer package based on the simplex method to solve the problem.

4.6-17. This chapter has described the simplex method as applied to linear programming problems where the objective function is to be maximized. Section 4.6 then described how to convert a minimization problem to an equivalent maximization problem for applying the simplex method. Another option with minimization problems is to make a few modifications in the instructions for the simplex method given in the chapter in order to apply the algorithm directly.

(a) Describe what these modifications would need to be.

(b) Using the Big M method, apply the modified algorithm developed in part (a) to solve the following problem directly by hand. (Do not use your OR Courseware.)

Minimize $Z = 3x_1 + 8x_2 + 5x_3,$

subject to

$$3x_2 + 4x_3 \geq 70$$
$$3x_1 + 5x_2 + 2x_3 \geq 70$$

and

$$x_1 \geq 0, \qquad x_2 \geq 0, \qquad x_3 \geq 0.$$

4.6-18. Consider the following problem.

Maximize $Z = -2x_1 + x_2 - 4x_3 + 3x_4,$

subject to

$$x_1 + x_2 + 3x_3 + 2x_4 \leq 4$$
$$x_1 \qquad - x_3 + x_4 \geq -1$$
$$2x_1 + x_2 \qquad \leq 2$$
$$x_1 + 2x_2 + x_3 + 2x_4 = 2$$

and

$$x_2 \geq 0, \qquad x_3 \geq 0, \qquad x_4 \geq 0$$

(no nonnegativity constraint for x_1).

(a) Reformulate this problem to fit our standard form for a linear programming model presented in Sec. 3.2.

(b) Using the Big M method, construct the complete first simplex tableau for the simplex method and identify the corresponding initial (artificial) BF solution. Also identify the initial entering basic variable and the leaving basic variable.

(c) Using the two-phase method, construct row 0 of the first simplex tableau for phase 1.

C (d) Use a computer package based on the simplex method to solve the problem.

I **4.6-19.** Consider the following problem.

Maximize $Z = 4x_1 + 5x_2 + 3x_3$,

subject to

$$x_1 + x_2 + 2x_3 \geq 20$$
$$15x_1 + 6x_2 - 5x_3 \leq 50$$
$$x_1 + 3x_2 + 5x_3 \leq 30$$

and

$$x_1 \geq 0, \qquad x_2 \geq 0, \qquad x_3 \geq 0.$$

Work through the simplex method step by step to demonstrate that this problem does not possess any feasible solutions.

4.7-1. Refer to Fig. 4.10 and the resulting *allowable range to stay feasible* for the respective right-hand sides of the Wyndor Glass Co. problem given in Sec. 3.1. Use graphical analysis to demonstrate that each given allowable range is correct.

4.7-2. Reconsider the model in Prob. 4.1-5. Interpret the right-hand side of the respective functional constraints as the amount available of the respective resources.
(a) Use graphical analysis as in Fig. 4.8 to determine the shadow prices for the respective resources.
(b) Use graphical analysis to perform sensitivity analysis on this model. In particular, check each parameter of the model to determine whether it is a *sensitive* parameter (a parameter whose value cannot be changed without changing the optimal solution) by examining the graph that identifies the optimal solution.
(c) Use graphical analysis as in Fig. 4.9 to determine the allowable range for each c_j value (coefficient of x_j in the objective function) over which the current optimal solution will remain optimal.
(d) Changing just one b_i value (the right-hand side of functional constraint i) will shift the corresponding constraint boundary. If the current optimal CPF solution lies on this constraint boundary, this CPF solution also will shift. Use graphical analysis to determine the allowable range for each b_i value over which this CPF solution will remain feasible.
c **(e)** Verify your answers in parts (*a*), (*c*), and (*d*) by using a computer package based on the simplex method to solve the problem and then to generate sensitivity analysis information.

4.7-3. Repeat Prob. 4.7-2 for the model in Prob. 4.1-6.

4.7-4. You are given the following linear programming problem.

Maximize $Z = 4x_1 + 2x_2$,

subject to

$$2x_1 \qquad \leq 16 \qquad \text{(resource 1)}$$
$$x_1 + 3x_2 \leq 17 \qquad \text{(resource 2)}$$
$$x_2 \leq 5 \qquad \text{(resource 3)}$$

and

$$x_1 \geq 0, \qquad x_2 \geq 0.$$

(a) Solve this problem graphically.
(b) Use graphical analysis to find the shadow prices for the resources.
(c) Determine how many additional units of resource 1 would be needed to increase the optimal value of Z by 15.

4.7-5. Consider the following problem.

Maximize $Z = x_1 - 7x_2 + 3x_3$,

subject to

$$2x_1 + x_2 - x_3 \leq 4 \qquad \text{(resource 1)}$$
$$4x_1 - 3x_2 \qquad \leq 2 \qquad \text{(resource 2)}$$
$$-3x_1 + 2x_2 + x_3 \leq 3 \qquad \text{(resource 3)}$$

and

$$x_1 \geq 0, \qquad x_2 \geq 0, \qquad x_3 \geq 0.$$

D,I **(a)** Work through the simplex method step by step to solve the problem.
(b) Identify the shadow prices for the three resources and describe their significance.
c **(c)** Use a software package based on the simplex method to solve the problem and then to generate sensitivity information. Use this information to identify the shadow price for each resource, the allowable range to stay optimal for each objective function coefficient, and the allowable range to stay feasible for each right-hand side.

4.7-6.* Consider the following problem.

Maximize $Z = 2x_1 - 2x_2 + 3x_3$,

subject to

$$-x_1 + x_2 + x_3 \leq 4 \qquad \text{(resource 1)}$$
$$2x_1 - x_2 + x_3 \leq 2 \qquad \text{(resource 2)}$$
$$x_1 + x_2 + 3x_3 \leq 12 \qquad \text{(resource 3)}$$

and

$$x_1 \geq 0, \qquad x_2 \geq 0, \qquad x_3 \geq 0.$$

D,I **(a)** Work through the simplex method step by step to solve the problem.
(b) Identify the shadow prices for the three resources and describe their significance.
c **(c)** Use a software package based on the simplex method to solve the problem and then to generate sensitivity information. Use this information to identify the shadow price for each resource, the allowable range to stay optimal for each objective function coefficient and the allowable range to stay feasible for each right-hand side.

4.7-7. Consider the following problem.

Maximize $Z = 2x_1 + 4x_2 - x_3$,

subject to

$$
\begin{aligned}
3x_2 - x_3 &\leq 30 \quad &\text{(resource 1)} \\
2x_1 - x_2 + x_3 &\leq 10 \quad &\text{(resource 2)} \\
4x_1 + 2x_2 - 2x_3 &\leq 40 \quad &\text{(resource 3)}
\end{aligned}
$$

and

$$x_1 \geq 0, \qquad x_2 \geq 0, \qquad x_3 \geq 0.$$

D,I **(a)** Work through the simplex method step by step to solve the problem.

(b) Identify the shadow prices for the three resources and describe their significance.

C **(c)** Use a software package based on the simplex method to solve the problem and then to generate sensitivity information. Use this information to identify the shadow price for each resource, the allowable range to stay optimal for each objective function coefficient, and the allowable range to stay feasible for each right-hand side.

4.7-8. Consider the following problem.

Maximize $Z = 5x_1 + 4x_2 - x_3 + 3x_4$,

subject to

$$
\begin{aligned}
3x_1 + 2x_2 - 3x_3 + x_4 &\leq 24 \quad &\text{(resource 1)} \\
3x_1 + 3x_2 + x_3 + 3x_4 &\leq 36 \quad &\text{(resource 2)}
\end{aligned}
$$

and

$$x_1 \geq 0, \qquad x_2 \geq 0, \qquad x_3 \geq 0, \qquad x_4 \geq 0.$$

D,I **(a)** Work through the simplex method step by step to solve the problem.

(b) Identify the shadow prices for the two resources and describe their significance.

C **(c)** Use a software package based on the simplex method to solve the problem and then to generate sensitivity information. Use this information to identify the shadow price for each resource, the allowable range to stay optimal for each objective function coefficient, and the allowable range to stay feasible for each right-hand side.

4.9-1. Use the interior-point algorithm in your OR Courseware to solve the model in Prob. 4.1-4. Choose $\alpha = 0.5$ from the Option menu, use $(x_1, x_2) = (0.1, 0.4)$ as the initial trial solution, and run 15 iterations. Draw a graph of the feasible region, and then plot the trajectory of the trial solutions through this feasible region.

4.9-2. Repeat Prob. 4.9-1 for the model in Prob. 4.1-5.

4.9-3. Repeat Prob. 4.9-1 for the model in Prob. 4.1-6.

CASE 4.1   FABRICS AND FALL FASHIONS

From the tenth floor of her office building, Katherine Rally watches the swarms of New Yorkers fight their way through the streets infested with yellow cabs and the sidewalks littered with hot dog stands. On this sweltering July day, she pays particular attention to the fashions worn by the various women and wonders what they will choose to wear in the fall. Her thoughts are not simply random musings; they are critical to her work since she owns and manages TrendLines, an elite women's clothing company.

Today is an especially important day because she must meet with Ted Lawson, the production manager, to decide upon next month's production plan for the fall line. Specifically, she must determine the quantity of each clothing item she should produce given the plant's production capacity, limited resources, and demand forecasts. Accurate planning for next month's production is critical to fall sales since the items produced next month will appear in stores during September, and women generally buy the majority of the fall fashions when they first appear in September.

She turns back to her sprawling glass desk and looks at the numerous papers covering it. Her eyes roam across the clothing patterns designed almost six months ago, the lists of materials requirements for each pattern, and the lists of demand forecasts for each pattern determined by customer surveys at fashion shows. She remembers the hectic and sometimes nightmarish days of designing the fall line and presenting it at fashion shows in New York, Milan, and Paris. Ultimately, she paid her team of six designers a total of $860,000 for their work on her fall line. With the cost of hiring runway models, hair stylists, and makeup artists, sewing and fitting clothes, building the set, choreographing and rehearsing the show, and renting the conference hall, each of the three fashion shows cost her an additional $2,700,000.

She studies the clothing patterns and material requirements. Her fall line consists of both professional and casual fashions. She determined the prices for each clothing item by taking into account the quality and cost of material, the cost of labor and machining, the demand for the item, and the prestige of the TrendLines brand name.

The fall professional fashions include:

Clothing Item	Materials Requirements	Price	Labor and Machine Cost
Tailored wool slacks	3 yards of wool 2 yards of acetate for lining	$300	$160
Cashmere sweater	1.5 yards of cashmere	$450	$150
Silk blouse	1.5 yards of silk	$180	$100
Silk camisole	0.5 yard of silk	$120	$ 60
Tailored skirt	2 yards of rayon 1.5 yards of acetate for lining	$270	$120
Wool blazer	2.5 yards of wool 1.5 yards of acetate for lining	$320	$140

The fall casual fashions include:

Clothing Item	Materials Requirements	Price	Labor and Machine Cost
Velvet pants	3 yards of velvet 2 yards of acetate for lining	$350	$175
Cotton sweater	1.5 yards of cotton	$130	$ 60
Cotton miniskirt	0.5 yard of cotton	$ 75	$ 40
Velvet shirt	1.5 yards of velvet	$200	$160
Button-down blouse	1.5 yards of rayon	$120	$ 90

She knows that for the next month, she has ordered 45,000 yards of wool, 28,000 yards of acetate, 9,000 yards of cashmere, 18,000 yards of silk, 30,000 yards of rayon, 20,000 yards of velvet, and 30,000 yards of cotton for production. The prices of the materials are listed on the next page.

Material	Price per yard
Wool	$ 9.00
Acetate	$ 1.50
Cashmere	$60.00
Silk	$13.00
Rayon	$ 2.25
Velvet	$12.00
Cotton	$ 2.50

Any material that is not used in production can be sent back to the textile wholesaler for a full refund, although scrap material cannot be sent back to the wholesaler.

She knows that the production of both the silk blouse and cotton sweater leaves leftover scraps of material. Specifically, for the production of one silk blouse or one cotton sweater, 2 yards of silk and cotton, respectively, are needed. From these 2 yards, 1.5 yards are used for the silk blouse or the cotton sweater and 0.5 yard is left as scrap material. She does not want to waste the material, so she plans to use the rectangular scrap of silk or cotton to produce a silk camisole or cotton miniskirt, respectively. Therefore, whenever a silk blouse is produced, a silk camisole is also produced. Likewise, whenever a cotton sweater is produced, a cotton miniskirt is also produced. Note that it is possible to produce a silk camisole without producing a silk blouse and a cotton miniskirt without producing a cotton sweater.

The demand forecasts indicate that some items have limited demand. Specifically, because the velvet pants and velvet shirts are fashion fads, TrendLines has forecasted that it can sell only 5,500 pairs of velvet pants and 6,000 velvet shirts. TrendLines does not want to produce more than the forecasted demand because once the pants and shirts go out of style, the company cannot sell them. TrendLines can produce less than the forecasted demand, however, since the company is not required to meet the demand. The cashmere sweater also has limited demand because it is quite expensive, and TrendLines knows it can sell at most 4,000 cashmere sweaters. The silk blouses and camisoles have limited demand because many women think silk is too hard to care for, and TrendLines projects that it can sell at most 12,000 silk blouses and 15,000 silk camisoles.

The demand forecasts also indicate that the wool slacks, tailored skirts, and wool blazers have a great demand because they are basic items needed in every professional wardrobe. Specifically, the demand for wool slacks is 7,000 pairs of slacks, and the demand for wool blazers is 5,000 blazers. Katherine wants to meet at least 60 percent of the demand for these two items in order to maintain her loyal customer base and not lose business in the future. Although the demand for tailored skirts could not be estimated, Katherine feels she should make at least 2,800 of them.

(a) Ted is trying to convince Katherine not to produce any velvet shirts since the demand for this fashion fad is quite low. He argues that this fashion fad alone accounts for $500,000 of the fixed design and other costs. The net contribution (price of clothing item − materials cost − labor cost) from selling the fashion fad should cover these fixed costs. Each velvet shirt generates a net contribution of $22. He argues that given the net contribution,

even satisfying the maximum demand will not yield a profit. What do you think of Ted's argument?
(b) Formulate and solve a linear programming problem to maximize profit given the production, resource, and demand constraints.

Before she makes her final decision, Katherine plans to explore the following questions independently except where otherwise indicated.

(c) The textile wholesaler informs Katherine that the velvet cannot be sent back because the demand forecasts show that the demand for velvet will decrease in the future. Katherine can therefore get no refund for the velvet. How does this fact change the production plan?
(d) What is an intuitive economic explanation for the difference between the solutions found in parts (b) and (c)?
(e) The sewing staff encounters difficulties sewing the arms and lining into the wool blazers since the blazer pattern has an awkward shape and the heavy wool material is difficult to cut and sew. The increased labor time to sew a wool blazer increases the labor and machine cost for each blazer by $80. Given this new cost, how many of each clothing item should TrendLines produce to maximize profit?
(f) The textile wholesaler informs Katherine that since another textile customer canceled his order, she can obtain an extra 10,000 yards of acetate. How many of each clothing item should TrendLines now produce to maximize profit?
(g) TrendLines assumes that it can sell every item that was not sold during September and October in a big sale in November at 60 percent of the original price. Therefore, it can sell all items in unlimited quantity during the November sale. (The previously mentioned upper limits on demand concern only the sales during September and October.) What should the new production plan be to maximize profit?

CASE 4.2   NEW FRONTIERS

Rob Richman, president of AmeriBank, takes off his glasses, rubs his eyes in exhaustion, and squints at the clock in his study. It reads 3 A.M. For the last several hours, Rob has been poring over AmeriBank's financial statements from the last three quarters of operation. AmeriBank, a medium-sized bank with branches throughout the United States, is headed for dire economic straits. The bank, which provides transaction, savings, and investment and loan services, has been experiencing a steady decline in its net income over the past year, and trends show that the decline will continue. The bank is simply losing customers to nonbank and foreign bank competitors.

AmeriBank is not alone in its struggle to stay out of the red. From his daily industry readings, Rob knows that many American banks have been suffering significant losses because of increasing competition from nonbank and foreign bank competitors offering services typically in the domain of American banks. Because the nonbank and foreign bank competitors specialize in particular services, they are able to better capture the market for those services by offering less expensive, more efficient, more convenient services. For example, large corporations now turn to foreign banks and commercial paper offerings for loans, and affluent Americans now turn to money-market funds for investment. Banks face the daunting challenge of distinguishing themselves from nonbank and foreign bank competitors.

Rob has concluded that one strategy for distinguishing AmeriBank from its competitors is to improve services that nonbank and foreign bank competitors do not readily provide: transaction services. He has decided that a more convenient transaction method must logically succeed the automatic teller machine, and he believes that electronic banking over the Internet allows this convenient transaction method. Over the Internet, customers are able to perform transactions on their desktop computers either at home or at work. The explosion of the Internet means that many potential customers understand and use the World Wide Web. He therefore feels that if AmeriBank offers Web banking (as the practice of Internet banking is commonly called), the bank will attract many new customers.

Before Rob undertakes the project to make Web banking possible, however, he needs to understand the market for Web banking and the services AmeriBank should provide over the Internet. For example, should the bank only allow customers to access account balances and historical transaction information over the Internet, or should the bank develop a strategy to allow customers to make deposits and withdrawals over the Internet? Should the bank try to recapture a portion of the investment market by continuously running stock prices and allowing customers to make stock transactions over the Internet for a minimal fee?

Because AmeriBank is not in the business of performing surveys, Rob has decided to outsource the survey project to a professional survey company. He has opened the project up for bidding by several survey companies and will award the project to the company which is willing to perform the survey for the least cost.

Sophisticated Surveys is one of three survey companies competing for the project. Rob provided each survey company with a list of survey requirements to ensure that AmeriBank receives the needed information for planning the Web banking project.

Because different age groups require different services, AmeriBank is interested in surveying four different age groups. The first group encompasses customers who are 18 to 25 years old. The bank assumes that this age group has limited yearly income and performs minimal transactions. The second group encompasses customers who are 26 to 40 years old. This age group has significant sources of income, performs many transactions, requires numerous loans for new houses and cars, and invests in various securities. The third group encompasses customers who are 41 to 50 years old. These customers typically have the same level of income and perform the same number of transactions as the second age group, but the bank assumes that these customers are less likely to use Web banking since they have not become as comfortable with the explosion of computers or the Internet. Finally, the fourth group encompasses customers who are 51 years of age and over. These customers commonly crave security and require continuous information on retirement funds. The banks believes that it is highly unlikely that customers in this age group will use Web banking, but the bank desires to learn the needs of this age group for the future. AmeriBank wants to interview 2,000 customers with at least 20 percent from the first age group, at least 27.5 percent from the second age group, at least 15 percent from the third age group, and at least 15 percent from the fourth age group.

Rob understands that the Internet is a recent phenomenon and that some customers may not have heard of the World Wide Web. He therefore wants to ensure that the survey includes a mix of customers who know the Internet well and those that have less exposure to the Internet. To ensure that AmeriBank obtains the correct mix, he wants to interview at least 15 percent of customers from the Silicon Valley where Internet use is high, at least 35 percent of customers from big cities where Internet use is medium, and at least 20 percent of customers from small towns where Internet use is low.

Sophisticated Surveys has performed an initial analysis of these survey requirements to determine the cost of surveying different populations. The costs per person surveyed are listed in the following table:

| Region | Age Group | | | |
	18 to 25	26 to 40	41 to 50	51 and over
Silicon Valley	$4.75	$6.50	$6.50	$5.00
Big cities	$5.25	$5.75	$6.25	$6.25
Small towns	$6.50	$7.50	$7.50	$7.25

Sophisticated Surveys explores the following options cumulatively.

(a) Formulate a linear programming model to minimize costs while meeting all survey constraints imposed by AmeriBank.
(b) If the profit margin for Sophisticated Surveys is 15 percent of cost, what bid will they submit?
(c) After submitting its bid, Sophisticated Surveys is informed that it has the lowest cost but that AmeriBank does not like the solution. Specifically, Rob feels that the selected survey population is not representative enough of the banking customer population. Rob wants at least 50 people of each age group surveyed in each region. What is the new bid made by Sophisticated Surveys?
(d) Rob feels that Sophisticated Survey oversampled the 18- to 25-year-old population and the Silicon Valley population. He imposes a new constraint that no more than 600 individuals can be surveyed from the 18- to 25-year-old population and no more than 650 individuals can be surveyed from the Silicon Valley population. What is the new bid?
(e) When Sophisticated Surveys calculated the cost of reaching and surveying particular individuals, the company thought that reaching individuals in young populations would be easiest. In a recently completed survey, however, Sophisticated Surveys learned that this assumption was wrong. The new costs for surveying the 18- to 25-year-old population are listed below.

Region survey cost per person

Silicon Valley	$6.50
Big cities	$6.75
Small towns	$7.00

Given the new costs, what is the new bid?

(f) To ensure the desired sampling of individuals, Rob imposes even stricter requirements. He fixes the exact percentage of people that should be surveyed from each population. The requirements are listed below:

Population percentage of people surveyed	
18 to 25	25%
26 to 40	35%
41 to 50	20%
51 and over	20%
Silicon Valley	20%
Big cities	50%
Small towns	30%

By how much would these new requirements increase the cost of surveying for Sophisticated Surveys? Given the 15 percent profit margin, what would Sophisticated Surveys bid?

CASE 4.3   ASSIGNING STUDENTS TO SCHOOLS

The Springfield school board has made the decision to close one of its middle schools (sixth, seventh, and eighth grades) at the end of this school year and reassign all of next year's middle school students to the three remaining middle schools. The school district provides bussing for all middle school students who must travel more than approximately a mile, so the school board wants a plan for reassigning the students that will minimize the total bussing cost. The annual cost per student of bussing from each of the six residential areas of the city to each of the schools is shown in the following table (along with other basic data for next year), where 0 indicates that bussing is not needed and a dash indicates an infeasible assignment.

Area	No. of Students	Percentage in 6th Grade	Percentage in 7th Grade	Percentage in 8th Grade	Bussing Cost per Student		
					School 1	School 2	School 3
1	450	32	38	30	$300	0	$700
2	600	37	28	35	—	$400	$500
3	550	30	32	38	$600	$300	$200
4	350	28	40	32	$200	$500	—
5	500	39	34	27	0	—	$400
6	450	34	28	38	$500	$300	0
				School capacity:	900	1,100	1,000

The school board also has imposed the restriction that each grade must constitute between 30 and 36 percent of each school's population. The above table shows the percentage of each area's middle school population for next year that falls into each of the three grades. The school attendance zone boundaries can be drawn so as to split any given area among more than one school, but assume that the percentages shown in the table will continue to hold for any partial assignment of an area to a school.

You have been hired as an operations research consultant to assist the school board in determining how many students in each area should be assigned to each school.

(a) Formulate a linear programming model for this problem.
(b) Solve the model.
(c) What is your resulting recommendation to the school board?

After seeing your recommendation, the school board expresses concern about all the splitting of residential areas among multiple schools. They indicate that they "would like to keep each neighborhood together."

(d) Adjust your recommendation as well as you can to enable each area to be assigned to just one school. (Adding this restriction may force you to fudge on some other constraints.) How much does this increase the total bussing cost? (This line of analysis will be pursued more rigorously in Case 12.4.)

The school board is considering eliminating some bussing to reduce costs. Option 1 is to eliminate bussing only for students traveling 1 to 1.5 miles, where the cost per student is given in the table as $200. Option 2 is to also eliminate bussing for students traveling 1.5 to 2 miles, where the estimated cost per student is $300.

(e) Revise the model from part (a) to fit Option 1, and solve. Compare these results with those from part (c), including the reduction in total bussing cost.
(f) Repeat part (e) for Option 2.

The school board now needs to choose among the three alternative bussing plans (the current one or Option 1 or Option 2). One important factor is bussing costs. However, the school board also wants to place equal weight on a second factor: the inconvenience and safety problems caused by forcing students to travel by foot or bicycle a substantial distance (more than a mile, and especially more than 1.5 miles). Therefore, they want to choose a plan that provides the best trade-off between these two factors.

(g) Use your results from parts (c), (e), and (f) to summarize the key information related to these two factors that the school board needs to make this decision.
(h) Which decision do you think should be made? Why?

Note: This case will be continued in later chapters (Cases 6.3 and 12.4), so we suggest that you save your analysis, including your basic model.

5

The Theory of the Simplex Method

Chapter 4 introduced the basic mechanics of the simplex method. Now we shall delve a little more deeply into this algorithm by examining some of its underlying theory. The first section further develops the general geometric and algebraic properties that form the foundation of the simplex method. We then describe the *matrix form* of the simplex method (called the *revised simplex method*), which streamlines the procedure considerably for computer implementation. Next we present a fundamental insight about a property of the simplex method that enables us to deduce how changes that are made in the original model get carried along to the final simplex tableau. This insight will provide the key to the important topics of Chap. 6 (duality theory and sensitivity analysis).

5.1 FOUNDATIONS OF THE SIMPLEX METHOD

Section 4.1 introduced *corner-point feasible (CPF) solutions* and the key role they play in the simplex method. These geometric concepts were related to the algebra of the simplex method in Secs. 4.2 and 4.3. However, all this was done in the context of the Wyndor Glass Co. problem, which has only *two decision variables* and so has a straightforward geometric interpretation. How do these concepts generalize to higher dimensions when we deal with larger problems? We address this question in this section.

We begin by introducing some basic terminology for any linear programming problem with n decision variables. While we are doing this, you may find it helpful to refer to Fig. 5.1 (which repeats Fig. 4.1) to interpret these definitions in two dimensions ($n = 2$).

Terminology

It may seem intuitively clear that optimal solutions for any linear programming problem must lie on the boundary of the feasible region, and in fact this is a general property. Because boundary is a geometric concept, our initial definitions clarify how the boundary of the feasible region is identified algebraically.

> The **constraint boundary equation** for any constraint is obtained by replacing its $\leq$, $=$, or $\geq$ sign by an $=$ sign.

Consequently, the form of a constraint boundary equation is $a_{i1}x_1 + a_{i2}x_2 + \cdots + a_{in}x_n = b_i$ for functional constraints and $x_j = 0$ for nonnegativity constraints. Each such

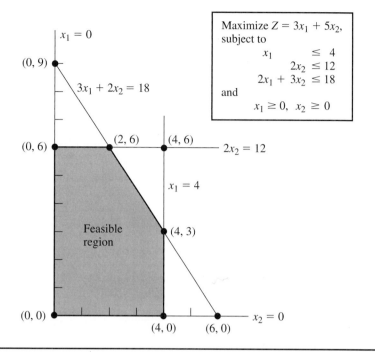

FIGURE 5.1
Constraint boundaries, constraint boundary equations, and corner-point solutions for the Wyndor Glass Co. problem.

equation defines a "flat" geometric shape (called a **hyperplane**) in n-dimensional space, analogous to the line in two-dimensional space and the plane in three-dimensional space. This hyperplane forms the **constraint boundary** for the corresponding constraint. When the constraint has either a $\leq$ or a $\geq$ sign, this *constraint boundary* separates the points that satisfy the constraint (all the points on one side up to and including the constraint boundary) from the points that violate the constraint (all those on the other side of the constraint boundary). When the constraint has an $=$ sign, only the points on the constraint boundary satisfy the constraint.

For example, the Wyndor Glass Co. problem has five constraints (three functional constraints and two nonnegativity constraints), so it has the five *constraint boundary equations* shown in Fig. 5.1. Because $n = 2$, the hyperplanes defined by these constraint boundary equations are simply lines. Therefore, the constraint boundaries for the five constraints are the five lines shown in Fig. 5.1.

> The **boundary** of the feasible region contains just those feasible solutions that satisfy one or more of the constraint boundary equations.

Geometrically, any point on the boundary of the feasible region lies on one or more of the hyperplanes defined by the respective constraint boundary equations. Thus, in Fig. 5.1, the boundary consists of the five darker line segments.

Next, we give a general definition of *CPF solution* in n-dimensional space.

> A **corner-point feasible (CPF) solution** is a feasible solution that does not lie on *any* line segment[1] connecting two *other* feasible solutions.

---

[1] An algebraic expression for a line segment is given in Appendix 2.

As this definition implies, a feasible solution that *does* lie on a line segment connecting two other feasible solutions is *not* a CPF solution. To illustrate when $n = 2$, consider Fig. 5.1. The point $(2, 3)$ is *not* a CPF solution, because it lies on various such line segments, e.g., the line segment connecting $(0, 3)$ and $(4, 3)$. Similarly, $(0, 3)$ is *not* a CPF solution, because it lies on the line segment connecting $(0, 0)$ and $(0, 6)$. However, $(0, 0)$ *is* a CPF solution, because it is impossible to find two *other* feasible solutions that lie on completely opposite sides of $(0, 0)$. (Try it.)

When the number of decision variables n is greater than 2 or 3, this definition for *CPF solution* is not a very convenient one for identifying such solutions. Therefore, it will prove most helpful to interpret these solutions algebraically. For the Wyndor Glass Co. example, each CPF solution in Fig. 5.1 lies at the intersection of two ($n = 2$) constraint lines; i.e., it is the *simultaneous solution* of a system of two constraint boundary equations. This situation is summarized in Table 5.1, where **defining equations** refer to the constraint boundary equations that yield (define) the indicated CPF solution.

> For any linear programming problem with n decision variables, each CPF solution lies at the intersection of n constraint boundaries; i.e., it is the *simultaneous solution* of a system of n constraint boundary equations.

However, this is not to say that *every* set of n constraint boundary equations chosen from the $n + m$ constraints (n nonnegativity and m functional constraints) yields a CPF solution. In particular, the simultaneous solution of such a system of equations might violate one or more of the other m constraints not chosen, in which case it is a corner-point *infeasible* solution. The example has three such solutions, as summarized in Table 5.2. (Check to see why they are infeasible.)

Furthermore, a system of n constraint boundary equations might have no solution at all. This occurs twice in the example, with the pairs of equations (1) $x_1 = 0$ and $x_1 = 4$ and (2) $x_2 = 0$ and $2x_2 = 12$. Such systems are of no interest to us.

The final possibility (which never occurs in the example) is that a system of n constraint boundary equations has multiple solutions because of redundant equations. You need not be concerned with this case either, because the simplex method circumvents its difficulties.

TABLE 5.1 Defining equations for each CPF solution for the Wyndor Glass Co. problem

CPF Solution	Defining Equations
$(0, 0)$	$x_1 = 0$ $x_2 = 0$
$(0, 6)$	$x_1 = 0$ $2x_2 = 12$
$(2, 6)$	$2x_2 = 12$ $3x_1 + 2x_2 = 18$
$(4, 3)$	$3x_1 + 2x_2 = 18$ $x_1 = 4$
$(4, 0)$	$x_1 = 4$ $x_2 = 0$

TABLE 5.2 Defining equations for each corner-point infeasible solution for the Wyndor Glass Co. problem

Corner-Point Infeasible Solution	Defining Equations
(0, 9)	$x_1 = 0$ $3x_1 + 2x_2 = 18$
(4, 6)	$2x_2 = 12$ $x_1 = 4$
(6, 0)	$3x_1 + 2x_2 = 18$ $x_2 = 0$

To summarize for the example, with five constraints and two variables, there are 10 pairs of constraint boundary equations. Five of these pairs became defining equations for CPF solutions (Table 5.1), three became defining equations for corner-point infeasible solutions (Table 5.2), and each of the final two pairs had no solution.

Adjacent CPF Solutions

Section 4.1 introduced adjacent CPF solutions and their role in solving linear programming problems. We now elaborate.

Recall from Chap. 4 that (when we ignore slack, surplus, and artificial variables) each iteration of the simplex method moves from the current CPF solution to an *adjacent* one. What is the *path* followed in this process? What really is meant by *adjacent* CPF solution? First we address these questions from a geometric viewpoint, and then we turn to algebraic interpretations.

These questions are easy to answer when $n = 2$. In this case, the *boundary* of the feasible region consists of several connected *line segments* forming a *polygon,* as shown in Fig. 5.1 by the five darker line segments. These line segments are the *edges* of the feasible region. Emanating from each CPF solution are *two* such edges leading to an adjacent CPF solution at the other end. (Note in Fig. 5.1 how each CPF solution has two adjacent ones.) The path followed in an iteration is to move along one of these edges from one end to the other. In Fig. 5.1, the first iteration involves moving along the edge from (0, 0) to (0, 6), and then the next iteration moves along the edge from (0, 6) to (2, 6). As Table 5.1 illustrates, each of these moves to an adjacent CPF solution involves just one change in the set of defining equations (constraint boundaries on which the solution lies).

When $n = 3$, the answers are slightly more complicated. To help you visualize what is going on, Fig. 5.2 shows a three-dimensional drawing of a typical feasible region when $n = 3$, where the dots are the CPF solutions. This feasible region is a *polyhedron* rather than the polygon we had with $n = 2$ (Fig. 5.1), because the constraint boundaries now are *planes* rather than lines. The faces of the polyhedron form the *boundary* of the feasible region, where each face is the portion of a constraint boundary that satisfies the other constraints as well. Note that each CPF solution lies at the intersection of three constraint boundaries (sometimes including some of the $x_1 = 0$, $x_2 = 0$, and $x_3 = 0$ constraint boundaries for the nonnegativity

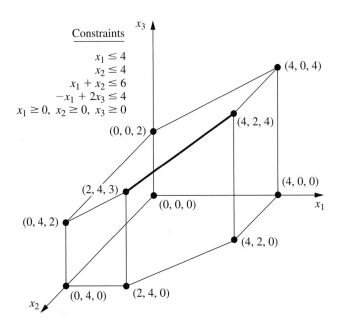

FIGURE 5.2
Feasible region and CPF solutions for a three-variable linear programming problem.

constraints), and the solution also satisfies the other constraints. Such intersections that do not satisfy one or more of the other constraints yield corner-point *infeasible* solutions instead.

The darker line segment in Fig. 5.2 depicts the path of the simplex method on a typical iteration. The point $(2, 4, 3)$ is the *current* CPF solution to begin the iteration, and the point $(4, 2, 4)$ will be the new CPF solution at the end of the iteration. The point $(2, 4, 3)$ lies at the intersection of the $x_2 = 4$, $x_1 + x_2 = 6$, and $-x_1 + 2x_3 = 4$ constraint boundaries, so these three equations are the *defining equations* for this CPF solution. If the $x_2 = 4$ defining equation were removed, the intersection of the other two constraint boundaries (planes) would form a line. One segment of this line, shown as the dark line segment from $(2, 4, 3)$ to $(4, 2, 4)$ in Fig. 5.2, lies on the boundary of the feasible region, whereas the rest of the line is infeasible. This line segment is an edge of the feasible region, and its endpoints $(2, 4, 3)$ and $(4, 2, 4)$ are adjacent CPF solutions.

For $n = 3$, all the *edges* of the feasible region are formed in this way as the feasible segment of the line lying at the intersection of two constraint boundaries, and the two endpoints of an edge are *adjacent* CPF solutions. In Fig. 5.2 there are 15 edges of the feasible region, and so there are 15 pairs of adjacent CPF solutions. For the current CPF solution $(2, 4, 3)$, there are three ways to remove one of its three defining equations to obtain an intersection of the other two constraint boundaries, so there are three edges emanating from $(2, 4, 3)$. These edges lead to $(4, 2, 4)$, $(0, 4, 2)$, and $(2, 4, 0)$, so these are the CPF solutions that are adjacent to $(2, 4, 3)$.

For the next iteration, the simplex method chooses one of these three edges, say, the darker line segment in Fig. 5.2, and then moves along this edge away from $(2, 4, 3)$ until it reaches the first new constraint boundary, $x_1 = 4$, at its other endpoint. [We cannot continue farther along this line to the next constraint boundary, $x_2 = 0$, because this leads to a corner-point infeasible solution—(6, 0, 5).] The intersection of this first new constraint boundary with the two constraint boundaries forming the edge yields the *new* CPF solution (4, 2, 4).

When $n > 3$, these same concepts generalize to higher dimensions, except the constraint boundaries now are *hyperplanes* instead of planes. Let us summarize.

> Consider any linear programming problem with n decision variables and a bounded feasible region. A CPF solution lies at the intersection of n constraint boundaries (and satisfies the other constraints as well). An **edge** of the feasible region is a feasible line segment that lies at the intersection of $n - 1$ constraint boundaries, where each endpoint lies on one additional constraint boundary (so that these endpoints are CPF solutions). Two CPF solutions are **adjacent** if the line segment connecting them is an edge of the feasible region. Emanating from each CPF solution are n such edges, each one leading to one of the n adjacent CPF solutions. Each iteration of the simplex method moves from the current CPF solution to an adjacent one by moving along one of these n edges.

When you shift from a geometric viewpoint to an algebraic one, *intersection of constraint boundaries* changes to *simultaneous solution of constraint boundary equations*. The n constraint boundary equations yielding (defining) a CPF solution are its defining equations, where deleting one of these equations yields a line whose feasible segment is an edge of the feasible region.

We next analyze some key properties of CPF solutions and then describe the implications of all these concepts for interpreting the simplex method. However, while the above summary is fresh in your mind, let us give you a preview of its implications. When the simplex method chooses an entering basic variable, the geometric interpretation is that it is choosing one of the edges emanating from the current CPF solution to move along. Increasing this variable from zero (and simultaneously changing the values of the other basic variables accordingly) corresponds to moving along this edge. Having one of the basic variables (the leaving basic variable) decrease so far that it reaches zero corresponds to reaching the first new constraint boundary at the other end of this edge of the feasible region.

Properties of CPF Solutions

We now focus on three key properties of CPF solutions that hold for *any* linear programming problem that has feasible solutions and a bounded feasible region.

> **Property 1:** (*a*) If there is exactly one optimal solution, then it must be a CPF solution. (*b*) If there are multiple optimal solutions (and a bounded feasible region), then at least two must be adjacent CPF solutions.

Property 1 is a rather intuitive one from a geometric viewpoint. First consider Case (*a*), which is illustrated by the Wyndor Glass Co. problem (see Fig. 5.1) where the one optimal solution (2, 6) is indeed a CPF solution. Note that there is nothing special about this example that led to this result. For any problem having just one optimal solution, it always is possible to keep raising the objective function line (hyperplane) until it just touches one point (the optimal solution) at a corner of the feasible region.

We now give an algebraic proof for this case.

> **Proof of Case (*a*) of Property 1:** We set up a *proof by contradiction* by assuming that there is exactly one optimal solution and that it is *not* a CPF solution.

We then show below that this assumption leads to a contradiction and so cannot be true. (The solution assumed to be optimal will be denoted by $\mathbf{x}^*$, and its objective function value by Z^*.)

Recall the definition of *CPF solution* (a feasible solution that does not lie on any line segment connecting two other feasible solutions). Since we have assumed that the optimal solution $\mathbf{x}^*$ is not a CPF solution, this implies that there must be two other feasible solutions such that the line segment connecting them contains the optimal solution. Let the vectors $\mathbf{x}'$ and $\mathbf{x}''$ denote these two other feasible solutions, and let Z_1 and Z_2 denote their respective objective function values. Like each other point on the line segment connecting $\mathbf{x}'$ and $\mathbf{x}''$,

$$\mathbf{x}^* = \alpha\mathbf{x}'' + (1 - \alpha)\mathbf{x}'$$

for some value of α such that $0 < \alpha < 1$. Thus,

$$Z^* = \alpha Z_2 + (1 - \alpha)Z_1.$$

Since the weights α and $1 - \alpha$ add to 1, the only possibilities for how Z^*, Z_1, and Z_2 compare are (1) $Z^* = Z_1 = Z_2$, (2) $Z_1 < Z^* < Z_2$, and (3) $Z_1 > Z^* > Z_2$. The first possibility implies that $\mathbf{x}'$ and $\mathbf{x}''$ also are optimal, which contradicts the assumption that there is exactly one optimal solution. Both the latter possibilities contradict the assumption that $\mathbf{x}^*$ (not a CPF solution) is optimal. The resulting conclusion is that it is impossible to have a single optimal solution that is not a CPF solution.

Now consider Case (*b*), which was demonstrated in Sec. 3.2 under the definition of *optimal solution* by changing the objective function in the example to $Z = 3x_1 + 2x_2$ (see Fig. 3.5 on page 35). What then happens when you are solving graphically is that the objective function line keeps getting raised until it contains the line segment connecting the two CPF solutions (2, 6) and (4, 3). The same thing would happen in higher dimensions except that an objective function *hyperplane* would keep getting raised until it contained the line segment(s) connecting two (or more) adjacent CPF solutions. As a consequence, *all* optimal solutions can be obtained as weighted averages of optimal CPF solutions. (This situation is described further in Probs. 4.5-5 and 4.5-6.)

The real significance of Property 1 is that it greatly simplifies the search for an optimal solution because now only CPF solutions need to be considered. The magnitude of this simplification is emphasized in Property 2.

Property 2: There are only a *finite* number of CPF solutions.

This property certainly holds in Figs. 5.1 and 5.2, where there are just 5 and 10 CPF solutions, respectively. To see why the number is finite in general, recall that each CPF solution is the simultaneous solution of a system of n out of the $m + n$ constraint boundary equations. The number of different combinations of $m + n$ equations taken n at a time is

$$\binom{m + n}{n} = \frac{(m + n)!}{m!n!},$$

which is a finite number. This number, in turn, in an *upper bound* on the number of CPF solutions. In Fig. 5.1, $m = 3$ and $n = 2$, so there are 10 different systems of two equations, but only half of them yield CPF solutions. In Fig. 5.2, $m = 4$ and $n = 3$, which gives 35 different systems of three equations, but only 10 yield CPF solutions.

Property 2 suggests that, in principle, an optimal solution can be obtained by exhaustive enumeration; i.e., find and compare all the finite number of CPF solutions. Unfortunately, there are finite numbers, and then there are finite numbers that (for all practical purposes) might as well be infinite. For example, a rather small linear programming problem with only $m = 50$ and $n = 50$ would have $100!/(50!)^2 \approx 10^{29}$ systems of equations to be solved! By contrast, the simplex method would need to examine only approximately 100 CPF solutions for a problem of this size. This tremendous savings can be obtained because of the optimality test given in Sec. 4.1 and restated here as Property 3.

> **Property 3:** If a CPF solution has no *adjacent* CPF solutions that are *better* (as measured by Z), then there are no *better* CPF solutions anywhere. Therefore, such a CPF solution is guaranteed to be an *optimal* solution (by Property 1), assuming only that the problem possesses at least one optimal solution (guaranteed if the problem possesses feasible solutions and a bounded feasible region).

To illustrate Property 3, consider Fig. 5.1 for the Wyndor Glass Co. example. For the CPF solution (2, 6), its adjacent CPF solutions are (0, 6) and (4, 3), and neither has a better value of Z than (2, 6) does. This outcome implies that none of the other CPF solutions—(0, 0) and (4, 0)—can be better than (2, 6), so (2, 6) must be optimal.

By contrast, Fig. 5.3 shows a feasible region that can *never* occur for a linear programming problem but that does violate Property 3. The problem shown is identical to the Wyndor Glass Co. example (including the same objective function) *except* for the en-

FIGURE 5.3
Modification of the Wyndor Glass Co. problem that violates both linear programming and Property 3 for CPF solutions in linear programming.

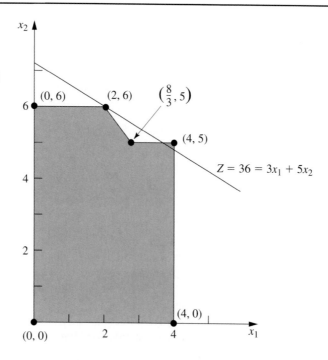

largement of the feasible region to the right of $(\frac{8}{3}, 5)$. Consequently, the adjacent CPF so-lutions for (2, 6) now are (0, 6) and $(\frac{8}{3}, 5)$, and again neither is better than (2, 6). How-ever, another CPF solution (4, 5) now is better than (2, 6), thereby violating Property 3. The reason is that the boundary of the feasible region goes down from (2, 6) to $(\frac{8}{3}, 5)$ and then "bends outward" to (4, 5), beyond the objective function line passing through (2, 6).

The key point is that the kind of situation illustrated in Fig. 5.3 can never occur in linear programming. The feasible region in Fig. 5.3 implies that the $2x_2 \leq 12$ and $3x_1 + 2x_2 \leq 18$ constraints apply for $0 \leq x_1 \leq \frac{8}{3}$. However, under the condition that $\frac{8}{3} \leq x_1 \leq 4$, the $3x_1 + 2x_2 \leq 18$ constraint is dropped and replaced by $x_2 \leq 5$. Such "conditional con-straints" just are not allowed in linear programming.

The basic reason that Property 3 holds for any linear programming problem is that the feasible region always has the property of being a *convex set,* as defined in Appendix 2 and illustrated in several figures there. For two-variable linear programming problems, this convex property means that the *angle* inside the feasible region at *every* CPF solu-tion is less than 180°. This property is illustrated in Fig. 5.1, where the angles at (0, 0), (0, 6), and (4, 0) are 90° and those at (2, 6) and (4, 3) are between 90° and 180°. By con-trast, the feasible region in Fig. 5.3 is *not* a convex set, because the angle at $(\frac{8}{3}, 5)$ is more than 180°. This is the kind of "bending outward" at an angle greater than 180° that can never occur in linear programming. In higher dimensions, the same intuitive notion of "never bending outward" continues to apply.

To clarify the significance of a convex feasible region, consider the objective func-tion hyperplane that passes through a CPF solution that has no adjacent CPF solutions that are better. [In the original Wyndor Glass Co. example, this hyperplane is the objec-tive function line passing through (2, 6).] All these adjacent solutions [(0, 6) and (4, 3) in the example] must lie either on the hyperplane or on the unfavorable side (as measured by Z) of the hyperplane. The feasible region being convex means that its boundary can-not "bend outward" beyond an adjacent CPF solution to give another CPF solution that lies on the favorable side of the hyperplane. So Property 3 holds.

Extensions to the Augmented Form of the Problem

For any linear programming problem in our standard form (including functional constraints in ≤ form), the appearance of the functional constraints after slack variables are intro-duced is as follows:

(1) $a_{11}x_1 + a_{12}x_2 + \cdots + a_{1n}x_n + x_{n+1} \qquad\qquad = b_1$
(2) $a_{21}x_1 + a_{22}x_2 + \cdots + a_{2n}x_n \qquad + x_{n+2} \qquad = b_2$

(m) $a_{m1}x_1 + a_{m2}x_2 + \cdots + a_{mn}x_n \qquad\qquad + x_{n+m} = b_m,$

where $x_{n+1}, x_{n+2}, \ldots, x_{n+m}$ are the slack variables. For other linear programming prob-lems, Sec. 4.6 described how essentially this same appearance (proper form from Gauss-ian elimination) can be obtained by introducing artificial variables, etc. Thus, the origi-nal solutions $(x_1, x_2, \ldots, x_n)$ now are augmented by the corresponding values of the slack or artificial variables $(x_{n+1}, x_{n+2}, \ldots, x_{n+m})$ and perhaps some surplus variables as well. This augmentation led in Sec. 4.2 to defining **basic solutions** as *augmented cor-ner-point solutions* and **basic feasible solutions (BF solutions)** as *augmented CPF so-*

lutions. Consequently, the preceding three properties of CPF solutions also hold for BF solutions.

Now let us clarify the algebraic relationships between basic solutions and corner-point solutions. Recall that each corner-point solution is the simultaneous solution of a system of n constraint boundary equations, which we called its *defining equations*. The key question is: How do we tell whether a particular constraint boundary equation is one of the defining equations when the problem is in augmented form? The answer, fortunately, is a simple one. Each constraint has an **indicating variable** that completely indicates (by whether its value is zero) whether that constraint's boundary equation is satisfied by the current solution. A summary appears in Table 5.3. For the type of constraint in each row of the table, note that the corresponding constraint boundary equation (fourth column) is satisfied if and only if this constraint's indicating variable (fifth column) equals zero. In the last row (functional constraint in $\geq$ form), the indicating variable $\bar{x}_{n+i} - x_{s_i}$ actually is the difference between the artificial variable $\bar{x}_{n+i}$ and the surplus variable x_{s_i}.

Thus, whenever a constraint boundary equation is one of the defining equations for a corner-point solution, its indicating variable has a value of zero in the augmented form of the problem. Each such indicating variable is called a *nonbasic variable* for the corresponding basic solution. The resulting conclusions and terminology (already introduced in Sec. 4.2) are summarized next.

Each **basic solution** has m **basic variables,** and the rest of the variables are **nonbasic variables** set equal to zero. (The number of nonbasic variables equals n plus the number of surplus variables.) The values of the **basic variables** are given by the simultaneous solution of the system of m equations for the problem in augmented form (after the nonbasic variables are set to zero). This basic solution is the augmented corner-point solution whose n defining equations are those indicated by the nonbasic variables. In particular, whenever an indicating variable in the fifth column of Table 5.3 is a nonbasic variable, the constraint boundary equation in the fourth column is a defining equation for the corner-point solution. (For functional constraints in $\geq$ form, at least one of the two supplementary variables $\bar{x}_{n+i}$ and x_{s_i} always is a nonbasic variable, but the constraint boundary equation becomes a defining equation only if *both* of these variables are nonbasic variables.)

TABLE 5.3 Indicating variables for constraint boundary equations*

Type of Constraint	Form of Constraint	Constraint in Augmented Form	Constraint Boundary Equation	Indicating Variable
Nonnegativity	$x_j \geq 0$	$x_j \geq 0$	$x_j = 0$	x_j
Functional ($\leq$)	$\sum_{j=1}^{n} a_{ij}x_j \leq b_i$	$\sum_{j=1}^{n} a_{ij}x_j + x_{n+i} = b_i$	$\sum_{j=1}^{n} a_{ij}x_j = b_i$	x_{n+i}
Functional ($=$)	$\sum_{j=1}^{n} a_{ij}x_j = b_i$	$\sum_{j=1}^{n} a_{ij}x_j + \bar{x}_{n+i} = b_i$	$\sum_{j=1}^{n} a_{ij}x_j = b_i$	$\bar{x}_{n+i}$
Functional ($\geq$)	$\sum_{j=1}^{n} a_{ij}x_j \geq b_i$	$\sum_{j=1}^{n} a_{ij}x_j + \bar{x}_{n+i} - x_{s_i} = b_i$	$\sum_{j=1}^{n} a_{ij}x_j = b_i$	$\bar{x}_{n+i} - x_{s_i}$

*Indicating variable $= 0 \Rightarrow$ constraint boundary equation satisfied;
indicating variable $\neq 0 \Rightarrow$ constraint boundary equation violated.

Now consider the basic *feasible* solutions. Note that the only requirements for a solution to be feasible in the augmented form of the problem are that it satisfy the system of equations and that *all* the variables be *nonnegative.*

A **BF solution** is a basic solution where all m basic variables are nonnegative (≥ 0). A BF solution is said to be **degenerate** if any of these m variables equals zero.

Thus, it is possible for a variable to be zero and still not be a nonbasic variable for the current BF solution. (This case corresponds to a CPF solution that satisfies another constraint boundary equation in addition to its n defining equations.) Therefore, it is necessary to keep track of which is the current set of nonbasic variables (or the current set of basic variables) rather than to rely upon their zero values.

We noted earlier that not every system of n constraint boundary equations yields a corner-point solution, because either the system has no solution or it has multiple solutions. For analogous reasons, not every set of n nonbasic variables yields a basic solution. However, these cases are avoided by the simplex method.

To illustrate these definitions, consider the Wyndor Glass Co. example once more. Its constraint boundary equations and indicating variables are shown in Table 5.4.

Augmenting each of the CPF solutions (see Table 5.1) yields the BF solutions listed in Table 5.5. This table places adjacent BF solutions next to each other, except for the pair consisting of the first and last solutions listed. Notice that in each case the nonbasic variables necessarily are the indicating variables for the defining equations. Thus, adjacent BF solutions differ by having just one different nonbasic variable. Also notice that each BF solution is the simultaneous solution of the system of equations for the problem in augmented form (see Table 5.4) when the nonbasic variables are set equal to zero.

Similarly, the three corner-point *infeasible* solutions (see Table 5.2) yield the three basic *infeasible* solutions shown in Table 5.6.

The other two sets of nonbasic variables, (1) x_1 and x_3 and (2) x_2 and x_4, do not yield a basic solution, because setting either pair of variables equal to zero leads to having no solution for the system of Eqs. (1) to (3) given in Table 5.4. This conclusion parallels the observation we made early in this section that the corresponding sets of constraint boundary equations do not yield a solution.

TABLE 5.4 Indicating variables for the constraint boundary equations of the Wyndor Glass Co. problem*

Constraint	Constraint in Augmented Form	Constraint Boundary Equation	Indicating Variable
$x_1 \geq 0$	$x_1 \geq 0$	$x_1 = 0$	x_1
$x_2 \geq 0$	$x_2 \geq 0$	$x_2 = 0$	x_2
$x_1 \leq 4$	(1) $x_1 + x_3 = 4$	$x_1 = 4$	x_3
$2x_2 \leq 12$	(2) $2x_2 + x_4 = 12$	$2x_2 = 12$	x_4
$3x_1 + x_2 \leq 18$	(3) $3x_1 + 2x_2 + x_5 = 18$	$3x_1 + 2x_2 = 18$	x_5

*Indicating variable $= 0 \Rightarrow$ constraint boundary equation satisfied; indicating variable $\neq 0 \Rightarrow$ constraint boundary equation violated.

TABLE 5.5 BF solutions for the Wyndor Glass Co. problem

CPF Solution	Defining Equations	BF Solution	Nonbasic Variables
(0, 0)	$x_1 = 0$ $x_2 = 0$	(0, 0, 4, 12, 18)	x_1 x_2
(0, 6)	$x_1 = 0$ $2x_2 = 12$	(0, 6, 4, 0, 6)	x_1 x_4
(2, 6)	$2x_2 = 12$ $3x_1 + 2x_2 = 18$	(2, 6, 2, 0, 0)	x_4 x_5
(4, 3)	$3x_1 + 2x_2 = 18$ $x_1 = 4$	(4, 3, 0, 6, 0)	x_5 x_3
(4, 0)	$x_1 = 4$ $x_2 = 0$	(4, 0, 0, 12, 6)	x_3 x_2

The *simplex method* starts at a BF solution and then iteratively moves to a better adjacent BF solution until an optimal solution is reached. At each iteration, how is the adjacent BF solution reached?

For the original form of the problem, recall that an adjacent CPF solution is reached from the current one by (1) deleting one constraint boundary (defining equation) from the set of n constraint boundaries defining the current solution, (2) moving away from the current solution in the feasible direction along the intersection of the remaining $n - 1$ constraint boundaries (an edge of the feasible region), and (3) stopping when the *first* new constraint boundary (defining equation) is reached.

Equivalently, in our new terminology, the simplex method reaches an adjacent BF solution from the current one by (1) deleting one variable (the entering basic variable) from the set of n nonbasic variables defining the current solution, (2) moving away from the current solution by *increasing* this one variable from zero (and adjusting the other basic variables to still satisfy the system of equations) while keeping the remaining $n - 1$ nonbasic variables at zero, and (3) stopping when the *first* of the basic variables (the leaving basic variable) reaches a value of zero (its constraint boundary). With either interpretation, the choice among the n alternatives in step 1 is made by selecting the one that would give the best rate of improvement in Z (per unit increase in the entering basic variable) during step 2.

TABLE 5.6 Basic infeasible solutions for the Wyndor Glass Co. problem

Corner-Point Infeasible Solution	Defining Equations	Basic Infeasible Solution	Nonbasic Variables
(0, 9)	$x_1 = 0$ $3x_1 + 2x_2 = 18$	(0, 9, 4, −6, 0)	x_1 x_5
(4, 6)	$2x_2 = 12$ $x_1 = 4$	(4, 6, 0, 0, −6)	x_4 x_3
(6, 0)	$3x_1 + 2x_2 = 18$ $x_2 = 0$	(6, 0, −2, 12, 0)	x_5 x_2

TABLE 5.7 Sequence of solutions obtained by the simplex method for the Wyndor Glass Co. problem

Iteration	CPF Solution	Defining Equations	BF Solution	Nonbasic Variables	Functional Constraints in Augmented Form
0	(0, 0)	$x_1 = 0$ $x_2 = 0$	(0, 0, 4, 12, 18)	$x_1 = 0$ $x_2 = 0$	$x_1 \qquad\quad + \mathbf{x}_3 = 4$ $\quad 2x_2 + \mathbf{x}_4 = 12$ $3x_1 + 2x_2 + \mathbf{x}_5 = 18$
1	(0, 6)	$x_1 = 0$ $2x_2 = 12$	(0, 6, 4, 0, 6)	$x_1 = 0$ $x_4 = 0$	$x_1 \qquad\quad + \mathbf{x}_3 = 4$ $\quad 2\mathbf{x}_2 + x_4 = 12$ $3x_1 + 2\mathbf{x}_2 + \mathbf{x}_5 = 18$
2	(2, 6)	$2x_2 = 12$ $3x_1 + 2x_2 = 18$	(2, 6, 2, 0, 0)	$x_4 = 0$ $x_5 = 0$	$\mathbf{x}_1 \qquad\quad + \mathbf{x}_3 = 4$ $\quad 2\mathbf{x}_2 + x_4 = 12$ $3\mathbf{x}_1 + 2\mathbf{x}_2 + x_5 = 18$

Table 5.7 illustrates the close correspondence between these geometric and algebraic interpretations of the simplex method. Using the results already presented in Secs. 4.3 and 4.4, the fourth column summarizes the sequence of BF solutions found for the Wyndor Glass Co. problem, and the second column shows the corresponding CPF solutions. In the third column, note how each iteration results in deleting one constraint boundary (defining equation) and substituting a new one to obtain the new CPF solution. Similarly, note in the fifth column how each iteration results in deleting one nonbasic variable and substituting a new one to obtain the new BF solution. Furthermore, the nonbasic variables being deleted and added are the indicating variables for the defining equations being deleted and added in the third column. The last column displays the initial system of equations [excluding Eq. (0)] for the augmented form of the problem, with the current basic variables shown in bold type. In each case, note how setting the nonbasic variables equal to zero and then solving this system of equations for the basic variables must yield the same solution for (x_1, x_2) as the corresponding pair of defining equations in the third column.

5.2 THE REVISED SIMPLEX METHOD

The simplex method as described in Chap. 4 (hereafter called the *original simplex method*) is a straightforward algebraic procedure. However, this way of executing the algorithm (in either algebraic or tabular form) is not the most efficient computational procedure for computers because it computes and stores many numbers that are not needed at the current iteration and that may not even become relevant for decision making at subsequent iterations. The only pieces of information relevant at each iteration are the coefficients of the nonbasic variables in Eq. (0), the coefficients of the entering basic variable in the other equations, and the right-hand sides of the equations. It would be very useful to have a procedure that could obtain this information efficiently without computing and storing all the other coefficients.

As mentioned in Sec. 4.8, these considerations motivated the development of the *revised simplex method*. This method was designed to accomplish exactly the same things as the original simplex method, but in a way that is more efficient for execution on a computer. Thus, it is a streamlined version of the original procedure. It computes and stores only the information that is currently needed, and it carries along the essential data in a more compact form.

The revised simplex method explicitly uses *matrix* manipulations, so it is necessary to describe the problem in matrix notation. (See Appendix 4 for a review of matrices.) To help you distinguish between matrices, vectors, and scalars, we consistently use **BOLD-FACE CAPITAL** letters to represent matrices, **boldface lowercase** letters to represent vectors, and *italicized* letters in ordinary print to represent scalars. We also use a boldface zero (**0**) to denote a *null vector* (a vector whose elements all are zero) in either column or row form (which one should be clear from the context), whereas a zero in ordinary print (0) continues to represent the number zero.

Using matrices, our standard form for the general linear programming model given in Sec. 3.2 becomes

$$
\begin{array}{ll}
\text{Maximize} & Z = \mathbf{cx}, \\
\text{subject to} \\
\mathbf{Ax} \le \mathbf{b} & \text{and} \quad \mathbf{x} \ge \mathbf{0},
\end{array}
$$

where **c** is the row vector

$$\mathbf{c} = [c_1, c_2, \ldots, c_n],$$

x, **b**, and **0** are the column vectors such that

$$
\mathbf{x} = \begin{bmatrix} x_1 \\ x_2 \\ \vdots \\ x_n \end{bmatrix}, \qquad
\mathbf{b} = \begin{bmatrix} b_1 \\ b_2 \\ \vdots \\ b_m \end{bmatrix}, \qquad
\mathbf{0} = \begin{bmatrix} 0 \\ 0 \\ \vdots \\ 0 \end{bmatrix},
$$

and **A** is the matrix

$$
\mathbf{A} = \begin{bmatrix}
a_{11} & a_{12} & \ldots & a_{1n} \\
a_{21} & a_{22} & \ldots & a_{2n} \\
\multicolumn{4}{c}{\dotfill} \\
a_{m1} & a_{m2} & \ldots & a_{mn}
\end{bmatrix}.
$$

To obtain the *augmented form* of the problem, introduce the column vector of slack variables

$$
\mathbf{x}_s = \begin{bmatrix} x_{n+1} \\ x_{n+2} \\ \vdots \\ x_{n+m} \end{bmatrix}
$$

so that the constraints become

$$
[\mathbf{A}, \mathbf{I}] \begin{bmatrix} \mathbf{x} \\ \mathbf{x}_s \end{bmatrix} = \mathbf{b}
\qquad \text{and} \qquad
\begin{bmatrix} \mathbf{x} \\ \mathbf{x}_s \end{bmatrix} \ge \mathbf{0},
$$

where $\mathbf{I}$ is the $m \times m$ identity matrix, and the null vector $\mathbf{0}$ now has $n + m$ elements. (We comment at the end of the section about how to deal with problems that are not in our standard form.)

Solving for a Basic Feasible Solution

Recall that the general approach of the simplex method is to obtain a sequence of *improving BF solutions* until an optimal solution is reached. One of the key features of the revised simplex method involves the way in which it solves for each new BF solution after identifying its basic and nonbasic variables. Given these variables, the resulting basic solution is the solution of the m equations

$$[\mathbf{A}, \mathbf{I}] \begin{bmatrix} \mathbf{x} \\ \mathbf{x}_s \end{bmatrix} = \mathbf{b},$$

in which the n *nonbasic variables* from the $n + m$ elements of

$$\begin{bmatrix} \mathbf{x} \\ \mathbf{x}_s \end{bmatrix}$$

are set equal to zero. Eliminating these n variables by equating them to zero leaves a set of m equations in m unknowns (the *basic variables*). This set of equations can be denoted by

$$\mathbf{B}\mathbf{x}_B = \mathbf{b},$$

where the **vector of basic variables**

$$\mathbf{x}_B = \begin{bmatrix} x_{B1} \\ x_{B2} \\ \vdots \\ x_{Bm} \end{bmatrix}$$

is obtained by eliminating the nonbasic variables from

$$\begin{bmatrix} \mathbf{x} \\ \mathbf{x}_s \end{bmatrix},$$

and the **basis matrix**

$$\mathbf{B} = \begin{bmatrix} B_{11} & B_{12} & \ldots & B_{1m} \\ B_{21} & B_{22} & \ldots & B_{2m} \\ \multicolumn{4}{c}{\ldots\ldots\ldots\ldots\ldots\ldots\ldots\ldots} \\ B_{m1} & B_{m2} & \ldots & B_{mm} \end{bmatrix}$$

is obtained by eliminating the columns corresponding to coefficients of nonbasic variables from $[\mathbf{A}, \mathbf{I}]$. (In addition, the elements of $\mathbf{x}_B$ and, therefore, the columns of $\mathbf{B}$ may be placed in a different order when the simplex method is executed.)

The simplex method introduces only basic variables such that $\mathbf{B}$ is *nonsingular*, so that $\mathbf{B}^{-1}$ always will exist. Therefore, to solve $\mathbf{B}\mathbf{x}_B = \mathbf{b}$, both sides are premultiplied by $\mathbf{B}^{-1}$:

$$\mathbf{B}^{-1}\mathbf{B}\mathbf{x}_B = \mathbf{B}^{-1}\mathbf{b}.$$

Since $\mathbf{B}^{-1}\mathbf{B} = \mathbf{I}$, the desired solution for the basic variables is

$$\mathbf{x}_B = \mathbf{B}^{-1}\mathbf{b}.$$

Let $\mathbf{c}_B$ be the vector whose elements are the objective function coefficients (including zeros for slack variables) for the corresponding elements of $\mathbf{x}_B$. The value of the objective function for this basic solution is then

$$Z = \mathbf{c}_B\mathbf{x}_B = \mathbf{c}_B\mathbf{B}^{-1}\mathbf{b}.$$

Example. To illustrate this method of solving for a BF solution, consider again the Wyndor Glass Co. problem presented in Sec. 3.1 and solved by the original simplex method in Table 4.8. In this case,

$$\mathbf{c} = [3, 5], \quad [\mathbf{A}, \mathbf{I}] = \begin{bmatrix} 1 & 0 & 1 & 0 & 0 \\ 0 & 2 & 0 & 1 & 0 \\ 3 & 2 & 0 & 0 & 1 \end{bmatrix}, \quad \mathbf{b} = \begin{bmatrix} 4 \\ 12 \\ 18 \end{bmatrix}, \quad \mathbf{x} = \begin{bmatrix} x_1 \\ x_2 \end{bmatrix}, \quad \mathbf{x}_s = \begin{bmatrix} x_3 \\ x_4 \\ x_5 \end{bmatrix}.$$

Referring to Table 4.8, we see that the sequence of BF solutions obtained by the simplex method (original or revised) is the following:

Iteration 0

$$\mathbf{x}_B = \begin{bmatrix} x_3 \\ x_4 \\ x_5 \end{bmatrix}, \quad \mathbf{B} = \begin{bmatrix} 1 & 0 & 0 \\ 0 & 1 & 0 \\ 0 & 0 & 1 \end{bmatrix} = \mathbf{B}^{-1}, \quad \text{so} \quad \begin{bmatrix} x_3 \\ x_4 \\ x_5 \end{bmatrix} = \begin{bmatrix} 1 & 0 & 0 \\ 0 & 1 & 0 \\ 0 & 0 & 1 \end{bmatrix}\begin{bmatrix} 4 \\ 12 \\ 18 \end{bmatrix} = \begin{bmatrix} 4 \\ 12 \\ 18 \end{bmatrix},$$

$$\mathbf{c}_B = [0, 0, 0], \quad \text{so} \quad Z = [0, 0, 0]\begin{bmatrix} 4 \\ 12 \\ 18 \end{bmatrix} = 0.$$

Iteration 1

$$\mathbf{x}_B = \begin{bmatrix} x_3 \\ x_2 \\ x_5 \end{bmatrix}, \quad \mathbf{B} = \begin{bmatrix} 1 & 0 & 0 \\ 0 & 2 & 0 \\ 0 & 2 & 1 \end{bmatrix}, \quad \mathbf{B}^{-1} = \begin{bmatrix} 1 & 0 & 0 \\ 0 & \frac{1}{2} & 0 \\ 0 & -1 & 1 \end{bmatrix},$$

so

$$\begin{bmatrix} x_3 \\ x_2 \\ x_5 \end{bmatrix} = \begin{bmatrix} 1 & 0 & 0 \\ 0 & \frac{1}{2} & 0 \\ 0 & -1 & 1 \end{bmatrix}\begin{bmatrix} 4 \\ 12 \\ 18 \end{bmatrix} = \begin{bmatrix} 4 \\ 6 \\ 6 \end{bmatrix},$$

$$\mathbf{c}_B = [0, 5, 0], \quad \text{so} \quad Z = [0, 5, 0]\begin{bmatrix} 4 \\ 6 \\ 6 \end{bmatrix} = 30.$$

Iteration 2

$$\mathbf{x}_B = \begin{bmatrix} x_3 \\ x_2 \\ x_1 \end{bmatrix}, \qquad \mathbf{B} = \begin{bmatrix} 1 & 0 & 1 \\ 0 & 2 & 0 \\ 0 & 2 & 3 \end{bmatrix}, \qquad \mathbf{B}^{-1} = \begin{bmatrix} 1 & \frac{1}{3} & -\frac{1}{3} \\ 0 & \frac{1}{2} & 0 \\ 0 & -\frac{1}{3} & \frac{1}{3} \end{bmatrix},$$

so

$$\begin{bmatrix} x_3 \\ x_2 \\ x_1 \end{bmatrix} = \begin{bmatrix} 1 & \frac{1}{3} & -\frac{1}{3} \\ 0 & \frac{1}{2} & 0 \\ 0 & -\frac{1}{3} & \frac{1}{3} \end{bmatrix} \begin{bmatrix} 4 \\ 12 \\ 18 \end{bmatrix} = \begin{bmatrix} 2 \\ 6 \\ 2 \end{bmatrix},$$

$$\mathbf{c}_B = [0, 5, 3], \qquad \text{so} \qquad Z = [0, 5, 3] \begin{bmatrix} 2 \\ 6 \\ 2 \end{bmatrix} = 36.$$

Matrix Form of the Current Set of Equations

The last preliminary before we summarize the revised simplex method is to show the matrix form of the set of equations appearing in the simplex tableau for any iteration of the original simplex method.

For the *original* set of equations, the matrix form is

$$\begin{bmatrix} 1 & -\mathbf{c} & \mathbf{0} \\ 0 & \mathbf{A} & \mathbf{I} \end{bmatrix} \begin{bmatrix} Z \\ \mathbf{x} \\ \mathbf{x}_s \end{bmatrix} = \begin{bmatrix} 0 \\ \mathbf{b} \end{bmatrix}.$$

This set of equations also is exhibited in the first simplex tableau of Table 5.8.

The algebraic operations performed by the simplex method (multiply an equation by a constant and add a multiple of one equation to another equation) are expressed in ma-

TABLE 5.8 Initial and later simplex tableaux in matrix form

Iteration	Basic Variable	Eq.	Z	Original Variables	Slack Variables	Right Side
0	Z	(0)	1	$-\mathbf{c}$	$\mathbf{0}$	0
	$\mathbf{x}_B$	$(1, 2, \ldots, m)$	0	$\mathbf{A}$	$\mathbf{I}$	$\mathbf{b}$
Any	Z	(0)	1	$\mathbf{c}_B \mathbf{B}^{-1} \mathbf{A} - \mathbf{c}$	$\mathbf{c}_B \mathbf{B}^{-1}$	$\mathbf{c}_B \mathbf{B}^{-1} \mathbf{b}$
	$\mathbf{x}_B$	$(1, 2, \ldots m)$	0	$\mathbf{B}^{-1} \mathbf{A}$	$\mathbf{B}^{-1}$	$\mathbf{B}^{-1} \mathbf{b}$

The "Coefficient of:" spans the Z, Original Variables, and Slack Variables columns.

trix form by premultiplying both sides of the original set of equations by the appropriate matrix. This matrix would have the same elements as the identity matrix, *except* that each multiple for an algebraic operation would go into the spot needed to have the matrix multiplication perform this operation. Even after a series of algebraic operations over several iterations, we still can deduce what this matrix must be (symbolically) for the entire series by using what we already know about the right-hand sides of the new set of equations. In particular, after any iteration, $\mathbf{x}_B = \mathbf{B}^{-1}\mathbf{b}$ and $Z = \mathbf{c}_B\mathbf{B}^{-1}\mathbf{b}$, so the right-hand sides of the new set of equations have become

$$\begin{bmatrix} Z \\ \mathbf{x}_B \end{bmatrix} = \begin{bmatrix} 1 & \mathbf{c}_B\mathbf{B}^{-1} \\ \mathbf{0} & \mathbf{B}^{-1} \end{bmatrix} \begin{bmatrix} 0 \\ \mathbf{b} \end{bmatrix} = \begin{bmatrix} \mathbf{c}_B\mathbf{B}^{-1}\mathbf{b} \\ \mathbf{B}^{-1}\mathbf{b} \end{bmatrix}.$$

Because we perform the same series of algebraic operations on *both* sides of the original set of operations, we use this same matrix that premultiplies the original right-hand side to premultiply the original left-hand side. Consequently, since

$$\begin{bmatrix} 1 & \mathbf{c}_B\mathbf{B}^{-1} \\ \mathbf{0} & \mathbf{B}^{-1} \end{bmatrix} \begin{bmatrix} 1 & -\mathbf{c} & \mathbf{0} \\ \mathbf{0} & \mathbf{A} & \mathbf{I} \end{bmatrix} = \begin{bmatrix} 1 & \mathbf{c}_B\mathbf{B}^{-1}\mathbf{A} - \mathbf{c} & \mathbf{c}_B\mathbf{B}^{-1} \\ \mathbf{0} & \mathbf{B}^{-1}\mathbf{A} & \mathbf{B}^{-1} \end{bmatrix},$$

the desired matrix form of the *set of equations after any iteration* is

$$\begin{bmatrix} 1 & \mathbf{c}_B\mathbf{B}^{-1}\mathbf{A} - \mathbf{c} & \mathbf{c}_B\mathbf{B}^{-1} \\ \mathbf{0} & \mathbf{B}^{-1}\mathbf{A} & \mathbf{B}^{-1} \end{bmatrix} \begin{bmatrix} Z \\ \mathbf{x} \\ \mathbf{x}_s \end{bmatrix} = \begin{bmatrix} \mathbf{c}_B\mathbf{B}^{-1}\mathbf{b} \\ \mathbf{B}^{-1}\mathbf{b} \end{bmatrix}.$$

The second simplex tableau of Table 5.8 also exhibits this same set of equations.

Example.   To illustrate this matrix form for the current set of equations, we will show how it yields the final set of equations resulting from iteration 2 for the Wyndor Glass Co. problem. Using the $\mathbf{B}^{-1}$ and $\mathbf{c}_B$ given for iteration 2 at the end of the preceding subsection, we have

$$\mathbf{B}^{-1}\mathbf{A} = \begin{bmatrix} 1 & \frac{1}{3} & -\frac{1}{3} \\ 0 & \frac{1}{2} & 0 \\ 0 & -\frac{1}{3} & \frac{1}{3} \end{bmatrix} \begin{bmatrix} 1 & 0 \\ 0 & 2 \\ 3 & 2 \end{bmatrix} = \begin{bmatrix} 0 & 0 \\ 0 & 1 \\ 1 & 0 \end{bmatrix},$$

$$\mathbf{c}_B\mathbf{B}^{-1} = [0, 5, 3] \begin{bmatrix} 1 & \frac{1}{3} & -\frac{1}{3} \\ 0 & \frac{1}{2} & 0 \\ 0 & -\frac{1}{3} & \frac{1}{3} \end{bmatrix} = [0, \tfrac{3}{2}, 1],$$

$$\mathbf{c}_B\mathbf{B}^{-1}\mathbf{A} - \mathbf{c} = [0, 5, 3] \begin{bmatrix} 0 & 0 \\ 0 & 1 \\ 1 & 0 \end{bmatrix} - [3, 5] = [0, 0].$$

Also, by using the values of $\mathbf{x}_B = \mathbf{B}^{-1}\mathbf{b}$ and $Z = \mathbf{c}_B\mathbf{B}^{-1}\mathbf{b}$ calculated at the end of the preceding subsection, these results give the following set of equations:

$$
\begin{bmatrix}
1 & 0 & 0 & 0 & \frac{3}{2} & 1 \\
0 & 0 & 0 & 1 & \frac{1}{3} & -\frac{1}{3} \\
0 & 0 & 1 & 0 & \frac{1}{2} & 0 \\
0 & 1 & 0 & 0 & -\frac{1}{3} & \frac{1}{3}
\end{bmatrix}
\begin{bmatrix}
Z \\ x_1 \\ x_2 \\ x_3 \\ x_4 \\ x_5
\end{bmatrix}
=
\begin{bmatrix}
36 \\ 2 \\ 6 \\ 2
\end{bmatrix},
$$

as shown in the final simplex tableau in Table 4.8.

The Overall Procedure

There are two key implications from the matrix form of the current set of equations shown at the bottom of Table 5.8. The first is that *only* $\mathbf{B}^{-1}$ needs to be derived to be able to calculate all the numbers in the simplex tableau from the original parameters ($\mathbf{A}$, $\mathbf{b}$, $\mathbf{c}_B$) of the problem. (This implication is the essence of the **fundamental insight** described in the next section.) The second is that *any one* of these numbers can be obtained *individually,* usually by performing *only* a vector multiplication (one row times one column) instead of a complete matrix multiplication. Therefore, the *required numbers* to perform an iteration of the simplex method can be obtained as needed *without* expending the computational effort to obtain *all* the numbers. These two key implications are incorporated into the following summary of the overall procedure.

Summary of the Revised Simplex Method.

1. *Initialization:* Same as for the original simplex method.
2. *Iteration:*
       Step 1   Determine the entering basic variable: Same as for the original simplex method.
       Step 2   Determine the leaving basic variable: Same as for the original simplex method, except calculate only the numbers required to do this [the coefficients of the entering basic variable in every equation but Eq. (0), and then, for each strictly positive coefficient, the right-hand side of that equation].[1]
       Step 3   Determine the new BF solution: Derive $\mathbf{B}^{-1}$ and set $\mathbf{x}_B = \mathbf{B}^{-1}\mathbf{b}$.
3. *Optimality test:* Same as for the original simplex method, except calculate only the numbers required to do this test, i.e., the coefficients of the *nonbasic variables* in Eq. (0).

In step 3 of an iteration, $\mathbf{B}^{-1}$ could be derived each time by using a standard computer routine for inverting a matrix. However, since $\mathbf{B}$ (and therefore $\mathbf{B}^{-1}$) changes so little from one iteration to the next, it is much more efficient to derive the new $\mathbf{B}^{-1}$ (denote it by $\mathbf{B}_{\text{new}}^{-1}$) from the $\mathbf{B}^{-1}$ at the preceding iteration (denote it by $\mathbf{B}_{\text{old}}^{-1}$). (For the initial BF solution,

---

[1]Because the value of $\mathbf{x}_B$ is the entire vector of right-hand sides except for Eq. (0), the relevant right-hand sides need not be calculated here if $\mathbf{x}_B$ was calculated in step 3 of the preceding iteration.

$\mathbf{B} = \mathbf{I} = \mathbf{B}^{-1}$.) One method for doing this derivation is based directly upon the interpretation of the elements of $\mathbf{B}^{-1}$ [the coefficients of the slack variables in the current Eqs. (1), (2), . . . , (m)] presented in the next section, as well as upon the procedure used by the original simplex method to obtain the new set of equations from the preceding set.

To describe this method formally, let

x_k = entering basic variable,

a'_{ik} = coefficient of x_k in current Eq. (i), for $i = 1, 2, \ldots , m$ (calculated in step 2 of an iteration),

r = number of equation containing the leaving basic variable.

Recall that the new set of equations [excluding Eq. (0)] can be obtained from the preceding set by subtracting a'_{ik}/a'_{rk} times Eq. (r) from Eq. (i), for all $i = 1, 2, \ldots , m$ except $i = r$, and then dividing Eq. (r) by a'_{rk}. Therefore, the element in row i and column j of $\mathbf{B}^{-1}_{\text{new}}$ is

$$(\mathbf{B}^{-1}_{\text{new}})_{ij} = \begin{cases} (\mathbf{B}^{-1}_{\text{old}})_{ij} - \dfrac{a'_{ik}}{a'_{rk}}(\mathbf{B}^{-1}_{\text{old}})_{rj} & \text{if } i \neq r, \\[2ex] \dfrac{1}{a'_{rk}}(\mathbf{B}^{-1}_{\text{old}})_{rj} & \text{if } i = r. \end{cases}$$

These formulas are expressed in matrix notation as

$$\mathbf{B}^{-1}_{\text{new}} = \mathbf{E}\mathbf{B}^{-1}_{\text{old}},$$

where matrix $\mathbf{E}$ is an identity matrix except that its rth column is replaced by the vector

$$\boldsymbol{\eta} = \begin{bmatrix} \eta_1 \\ \eta_2 \\ \vdots \\ \eta_m \end{bmatrix}, \qquad \text{where} \qquad \eta_i = \begin{cases} -\dfrac{a'_{ik}}{a'_{rk}} & \text{if } i \neq r, \\[2ex] \dfrac{1}{a'_{rk}} & \text{if } i = r. \end{cases}$$

Thus, $\mathbf{E} = [\mathbf{U}_1, \mathbf{U}_2, \ldots , \mathbf{U}_{r-1}, \boldsymbol{\eta}, \mathbf{U}_{r+1}, \ldots , \mathbf{U}_m]$, where the m elements of each of the $\mathbf{U}_i$ column vectors are 0 except for a 1 in the ith position.

Example. We shall illustrate the revised simplex method by applying it to the Wyndor Glass Co. problem. The initial basic variables are the slack variables

$$\mathbf{x}_B = \begin{bmatrix} x_3 \\ x_4 \\ x_5 \end{bmatrix}.$$

Iteration 1

Because the initial $\mathbf{B}^{-1} = \mathbf{I}$, no calculations are needed to obtain the numbers required to identify the entering basic variable x_2 ($-c_2 = -5 < -3 = -c_1$) and the leaving basic variable x_4 ($a_{12} = 0$, $b_2/a_{22} = \frac{12}{2} < \frac{18}{2} = b_3/a_{32}$, so $r = 2$). Thus, the new set of basic variables is

$$\mathbf{x}_B = \begin{bmatrix} x_3 \\ x_2 \\ x_5 \end{bmatrix}.$$

To obtain the new $\mathbf{B}^{-1}$,

$$\boldsymbol{\eta} = \begin{bmatrix} -\dfrac{a_{12}}{a_{22}} \\ \dfrac{1}{a_{22}} \\ -\dfrac{a_{32}}{a_{22}} \end{bmatrix} = \begin{bmatrix} 0 \\ \dfrac{1}{2} \\ -1 \end{bmatrix},$$

so

$$\mathbf{B}^{-1} = \begin{bmatrix} 1 & 0 & 0 \\ 0 & \frac{1}{2} & 0 \\ 0 & -1 & 1 \end{bmatrix} \begin{bmatrix} 1 & 0 & 0 \\ 0 & 1 & 0 \\ 0 & 0 & 1 \end{bmatrix} = \begin{bmatrix} 1 & 0 & 0 \\ 0 & \frac{1}{2} & 0 \\ 0 & -1 & 1 \end{bmatrix},$$

so that

$$\mathbf{x}_B = \begin{bmatrix} 1 & 0 & 0 \\ 0 & \frac{1}{2} & 0 \\ 0 & -1 & 1 \end{bmatrix} \begin{bmatrix} 4 \\ 12 \\ 18 \end{bmatrix} = \begin{bmatrix} 4 \\ 6 \\ 6 \end{bmatrix}.$$

To test whether this solution is optimal, we calculate the coefficients of the nonbasic variables (x_1 and x_4) in Eq. (0). Performing only the relevant parts of the matrix multiplications, we obtain

$$\mathbf{c}_B\mathbf{B}^{-1}\mathbf{A} - \mathbf{c} = [0, 5, 0]\begin{bmatrix} 1 & 0 & 0 \\ 0 & \frac{1}{2} & 0 \\ 0 & -1 & 1 \end{bmatrix}\begin{bmatrix} 1 & - \\ 0 & - \\ 3 & - \end{bmatrix} - [3, -] = [-3, -],$$

$$\mathbf{c}_B\mathbf{B}^{-1} = [0, 5, 0]\begin{bmatrix} - & 0 & - \\ - & \frac{1}{2} & - \\ - & -1 & - \end{bmatrix} = [-, \tfrac{5}{2}, -],$$

so the coefficients of x_1 and x_4 are -3 and $\frac{5}{2}$, respectively. Since x_1 has a negative coefficient, this solution is *not* optimal.

Iteration 2
Using these coefficients of the nonbasic variables in Eq. (0), since only x_1 has a negative coefficient, we begin the next iteration by identifying x_1 as the entering basic variable. To determine the leaving basic variable, we must calculate the other coefficients of x_1:

$$\mathbf{B}^{-1}\mathbf{A} = \begin{bmatrix} 1 & 0 & 0 \\ 0 & \frac{1}{2} & 0 \\ 0 & -1 & 1 \end{bmatrix}\begin{bmatrix} 1 & - \\ 0 & - \\ 3 & - \end{bmatrix} = \begin{bmatrix} 1 & - \\ 0 & - \\ 3 & - \end{bmatrix}.$$

By using the *right side* column for the current BF solution (the value of $\mathbf{x}_B$) just given for iteration 1, the ratios $4/1 > 6/3$ indicate that x_5 is the leaving basic variable, so the new set of basic variables is

$$\mathbf{x}_B = \begin{bmatrix} x_3 \\ x_2 \\ x_1 \end{bmatrix} \quad \text{with} \quad \boldsymbol{\eta} = \begin{bmatrix} -\dfrac{a'_{11}}{a'_{31}} \\ -\dfrac{a'_{21}}{a'_{31}} \\ \dfrac{1}{a'_{31}} \end{bmatrix} = \begin{bmatrix} -\dfrac{1}{3} \\ 0 \\ \dfrac{1}{3} \end{bmatrix}.$$

Therefore, the new $\mathbf{B}^{-1}$ is

$$\mathbf{B}^{-1} = \begin{bmatrix} 1 & 0 & -\frac{1}{3} \\ 0 & 1 & 0 \\ 0 & 0 & \frac{1}{3} \end{bmatrix} \begin{bmatrix} 1 & 0 & 0 \\ 0 & \frac{1}{2} & 0 \\ 0 & -1 & 1 \end{bmatrix} = \begin{bmatrix} 1 & \frac{1}{3} & -\frac{1}{3} \\ 0 & \frac{1}{2} & 0 \\ 0 & -\frac{1}{3} & \frac{1}{3} \end{bmatrix},$$

so that

$$\mathbf{x}_B = \begin{bmatrix} 1 & \frac{1}{3} & -\frac{1}{3} \\ 0 & \frac{1}{2} & 0 \\ 0 & -\frac{1}{3} & \frac{1}{3} \end{bmatrix} \begin{bmatrix} 4 \\ 12 \\ 18 \end{bmatrix} = \begin{bmatrix} 2 \\ 6 \\ 2 \end{bmatrix}.$$

Applying the optimality test, we find that the coefficients of the nonbasic variables (x_4 and x_5) in Eq. (0) are

$$\mathbf{c}_B \mathbf{B}^{-1} = [0, 5, 3] \begin{bmatrix} - & \frac{1}{3} & -\frac{1}{3} \\ - & \frac{1}{2} & 0 \\ - & -\frac{1}{3} & \frac{1}{3} \end{bmatrix} = [-, \tfrac{3}{2}, 1].$$

Because both coefficients ($\frac{3}{2}$ and 1) are nonnegative, the current solution ($x_1 = 2$, $x_2 = 6$, $x_3 = 2$, $x_4 = 0$, $x_5 = 0$) is optimal and the procedure terminates.

General Observations

The preceding discussion was limited to the case of linear programming problems fitting our standard form given in Sec. 3.2. However, the modifications for other forms are relatively straightforward. The initialization would be conducted just as it would for the original simplex method (see Sec. 4.6). When this step involves introducing artificial variables to obtain an initial BF solution (and thereby to obtain an *identity matrix* as the *initial basis matrix*), these variables are included among the m elements of x_s.

Let us summarize the advantages of the revised simplex method over the original simplex method. One advantage is that the number of arithmetic computations may be reduced. This is especially true when the $\mathbf{A}$ matrix contains a large number of zero elements (which is usually the case for the large problems arising in practice). The amount of information that must be stored at each iteration is less, sometimes considerably so. The revised simplex method also permits the control of the rounding errors inevitably generated by computers. This control can be exercised by periodically obtaining the current $\mathbf{B}^{-1}$ by directly inverting $\mathbf{B}$. Furthermore, some of the postoptimality analysis problems discussed in Sec. 4.7 can be handled more conveniently with the revised simplex method. For all these reasons, the revised simplex method is usually preferable to the original simplex method for computer execution.

5.3 A FUNDAMENTAL INSIGHT

We shall now focus on a property of the simplex method (in any form) that has been revealed by the revised simplex method in the preceding section.[1] This fundamental insight provides the key to both duality theory and sensitivity analysis (Chap. 6), two very important parts of linear programming.

The insight involves the coefficients of the *slack* variables and the information they give. It is a direct result of the initialization, where the *i*th slack variable x_{n+i} is given a coefficient of $+1$ in Eq. (*i*) and a coefficient of 0 in *every other equation* [including Eq. (0)] for $i = 1, 2, \ldots, m$, as shown by the null vector $\mathbf{0}$ and the identity matrix $\mathbf{I}$ in the *slack variables* column for iteration 0 in Table 5.8. (For most of this section, we are assuming that the problem is in *our standard form*, with $b_i \geq 0$ for all $i = 1, 2, \ldots, m$, so that no additional adjustments are needed in the initialization.) The other key factor is that subsequent iterations change the initial equations *only* by

1. Multiplying (or dividing) an *entire* equation by a nonzero constant
2. Adding (or subtracting) a multiple of one *entire* equation to another *entire* equation

As already described in the preceding section, a sequence of these kinds of elementary algebraic operations is equivalent to premultiplying the initial simplex tableau by some matrix. (See Appendix 4 for a review of matrices.) The consequence can be summarized as follows.

> **Verbal description of fundamental insight:** After any iteration, the coefficients of the *slack* variables in each equation immediately reveal how that equation has been obtained from the *initial* equations.

As one example of the importance of this insight, recall from Table 5.8 that the matrix formula for the optimal solution obtained by the simplex method is

$$\mathbf{x}_B = \mathbf{B}^{-1}\mathbf{b},$$

where $\mathbf{x}_B$ is the vector of basic variables, $\mathbf{B}^{-1}$ is the matrix of coefficients of slack variables for rows 1 to m of the final tableau, and $\mathbf{b}$ is the vector of original right-hand sides (resource availabilities). (We soon will denote this particular $\mathbf{B}^{-1}$ by $\mathbf{S}^*$.) Postoptimality analysis normally includes an investigation of possible changes in $\mathbf{b}$. By using this formula, you can see exactly how the optimal BF solution changes (or whether it becomes infeasible because of negative variables) as a function of $\mathbf{b}$. You do *not* have to reapply the simplex method over and over for each new $\mathbf{b}$, because the coefficients of the slack

---

[1]However, since some instructors do not cover the preceding section, we have written this section in a way that can be understood without first reading Sec. 5.2. It is helpful to take a brief look at the matrix notation introduced at the beginning of Sec. 5.2, including the resulting key equation, $\mathbf{x}_B = \mathbf{B}^{-1}\mathbf{b}$.

variables tell all! In a similar fashion, this fundamental insight provides a tremendous computational saving for the rest of sensitivity analysis as well.

To spell out the how and the why of this insight, let us look again at the Wyndor Glass Co. example. (The OR Tutor also includes another demonstration example.)

Example. Table 5.9 shows the relevant portion of the simplex tableau for demonstrating this fundamental insight. Light lines have been drawn around the coefficients of the slack variables in all the tableaux in this table because these are the crucial coefficients for applying the insight. To avoid clutter, we then identify the pivot row and pivot column by a single box around the pivot number only.

Iteration 1

To demonstrate the fundamental insight, our focus is on the algebraic operations performed by the simplex method while using Gaussian elimination to obtain the new BF solution. If we do all the algebraic operations with the *old* row 2 (the pivot row) rather than the new one, then the algebraic operations spelled out in Chap. 4 for iteration 1 are

$$\text{New row 0} = \text{old row 0} + \quad (\tfrac{5}{2})(\text{old row 2}),$$
$$\text{New row 1} = \text{old row 1} + \quad (0)(\text{old row 2}),$$
$$\text{New row 2} = \qquad\qquad\quad (\tfrac{1}{2})(\text{old row 2}),$$
$$\text{New row 3} = \text{old row 3} + (-1)(\text{old row 2}).$$

TABLE 5.9 Simplex tableaux without leftmost columns for the Wyndor Glass Co. problem

Iteration	Coefficient of:					Right Side
	x_1	x_2	x_3	x_4	x_5	Right Side
0	-3	-5	0	0	0	0
	1	0	1	0	0	4
	0	$\boxed{2}$	0	1	0	12
	3	2	0	0	1	18
1	-3	0	0	$\frac{5}{2}$	0	30
	1	0	1	0	0	4
	0	1	0	$\frac{1}{2}$	0	6
	$\boxed{3}$	0	0	-1	1	6
2	0	0	0	$\frac{3}{2}$	1	36
	0	0	1	$\frac{1}{3}$	$-\frac{1}{3}$	2
	0	1	0	$\frac{1}{2}$	0	6
	1	0	0	$-\frac{1}{3}$	$\frac{1}{3}$	2

Ignoring row 0 for the moment, we see that these algebraic operations amount to premultiplying rows 1 to 3 of the initial tableau by the matrix

$$
\begin{bmatrix}
1 & 0 & 0 \\
0 & \frac{1}{2} & 0 \\
0 & -1 & 1
\end{bmatrix}.
$$

Rows 1 to 3 of the initial tableau are

$$
\text{Old rows 1–3} =
\begin{bmatrix}
1 & 0 & \vdots & 1 & 0 & 0 & \vdots & 4 \\
0 & 2 & \vdots & 0 & 1 & 0 & \vdots & 12 \\
3 & 2 & \vdots & 0 & 0 & 1 & \vdots & 18
\end{bmatrix},
$$

where the third, fourth, and fifth columns (the coefficients of the slack variables) form an *identity matrix*. Therefore,

$$
\text{New rows 1–3} =
\begin{bmatrix}
1 & 0 & 0 \\
0 & \frac{1}{2} & 0 \\
0 & -1 & 1
\end{bmatrix}
\begin{bmatrix}
1 & 0 & \vdots & 1 & 0 & 0 & \vdots & 4 \\
0 & 2 & \vdots & 0 & 1 & 0 & \vdots & 12 \\
3 & 2 & \vdots & 0 & 0 & 1 & \vdots & 18
\end{bmatrix}
$$

$$
=
\begin{bmatrix}
1 & 0 & \boxed{1 & 0 & 0} & 4 \\
0 & 1 & \boxed{0 & \frac{1}{2} & 0} & 6 \\
3 & 0 & \boxed{0 & -1 & 1} & 6
\end{bmatrix}.
$$

Note how the first matrix is reproduced exactly in the box below it as the coefficients of the slack variables in rows 1 to 3 of the new tableau, because the coefficients of the slack variables in rows 1 to 3 of the initial tableau form an identity matrix. Thus, just as stated in the verbal description of the fundamental insight, the coefficients of the slack variables in the new tableau do indeed provide a record of the algebraic operations performed.

This insight is not much to get excited about after just one iteration, since you can readily see from the initial tableau what the algebraic operations had to be, but it becomes invaluable after all the iterations are completed.

For row 0, the algebraic operation performed amounts to the following matrix calculations, where now our focus is on the vector $[0, \frac{5}{2}, 0]$ that premultiplies rows 1 to 3 of the initial tableau.

$$
\text{New row 0} = [-3, \ -5 \mathbin{\vdots} 0, \ 0, \ 0 \mathbin{\vdots} 0] + [0, \ \tfrac{5}{2}, \ 0]
\begin{bmatrix}
1 & 0 & \vdots & 1 & 0 & 0 & \vdots & 4 \\
0 & 2 & \vdots & 0 & 1 & 0 & \vdots & 12 \\
3 & 2 & \vdots & 0 & 0 & 1 & \vdots & 18
\end{bmatrix}
$$

$$
= [-3, \ 0, \ \boxed{0, \ \tfrac{5}{2}, \ 0,} \ 30].
$$

Note how this vector is reproduced exactly in the box below it as the coefficients of the slack variables in row 0 of the new tableau, just as was claimed in the statement of the fundamental insight. (Once again, the reason is the identity matrix for the coefficients of the slack variables in rows 1 to 3 of the initial tableau, along with the zeros for these coefficients in row 0 of the initial tableau.)

Iteration 2

The algebraic operations performed on the second tableau of Table 5.9 for iteration 2 are

$$\text{New row } 0 = \text{old row } 0 + \quad (1)(\text{old row } 3),$$

$$\text{New row } 1 = \text{old row } 1 + (-\tfrac{1}{3})(\text{old row } 3),$$

$$\text{New row } 2 = \text{old row } 2 + \quad (0)(\text{old row } 3),$$

$$\text{New row } 3 = \qquad\qquad (\tfrac{1}{3})(\text{old row } 3).$$

Ignoring row 0 for the moment, we see that these operations amount to premultiplying rows 1 to 3 of this tableau by the matrix

$$\begin{bmatrix} 1 & 0 & -\tfrac{1}{3} \\ 0 & 1 & 0 \\ 0 & 0 & \tfrac{1}{3} \end{bmatrix}.$$

Writing this second tableau as the matrix product shown for iteration 1 (namely, the corresponding matrix times rows 1 to 3 of the initial tableau) then yields

$$\text{Final rows } 1\text{–}3 = \begin{bmatrix} 1 & 0 & -\tfrac{1}{3} \\ 0 & 1 & 0 \\ 0 & 0 & \tfrac{1}{3} \end{bmatrix} \begin{bmatrix} 1 & 0 & 0 \\ 0 & \tfrac{1}{2} & 0 \\ 0 & -1 & 1 \end{bmatrix} \left[\begin{array}{ccc:ccc} 1 & 0 & 1 & 0 & 0 & 4 \\ 0 & 2 & 0 & 1 & 0 & 12 \\ 3 & 2 & 0 & 0 & 1 & 18 \end{array}\right]$$

$$= \begin{bmatrix} 1 & \tfrac{1}{3} & -\tfrac{1}{3} \\ 0 & \tfrac{1}{2} & 0 \\ 0 & -\tfrac{1}{3} & \tfrac{1}{3} \end{bmatrix} \left[\begin{array}{cc:ccc} 1 & 0 & 1 & 0 & 0 & 4 \\ 0 & 2 & 0 & 1 & 0 & 12 \\ 3 & 2 & 0 & 0 & 1 & 18 \end{array}\right]$$

$$= \begin{bmatrix} 0 & 0 & \boxed{1 \quad \tfrac{1}{3} \quad -\tfrac{1}{3}} & 2 \\ 0 & 1 & \boxed{0 \quad \tfrac{1}{2} \quad 0} & 6 \\ 1 & 0 & \boxed{0 \quad -\tfrac{1}{3} \quad \tfrac{1}{3}} & 2 \end{bmatrix}.$$

The first two matrices shown on the first line of these calculations summarize the algebraic operations of the second and first iterations, respectively. Their product, shown as the first matrix on the second line, then combines the algebraic operations of the two iterations. Note how this matrix is reproduced exactly in the box below it as the coefficients of the slack variables in rows 1 to 3 of the new (final) tableau shown on the third line. What this portion of the tableau reveals is how the *entire* final tableau (except row 0) has been obtained from the initial tableau, namely,

$$\text{Final row } 1 = (1)(\text{initial row } 1) + \quad (\tfrac{1}{3})(\text{initial row } 2) + (-\tfrac{1}{3})(\text{initial row } 3),$$

$$\text{Final row } 2 = (0)(\text{initial row } 1) + \quad (\tfrac{1}{2})(\text{initial row } 2) + \quad (0)(\text{initial row } 3),$$

$$\text{Final row } 3 = (0)(\text{initial row } 1) + (-\tfrac{1}{3})(\text{initial row } 2) + \quad (\tfrac{1}{3})(\text{initial row } 3).$$

To see why these multipliers of the initial rows are correct, you would have to trace through all the algebraic operations of both iterations. For example, why does final row 1 include $(\tfrac{1}{3})$(initial row 2), even though a multiple of row 2 has never been added directly to row 1? The reason is that initial row 2 was subtracted from initial row 3 in iteration 1, and then $(\tfrac{1}{3})$(old row 3) was subtracted from old row 1 in iteration 2.

However, there is no need for you to trace through. Even when the simplex method has gone through hundreds or thousands of iterations, the coefficients of the slack variables in the final tableau will reveal how this tableau has been obtained from the initial tableau. Furthermore, the same algebraic operations would give these same coefficients even if the values of some of the parameters in the original model (initial tableau) were changed, so these coefficients also reveal how the *rest* of the final tableau changes with changes in the initial tableau.

To complete this story for row 0, the fundamental insight reveals that the entire final row 0 can be calculated from the initial tableau by using just the coefficients of the slack variables in the final row 0—$[0, \frac{3}{2}, 1]$. This calculation is shown below, where the first vector is row 0 of the initial tableau and the matrix is rows 1 to 3 of the initial tableau.

$$\text{Final row } 0 = [-3, \quad -5 \mid 0, \quad 0, \quad 0 \mid 0] + [0, \quad \tfrac{3}{2}, \quad 1]\begin{bmatrix} 1 & 0 & 1 & 0 & 0 & 4 \\ 0 & 2 & 0 & 1 & 0 & 12 \\ 3 & 2 & 0 & 0 & 1 & 18 \end{bmatrix}$$

$$= [0, \quad 0, \quad \boxed{0, \quad \tfrac{3}{2}, \quad 1,} \quad 36].$$

Note again how the vector premultiplying rows 1 to 3 of the initial tableau is reproduced exactly as the coefficients of the slack variables in the final row 0. These quantities must be identical because of the coefficients of the slack variables in the initial tableau (an identity matrix below a null vector). This conclusion is the row 0 part of the fundamental insight.

Mathematical Summary

Because its primary applications involve the *final* tableau, we shall now give a general mathematical expression for the fundamental insight just in terms of this tableau, using matrix notation. If you have not read Sec. 5.2, you now need to know that the *parameters* of the model are given by the matrix $\mathbf{A} = \|a_{ij}\|$ and the vectors $\mathbf{b} = \|b_i\|$ and $\mathbf{c} = \|c_j\|$, as displayed at the beginning of that section.

The only other notation needed is summarized and illustrated in Table 5.10. Notice how vector $\mathbf{t}$ (representing row 0) and matrix $\mathbf{T}$ (representing the other rows) together correspond to the rows of the initial tableau in Table 5.9, whereas vector $\mathbf{t}^*$ and matrix $\mathbf{T}^*$ together correspond to the rows of the final tableau in Table 5.9. This table also shows these vectors and matrices partitioned into three parts: the coefficients of the original variables, the coefficients of the slack variables (our focus), and the right-hand side. Once again, the notation distinguishes between parts of the initial tableau and the final tableau by using an asterisk only in the latter case.

For the coefficients of the slack variables (the middle part) in the initial tableau of Table 5.10, notice the null vector $\mathbf{0}$ in row 0 and the identity matrix $\mathbf{I}$ below, which provide the keys for the fundamental insight. The vector and matrix in the same location of the final tableau, $\mathbf{y}^*$ and $\mathbf{S}^*$, then play a prominent role in the equations for the fundamental insight. $\mathbf{A}$ and $\mathbf{b}$ in the initial tableau turn into $\mathbf{A}^*$ and $\mathbf{b}^*$ in the final tableau. For row 0 of the final tableau, the coefficients of the decision variables are $\mathbf{z}^* - \mathbf{c}$ (so the vector $\mathbf{z}^*$ is what has been added to the vector of initial coefficients, $-\mathbf{c}$), and the right-hand side Z^* denotes the optimal value of Z.

TABLE 5.10 General notation for initial and final simplex tableaux in matrix form, illustrated by the Wyndor Glass Co. problem

Initial Tableau

Row 0: $\mathbf{t} = [-3, -5 \mathbin{\vdots} 0, 0, 0 \mathbin{\vdots} 0] = [-\mathbf{c} \mathbin{\vdots} \mathbf{0} \mathbin{\vdots} 0]$.

Other rows: $\mathbf{T} = \begin{bmatrix} 1 & 0 & 1 & 0 & 0 & 4 \\ 0 & 2 & 0 & 1 & 0 & 12 \\ 3 & 2 & 0 & 0 & 1 & 18 \end{bmatrix} = [\mathbf{A} \mathbin{\vdots} \mathbf{I} \mathbin{\vdots} \mathbf{b}]$.

Combined: $\begin{bmatrix} \mathbf{t} \\ \mathbf{T} \end{bmatrix} = \begin{bmatrix} -\mathbf{c} & \mathbf{0} & 0 \\ \mathbf{A} & \mathbf{I} & \mathbf{b} \end{bmatrix}$.

Final Tableau

Row 0: $\mathbf{t}^* = [0, 0 \mathbin{\vdots} 0, \frac{3}{2}, 1 \mathbin{\vdots} 36] = [\mathbf{z}^* - \mathbf{c} \mathbin{\vdots} \mathbf{y}^* \mathbin{\vdots} Z^*]$.

Other rows: $\mathbf{T}^* = \begin{bmatrix} 0 & 0 & 1 & \frac{1}{3} & -\frac{1}{3} & 2 \\ 0 & 1 & 0 & \frac{1}{2} & 0 & 6 \\ 1 & 0 & 0 & -\frac{1}{3} & \frac{1}{3} & 2 \end{bmatrix} = [\mathbf{A}^* \mathbin{\vdots} \mathbf{S}^* \mathbin{\vdots} \mathbf{b}^*]$.

Combined: $\begin{bmatrix} \mathbf{t}^* \\ \mathbf{T}^* \end{bmatrix} = \begin{bmatrix} \mathbf{z}^* - \mathbf{c} & \mathbf{y}^* & Z^* \\ \mathbf{A}^* & \mathbf{S}^* & \mathbf{b}^* \end{bmatrix}$.

It is helpful at this point to look back at Table 5.8 in Sec. 5.2 and compare it with Table 5.10. (If you haven't previously studied Sec. 5.2, you will need to read the definition of the basis matrix $\mathbf{B}$ and the vectors $\mathbf{x}_B$ and $\mathbf{c}_B$ given early in that section before looking at Table 5.8.) The notation for the components of the *initial* simplex tableau is the same in the two tables. The lower part of Table 5.8 shows *any* later simplex tableau in matrix form, whereas the lower part of Table 5.10 gives the *final* tableau in matrix form. Note that the matrix $\mathbf{B}^{-1}$ in Table 5.8 is in the same location as $\mathbf{S}^*$ in Table 5.10. Thus,

$$\mathbf{S}^* = \mathbf{B}^{-1}$$

when $\mathbf{B}$ is the basis matrix for the *optimal* solution found by the simplex method.

Referring to Table 5.10 again, suppose now that you are given the initial tableau, $\mathbf{t}$ and $\mathbf{T}$, and just $\mathbf{y}^*$ and $\mathbf{S}^*$ from the final tableau. How can this information alone be used to calculate the rest of the final tableau? The answer is provided by Table 5.8. This table includes some information that is not directly relevant to our current discussion, namely, how $\mathbf{y}^*$ and $\mathbf{S}^*$ themselves can be calculated ($\mathbf{y}^* = \mathbf{c}_B \mathbf{B}^{-1}$ and $\mathbf{S}^* = \mathbf{B}^{-1}$) by knowing the set of basic variables and so the basis matrix $\mathbf{B}$ for the optimal solution found by the simplex method. However, the lower part of this table also shows how the rest of the final tableau can be obtained from the coefficients of the slack variables, which is summarized as follows.

Fundamental Insight

(1) $\mathbf{t}^* = \mathbf{t} + \mathbf{y}^*\mathbf{T} = [\mathbf{y}^*\mathbf{A} - \mathbf{c} \mathbin{\vdots} \mathbf{y}^* \mathbin{\vdots} \mathbf{y}^*\mathbf{b}]$.
(2) $\mathbf{T}^* = \mathbf{S}^*\mathbf{T} = [\mathbf{S}^*\mathbf{A} \mathbin{\vdots} \mathbf{S}^* \mathbin{\vdots} \mathbf{S}^*\mathbf{b}]$.

Thus, by knowing the parameters of the model in the initial tableau (**c**, **A**, and **b**) and *only* the coefficients of the slack variables in the final tableau (**y*** and **S***), these equations enable calculating *all* the other numbers in the final tableau.

We already used these two equations when dealing with iteration 2 for the Wyndor Glass Co. problem in the preceding subsection. In particular, the right-hand side of the expression for final row 0 for iteration 2 is just **t** + **y*T**, and the second line of the expression for final rows 1 to 3 is just **S*T**.

Now let us summarize the mathematical logic behind the two equations for the fundamental insight. To derive Eq. (2), recall that the entire sequence of algebraic operations performed by the simplex method (excluding those involving row 0) is equivalent to premultiplying **T** by some matrix, call it **M**. Therefore,

$$\mathbf{T^*} = \mathbf{MT},$$

but now we need to identify **M**. By writing out the component parts of **T** and **T***, this equation becomes

$$[\mathbf{A^*} \vdots \mathbf{S^*} \vdots \mathbf{b^*}] = \mathbf{M}\,[\mathbf{A} \vdots \mathbf{I} \vdots \mathbf{b}]$$
$$= [\mathbf{MA} \vdots \mathbf{M} \vdots \mathbf{Mb}].$$

Because the middle (or any other) component of these equal matrices must be the same, it follows that **M** = **S***, so Eq. (2) is a valid equation.

Equation (1) is derived in a similar fashion by noting that the entire sequence of algebraic operations involving row 0 amounts to adding some linear combination of the rows in **T** to **t**, which is equivalent to adding to **t** some *vector* times **T**. Denoting this vector by **v**, we thereby have

$$\mathbf{t^*} = \mathbf{t} + \mathbf{vT},$$

but **v** still needs to be identified. Writing out the component parts of **t** and **t*** yields

$$[\mathbf{z^*} - \mathbf{c} \vdots \mathbf{y^*} \vdots Z^*] = [-\mathbf{c} \vdots \mathbf{0} \vdots 0] + \mathbf{v}\,[\mathbf{A} \vdots \mathbf{I} \vdots \mathbf{b}]$$
$$= [-\mathbf{c} + \mathbf{vA} \vdots \mathbf{v} \vdots \mathbf{vb}].$$

Equating the middle component of these equal vectors gives **v** = **y***, which validates Eq. (1).

Adapting to Other Model Forms

Thus far, the fundamental insight has been described under the assumption that the original model is in our standard form, described in Sec. 3.2. However, the above mathematical logic now reveals just what adjustments are needed for other forms of the original model. The key is the identity matrix **I** in the initial tableau, which turns into **S*** in the final tableau. If some artificial variables must be introduced into the initial tableau to serve as initial basic variables, then it is the set of columns (appropriately ordered) for *all* the initial basic variables (both slack and artificial) that forms **I** in this tableau. (The columns for any surplus variables are extraneous.) The *same* columns in the final tableau provide **S*** for the **T*** = **S*T** equation and **y*** for the **t*** = **t** + **y*T** equation. If *M*'s were introduced into the preliminary row 0 as coefficients for artificial variables, then the $\mathbf{t}$ for the $\mathbf{t}^* = \mathbf{t} + \mathbf{y}^*\mathbf{T}$ equation is the row 0 for the initial tableau after these nonzero coefficients for basic variables are algebraically eliminated. (Alternatively, the preliminary row 0 can be used for $\mathbf{t}$, but then these M's must be subtracted from the final row 0 to give $\mathbf{y}^*$.) (See Prob. 5.3-11.)

Applications

The fundamental insight has a variety of important applications in linear programming. One of these applications involves the revised simplex method. As described in the preceding section (see Table 5.8), this method used $\mathbf{B}^{-1}$ and the initial tableau to calculate all the relevant numbers in the current tableau for *every* iteration. It goes even further than the fundamental insight by using $\mathbf{B}^{-1}$ to calculate $\mathbf{y}^*$ itself as $\mathbf{y}^* = \mathbf{c}_B\mathbf{B}^{-1}$.

Another application involves the interpretation of the *shadow prices* $(y_1^*, y_2^*, \ldots, y_m^*)$ described in Sec. 4.7. The fundamental insight reveals that Z^* (the value of Z for the optimal solution) is

$$Z^* = \mathbf{y}^*\mathbf{b} = \sum_{i=1}^{m} y_i^* b_i,$$

so, e.g.,

$$Z^* = 0b_1 + \frac{3}{2}b_2 + b_3$$

for the Wyndor Glass Co. problem. This equation immediately yields the interpretation for the y_i^* values given in Sec. 4.7.

Another group of extremely important applications involves various *postoptimality tasks* (reoptimization technique, sensitivity analysis, parametric linear programming— described in Sec. 4.7) that investigate the effect of making one or more changes in the original model. In particular, suppose that the simplex method already has been applied to obtain an optimal solution (as well as $\mathbf{y}^*$ and $\mathbf{S}^*$) for the original model, and then these changes are made. If exactly the same sequence of algebraic operations were to be applied to the revised initial tableau, what would be the resulting changes in the final tableau? Because $\mathbf{y}^*$ and $\mathbf{S}^*$ don't change, the fundamental insight reveals the answer immediately.

For example, consider the change from $b_2 = 12$ to $b_2 = 13$ as illustrated in Fig. 4.8 for the Wyndor Glass Co. problem. It is not necessary to *solve* for the new optimal solution $(x_1, x_2) = (\frac{5}{3}, \frac{13}{2})$ because the values of the basic variables in the final tableau ($\mathbf{b}^*$) are immediately revealed by the fundamental insight:

$$\begin{bmatrix} x_3 \\ x_2 \\ x_1 \end{bmatrix} = \mathbf{b}^* = \mathbf{S}^*\mathbf{b} = \begin{bmatrix} 1 & \frac{1}{3} & -\frac{1}{3} \\ 0 & \frac{1}{2} & 0 \\ 0 & -\frac{1}{3} & \frac{1}{3} \end{bmatrix} \begin{bmatrix} 4 \\ 13 \\ 18 \end{bmatrix} = \begin{bmatrix} \frac{7}{3} \\ \frac{13}{2} \\ \frac{5}{3} \end{bmatrix}.$$

There is an even easier way to make this calculation. Since the only change is in the *second* component of $\mathbf{b}$ ($\Delta b_2 = 1$), which gets premultiplied by only the *second* column of $\mathbf{S}^*$, the *change* in $\mathbf{b}^*$ can be calculated as simply

$$\Delta \mathbf{b}^* = \begin{bmatrix} \frac{1}{3} \\ \frac{1}{2} \\ -\frac{1}{3} \end{bmatrix} \Delta b_2 = \begin{bmatrix} \frac{1}{3} \\ \frac{1}{2} \\ -\frac{1}{3} \end{bmatrix},$$

so the original values of the basic variables in the final tableau ($x_3 = 2$, $x_2 = 6$, $x_1 = 2$) now become

$$\begin{bmatrix} x_3 \\ x_2 \\ x_1 \end{bmatrix} = \begin{bmatrix} 2 \\ 6 \\ 2 \end{bmatrix} + \begin{bmatrix} \frac{1}{3} \\ \frac{1}{2} \\ -\frac{1}{3} \end{bmatrix} = \begin{bmatrix} \frac{7}{13} \\ \frac{13}{2} \\ \frac{5}{3} \end{bmatrix}.$$

(If any of these new values were *negative,* and thus infeasible, then the reoptimization technique described in Sec. 4.7 would be applied, starting from this revised final tableau.) Applying *incremental analysis* to the preceding equation for $Z*$ also immediately yields

$$\Delta Z* = \frac{3}{2}\Delta b_2 = \frac{3}{2}.$$

The fundamental insight can be applied to investigating other kinds of changes in the original model in a very similar fashion; it is the crux of the sensitivity analysis procedure described in the latter part of Chap. 6.

You also will see in the next chapter that the fundamental insight plays a key role in the very useful duality theory for linear programming.

5.4 CONCLUSIONS

Although the simplex method is an algebraic procedure, it is based on some fairly simple geometric concepts. These concepts enable one to use the algorithm to examine only a relatively small number of BF solutions before reaching and identifying an optimal solution.

Chapter 4 describes how *elementary algebraic operations* are used to execute the *algebraic form* of the simplex method, and then how the *tableau form* of the simplex method uses the equivalent *elementary row operations* in the same way. Studying the simplex method in these forms is a good way of getting started in learning its basic concepts. However, these forms of the simplex method do not provide the most efficient form for execution on a computer. *Matrix operations* are a faster way of combining and executing elementary algebraic operations or row operations. Therefore, by using the *matrix form* of the simplex method, the revised simplex method provides an effective way of adapting the simplex method for computer implementation.

The final simplex tableau includes complete information on how it can be algebraically reconstructed directly from the initial simplex tableau. This fundamental insight has some very important applications, especially for postoptimality analysis.

SELECTED REFERENCES

1. Bazaraa, M. S., J. J. Jarvis, and H. D. Sherali: *Linear Programming and Network Flows,* 2d ed., Wiley, New York, 1990.

2. Dantzig, G. B., and M. N. Thapa: *Linear Programming 1: Introduction,* Springer, New York, 1997.

3. Schriver, A: *Theory of Linear and Integer Programming,* Wiley, New York, 1986.

4. Vanderbei, R. J.: *Linear Programming: Foundations and Extensions,* Kluwer Academic Publishers, Boston, MA, 1996.

LEARNING AIDS FOR THIS CHAPTER IN YOUR OR COURSEWARE

A Demonstration Example in OR Tutor:

Fundamental Insight

Interactive Routines:

Enter or Revise a General Linear Programming Model
Set Up for the Simplex Method—Interactive Only
Solve Interactively by the Simplex Method

Files (Chapter 3) for Solving the Wyndor Example:

Excel File
LINGO/LINDO File
MPL/CPLEX File

See Appendix 1 for documentation of the software.

PROBLEMS

The symbols to the left of some of the problems (or their parts) have the following meaning:

D: The demonstration example listed above may be helpful.
I: You can check some of your work by using the interactive routines listed above for the original simplex method.

An asterisk on the problem number indicates that at least a partial answer is given in the back of the book.

5.1-1.* Consider the following problem.

Maximize $Z = 3x_1 + 2x_2$,

subject to

$$2x_1 + x_2 \le 6$$
$$x_1 + 2x_2 \le 6$$

and

$$x_1 \ge 0, \qquad x_2 \ge 0.$$

(a) Solve this problem graphically. Identify the CPF solutions by circling them on the graph.
(b) Identify all the sets of two defining equations for this problem. For each set, solve (if a solution exists) for the corresponding corner-point solution, and classify it as a CPF solution or corner-point infeasible solution.
(c) Introduce slack variables in order to write the functional constraints in augmented form. Use these slack variables to identify the basic solution that corresponds to each corner-point solution found in part (b).

(d) Do the following for *each* set of two defining equations from part (b): Identify the indicating variable for each defining equation. Display the set of equations from part (c) *after* deleting these two indicating (nonbasic) variables. Then use the latter set of equations to solve for the two remaining variables (the basic variables). Compare the resulting basic solution to the corresponding basic solution obtained in part (c).
(e) Without executing the simplex method, use its geometric interpretation (and the objective function) to identify the path (sequence of CPF solutions) it would follow to reach the optimal solution. For each of these CPF solutions in turn, identify the following decisions being made for the next iteration: (*i*) which defining equation is being deleted and which is being added; (*ii*) which indicating variable is being deleted (the entering basic variable) and which is being added (the leaving basic variable).

5.1-2. Repeat Prob. 5.1-1 for the model in Prob. 3.1-5.

5.1-3. Consider the following problem.

Maximize $Z = 2x_1 + 3x_2$,

subject to

$$-3x_1 + x_2 \le 1$$
$$4x_1 + 2x_2 \le 20$$
$$4x_1 - x_2 \le 10$$
$$-x_1 + 2x_2 \le 5$$

and

$$x_1 \ge 0, \qquad x_2 \ge 0.$$

(a) Solve this problem graphically. Identify the CPF solutions by circling them on the graph.

(b) Develop a table giving each of the CPF solutions and the corresponding defining equations, BF solution, and nonbasic variables. Calculate Z for each of these solutions, and use just this information to identify the optimal solution.

(c) Develop the corresponding table for the corner-point infeasible solutions, etc. Also identify the sets of defining equations and nonbasic variables that do not yield a solution.

5.1-4. Consider the following problem.

Maximize $Z = 2x_1 - x_2 + x_3,$

subject to

$$3x_1 + x_2 + x_3 \leq 60$$
$$x_1 - x_2 + 2x_3 \leq 10$$
$$x_1 + x_2 - x_3 \leq 20$$

and

$$x_1 \geq 0, \qquad x_2 \geq 0, \qquad x_3 \geq 0.$$

After slack variables are introduced and then one complete iteration of the simplex method is performed, the following simplex tableau is obtained.

						Coefficient of:				
Iteration	Basic Variable	Eq.	Z	x_1	x_2	x_3	x_4	x_5	x_6	Right Side
	Z	(0)	1	0	−1	3	0	2	0	20
1	x_4	(1)	0	0	4	−5	1	−3	0	30
	x_1	(2)	0	1	−1	2	0	1	0	10
	x_6	(3)	0	0	2	−3	0	−1	1	10

(a) Identify the CPF solution obtained at iteration 1.

(b) Identify the constraint boundary equations that define this CPF solution.

5.1-5. Consider the three-variable linear programming problem shown in Fig. 5.2.

(a) Construct a table like Table 5.1, giving the set of defining equations for each CPF solution.

(b) What are the defining equations for the corner-point infeasible solution (6, 0, 5)?

(c) Identify one of the systems of three constraint boundary equations that yields neither a CPF solution nor a corner-point infeasible solution. Explain why this occurs for this system.

5.1-6. Consider the linear programming problem given in Table 6.1 as the dual problem for the Wyndor Glass Co. example.

(a) Identify the 10 sets of defining equations for this problem. For each one, solve (if a solution exists) for the corresponding corner-point solution, and classify it as a CPF solution or corner-point infeasible solution.

(b) For each corner-point solution, give the corresponding basic solution and its set of nonbasic variables. (Compare with Table 6.9.)

5.1-7. Consider the following problem.

Minimize $Z = x_1 + 2x_2,$

subject to

$$-x_1 + x_2 \leq 15$$
$$2x_1 + x_2 \leq 90$$
$$x_2 \geq 30$$

and

$$x_1 \geq 0, \qquad x_2 \geq 0.$$

(a) Solve this problem graphically.

(b) Develop a table giving each of the CPF solutions and the corresponding defining equations, BF solution, and nonbasic variables.

5.1-8. Reconsider the model in Problem 4.6-3.

(a) Identify the 10 sets of defining equations for this problem. For each one, solve (if a solution exists) for the corresponding corner-point solution, and classify it as a CPF solution or a corner-point infeasible solution.

(b) For each corner-point solution, give the corresponding basic solution and its set of nonbasic variables.

5.1-9. Reconsider the model in Prob. 3.1-4.

(a) Identify the 15 sets of defining equations for this problem. For each one, solve (if a solution exists) for the corresponding corner-point solution, and classify it as a CPF solution or a corner-point infeasible solution.

(b) For each corner-point solution, give the corresponding basic solution and its set of nonbasic variables.

5.1-10. Each of the following statements is true under most circumstances, but not always. In each case, indicate when the statement will not be true and why.

(a) The best CPF solution is an optimal solution.

(b) An optimal solution is a CPF solution.

(c) A CPF solution is the only optimal solution if none of its adjacent CPF solutions are better (as measured by the value of the objective function).

5.1-11. Consider the original form (before augmenting) of a linear programming problem with n decision variables (each with a nonnegativity constraint) and m functional constraints. Label each of the following statements as true or false, and then justify your answer with specific references (including page citations) to material in the chapter.

(a) If a feasible solution is optimal, it must be a CPF solution.

(b) The number of CPF solutions is at least

$$\frac{(m + n)!}{m!n!}.$$

(c) If a CPF solution has adjacent CPF solutions that are better (as measured by Z), then one of these adjacent CPF solutions must be an optimal solution.

5.1-12. Label each of the following statements about linear programming problems as true or false, and then justify your answer.

(a) If a feasible solution is optimal but not a CPF solution, then infinitely many optimal solutions exist.

(b) If the value of the objective function is equal at two different feasible points x^* and x^{**}, then all points on the line segment connecting x^* and x^{**} are feasible and Z has the same value at all those points.

(c) If the problem has n variables (before augmenting), then the simultaneous solution of any set of n constraint boundary equations is a CPF solution.

5.1-13. Consider the augmented form of linear programming problems that have feasible solutions and a bounded feasible region. Label each of the following statements as true or false, and then justify your answer by referring to specific statements (with page citations) in the chapter.

(a) There must be at least one optimal solution.

(b) An optimal solution must be a BF solution.

(c) The number of BF solutions is finite.

5.1-14.* Reconsider the model in Prob. 4.6-10. Now you are given the information that the basic variables in the optimal solution are x_2 and x_3. Use this information to identify a system of three constraint boundary equations whose simultaneous solution must be this optimal solution. Then solve this system of equations to obtain this solution.

5.1-15. Reconsider Prob. 4.3-7. Now use the given information and the theory of the simplex method to identify a system of three constraint boundary equations (in x_1, x_2, x_3) whose simultaneous solution must be the optimal solution, without applying the simplex method. Solve this system of equations to find the optimal solution.

5.1-16. Reconsider Prob. 4.3-8. Using the given information and the theory of the simplex method, analyze the constraints of the problem in order to identify a system of three constraint boundary equations whose simultaneous solution must be the optimal solution (not augmented). Then solve this system of equations to obtain this solution.

5.1-17. Consider the following problem.

$$\text{Maximize} \quad Z = 2x_1 + 2x_2 + 3x_3,$$

subject to

$$2x_1 + x_2 + 2x_3 \le 4$$
$$x_1 + x_2 + x_3 \le 3$$

and

$$x_1 \ge 0, \qquad x_2 \ge 0, \qquad x_3 \ge 0.$$

Let x_4 and x_5 be the slack variables for the respective functional constraints. Starting with these two variables as the basic variables for the initial BF solution, you now are given the information that the simplex method proceeds as follows to obtain the optimal solution in two iterations: (1) In iteration 1, the entering basic variable is x_3 and the leaving basic variable is x_4; (2) in iteration 2, the entering basic variable is x_2 and the leaving basic variable is x_5.

(a) Develop a three-dimensional drawing of the feasible region for this problem, and show the path followed by the simplex method.

(b) Give a geometric interpretation of why the simplex method followed this path.

(c) For each of the two edges of the feasible region traversed by the simplex method, give the equation of each of the two constraint boundaries on which it lies, and then give the equation of the additional constraint boundary at each endpoint.

(d) Identify the set of defining equations for each of the three CPF solutions (including the initial one) obtained by the simplex method. Use the defining equations to solve for these solutions.

(e) For each CPF solution obtained in part (d), give the corresponding BF solution and its set of nonbasic variables. Explain how these nonbasic variables identify the defining equations obtained in part (d).

5.1-18. Consider the following problem.

$$\text{Maximize} \quad Z = 3x_1 + 4x_2 + 2x_3,$$

subject to

$$x_1 + x_2 + x_3 \le 20$$
$$x_1 + 2x_2 + x_3 \le 30$$

and

$$x_1 \ge 0, \qquad x_2 \ge 0, \qquad x_3 \ge 0.$$

Let x_4 and x_5 be the slack variables for the respective functional constraints. Starting with these two variables as the basic variables for the initial BF solution, you now are given the information that the simplex method proceeds as follows to obtain the optimal solution in two iterations: (1) In iteration 1, the entering basic variable is x_2 and the leaving basic variable is x_5; (2) in iteration 2, the entering basic variable is x_1 and the leaving basic variable is x_4.

Follow the instructions of Prob. 5.1-17 for this situation.

5.1-19. By inspecting Fig. 5.2, explain why Property 1*b* for CPF solutions holds for this problem if it has the following objective function.
(a) Maximize $Z = x_3$.
(b) Maximize $Z = -x_1 + 2x_3$.

5.1-20. Consider the three-variable linear programming problem shown in Fig. 5.2.
(a) Explain in geometric terms why the set of solutions satisfying any individual constraint is a convex set, as defined in Appendix 2.
(b) Use the conclusion in part (*a*) to explain why the entire feasible region (the set of solutions that simultaneously satisfies every constraint) is a convex set.

5.1-21. Suppose that the three-variable linear programming problem given in Fig. 5.2 has the objective function

Maximize $Z = 3x_1 + 4x_2 + 3x_3$.

Without using the algebra of the simplex method, apply just its geometric reasoning (including choosing the edge giving the maximum rate of increase of Z) to determine and explain the path it would follow in Fig. 5.2 from the origin to the optimal solution.

5.1-22. Consider the three-variable linear programming problem shown in Fig. 5.2.
(a) Construct a table like Table 5.4, giving the indicating variable for each constraint boundary equation and original constraint.
(b) For the CPF solution (2, 4, 3) and its three adjacent CPF solutions (4, 2, 4), (0, 4, 2), and (2, 4, 0), construct a table like Table 5.5, showing the corresponding defining equations, BF solution, and nonbasic variables.
(c) Use the sets of defining equations from part (*b*) to demonstrate that (4, 2, 4), (0, 4, 2), and (2, 4, 0) are indeed adjacent to (2, 4, 3), but that none of these three CPF solutions are adjacent to each other. Then use the sets of nonbasic variables from part (*b*) to demonstrate the same thing.

5.1-23. The formula for the line passing through (2, 4, 3) and (4, 2, 4) in Fig. 5.2 can be written as

(2, 4, 3) + α[(4, 2, 4) − (2, 4, 3)] = (2, 4, 3) + α(2, −2, 1),

where $0 \le \alpha \le 1$ for just the line segment between these points. After augmenting with the slack variables x_4, x_5, x_6, x_7 for the respective functional constraints, this formula becomes

(2, 4, 3, 2, 0, 0, 0) + α(2, −2, 1, −2, 2, 0, 0).

Use this formula directly to answer each of the following questions, and thereby relate the algebra and geometry of the simplex

method as it goes through one iteration in moving from (2, 4, 3) to (4, 2, 4). (You are given the information that it is moving along this line segment.)
(a) What is the entering basic variable?
(b) What is the leaving basic variable?
(c) What is the new BF solution?

5.1-24. Consider a two-variable mathematical programming problem that has the feasible region shown on the graph, where the six dots correspond to CPF solutions. The problem has a linear objective function, and the two dashed lines are objective function lines passing through the optimal solution (4, 5) and the second-best CPF solution (2, 5). Note that the nonoptimal solution (2, 5) is better than both of its adjacent CPF solutions, which violates Property 3 in Sec. 5.1 for CPF solutions in linear programming. Demonstrate that this problem *cannot* be a linear programming problem by constructing the feasible region that would result if the six line segments on the boundary were constraint boundaries for linear programming constraints.

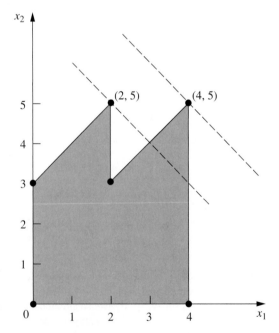

5.2-1. Consider the following problem.

Maximize $Z = 8x_1 + 4x_2 + 6x_3 + 3x_4 + 9x_5$,

subject to

$$
\begin{aligned}
x_1 + 2x_2 + 3x_3 + 3x_4 \quad\quad &\le 180 \quad \text{(resource 1)} \\
4x_1 + 3x_2 + 2x_3 + x_4 + x_5 &\le 270 \quad \text{(resource 2)} \\
x_1 + 3x_2 \quad\quad\quad + x_4 + 3x_5 &\le 180 \quad \text{(resource 3)}
\end{aligned}
$$

and

$$x_j \geq 0, \qquad j = 1, \ldots, 5.$$

You are given the facts that the basic variables in the optimal solution are x_3, x_1, and x_5 and that

$$\begin{bmatrix} 3 & 1 & 0 \\ 2 & 4 & 1 \\ 0 & 1 & 3 \end{bmatrix}^{-1} = \frac{1}{27} \begin{bmatrix} 11 & -3 & 1 \\ -6 & 9 & -3 \\ 2 & -3 & 10 \end{bmatrix}.$$

(a) Use the given information to identify the optimal solution.
(b) Use the given information to identify the shadow prices for the three resources.

I **5.2-2.*** Work through the revised simplex method step by step to solve the following problem.

Maximize $Z = 5x_1 + 8x_2 + 7x_3 + 4x_4 + 6x_5,$

subject to

$$2x_1 + 3x_2 + 3x_3 + 2x_4 + 2x_5 \leq 20$$
$$3x_1 + 5x_2 + 4x_3 + 2x_4 + 4x_5 \leq 30$$

and

$$x_j \geq 0, \qquad j = 1, 2, 3, 4, 5.$$

I **5.2-3.** Work through the revised simplex method step by step to solve the model given in Prob. 4.3-4.

5.2-4. Reconsider Prob. 5.1-1. For the sequence of CPF solutions identified in part (*e*), construct the basis matrix **B** for each of the corresponding BF solutions. For each one, invert **B** manually, use this $\mathbf{B}^{-1}$ to calculate the current solution, and then perform the next iteration (or demonstrate that the current solution is optimal).

I **5.2-5.** Work through the revised simplex method step by step to solve the model given in Prob. 4.1-5.

I **5.2-6.** Work through the revised simplex method step by step to solve the model given in Prob. 4.7-6.

I **5.2-7.** Work through the revised simplex method step by step to solve each of the following models:
(a) Model given in Prob. 3.1-5.
(b) Model given in Prob. 4.7-8.

D **5.3-1.*** Consider the following problem.

Maximize $Z = x_1 - x_2 + 2x_3,$

subject to

$$2x_1 - 2x_2 + 3x_3 \leq 5$$
$$x_1 + x_2 - x_3 \leq 3$$
$$x_1 - x_2 + x_3 \leq 2$$

and

$$x_1 \geq 0, \qquad x_2 \geq 0, \qquad x_3 \geq 0.$$

Let x_4, x_5, and x_6 denote the slack variables for the respective constraints. After you apply the simplex method, a portion of the final simplex tableau is as follows:

Basic Variable	Eq.	Z	\multicolumn{6}{c}{Coefficient of:}	Right Side
			x_1	x_2	x_3	x_4	x_5	x_6	
Z	(0)	1				1	1	0	
x_2	(1)	0				1	3	0	
x_6	(2)	0				0	1	1	
x_3	(3)	0				1	2	0	

(a) Use the fundamental insight presented in Sec. 5.3 to identify the missing numbers in the final simplex tableau. Show your calculations.
(b) Identify the defining equations of the CPF solution corresponding to the optimal BF solution in the final simplex tableau.

D **5.3-2.** Consider the following problem.

Maximize $Z = 4x_1 + 3x_2 + x_3 + 2x_4,$

subject to

$$4x_1 + 2x_2 + x_3 + x_4 \leq 5$$
$$3x_1 + x_2 + 2x_3 + x_4 \leq 4$$

and

$$x_1 \geq 0, \qquad x_2 \geq 0, \qquad x_3 \geq 0, \qquad x_4 \geq 0.$$

Let x_5 and x_6 denote the slack variables for the respective constraints. After you apply the simplex method, a portion of the final simplex tableau is as follows:

Basic Variable	Eq.	Z	\multicolumn{6}{c}{Coefficient of:}	Right Side
			x_1	x_2	x_3	x_4	x_5	x_6	
Z	(0)	1					1	1	
x_2	(1)	0					1	-1	
x_4	(2)	0					-1	2	

(a) Use the fundamental insight presented in Sec. 5.3 to identify the missing numbers in the final simplex tableau. Show your calculations.
(b) Identify the defining equations of the CPF solution corresponding to the optimal BF solution in the final simplex tableau.

D **5.3-3.** Consider the following problem.

Maximize $Z = 6x_1 + x_2 + 2x_3,$

subject to

$$2x_1 + 2x_2 + \frac{1}{2}x_3 \le 2$$

$$-4x_1 - 2x_2 - \frac{3}{2}x_3 \le 3$$

$$x_1 + 2x_2 + \frac{1}{2}x_3 \le 1$$

and

$$x_1 \ge 0, \qquad x_2 \ge 0, \qquad x_3 \ge 0.$$

Let x_4, x_5, and x_6 denote the slack variables for the respective constraints. After you apply the simplex method, a portion of the final simplex tableau is as follows:

Basic Variable	Eq.	Z	x_1	x_2	x_3	x_4	x_5	x_6	Right Side
Z	(0)	1				2	0	2	
x_5	(1)	0				1	1	2	
x_3	(2)	0				-2	0	4	
x_1	(3)	0				1	0	-1	

Use the fundamental insight presented in Sec. 5.3 to identify the missing numbers in the final simplex tableau. Show your calculations.

D **5.3-4.** Consider the following problem.

Maximize $Z = x_1 - x_2 + 2x_3,$

subject to

$$x_1 + x_2 + 3x_3 \le 15$$
$$2x_1 - x_2 + x_3 \le 2$$
$$-x_1 + x_2 + x_3 \le 4$$

and

$$x_1 \ge 0, \qquad x_2 \ge 0, \qquad x_3 \ge 0.$$

Let x_4, x_5, and x_6 denote the slack variables for the respective constraints. After the simplex method is applied, a portion of the final simplex tableau is as follows:

Basic Variable	Eq.	Z	x_1	x_2	x_3	x_4	x_5	x_6	Right Side
Z	(0)	1					$\frac{3}{2}$	$\frac{1}{2}$	
x_4	(1)	0					-1	-2	
x_3	(2)	0					$\frac{1}{2}$	$\frac{1}{2}$	
x_2	(3)	0					$-\frac{1}{2}$	$\frac{1}{2}$	

(a) Use the fundamental insight presented in Sec. 5.3 to identify the missing numbers in the final simplex tableau. Show your calculations.
(b) Identify the defining equations of the CPF solution corresponding to the optimal BF solution in the final simplex tableau.

D **5.3-5.** Consider the following problem.

Maximize $Z = 20x_1 + 6x_2 + 8x_3,$

subject to

$$8x_1 + 2x_2 + 3x_3 \le 200$$
$$4x_1 + 3x_2 + 3x_3 \le 100$$
$$2x_1 + 3x_2 + x_3 \le 50$$
$$x_3 \le 20$$

and

$$x_1 \ge 0, \qquad x_2 \ge 0, \qquad x_3 \ge 0.$$

Let x_4, x_5, x_6, and x_7 denote the slack variables for the first through fourth constraints, respectively. Suppose that after some number of iterations of the simplex method, a portion of the current simplex tableau is as follows:

Basic Variable	Eq.	Z	x_1	x_2	x_3	x_4	x_5	x_6	x_7	Right Side
Z	(0)	1				$\frac{9}{4}$	$\frac{1}{2}$	0	0	
x_1	(1)	0				$\frac{3}{16}$	$-\frac{1}{8}$	0	0	
x_2	(2)	0				$-\frac{1}{4}$	$\frac{1}{2}$	0	0	
x_6	(3)	0				$-\frac{3}{8}$	$\frac{1}{4}$	1	0	
x_7	(4)	0				0	0	0	1	

(a) Use the fundamental insight presented in Sec. 5.3 to identify the missing numbers in the current simplex tableau. Show your calculations.

(b) Indicate which of these missing numbers would be generated by the revised simplex method in order to perform the next iteration.

(c) Identify the defining equations of the CPF solution corresponding to the BF solution in the current simplex tableau.

D **5.3-6.** You are using the simplex method to solve the following linear programming problem.

Maximize $Z = 6x_1 + 5x_2 - x_3 + 4x_4,$

subject to

$$3x_1 + 2x_2 - 3x_3 + x_4 \le 120$$
$$3x_1 + 3x_2 + x_3 + 3x_4 \le 180$$

and

$$x_1 \ge 0, \qquad x_2 \ge 0, \qquad x_3 \ge 0, \qquad x_4 \ge 0.$$

You have obtained the following final simplex tableau where x_5 and x_6 are the slack variables for the respective constraints.

Basic Variable	Eq.	Z				Coefficient of:			Right Side
			x_1	x_2	x_3	x_4	x_5	x_6	
Z	(0)	1	0	$\frac{1}{4}$	0	$\frac{1}{2}$	$\frac{3}{4}$	$\frac{5}{4}$	Z^*
x_1	(1)	0	1	$\frac{11}{12}$	0	$\frac{5}{6}$	$\frac{1}{12}$	$\frac{1}{4}$	b_1^*
x_3	(2)	0	0	$\frac{1}{4}$	1	$\frac{1}{2}$	$-\frac{1}{4}$	$\frac{1}{4}$	b_2^*

Use the fundamental insight presented in Sec. 5.3 to identify Z^*, b_1^*, and b_2^*. Show your calculations.

D **5.3-7.** Consider the following problem.

Maximize $Z = c_1x_1 + c_2x_2 + c_3x_3,$

subject to

$$x_1 + 2x_2 + x_3 \le b$$
$$2x_1 + x_2 + 3x_3 \le 2b$$

and

$$x_1 \ge 0, \qquad x_2 \ge 0, \qquad x_3 \ge 0.$$

Note that values have not been assigned to the coefficients in the objective function (c_1, c_2, c_3), and that the only specification for the right-hand side of the functional constraints is that the second one $(2b)$ be twice as large as the first (b).

Now suppose that your boss has inserted her best estimate of the values of c_1, c_2, c_3, and b without informing you and then has run the simplex method. You are given the resulting final simplex tableau below (where x_4 and x_5 are the slack variables for the respective functional constraints), but you are unable to read the value of Z^*.

Basic Variable	Eq.	Z			Coefficient of:			Right Side
			x_1	x_2	x_3	x_4	x_5	
Z	(0)	1	$\frac{7}{10}$	0	0	$\frac{3}{5}$	$\frac{4}{5}$	Z^*
x_2	(1)	0	$\frac{1}{5}$	1	0	$\frac{3}{5}$	$-\frac{1}{5}$	1
x_3	(2)	0	$\frac{3}{5}$	0	1	$-\frac{1}{5}$	$\frac{2}{5}$	3

(a) Use the fundamental insight presented in Sec. 5.3 to identify the value of (c_1, c_2, c_3) that was used.

(b) Use the fundamental insight presented in Sec. 5.3 to identify the value of b that was used.

(c) Calculate the value of Z^* in two ways, where one way uses your results from part (a) and the other way uses your result from part (b). Show your two methods for finding Z^*.

5.3-8. For iteration 2 of the example in Sec. 5.3, the following expression was shown:

Final row $0 = [-3, \quad -5 \mid 0, \quad 0, \quad 0 \mid 0]$

$$+ [0, \tfrac{3}{2}, 1] \begin{bmatrix} 1 & 0 \mid 1 & 0 & 0 \mid 4 \\ 0 & 2 \mid 0 & 1 & 0 \mid 12 \\ 3 & 2 \mid 0 & 0 & 1 \mid 18 \end{bmatrix}.$$

Derive this expression by combining the algebraic operations (in matrix form) for iterations 1 and 2 that affect row 0.

5.3-9. Most of the description of the fundamental insight presented in Sec. 5.3 assumes that the problem is in our standard form. Now consider each of the following other forms, where the additional adjustments in the initialization step are those presented in Sec. 4.6, including the use of artificial variables and the Big M method where appropriate. Describe the resulting adjustments in the fundamental insight.

(a) Equality constraints

(b) Functional constraints in $\ge$ form

(c) Negative right-hand sides

(d) Variables allowed to be negative (with no lower bound)

5.3-10. Reconsider the model in Prob. 4.6-6. Use artificial variables and the Big M method to construct the complete first simplex tableau for the simplex method, and then identify the columns that will contains $\mathbf{S}^*$ for applying the fundamental insight in the final tableau. Explain why these are the appropriate columns.

5.3-11. Consider the following problem.

$$\text{Minimize} \quad Z = 2x_1 + 3x_2 + 2x_3,$$

subject to

$$x_1 + 4x_2 + 2x_3 \geq 8$$
$$3x_1 + 2x_2 + 2x_3 \geq 6$$

and

$$x_1 \geq 0, \qquad x_2 \geq 0, \qquad x_3 \geq 0.$$

Let x_4 and x_6 be the surplus variables for the first and second constraints, respectively. Let $\bar{x}_5$ and $\bar{x}_7$ be the corresponding artificial variables. After you make the adjustments described in Sec. 4.6 for this model form when using the Big M method, the initial simplex tableau ready to apply the simplex method is as follows:

Basic Variable	Eq.	Z	x_1	x_2	x_3	x_4	$\bar{x}_5$	x_6	$\bar{x}_7$	Right Side
					Coefficient of:					
Z	(0)	-1	$-4M+2$	$-6M+3$	$-2M+2$	M	0	M	0	$-14M$
$\bar{x}_5$	(1)	0	1	4	2	-1	1	0	0	8
$\bar{x}_7$	(2)	0	3	2	2	0	0	-1	1	6

After you apply the simplex method, a portion of the final simplex tableau is as follows:

Basic Variable	Eq.	Z	x_1	x_2	x_3	x_4	$\bar{x}_5$	x_6	$\bar{x}_7$	Right Side
					Coefficient of:					
Z	(0)	-1					$M-0.5$		$M-0.5$	
x_2	(1)	0					0.3		-0.1	
x_1	(2)	0					-0.2		0.4	

(a) Based on the above tableaux, use the fundamental insight presented in Sec. 5.3 to identify the missing numbers in the final simplex tableau. Show your calculations.

(b) Examine the mathematical logic presented in Sec. 5.3 to validate the fundamental insight (see the $\mathbf{T}^* = \mathbf{MT}$ and $\mathbf{t}^* = \mathbf{t} + \mathbf{vT}$ equations and the subsequent derivations of $\mathbf{M}$ and $\mathbf{v}$). This logic assumes that the original model fits our standard form, whereas the current problem does not fit this form. Show how, with minor adjustments, this same logic applies to the current problem when $\mathbf{t}$ is row 0 and $\mathbf{T}$ is rows 1 and 2 in the initial simplex tableau given above. Derive $\mathbf{M}$ and $\mathbf{v}$ for this problem.

(c) When you apply the $\mathbf{t}^* = \mathbf{t} + \mathbf{vT}$ equation, another option is to use $\mathbf{t} = [2, 3, 2, 0, M, 0, M, 0]$, which is the *preliminary* row 0 before the algebraic elimination of the nonzero coefficients of the initial basic variables $\bar{x}_5$ and $\bar{x}_7$. Repeat part (b) for this equation with this new $\mathbf{t}$. After you derive the new $\mathbf{v}$, show that this equation yields the same final row 0 for this problem as the equation derived in part (b).

(d) Identify the defining equations of the CPF solution corresponding to the optimal BF solution in the final simplex tableau.

5.3-12. Consider the following problem.

$$\text{Maximize} \quad Z = 2x_1 + 4x_2 + 3x_3,$$

subject to

$$x_1 + 3x_2 + 2x_3 = 20$$
$$x_1 + 5x_2 \qquad \geq 10$$

and

$$x_1 \geq 0, \qquad x_2 \geq 0, \qquad x_3 \geq 0.$$

Let $\bar{x}_4$ be the artificial variable for the first constraint. Let x_5 and $\bar{x}_6$ be the surplus variable and artificial variable, respectively, for the second constraint.

You are now given the information that a portion of the final simplex tableau is as follows:

Basic Variable	Eq.	Z	x_1	x_2	x_3	$\bar{x}_4$	x_5	$\bar{x}_6$	Right Side
					Coefficient of:				
Z	(0)	1				$M+2$	0	M	
x_1	(1)	0				1	0	0	
x_5	(2)	0				1	1	-1	

(a) Extend the fundamental insight presented in Sec. 5.3 to identify the missing numbers in the final simplex tableau. Show your calculations.

(b) Identify the defining equations of the CPF solution corresponding to the optimal solution in the final simplex tableau.

5.3-13. Consider the following problem.

$$\text{Maximize} \quad Z = 3x_1 + 7x_2 + 2x_3,$$

subject to

$$-2x_1 + 2x_2 + x_3 \leq 10$$
$$3x_1 + x_2 - x_3 \leq 20$$

and

$$x_1 \geq 0, \qquad x_2 \geq 0, \qquad x_3 \geq 0.$$

You are given the fact that the basic variables in the optimal solution are x_1 and x_3.

(a) Introduce slack variables, and then use the given information to find the optimal solution directly by Gaussian elimination.

(b) Extend the work in part (a) to find the shadow prices.

(c) Use the given information to identify the defining equations of the optimal CPF solution, and then solve these equations to obtain the optimal solution.

(d) Construct the basis matrix $\mathbf{B}$ for the optimal BF solution, invert $\mathbf{B}$ manually, and then use this $\mathbf{B}^{-1}$ to solve for the optimal solution and the shadow prices $\mathbf{y}^*$. Then apply the optimality test for the revised simplex method to verify that this solution is optimal.

(e) Given $\mathbf{B}^{-1}$ and $\mathbf{y}^*$ from part (d), use the fundamental insight presented in Sec. 5.3 to construct the complete final simplex tableau.

6

Duality Theory and Sensitivity Analysis

One of the most important discoveries in the early development of linear programming was the concept of duality and its many important ramifications. This discovery revealed that every linear programming problem has associated with it another linear programming problem called the **dual.** The relationships between the dual problem and the original problem (called the **primal**) prove to be extremely useful in a variety of ways. For example, you soon will see that the shadow prices described in Sec. 4.7 actually are provided by the optimal solution for the dual problem. We shall describe many other valuable applications of duality theory in this chapter as well.

One of the key uses of duality theory lies in the interpretation and implementation of *sensitivity analysis.* As we already mentioned in Secs. 2.3, 3.3, and 4.7, sensitivity analysis is a very important part of almost every linear programming study. Because most of the parameter values used in the original model are just *estimates* of future conditions, the effect on the optimal solution if other conditions prevail instead needs to be investigated. Furthermore, certain parameter values (such as resource amounts) may represent *managerial decisions,* in which case the choice of the parameter values may be the main issue to be studied, which can be done through sensitivity analysis.

For greater clarity, the first three sections discuss duality theory under the assumption that the *primal* linear programming problem is in *our standard form* (but with no restriction that the b_i values need to be positive). Other forms are then discussed in Sec. 6.4. We begin the chapter by introducing the essence of duality theory and its applications. We then describe the economic interpretation of the dual problem (Sec. 6.2) and delve deeper into the relationships between the primal and dual problems (Sec. 6.3). Section 6.5 focuses on the role of duality theory in sensitivity analysis. The basic procedure for sensitivity analysis (which is based on the fundamental insight of Sec. 5.3) is summarized in Sec. 6.6 and illustrated in Sec. 6.7.

6.1 THE ESSENCE OF DUALITY THEORY

Given our standard form for the *primal problem* at the left (perhaps after conversion from another form), its *dual problem* has the form shown to the right.

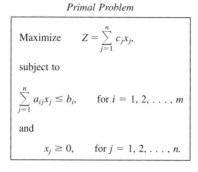

Primal Problem

Maximize $\quad Z = \sum_{j=1}^{n} c_j x_j,$

subject to

$\quad \sum_{j=1}^{n} a_{ij} x_j \leq b_i, \qquad$ for $i = 1, 2, \ldots, m$

and

$\quad x_j \geq 0, \qquad$ for $j = 1, 2, \ldots, n.$

Dual Problem

Minimize $\quad W = \sum_{i=1}^{m} b_i y_i,$

subject to

$\quad \sum_{i=1}^{m} a_{ij} y_i \geq c_j, \qquad$ for $j = 1, 2, \ldots, n$

and

$\quad y_i \geq 0, \qquad$ for $i = 1, 2, \ldots, m.$

Thus, the dual problem uses exactly the same *parameters* as the primal problem, but in different locations. To highlight the comparison, now look at these same two problems in matrix notation (as introduced at the beginning of Sec. 5.2), where **c** and $\mathbf{y} = [y_1, y_2, \ldots, y_m]$ are row vectors but **b** and **x** are column vectors.

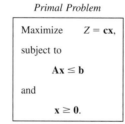

Primal Problem

Maximize $\quad Z = \mathbf{cx},$

subject to

$\quad \mathbf{Ax} \leq \mathbf{b}$

and

$\quad \mathbf{x} \geq \mathbf{0}.$

Dual Problem

Minimize $\quad W = \mathbf{yb},$

subject to

$\quad \mathbf{yA} \geq \mathbf{c}$

and

$\quad \mathbf{y} \geq \mathbf{0}.$

To illustrate, the primal and dual problems for the Wyndor Glass Co. example of Sec. 3.1 are shown in Table 6.1 in both algebraic and matrix form.

The **primal-dual table** for linear programming (Table 6.2) also helps to highlight the correspondence between the two problems. It shows all the linear programming parameters (the a_{ij}, b_i, and c_j) and how they are used to construct the two problems. All the headings for the primal problem are horizontal, whereas the headings for the dual problem are read by turning the book sideways. For the primal problem, each *column* (except the Right Side column) gives the coefficients of a single variable in the respective constraints and then in the objective function, whereas each *row* (except the bottom one) gives the parameters for a single contraint. For the dual problem, each *row* (except the Right Side row) gives the coefficients of a single variable in the respective constraints and then in the objective function, whereas each *column* (except the rightmost one) gives the parameters for a single constraint. In addition, the Right Side column gives the right-hand sides for the primal problem and the objective function coefficients for the dual problem, whereas the bottom row gives the objective function coefficients for the primal problem and the right-hand sides for the dual problem.

TABLE 6.1 Primal and dual problems for the Wyndor Glass Co. example

Primal Problem in Algebraic Form	Dual Problem in Algebraic Form

Maximize $Z = 3x_1 + 5x_2,$

subject to

$$x_1 \leq 4$$
$$2x_2 \leq 12$$
$$3x_1 + 2x_2 \leq 18$$

and $x_1 \geq 0,$ $x_2 \geq 0.$

Minimize $W = 4y_1 + 12y_2 + 18y_3,$

subject to

$$y_1 + 3y_3 \geq 3$$
$$2y_2 + 2y_3 \geq 5$$

and

$$y_1 \geq 0, \qquad y_2 \geq 0, \qquad y_3 \geq 0.$$

Primal Problem in Matrix Form	Dual Problem in Matrix Form

Maximize $Z = [3, \ 5] \begin{bmatrix} x_1 \\ x_2 \end{bmatrix},$

subject to

$$\begin{bmatrix} 1 & 0 \\ 0 & 2 \\ 3 & 2 \end{bmatrix} \begin{bmatrix} x_1 \\ x_2 \end{bmatrix} \leq \begin{bmatrix} 4 \\ 12 \\ 18 \end{bmatrix}$$

and

$$\begin{bmatrix} x_1 \\ x_2 \end{bmatrix} \geq \begin{bmatrix} 0 \\ 0 \end{bmatrix}.$$

Minimize $W = [y_1, y_2, y_3] \begin{bmatrix} 4 \\ 12 \\ 18 \end{bmatrix}$

subject to

$$[y_1, \ y_2, \ y_3] \begin{bmatrix} 1 & 0 \\ 0 & 2 \\ 3 & 2 \end{bmatrix} \geq [3, \ 5]$$

and

$$[y_1, \ y_2, \ y_3] \geq [0, \ 0, \ 0].$$

Consequently, (1) the parameters for a *constraint* in either problem are the coefficients of a *variable* in the other problem and (2) the coefficients for the *objective function* of either problem are the *right sides* for the other problem. Thus, there is a direct correspondence between these entities in the two problems, as summarized in Table 6.3. These correspondences are a key to some of the applications of duality theory, including sensitivity analysis.

Origin of the Dual Problem

Duality theory is based directly on the fundamental insight (particularly with regard to row 0) presented in Sec. 5.3. To see why, we continue to use the notation introduced in Table 5.10 for row 0 of the *final* tableau, except for replacing Z^* by W^* and dropping the asterisks from z^* and y^* when referring to *any* tableau. Thus, at *any* given iteration of the simplex method for the primal problem, the current numbers in row 0 are denoted as shown in the (partial) tableau given in Table 6.4. For the coefficients of $x_1, x_2, \ldots, x_n$, recall that $\mathbf{z} = (z_1, z_2, \ldots, z_n)$ denotes the vector that the simplex method added to the vector of *initial* coefficients, $-\mathbf{c}$, in the process of reaching the current tableau. (Do not confuse $\mathbf{z}$ with the value of the objective function Z.) Similarly, since the *initial* coefficients of $x_{n+1}, x_{n+2}, \ldots, x_{n+m}$ in row 0 all are 0, $\mathbf{y} = (y_1, y_2, \ldots, y_m)$ denotes the vector that the simplex method has added to these coefficients. Also recall [see Eq. (1) in the

TABLE 6.2 Primal-dual table for linear programming, illustrated by the Wyndor Glass Co. example

(a) General Case

			\multicolumn{4}{c}{Primal Problem}		
			\multicolumn{4}{c}{Coefficient of:}	Right Side	
			x_1	x_2	$\cdots$	x_n		
Dual Problem	Coefficient of:	y_1	a_{11}	a_{12}	$\cdots$	a_{1n}	$\leq b_1$	Coefficients for Objective Function (Minimize)
		y_2	a_{21}	a_{22}	$\cdots$	a_{2n}	$\leq b_2$	
		$\vdots$					$\vdots$	
		y_m	a_{m1}	a_{m2}	$\cdots$	a_{mn}	$\leq b_m$	
	Right Side		VI c_1	VI c_2	$\cdots$	VI c_n		

Coefficients for Objective Function (Maximize)

(b) Wyndor Glass Co. Example

	x_1	x_2	
y_1	1	0	≤ 4
y_2	0	2	≤ 12
y_3	3	2	≤ 18
	VI	VI	
	3	5	

"Mathematical Summary" subsection of Sec. 5.3] that the fundamental insight led to the following relationships between these quantities and the parameters of the original model:

$$W = \mathbf{yb} = \sum_{i=1}^{m} b_i y_i,$$

$$\mathbf{z} = \mathbf{yA}, \quad \text{so} \quad z_j = \sum_{i=1}^{m} a_{ij} y_i, \quad \text{for } j = 1, 2, \ldots, n.$$

To illustrate these relationships with the Wyndor example, the first equation gives $W = 4y_1 + 12y_2 + 18y_3$, which is just the objective function for the dual problem shown

TABLE 6.3 Correspondence between entities in primal and dual problems

One Problem	Other Problem
Constraint i $\longleftrightarrow$	Variable i
Objective function $\longleftrightarrow$	Right sides

TABLE 6.4 Notation for entries in row 0 of a simplex tableau

Iteration	Basic Variable	Eq.	Z	x_1	x_2	$\cdots$	x_n	x_{n+1}	x_{n+2}	$\cdots$	x_{n+m}	Right Side
				Coefficient of:								
Any	Z	(0)	1	$z_1 - c_1$	$z_2 - c_2$	$\cdots$	$z_n - c_n$	y_1	y_2	$\cdots$	y_m	W

in the upper right-hand box of Table 6.1. The second set of equations give $z_1 = y_1 + 3y_3$ and $z_2 = 2y_2 + 2y_3$, which are the left-hand sides of the functional constraints for this dual problem. Thus, by subtracting the right-hand sides of these $\geq$ constraints ($c_1 = 3$ and $c_2 = 5$), ($z_1 - c_1$) and ($z_2 - c_2$) can be interpreted as being the *surplus variables* for these functional constraints.

The remaining key is to express what the simplex method tries to accomplish (according to the optimality test) in terms of these symbols. Specifically, it seeks a set of basic variables, and the corresponding BF solution, such that *all* coefficients in row 0 are *nonnegative*. It then stops with this optimal solution. Using the notation in Table 6.4, this goal is expressed symbolically as follows:

Condition for Optimality:
$$z_j - c_j \geq 0 \qquad \text{for } j = 1, 2, \ldots, n,$$
$$y_i \geq 0 \qquad \text{for } i = 1, 2, \ldots, m.$$

After we substitute the preceding expression for z_j, the condition for optimality says that the simplex method can be interpreted as seeking values for $y_1, y_2, \ldots, y_m$ such that

$$W = \sum_{i=1}^{m} b_i y_i,$$

subject to

$$\sum_{i=1}^{m} a_{ij} y_i \geq c_j, \qquad \text{for } j = 1, 2, \ldots, n$$

and

$$y_i \geq 0, \qquad \text{for } i = 1, 2, \ldots, m.$$

But, except for lacking an objective for W, this problem is precisely the *dual problem*! To complete the formulation, let us now explore what the missing objective should be.

Since W is just the current value of Z, and since the objective for the primal problem is to maximize Z, a natural first reaction is that W should be maximized also. However, this is not correct for the following rather subtle reason: The only *feasible* solutions for this new problem are those that satisfy the condition for *optimality* for the primal problem. Therefore, it is *only* the optimal solution for the primal problem that corresponds to a feasible solution for this new problem. As a consequence, the optimal value of Z in the primal problem is the *minimum* feasible value of W in the new problem, so W should be minimized. (The full justification for this conclusion is provided by the relationships we develop in Sec. 6.3.) Adding this objective of minimizing W gives the *complete* dual problem.

Consequently, the dual problem may be viewed as a restatement in linear programming terms of the *goal* of the simplex method, namely, to reach a solution for the primal problem that *satisfies the optimality test. Before* this goal has been reached, the corresponding **y** in row 0 (coefficients of slack variables) of the current tableau must be *infeasible* for the *dual problem.* However, *after* the goal is reached, the corresponding **y** must be an *optimal solution* (labeled **y***) for the *dual problem,* because it is a feasible solution that attains the minimum feasible value of W. This optimal solution $(y_1^*, y_2^*, \ldots, y_m^*)$ provides for the primal problem the shadow prices that were described in Sec. 4.7. Furthermore, this optimal W is just the optimal value of Z, so the *optimal objective function values are equal* for the two problems. This fact also implies that $\mathbf{cx} \leq \mathbf{yb}$ for any **x** and **y** that are *feasible* for the primal and dual problems, respectively.

To illustrate, the left-hand side of Table 6.5 shows row 0 for the respective iterations when the simplex method is applied to the Wyndor Glass Co. example. In each case, row 0 is partitioned into three parts: the coefficients of the decision variables (x_1, x_2), the coefficients of the slack variables (x_3, x_4, x_5), and the right-hand side (value of Z). Since the coefficients of the slack variables give the corresponding values of the dual variables (y_1, y_2, y_3), each row 0 identifies a corresponding solution for the dual problem, as shown in the y_1, y_2, and y_3 columns of Table 6.5. To interpret the next two columns, recall that $(z_1 - c_1)$ and $(z_2 - c_2)$ are the surplus variables for the functional constraints in the dual problem, so the full dual problem after augmenting with these surplus variables is

$$\text{Minimize} \quad W = 4y_1 + 12y_2 + 18y_3,$$

subject to

$$
\begin{aligned}
y_1 \quad\quad + 3y_3 - (z_1 - c_1) &= 3 \\
2y_2 + 2y_3 - (z_2 - c_2) &= 5
\end{aligned}
$$

and

$$y_1 \geq 0, \qquad y_2 \geq 0, \qquad y_3 \geq 0.$$

Therefore, by using the numbers in the y_1, y_2, and y_3 columns, the values of these surplus variables can be calculated as

$$
\begin{aligned}
z_1 - c_1 &= y_1 + 3y_3 - 3, \\
z_2 - c_2 &= 2y_2 + 2y_3 - 5.
\end{aligned}
$$

TABLE 6.5 Row 0 and corresponding dual solution for each iteration for the Wyndor Glass Co. example

Iteration	Primal Problem						Dual Problem					
	Row 0						y_1	y_2	y_3	$z_1 - c_1$	$z_2 - c_2$	W
0	[−3,	−5	0,	0,	0	0]	0	0	0	−3	−5	0
1	[−3,	0	0,	$\frac{5}{2}$,	0	30]	0	$\frac{5}{2}$	0	−3	0	30
2	[0,	0	0,	$\frac{3}{2}$,	1	36]	0	$\frac{3}{2}$	1	0	0	36

Thus, a negative value for either surplus variable indicates that the corresponding constraint is violated. Also included in the rightmost column of the table is the calculated value of the dual objective function $W = 4y_1 + 12y_2 + 18y_3$.

As displayed in Table 6.4, *all* these quantities to the right of row 0 in Table 6.5 already are identified by row 0 without requiring any new calculations. In particular, note in Table 6.5 how *each* number obtained for the dual problem already appears in row 0 in the spot indicated by Table 6.4.

For the initial row 0, Table 6.5 shows that the corresponding dual solution $(y_1, y_2, y_3) = (0, 0, 0)$ is infeasible because both surplus variables are negative. The first iteration succeeds in eliminating one of these negative values, but not the other. After two iterations, the optimality test is satisfied for the primal problem because all the dual variables and surplus variables are nonnegative. This dual solution $(y_1^*, y_2^*, y_3^*) = (0, \frac{3}{2}, 1)$ is optimal (as could be verified by applying the simplex method directly to the dual problem), so the optimal value of Z and W is $Z^* = 36 = W^*$.

Summary of Primal-Dual Relationships

Now let us summarize the newly discovered key relationships between the primal and dual problems.

> **Weak duality property:** If $\mathbf{x}$ is a feasible solution for the primal problem and $\mathbf{y}$ is a feasible solution for the dual problem, then
>
> $$\mathbf{cx} \leq \mathbf{yb}.$$

For example, for the Wyndor Glass Co. problem, one feasible solution is $x_1 = 3$, $x_2 = 3$, which yields $Z = \mathbf{cx} = 24$, and one feasible solution for the dual problem is $y_1 = 1$, $y_2 = 1$, $y_3 = 2$, which yields a larger objective function value $W = \mathbf{yb} = 52$. These are just sample feasible solutions for the two problems. For *any* such pair of feasible solutions, this inequality must hold because the *maximum* feasible value of $Z = \mathbf{cx}$ (36) *equals* the *minimum* feasible value of the dual objective function $W = \mathbf{yb}$, which is our next property.

> **Strong duality property:** If $\mathbf{x}^*$ is an optimal solution for the primal problem and $\mathbf{y}^*$ is an optimal solution for the dual problem, then
>
> $$\mathbf{cx}^* = \mathbf{y}^*\mathbf{b}.$$

Thus, these two properties imply that $\mathbf{cx} < \mathbf{yb}$ for feasible solutions if one or both of them are *not optimal* for their respective problems, whereas equality holds when both are optimal.

The *weak duality property* describes the relationship between any pair of solutions for the primal and dual problems where *both* solutions are *feasible* for their respective problems. At each iteration, the simplex method finds a specific pair of solutions for the two problems, where the primal solution is feasible but the dual solution is *not feasible* (except at the final iteration). Our next property describes this situation and the relationship between this pair of solutions.

> **Complementary solutions property:** At each iteration, the simplex method simultaneously identifies a CPF solution $\mathbf{x}$ for the primal problem and a **complementary solution** $\mathbf{y}$ for the dual problem (found in row 0, the coefficients of the slack variables), where
>
> $$\mathbf{cx} = \mathbf{yb}.$$

If **x** is *not optimal* for the primal problem, then **y** is *not feasible* for the dual problem.

To illustrate, after one iteration for the Wyndor Glass Co. problem, $x_1 = 0$, $x_2 = 6$, and $y_1 = 0$, $y_2 = \frac{5}{2}$, $y_3 = 0$, with $\mathbf{cx} = 30 = \mathbf{yb}$. This **x** is feasible for the primal problem, but this **y** is not feasible for the dual problem (since it violates the constraint, $y_1 + 3y_3 \geq 3$).

The complementary solutions property also holds at the final iteration of the simplex method, where an optimal solution is found for the primal problem. However, more can be said about the complementary solution **y** in this case, as presented in the next property.

> **Complementary optimal solutions property:** At the final iteration, the simplex method simultaneously identifies an optimal solution **x*** for the primal problem and a **complementary optimal solution y*** for the dual problem (found in row 0, the coefficients of the slack variables), where
>
> $$\mathbf{cx^*} = \mathbf{y^*b}.$$
>
> The y_i^* are the shadow prices for the primal problem.

For the example, the final iteration yields $x_1^* = 2$, $x_2^* = 6$, and $y_1^* = 0$, $y_2^* = \frac{3}{2}$, $y_3^* = 1$, with $\mathbf{cx^*} = 36 = \mathbf{y^*b}$.

We shall take a closer look at some of these properties in Sec. 6.3. There you will see that the complementary solutions property can be extended considerably further. In particular, after slack and surplus variables are introduced to augment the respective problems, every *basic* solution in the primal problem has a complementary *basic* solution in the dual problem. We already have noted that the simplex method identifies the values of the surplus variables for the dual problem as $z_j - c_j$ in Table 6.4. This result then leads to an additional *complementary slackness property* that relates the basic variables in one problem to the nonbasic variables in the other (Tables 6.7 and 6.8), but more about that later.

In Sec. 6.4, after describing how to construct the dual problem when the primal problem is *not* in our standard form, we discuss another very useful property, which is summarized as follows:

> **Symmetry property:** For *any* primal problem and its dual problem, all relationships between them must be *symmetric* because the dual of this dual problem is this primal problem.

Therefore, all the preceding properties hold regardless of which of the two problems is labeled as the primal problem. (The direction of the inequality for the weak duality property does require that the primal problem be expressed or reexpressed in maximization form and the dual problem in minimization form.) Consequently, the simplex method can be applied to either problem, and it simultaneously will identify complementary solutions (ultimately a complementary optimal solution) for the other problem.

So far, we have focused on the relationships between *feasible* or *optimal* solutions in the primal problem and corresponding solutions in the dual problem. However, it is possible that the primal (or dual) problem either has *no feasible solutions* or has feasible solutions but *no optimal solution* (because the objective function is unbounded). Our final property summarizes the primal-dual relationships under all these possibilities.

Duality theorem: The following are the only possible relationships between the primal and dual problems.

1. If one problem has *feasible solutions* and a *bounded* objective function (and so has an optimal solution), then so does the other problem, so both the weak and strong duality properties are applicable.
2. If one problem has *feasible solutions* and an *unbounded* objective function (and so *no optimal solution*), then the other problem has *no feasible solutions*.
3. If one problem has *no feasible solutions,* then the other problem has either *no feasible solutions* or an *unbounded* objective function.

Applications

As we have just implied, one important application of duality theory is that the *dual* problem can be solved directly by the simplex method in order to identify an optimal solution for the primal problem. We discussed in Sec. 4.8 that the number of functional constraints affects the computational effort of the simplex method far more than the number of variables does. If $m > n$, so that the dual problem has fewer functional constraints (n) than the primal problem (m), then applying the simplex method directly to the dual problem instead of the primal problem probably will achieve a substantial reduction in computational effort.

The *weak* and *strong duality properties* describe key relationships between the primal and dual problems. One useful application is for evaluating a proposed solution for the primal problem. For example, suppose that **x** is a feasible solution that has been proposed for implementation and that a feasible solution **y** has been found by inspection for the dual problem such that **cx** = **yb**. In this case, **x** must be *optimal* without the simplex method even being applied! Even if **cx** < **yb**, then **yb** still provides an upper bound on the optimal value of Z, so if **yb** − **cx** is small, intangible factors favoring **x** may lead to its selection without further ado.

One of the key applications of the complementary solutions property is its use in the dual simplex method presented in Sec. 7.1. This algorithm operates on the primal problem exactly as if the simplex method were being applied simultaneously to the dual problem, which can be done because of this property. Because the roles of row 0 and the right side in the simplex tableau have been reversed, the dual simplex method requires that row 0 *begin and remain nonnegative* while the right side *begins* with some *negative* values (subsequent iterations strive to reach a nonnegative right side). Consequently, this algorithm occasionally is used because it is more convenient to set up the initial tableau in this form than in the form required by the simplex method. Furthermore, it frequently is used for reoptimization (discussed in Sec. 4.7), because changes in the original model lead to the revised final tableau fitting this form. This situation is common for certain types of sensitivity analysis, as you will see later in the chapter.

In general terms, duality theory plays a central role in sensitivity analysis. This role is the topic of Sec. 6.5.

Another important application is its use in the economic interpretation of the dual problem and the resulting insights for analyzing the primal problem. You already have seen one example when we discussed shadow prices in Sec. 4.7. The next section describes how this interpretation extends to the entire dual problem and then to the simplex method.

6.2 ECONOMIC INTERPRETATION OF DUALITY

The economic interpretation of duality is based directly upon the typical interpretation for the primal problem (linear programming problem in our standard form) presented in Sec. 3.2. To refresh your memory, we have summarized this interpretation of the primal problem in Table 6.6.

Interpretation of the Dual Problem

To see how this interpretation of the primal problem leads to an economic interpretation for the dual problem,[1] note in Table 6.4 that W is the value of Z (total profit) at the current iteration. Because

$$W = b_1 y_1 + b_2 y_2 + \cdots + b_m y_m,$$

each $b_i y_i$ can thereby be interpreted as the current *contribution to profit* by having b_i units of resource i available for the primal problem. Thus,

> The dual variable y_i is interpreted as the contribution to profit per unit of resource i ($i = 1, 2, \ldots, m$), when the current set of basic variables is used to obtain the primal solution.

In other words, the y_i values (or y_i^* values in the optimal solution) are just the shadow prices discussed in Sec. 4.7.

For example, when iteration 2 of the simplex method finds the optimal solution for the Wyndor problem, it also finds the optimal values of the dual variables (as shown in the bottom row of Table 6.5) to be $y_1^* = 0$, $y_2^* = \frac{3}{2}$, and $y_3^* = 1$. These are precisely the shadow prices found in Sec. 4.7 for this problem through graphical analysis. Recall that the resources for the Wyndor problem are the production capacities of the three plants being made available to the two new products under consideration, so that b_i is the number of hours of production time per week being made available in Plant i for these new products, where $i = 1, 2, 3$. As discussed in Sec. 4.7, the shadow prices indicate that individually increasing any b_i by 1 would increase the optimal value of the objective function (total weekly profit in units of thousands of dollars) by y_i^*. Thus, y_i^* can be interpreted as the contribution to profit per unit of resource i when using the optimal solution.

[1]Actually, several slightly different interpretations have been proposed. The one presented here seems to us to be the most useful because it also directly interprets what the simplex method does in the primal problem.

TABLE 6.6 Economic interpretation of the primal problem

Quantity	Interpretation
x_j	Level of activity j ($j = 1, 2, \ldots, n$)
c_j	Unit profit from activity j
Z	Total profit from all activities
b_i	Amount of resource i available ($i = 1, 2, \ldots, m$)
a_{ij}	Amount of resource i consumed by each unit of activity j

This interpretation of the dual variables leads to our interpretation of the overall dual problem. Specifically, since each unit of activity j in the primal problem consumes a_{ij} units of resource i,

$\sum_{i=1}^{m} a_{ij} y_i$ is interpreted as the current contribution to profit of the mix of resources that would be consumed if 1 unit of activity j were used ($j = 1, 2, \ldots, n$).

For the Wyndor problem, 1 unit of activity j corresponds to producing 1 batch of product j per week, where $j = 1, 2$. The mix of resources consumed by producing 1 batch of product 1 is 1 hour of production time in Plant 1 and 3 hours in Plant 3. The corresponding mix per batch of product 2 is 2 hours each in Plants 2 and 3. Thus, $y_1 + 3y_3$ and $2y_2 + 2y_3$ are interpreted as the current contributions to profit (in thousands of dollars per week) of these respective mixes of resources per batch produced per week of the respective products.

For each activity j, this same mix of resources (and more) probably can be used in other ways as well, but no alternative use should be considered if it is less profitable than 1 unit of activity j. Since c_j is interpreted as the unit profit from activity j, each functional constraint in the dual problem is interpreted as follows:

$\sum_{i=1}^{m} a_{ij} y_i \geq c_j$ says that the actual contribution to profit of the above mix of resources must be at least as much as if they were used by 1 unit of activity j; otherwise, we would not be making the best possible use of these resources.

For the Wyndor problem, the unit profits (in thousands of dollars per week) are $c_1 = 3$ and $c_2 = 5$, so the dual functional constraints with this interpretation are $y_1 + y_3 \geq 3$ and $2y_2 + 2y_3 \geq 5$. Similarly, the interpretation of the nonnegativity constraints is the following:

$y_i \geq 0$ says that the contribution to profit of resource i ($i = 1, 2, \ldots, m$) must be nonnegative: otherwise, it would be better not to use this resource at all.

The objective

$$\text{Minimize} \quad W = \sum_{i=1}^{m} b_i y_i$$

can be viewed as minimizing the total implicit value of the resources consumed by the activities. For the Wyndor problem, the total implicit value (in thousands of dollars per week) of the resources consumed by the two products is $W = 4y_1 + 12y_2 + 18y_3$.

This interpretation can be sharpened somewhat by differentiating between basic and nonbasic variables in the primal problem for any given BF solution ($x_1, x_2, \ldots, x_{n+m}$). Recall that the *basic* variables (the only variables whose values can be nonzero) *always* have a coefficient of *zero* in row 0. Therefore, referring again to Table 6.4 and the accompanying equation for z_j, we see that

$$\sum_{i=1}^{m} a_{ij} y_i = c_j, \quad \text{if } x_j > 0 \quad (j = 1, 2, \ldots, n),$$

$$y_i = 0, \quad \text{if } x_{n+i} > 0 \quad (i = 1, 2, \ldots, m).$$

(This is one version of the complementary slackness property discussed in the next section.) The economic interpretation of the first statement is that whenever an activity j operates at a strictly positive level ($x_j > 0$), the marginal value of the resources it consumes *must equal* (as opposed to exceeding) the unit profit from this activity. The second statement implies that the marginal value of resource i is *zero* ($y_i = 0$) whenever the supply of this resource is not exhausted by the activities ($x_{n+i} > 0$). In economic terminology, such a resource is a "free good"; the price of goods that are oversupplied must drop to zero by the law of supply and demand. This fact is what justifies interpreting the objective for the dual problem as minimizing the total implicit value of the resources *consumed,* rather than the resources *allocated.*

To illustrate these two statements, consider the optimal BF solution (2, 6, 2, 0, 0) for the Wyndor problem. The basic variables are x_1, x_2, and x_3, so their coefficients in row 0 are zero, as shown in the bottom row of Table 6.5. This bottom row also gives the corresponding dual solution: $y_1^* = 0$, $y_2^* = \frac{3}{2}$, $y_3^* = 1$, with surplus variables $(z_1^* - c_1) = 0$ and $(z_2^* - c_2) = 0$. Since $x_1 > 0$ and $x_2 > 0$, both these surplus variables and direct calculations indicate that $y_1^* + 3y_3^* = c_1 = 3$ and $2y_2^* + 2y_3^* = c_2 = 5$. Therefore, the value of the resources consumed per batch of the respective products produced does indeed equal the respective unit profits. The slack variable for the constraint on the amount of Plant 1 capacity used is $x_3 > 0$, so the marginal value of adding any Plant 1 capacity would be zero ($y_1^* = 0$).

Interpretation of the Simplex Method

The interpretation of the dual problem also provides an economic interpretation of what the simplex method does in the primal problem. The *goal* of the simplex method is to find how to use the available resources in the most profitable feasible way. To attain this goal, we must reach a BF solution that satisfies all the *requirements* on profitable use of the resources (the constraints of the dual problem). These requirements comprise the *condition for optimality* for the algorithm. For any given BF solution, the requirements (dual constraints) associated with the basic variables are automatically satisfied (with equality). However, those associated with nonbasic variables may or may not be satisfied.

In particular, if an original variable x_j is nonbasic so that activity j is not used, then the current contribution to profit of the resources that would be required to undertake each unit of activity j

$$\sum_{i=1}^{m} a_{ij} y_i$$

may be smaller than, larger than, or equal to the unit profit c_j obtainable from the activity. If it is smaller, so that $z_j - c_j < 0$ in row 0 of the simplex tableau, then these resources can be used more profitably by initiating this activity. If it is larger ($z_j - c_j > 0$), then these resources already are being assigned elsewhere in a more profitable way, so they should not be diverted to activity j. If $z_j - c_j = 0$, there would be no change in profitability by initiating activity j.

Similarly, if a slack variable x_{n+i} is nonbasic so that the total allocation b_i of resource i is being used, then y_i is the current contribution to profit of this resource on a marginal basis. Hence, if $y_i < 0$, profit can be increased by cutting back on the use of this resource (i.e., increasing x_{n+i}). If $y_i > 0$, it is worthwhile to continue fully using this resource, whereas this decision does not affect profitability if $y_i = 0$.

Therefore, what the simplex method does is to examine all the nonbasic variables in the current BF solution to see which ones can provide a *more profitable use of the resources* by being increased. If *none* can, so that no feasible shifts or reductions in the current proposed use of the resources can increase profit, then the current solution must be optimal. If one or more can, the simplex method selects the variable that, if increased by 1, would *improve the profitability* of the use of the resources the most. It then actually increases this variable (the entering basic variable) as much as it can until the marginal values of the resources change. This increase results in a new BF solution with a new row 0 (dual solution), and the whole process is repeated.

The economic interpretation of the dual problem considerably expands our ability to analyze the primal problem. However, you already have seen in Sec. 6.1 that this interpretation is just one ramification of the relationships between the two problems. In the next section, we delve into these relationships more deeply.

6.3   PRIMAL-DUAL RELATIONSHIPS

Because the dual problem is a linear programming problem, it also has corner-point solutions. Furthermore, by using the augmented form of the problem, we can express these corner-point solutions as basic solutions. Because the functional constraints have the $\geq$ form, this augmented form is obtained by *subtracting* the surplus (rather than adding the slack) from the left-hand side of each constraint j ($j = 1, 2, \ldots, n$).[1] This surplus is

$$z_j - c_j = \sum_{i=1}^{m} a_{ij} y_i - c_j, \qquad \text{for } j = 1, 2, \ldots, n.$$

Thus, $z_j - c_j$ plays the role of the *surplus variable* for constraint j (or its slack variable if the constraint is multiplied through by -1). Therefore, augmenting each corner-point solution $(y_1, y_2, \ldots, y_m)$ yields a basic solution $(y_1, y_2, \ldots, y_m, z_1 - c_1, z_2 - c_2, \ldots, z_n - c_n)$ by using this expression for $z_j - c_j$. Since the augmented form of the dual problem has n functional constraints and $n + m$ variables, each basic solution has n basic variables and m nonbasic variables. (Note how m and n reverse their previous roles here because, as Table 6.3 indicates, dual constraints correspond to primal variables and dual variables correspond to primal constraints.)

Complementary Basic Solutions

One of the important relationships between the primal and dual problems is a direct correspondence between their basic solutions. The key to this correspondence is row 0 of the simplex tableau for the primal basic solution, such as shown in Table 6.4 or 6.5. Such a row 0 can be obtained for *any* primal basic solution, feasible or not, by using the formulas given in the bottom part of Table 5.8.

Note again in Tables 6.4 and 6.5 how a complete solution for the dual problem (including the surplus variables) can be read directly from row 0. Thus, because of its coefficient in

---

[1]You might wonder why we do not also introduce *artificial variables* into these constraints as discussed in Sec. 4.6. The reason is that these variables have no purpose other than to change the feasible region temporarily as a convenience in starting the simplex method. We are not interested now in applying the simplex method to the dual problem, and we do not want to change its feasible region.

TABLE 6.7 Association between variables in primal and dual problems

	Primal Variable	Associated Dual Variable
Any problem	(Decision variable) x_j (Slack variable) x_{n+i}	$z_j - c_j$ (surplus variable) $j = 1, 2, \ldots, n$ y_i (decision variable) $i = 1, 2, \ldots, m$

Wyndor problem	Decision variables: x_1
	                 x_2
	Slack variables: x_3
	                 x_4
	                 x_5
		$z_1 - c_1$ (surplus variables)
		$z_2 - c_2$
		y_1 (decision variables)
		y_2
		y_3

row 0, each variable in the primal problem has an associated variable in the dual problem, as summarized in Table 6.7, first for any problem and then for the Wyndor problem.

A key insight here is that the dual solution read from row 0 must also be a basic solution! The reason is that the m basic variables for the primal problem are required to have a coefficient of zero in row 0, which thereby requires the m associated dual variables to be zero, i.e., nonbasic variables for the dual problem. The values of the remaining n (basic) variables then will be the simultaneous solution to the system of equations given at the beginning of this section. In matrix form, this system of equations is $\mathbf{z} - \mathbf{c} = \mathbf{y}\mathbf{A} - \mathbf{c}$, and the fundamental insight of Sec. 5.3 actually identifies its solution for $\mathbf{z} - \mathbf{c}$ and $\mathbf{y}$ as being the corresponding entries in row 0.

Because of the symmetry property quoted in Sec. 6.1 (and the direct association between variables shown in Table 6.7), the correspondence between basic solutions in the primal and dual problems is a symmetric one. Furthermore, a pair of complementary basic solutions has the same objective function value, shown as W in Table 6.4.

Let us now summarize our conclusions about the correspondence between primal and dual basic solutions, where the first property extends the complementary solutions property of Sec. 6.1 to the augmented forms of the two problems and then to any basic solution (feasible or not) in the primal problem.

> **Complementary basic solutions property:** Each *basic* solution in the *primal problem* has a **complementary basic solution** in the *dual problem,* where their respective objective function values (Z and W) are equal. Given row 0 of the simplex tableau for the primal basic solution, the complementary dual basic solution $(\mathbf{y}, \mathbf{z} - \mathbf{c})$ is found as shown in Table 6.4.

The next property shows how to identify the basic and nonbasic variables in this complementary basic solution.

> **Complementary slackness property:** Given the association between variables in Table 6.7, the variables in the primal basic solution and the complementary dual basic solution satisfy the **complementary slackness** relationship shown in Table 6.8. Furthermore, this relationship is a symmetric one, so that these two basic solutions are complementary to each other.

The reason for using the name *complementary slackness* for this latter property is that it says (in part) that for each pair of associated variables, if one of them has *slack* in its

TABLE 6.8 Complementary slackness relationship for complementary basic solutions

Primal Variable	Associated Dual Variable	
Basic	Nonbasic	(*m* variables)
Nonbasic	Basic	(*n* variables)

nonnegativity constraint (a basic variable > 0), then the other one must have *no slack* (a nonbasic variable $= 0$). We mentioned in Sec. 6.2 that this property has a useful economic interpretation for linear programming problems.

Example.   To illustrate these two properties, again consider the Wyndor Glass Co. problem of Sec. 3.1. All eight of its basic solutions (five feasible and three infeasible) are shown in Table 6.9. Thus, its dual problem (see Table 6.1) also must have eight basic solutions, each complementary to one of these primal solutions, as shown in Table 6.9.

The three BF solutions obtained by the simplex method for the primal problem are the first, fifth, and sixth primal solutions shown in Table 6.9. You already saw in Table 6.5 how the complementary basic solutions for the dual problem can be read directly from row 0, starting with the coefficients of the slack variables and then the original variables. The other dual basic solutions also could be identified in this way by constructing row 0 for each of the other primal basic solutions, using the formulas given in the bottom part of Table 5.8.

Alternatively, for each primal basic solution, the complementary slackness property can be used to identify the basic and nonbasic variables for the complementary dual basic solution, so that the system of equations given at the beginning of the section can be

TABLE 6.9 Complementary basic solutions for the Wyndor Glass Co. example

| No. | Primal Problem | | | Dual Problem | |
	Basic Solution	Feasible?	$Z = W$	Feasible?	Basic Solution
1	$(0, 0, 4, 12, 18)$	Yes	0	No	$(0, 0, 0, -3, -5)$
2	$(4, 0, 0, 12, 6)$	Yes	12	No	$(3, 0, 0, 0, -5)$
3	$(6, 0, -2, 12, 0)$	No	18	No	$(0, 0, 1, 0, -3)$
4	$(4, 3, 0, 6, 0)$	Yes	27	No	$\left(-\frac{9}{2}, 0, \frac{5}{2}, 0, 0\right)$
5	$(0, 6, 4, 0, 6)$	Yes	30	No	$\left(0, \frac{5}{2}, 0, -3, 0\right)$
6	$(2, 6, 2, 0, 0)$	Yes	36	Yes	$\left(0, \frac{3}{2}, 1, 0, 0\right)$
7	$(4, 6, 0, 0, -6)$	No	42	Yes	$\left(3, \frac{5}{2}, 0, 0, 0\right)$
8	$(0, 9, 4, -6, 0)$	No	45	Yes	$\left(0, 0, \frac{5}{2}, \frac{9}{2}, 0\right)$

solved directly to obtain this complementary solution. For example, consider the next-to-last primal basic solution in Table 6.9, (4, 6, 0, 0, −6). Note that x_1, x_2, and x_5 are *basic variables*, since these variables are not equal to 0. Table 6.7 indicates that the associated dual variables are $(z_1 - c_1)$, $(z_2 - c_2)$, and y_3. Table 6.8 specifies that these associated dual variables are *nonbasic variables* in the complementary basic solution, so

$$z_1 - c_1 = 0, \qquad z_2 - c_2 = 0, \qquad y_3 = 0.$$

Consequently, the augmented form of the functional constraints in the dual problem,

$$\begin{aligned} y_1 \quad &+ 3y_3 - (z_1 - c_1) = 3 \\ 2y_2 &+ 2y_3 - (z_2 - c_2) = 5, \end{aligned}$$

reduce to

$$\begin{aligned} y_1 \quad &+ 0 - 0 = 3 \\ 2y_2 &+ 0 - 0 = 5, \end{aligned}$$

so that $y_1 = 3$ and $y_2 = \frac{5}{2}$. Combining these values with the values of 0 for the nonbasic variables gives the basic solution $(3, \frac{5}{2}, 0, 0, 0)$, shown in the rightmost column and next-to-last row of Table 6.9. Note that this dual solution is feasible for the dual problem because all five variables satisfy the nonnegativity constraints.

Finally, notice that Table 6.9 demonstrates that $(0, \frac{3}{2}, 1, 0, 0)$ is the optimal solution for the dual problem, because it is the basic *feasible* solution with minimal W (36).

Relationships between Complementary Basic Solutions

We now turn our attention to the relationships between complementary basic solutions, beginning with their *feasibility* relationships. The middle columns in Table 6.9 provide some valuable clues. For the pairs of complementary solutions, notice how the yes or no answers on feasibility also satisfy a complementary relationship in most cases. In particular, with one exception, whenever one solution is feasible, the other is not. (It also is possible for *neither* solution to be feasible, as happened with the third pair.) The one exception is the sixth pair, where the primal solution is known to be optimal. The explanation is suggested by the $Z = W$ column. Because the sixth dual solution also is optimal (by the complementary optimal solutions property), with $W = 36$, the first five dual solutions *cannot be feasible* because $W < 36$ (remember that the dual problem objective is to *minimize* W). By the same token, the last two primal solutions cannot be feasible because $Z > 36$.

This explanation is further supported by the strong duality property that optimal primal and dual solutions have $Z = W$.

Next, let us state the *extension* of the complementary optimal solutions property of Sec. 6.1 for the augmented forms of the two problems.

> **Complementary optimal basic solutions property:** Each *optimal* basic solution in the *primal problem* has a **complementary optimal basic solution** in the dual problem, where their respective objective function values (Z and W) are equal. Given row 0 of the simplex tableau for the optimal primal solution, the complementary optimal dual solution ($\mathbf{y}^*$, $\mathbf{z}^* - \mathbf{c}$) is found as shown in Table 6.4.

TABLE 6.10 Classification of basic solutions

		Satisfies Condition for Optimality?	
		Yes	**No**
Feasible?	**Yes**	Optimal	Suboptimal
	No	Superoptimal	Neither feasible nor superoptimal

To review the reasoning behind this property, note that the dual solution $(\mathbf{y}^*, \mathbf{z}^* - \mathbf{c})$ must be feasible for the dual problem because the condition for optimality for the primal problem requires that *all* these dual variables (including surplus variables) be *nonnegative*. Since this solution is *feasible,* it must be *optimal* for the dual problem by the weak duality property (since $W = Z$, so $\mathbf{y}^*\mathbf{b} = \mathbf{c}\mathbf{x}^*$ where $\mathbf{x}^*$ is optimal for the primal problem).

Basic solutions can be classified according to whether they satisfy each of two conditions. One is the *condition for feasibility,* namely, whether *all* the variables (including slack variables) in the augmented solution are *nonnegative.* The other is the *condition for optimality,* namely, whether *all* the coefficients in row 0 (i.e., all the variables in the complementary basic solution) are *nonnegative.* Our names for the different types of basic solutions are summarized in Table 6.10. For example, in Table 6.9, primal basic solutions 1, 2, 4, and 5 are suboptimal, 6 is optimal, 7 and 8 are superoptimal, and 3 is neither feasible nor superoptimal.

Given these definitions, the general relationships between complementary basic solutions are summarized in Table 6.11. The resulting range of possible (common) values for the objective functions $(Z = W)$ for the first three pairs given in Table 6.11 (the last pair can have any value) is shown in Fig. 6.1. Thus, while the simplex method is dealing directly with suboptimal basic solutions and working toward optimality in the primal problem, it is simultaneously dealing indirectly with complementary superoptimal solutions and working toward feasibility in the dual problem. Conversely, it sometimes is more convenient (or necessary) to work directly with superoptimal basic solutions and to move toward feasibility in the primal problem, which is the purpose of the dual simplex method described in Sec. 7.1.

The third and fourth columns of Table 6.11 introduce two other common terms that are used to describe a pair of complementary basic solutions. The two solutions are said to be **primal feasible** if the primal basic solution is feasible, whereas they are called **dual feasible** if the complementary dual basic solution is feasible for the dual problem. Using

TABLE 6.11 Relationships between complementary basic solutions

Primal Basic Solution	**Complementary Dual Basic Solution**	**Both Basic Solutions**	
		Primal Feasible?	**Dual Feasible?**
Suboptimal	Superoptimal	Yes	No
Optimal	Optimal	Yes	Yes
Superoptimal	Suboptimal	No	Yes
Neither feasible nor superoptimal	Neither feasible nor superoptimal	No	No

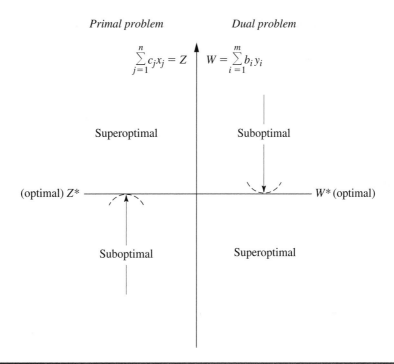

Primal problem   *Dual problem*

$$\sum_{j=1}^{n} c_j x_j = Z \qquad W = \sum_{i=1}^{m} b_i y_i$$

Superoptimal   Suboptimal

(optimal) Z^* ————————————————— W^* (optimal)

Suboptimal   Superoptimal

FIGURE 6.1
Range of possible values of $Z = W$ for certain types of complementary basic solutions.

this terminology, the simplex method deals with primal feasible solutions and strives toward achieving dual feasibility as well. When this is achieved, the two complementary basic solutions are optimal for their respective problems.

These relationships prove very useful, particularly in sensitivity analysis, as you will see later in the chapter.

6.4 ADAPTING TO OTHER PRIMAL FORMS

Thus far it has been assumed that the model for the primal problem is in our standard form. However, we indicated at the beginning of the chapter that any linear programming problem, whether in our standard form or not, possesses a dual problem. Therefore, this section focuses on how the dual problem changes for other primal forms.

Each nonstandard form was discussed in Sec. 4.6, and we pointed out how it is possible to convert each one to an equivalent standard form if so desired. These conversions are summarized in Table 6.12. Hence, you always have the option of converting any model to our standard form and *then* constructing its dual problem in the usual way. To illustrate, we do this for our standard dual problem (it must have a dual also) in Table 6.13. Note that what we end up with is just our standard primal problem! Since any pair of primal and dual problems can be converted to these forms, this fact implies that the dual of the dual problem always is the primal problem. Therefore, for any primal problem and its dual problem, all relationships between them must be symmetric. This is just the symmetry property already stated in Sec. 6.1 (without proof), but now Table 6.13 demonstrates why it holds.

TABLE 6.12 Conversions to standard form for linear programming models

Nonstandard Form	Equivalent Standard Form
Minimize $\quad Z$	Maximize $\quad (-Z)$
$\displaystyle\sum_{j=1}^{n} a_{ij}x_j \geq b_i$	$\displaystyle -\sum_{j=1}^{n} a_{ij}x_j \leq -b_i$
$\displaystyle\sum_{j=1}^{n} a_{ij}x_j = b_i$	$\displaystyle\sum_{j=1}^{n} a_{ij}x_j \leq b_i \quad$ and $\quad \displaystyle -\sum_{j=1}^{n} a_{ij}x_j \leq -b_i$
x_j unconstrained in sign	$x_j^+ - x_j^-, \quad x_j^+ \geq 0, \quad x_j^- \geq 0$

One consequence of the symmetry property is that all the statements made earlier in the chapter about the relationships of the dual problem to the primal problem also hold in reverse.

Another consequence is that it is immaterial which problem is called the primal and which is called the dual. In practice, you might see a linear programming problem fitting our standard form being referred to as the dual problem. The convention is that the model formulated to fit the actual problem is called the primal problem, regardless of its form.

Our illustration of how to construct the dual problem for a nonstandard primal problem did not involve either equality constraints or variables unconstrained in sign. Actually, for these two forms, a shortcut is available. It is possible to show (see Probs. 6.4-7 and 6.4-2*a*) that an *equality constraint* in the primal problem should be treated just like a $\leq$ constraint in

TABLE 6.13 Constructing the dual of the dual problem

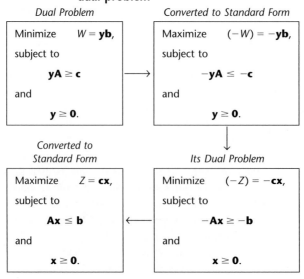

constructing the dual problem except that the nonnegativity constraint for the corresponding dual variable should be *deleted* (i.e., this variable is unconstrained in sign). By the symmetry property, deleting a nonnegativity constraint in the primal problem affects the dual problem only by changing the corresponding inequality constraint to an equality constraint.

Another shortcut involves functional constraints in $\geq$ form for a maximization problem. The straightforward (but longer) approach would begin by converting each such constraint to $\leq$ form

$$\sum_{j=1}^{n} a_{ij}x_j \geq b_i \longrightarrow -\sum_{j=1}^{n} a_{ij}x_j \leq -b_i.$$

Constructing the dual problem in the usual way then gives $-a_{ij}$ as the coefficient of y_i in functional constraint j (which has $\geq$ form) and a coefficient of $-b_i$ in the objective function (which is to be minimized), where y_i also has a nonnegativity constraint $y_i \geq 0$. Now suppose we define a new variable $y_i' = -y_i$. The changes caused by expressing the dual problem in terms of y_i' instead of y_i are that (1) the coefficients of the variable become a_{ij} for functional constraint j and b_i for the objective function and (2) the constraint on the variable becomes $y_i' \leq 0$ (a *nonpositivity constraint*). The shortcut is to use y_i' instead of y_i as a dual variable so that the parameters in the original constraint (a_{ij} and b_i) immediately become the coefficients of this variable in the dual problem.

Here is a useful mnemonic device for remembering what the forms of dual constraints should be. With a maximization problem, it might seem *sensible* for a functional constraint to be in $\leq$ form, slightly *odd* to be in $=$ form, and somewhat *bizarre* to be in $\geq$ form. Similarly, for a minimization problem, it might seem *sensible* to be in $\geq$ form, slightly *odd* to be in $=$ form, and somewhat *bizarre* to be in $\leq$ form. For the constraint on an individual variable in either kind of problem, it might seem *sensible* to have a nonnegativity constraint, somewhat *odd* to have no constraint (so the variable is unconstrained in sign), and quite *bizarre* for the variable to be restricted to be *less* than or equal to zero. Now recall the correspondence between entities in the primal and dual problems indicated in Table 6.3; namely, functional constraint i in one problem corresponds to variable i in the other problem, and vice versa. The *sensible-odd-bizarre method,* or **SOB method** for short, says that the form of a functional constraint or the constraint on a variable in the dual problem should be sensible, odd, or bizarre, depending on whether the form for the corresponding entity in the primal problem is sensible, odd, or bizarre. Here is a summary.

The SOB Method for Determining the Form of Constraints in the Dual.[1]

1. Formulate the primal problem in either maximization form or minimization form, and then the dual problem automatically will be in the other form.
2. Label the different forms of functional constraints and of constraints on individual variables in the primal problem as being sensible, odd, or bizarre according to Table 6.14.

---

[1]This particular mnemonic device (and a related one) for remembering what the forms of dual constraints should be has been suggested by Arthur T. Benjamin, a mathematics professor at Harvey Mudd College. An interesting and wonderfully bizarre fact about Professor Benjamin himself is that he is one of the world's great human calculators who can perform such feats as quickly multiplying six-digit numbers in his head.

TABLE 6.14 Corresponding primal-dual forms

Label	Primal Problem (or Dual Problem)	Dual Problem (or Primal Problem)
	Maximize　　Z (or W)	Minimize　　W (or Z)
	Constraint i:	Variable y_i (or x_i):
Sensible	$\leq$ form ⟵⟶	$y_i \geq 0$
Odd	$=$ form ⟵⟶	Unconstrained
Bizarre	$\geq$ form ⟵	$y_i' \leq 0$
	Variable x_j (or y_j):	Constraint j:
Sensible	$x_j \geq 0$ ⟵⟶	$\geq$ form
Odd	Unconstrained ⟵⟶	$=$ form
Bizarre	$x_j' \leq 0$ ⟵⟶	$\leq$ form

The labeling of the functional constraints depends on whether the problem is a *maximization* problem (use the second column) or a *minimization* problem (use the third column).

3. For each constraint on an *individual variable* in the dual problem, use the form that has the same label as for the functional constraint in the primal problem that corresponds to this dual variable (as indicated by Table 6.3).

4. For each *functional constraint* in the dual problem, use the form that has the same label as for the constraint on the corresponding individual variable in the primal problem (as indicated by Table 6.3).

The arrows between the second and third columns of Table 6.14 spell out the correspondence between the forms of constraints in the primal and dual. Note that the correspondence always is between a functional constraint in one problem and a constraint on an individual variable in the other problem. Since the primal problem can be either a maximization or minimization problem, where the dual then will be of the opposite type, the second column of the table gives the form for whichever is the maximization problem and the third column gives the form for the other problem (a minimization problem).

To illustrate, consider the radiation therapy example presented in Sec. 3.4. (Its model is shown on p. 46.) To show the conversion in both directions in Table 6.14, we begin with the maximization form of this model as the primal problem, before using the (original) minimization form.

The primal problem in maximization form is shown on the left side of Table 6.15. By using the second column of Table 6.14 to represent this problem, the arrows in this table indicate the form of the dual problem in the third column. These same arrows are used in Table 6.15 to show the resulting dual problem. (Because of these arrows, we have placed the functional constraints last in the dual problem rather than in their usual top position.) Beside each constraint in both problems, we have inserted (in parentheses) an S, O, or B to label the form as sensible, odd, or bizarre. As prescribed by the SOB method, the label for each dual constraint always is the same as for the corresponding primal constraint.

TABLE 6.15 One primal-dual form for the radiation therapy example

Primal Problem	Dual Problem
Maximize $\quad -Z = -0.4x_1 - 0.5x_2,$	Minimize $\quad W = 2.7y_1 + 6y_2 + 6y_3',$
subject to	subject to
(S) $\quad 0.3x_1 + 0.1x_2 \leq 2.7$	$\rightarrow y_1 \geq 0$ (S)
(O) $\quad 0.5x_1 + 0.5x_2 = 6$	$\rightarrow y_2$ unconstrained in sign (O)
(B) $\quad 0.6x_1 + 0.4x_2 \geq 6$	$\rightarrow y_3' \leq 0$ (B)
and	and
(S) $\qquad x_1 \geq 0$	$\rightarrow 0.3y_1 + 0.5y_2 + 0.6y_3' \geq -0.4$ (S)
(S) $\qquad x_2 \geq 0$	$\rightarrow 0.1y_1 + 0.5y_2 + 0.4y_3' \geq -0.5$ (S)

However, there was no need (other than for illustrative purposes) to convert the primal problem to maximization form. Using the original minimization form, the equivalent primal problem is shown on the left side of Table 6.16. Now we use the *third column* of Table 6.14 to represent this primal problem, where the arrows indicate the form of the dual problem in the *second column*. These same arrows in Table 6.16 show the resulting dual problem on the right side. Again, the labels on the constraints show the application of the SOB method.

Just as the primal problems in Tables 6.15 and 6.16 are equivalent, the two dual problems also are completely equivalent. The key to recognizing this equivalency lies in the fact that the variables in each version of the dual problem are the negative of those in the other version ($y_1' = -y_1$, $y_2' = -y_2$, $y_3 = -y_3'$). Therefore, for each version, if the variables in the other version are used instead, and if both the objective function and the constraints are multiplied through by -1, then the other version is obtained. (Problem 6.4-5 asks you to verify this.)

If the simplex method is to be applied to either a primal or a dual problem that has any variables constrained to be *nonpositive* (for example, $y_3' \leq 0$ in the dual problem of Table 6.15), this variable may be replaced by its *nonnegative* counterpart (for example, $y_3 = -y_3'$).

TABLE 6.16 The other primal-dual form for the radiation therapy example

Primal Problem	Dual Problem
Minimize $\quad Z = 0.4x_1 + 0.5x_2,$	Maximize $\quad W = 2.7y_1' + 6y_2' + 6y_3,$
subject to	subject to
(B) $\quad 0.3x_1 + 0.1x_2 \leq 2.7$	$\rightarrow y_1' \leq 0$ (B)
(O) $\quad 0.5x_1 + 0.5x_2 = 6$	$\rightarrow y_2'$ unconstrained in sign (O)
(S) $\quad 0.6x_1 + 0.4x_2 \geq 6$	$\rightarrow y_3 \geq 0$ (S)
and	and
(S) $\qquad x_1 \geq 0$	$\rightarrow 0.3y_1' + 0.5y_2' + 0.6y_3 \leq 0.4$ (S)
(S) $\qquad x_2 \geq 0$	$\rightarrow 0.1y_1' + 0.5y_2' + 0.4y_3 \leq 0.6$ (S)

When artificial variables are used to help the simplex method solve a primal problem, the duality interpretation of row 0 of the simplex tableau is the following: Since artificial variables play the role of slack variables, their coefficients in row 0 now provide the values of the corresponding dual variables in the complementary basic solution for the dual problem. Since artificial variables are used to replace the real problem with a more convenient artificial problem, this dual problem actually is the dual of the artificial problem. However, after all the artificial variables become nonbasic, we are back to the real primal and dual problems. With the two-phase method, the artificial variables would need to be retained in phase 2 in order to read off the complete dual solution from row 0. With the Big M method, since M has been added initially to the coefficient of each artificial variable in row 0, the current value of each corresponding dual variable is the current coefficient of this artificial variable *minus* M.

For example, look at row 0 in the final simplex tableau for the radiation therapy example, given at the bottom of Table 4.12 on p. 142. After M is subtracted from the coefficients of the artificial variables $\bar{x}_4$ and $\bar{x}_6$, the optimal solution for the corresponding dual problem given in Table 6.15 is read from the coefficients of x_3, $\bar{x}_4$, and $\bar{x}_6$ as $(y_1, y_2, y_3') = (0.5, -1.1, 0)$. As usual, the surplus variables for the two functional constraints are read from the coefficients of x_1 and x_2 as $z_1 - c_1 = 0$ and $z_2 - c_2 = 0$.

6.5   THE ROLE OF DUALITY THEORY IN SENSITIVITY ANALYSIS

As described further in the next two sections, sensitivity analysis basically involves investigating the effect on the optimal solution of making changes in the values of the model parameters a_{ij}, b_i, and c_j. However, changing parameter values in the primal problem also changes the corresponding values in the dual problem. Therefore, you have your choice of which problem to use to investigate each change. Because of the primal-dual relationships presented in Secs. 6.1 and 6.3 (especially the complementary basic solutions property), it is easy to move back and forth between the two problems as desired. In some cases, it is more convenient to analyze the dual problem directly in order to determine the complementary effect on the primal problem. We begin by considering two such cases.

Changes in the Coefficients of a Nonbasic Variable

Suppose that the changes made in the original model occur in the coefficients of a variable that was nonbasic in the original optimal solution. What is the effect of these changes on this solution? Is it still feasible? Is it still optimal?

Because the variable involved is nonbasic (value of zero), changing its coefficients cannot affect the feasibility of the solution. Therefore, the open question in this case is whether it is still optimal. As Tables 6.10 and 6.11 indicate, an equivalent question is whether the complementary basic solution for the dual problem is still feasible after these changes are made. Since these changes affect the dual problem by changing only one constraint, this question can be answered simply by checking whether this complementary basic solution still satisfies this revised constraint.

We shall illustrate this case in the corresponding subsection of Sec. 6.7 after developing a relevant example.

Introduction of a New Variable

As indicated in Table 6.6, the decision variables in the model typically represent the levels of the various activities under consideration. In some situations, these activities were selected from a larger group of *possible* activities, where the remaining activities were not included in the original model because they seemed less attractive. Or perhaps these other activities did not come to light until after the original model was formulated and solved. Either way, the key question is whether any of these previously unconsidered activities are sufficiently worthwhile to warrant initiation. In other words, would adding any of these activities to the model change the original optimal solution?

Adding another activity amounts to introducing a new variable, with the appropriate coefficients in the functional constraints and objective function, into the model. The only resulting change in the dual problem is to add a *new constraint* (see Table 6.3).

After these changes are made, would the original optimal solution, along with the new variable equal to zero (nonbasic), still be optimal for the primal problem? As for the preceding case, an equivalent question is whether the complementary basic solution for the dual problem is still feasible. And, as before, this question can be answered simply by checking whether this complementary basic solution satisfies one constraint, which in this case is the new constraint for the dual problem.

To illustrate, suppose for the Wyndor Glass Co. problem of Sec. 3.1 that a possible third new product now is being considered for inclusion in the product line. Letting x_{new} represent the production rate for this product, we show the resulting revised model as follows:

$$\text{Maximize} \quad Z = 3x_1 + 5x_2 + 4x_{new},$$

subject to

$$
\begin{aligned}
x_1 \quad\quad\quad + 2x_{new} &\leq 4 \\
2x_2 + 3x_{new} &\leq 12 \\
3x_1 + 2x_2 + \quad x_{new} &\leq 18
\end{aligned}
$$

and

$$x_1 \geq 0, \qquad x_2 \geq 0, \qquad x_{new} \geq 0.$$

After we introduced slack variables, the original optimal solution for this problem without x_{new} (given by Table 4.8) was $(x_1, x_2, x_3, x_4, x_5) = (2, 6, 2, 0, 0)$. Is this solution, along with $x_{new} = 0$, still optimal?

To answer this question, we need to check the complementary basic solution for the dual problem. As indicated by the *complementary optimal basic solutions property* in Sec. 6.3, this solution is given in row 0 of the *final* simplex tableau for the primal problem, using the locations shown in Table 6.4 and illustrated in Table 6.5. Therefore, as given in both the bottom row of Table 6.5 and the sixth row of Table 6.9, the solution is

$$(y_1, y_2, y_3, z_1 - c_1, z_2 - c_2) = \left(0, \frac{3}{2}, 1, 0, 0\right).$$

(Alternatively, this complementary basic solution can be derived in the way that was illustrated in Sec. 6.3 for the complementary basic solution in the next-to-last row of Table 6.9.)

Since this solution was optimal for the original dual problem, it certainly satisfies the original dual constraints shown in Table 6.1. But does it satisfy this new dual constraint?

$$2y_1 + 3y_2 + y_3 \geq 4$$

Plugging in this solution, we see that

$$2(0) + 3\left(\frac{3}{2}\right) + (1) \geq 4$$

is satisfied, so this dual solution is still feasible (and thus still optimal). Consequently, the original primal solution (2, 6, 2, 0, 0), along with $x_{\text{new}} = 0$, is still optimal, so this third possible new product should *not* be added to the product line.

This approach also makes it very easy to conduct sensitivity analysis on the coefficients of the new variable added to the primal problem. By simply checking the new dual constraint, you can immediately see how far any of these parameter values can be changed before they affect the feasibility of the dual solution and so the optimality of the primal solution.

Other Applications

Already we have discussed two other key applications of duality theory to sensitivity analysis, namely, shadow prices and the dual simplex method. As described in Secs. 4.7 and 6.2, the optimal dual solution $(y_1^*, y_2^*, \ldots, y_m^*)$ provides the shadow prices for the respective resources that indicate how Z would change if (small) changes were made in the b_i (the resource amounts). The resulting analysis will be illustrated in some detail in Sec. 6.7.

In more general terms, the economic interpretation of the dual problem and of the simplex method presented in Sec. 6.2 provides some useful insights for sensitivity analysis.

When we investigate the effect of changing the b_i or the a_{ij} values (for basic variables), the original optimal solution may become a *superoptimal* basic solution (as defined in Table 6.10) instead. If we then want to *reoptimize* to identify the new optimal solution, the dual simplex method (discussed at the end of Secs. 6.1 and 6.3) should be applied, starting from this basic solution.

We mentioned in Sec. 6.1 that sometimes it is more efficient to solve the dual problem directly by the simplex method in order to identify an optimal solution for the primal problem. When the solution has been found in this way, sensitivity analysis for the primal problem then is conducted by applying the procedure described in the next two sections directly to the dual problem and then inferring the complementary effects on the primal problem (e.g., see Table 6.11). This approach to sensitivity analysis is relatively straightforward because of the close primal-dual relationships described in Secs. 6.1 and 6.3. (See Prob. 6.6-3.)

6.6   THE ESSENCE OF SENSITIVITY ANALYSIS

The work of the operations research team usually is not even nearly done when the simplex method has been successfully applied to identify an optimal solution for the model. As we pointed out at the end of Sec. 3.3, one assumption of linear programming is that all the parameters of the model (a_{ij}, b_i, and c_j) are *known constants*. Actually, the parameter values used in the model normally are just *estimates* based on a *prediction of future conditions*. The data obtained to develop these estimates often are rather crude or nonexistent, so that the parameters in the original formulation may represent little more than quick rules of thumb provided by harassed line personnel. The data may even represent deliberate overestimates or underestimates to protect the interests of the estimators.

Thus, the successful manager and operations research staff will maintain a healthy skepticism about the original numbers coming out of the computer and will view them in many cases as only a starting point for further analysis of the problem. An "optimal" solution is optimal only with respect to the specific model being used to represent the real problem, and such a solution becomes a reliable guide for action only after it has been verified as performing well for other reasonable representations of the problem. Furthermore, the model parameters (particularly b_i) sometimes are set as a result of managerial policy decisions (e.g., the amount of certain resources to be made available to the activities), and these decisions should be reviewed after their potential consequences are recognized.

For these reasons it is important to perform **sensitivity analysis** to investigate the effect on the optimal solution provided by the simplex method if the parameters take on other possible values. Usually there will be some parameters that can be assigned any reasonable value without the optimality of this solution being affected. However, there may also be parameters with likely alternative values that would yield a new optimal solution. This situation is particularly serious if the original solution would then have a substantially inferior value of the objective function, or perhaps even be infeasible!

Therefore, one main purpose of sensitivity analysis is to identify the **sensitive parameters** (i.e., the parameters whose values cannot be changed without changing the optimal solution). For certain parameters that are not categorized as sensitive, it is also very helpful to determine the *range of values* of the parameter over which the optimal solution will remain unchanged. (We call this range of values the *allowable range to stay optimal.*) In some cases, changing a parameter value can affect the *feasibility* of the optimal BF solution. For such parameters, it is useful to determine the range of values over which the optimal BF solution (with adjusted values for the basic variables) will remain feasible. (We call this range of values the *allowable range to stay feasible.*) In the next section, we will describe the specific procedures for obtaining this kind of information.

Such information is invaluable in two ways. First, it identifies the more important parameters, so that special care can be taken to estimate them closely and to select a solution that performs well for most of their likely values. Second, it identifies the parameters that will need to be monitored particularly closely as the study is implemented. If it is discovered that the true value of a parameter lies outside its allowable range, this immediately signals a need to change the solution.

For small problems, it would be straightforward to check the effect of a variety of changes in parameter values simply by reapplying the simplex method each time to see if the optimal solution changes. This is particularly convenient when using a spreadsheet formulation. Once the Solver has been set up to obtain an optimal solution, all you have to do is make any desired change on the spreadsheet and then click on the Solve button again.

However, for larger problems of the size typically encountered in practice, sensitivity analysis would require an exorbitant computational effort if it were necessary to reapply the simplex method from the beginning to investigate each new change in a parameter value. Fortunately, the fundamental insight discussed in Sec. 5.3 virtually eliminates computational effort. The basic idea is that the fundamental insight *immediately* reveals just how any changes in the original model would change the numbers in the final simplex tableau (assuming that the *same* sequence of algebraic operations originally performed by the simplex method were to be *duplicated*). Therefore, after making a few simple calculations to revise this tableau, we can check easily whether the original optimal BF solution is now nonoptimal (or infeasible). If so, this solution would be used as the initial basic solution to restart the simplex method (or dual simplex method) to find the new optimal solution, if desired. If the changes in the model are not major, only a very few iterations should be required to reach the new optimal solution from this "advanced" initial basic solution.

To describe this procedure more specifically, consider the following situation. The simplex method already has been used to obtain an optimal solution for a linear programming model with specified values for the b_i, c_j, and a_{ij} parameters. To initiate sensitivity analysis, at least one of the parameters is changed. After the changes are made, let $\bar{b}_i$, $\bar{c}_j$, and $\bar{a}_{ij}$ denote the values of the various parameters. Thus, in matrix notation,

$$\mathbf{b} \to \overline{\mathbf{b}}, \qquad \mathbf{c} \to \overline{\mathbf{c}}, \qquad \mathbf{A} \to \overline{\mathbf{A}},$$

for the revised model.

The first step is to revise the final simplex tableau to reflect these changes. Continuing to use the notation presented in Table 5.10, as well as the accompanying formulas for the fundamental insight [(1) $\mathbf{t}^* = \mathbf{t} + \mathbf{y}^*\mathbf{T}$ and (2) $\mathbf{T}^* = \mathbf{S}^*\mathbf{T}$], we see that the revised final tableau is calculated from $\mathbf{y}^*$ and $\mathbf{S}^*$ (which have not changed) and the new initial tableau, as shown in Table 6.17.

Example (Variation 1 of the Wyndor Model).   To illustrate, suppose that the first revision in the model for the Wyndor Glass Co. problem of Sec. 3.1 is the one shown in Table 6.18.

Thus, the changes from the original model are $c_1 = 3 \to 4$, $a_{31} = 3 \to 2$, and $b_2 = 12 \to 24$. Figure 6.2 shows the graphical effect of these changes. For the original model, the simplex method already has identified the optimal CPF solution as (2, 6), lying at the intersection of the two constraint boundaries, shown as dashed lines $2x_2 = 12$ and $3x_1 + 2x_2 = 18$. Now the revision of the model has shifted both of these constraint boundaries as shown by the dark lines $2x_2 = 24$ and $2x_1 + 2x_2 = 18$. Consequently, the previous

TABLE 6.17 Revised final simplex tableau resulting from changes in original model

	Eq.	Z	Coefficient of:		Right Side
			Original Variables	**Slack Variables**	
New initial tableau	(0)	1	$-\overline{\mathbf{c}}$	**0**	0
	(1, 2, . . . , m)	**0**	$\overline{\mathbf{A}}$	**I**	$\overline{\mathbf{b}}$
Revised final tableau	(0)	1	$\mathbf{z}^* - \overline{\mathbf{c}} = \mathbf{y}^*\overline{\mathbf{A}} - \overline{\mathbf{c}}$	$\mathbf{y}^*$	$Z^* = \mathbf{y}^*\overline{\mathbf{b}}$
	(1, 2, . . . , m)	**0**	$\mathbf{A}^* = \mathbf{S}^*\overline{\mathbf{A}}$	$\mathbf{S}^*$	$\mathbf{b}^* = \mathbf{S}^*\overline{\mathbf{b}}$

TABLE 6.18 The original model and the first revised model (variation 1) for conducting sensitivity analysis on the Wyndor Glass Co. model

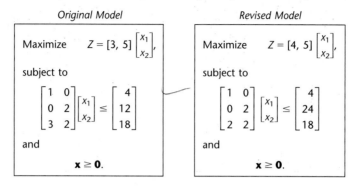

Original Model

Maximize $\quad Z = [3, 5] \begin{bmatrix} x_1 \\ x_2 \end{bmatrix}$,

subject to

$$\begin{bmatrix} 1 & 0 \\ 0 & 2 \\ 3 & 2 \end{bmatrix} \begin{bmatrix} x_1 \\ x_2 \end{bmatrix} \leq \begin{bmatrix} 4 \\ 12 \\ 18 \end{bmatrix}$$

and

$$\mathbf{x} \geq \mathbf{0}.$$

Revised Model

Maximize $\quad Z = [4, 5] \begin{bmatrix} x_1 \\ x_2 \end{bmatrix}$,

subject to

$$\begin{bmatrix} 1 & 0 \\ 0 & 2 \\ 2 & 2 \end{bmatrix} \begin{bmatrix} x_1 \\ x_2 \end{bmatrix} \leq \begin{bmatrix} 4 \\ 24 \\ 18 \end{bmatrix}$$

and

$$\mathbf{x} \geq \mathbf{0}.$$

FIGURE 6.2
Shift of the final corner-point solution from (2, 6) to (−3, 12) for Variation 1 of the Wyndor Glass Co. model where $c_1 = 3 \rightarrow 4$, $a_{31} = 3 \rightarrow 2$, and $b_2 = 12 \rightarrow 24$.

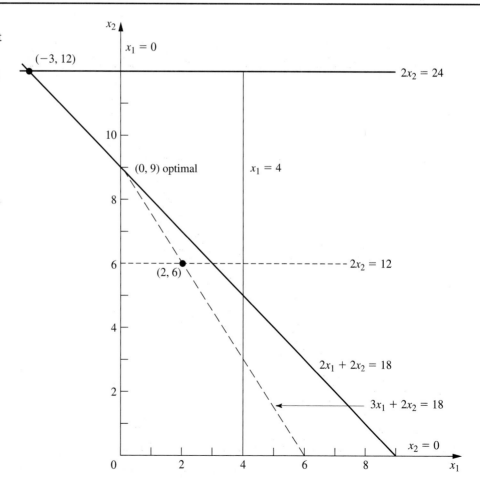

CPF solution (2, 6) now shifts to the new intersection $(-3, 12)$, which is a corner-point *infeasible* solution for the revised model. The procedure described in the preceding paragraphs finds this shift *algebraically* (in augmented form). Furthermore, it does so in a manner that is very efficient even for huge problems where graphical analysis is impossible.

To carry out this procedure, we begin by displaying the parameters of the revised model in matrix form:

$$\bar{\mathbf{c}} = [4, 5], \qquad \bar{\mathbf{A}} = \begin{bmatrix} 1 & 0 \\ 0 & 2 \\ 2 & 2 \end{bmatrix}, \qquad \bar{\mathbf{b}} = \begin{bmatrix} 4 \\ 24 \\ 18 \end{bmatrix}.$$

The resulting new initial simplex tableau is shown at the top of Table 6.19. Below this tableau is the original final tableau (as first given in Table 4.8). We have drawn dark boxes around the portions of this final tableau that the changes in the model definitely *do not change,* namely, the coefficients of the slack variables in both row 0 ($\mathbf{y}^*$) and the rest of the rows ($\mathbf{S}^*$). Thus,

$$\mathbf{y}^* = [0, \tfrac{3}{2}, 1], \qquad \mathbf{S}^* = \begin{bmatrix} 1 & \tfrac{1}{3} & -\tfrac{1}{3} \\ 0 & \tfrac{1}{2} & 0 \\ 0 & -\tfrac{1}{3} & \tfrac{1}{3} \end{bmatrix}.$$

TABLE 6.19 Obtaining the revised final simplex tableau for Variation 1 of the Wyndor Glass Co. model

	Basic Variable	Eq.	Coefficient of:							Right Side
			Z	x_1	x_2	x_3	x_4	x_5		
New initial tableau	Z	(0)	1	-4	-5	0	0	0		0
	x_3	(1)	0	1	0	1	0	0		4
	x_4	(2)	0	0	2	0	1	0		24
	x_5	(3)	0	2	2	0	0	1		18
Final tableau for original model	Z	(0)	1	0	0	0	$\tfrac{3}{2}$	1		36
	x_3	(1)	0	0	0	1	$\tfrac{1}{3}$	$-\tfrac{1}{3}$		2
	x_2	(2)	0	0	1	0	$\tfrac{1}{2}$	0		6
	x_1	(3)	0	1	0	0	$-\tfrac{1}{3}$	$\tfrac{1}{3}$		2
Revised final tableau	Z	(0)	1	-2	0	0	$\tfrac{3}{2}$	1		54
	x_3	(1)	0	$\tfrac{1}{3}$	0	1	$\tfrac{1}{3}$	$-\tfrac{1}{3}$		6
	x_2	(2)	0	0	1	0	$\tfrac{1}{2}$	0		12
	x_1	(3)	0	$\tfrac{2}{3}$	0	0	$-\tfrac{1}{3}$	$\tfrac{1}{3}$		-2

These coefficients of the slack variables necessarily are unchanged with the same algebraic operations originally performed by the simplex method because the coefficients of these same variables in the initial tableau are unchanged.

However, because other portions of the initial tableau have changed, there will be changes in the rest of the final tableau as well. Using the formulas in Table 6.17, we calculate the revised numbers in the rest of the final tableau as follows:

$$\mathbf{z}^* - \bar{\mathbf{c}} = [0, \tfrac{3}{2}, 1] \begin{bmatrix} 1 & 0 \\ 0 & 2 \\ 2 & 2 \end{bmatrix} - [4, 5] = [-2, 0], \qquad Z^* = [0, \tfrac{3}{2}, 1] \begin{bmatrix} 4 \\ 24 \\ 18 \end{bmatrix} = 54,$$

$$\mathbf{A}^* = \begin{bmatrix} 1 & \tfrac{1}{3} & -\tfrac{1}{3} \\ 0 & \tfrac{1}{2} & 0 \\ 0 & -\tfrac{1}{3} & \tfrac{1}{3} \end{bmatrix} \begin{bmatrix} 1 & 0 \\ 0 & 2 \\ 2 & 2 \end{bmatrix} = \begin{bmatrix} \tfrac{1}{3} & 0 \\ 0 & 1 \\ \tfrac{2}{3} & 0 \end{bmatrix},$$

$$\mathbf{b}^* = \begin{bmatrix} 1 & \tfrac{1}{3} & -\tfrac{1}{3} \\ 0 & \tfrac{1}{2} & 0 \\ 0 & -\tfrac{1}{3} & \tfrac{1}{3} \end{bmatrix} \begin{bmatrix} 4 \\ 24 \\ 18 \end{bmatrix} = \begin{bmatrix} 6 \\ 12 \\ -2 \end{bmatrix}.$$

The resulting revised final tableau is shown at the bottom of Table 6.19.

Actually, we can substantially streamline these calculations for obtaining the revised final tableau. Because none of the coefficients of x_2 changed in the original model (tableau), none of them can change in the final tableau, so we can delete their calculation. Several other original parameters (a_{11}, a_{21}, b_1, b_3) also were not changed, so another shortcut is to calculate only the *incremental changes* in the final tableau in terms of the incremental changes in the initial tableau, ignoring those terms in the vector or matrix multiplication that involve zero change in the initial tableau. In particular, the only incremental changes in the initial tableau are $\Delta c_1 = 1$, $\Delta a_{31} = -1$, and $\Delta b_2 = 12$, so these are the only terms that need be considered. This streamlined approach is shown below, where a zero or dash appears in each spot where no calculation is needed.

$$\Delta(\mathbf{z}^* - \mathbf{c}) = \mathbf{y}^* \, \Delta\mathbf{A} - \Delta\mathbf{c} = [0, \tfrac{3}{2}, 1] \begin{bmatrix} 0 & — \\ 0 & — \\ -1 & — \end{bmatrix} - [1, —] = [-2, —].$$

$$\Delta Z^* = \mathbf{y}^* \, \Delta\mathbf{b} = [0, \tfrac{3}{2}, 1] \begin{bmatrix} 0 \\ 12 \\ 0 \end{bmatrix} = 18.$$

$$\Delta\mathbf{A}^* = \mathbf{S}^* \, \Delta\mathbf{A} = \begin{bmatrix} 1 & \tfrac{1}{3} & -\tfrac{1}{3} \\ 0 & \tfrac{1}{2} & 0 \\ 0 & -\tfrac{1}{3} & \tfrac{1}{3} \end{bmatrix} \begin{bmatrix} 0 & — \\ 0 & — \\ -1 & — \end{bmatrix} = \begin{bmatrix} \tfrac{1}{3} & — \\ 0 & — \\ -\tfrac{1}{3} & — \end{bmatrix}.$$

$$\Delta\mathbf{b}^* = \mathbf{S}^* \, \Delta\mathbf{b} = \begin{bmatrix} 1 & \tfrac{1}{3} & -\tfrac{1}{3} \\ 0 & \tfrac{1}{2} & 0 \\ 0 & -\tfrac{1}{3} & \tfrac{1}{3} \end{bmatrix} \begin{bmatrix} 0 \\ 12 \\ 0 \end{bmatrix} = \begin{bmatrix} 4 \\ 6 \\ -4 \end{bmatrix}.$$

Adding these increments to the original quantities in the final tableau (middle of Table 6.19) then yields the revised final tableau (bottom of Table 6.19).

This *incremental analysis* also provides a useful general insight, namely, that changes in the final tableau must be *proportional* to each change in the initial tableau. We illustrate in the next section how this property enables us to use linear interpolation or extrapolation to determine the range of values for a given parameter over which the final basic solution remains both feasible and optimal.

After obtaining the revised final simplex tableau, we next convert the tableau to proper form from Gaussian elimination (as needed). In particular, the basic variable for row i must have a coefficient of 1 in that row and a coefficient of 0 in every other row (including row 0) for the tableau to be in the proper form for identifying and evaluating the current basic solution. Therefore, if the changes have violated this requirement (which can occur only if the original constraint coefficients of a basic variable have been changed), further changes must be made to restore this form. This restoration is done by using Gaussian elimination, i.e., by successively applying step 3 of an iteration for the simplex method (see Chap. 4) as if each violating basic variable were an entering basic variable. Note that these algebraic operations may also cause further changes in the *right side* column, so that the current basic solution can be read from this column only when the proper form from Gaussian elimination has been fully restored.

For the example, the revised final simplex tableau shown in the top half of Table 6.20 is not in proper form from Gaussian elimination because of the column for the basic variable x_1. Specifically, the coefficient of x_1 in *its* row (row 3) is $\frac{2}{3}$ instead of 1, and it has nonzero coefficients (-2 and $\frac{1}{3}$) in rows 0 and 1. To restore proper form, row 3 is multiplied by $\frac{3}{2}$; then 2 times this new row 3 is added to row 0 and $\frac{1}{3}$ times new row 3 is subtracted from row 1. This yields the proper form from Gaussian elimination shown in

TABLE 6.20 Converting the revised final simplex tableau to proper form from Gaussian elimination for Variation 1 of the Wyndor Glass Co. model

	Basic Variable	Eq.	Z	x_1	x_2	x_3	x_4	x_5	Right Side
						Coefficient of:			
Revised final tableau	Z	(0)	1	-2	0	0	$\frac{3}{2}$	1	54
	x_3	(1)	0	$\frac{1}{3}$	0	1	$\frac{1}{3}$	$-\frac{1}{3}$	6
	x_2	(2)	0	0	1	0	$\frac{1}{2}$	0	12
	x_1	(3)	0	$\frac{2}{3}$	0	0	$-\frac{1}{3}$	$\frac{1}{3}$	-2
Converted to proper form	Z	(0)	1	0	0	0	$\frac{1}{2}$	2	48
	x_3	(1)	0	0	0	1	$\frac{1}{2}$	$-\frac{1}{2}$	7
	x_2	(2)	0	0	1	0	$\frac{1}{2}$	0	12
	x_1	(3)	0	1	0	0	$-\frac{1}{2}$	$\frac{1}{2}$	-3

the bottom half of Table 6.20, which now can be used to identify the new values for the current (previously optimal) basic solution:

$$(x_1, x_2, x_3, x_4, x_5) = (-3, 12, 7, 0, 0).$$

Because x_1 is negative, this basic solution no longer is feasible. However, it is *superoptimal* (as defined in Table 6.10), and so *dual feasible*, because *all* the coefficients in row 0 still are *nonnegative*. Therefore, the dual simplex method can be used to reoptimize (if desired), by starting from this basic solution. (The sensitivity analysis routine in the OR Courseware includes this option.) Referring to Fig. 6.2 (and ignoring slack variables), the dual simplex method uses just one iteration to move from the corner-point solution $(-3, 12)$ to the optimal CPF solution $(0, 9)$. (It is often useful in sensitivity analysis to identify the solutions that are optimal for some set of likely values of the model parameters and then to determine which of these solutions most *consistently* performs well for the various likely parameter values.)

If the basic solution $(-3, 12, 7, 0, 0)$ had been *neither* primal feasible nor dual feasible (i.e., if the tableau had negative entries in *both* the *right side* column and row 0), artificial variables could have been introduced to convert the tableau to the proper form for an initial simplex tableau.[1]

The General Procedure. When one is testing to see how *sensitive* the original optimal solution is to the various parameters of the model, the common approach is to check each parameter (or at least c_j and b_i) individually. In addition to finding allowable ranges as described in the next section, this check might include changing the value of the parameter from its initial estimate to other possibilities in the *range of likely values* (including the endpoints of this range). Then some combinations of simultaneous changes of parameter values (such as changing an entire functional constraint) may be investigated. *Each* time one (or more) of the parameters is changed, the procedure described and illustrated here would be applied. Let us now summarize this procedure.

Summary of Procedure for Sensitivity Analysis

1. *Revision of model:* Make the desired change or changes in the model to be investigated next.
2. *Revision of final tableau:* Use the fundamental insight (as summarized by the formulas on the bottom of Table 6.17) to determine the resulting changes in the final simplex tableau. (See Table 6.19 for an illustration.)
3. *Conversion to proper form from Gaussian elimination:* Convert this tableau to the proper form for identifying and evaluating the current basic solution by applying (as necessary) Gaussian elimination. (See Table 6.20 for an illustration.)
4. *Feasibility test:* Test this solution for feasibility by checking whether all its basic variable values in the right-side column of the tableau still are nonnegative.
5. *Optimality test:* Test this solution for optimality (if feasible) by checking whether all its nonbasic variable coefficients in row 0 of the tableau still are nonnegative.
6. *Reoptimization:* If this solution fails either test, the new optimal solution can be obtained (if desired) by using the current tableau as the initial simplex tableau (and making any necessary conversions) for the simplex method or dual simplex method.

---

[1]There also exists a primal-dual algorithm that can be directly applied to such a simplex tableau without any conversion.

The interactive routine entitled *sensitivity analysis* in the OR Courseware will enable you to efficiently practice applying this procedure. In addition, a demonstration in OR Tutor (also entitled *sensitivity analysis*) provides you with another example.

In the next section, we shall discuss and illustrate the application of this procedure to each of the major categories of revisions in the original model. This discussion will involve, in part, expanding upon the example introduced in this section for investigating changes in the Wyndor Glass Co. model. In fact, we shall begin by *individually* checking each of the preceding changes. At the same time, we shall integrate some of the applications of duality theory to sensitivity analysis discussed in Sec. 6.5.

6.7 APPLYING SENSITIVITY ANALYSIS

Sensitivity analysis often begins with the investigation of changes in the values of b_i, the amount of resource i ($i = 1, 2, \ldots, m$) being made available for the activities under consideration. The reason is that there generally is more flexibility in setting and adjusting these values than there is for the other parameters of the model. As already discussed in Secs. 4.7 and 6.2, the economic interpretation of the dual variables (the y_i) as shadow prices is extremely useful for deciding which changes should be considered.

Case 1—Changes in b_i

Suppose that the only changes in the current model are that one or more of the b_i parameters ($i = 1, 2, \ldots, m$) has been changed. In this case, the *only* resulting changes in the final simplex tableau are in the *right-side* column. Consequently, the tableau still will be in proper form from Gaussian elimination and all the nonbasic variable coefficients in row 0 still will be nonnegative. Therefore, both the *conversion to proper form from Gaussian elimination* and the *optimality test* steps of the general procedure can be skipped. After revising the right-side column of the tableau, the only question will be whether all the basic variable values in this column still are nonnegative (the feasibility test).

As shown in Table 6.17, when the vector of the b_i values is changed from $\mathbf{b}$ to $\overline{\mathbf{b}}$, the formulas for calculating the new *right-side* column in the final tableau are

Right side of final row 0: $Z^* = \mathbf{y}^* \overline{\mathbf{b}}$,
Right side of final rows 1, 2, $\ldots$, m: $\mathbf{b}^* = \mathbf{S}^* \overline{\mathbf{b}}$.

(See the bottom of Table 6.17 for the location of the unchanged vector $\mathbf{y}^*$ and matrix $\mathbf{S}^*$ in the final tableau.)

Example (Variation 2 of the Wyndor Model). Sensitivity analysis is begun for the original Wyndor Glass Co. problem of Sec. 3.1 by examining the optimal values of the y_i dual variables ($y_1^* = 0$, $y_2^* = \frac{3}{2}$, $y_3^* = 1$). These shadow prices give the marginal value of each resource i for the activities (two new products) under consideration, where marginal value is expressed in the units of Z (thousands of dollars of profit per week). As discussed in Sec. 4.7 (see Fig. 4.8), the total profit from these activities can be increased $1,500 per week ($y_2^*$ times $1,000 per week) for each additional unit of resource 2 (hour of production time per week in Plant 2) that is made available. This increase in profit holds for relatively small changes that do not affect the feasibility of the current basic solution (and so do not affect the y_i^* values).

Consequently, the OR team has investigated the marginal profitability from the other current uses of this resource to determine if any are less than \$1,500 per week. This investigation reveals that one old product is far less profitable. The production rate for this product already has been reduced to the minimum amount that would justify its marketing expenses. However, it can be discontinued altogether, which would provide an additional 12 units of resource 2 for the new products. Thus, the next step is to determine the profit that could be obtained from the new products if this shift were made. This shift changes b_2 from 12 to 24 in the linear programming model. Figure 6.3 shows the graphical effect of this change, including the shift in the final corner-point solution from (2, 6) to (−2, 12). (Note that this figure differs from Fig. 6.2, which depicts Variation 1 of the Wyndor model, because the constraint $3x_1 + 2x_2 \leq 18$ has not been changed here.)

Thus, for Variation 2 of the Wyndor model, the only revision in the original model is the following change in the vector of the b_i values:

$$\mathbf{b} = \begin{bmatrix} 4 \\ 12 \\ 18 \end{bmatrix} \longrightarrow \bar{\mathbf{b}} = \begin{bmatrix} 4 \\ 24 \\ 18 \end{bmatrix}.$$

so only b_2 has a new value.

FIGURE 6.3
Feasible region for Variation 2 of the Wyndor Glass Co. model where $b_2 = 12 \rightarrow 24$.

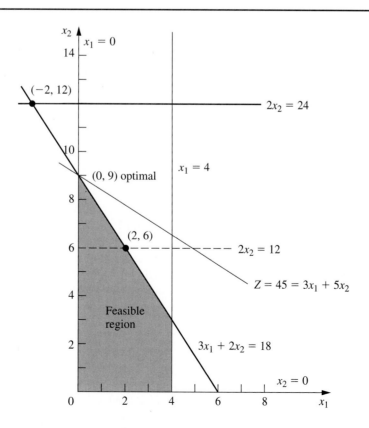

Analysis of Variation 2. When the fundamental insight (Table 6.17) is applied, the effect of this change in b_2 on the original final simplex tableau (middle of Table 6.19) is that the entries in the right-side column change to the following values:

$$Z^* = \mathbf{y}^*\overline{\mathbf{b}} = [0, \tfrac{3}{2}, 1] \begin{bmatrix} 4 \\ 24 \\ 18 \end{bmatrix} = 54,$$

$$\mathbf{b}^* = \mathbf{S}^*\overline{\mathbf{b}} = \begin{bmatrix} 1 & \tfrac{1}{3} & -\tfrac{1}{3} \\ 0 & \tfrac{1}{2} & 0 \\ 0 & -\tfrac{1}{3} & \tfrac{1}{3} \end{bmatrix} \begin{bmatrix} 4 \\ 24 \\ 18 \end{bmatrix} = \begin{bmatrix} 6 \\ 12 \\ -2 \end{bmatrix}, \quad \text{so} \quad \begin{bmatrix} x_3 \\ x_2 \\ x_1 \end{bmatrix} = \begin{bmatrix} 6 \\ 12 \\ -2 \end{bmatrix}.$$

Equivalently, because the only change in the original model is $\Delta b_2 = 24 - 12 = 12$, incremental analysis can be used to calculate these same values more quickly. Incremental analysis involves calculating just the *increments* in the tableau values caused by the change (or changes) in the original model, and then adding these increments to the original values. In this case, the increments in Z^* and $\mathbf{b}^*$ are

$$\Delta Z^* = \mathbf{y}^*\Delta\mathbf{b} = \mathbf{y}^* \begin{bmatrix} \Delta b_1 \\ \Delta b_2 \\ \Delta b_3 \end{bmatrix} = \mathbf{y}^* \begin{bmatrix} 0 \\ 12 \\ 0 \end{bmatrix},$$

$$\Delta\mathbf{b}^* = \mathbf{S}^* \Delta\mathbf{b} = \mathbf{S}^* \begin{bmatrix} \Delta b_1 \\ \Delta b_2 \\ \Delta b_3 \end{bmatrix} = \mathbf{S}^* \begin{bmatrix} 0 \\ 12 \\ 0 \end{bmatrix}.$$

Therefore, using the second component of $\mathbf{y}^*$ and the second column of $\mathbf{S}^*$, the only calculations needed are

$$\Delta Z^* = \frac{3}{2}(12) = 18, \qquad \text{so } Z^* = 36 + 18 = 54,$$

$$\Delta b_1^* = \frac{1}{3}(12) = 4, \qquad \text{so } b_1^* = 2 + 4 = 6,$$

$$\Delta b_2^* = \frac{1}{2}(12) = 6, \qquad \text{so } b_2^* = 6 + 6 = 12,$$

$$\Delta b_3^* = -\frac{1}{3}(12) = -4, \qquad \text{so } b_3^* = 2 - 4 = -2,$$

where the original values of these quantities are obtained from the right-side column in the original final tableau (middle of Table 6.19). The resulting revised final tableau corresponds completely to this original final tableau except for replacing the right-side column with these new values.

Therefore, the current (previously optimal) basic solution has become

$$(x_1, x_2, x_3, x_4, x_5) = (-2, 12, 6, 0, 0),$$

which fails the feasibility test because of the negative value. The dual simplex method now can be applied, starting with this revised simplex tableau, to find the new optimal so-

TABLE 6.21 Data for Variation 2 of the Wyndor Glass Co. model

| | | | | **Final Simplex Tableau after Reoptimization** | | | | | | |
| | | | | | **Coefficient of:** | | | | | |
		Basic Variable	**Eq.**	**Z**	x_1	x_2	x_3	x_4	x_5	**Right Side**
Model Parameters		Z	(0)	1	$\frac{9}{2}$	0	0	0	$\frac{5}{2}$	45
$c_1 = 3,$ $c_2 = 5$ $(n = 2)$		x_3	(1)	0	1	0	1	0	0	4
$a_{11} = 1,$ $a_{12} = 0,$ $b_1 = 4$		x_2	(2)	0	$\frac{3}{2}$	1	0	0	$\frac{1}{2}$	9
$a_{21} = 0,$ $a_{22} = 2,$ $b_2 = 24$		x_4	(3)	0	-3	0	0	1	-1	6
$a_{31} = 3,$ $a_{32} = 2,$ $b_3 = 18$										

lution. This method leads in just one iteration to the new final simplex tableau shown in Table 6.21. (Alternatively, the simplex method could be applied from the beginning, which also would lead to this final tableau in just one iteration in this case.) This tableau indicates that the new optimal solution is

$$(x_1, x_2, x_3, x_4, x_5) = (0, 9, 4, 6, 0),$$

with $Z = 45$, thereby providing an increase in profit from the new products of 9 units ($9,000 per week) over the previous $Z = 36$. The fact that $x_4 = 6$ indicates that 6 of the 12 additional units of resource 2 are unused by this solution.

Based on the results with $b_2 = 24$, the relatively unprofitable old product will be discontinued and the unused 6 units of resource 2 will be saved for some future use. Since y_3^* still is positive, a similar study is made of the possibility of changing the allocation of resource 3, but the resulting decision is to retain the current allocation. Therefore, the current linear programming model at this point (Variation 2) has the parameter values and optimal solution shown in Table 6.21. This model will be used as the starting point for investigating other types of changes in the model later in this section. However, before turning to these other cases, let us take a broader look at the current case.

The Allowable Range to Stay Feasible. Although $\Delta b_2 = 12$ proved to be too large an increase in b_2 to retain feasibility (and so optimality) with the basic solution where x_1, x_2, and x_3 are the basic variables (middle of Table 6.19), the above incremental analysis shows immediately just how large an increase is feasible. In particular, note that

$$b_1^* = 2 + \frac{1}{3} \Delta b_2,$$

$$b_2^* = 6 + \frac{1}{2} \Delta b_2,$$

$$b_3^* = 2 - \frac{1}{3} \Delta b_2,$$

where these three quantities are the values of x_3, x_2, and x_1, respectively, for this basic solution. The solution remains feasible, and so optimal, as long as all three quantities remain nonnegative.

$$2 + \frac{1}{3}\Delta b_2 \geq 0 \Rightarrow \frac{1}{3}\Delta b_2 \geq -2 \Rightarrow \Delta b_2 \geq -6,$$

$$6 + \frac{1}{2}\Delta b_2 \geq 0 \Rightarrow \frac{1}{2}\Delta b_2 \geq -6 \Rightarrow \Delta b_2 \geq -12,$$

$$2 - \frac{1}{3}\Delta b_2 \geq 0 \Rightarrow 2 \geq \frac{1}{3}\Delta b_2 \Rightarrow \Delta b_2 \leq 6.$$

Therefore, since $b_2 = 12 + \Delta b_2$, the solution remains feasible only if

$$-6 \leq \Delta b_2 \leq 6, \quad \text{that is,} \quad 6 \leq b_2 \leq 18.$$

(Verify this graphically in Fig. 6.3.) As introduced in Sec. 4.7, this range of values for b_2 is referred to as its *allowable range to stay feasible.*

> For any b_i, recall from Sec. 4.7 that its **allowable range to stay feasible** is the range of values over which the current optimal BF solution[1] (with adjusted values for the basic variables) remains feasible. Thus, the shadow price for b_i remains valid for evaluating the effect on Z of changing b_i only as long as b_i remains within this allowable range. (It is assumed that the change in this one b_i value is the only change in the model.) The adjusted values for the basic variables are obtained from the formula $\mathbf{b}^* = \mathbf{S}^*\mathbf{b}$. The calculation of the allowable range to stay feasible then is based on finding the range of values of b_i such that $\mathbf{b}^* \geq \mathbf{0}$.

Many linear programming software packages use this same technique for automatically generating the allowable range to stay feasible for each b_i. (A similar technique, discussed under Cases 2a and 3, also is used to generate an *allowable range to stay optimal* for each c_j.) In Chap. 4, we showed the corresponding output for the Excel Solver and LINDO in Figs. 4.10 and 4.13, respectively. Table 6.22 summarizes this same output with respect to the b_i for the original Wyndor Glass Co. model. For example, both the *allowable increase* and *allowable decrease* for b_2 are 6, that is, $-6 \leq \Delta b_2 \leq 6$. The above analysis shows how these quantities were calculated.

---

[1]When there is more than one optimal BF solution for the current model (before changing b_i), we are referring here to the one obtained by the simplex method.

TABLE 6.22 Typical software output for sensitivity analysis of the right-hand sides for the original Wyndor Glass Co. model

Constraint	Shadow Price	Current RHS	Allowable Increase	Allowable Decrease
Plant 1	0	4	∞	2
Plant 2	1.5	12	6	6
Plant 3	1	18	6	6

Analyzing Simultaneous Changes in Right-Hand Sides. When multiple b_i values are changed simultaneously, the formula $\mathbf{b}^* = \mathbf{S}^*\overline{\mathbf{b}}$ can again be used to see how the right-hand sides change in the final tableau. If all these right-hand sides still are nonnegative, the feasibility test will indicate that the revised solution provided by this tableau still is feasible. Since row 0 has not changed, being feasible implies that this solution also is optimal.

Although this approach works fine for checking the effect of a *specific* set of changes in the b_i, it does not give much insight into how far the b_i can be simultaneously changed from their original values before the revised solution will no longer be feasible. As part of postoptimality analysis, the management of an organization often is interested in investigating the effect of various changes in policy decisions (e.g., the amounts of resources being made available to the activities under consideration) that determine the right-hand sides. Rather than considering just one specific set of changes, management may want to explore *directions* of changes where some right-hand sides increase while others decrease. Shadow prices are invaluable for this kind of exploration. However, shadow prices remain valid for evaluating the effect of such changes on Z only within certain ranges of changes. For each b_i, the *allowable range to stay feasible* gives this range if *none* of the other b_i are changing at the same time. What do these *allowable ranges* become when some of the b_i are changing simultaneously?

A partial answer to this question is provided by the following 100 percent rule, which combines the *allowable changes* (increase or decrease) for the individual b_i that are given by the last two columns of a table like Table 6.22.

> **The 100 Percent Rule for Simultaneous Changes in Right-Hand Sides:** The shadow prices remain valid for predicting the effect of simultaneously changing the right-hand sides of some of the functional constraints as long as the changes are not too large. To check whether the changes are small enough, calculate for each change the percentage of the allowable change (increase or decrease) for that right-hand side to remain within its allowable range to stay feasible. If the *sum* of the percentage changes does *not* exceed 100 percent, the shadow prices definitely will still be valid. (If the sum *does* exceed 100 percent, then we cannot be sure.)

Example (Variation 3 of the Wyndor Model). To illustrate this rule, consider *Variation* 3 of the Wyndor Glass Co. model, which revises the original model by changing the right-hand side vector as follows:

$$\mathbf{b} = \begin{bmatrix} 4 \\ 12 \\ 18 \end{bmatrix} \rightarrow \overline{\mathbf{b}} = \begin{bmatrix} 4 \\ 15 \\ 15 \end{bmatrix}.$$

The calculations for the 100 percent rule in this case are

$$b_2: 12 \rightarrow 15. \quad \text{Percentage of allowable increase} = 100\left(\frac{15-12}{6}\right) = 50\%$$

$$b_3: 18 \rightarrow 15. \quad \text{Percentage of allowable decrease} = 100\left(\frac{18-15}{6}\right) = \underline{50\%}$$

$$\text{Sum} = 100\%$$

Since the sum of 100 percent barely does *not* exceed 100 percent, the shadow prices definitely are valid for predicting the effect of these changes on Z. In particular, since the shadow prices of b_2 and b_3 are 1.5 and 1, respectively, the resulting change in Z would be

$$\Delta Z = 1.5(3) + 1(-3) = 1.5,$$

so Z^* would increase from 36 to 37.5.

Figure 6.4 shows the feasible region for this revised model. (The dashed lines show the original locations of the revised constraint boundary lines.) The optimal solution now is the CPF solution $(0, 7.5)$, which gives

$$Z = 3x_1 + 5x_2 = 0 + 5(7.5) = 37.5,$$

just as predicted by the shadow prices. However, note what would happen if either b_2 were further increased above 15 or b_3 were further decreased below 15, so that the sum of the percentages of allowable changes would exceed 100 percent. This would cause the previously optimal corner-point solution to slide to the left of the x_2 axis ($x_1 < 0$), so this *infeasible* solution would no longer be optimal. Consequently, the old shadow prices would no longer be valid for predicting the new value of Z^*.

FIGURE 6.4
Feasible region for Variation 3 of the Wyndor Glass Co. model where $b_2 = 12 \rightarrow 15$ and $b_3 = 18 \rightarrow 15$.

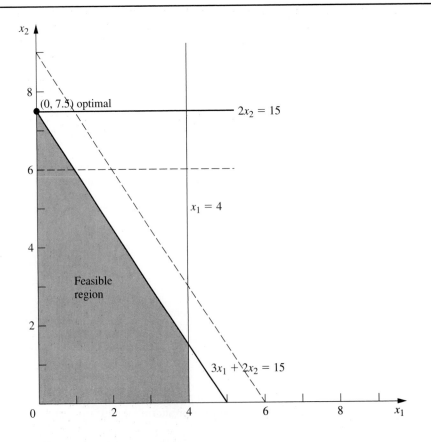

Case 2a—Changes in the Coefficients of a Nonbasic Variable

Consider a particular variable x_j (fixed j) that is a nonbasic variable in the optimal solution shown by the final simplex tableau. In Case 2a, the only change in the current model is that one or more of the coefficients of this variable—c_j, a_{1j}, a_{2j}, ..., a_{mj}—have been changed. Thus, letting $\bar{c}_j$ and $\bar{a}_{ij}$ denote the new values of these parameters, with $\bar{\mathbf{A}}_j$ (column j of matrix $\bar{\mathbf{A}}$) as the vector containing the $\bar{a}_{ij}$, we have

$$c_j \longrightarrow \bar{c}_j, \qquad \mathbf{A}_j \longrightarrow \bar{\mathbf{A}}_j$$

for the revised model.

As described at the beginning of Sec. 6.5, duality theory provides a very convenient way of checking these changes. In particular, if the *complementary* basic solution $\mathbf{y}^*$ in the dual problem still satisfies the single dual constraint that has changed, then the original optimal solution in the primal problem *remains optimal* as is. Conversely, if $\mathbf{y}^*$ violates this dual constraint, then this primal solution is *no longer optimal.*

If the optimal solution has changed and you wish to find the new one, you can do so rather easily. Simply apply the fundamental insight to revise the x_j column (the only one that has changed) in the final simplex tableau. Specifically, the formulas in Table 6.17 reduce to the following:

Coefficient of x_j in final row 0: $\qquad z_j^* - \bar{c}_j = \mathbf{y}^* \bar{\mathbf{A}}_j - \bar{c}_j,$
Coefficient of x_j in final rows 1 to m: $\qquad \mathbf{A}_j^* = \mathbf{S}^* \bar{\mathbf{A}}_j.$

With the current basic solution no longer optimal, the new value of $z_j^* - c_j$ now will be the one negative coefficient in row 0, so restart the simplex method with x_j as the initial entering basic variable.

Note that this procedure is a streamlined version of the general procedure summarized at the end of Sec. 6.6. Steps 3 and 4 (conversion to proper form from Gaussian elimination and the feasibility test) have been deleted as irrelevant, because the only column being changed in the revision of the final tableau (before reoptimization) is for the nonbasic variable x_j. Step 5 (optimality test) has been replaced by a quicker test of optimality to be performed right after step 1 (revision of model). It is only if this test reveals that the optimal solution has changed, and you wish to find the new one, that steps 2 and 6 (revision of final tableau and reoptimization) are needed.

Example (Variation 4 of the Wyndor Model).

Since x_1 is nonbasic in the current optimal solution (see Table 6.21) for Variation 2 of the Wyndor Glass Co. model, the next step in its sensitivity analysis is to check whether any reasonable changes in the estimates of the coefficients of x_1 could still make it advisable to introduce product 1. The set of changes that goes as far as realistically possible to make product 1 more attractive would be to reset $c_1 = 4$ and $a_{31} = 2$. Rather than exploring each of these changes independently (as is often done in sensitivity analysis), we will consider them together. Thus, the changes under consideration are

$$c_1 = 3 \longrightarrow \bar{c}_1 = 4, \qquad \mathbf{A}_1 = \begin{bmatrix} 1 \\ 0 \\ 3 \end{bmatrix} \longrightarrow \bar{\mathbf{A}}_1 = \begin{bmatrix} 1 \\ 0 \\ 2 \end{bmatrix}.$$

These two changes in Variation 2 give us *Variation* 4 of the Wyndor model. Variation 4 actually is equivalent to Variation 1 considered in Sec. 6.6 and depicted in Fig. 6.2, since Variation 1 combined these two changes with the change in the original Wyndor model ($b_2 = 12 \rightarrow 24$) that gave Variation 2. However, the key difference from the treatment of Variation 1 in Sec. 6.6 is that the analysis of Variation 4 treats Variation 2 as being the original model, so our starting point is the final simplex tableau given in Table 6.21 where x_1 now is a nonbasic variable.

The change in a_{31} revises the feasible region from that shown in Fig. 6.3 to the corresponding region in Fig. 6.5. The change in c_1 revises the objective function from $Z = 3x_1 + 5x_2$ to $Z = 4x_1 + 5x_2$. Figure 6.5 shows that the optimal objective function line $Z = 45 = 4x_1 + 5x_2$ still passes through the current optimal solution $(0, 9)$, so this solution remains optimal after these changes in a_{31} and c_1.

To use duality theory to draw this same conclusion, observe that the changes in c_1 and a_{31} lead to a single revised constraint for the dual problem, namely, the constraint that $a_{11}y_1 + a_{21}y_2 + a_{31}y_3 \geq c_1$. Both this revised constraint and the current $\mathbf{y}^*$ (coefficients of the slack variables in row 0 of Table 6.21) are shown below.

$$y_1^* = 0, \qquad y_2^* = 0, \qquad y_3^* = \frac{5}{2},$$

$$y_1 + 3y_3 \geq 3 \longrightarrow y_1 + 2y_3 \geq 4,$$

$$0 + 2\left(\frac{5}{2}\right) \geq 4.$$

Since $\mathbf{y}^*$ *still* satisfies the revised constraint, the current primal solution (Table 6.21) is still optimal.

Because this solution is still optimal, there is no need to revise the x_j column in the final tableau (step 2). Nevertheless, we do so below for illustrative purposes.

$$z_1^* - \overline{c}_1 = \mathbf{y}^*\overline{\mathbf{A}}_1 - c_1 = [0, 0, \tfrac{5}{2}]\begin{bmatrix} 1 \\ 0 \\ 2 \end{bmatrix} - 4 = 1.$$

$$\mathbf{A}_1^* = \mathbf{S}^*\overline{\mathbf{A}}_1 = \begin{bmatrix} 1 & 0 & 0 \\ 0 & 0 & \frac{1}{2} \\ 0 & 1 & -1 \end{bmatrix}\begin{bmatrix} 1 \\ 0 \\ 2 \end{bmatrix} = \begin{bmatrix} 1 \\ 1 \\ -2 \end{bmatrix}.$$

The fact that $z_1^* - \overline{c}_1 \geq 0$ again confirms the optimality of the current solution. Since $z_1^* - c_1$ is the surplus variable for the revised constraint in the dual problem, this way of testing for optimality is equivalent to the one used above.

This completes the analysis of the effect of changing the current model (Variation 2) to Variation 4. Because any larger changes in the original estimates of the coefficients of x_1 would be unrealistic, the OR team concludes that these coefficients are *insensitive* parameters in the current model. Therefore, they will be kept fixed at their best estimates shown in Table 6.21—$c_1 = 3$ and $a_{31} = 3$—for the remainder of the sensitivity analysis.

The Allowable Range to Stay Optimal.   We have just described and illustrated how to analyze *simultaneous* changes in the coefficients of a nonbasic variable x_j. It is common practice in sensitivity analysis to also focus on the effect of changing just *one* param-

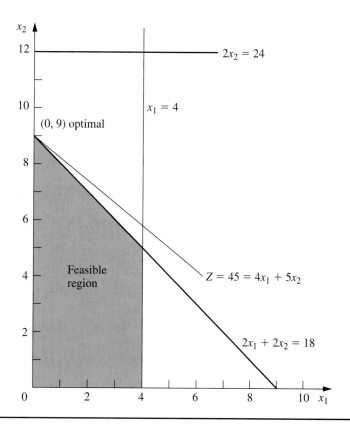

FIGURE 6.5
Feasible region for Variation 4 of the Wyndor model where Variation 2 (Fig. 6.3) has been revised so $a_{31} = 3 \rightarrow 2$ and $c_1 = 3 \rightarrow 4$.

eter, c_j. As introduced in Sec. 4.7, this involves streamlining the above approach to find the *allowable range to stay optimal* for c_j.

For any c_j, recall from Sec. 4.7 that its **allowable range to stay optimal** is the range of values over which the current optimal solution (as obtained by the simplex method for the current model before c_j is changed) remains optimal. (It is assumed that the change in this one c_j is the only change in the current model.) When x_j is a nonbasic variable for this solution, the solution remains optimal as long as $z_j^* - c_j \geq 0$, where $z_j^* = \mathbf{y}^* \mathbf{A}_j$ is a constant unaffected by any change in the value of c_j. Therefore, the allowable range to stay optimal for c_j can be calculated as $c_j \leq \mathbf{y}^* \mathbf{A}_j$.

For example, consider the current model (Variation 2) for the Wyndor Glass Co. problem summarized on the left side of Table 6.21, where the current optimal solution (with $c_1 = 3$) is given on the right side. When considering only the decision variables, x_1 and x_2, this optimal solution is $(x_1, x_2) = (0, 9)$, as displayed in Fig. 6.3. When just c_1 is changed, this solution remains optimal as long as

$$c_1 \leq \mathbf{y}^* \mathbf{A}_1 = [0, 0, \tfrac{5}{2}] \begin{bmatrix} 1 \\ 0 \\ 3 \end{bmatrix} = 7\tfrac{1}{2},$$

so $c_1 \leq 7\tfrac{1}{2}$ is the allowable range to stay optimal.

An alternative to performing this vector multiplication is to note in Table 6.21 that $z_1^* - c_1 = \frac{9}{2}$ (the coefficient of x_1 in row 0) when $c_1 = 3$, so $z_1^* = 3 + \frac{9}{2} = 7\frac{1}{2}$. Since $z_1^* = y^* A_1$, this immediately yields the same allowable range.

Figure 6.3 provides graphical insight into why $c_1 \leq 7\frac{1}{2}$ is the allowable range. At $c_1 = 7\frac{1}{2}$, the objective function becomes $Z = 7.5x_1 + 5x_2 = 2.5(3x_1 + 2x_2)$, so the optimal objective line will lie on top of the constraint boundary line $3x_1 + 2x_2 = 18$ shown in the figure. Thus, at this endpoint of the allowable range, we have multiple optimal solutions consisting of the line segment between $(0, 9)$ and $(4, 3)$. If c_1 were to be increased any further ($c_1 > 7\frac{1}{2}$), only $(4, 3)$ would be optimal. Consequently, we need $c_1 \leq 7\frac{1}{2}$ for $(0, 9)$ to remain optimal.

For any nonbasic decision variable x_j, the value of $z_j^* - c_j$ sometimes is referred to as the **reduced cost** for x_j, because it is the minimum amount by which the unit *cost* of activity j would have to be *reduced* to make it worthwhile to undertake activity j (increase x_j from zero). Interpreting c_j as the unit profit of activity j (so reducing the unit cost increases c_j by the same amount), the value of $z_j^* - c_j$ thereby is the maximum allowable increase in c_j to keep the current BF solution optimal.

The sensitivity analysis information generated by linear programming software packages normally includes both the reduced cost and the allowable range to stay optimal for each coefficient in the objective function (along with the types of information displayed in Table 6.22). This was illustrated in Figs. 4.10, 4.12, and 4.13 for the Excel Solver and LINDO. Table 6.23 displays this information in a typical form for our current model (Variation 2 of the Wyndor Glass Co. model). The last three columns are used to calculate the allowable range to stay optimal for each coefficient, so these allowable ranges are

$$c_1 \leq 3 + 4.5 = 7.5,$$
$$c_2 \geq 5 - 3 = 2.$$

As was discussed in Sec. 4.7, if any of the allowable increases or decreases had turned out to be zero, this would have been a signpost that the optimal solution given in the table is only one of multiple optimal solutions. In this case, changing the corresponding coefficient a tiny amount beyond the zero allowed and re-solving would provide another optimal CPF solution for the original model.

Thus far, we have described how to calculate the type of information in Table 6.23 for only nonbasic variables. For a basic variable like x_2, the reduced cost automatically is 0. We will discuss how to obtain the allowable range to stay optimal for c_j when x_j is a basic variable under Case 3.

TABLE 6.23 Typical software output for sensitivity analysis of the objective function coefficients for Variation 2 of the Wyndor Glass Co. model

Variable	Value	Reduced Cost	Current Coefficient	Allowable Increase	Allowable Decrease
x_1	0	4.5	3	4.5	∞
x_2	9	0	5	∞	3

Analyzing Simultaneous Changes in Objective Function Coefficients. Regardless of whether x_j is a basic or nonbasic variable, the allowable range to stay optimal for c_j is valid only if this objective function coefficient is the only one being changed. However, when simultaneous changes are made in the coefficients of the objective function, a 100 percent rule is available for checking whether the original solution must still be optimal. Much like the 100 percent rule for simultaneous changes in right-hand sides, this 100 percent rule combines the *allowable changes* (increase or decrease) for the individual c_j that are given by the last two columns of a table like Table 6.23, as described below.

> **The 100 Percent Rule for Simultaneous Changes in Objective Function Coefficients:** If simultaneous changes are made in the coefficients of the objective function, calculate for each change the percentage of the allowable change (increase or decrease) for that coefficient to remain within its allowable range to stay optimal. If the *sum* of the percentage changes does *not* exceed 100 percent, the original optimal solution definitely will still be optimal. (If the sum *does* exceed 100 percent, then we cannot be sure.)

Using Table 6.23 (and referring to Fig. 6.3 for visualization), this 100 percent rule says that (0, 9) will remain optimal for Variation 2 of the Wyndor Glass Co. model even if we simultaneously increase c_1 from 3 and decrease c_2 from 5 as long as these changes are not too large. For example, if c_1 is increased by 1.5 ($33\frac{1}{3}$ percent of the allowable change), then c_2 can be decreased by as much as 2 ($66\frac{2}{3}$ percent of the allowable change). Similarly, if c_1 is increased by 3 ($66\frac{2}{3}$ percent of the allowable change), then c_2 can only be decreased by as much as 1 ($33\frac{1}{3}$ percent of the allowable change). These maximum changes revise the objective function to either $Z = 4.5x_1 + 3x_2$ or $Z = 6x_1 + 4x_2$, which causes the optimal objective function line in Fig. 6.3 to rotate clockwise until it coincides with the constraint boundary equation $3x_1 + 2x_2 = 18$.

In general, when objective function coefficients change in the *same* direction, it is possible for the percentages of allowable changes to sum to more than 100 percent without changing the optimal solution. We will give an example at the end of the discussion of Case 3.

Case 2b—Introduction of a New Variable

After solving for the optimal solution, we may discover that the linear programming formulation did not consider all the attractive alternative activities. Considering a new activity requires introducing a new variable with the appropriate coefficients into the objective function and constraints of the current model—which is Case 2b.

The convenient way to deal with this case is to treat it just as if it were Case 2a! This is done by pretending that the new variable x_j actually was in the original model with all its coefficients equal to zero (so that they still are zero in the final simplex tableau) and that x_j is a nonbasic variable in the current BF solution. Therefore, if we change these zero coefficients to their actual values for the new variable, the procedure (including any reoptimization) does indeed become identical to that for Case 2a.

In particular, all you have to do to check whether the current solution still is optimal is to check whether the complementary basic solution $\mathbf{y}^*$ satisfies the one new dual constraint that corresponds to the new variable in the primal problem. We already have described this approach and then illustrated it for the Wyndor Glass Co. problem in Sec. 6.5.

Case 3—Changes in the Coefficients of a Basic Variable

Now suppose that the variable x_j (fixed j) under consideration is a *basic* variable in the optimal solution shown by the final simplex tableau. Case 3 assumes that the only changes in the current model are made to the coefficients of this variable.

Case 3 differs from Case 2a because of the requirement that a simplex tableau be in proper form from Gaussian elimination. This requirement allows the column for a nonbasic variable to be anything, so it does not affect Case 2a. However, for Case 3, the basic variable x_j must have a coefficient of 1 in its row of the simplex tableau and a coefficient of 0 in every other row (including row 0). Therefore, after the changes in the x_j column of the final simplex tableau have been calculated,[1] it probably will be necessary to apply Gaussian elimination to restore this form, as illustrated in Table 6.20. In turn, this step probably will change the value of the current basic solution and may make it either infeasible or nonoptimal (so reoptimization may be needed). Consequently, all the steps of the overall procedure summarized at the end of Sec. 6.6 are required for Case 3.

Before Gaussian elimination is applied, the formulas for revising the x_j column are the same as for Case 2a, as summarized below.

Coefficient of x_j in final row 0: $z_j^* - \bar{c}_j = \mathbf{y}^*\overline{\mathbf{A}}_j - \bar{c}_j.$

Coefficient of x_j in final rows 1 to m: $\mathbf{A}_j^* = \mathbf{S}^*\mathbf{A}_j.$

Example (Variation 5 of the Wyndor Model).   Because x_2 is a basic variable in Table 6.21 for Variation 2 of the Wyndor Glass Co. model, sensitivity analysis of its coefficients fits Case 3. Given the current optimal solution ($x_1 = 0$, $x_2 = 9$), product 2 is the *only* new product that should be introduced, and its production rate should be relatively large. Therefore, the key question now is whether the initial estimates that led to the coefficients of x_2 in the current model (Variation 2) could have *overestimated* the attractiveness of product 2 so much as to invalidate this conclusion. This question can be tested by checking the *most pessimistic* set of reasonable estimates for these coefficients, which turns out to be $c_2 = 3$, $a_{22} = 3$, and $a_{32} = 4$. Consequently, the changes to be investigated (Variation 5 of the Wyndor model) are

$$c_2 = 5 \longrightarrow \bar{c}_2 = 3, \qquad \mathbf{A}_2 = \begin{bmatrix} 0 \\ 2 \\ 2 \end{bmatrix} \longrightarrow \overline{\mathbf{A}}_2 = \begin{bmatrix} 0 \\ 3 \\ 4 \end{bmatrix}.$$

The graphical effect of these changes is that the feasible region changes from the one shown in Fig. 6.3 to the one in Fig. 6.6. The optimal solution in Fig. 6.3 is (x_1, x_2) = (0, 9), which is the corner-point solution lying at the intersection of the $x_1 = 0$ and $3x_1 + 2x_2 = 18$ constraint boundaries. With the revision of the constraints, the corre-

---

[1]For the relatively sophisticated reader, we should point out a possible pitfall for Case 3 that would be discovered at this point. Specifically, the changes in the initial tableau can destroy the linear independence of the columns of coefficients of basic variables. This event occurs only if the unit coefficient of the basic variable x_j in the final tableau has been changed to zero at this point, in which case more extensive simplex method calculations must be used for Case 3.

sponding corner-point solution in Fig. 6.6 is $(0, \frac{9}{2})$. However, this solution no longer is optimal, because the revised objective function of $Z = 3x_1 + 3x_2$ now yields a new optimal solution of $(x_1, x_2) = (4, \frac{3}{2})$.

Analysis of Variation 5. Now let us see how we draw these same conclusions algebraically. Because the only changes in the model are in the coefficients of x_2, the *only* resulting changes in the final simplex tableau (Table 6.21) are in the x_2 column. Therefore, the above formulas are used to recompute just this column.

$$z_2 - \bar{c}_2 = \mathbf{y}^*\overline{\mathbf{A}}_2 - \bar{c}_2 = [0, 0, \tfrac{5}{2}] \begin{bmatrix} 0 \\ 3 \\ 4 \end{bmatrix} - 3 = 7.$$

$$\mathbf{A}_2^* = \mathbf{S}^*\overline{\mathbf{A}}_2 = \begin{bmatrix} 1 & 0 & 0 \\ 0 & 0 & \tfrac{1}{2} \\ 0 & 1 & -1 \end{bmatrix} \begin{bmatrix} 0 \\ 3 \\ 4 \end{bmatrix} = \begin{bmatrix} 0 \\ 2 \\ -1 \end{bmatrix}.$$

FIGURE 6.6
Feasible region for Variation 5 of the Wyndor model where Variation 2 (Fig. 6.3) has been revised so $c_2 = 5 \rightarrow 3$, $a_{22} = 2 \rightarrow 3$, and $a_{32} = 2 \rightarrow 4$.

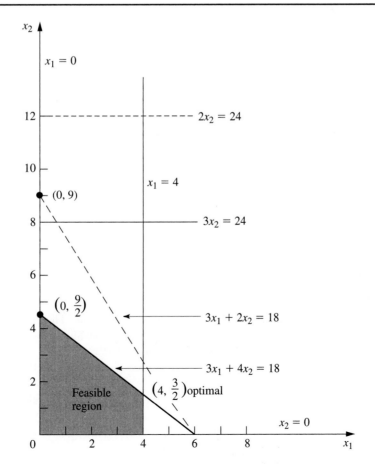

TABLE 6.24 Sensitivity analysis procedure applied to Variation 5 of the Wyndor Glass Co. model

	Basic Variable	Eq.	Z	Coefficient of:					Right Side
				x_1	x_2	x_3	x_4	x_5	
Revised final tableau	Z	(0)	1	$\frac{9}{2}$	7	0	0	$\frac{5}{2}$	45
	x_3	(1)	0	1	0	1	0	0	4
	x_2	(2)	0	$\frac{3}{2}$	2	0	0	$\frac{1}{2}$	9
	x_4	(3)	0	-3	-1	0	1	-1	6
Converted to proper form	Z	(0)	1	$-\frac{3}{4}$	0	0	0	$\frac{3}{4}$	$\frac{27}{2}$
	x_3	(1)	0	1	0	1	0	0	4
	x_2	(2)	0	$\frac{3}{4}$	1	0	0	$\frac{1}{4}$	$\frac{9}{2}$
	x_4	(3)	0	$-\frac{9}{4}$	0	0	1	$-\frac{3}{4}$	$\frac{21}{2}$
New final tableau after reoptimization (only one iteration of the simplex method needed in this case)	Z	(0)	1	0	0	$\frac{3}{4}$	0	$\frac{3}{4}$	$\frac{33}{2}$
	x_1	(1)	0	1	0	1	0	0	4
	x_2	(2)	0	0	1	$-\frac{3}{4}$	0	$\frac{1}{4}$	$\frac{3}{2}$
	x_4	(3)	0	0	0	$\frac{9}{4}$	1	$-\frac{3}{4}$	$\frac{39}{2}$

(Equivalently, incremental analysis with $\Delta c_2 = -2$, $\Delta a_{22} = 1$, and $\Delta a_{32} = 2$ can be used in the same way to obtain this column.)

The resulting revised final tableau is shown at the top of Table 6.24. Note that the new coefficients of the basic variable x_2 do not have the required values, so the conversion to proper form from Gaussian elimination must be applied next. This step involves dividing row 2 by 2, subtracting 7 times the new row 2 from row 0, and adding the new row 2 to row 3.

The resulting second tableau in Table 6.24 gives the new value of the current basic solution, namely, $x_3 = 4$, $x_2 = \frac{9}{2}$, $x_4 = \frac{21}{2}$ ($x_1 = 0$, $x_5 = 0$). Since all these variables are nonnegative, the solution is still feasible. However, because of the negative coefficient of x_1 in row 0, we know that it is no longer optimal. Therefore, the simplex method would be applied to this tableau, with this solution as the initial BF solution, to find the new optimal solution. The initial entering basic variable is x_1, with x_3 as the leaving basic variable. Just one iteration is needed in this case to reach the new optimal solution $x_1 = 4$, $x_2 = \frac{3}{2}$, $x_4 = \frac{39}{2}$ ($x_3 = 0$, $x_5 = 0$), as shown in the last tableau of Table 6.24.

All this analysis suggests that c_2, a_{22}, and a_{32} are relatively sensitive parameters. However, additional data for estimating them more closely can be obtained only by conducting a pilot run. Therefore, the OR team recommends that production of product 2 be initiated immediately on a small scale ($x_2 = \frac{3}{2}$) and that this experience be used to guide the decision on whether the remaining production capacity should be allocated to product 2 or product 1.

The Allowable Range to Stay Optimal. For Case 2a, we described how to find the allowable range to stay optimal for any c_j such that x_j is a nonbasic variable for the current optimal solution (before c_j is changed). When x_j is a basic variable instead, the procedure is somewhat more involved because of the need to convert to proper form from Gaussian elimination before testing for optimality.

To illustrate the procedure, consider Variation 5 of the Wyndor Glass Co. model (with $c_2 = 3$, $a_{22} = 3$, $a_{23} = 4$) that is graphed in Fig. 6.6 and solved in Table 6.24. Since x_2 is a basic variable for the optimal solution (with $c_2 = 3$) given at the bottom of this table, the steps needed to find the allowable range to stay optimal for c_2 are the following:

1. Since x_2 is a basic variable, note that its coefficient in the new final row 0 (see the bottom tableau in Table 6.24) is automatically $z_2^* - c_2 = 0$ before c_2 is changed from its current value of 3.

2. Now increment $c_2 = 3$ by Δc_2 (so $c_2 = 3 + \Delta c_2$). This changes the coefficient noted in step 1 to $z_2^* - c_2 = -\Delta c_2$, which changes row 0 to

$$\text{Row } 0 = \left[0, -\Delta c_2, \frac{3}{4}, 0, \frac{3}{4} \ \middle| \ \frac{33}{2}\right].$$

3. With this coefficient now not zero, we must perform elementary row operations to restore proper form from Gaussian elimination. In particular, add to row 0 the product, Δc_2 times row 2, to obtain the new row 0, as shown below.

$$\left[0, -\Delta c_2, \frac{3}{4}, \quad 0, \frac{3}{4} \quad \middle| \quad \frac{33}{2}\right]$$

$$+ \left[0, \quad \Delta c_2, -\frac{3}{4}\Delta c_2, 0, \frac{1}{4}\Delta c_2 \quad \middle| \quad \frac{3}{2}\Delta c_2\right]$$

$$\text{New row } 0 = \left[0, \quad 0, \frac{3}{4} - \frac{3}{4}\Delta c_2, 0, \frac{3}{4} + \frac{1}{4}\Delta c_2 \quad \middle| \quad \frac{33}{2} + \frac{3}{2}\Delta c_2\right]$$

4. Using this new row 0, solve for the range of values of Δc_2 that keeps the coefficients of the nonbasic variables (x_3 and x_5) nonnegative.

$$\frac{3}{4} - \frac{3}{4}\Delta c_2 \geq 0 \quad \Rightarrow \quad \frac{3}{4} \geq \frac{3}{4}\Delta c_2 \quad \Rightarrow \quad \Delta c_2 \leq 1.$$

$$\frac{3}{4} + \frac{1}{4}\Delta c_2 \geq 0 \quad \Rightarrow \quad \frac{1}{4}\Delta c_2 \geq -\frac{3}{4} \quad \Rightarrow \quad \Delta c_2 \geq -3.$$

Thus, the range of values is $-3 \leq \Delta c_2 \leq 1$.

5. Since $c_2 = 3 + \Delta c_2$, add 3 to this range of values, which yields

$$0 \leq c_2 \leq 4$$

as the allowable range to stay optimal for c_2.

With just two decision variables, this allowable range can be verified graphically by using Fig. 6.6 with an objective function of $Z = 3x_1 + c_2x_2$. With the current value of $c_2 = 3$, the optimal solution is $(4, \frac{3}{2})$. When c_2 is increased, this solution remains optimal only for $c_2 \leq 4$. For $c_2 \geq 4$, $(0, \frac{9}{2})$ becomes optimal (with a tie at $c_2 = 4$), because of the constraint boundary $3x_1 + 4x_2 = 18$. When c_2 is decreased instead, $(4, \frac{3}{2})$ remains optimal only for $c_2 \geq 0$. For $c_2 \leq 0$, $(4, 0)$ becomes optimal because of the constraint boundary $x_1 = 4$.

In a similar manner, the allowable range to stay optimal for c_1 (with c_2 fixed at 3) can be derived either algebraically or graphically to be $c_1 \geq \frac{9}{4}$. (Problem 6.7-13 asks you to verify this both ways.)

Thus, the *allowable decrease* for c_1 from its current value of 3 is only $\frac{3}{4}$. However, it is possible to decrease c_1 by a larger amount without changing the optimal solution if c_2 also decreases sufficiently. For example, suppose that *both* c_1 and c_2 are decreased by 1 from their current value of 3, so that the objective function changes from $Z = 3x_1 + 3x_2$ to $Z = 2x_1 + 2x_2$. According to the 100 percent rule for simultaneous changes in objective function coefficients, the percentages of allowable changes are $133\frac{1}{3}$ percent and $33\frac{1}{3}$ percent, respectively, which sum to far over 100 percent. However, the slope of the objective function line has not changed at all, so $(4, \frac{3}{2})$ still is optimal.

Case 4—Introduction of a New Constraint

In this case, a new constraint must be introduced to the model after it has already been solved. This case may occur because the constraint was overlooked initially or because new considerations have arisen since the model was formulated. Another possibility is that the constraint was deleted purposely to decrease computational effort because it appeared to be less restrictive than other constraints already in the model, but now this impression needs to be checked with the optimal solution actually obtained.

To see if the current optimal solution would be affected by a new constraint, all you have to do is to check directly whether the optimal solution satisfies the constraint. If it does, then it would still be the *best feasible solution* (i.e., the optimal solution), even if the constraint were added to the model. The reason is that a new constraint can only eliminate some previously feasible solutions without adding any new ones.

If the new constraint does eliminate the current optimal solution, and if you want to find the new solution, then introduce this constraint into the final simplex tableau (as an additional row) *just* as if this were the initial tableau, where the usual additional variable (slack variable or artificial variable) is designated to be the basic variable for this new row. Because the new row probably will have *nonzero* coefficients for some of the other basic variables, the conversion to proper form from Gaussian elimination is applied next, and then the reoptimization step is applied in the usual way.

Just as for some of the preceding cases, this procedure for Case 4 is a streamlined version of the general procedure summarized at the end of Sec. 6.6. The only question to be addressed for this case is whether the previously optimal solution still is *feasible,* so step 5 (optimality test) has been deleted. Step 4 (feasibility test) has been replaced by a much quicker test of feasibility (does the previously optimal solution satisfy the new constraint?) to be performed right after step 1 (revision of model). It is only if this test provides a negative answer, and you wish to reoptimize, that steps 2, 3, and 6 are used (revision of final tableau, conversion to proper form from Gaussian elimination, and reoptimization).

Example (Variation 6 of the Wyndor Model).   To illustrate this case, we consider Variation 6 of the Wyndor Glass Co. model, which simply introduces the new constraint

$$2x_1 + 3x_2 \leq 24$$

into the Variation 2 model given in Table 6.21. The graphical effect is shown in Fig. 6.7. The previous optimal solution (0, 9) violates the new constraint, so the optimal solution changes to (0, 8).

To analyze this example algebraically, note that (0, 9) yields $2x_1 + 3x_2 = 27 > 24$, so this previous optimal solution is no longer feasible. To find the new optimal solution, add the new constraint to the current final simplex tableau as just described, with the slack variable x_6 as its initial basic variable. This step yields the first tableau shown in Table 6.25. The conversion to proper form from Gaussian elimination then requires subtracting from the new row the product, 3 times row 2, which identifies the current basic solution $x_3 = 4$, $x_2 = 9$, $x_4 = 6$, $x_6 = -3$ ($x_1 = 0$, $x_5 = 0$), as shown in the second tableau. Applying the dual simplex method (described in Sec. 7.1) to this tableau then leads in just one iteration (more are sometimes needed) to the new optimal solution in the last tableau of Table 6.25.

FIGURE 6.7
Feasible region for Variation 6 of the Wyndor model where Variation 2 (Fig. 6.3) has been revised by adding the new constraint,
$2x_1 + 3x_2 \leq 24$.

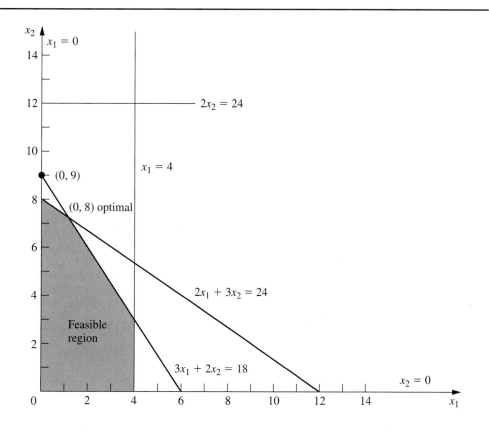

TABLE 6.25 Sensitivity analysis procedure applied to Variation 6 of the Wyndor Glass Co. model

	Basic Variable	Eq.	Z	x_1	x_2	x_3	x_4	x_5	x_6	Right Side
Revised final tableau	Z	(0)	1	$\frac{9}{2}$	0	0	0	$\frac{5}{2}$	0	45
	x_3	(1)	0	1	0	1	0	0	0	4
	x_2	(2)	0	$\frac{3}{2}$	1	0	0	$\frac{1}{2}$	0	9
	x_4	(3)	0	-3	0	0	1	-1	0	6
	x_6	New	0	2	3	0	0	0	1	24
Converted to proper form	Z	(0)	1	$\frac{9}{2}$	0	0	0	$\frac{5}{2}$	0	45
	x_3	(1)	0	1	0	1	0	0	0	4
	x_2	(2)	0	$\frac{3}{2}$	1	0	0	$\frac{1}{2}$	0	9
	x_4	(3)	0	-3	0	0	1	-1	0	6
	x_6	New	0	$-\frac{5}{2}$	0	0	0	$-\frac{3}{2}$	1	-3
New final tableau after reoptimization (only one iteration of dual simplex method needed in this case)	Z	(0)	1	$\frac{1}{3}$	0	0	0	0	$\frac{5}{3}$	40
	x_3	(1)	0	1	0	1	0	0	0	4
	x_2	(2)	0	$\frac{2}{3}$	1	0	0	0	$\frac{1}{3}$	8
	x_4	(3)	0	$-\frac{4}{3}$	0	0	1	0	$-\frac{2}{3}$	8
	x_5	New	0	$\frac{5}{3}$	0	0	0	1	$-\frac{2}{3}$	2

Systematic Sensitivity Analysis—Parametric Programming

So far we have described how to test specific changes in the model parameters. Another common approach to sensitivity analysis is to vary one or more parameters continuously over some interval(s) to see when the optimal solution changes.

For example, with Variation 2 of the Wyndor Glass Co. model, rather than beginning by testing the specific change from $b_2 = 12$ to $\bar{b}_2 = 24$, we might instead set

$$\bar{b}_2 = 12 + \theta$$

and then vary θ continuously from 0 to 12 (the maximum value of interest). The geometric interpretation in Fig. 6.3 is that the $2x_2 = 12$ constraint line is being shifted upward to $2x_2 = 12 + \theta$, with θ being increased from 0 to 12. The result is that the original optimal CPF solution (2, 6) shifts up the $3x_1 + 2x_2 = 18$ constraint line toward $(-2, 12)$. This corner-point solution remains optimal as long as it is still feasible ($x_1 \geq 0$), after which (0, 9) becomes the optimal solution.

The algebraic calculations of the effect of having $\Delta b_2 = \theta$ are directly analogous to those for the Case 1 example where $\Delta b_2 = 12$. In particular, we use the expressions for Z^* and $\mathbf{b}^*$ given for Case 1,

$$Z^* = \mathbf{y}^* \overline{\mathbf{b}}$$
$$\mathbf{b}^* = \mathbf{S}^* \overline{\mathbf{b}}$$

where $\overline{\mathbf{b}}$ now is

$$\overline{\mathbf{b}} = \begin{bmatrix} 4 \\ 12 + \theta \\ 18 \end{bmatrix}$$

and where $\mathbf{y}^*$ and $\mathbf{S}^*$ are given in the boxes in the middle tableau in Table 6.19. These equations indicate that the optimal solution is

$$Z^* = 36 + \frac{3}{2}\theta$$

$$x_3 = 2 + \frac{1}{3}\theta$$

$$x_2 = 6 + \frac{1}{2}\theta \qquad (x_4 = 0, x_5 = 0)$$

$$x_1 = 2 - \frac{1}{3}\theta$$

for θ small enough that this solution still is feasible, i.e., for $\theta \leq 6$. For $\theta > 6$, the dual simplex method (described in Sec. 7.1) yields the tableau shown in Table 6.21 except for the value of x_4. Thus, $Z = 45$, $x_3 = 4$, $x_2 = 9$ (along with $x_1 = 0$, $x_5 = 0$), and the expression for $\mathbf{b}^*$ yields

$$x_4 = b_3^* = 0(4) + 1(12 + \theta) - 1(18) = -6 + \theta.$$

This information can then be used (along with other data not incorporated into the model on the effect of increasing b_2) to decide whether to retain the original optimal solution and, if not, how much to increase b_2.

In a similar way, we can investigate the effect on the optimal solution of varying several parameters simultaneously. When we vary just the b_i parameters, we express the new value $\overline{b}_i$ in terms of the original value b_i as follows:

$$\overline{b}_i = b_i + \alpha_i \theta, \qquad \text{for } i = 1, 2, \ldots, m,$$

where the α_i values are input constants specifying the desired rate of increase (positive or negative) of the corresponding right-hand side as θ is increased.

For example, suppose that it is possible to shift some of the production of a current Wyndor Glass Co. product from Plant 2 to Plant 3, thereby increasing b_2 by decreasing b_3. Also suppose that b_3 decreases twice as fast as b_2 increases. Then

$$\overline{b}_2 = 12 + \theta$$
$$\overline{b}_3 = 18 - 2\theta,$$

where the (nonnegative) value of θ measures the amount of production shifted. (Thus, $\alpha_1 = 0$, $\alpha_2 = 1$, and $\alpha_3 = -2$ in this case.) In Fig. 6.3, the geometric interpretation is that as θ is increased from 0, the $2x_2 = 12$ constraint line is being pushed up to $2x_2 = 12 + \theta$ (ignore the $2x_2 = 24$ line) and simultaneously the $3x_1 + 2x_2 = 18$ constraint line is being pushed down to $3x_1 + 2x_2 = 18 - 2\theta$. The original optimal CPF solution (2, 6) lies at the intersection of the $2x_2 = 12$ and $3x_1 + 2x_2 = 18$ lines, so shifting these lines causes this corner-point solution to shift. However, with the objective function of $Z = 3x_1 + 5x_2$, this corner-point solution will remain optimal as long as it is still feasible ($x_1 \geq 0$).

An algebraic investigation of simultaneously changing b_2 and b_3 in this way again involves using the formulas for Case 1 (treating θ as representing an unknown number) to calculate the resulting changes in the final tableau (middle of Table 6.19), namely,

$$Z^* = \mathbf{y}^*\overline{\mathbf{b}} = [0, \tfrac{3}{2}, 1]\begin{bmatrix} 4 \\ 12 + \theta \\ 18 - 2\theta \end{bmatrix} = 36 - \tfrac{1}{2}\theta,$$

$$\mathbf{b}^* = \mathbf{S}^*\overline{\mathbf{b}} = \begin{bmatrix} 1 & \tfrac{1}{3} & -\tfrac{1}{3} \\ 0 & \tfrac{1}{2} & 0 \\ 0 & -\tfrac{1}{3} & \tfrac{1}{3} \end{bmatrix}\begin{bmatrix} 4 \\ 12 + \theta \\ 18 - 2\theta \end{bmatrix} = \begin{bmatrix} 2 + \theta \\ 6 + \tfrac{1}{2}\theta \\ 2 - \theta \end{bmatrix}.$$

Therefore, the optimal solution becomes

$$Z^* = 36 - \frac{1}{2}\theta$$

$$x_3 = 2 + \theta$$

$$x_2 = 6 + \frac{1}{2}\theta \qquad (x_4 = 0, \qquad x_5 = 0)$$

$$x_1 = 2 - \theta$$

for θ small enough that this solution still is feasible, i.e., for $\theta \leq 2$. (Check this conclusion in Fig. 6.3.) However, the fact that Z decreases as θ increases from 0 indicates that the best choice for θ is $\theta = 0$, so none of the possible shifting of production should be done.

The approach to varying several c_j parameters simultaneously is similar. In this case, we express the new value $\overline{c}_j$ in terms of the original value of c_j as

$$\overline{c}_j = c_j + \alpha_j\theta, \qquad \text{for } j = 1, 2, \ldots, n,$$

where the α_j are input constants specifying the desired rate of increase (positive or negative) of c_j as θ is increased.

To illustrate this case, reconsider the sensitivity analysis of c_1 and c_2 for the Wyndor Glass Co. problem that was performed earlier in this section. Starting with Variation 2 of the Wyndor model presented in Table 6.21 and Fig. 6.3, we separately considered the effect of changing c_1 from 3 to 4 (its most optimistic estimate) and c_2 from 5 to 3 (its most pessimistic estimate). Now we can simultaneously consider both changes, as well as various intermediate cases with smaller changes, by setting

$$\overline{c}_1 = 3 + \theta \qquad \text{and} \qquad \overline{c}_2 = 5 - 2\theta,$$

where the value of θ measures the *fraction* of the maximum possible change that is made. The result is to replace the original objective function $Z = 3x_1 + 5x_2$ by a *function* of θ

$$Z(\theta) = (3 + \theta)x_1 + (5 - 2\theta)x_2,$$

so the optimization now can be performed for any desired (fixed) value of θ between 0 and 1. By checking the effect as θ increases from 0 to 1, we can determine just when and how the optimal solution changes as the error in the original estimates of these parameters increases.

Considering these changes simultaneously is especially appropriate if there are factors that cause the parameters to change together. Are the two products competitive in some sense, so that a larger-than-expected unit profit for one implies a smaller-than-expected unit profit for the other? Are they both affected by some exogenous factor, such as the advertising emphasis of a competitor? Is it possible to simultaneously change both unit profits through appropriate shifting of personnel and equipment?

In the feasible region shown in Fig. 6.3, the geometric interpretation of changing the objective function from $Z = 3x_1 + 5x_2$ to $Z(\theta) = (3 + \theta)x_1 + (5 - 2\theta)x_2$ is that we are changing the *slope* of the original objective function line ($Z = 45 = 3x_1 + 5x_2$) that passes through the optimal solution (0, 9). If θ is increased enough, this slope will change sufficiently that the optimal solution will switch from (0, 9) to another CPF solution (4, 3). (Check graphically whether this occurs for $\theta \leq 1$.)

The algebraic procedure for dealing simultaneously with these two changes ($\Delta c_1 = \theta$ and $\Delta c_2 = -2\theta$) is shown in Table 6.26. Although the changes now are expressed in terms of θ rather than specific numerical amounts, θ is treated just as an unknown number. The table displays just the relevant rows of the tableaux involved (row 0 and the row for the basic variable x_2). The first tableau shown is just the final tableau for the current version of the model (before c_1 and c_2 are changed) as given in Table 6.21. Refer to the formulas in Table 6.17. The only changes in the *revised* final tableau shown next are that Δc_1 and Δc_2 are subtracted from the row 0 coefficients of x_1 and x_2, respectively. To convert this tableau to proper form from Gaussian elimination, we subtract 2θ times row 2 from row 0, which yields the last tableau shown. The expressions in terms of θ for the coeffi-

TABLE 6.26 Dealing with $\Delta c_1 = \theta$ and $\Delta c_2 = -2\theta$ for Variation 2 of the Wyndor model as given in Table 6.21

	Basic Variable	Eq.	Z	Coefficient of:					Right Side
				x_1	x_2	x_3	x_4	x_5	
Final tableau	Z	(0)	1	$\frac{9}{2}$	0	0	0	$\frac{5}{2}$	45
	x_2	(2)	0	$\frac{3}{2}$	1	0	0	$\frac{1}{2}$	9
Revised final tableau when $\Delta c_1 = \theta$ and $\Delta c_2 = -2\theta$	$Z(\theta)$	(0)	1	$\frac{9}{2} - \theta$	2θ	0	0	$\frac{5}{2}$	45
	x_2	(2)	0	$\frac{3}{2}$	1	0	0	$\frac{1}{2}$	9
Converted to proper form	$Z(\theta)$	(0)	1	$\frac{9}{2} - 4\theta$	0	0	0	$\frac{5}{2} - \theta$	$45 - 18\theta$
	x_2	(2)	0	$\frac{3}{2}$	1	0	0	$\frac{1}{2}$	9

cients of nonbasic variables x_1 and x_5 in row 0 of this tableau show that the current BF solution remains optimal for $\theta \leq \frac{9}{8}$. Because $\theta = 1$ is the maximum realistic value of θ, this indicates that c_1 and c_2 together are insensitive parameters with respect to the Variation 2 model in Table 6.21. There is no need to try to estimate these parameters more closely unless other parameters change (as occurred for Variation 5 of the Wyndor model).

As we discussed in Sec. 4.7, this way of continuously varying several parameters simultaneously is referred to as *parametric linear programming*. Section 7.2 presents the complete parametric linear programming procedure (including identifying new optimal solutions for larger values of θ) when just the c_j parameters are being varied and then when just the b_i parameters are being varied. Some linear programming software packages also include routines for varying just the coefficients of a single variable or just the parameters of a single constraint. In addition to the other applications discussed in Sec. 4.7, these procedures provide a convenient way of conducting sensitivity analysis systematically.

6.8 CONCLUSIONS

Every linear programming problem has associated with it a dual linear programming problem. There are a number of very useful relationships between the original (primal) problem and its dual problem that enhance our ability to analyze the primal problem. For example, the economic interpretation of the dual problem gives shadow prices that measure the marginal value of the resources in the primal problem and provides an interpretation of the simplex method. Because the simplex method can be applied directly to either problem in order to solve both of them simultaneously, considerable computational effort sometimes can be saved by dealing directly with the dual problem. Duality theory, including the dual simplex method for working with superoptimal basic solutions, also plays a major role in sensitivity analysis.

The values used for the parameters of a linear programming model generally are just estimates. Therefore, sensitivity analysis needs to be performed to investigate what happens if these estimates are wrong. The fundamental insight of Sec. 5.3 provides the key to performing this investigation efficiently. The general objectives are to identify the sensitive parameters that affect the optimal solution, to try to estimate these sensitive parameters more closely, and then to select a solution that remains good over the range of likely values of the sensitive parameters. This analysis is a very important part of most linear programming studies.

SELECTED REFERENCES

1. Bazaraa, M. S., J. J. Jarvis, and H. D. Sherali: *Linear Programming and Network Flows,* 2d ed., Wiley, New York, 1990.
2. Dantzig, G. B., and M. N. Thapa: *Linear Programming* 1: *Introduction*, Springer, New York, 1997.
3. Hillier, F. S., M. S. Hillier, and G. J. Lieberman: *Introduction to Management Science*: *A Modeling and Case Studies Approach with Spreadsheets*, Irwin/McGraw-Hill, Burr Ridge, IL, 2000, chap. 4.
4. Vanderbei, R. J.: *Linear Programming*: *Foundations and Extensions*, Kluwer Academic Publishers, Boston, MA, 1996.

LEARNING AIDS FOR THIS CHAPTER IN YOUR OR COURSEWARE

A Demonstration Example in OR Tutor:

Sensitivity Analysis

Interactive Routines:

Enter or Revise a General Linear Programming Model
Solve Interactively by the Simplex Method
Sensitivity Analysis

An Excel Add-In:

Premium Solver

Files (Chapter 3) for Solving the Wyndor Example:

Excel File
LINGO/LINDO File
MPL/CPLEX File

See Appendix 1 for documentation of the software.

PROBLEMS

The symbols to the left of some of the problems (or their parts) have the following meaning:

D: The demonstration example listed above may be helpful.
I: We suggest that you use the corresponding interactive routine listed above (the printout records your work).
C: Use the computer with any of the software options available to you (or as instructed by your instructor) to solve the problem automatically.

An asterisk on the problem number indicates that at least a partial answer is given in the back of the book.

6.1-1. Construct the primal-dual table and the dual problem for each of the following linear programming models fitting our standard form.
(a) Model in Prob. 4.1-6
(b) Model in Prob. 4.7-8

6.1-2.* Construct the dual problem for each of the following linear programming models fitting our standard form.
(a) Model in Prob. 3.1-5
(b) Model in Prob. 4.7-6

6.1-3. Consider the linear programming model in Prob. 4.5-4.
(a) Construct the primal-dual table and the dual problem for this model.
(b) What does the fact that Z is unbounded for this model imply about its dual problem?

6.1-4. For each of the following linear programming models, give your recommendation on which is the more efficient way (probably) to obtain an optimal solution: by applying the simplex method directly to this primal problem or by applying the simplex method directly to the dual problem instead. Explain.
(a) Maximize $\quad Z = 10x_1 - 4x_2 + 7x_3,$

subject to

$$3x_1 - x_2 + 2x_3 \le 25$$
$$x_1 - 2x_2 + 3x_3 \le 25$$
$$5x_1 + x_2 + 2x_3 \le 40$$
$$x_1 + x_2 + x_3 \le 90$$
$$2x_1 - x_2 + x_3 \le 20$$

and

$$x_1 \ge 0, \qquad x_2 \ge 0, \qquad x_3 \ge 0.$$

(b) Maximize $Z = 2x_1 + 5x_2 + 3x_3 + 4x_4 + x_5$,

subject to

$$x_1 + 3x_2 + 2x_3 + 3x_4 + x_5 \leq 6$$
$$4x_1 + 6x_2 + 5x_3 + 7x_4 + x_5 \leq 15$$

and

$$x_j \geq 0, \qquad \text{for } j = 1, 2, 3, 4, 5.$$

6.1-5. Consider the following problem.

Maximize $Z = -x_1 - 2x_2 - x_3$,

subject to

$$x_1 + x_2 + 2x_3 \leq 12$$
$$x_1 + x_2 - x_3 \leq 1$$

and

$$x_1 \geq 0, \qquad x_2 \geq 0, \qquad x_3 \geq 0.$$

(a) Construct the dual problem.
(b) Use duality theory to show that the optimal solution for the primal problem has $Z \leq 0$.

6.1-6. Consider the following problem.

Maximize $Z = 2x_1 + 6x_2 + 9x_3$,

subject to

$$x_1 \quad + \quad x_3 \leq 3 \qquad \text{(resource 1)}$$
$$x_2 + 2x_3 \leq 5 \qquad \text{(resource 2)}$$

and

$$x_1 \geq 0, \qquad x_2 \geq 0, \qquad x_3 \geq 0.$$

(a) Construct the dual problem for this primal problem.
(b) Solve the dual problem graphically. Use this solution to identify the shadow prices for the resources in the primal problem.
C **(c)** Confirm your results from part (b) by solving the primal problem automatically by the simplex method and then identifying the shadow prices.

6.1-7. Follow the instructions of Prob. 6.1-6 for the following problem.

Maximize $Z = x_1 - 3x_2 + 2x_3$,

subject to

$$2x_1 + 2x_2 - 2x_3 \leq 6 \qquad \text{(resource 1)}$$
$$-x_2 + 2x_3 \leq 4 \qquad \text{(resource 2)}$$

and

$$x_1 \geq 0, \qquad x_2 \geq 0, \qquad x_3 \geq 0.$$

6.1-8. Consider the following problem.

Maximize $Z = x_1 + 2x_2$,

subject to

$$-x_1 + x_2 \leq -2$$
$$4x_1 + x_2 \leq 4$$

and

$$x_1 \geq 0, \qquad x_2 \geq 0.$$

(a) Demonstrate graphically that this problem has no feasible solutions.
(b) Construct the dual problem.
(c) Demonstrate graphically that the dual problem has an unbounded objective function.

6.1-9. Construct and graph a primal problem with two decision variables and two functional constraints that has feasible solutions and an unbounded objective function. Then construct the dual problem and demonstrate graphically that it has no feasible solutions.

6.1-10. Construct a pair of primal and dual problems, each with two decision variables and two functional constraints, such that both problems have no feasible solutions. Demonstrate this property graphically.

6.1-11. Construct a pair of primal and dual problems, each with two decision variables and two functional constraints, such that the primal problem has no feasible solutions and the dual problem has an unbounded objective function.

6.1-12. Use the weak duality property to prove that if both the primal and the dual problem have feasible solutions, then both must have an optimal solution.

6.1-13. Consider the primal and dual problems in our standard form presented in matrix notation at the beginning of Sec. 6.1. Use only this definition of the dual problem for a primal problem in this form to prove each of the following results.
(a) The weak duality property presented in Sec. 6.1.
(b) If the primal problem has an unbounded feasible region that permits increasing Z indefinitely, then the dual problem has no feasible solutions.

6.1-14. Consider the primal and dual problems in our standard form presented in matrix notation at the beginning of Sec. 6.1. Let $\mathbf{y}^*$ denote the optimal solution for this dual problem. Suppose that $\mathbf{b}$ is then replaced by $\bar{\mathbf{b}}$. Let $\bar{\mathbf{x}}$ denote the optimal solution for the new primal problem. Prove that

$$\mathbf{c}\bar{\mathbf{x}} \leq \mathbf{y}^*\bar{\mathbf{b}}.$$

6.1-15. For any linear programming problem in our standard form and its dual problem, label each of the following statements as true or false and then justify your answer.

(a) The sum of the number of functional constraints and the number of variables (before augmenting) is the same for both the primal and the dual problems.

(b) At each iteration, the simplex method simultaneously identifies a CPF solution for the primal problem and a CPF solution for the dual problem such that their objective function values are the same.

(c) If the primal problem has an unbounded objective function, then the optimal value of the objective function for the dual problem must be zero.

6.2-1. Consider the simplex tableaux for the Wyndor Glass Co. problem given in Table 4.8. For each tableau, give the economic interpretation of the following items:

(a) Each of the coefficients of the slack variables (x_3, x_4, x_5) in row 0

(b) Each of the coefficients of the decision variables (x_1, x_2) in row 0

(c) The resulting choice for the entering basic variable (or the decision to stop after the final tableau)

6.3-1.* Consider the following problem.

$$\text{Maximize} \qquad Z = 6x_1 + 8x_2,$$

subject to

$$5x_1 + 2x_2 \leq 20$$
$$x_1 + 2x_2 \leq 10$$

and

$$x_1 \geq 0, \qquad x_2 \geq 0.$$

(a) Construct the dual problem for this primal problem.

(b) Solve both the primal problem and the dual problem graphically. Identify the CPF solutions and corner-point infeasible solutions for both problems. Calculate the objective function values for all these solutions.

(c) Use the information obtained in part (b) to construct a table listing the complementary basic solutions for these problems. (Use the same column headings as for Table 6.9.)

I (d) Work through the simplex method step by step to solve the primal problem. After each iteration (including iteration 0), identify the BF solution for this problem and the complementary basic solution for the dual problem. Also identify the corresponding corner-point solutions.

6.3-2. Consider the model with two functional constraints and two variables given in Prob. 4.1-5. Follow the instructions of Prob. 6.3-1 for this model.

6.3-3. Consider the primal and dual problems for the Wyndor Glass Co. example given in Table 6.1. Using Tables 5.5, 5.6, 6.8, and 6.9, construct a new table showing the eight sets of nonbasic variables for the primal problem in column 1, the corresponding sets of associated variables for the dual problem in column 2, and the set of nonbasic variables for each complementary basic solution in the dual problem in column 3. Explain why this table demonstrates the complementary slackness property for this example.

6.3-4. Suppose that a primal problem has a *degenerate* BF solution (one or more basic variables equal to zero) as its optimal solution. What does this degeneracy imply about the dual problem? Why? Is the converse also true?

6.3-5. Consider the following problem.

$$\text{Maximize} \qquad Z = 2x_1 - 4x_2,$$

subject to

$$x_1 - x_2 \leq 1$$

and

$$x_1 \geq 0, \qquad x_2 \geq 0.$$

(a) Construct the dual problem, and then find its optimal solution by inspection.

(b) Use the complementary slackness property and the optimal solution for the dual problem to find the optimal solution for the primal problem.

(c) Suppose that c_1, the coefficient of x_1 in the primal objective function, actually can have any value in the model. For what values of c_1 does the dual problem have no feasible solutions? For these values, what does duality theory then imply about the primal problem?

6.3-6. Consider the following problem.

$$\text{Maximize} \qquad Z = 2x_1 + 7x_2 + 4x_3,$$

subject to

$$x_1 + 2x_2 + x_3 \leq 10$$
$$3x_1 + 3x_2 + 2x_3 \leq 10$$

and

$$x_1 \geq 0, \qquad x_2 \geq 0, \qquad x_3 \geq 0.$$

(a) Construct the dual problem for this primal problem.

(b) Use the dual problem to demonstrate that the optimal value of Z for the primal problem cannot exceed 25.

(c) It has been conjectured that x_2 and x_3 should be the basic variables for the optimal solution of the primal problem. Directly derive this basic solution (and Z) by using Gaussian elimination. Simultaneously derive and identify the complementary basic solution for the dual problem by using Eq. (0) for the primal problem. Then draw your conclusions about whether these two basic solutions are optimal for their respective problems.

I **(d)** Solve the dual problem graphically. Use this solution to identify the basic variables and the nonbasic variables for the optimal solution of the primal problem. Directly derive this solution, using Gaussian elimination.

6.3-7.* Reconsider the model of Prob. 6.1-4*b*.
(a) Construct its dual problem.
(b) Solve this dual problem graphically.
(c) Use the result from part (*b*) to identify the nonbasic variables and basic variables for the optimal BF solution for the primal problem.
(d) Use the results from part (*c*) to obtain the optimal solution for the primal problem directly by using Gaussian elimination to solve for its basic variables, starting from the initial system of equations [excluding Eq. (0)] constructed for the simplex method and setting the nonbasic variables to zero.
(e) Use the results from part (*c*) to identify the defining equations (see Sec. 5.1) for the optimal CPF solution for the primal problem, and then use these equations to find this solution.

6.3-8. Consider the model given in Prob. 5.3-13.
(a) Construct the dual problem.
(b) Use the given information about the basic variables in the optimal primal solution to identify the nonbasic variables and basic variables for the optimal dual solution.
(c) Use the results from part (*b*) to identify the defining equations (see Sec. 5.1) for the optimal CPF solution for the dual problem, and then use these equations to find this solution.
(d) Solve the dual problem graphically to verify your results from part (*c*).

6.3-9. Consider the model given in Prob. 3.1-4.
(a) Construct the dual problem for this model.
(b) Use the fact that $(x_1, x_2) = (13, 5)$ is optimal for the primal problem to identify the nonbasic variables and basic variables for the optimal BF solution for the dual problem.
(c) Identify this optimal solution for the dual problem by directly deriving Eq. (0) corresponding to the optimal primal solution identified in part (*b*). Derive this equation by using Gaussian elimination.
(d) Use the results from part (*b*) to identify the defining equations (see Sec. 5.1) for the optimal CPF solution for the dual problem. Verify your optimal dual solution from part (*c*) by checking to see that it satisfies this system of equations.

6.3-10. Suppose that you also want information about the dual problem when you apply the revised simplex method (see Sec. 5.2) to the primal problem in our standard form.

(a) How would you identify the optimal solution for the dual problem?
(b) After obtaining the BF solution at each iteration, how would you identify the complementary basic solution in the dual problem?

6.4-1. Consider the following problem.

$$\text{Maximize} \quad Z = x_1 + x_2,$$

subject to

$$x_1 + 2x_2 = 10$$
$$2x_1 + x_2 \geq 2$$

and

$$x_2 \geq 0 \quad (x_1 \text{ unconstrained in sign}).$$

(a) Use the SOB method to construct the dual problem.
(b) Use Table 6.12 to convert the primal problem to our standard form given at the beginning of Sec. 6.1, and construct the corresponding dual problem. Then show that this dual problem is equivalent to the one obtained in part (*a*).

6.4-2. Consider the primal and dual problems in our standard form presented in matrix notation at the beginning of Sec. 6.1. Use only this definition of the dual problem for a primal problem in this form to prove each of the following results.
(a) If the functional constraints for the primal problem $\mathbf{Ax} \leq \mathbf{b}$ are changed to $\mathbf{Ax} = \mathbf{b}$, the only resulting change in the dual problem is to *delete* the nonnegativity constraints, $\mathbf{y} \geq \mathbf{0}$. (*Hint:* The constraints $\mathbf{Ax} = \mathbf{b}$ are equivalent to the set of constraints $\mathbf{Ax} \leq \mathbf{b}$ *and* $\mathbf{Ax} \geq \mathbf{b}$.)
(b) If the functional constraints for the primal problem $\mathbf{Ax} \leq \mathbf{b}$ are changed to $\mathbf{Ax} \geq \mathbf{b}$, the only resulting change in the dual problem is that the nonnegativity constraints $\mathbf{y} \geq \mathbf{0}$ are replaced by nonpositivity constraints $\mathbf{y} \leq \mathbf{0}$, where the current dual variables are interpreted as the negative of the original dual variables. (*Hint:* The constraints $\mathbf{Ax} \geq \mathbf{b}$ are equivalent to $-\mathbf{Ax} \leq -\mathbf{b}$.)
(c) If the nonnegativity constraints for the primal problem $\mathbf{x} \geq \mathbf{0}$ are deleted, the only resulting change in the dual problem is to replace the functional constraints $\mathbf{yA} \geq \mathbf{c}$ by $\mathbf{yA} = \mathbf{c}$. (*Hint:* A variable unconstrained in sign can be replaced by the difference of two nonnegative variables.)

6.4-3.* Construct the dual problem for the linear programming problem given in Prob. 4.6-4.

6.4-4. Consider the following problem.

$$\text{Minimize} \quad Z = x_1 + 2x_2,$$

subject to

$$-2x_1 + x_2 \geq 1$$
$$x_1 - 2x_2 \geq 1$$

and

$$x_1 \geq 0, \qquad x_2 \geq 0.$$

(a) Construct the dual problem.
(b) Use graphical analysis of the dual problem to determine whether the primal problem has feasible solutions and, if so, whether its objective function is bounded.

6.4-5. Consider the two versions of the dual problem for the radiation therapy example that are given in Tables 6.15 and 6.16. Review in Sec. 6.4 the general discussion of why these two versions are completely equivalent. Then fill in the details to verify this equivalency by proceeding step by step to convert the version in Table 6.15 to equivalent forms until the version in Table 6.16 is obtained.

6.4-6. For each of the following linear programming models, use the SOB method to construct its dual problem.
(a) Model in Prob. 4.6-3
(b) Model in Prob. 4.6-8
(c) Model in Prob. 4.6-18

6.4-7. Consider the model with equality constraints given in Prob. 4.6-2.
(a) Construct its dual problem.
(b) Demonstrate that the answer in part (a) is correct (i.e., equality constraints yield dual variables without nonnegativity constraints) by first converting the primal problem to our standard form (see Table 6.12), then constructing its dual problem, and next converting this dual problem to the form obtained in part (a).

6.4-8.* Consider the model without nonnegativity constraints given in Prob. 4.6-16.
(a) Construct its dual problem.
(b) Demonstrate that the answer in part (a) is correct (i.e., variables without nonnegativity constraints yield equality constraints in the dual problem) by first converting the primal problem to our standard form (see Table 6.12), then constructing its dual problem, and finally converting this dual problem to the form obtained in part (a).

6.4-9. Consider the dual problem for the Wyndor Glass Co. example given in Table 6.1. Demonstrate that *its* dual problem is the primal problem given in Table 6.1 by going through the conversion steps given in Table 6.13.

6.4-10. Consider the following problem.

Minimize $Z = -x_1 - 3x_2,$

subject to

$$x_1 - 2x_2 \leq 2$$
$$-x_1 + x_2 \leq 4$$

and

$$x_1 \geq 0, \qquad x_2 \geq 0.$$

(a) Demonstrate graphically that this problem has an unbounded objective function.
(b) Construct the dual problem.
(c) Demonstrate graphically that the dual problem has no feasible solutions.

6.5-1. Consider the model of Prob. 6.7-1. Use duality theory directly to determine whether the current basic solution remains optimal after each of the following independent changes.
(a) The change in part (e) of Prob. 6.7-1
(b) The change in part (g) of Prob. 6.7-1

6.5-2. Consider the model of Prob. 6.7-3. Use duality theory directly to determine whether the current basic solution remains optimal after each of the following independent changes.
(a) The change in part (c) of Prob. 6.7-3
(b) The change in part (f) of Prob. 6.7-3

6.5-3. Consider the model of Prob. 6.7-4. Use duality theory directly to determine whether the current basic solution remains optimal after each of the following independent changes.
(a) The change in part (b) of Prob. 6.7-4
(b) The change in part (d) of Prob. 6.7-4

6.5-4. Reconsider part (d) of Prob. 6.7-6. Use duality theory directly to determine whether the original optimal solution is still optimal.

6.6-1.* Consider the following problem.

Maximize $Z = 3x_1 + x_2 + 4x_3,$

subject to

$$6x_1 + 3x_2 + 5x_3 \leq 25$$
$$3x_1 + 4x_2 + 5x_3 \leq 20$$

and

$$x_1 \geq 0, \qquad x_2 \geq 0, \qquad x_3 \geq 0.$$

The corresponding final set of equations yielding the optimal solution is

$$(0) \quad Z \quad + 2x_2 \quad\quad + \frac{1}{5}x_4 + \frac{3}{5}x_5 = 17$$

$$(1) \quad x_1 - \frac{1}{3}x_2 \quad\quad + \frac{1}{3}x_4 - \frac{1}{3}x_5 = \frac{5}{3}$$

$$(2) \quad x_2 + x_3 - \frac{1}{5}x_4 + \frac{2}{5}x_5 = 3.$$

(a) Identify the optimal solution from this set of equations.
(b) Construct the dual problem.

(c) Identify the optimal solution for the dual problem from the final set of equations. Verify this solution by solving the dual problem graphically.

(d) Suppose that the original problem is changed to

$$\text{Maximize} \quad Z = 3x_1 + 3x_2 + 4x_3,$$

subject to

$$6x_1 + 2x_2 + 5x_3 \le 25$$
$$3x_1 + 3x_2 + 5x_3 \le 20$$

and

$$x_1 \ge 0, \quad x_2 \ge 0, \quad x_3 \ge 0.$$

Use duality theory to determine whether the previous optimal solution is still optimal.

(e) Use the fundamental insight presented in Sec. 5.3 to identify the new coefficients of x_2 in the final set of equations after it has been adjusted for the changes in the original problem given in part (d).

(f) Now suppose that the only change in the original problem is that a new variable x_{new} has been introduced into the model as follows:

$$\text{Maximize} \quad Z = 3x_1 + x_2 + 4x_3 + 2x_{\text{new}},$$

subject to

$$6x_1 + 3x_2 + 5x_3 + 3x_{\text{new}} \le 25$$
$$3x_1 + 4x_2 + 5x_3 + 2x_{\text{new}} \le 20$$

and

$$x_1 \ge 0, \quad x_2 \ge 0, \quad x_3 \ge 0, \quad x_{\text{new}} \ge 0.$$

Use duality theory to determine whether the previous optimal solution, along with $x_{\text{new}} = 0$, is still optimal.

(g) Use the fundamental insight presented in Sec. 5.3 to identify the coefficients of x_{new} as a nonbasic variable in the final set of equations resulting from the introduction of x_{new} into the original model as shown in part (f).

D,I **6.6-2.** Reconsider the model of Prob. 6.6-1. You are now to conduct sensitivity analysis by *independently* investigating each of the following six changes in the original model. For each change, use the sensitivity analysis procedure to revise the given final set of equations (in tableau form) and convert it to proper form from Gaussian elimination. Then test this solution for feasibility and for optimality. (Do not reoptimize.)

(a) Change the right-hand side of constraint 1 to $b_1 = 15$.

(b) Change the right-hand side of constraint 2 to $b_2 = 5$.

(c) Change the coefficient of x_2 in the objective function to $c_2 = 4$.

(d) Change the coefficient of x_3 in the objective function to $c_3 = 3$.

(e) Change the coefficient of x_2 in constraint 2 to $a_{22} = 1$.

(f) Change the coefficient of x_1 in constraint 1 to $a_{11} = 10$.

D,I **6.6-3.** Consider the following problem.

$$\text{Minimize} \quad W = 5y_1 + 4y_2,$$

subject to

$$4y_1 + 3y_2 \ge 4$$
$$2y_1 + y_2 \ge 3$$
$$y_1 + 2y_2 \ge 1$$
$$y_1 + y_2 \ge 2$$

and

$$y_1 \ge 0, \quad y_2 \ge 0.$$

Because this primal problem has more functional constraints than variables, suppose that the simplex method has been applied directly to its dual problem. If we let x_5 and x_6 denote the slack variables for this dual problem, the resulting final simplex tableau is

Basic Variable	Eq.	Coefficient of:							Right Side
		Z	x_1	x_2	x_3	x_4	x_5	x_6	
Z	(0)	1	3	0	2	0	1	1	9
x_2	(1)	0	1	1	-1	0	1	-1	1
x_4	(2)	0	2	0	3	1	-1	2	3

For each of the following independent changes in the original primal model, you now are to conduct sensitivity analysis by directly investigating the effect on the dual problem and then inferring the complementary effect on the primal problem. For each change, apply the procedure for sensitivity analysis summarized at the end of Sec. 6.6 to the dual problem (do *not* reoptimize), and then give your conclusions as to whether the current basic solution for the primal problem still is feasible and whether it still is optimal. Then check your conclusions by a direct graphical analysis of the primal problem.

(a) Change the objective function to $W = 3y_1 + 5y_2$.

(b) Change the right-hand sides of the functional constraints to 3, 5, 2, and 3, respectively.

(c) Change the first constraint to $2y_1 + 4y_2 \ge 7$.

(d) Change the second constraint to $5y_1 + 2y_2 \ge 10$.

D,I **6.7-1.*** Consider the following problem.

$$\text{Maximize} \quad Z = -5x_1 + 5x_2 + 13x_3,$$

subject to

$$-x_1 + x_2 + 3x_3 \le 20$$
$$12x_1 + 4x_2 + 10x_3 \le 90$$

and

$$x_j \ge 0 \quad (j = 1, 2, 3).$$

If we let x_4 and x_5 be the slack variables for the respective constraints, the simplex method yields the following final set of equations:

$$
\begin{array}{llll}
(0) & Z & + 2x_3 + 5x_4 & = 100 \\
(1) & -x_1 + x_2 + 3x_3 + x_4 & = 20 \\
(2) & 16x_1 \quad - 2x_3 - 4x_4 + x_5 = & 10.
\end{array}
$$

Now you are to conduct sensitivity analysis by *independently* investigating each of the following nine changes in the original model. For each change, use the sensitivity analysis procedure to revise this set of equations (in tableau form) and convert it to proper form from Gaussian elimination for identifying and evaluating the current basic solution. Then test this solution for feasibility and for optimality. (Do not reoptimize.)

(a) Change the right-hand side of constraint 1 to

$b_1 = 30.$

(b) Change the right-hand side of constraint 2 to

$b_2 = 70.$

(c) Change the right-hand sides to

$$
\begin{bmatrix} b_1 \\ b_2 \end{bmatrix} = \begin{bmatrix} 10 \\ 100 \end{bmatrix}.
$$

(d) Change the coefficient of x_3 in the objective function to

$c_3 = 8.$

(e) Change the coefficients of x_1 to

$$
\begin{bmatrix} c_1 \\ a_{11} \\ a_{21} \end{bmatrix} = \begin{bmatrix} -2 \\ 0 \\ 5 \end{bmatrix}.
$$

(f) Change the coefficients of x_2 to

$$
\begin{bmatrix} c_2 \\ a_{12} \\ a_{22} \end{bmatrix} = \begin{bmatrix} 6 \\ 2 \\ 5 \end{bmatrix}.
$$

(g) Introduce a new variable x_6 with coefficients

$$
\begin{bmatrix} c_6 \\ a_{16} \\ a_{26} \end{bmatrix} = \begin{bmatrix} 10 \\ 3 \\ 5 \end{bmatrix}.
$$

(h) Introduce a new constraint $2x_1 + 3x_2 + 5x_3 \leq 50$. (Denote its slack variable by x_6.)

(i) Change constraint 2 to

$10x_1 + 5x_2 + 10x_3 \leq 100.$

6.7-2.* Reconsider the model of Prob. 6.7-1. Suppose that we now want to apply parametric linear programming analysis to this problem. Specifically, the right-hand sides of the functional constraints are changed to

$20 + 2\theta$ (for constraint 1)

and

$90 - \theta$ (for constraint 2),

where θ can be assigned any positive or negative values.

Express the basic solution (and Z) corresponding to the original optimal solution as a function of θ. Determine the lower and upper bounds on θ before this solution would become infeasible.

D,I **6.7-3.** Consider the following problem.

$$\text{Maximize} \quad Z = 2x_1 - x_2 + x_3,$$

subject to

$$
\begin{array}{rcl}
3x_1 + x_2 + x_3 & \leq & 60 \\
x_1 - x_2 + 2x_3 & \leq & 10 \\
x_1 + x_2 - x_3 & \leq & 20
\end{array}
$$

and

$$x_1 \geq 0, \qquad x_2 \geq 0, \qquad x_3 \geq 0.$$

Let x_4, x_5, and x_6 denote the slack variables for the respective constraints. After we apply the simplex method, the final simplex tableau is

Basic Variable	Eq.	Z	x_1	x_2	x_3	x_4	x_5	x_6	Right Side
Z	(0)	1	0	0	$\frac{3}{2}$	0	$\frac{3}{2}$	$\frac{1}{2}$	25
x_4	(1)	0	0	0	1	1	-1	-2	10
x_1	(2)	0	1	0	$\frac{1}{2}$	0	$\frac{1}{2}$	$\frac{1}{2}$	15
x_2	(3)	0	0	1	$-\frac{3}{2}$	0	$-\frac{1}{2}$	$\frac{1}{2}$	5

The table header spans: **Coefficient of:** over columns Z, x_1, x_2, x_3, x_4, x_5, x_6.

Now you are to conduct sensitivity analysis by *independently* investigating each of the following six changes in the original model. For each change, use the sensitivity analysis procedure to revise this final tableau and convert it to proper form from Gaussian elimination for identifying and evaluating the current basic solution. Then test this solution for feasibility and for optimality. If either test fails, reoptimize to find a new optimal solution.

(a) Change the right-hand sides

$$\text{from} \quad \begin{bmatrix} b_1 \\ b_2 \\ b_3 \end{bmatrix} = \begin{bmatrix} 60 \\ 10 \\ 20 \end{bmatrix} \quad \text{to} \quad \begin{bmatrix} b_1 \\ b_2 \\ b_3 \end{bmatrix} = \begin{bmatrix} 70 \\ 20 \\ 10 \end{bmatrix}.$$

(b) Change the coefficients of x_1

$$\text{from} \quad \begin{bmatrix} c_1 \\ a_{11} \\ a_{21} \\ a_{31} \end{bmatrix} = \begin{bmatrix} 2 \\ 3 \\ 1 \\ 1 \end{bmatrix} \quad \text{to} \quad \begin{bmatrix} c_1 \\ a_{11} \\ a_{21} \\ a_{31} \end{bmatrix} = \begin{bmatrix} 1 \\ 2 \\ 2 \\ 0 \end{bmatrix}.$$

(c) Change the coefficients of x_3

$$\text{from} \quad \begin{bmatrix} c_3 \\ a_{13} \\ a_{23} \\ a_{33} \end{bmatrix} = \begin{bmatrix} 1 \\ 1 \\ 2 \\ -1 \end{bmatrix} \quad \text{to} \quad \begin{bmatrix} c_3 \\ a_{13} \\ a_{23} \\ a_{33} \end{bmatrix} = \begin{bmatrix} 2 \\ 3 \\ 1 \\ -2 \end{bmatrix}.$$

(d) Change the objective function to $Z = 3x_1 - 2x_2 + 3x_3$.

(e) Introduce a new constraint $3x_1 - 2x_2 + x_3 \le 30$. (Denote its slack variable by x_7.)

(f) Introduce a new variable x_8 with coefficients

$$\begin{bmatrix} c_8 \\ a_{18} \\ a_{28} \\ a_{38} \end{bmatrix} = \begin{bmatrix} -1 \\ -2 \\ 1 \\ 2 \end{bmatrix}.$$

D,I **6.7-4.** Consider the following problem.

Maximize $Z = 2x_1 + 7x_2 - 3x_3$,

subject to

$$x_1 + 3x_2 + 4x_3 \le 30$$
$$x_1 + 4x_2 - x_3 \le 10$$

and

$$x_1 \ge 0, \qquad x_2 \ge 0, \qquad x_3 \ge 0.$$

By letting x_4 and x_5 be the slack variables for the respective constraints, the simplex method yields the following final set of equations:

(0) $Z \quad + \; x_2 + \; x_3 \qquad\qquad + 2x_5 = 20$
(1) $\qquad - \; x_2 + 5x_3 + x_4 - \; x_5 = 20$
(2) $\qquad x_1 + 4x_2 - \; x_3 \qquad + \; x_5 = 10.$

Now you are to conduct sensitivity analysis by *independently* investigating each of the following seven changes in the original model. For each change, use the sensitivity analysis procedure to revise this set of equations (in tableau form) and convert it to proper

form from Gaussian elimination for identifying and evaluating the current basic solution. Then test this solution for feasibility and for optimality. If either test fails, reoptimize to find a new optimal solution.

(a) Change the right-hand sides to

$$\begin{bmatrix} b_1 \\ b_2 \end{bmatrix} = \begin{bmatrix} 20 \\ 30 \end{bmatrix}.$$

(b) Change the coefficients of x_3 to

$$\begin{bmatrix} c_3 \\ a_{13} \\ a_{23} \end{bmatrix} = \begin{bmatrix} -2 \\ 3 \\ -2 \end{bmatrix}.$$

(c) Change the coefficients of x_1 to

$$\begin{bmatrix} c_1 \\ a_{11} \\ a_{21} \end{bmatrix} = \begin{bmatrix} 4 \\ 3 \\ 2 \end{bmatrix}.$$

(d) Introduce a new variable x_6 with coefficients

$$\begin{bmatrix} c_6 \\ a_{16} \\ a_{26} \end{bmatrix} = \begin{bmatrix} -3 \\ 1 \\ 2 \end{bmatrix}.$$

(e) Change the objective function to $Z = x_1 + 5x_2 - 2x_3$.

(f) Introduce a new constraint $3x_1 + 2x_2 + 3x_3 \le 25$.

(g) Change constraint 2 to $x_1 + 2x_2 + 2x_3 \le 35$.

6.7-5. Reconsider the model of Prob. 6.7-4. Suppose that we now want to apply parametric linear programming analysis to this problem. Specifically, the right-hand sides of the functional constraints are changed to

$$30 + 3\theta \qquad \text{(for constraint 1)}$$

and

$$10 - \theta \qquad \text{(for constraint 2)},$$

where θ can be assigned any positive or negative values.

Express the basic solution (and Z) corresponding to the original optimal solution as a function of θ. Determine the lower and upper bounds on θ before this solution would become infeasible.

D,I **6.7-6.** Consider the following problem.

Maximize $Z = 2x_1 - x_2 + x_3$,

subject to

$$3x_1 - 2x_2 + 2x_3 \le 15$$
$$-x_1 + x_2 + x_3 \le 3$$
$$x_1 - x_2 + x_3 \le 4$$

and

$$x_1 \geq 0, \qquad x_2 \geq 0, \qquad x_3 \geq 0.$$

If we let x_4, x_5, and x_6 be the slack variables for the respective constraints, the simplex method yields the following final set of equations:

(0) $Z \quad + 2x_3 + x_4 + \quad x_5 \qquad = 18$
(1) $\qquad x_2 + 5x_3 + x_4 + 3x_5 \qquad = 24$
(2) $\qquad\qquad 2x_3 \quad + \quad x_5 + x_6 = 7$
(3) $x_1 \quad + 4x_3 + x_4 + 2x_5 \qquad = 21.$

Now you are to conduct sensitivity analysis by *independently* investigating each of the following eight changes in the original model. For each change, use the sensitivity analysis procedure to revise this set of equations (in tableau form) and convert it to proper form from Gaussian elimination for identifying and evaluating the current basic solution. Then test this solution for feasibility and for optimality. If either test fails, reoptimize to find a new optimal solution.

(a) Change the right-hand sides to

$$\begin{bmatrix} b_1 \\ b_2 \\ b_3 \end{bmatrix} = \begin{bmatrix} 10 \\ 4 \\ 2 \end{bmatrix}.$$

(b) Change the coefficient of x_3 in the objective function to $c_3 = 2$.
(c) Change the coefficient of x_1 in the objective function to $c_1 = 3$.
(d) Change the coefficients of x_3 to

$$\begin{bmatrix} c_3 \\ a_{13} \\ a_{23} \\ a_{33} \end{bmatrix} = \begin{bmatrix} 4 \\ 3 \\ 2 \\ 1 \end{bmatrix}.$$

(e) Change the coefficients of x_1 and x_2 to

$$\begin{bmatrix} c_1 \\ a_{11} \\ a_{21} \\ a_{31} \end{bmatrix} = \begin{bmatrix} 1 \\ 1 \\ -2 \\ 3 \end{bmatrix} \quad \text{and} \quad \begin{bmatrix} c_2 \\ a_{12} \\ a_{22} \\ a_{32} \end{bmatrix} = \begin{bmatrix} -2 \\ -2 \\ 3 \\ 2 \end{bmatrix},$$

respectively.
(f) Change the objective function to $Z = 5x_1 + x_2 + 3x_3$.
(g) Change constraint 1 to $2x_1 - x_2 + 4x_3 \leq 12$.
(h) Introduce a new constraint $2x_1 + x_2 + 3x_3 \leq 60$.

6.7-7. One of the products of the G. A. Tanner Company is a special kind of toy that provides an estimated unit profit of $3. Because of a large demand for this toy, management would like to increase its production rate from the current level of 1,000 per day. However, a limited supply of two subassemblies (A and B) from vendors makes this difficult. Each toy requires two subassemblies

of type A, but the vendor providing these subassemblies would only be able to increase its supply rate from the current 2,000 per day to a maximum of 3,000 per day. Each toy requires only one subassembly of type B, but the vendor providing these subassemblies would be unable to increase its supply rate above the current level of 1,000 per day.

Because no other vendors currently are available to provide these subassemblies, management is considering initiating a new production process internally that would simultaneously produce an equal number of subassemblies of the two types to supplement the supply from the two vendors. It is estimated that the company's cost for producing one subassembly of each type would be $2.50 more than the cost of purchasing these subassemblies from the two vendors. Management wants to determine both the production rate of the toy and the production rate of each pair of subassemblies (one A and one B) that would maximize the total profit.

The following table summarizes the data for the problem.

Resource	Resource Usage per Unit of Each Activity		Amount of Resource Available
	Produce Toys	Produce Subassemblies	
Subassembly A	2	−1	3,000
Subassembly B	1	−1	1,000
Unit profit	$3	−$2.50	

(a) Formulate a linear programming model for this problem and use the graphical method to obtain its optimal solution.
C **(b)** Use a software package based on the simplex method to solve for an optimal solution.
C **(c)** Since the stated unit profits for the two activities are only estimates, management wants to know how much each of these estimates can be off before the optimal solution would change. Begin exploring this question for the first activity (producing toys) by using the same software package to re-solve for an optimal solution and total profit as the unit profit for this activity increases in 50-cent increments from $2.00 to $4.00. What conclusion can be drawn about how much the estimate of this unit profit can differ in each direction from its original value of $3.00 before the optimal solution would change?
C **(d)** Repeat part (c) for the second activity (producing subassemblies) by re-solving as the unit profit for this activity increases in 50-cent increments from −$3.50 to −$1.50 (with the unit profit for the first activity fixed at $3).
C **(e)** Use the same software package to generate the usual output (as in Table 6.23) for sensitivity analysis of the unit profits.

Use this output to obtain the allowable range to stay optimal for each unit profit.

(f) Use graphical analysis to verify the allowable ranges obtained in part (e).

(g) For each of the 16 combinations of unit profits considered in parts (c) and (d) where both unit profits differ from their original estimates, use the 100 percent rule for simultaneous changes in objective function coefficients to determine if the original optimal solution must still be optimal.

(h) For each of the combinations of unit profits considered in part (g) where it was found that the original optimal solution is not guaranteed to still be optimal, use graphical analysis to determine whether this solution is still optimal.

6.7-8. Reconsider Prob. 6.7-7. After further negotiations with each vendor, management of the G. A. Tanner Co. has learned that either of them would be willing to consider increasing their supply of their respective subassemblies over the previously stated maxima (3,000 subassemblies of type A per day and 1,000 of type B per day) if the company would pay a small premium over the regular price for the extra subassemblies. The size of the premium for each type of subassembly remains to be negotiated. The demand for the toy being produced is sufficiently high that 2,500 per day could be sold if the supply of subassemblies could be increased enough to support this production rate. Assume that the original estimates of unit profits given in Prob. 6.7-7 are accurate.

(a) Formulate a linear programming model for this problem with the original maximum supply levels and the additional constraint that no more than 2,500 toys should be produced per day. Then use the graphical method to obtain its optimal solution.

C **(b)** Use a software package based on the simplex method to solve for an optimal solution.

C **(c)** Without considering the premium, use the same software package to determine the shadow price for the subassembly A constraint by solving the model again after increasing the maximum supply by 1. Use this shadow price to determine the maximum premium that the company should be willing to pay for each subassembly of this type.

C **(d)** Repeat part (c) for the subassembly B constraint.

C **(e)** Estimate how much the maximum supply of subassemblies of type A could be increased before the shadow price (and the corresponding premium) found in part (c) would no longer be valid by using the same software package to re-solve for an optimal solution and the total profit (excluding the premium) as the maximum supply increases in increments of 100 from 3,000 to 4,000.

C **(f)** Repeat part (e) for subassemblies of type B by re-solving as the maximum supply increases in increments of 100 from 1,000 to 2,000.

C **(g)** Use the same software package to generate the usual output (as in Table 6.23) for sensitivity analysis of the supplies being made available of the subassemblies. Use this output to obtain the allowable range to stay feasible for each subassembly supply.

(h) Use graphical analysis to verify the allowable ranges obtained in part (g).

(i) For each of the four combinations where the maximum supply of subassembly A is either 3,500 or 4,000 and the maximum supply of subassembly B is either 1,500 or 2,000, use the 100 percent rule for simultaneous changes in right-hand sides to determine whether the original shadow prices definitely will still be valid.

(j) For each of the combinations considered in part (i) where it was found that the original shadow prices are not guaranteed to still be valid, use graphical analysis to determine whether these shadow prices actually are still valid for predicting the effect of changing the right-hand sides.

C **6.7-9** Consider the Distribution Unlimited Co. problem presented in Sec. 3.4 and summarized in Fig. 3.13.

Although Fig. 3.13 gives estimated unit costs for shipping through the various shipping lanes, there actually is some uncertainty about what these unit costs will turn out to be. Therefore, before adopting the optimal solution given at the end of Sec. 3.4, management wants additional information about the effect of inaccuracies in estimating these unit costs.

Use a computer package based on the simplex method to generate sensitivity analysis information preparatory to addressing the following questions.

(a) Which of the unit shipping costs given in Fig. 3.13 has the smallest margin for error without invalidating the optimal solution given in Sec. 3.4? Where should the greatest effort be placed in estimating the unit shipping costs?

(b) What is the allowable range to stay optimal for each of the unit shipping costs?

(c) How should these allowable ranges be interpreted to management?

(d) If the estimates change for more than one of the unit shipping costs, how can you use the generated sensitivity analysis information to determine whether the optimal solution might change?

C **6.7-10.** Consider the Union Airways problem presented in Sec. 3.4, including the data given in Table 3.19.

Management is about to begin negotiations on a new contract with the union that represents the company's customer service agents. This might result in some small changes in the daily costs per agent given in Table 3.19 for the various shifts. Several possible changes listed below are being considered separately. In each case, management would like to know whether the change might result in the original optimal solution (given in Sec. 3.4) no longer being optimal. Answer this question in parts (a) to (e) by using a software package based on the simplex method to generate sensitivity analysis information. If the optimal solution might change, use the software package to re-solve for the optimal solution.

(a) The daily cost per agent for Shift 2 changes from $160 to $165.
(b) The daily cost per agent for Shift 4 changes from $180 to $170.
(c) The changes in parts (a) and (b) both occur.
(d) The daily cost per agent increases by $4 for shifts 2, 4, and 5, but decreases by $4 for shifts 1 and 3.
(e) The daily cost per agent increases by 2 percent for each shift.

6.7-11. Consider the following problem.

$$\text{Maximize} \quad Z = c_1 x_1 + c_2 x_2,$$

subject to

$$2x_1 - x_2 \le b_1$$
$$x_1 - x_2 \le b_2$$

and

$$x_1 \ge 0, \qquad x_2 \ge 0.$$

Let x_3 and x_4 denote the slack variables for the respective functional constraints. When $c_1 = 3$, $c_2 = -2$, $b_1 = 30$, and $b_2 = 10$, the simplex method yields the following final simplex tableau.

Basic Variable	Eq.	Z	Coefficient of: x_1	x_2	x_3	x_4	Right Side
Z	(0)	1	0	0	1	1	40
x_2	(1)	0	0	1	1	-2	10
x_1	(2)	0	1	0	1	-1	20

(a) Use graphical analysis to determine the allowable range to stay optimal for c_1 and c_2.
(b) Use algebraic analysis to derive and verify your answers in part (a).
(c) Use graphical analysis to determine the allowable range to stay feasible for b_1 and b_2.
(d) Use algebraic analysis to derive and verify your answers in part (c)
C (e) Use a software package based on the simplex method to find these allowable ranges.

6.7-12. Consider Variation 5 of the Wyndor Glass Co. model (see Fig. 6.6 and Table 6.24), where the changes in the parameter values given in Table 6.21 are $\bar{c}_2 = 3$, $\bar{a}_{22} = 3$, and $\bar{a}_{32} = 4$. Use the formula $\mathbf{b^*} = \mathbf{S^* b}$ to find the allowable range to stay feasible for each b_i. Then interpret each allowable range graphically.

6.7-13. Consider Variation 5 of the Wyndor Glass Co. model (see Fig. 6.6 and Table 6.24), where the changes in the parameter values given in Table 6.21 are $\bar{c}_2 = 3$, $\bar{a}_{22} = 3$, and $\bar{a}_{32} = 4$. Verify both algebraically and graphically that the allowable range to stay optimal for c_1 is $c_1 \ge \frac{9}{4}$.

6.7-14. Consider the following problem.

$$\text{Maximize} \quad Z = 3x_1 + x_2 + 2x_3,$$

subject to

$$x_1 - x_2 + 2x_3 \le 20$$
$$2x_1 + x_2 - x_3 \le 10$$

and

$$x_1 \ge 0, \qquad x_2 \ge 0, \qquad x_3 \ge 0.$$

Let x_4 and x_5 denote the slack variables for the respective functional constraints. After we apply the simplex method, the final simplex tableau is

Basic Variable	Eq.	Z	Coefficient of: x_1	x_2	x_3	x_4	x_5	Right Side
Z	(0)	1	8	0	0	3	4	100
x_3	(1)	0	3	0	1	1	1	30
x_2	(2)	0	5	1	0	1	2	40

(a) Perform sensitivity analysis to determine which of the 11 parameters of the model are sensitive parameters in the sense that *any* change in just that parameter's value will change the optimal solution.
(b) Use algebraic analysis to find the allowable range to stay optimal for each c_j.
(c) Use algebraic analysis to find the allowable range to stay feasible for each b_i.
C (d) Use a software package based on the simplex method to find these allowable ranges.

6.7-15. For the problem given in Table 6.21, find the allowable range to stay optimal for c_2. Show your work algebraically, using the tableau given in Table 6.21. Then justify your answer from a geometric viewpoint, referring to Fig. 6.3.

6.7-16.* For the original Wyndor Glass Co. problem, use the last tableau in Table 4.8 to do the following.
(a) Find the allowable range to stay feasible for each b_i.
(b) Find the allowable range to stay optimal for c_1 and c_2.
C (c) Use a software package based on the simplex method to find these allowable ranges.

6.7-17. For Variation 6 of the Wyndor Glass Co. model presented in Sec. 6.7, use the last tableau in Table 6.25 to do the following.
(a) Find the allowable range to stay feasible for each b_i.
(b) Find the allowable range to stay optimal for c_1 and c_2.
C **(c)** Use a software package based on the simplex method to find these allowable ranges.

6.7-18. Ken and Larry, Inc., supplies its ice cream parlors with three flavors of ice cream: chocolate, vanilla, and banana. Because of extremely hot weather and a high demand for its products, the company has run short of its supply of ingredients: milk, sugar, and cream. Hence, they will not be able to fill all the orders received from their retail outlets, the ice cream parlors. Owing to these circumstances, the company has decided to choose the amount of each flavor to produce that will maximize total profit, given the constraints on supply of the basic ingredients.

The chocolate, vanilla, and banana flavors generate, respectively, $1.00, $0.90, and $0.95 of profit per gallon sold. The company has only 200 gallons of milk, 150 pounds of sugar, and 60

gallons of cream left in its inventory. The linear programming formulation for this problem is shown below in algebraic form.

Let C = gallons of chocolate ice cream produced,
       V = gallons of vanilla ice cream produced,
       B = gallons of banana ice cream produced.

Maximize   profit $= 1.00\, C + 0.90\, V + 0.95\, B$,

subject to

Milk: $0.45\, C + 0.50\, V + 0.40\, B \leq 200$ gallons
Sugar: $0.50\, C + 0.40\, V + 0.40\, B \leq 150$ pounds
Cream: $0.10\, C + 0.15\, V + 0.20\, B \leq\ 60$ gallons

and

$$C \geq 0, \qquad V \geq 0, \qquad B \geq 0.$$

This problem was solved using the Excel Solver. The spreadsheet (already solved) and the sensitivity report are shown below. [*Note:* The numbers in the sensitivity report for the milk constraint are missing on purpose, since you will be asked to fill in these numbers in part (f).]

	A	B	C	D	E	F	G
1		Resource Usage Per Unit of Each Activity					Resource
2			Activity				Resource
3	Resource	Chocolate	Vanilla	Banana	Totals		Available
4	Milk	0.45	0.5	0.4	180	≤	200
5	Sugar	0.5	0.4	0.4	150	≤	150
6	Cream	0.1	0.15	0.2	60	≤	60
7	Unit Profit	1	0.9	0.95	$341.25		
8	Solution	0	300	75			

Changing Cells

Cell	Name	Final Value	Reduced Cost	Objective Coefficient	Allowable Increase	Allowable Decrease
$B$8	Solution Chocolate	0	-0.0375	1	0.0375	1E+30
$C$8	Solution Vanilla	300	0	0.9	0.05	0.0125
$D$8	Solution Banana	75	0	0.95	0.021429	0.05

Constraints

Cell	Name	Final Value	Shadow Price	Constraint R.H. Side	Allowable Increase	Allowable Decrease
$E$4	Milk Totals					
$E$5	Sugar Totals	150	1.875	150	10	30
$E$6	Cream Totals	60	1	60	15	3.75

For each of the following parts, answer the question as specifically and completely as is possible without solving the problem again on the Excel Solver. *Note:* Each part is independent (i.e., any change made to the model in one part does not apply to any other parts).

(a) What is the optimal solution and total profit?

(b) Suppose the profit per gallon of banana changes to $1.00. Will the optimal solution change, and what can be said about the effect on total profit?

(c) Suppose the profit per gallon of banana changes to 92 cents. Will the optimal solution change, and what can be said about the effect on total profit?

(d) Suppose the company discovers that 3 gallons of cream have gone sour and so must be thrown out. Will the optimal solution change, and what can be said about the effect on total profit?

(e) Suppose the company has the opportunity to buy an additional 15 pounds of sugar at a total cost of $15. Should they? Explain.

(f) Fill in all the sensitivity report information for the milk constraint, given just the optimal solution for the problem. Explain how you were able to deduce each number.

6.7-19. David, LaDeana, and Lydia are the sole partners and workers in a company which produces fine clocks. David and LaDeana each are available to work a maximum of 40 hours per week at the company, while Lydia is available to work a maximum of 20 hours per week.

The company makes two different types of clocks: a grandfather clock and a wall clock. To make a clock, David (a mechanical engineer) assembles the inside mechanical parts of the clock while LaDeana (a woodworker) produces the hand-carved wood casings. Lydia is responsible for taking orders and shipping the clocks. The amount of time required for each of these tasks is shown below.

Task	Time Required	
	Grandfather Clock	**Wall Clock**
Assemble clock mechanism	6 hours	4 hours
Carve wood casing	8 hours	4 hours
Shipping	3 hours	3 hours

Each grandfather clock built and shipped yields a profit of $300, while each wall clock yields a profit of $200.

The three partners now want to determine how many clocks of each type should be produced per week to maximize the total profit.

(a) Formulate a linear programming model for this problem.

(b) Use the graphical method to solve the model.

C **(c)** Use a software package based on the simplex method to solve the model.

C **(d)** Use this same software package to generate sensitivity analysis information.

(e) Use this sensitivity analysis information to determine whether the optimal solution must remain optimal if the estimate of the unit profit for grandfather clocks is changed from $300 to $375 (with no other changes in the model).

(f) Repeat part (*e*) if, in addition to this change in the unit profit for grandfather clocks, the estimated unit profit for wall clocks also changes from $200 to $175.

(g) Use graphical analysis to verify your answers in parts (*e*) and (*f*).

(h) To increase the total profit, the three partners have agreed that one of them will slightly increase the maximum number of hours available to work per week. The choice of which one will be based on which one would increase the total profit the most. Use the sensitivity analysis information to make this choice. (Assume no change in the original estimates of the unit profits.)

(i) Explain why one of the shadow prices is equal to zero.

(j) Can the shadow prices given in the sensitivity analysis information be validly used to determine the effect if Lydia were to change her maximum number of hours available to work per week from 20 to 25? If so, what would be the increase in the total profit?

(k) Repeat part (*j*) if, in addition to the change for Lydia, David also were to change his maximum number of hours available to work per week from 40 to 35.

(l) Use graphical analysis to verify your answer in part (*k*).

C **6.7-20.** Consider the Union Airways problem presented in Sec. 3.4, including the data given in Table 3.19.

Management now is considering increasing the level of service provided to customers by increasing one or more of the numbers in the rightmost column of Table 3.19 for the minimum number of agents needed in the various time periods. To guide them in making this decision, they would like to know what impact this change would have on total cost.

Use a software package based on the simplex method to generate sensitivity analysis information in preparation for addressing the following questions.

(a) Which of the numbers in the rightmost column of Table 3.19 can be increased without increasing total cost? In each case, indicate how much it can be increased (if it is the only one being changed) without increasing total cost.

(b) For each of the other numbers, how much would the total cost increase per increase of 1 in the number? For each answer, indicate how much the number can be increased (if it is the only one being changed) before the answer is no longer valid.

(c) Do your answers in part (b) definitely remain valid if all the numbers considered in part (b) are simultaneously increased by 1?

(d) Do your answers in part (b) definitely remain valid if all 10 numbers are simultaneously increased by 1?

(e) How far can all 10 numbers be simultaneously increased by the same amount before your answers in part (b) may no longer be valid?

6.7-21. Consider the following problem.

$$\text{Maximize} \quad Z = 2x_1 + 5x_2,$$

subject to

$$x_1 + 2x_2 \leq 10$$
$$x_1 + 3x_2 \leq 12$$

and

$$x_1 \geq 0, \quad x_2 \geq 0.$$

Let x_3 and x_4 denote the slack variables for the respective functional constraints. After we apply the simplex method, the final simplex tableau is

Basic Variable	Eq.	Z	x_1	x_2	x_3	x_4	Right Side
Z	(0)	1	0	0	1	1	22
x_1	(1)	0	1	0	3	-2	6
x_2	(2)	0	0	1	-1	1	2

While doing postoptimality analysis, you learn that all four b_i and c_j values used in the original model just given are accurate only to within ±50 percent. In other words, their ranges of *likely values* are $5 \leq b_1 \leq 15$, $6 \leq b_2 \leq 18$, $1 \leq c_1 \leq 3$, and $2.5 \leq c_2 \leq 7.5$. Your job now is to perform sensitivity analysis to determine for each parameter individually (assuming the other three parameters equal their values in the original model) whether this uncertainty might affect either the feasibility or the optimality of the above basic solution (perhaps with new values for the basic variables). Specifically, determine the allowable range to stay feasible for each b_i and the allowable range to stay optimal for each c_j. Then, for each parameter and its range of likely values, indicate which part of this range lies within the allowable range and which parts correspond to values for which the current basic solution will no longer be both feasible and optimal.

(a) Perform this sensitivity analysis graphically on the original model.

(b) Now perform this sensitivity analysis as described and illustrated in Sec. 6.7 for b_1 and c_1.

(c) Repeat part (b) for b_2.

(d) Repeat part (b) for c_2.

6.7-22. Reconsider Prob. 6.7-21. Now use a software package based on the simplex method to generate sensitivity analysis information preparatory to doing parts (a) and (c) below.

C (a) Suppose that the estimates for c_1 and c_2 are correct but the estimates for both b_1 and b_2 are incorrect. Consider the following four cases where the true values of b_1 and b_2 differ from their estimates by the same percentage: (1) both b_1 and b_2 are smaller than their estimates, (2) both b_1 and b_2 are larger than their estimates, (3) b_1 is smaller and b_2 is larger than their estimates, and (4) b_1 is larger and b_2 is smaller than their estimates. For each of these cases, use the 100 percent rule for simultaneous changes in right-hand sides to determine how large the percentage error can be while guaranteeing that the original shadow prices still will be valid.

(b) For each of the four cases considered in part (a), start with the final simplex tableau given in Prob. 6.7-21 and use algebraic analysis based on the fundamental insight presented in Sec. 5.3 to determine how large the percentage error can be without invalidating the original shadow prices.

C (c) Suppose that the estimates for b_1 and b_2 are correct but the estimates for both c_1 and c_2 are incorrect. Consider the following four cases where the true values of c_1 and c_2 differ from their estimates by the same percentage: (1) both c_1 and c_2 are smaller than their estimates, (2) both c_1 and c_2 are larger than their estimates, (3) c_1 is smaller and c_2 is larger than their estimates, and (4) c_1 is larger and c_2 is smaller than their estimates. For each of these cases, use the 100 percent rule for simultaneous changes in objective function coefficients to determine how large the percentage error can be while guaranteeing that the original optimal solution must still be optimal.

(d) For each of the four cases considered in part (c), start with the final simplex tableau given in Prob. 6.7-21 and use algebraic analysis based on the fundamental insight presented in Sec. 5.3 to determine how large the percentage error can be without invalidating the original optimal solution.

6.7-23. Consider the following problem.

$$\text{Maximize} \quad Z = 3x_1 + 4x_2 + 8x_3,$$

subject to

$$2x_1 + 3x_2 + 5x_3 \leq 9$$
$$x_1 + 2x_2 + 3x_3 \leq 5$$

and

$$x_1 \geq 0, \quad x_2 \geq 0, \quad x_3 \geq 0.$$

Let x_4 and x_5 denote the slack variables for the respective functional constraints. After we apply the simplex method, the final simplex tableau is

Basic Variable	Eq.	Z	x_1	x_2	x_3	x_4	x_5	Right Side
			Coefficient of:					
Z	(0)	1	0	1	0	1	1	14
x_1	(1)	0	1	-1	0	3	-5	2
x_3	(2)	0	0	1	1	-1	2	1

While doing postoptimality analysis, you learn that some of the parameter values used in the original model just given are just rough estimates, where the range of likely values in each case is within ± 50 percent of the value used here. For each of these following parameters, perform sensitivity analysis to determine whether this uncertainty might affect either the feasibility or the optimality of the above basic solution. Specifically, for each parameter, determine the allowable range of values for which the current basic solution (perhaps with new values for the basic variables) will remain both feasible and optimal. Then, for each parameter and its range of likely values, indicate which part of this range lies within the allowable range and which parts correspond to values for which the current basic solution will no longer be both feasible and optimal.
(a) Parameter b_2
(b) Parameter c_2
(c) Parameter a_{22}
(d) Parameter c_3
(e) Parameter a_{12}
(f) Parameter b_1

6.7-24. Consider Variation 5 of the Wyndor Glass Co. model presented in Sec. 6.7, where $\bar{c}_2 = 3$, $\bar{a}_{22} = 3$, $\bar{a}_{32} = 4$, and where the other parameters are given in Table 6.21. Starting from the resulting final tableau given at the bottom of Table 6.24, construct a table like Table 6.26 to perform parametric linear programming analysis, where

$$c_1 = 3 + \theta \quad \text{and} \quad c_2 = 3 + 2\theta.$$

How far can θ be increased above 0 before the current basic solution is no longer optimal?

6.7-25. Reconsider the model of Prob. 6.7-6. Suppose that you now have the option of making trade-offs in the profitability of the first two activities, whereby the objective function coefficient of x_1 can be increased by any amount by simultaneously decreasing the objective function coefficient of x_2 by the same amount. Thus, the alternative choices of the objective function are

$$Z(\theta) = (2 + \theta)x_1 - (1 + \theta)x_2 + x_3,$$

where any nonnegative value of θ can be chosen.

Construct a table like Table 6.26 to perform parametric linear programming analysis on this problem. Determine the upper bound on θ before the original optimal solution would become nonoptimal. Then determine the best choice of θ over this range.

6.7-26. Consider the following parametric linear programming problem.

$$\text{Maximize} \quad Z(\theta) = (10 - 4\theta)x_1 + (4 - \theta)x_2 + (7 + \theta)x_3,$$

subject to

$$3x_1 + x_2 + 2x_3 \leq 7 \quad \text{(resource 1)},$$
$$2x_1 + x_2 + 3x_3 \leq 5 \quad \text{(resource 2)},$$

and

$$x_1 \geq 0, \qquad x_2 \geq 0, \qquad x_3 \geq 0,$$

where θ can be assigned any positive or negative values. Let x_4 and x_5 be the slack variables for the respective constraints. After we apply the simplex method with $\theta = 0$, the final simplex tableau is

Basic Variable	Eq.	Z	x_1	x_2	x_3	x_4	x_5	Right Side
			Coefficient of:					
Z	(0)	1	0	0	3	2	2	24
x_1	(1)	0	1	0	-1	1	-1	2
x_2	(2)	0	0	1	5	-2	3	1

(a) Determine the range of values of θ over which the above BF solution will remain optimal. Then find the best choice of θ within this range.
(b) Given that θ is within the range of values found in part (a), find the allowable range to stay feasible for b_1 (the available amount of resource 1). Then do the same for b_2 (the available amount of resource 2).
(c) Given that θ is within the range of values found in part (a), identify the shadow prices (as a function of θ) for the two resources. Use this information to determine how the optimal value of the objective function would change (as a function of θ) if the available amount of resource 1 were decreased by 1 and the available amount of resource 2 simultaneously were increased by 1.
(d) Construct the dual of this parametric linear programming problem. Set $\theta = 0$ and solve this dual problem graphically to find the corresponding shadow prices for the two resources of the primal problem. Then find these shadow prices as a function of θ [within the range of values found in part (a)] by algebraically solving for this same optimal CPF solution for the dual problem as a function of θ.

6.7-27. Consider the following parametric linear programming problem.

$$\text{Maximize} \quad Z(\theta) = 2x_1 + 4x_2 + 5x_3,$$

subject to

$$x_1 + 3x_2 + 2x_3 \le 5 + \theta$$
$$x_1 + 2x_2 + 3x_3 \le 6 + 2\theta$$

and

$$x_1 \ge 0, \qquad x_2 \ge 0, \qquad x_3 \ge 0,$$

where θ can be assigned any positive or negative values. Let x_4 and x_5 be the slack variables for the respective functional constraints. After we apply the simplex method with $\theta = 0$, the final simplex tableau is

Basic Variable	Eq.	Z		Coefficient of:					Right Side
			x_1	x_2	x_3	x_4	x_5		
Z	(0)	0	0	1	0	1	1		11
x_1	(1)	1	1	5	0	3	-2		3
x_3	(2)	2	0	-1	1	-1	1		1

(a) Express the BF solution (and Z) given in this tableau as a function of θ. Determine the lower and upper bounds on θ before this optimal solution would become infeasible. Then determine the best choice of θ between these bounds.

(b) Given that θ is between the bounds found in part (a), determine the allowable range to stay optimal for c_1 (the coefficient of x_1 in the objective function).

6.7-28. Consider the following parametric linear programming problem, where the parameter θ must be nonnegative:

$$\text{Maximize} \quad Z(\theta) = (5 + 2\theta)x_1 + (2 - \theta)x_2 + (3 + \theta)x_3,$$

subject to

$$4x_1 + x_2 \qquad \ge 5 + 5\theta$$
$$3x_1 + x_2 + 2x_3 = 10 - 10\theta$$

and

$$x_1 \ge 0, \qquad x_2 \ge 0, \qquad x_3 \ge 0.$$

Let x_4 be the surplus variable for the first functional constraint, and let $\bar{x}_5$ and $\bar{x}_6$ be the artificial variables for the respective functional constraints. After we apply the simplex method with the Big M method and with $\theta = 0$, the final simplex tableau is

Basic Variable	Eq.	Z		Coefficient of:						Right Side
			x_1	x_2	x_3	x_4	$\bar{x}_5$	$\bar{x}_6$	
Z	(0)	1	1	0	1	0	M	$M+2$	20
x_2	(1)	0	3	1	2	0	0	1	10
x_4	(2)	0	-1	0	2	1	-1	1	5

(a) Use the fundamental insight (Sec. 5.3) to revise this tableau to reflect the inclusion of the parameter θ in the original model. Show the complete tableau needed to apply the feasibility test and the optimality test for any value of θ. Express the corresponding basic solution (and Z) as a function of θ.

(b) Determine the range of nonnegative values of θ over which this basic solution is feasible.

(c) Determine the range of nonnegative values of θ over which this basic solution is both feasible and optimal. Determine the best choice of θ over this range.

6.7-29. Consider the following problem.

$$\text{Maximize} \quad Z = 10x_1 + 4x_2,$$

subject to

$$3x_1 + x_2 \le 30$$
$$2x_1 + x_2 \le 25$$

and

$$x_1 \ge 0, \qquad x_2 \ge 0.$$

Let x_3 and x_4 denote the slack variables for the respective functional constraints. After we apply the simplex method, the final simplex tableau is

Basic Variable	Eq.	Z		Coefficient of:			Right Side
			x_1	x_2	x_3	x_4	
Z	(0)	1	0	0	2	2	110
x_2	(1)	0	0	1	-2	3	15
x_1	(2)	0	1	0	1	-1	5

Now suppose that both of the following changes are made simultaneously in the original model:

1. The first constraint is changed to $4x_1 + x_2 \le 40$.
2. Parametric programming is introduced to change the objective function to the alternative choices of

$$Z(\theta) = (10 - 2\theta)x_1 + (4 + \theta)x_2,$$

where any nonnegative value of θ can be chosen.

(a) Construct the resulting revised final tableau (as a function of θ), and then convert this tableau to proper form from Gaussian elimination. Use this tableau to identify the new optimal solution that applies for either $\theta = 0$ or sufficiently small values of θ.

(b) What is the upper bound on θ before this optimal solution would become nonoptimal?

(c) Over the range of θ from zero to this upper bound, which choice of θ gives the largest value of the objective function?

6.7-30. Consider the following problem.

Maximize $\quad Z = 9x_1 + 8x_2 + 5x_3,$

subject to

$$2x_1 + 3x_2 + x_3 \leq 4$$
$$5x_1 + 4x_2 + 3x_3 \leq 11$$

and

$$x_1 \geq 0, \qquad x_2 \geq 0, \qquad x_3 \geq 0.$$

Let x_4 and x_5 denote the slack variables for the respective functional constraints. After we apply the simplex method, the final simplex tableau is

Basic Variable	Eq.		Coefficient of:					Right Side
		Z	x_1	x_2	x_3	x_4	x_5	
Z	(0)	1	0	2	0	2	1	19
x_1	(1)	0	1	5	0	3	−1	1
x_3	(2)	0	0	−7	1	−5	2	2

D,I **(a)** Suppose that a new technology has become available for conducting the first activity considered in this problem. If the new technology were adopted to replace the existing one, the coefficients of x_1 in the model would change

from $\quad \begin{bmatrix} c_1 \\ a_{11} \\ a_{21} \end{bmatrix} = \begin{bmatrix} 9 \\ 2 \\ 5 \end{bmatrix} \quad$ to $\quad \begin{bmatrix} c_1 \\ a_{11} \\ a_{21} \end{bmatrix} = \begin{bmatrix} 18 \\ 3 \\ 6 \end{bmatrix}.$

Use the sensitivity analysis procedure to investigate the potential effect and desirability of adopting the new technology. Specifically, assuming it were adopted, construct the resulting revised final tableau, convert this tableau to proper form from Gaussian elimination, and then reoptimize (if necessary) to find the new optimal solution.

(b) Now suppose that you have the option of mixing the old and new technologies for conducting the first activity. Let θ denote the fraction of the technology used that is from the new tech-

nology, so $0 \leq \theta \leq 1$. Given θ, the coefficients of x_1 in the model become

$$\begin{bmatrix} c_1 \\ a_{11} \\ a_{21} \end{bmatrix} = \begin{bmatrix} 9 + 9\theta \\ 2 + \theta \\ 5 + \theta \end{bmatrix}.$$

Construct the resulting revised final tableau (as a function of θ), and convert this tableau to proper form from Gaussian elimination. Use this tableau to identify the current basic solution as a function of θ. Over the allowable values of $0 \leq \theta \leq 1$, give the range of values of θ for which this solution is both feasible and optimal. What is the best choice of θ within this range?

6.7-31. Consider the following problem.

Maximize $\quad Z = 3x_1 + 5x_2 + 2x_3,$

subject to

$$-2x_1 + 2x_2 + x_3 \leq 5$$
$$3x_1 + x_2 - x_3 \leq 10$$

and

$$x_1 \geq 0, \qquad x_2 \geq 0, \qquad x_3 \geq 0.$$

Let x_4 and x_5 be the slack variables for the respective functional constraints. After we apply the simplex method, the final simplex tableau is

Basic Variable	Eq.		Coefficient of:					Right Side
		Z	x_1	x_2	x_3	x_4	x_5	
Z	(0)	1	0	20	0	9	7	115
x_1	(1)	0	1	3	0	1	1	15
x_3	(2)	0	0	8	1	3	2	35

Parametric linear programming analysis now is to be applied simultaneously to the objective function and right-hand sides, where the model in terms of the new parameter is the following:

Maximize $\quad Z(\theta) = (3 + 2\theta)x_1 + (5 + \theta)x_2 + (2 - \theta)x_3,$

subject to

$$-2x_1 + 2x_2 + x_3 \leq 5 + 6\theta$$
$$3x_1 + x_2 - x_3 \leq 10 - 8\theta$$

and

$$x_1 \geq 0, \qquad x_2 \geq 0, \qquad x_3 \geq 0.$$

Construct the resulting revised final tableau (as a function of θ), and convert this tableau to proper form from Gaussian elimination.

Use this tableau to identify the current basic solution as a function of θ. For $\theta \geq 0$, give the range of values of θ for which this solution is both feasible and optimal. What is the best choice of θ within this range?

6.7-32. Consider the Wyndor Glass Co. problem described in Sec. 3.1. Suppose that, in addition to considering the introduction of two new products, management now is considering changing the production rate of a certain old product that is still profitable. Refer to Table 3.1. The number of production hours per week used per unit production rate of this old product is 1, 4, and 3 for Plants 1, 2, and 3, respectively. Therefore, if we let θ denote the *change* (positive or negative) in the production rate of this old product, the right-hand sides of the three functional constraints in Sec. 3.1 become $4 - \theta$, $12 - 4\theta$, and $18 - 3\theta$, respectively. Thus, choosing a negative value of θ would free additional capacity for producing more of the two new products, whereas a positive value would have the opposite effect.

(a) Use a parametric linear programming formulation to determine the effect of different choices of θ on the optimal solution for the product mix of the two new products given in the final tableau of Table 4.8. In particular, use the fundamental insight of Sec. 5.3 to obtain expressions for Z and the basic variables $x_3, x_2,$ and x_1 in terms of θ, assuming that θ is sufficiently close to zero that this "final" basic solution still is feasible and thus optimal for the given value of θ.

(b) Now consider the broader question of the choice of θ along with the product mix for the two new products. What is the breakeven unit profit for the old product (in comparison with the two new products) below which its production rate should be decreased ($\theta < 0$) in favor of the new products and above which its production rate should be increased ($\theta > 0$)?

(c) If the unit profit is above this breakeven point, how much can the old product's production rate be increased before the final BF solution would become infeasible?

(d) If the unit profit is below this breakeven point, how much can the old product's production rate be decreased (assuming its previous rate was larger than this decrease) before the final BF solution would become infeasible?

6.7-33. Consider the following problem.

Maximize $Z = 2x_1 - x_2 + 3x_3,$

subject to

$$x_1 + x_2 + x_3 = 3$$
$$x_1 - 2x_2 + x_3 \geq 1$$
$$2x_2 + x_3 \leq 2$$

and

$$x_1 \geq 0, \qquad x_2 \geq 0, \qquad x_3 \geq 0.$$

Suppose that the Big M method (see Sec. 4.6) is used to obtain the initial (artificial) BF solution. Let $\bar{x}_4$ be the artificial slack variable for the first constraint, x_5 the surplus variable for the second constraint, $\bar{x}_6$ the artificial variable for the second constraint, and x_7 the slack variable for the third constraint. The corresponding final set of equations yielding the optimal solution is

(0)	Z	$+ 5x_2$		$+ (M + 2)\bar{x}_4$		$+ M\bar{x}_6 + x_7 = 8$
(1)		$x_1 - x_2$	$+$	$\bar{x}_4$		$- x_7 = 1$
(2)		$2x_2 + x_3$				$+ x_7 = 2$
(3)		$3x_2$	$+$	$\bar{x}_4 + x_5 -$	$\bar{x}_6$	$= 2.$

Suppose that the original objective function is changed to $Z = 2x_1 + 3x_2 + 4x_3$ and that the original third constraint is changed to $2x_2 + x_3 \leq 1$. Use the sensitivity analysis procedure to revise the final set of equations (in tableau form) and convert it to proper form from Gaussian elimination for identifying and evaluating the current basic solution. Then test this solution for feasibility and for optimality. (Do not reoptimize.)

CASE 6.1   CONTROLLING AIR POLLUTION

Refer to Sec. 3.4 (subsection entitled "Controlling Air Pollution") for the Nori & Leets Co. problem. After the OR team obtained an optimal solution, we mentioned that the team then conducted sensitivity analysis. We now continue this story by having you retrace the steps taken by the OR team, after we provide some additional background.

The values of the various parameters in the original formulation of the model are given in Tables 3.12, 3.13, and 3.14. Since the company does not have much prior experience with the pollution abatement methods under consideration, the cost estimates given in Table 3.14 are fairly rough, and each one could easily be off by as much as 10 percent in either direction. There also is some uncertainty about the parameter values given in Table 3.13, but less so than for Table 3.14. By contrast, the values in Table 3.12 are policy standards, and so are prescribed constants.

However, there still is considerable debate about where to set these policy standards on the required reductions in the emission rates of the various pollutants. The numbers in Table 3.12 actually are preliminary values tentatively agreed upon before learning what the total cost would be to meet these standards. Both the city and company officials agree that the final decision on these policy standards should be based on the *trade-off* between costs and benefits. With this in mind, the city has concluded that each 10 percent increase in the policy standards over the current values (all the numbers in Table 3.12) would be worth $3.5 million to the city. Therefore, the city has agreed to reduce the company's tax payments to the city by $3.5 million for *each* 10 percent reduction in the policy standards (up to 50 percent) that is accepted by the company.

Finally, there has been some debate about the *relative* values of the policy standards for the three pollutants. As indicated in Table 3.12, the required reduction for particulates now is less than half of that for either sulfur oxides or hydrocarbons. Some have argued for decreasing this disparity. Others contend that an even greater disparity is justified because sulfur oxides and hydrocarbons cause considerably more damage than particulates. Agreement has been reached that this issue will be reexamined after information is obtained about which trade-offs in policy standards (increasing one while decreasing another) are available without increasing the total cost.

(a) Use any available linear programming software to solve the model for this problem as formulated in Sec. 3.4. In addition to the optimal solution, obtain the additional output provided for performing postoptimality analysis (e.g., the Sensitivity Report when using Excel). This output provides the basis for the following steps.

(b) Ignoring the constraints with no uncertainty about their parameter values (namely, $x_j \leq 1$ for $j = 1, 2, \ldots, 6$), identify the parameters of the model that should be classified as *sensitive parameters*. (*Hint:* See the subsection "Sensitivity Analysis" in Sec. 4.7.) Make a resulting recommendation about which parameters should be estimated more closely, if possible.

(c) Analyze the effect of an inaccuracy in estimating each cost parameter given in Table 3.14. If the true value is 10 percent *less* than the estimated value, would this alter the optimal solution? Would it change if the true value were 10 percent *more* than the estimated value? Make a resulting recommendation about where to focus further work in estimating the cost parameters more closely.

(d) Consider the case where your model has been converted to maximization form before applying the simplex method. Use Table 6.14 to construct the corresponding dual problem, and use the output from applying the simplex method to the primal problem to identify an optimal solution for this dual problem. If the primal problem had been left in minimization form, how would this affect the form of the dual problem and the sign of the optimal dual variables?

(e) For each pollutant, use your results from part (*d*) to specify the rate at which the total cost of an optimal solution would change with any small change in the required reduction in the annual emission rate of the pollutant. Also specify how much this required reduction can be changed (up or down) without affecting the rate of change in the total cost.

(f) For each unit change in the policy standard for particulates given in Table 3.12, determine the change in the opposite direction for sulfur oxides that would keep the total cost of an optimal solution unchanged. Repeat this for hydrocarbons instead of sulfur oxides. Then do it for a simultaneous and equal change for both sulfur oxides and hydrocarbons in the opposite direction from particulates.

(g) Letting θ denote the percentage increase in all the policy standards given in Table 3.12, formulate the problem of analyzing the effect of simultaneous proportional increases in these standards as a parametric linear programming problem. Then use your results from part (e) to determine the rate at which the total cost of an optimal solution would increase with a small increase in θ from zero.

(h) Use the simplex method to find an optimal solution for the parametric linear programming problem formulated in part (g) for each $\theta = 10, 20, 30, 40, 50$. Considering the tax incentive offered by the city, use these results to determine which value of θ (including the option of $\theta = 0$) should be chosen to minimize the company's total cost of both pollution abatement and taxes.

(i) For the value of θ chosen in part (h), repeat parts (e) and (f) so that the decision makers can make a final decision on the *relative* values of the policy standards for the three pollutants.

CASE 6.2   FARM MANAGEMENT

The Ploughman family owns and operates a 640-acre farm that has been in the family for several generations. The Ploughmans always have had to work hard to make a decent living from the farm and have had to endure some occasional difficult years. Stories about earlier generations overcoming hardships due to droughts, floods, etc., are an important part of the family history. However, the Ploughmans enjoy their self-reliant lifestyle and gain considerable satisfaction from continuing the family tradition of successfully living off the land during an era when many family farms are being abandoned or taken over by large agricultural corporations.

John Ploughman is the current manager of the farm while his wife Eunice runs the house and manages the farm's finances. John's father, Grandpa Ploughman, lives with them and still puts in many hours working on the farm. John and Eunice's older children, Frank, Phyllis, and Carl, also are given heavy chores before and after school.

The entire famiy can produce a total of 4,000 person-hours worth of labor during the winter and spring months and 4,500 person-hours during the summer and fall. If any of these person-hours are not needed, Frank, Phyllis, and Carl will use them to work on a neighboring farm for $5 per hour during the winter and spring months and $5.50 per hour during the summer and fall.

The farm supports two types of livestock: dairy cows and laying hens, as well as three crops: soybeans, corn, and wheat. (All three are cash crops, but the corn also is a feed crop for the cows and the wheat also is used for chicken feed.) The crops are harvested during the late summer and fall. During the winter months, John, Eunice, and Grandpa make a decision about the mix of livestock and crops for the coming year.

Currently, the family has just completed a particularly successful harvest which has provided an investment fund of $20,000 that can be used to purchase more livestock. (Other money is available for ongoing expenses, including the next planting of crops.) The family currently has 30 cows valued at $35,000 and 2,000 hens valued at $5,000. They wish to keep all this livestock and perhaps purchase more. Each new cow would cost $1,500, and each new hen would cost $3.

Over a year's time, the value of a herd of cows will decrease by about 10 percent and the value of a flock of hens will decrease by about 25 percent due to aging.

Each cow will require 2 acres of land for grazing and 10 person-hours of work per month, while producing a net annual cash income of $850 for the family. The corresponding figures for each hen are: no significant acreage, 0.05 person-hour per month, and an annual net cash income of $4.25. The chicken house can accommodate a maximum of 5,000 hens, and the size of the barn limits the herd to a maximum of 42 cows.

For each acre planted in each of the three crops, the following table gives the number of person-hours of work that will be required during the first and second halves of the year, as well as a rough estimate of the crop's net value (in either income or savings in purchasing feed for the livestock).

Data per acre planted

	Soybeans	Corn	Wheat
Winter and spring, person-hours	1.0	0.9	0.6
Summer and fall, person-hours	1.4	1.2	0.7
Net value	$70	$60	$40

To provide much of the feed for the livestock, John wants to plant at least 1 acre of corn for each cow in the coming year's herd and at least 0.05 acre of wheat for each hen in the coming year's flock.

John, Eunice, and Grandpa now are discussing how much acreage should be planted in each of the crops and how many cows and hens to have for the coming year. Their objective is to maximize the family's monetary worth at the end of the coming year (the *sum* of the net income from the livestock for the coming year *plus* the net value of the crops for the coming year *plus* what remains from the investment fund *plus* the value of the livestock at the end of the coming year *plus* any income from working on a neighboring farm, *minus* living expenses of $40,000 for the year).

(a) Identify verbally the components of a linear programming model for this problem.
(b) Formulate this model. (Either an algebraic or a spreadsheet formulation is acceptable.)
(c) Obtain an optimal solution and generate the additional output provided for performing postoptimality analysis (e.g., the Sensitivity Report when using Excel). What does the model predict regarding the family's monetary worth at the end of the coming year?
(d) Find the allowable range to stay optimal for the net value per acre planted for each of the three crops.

The above estimates of the net value per acre planted in each of the three crops assumes good weather conditions. Adverse weather conditions would harm the crops and greatly reduce the resulting value. The scenarios particularly feared by the family are a drought, a flood, an early frost, *both* a drought and an early frost, and *both* a flood and an early frost. The estimated net values for the year under these scenarios are shown on the next page.

| Scenario | Net Value per Acre Planted | | |
	Soybeans	Corn	Wheat
Drought	−$10	−$15	0
Flood	$15	$20	$10
Early frost	$50	$40	$30
Drought and early frost	−$15	−$20	−$10
Flood and early frost	$10	$10	$ 5

(e) Find an optimal solution under each scenario after making the necessary adjustments to the linear programming model formulated in part (b). In each case, what is the prediction regarding the family's monetary worth at the end of the year?

(f) For the optimal solution obtained under each of the six scenarios [including the good weather scenario considered in parts (a) to (d)], calculate what the family's monetary worth would be at the end of the year if each of the other five scenarios occur instead. In your judgment, which solution provides the best balance between yielding a large monetary worth under good weather conditions and avoiding an overly small monetary worth under adverse weather conditions.

Grandpa has researched what the weather conditions were in past years as far back as weather records have been kept, and obtained the following data.

Scenario	Frequency
Good weather	40%
Drought	20%
Flood	10%
Early frost	15%
Drought and early frost	10%
Flood and early frost	5%

With these data, the family has decided to use the following approach to making its planting and livestock decisions. Rather than the optimistic approach of assuming that good weather conditions will prevail [as done in parts (a) to (d)], the *average* net value under all weather conditions will be used for each crop (weighting the net values under the various scenarios by the frequencies in the above table).

(g) Modify the linear programming model formulated in part (b) to fit this new approach.

(h) Repeat part (c) for this modified model.

(i) Use a shadow price obtained in part (h) to analyze whether it would be worthwhile for the family to obtain a bank loan with a 10 percent interest rate to purchase more livestock now beyond what can be obtained with the $20,000 from the investment fund.

(j) For each of the three crops, use the postoptimality analysis information obtained in part (h) to identify how much latitude for error is available in estimating the net value per acre planted for that crop without changing the optimal solution. Which two net values need to be estimated most carefully? If both estimates are incorrect simultaneously, how close do the estimates need to be to guarantee that the optimal solution will not change?

This problem illustrates a kind of situation that is frequently faced by various kinds of organizations. To describe the situation in general terms, an organization faces an uncertain future where any one of a number of scenarios may unfold. Which one will occur depends on conditions that are outside the control of the organization. The organization needs to choose the levels of various activities, but the unit contribution of each activity to the overall measure of performance is greatly affected by which scenario unfolds. Under these circumstances, what is the best mix of activities?

(k) Think about specific situations outside of farm management that fit this description. Describe one.

CASE 6.3   ASSIGNING STUDENTS TO SCHOOLS (REVISITED)

Reconsider Case 4.3.

The Springfield School Board still has the policy of providing bussing for all middle school students who must travel more than approximately 1 mile. Another current policy is to allow splitting residential areas among multiple schools if this will reduce the total bussing cost. (This latter policy will be reversed in Case 12.4.) However, before adopting a bussing plan based on parts (a) and (b) of Case 4.3, the school board now wants to conduct some postoptimality analysis.

(a) If you have not already done so for parts (a) and (b) of Case 4.3, formulate and solve a linear programming model for this problem. (Either an algebraic or a spreadsheet formulation is acceptable.)
(b) Generate a sensitivity analysis report with the same software package as used in part (a).

One concern of the school board is the ongoing road construction in area 6. These construction projects have been delaying traffic considerably and are likely to affect the cost of bussing students from area 6, perhaps increasing them as much as 10 percent.

(c) Use the report from part (b) to check how much the bussing cost from area 6 to school 1 can increase (assuming no change in the costs for the other schools) before the current optimal solution would no longer be optimal. If the allowable increase is less than 10 percent, re-solve to find the new optimal solution with a 10 percent increase.
(d) Repeat part (c) for school 2 (assuming no change in the costs for the other schools).
(e) Now assume that the bussing cost from area 6 would increase by the same percentage for all the schools. Use the report from part (b) to determine how large this percentage can be before the current optimal solution might no longer be optimal. If the allowable increase is less than 10 percent, re-solve to find the new optimal solution with a 10 percent increase.

The school board has the option of adding portable classrooms to increase the capacity of one or more of the middle schools for a few years. However, this is a costly move that the board would consider only if it would significantly decrease bussing costs. Each portable classroom holds 20 students and has a leasing cost of $2,500 per year. To analyze this option, the school board decides to assume that the road construction in area 6 will wind down without significantly increasing the bussing costs from that area.

(f) For each school, use the corresponding shadow price from the report obtained in part (b) to determine whether it would be worthwhile to add any portable classrooms.

(g) For each school where it is worthwhile to add any portable classrooms, use the report from part (b) to determine how many could be added before the shadow price would no longer be valid (assuming this is the only school receiving portable classrooms).

(h) If it would be worthwhile to add portable classrooms to more than one school, use the report from part (b) to determine the combinations of the number to add for which the shadow prices definitely would still be valid. Then use the shadow prices to determine which of these combinations is best in terms of minimizing the total cost of bussing students and leasing portable classrooms. Re-solve to find the corresponding optimal solution for assigning students to schools.

(i) If part (h) was applicable, modify the best combination of portable classrooms found there by adding one more to the school with the most favorable shadow price. Find the corresponding optimal solution for assigning students to schools and generate the corresponding sensitivity analysis report. Use this information to assess whether the plan developed in part (h) is the best one available for minimizing the total cost of bussing students and leasing portable classrooms. If not, find the best plan.

7

Other Algorithms for Linear Programming

The key to the extremely widespread use of linear programming is the availability of an exceptionally efficient algorithm—the simplex method—that will routinely solve the large-size problems that typically arise in practice. However, the simplex method is only part of the arsenal of algorithms regularly used by linear programming practitioners. We now turn to these other algorithms.

This chapter focuses first on three particularly important algorithms that are, in fact, *variants* of the simplex method. In particular, the next three sections present the *dual simplex method* (a modification particularly useful for sensitivity analysis), *parametric linear programming* (an extension for systematic sensitivity analysis), and the *upper bound technique* (a streamlined version of the simplex method for dealing with variables having upper bounds).

Section 4.9 introduced another algorithmic approach to linear programming—a type of algorithm that moves through the interior of the feasible region. We describe this *interior-point approach* further in Sec. 7.4.

We next introduce *linear goal programming* where, rather than having a *single objective* (maximize or minimize Z) as for linear programming, the problem instead has *several goals* toward which we must strive simultaneously. Certain formulation techniques enable converting a linear goal programming problem back into a linear programming problem so that solution procedures based on the simplex method can still be used. Section 7.5 describes these techniques and procedures.

7.1 THE DUAL SIMPLEX METHOD

The *dual simplex method* is based on the duality theory presented in the first part of Chap. 6. To describe the basic idea behind this method, it is helpful to use some terminology introduced in Tables 6.10 and 6.11 of Sec. 6.3 for describing any pair of complementary basic solutions in the primal and dual problems. In particular, recall that both solutions are said to be *primal feasible* if the primal basic solution is feasible, whereas they are called *dual feasible* if the complementary dual basic solution is feasible for the dual problem. Also recall (as indicated on the right side of Table 6.11) that each complementary basic solution is optimal for its problem only if it is *both* primal feasible and dual feasible.

The dual simplex method can be thought of as the *mirror image* of the simplex method. The simplex method deals directly with basic solutions in the primal problem that are *primal feasible* but not dual feasible. It then moves toward an optimal solution by striving to achieve dual feasibility as well (the optimality test for the simplex method). By contrast, the dual simplex method deals with basic solutions in the primal problem that are *dual feasible* but not primal feasible. It then moves toward an optimal solution by striving to achieve primal feasibility as well.

Furthermore, the dual simplex method deals with a problem as if the simplex method were being applied simultaneously to its dual problem. If we make their *initial* basic solutions *complementary,* the two methods move in complete sequence, obtaining *complementary* basic solutions with each iteration.

The dual simplex method is very useful in certain special types of situations. Ordinarily it is easier to find an initial basic solution that is feasible than one that is dual feasible. However, it is occasionally necessary to introduce many *artificial* variables to construct an initial BF solution artificially. In such cases it may be easier to begin with a dual feasible basic solution and use the dual simplex method. Furthermore, fewer iterations may be required when it is not necessary to drive many artificial variables to zero.

As we mentioned several times in Chap. 6 as well as in Sec. 4.7, another important primary application of the dual simplex method is its use in conjunction with sensitivity analysis. Suppose that an optimal solution has been obtained by the simplex method but that it becomes necessary (or of interest for sensitivity analysis) to make minor changes in the model. If the formerly optimal basic solution is *no longer primal feasible* (but still satisfies the optimality test), you can immediately apply the dual simplex method by starting with this *dual feasible* basic solution. Applying the dual simplex method in this way usually leads to the new optimal solution much more quickly than would solving the new problem from the beginning with the simplex method.

The dual simplex method also can be useful in solving huge linear programming problems from scratch because it is such an efficient algorithm. Recent computational experience with the latest versions of CPLEX indicates that the dual simplex method often is more efficient than the simplex method for solving particularly massive problems encountered in practice.

The rules for the dual simplex method are very similar to those for the simplex method. In fact, once the methods are started, the only difference between them is in the criteria used for selecting the entering and leaving basic variables and for stopping the algorithm.

To start the dual simplex method (for a maximization problem), we must have all the coefficients in Eq. (0) *nonnegative* (so that the basic solution is dual feasible). The basic solutions will be infeasible (except for the last one) only because some of the variables are negative. The method continues to decrease the value of the objective function, always retaining *nonnegative coefficients* in Eq. (0), until all the *variables* are nonnegative. Such a basic solution is feasible (it satisfies all the equations) and is, therefore, optimal by the simplex method criterion of nonnegative coefficients in Eq. (0).

The details of the dual simplex method are summarized next.

Summary of the Dual Simplex Method.

1. *Initialization:*   After converting any functional constraints in $\geq$ form to $\leq$ form (by multiplying through both sides by -1), introduce slack variables as needed to construct a set of equations describing the problem. Find a basic solution such that the coefficients in Eq. (0) are zero for basic variables and nonnegative for nonbasic variables (so the solution is optimal if it is feasible). Go to the feasibility test.

2. *Feasibility test:* Check to see whether all the basic variables are *nonnegative.* If they are, then this solution is feasible, and therefore optimal, so stop. Otherwise, go to an iteration.
3. *Iteration:*

Step 1 Determine the *leaving basic variable:* Select the *negative* basic variable that has the largest absolute value.

Step 2 Determine the *entering basic variable:* Select the nonbasic variable whose coefficient in Eq. (0) reaches zero first as an increasing multiple of the equation containing the leaving basic variable is added to Eq. (0). This selection is made by checking the nonbasic variables with *negative coefficients* in that equation (the one containing the leaving basic variable) and selecting the one with the smallest absolute value of the ratio of the Eq. (0) coefficient to the coefficient in that equation.

Step 3 Determine the *new basic solution:* Starting from the current set of equations, solve for the basic variables in terms of the nonbasic variables by Gaussian elimination. When we set the nonbasic variables equal to zero, each basic variable (and Z) equals the new right-hand side of the one equation in which it appears (with a coefficient of $+1$). Return to the feasibility test.

To fully understand the dual simplex method, you must realize that the method proceeds just as if the *simplex method* were being applied to the complementary basic solutions in the *dual problem.* (In fact, this interpretation was the motivation for constructing the method as it is.) Step 1 of an iteration, determining the leaving basic variable, is equivalent to determining the entering basic variable in the dual problem. The negative variable with the largest absolute value corresponds to the negative coefficient with the largest absolute value in Eq. (0) of the dual problem (see Table 6.3). Step 2, determining the entering basic variable, is equivalent to determining the leaving basic variable in the dual problem. The coefficient in Eq. (0) that reaches zero first corresponds to the variable in the dual problem that reaches zero first. The two criteria for stopping the algorithm are also complementary.

We shall now illustrate the dual simplex method by applying it to the *dual problem* for the Wyndor Glass Co. (see Table 6.1). Normally this method is applied directly to the problem of concern (a primal problem). However, we have chosen this problem because you have already seen the simplex method applied to *its* dual problem (namely, the primal problem[1]) in Table 4.8 so you can compare the two. To facilitate the comparison, we shall continue to denote the decision variables in the problem being solved by y_i rather than x_j.

In *maximization* form, the problem to be solved is

Maximize $Z = -4y_1 - 12y_2 - 18y_3,$

subject to

$$y_1 \quad + 3y_3 \geq 3$$
$$2y_2 + 2y_3 \geq 5$$

and

$$y_1 \geq 0, \qquad y_2 \geq 0, \qquad y_3 \geq 0.$$

---

[1]Recall that the symmetry property in Sec. 6.1 points out that the dual of a dual problem is the original primal problem.

TABLE 7.1 Dual simplex method applied to the Wyndor Glass Co. dual problem

Iteration	Basic Variable	Eq.	Z	y_1	y_2	y_3	y_4	y_5	Right Side
0	Z	(0)	1	4	12	18	0	0	0
	y_4	(1)	0	-1	0	-3	1	0	-3
	y_5	(2)	0	0	-2	-2	0	1	-5
1	Z	(0)	1	4	0	6	0	6	-30
	y_4	(1)	0	-1	0	-3	1	0	-3
	y_2	(2)	0	0	1	1	0	$-\frac{1}{2}$	$\frac{5}{2}$
2	Z	(0)	1	2	0	0	2	6	-36
	y_3	(1)	0	$\frac{1}{3}$	0	1	$-\frac{1}{3}$	0	1
	y_2	(2)	0	$-\frac{1}{3}$	1	0	$\frac{1}{3}$	$-\frac{1}{2}$	$\frac{3}{2}$

Since negative right-hand sides are now allowed, we do not need to introduce artificial variables to be the initial basic variables. Instead, we simply convert the functional constraints to $\leq$ form and introduce slack variables to play this role. The resulting initial set of equations is that shown for iteration 0 in Table 7.1. Notice that all the coefficients in Eq. (0) are nonnegative, so the solution is optimal if it is feasible.

The initial basic solution is $y_1 = 0$, $y_2 = 0$, $y_3 = 0$, $y_4 = -3$, $y_5 = -5$, with $Z = 0$, which is not feasible because of the negative values. The leaving basic variable is y_5 ($5 > 3$), and the entering basic variable is y_2 ($12/2 < 18/2$), which leads to the second set of equations, labeled as iteration 1 in Table 7.1. The corresponding basic solution is $y_1 = 0$, $y_2 = \frac{5}{2}$, $y_3 = 0$, $y_4 = -3$, $y_5 = 0$, with $Z = -30$, which is not feasible.

The next leaving basic variable is y_4, and the entering basic variable is y_3 ($6/3 < 4/1$), which leads to the final set of equations in Table 7.1. The corresponding basic solution is $y_1 = 0$, $y_2 = \frac{3}{2}$, $y_3 = 1$, $y_4 = 0$, $y_5 = 0$, with $Z = -36$, which is feasible and therefore optimal.

Notice that the optimal solution for the dual of this problem[1] is $x_1^* = 2$, $x_2^* = 6$, $x_3^* = 2$, $x_4^* = 0$, $x_5^* = 0$, as was obtained in Table 4.8 by the simplex method. We suggest that you now trace through Tables 7.1 and 4.8 simultaneously and compare the complementary steps for the two mirror-image methods.

7.2 PARAMETRIC LINEAR PROGRAMMING

At the end of Sec. 6.7 we described *parametric linear programming* and its use for conducting sensitivity analysis systematically by gradually changing various model parameters simultaneously. We shall now present the algorithmic procedure, first for the case where the c_j parameters are being changed and then where the b_i parameters are varied.

---

[1] The *complementary optimal basic solutions property* presented in Sec. 6.3 indicates how to read the optimal solution for the dual problem from row 0 of the final simplex tableau for the primal problem. This same conclusion holds regardless of whether the simplex method or the dual simplex method is used to obtain the final tableau.

Systematic Changes in the c_j Parameters

For the case where the c_j parameters are being changed, the *objective function* of the ordinary linear programming model

$$Z = \sum_{j=1}^{n} c_j x_j$$

is replaced by

$$Z(\theta) = \sum_{j=1}^{n} (c_j + \alpha_j \theta) x_j,$$

where the α_j are given input constants representing the *relative* rates at which the coefficients are to be changed. Therefore, gradually increasing θ from zero changes the coefficients at these relative rates.

The values assigned to the α_j may represent interesting simultaneous changes of the c_j for systematic sensitivity analysis of the effect of increasing the magnitude of these changes. They may also be based on how the coefficients (e.g., unit profits) would change together with respect to some factor measured by θ. This factor might be uncontrollable, e.g., the state of the economy. However, it may also be under the control of the decision maker, e.g., the amount of personnel and equipment to shift from some of the activities to others.

For any given value of θ, the optimal solution of the corresponding linear programming problem can be obtained by the simplex method. This solution may have been obtained already for the original problem where $\theta = 0$. However, the objective is to *find the optimal solution* of the modified linear programming problem [maximize $Z(\theta)$ subject to the original constraints] *as a function of θ*. Therefore, in the solution procedure you need to be able to determine when and how the optimal solution changes (if it does) as θ increases from zero to any specified positive number.

Figure 7.1 illustrates how $Z^*(\theta)$, the objective function value for the optimal solution (given θ), changes as θ increases. In fact, $Z^*(\theta)$ always has this *piecewise linear* and *con-*

FIGURE 7.1
The objective function value for an optimal solution as a function of θ for parametric linear programming with systematic changes in the c_j parameters.

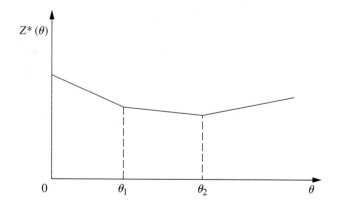

vex[1] form (see Prob. 7.2-7). The corresponding optimal solution changes (as θ increases) *just* at the values of θ where the slope of the $Z^*(\theta)$ function changes. Thus, Fig. 7.1 depicts a problem where three different solutions are optimal for different values of θ, the first for $0 \leq \theta \leq \theta_1$, the second for $\theta_1 \leq \theta \leq \theta_2$, and the third for $\theta \geq \theta_2$. Because the value of each x_j remains the same within each of these intervals for θ, the value of $Z^*(\theta)$ varies with θ only because the *coefficients* of the x_j are changing as a linear function of θ. The solution procedure is based directly upon the sensitivity analysis procedure for investigating changes in the c_j parameters (Cases 2a and 3, Sec. 6.7). As described in the last subsection of Sec. 6.7, the only basic difference with parametric linear programming is that the changes now are expressed in terms of θ rather than as specific numbers.

To illustrate, suppose that $\alpha_1 = 2$ and $\alpha_2 = -1$ for the original Wyndor Glass Co. problem presented in Sec. 3.1, so that

$$Z(\theta) = (3 + 2\theta)x_1 + (5 - \theta)x_2.$$

Beginning with the final simplex tableau for $\theta = 0$ (Table 4.8), we see that its Eq. (0)

$$(0) \quad Z + \frac{3}{2}x_4 + x_5 = 36$$

would first have these changes from the original ($\theta = 0$) coefficients added into it on the left-hand side:

$$(0) \quad Z - 2\theta x_1 + \theta x_2 + \frac{3}{2}x_4 + x_5 = 36.$$

Because both x_1 and x_2 are basic variables [appearing in Eqs. (3) and (2), respectively], they both need to be eliminated algebraically from Eq. (0):

$$Z - 2\theta x_1 + \theta x_2 + \frac{3}{2}x_4 + x_5 = 36$$
$$+ \ 2\theta \text{ times Eq. (3)}$$
$$- \ \ \theta \text{ times Eq. (2)}$$
$$\overline{}$$

$$(0) \quad Z + \left(\frac{3}{2} - \frac{7}{6}\theta\right)x_4 + \left(1 + \frac{2}{3}\theta\right)x_5 = 36 - 2\theta.$$

The optimality test says that the current BF solution will remain optimal as long as these coefficients of the nonbasic variables remain nonnegative:

$$\frac{3}{2} - \frac{7}{6}\theta \geq 0, \quad \text{for } 0 \leq \theta \leq \frac{9}{7},$$

$$1 + \frac{2}{3}\theta \geq 0, \quad \text{for all } \theta \geq 0.$$

Therefore, after θ is increased past $\theta = \frac{9}{7}$, x_4 would need to be the entering basic variable for another iteration of the simplex method to find the new optimal solution. Then θ would be increased further until another coefficient goes negative, and so on until θ has been increased as far as desired.

This entire procedure is now summarized, and the example is completed in Table 7.2.

---

[1]See Appendix 2 for a definition and discussion of convex functions.

TABLE 7.2 The c_j parametric linear programming procedure applied to the Wyndor Glass Co. example

Range of θ	Basic Variable	Eq.	Z	x_1	x_2	x_3	x_4	x_5	Right Side	Optimal Solution
	$Z(\theta)$	(0)	1	0	0	0	$\dfrac{9-7\theta}{6}$	$\dfrac{3+2\theta}{3}$	$36-2\theta$	$x_4 = 0$
										$x_5 = 0$
$0 \le \theta \le \dfrac{9}{7}$	x_3	(1)	0	0	0	1	$\dfrac{1}{3}$	$-\dfrac{1}{3}$	2	$x_3 = 2$
	x_2	(2)	0	0	1	0	$\dfrac{1}{2}$	0	6	$x_2 = 6$
	x_1	(3)	0	1	0	0	$-\dfrac{1}{3}$	$\dfrac{1}{3}$	2	$x_1 = 2$
	$Z(\theta)$	(0)	1	0	0	$\dfrac{-9+7\theta}{2}$	0	$\dfrac{5-\theta}{2}$	$27+5\theta$	$x_3 = 0$
										$x_5 = 0$
$\dfrac{9}{7} \le \theta \le 5$	x_4	(1)	0	0	0	3	1	-1	6	$x_4 = 6$
	x_2	(2)	0	0	1	$-\dfrac{3}{2}$	0	$\dfrac{1}{2}$	3	$x_2 = 3$
	x_1	(3)	0	1	0	1	0	0	4	$x_1 = 4$
	$Z(\theta)$	(0)	1	0	$-5+\theta$	$3+2\theta$	0	0	$12+8\theta$	$x_2 = 0$
										$x_3 = 0$
$\theta \ge 5$	x_4	(1)	0	0	2	0	1	0	12	$x_4 = 12$
	x_5	(2)	0	0	2	-3	0	1	6	$x_5 = 6$
	x_1	(3)	0	1	0	1	0	0	4	$x_1 = 4$

Summary of the Parametric Linear Programming Procedure for Systematic Changes in the c_j Parameters.

1. Solve the problem with $\theta = 0$ by the simplex method.
2. Use the sensitivity analysis procedure (Cases 2a and 3, Sec. 6.7) to introduce the $\Delta c_j = \alpha_j \theta$ changes into Eq. (0).
3. Increase θ until one of the nonbasic variables has its coefficient in Eq. (0) go negative (or until θ has been increased as far as desired).
4. Use this variable as the entering basic variable for an iteration of the simplex method to find the new optimal solution. Return to step 3.

Systematic Changes in the b_i Parameters

For the case where the b_i parameters change systematically, the one modification made in the original linear programming model is that b_i is replaced by $b_i + \alpha_i \theta$, for $i = 1, 2, \ldots, m$, where the α_i are given input constants. Thus, the problem becomes

$$\text{Maximize} \qquad Z(\theta) = \sum_{j=1}^{n} c_j x_j,$$

subject to

$$\sum_{j=1}^{n} a_{ij}x_j \le b_i + \alpha_i\theta \qquad \text{for } i = 1, 2, \ldots, m$$

and

$$x_j \ge 0 \qquad \text{for } j = 1, 2, \ldots, n.$$

The goal is to identify the optimal solution as a function of θ.

With this formulation, the corresponding objective function value $Z^*(\theta)$ always has the *piecewise linear* and *concave*[1] form shown in Fig. 7.2. (See Prob. 7.2-8.) The set of basic variables in the optimal solution still changes (as θ increases) *only* where the slope of $Z^*(\theta)$ changes. However, in contrast to the preceding case, the values of these variables now change as a (linear) function of θ between the slope changes. The reason is that increasing θ changes the right-hand sides in the initial set of equations, which then causes changes in the right-hand sides in the final set of equations, i.e., in the values of the final set of basic variables. Figure 7.2 depicts a problem with three sets of basic variables that are optimal for different values of θ, the first for $0 \le \theta \le \theta_1$, the second for $\theta_1 \le \theta \le \theta_2$, and the third for $\theta \ge \theta_2$. Within each of these intervals of θ, the value of $Z^*(\theta)$ varies with θ despite the fixed coefficients c_j because the x_j values are changing.

The following solution procedure summary is very similar to that just presented for systematic changes in the c_j parameters. The reason is that changing the b_i values is equivalent to changing the coefficients in the objective function of the *dual* model. Therefore, the procedure for the primal problem is exactly *complementary* to applying simultaneously the procedure for systematic changes in the c_j parameters to the *dual* problem. Consequently, the *dual simplex method* (see Sec. 7.1) now would be used to obtain each new optimal solution, and the applicable sensitivity analysis case (see Sec. 6.7) now is Case 1, but these differences are the only major differences.

---

[1]See Appendix 2 for a definition and discussion of concave functions.

FIGURE 7.2
The objective function value for an optimal solution as a function of θ for parametric linear programming with systematic changes in the b_i parameters.

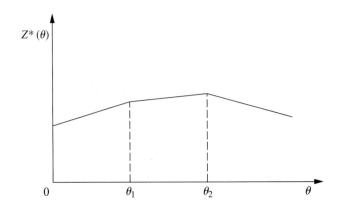

Summary of the Parametric Linear Programming Procedure for Systematic Changes in the b_i Parameters.

1. Solve the problem with $\theta = 0$ by the simplex method.
2. Use the sensitivity analysis procedure (Case 1, Sec. 6.7) to introduce the $\Delta b_i = \alpha_i \theta$ changes to the *right side* column.
3. Increase θ until one of the basic variables has its value in the *right side* column go negative (or until θ has been increased as far as desired).
4. Use this variable as the leaving basic variable for an iteration of the dual simplex method to find the new optimal solution. Return to step 3.

To illustrate this procedure in a way that demonstrates its *duality* relationship with the procedure for systematic changes in the c_j parameters, we now apply it to the dual problem for the Wyndor Glass Co. (see Table 6.1). In particular, suppose that $\alpha_1 = 2$ and $\alpha_2 = -1$ so that the functional constraints become

$$
\begin{aligned}
y_1 \quad + 3y_3 &\geq 3 + 2\theta \quad &\text{or} \quad &-y_1 \quad - 3y_3 \leq -3 - 2\theta \\
2y_2 + 2y_3 &\geq 5 - \theta \quad &\text{or} \quad &-2y_2 - 2y_3 \leq -5 + \theta.
\end{aligned}
$$

Thus, the dual of *this* problem is just the example considered in Table 7.2.

This problem with $\theta = 0$ has already been solved in Table 7.1, so we begin with the final simplex tableau given there. Using the sensitivity analysis procedure for Case 1, Sec. 6.7, we find that the entries in the *right side* column of the tableau change to the values given below.

$$
Z^* = \mathbf{y^*\bar{b}} = [2, 6] \begin{bmatrix} -3 - 2\theta \\ -5 + \theta \end{bmatrix} = -36 + 2\theta,
$$

$$
\mathbf{b^*} = \mathbf{S^*\bar{b}} = \begin{bmatrix} -\dfrac{1}{3} & 0 \\ \dfrac{1}{3} & -\dfrac{1}{2} \end{bmatrix} \begin{bmatrix} -3 - 2\theta \\ -5 + \theta \end{bmatrix} = \begin{bmatrix} 1 + \dfrac{2\theta}{3} \\ \dfrac{3}{2} - \dfrac{7\theta}{6} \end{bmatrix}.
$$

Therefore, the two basic variables in this tableau

$$
y_3 = \frac{3 + 2\theta}{3} \quad \text{and} \quad y_2 = \frac{9 - 7\theta}{6}
$$

remain nonnegative for $0 \leq \theta \leq \frac{9}{7}$. Increasing θ past $\theta = \frac{9}{7}$ requires making y_2 a leaving basic variable for another iteration of the dual simplex method, and so on, as summarized in Table 7.3.

We suggest that you now trace through Tables 7.2 and 7.3 simultaneously to note the duality relationship between the two procedures.

7.3 THE UPPER BOUND TECHNIQUE

It is fairly common in linear programming problems for some of or all the *individual* x_j variables to have *upper bound constraints*

$$
x_j \leq u_j,
$$

where u_j is a positive constant representing the maximum *feasible* value of x_j. We pointed out in Sec. 4.8 that the most important determinant of computation time for the simplex

TABLE 7.3 The b_i parametric linear programming procedure applied to the dual of the Wyndor Glass Co. example

Range of θ	Basic Variable	Eq.	Z	y_1	y_2	y_3	y_4	y_5	Right Side	Optimal Solution
$0 \leq \theta \leq \frac{9}{7}$	$Z(\theta)$	(0)	1	2	0	0	2	6	$-36 + 2\theta$	$y_1 = y_4 = y_5 = 0$
	y_3	(1)	0	$\frac{1}{3}$	0	1	$-\frac{1}{3}$	0	$\frac{3 + 2\theta}{3}$	$y_3 = \frac{3 + 2\theta}{3}$
	y_2	(2)	0	$-\frac{1}{3}$	1	0	$\frac{1}{3}$	$-\frac{1}{2}$	$\frac{9 - 7\theta}{6}$	$y_2 = \frac{9 - 7\theta}{6}$
$\frac{9}{7} \leq \theta \leq 5$	$Z(\theta)$	(0)	1	0	6	0	4	3	$-27 - 5\theta$	$y_2 = y_4 = y_5 = 0$
	y_3	(1)	0	0	1	1	0	$-\frac{1}{2}$	$\frac{5 - \theta}{2}$	$y_3 = \frac{5 - \theta}{2}$
	y_1	(2)	0	1	-3	0	-1	$\frac{3}{2}$	$\frac{-9 + 7\theta}{2}$	$y_1 = \frac{-9 + 7\theta}{2}$
$\theta \geq 5$	$Z(\theta)$	(0)	1	0	12	6	4	0	$-12 - 8\theta$	$y_2 = y_3 = y_4 = 0$
	y_5	(1)	0	0	-2	-2	0	1	$-5 + \theta$	$y_5 = -5 + \theta$
	y_1	(2)	0	1	0	3	-1	0	$3 + 2\theta$	$y_1 = 3 + 2\theta$

method is the *number of functional constraints,* whereas the number of *nonnegativity* constraints is relatively unimportant. Therefore, having a large number of upper bound constraints among the functional constraints greatly increases the computational effort required.

The *upper bound technique* avoids this increased effort by removing the upper bound constraints from the functional constraints and treating them separately, essentially like nonnegativity constraints. Removing the upper bound constraints in this way causes no problems as long as none of the variables gets increased over its upper bound. The only time the simplex method increases some of the variables is when the entering basic variable is increased to obtain a new BF solution. Therefore, the upper bound technique simply applies the simplex method in the usual way to the *remainder* of the problem (i.e., without the upper bound constraints) but with the one additional restriction that each new BF solution must satisfy the upper bound constraints in addition to the usual lower bound (nonnegativity) constraints.

To implement this idea, note that a decision variable x_j with an upper bound constraint $x_j \leq u_j$ can always be replaced by

$$x_j = u_j - y_j,$$

where y_j would then be the decision variable. In other words, you have a choice between letting the decision variable be the *amount above zero* (x_j) or the *amount below* u_j ($y_j = u_j - x_j$). (We shall refer to x_j and y_j as *complementary* decision variables.) Because

$$0 \leq x_j \leq u_j$$

it also follows that

$$0 \leq y_j \leq u_j.$$

Thus, at any point during the simplex method, you can either

  1. Use x_j, where $0 \leq x_j \leq u_j$,
or **2.** Replace x_j by $u_j - y_j$, where $0 \leq y_j \leq u_j$.

The upper bound technique uses the following rule to make this choice:

Rule: Begin with choice 1.
Whenever $x_j = 0$, use choice 1, so x_j is *nonbasic*.
Whenever $x_j = u_j$, use choice 2, so $y_j = 0$ is *nonbasic*.
Switch choices only when the other extreme value of x_j is reached.

Therefore, whenever a basic variable reaches its upper bound, you should switch choices and use its complementary decision variable as the new nonbasic variable (the leaving basic variable) for identifying the new BF solution. Thus, the one substantive modification being made in the simplex method is in the rule for selecting the leaving basic variable.

  Recall that the simplex method selects as the leaving basic variable the one that would be the first to become infeasible by going negative as the entering basic variable is increased. The modification now made is to select instead the variable that would be the first to become infeasible *in any way,* either by going negative or by going over the upper bound, as the entering basic variable is increased. (Notice that one possibility is that the entering basic variable may become infeasible first by going over its upper bound, so that its complementary decision variable becomes the leaving basic variable.) If the leaving basic variable reaches zero, then proceed as usual with the simplex method. However, if it reaches its upper bound instead, then switch choices and make its complementary decision variable the leaving basic variable.

  To illustrate, consider this problem:

  Maximize $Z = 2x_1 + x_2 + 2x_3$,

subject to

$$4x_1 + x_2 \qquad = 12$$
$$-2x_1 \qquad + x_3 = \quad 4$$

and

$$0 \leq x_1 \leq 4, \qquad 0 \leq x_2 \leq 15, \qquad 0 \leq x_3 \leq 6.$$

Thus, all three variables have upper bound constraints ($u_1 = 4$, $u_2 = 15$, $u_3 = 6$).

  The two equality constraints are already in proper form from Gaussian elimination for identifying the initial BF solution ($x_1 = 0$, $x_2 = 12$, $x_3 = 4$), and none of the variables in this solution exceeds its upper bound, so x_2 and x_3 can be used as the initial basic variables without artificial variables being introduced. However, these variables then need to be eliminated algebraically from the objective function to obtain the initial Eq. (0), as follows:

$$
\begin{array}{llll}
Z & - \ 2x_1 - x_2 - 2x_3 = & 0 \\
  & + \ (4x_1 + x_2 \qquad = & 12) \\
  & \underline{+ \ 2(- \ 2x_1 \qquad + \ x_3 = \quad 4)} \\
\text{(0)} \quad Z & - \ 2x_1 \qquad\qquad\quad = & 20.
\end{array}
$$

TABLE 7.4 Equations and calculations for the initial leaving basic variable in the example for the upper bound technique

Initial Set of Equations	Maximum Feasible Value of x_1
(0) $Z - 2x_1 \qquad = 20$	$x_1 \leq 4 \quad$ (since $u_1 = 4$)
(1) $\quad 4x_1 + x_2 \quad = 12$	$x_1 \leq \dfrac{12}{4} = 3$
(2) $\quad -2x_1 \qquad + x_3 = 4$	$x_1 \leq \dfrac{6-4}{2} = 1 \leftarrow$ minimum (because $u_3 = 6$)

To start the first iteration, this initial Eq. (0) indicates that the initial *entering* basic variable is x_1. Since the upper bound constraints are not to be included, the entire initial set of equations and the corresponding calculations for selecting the leaving basic variables are those shown in Table 7.4. The second column shows how much the entering basic variable x_1 can be *increased* from zero before some basic variable (including x_1) becomes infeasible. The maximum value given next to Eq. (0) is just the upper bound constraint for x_1. For Eq. (1), since the coefficient of x_1 is *positive, increasing* x_1 to 3 decreases the basic variable in this equation (x_2) from 12 to its *lower* bound of *zero*. For Eq. (2), since the coefficient of x_1 is *negative, increasing* x_1 to 1 *increases* the basic variable in this equation (x_3) from 4 to its *upper bound* of 6.

Because Eq. (2) has the *smallest* maximum feasible value of x_1 in Table 7.4, the basic variable in this equation (x_3) provides the *leaving* basic variable. However, because x_3 reached its *upper* bound, replace x_3 by $6 - y_3$, so that $y_3 = 0$ becomes the new nonbasic variable for the next BF solution and x_1 becomes the new basic variable in Eq. (2). This replacement leads to the following changes in this equation:

$$
\begin{aligned}
(2) \qquad & -2x_1 + x_3 && = && 4 \\
\rightarrow \quad & -2x_1 + 6 - y_3 && = && 4 \\
\rightarrow \quad & -2x_1 - \quad y_3 && = && -2 \\
\rightarrow \quad & x_1 + \tfrac{1}{2}y_3 && = && 1
\end{aligned}
$$

Therefore, after we eliminate x_1 algebraically from the other equations, the *second* complete set of equations becomes

$$
\begin{aligned}
(0) \quad & Z \quad + \quad y_3 = 22 \\
(1) \quad & x_2 - 2y_3 = 8 \\
(2) \quad & x_1 + \tfrac{1}{2}y_3 = 1.
\end{aligned}
$$

The resulting BF solution is $x_1 = 1$, $x_2 = 8$, $y_3 = 0$. By the optimality test, it also is an optimal solution, so $x_1 = 1$, $x_2 = 8$, $x_3 = 6 - y_3 = 6$ is the desired solution for the original problem.

7.4 AN INTERIOR-POINT ALGORITHM

In Sec. 4.9 we discussed a dramatic development in linear programming that occurred in 1984, the invention by Narendra Karmarkar of AT&T Bell Laboratories of a powerful algorithm for solving huge linear programming problems with an approach very different from the simplex method. We now introduce the nature of Karmarkar's approach by describing a relatively elementary variant (the "affine" or "affine-scaling" variant) of his algorithm.[1] (Your OR Courseware also includes this variant under the title, *Solve Automatically by the Interior-Point Algorithm.*)

Throughout this section we shall focus on Karmarkar's main ideas on an intuitive level while avoiding mathematical details. In particular, we shall bypass certain details that are needed for the full implementation of the algorithm (e.g., how to find an initial feasible trial solution) but are not central to a basic conceptual understanding. The ideas to be described can be summarized as follows:

Concept 1: Shoot through the *interior* of the feasible region toward an optimal solution.
Concept 2: Move in a direction that improves the objective function value at the fastest possible rate.
Concept 3: Transform the feasible region to place the current trial solution near its center, thereby enabling a large improvement when concept 2 is implemented.

To illustrate these ideas throughout the section, we shall use the following example:

$$\text{Maximize} \quad Z = x_1 + 2x_2,$$

subject to

$$x_1 + x_2 \leq 8$$

and

$$x_1 \geq 0, \quad x_2 \geq 0.$$

This problem is depicted graphically in Fig. 7.3, where the optimal solution is seen to be $(x_1, x_2) = (0, 8)$ with $Z = 16$.

The Relevance of the Gradient for Concepts 1 and 2

The algorithm begins with an initial trial solution that (like all subsequent trial solutions) lies in the *interior* of the feasible region, i.e., *inside the boundary* of the feasible region. Thus, for the example, the solution must not lie on any of the three lines ($x_1 = 0$, $x_2 = 0$, $x_1 + x_2 = 8$) that form the boundary of this region in Fig. 7.3. (A trial solution that lies on the boundary cannot be used because this would lead to the undefined mathematical operation of division by zero at one point in the algorithm.) We have arbitrarily chosen $(x_1, x_2) = (2, 2)$ to be the initial trial solution.

To begin implementing concepts 1 and 2, note in Fig. 7.3 that the direction of movement from (2, 2) that increases Z at the fastest possible rate is *perpendicular* to (and toward) the objective function line $Z = 16 = x_1 + 2x_2$. We have shown this direction by the arrow from (2, 2) to (3, 4). Using vector addition, we have

$$(3, 4) = (2, 2) + (1, 2),$$

---

[1]The basic approach for this variant actually was proposed in 1967 by a Russian mathematician I. I. Dikin and then rediscovered soon after the appearance of Karmarkar's work by a number of researchers, including E. R. Barnes, T. M. Cavalier, and A. L. Soyster. Also see R. J. Vanderbei, M. S. Meketon, and B. A. Freedman, "A Modification of Karmarkar's Linear Programming Algorithm," *Algorithmica*, **1**(4) (Special Issue on New Approaches to Linear Programming): 395–407, 1986.

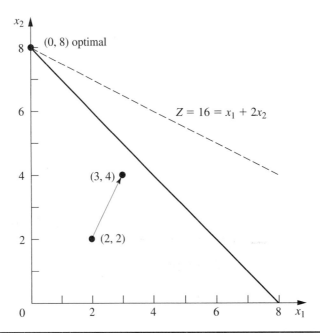

FIGURE 7.3
Example for the interior-point algorithm.

where the vector $(1, 2)$ is the **gradient** of the objective function. (We will discuss gradients further in Sec. 13.5 in the broader context of *nonlinear programming,* where algorithms similar to Karmarkar's have long been used.) The components of $(1, 2)$ are just the coefficients in the objective function. Thus, with one subsequent modification, the gradient $(1, 2)$ defines the ideal direction to which to move, where the question of the *distance to move* will be considered later.

The algorithm actually operates on linear programming problems after they have been rewritten in augmented form. Letting x_3 be the slack variable for the functional constraint of the example, we see that this form is

Maximize $Z = x_1 + 2x_2,$

subject to

$x_1 + x_2 + x_3 = 8$

and

$x_1 \geq 0, \qquad x_2 \geq 0, \qquad x_3 \geq 0.$

In matrix notation (slightly different from Chap. 5 because the slack variable now is incorporated into the notation), the augmented form can be written in general as

Maximize $Z = \mathbf{c}^T\mathbf{x},$

subject to

$\mathbf{Ax} = \mathbf{b}$

and

$$\mathbf{x} \geq \mathbf{0},$$

where

$$\mathbf{c} = \begin{bmatrix} 1 \\ 2 \\ 0 \end{bmatrix}, \qquad \mathbf{x} = \begin{bmatrix} x_1 \\ x_2 \\ x_3 \end{bmatrix}, \qquad \mathbf{A} = [1, \quad 1, \quad 1], \qquad \mathbf{b} = [8], \qquad \mathbf{0} = \begin{bmatrix} 0 \\ 0 \\ 0 \end{bmatrix}$$

for the example. Note that $\mathbf{c}^T = [1, 2, 0]$ now is the gradient of the objective function.

The augmented form of the example is depicted graphically in Fig. 7.4. The feasible region now consists of the triangle with vertices $(8, 0, 0)$, $(0, 8, 0)$, and $(0, 0, 8)$. Points in the interior of this feasible region are those where $x_1 > 0$, $x_2 > 0$, and $x_3 > 0$. Each of these three $x_j > 0$ conditions has the effect of forcing (x_1, x_2) away from one of the three lines forming the boundary of the feasible region in Fig. 7.3.

Using the Projected Gradient to Implement Concepts 1 and 2

In augmented form, the initial trial solution for the example is $(x_1, x_2, x_3) = (2, 2, 4)$. Adding the gradient $(1, 2, 0)$ leads to

$$(3, 4, 4) = (2, 2, 4) + (1, 2, 0).$$

However, now there is a complication. The algorithm cannot move from $(2, 2, 4)$ toward $(3, 4, 4)$, because $(3, 4, 4)$ is infeasible! When $x_1 = 3$ and $x_2 = 4$, then $x_3 = 8 - x_1 - x_2 = 1$ instead of 4. The point $(3, 4, 4)$ lies on the near side as you look down on the feasible triangle in Fig. 7.4. Therefore, to remain feasible, the algorithm (indirectly) *projects* the point $(3, 4, 4)$ down onto the feasible triangle by dropping a line that is *perpendicular* to this triangle. A vector from $(0, 0, 0)$ to $(1, 1, 1)$ is perpendicular to this triangle, so the perpendicular line through $(3, 4, 4)$ is given by the equation

$$(x_1, x_2, x_3) = (3, 4, 4) - \theta(1, 1, 1),$$

where θ is a scalar. Since the triangle satisfies the equation $x_1 + x_2 + x_3 = 8$, this perpendicular line intersects the triangle at $(2, 3, 3)$. Because

$$(2, 3, 3) = (2, 2, 4) + (0, 1, -1),$$

the **projected gradient** of the objective function (the gradient projected onto the feasible region) is $(0, 1, -1)$. It is this projected gradient that defines the direction of movement for the algorithm, as shown by the arrow in Fig. 7.4.

A formula is available for computing the projected gradient directly. By defining the *projection matrix* $\mathbf{P}$ as

$$\mathbf{P} = \mathbf{I} - \mathbf{A}^T(\mathbf{A}\mathbf{A}^T)^{-1}\mathbf{A},$$

the *projected gradient* (in column form) is

$$\mathbf{c}_p = \mathbf{P}\mathbf{c}.$$

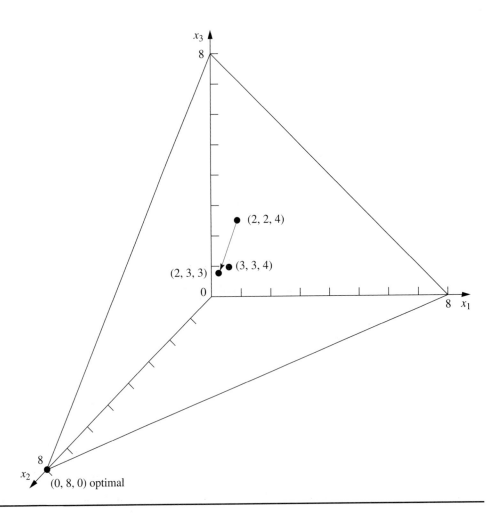

FIGURE 7.4
Example in augmented form for the interior-point algorithm.

Thus, for the example,

$$\mathbf{P} = \begin{bmatrix} 1 & 0 & 0 \\ 0 & 1 & 0 \\ 0 & 0 & 1 \end{bmatrix} - \begin{bmatrix} 1 \\ 1 \\ 1 \end{bmatrix} \left(\begin{bmatrix} 1 & 1 & 1 \end{bmatrix} \begin{bmatrix} 1 \\ 1 \\ 1 \end{bmatrix} \right)^{-1} \begin{bmatrix} 1 & 1 & 1 \end{bmatrix}$$

$$= \begin{bmatrix} 1 & 0 & 0 \\ 0 & 1 & 0 \\ 0 & 0 & 1 \end{bmatrix} - \frac{1}{3} \begin{bmatrix} 1 \\ 1 \\ 1 \end{bmatrix} \begin{bmatrix} 1 & 1 & 1 \end{bmatrix}$$

$$= \begin{bmatrix} 1 & 0 & 0 \\ 0 & 1 & 0 \\ 0 & 0 & 1 \end{bmatrix} - \frac{1}{3} \begin{bmatrix} 1 & 1 & 1 \\ 1 & 1 & 1 \\ 1 & 1 & 1 \end{bmatrix} = \begin{bmatrix} \frac{2}{3} & -\frac{1}{3} & -\frac{1}{3} \\ -\frac{1}{3} & \frac{2}{3} & -\frac{1}{3} \\ -\frac{1}{3} & -\frac{1}{3} & \frac{2}{3} \end{bmatrix},$$

so

$$
\mathbf{c}_p = \begin{bmatrix} \frac{2}{3} & -\frac{1}{3} & -\frac{1}{3} \\ -\frac{1}{3} & \frac{2}{3} & -\frac{1}{3} \\ -\frac{1}{3} & -\frac{1}{3} & \frac{2}{3} \end{bmatrix} \begin{bmatrix} 1 \\ 2 \\ 0 \end{bmatrix} = \begin{bmatrix} 0 \\ 1 \\ -1 \end{bmatrix}.
$$

Moving from (2, 2, 4) in the direction of the projected gradient (0, 1, −1) involves increasing α from zero in the formula

$$
\mathbf{x} = \begin{bmatrix} 2 \\ 2 \\ 4 \end{bmatrix} + 4\alpha\mathbf{c}_p = \begin{bmatrix} 2 \\ 2 \\ 4 \end{bmatrix} + 4\alpha \begin{bmatrix} 0 \\ 1 \\ -1 \end{bmatrix},
$$

where the coefficient 4 is used simply to give an upper bound of 1 for α to maintain feasibility (all $x_j \geq 0$). Note that increasing α to $\alpha = 1$ would cause x_3 to decrease to $x_3 = 4 + 4(1)(-1) = 0$, where $\alpha > 1$ yields $x_3 < 0$. Thus, α measures the fraction used of the distance that could be moved before the feasible region is left.

How large should α be made for moving to the next trial solution? Because the increase in Z is proportional to α, a value close to the upper bound of 1 is good for giving a relatively large step toward optimality on the current iteration. However, the problem with a value too close to 1 is that the next trial solution then is jammed against a constraint boundary, thereby making it difficult to take large improving steps during subsequent iterations. Therefore, it is very helpful for trial solutions to be near the center of the feasible region (or at least near the center of the portion of the feasible region in the vicinity of an optimal solution), and not too close to any constraint boundary. With this in mind, Karmarkar has stated for his algorithm that a value as large as $\alpha = 0.25$ should be "safe." In practice, much larger values (for example, $\alpha = 0.9$) sometimes are used. For the purposes of this example (and the problems at the end of the chapter), we have chosen $\alpha = 0.5$. (Your OR Courseware uses $\alpha = 0.5$ as the default value, but also has $\alpha = 0.9$ available.)

A Centering Scheme for Implementing Concept 3

We now have just one more step to complete the description of the algorithm, namely, a special scheme for transforming the feasible region to place the current trial solution near its center. We have just described the benefit of having the trial solution near the center, but another important benefit of this centering scheme is that it keeps turning the direction of the projected gradient to point more nearly toward an optimal solution as the algorithm converges toward this solution.

The basic idea of the centering scheme is straightforward—simply change the scale (units) for each of the variables so that the trial solution becomes equidistant from the constraint boundaries in the new coordinate system. (Karmarkar's original algorithm uses a more sophisticated centering scheme.)

For the example, there are three constraint boundaries in Fig. 7.3, each one corresponding to a zero value for one of the three variables of the problem in augmented form, namely, $x_1 = 0$, $x_2 = 0$, and $x_3 = 0$. In Fig. 7.4, see how these three constraint boundaries intersect the $\mathbf{Ax} = \mathbf{b}$ ($x_1 + x_2 + x_3 = 8$) plane to form the boundary of the feasible region. The initial trial solution is $(x_1, x_2, x_3) = (2, 2, 4)$, so this solution is 2 units away from the $x_1 = 0$ and $x_2 = 0$ constraint boundaries and 4 units away from the $x_3 = 0$ constraint boundary, when the units of the respective variables are used. However, whatever these units are in each case, they are quite arbitrary and can be changed as desired without changing the problem. Therefore, let us rescale the variables as follows:

$$\tilde{x}_1 = \frac{x_1}{2}, \qquad \tilde{x}_2 = \frac{x_2}{2}, \qquad \tilde{x}_3 = \frac{x_3}{4}$$

in order to make the current trial solution of $(x_1, x_2, x_3) = (2, 2, 4)$ become

$$(\tilde{x}_1, \tilde{x}_2, \tilde{x}_3) = (1, 1, 1).$$

In these new coordinates (substituting $2\tilde{x}_1$ for x_1, $2\tilde{x}_2$ for x_2, and $4\tilde{x}_3$ for x_3), the problem becomes

$$\text{Maximize} \qquad Z = 2\tilde{x}_1 + 4\tilde{x}_2,$$

subject to

$$2\tilde{x}_1 + 2\tilde{x}_2 + 4\tilde{x}_3 = 8$$

and

$$\tilde{x}_1 \geq 0, \qquad \tilde{x}_2 \geq 0, \qquad \tilde{x}_3 \geq 0,$$

as depicted graphically in Fig. 7.5.

Note that the trial solution $(1, 1, 1)$ in Fig. 7.5 is equidistant from the three constraint boundaries $\tilde{x}_1 = 0$, $\tilde{x}_2 = 0$, $\tilde{x}_3 = 0$. For each subsequent iteration as well, the problem is rescaled again to achieve this same property, so that the current trial solution always is $(1, 1, 1)$ in the current coordinates.

FIGURE 7.5
Example after rescaling for iteration 1.

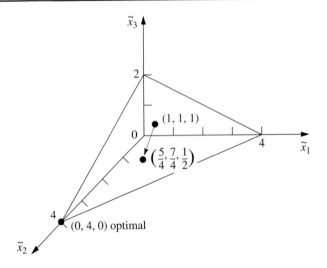

Summary and Illustration of the Algorithm

Now let us summarize and illustrate the algorithm by going through the first iteration for the example, then giving a summary of the general procedure, and finally applying this summary to a second iteration.

Iteration 1. Given the initial trial solution $(x_1, x_2, x_3) = (2, 2, 4)$, let $\mathbf{D}$ be the corresponding *diagonal matrix* such that $\mathbf{x} = \mathbf{D\tilde{x}}$, so that

$$\mathbf{D} = \begin{bmatrix} 2 & 0 & 0 \\ 0 & 2 & 0 \\ 0 & 0 & 4 \end{bmatrix}.$$

The rescaled variables then are the components of

$$\tilde{\mathbf{x}} = \mathbf{D}^{-1}\mathbf{x} = \begin{bmatrix} \frac{1}{2} & 0 & 0 \\ 0 & \frac{1}{2} & 0 \\ 0 & 0 & \frac{1}{4} \end{bmatrix} \begin{bmatrix} x_1 \\ x_2 \\ x_3 \end{bmatrix} = \begin{bmatrix} \frac{x_1}{2} \\ \frac{x_2}{2} \\ \frac{x_3}{4} \end{bmatrix}.$$

In these new coordinates, $\mathbf{A}$ and $\mathbf{c}$ have become

$$\tilde{\mathbf{A}} = \mathbf{AD} = \begin{bmatrix} 1 & 1 & 1 \end{bmatrix} \begin{bmatrix} 2 & 0 & 0 \\ 0 & 2 & 0 \\ 0 & 0 & 4 \end{bmatrix} = \begin{bmatrix} 2 & 2 & 4 \end{bmatrix},$$

$$\tilde{\mathbf{c}} = \mathbf{Dc} = \begin{bmatrix} 2 & 0 & 0 \\ 0 & 2 & 0 \\ 0 & 0 & 4 \end{bmatrix} \begin{bmatrix} 1 \\ 2 \\ 0 \end{bmatrix} = \begin{bmatrix} 2 \\ 4 \\ 0 \end{bmatrix}.$$

Therefore, the projection matrix is

$$\mathbf{P} = \mathbf{I} - \tilde{\mathbf{A}}^T(\tilde{\mathbf{A}}\tilde{\mathbf{A}}^T)^{-1}\tilde{\mathbf{A}}$$

$$= \begin{bmatrix} 1 & 0 & 0 \\ 0 & 1 & 0 \\ 0 & 0 & 1 \end{bmatrix} - \begin{bmatrix} 2 \\ 2 \\ 4 \end{bmatrix} \left(\begin{bmatrix} 2 & 2 & 4 \end{bmatrix} \begin{bmatrix} 2 \\ 2 \\ 4 \end{bmatrix} \right)^{-1} \begin{bmatrix} 2 & 2 & 4 \end{bmatrix}$$

$$= \begin{bmatrix} 1 & 0 & 0 \\ 0 & 1 & 0 \\ 0 & 0 & 1 \end{bmatrix} - \frac{1}{24}\begin{bmatrix} 4 & 4 & 8 \\ 4 & 4 & 8 \\ 8 & 8 & 16 \end{bmatrix} = \begin{bmatrix} \frac{5}{6} & -\frac{1}{6} & -\frac{1}{3} \\ -\frac{1}{6} & \frac{5}{6} & -\frac{1}{3} \\ -\frac{1}{3} & -\frac{1}{3} & \frac{1}{3} \end{bmatrix},$$

so that the projected gradient is

$$\mathbf{c}_p = \mathbf{P\tilde{c}} = \begin{bmatrix} \frac{5}{6} & -\frac{1}{6} & -\frac{1}{3} \\ -\frac{1}{6} & \frac{5}{6} & -\frac{1}{3} \\ -\frac{1}{3} & -\frac{1}{3} & \frac{1}{3} \end{bmatrix} \begin{bmatrix} 2 \\ 4 \\ 0 \end{bmatrix} = \begin{bmatrix} 1 \\ 3 \\ -2 \end{bmatrix}.$$

Define v as the *absolute value* of the *negative* component of $\mathbf{c}_p$ having the *largest* absolute value, so that $v = |-2| = 2$ in this case. Consequently, in the current coordinates, the algorithm now moves from the current trial solution $(\tilde{x}_1, \tilde{x}_2, \tilde{x}_3) = (1, 1, 1)$ to the next trial solution

$$\tilde{\mathbf{x}} = \begin{bmatrix} 1 \\ 1 \\ 1 \end{bmatrix} + \frac{\alpha}{v}\mathbf{c}_p = \begin{bmatrix} 1 \\ 1 \\ 1 \end{bmatrix} + \frac{0.5}{2}\begin{bmatrix} 1 \\ 3 \\ -2 \end{bmatrix} = \begin{bmatrix} \frac{5}{4} \\ \frac{7}{4} \\ \frac{1}{2} \end{bmatrix},$$

as shown in Fig. 7.5. (The definition of v has been chosen to make the smallest component of $\tilde{\mathbf{x}}$ equal to zero when $\alpha = 1$ in this equation for the next trial solution.) In the original coordinates, this solution is

$$\begin{bmatrix} x_1 \\ x_2 \\ x_3 \end{bmatrix} = \mathbf{D}\tilde{\mathbf{x}} = \begin{bmatrix} 2 & 0 & 0 \\ 0 & 2 & 0 \\ 0 & 0 & 4 \end{bmatrix}\begin{bmatrix} \frac{5}{4} \\ \frac{7}{4} \\ \frac{1}{2} \end{bmatrix} = \begin{bmatrix} \frac{5}{2} \\ \frac{7}{2} \\ 2 \end{bmatrix}.$$

This completes the iteration, and this new solution will be used to start the next iteration.

These steps can be summarized as follows for any iteration.

Summary of the Interior-Point Algorithm.

1. Given the current trial solution $(x_1, x_2, \ldots, x_n)$, set

$$\mathbf{D} = \begin{bmatrix} x_1 & 0 & 0 & \cdots & 0 \\ 0 & x_2 & 0 & \cdots & 0 \\ 0 & 0 & x_3 & \cdots & 0 \\ \cdots\cdots\cdots\cdots\cdots\cdots\cdots\cdots \\ 0 & 0 & 0 & \cdots & x_n \end{bmatrix}$$

2. Calculate $\tilde{\mathbf{A}} = \mathbf{AD}$ and $\tilde{\mathbf{c}} = \mathbf{Dc}$.
3. Calculate $\mathbf{P} = \mathbf{I} - \tilde{\mathbf{A}}^T(\tilde{\mathbf{A}}\tilde{\mathbf{A}}^T)^{-1}\tilde{\mathbf{A}}$ and $\mathbf{c}_p = \mathbf{P}\tilde{\mathbf{c}}$.
4. Identify the negative component of $\mathbf{c}_p$ having the largest absolute value, and set v equal to this absolute value. Then calculate

$$\tilde{\mathbf{x}} = \begin{bmatrix} 1 \\ 1 \\ \vdots \\ 1 \end{bmatrix} + \frac{\alpha}{v}\mathbf{c}_p,$$

where α is a selected constant between 0 and 1 (for example, $\alpha = 0.5$).
5. Calculate $\mathbf{x} = \mathbf{D}\tilde{\mathbf{x}}$ as the trial solution for the next iteration (step 1). (If this trial solution is virtually unchanged from the preceding one, then the algorithm has virtually converged to an optimal solution, so stop.)

Now let us apply this summary to iteration 2 for the example.

Iteration 2.

Step 1:
Given the current trial solution $(x_1, x_2, x_3) = (\frac{5}{2}, \frac{7}{2}, 2)$, set

$$\mathbf{D} = \begin{bmatrix} \frac{5}{2} & 0 & 0 \\ 0 & \frac{7}{2} & 0 \\ 0 & 0 & 2 \end{bmatrix}.$$

(Note that the rescaled variables are

$$\begin{bmatrix} \tilde{x}_1 \\ \tilde{x}_2 \\ \tilde{x}_3 \end{bmatrix} = \mathbf{D}^{-1}\mathbf{x} = \begin{bmatrix} \frac{2}{5} & 0 & 0 \\ 0 & \frac{2}{7} & 0 \\ 0 & 0 & \frac{1}{2} \end{bmatrix} \begin{bmatrix} x_1 \\ x_2 \\ x_3 \end{bmatrix} = \begin{bmatrix} \frac{2}{5}x_1 \\ \frac{2}{7}x_2 \\ \frac{1}{2}x_3 \end{bmatrix},$$

so that the BF solutions in these new coordinates are

$$\tilde{\mathbf{x}} = \mathbf{D}^{-1}\begin{bmatrix} 8 \\ 0 \\ 0 \end{bmatrix} = \begin{bmatrix} \frac{16}{5} \\ 0 \\ 0 \end{bmatrix}, \qquad \tilde{\mathbf{x}} = \mathbf{D}^{-1}\begin{bmatrix} 0 \\ 8 \\ 0 \end{bmatrix} = \begin{bmatrix} 0 \\ \frac{16}{7} \\ 0 \end{bmatrix},$$

and

$$\tilde{\mathbf{x}} = \mathbf{D}^{-1}\begin{bmatrix} 0 \\ 0 \\ 8 \end{bmatrix} = \begin{bmatrix} 0 \\ 0 \\ 4 \end{bmatrix},$$

as depicted in Fig. 7.6.)

Step 2:

$$\tilde{\mathbf{A}} = \mathbf{AD} = [\tfrac{5}{2}, \tfrac{7}{2}, 2] \qquad \text{and} \qquad \tilde{\mathbf{c}} = \mathbf{Dc} = \begin{bmatrix} \frac{5}{2} \\ 7 \\ 0 \end{bmatrix}.$$

FIGURE 7.6
Example after rescaling for iteration 2.

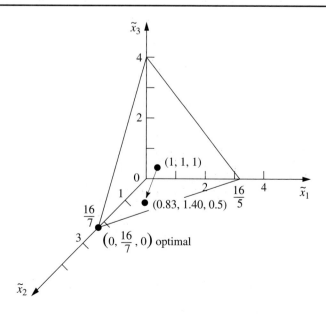

Step 3:

$$\mathbf{P} = \begin{bmatrix} \frac{13}{18} & -\frac{7}{18} & -\frac{2}{9} \\ -\frac{7}{18} & \frac{41}{90} & -\frac{14}{45} \\ -\frac{2}{9} & -\frac{14}{45} & \frac{37}{45} \end{bmatrix} \qquad \text{and} \qquad \mathbf{c}_p = \begin{bmatrix} -\frac{11}{12} \\ \frac{133}{60} \\ -\frac{41}{15} \end{bmatrix}.$$

Step 4:

$\left| -\frac{41}{15} \right| > \left| -\frac{11}{12} \right|$, so $v = \frac{41}{15}$ and

$$\tilde{\mathbf{x}} = \begin{bmatrix} 1 \\ 1 \\ 1 \end{bmatrix} + \frac{0.5}{\frac{41}{15}} \begin{bmatrix} -\frac{11}{12} \\ \frac{133}{60} \\ -\frac{41}{15} \end{bmatrix} = \begin{bmatrix} \frac{273}{328} \\ \frac{461}{328} \\ \frac{1}{2} \end{bmatrix} \approx \begin{bmatrix} 0.83 \\ 1.40 \\ 0.50 \end{bmatrix}.$$

Step 5:

$$\mathbf{x} = \mathbf{D}\tilde{\mathbf{x}} = \begin{bmatrix} \frac{1365}{656} \\ \frac{3227}{656} \\ 1 \end{bmatrix} \approx \begin{bmatrix} 2.08 \\ 4.92 \\ 1.00 \end{bmatrix}$$

is the trial solution for iteration 3.

Since there is little to be learned by repeating these calculations for additional iterations, we shall stop here. However, we do show in Fig. 7.7 the reconfigured feasible region after rescaling based on the trial solution just obtained for iteration 3. As always, the rescaling has placed the trial solution at $(\tilde{x}_1, \tilde{x}_2, \tilde{x}_3) = (1, 1, 1)$, equidistant from the $\tilde{x}_1 = 0$, $\tilde{x}_2 = 0$, and $\tilde{x}_3 = 0$ constraint boundaries. Note in Figs. 7.5, 7.6, and 7.7 how the sequence of iterations and rescaling have the effect of "sliding" the optimal solution toward $(1, 1, 1)$ while the other BF solutions tend to slide away. Eventually, after enough iterations, the optimal solution will lie very near $(\tilde{x}_1, \tilde{x}_2, \tilde{x}_3) = (0, 1, 0)$ after rescaling, while the other two BF solutions will be *very* far from the origin on the $\tilde{x}_1$ and $\tilde{x}_3$ axes. Step 5 of that iteration then will yield a solution in the original coordinates very near the optimal solution of $(x_1, x_2, x_3) = (0, 8, 0)$.

Figure 7.8 shows the progress of the algorithm in the original $x_1 = x_2$ coordinate system before the problem is augmented. The three points—$(x_1, x_2) = (2, 2)$, $(2.5, 3.5)$, and $(2.08, 4.92)$—are the trial solutions for initiating iterations 1, 2, and 3, respectively. We then have drawn a smooth curve through and beyond these points to show the trajectory of the algorithm in subsequent iterations as it approaches $(x_1, x_2) = (0, 8)$.

The functional constraint for this particular example happened to be an inequality constraint. However, equality constraints cause no difficulty for the algorithm, since it deals with the constraints only after any necessary augmenting has been done to convert them to equality form $(\mathbf{Ax} = \mathbf{b})$ anyway. To illustrate, suppose that the only change in the example is that the constraint $x_1 + x_2 \leq 8$ is changed to $x_1 + x_2 = 8$. Thus, the feasible region in Fig. 7.3 changes to just the line segment between $(8, 0)$ and $(0, 8)$. Given an initial feasible trial solution in the interior $(x_1 > 0$ and $x_2 > 0)$ of this line segment—say, $(x_1, x_2) = (4, 4)$—the algorithm can proceed just as presented in the five-step summary with just the two variables and $\mathbf{A} = [1, 1]$. For each iteration, the projected gradient points along this line segment in the direction of $(0, 8)$. With $\alpha = \frac{1}{2}$, iteration 1 leads from $(4, 4)$

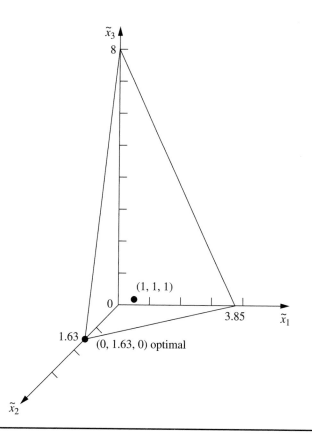

FIGURE 7.7
Example after rescaling for iteration 3.

to (2, 6), iteration 2 leads from (2, 6) to (1, 7), etc. (Problem 7.4-3 asks you to verify these results.)

Although either version of the example has only one functional constraint, having more than one leads to just one change in the procedure as already illustrated (other than more extensive calculations). Having a single functional constraint in the example meant that $\mathbf{A}$ had only a single row, so the $(\tilde{\mathbf{A}}\tilde{\mathbf{A}}^T)^{-1}$ term in step 3 only involved taking the reciprocal of the number obtained from the vector product $\tilde{\mathbf{A}}\tilde{\mathbf{A}}^T$. Multiple functional constraints mean that $\mathbf{A}$ has multiple rows, so then the $(\tilde{\mathbf{A}}\tilde{\mathbf{A}}^T)^{-1}$ term involves finding the *inverse* of the matrix obtained from the matrix product $\tilde{\mathbf{A}}\tilde{\mathbf{A}}^T$.

To conclude, we need to add a comment to place the algorithm into better perspective. For our extremely small example, the algorithm requires relatively extensive calculations and then, after many iterations, obtains only an approximation of the optimal solution. By contrast, the graphical procedure of Sec. 3.1 finds the optimal solution in Fig. 7.3 immediately, and the simplex method requires only one quick iteration. However, do not let this contrast fool you into downgrading the efficiency of the interior-point algorithm. This algorithm is designed for dealing with *big* problems having many hundreds or thousands of functional constraints. The simplex method typically requires thousands of iterations on such problems. By "shooting" through the interior of the feasible region, the interior-point algorithm tends to require a substantially smaller number of iterations

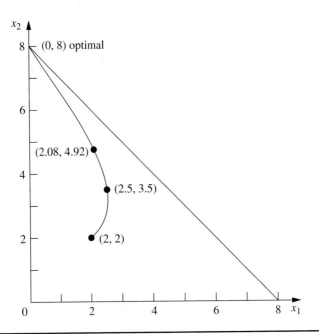

FIGURE 7.8
Trajectory of the interior-point algorithm for the example in the original x_1-x_2 coordinate system.

(although with considerably more work per iteration). Therefore, interior-point algorithms similar to the one presented here should play an important role in the future of linear programming.

See Sec. 4.9 for a further discussion of this role and a comparison of the interior-point approach with the simplex method.

7.5 LINEAR GOAL PROGRAMMING AND ITS SOLUTION PROCEDURES

We have assumed throughout the preceding chapters that the objectives of the organization conducting the linear programming study can be encompassed within a single overriding objective, such as maximizing total profit or minimizing total cost. However, this assumption is not always realistic. In fact, as we discussed in Sec. 2.1, studies have found that the management of U.S. corporations frequently focuses on a variety of other objectives, e.g., to maintain stable profits, increase (or maintain) market share, diversify products, maintain stable prices, improve worker morale, maintain family control of the business, and increase company prestige. *Goal programming* provides a way of striving toward several such objectives *simultaneously*.

The basic approach of **goal programming** is to establish a specific numeric goal for each of the objectives, formulate an objective function for each objective, and then seek a solution that minimizes the (weighted) sum of deviations of these objective functions from their respective goals. There are three possible types of goals:

1. A **lower, one-sided goal** sets a *lower limit* that we do not want to fall under (but exceeding the limit is fine).

2. An **upper, one-sided goal** sets an *upper limit* that we do not want to exceed (but falling under the limit is fine).
3. A **two-sided goal** sets a *specific target* that we do not want to miss on either side.

Goal programming problems can be categorized according to the type of mathematical programming model (linear programming, integer programming, nonlinear programming, etc.) that it fits except for having multiple goals instead of a single objective. In this book, we only consider *linear* goal programming—those goal programming problems that fit linear programming otherwise (each objective function is linear, etc.) and so we will drop the adjective *linear* from now on.

Another categorization is according to how the goals compare in importance. In one case, called **nonpreemptive goal programming,** all the goals are of *roughly comparable importance*. In another case, called **preemptive goal programming,** there is a *hierarchy of priority levels* for the goals, so that the goals of primary importance receive first-priority attention, those of secondary importance receive second-priority attention, and so forth (if there are more than two priority levels).

We begin with an example that illustrates the basic features of nonpreemptive goal programming and then discuss the preemptive case.

Prototype Example for Nonpreemptive Goal Programming

The DEWRIGHT COMPANY is considering three new products to replace current models that are being discontinued, so their OR department has been assigned the task of determining which mix of these products should be produced. Management wants primary consideration given to three factors: long-run profit, stability in the workforce, and the level of capital investment that would be required now for new equipment. In particular, management has established the goals of (1) achieving a long-run profit (net present value) of at least $125 million from these products, (2) maintaining the current employment level of 4,000 employees, and (3) holding the capital investment to less than $55 million. However, management realizes that it probably will not be possible to attain all these goals simultaneously, so it has discussed priorities with the OR department. This discussion has led to setting *penalty weights* of 5 for missing the profit goal (per $1 million under), 2 for going over the employment goal (per 100 employees), 4 for going under this same goal, and 3 for exceeding the capital investment goal (per $1 million over). Each new product's contribution to profit, employment level, and capital investment level is *proportional* to the rate of production. These contributions per unit rate of production are shown in Table 7.5, along with the goals and penalty weights.

Formulation. The Dewright Company problem includes all three possible types of goals: a lower, one-sided goal (long-run profit); a two-sided goal (employment level); and an upper, one-sided goal (capital investment). Letting the decision variables x_1, x_2, x_3 be the production rates of products 1, 2, and 3, respectively, we see that these goals can be stated as

$$12x_1 + 9x_2 + 15x_3 \geq 125 \qquad \text{profit goal}$$
$$5x_1 + 3x_2 + 4x_3 = 40 \qquad \text{employment goal}$$
$$5x_1 + 7x_2 + 8x_3 \leq 55 \qquad \text{investment goal.}$$

TABLE 7.5 Data for the Dewright Co. nonpreemptive goal programming problem

Factor	Unit Contribution Product: 1	2	3	Goal (Units)	Penalty Weight
Long-run profit	12	9	15	≥ 125 (millions of dollars)	5
Employment level	5	3	4	$= 40$ (hundreds of employees)	2(+), 4(−)
Capital investment	5	7	8	≤ 55 (millions of dollars)	3

More precisely, given the penalty weights in the rightmost column of Table 7.5, let Z be the *number of penalty points* incurred by missing these goals. The overall objective then is to choose the values of x_1, x_2, and x_3 so as to

Minimize $Z = 5$(amount under the long-run profit goal)
+ 2(amount over the employment level goal)
+ 4(amount under the employment level goal)
+ 3(amount over the capital investment goal),

where no penalty points are incurred for being over the long-run profit goal or for being under the capital investment goal. To express this overall objective mathematically, we introduce some *auxiliary variables* (extra variables that are helpful for formulating the model) y_1, y_2, and y_3, defined as follows:

$$y_1 = 12x_1 + 9x_2 + 15x_3 - 125 \quad \text{(long-run profit minus the target).}$$
$$y_2 = 5x_1 + 3x_2 + 4x_3 - 40 \quad \text{(employment level minus the target).}$$
$$y_3 = 5x_1 + 7x_2 + 8x_3 - 55 \quad \text{(capital investment minus the target).}$$

Since each y_i can be either positive or negative, we next use the technique described at the end of Sec. 4.6 for dealing with such variables; namely, we replace each one by the difference of two nonnegative variables:

$$y_1 = y_1^+ - y_1^-, \quad \text{where } y_1^+ \geq 0, y_1^- \geq 0,$$
$$y_2 = y_2^+ - y_2^-, \quad \text{where } y_2^+ \geq 0, y_2^- \geq 0,$$
$$y_3 = y_3^+ - y_3^-, \quad \text{where } y_3^+ \geq 0, y_3^- \geq 0.$$

As discussed in Sec. 4.6, for any BF solution, these new auxiliary variables have the interpretation

$$y_j^+ = \begin{cases} y_j & \text{if } y_j \geq 0, \\ 0 & \text{otherwise;} \end{cases}$$
$$y_j^- = \begin{cases} |y_j| & \text{if } y_j \leq 0, \\ 0 & \text{otherwise;} \end{cases}$$

so that y_j^+ represents the positive part of the variable y_j and y_j^- its negative part (as suggested by the superscripts).

Given these new auxiliary variables, the overall objective can be expressed mathematically as

Minimize $Z = 5y_1^- + 2y_2^+ + 4y_2^- + 3y_3^+,$

which now is a legitimate objective function for a linear programming model. (Because there is no penalty for exceeding the profit goal of 125 or being under the investment goal of 55, neither y_1^+ nor y_3^- should appear in this objective function representing the total penalty for deviations from the goals.)

To complete the conversion of this goal programming problem to a linear programming model, we must incorporate the above definitions of the y_j^+ and y_j^- directly into the model. (It is not enough to simply record the definitions, as we just did, because the simplex method considers only the objective function and constraints that constitute the model.) For example, since $y_1^+ - y_1^- = y_1$, the above expression for y_1 gives

$$12x_1 + 9x_2 + 15x_3 - 125 = y_1^+ - y_1^-.$$

After we move the variables $(y_1^+ - y_1^-)$ to the left-hand side and the constant (125) to the right-hand side,

$$12x_1 + 9x_2 + 15x_3 - (y_1^+ - y_1^-) = 125$$

becomes a legitimate equality constraint for a linear programming model. Furthermore, this constraint forces the auxiliary variables $(y_1^+ - y_1^-)$ to satisfy their definition in terms of the decision variables (x_1, x_2, x_3).

Proceeding in the same way for $y_2^+ - y_2^-$ and $y_3^+ - y_3^-$, we obtain the following linear programming formulation of this goal programming problem:

Minimize $Z = 5y_1^- + 2y_2^+ + 4y_2^- + 3y_3^+,$

subject to

$$\begin{aligned}
12x_1 + 9x_2 + 15x_3 - (y_1^+ - y_1^-) &= 125 \\
5x_1 + 3x_2 + 4x_3 - (y_2^+ - y_2^-) &= 40 \\
5x_1 + 7x_2 + 8x_3 - (y_3^+ - y_3^-) &= 55
\end{aligned}$$

and

$$x_j \geq 0, \qquad y_k^+ \geq 0, \qquad y_k^- \geq 0 \qquad (j = 1, 2, 3; k = 1, 2, 3).$$

(If the original problem had any actual linear programming constraints, such as constraints on fixed amounts of certain resources being available, these would be included in the model.)

Applying the simplex method to this formulation yields an optimal solution $x_1 = \frac{25}{3}$, $x_2 = 0$, $x_3 = \frac{5}{3}$, with $y_1^+ = 0$, $y_1^- = 0$, $y_2^+ = \frac{25}{3}$, $y_2^- = 0$, $y_3^+ = 0$, and $y_3^- = 0$. Therefore, $y_1 = 0$, $y_2 = \frac{25}{3}$, and $y_3 = 0$, so the first and third goals are fully satisfied, but the employment level goal of 40 is exceeded by $8\frac{1}{3}$ (833 employees). The resulting penalty for deviating from the goals is $Z = 16\frac{2}{3}$.

As usual, you can see how Excel, LINGO/LINDO, and MPL/CPLEX are used to set up and solve this example by referring to their files for this chapter in your OR Courseware.

Preemptive Goal Programming

In the preceding example we assume that all the goals are of roughly comparable importance. Now consider the case of *preemptive* goal programming, where there is a hierarchy of priority levels for the goals. Such a case arises when one or more of the goals clearly are far more important than the others. Thus, the initial focus should be on achieving as closely as possible these *first-priority* goals. The other goals also might naturally divide further into second-priority goals, third-priority goals, and so on. After we find an optimal solution with respect to the first-priority goals, we can break any ties for the optimal solution by considering the second-priority goals. Any ties that remain after this re-optimization can be broken by considering the third-priority goals, and so on.

When we deal with goals on the *same* priority level, our approach is just like the one described for nonpreemptive goal programming. Any of the same three types of goals (lower one-sided, two-sided, upper one-sided) can arise. Different penalty weights for deviations from different goals still can be included, if desired. The same formulation technique of introducing auxiliary variables again is used to reformulate this portion of the problem to fit the linear programming format.

There are two basic methods based on linear programming for solving preemptive goal programming problems. One is called the *sequential procedure,* and the other is the *streamlined procedure.* We shall illustrate these procedures in turn by solving the following example.

Example.   Faced with the unpleasant recommendation to increase the company's workforce by more than 20 percent, the management of the Dewright Company has reconsidered the original formulation of the problem that was summarized in Table 7.5. This increase in workforce probably would be a rather temporary one, so the very high cost of training 833 new employees would be largely wasted, and the large (undoubtedly well-publicized) layoffs would make it more difficult for the company to attract high-quality employees in the future. Consequently, management has concluded that a very high priority should be placed on avoiding an increase in the workforce. Furthermore, management has learned that raising *more than* $55 million for capital investment for the new products would be extremely difficult, so a very high priority also should be placed on avoiding capital investment above this level.

Based on these considerations, management has concluded that a *preemptive goal programming* approach now should be used, where the two goals just discussed should be the first-priority goals, and the other two original goals (exceeding $125 million in long-run profit and avoiding a decrease in the employment level) should be the second-priority goals. Within the two priority levels, management feels that the relative penalty weights still should be the same as those given in the rightmost column of Table 7.5. This reformulation is summarized in Table 7.6, where a factor of M (representing a huge positive number) has been included in the penalty weights for the first-priority goals to emphasize that these goals preempt the second-priority goals. (The portions of Table 7.5 that are not included in Table 7.6 are *unchanged.*)

The Sequential Procedure for Preemptive Goal Programming

The *sequential procedure* solves a preemptive goal programming problem by solving a *sequence* of linear programming models.

At the first stage of the sequential procedure, the only goals included in the linear programming model are the first-priority goals, and the simplex method is applied in the

TABLE 7.6 Revised formulation for the Dewright Co. preemptive goal
programming problem

Priority Level	Factor	Goal	Penalty Weight
First priority	Employment level	≤ 40	$2M$
	Capital investment	≤ 55	$3M$
Second priority	Long-run profit	≥ 125	5
	Employment level	≥ 40	4

usual way. If the resulting optimal solution is *unique,* we adopt it immediately without considering any additional goals.

However, if there are *multiple* optimal solutions with the same optimal value of Z (call it Z^*), we prepare to break the tie among these solutions by moving to the second stage and adding the second-priority goals to the model. If $Z^* = 0$, all the auxiliary variables representing the *deviations from first-priority goals* must equal zero (full achievement of these goals) for the solutions remaining under consideration. Thus, in this case, all these auxiliary variables now can be completely deleted from the model, where the equality constraints that contain these variables are replaced by the mathematical expressions (inequalities or equations) for these first-priority goals, to ensure that they continue to be fully achieved. On the other hand, if $Z^* > 0$, the second-stage model simply adds the second-priority goals to the first-stage model (as if these additional goals actually were first-priority goals), but then it also adds the constraint that the *first-stage objective function* equals Z^* (which enables us again to delete the terms involving first-priority goals from the second-stage objective function). After we apply the simplex method again, if there still are multiple optimal solutions, we repeat the same process for any lower-priority goals.

Example. We now illustrate this procedure by applying it to the example summarized in Table 7.6.

At the first stage, only the two *first-priority* goals are included in the linear programming model. Therefore, we can drop the common factor M for their penalty weights, shown in Table 7.6. By proceeding just as for the nonpreemptive model if these were the only goals, the resulting linear programming model is

$$\text{Minimize} \quad Z = 2y_2^+ + 3y_3^+,$$

subject to

$$5x_1 + 3x_2 + 4x_3 - (y_2^+ - y_2^-) = 40$$
$$5x_1 + 7x_2 + 8x_3 - (y_3^+ - y_3^-) = 55$$

and

$$x_j \geq 0, \quad y_k^+ \geq 0, \quad y_k^- \geq 0 \quad (j = 1, 2, 3; k = 2, 3).$$

(For ease of comparison with the nonpreemptive model with all four goals, we have kept the same subscripts on the auxiliary variables.)

By using the simplex method (or inspection), an optimal solution for this linear programming model has $y_2^+ = 0$ and $y_3^+ = 0$, with $Z = 0$ (so $Z^* = 0$), because there are innumerable solutions for (x_1, x_2, x_3) that satisfy the relationships

$$5x_1 + 3x_2 + 4x_3 \leq 40$$
$$5x_1 + 7x_2 + 8x_3 \leq 55$$

as well as the nonnegativity constraints. Therefore, these two first-priority goals should be used as *constraints* hereafter. Using them as constraints will force y_2^+ and y_3^+ to remain zero and thereby disappear from the model automatically.

If we drop y_2^+ and y_3^+ but add the second-priority goals, the second-stage linear programming model becomes

Minimize $Z = 5y_1^- + 4y_2^-$,

subject to

$$12x_1 + 9x_2 + 15x_3 - (y_1^+ - y_1^-) \qquad\qquad = 125$$
$$5x_1 + 3x_2 + 4x_3 \qquad\quad + y_2^- \qquad = 40$$
$$5x_1 + 7x_2 + 8x_3 \qquad\qquad\quad + y_3^- = 55$$

and

$$x_j \geq 0, \qquad y_1^+ \geq 0, \qquad y_k^- \geq 0 \qquad (j = 1, 2, 3; k = 1, 2, 3).$$

Applying the simplex method to this model yields the unique optimal solution $x_1 = 5$, $x_2 = 0$, $x_3 = 3\frac{3}{4}$, $y_1^+ = 0$, $y_1^- = 8\frac{3}{4}$, $y_2^- = 0$, and $y_3^- = 0$, with $Z = 43\frac{3}{4}$.

Because this solution is unique (*or* because there are no more priority levels), the procedure can now stop, with $(x_1, x_2, x_3) = (5, 0, 3\frac{3}{4})$ as the optimal solution for the *overall* problem. This solution fully achieves both first-priority goals as well as one of the second-priority goals (no decrease in employment level), and it falls short of the other second-priority goal (long-run profit ≥ 125) by just $8\frac{3}{4}$.

The Streamlined Procedure for Preemptive Goal Programming

Instead of solving a sequence of linear programming models, like the sequential procedure, the *streamlined procedure* finds an optimal solution for a preemptive goal programming problem by solving just *one* linear programming model. Thus, the streamlined procedure is able to duplicate the work of the sequential procedure with just *one run* of the simplex method. This one run *simultaneously* finds optimal solutions based just on first-priority goals and breaks ties among these solutions by considering lower-priority goals. However, this does require a slight modification of the simplex method.

If there are just *two* priority levels, the modification of the simplex method is one you already have seen, namely, the form of the *Big M method* illustrated throughout Sec. 4.6. In this form, instead of replacing M throughout the model by some huge positive number before running the simplex method, we retain the *symbolic* quantity M in the sequence of simplex tableaux. Each coefficient in row 0 (for each iteration) is some linear function $aM + b$, where a is the current *multiplicative factor* and b is the current *additive term*. The usual decisions based on these coefficients (entering basic variable and optimality test) now are based solely on the *multiplicative* factors, except that any ties would be broken by using the *additive* terms. This is how the OR Courseware operates when solving interactively by the simplex method (and choosing the Big M method).

The linear programming formulation for the streamlined procedure with two priority levels would include *all* the goals in the model in the usual manner, but with basic penalty weights of M and 1 assigned to deviations from first-priority and second-priority goals, respectively. If different penalty weights are desired within the same priority level, these basic penalty weights then are multiplied by the individual penalty weights assigned within the level. This approach is illustrated by the following example.

Example. For the Dewright Co. preemptive goal programming problem summarized in Table 7.6, note that (1) different penalty weights are assigned within each of the two priority levels and (2) the individual penalty weights (2 and 3) for the first-priority goals have been multiplied by M. These penalty weights yield the following single linear programming model that incorporates all the goals.

$$\text{Minimize} \quad Z = 5y_1^- + 2My_2^+ + 4y_2^- + 3My_3^+,$$

subject to

$$
\begin{aligned}
12x_1 + 9x_2 + 15x_3 - (y_1^+ - y_1^-) &= 125 \\
5x_1 + 3x_2 + 4x_3 - (y_2^+ - y_2^-) &= 40 \\
5x_1 + 7x_2 + 8x_3 - (y_3^+ - y_3^-) &= 55
\end{aligned}
$$

and

$$x_j \geq 0, \qquad y_k^+ \geq 0, \qquad y_k^- \geq 0 \qquad (j = 1, 2, 3; k = 1, 2, 3).$$

Because this model uses M to symbolize a huge positive number, the simplex method can be applied as described and illustrated throughout Sec. 4.6. Alternatively, a very large positive number can be substituted for M in the model and then any software package based on the simplex method can be applied. Doing either naturally yields the same unique optimal solution obtained by the sequential procedure.

More than Two Priority Levels. When there are more than two priority levels (say, p of them), the streamlined procedure generalizes in a straightforward way. The basic penalty weights for the respective levels now are $M_1, M_2, \ldots, M_{p-1}, 1$, where M_1 represents a number that is vastly larger than M_2, M_2 is vastly larger than $M_3, \ldots$, and M_{p-1} is vastly larger than 1. Each coefficient in row 0 of each simplex tableau is now a linear function of all of these quantities, where the multiplicative factor of M_1 is used to make the necessary decisions, with tie breakers beginning with the multiplicative factor of M_2 and ending with the additive term.

7.6 CONCLUSIONS

The *dual simplex method* and *parametric linear programming* are especially valuable for postoptimality analysis, although they also can be very useful in other contexts.

The *upper bound technique* provides a way of streamlining the simplex method for the common situation in which many or all of the variables have explicit upper bounds. It can greatly reduce the computational effort for large problems.

Mathematical-programming computer packages usually include all three of these procedures, and they are widely used. Because their basic structure is based largely upon the simplex method as presented in Chap. 4, they retain the exceptional computational efficiency to handle very large problems of the sizes described in Sec. 4.8.

Various other special-purpose algorithms also have been developed to exploit the special structure of particular types of linear programming problems (such as those to be discussed in Chaps. 8 and 9). Much research is currently being done in this area.

Karmarkar's interior-point algorithm has been an exciting development in linear programming. Variants of this algorithm now provide a powerful approach for efficiently solving some very large problems.

Linear goal programming and its solution procedures provide an effective way of dealing with problems where management wishes to strive toward several goals simultaneously. The key is a formulation technique of introducing auxiliary variables that enable converting the problem into a linear programming format.

SELECTED REFERENCES

1. Hooker, J. N.: "Karmarkar's Linear Programming Algorithm," *Interfaces,* **16:** 75–90, July–August 1986.
2. Lustig, I. J., R. E. Marsten, and D. F. Shanno: "Interior-Point Methods for Linear Programming: Computational State of the Art," *ORSA Journal on Computing,* **6:** 1–14, 1994. (Also see pp. 15–86 of this issue for commentaries on this article.)
3. Marsten, R., R. Subramanian, M. Saltzman, I. Lustig, and D. Shanno: "Interior-Point Methods for Linear Programming: Just Call Newton, Lagrange, and Fiacco and McCormick!," *Interfaces,* **20:** 105–116, July–August 1990.
4. Saigal, R.: *Linear Programming: A Modern Integrated Analysis,* Kluwer Academic Publishers, Boston, 1995.
5. Schneiderjans, M.: *Goal Programming: Methodology and Applications,* Kluwer Academic Publishers, Boston, 1995.
6. Terlaky, T. (ed.): *Interior Point Methods in Mathematical Programming,* Kluwer Academic Publishers, Boston, 1996.
7. Vanderbei, R. J.: "Affine-Scaling for Linear Programs with Free Variables," *Mathematical Programming,* **43:** 31–44, 1989.
8. Vanderbei, R. J.: *Linear Programming: Foundations and Extensions,* Kluwer Academic Publishers, Boston, 1996.

LEARNING AIDS FOR THIS CHAPTER IN YOUR OR COURSEWARE

Interactive Routines:

Enter or Revise a General Linear Programming Model
Set Up for the Simplex Method—Interactive Only
Solve Interactively by the Simplex Method

An Automatic Routine:

Solve Automatically by the Interior-Point Algorithm

An Excel Add-In:

Premium Solver

"Ch. 7—Other Algorithms for LP" Files for Solving the Examples:

Excel File
LINGO/LINDO File
MPL/CPLEX File

See Appendix 1 for documentation of the software.

PROBLEMS

The symbols to the left of some of the problems (or their parts) have the following meaning:

I: We suggest that you use the above interactive routines (the printout records your work). For parametric linear programming, this only applies to $\theta = 0$, after which you should proceed manually.

C: Use the computer to solve the problem.

An asterisk on the problem number indicates that at least a partial answer is given in the back of the book.

7.1-1. Consider the following problem.

   Maximize $Z = -x_1 - x_2,$

subject to

$$x_1 + x_2 \leq 8$$
$$x_2 \geq 3$$
$$-x_1 + x_2 \leq 2$$

and

$$x_1 \geq 0, \qquad x_2 \geq 0.$$

(a) Solve this problem graphically.
(b) Use the *dual simplex method* manually to solve this problem.
(c) Trace graphically the path taken by the dual simplex method.

7.1-2.* Use the *dual simplex method* manually to solve the following problem.

   Minimize $Z = 5x_1 + 2x_2 + 4x_3,$

subject to

$$3x_1 + x_2 + 2x_3 \geq 4$$
$$6x_1 + 3x_2 + 5x_3 \geq 10$$

and

$$x_1 \geq 0, \qquad x_2 \geq 0, \qquad x_3 \geq 0.$$

7.1-3. Use the *dual simplex method* manually to solve the following problem.

   Minimize $Z = 7x_1 + 2x_2 + 5x_3 + 4x_4,$

subject to

$$2x_1 + 4x_2 + 7x_3 + x_4 \geq 5$$
$$8x_1 + 4x_2 + 6x_3 + 4x_4 \geq 8$$
$$3x_1 + 8x_2 + x_3 + 4x_4 \geq 4$$

and

$$x_j \geq 0, \qquad \text{for } j = 1, 2, 3, 4.$$

7.1-4. Consider the following problem.

   Maximize $Z = 3x_1 + 2x_2,$

subject to

$$3x_1 + x_2 \leq 12$$
$$x_1 + x_2 \leq 6$$
$$5x_1 + 3x_2 \leq 27$$

and

$$x_1 \geq 0, \qquad x_2 \geq 0.$$

I (a) Solve by the *original simplex method* (in tabular form). Identify the *complementary* basic solution for the dual problem obtained at each iteration.

(b) Solve the *dual* of this problem manually by the *dual simplex method*. Compare the resulting sequence of basic solutions with the complementary basic solutions obtained in part (a).

7.1-5. Consider the example for case 1 of sensitivity analysis given in Sec. 6.7, where the initial simplex tableau of Table 4.8 is modified by changing b_2 from 12 to 24, thereby changing the respective entries in the right-side column of the *final* simplex tableau to 54, 6, 12, and -2. Starting from this revised final simplex tableau, use the *dual simplex method* to obtain the new optimal solution shown in Table 6.21. Show your work.

7.1-6.* Consider parts (*a*) and (*b*) of Prob. 6.7-1. Use the *dual simplex method* manually to reoptimize for each of these two cases, starting from the revised final tableau.

7.2-1.* Consider the following problem.

Maximize $Z = 8x_1 + 24x_2$,

subject to

$$x_1 + 2x_2 \leq 10$$
$$2x_1 + x_2 \leq 10$$

and

$$x_1 \geq 0, \quad x_2 \geq 0.$$

Suppose that Z represents profit and that it is possible to modify the objective function somewhat by an appropriate shifting of key personnel between the two activities. In particular, suppose that the unit profit of activity 1 can be increased above 8 (to a maximum of 18) at the expense of decreasing the unit profit of activity 2 below 24 by twice the amount. Thus, Z can actually be represented as

$$Z(\theta) = (8 + \theta)x_1 + (24 - 2\theta)x_2,$$

where θ is also a decision variable such that $0 \leq \theta \leq 10$.
(a) Solve the original form of this problem graphically. Then extend this graphical procedure to solve the parametric extension of the problem; i.e., find the optimal solution and the optimal value of $Z(\theta)$ as a function of θ, for $0 \leq \theta \leq 10$.
I **(b)** Find an optimal solution for the original form of the problem by the simplex method. Then use *parametric linear programming* to find an optimal solution and the optimal value of $Z(\theta)$ as a function of θ, for $0 \leq \theta \leq 10$. Plot $Z(\theta)$.
(c) Determine the optimal value of θ. Then indicate how this optimal value could have been identified directly by solving only two ordinary linear programming problems. (*Hint:* A convex function achieves its maximum at an endpoint.)

I **7.2-2.** Use *parametric linear programming* to find the optimal solution for the following problem as a function of θ, for $0 \leq \theta \leq 20$.

Maximize $Z(\theta) = (20 + 4\theta)x_1 + (30 - 3\theta)x_2 + 5x_3$,

subject to

$$3x_1 + 3x_2 + x_3 \leq 30$$
$$8x_1 + 6x_2 + 4x_3 \leq 75$$
$$6x_1 + x_2 + x_3 \leq 45$$

and

$$x_1 \geq 0, \quad x_2 \geq 0, \quad x_3 \geq 0.$$

7.2-3. Consider the following problem.

Maximize $Z(\theta) = (10 - \theta)x_1 + (12 + \theta)x_2 + (7 + 2\theta)x_3$,

subject to

$$x_1 + 2x_2 + 2x_3 \leq 30$$
$$x_1 + x_2 + x_3 \leq 20$$

and

$$x_1 \geq 0, \quad x_2 \geq 0, \quad x_3 \geq 0.$$

I **(a)** Use *parametric linear programming* to find an optimal solution for this problem as a function of θ, for $\theta \geq 0$.
(b) Construct the dual model for this problem. Then find an optimal solution for this dual problem as a function of θ, for $\theta \geq 0$, by the method described in the latter part of Sec. 7.2. Indicate graphically what this algebraic procedure is doing. Compare the basic solutions obtained with the complementary basic solutions obtained in part (*a*).

I **7.2-4.*** Use the *parametric linear programming* procedure for making systematic changes in the b_i parameters to find an optimal solution for the following problem as a function of θ, for $0 \leq \theta \leq 25$.

Maximize $Z(\theta) = 2x_1 + x_2$,

subject to

$$x_1 \leq 10 + 2\theta$$
$$x_1 + x_2 \leq 25 - \theta$$
$$x_2 \leq 10 + 2\theta$$

and

$$x_1 \geq 0, \quad x_2 \geq 0.$$

Indicate graphically what this algebraic procedure is doing.

I **7.2-5.** Use *parametric linear programming* to find an optimal solution for the following problem as a function of θ, for $0 \leq \theta \leq 30$.

Maximize $Z(\theta) = 5x_1 + 6x_2 + 4x_3 + 7x_4$,

subject to

$$3x_1 - 2x_2 + x_3 + 3x_4 \leq 135 - 2\theta$$
$$2x_1 + 4x_2 - x_3 + 2x_4 \leq 78 - \theta$$
$$x_1 + 2x_2 + x_3 + 2x_4 \leq 30 + \theta$$

and

$$x_j \geq 0, \quad \text{for } j = 1, 2, 3, 4.$$

Then identify the value of θ that gives the largest optimal value of $Z(\theta)$.

7.2-6. Consider Prob. 6.7-2. Use *parametric linear programming* to find an optimal solution as a function of θ over the following ranges of θ.
(a) $0 \le \theta \le 20$.
(b) $-20 \le \theta \le 0$. (*Hint:* Substitute $-\theta'$ for θ, and then increase θ' from zero.)

7.2-7. Consider the $Z^*(\theta)$ function shown in Fig. 7.1 for *parametric linear programming* with systematic changes in the c_j parameters.
(a) Explain why this function is piecewise linear.
(b) Show that this function must be convex.

7.2-8. Consider the $Z^*(\theta)$ function shown in Fig. 7.2 for *parametric linear programming* with systematic changes in the b_i parameters.
(a) Explain why this function is piecewise linear.
(b) Show that this function must be concave.

7.2-9. Let

$$Z^* = \max \left\{ \sum_{j=1}^{n} c_j x_j \right\},$$

subject to

$$\sum_{j=1}^{n} a_{ij} x_j \le b_i, \quad \text{for } i = 1, 2, \ldots, m,$$

and

$$x_j \ge 0, \quad \text{for } j = 1, 2, \ldots, n$$

(where the a_{ij}, b_i, and c_j are fixed constants), and let $(y_1^*, y_2^*, \ldots, y_m^*)$ be the corresponding optimal dual solution. Then let

$$Z^{**} = \max \left\{ \sum_{j=1}^{n} c_j x_j \right\},$$

subject to

$$\sum_{j=1}^{n} a_{ij} x_j \le b_i + k_i, \quad \text{for } i = 1, 2, \ldots, m,$$

and

$$x_j \ge 0, \quad \text{for } j = 1, 2, \ldots, n,$$

where $k_1, k_2, \ldots, k_m$ are given constants. Show that

$$Z^{**} \le Z^* + \sum_{i=1}^{m} k_i y_i^*.$$

7.3-1. Use the *upper bound technique* manually to solve the Wyndor Glass Co. problem presented in Sec. 3.1.

7.3-2. Consider the following problem.

Maximize $Z = 2x_1 + x_2,$

subject to

$$x_1 - x_2 \le 5$$
$$x_1 \le 10$$
$$x_2 \le 10$$

and

$$x_1 \ge 0, \quad x_2 \ge 0.$$

(a) Solve this problem graphically.
(b) Use the *upper bound technique* manually to solve this problem.
(c) Trace graphically the path taken by the upper bound technique.

7.3-3.* Use the *upper bound technique* manually to solve the following problem.

Maximize $Z = x_1 + 3x_2 - 2x_3,$

subject to

$$x_2 - 2x_3 \le 1$$
$$2x_1 + x_2 + 2x_3 \le 8$$
$$x_1 \le 1$$
$$x_2 \le 3$$
$$x_3 \le 2$$

and

$$x_1 \ge 0, \quad x_2 \ge 0, \quad x_3 \ge 0.$$

7.3-4. Use the *upper bound technique* manually to solve the following problem.

Maximize $Z = 2x_1 + 3x_2 - 2x_3 + 5x_4,$

subject to

$$2x_1 + 2x_2 + x_3 + 2x_4 \le 5$$
$$x_1 + 2x_2 - 3x_3 + 4x_4 \le 5$$

and

$$0 \le x_j \le 1, \quad \text{for } j = 1, 2, 3, 4.$$

7.3-5. Use the *upper bound technique* manually to solve the following problem.

Maximize $Z = 2x_1 + 5x_2 + 3x_3 + 4x_4 + x_5,$

subject to

$$x_1 + 3x_2 + 2x_3 + 3x_4 + x_5 \le 6$$
$$4x_1 + 6x_2 + 5x_3 + 7x_4 + x_5 \le 15$$

and

$$0 \le x_j \le 1, \quad \text{for } j = 1, 2, 3, 4, 5.$$

7.3-6. Simultaneously use the *upper bound technique* and the *dual simplex method* manually to solve the following problem.

Minimize $\quad Z = 3x_1 + 4x_2 + 2x_3,$

subject to

$$x_1 + x_2 + x_3 \ge 15$$
$$x_2 + x_3 \ge 10$$

and

$$0 \le x_1 \le 25, \quad 0 \le x_2 \le 5, \quad 0 \le x_3 \le 15.$$

C **7.4-1.** Reconsider the example used to illustrate the interior-point algorithm in Sec. 7.4. Suppose that $(x_1, x_2) = (1, 3)$ were used instead as the initial feasible trial solution. Perform two iterations manually, starting from this solution. Then use the automatic routine in your OR Courseware to check your work.

7.4-2. Consider the following problem.

Maximize $\quad Z = 3x_1 + x_2,$

subject to

$$x_1 + x_2 \le 4$$

and

$$x_1 \ge 0, \quad x_2 \ge 0.$$

(a) Solve this problem graphically. Also identify all CPF solutions.
C (b) Starting from the initial trial solution $(x_1, x_2) = (1, 1)$, perform four iterations of the interior-point algorithm presented in Sec. 7.4 manually. Then use the automatic routine in your OR Courseware to check your work.
(c) Draw figures corresponding to Figs. 7.4, 7.5, 7.6, 7.7, and 7.8 for this problem. In each case, identify the basic (or corner-point) feasible solutions in the current coordinate system. (Trial solutions can be used to determine projected gradients.)

7.4-3. Consider the following problem.

Maximize $\quad Z = x_1 + 2x_2,$

subject to

$$x_1 + x_2 = 8$$

and

$$x_1 \ge 0, \quad x_2 \ge 0.$$

C (a) Near the end of Sec. 7.4, there is a discussion of what the interior-point algorithm does on this problem when starting from the initial feasible trial solution $(x_1, x_2) = (4, 4)$. Verify the results presented there by performing two iterations manually. Then use the automatic routine in your OR Courseware to check your work.
(b) Use these results to predict what subsequent trial solutions would be if additional iterations were to be performed.
(c) Suppose that the stopping rule adopted for the algorithm in this application is that the algorithm stops when two successive trial solutions differ by no more than 0.01 in any component. Use your predictions from part (b) to predict the final trial solution and the total number of iterations required to get there. How close would this solution be to the optimal solution $(x_1, x_2) = (0, 8)$?

7.4-4. Consider the following problem.

Maximize $\quad Z = x_1 + x_2,$

subject to

$$x_1 + 2x_2 \le 9$$
$$2x_1 + x_2 \le 9$$

and

$$x_1 \ge 0, \quad x_2 \ge 0.$$

(a) Solve the problem graphically.
(b) Find the *gradient* of the objective function in the original x_1-x_2 coordinate system. If you move from the origin in the direction of the gradient until you reach the boundary of the feasible region, where does it lead relative to the optimal solution?
C (c) Starting from the initial trial solution $(x_1, x_2) = (1, 1)$, use your OR Courseware to perform 10 iterations of the interior-point algorithm presented in Sec. 7.4.
C (d) Repeat part (c) with $\alpha = 0.9$.

7.4-5. Consider the following problem.

Maximize $\quad Z = 2x_1 + 5x_2 + 7x_3,$

subject to

$$x_1 + 2x_2 + 3x_3 = 6$$

and

$$x_1 \ge 0, \quad x_2 \ge 0, \quad x_3 \ge 0.$$

(a) Graph the feasible region.
(b) Find the *gradient* of the objective function, and then find the *projected gradient* onto the feasible region.
(c) Starting from the initial trial solution $(x_1, x_2, x_3) = (1, 1, 1)$, perform two iterations of the interior-point algorithm presented in Sec. 7.4 manually.

c **(d)** Starting from this same initial trial solution, use your OR Courseware to perform 10 iterations of this algorithm.

c **7.4-6.** Starting from the initial trial solution $(x_1, x_2) = (2, 2)$, use your OR Courseware to apply 15 iterations of the interior-point algorithm presented in Sec. 7.4 to the Wyndor Glass Co. problem presented in Sec. 3.1. Also draw a figure like Fig. 7.8 to show the trajectory of the algorithm in the original x_1-x_2 coordinate system.

7.5-1. One of management's goals in a goal programming problem is expressed algebraically as

$$3x_1 + 4x_2 + 2x_3 = 60,$$

where 60 is the specific numeric goal and the left-hand side gives the level achieved toward meeting this goal.
(a) Letting y^+ be the amount by which the level achieved exceeds this goal (if any) and y^- the amount under the goal (if any), show how this goal would be expressed as an equality constraint when reformulating the problem as a linear programming model.
(b) If each unit over the goal is considered twice as serious as each unit under the goal, what is the relationship between the coefficients of y^+ and y^- in the objective function being minimized in this linear programming model.

7.5-2. Management of the Albert Franko Co. has established goals for the market share it wants each of the company's two new products to capture in their respective markets. Specifically, management wants Product 1 to capture at least 15 percent of its market and Product 2 to capture at least 10 percent of its market. Three advertising campaigns are being planned to try to achieve these market shares. One is targeted directly on the first product. The second targets the second product. The third is intended to enhance the general reputation of the company and its products. Letting x_1, x_2, and x_3 be the amount of money allocated (in millions of dollars) to these respective campaigns, the resulting market share (expressed as a percentage) for the two products are estimated to be

Market share for Product 1 = $0.5x_1 + 0.2x_3$,
Market share for Product 2 = $0.3x_2 + 0.2x_3$.

A total of $55 million is available for the three advertising campaigns, but management wants at least $10 million devoted to the third campaign. If both market share goals cannot be achieved, management considers each 1 percent decrease in the market share from the goal to be equally serious for the two products. In this light, management wants to know how to most effectively allocate the available money to the three campaigns.
(a) Formulate a goal programming model for this problem.
(b) Reformulate this model as a linear programming model.
c **(c)** Use the simplex method to solve this model.

7.5-3. The Research and Development Division of the Emax Corporation has developed three new products. A decision now needs to be made on which mix of these products should be produced. Management wants primary consideration given to three factors: total profit, stability in the workforce, and achieving an increase in the company's earnings next year from the $75 million achieved this year. In particular, using the units given in the following table, they want to

Maximize $Z = P - 6C - 3D,$

where P = total (discounted) profit over the life of the new products,
C = change (in either direction) in the current level of employment,
D = decrease (if any) in next year's earnings from the current year's level.

The amount of any increase in earnings does not enter into Z, because management is concerned primarily with just achieving some increase to keep the stockholders happy. (It has mixed feelings about a large increase that then would be difficult to surpass in subsequent years.)

The impact of each of the new products (per unit rate of production) on each of these factors is shown in the following table:

Factor	Unit Contribution Product: 1	2	3	Goal	Units
Total profit	20	15	25	Maximize	Millions of dollars
Employment level	6	4	5	= 50	Hundreds of employees
Earnings next year	8	7	5	≥ 75	Millions of dollars

(a) Define y_1^+ and y_1^-, respectively, as the amount over (if any) and the amount under (if any) the employment level goal. Define y_2^+ and y_2^- in the same way for the goal regarding earnings next year. Define x_1, x_2, and x_3 as the production rates of Products 1, 2, and 3, respectively. With these definitions, use the goal programming technique to express y_1^+, y_1^-, y_2^+, and y_2^- algebraically in terms of x_1, x_2, and x_3. Also express P in terms of x_1, x_2, and x_3.
(b) Express management's objective function in terms of x_1, x_2, x_3, y_1^+, y_1^-, y_2^+, and y_2^-.
(c) Formulate a linear programming model for this problem.
c **(d)** Use the simplex method to solve this model.

7.5-4. Reconsider the original version of the Dewright Co. problem presented in Sec. 7.5 and summarized in Table 7.5. After further reflection about the solution obtained by the simplex method, management now is asking some what-if questions.

(a) Management wonders what would happen if the penalty weights in the rightmost column of Table 7.5 were to be changed to 7, 4, 1, and 3, respectively. Would you expect the optimal solution to change? Why?

c (b) Management is wondering what would happen if the total profit goal were to be increased to wanting at least $140 million (without any change in the original penalty weights). Solve the revised model with this change.

c (c) Solve the revised model if both changes are made.

7.5-5. Montega is a developing country which has 15,000,000 acres of publicly controlled agricultural land in active use. Its government currently is planning a way to divide this land among three basic crops (labeled 1, 2, and 3) next year. A certain percentage of each of these crops is exported to obtain badly needed foreign capital (dollars), and the rest of each of these crops is used to feed the populace. Raising these crops also provides employment for a significant proportion of the population. Therefore, the main factors to be considered in allocating the land to these crops are (1) the amount of foreign capital generated, (2) the number of citizens fed, and (3) the number of citizens employed in raising these crops. The following table shows how much each 1,000 acres of each crop contributes toward these factors, and the last column gives the goal established by the government for each of these factors.

| | Contribution per 1,000 Acres | | | |
| | Crop: | | | |
Factor	1	2	3	Goal
Foreign capital	$3,000	$5,000	$4,000	$\geq$ $70,000,000
Citizens fed	150	75	100	$\geq$ 1,750,000
Citizens employed	10	15	12	= 200,000

In evaluating the relative seriousness of *not* achieving these goals, the government has concluded that the following deviations from the goals should be considered *equally undesirable:* (1) each $100 under the foreign-capital goal, (2) each person under the citizens-fed goal, and (3) each deviation of one (in either direction) from the citizens-employed goal.

(a) Formulate a goal programming model for this problem.
(b) Reformulate this model as a linear programming model.
c (c) Use the simplex method to solve this model.
(d) Now suppose that the government concludes that the importance of the various goals differs greatly so that a preemptive goal programming approach should be used. In particular, the

first-priority goal is citizens fed $\geq$ 1,750,000, the second-priority goal is foreign capital $\geq$ $70,000,000, and the third-priority goal is citizens employed = 200,000. Use the goal programming technique to formulate one complete linear programming model for this problem.

(e) Use the streamlined procedure to solve the problem as formulated in part (*d*).

c (f) Use the sequential procedure to solve the problem as presented in part (*d*).

7.5-6.* Consider a *preemptive goal programming* problem with three priority levels, just one goal for each priority level, and just two activities to contribute toward these goals, as summarized in the following table:

| | Unit Contribution | | |
| | Activity: | | |
Priority Level	1	2	Goal
First priority	1	2	$\leq$ 20
Second priority	1	1	= 15
Third priority	2	1	$\geq$ 40

(a) Use the *goal programming technique* to formulate one complete linear programming model for this problem.
(b) Construct the initial simplex tableau for applying the *streamlined procedure.* Identify the *initial BF solution* and the *initial entering basic variable,* but do not proceed further.
(c) Starting from (*b*), use the *streamlined procedure* to solve the problem.
(d) Use the logic of preemptive goal programming to solve the problem graphically by focusing on just the two decision variables. Explain the logic used.
(e) Use the *sequential procedure* to solve this problem. After using the *goal programming technique* to formulate the linear programming model (including auxiliary variables) at each stage, solve the model *graphically* by focusing on just the two decision variables. Identify *all* optimal solutions obtained for each stage.

7.5-7. Redo Prob. 7.5-6 with the following revised table:

| | Unit Contribution | | |
| | Activity: | | |
Priority Level	1	2	Goal
First priority	1	1	$\leq$ 20
Second priority	1	1	$\geq$ 30
Third priority	1	2	$\geq$ 50

7.5-8. One of the most important problems in the field of *statistics* is the *linear regression problem*. Roughly speaking, this problem involves fitting a straight line to statistical data represented by points—$(x_1, y_1), (x_2, y_2), \ldots, (x_n, y_n)$—on a graph. If we denote the line by $y = a + bx$, the objective is to choose the constants a and b to provide the "best" fit according to some criterion. The criterion usually used is the *method of least squares*, but there are other interesting criteria where linear programming can be used to solve for the optimal values of a and b.

Formulate a linear programming model for this problem under the following criterion:

Minimize the sum of the absolute deviations of the data from the line; that is,

$$\text{Minimize} \quad \sum_{i=1}^{n} \left| y_i - (a + bx_i) \right|.$$

(*Hint:* Note that this problem can be viewed as a nonpreemptive goal programming problem where each data point represents a "goal" for the regression line.)

CASE 7.1   A CURE FOR CUBA

Fulgencio Batista led Cuba with a cold heart and iron fist—greedily stealing from poor citizens, capriciously ruling the Cuban population that looked to him for guidance, and violently murdering the innocent critics of his politics. In 1958, tired of watching his fellow Cubans suffer from corruption and tyranny, Fidel Castro led a guerilla attack against the Batista regime and wrested power from Batista in January 1959. Cubans, along with members of the international community, believed that political and economic freedom had finally triumphed on the island. The next two years showed, however, that Castro was leading a Communist dictatorship—killing his political opponents and nationalizing all privately held assets. The United States responded to Castro's leadership in 1961 by invoking a trade embargo against Cuba. The embargo forbade any country from selling Cuban products in the United States and forbade businesses from selling American products to Cuba. Cubans did not feel the true impact of the embargo until 1989 when the Soviet economy collapsed. Prior to the disintegration of the Soviet Union, Cuba had received an average of $5 billion in annual economic assistance from the Soviet Union. With the disappearance of the economy that Cuba had almost exclusively depended upon for trade, Cubans had few avenues from which to purchase food, clothes, and medicine. The avenues narrowed even further when the United States passed the Torricelli Act in 1992 that forbade American subsidiaries in third countries from doing business with Cuba that had been worth a total of $700 million annually.

Since 1989, the Cuban economy has certainly felt the impact from decades of frozen trade. Today poverty ravages the island of Cuba. Families do not have money to purchase bare necessities, such as food, milk, and clothing. Children die from malnutrition or exposure. Disease infects the island because medicine is unavailable. Optical neuritis, tuberculosis, pneumonia, and influenza run rampant among the population.

Few Americans hold sympathy for Cuba, but Robert Baker, director of Helping Hand, leads a handful of tender souls on Capitol Hill who cannot bear to see politics destroy so many human lives. His organization distributes humanitarian aid annually to needy countries around the world. Mr. Baker recognizes the dire situation in Cuba, and he wants to allocate aid to Cuba for the coming year.

Mr. Baker wants to send numerous aid packages to Cuban citizens. Three different types of packages are available. The basic package contains only food, such as grain and powdered milk. Each basic package costs $300, weighs 120 pounds, and aids 30 people. The advanced package contains food and clothing, such as blankets and fabrics. Each advanced package costs $350, weighs 180 pounds, and aids 35 people. The supreme package contains food, clothing, and medicine. Each supreme package costs $720, weighs 220 pounds, and aids 54 people.

Mr. Baker has several goals he wants to achieve when deciding upon the number and types of aid packages to allocate to Cuba. First, he wants to aid at least 20 percent of Cuba's 11 million citizens. Second, because disease runs rampant among the Cuban population, he wants at least 3,000 of the aid packages sent to Cuba to be the supreme packages. Third, because he knows many other nations also require humanitarian aid, he wants to keep the cost of aiding Cuba below $20 million.

Mr. Baker places different levels of importance on his three goals. He believes the most important goal is keeping costs down since low costs mean that his organization is able to aid a larger number of needy nations. He decides to penalize his plan by 1 point for every $1 million above his $20 million goal. He believes the second most important goal is ensuring that at least 3,000 of the aid packages sent to Cuba are supreme packages, since he does not want to see an epidemic develop and completely destroy the Cuban population. He decides to penalize his plan by 1 point for every 1,000 packages below his goal of 3,000 packages. Finally, he believes the least important goal is reaching at least 20 percent of the population, since he would rather give a smaller number of individuals all they need to thrive instead of a larger number of individuals only some of what they need to thrive. He therefore decides to penalize his plan by 7 points for every 100,000 people below his 20 percent goal.

Mr. Baker realizes that he has certain limitations on the aid packages that he delivers to Cuba. Each type of package is approximately the same size, and because only a limited number of cargo flights from the United States are allowed into Cuba, he is only able to send a maximum of 40,000 packages. Along with a size limitation, he also encounters a weight restriction. He cannot ship more that 6 million pounds of cargo. Finally, he has a safety restriction. When sending medicine, he needs to ensure that the Cubans know how to use the medicine properly. Therefore, for every 100 supreme packages, Mr. Baker must send one doctor to Cuba at a cost of $33,000 per doctor.

(a) Identify one of the techniques described in this chapter that is applicable to Mr. Baker's problem.

(b) How many basic, advanced, and supreme packages should Mr. Baker send to Cuba?

(c) Mr. Baker reevaluates the levels of importance he places on each of the three goals. To sell his efforts to potential donors, he must show that his program is effective. Donors generally judge the effectiveness of a program on the number of people reached by aid packages. Mr. Baker therefore decides that he must put more importance on the goal of reaching at least 20 percent of the population. He decides to penalize his plan by 10 points for every half a percentage point below his 20 percent goal. The penalties for his other two goals remain the same. Under this scenario, how many basic, advanced, and supreme packages should Mr. Baker send to Cuba? How sensitive is the plan to changes in the penalty weights?

(d) Mr. Baker realizes that sending more doctors along with the supreme packages will improve the proper use and distribution of the packages' contents, which in turn will increase the effectiveness of the program. He therefore decides to send one doctor with every 75 supreme packages. The penalties for the goals remain the same as in part (c). Under this scenario, how many basic, advanced, and supreme packages should Mr. Baker send to Cuba?

(e) The aid budget is cut, and Mr. Baker learns that he definitely cannot allocate more than $20 million in aid to Cuba. Due to the budget cut, Mr. Baker decides to stay with his original policy of sending one doctor with every 100 supreme packages. How many basic, advanced, and supreme packages should Mr. Baker send to Cuba assuming that the penalties for not meeting the other two goals remain the same as in part (b)?

8

The Transportation and Assignment Problems

Chapter 3 emphasized the wide applicability of linear programming. We continue to broaden our horizons in this chapter by discussing two particularly important (and related) types of linear programming problems. One type, called the *transportation problem*, received this name because many of its applications involve determining how to optimally transport goods. However, some of its important applications (e.g., production scheduling) actually have nothing to do with transportation.

The second type, called the *assignment problem*, involves such applications as assigning people to tasks. Although its applications appear to be quite different from those for the transportation problem, we shall see that the assignment problem can be viewed as a special type of transportation problem.

The next chapter will introduce additional special types of linear programming problems involving *networks*, including the *minimum cost flow problem* (Sec. 9.6). There we shall see that both the transportation and assignment problems actually are special cases of the minimum cost flow problem. We introduce the network representation of the transportation and assignment problems in this chapter.

Applications of the transportation and assignment problems tend to require a very large number of constraints and variables, so a straightforward computer application of the simplex method may require an exorbitant computational effort. Fortunately, a key characteristic of these problems is that most of the a_{ij} coefficients in the constraints are zeros, and the relatively few nonzero coefficients appear in a distinctive pattern. As a result, it has been possible to develop special *streamlined* algorithms that achieve dramatic computational savings by exploiting this special structure of the problem. Therefore, it is important to become sufficiently familiar with these special types of problems that you can recognize them when they arise and apply the proper computational procedure.

To describe special structures, we shall introduce the table (matrix) of constraint coefficients shown in Table 8.1, where a_{ij} is the coefficient of the jth variable in the ith functional constraint. Later, portions of the table containing only coefficients equal to zero will be indicated by leaving them blank, whereas blocks containing nonzero coefficients will be shaded.

After presenting a prototype example for the transportation problem, we describe the special structure in its model and give additional examples of its applications. Section 8.2 presents the *transportation simplex method*, a special streamlined version of the simplex

TABLE 8.1 Table of
constraint coefficients
for linear
programming

$$
\mathbf{A} = \begin{bmatrix} a_{11} & a_{12} & \dots & a_{1n} \\ a_{21} & a_{22} & \dots & a_{2n} \\ \multicolumn{4}{c}{\dotfill} \\ a_{m1} & a_{m2} & \dots & a_{mn} \end{bmatrix}
$$

method for efficiently solving transportation problems. (You will see in Sec. 9.7 that this algorithm is related to the *network simplex method,* another streamlined version of the simplex method for efficiently solving any minimum cost flow problem, including both transportation and assignment problems.) Section 8.3 then focuses on the assignment problem.

8.1 THE TRANSPORTATION PROBLEM

Prototype Example

One of the main products of the P & T COMPANY is canned peas. The peas are prepared at three canneries (near Bellingham, Washington; Eugene, Oregon; and Albert Lea, Minnesota) and then shipped by truck to four distributing warehouses in the western United States (Sacramento, California; Salt Lake City, Utah; Rapid City, South Dakota; and Albuquerque, New Mexico), as shown in Fig. 8.1. Because the shipping costs are a major expense, management is initiating a study to reduce them as much as possible. For the upcoming season, an estimate has been made of the output from each cannery, and each warehouse has been allocated a certain amount from the total supply of peas. This information (in units of truckloads), along with the shipping cost per truckload for each cannery-warehouse combination, is given in Table 8.2. Thus, there are a total of 300 truckloads to be shipped. The problem now is to determine which plan for assigning these shipments to the various cannery-warehouse combinations would *minimize the total shipping cost.*

By ignoring the geographical layout of the canneries and warehouses, we can provide a *network representation* of this problem in a simple way by lining up all the canneries in one column on the left and all the warehouses in one column on the right. This representation is shown in Fig. 8.2. The arrows show the possible routes for the truckloads, where the number next to each arrow is the shipping cost per truckload for that route. A square bracket next to each location gives the number of truckloads to be shipped *out* of that location (so that the allocation into each warehouse is given as a negative number).

The problem depicted in Fig. 8.2 is actually a linear programming problem of the *transportation problem type.* To formulate the model, let Z denote total shipping cost, and let x_{ij} ($i = 1, 2, 3; j = 1, 2, 3, 4$) be the number of truckloads to be shipped from cannery i to warehouse j. Thus, the objective is to choose the values of these 12 decision variables (the x_{ij}) so as to

$$
\begin{aligned} \text{Minimize} \quad Z = {} & 464x_{11} + 513x_{12} + 654x_{13} + 867x_{14} + 352x_{21} + 416x_{22} \\ & + 690x_{23} + 791x_{24} + 995x_{31} + 682x_{32} + 388x_{33} + 685x_{34}, \end{aligned}
$$

FIGURE 8.1
Location of canneries and warehouses for the P & T Co. problem.

TABLE 8.2 Shipping data for P & T Co.

		Shipping Cost ($) per Truckload				
		Warehouse				
		1	**2**	**3**	**4**	**Output**
	1	464	513	654	867	75
Cannery	2	352	416	690	791	125
	3	995	682	388	685	100
Allocation		80	65	70	85	

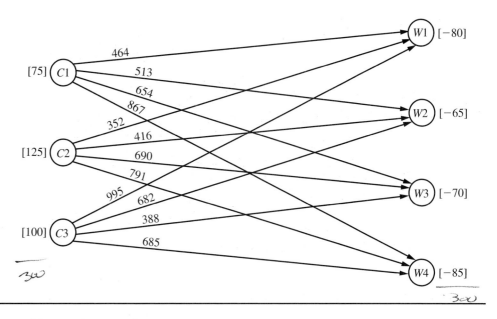

FIGURE 8.2
Network representation of
the P & T Co. problem.

subject to the constraints

$$
\begin{array}{llll}
x_{11} + x_{12} + x_{13} + x_{14} & & & = 75 \\
& x_{21} + x_{22} + x_{23} + x_{24} & & = 125 \\
& & x_{31} + x_{32} + x_{33} + x_{34} & = 100 \\
x_{11} & + x_{21} & + x_{31} & = 80 \\
\quad x_{12} & \quad + x_{22} & \quad + x_{32} & = 65 \\
\quad\quad x_{13} & \quad\quad + x_{23} & \quad\quad + x_{33} & = 70 \\
\quad\quad\quad x_{14} & \quad\quad\quad + x_{24} & \quad\quad\quad + x_{34} & = 85
\end{array}
$$

and

$$
x_{ij} \geq 0 \qquad (i = 1, 2, 3; j = 1, 2, 3, 4).
$$

Table 8.3 shows the constraint coefficients. As you will see later in this section, it is the special structure in the pattern of these coefficients that distinguishes this problem as a transportation problem, not its context.

TABLE 8.3 Constraint coefficients for P & T Co.

						Coefficient of:							
	x_{11}	x_{12}	x_{13}	x_{14}	x_{21}	x_{22}	x_{23}	x_{24}	x_{31}	x_{32}	x_{33}	x_{34}	
	1	1	1	1									Cannery
					1	1	1	1					constraints
$\mathbf{A} =$									1	1	1	1	
	1				1				1				Warehouse
		1				1				1			constraints
			1				1				1		
				1				1				1	

However, before examining the special structure of the transportation problem model, let us pause to look at an actual application that resembles the P&T Co. problem but on a vastly larger scale.

An Award Winning Application of a Transportation Problem

Except for its small size, the P & T Co. problem is typical of the problems faced by many corporations which must ship goods from their manufacturing plants to their customers.

For example, consider an award winning OR study conducted at *Proctor & Gamble* (as described in the January–February 1997 issue of *Interfaces*). Prior to the study, the company's supply chain consisted of hundreds of suppliers, over 50 product categories, over 60 plants, 15 distribution centers, and over 1,000 customer zones. However, as the company moved toward global brands, management realized that it needed to consolidate plants to reduce manufacturing expenses, improve speed to market, and reduce capital investment. Therefore, the study focused on redesigning the company's production and distribution system for its North American operations. The result was a reduction in the number of North American plants by almost 20 percent, saving over $200 million in pretax costs per year.

A major part of the study revolved around formulating and solving transportation problems for individual product categories. For each option regarding the plants to keep open, etc., solving the corresponding transportation problem for a product category shows what the distribution cost would be for shipping the product category from those plants to the distribution centers and customer zones. Numerous such transportation problems were solved in the process of identifying the best new production and distribution system.

The Transportation Problem Model

To describe the general model for the transportation problem, we need to use terms that are considerably less specific than those for the components of the prototype example. In particular, the general transportation problem is concerned (literally or figuratively) with distributing *any* commodity from *any* group of supply centers, called **sources**, to *any* group of receiving centers, called **destinations**, in such a way as to minimize the total distribution cost. The correspondence in terminology between the prototype example and the general problem is summarized in Table 8.4.

As indicated by the fourth and fifth rows of the table, each source has a certain **supply** of units to distribute to the destinations, and each destination has a certain **demand**

TABLE 8.4 Terminology for the transportation problem

Prototype Example	General Problem
Truckloads of canned peas	Units of a commodity
Three canneries	m sources
Four warehouses	n destinations
Output from cannery i	Supply s_i from source i
Allocation to warehouse j	Demand d_j at destination j
Shipping cost per truckload from cannery i to warehouse j	Cost c_{ij} per unit distributed from source i to destination j

for units to be received from the sources. The model for a transportation problem makes the following assumption about these supplies and demands.

> **The requirements assumption:** Each source has a fixed *supply* of units, where this entire supply must be distributed to the destinations. (We let s_i denote the number of units being supplied by source i, for $i = 1, 2, \ldots, m$.) Similarly, each destination has a fixed *demand* for units, where this entire demand must be received from the sources. (We let d_j denote the number of units being received by destination j, for $j = 1, 2, \ldots, n$.)

This assumption that there is no leeway in the amounts to be sent or received means that there needs to be a balance between the total supply from all sources and the total demand at all destinations.

> **The feasible solutions property:** A transportation problem will have feasible solutions if and only if

$$\sum_{i=1}^{m} s_i = \sum_{j=1}^{n} d_j.$$

Fortunately, these sums are equal for the P & T Co. since Table 8.2 indicates that the supplies (outputs) sum to 300 truckloads and so do the demands (allocations).

In some real problems, the supplies actually represent *maximum* amounts (rather than fixed amounts) to be distributed. Similarly, in other cases, the demands represent maximum amounts (rather than fixed amounts) to be received. Such problems do not quite fit the model for a transportation problem because they violate the *requirements assumption.* However, it is possible to *reformulate* the problem so that they then fit this model by introducing a *dummy destination* or a *dummy source* to take up the slack between the actual amounts and maximum amounts being distributed. We will illustrate how this is done with two examples at the end of this section.

The last row of Table 8.4 refers to a cost per unit distributed. This reference to a *unit cost* implies the following basic assumption for any transportation problem.

> **The cost assumption:** The cost of distributing units from any particular source to any particular destination is *directly proportional* to the number of units distributed. Therefore, this cost is just the *unit cost* of distribution *times the number of units distributed.* (We let c_{ij} denote this unit cost for source i and destination j.)

The only data needed for a transportation problem model are the supplies, demands, and unit costs. These are the *parameters of the model.* All these parameters can be summarized conveniently in a single *parameter table* as shown in Table 8.5.

> **The model:** Any problem (whether involving transportation or not) fits the model for a transportation problem if it can be described completely in terms of a *parameter table* like Table 8.5 and it satisfies both the *requirements assumption* and the *cost assumption.* The objective is to minimize the total cost of distributing the units. All the parameters of the model are included in this parameter table.

TABLE 8.5 Parameter table for the transportation problem

		Cost per Unit Distributed				
		Destination				
		1	**2**	...	**n**	**Supply**
	1	c_{11}	c_{12}	...	c_{1n}	s_1
Source	2	c_{21}	c_{22}	...	c_{2n}	s_2
	⋮					⋮
	m	c_{m1}	c_{m2}	...	c_{mn}	s_m
Demand		d_1	d_2	...	d_n	

Therefore, formulating a problem as a transportation problem only requires filling out a parameter table in the format of Table 8.5. Alternatively, the same information can be provided by using the network representation of the problem shown in Fig. 8.3. It is not necessary to write out a formal mathematical model.

However, we will go ahead and show you this model once for the general transportation problem just to emphasize that it is indeed a special type of linear programming problem.

Letting Z be the total distribution cost and x_{ij} ($i = 1, 2, \ldots, m$; $j = 1, 2, \ldots, n$) be the number of units to be distributed from source i to destination j, the linear programming formulation of this problem is

Minimize $$Z = \sum_{i=1}^{m} \sum_{j=1}^{n} c_{ij}x_{ij},$$

subject to

$$\sum_{j=1}^{n} x_{ij} = s_i \qquad \text{for } i = 1, 2, \ldots, m,$$

$$\sum_{i=1}^{m} x_{ij} = d_j \qquad \text{for } j = 1, 2, \ldots, n,$$

and

$$x_{ij} \geq 0, \qquad \text{for all } i \text{ and } j.$$

Note that the resulting table of constraint coefficients has the special structure shown in Table 8.6. *Any* linear programming problem that fits this special formulation is of the transportation problem type, regardless of its physical context. In fact, there have been numerous applications unrelated to transportation that have been fitted to this special structure, as we shall illustrate in the next example later in this section. (The assignment problem described in Sec. 8.3 is an additional example.) This is one of the reasons why the transportation problem is considered such an important special type of linear programming problem.

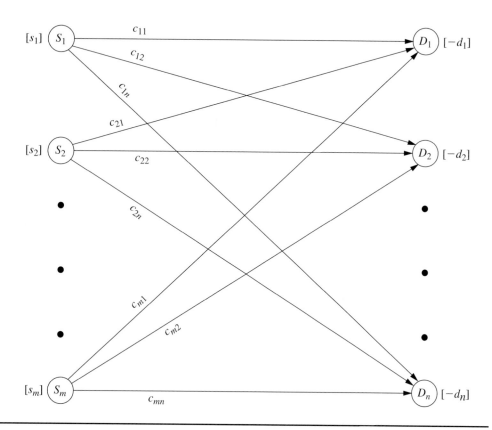

FIGURE 8.3
Network representation of
the transportation problem.

For many applications, the supply and demand quantities in the model (the s_i and d_i) have integer values, and implementation will require that the distribution quantities (the x_{ij}) also have integer values. Fortunately, because of the special structure shown in Table 8.6, all such problems have the following property.

Integer solutions property: For transportation problems where every s_i and d_j have an integer value, all the basic variables (allocations) in *every* basic feasible (BF) solution (including an optimal one) also have *integer* values.

The solution procedure described in Sec. 8.2 deals only with BF solutions, so it automatically will obtain an *integer* optimal solution for this case. (You will be able to see why this solution procedure actually gives a proof of the integer solutions property after you learn the procedure; Prob. 8.2-22 guides you through the reasoning involved.) Therefore, it is unnecessary to add a constraint to the model that the x_{ij} must have integer values.

As with other linear programming problems, the usual software options (Excel, LINGO/LINDO, MPL/CPLEX) are available to you for setting up and solving transportation problems (and assignment problems), as demonstrated in the files for this chapter in your OR Courseware. However, because the Excel approach now is somewhat different from what you have seen previously, we next describe this approach.

TABLE 8.6 Constraint coefficients for the transportation problem

Using Excel to Formulate and Solve Transportation Problems

To formulate and solve a transportation problem using Excel, two separate tables need to be entered on a spreadsheet. The first one is the parameter table. The second is a solution table, containing the quantities to distribute from each source to each destination. Figure 8.4 shows these two tables in rows 3–9 and 12–18 for the P&T Co. problem.

The two types of functional constraints need to be included in the spreadsheet. For the supply constraints, the total amount shipped from each source is calculated in column H of the solution table in Fig. 8.4. It is the sum of all the decision variable cells in the corresponding row. For example, the equation in cell H15 is "=D15+E15+F15+G15" or "=SUM(D15:G15)." The supply at each source is included in column J. Hence, the cells in column H must equal the corresponding cells in column J.

For the demand constraints, the total amount shipped to each destination is calculated in row 18 of the spreadsheet. For example, the equation in cell D18 is "=SUM(D15:D17)." The demand at each destination is then included in row 20.

The total cost is calculated in cell H18. This cost is the sum of the products of the corresponding cells in the main bodies of the parameter table and the solution table. Hence, the equation contained in cell H18 is "=SUMPRODUCT(D6:G8,D15:G17)."

Now let us look at the entries in the Solver dialogue box shown at the bottom of Fig. 8.4. These entries indicate that we are minimizing the total cost (calculated in cell H18) by changing the shipment quantities (in cells D15 through G17), subject to the constraints that the total amount shipped to each destination equals its demand (D18:G18=D20:G20) and that the total amount shipped from each source equals its supply (H15:H17=J15:J17). One of the selected Solver options (Assume Non-Negative) specifies that all shipment quantities must be nonnegative. The other one (Assume Linear Model) indicates that this transportation problem is a linear programming problem.

The values of the x_{ij} decision variables (the shipment quantities) are contained in the changing cells (D15:G17). To begin, any value (such as 0) can be entered in each of these cells. After clicking on the Solve button, the Solver will use the simplex method to solve the problem. The optimal solution obtained in this way is shown in the changing cells in Fig. 8.4, along with the resulting total cost in cell H18.

Note that the Solver simply uses the general simplex method to solve a transportation problem rather than a streamlined version that is specially designed for solving trans-

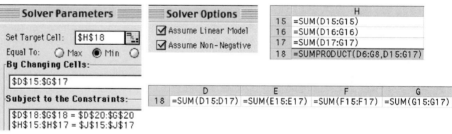

FIGURE 8.4
A spreadsheet formulation of the P & T Co. problem as a transportation problem, where rows 3 to 9 show the parameter table and rows 12 to 18 display the solution table after using the Excel Solver to obtain an optimal shipping plan. Both the formulas for the output cells and the specifications needed to set up the Solver are given at the bottom.

portation problems very efficiently, such as the transportation simplex method presented in the next section. Therefore, a software package that includes such a streamlined version should solve a large transportation problem much faster than the Excel Solver.

We mentioned earlier that some problems do not quite fit the model for a transportation problem because they violate the requirements assumption, but that it is possible to reformulate such a problem to fit this model by introducing a dummy destination or a dummy source. When using the Excel Solver, it is not necessary to do this reformulation since the simplex method can solve the original model where the supply constraints are in ≤ form or the demand constraints are in ≥ form. However, the larger the problem, the more worthwhile it becomes to do the reformulation and use the transportation simplex method (or equivalent) instead with another software package.

The next two examples illustrate how to do this kind of reformulation.

An Example with a Dummy Destination

The NORTHERN AIRPLANE COMPANY builds commercial airplanes for various airline companies around the world. The last stage in the production process is to produce the jet engines and then to install them (a very fast operation) in the completed airplane frame. The company has been working under some contracts to deliver a considerable number of airplanes in the near future, and the production of the jet engines for these planes must now be scheduled for the next 4 months.

TABLE 8.7 Production scheduling data for Northern Airplane Co.

Month	Scheduled Installations	Maximum Production	Unit Cost* of Production	Unit Cost* of Storage
1	10	25	1.08	0.015
2	15	35	1.11	0.015
3	25	30	1.10	0.015
4	20	10	1.13	

*Cost is expressed in millions of dollars.

To meet the contracted dates for delivery, the company must supply engines for installation in the quantities indicated in the second column of Table 8.7. Thus, the cumulative number of engines produced by the end of months 1, 2, 3, and 4 must be at least 10, 25, 50, and 70, respectively.

The facilities that will be available for producing the engines vary according to other production, maintenance, and renovation work scheduled during this period. The resulting monthly differences in the maximum number that can be produced and the cost (in millions of dollars) of producing each one are given in the third and fourth columns of Table 8.7.

Because of the variations in production costs, it may well be worthwhile to produce some of the engines a month or more before they are scheduled for installation, and this possibility is being considered. The drawback is that such engines must be stored until the scheduled installation (the airplane frames will not be ready early) at a storage cost of $15,000 per month (including interest on expended capital) for each engine,[1] as shown in the rightmost column of Table 8.7.

The production manager wants a schedule developed for the number of engines to be produced in each of the 4 months so that the total of the production and storage costs will be minimized.

Formulation.   One way to formulate a mathematical model for this problem is to let x_j be the number of jet engines to be produced in month j, for $j = 1, 2, 3, 4$. By using only these four decision variables, the problem can be formulated as a linear programming problem that does *not* fit the transportation problem type. (See Prob. 8.2-20.)

On the other hand, by adopting a different viewpoint, we can instead formulate the problem as a transportation problem that requires *much* less effort to solve. This viewpoint will describe the problem in terms of sources and destinations and then identify the corresponding x_{ij}, c_{ij}, s_i, and d_j. (See if you can do this before reading further.)

Because the units being distributed are jet engines, each of which is to be scheduled for production in a particular month and then installed in a particular (perhaps different) month,

Source i = production of jet engines in month i ($i = 1, 2, 3, 4$)

Destination j = installation of jet engines in month j ($j = 1, 2, 3, 4$)

---

[1] For modeling purposes, assume that this storage cost is incurred at the *end of the month* for just those engines that are being held over into the next month. Thus, engines that are produced in a given month for installation in the same month are assumed to incur no storage cost.

$$x_{ij} = \text{number of engines produced in month } i \text{ for installation in month } j$$

$$c_{ij} = \text{cost associated with each unit of } x_{ij}$$

$$= \begin{cases} \text{cost per unit for production and any storage} & \text{if } i \le j \\ ? & \text{if } i > j \end{cases}$$

$$s_i = ?$$

$$d_j = \text{number of scheduled installations in month } j.$$

The corresponding (incomplete) parameter table is given in Table 8.8. Thus, it remains to identify the missing costs and the supplies.

Since it is impossible to produce engines in one month for installation in an earlier month, x_{ij} must be zero if $i > j$. Therefore, there is no real cost that can be associated with such x_{ij}. Nevertheless, in order to have a well-defined transportation problem to which the solution procedure of Sec. 8.2 can be applied, it is necessary to assign some value for the unidentified costs. Fortunately, we can use the *Big M method* introduced in Sec. 4.6 to assign this value. Thus, we assign a *very* large number (denoted by M for convenience) to the unidentified cost entries in Table 8.8 to force the corresponding values of x_{ij} to be zero in the final solution.

The numbers that need to be inserted into the supply column of Table 8.8 are not obvious because the "supplies," the amounts produced in the respective months, are not fixed quantities. In fact, the objective is to solve for the most desirable values of these production quantities. Nevertheless, it is necessary to assign some fixed number to every entry in the table, including those in the supply column, to have a transportation problem. A clue is provided by the fact that although the supply constraints are not present in the usual form, these constraints do exist in the form of upper bounds on the amount that can be supplied, namely,

$$x_{11} + x_{12} + x_{13} + x_{14} \le 25,$$
$$x_{21} + x_{22} + x_{23} + x_{24} \le 35,$$
$$x_{31} + x_{32} + x_{33} + x_{34} \le 30,$$
$$x_{41} + x_{42} + x_{43} + x_{44} \le 10.$$

The only change from the standard model for the transportation problem is that these constraints are in the form of inequalities instead of equalities.

TABLE 8.8 Incomplete parameter table for Northern Airplane Co.

		Cost per Unit Distributed				
		Destination				
		1	2	3	4	Supply
	1	1.080	1.095	1.110	1.125	?
Source	2	?	1.110	1.125	1.140	?
	3	?	?	1.100	1.115	?
	4	?	?	?	1.130	?
Demand		10	15	25	20	

TABLE 8.9 Complete parameter table for Northern Airplane Co.

		Cost per Unit Distributed					
		Destination					
		1	2	3	4	5(D)	Supply
	1	1.080	1.095	1.110	1.125	0	25
	2	M	1.110	1.125	1.140	0	35
Source	3	M	M	1.100	1.115	0	30
	4	M	M	M	1.130	0	10
Demand		10	15	25	20	30	

To convert these inequalities to equations in order to fit the transportation problem model, we use the familiar device of *slack variables,* introduced in Sec. 4.2. In this context, the slack variables are allocations to a single **dummy destination** that represent the *unused production capacity* in the respective months. This change permits the supply in the transportation problem formulation to be the total production capacity in the given month. Furthermore, because the demand for the dummy destination is the total unused capacity, this demand is

$$(25 + 35 + 30 + 10) - (10 + 15 + 25 + 20) = 30.$$

With this demand included, the sum of the supplies now equals the sum of the demands, which is the condition given by the *feasible solutions property* for having feasible solutions.

The cost entries associated with the dummy destination should be zero because there is no cost incurred by a fictional allocation. (Cost entries of M would be *inappropriate* for this column because we do not want to force the corresponding values of x_{ij} to be zero. In fact, these values need to sum to 30.)

The resulting final parameter table is given in Table 8.9, with the dummy destination labeled as destination 5(D). By using this formulation, it is quite easy to find the optimal production schedule by the solution procedure described in Sec. 8.2. (See Prob. 8.2-11 and its answer in the back of the book.)

An Example with a Dummy Source

METRO WATER DISTRICT is an agency that administers water distribution in a large geographic region. The region is fairly arid, so the district must purchase and bring in water from outside the region. The sources of this imported water are the Colombo, Sacron, and Calorie rivers. The district then resells the water to users in the region. Its main customers are the water departments of the cities of Berdoo, Los Devils, San Go, and Hollyglass.

It is possible to supply any of these cities with water brought in from any of the three rivers, with the exception that no provision has been made to supply Hollyglass with Calorie River water. However, because of the geographic layouts of the aqueducts and the cities in the region, the cost to the district of supplying water depends upon both the source of

TABLE 8.10 Water resources data for Metro Water District

	Cost (Tens of Dollars) per Acre Foot				
	Berdoo	Los Devils	San Go	Hollyglass	Supply
Colombo River	16	13	22	17	50
Sacron River	14	13	19	15	60
Calorie River	19	20	23	—	50
Minimum needed	30	70	0	10	(in units of 1
Requested	50	70	30	∞	million acre feet)

the water and the city being supplied. The variable cost per acre foot of water (in tens of dollars) for each combination of river and city is given in Table 8.10. Despite these variations, the price per acre foot charged by the district is independent of the source of the water and is the same for all cities.

The management of the district is now faced with the problem of how to allocate the available water during the upcoming summer season. In units of 1 million acre feet, the amounts available from the three rivers are given in the rightmost column of Table 8.10. The district is committed to providing a certain minimum amount to meet the essential needs of each city (with the exception of San Go, which has an independent source of water), as shown in the *minimum needed* row of the table. The *requested* row indicates that Los Devils desires no more than the minimum amount, but that Berdoo would like to buy as much as 20 more, San Go would buy up to 30 more, and Hollyglass will take as much as it can get.

Management wishes to allocate *all* the available water from the three rivers to the four cities in such a way as to at least meet the essential needs of each city while minimizing the total cost to the district.

Formulation. Table 8.10 already is close to the proper form for a parameter table, with the rivers being the sources and the cities being the destinations. However, the one basic difficulty is that it is not clear what the demands at the destinations should be. The amount to be received at each destination (except Los Devils) actually is a decision variable, with both a lower bound and an upper bound. This upper bound is the amount requested unless the request exceeds the total supply remaining after the minimum needs of the other cities are met, in which case this *remaining supply* becomes the upper bound. Thus, insatiably thirsty Hollyglass has an upper bound of

$$(50 + 60 + 50) - (30 + 70 + 0) = 60.$$

Unfortunately, just like the other numbers in the parameter table of a transportation problem, the demand quantities must be *constants*, not bounded decision variables. To begin resolving this difficulty, temporarily suppose that it is not necessary to satisfy the minimum needs, so that the upper bounds are the only constraints on amounts to be allocated to the cities. In this circumstance, can the requested allocations be viewed as the demand quantities for a transportation problem formulation? After one adjustment, yes! (Do you see already what the needed adjustment is?)

The situation is analogous to Northern Airplane Co.'s production scheduling problem, where there was *excess supply capacity*. Now there is *excess demand capacity*. Consequently, rather than introducing a *dummy destination* to "receive" the unused supply capacity, the adjustment needed here is to introduce a **dummy source** to "send" the *unused demand capacity*. The imaginary supply quantity for this dummy source would be the amount by which the sum of the demands exceeds the sum of the real supplies:

$$(50 + 70 + 30 + 60) - (50 + 60 + 50) = 50.$$

This formulation yields the parameter table shown in Table 8.11, which uses units of million acre feet and tens of millions of dollars. The cost entries in the *dummy* row are zero because there is no cost incurred by the fictional allocations from this dummy source. On the other hand, a huge unit cost of M is assigned to the Calorie River–Hollyglass spot. The reason is that Calorie River water cannot be used to supply Hollyglass, and assigning a cost of M will prevent any such allocation.

Now let us see how we can take each city's minimum needs into account in this kind of formulation. Because San Go has no minimum need, it is all set. Similarly, the formulation for Hollyglass does not require any adjustments because its demand (60) exceeds the dummy source's supply (50) by 10, so the amount supplied to Hollyglass from the *real* sources will be *at least 10* in any feasible solution. Consequently, its minimum need of 10 from the rivers is guaranteed. (If this coincidence had not occurred, Hollyglass would need the same adjustments that we shall have to make for Berdoo.)

Los Devils' minimum need equals its requested allocation, so its *entire* demand of 70 must be filled from the real sources rather than the dummy source. This requirement calls for the Big M method! Assigning a huge unit cost of M to the allocation from the dummy source to Los Devils ensures that this allocation will be zero in an optimal solution.

Finally, consider Berdoo. In contrast to Hollyglass, the dummy source has an adequate (fictional) supply to "provide" at least some of Berdoo's minimum need in addition to its extra requested amount. Therefore, since Berdoo's minimum need is 30, adjustments must be made to prevent the dummy source from contributing more than 20 to Berdoo's total demand of 50. This adjustment is accomplished by splitting Berdoo into two destinations, one having a demand of 30 with a unit cost of M for any allocation from the dummy source and the other having a demand of 20 with a unit cost of zero for the dummy source allocation. This formulation gives the final parameter table shown in Table 8.12.

TABLE 8.11 Parameter table without minimum needs for Metro Water District

		Cost (Tens of Millions of Dollars) per Unit Distributed				
		Destination				
		Berdoo	Los Devils	San Go	Hollyglass	Supply
Source	Colombo River	16	13	22	17	50
	Sacron River	14	13	19	15	60
	Calorie River	19	20	23	M	50
	Dummy	0	0	0	0	50
Demand		50	70	30	60	

TABLE 8.12 Parameter table for Metro Water District

			Cost (Tens of Millions of Dollars) per Unit Distributed					
			Destination					
			Berdoo (min.) 1	Berdoo (extra) 2	Los Devils 3	San Go 4	Hollyglass 5	Supply
	Colombo River	1	16	16	13	22	17	50
Source	Sacron River	2	14	14	13	19	15	60
	Calorie River	3	19	19	20	23	M	50
	Dummy	4(D)	M	0	M	0	0	50
Demand			30	20	70	30	60	

> This problem will be solved in the next section to illustrate the solution procedure presented there.

8.2 A STREAMLINED SIMPLEX METHOD FOR THE TRANSPORTATION PROBLEM

Because the transportation problem is just a special type of linear programming problem, it can be solved by applying the simplex method as described in Chap. 4. However, you will see in this section that some tremendous computational shortcuts can be taken in this method by exploiting the special structure shown in Table 8.6. We shall refer to this streamlined procedure as the **transportation simplex method.**

As you read on, note particularly how the special structure is exploited to achieve great computational savings. This will illustrate an important OR technique—streamlining an algorithm to exploit the special structure in the problem at hand.

Setting Up the Transportation Simplex Method

To highlight the streamlining achieved by the transportation simplex method, let us first review how the general (unstreamlined) simplex method would set up a transportation problem in tabular form. After constructing the table of constraint coefficients (see Table 8.6), converting the objective function to maximization form, and using the Big M method to introduce artificial variables $z_1, z_2, \ldots, z_{m+n}$ into the $m + n$ respective equality constraints (see Sec. 4.6), typical columns of the simplex tableau would have the form shown in Table 8.13, where all entries *not shown* in these columns are *zeros*. [The one remaining adjustment to be made before the first iteration of the simplex method is to algebraically eliminate the nonzero coefficients of the initial (artificial) basic variables in row 0.]

After any subsequent iteration, row 0 then would have the form shown in Table 8.14. Because of the pattern of 0s and 1s for the coefficients in Table 8.13, by the *fundamental insight* presented in Sec. 5.3, u_i and v_j would have the following interpretation:

u_i = multiple of *original* row i that has been subtracted (directly or indirectly) from *original* row 0 by the simplex method during all iterations leading to the current simplex tableau.

TABLE 8.13 Original simplex tableau before simplex method is applied to transportation problem

Basic Variable	Eq.	Coefficient of:						Right side
		Z	$\cdots$	x_{ij}	$\cdots$	z_i	$\cdots$	z_{m+j}	$\cdots$	
Z	(0)	-1		c_{ij}		M		M		0
	(1)									
	$\vdots$									
z_i	(i)	0		1		1				s_i
	$\vdots$									
z_{m+j}	$(m+j)$	0		1				1		d_j
	$\vdots$									
	$(m+n)$									

v_j = multiple of *original* row $m + j$ that has been subtracted (directly or indirectly) from *original* row 0 by the simplex method during all iterations leading to the current simplex tableau.

Using the duality theory introduced in Chap. 6, another property of the u_i and v_j is that they are the *dual variables*.[1] If x_{ij} is a nonbasic variable, $c_{ij} - u_i - v_j$ is interpreted as the rate at which Z will change as x_{ij} is increased.

To lay the groundwork for simplifying this setup, recall what information is needed by the simplex method. In the initialization, an initial BF solution must be obtained, which is done artificially by introducing artificial variables as the initial basic variables and setting them equal to s_i and d_j. The optimality test and step 1 of an iteration (selecting an entering basic variable) require knowing the current row 0, which is obtained by subtracting a certain multiple of another row from the preceding row 0. Step 2 (determining the leaving basic variable) must identify the basic variable that reaches zero first as the entering basic variable is increased, which is done by comparing the current coefficients of the entering basic variable and the corresponding right side. Step 3 must determine the new BF solution, which is found by subtracting certain multiples of one row from the other rows in the current simplex tableau.

Now, how does the *transportation simplex method* obtain the same information in much simpler ways? This story will unfold fully in the coming pages, but here are some preliminary answers.

First, *no artificial variables* are needed, because a simple and convenient procedure (with several variations) is available for constructing an initial BF solution.

Second, the current row 0 can be obtained *without using any other row* simply by calculating the current values of u_i and v_j directly. Since each basic variable must have a coefficient of zero in row 0, the current u_i and v_j are obtained by solving the set of equations

$$c_{ij} - u_i - v_j = 0 \qquad \text{for each } i \text{ and } j \text{ such that } x_{ij} \text{ is a basic variable.}$$

[1] It would be easier to recognize these variables as dual variables by relabeling all these variables as y_i and then changing all the signs in row 0 of Table 8.14 by converting the objective function back to its original minimization form.

TABLE 8.14 Row 0 of simplex tableau when simplex method is applied to transportation problem

Basic Variable	Eq.	Z	$\cdots$	x_{ij}	$\cdots$	z_i	$\cdots$	z_{m+j}	$\cdots$	Right Side
				Coefficient of:						
Z	(0)	-1		$c_{ij} - u_i - v_j$		$M - u_i$		$M - v_j$		$-\sum_{i=1}^{m} s_i u_i - \sum_{j=1}^{n} d_j v_j$

(We will illustrate this straightforward procedure later when discussing the optimality test for the transportation simplex method.) The special structure in Table 8.13 makes this convenient way of obtaining row 0 possible by yielding $c_{ij} - u_i - v_j$ as the coefficient of x_{ij} in Table 8.14.

Third, the leaving basic variable can be identified in a simple way without (explicitly) using the coefficients of the entering basic variable. The reason is that the special structure of the problem makes it easy to see how the solution must change as the entering basic variable is increased. As a result, the new BF solution also can be identified immediately *without any algebraic manipulations* on the rows of the simplex tableau. (You will see the details when we describe how the transportation simplex method performs an iteration.)

The grand conclusion is that *almost the entire simplex tableau* (and the work of maintaining it) *can be eliminated*! Besides the input data (the c_{ij}, s_i, and d_j values), the only information needed by the transportation simplex method is the current BF solution,[1] the current values of u_i and v_j, and the resulting values of $c_{ij} - u_i - v_j$ for nonbasic variables x_{ij}. When you solve a problem by hand, it is convenient to record this information for each iteration in a **transportation simplex tableau**, such as shown in Table 8.15. (Note carefully that the values of x_{ij} and $c_{ij} - u_i - v_j$ are distinguished in these tableaux by circling the former but not the latter.)

You can gain a fuller appreciation for the great difference in efficiency and convenience between the simplex and the transportation simplex methods by applying both to the same small problem (see Prob. 8.2-19). However, the difference becomes even more pronounced for large problems that must be solved on a computer. This pronounced difference is suggested somewhat by comparing the sizes of the simplex and the transportation simplex tableaux. Thus, for a transportation problem having m sources and n destinations, the simplex tableau would have $m + n + 1$ rows and $(m + 1)(n + 1)$ columns (excluding those to the left of the x_{ij} columns), and the transportation simplex tableau would have m rows and n columns (excluding the two extra informational rows and columns). Now try plugging in various values for m and n (for example, $m = 10$ and $n = 100$ would be a rather typical medium-size transportation problem), and note how the ratio of the number of cells in the simplex tableau to the number in the transportation simplex tableau increases as m and n increase.

---

[1]Since nonbasic variables are automatically zero, the current BF solution is fully identified by recording just the values of the basic variables. We shall use this convention from now on.

TABLE 8.15 Format of a transportation simplex tableau

		Destination				Supply	u_i
		1	**2**	$\cdots$	**n**		
Source	1	c_{11}	c_{12}	$\cdots$	c_{1n}	s_1	
	2	c_{21}	c_{22}	$\cdots$	c_{2n}	s_2	
	$\vdots$	$\cdots$	$\cdots$	$\cdots$	$\cdots$	$\vdots$	
	m	c_{m1}	c_{m2}	$\cdots$	c_{mn}	s_m	
Demand		d_1	d_2	$\cdots$	d_n	$Z =$	
v_j							

Additional information to be added to each cell:

If x_{ij} is a basic variable

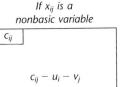
If x_{ij} is a nonbasic variable

Initialization

Recall that the objective of the initialization is to obtain an initial BF solution. Because all the functional constraints in the transportation problem are *equality* constraints, the simplex method would obtain this solution by introducing artificial variables and using them as the initial basic variables, as described in Sec. 4.6. The resulting basic solution actually is feasible only for a revised version of the problem, so a number of iterations are needed to drive these artificial variables to zero in order to reach the real BF solutions. The transportation simplex method bypasses all this by instead using a simpler procedure to directly construct a real BF solution on a transportation simplex tableau.

Before outlining this procedure, we need to point out that the number of basic variables in any basic solution of a transportation problem is one fewer than you might expect. Ordinarily, there is one basic variable for each functional constraint in a linear programming problem. For transportation problems with m sources and n destinations, the number of functional constraints is $m + n$. However,

> Number of basic variables $= m + n - 1$.

The reason is that the functional constraints are equality constraints, and this set of $m + n$ equations has one *extra* (or *redundant*) equation that can be deleted without changing the feasible region; i.e., any one of the constraints is automatically satisfied whenever the other $m + n - 1$ constraints are satisfied. (This fact can be verified by showing that any supply constraint exactly equals the sum of the demand constraints minus the sum of the *other* supply constraints, and that any demand equation also can be reproduced by summing the supply equations and subtracting the other demand equations. See Prob.

8.2-21.) Therefore, any *BF solution* appears on a transportation simplex tableau with exactly $m + n - 1$ circled *nonnegative* allocations, where the sum of the allocations for each row or column equals its supply or demand.[1]

The procedure for constructing an initial BF solution selects the $m + n - 1$ basic variables one at a time. After each selection, a value that will satisfy one additional constraint (thereby eliminating that constraint's row or column from further consideration for providing allocations) is assigned to that variable. Thus, after $m + n - 1$ selections, an entire basic solution has been constructed in such a way as to satisfy all the constraints. A number of different criteria have been proposed for selecting the basic variables. We present and illustrate three of these criteria here, after outlining the general procedure.

General Procedure[2] for Constructing an Initial BF Solution.
To begin, all source rows and destination columns of the transportation simplex tableau are initially under consideration for providing a basic variable (allocation).

1. From the rows and columns still under consideration, select the next basic variable (allocation) according to some criterion.
2. Make that allocation large enough to exactly use up the remaining supply in its row or the remaining demand in its column (whichever is smaller).
3. Eliminate that row or column (whichever had the smaller remaining supply or demand) from further consideration. (If the row and column have the same remaining supply and demand, then arbitrarily select the *row* as the one to be eliminated. The column will be used later to provide a *degenerate* basic variable, i.e., a circled allocation of zero.)
4. If only one row or only one column remains under consideration, then the procedure is completed by selecting every *remaining* variable (i.e., those variables that were neither previously selected to be basic nor eliminated from consideration by eliminating their row or column) associated with that row or column to be basic with the only feasible allocation. Otherwise, return to step 1.

Alternative Criteria for Step 1

1. *Northwest corner rule:* Begin by selecting x_{11} (that is, start in the northwest corner of the transportation simplex tableau). Thereafter, if x_{ij} was the last basic variable selected, then next select $x_{i,j+1}$ (that is, move one column to the *right*) if source i has any supply remaining. Otherwise, next select $x_{i+1,j}$ (that is, move one row *down*).

Example.
To make this description more concrete, we now illustrate the general procedure on the Metro Water District problem (see Table 8.12) with the northwest corner rule being used in step 1. Because $m = 4$ and $n = 5$ in this case, the procedure would find an initial BF solution having $m + n - 1 = 8$ basic variables.

---

[1]However, note that any feasible solution with $m + n - 1$ nonzero variables is *not necessarily* a basic solution because it might be the weighted average of two or more degenerate BF solutions (i.e., BF solutions having some basic variables equal to zero). We need not be concerned about mislabeling such solutions as being basic, however, because the transportation simplex method constructs only legitimate BF solutions.

[2]In Sec. 4.1 we pointed out that the simplex method is an example of the algorithms (systematic solution procedures) so prevalent in OR work. Note that this procedure also is an algorithm, where each successive execution of the (four) steps constitutes an iteration.

TABLE 8.16 Initial BF solution from the Northwest Corner Rule

		Destination						
		1	**2**	**3**	**4**	**5**	**Supply**	u_i
Source	1	16 (30)	16 (20)	13	22	17	50	
	2	14	14 (0)	13 (60)	19	15	60	
	3	19	19	20 (10)	23 (30)	M (10)	50	
	4(D)	M	0	M	0	0 (50)	50	
Demand		30	20	70	30	60	$Z = 2{,}470 + 10M$	
	v_j							

As shown in Table 8.16, the first allocation is $x_{11} = 30$, which exactly uses up the demand in column 1 (and eliminates this column from further consideration). This first iteration leaves a supply of 20 remaining in row 1, so next select $x_{1,1+1} = x_{12}$ to be a basic variable. Because this supply is no larger than the demand of 20 in column 2, all of it is allocated, $x_{12} = 20$, and this row is eliminated from further consideration. (Row 1 is chosen for elimination rather than column 2 because of the parenthetical instruction in step 3.) Therefore, select $x_{1+1,2} = x_{22}$ next. Because the remaining demand of 0 in column 2 is less than the supply of 60 in row 2, allocate $x_{22} = 0$ and eliminate column 2.

Continuing in this manner, we eventually obtain the entire *initial BF solution* shown in Table 8.16, where the circled numbers are the values of the basic variables ($x_{11} = 30$, $\ldots$, $x_{45} = 50$) and all the other variables (x_{13}, etc.) are nonbasic variables equal to zero. Arrows have been added to show the order in which the basic variables (allocations) were selected. The value of Z for this solution is

$$Z = 16(30) + 16(20) + \cdots + 0(50) = 2{,}470 + 10M.$$

2. *Vogel's approximation method:* For each row and column remaining under consideration, calculate its **difference,** which is defined as *the arithmetic difference between the smallest and next-to-the-smallest unit cost* c_{ij} *still remaining in that row or column.* (If two unit costs tie for being the smallest remaining in a row or column, then the *difference* is 0.) In that row or column having the *largest difference,* select the variable having the *smallest remaining unit cost.* (Ties for the largest difference, or for the smallest remaining unit cost, may be broken arbitrarily.)

Example. Now let us apply the general procedure to the Metro Water District problem by using the criterion for Vogel's approximation method to select the next basic variable in step 1. With this criterion, it is more convenient to work with parameter tables (rather than with complete transportation simplex tableaux), beginning with the one shown in Table 8.12. At each iteration, after the difference for every row and column remaining under consideration is calculated and displayed, the largest difference is circled and the smallest unit cost in its row or column is enclosed in a box. The resulting selection (and value) of the variable having this unit cost as the next basic variable is indicated in the lower right-hand corner of the current table, along with the row or column thereby being eliminated from further consideration (see steps 2 and 3 of the general procedure). The table for the next iteration is exactly the same except for deleting this row or column and subtracting the last allocation from its supply or demand (whichever remains).

Applying this procedure to the Metro Water District problem yields the sequence of parameter tables shown in Table 8.17, where the resulting initial BF solution consists of the eight basic variables (allocations) given in the lower right-hand corner of the respective parameter tables.

This example illustrates two relatively subtle features of the general procedure that warrant special attention. First, note that the final iteration selects *three* variables (x_{31}, x_{32}, and x_{33}) to become basic instead of the single selection made at the other iterations. The reason is that only *one* row (row 3) remains under consideration at this point. Therefore, step 4 of the general procedure says to select *every* remaining variable associated with row 3 to be basic.

Second, note that the allocation of $x_{23} = 20$ at the next-to-last iteration exhausts *both* the remaining supply in its row *and* the remaining demand in its column. However, rather than eliminate both the row and column from further consideration, step 3 says to eliminate *only the row,* saving the column to provide a *degenerate* basic variable later. Column 3 is, in fact, used for just this purpose at the final iteration when $x_{33} = 0$ is selected as one of the basic variables. For another illustration of this same phenomenon, see Table 8.16 where the allocation of $x_{12} = 20$ results in eliminating only row 1, so that column 2 is saved to provide a degenerate basic variable, $x_{22} = 0$, at the next iteration.

Although a zero allocation might seem irrelevant, it actually plays an important role. You will see soon that the transportation simplex method must know *all* $m + n - 1$ basic variables, including those with value zero, in the current BF solution.

---

3. *Russell's approximation method:* For each source row i remaining under consideration, determine its $\bar{u}_i$, which is the largest unit cost c_{ij} still remaining in that row. For each destination column j remaining under consideration, determine its $\bar{v}_j$, which is the largest unit cost c_{ij} still remaining in that column. For each variable x_{ij} not previously selected in these rows and columns, calculate $\Delta_{ij} = c_{ij} - \bar{u}_i - \bar{v}_j$. Select the variable having the *largest* (in absolute terms) *negative* value of Δ_{ij}. (Ties may be broken arbitrarily.)

Example.   Using the criterion for Russell's approximation method in step 1, we again apply the general procedure to the Metro Water District problem (see Table 8.12). The results, including the sequence of basic variables (allocations), are shown in Table 8.18.

At iteration 1, the largest unit cost in row 1 is $\bar{u}_1 = 22$, the largest in column 1 is $\bar{v}_1 = M$, and so forth. Thus,

$$\Delta_{11} = c_{11} - \bar{u}_1 - \bar{v}_1 = 16 - 22 - M = -6 - M.$$

TABLE 8.17 Initial BF solution from Vogel's approximation method

		Destination					Supply	Row Difference
		1	**2**	**3**	**4**	**5**		
	1	16	16	13	22	17	50	3
Source	2	14	14	13	19	15	60	1
	3	19	19	20	23	M	50	0
	4(D)	M	0	M	⬚0	0	50	0
Demand		30	20	70	30	60	Select $x_{44} = 30$	
Column difference		2	14	0	ⓘ19	15	Eliminate column 4	

		Destination				Supply	Row Difference
		1	**2**	**3**	**5**		
	1	16	16	13	17	50	3
Source	2	14	14	13	15	60	1
	3	19	19	20	M	50	0
	4(D)	M	0	M	⬚0	20	0
Demand		30	20	70	60	Select $x_{45} = 20$	
Column difference		2	14	0	ⓘ15	Eliminate row 4(D)	

		Destination				Supply	Row Difference
		1	**2**	**3**	**5**		
	1	16	16	⬚13	17	50	③
Source	2	14	14	13	15	60	1
	3	19	19	20	M	50	0
Demand		30	20	70	40	Select $x_{13} = 50$	
Column difference		2	2	0	2	Eliminate row 1	

		Destination				Supply	Row Difference
		1	**2**	**3**	**5**		
Source	2	14	14	13	⬚15	60	1
	3	19	19	20	M	50	0
Demand		30	20	20	40	Select $x_{25} = 40$	
Column difference		5	5	7	ⓘ$M-15$	Eliminate column 5	

		Destination			Supply	Row Difference
		1	**2**	**3**		
Source	2	14	14	⬚13	20	1
	3	19	19	20	50	0
Demand		30	20	20	Select $x_{23} = 20$	
Column difference		5	5	ⓘ7	Eliminate row 2	

		Destination			Supply
		1	**2**	**3**	
Source	3	19	19	20	50
Demand		30	20	0	Select $x_{31} = 30$
					$x_{32} = 20$ $Z = 2{,}460$
					$x_{33} = 0$

TABLE 8.18 Initial BF solution from Russell's approximation method

Iteration	$\bar{u}_1$	$\bar{u}_2$	$\bar{u}_3$	$\bar{u}_4$	$\bar{v}_1$	$\bar{v}_2$	$\bar{v}_3$	$\bar{v}_4$	$\bar{v}_5$	Largest Negative Δ_{ij}	Allocation
1	22	19	M	M	M	19	M	23	M	$\Delta_{45} = -2M$	$x_{45} = 50$
2	22	19	M		19	19	20	23	M	$\Delta_{15} = -5 - M$	$x_{15} = 10$
3	22	19	23		19	19	20	23		$\Delta_{13} = -29$	$x_{13} = 40$
4		19	23		19	19	20	23		$\Delta_{23} = -26$	$x_{23} = 30$
5		19	23		19	19		23		$\Delta_{21} = -24*$	$x_{21} = 30$
6										Irrelevant	$x_{31} = 0$
											$x_{32} = 20$
											$x_{34} = 30$
											$Z = 2{,}570$

*Tie with $\Delta_{22} = -24$ broken arbitrarily.

Calculating all the Δ_{ij} values for $i = 1, 2, 3, 4$ and $j = 1, 2, 3, 4, 5$ shows that $\Delta_{45} = 0 - 2M$ has the largest negative value, so $x_{45} = 50$ is selected as the first basic variable (allocation). This allocation exactly uses up the supply in row 4, so this row is eliminated from further consideration.

Note that eliminating this row changes $\bar{v}_1$ and $\bar{v}_3$ for the next iteration. Therefore, the second iteration requires recalculating the Δ_{ij} with $j = 1, 3$ as well as eliminating $i = 4$. The largest negative value now is

$$\Delta_{15} = 17 - 22 - M = -5 - M,$$

so $x_{15} = 10$ becomes the second basic variable (allocation), eliminating column 5 from further consideration.

The subsequent iterations proceed similarly, but you may want to test your understanding by verifying the remaining allocations given in Table 8.18. As with the other procedures in this (and other) section(s), you should find your OR Courseware useful for doing the calculations involved and illuminating the approach. (See the interactive routine for finding an initial BF solution.)

Comparison of Alternative Criteria for Step 1. Now let us compare these three criteria for selecting the next basic variable. The main virtue of the northwest corner rule is that it is quick and easy. However, because it pays no attention to unit costs c_{ij}, usually the solution obtained will be far from optimal. (Note in Table 8.16 that $x_{35} = 10$ even though $c_{35} = M$.) Expending a little more effort to find a good initial BF solution might greatly reduce the number of iterations then required by the transportation simplex method to reach an optimal solution (see Probs. 8.2-8 and 8.2-10). Finding such a solution is the objective of the other two criteria.

Vogel's approximation method has been a popular criterion for many years,[1] partially because it is relatively easy to implement by hand. Because the *difference* represents the minimum extra unit cost incurred by failing to make an allocation to the cell having the

[1]N. V. Reinfeld and W. R. Vogel, *Mathematical Programming,* Prentice-Hall, Englewood Cliffs, NJ, 1958.

smallest unit cost in that row or column, this criterion does take costs into account in an effective way.

Russell's approximation method provides another excellent criterion[1] that is still quick to implement on a computer (but not manually). Although is is unclear as to which is more effective *on average,* this criterion *frequently* does obtain a better solution than Vogel's. (For the example, Vogel's approximation method happened to find the optimal solution with $Z = 2,460$, whereas Russell's misses slightly with $Z = 2,570$.) For a large problem, it may be worthwhile to apply both criteria and then use the better solution to start the iterations of the transportation simplex method.

One distinct advantage of Russell's approximation method is that it is patterned directly after step 1 for the transportation simplex method (as you will see soon), which somewhat simplifies the overall computer code. In particular, the $\bar{u}_i$ and $\bar{v}_j$ values have been defined in such a way that the relative values of the $c_{ij} - \bar{u}_i - \bar{v}_j$ *estimate* the relative values of $c_{ij} - u_i - v_j$ that will be obtained when the transportation simplex method reaches an optimal solution.

We now shall use the initial BF solution obtained in Table 8.18 by Russell's approximation method to illustrate the remainder of the transportation simplex method. Thus, our *initial transportation simplex tableau* (before we solve for u_i and v_j) is shown in Table 8.19.

The next step is to check whether this initial solution is optimal by applying the *optimality test.*

[1]E. J. Russell, "Extension of Dantzig's Algorithm to Finding an Initial Near-Optimal Basis for the Transportation Problem," *Operations Research,* **17:** 187–191, 1969.

TABLE 8.19 Initial transportation simplex tableau (before we obtain $c_{ij} - u_i - v_j$) from Russell's approximation method

Iteration 0		Destination					Supply	u_i
		1	2	3	4	5		
Source	1	16	16	13 (40)	22	17 (10)	50	
	2	14 (30)	14	13 (30)	19	15	60	
	3	19 (0)	19 (20)	20	23 (30)	M	50	
	4(D)	M	0	M	0	0 (50)	50	
Demand		30	20	70	30	60	Z = 2,570	
v_j								

Optimality Test

Using the notation of Table 8.14, we can reduce the standard optimality test for the simplex method (see Sec. 4.3) to the following for the transportation problem:

> **Optimality test:** A BF solution is optimal if and only if $c_{ij} - u_i - v_j \geq 0$ for every (i, j) such that x_{ij} is nonbasic.[1]

Thus, the only work required by the optimality test is the derivation of the values of u_i and v_j for the current BF solution and then the calculation of these $c_{ij} - u_i - v_j$, as described below.

Since $c_{ij} - u_i - v_j$ is required to be zero if x_{ij} is a basic variable, u_i and v_j satisfy the set of equations

$$c_{ij} = u_i + v_j \qquad \text{for each } (i, j) \text{ such that } x_{ij} \text{ is basic.}$$

There are $m + n - 1$ basic variables, and so there are $m + n - 1$ of these equations. Since the number of unknowns (the u_i and v_j) is $m + n$, one of these variables can be assigned a value arbitrarily without violating the equations. The choice of this one variable and its value does not affect the value of any $c_{ij} - u_i - v_j$, even when x_{ij} is nonbasic, so the only (minor) difference it makes is in the ease of solving these equations. A convenient choice for this purpose is to select the u_i that has the *largest number of allocations in its row* (break any tie arbitrarily) and to assign to it the value zero. Because of the simple structure of these equations, it is then very simple to solve for the remaining variables algebraically.

To demonstrate, we give each equation that corresponds to a basic variable in our initial BF solution.

x_{31}:	$19 = u_3 + v_1$.	Set $u_3 = 0$, so $v_1 = 19$,
x_{32}:	$19 = u_3 + v_2$.	$v_2 = 19$,
x_{34}:	$23 = u_3 + v_4$.	$v_4 = 23$.
x_{21}:	$14 = u_2 + v_1$.	Know $v_1 = 19$, so $u_2 = -5$.
x_{23}:	$13 = u_2 + v_3$.	Know $u_2 = -5$, so $v_3 = 18$.
x_{13}:	$13 = u_1 + v_3$.	Know $v_3 = 18$, so $u_1 = -5$.
x_{15}:	$17 = u_1 + v_5$.	Know $u_1 = -5$, so $v_5 = 22$.
x_{45}:	$0 = u_4 + v_5$.	Know $v_5 = 22$, so $u_4 = -22$.

Setting $u_3 = 0$ (since row 3 of Table 8.19 has the largest number of allocations—3) and moving down the equations one at a time immediately give the derivation of values for the unknowns shown to the right of the equations. (Note that this derivation of the u_i and v_j values depends on which x_{ij} variables are *basic variables* in the current BF solution, so this derivation will need to be repeated each time a new BF solution is obtained.)

---

[1]The one exception is that two or more equivalent degenerate BF solutions (i.e., identical solutions having different degenerate basic variables equal to zero) can be optimal with only some of these basic solutions satisfying the optimality test. This exception is illustrated later in the example (see the identical solutions in the last two tableaux of Table 8.23, where only the latter solution satisfies the criterion for optimality).

Once you get the hang of it, you probably will find it even more convenient to solve these equations without writing them down by working directly on the transportation simplex tableau. Thus, in Table 8.19 you begin by writing in the value $u_3 = 0$ and then picking out the circled allocations (x_{31}, x_{32}, x_{34}) in that row. For each one you set $v_j = c_{3j}$ and then look for circled allocations (except in row 3) in these columns (x_{21}). Mentally calculate $u_2 = c_{21} - v_1$, pick out x_{23}, set $v_3 = c_{23} - u_2$, and so on until you have filled in all the values for u_i and v_j. (Try it.) Then calculate and fill in the value of $c_{ij} - u_i - v_j$ for each nonbasic variable x_{ij} (that is, for each cell without a circled allocation), and you will have the completed initial transportation simplex tableau shown in Table 8.20.

We are now in a position to apply the optimality test by checking the values of $c_{ij} - u_i - v_j$ given in Table 8.20. Because two of these values ($c_{25} - u_2 - v_5 = -2$ and $c_{44} - u_4 - v_4 = -1$) are negative, we conclude that the current BF solution is not optimal. Therefore, the transportation simplex method must next go to an iteration to find a better BF solution.

An Iteration

As with the full-fledged simplex method, an iteration for this streamlined version must determine an entering basic variable (step 1), a leaving basic variable (step 2), and then identify the resulting new BF solution (step 3).

Step 1. Since $c_{ij} - u_i - v_j$ represents the rate at which the objective function will change as the nonbasic variable x_{ij} is increased, the entering basic variable must have a *negative* $c_{ij} - u_i - v_j$ value to decrease the total cost Z. Thus, the candidates in Table 8.20 are x_{25} and x_{44}. To choose between the candidates, select the one having the larger (in absolute terms) negative value of $c_{ij} - u_i - v_j$ to be the entering basic variable, which is x_{25} in this case.

TABLE 8.20 Completed initial transportation simplex tableau

Iteration 0		Destination 1	2	3	4	5	Supply	u_i
Source	1	16 +2	16 +2	13 (40)	22 +4	17 (10)	50	−5
	2	14 (30)	14 0	13 (30)	19 +1	15 −2	60	−5
	3	19 (0)	19 (20)	20 +2	23 (30)	M M−22	50	0
	4(D)	M M+3	0 +3	M M+4	0 −1	0 (50)	50	−22
Demand		30	20	70	30	60	Z = 2,570	
v_j		19	19	18	23	22		

Step 2. Increasing the entering basic variable from zero sets off a *chain reaction* of compensating changes in other basic variables (allocations), in order to continue satisfying the supply and demand constraints. The first basic variable to be decreased to zero then becomes the leaving basic variable.

With x_{25} as the entering basic variable, the chain reaction in Table 8.20 is the relatively simple one summarized in Table 8.21. (We shall always indicate the entering basic variable by placing a boxed plus sign in the center of its cell while leaving the corresponding value of $c_{ij} - u_i - v_j$ in the lower right-hand corner of this cell.) Increasing x_{25} by some amount requires decreasing x_{15} by the same amount to restore the demand of 60 in column 5. This change then requires increasing x_{13} by this same amount to restore the supply of 50 in row 1. This change then requires decreasing x_{23} by this amount to restore the demand of 70 in column 3. This decrease in x_{23} successfully completes the chain reaction because it also restores the supply of 60 in row 2. (Equivalently, we could have started the chain reaction by restoring this supply in row 2 with the decrease in x_{23}, and then the chain reaction would continue with the increase in x_{13} and decrease in x_{15}.)

The net result is that cells (2, 5) and (1, 3) become **recipient cells,** each receiving its additional allocation from one of the **donor cells,** (1, 5) and (2, 3). (These cells are indicated in Table 8.21 by the plus and minus signs.) Note that cell (1, 5) had to be the donor cell for column 5 rather than cell (4, 5), because cell (4, 5) would have no recipient cell in row 4 to continue the chain reaction. [Similarly, if the chain reaction had been started in row 2 instead, cell (2, 1) could not be the donor cell for this row because the chain reaction could not then be completed successfully after necessarily choosing cell (3, 1) as the next recipient cell and either cell (3, 2) or (3, 4) as its donor cell.] Also note that, except for the entering basic variable, *all* recipient cells and donor cells in the chain reaction must correspond to *basic* variables in the current BF solution.

Each donor cell decreases its allocation by exactly the same amount as the entering basic variable (and other recipient cells) is increased. Therefore, the donor cell that starts with the smallest allocation—cell (1, 5) in this case (since $10 < 30$ in Table 8.21)—must reach a zero allocation first as the entering basic variable x_{25} is increased. Thus, x_{15} becomes the leaving basic variable.

TABLE 8.21 Part of initial transportation simplex tableau showing the chain reaction caused by increasing the entering basic variable x_{25}

			Destination			
			3	**4**	**5**	**Supply**
Source	1	...	[13] (40)+	[22] +4	[17] (10)−	50
	2	...	[13] (30)−	[19] +1	[15] ☐+ −2	60
		...	...	...	...	
Demand			70	30	60	

In general, there always is just *one* chain reaction (in either direction) that can be completed successfully to maintain feasibility when the entering basic variable is increased from zero. This chain reaction can be identified by selecting from the cells having a basic variable: first the donor cell in the *column* having the entering basic variable, then the recipient cell in the row having this donor cell, then the donor cell in the column having this recipient cell, and so on until the chain reaction yields a donor cell in the *row* having the entering basic variable. When a column or row has more than one additional basic variable cell, it may be necessary to trace them all further to see which one must be selected to be the donor or recipient cell. (All but this one eventually will reach a dead end in a row or column having no additional basic variable cell.) After the chain reaction is identified, the donor cell having the *smallest* allocation automatically provides the leaving basic variable. (In the case of a tie for the donor cell having the smallest allocation, any one can be chosen arbitrarily to provide the leaving basic variable.)

Step 3.   The *new BF solution* is identified simply by adding the value of the leaving basic variable (before any change) to the allocation for each recipient cell and subtracting *this same amount* from the allocation for each donor cell. In Table 8.21 the value of the leaving basic variable x_{15} is 10, so the portion of the transportation simplex tableau in this table changes as shown in Table 8.22 for the new solution. (Since x_{15} is nonbasic in the new solution, its new allocation of zero is no longer shown in this new tableau.)

We can now highlight a useful interpretation of the $c_{ij} - u_i - v_j$ quantities derived during the optimality test. Because of the shift of 10 allocation units from the donor cells to the recipient cells (shown in Tables 8.21 and 8.22), the total cost changes by

$$\Delta Z = 10(15 - 17 + 13 - 13) = 10(-2) = 10(c_{25} - u_2 - v_5).$$

Thus, the effect of increasing the entering basic variable x_{25} from zero has been a cost change at the rate of -2 per unit increase in x_{25}. This is precisely what the value of $c_{25} - u_2 - v_5 = -2$ in Table 8.20 indicates would happen. In fact, another (but less efficient) way of deriving $c_{ij} - u_i - v_j$ for each nonbasic variable x_{ij} is to identify the chain reaction caused by increasing this variable from 0 to 1 and then to calculate the resulting cost change. This intuitive interpretation sometimes is useful for checking calculations during the optimality test.

TABLE 8.22 Part of second transportation simplex tableau showing the changes in the BF solution

		Destination			
		3	4	5	Supply
Source	1	...	[13] (50)	[22]	[17]	50
	2	...	[13] (20)	[19]	[15] (10)	60
		...	...	...	...	
Demand			70	30	60	

Before completing the solution of the Metro Water District problem, we now summarize the rules for the transportation simplex method.

Summary of the Transportation Simplex Method.

Initialization: Construct an initial BF solution by the procedure outlined earlier in this section. Go to the optimality test.

Optimality test: Derive u_i and v_j by selecting the row having the largest number of allocations, setting its $u_i = 0$, and then solving the set of equations $c_{ij} = u_i + v_j$ for each (i, j) such that x_{ij} is basic. If $c_{ij} - u_i - v_j \geq 0$ for every (i, j) such that x_{ij} is *nonbasic,* then the current solution is optimal, so stop. Otherwise, go to an iteration.

Iteration:

1. Determine the entering basic variable: Select the nonbasic variable x_{ij} having the *largest* (in absolute terms) *negative* value of $c_{ij} - u_i - v_j$.
2. Determine the leaving basic variable: Identify the chain reaction required to retain feasibility when the entering basic variable is increased. From the donor cells, select the basic variable having the *smallest* value.
3. Determine the new BF solution: Add the value of the leaving basic variable to the allocation for each recipient cell. Subtract this value from the allocation for each donor cell.

Continuing to apply this procedure to the Metro Water District problem yields the complete set of transportation simplex tableaux shown in Table 8.23. Since all the $c_{ij} - u_i - v_j$ values are nonnegative in the fourth tableau, the optimality test identifies the set of allocations in this tableau as being optimal, which concludes the algorithm.

It would be good practice for you to derive the values of u_i and v_j given in the second, third, and fourth tableaux. Try doing this by working directly on the tableaux. Also

TABLE 8.23 Complete set of transportation simplex tableaux for the Metro Water District problem

Iteration 0		Destination					Supply	u_i
		1	2	3	4	5		
Source	1	16 +2	16 +2	13 (40)+	22 +4	17 (10)−	50	−5
	2	14 (30)	14 0	13 (30)−	19 +1	15 +−2	60	−5
	3	19 (0)	19 (20)	20 +2	23 (30)	M M − 22	50	0
	4(D)	M M + 3	0 +3	M M + 4	0 −1	0 (50)	50	−22
Demand		30	20	70	30	60	Z = 2,570	
v_j		19	19	18	23	22		

TABLE 8.23   (*Continued*)

Iteration 1

Source \ Destination	1	2	3	4	5	Supply	u_i
1	16 +2	16 +2	13 (50)	22 +4	17 +2	50	−5
2	14 (30)−	14 —0—	13 (20)	19 +1	15 (10)+	60	−5
3	19 (0)+	19 (20)	20 +2	23 (30)−	M, M−20	50	0
4(D)	M, M+1	0 +1	M, M+2	0, + −3	0 (50)−	50	−20
Demand	30	20	70	30	60	Z = 2,550	
v_j	19	19	18	23	20		

Iteration 2

Source \ Destination	1	2	3	4	5	Supply	u_i
1	16 +5	16 +5	13 (50)	22 +7	17 +2	50	−8
2	14 +3	14 +3	13 (20)−	19 +4	15 (40)+	60	−8
3	19 (30)	19 (20)	20 + −1	23 (0)−	M, M−23	50	0
4(D)	M, M+4	0 +4	M, M+2	0 (30)+	0 (20)−	50	−23
Demand	30	20	70	30	60	Z = 2,460	
v_j	19	19	21	23	23		

Iteration 3

Source \ Destination	1	2	3	4	5	Supply	u_i
1	16 +4	16 +4	13 (50)	22 +7	17 +2	50	−7
2	14 +2	14 +2	13 (20)	19 +4	15 (40)	60	−7
3	19 (30)	19 (20)	20 (0)	23 +1	M, M−22	50	0
4(D)	M, M+3	0 +3	M, M+2	0 (30)	0 (20)	50	−22
Demand	30	20	70	30	60	Z = 2,460	
v_j	19	19	20	22	22		

check out the chain reactions in the second and third tableaux, which are somewhat more complicated than the one you have seen in Table 8.21.

Note three special points that are illustrated by this example. First, the initial BF solution is *degenerate* because the basic variable $x_{31} = 0$. However, this degenerate basic variable causes no complication, because cell (3, 1) becomes a *recipient cell* in the second tableau, which increases x_{31} to a value greater than zero.

Second, another degenerate basic variable (x_{34}) arises in the third tableau because the basic variables for *two* donor cells in the second tableau, cells (2, 1) and (3, 4), *tie* for having the smallest value (30). (This tie is broken arbitrarily by selecting x_{21} as the leaving basic variable; if x_{34} had been selected instead, then x_{21} would have become the degenerate basic variable.) This degenerate basic variable does appear to create a complication subsequently, because cell (3, 4) becomes a *donor cell* in the third tableau but has nothing to donate! Fortunately, such an event actually gives no cause for concern. Since zero is the amount to be added to or subtracted from the allocations for the recipient and donor cells, these allocations do not change. However, the degenerate basic variable does become the leaving basic variable, so it is replaced by the entering basic variable as the circled allocation of zero in the fourth tableau. This change in the set of basic variables changes the values of u_i and v_j. Therefore, if any of the $c_{ij} - u_i - v_j$ had been negative in the fourth tableau, the algorithm would have gone on to make *real* changes in the allocations (whenever all donor cells have nondegenerate basic variables).

Third, because none of the $c_{ij} - u_i - v_j$ turned out to be negative in the fourth tableau, the equivalent set of allocations in the third tableau is optimal also. Thus, the algorithm executed one more iteration than was necessary. This extra iteration is a flaw that occasionally arises in both the transportation simplex method and the simplex method because of degeneracy, but it is not sufficiently serious to warrant any adjustments to these algorithms.

For another (smaller) example of the application of the transportation simplex method, refer to the demonstration provided for the transportation problem area in your OR Tutor. Also provided in your OR Courseware is an interactive routine for the transportation simplex method.

Now that you have studied the transportation simplex method, you are in a position to check for yourself how the algorithm actually provides a proof of the *integer solutions property* presented in Sec. 8.1. Problem 8.2-22 helps to guide you through the reasoning.

8.3 THE ASSIGNMENT PROBLEM

The **assignment problem** is a special type of linear programming problem where **assignees** are being assigned to perform **tasks.** For example, the assignees might be employees who need to be given work assignments. Assigning people to jobs is a common application of the assignment problem. However, the assignees need not be people. They also could be machines, or vehicles, or plants, or even time slots to be assigned tasks. The first example below involves machines being assigned to locations, so the tasks in this case simply involve holding a machine. A subsequent example involves plants being assigned products to be produced.

To fit the definition of an assignment problem, these kinds of applications need to be formulated in a way that satisfies the following assumptions.

1. The number of assignees and the number of tasks are the same. (This number is denoted by n.)
2. Each assignee is to be assigned to exactly *one* task.
3. Each task is to be performed by exactly *one* assignee.
4. There is a cost c_{ij} associated with assignee i ($i = 1, 2, \ldots, n$) performing task j ($j = 1, 2, \ldots, n$).
5. The objective is to determine how all n assignments should be made to minimize the total cost.

Any problem satisfying all these assumptions can be solved extremely efficiently by algorithms designed specifically for assignment problems.

The first three assumptions are fairly restrictive. Many potential applications do not quite satisfy these assumptions. However, it often is possible to reformulate the problem to make it fit. For example, *dummy assignees* or *dummy tasks* frequently can be used for this purpose. We illustrate these formulation techniques in the examples.

Prototype Example

The JOB SHOP COMPANY has purchased three new machines of different types. There are four available locations in the shop where a machine could be installed. Some of these locations are more desirable than others for particular machines because of their proximity to work centers that will have a heavy work flow to and from these machines. (There will be no work flow *between* the new machines.) Therefore, the objective is to assign the new machines to the available locations to minimize the total cost of materials handling. The estimated cost in dollars per hour of materials handling involving each of the machines is given in Table 8.24 for the respective locations. Location 2 is not considered suitable for machine 2, so no cost is given for this case.

To formulate this problem as an assignment problem, we must introduce a *dummy machine* for the extra location. Also, an extremely large cost M should be attached to the assignment of machine 2 to location 2 to prevent this assignment in the optimal solution. The resulting assignment problem *cost table* is shown in Table 8.25. This cost table contains all the necessary data for solving the problem. The optimal solution is to assign machine 1 to location 4, machine 2 to location 3, and machine 3 to location 1, for a total cost of $29 per hour. The dummy machine is assigned to location 2, so this location is available for some future real machine.

We shall discuss how this solution is obtained after we formulate the mathematical model for the general assignment problem.

TABLE 8.24 Materials-handling cost data
($) for Job Shop Co.

		Location			
		1	**2**	**3**	**4**
Machine	1	13	16	12	11
	2	15	—	13	20
	3	5	7	10	6

TABLE 8.25 Cost table for the Job Shop Co. assignment problem

		Task (Location)			
		1	**2**	**3**	**4**
	1	13	16	12	11
Assignee	2	15	M	13	20
(Machine)	3	5	7	10	6
	4(D)	0	0	0	0

The Assignment Problem Model and Solution Procedures

The mathematical model for the assignment problem uses the following decision variables:

$$x_{ij} = \begin{cases} 1 & \text{if assignee } i \text{ performs task } j, \\ 0 & \text{if not,} \end{cases}$$

for $i = 1, 2, \ldots, n$ and $j = 1, 2, \ldots, n$. Thus, each x_{ij} is a *binary variable* (it has value 0 or 1). As discussed at length in the chapter on integer programming (Chap. 12), binary variables are important in OR for representing *yes/no decisions*. In this case, the yes/no decision is: Should assignee i perform task j?

By letting Z denote the total cost, the assignment problem model is

Minimize $$Z = \sum_{i=1}^{n} \sum_{j=1}^{n} c_{ij}x_{ij},$$

subject to

$$\sum_{j=1}^{n} x_{ij} = 1 \qquad \text{for } i = 1, 2, \ldots, n,$$

$$\sum_{i=1}^{n} x_{ij} = 1 \qquad \text{for } j = 1, 2, \ldots, n,$$

and

$$x_{ij} \geq 0, \qquad \text{for all } i \text{ and } j$$
$$(x_{ij} \text{ binary}, \qquad \text{for all } i \text{ and } j).$$

The first set of functional constraints specifies that each assignee is to perform exactly one task, whereas the second set requires each task to be performed by exactly one assignee. If we delete the parenthetical restriction that the x_{ij} be binary, the model clearly is a special type of linear programming problem and so can be readily solved. Fortunately, for reasons about to unfold, we *can* delete this restriction. (This deletion is the reason that the assignment problem appears in this chapter rather than in the integer programming chapter.)

Now compare this model (without the binary restriction) with the transportation problem model presented in the third subsection of Sec. 8.1 (including Table 8.6). Note how similar their structures are. In fact, the assignment problem is just a special type of transportation problem where the *sources* now are *assignees* and the *destinations* now are *tasks* and where

Number of sources m = number of destinations n,

Every supply $s_i = 1$,

Every demand $d_j = 1$.

Now focus on the *integer solutions property* in the subsection on the transportation problem model. Because s_i and d_j are integers (= 1) now, this property implies that *every BF solution* (including an optimal one) is an *integer* solution for an assignment problem. The functional constraints of the assignment problem model prevent any variable from being greater than 1, and the nonnegativity constraints prevent values less than 0. Therefore, by deleting the binary restriction to enable us to solve an assignment problem as a linear programming problem, the resulting BF solutions obtained (including the final optimal solution) *automatically* will satisfy the binary restriction anyway.

Just as the transportation problem has a network representation (see Fig. 8.3), the assignment problem can be depicted in a very similar way, as shown in Fig. 8.5. The first column now lists the n assignees and the second column the n tasks. Each number in a

FIGURE 8.5
Network representation of the assignment problem.

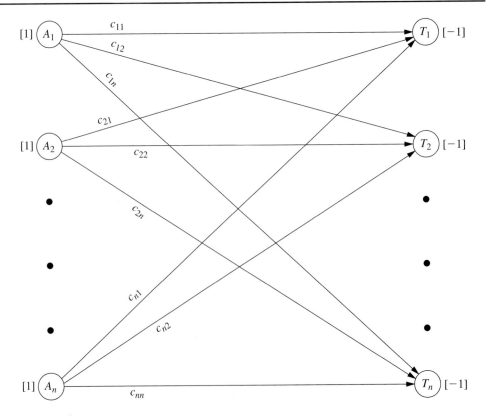

square bracket indicates the number of assignees being provided at that location in the network, so the values are automatically 1 on the left, whereas the values of -1 on the right indicate that each task is using up one assignee.

For any particular assignment problem, practitioners normally do not bother writing out the full mathematical model. It is simpler to formulate the problem by filling out a cost table (e.g., Table 8.25), including identifying the assignees and tasks, since this table contains all the essential data in a far more compact form.

Alternative solution procedures are available for solving assignment problems. Problems that aren't much larger than the Job Shop Co. example can be solved very quickly by the general simplex method, so it may be convenient to simply use a basic software package (such as Excel and its Solver) that only employs this method. If this were done for the Job Shop Co. problem, it would not have been necessary to add the dummy machine to Table 8.25 to make it fit the assignment problem model. The constraints on the number of machines assigned to each location would be expressed instead as

$$\sum_{i=1}^{3} x_{ij} \leq 1 \qquad \text{for } j = 1, 2, 3, 4.$$

As shown in the Excel file for this chapter, a spreadsheet formulation for this example would be very similar to the formulation for a transportation problem displayed in Fig. 8.4 except now all the supplies and demands would be 1 and the demand constraints would be ≤ 1 instead of $= 1$.

However, large assignment problems can be solved much faster by using more specialized solution procedures, so we recommend using such a procedure instead of the general simplex method for big problems.

Because the assignment problem is a special type of transportation problem, one convenient and relatively fast way to solve any particular assignment problem is to apply the transportation simplex method described in Sec. 8.2. This approach requires converting the cost table to a parameter table for the equivalent transportation problem, as shown in Table 8.26a.

TABLE 8.26 Parameter table for the assignment problem formulated as a transportation problem, illustrated by the Job Shop Co. example

(a) General Case

		Cost per Unit Distributed				
		Destination				Supply
		1	2	...	n	
Source	1	c_{11}	c_{12}	...	c_{1n}	1
	2	c_{21}	c_{22}	...	c_{2n}	1
	:	...	...	...	...	:
	$m = n$	c_{n1}	c_{n2}	...	c_{nn}	1
Demand		1	1	...	1	

(b) Job Shop Co. Example

		Cost per Unit Distributed				
		Destination (Location)				Supply
		1	2	3	4	
Source (Machine)	1	13	16	12	11	1
	2	15	M	13	20	1
	3	5	7	10	6	1
	4(D)	0	0	0	0	1
Demand		1	1	1	1	

For example, Table 8.26b shows the parameter table for the Job Shop Co. problem that is obtained from the cost table of Table 8.25. When the transportation simplex method is applied to this transportation problem formulation, the resulting optimal solution has basic variables $x_{13} = 0$, $x_{14} = 1$, $x_{23} = 1$, $x_{31} = 1$, $x_{41} = 0$, $x_{42} = 1$, $x_{43} = 0$. (You are asked to verify this solution in Prob. 8.3-7.). The degenerate basic variables $(x_{ij} = 0)$ and the assignment for the dummy machine $(x_{42} = 1)$ do not mean anything for the original problem, so the real assignments are machine 1 to location 4, machine 2 to location 3, and machine 3 to location 1.

It is no coincidence that this optimal solution provided by the transportation simplex method has so many degenerate basic variables. For any assignment problem with n assignments to be made, the transportation problem formulation shown in Table 8.26a has $m = n$, that is, both the number of sources (m) and the number of destinations (n) in this formulation equal the number of assignments (n). Transportation problems in general have $m + n - 1$ basic variables (allocations), so every BF solution for this particular kind of transportation problem has $2n - 1$ basic variables, but exactly n of these x_{ij} equal 1 (corresponding to the n assignments being made). Therefore, since all the variables are binary variables, there always are $n - 1$ degenerate basic variables $(x_{ij} = 0)$. As discussed at the end of Sec. 8.2, degenerate basic variables do not cause any major complication in the execution of the algorithm. However, they do frequently cause *wasted iterations,* where nothing changes (same allocations) except for the labeling of which allocations of zero correspond to degenerate basic variables rather than nonbasic variables. These wasted iterations are a major drawback to applying the transportation simplex method in this kind of situation, where there *always* are so many degenerate basic variables.

Another drawback of the transportation simplex method here is that it is purely a *general-purpose* algorithm for solving all transportation problems. Therefore, it does nothing to exploit the additional special structure in this special type of transportation problem ($m = n$, every $s_i = 1$, and every $d_j = 1$). Although we will not take the space to describe them,[1] specialized algorithms have been developed to fully streamline the procedure for solving just assignment problems. These algorithms operate directly on the cost table and do not bother with degenerate basic variables. When a computer code is available for one of these algorithms, it generally should be used in preference to the transportation simplex method, especially for really big problems. (The supplement to this chapter on the book's website, www.mhhe.com/hillier, describes one such algorithm.)

Example—Assigning Products to Plants

The BETTER PRODUCTS COMPANY has decided to initiate the production of four new products, using three plants that currently have excess production capacity. The products require a comparable production effort per unit, so the available production capacity of the plants is measured by the number of units of any product that can be produced per day, as given in the rightmost column of Table 8.27. The bottom row gives the required production rate per day to meet projected sales. Each plant can produce any of these prod-

---

[1]For an article comparing various algorithms for the assignment problem, see J. L. Kennington and Z. Wang, "An Empirical Analysis of the Dense Assignment Problem: Sequential and Parallel Implementations," *ORSA Journal on Computing,* **3:** 299–306, 1991.

TABLE 8.27 Data for the Better Products Co. problem

		Unit Cost ($) for Product				Capacity Available
		1	**2**	**3**	**4**	
	1	41	27	28	24	75
Plant	2	40	29	—	23	75
	3	37	30	27	21	45
Production rate		20	30	30	40	

ucts, *except* that Plant 2 *cannot* produce product 3. However, the variable costs per unit of each product differ from plant to plant, as shown in the main body of Table 8.27.

Management now needs to make a decision on how to split up the production of the products among plants. Two kinds of options are available.

Option 1: Permit *product splitting,* where the same product is produced in more than one plant.

Option 2: Prohibit *product splitting.*

This second option imposes a constraint that can only increase the cost of an optimal solution based on Table 8.27. On the other hand, the key advantage of Option 2 is that it eliminates some *hidden costs* associated with product splitting that are not reflected in Table 8.27, including extra setup, distribution, and administration costs. Therefore, management wants both options analyzed before a final decision is made. For Option 2, management further specifies that every plant should be assigned at least one of the products.

We will formulate and solve the model for each option in turn, where Option 1 leads to a transportation problem and Option 2 leads to an assignment problem.

Formulation of Option 1. With product splitting permitted, Table 8.27 can be converted directly to a parameter table for a transportation problem. The plants become the sources, and the products become the destinations (or vice versa), so the supplies are the available production capacities and the demands are the required production rates. Only two changes need to be made in Table 8.27. First, because Plant 2 cannot produce product 3, such an allocation is prevented by assigning to it a huge unit cost of M. Second, the total capacity $(75 + 75 + 45 = 195)$ exceeds the total required production $(20 + 30 + 30 + 40 = 120)$, so a dummy destination with a demand of 75 is needed to balance these two quantities. The resulting parameter table is shown in Table 8.28.

The optimal solution for this transportation problem has basic variables (allocations) $x_{12} = 30$, $x_{13} = 30$, $x_{15} = 15$, $x_{24} = 15$, $x_{25} = 60$, $x_{31} = 20$, and $x_{34} = 25$, so

Plant 1 produces all of products 2 and 3.
Plant 2 produces 37.5 percent of product 4.
Plant 3 produces 62.5 percent of product 4 and all of product 1.

The total cost is $Z = \$3,260$ per day.

Formulation of Option 2. Without product splitting, each product must be assigned to just one plant. Therefore, producing the products can be interpreted as the tasks for an assignment problem, where the plants are the assignees.

TABLE 8.28 Parameter table for the transportation problem formulation of Option 1 for the Better Products Co. problem

		Cost per Unit Distributed					
		Destination (Product)					
		1	2	3	4	5(D)	Supply
Source (Plant)	1	41	27	28	24	0	75
	2	40	29	M	23	0	75
	3	37	30	27	21	0	45
Demand		20	30	30	40	75	

Management has specified that every plant should be assigned at least one of the products. There are more products (four) than plants (three), so one of the plants will need to be assigned two products. Plant 3 has only enough excess capacity to produce one product (see Table 8.27), so *either* Plant 1 or Plant 2 will take the extra product.

To make this assignment of an extra product possible within an assignment problem formulation, Plants 1 and 2 each are split into two assignees, as shown in Table 8.29.

The number of assignees (now five) must equal the number of tasks (now four), so a *dummy task* (product) is introduced into Table 8.29 as 5(D). The role of this dummy task is to provide the fictional second product to either Plant 1 or Plant 2, whichever one receives only one real product. There is no cost for producing a fictional product so, as usual, the cost entries for the dummy task are zero. The one exception is the entry of M in the last row of Table 8.29. The reason for M here is that Plant 3 must be assigned a real product (a choice of product 1, 2, 3, or 4), so the Big M method is needed to prevent the assignment of the fictional product to Plant 3 instead. (As in Table 8.28, M also is used to prevent the infeasible assignment of product 3 to Plant 2.)

The remaining cost entries in Table 8.29 are *not* the unit costs shown in Table 8.27 or 8.28. Table 8.28 gives a transportation problem formulation (for Option 1), so unit costs are appropriate there, but now we are formulating an assignment problem (for Option 2). For an assignment problem, the cost c_{ij} is the *total* cost associated with assignee i performing task j. For Table 8.29, the *total cost* (per day) for Plant i to produce product j is the unit cost

TABLE 8.29 Cost table for the assignment problem formulation of Option 2 for the Better Products Co. problem

		Task (Product)				
		1	2	3	4	5(D)
Assignee (Plant)	1a	820	810	840	960	0
	1b	820	810	840	960	0
	2a	800	870	M	920	0
	2b	800	870	M	920	0
	3	740	900	810	840	M

of production *times* the number of units produced (per day), where these two quantities for the multiplication are given separately in Table 8.27. For example, consider the assignment of Plant 1 to product 1. By using the corresponding unit cost in Table 8.28 ($41) and the corresponding demand (number of units produced per day) in Table 8.28 (20), we obtain

Cost of Plant 1 producing one unit of product 1 = $41

Required (daily) production of product 1 = 20 units

Total (daily) cost of assigning plant 1 to product 1 = 20 ($41)

= $820

so 820 is entered into Table 8.29 for the cost of either Assignee 1a or 1b performing Task 1.

The optimal solution for this assignment problem is as follows:

Plant 1 produces products 2 and 3.
Plant 2 produces product 1.
Plant 3 produces product 4.

Here the dummy assignment is given to Plant 2. The total cost is $Z = \$3,290$ per day.

As usual, one way to obtain this optimal solution is to convert the cost table of Table 8.29 to a parameter table for the equivalent transportation problem (see Table 8.26) and then apply the transportation simplex method. Because of the identical rows in Table 8.29, this approach can be streamlined by combining the five assignees into three sources with supplies 2, 2, and 1, respectively. (See Prob. 8.3-6.) This streamlining also decreases by two the number of degenerate basic variables in every BF solution. Therefore, even though this streamlined formulation no longer fits the format presented in Table 8.26a for an assignment problem, it is a more efficient formulation for applying the transportation simplex method.

Figure 8.6 shows how Excel and its Solver can be used to obtain this optimal solution, which is displayed in the changing cells (D24:G26) of the spreadsheet. Since the general simplex method is being used, there is no need to fit this formulation into the format for either the assignment problem or transportation problem model. Therefore, the formulation does not bother to split Plants 1 and 2 into two assignees each, or to add a dummy task. Instead, Plants 1 and 2 are given a supply of 2 each, and then $\leq$ signs are entered into cells I24 and I25 as well as into the corresponding constraints in the Solver dialogue box. There also is no need to include the Big M method to prohibit assigning product 3 to Plant 2 in cell F25, since this dialogue box includes the constraint that F25 = 0. The target cell (H27) shows the total cost of $3,290 per day.

Now look back and compare this solution to the one obtained for Option 1, which included the splitting of product 4 between Plants 2 and 3. The allocations are somewhat different for the two solutions, but the total daily costs are virtually the same ($3,260 for Option 1 versus $3,290 for Option 2). However, there are hidden costs associated with product splitting (including the cost of extra setup, distribution, and administration) that are not included in the objective function for Option 1. As with any application of OR, the mathematical model used can provide only an approximate representation of the total problem, so management needs to consider factors that cannot be incorporated into the model before it makes a final decision. In this case, after evaluating the disadvantages of product splitting, management decided to adopt the Option 2 solution.

FIGURE 8.6
A spreadsheet formulation of Option 2 for the Better Products Co. problem as a variant of an assignment problem, where rows 12 to 18 show the cost table and the changing cells (D24:G26) display the optimal production plan obtained by the Solver.

	A	B	C	D	E	F	G	H	I	J
1		Better Products Co. Production-Planning Problem (Option 2)								
2										
3					Unit Cost					
4					Product					
5				1	2	3	4			
6			1	$41	$27	$28	$24			
7		Plant	2	$40	$29	-	$23			
8			3	$37	$30	$27	$21			
9		Required Production		20	30	30	40			
10										
11										
12					Cost ($/day)					
13					Task (Product)					
14				1	2	3	4	Supply		
15		Assignee	1	$820	$810	$840	$960	2		
16		(Plant)	2	$800	$870	-	$920	2		
17			3	$740	$900	$810	$840	1		
18		Demand		1	1	1	1			
19										
20										
21					Assignments					
22					Task (Product)					
23				1	2	3	4	Totals		Supply
24		Assignee	1	0	1	1	0	2	≤	2
25		(Plant)	2	1	0	0	0	1	≤	2
26			3	0	0	0	1	1	=	1
27		Totals		1	1	1	1	$ 3,290	=	Total Cost
28				=	=	=	=			
29		Demand		1	1	1	1			

Solver Parameters

Set Target Cell: $H$27

Equal To: ○ Max ● Min ○

By Changing Cells:

$D$24:$G$26

Subject to the Constraints:

$D$27:$G$27 = $D$29:$G$29
$F$25 = 0
$H$24:$H$25 <= $J$24:$J$25
$H$26 = $J$26

Solver Options

☑ Assume Linear Model
☑ Assume Non-Negative

	H
24	=SUM(D24:G24)
25	=SUM(D25:G25)
26	=SUM(D26:G26)
27	=SUMPRODUCT(D15:G17,D24:G26)

	D	E	F	G
15	=D6*D$9	=E6*E$9	=F6*F$9	=G6*G$9
16	=D7*D$9	=E7*E$9	-	=G7*G$9
17	=D8*D$9	=E8*E$9	=F8*F$9	=G8*G$9
27	=SUM(D24:D26)	=SUM(E24:E26)	=SUM(F24:F26)	=SUM(G24:G26)

8.4 CONCLUSIONS

The linear programming model encompasses a wide variety of specific types of problems. The general simplex method is a powerful algorithm that can solve surprisingly large versions of any of these problems. However, some of these problem types have such simple formulations that they can be solved much more efficiently by *streamlined* algorithms that exploit their *special structure.* These streamlined algorithms can cut down tremendously on the computer time required for large problems, and they sometimes make it computationally feasible to solve huge problems. This is particularly true for the two types of linear programming problems studied in this chapter, namely, the transportation problem and the assignment problem. Both types have a number of common applications, so it is important to recognize them when they arise and to use the best available algorithms. These special-purpose algorithms are included in some linear programming software packages.

We shall reexamine the special structure of the transportation and assignment problems in Sec. 9.6. There we shall see that these problems are special cases of an important class of linear programming problems known as the *minimum cost flow problem.* This problem has the interpretation of minimizing the cost for the flow of goods through a network. A streamlined version of the simplex method called the *network simplex method* (described in Sec. 9.7) is widely used for solving this type of problem, including its various special cases.

A supplementary chapter (Chap. 23) on the book's website, www.mhhe.com/hillier, describes various additional special types of linear programming problems. One of these, called the *transshipment problem,* is a generalization of the transportation problem which allows shipments from any source to any destination to first go through intermediate transfer points. Since the transshipment problem also is a special case of the minimum cost flow problem, we will describe it further in Sec. 9.6.

Much research continues to be devoted to developing streamlined algorithms for special types of linear programming problems, including some not discussed here. At the same time, there is widespread interest in applying linear programming to optimize the operation of complicated large-scale systems. The resulting formulations usually have special structures that can be exploited. Being able to recognize and exploit special structures is an important factor in the successful application of linear programming.

SELECTED REFERENCES

1. Bazaraa, M. S., J. J. Jarvis, and H. D. Sherali: *Linear Programming and Network Flows,* 2d ed., Wiley, New York, 1990, chap. 10.
2. Dantzig, G. B., and M. N. Thapa: *Linear Programming 1: Introduction,* Springer, New York, 1997, chap. 8.
3. Geoffrion, A. M.: "Elements of Large-Scale Mathematical Programming," *Management Science,* **16:** 652–691, 1970.
4. Hillier, F. S., M. S. Hillier, and G. J. Lieberman: *Introduction to Management Science: A Modeling and Case Studies Approach with Spreadsheets,* Irwin/McGraw-Hill, Burr Ridge, IL, 2000, chap. 6.
5. Murthy, D. N. P., N. W. Page, and E. Y. Rodin: *Mathematical Modeling: A Tool for Problem Solving in Engineering, Physical, Biological and Social Sciences,* Pergamon Press, Oxford, England, 1990.

LEARNING AIDS FOR THIS CHAPTER IN YOUR OR COURSEWARE

A Demonstration Example in OR Tutor:

The Transportation Problem

Interactive Routines:

Enter or Revise a Transportation Problem
Find Initial Basic Feasible Solution—for Interactive Method
Solve Interactively by the Transportation Simplex Method

An Excel Add-in:

Premium Solver

"Ch. 8—Transp. & Assignment" Files for Solving the Examples:

Excel File
LINGO/LINDO File
MPL/CPLEX File

Supplement to this Chapter:

An Algorithm for the Assignment Problem (appears on the book's website, www.mhhe.com/hillier)

See Appendix 1 for documentation of the software.

PROBLEMS

The symbols to the left of some of the problems (or their parts) have the following meaning:

D: The demonstration example listed above may be helpful.
I: We suggest that you use the corresponding interactive routines listed above (the printout records your work).
C: Use the computer with any of the software options available to you (or as instructed by your instructor) to solve the problem.

An asterisk on the problem number indicates that at least a partial answer is given in the back of the book.

8.1-1. The Childfair Company has three plants producing child push chairs that are to be shipped to four distribution centers. Plants 1, 2, and 3 produce 12, 17, and 11 shipments per month, respectively. Each distribution center needs to receive 10 shipments per month. The distance from each plant to the respective distributing centers is given to the right:

		Distance			
		Distribution Center			
		1	2	3	4
Plant	1	800 miles	1,300 miles	400 miles	700 miles
	2	1,100 miles	1,400 miles	600 miles	1,000 miles
	3	600 miles	1,200 miles	800 miles	900 miles

The freight cost for each shipment is $100 plus 50 cents per mile.

How much should be shipped from each plant to each of the distribution centers to minimize the total shipping cost?
(a) Formulate this problem as a transportation problem by constructing the appropriate parameter table.
(b) Draw the network representation of this problem.
C (c) Obtain an optimal solution.

8.1-2.* Tom would like 3 pints of home brew today and an additional 4 pints of home brew tomorrow. Dick is willing to sell a maximum of 5 pints total at a price of $3.00 per pint today and $2.70 per pint tomorrow. Harry is willing to sell a maximum of 4 pints total at a price of $2.90 per pint today and $2.80 per pint tomorrow.

Tom wishes to know what his purchases should be to minimize his cost while satisfying his thirst requirements.

(a) Formulate a *linear programming* model for this problem, and construct the initial simplex tableau (see Chaps. 3 and 4).
(b) Formulate this problem as a *transportation problem* by constructing the appropriate parameter table.
C (c) Obtain an optimal solution.

8.1-3. The Versatech Corporation has decided to produce three new products. Five branch plants now have excess product capacity. The unit manufacturing cost of the first product would be $31, $29, $32, $28, and $29 in Plants 1, 2, 3, 4, and 5, respectively. The unit manufacturing cost of the second product would be $45, $41, $46, $42, and $43 in Plants 1, 2, 3, 4, and 5, respectively. The unit manufacturing cost of the third product would be $38, $35, and $40 in Plants 1, 2, and 3, respectively, whereas Plants 4 and 5 do not have the capability for producing this product. Sales forecasts indicate that 600, 1,000, and 800 units of products 1, 2, and 3, respectively, should be produced per day. Plants 1, 2, 3, 4, and 5 have the capacity to produce 400, 600, 400, 600, and 1,000 units daily, respectively, regardless of the product or combination of products involved. Assume that any plant having the capability and capacity to produce them can produce any combination of the products in any quantity.

Management wishes to know how to allocate the new products to the plants to minimize total manufacturing cost.

(a) Formulate this problem as a *transportation problem* by constructing the appropriate parameter table.
C (b) Obtain an optimal solution.

8.1-4. Suppose that England, France, and Spain produce all the wheat, barley, and oats in the world. The world demand for wheat requires 125 million acres of land devoted to wheat production. Similarly, 60 million acres of land are required for barley and 75 million acres of land for oats. The total amount of land available for these purposes in England, France, and Spain is 70 million acres, 110 million acres, and 80 million acres, respectively. The number of hours of labor needed in England, France, and Spain to produce an acre of wheat is 18, 13, and 16, respectively. The number of hours of labor needed in England, France, and Spain to produce an acre of barley is 15, 12, and 12, respectively. The number of hours of labor needed in England, France, and Spain to produce an acre of oats is 12, 10, and 16, respectively. The labor cost per hour in producing wheat is $9.00, $7.20, and $9.90 in England, France, and Spain, respectively. The labor cost per hour in pro-

ducing barley is $8.10, $9.00, and $8.40 in England, France, and Spain, respectively. The labor cost per hour in producing oats is $6.90, $7.50, and $6.30 in England, France, and Spain, respectively. The problem is to allocate land use in each country so as to meet the world food requirement and minimize the total labor cost.

(a) Formulate this problem as a transportation problem by constructing the appropriate parameter table.
(b) Draw the network representation of this problem.
C (c) Obtain an optimal solution.

8.1-5. Reconsider the P & T Co. problem presented in Sec. 8.1. You now learn that one or more of the shipping costs per truckload given in Table 8.2 may change slightly before shipments begin.

Use the Excel Solver to generate the Sensitivity Report for this problem. Use this report to determine the allowable range to stay optimal for each of the unit costs. What do these allowable ranges tell P & T management?

8.1-6. The Onenote Co. produces a single product at three plants for four customers. The three plants will produce 60, 80, and 40 units, respectively, during the next time period. The firm has made a commitment to sell 40 units to customer 1, 60 units to customer 2, and at least 20 units to customer 3. Both customers 3 and 4 also want to buy as many of the remaining units as possible. The net profit associated with shipping a unit from plant i for sale to customer j is given by the following table:

		Customer			
		1	**2**	**3**	**4**
	1	$800	$700	$500	$200
Plant	2	$500	$200	$100	$300
	3	$600	$400	$300	$500

Management wishes to know how many units to sell to customers 3 and 4 and how many units to ship from each of the plants to each of the customers to maximize profit.

(a) Formulate this problem as a transportation problem where the objective function is to be maximized by constructing the appropriate parameter table that gives unit profits.
(b) Now formulate this transportation problem with the usual objective of minimizing total cost by converting the parameter table from part (*a*) into one that gives unit costs instead of unit profits.
(c) Display the formulation in part (*a*) on an Excel spreadsheet.
C (d) Use this information and the Excel Solver to obtain an optimal solution.
C (e) Repeat parts (*c*) and (*d*) for the formulation in part (*b*). Compare the optimal solutions for the two formulations.

8.1-7. The Move-It Company has two plants producing forklift trucks that then are shipped to three distribution centers. The production costs are the same at the two plants, and the cost of shipping for each truck is shown for each combination of plant and distribution center:

		Distribution Center		
		1	2	3
Plant	A	$800	$700	$400
	B	$600	$800	$500

A total of 60 forklift trucks are produced and shipped per week. Each plant can produce and ship any amount up to a maximum of 50 trucks per week, so there is considerable flexibility on how to divide the total production between the two plants so as to reduce shipping costs. However, each distribution center must receive exactly 20 trucks per week.

Management's objective is to determine how many forklift trucks should be produced at each plant, and then what the overall shipping pattern should be to minimize total shipping cost.

(a) Formulate this problem as a transportation problem by constructing the appropriate parameter table.

(b) Display the transportation problem on an Excel spreadsheet.

c **(c)** Use the Excel Solver to obtain an optimal solution.

8.1-8. Redo Prob. 8.1-7 when any distribution center may receive any quantity between 10 and 30 forklift trucks per week in order to further reduce total shipping cost, provided only that the total shipped to all three distribution centers must still equal 60 trucks per week.

8.1-9. The Build-Em-Fast Company has agreed to supply its best customer with three widgets during *each* of the next 3 weeks, even though producing them will require some overtime work. The relevant production data are as follows:

Week	Maximum Production, Regular Time	Maximum Production, Overtime	Production Cost per Unit, Regular Time
1	2	2	$300
2	3	2	$500
3	1	2	$400

The cost per unit produced with overtime for each week is $100 more than for regular time. The cost of storage is $50 per unit for each week it is stored. There is already an inventory of two wid-

gets on hand currently, but the company does not want to retain any widgets in inventory after the 3 weeks.

Management wants to know how many units should be produced in each week to minimize the total cost of meeting the delivery schedule.

(a) Formulate this problem as a transportation problem by constructing the appropriate parameter table.

c **(b)** Obtain an optimal solution.

8.1-10. The MJK Manufacturing Company must produce two products in sufficient quantity to meet contracted sales in each of the next three months. The two products share the same production facilities, and each unit of both products requires the same amount of production capacity. The available production and storage facilities are changing month by month, so the production capacities, unit production costs, and unit storage costs vary by month. Therefore, it may be worthwhile to overproduce one or both products in some months and store them until needed.

For each of the three months, the second column of the following table gives the maximum number of units of the two products combined that can be produced on Regular Time (RT) and on Overtime (O). For each of the two products, the subsequent columns give (1) the number of units needed for the contracted sales, (2) the cost (in thousands of dollars) per unit produced on Regular Time, (3) the cost (in thousands of dollars) per unit produced on Overtime, and (4) the cost (in thousands of dollars) of storing each extra unit that is held over into the next month. In each case, the numbers for the two products are separated by a slash /, with the number for Product 1 on the left and the number for Product 2 on the right.

	Maximum Combined Production			Product 1/Product 2		
					Unit Cost of Production ($1,000's)		Unit Cost of Storage
Month	RT	OT	Sales	RT	OT	($1,000's)
1	10	3	5/3	15/16	18/20	1/2
2	8	2	3/5	17/15	20/18	2/1
3	10	3	4/4	19/17	22/22	

The production manager wants a schedule developed for the number of units of each of the two products to be produced on Regular Time and (if Regular Time production capacity is used up) on Overtime in each of the three months. The objective is to minimize the total of the production and storage costs while meeting the contracted sales for each month. There is no initial inventory, and no final inventory is desired after the three months.

(a) Formulate this problem as a transportation problem by constructing the appropriate parameter table.

C **(b)** Obtain an optimal solution.

8.2-1. Consider the transportation problem having the following parameter table:

		Destination			Supply
		1	**2**	**3**	
Source	1	6	3	5	4
	2	4	M	7	3
	3	3	4	3	2
Demand		4	2	3	

(a) Use Vogel's approximation method manually (don't use the interactive routine in your OR Courseware) to select the first basic variable for an initial BF solution.

(b) Use Russell's approximation method manually to select the first basic variable for an initial BF solution.

(c) Use the northwest corner rule manually to construct a complete initial BF solution.

D,I **8.2-2.*** Consider the transportation problem having the following parameter table:

		Destination					Supply
		1	**2**	**3**	**4**	**5**	
Source	1	2	4	6	5	7	4
	2	7	6	3	M	4	6
	3	8	7	5	2	5	6
	4	0	0	0	0	0	4
Demand		4	4	2	5	5	

Use each of the following criteria to obtain an initial BF solution. Compare the values of the objective function for these solutions.

(a) Northwest corner rule.

(b) Vogel's approximation method.

(c) Russell's approximation method.

D,I **8.2-3.** Consider the transportation problem having the following parameter table:

		Destination						Supply
		1	**2**	**3**	**4**	**5**	**6**	
Source	1	13	10	22	29	18	0	5
	2	14	13	16	21	M	0	6
	3	3	0	M	11	6	0	7
	4	18	9	19	23	11	0	4
	5	30	24	34	36	28	0	3
Demand		3	5	4	5	6	2	

Use each of the following criteria to obtain an initial BF solution. Compare the values of the objective function for these solutions.

(a) Northwest corner rule.

(b) Vogel's approximation method.

(c) Russell's approximation method.

8.2-4. Consider the transportation problem having the following parameter table:

		Destination				Supply
		1	**2**	**3**	**4**	
Source	1	7	4	1	4	1
	2	4	6	7	2	1
	3	8	5	4	6	1
	4	6	7	6	3	1
Demand		1	1	1	1	

(a) Notice that this problem has three special characteristics: (1) number of sources = number of destinations, (2) each supply = 1, and (3) each demand = 1. Transportation problems with these characteristics are of a special type called the assignment problem (as described in Sec. 8.3). Use the integer solutions property to explain why this type of transportation problem can be interpreted as assigning sources to destinations as a one-to-one basis.

(b) How many basic variables are there in every BF solution? How many of these are degenerate basic variables ($= 0$)?

D,I **(c)** Use the northwest corner rule to obtain an initial BF solution.

I **(d)** Construct an initial BF solution by applying the general procedure for the initialization step of the transportation simplex method. However, rather than using one of the three criteria for step 1 presented in Sec. 8.2, use the minimum cost criterion given next for selecting the next basic variable. (With the corresponding interactive routine in your OR Courseware, choose the *Northwest Corner Rule,* since this choice actually allows the use of any criterion.)

Minimum cost criterion: From among the rows and columns still under consideration, select the variable x_{ij} having the smallest unit cost c_{ij} to be the next basic variable. (Ties may be broken arbitrarily.)

D,I **(e)** Starting with the initial BF solution from part (c), interactively apply the transportation simplex method to obtain an optimal solution.

8.2-5. Consider the prototype example for the transportation problem (the P & T Co. problem) presented at the beginning of Sec. 8.1. Verify that the solution given there actually is optimal by applying just the *optimality test* portion of the transportation simplex method to this solution.

8.2-6. Consider the transportation problem formulation of Option 1 for the Better Products Co. problem presented in Table 8.28. Verify that the optimal solution given in Sec. 8.3 actually is optimal by applying just the *optimality test* portion of the transportation simplex method to this solution.

8.2-7. Consider the transportation problem having the following parameter table:

		Destination					
		1	**2**	**3**	**4**	**5**	**Supply**
	1	8	6	3	7	5	20
Source	2	5	M	8	4	7	30
	3	6	3	9	6	8	30
	4(D)	0	0	0	0	0	20
Demand		25	25	20	10	20	

After several iterations of the transportation simplex method, a BF solution is obtained that has the following basic variables: $x_{13} = 20$, $x_{21} = 25$, $x_{24} = 5$, $x_{32} = 25$, $x_{34} = 5$, $x_{42} = 0$, $x_{43} = 0$, $x_{45} = 20$. Continue the transportation simplex method for *two more* iterations by hand. After two iterations, state whether the solution is optimal and, if so, why.

D,I **8.2-8.*** Consider the transportation problem having the following parameter table:

		Destination				Supply
		1	**2**	**3**	**4**	
	1	3	7	6	4	5
Source	2	2	4	3	2	2
	3	4	3	8	5	3
Demand		3	3	2	2	

Use each of the following criteria to obtain an initial BF solution. In each case, interactively apply the transportation simplex method, starting with this initial solution, to obtain an optimal solution. Compare the resulting number of iterations for the transportation simplex method.

(a) Northwest corner rule.
(b) Vogel's approximation method.
(c) Russell's approximation method.

D,I **8.2-9.** The Cost-Less Corp. supplies its four retail outlets from its four plants. The shipping cost per shipment from each plant to each retail outlet is given below.

		Unit Shipping Cost Retail Outlet			
		1	**2**	**3**	**4**
	1	$500	$600	$400	$200
	2	$200	$900	$100	$300
Plant	3	$300	$400	$200	$100
	4	$200	$100	$300	$200

Plants 1, 2, 3, and 4 make 10, 20, 20, and 10 shipments per month, respectively. Retail outlets 1, 2, 3, and 4 need to receive 20, 10, 10, and 20 shipments per month, respectively.

The distribution manager, Randy Smith, now wants to determine the best plan for how many shipments to send from each plant to the respective retail outlets each month. Randy's objective is to minimize the total shipping cost.

(a) Formulate this problem as a transportation problem by constructing the appropriate parameter table.
(b) Use the northwest corner rule to construct an initial BF solution.
(c) Starting with the initial basic solution from part (b), interactively apply the transportation simplex method to obtain an optimal solution.

8.2-10. The Energetic Company needs to make plans for the energy systems for a new building.

The energy needs in the building fall into three categories: (1) electricity, (2) heating water, and (3) heating space in the building. The daily requirements for these three categories (all measured in the same units) are

Electricity	20 units
Water heating	10 units
Space heating	30 units.

The three possible sources of energy to meet these needs are electricity, natural gas, and a solar heating unit that can be installed on the roof. The size of the roof limits the largest possible solar heater to 30 units, but there is no limit to the electricity and natural gas available. Electricity needs can be met only by purchasing electricity (at a cost of $50 per unit). Both other energy needs can be met by any source or combination of sources. The unit costs are

	Electricity	Natural Gas	Solar Heater
Water heating	$90	$60	$30
Space heating	$80	$50	$40

The objective is to minimize the total cost of meeting the energy needs.

(a) Formulate this problem as a transportation problem by constructing the appropriate parameter table.

D,I (b) Use the northwest corner rule to obtain an initial BF solution for this problem.

D,I (c) Starting with the initial BF solution from part (b), interactively apply the transportation simplex method to obtain an optimal solution.

D,I (d) Use Vogel's approximation method to obtain an initial BF solution for this problem.

D,I (e) Starting with the initial BF solution from part (d), interactively apply the transportation simplex method to obtain an optimal solution.

I (f) Use Russell's approximation method to obtain an initial BF solution for this problem.

D,I (g) Starting with the initial BF solution obtained from part (f), interactively apply the transportation simplex method to obtain an optimal solution. Compare the number of iterations required by the transportation simplex method here and in parts (c) and (e).

D,I **8.2-11.*** Interactively apply the transportation simplex method to solve the Northern Airplane Co. production scheduling problem as it is formulated in Table 8.9.

D,I **8.2-12.*** Reconsider Prob. 8.1-1.

(a) Use the northwest corner rule to obtain an initial BF solution.

(b) Starting with the initial BF solution from part (a), interactively apply the transportation simplex method to obtain an optimal solution.

D,I **8.2-13.** Reconsider Prob. 8.1-2b. Starting with the northwest corner rule, interactively apply the transportation simplex method to obtain an optimal solution for this problem.

D,I **8.2-14.** Reconsider Prob. 8.1-3. Starting with the northwest corner rule, interactively apply the transportation simplex method to obtain an optimal solution for this problem.

D,I **8.2-15.** Reconsider Prob. 8.1-4. Starting with the northwest corner rule, interactively apply the transportation simplex method to obtain an optimal solution for this problem.

D,I **8.2-16.** Reconsider Prob. 8.1-6. Starting with Russell's approximation method, interactively apply the transportation simplex method to obtain an optimal solution for this problem.

8.2-17. Reconsider the transportation problem formulated in Prob. 8.1-7a.

D,I (a) Use each of the three criteria presented in Sec. 8.2 to obtain an initial BF solution, and time how long you spend for each one. Compare both these times and the values of the objective function for these solutions.

C (b) Obtain an optimal solution for this problem. For each of the three initial BF solutions obtained in part (a), calculate the percentage by which its objective function value exceeds the optimal one.

D,I (c) For each of the three initial BF solutions obtained in part (a), interactively apply the transportation simplex method to obtain (and verify) an optimal solution. Time how long you spend in each of the three cases. Compare both these times and the number of iterations needed to reach an optimal solution.

8.2-18. Follow the instructions of Prob. 8.2-17 for the transportation problem formulated in Prob. 8.1-8a.

8.2-19. Consider the transportation problem having the following parameter table:

		Destination		
		1	2	Supply
Source	1	8	5	4
	2	6	4	2
Demand		3	3	

(a) Using your choice of a criterion from Sec. 8.2 for obtaining the initial BF solution, solve this problem manually by the transportation simplex method. (Keep track of your time.)

(b) Reformulate this problem as a general linear programming problem, and then solve it manually by the *simplex method.* Keep track of how long this takes you, and contrast it with the computation time for part (a).

8.2-20. Consider the Northern Airplane Co. production scheduling problem presented in Sec. 8.1 (see Table 8.7). Formulate this problem as a general linear programming problem by letting the decision variables be x_j = number of jet engines to be produced in month j ($j = 1, 2, 3, 4$). Construct the initial simplex tableau for this formulation, and then contrast the size (number of rows and columns) of this tableau and the corresponding tableaux used to solve the transportation problem formulation of the problem (see Table 8.9).

8.2-21. Consider the general linear programming formulation of the transportation problem (see Table 8.6). Verify the claim in Sec. 8.2 that the set of ($m + n$) functional constraint equations (m supply constraints and n demand constraints) has one *redundant* equation; i.e., any one equation can be reproduced from a linear combination of the other ($m + n - 1$) equations.

8.2-22. When you deal with a transportation problem where the supply and demand quantities have *integer* values, explain why the steps of the transportation simplex method guarantee that all the basic variables (allocations) in the BF solutions obtained must have integer values. Begin with why this occurs with the initialization step when the general procedure for constructing an *initial* BF solution is used (regardless of the criterion for selecting the next basic variable). Then given a *current* BF solution that is integer, next explain why Step 3 of an iteration must obtain a new BF solution that also is integer. Finally, explain how the initialization step can be used to construct *any* initial BF solution, so the transportation simplex method actually gives a proof of the integer solutions property presented in Sec. 8.1.

8.2-23. A contractor, Susan Meyer, has to haul gravel to three building sites. She can purchase as much as 18 tons at a gravel pit in the north of the city and 14 tons at one in the south. She needs 10, 5, and 10 tons at sites 1, 2, and 3, respectively. The purchase price per ton at each gravel pit and the hauling cost per ton are given in the table below.

Pit	Hauling Cost per Ton at Site			Price per Ton
	1	2	3	
North	$30	$60	$50	$100
South	$60	$30	$40	$120

Susan wishes to determine how much to haul from each pit to each site to minimize the total cost for purchasing and hauling gravel.

(a) Formulate a linear programming model for this problem. Using the Big M method, construct the initial simplex tableau ready to apply the simplex method (but do not actually solve).

(b) Now formulate this problem as a transportation problem by constructing the appropriate parameter table. Compare the size

of this table (and the corresponding transportation simplex tableau) used by the transportation simplex method with the size of the simplex tableaux from part (a) that would be needed by the simplex method.

D (c) Susan Meyer notices that she can supply sites 1 and 2 completely from the north pit and site 3 completely from the south pit. Use the optimality test (but no iterations) of the transportation simplex method to check whether the corresponding BF solution is optimal.

D,I (d) Starting with the northwest corner rule, interactively apply the transportation simplex method to solve the problem as formulated in part (b).

(e) As usual, let c_{ij} denote the unit cost associated with source i and destination j as given in the parameter table constructed in part (b). For the optimal solution obtained in part (d), suppose that the value of c_{ij} for each basic variable x_{ij} is fixed at the value given in the parameter table, but that the value of c_{ij} for each nonbasic variable x_{ij} possibly can be altered through bargaining because the site manager wants to pick up the business. Use sensitivity analysis to determine the *allowable range to stay optimal* for each of the latter c_{ij}, and explain how this information is useful to the contractor.

C **8.2-24.** Consider the transportation problem formulation and solution of the Metro Water District problem presented in Secs. 8.1 and 8.2 (see Tables 8.12 and 8.23).

The numbers given in the parameter table are only estimates that may be somewhat inaccurate, so management now wishes to do some what-if analysis. Use the Excel Solver to generate the Sensitivity Report. Then use this report to address the following questions. (In each case, assume that the indicated change is the only change in the model.)

(a) Would the optimal solution in Table 8.23 remain optimal if the cost per acre foot of shipping Calorie River water to San Go were actually $200 rather than $230?

(b) Would this solution remain optimal if the cost per acre foot of shipping Sacron River water to Los Devils were actually $160 rather than $130?

(c) Must this solution remain optimal if the costs considered in parts (a) and (b) were simultaneously changed from their original values to $215 and $145, respectively?

(d) Suppose that the supply from the Sacron River and the demand at Hollyglass are decreased simultaneously by the same amount. Must the shadow prices for evaluating these changes remain valid if the decrease were 0.5 million acre feet?

8.2-25. Without generating the Sensitivity Report, adapt the sensitivity analysis procedure presented in Secs. 6.6 and 6.7 to conduct the sensitivity analysis specified in the four parts of Prob. 8.2-24.

8.3-1. Consider the assignment problem having the following cost table.

		Task			
		1	**2**	**3**	**4**
	A	8	6	5	7
Assignee	B	6	5	3	4
	C	7	8	4	6
	D	6	7	5	6

(a) Draw the network representation of this assignment problem.
(b) Formulate this problem as a transportation problem by constructing the appropriate parameter table.
(c) Display this formulation on an Excel spreadsheet.
C (d) Use the Excel Solver to obtain an optimal solution.

8.3-2. Four cargo ships will be used for shipping goods from one port to four other ports (labeled 1, 2, 3, 4). Any ship can be used for making any one of these four trips. However, because of differences in the ships and cargoes, the total cost of loading, transporting, and unloading the goods for the different ship-port combinations varies considerably, as shown in the following table:

		Port			
		1	**2**	**3**	**4**
	1	$500	$400	$600	$700
Ship	2	$600	$600	$700	$500
	3	$700	$500	$700	$600
	4	$500	$400	$600	$600

The objective is to assign the four ships to four different ports in such a way as to minimize the total cost for all four shipments.
(a) Describe how this problem fits into the general format for the assignment problem.
C (b) Obtain an optimal solution.
(c) Reformulate this problem as an equivalent transportation problem by constructing the appropriate parameter table.
D,I (d) Use the northwest corner rule to obtain an initial BF solution for the problem as formulated in part (c).
D,I (e) Starting with the initial BF solution from part (d), interactively apply the transportation simplex method to obtain an optimal set of assignments for the original problem.
D,I (f) Are there other optimal solutions in addition to the one obtained in part (e)? If so, use the transportation simplex method to identify them.

8.3-3. Reconsider Prob. 8.1-3. Suppose that the sales forecasts have been revised downward to 240, 400, and 320 units per day of products 1, 2, and 3, respectively, and that each plant now has the capacity to produce all that is required of any one product. Therefore, management has decided that each new product should be assigned to only one plant and that no plant should be assigned more than one product (so that three plants are each to be assigned one product, and two plants are to be assigned none). The objective is to make these assignments so as to minimize the *total* cost of producing these amounts of the three products.
(a) Formulate this problem as an assignment problem by constructing the appropriate cost table.
C (b) Obtain an optimal solution.
(c) Reformulate this assignment problem as an equivalent transportation problem by constructing the appropriate parameter table.
D,I (d) Starting with Vogel's approximation method, interactively apply the transportation simplex method to solve the problem as formulated in part (c).

8.3-4.* The coach of an age group swim team needs to assign swimmers to a 200-yard medley relay team to send to the Junior Olympics. Since most of his best swimmers are very fast in more than one stroke, it is not clear which swimmer should be assigned to each of the four strokes. The five fastest swimmers and the best times (in seconds) they have achieved in each of the strokes (for 50 yards) are

Stroke	Carl	Chris	David	Tony	Ken
Backstroke	37.7	32.9	33.8	37.0	35.4
Breaststroke	43.4	33.1	42.2	34.7	41.8
Butterfly	33.3	28.5	38.9	30.4	33.6
Freestyle	29.2	26.4	29.6	28.5	31.1

The coach wishes to determine how to assign four swimmers to the four different strokes to minimize the sum of the corresponding best times.
(a) Formulate this problem as an assignment problem.
C (b) Obtain an optimal solution.

8.3-5. Reconsider Prob. 8.2-23. Now suppose that trucks (and their drivers) need to be hired to do the hauling, where each truck can only be used to haul gravel from a single pit to a single site. Each truck can haul 5 tons, and the cost per truck is five times the hauling cost per ton given earlier. Only full trucks would be used to supply each site.
(a) Formulate this problem as an assignment problem by constructing the appropriate cost table, including identifying the assignees and tasks.

C **(b)** Obtain an optimal solution.

(c) Reformulate this assignment problem as an equivalent transportation problem with two sources and three destinations by constructing the appropriate parameter table.

C **(d)** Obtain an optimal solution for the problem as formulated in part (c).

8.3-6. Consider the assignment problem formulation of Option 2 for the Better Products Co. problem presented in Table 8.29.

(a) Reformulate this problem as an equivalent transportation problem with three sources and five destinations by constructing the appropriate parameter table.

(b) Convert the optimal solution given in Sec. 8.3 for this assignment problem into a complete BF solution (including degenerate basic variables) for the transportation problem formulated in part (a). Specifically, apply the "General Procedure for Constructing an Initial BF Solution" given in Sec. 8.2. For each iteration of the procedure, rather than using any of the three alternative criteria presented for step 1, select the next basic variable to correspond to the next assignment of a plant to a product given in the optimal solution. When only one row or only one column remains under consideration, use step 4 to select the remaining basic variables.

(c) Verify that the optimal solution given in Sec. 8.3 for this assignment problem actually is optimal by applying just the optimality test portion of the transportation simplex method to the complete BF solution obtained in part (b).

(d) Now reformulate this assignment problem as an equivalent transportation problem with five sources and five destinations by constructing the appropriate parameter table. Compare this transportation problem with the one formulated in part (a).

(e) Repeat part (b) for the problem as formulated in part (d). Compare the BF solution obtained with the one from part (b).

D,I **8.3-7.** Starting with Vogel's approximation method, interactively apply the transportation simplex method to solve the Job Shop Co. assignment problem as formulated in Table 8.26b. (As stated in Sec. 8.3, the resulting optimal solution has $x_{14} = 1$, $x_{23} = 1$, $x_{31} = 1$, $x_{42} = 1$, and all other $x_{ij} = 0$.)

8.3-8. Reconsider Prob. 8.1-7. Now assume that distribution centers 1, 2, and 3 must receive exactly 10, 20, and 30 units per week, respectively. For administrative convenience, management has decided that each distribution center will be supplied totally by a single plant, so that one plant will supply one distribution center and the other plant will supply the other two distribution centers. The

choice of these assignments of plants to distribution centers is to be made solely on the basis of minimizing total shipping cost.

(a) Formulate this problem as an assignment problem by constructing the appropriate cost table, including identifying the corresponding assignees and tasks.

C **(b)** Obtain an optimal solution.

(c) Reformulate this assignment problem as an equivalent transportation problem (with four sources) by constructing the appropriate parameter table.

C **(d)** Solve the problem as formulated in part (c).

(e) Repeat part (c) with just two sources.

C **(f)** Solve the problem as formulated in part (e).

8.3-9. Consider the assignment problem having the following cost table.

		\multicolumn{3}{c}{Job}
		1	**2**	**3**
	A	5	7	4
Person	B	3	6	5
	C	2	3	4

The optimal solution is A-3, B-1, C-2, with $Z = 10$.

C **(a)** Use the computer to verify this optimal solution.

(b) Reformulate this problem as an equivalent transportation problem by constructing the appropriate parameter table.

C **(c)** Obtain an optimal solution for the transportation problem formulated in part (b).

(d) Why does the optimal BF solution obtained in part (c) include some (degenerate) basic variables that are not part of the optimal solution for the assignment problem?

(e) Now consider the *nonbasic* variables in the optimal BF solution obtained in part (c). For each nonbasic variable x_{ij} and the corresponding cost c_{ij}, adapt the sensitivity analysis procedure for general linear programming (see Case 2a in Sec. 6.7) to determine the *allowable range to stay optimal for* c_{ij}.

8.3-10. Consider the linear programming model for the general assignment problem given in Sec. 8.3. Construct the table of constraint coefficients for this model. Compare this table with the one for the general transportation problem (Table 8.6). In what ways does the general assignment problem have more special structure than the general transportation problem?

CASE 8.1   SHIPPING WOOD TO MARKET

Alabama Atlantic is a lumber company that has three sources of wood and five markets to be supplied. The annual availability of wood at sources 1, 2, and 3 is 15, 20, and 15 million board feet, respectively. The amount that can be sold annually at markets 1, 2, 3, 4, and 5 is 11, 12, 9, 10, and 8 million board feet, respectively.

In the past the company has shipped the wood by train. However, because shipping costs have been increasing, the alternative of using ships to make some of the deliveries is being investigated. This alternative would require the company to invest in some ships. Except for these investment costs, the shipping costs in thousands of dollars per million board feet by rail and by water (when feasible) would be the following for each route:

Source	Unit Cost by Rail ($1,000's) Market					Unit Cost by Ship ($1,000's) Market				
	1	2	3	4	5	1	2	3	4	5
1	61	72	45	55	66	31	38	24	—	35
2	69	78	60	49	56	36	43	28	24	31
3	59	66	63	61	47	—	33	36	32	26

The capital investment (in thousands of dollars) in ships required for each million board feet to be transported annually by ship along each route is given as follows:

Source	Investment for Ships ($1,000's) Market				
	1	2	3	4	5
1	275	303	238	—	285
2	293	318	270	250	265
3	—	283	275	268	240

Considering the expected useful life of the ships and the time value of money, the equivalent uniform annual cost of these investments is one-tenth the amount given in the table. The objective is to determine the overall shipping plan that minimizes the total equivalent uniform annual cost (including shipping costs).

You are the head of the OR team that has been assigned the task of determining this shipping plan for each of the following three options.

Option 1: Continue shipping exclusively by rail.
Option 2: Switch to shipping exclusively by water (except where only rail is feasible).
Option 3: Ship by either rail or water, depending on which is less expensive for the particular route.

Present your results for each option. Compare.

Finally, consider the fact that these results are based on *current* shipping and investment costs, so that the decision on the option to adopt now should take into account management's projection of how these costs are likely to change in the future. For each option, describe a scenario of future cost changes that would justify adopting that option now.

CASE 8.2   PROJECT PICKINGS

Tazer, a pharmaceutical manufacturing company, entered the pharmaceutical market 12 years ago with the introduction of six new drugs. Five of the six drugs were simply permutations of existing drugs and therefore did not sell very heavily. The sixth drug, however, addressed hypertension and was a huge success. Since Tazer had a patent on the hypertension drug, it experienced no competition, and profits from the hypertension drug alone kept Tazer in business.

During the past 12 years, Tazer continued a moderate amount of research and development, but it never stumbled upon a drug as successful as the hypertension drug. One reason is that the company never had the motivation to invest heavily in innovative research and development. The company was riding the profit wave generated by its hypertension drug and did not feel the need to commit significant resources to finding new drug breakthroughs.

Now Tazer is beginning to fear the pressure of competition. The patent for the hypertension drug expires in 5 years,[1] and Tazer knows that once the patent expires, generic drug manufacturing companies will swarm into the market like vultures. Historical trends show that generic drugs decreased sales of branded drugs by 75 percent.

Tazer is therefore looking to invest significant amounts of money in research and development this year to begin the search for a new breakthrough drug that will offer the company the same success as the hypertension drug. Tazer believes that if the company begins extensive research and development now, the probability of finding a successful drug shortly after the expiration of the hypertension patent will be high.

As head of research and development at Tazer, you are responsible for choosing potential projects and assigning project directors to lead each of the projects. After researching the needs of the market, analyzing the shortcomings of current drugs, and interviewing numerous scientists concerning the promising areas of medical research, you have decided that your department will pursue five separate projects, which are listed below:

Project Up   Develop an antidepressant that does not cause serious mood swings.
Project Stable   Develop a drug that addresses manic-depression.
Project Choice   Develop a less intrusive birth control method for women.
Project Hope   Develop a vaccine to prevent HIV infection.
Project Release   Develop a more effective drug to lower blood pressure.

---

[1]In general, patents protect inventions for 17 years. In 1995, GATT legislation extending the protection given by new pharmaceutical patents to 20 years became effective. The patent for Tazer's hypertension drug was issued prior to the GATT legislation, however. Thus, the patent only protects the drug for 17 years.

For each of the five projects, you are only able to specify the medical ailment the research should address, since you do not know what compounds will exist and be effective without research.

You also have five senior scientists to lead the five projects. You know that scientists are very temperamental people and will work well only if they are challenged and motivated by the project. To ensure that the senior scientists are assigned to projects they find motivating, you have established a bidding system for the projects. You have given each of the five scientists 1000 bid points. They assign bids to each project, giving a higher number of bid points to projects they most prefer to lead. The following table provides the bids from the five individual senior scientists for the five individual projects:

Project	Dr. Kvaal	Dr. Zuner	Dr. Tsai	Dr. Mickey	Dr. Rollins
Project Up	100	0	100	267	100
Project Stable	400	200	100	153	33
Project Choice	200	800	100	99	33
Project Hope	200	0	100	451	34
Project Release	100	0	600	30	800

You decide to evaluate a variety of scenarios you think are likely.

(a) Given the bids, you need to assign one senior scientist to each of the five projects to maximize the preferences of the scientists. What are the assignments?
(b) Dr. Rollins is being courted by Harvard Medical School to accept a teaching position. You are fighting desperately to keep her at Tazer, but the prestige of Harvard may lure her away. If this were to happen, the company would give up the project with the least enthusiasm. Which project would not be done?
(c) You do not want to sacrifice any project, since researching only four projects decreases the probability of finding a breakthrough new drug. You decide that either Dr. Zuner or Dr. Mickey could lead two projects. Under these new conditions with just four senior scientists, which scientists will lead which projects to maximize preferences?
(d) After Dr. Zuner was informed that she and Dr. Mickey are being considered for two projects, she decided to change her bids. The following table shows Dr. Zuner's new bids for each of the projects:

Project Up	20
Project Stable	450
Project Choice	451
Project Hope	39
Project Release	40

Under these new conditions with just four scientists, which scientists will lead which projects to maximize preferences?
(e) Do you support the assignment found in part (d)? Why or why not?
(f) Now you again consider all five scientists. You decide, however, that several scientists cannot lead certain projects. In particular, Dr. Mickey does not have experience with research on the immune system, so he cannot lead Project Hope. His family also has a history of manic-depression, and you feel that he would be too personally involved in Project Stable

to serve as an effective project leader. Dr. Mickey therefore cannot lead Project Stable. Dr. Kvaal also does not have experience with research on the immune systems and cannot lead Project Hope. In addition, Dr. Kvaal cannot lead Project Release because he does not have experience with research on the cardiovascular system. Finally, Dr. Rollins cannot lead Project Up because her family has a history of depression and you feel she would be too personally involved in the project to serve as an effective leader. Because Dr. Mickey and Dr. Kvaal cannot lead two of the five projects, they each have only 600 bid points. Dr. Rollins has only 800 bid points because she cannot lead one of the five projects. The following table provides the new bids of Dr. Mickey, Dr. Kvaal, and Dr. Rollins:

Project	Dr. Mickey	Dr. Kvaal	Dr. Rollins.
Project Up	300	86	Can't lead
Project Stable	Can't lead	343	50
Project Choice	125	171	50
Project Hope	Can't lead	Can't lead	100
Project Release	175	Can't lead	600

Which scientists should lead which projects to maximize preferences?

(g) You decide that Project Hope and Project Release are too complex to be led by only one scientist. Therefore, each of these projects will be assigned two scientists as project leaders. You decide to hire two more scientists in order to staff all projects: Dr. Arriaga and Dr. Santos. Because of religious reasons, the two doctors both do not want to lead Project Choice. The following table lists all projects, scientists, and their bids.

	Kvaal	Zuner	Tsai	Mickey	Rollins	Arriaga	Santos
Up	86	0	100	300	Can't lead	250	111
Stable	343	200	100	Can't lead	50	250	1
Choice	171	800	100	125	50	Can't lead	Can't lead
Hope	Can't lead	0	100	Can't lead	100	250	333
Release	Can't lead	0	600	175	600	250	555

Which scientists should lead which projects to maximize preferences?

(h) Do you think it is wise to base your decision in part (g) only on an optimal solution for an assignment problem?

9

Network Optimization Models

Networks arise in numerous settings and in a variety of guises. Transportation, electrical, and communication networks pervade our daily lives. Network representations also are widely used for problems in such diverse areas as production, distribution, project planning, facilities location, resource management, and financial planning—to name just a few examples. In fact, a network representation provides such a powerful visual and conceptual aid for portraying the relationships between the components of systems that it is used in virtually every field of scientific, social, and economic endeavor.

One of the most exciting developments in operations research (OR) in recent years has been the unusually rapid advance in both the methodology and application of network optimization models. A number of algorithmic breakthroughs have had a major impact, as have ideas from computer science concerning data structures and efficient data manipulation. Consequently, algorithms and software now are available *and are being used* to solve huge problems on a routine basis that would have been completely intractable two or three decades ago.

Many network optimization models actually are special types of *linear programming* problems. For example, both the transportation problem and the assignment problem discussed in the preceding chapter fall into this category because of their network representations presented in Figs. 8.3 and 8.5.

One of the linear programming examples presented in Sec. 3.4 also is a network optimization problem. This is the Distribution Unlimited Co. problem of how to distribute its goods through the distribution network shown in Fig. 3.13. This special type of linear programming problem, called the *minimum cost flow* problem, is presented in Sec. 9.6. We shall return to this specific example in that section and then solve it with network methodology in the following section.

The third linear programming case study presented in Sec. 3.5 also features an application of the minimum cost flow problem. This case study involved planning the supply, distribution, and marketing of goods at Citgo Petroleum Corp. The OR team at Citgo developed an optimization-based decision support system, using a minimum cost flow problem model for each product, and coupled this system with an on-line corporate database. Each product's model has about 3,000 equations (nodes) and 15,000 variables (arcs), which is a very modest size by today's standards for the application of network optimization models. The model takes in all aspects of the business, helping management decide everything from run levels at the various refineries to what prices to pay or charge. A network representation is essential because of the flow of goods through several stages: purchase of crude oil from various suppliers, shipping it to refineries, refining it into various products, and sending the products to distribution centers and product storage terminals for subsequent sale. As discussed in Sec. 3.5, the modeling system enabled the company to reduce its petroleum products inventory by over $116 million with no drop in service levels. This resulted in a savings in annual interest of $14 million as well as improvements in coordination, pricing, and purchasing decisions worth another $2.5 million each year, along with many indirect benefits.

In this one chapter we only scratch the surface of the current state of the art of network methodology. However, we shall introduce you to four important kinds of network problems and some basic ideas of how to solve them (without delving into issues of data structures that are so vital to successful large-scale implementations). Each of the first three problem types—the *shortest-path problem,* the *minimum spanning tree problem,* and the *maximum flow problem*—has a very specific structure that arises frequently in applications.

The fourth type—the *minimum cost flow problem*—provides a unified approach to many other applications because of its far more general structure. In fact, this structure is so general that it includes as special cases both the shortest-path problem and the maximum flow problem as well as the transportation problem and the assignment problem from Chap. 8. Because the minimum cost flow problem is a special type of linear programming problem, it can be solved extremely efficiently by a streamlined version of the simplex method called the *network simplex method.* (We shall not discuss even more general network problems that are more difficult to solve.)

The first section introduces a prototype example that will be used subsequently to illustrate the approach to the first three of these problems. Section 9.2 presents some basic terminology for networks. The next four sections deal with the four problems in turn. Section 9.7 then is devoted to the network simplex method.

9.1 PROTOTYPE EXAMPLE

SEERVADA PARK has recently been set aside for a limited amount of sightseeing and backpack hiking. Cars are not allowed into the park, but there is a narrow, winding road system for trams and for jeeps driven by the park rangers. This road system is shown (without the curves) in Fig. 9.1, where location O is the entrance into the park; other letters designate the locations of ranger stations (and other limited facilities). The numbers give the distances of these winding roads in miles.

The park contains a scenic wonder at station T. A small number of trams are used to transport sightseers from the park entrance to station T and back.

The park management currently faces three problems. One is to determine which route from the park entrance to station T has the *smallest total distance* for the operation of the trams. (This is an example of the shortest-path problem to be discussed in Sec. 9.3.)

A second problem is that telephone lines must be installed under the roads to establish telephone communication among all the stations (including the park entrance). Because the installation is both expensive and disruptive to the natural environment, lines

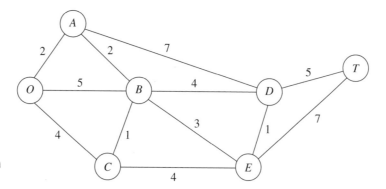

FIGURE 9.1
The road system for Seervada Park.

will be installed under just enough roads to provide some connection between every pair of stations. The question is where the lines should be laid to accomplish this with a *minimum* total number of miles of line installed. (This is an example of the minimum spanning tree problem to be discussed in Sec. 9.4.)

The third problem is that more people want to take the tram ride from the park entrance to station *T* than can be accommodated during the peak season. To avoid unduly disturbing the ecology and wildlife of the region, a strict ration has been placed on the number of tram trips that can be made on each of the roads per day. (These limits differ for the different roads, as we shall describe in detail in Sec. 9.5.) Therefore, during the peak season, various routes might be followed regardless of distance to increase the number of tram trips that can be made each day. The question pertains to how to route the various trips to *maximize* the number of trips that can be made per day without violating the limits on any individual road. (This is an example of the maximum flow problem to be discussed in Sec. 9.5.)

9.2 THE TERMINOLOGY OF NETWORKS

A relatively extensive terminology has been developed to describe the various kinds of networks and their components. Although we have avoided as much of this special vocabulary as we could, we still need to introduce a considerable number of terms for use throughout the chapter. We suggest that you read through this section once at the outset to understand the definitions and then plan to return to refresh your memory as the terms are used in subsequent sections. To assist you, each term is highlighted in **boldface** at the point where it is defined.

A network consists of a set of *points* and a set of *lines* connecting certain pairs of the points. The points are called **nodes** (or vertices); e.g., the network in Fig. 9.1 has seven nodes designated by the seven circles. The lines are called **arcs** (or links or edges or branches); e.g., the network in Fig. 9.1 has 12 arcs corresponding to the 12 roads in the road system. Arcs are labeled by naming the nodes at either end; for example, *AB* is the arc between nodes *A* and *B* in Fig. 9.1.

The arcs of a network may have a flow of some type through them, e.g., the flow of trams on the roads of Seervada Park in Sec. 9.1. Table 9.1 gives several examples of flow in typical networks. If flow through an arc is allowed in only one direction (e.g., a one-way street), the arc is said to be a **directed arc.** The direction is indicated by adding an arrowhead at the end of the line representing the arc. When a directed arc is labeled by listing two nodes it connects, the *from* node always is given before the *to* node; e.g., an arc that is directed *from* node A *to* node B must be labeled as AB rather than BA. Alternatively, this arc may be labeled as $A \rightarrow B$.

If flow through an arc is allowed in either direction (e.g., a pipeline that can be used to pump fluid in either direction), the arc is said to be an **undirected arc.** To help you distinguish between the two kinds of arcs, we shall frequently refer to undirected arcs by the suggestive name of **links.**

Although the flow through an undirected arc is allowed to be in either direction, we do assume that the flow will be one way in the direction of choice rather than having simultaneous flows in opposite directions. (The latter case requires the use of a *pair of directed arcs* in opposite directions.) However, in the process of making the decision on the flow through an undirected arc, it is permissible to make a sequence of assignments of flows in opposite directions, but with the understanding that the actual flow will be the *net flow* (the difference of the assigned flows in the two directions). For example, if a flow of 10 has been assigned in one direction and then a flow of 4 is assigned in the opposite direction, the actual effect is to *cancel* 4 units of the original assignment by reducing the flow in the original direction from 10 to 6. Even for a directed arc, the same technique sometimes is used as a convenient device to reduce a previously assigned flow. In particular, you are allowed to make a fictional assignment of flow in the "wrong" direction through a directed arc to record a reduction of that amount in the flow in the "right" direction.

A network that has only directed arcs is called a **directed network.** Similarly, if all its arcs are undirected, the network is said to be an **undirected network.** A network with a mixture of directed and undirected arcs (or even all undirected arcs) can be converted to a directed network, if desired, by replacing each undirected arc by a pair of directed arcs in opposite directions. (You then have the choice of interpreting the flows through each pair of directed arcs as being simultaneous flows in opposite directions or providing a net flow in one direction, depending on which fits your application.)

When two nodes are not connected by an arc, a natural question is whether they are connected by a series of arcs. A **path** between two nodes is a *sequence of distinct arcs* connecting these nodes. For example, one of the paths connecting nodes O and T in Fig. 9.1 is the sequence of arcs OB–BD–DT ($O \rightarrow B \rightarrow D \rightarrow T$), or vice versa. When some

TABLE 9.1 Components of typical networks

Nodes	Arcs	Flow
Intersections	Roads	Vehicles
Airports	Air lanes	Aircraft
Switching points	Wires, channels	Messages
Pumping stations	Pipes	Fluids
Work centers	Materials-handling routes	Jobs

of or all the arcs in the network are directed arcs, we then distinguish between directed paths and undirected paths. A **directed path** from node i to node j is a sequence of connecting arcs whose direction (if any) is *toward* node j, so that flow from node i to node j along this path is feasible. An **undirected path** from node i to node j is a sequence of connecting arcs whose direction (if any) can be *either* toward or away from node j. (Notice that a directed path also satisfies the definition of an undirected path, but not vice versa.) Frequently, an undirected path will have some arcs directed toward node j but others directed away (i.e., toward node i). You will see in Secs. 9.5 and 9.7 that, perhaps surprisingly, *undirected* paths play a major role in the analysis of *directed* networks.

To illustrate these definitions, Fig. 9.2 shows a typical directed network. (Its nodes and arcs are the same as in Fig. 3.13, where nodes A and B represent two factories, nodes D and E represent two warehouses, node C represents a distribution center, and the arcs represent shipping lanes.) The sequence of arcs $AB–BC–CE$ ($A \rightarrow B \rightarrow C \rightarrow E$) is a directed path from node A to E, since flow toward node E along this entire path is feasible. On the other hand, $BC–AC–AD$ ($B \rightarrow C \rightarrow A \rightarrow D$) is *not* a directed path from node B to node D, because the direction of arc AC is away from node D (on this path). However, $B \rightarrow C \rightarrow A \rightarrow D$ is an undirected path from node B to node D, because the sequence of arcs $BC–AC–AD$ does *connect* these two nodes (even though the direction of arc AC prevents flow through this path).

As an example of the relevance of undirected paths, suppose that 2 units of flow from node A to node C had previously been assigned to arc AC. Given this previous assignment, it now is feasible to assign a smaller flow, say, 1 unit, to the entire undirected path $B \rightarrow C \rightarrow A \rightarrow D$, even though the direction of arc AC prevents positive flow through $C \rightarrow A$. The reason is that this assignment of flow in the "wrong" direction for arc AC actually just *reduces* the flow in the "right" direction by 1 unit. Sections 9.5 and 9.7 make heavy use of this technique of assigning a flow through an undirected path that includes arcs whose direction is opposite to this flow, where the real effect for these arcs is to reduce previously assigned positive flows in the "right" direction.

A path that begins and ends at the same node is called a **cycle.** In a *directed* network, a cycle is either a directed or an undirected cycle, depending on whether the path involved

FIGURE 9.2

The distribution network for Distribution Unlimited Co., first shown in Fig. 3.13, illustrates a directed network.

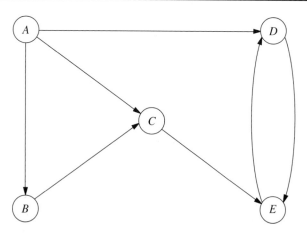

is a directed or an undirected path. (Since a directed path also is an undirected path, a directed cycle is an undirected cycle, but not vice versa in general.) In Fig. 9.2, for example, *DE–ED* is a directed cycle. By contrast, *AB–BC–AC* is *not* a directed cycle, because the direction of arc *AC* opposes the direction of arcs *AB* and *BC*. On the other hand, *AB–BC–AC* is an undirected cycle, because $A \rightarrow B \rightarrow C \rightarrow A$ is an undirected path. In the undirected network shown in Fig. 9.1, there are many cycles, for example, *OA–AB–BC–CO*. However, note that the definition of *path* (a sequence of *distinct* arcs) rules out retracing one's steps in forming a cycle. For example, *OB–BO* in Fig. 9.1 does not qualify as a cycle, because *OB* and *BO* are two labels for the *same* arc (link). On the other hand, *DE–ED* is a (directed) cycle in Fig. 9.2, because *DE* and *ED* are distinct arcs.

Two nodes are said to be **connected** if the network contains at least one *undirected* path between them. (Note that the path does not need to be directed even if the network is directed.) A **connected network** is a network where every pair of nodes is connected. Thus, the networks in Figs. 9.1 and 9.2 are both connected. However, the latter network would not be connected if arcs *AD* and *CE* were removed.

Consider a connected network with *n* nodes (e.g., the $n = 5$ nodes in Fig. 9.2) where all the arcs have been deleted. A "tree" can then be "grown" by adding one arc (or "branch") at a time from the original network in a certain way. The first arc can go anywhere to connect some pair of nodes. Thereafter, each new arc should be between a node that already is connected to other nodes and a new node not previously connected to any other nodes. Adding an arc in this way avoids creating a cycle and ensures that the number of connected nodes is 1 greater than the number of arcs. Each new arc creates a larger **tree,** which is a *connected network* (for some subset of the *n* nodes) that contains *no undirected cycles*. Once the $(n - 1)$st arc has been added, the process stops because the resulting tree *spans* (connects) all *n* nodes. This tree is called a **spanning tree,** i.e., a *connected network* for all *n* nodes that contains *no undirected cycles*. Every spanning tree has exactly $n - 1$ arcs, since this is the *minimum* number of arcs needed to have a connected network and the *maximum* number possible without having undirected cycles.

Figure 9.3 uses the five nodes and some of the arcs of Fig. 9.2 to illustrate this process of growing a tree one arc (branch) at a time until a spanning tree has been obtained. There are several alternative choices for the new arc at each stage of the process, so Fig. 9.3 shows only one of many ways to construct a spanning tree in this case. Note, however, how each new added arc satisfies the conditions specified in the preceding paragraph. We shall discuss and illustrate spanning trees further in Sec. 9.4.

Spanning trees play a key role in the analysis of many networks. For example, they form the basis for the *minimum spanning tree problem* discussed in Sec. 9.4. Another prime example is that (feasible) spanning trees correspond to the BF solutions for the *network simplex method* discussed in Sec. 9.7.

Finally, we shall need a little additional terminology about *flows* in networks. The maximum amount of flow (possibly infinity) that can be carried on a directed arc is referred to as the **arc capacity.** For nodes, a distinction is made among those that are net generators of flow, net absorbers of flow, or neither. A **supply node** (or source node or source) has the property that the flow *out* of the node exceeds the flow *into* the node. The reverse case is a **demand node** (or sink node or sink), where the flow *into* the node exceeds the flow *out* of the node. A **transshipment node** (or intermediate node) satisfies *conservation of flow,* so flow in equals flow out.

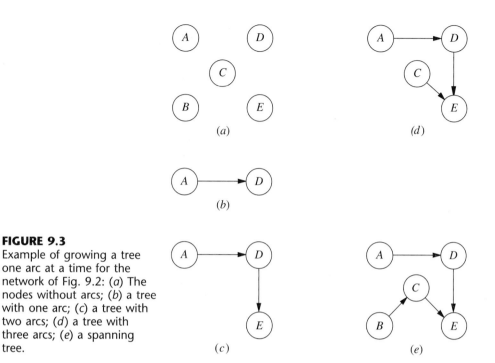

FIGURE 9.3
Example of growing a tree one arc at a time for the network of Fig. 9.2: (a) The nodes without arcs; (b) a tree with one arc; (c) a tree with two arcs; (d) a tree with three arcs; (e) a spanning tree.

9.3 THE SHORTEST-PATH PROBLEM

Although several other versions of the shortest-path problem (including some for directed networks) are mentioned at the end of the section, we shall focus on the following simple version. Consider an *undirected* and *connected* network with two special nodes called the *origin* and the *destination.* Associated with each of the *links* (undirected arcs) is a non-negative *distance.* The objective is to find the shortest path (the path with the minimum total distance) from the origin to the destination.

A relatively straightforward algorithm is available for this problem. The essence of this procedure is that it fans out from the origin, successively identifying the shortest path to each of the nodes of the network in the ascending order of their (shortest) distances from the origin, thereby solving the problem when the destination node is reached. We shall first outline the method and then illustrate it by solving the shortest-path problem encountered by the Seervada Park management in Sec. 9.1.

Algorithm for the Shortest-Path Problem.

Objective of nth iteration: Find the *n*th nearest node to the origin (to be repeated for $n = 1, 2, \ldots$ until the *n*th nearest node is the destination.

Input for nth iteration: $n - 1$ nearest nodes to the origin (solved for at the previous iterations), including their shortest path and distance from the origin. (These nodes, plus the origin, will be called *solved nodes;* the others are *unsolved nodes.*)

Candidates for nth nearest node: Each solved node that is directly connected by a link to one or more unsolved nodes provides *one* candidate—the unsolved node with the *shortest* connecting link. (Ties provide additional candidates.)

Calculation of nth nearest node: For each such solved node and its candidate, add the distance between them and the distance of the shortest path from the origin to this solved node. The candidate with the smallest such total distance is the *n*th nearest node (ties provide additional solved nodes), and its shortest path is the one generating this distance.

Applying This Algorithm to the Seervada Park Shortest-Path Problem

The Seervada Park management needs to find the shortest path from the park entrance (node *O*) to the scenic wonder (node *T*) through the road system shown in Fig. 9.1. Applying the above algorithm to this problem yields the results shown in Table 9.2 (where the tie for the second nearest node allows skipping directly to seeking the fourth nearest node next). The first column (*n*) indicates the iteration count. The second column simply lists the *solved nodes* for beginning the current iteration after deleting the irrelevant ones (those not connected directly to any unsolved node). The third column then gives the *candidates* for the *n*th nearest node (the unsolved nodes with the *shortest* connecting link to a solved node). The fourth column calculates the distance of the shortest path from the origin to each of these candidates (namely, the distance to the solved node plus the link distance to the candidate). The candidate with the smallest such distance is the *n*th nearest node to the origin, as listed in the fifth column. The last two columns summarize the information for this *newest solved node* that is needed to proceed to subsequent iterations (namely, the distance of the shortest path from the origin to this node and the last link on this shortest path).

TABLE 9.2 Applying the shortest-path algorithm to the Seervada Park problem

n	Solved Nodes Directly Connected to Unsolved Nodes	Closest Connected Unsolved Node	Total Distance Involved	nth Nearest Node	Minimum Distance	Last Connection
1	O	A	2	A	2	OA
2, 3	O	C	4	C	4	OC
	A	B	2 + 2 = 4	B	4	AB
4	A	D	2 + 7 = 9			
	B	E	4 + 3 = 7	E	7	BE
	C	E	4 + 4 = 8			
5	A	D	2 + 7 = 9			
	B	D	4 + 4 = 8	D	8	BD
	E	D	7 + 1 = 8	D	8	ED
6	D	T	8 + 5 = 13	T	13	DT
	E	T	7 + 7 = 14			

Now let us relate these columns directly to the outline given for the algorithm. The *input for nth iteration* is provided by the fifth and sixth columns for the preceding iterations, where the solved nodes in the fifth column are then listed in the second column for the current iteration after deleting those that are no longer directly connected to unsolved nodes. The *candidates for nth nearest node* next are listed in the third column for the current iteration. The *calculation of nth nearest node* is performed in the fourth column, and the results are recorded in the last three columns for the current iteration.

After the work shown in Table 9.2 is completed, the shortest path *from the destination to the origin* can be traced back through the last column of Table 9.2 as *either* $T \rightarrow D \rightarrow E \rightarrow B \rightarrow A \rightarrow O$ or $T \rightarrow D \rightarrow B \rightarrow A \rightarrow O$. Therefore, the two alternates for the shortest path *from the origin to the destination* have been identified as $O \rightarrow A \rightarrow B \rightarrow E \rightarrow D \rightarrow T$ and $O \rightarrow A \rightarrow B \rightarrow D \rightarrow T$, with a total distance of 13 miles on either path.

Using Excel to Formulate and Solve Shortest-Path Problems

This algorithm provides a particularly efficient way of solving large shortest-path problems. However, some mathematical programming software packages do not include this algorithm. If not, they often will include the *network simplex method* described in Sec. 9.7, which is another good option for these problems.

Since the shortest-path problem is a special type of linear programming problem, the general simplex method also can be used when better options are not readily available. Although not nearly as efficient as these specialized algorithms on large shortest-path problems, it is quite adequate for problems of even very substantial size (much larger than the Seervada Park problem). Excel, which relies on the general simplex method, provides a convenient way of formulating and solving shortest-path problems with dozens of arcs and nodes.

Figure 9.4 shows an appropriate spreadsheet formulation for the Seervada Park shortest-path problem. Rather than using the kind of formulation presented in Sec. 3.6 that uses a separate row for each functional constraint of the linear programming model, this formulation exploits the special structure by listing the *nodes* in column G and the *arcs* in columns B and C, as well as the distance (in miles) along each arc in column E. Since each *link* in the network is an *undirected arc,* whereas travel through the shortest path is in one direction, each link can be replaced by a pair of *directed* arcs in opposite directions. Thus, columns B and C together list both of the nearly vertical links in Fig. 9.1 (A–B and D–E) twice, once as a downward arc and once as an upward arc, since either direction might be on the chosen path. However, the other links are only listed as left-to-right arcs, since this is the only direction of interest for choosing a shortest path from the origin to the destination.

A trip from the origin to the destination is interpreted to be a "flow" of 1 on the chosen path through the network. The decisions to be made are which arcs should be included in the path to be traversed. A flow of 1 is assigned to an arc if it is included, whereas the flow is 0 if it is not included. Thus, the decision variables are

$$x_{ij} = \begin{cases} 0 & \text{if arc } i \rightarrow j \text{ is not included} \\ 1 & \text{if arc } i \rightarrow j \text{ is included} \end{cases}$$

for each of the arcs under consideration. The values of these decision variables are entered in the changing cells in column D (cells D4:D17).

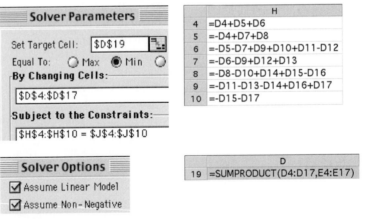

	A	B	C	D	E	F	G	H	I	J
1	Seervada Park Shortest-Path Problem									
2										
3		From	To	On Route	Distance		Nodes	Net Flow		Supply/Demand
4		O	A	1	2		O	1	=	1
5		O	B	0	5		A	0	=	0
6		O	C	0	4		B	0	=	0
7		A	B	1	2		C	0	=	0
8		A	D	0	7		D	0	=	0
9		B	C	0	1		E	0	=	0
10		B	D	0	4		T	-1	=	-1
11		B	E	1	3					
12		C	B	0	1					
13		C	E	0	4					
14		D	E	0	1					
15		D	T	1	5					
16		E	D	1	1					
17		E	T	0	7					
18										
19			Total Distance =	13						

Solver Parameters

Set Target Cell: $D$19

Equal To: ○ Max   ● Min   ○

By Changing Cells:

$D$4:$D$17

Subject to the Constraints:

$H$4:$H$10 = $J$4:$J$10

	H
4	=D4+D5+D6
5	=-D4+D7+D8
6	=-D5-D7+D9+D10+D11-D12
7	=-D6-D9+D12+D13
8	=-D8-D10+D14+D15-D16
9	=-D11-D13-D14+D16+D17
10	=-D15-D17

Solver Options

☑ Assume Linear Model

☑ Assume Non-Negative

	D
19	=SUMPRODUCT(D4:D17,E4:E17)

FIGURE 9.4
A spreadsheet formulation for the Seervada Park shortest-path problem, where the changing cells (D4:D17) show the optimal solution obtained by the Excel Solver and the target cell (D19) gives the total distance (in miles) of this shortest path.

Each node can be thought of as having a flow of 1 passing through it if it is on the selected path, but no flow otherwise. The *net flow* generated at a node is the *flow out* minus the *flow in*, so the net flow is 1 at the origin, −1 at the destination, and 0 at every other node. These requirements for the net flows are specified in column J of Fig. 9.4. Using the equations at the bottom of the figure, each column H cell then calculates the *actual* net flow at that node by adding the flow out and subtracting the flow in. The corresponding constraints, H4:H10 = J4:J10, are specified in the Solver dialogue box.

The target cell (D19) gives the total distance in miles of the chosen path by using the equation for this cell given at the bottom of Fig. 9.4. The objective of *minimizing* this target cell has been specified in the Solver dialogue box. The solution shown in column D is an optimal solution obtained after clicking on the Solve button. This solution is, of course, one of the two shortest paths identified earlier by the algorithm for the shortest-path algorithm.

Other Applications

Not all applications of the shortest-path problem involve minimizing the distance traveled from the origin to the destination. In fact, they might not even involve travel at all. The links (or arcs) might instead represent activities of some other kind, so choosing a path through the network corresponds to selecting the best sequence of activities. The numbers giving the "lengths" of the links might then be, for example, the *costs* of the activities, in which case the objective would be to determine which sequence of activities minimizes the total cost.

Here are three categories of applications.

1. Minimize the total *distance* traveled, as in the Seervada Park example.
2. Minimize the total *cost* of a sequence of activities. (Problem 9.3-2 is of this type.)
3. Minimize the total *time* of a sequence of activities. (Problems 9.3-5 and 9.3-6 are of this type.)

It is even possible for all three categories to arise in the *same* application. For example, suppose you wish to find the best route for driving from one town to another through a number of intermediate towns. You then have the choice of defining the best route as being the one that minimizes the total *distance* traveled or that minimizes the total *cost* incurred or that minimizes the total *time* required. (Problem 9.3-1 illustrates such an application.)

Many applications require finding the shortest *directed* path from the origin to the destination through a *directed* network. The algorithm already presented can be easily modified to deal just with directed paths at each iteration. In particular, when candidates for the *n*th nearest node are identified, only directed arcs *from* a solved node *to* an unsolved node are considered.

Another version of the shortest-path problem is to find the shortest paths from the origin to *all* the other nodes of the network. Notice that the algorithm already solves for the shortest path to each node that is closer to the origin than the destination. Therefore, when all nodes are potential destinations, the only modification needed in the algorithm is that it does not stop until all nodes are solved nodes.

An even more general version of the shortest-path problem is to find the shortest paths from *every* node to every other node. Another option is to drop the restriction that "distances" (arc values) be nonnegative. Constraints also can be imposed on the paths that can be followed. All these variations occasionally arise in applications and so have been studied by researchers.

The algorithms for a wide variety of combinatorial optimization problems, such as certain vehicle routing or network design problems, often call for the solution of a large number of shortest-path problems as subroutines. Although we lack the space to pursue this topic further, this use may now be the most important kind of application of the shortest-path problem.

9.4 THE MINIMUM SPANNING TREE PROBLEM

The minimum spanning tree problem bears some similarities to the main version of the shortest-path problem presented in the preceding section. In both cases, an *undirected* and *connected* network is being considered, where the given information includes some measure of the positive *length* (distance, cost, time, etc.) associated with each link. Both problems also involve choosing a set of links that have the *shortest total length* among all sets of links that satisfy a certain property. For the shortest-path problem, this property is that the chosen links must provide a path between the origin and the destination. For the minimum spanning tree problem, the required property is that the chosen links must provide a path between *each* pair of nodes.

The minimum spanning tree problem can be summarized as follows.

1. You are given the *nodes* of a network but *not* the *links*. Instead, you are given the *potential links* and the positive *length* for each if it is inserted into the network. (Alternative measures for the length of a link include distance, cost, and time.)
2. You wish to design the network by inserting enough links to satisfy the requirement that there be a path between *every* pair of nodes.
3. The objective is to satisfy this requirement in a way that minimizes the total length of the links inserted into the network.

A network with n nodes requires only $(n - 1)$ links to provide a path between each pair of nodes. No extra links should be used, since this would needlessly increase the total length of the chosen links. The $(n - 1)$ links need to be chosen in such a way that the resulting network (with just the chosen links) forms a *spanning tree* (as defined in Sec. 9.2). Therefore, the problem is to find the spanning tree with a minimum total length of the links.

Figure 9.5 illustrates this concept of a spanning tree for the Seervada Park problem (see Sec. 9.1). Thus, Fig. 9.5a is *not* a spanning tree because nodes *O, A, B,* and *C* are not connected with nodes *D, E,* and *T.* It needs another link to make this connection. This network actually consists of two trees, one for each of these two sets of nodes. The links in Fig. 9.5b do *span* the network (i.e., the network is connected as defined in Sec. 9.2), but it is *not* a tree because there are two *cycles* (*O–A–B–C–O* and *D–T–E–D*). It has too many links. Because the Seervada Park problem has $n = 7$ nodes, Sec. 9.2 indicates that the network must have exactly $n - 1 = 6$ links, with *no cycles,* to qualify as a spanning tree. This condition is achieved in Fig. 9.5c, so this network is a *feasible* solution (with a value of 24 miles for the total length of the links) for the minimum spanning tree problem. (You soon will see that this solution is not *optimal* because it is possible to construct a spanning tree with only 14 miles of links.)

Some Applications

Here is a list of some key types of applications of the minimum spanning tree problem.

1. Design of telecommunication networks (fiber-optic networks, computer networks, leased-line telephone networks, cable television networks, etc.)
2. Design of a lightly used transportation network to minimize the total cost of providing the links (rail lines, roads, etc.)
3. Design of a network of high-voltage electrical power transmission lines
4. Design of a network of wiring on electrical equipment (e.g., a digital computer system) to minimize the total length of the wire
5. Design of a network of pipelines to connect a number of locations

In this age of the information superhighway, applications of this first type have become particularly important. In a telecommunication network, it is only necessary to in-

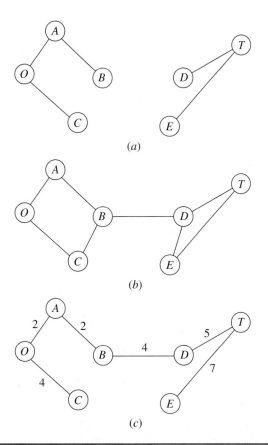

(a)

(b)

(c)

FIGURE 9.5
Illustrations of the spanning tree concept for the Seervada Park problem: (a) Not a spanning tree; (b) not a spanning tree; (c) a spanning tree.

sert enough links to provide a path between every pair of nodes, so designing such a network is a classic application of the minimum spanning tree problem. Because some telecommunication networks now cost many millions of dollars, it is very important to optimize their design by finding the minimum spanning tree for each one.

An Algorithm

The minimum spanning tree problem can be solved in a very straightforward way because it happens to be one of the few OR problems where being *greedy* at each stage of the solution procedure still leads to an overall optimal solution at the end! Thus, beginning with any node, the first stage involves choosing the shortest possible link to another node, without worrying about the effect of this choice on subsequent decisions. The second stage involves identifying the unconnected node that is closest to either of these connected nodes and then adding the corresponding link to the network. This process is repeated, per the following summary, until all the nodes have been connected. (Note that this is the same process already illustrated in Fig. 9.3 for constructing a spanning tree, but now with a specific rule for selecting each new link.) The resulting network is guaranteed to be a minimum spanning tree.

Algorithm for the Minimum Spanning Tree Problem.

1. Select any node arbitrarily, and then connect it (i.e., add a link) to the nearest distinct node.
2. Identify the unconnected node that is closest to a connected node, and then connect these two nodes (i.e., add a link between them). Repeat this step until all nodes have been connected.
3. Tie breaking: Ties for the nearest distinct node (step 1) or the closest unconnected node (step 2) may be broken arbitrarily, and the algorithm must still yield an optimal solution. However, such ties are a signal that there may be (but need not be) multiple optimal solutions. All such optimal solutions can be identified by pursuing all ways of breaking ties to their conclusion.

The fastest way of executing this algorithm manually is the graphical approach illustrated next.

Applying This Algorithm to the Seervada Park Minimum Spanning Tree Problem

The Seervada Park management (see Sec. 9.1) needs to determine under which roads telephone lines should be installed to connect all stations with a minimum total length of line. Using the data given in Fig. 9.1, we outline the step-by-step solution of this problem.

Nodes and distances for the problem are summarized below, where the thin lines now represent *potential* links.

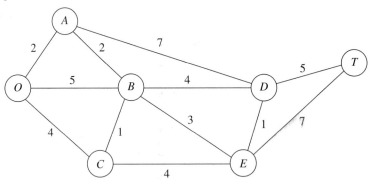

Arbitrarily select node O to start. The unconnected node closest to node O is node A. Connect node A to node O.

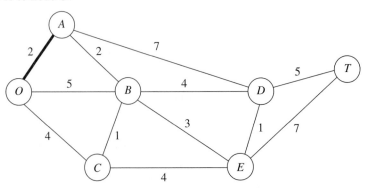

The unconnected node closest to either node O or node A is node B (closest to A). Connect node B to node A.

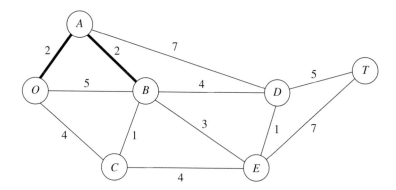

The unconnected node closest to node O, A, or B is node C (closest to B). Connect node C to node B.

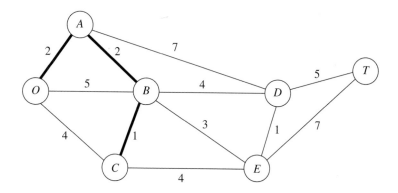

The unconnected node closest to node O, A, B, or C is node E (closest to B). Connect node E to node B.

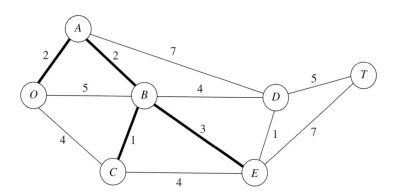

The unconnected node closest to node O, A, B, C, or E is node D (closest to E). Connect node D to node E.

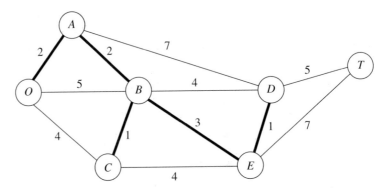

The only remaining unconnected node is node T. It is closest to node D. Connect node T to node D.

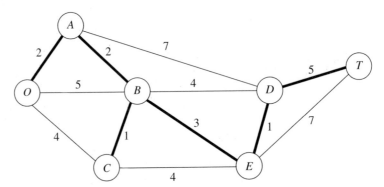

All nodes are now connected, so this solution to the problem is the desired (optimal) one. The total length of the links is 14 miles.

Although it may appear at first glance that the choice of the initial node will affect the resulting final solution (and its total link length) with this procedure, it really does not. We suggest you verify this fact for the example by reapplying the algorithm, starting with nodes other than node O.

The minimum spanning tree problem is the one problem we consider in this chapter that falls into the broad category of *network design*. In this category, the objective is to design the most appropriate network for the given application (frequently involving transportation systems) rather than analyzing an already designed network. Selected Reference 7 provides a survey of this important area.

9.5   THE MAXIMUM FLOW PROBLEM

Now recall that the third problem facing the Seervada Park management (see Sec. 9.1) during the peak season is to determine how to route the various tram trips from the park entrance (station O in Fig. 9.1) to the scenic wonder (station T) to maximize the number of trips per day. (Each tram will return by the same route it took on the outgoing trip, so

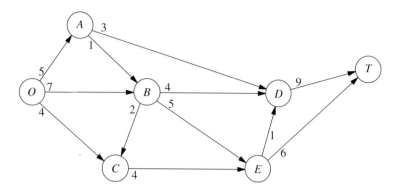

FIGURE 9.6
The Seervada Park maximum
flow problem.

the analysis focuses on outgoing trips only.) To avoid unduly disturbing the ecology and
wildlife of the region, strict upper limits have been imposed on the number of outgoing
trips allowed per day in the outbound direction on each individual road. For each road,
the direction of travel for outgoing trips is indicated by an arrow in Fig. 9.6. The number
at the base of the arrow gives the upper limit on the number of outgoing trips allowed per
day. Given the limits, one *feasible solution* is to send 7 trams per day, with 5 using the
route $O \rightarrow B \rightarrow E \rightarrow T$, 1 using $O \rightarrow B \rightarrow C \rightarrow E \rightarrow T$, and 1 using $O \rightarrow B \rightarrow C \rightarrow$
$E \rightarrow D \rightarrow T$. However, because this solution blocks the use of any routes starting with
$O \rightarrow C$ (because the $E \rightarrow T$ and $E \rightarrow D$ capacities are fully used), it is easy to find better feasible solutions. Many *combinations* of routes (and the number of trips to assign to
each one) need to be considered to find the one(s) maximizing the number of trips made
per day. This kind of problem is called a *maximum flow problem.*

In general terms, the maximum flow problem can be described as follows.

1. All flow through a directed and connected network originates at one node, called the
   source, and terminates at one other node, called the **sink.** (The source and sink in the
   Seervada Park problem are the park entrance at node O and the scenic wonder at node
   T, respectively.)
2. All the remaining nodes are *transshipment nodes.* (These are nodes A, B, C, D, and E
   in the Seervada Park problem.)
3. Flow through an arc is allowed only in the direction indicated by the arrowhead, where
   the maximum amount of flow is given by the *capacity* of that arc. At the *source,* all
   arcs point away from the node. At the *sink,* all arcs point into the node.
4. The objective is to maximize the total amount of flow from the source to the sink. This
   amount is measured in either of two equivalent ways, namely, either the amount *leaving the source* or the amount *entering the sink.*

Some Applications

Here are some typical kinds of applications of the maximum flow problem.

1. Maximize the flow through a company's distribution network from its factories to its
   customers.
2. Maximize the flow through a company's supply network from its vendors to its factories.

3. Maximize the flow of oil through a system of pipelines.
4. Maximize the flow of water through a system of aqueducts.
5. Maximize the flow of vehicles through a transportation network.

For some of these applications, the flow through the network may originate at more than one node and may also terminate at more than one node, even though a maximum flow problem is allowed to have only a single source and a single sink. For example, a company's distribution network commonly has multiple factories and multiple customers. A clever reformulation is used to make such a situation fit the maximum flow problem. This reformulation involves expanding the original network to include a *dummy source,* a *dummy sink,* and some new arcs. The dummy source is treated as the node that originates all the flow that, in reality, originates from some of the other nodes. For each of these other nodes, a new arc is inserted that leads from the dummy source to this node, where the capacity of this arc equals the maximum flow that, in reality, can originate from this node. Similarly, the dummy sink is treated as the node that absorbs all the flow that, in reality, terminates at some of the other nodes. Therefore, a new arc is inserted from each of these other nodes to the dummy sink, where the capacity of this arc equals the maximum flow that, in reality, can terminate at this node. Because of all these changes, all the nodes in the original network now are transshipment nodes, so the expanded network has the required single source (the dummy source) and single sink (the dummy sink) to fit the maximum flow problem.

An Algorithm

Because the maximum flow problem can be formulated as a *linear programming problem* (see Prob. 9.5-2), it can be solved by the simplex method, so any of the linear programming software packages introduced in Chaps. 3 and 4 can be used. However, an even more efficient *augmenting path algorithm* is available for solving this problem. This algorithm is based on two intuitive concepts, a *residual network* and an *augmenting path*.

After some flows have been assigned to the arcs, the **residual network** shows the *remaining* arc capacities (called **residual capacities**) for assigning *additional* flows. For example, consider arc $O \rightarrow B$ in Fig. 9.6, which has an arc capacity of 7. Now suppose that the assigned flows include a flow of 5 through this arc, which leaves a residual capacity of $7 - 5 = 2$ for any additional flow assignment through $O \rightarrow B$. This status is depicted as follows in the residual network.

The number on an arc next to a node gives the residual capacity for flow *from* that node *to* the other node. Therefore, in addition to the residual capacity of 2 for flow from O to B, the 5 on the right indicates a residual capacity of 5 for assigning some flow from B to O (that is, for canceling some previously assigned flow from O to B).

Initially, before any flows have been assigned, the residual network for the Seervada Park problem has the appearance shown in Fig. 9.7. Every arc in the original network (Fig. 9.6) has been changed from a *directed* arc to an *undirected arc*. However, the arc

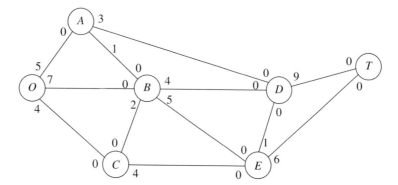

FIGURE 9.7
The initial residual network for the Seervada Park maximum flow problem.

capacity in the original direction remains the same and the arc capacity in the opposite direction is *zero,* so the constraints on flows are unchanged.

Subsequently, whenever some amount of flow is assigned to an arc, that amount is *subtracted* from the residual capacity in the same direction and *added* to the residual capacity in the opposite direction.

An **augmenting path** is a directed path from the source to the sink in the residual network such that *every* arc on this path has *strictly positive* residual capacity. The *minimum* of these residual capacities is called the *residual capacity of the augmenting path* because it represents the amount of flow that can feasibly be added to the entire path. Therefore, each augmenting path provides an opportunity to further augment the flow through the original network.

The augmenting path algorithm repeatedly selects some augmenting path and adds a flow equal to its residual capacity to that path in the original network. This process continues until there are no more augmenting paths, so the flow from the source to the sink cannot be increased further. The key to ensuring that the final solution necessarily is optimal is the fact that augmenting paths can cancel some previously assigned flows in the original network, so an indiscriminate selection of paths for assigning flows cannot prevent the use of a better combination of flow assignments.

To summarize, each *iteration* of the algorithm consists of the following three steps.

The Augmenting Path Algorithm for the Maximum Flow Problem.[1]

1. Identify an augmenting path by finding some directed path from the source to the sink in the residual network such that every arc on this path has strictly positive residual capacity. (If no augmenting path exists, the net flows already assigned constitute an optimal flow pattern.)
2. Identify the residual capacity c^* of this augmenting path by finding the *minimum* of the residual capacities of the arcs on this path. *Increase* the flow in this path by c^*.
3. *Decrease* by c^* the residual capacity of each arc on this augmenting path. *Increase* by c^* the residual capacity of each arc in the opposite direction on this augmenting path. Return to step 1.

---

[1]It is assumed that the arc capacities are either integers or rational numbers.

When step 1 is carried out, there often will be a number of alternative augmenting paths from which to choose. Although the algorithmic strategy for making this selection is important for the efficiency of large-scale implementations, we shall not delve into this relatively specialized topic. (Later in the section, we do describe a systematic procedure for finding some augmenting path.) Therefore, for the following example (and the problems at the end of the chapter), the selection is just made arbitrarily.

Applying This Algorithm to the Seervada Park Maximum Flow Problem

Applying this algorithm to the Seervada Park problem (see Fig. 9.6 for the original network) yields the results summarized next. Starting with the initial residual network given in Fig. 9.7, we give the new residual network after each one or two iterations, where the total amount of flow from O to T achieved thus far is shown in **boldface** (next to nodes O and T).

Iteration 1: In Fig. 9.7, one of several augmenting paths is $O \rightarrow B \rightarrow E \rightarrow T$, which has a residual capacity of min$\{7, 5, 6\} = 5$. By assigning a flow of 5 to this path, the resulting residual network is

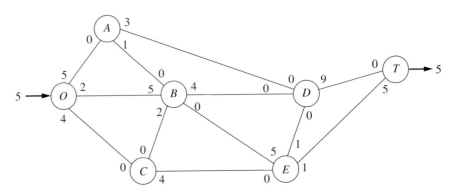

Iteration 2: Assign a flow of 3 to the augmenting path $O \rightarrow A \rightarrow D \rightarrow T$. The resulting residual network is

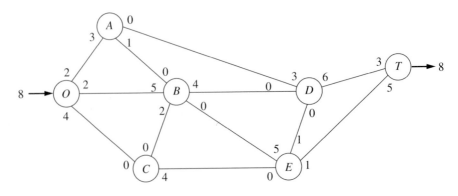

Iteration 3: Assign a flow of 1 to the augmenting path $O \rightarrow A \rightarrow B \rightarrow D \rightarrow T$.

Iteration 4: Assign a flow of 2 to the augmenting path $O \rightarrow B \rightarrow D \rightarrow T$. The resulting residual network is

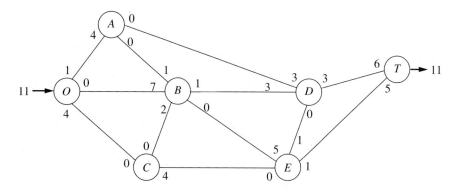

Iteration 5: Assign a flow of 1 to the augmenting path $O \rightarrow C \rightarrow E \rightarrow D \rightarrow T$.

Iteration 6: Assign a flow of 1 to the augmenting path $O \rightarrow C \rightarrow E \rightarrow T$. The resulting residual network is

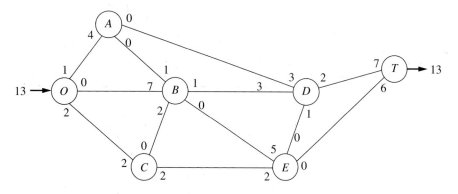

Iteration 7: Assign a flow of 1 to the augmenting path $O \rightarrow C \rightarrow E \rightarrow B \rightarrow D \rightarrow T$. The resulting residual network is

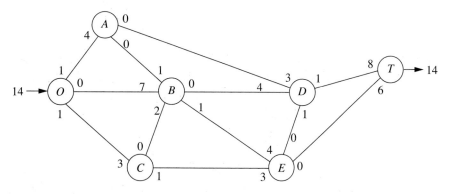

There are no more augmenting paths, so the current flow pattern is optimal.

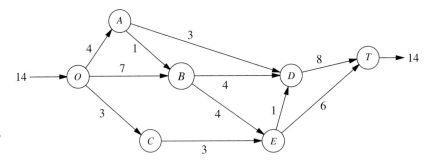

FIGURE 9.8
Optimal solution for the
Seervada Park maximum flow
problem.

The current flow pattern may be identified by either cumulating the flow assignments or comparing the final residual capacities with the original arc capacities. If we use the latter method, there is flow along an arc if the final residual capacity is less than the original capacity. The magnitude of this flow equals the difference in these capacities. Applying this method by comparing the residual network obtained from the last iteration with either Fig. 9.6 or 9.7 yields the optimal flow pattern shown in Fig. 9.8.

This example nicely illustrates the reason for replacing each directed arc $i \rightarrow j$ in the original network by an undirected arc in the residual network and then increasing the residual capacity for $j \rightarrow i$ by c^* when a flow of c^* is assigned to $i \rightarrow j$. Without this refinement, the first six iterations would be unchanged. However, at that point it would appear that no augmenting paths remain (because the real unused arc capacity for $E \rightarrow B$ is zero). Therefore, the refinement permits us to add the flow assignment of 1 for $O \rightarrow C \rightarrow E \rightarrow B \rightarrow D \rightarrow T$ in iteration 7. In effect, this additional flow assignment cancels 1 unit of flow assigned at iteration 1 ($O \rightarrow B \rightarrow E \rightarrow T$) and replaces it by assignments of 1 unit of flow to *both* $O \rightarrow B \rightarrow D \rightarrow T$ and $O \rightarrow C \rightarrow E \rightarrow T$.

Finding an Augmenting Path

The most difficult part of this algorithm when *large* networks are involved is finding an augmenting path. This task may be simplified by the following systematic procedure. Begin by determining all nodes that can be reached from the source along a single arc with strictly positive residual capacity. Then, for each of these nodes that were reached, determine all *new* nodes (those not yet reached) that can be reached from this node along an arc with strictly positive residual capacity. Repeat this successively with the new nodes as they are reached. The result will be the identification of a tree of all the nodes that can be reached from the source along a path with strictly positive residual flow capacity. Hence, this *fanning-out procedure* will always identify an augmenting path if one exists. The procedure is illustrated in Fig. 9.9 for the residual network that results from *iteration 6* in the preceding example.

Although the procedure illustrated in Fig. 9.9 is a relatively straightforward one, it would be helpful to be able to recognize when optimality has been reached without an exhaustive search for a nonexistent path. It is sometimes possible to recognize this event because of an important theorem of network theory known as the *max-flow min-cut theorem*. A **cut** may be defined as any set of directed arcs containing at least one arc from

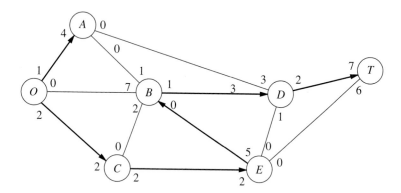

FIGURE 9.9
Procedure for finding an augmenting path for iteration 7 of the Seervada Park maximum flow problem.

every directed path from the source to the sink. There normally are many ways to slice through a network to form a cut to help analyze the network. For any particular cut, the **cut value** is the sum of the arc capacities of the arcs (in the specified direction) of the cut. The **max-flow min-cut theorem** states that, for any network with a single source and sink, the *maximum feasible flow* from the source to the sink *equals* the *minimum cut value* for all cuts of the network. Thus, if we let F denote the amount of flow from the source to the sink for any feasible flow pattern, the value of any cut provides an upper bound to F, and the smallest of the cut values is equal to the maximum value of F. Therefore, if a cut whose value equals the value of F currently attained by the solution procedure can be found in the original network, the current flow pattern must be *optimal*. Eventually, optimality has been attained whenever there exists a cut in the residual network whose value is zero.

To illustrate, consider the network of Fig. 9.7. One interesting cut through this network is shown in Fig. 9.10. Notice that the value of the cut is $3 + 4 + 1 + 6 = 14$, which was found to be the maximum value of F, so this cut is a minimum cut. Notice also that, in the residual network resulting from iteration 7, where $F = 14$, the corresponding cut has a value of zero. If this had been noticed, it would not have been necessary to search for additional augmenting paths.

FIGURE 9.10
A minimum cut for the Seervada Park maximum flow problem.

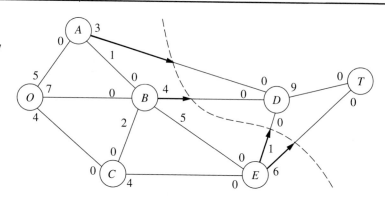

Using Excel to Formulate and Solve Maximum Flow Problems

Most maximum flow problems that arise in practice are considerably larger, and occasionally vastly larger, than the Seervada Park problem. Some problems have thousands of nodes and arcs. The augmenting path algorithm just presented is far more efficient than the general simplex method for solving such large problems. However, for problems of modest size, a reasonable and convenient alternative is to use Excel and its Solver based on the general simplex method.

Figure 9.11 shows a spreadsheet formulation for the Seervada Park maximum flow problem. The format is similar to that for the Seervada Park shortest-path problem displayed in Fig. 9.4. The arcs are listed in columns B and C, and the corresponding arc capacities are given in column F. Since the decision variables are the flows through the re-

FIGURE 9.11
A spreadsheet formulation for the Seervada Park maximum flow problem, where the changing cells (D4:D15) show the optimal solution obtained by the Excel Solver and the target cell (D17) gives the resulting maximum flow through the network.

	A	B	C	D	E	F	G	H	I	J	K
1		Seervada Park Maximum Flow Problem									
2											
3		From	To	Flow		Capacity		Nodes	Net Flow		Supply/Demand
4		O	A	4	≤	5		O	14		
5		O	B	7	≤	7		A	0	=	0
6		O	C	3	≤	4		B	0	=	0
7		A	B	1	≤	1		C	0	=	0
8		A	D	3	≤	3		D	0	=	0
9		B	C	0	≤	2		E	0	=	0
10		B	D	4	≤	4		T	-14		
11		B	E	4	≤	5					
12		C	E	3	≤	4					
13		D	T	8	≤	9					
14		E	D	1	≤	1					
15		E	T	6	≤	6					
16											
17		Maximum Flow =		14							

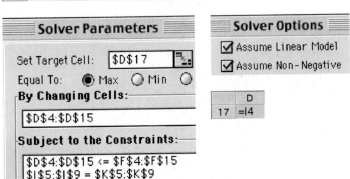

	Solver Parameters
Set Target Cell:	$D$17
Equal To:	● Max ○ Min ○
By Changing Cells:	
	$D$4:$D$15
Subject to the Constraints:	
	$D$4:$D$15 <= $F$4:$F$15
	$I$5:$I$9 = $K$5:$K$9

Solver Options
☑ Assume Linear Model
☑ Assume Non-Negative

	D
17	=I4

	I
4	=D4+D5+D6
5	=-D4+D7+D8
6	=-D5-D7+D9+D10+D11
7	=-D6-D9+D12
8	=-D8-D10+D13-D14
9	=-D11-D12+D14+D15
10	=-D13-D15

spective arcs, these quantities are entered in the changing cells in column D (cells D4:D15). Employing the equations given in the bottom right-hand corner of the figure, these flows then are used to calculate the net flow generated at each of the nodes (see columns H and I). These net flows are required to be 0 for the transshipment nodes (A, B, C, D, and E), as indicated by the second set of constraints (I5:I9 = K5:K9) in the Solver dialogue box. The first set of constraints (D4:D15 ≤ F4:F15) specifies the arc capacity constraints. The total amount of flow from the source (node O) to the sink (node T) equals the flow generated at the source (cell I4), so the target cell (D17) is set equal to I4. After specifying *maximization* of the target cell in the Solver dialogue box and then clicking on the Solve button, the optimal solution shown in cells D4:D15 is obtained.

9.6 THE MINIMUM COST FLOW PROBLEM

The minimum cost flow problem holds a central position among network optimization models, both because it encompasses such a broad class of applications and because it can be solved extremely efficiently. Like the maximum flow problem, it considers flow through a network with limited arc capacities. Like the shortest-path problem, it considers a cost (or distance) for flow through an arc. Like the transportation problem or assignment problem of Chap. 8, it can consider multiple sources (supply nodes) and multiple destinations (demand nodes) for the flow, again with associated costs. In fact, all four of these previously studied problems are special cases of the minimum cost flow problem, as we will demonstrate shortly.

The reason that the minimum cost flow problem can be solved so efficiently is that it can be formulated as a linear programming problem so it can be solved by a streamlined version of the simplex method called the *network simplex method*. We describe this algorithm in the next section.

The minimum cost flow problem is described below.

1. The network is a *directed* and *connected* network.
2. *At least one* of the nodes is a *supply node*.
3. *At least one* of the other nodes is a *demand node*.
4. All the remaining nodes are *transshipment nodes*.
5. Flow through an arc is allowed only in the direction indicated by the arrowhead, where the maximum amount of flow is given by the *capacity* of that arc. (If flow can occur in both directions, this would be represented by a pair of arcs pointing in opposite directions.)
6. The network has enough arcs with sufficient capacity to enable all the flow generated at the *supply nodes* to reach all the *demand nodes*.
7. The cost of the flow through each arc is *proportional* to the amount of that flow, where the cost per unit flow is known.
8. The objective is to minimize the total cost of sending the available supply through the network to satisfy the given demand. (An alternative objective is to maximize the total profit from doing this.)

Some Applications

Probably the most important kind of application of minimum cost flow problems is to the operation of a company's distribution network. As summarized in the first row of Table 9.3, this kind of application always involves determining a plan for shipping goods from

TABLE 9.3 Typical kinds of applications of minimum cost flow problems

Kind of Application	Supply Nodes	Transshipment Nodes	Demand Nodes
Operation of a distribution network	Sources of goods	Intermediate storage facilities	Customers
Solid waste management	Sources of solid waste	Processing facilities	Landfill locations
Operation of a supply network	Vendors	Intermediate warehouses	Processing facilities
Coordinating product mixes at plants	Plants	Production of a specific product	Market for a specific product
Cash flow management	Sources of cash at a specific time	Short-term investment options	Needs for cash at a specific time

its *sources* (factories, etc.) to *intermediate storage facilities* (as needed) and then on to the *customers.*

For example, consider the distribution network for the *International Paper Company* (as described in the March–April 1988 issue of *Interfaces*). This company is the world's largest manufacturer of pulp, paper, and paper products, as well as a major producer of lumber and plywood. It also either owns or has rights over about 20 million acres of woodlands. The supply nodes in its distribution network are these woodlands in their various locations. However, before the company's goods can eventually reach the demand nodes (the customers), the wood must pass through a long sequence of transshipment nodes. A typical path through the distribution network is

Woodlands → woodyards → sawmills
→ paper mills → converting plants
→ warehouses → customers.

Another example of a complicated distribution network is the one for the *Citgo Petroleum Corporation* described in Sec. 3.5. Applying a minimum cost flow problem formulation to improve the operation of this distribution network saved Citgo at least $16.5 million annually.

For some applications of minimum cost flow problems, all the transshipment nodes are *processing facilities* rather than intermediate storage facilities. This is the case for *solid waste management,* as indicated in the second row of Table 9.3. Here, the flow of materials through the network begins at the sources of the solid waste, then goes to the facilities for processing these waste materials into a form suitable for landfill, and then sends them on to the various landfill locations. However, the objective still is to determine the flow plan that minimizes the total cost, where the cost now is for both shipping and processing.

In other applications, the *demand nodes* might be processing facilities. For example, in the third row of Table 9.3, the objective is to find the minimum cost plan for obtaining supplies from various possible vendors, storing these goods in warehouses (as needed), and then shipping the supplies to the company's processing facilities (factories, etc.). Since the total amount that could be supplied by all the vendors is more than the company needs, the network includes a *dummy demand node* that receives (at zero cost) all the unused supply capacity at the vendors.

The July–August 1987 issue of *Interfaces* describes how, even back then, *microcomputers* were being used by *Marshalls, Inc.* (an off-price retail chain) to deal with a minimum cost flow problem this way. In this application, Marshalls was optimizing the flow of freight from vendors to processing centers and then on to retail stores. Some of their networks had over 20,000 arcs.

The next kind of application in Table 9.3 (coordinating product mixes at plants) illustrates that arcs can represent something other than a shipping lane for a physical flow of materials. This application involves a company with several plants (the supply nodes) that can produce the same products but at different costs. Each arc from a supply node represents the production of one of the possible products at that plant, where this arc leads to the transshipment node that corresponds to this product. Thus, this transshipment node has an arc coming in from each plant capable of producing this product, and then the arcs leading out of this node go to the respective customers (the demand nodes) for this product. The objective is to determine how to divide each plant's production capacity among the products so as to minimize the total cost of meeting the demand for the various products.

The last application in Table 9.3 (cash flow management) illustrates that different nodes can represent some event that occurs at different times. In this case, each supply node represents a specific time (or time period) when some cash will become available to the company (through maturing accounts, notes receivable, sales of securities, borrowing, etc.). The supply at each of these nodes is the amount of cash that will become available then. Similarly, each demand node represents a specific time (or time period) when the company will need to draw on its cash reserves. The demand at each such node is the amount of cash that will be needed then. The objective is to maximize the company's income from investing the cash between each time it becomes available and when it will be used. Therefore, each transshipment node represents the choice of a specific short-term investment option (e.g., purchasing a certificate of deposit from a bank) over a specific time interval. The resulting network will have a succession of flows representing a schedule for cash becoming available, being invested, and then being used after the maturing of the investment.

Formulation of the Model

Consider a directed and connected network where the n nodes include at least one supply node and at least one demand node. The decision variables are

$$x_{ij} = \text{flow through arc } i \rightarrow j,$$

and the given information includes

$$c_{ij} = \text{cost per unit flow through arc } i \rightarrow j,$$
$$u_{ij} = \text{arc capacity for arc } i \rightarrow j,$$
$$b_i = \text{net flow generated at node } i.$$

The value of b_i depends on the nature of node i, where

$$b_i > 0 \quad \text{if node } i \text{ is a supply node,}$$
$$b_i < 0 \quad \text{if node } i \text{ is a demand node,}$$
$$b_i = 0 \quad \text{if node } i \text{ is a transshipment node.}$$

The objective is to minimize the total cost of sending the available supply through the network to satisfy the given demand.

By using the convention that summations are taken only over existing arcs, the linear programming formulation of this problem is

$$\text{Minimize} \quad Z = \sum_{i=1}^{n} \sum_{j=1}^{n} c_{ij} x_{ij},$$

subject to

$$\sum_{j=1}^{n} x_{ij} - \sum_{j=1}^{n} x_{ji} = b_i, \quad \text{for each node } i,$$

and

$$0 \le x_{ij} \le u_{ij}, \quad \text{for each arc } i \to j.$$

The first summation in the *node constraints* represents the total flow *out* of node i, whereas the second summation represents the total flow *into* node i, so the difference is the net flow generated at this node.

In some applications, it is necessary to have a lower bound $L_{ij} > 0$ for the flow through each arc $i \to j$. When this occurs, use a translation of variables $x'_{ij} = x_{ij} - L_{ij}$, with $x'_{ij} + L_{ij}$ substituted for x_{ij} throughout the model, to convert the model back to the above format with nonnegativity constraints.

It is not guaranteed that the problem actually will possess *feasible* solutions, depending partially upon which arcs are present in the network and their arc capacities. However, for a reasonably designed network, the main condition needed is the following.

Feasible solutions property: A necessary condition for a minimum cost flow problem to have any feasible solutions is that

$$\sum_{i=1}^{n} b_i = 0.$$

That is, the total flow being generated at the supply nodes equals the total flow being absorbed at the demand nodes.

If the values of b_i provided for some application violate this condition, the usual interpretation is that either the supplies or the demands (whichever are in excess) actually represent upper bounds rather than exact amounts. When this situation arose for the transportation problem in Sec. 8.1, either a dummy destination was added to receive the excess supply or a dummy source was added to send the excess demand. The analogous step now is that either a dummy demand node should be added to absorb the excess supply (with $c_{ij} = 0$ arcs added from every supply node to this node) or a dummy supply node should be added to generate the flow for the excess demand (with $c_{ij} = 0$ arcs added from this node to every demand node).

For many applications, b_i and u_{ij} will have *integer* values, and implementation will require that the flow quantities x_{ij} also be integer. Fortunately, just as for the transportation problem, this outcome is guaranteed without explicitly imposing integer constraints on the variables because of the following property.

Integer solutions property: For minimum cost flow problems where every b_i and u_{ij} have integer values, all the basic variables in *every* basic feasible (BF) solution (including an optimal one) also have integer values.

An Example

An example of a minimum cost flow problem is shown in Fig. 9.12. This network actually is the *distribution network* for the Distribution Unlimited Co. problem presented in Sec. 3.4 (see Fig. 3.13). The quantities given in Fig. 3.13 provide the values of the b_i, c_{ij}, and u_{ij} shown here. The b_i values in Fig. 9.12 are shown in square brackets by the nodes, so the supply nodes ($b_i > 0$) are A and B (the company's two factories), the demand nodes ($b_i < 0$) are D and E (two warehouses), and the one transshipment node ($b_i = 0$) is C (a distribution center). The c_{ij} values are shown next to the arcs. In this example, all but two of the arcs have arc capacities exceeding the total flow generated (90), so $u_{ij} = \infty$ for all practical purposes. The two exceptions are arc $A \rightarrow B$, where $u_{AB} = 10$, and arc $C \rightarrow E$, which has $u_{CE} = 80$.

The linear programming model for this example is

Minimize $\quad Z = 2x_{AB} + 4x_{AC} + 9x_{AD} + 3x_{BC} + x_{CE} + 3x_{DE} + 2x_{ED},$

subject to

$$
\begin{array}{rcrcrcrcrcrcr}
x_{AB} &+& x_{AC} &+& x_{AD} & & & & & & & & &=& 50 \\
-x_{AB} & & & & &+& x_{BC} & & & & & & &=& 40 \\
& & -x_{AC} & & &-& x_{BC} &+& x_{CE} & & & & &=& 0 \\
& & & & -x_{AD} & & & & &+& x_{DE} &-& x_{ED} &=& -30 \\
& & & & & & &-& x_{CE} &-& x_{DE} &+& x_{ED} &=& -60
\end{array}
$$

and

$$x_{AB} \leq 10, \qquad x_{CE} \leq 80, \qquad \text{all } x_{ij} \geq 0.$$

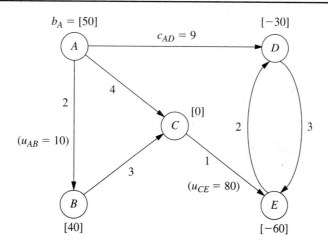

Now note the pattern of coefficients for each variable in the set of five *node constraints* (the equality constraints). Each variable has exactly *two* nonzero coefficients, where one is +1 and the other is −1. This pattern recurs in *every* minimum cost flow problem, and it is this special structure that leads to the integer solutions property.

Another implication of this special structure is that (any) one of the node constraints is *redundant*. The reason is that summing all these constraint equations yields nothing but zeros on both sides (assuming feasible solutions exist, so the b_i values sum to zero), so the negative of any one of these equations equals the sum of the rest of the equations. With just $n - 1$ nonredundant node constraints, these equations provide just $n - 1$ basic variables for a BF solution. In the next section, you will see that the network simplex method treats the $x_{ij} \leq u_{ij}$ constraints as mirror images of the nonnegativity constraints, so the *total* number of basic variables is $n - 1$. This leads to a direct correspondence between the $n - 1$ arcs of a *spanning tree* and the $n - 1$ basic variables—but more about that story later.

Using Excel to Formulate and Solve Minimum Cost Flow Problems

Excel provides a convenient way of formulating and solving small minimum cost flow problems like this one, as well as somewhat larger problems. Figure 9.13 shows how this can be done. The format is almost the same as displayed in Fig. 9.11 for a maximum flow problem. One difference is that the unit costs (c_{ij}) now need to be included (in column

FIGURE 9.13
A spreadsheet formulation for the Distribution Unlimited Co. minimum cost flow problem, where the changing cells (D4:D10) show the optimal solution obtained by the Excel Solver and the target cell (D12) gives the resulting total cost of the flow of shipments through the network.

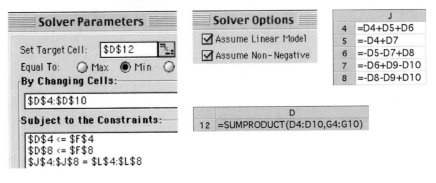

	From	To	Ship		Capacity	Unit Cost		Nodes	Net Flow		Supply/Demand
Distribution Unlimited Co. Minimum Cost Flow Problem											
	A	B	0	≤	10	2		A	50	=	50
	A	C	40			4		B	40	=	40
	A	D	10			9		C	0	=	0
	B	C	40			3		D	−30	=	−30
	C	E	80	≤	80	1		E	−60	=	−60
	D	E	0			3					
	E	D	20			2					
	Total Cost =		490								

Solver Parameters

Set Target Cell: $D$12

Equal To: ○ Max   ● Min   ○

By Changing Cells:

$D$4:$D$10

Subject to the Constraints:

$D$4 <= $F$4
$D$8 <= $F$8
$J$4:$J$8 = $L$4:$L$8

Solver Options

☑ Assume Linear Model
☑ Assume Non-Negative

	J
4	=D4+D5+D6
5	=-D4+D7
6	=-D5-D7+D8
7	=-D6+D9-D10
8	=-D8-D9+D10

	D
12	=SUMPRODUCT(D4:D10,G4:G10)

G). Because b_i values are specified for every node, net flow constraints are needed for all the nodes. However, only two of the arcs happen to need arc capacity constraints. The target cell (D12) now gives the total cost of the flow (shipments) through the network (see its equation at the bottom of the figure), so the objective specified in the Solver dialogue box is to *minimize* this quantity. The changing cells (D4:D10) in this spreadsheet show the optimal solution obtained after clicking on the Solve button.

For much larger minimum cost flow problems, the *network simplex method* described in the next section provides a considerably more efficient solution procedure. It also is an attractive option for solving various special cases of the minimum cost flow problem outlined below. This algorithm is commonly included in mathematical programming software packages. For example, it is one of the options with CPLEX.

We shall soon solve this same example by the network simplex method. However, let us first see how some special cases fit into the network format of the minimum cost flow problem.

Special Cases

The Transportation Problem. To formulate the transportation problem presented in Sec. 8.1 as a minimum cost flow problem, a *supply node* is provided for each *source,* as well as a *demand node* for each *destination,* but no transshipment nodes are included in the network. All the arcs are directed from a supply node to a demand node, where distributing x_{ij} units from source i to destination j corresponds to a flow of x_{ij} through arc $i \rightarrow j$. The cost c_{ij} per unit distributed becomes the cost c_{ij} per unit of flow. Since the transportation problem does not impose upper bound constraints on individual x_{ij}, all the $u_{ij} = \infty$.

Using this formulation for the P & T Co. transportation problem presented in Table 8.2 yields the network shown in Fig. 8.2. The corresponding network for the general transportation problem is shown in Fig. 8.3.

The Assignment Problem. Since the assignment problem discussed in Sec. 8.3 is a special type of transportation problem, its formulation as a minimum cost flow problem fits into the same format. The additional factors are that (1) the number of supply nodes equals the number of demand nodes, (2) $b_i = 1$ for each supply node, and (3) $b_i = -1$ for each demand node.

Figure 8.5 shows this formulation for the general assignment problem.

The Transshipment Problem. This special case actually includes all the general features of the minimum cost flow problem except for not having (finite) arc capacities. Thus, any minimum cost flow problem where each arc can carry any desired amount of flow is also called a transshipment problem.

For example, the Distribution Unlimited Co. problem shown in Fig. 9.13 would be a transshipment problem if the upper bounds on the flow through arcs $A \rightarrow B$ and $C \rightarrow E$ were removed.

Transshipment problems frequently arise as generalizations of transportation problems where units being distributed from each source to each destination can first pass through intermediate points. These intermediate points may include other sources and destinations, as well as additional transfer points that would be represented by transshipment nodes in the network representation of the problem. For example, the Distribution Unlimited Co. problem can be viewed as a generalization of a transportation problem with two sources (the two factories represented by nodes A and B in Fig. 9.13), two destinations (the two warehouses represented by nodes D and E), and one additional intermediate transfer point (the distribution center represented by node C).

(Chapter 23 on our website includes a further discussion of the transshipment problem.)

The Shortest-Path Problem. Now consider the main version of the shortest-path problem presented in Sec. 9.3 (finding the shortest path from one origin to one destination through an *undirected* network). To formulate this problem as a minimum cost flow problem, one supply node with a supply of 1 is provided for the origin, one demand node with a demand of 1 is provided for the destination, and the rest of the nodes are transshipment nodes. Because the network of our shortest-path problem is undirected, whereas the minimum cost flow problem is assumed to have a directed network, we replace each link by a pair of directed arcs in opposite directions (depicted by a single line with arrowheads at both ends). The only exceptions are that there is no need to bother with arcs *into* the supply node or *out of* the demand node. The distance between nodes i and j becomes the unit cost c_{ij} or c_{ji} for flow in either direction between these nodes. As with the preceding special cases, no arc capacities are imposed, so all $u_{ij} = \infty$.

Figure 9.14 depicts this formulation for the Seervada Park shortest-path problem shown in Fig. 9.1, where the numbers next to the lines now represent the unit cost of flow in either direction.

The Maximum Flow Problem. The last special case we shall consider is the maximum flow problem described in Sec. 9.5. In this case a network already is provided with one supply node (the source), one demand node (the sink), and various transshipment nodes, as well as the various arcs and arc capacities. Only three adjustments are needed to fit this problem into the format for the minimum cost flow problem. First, set $c_{ij} = 0$ for all existing arcs to reflect the absence of costs in the maximum flow problem. Second, select a quantity $\overline{F}$, which is a safe upper bound on the maximum feasible flow

FIGURE 9.14

Formulation of the Seervada Park shortest-path problem as a minimum cost flow problem.

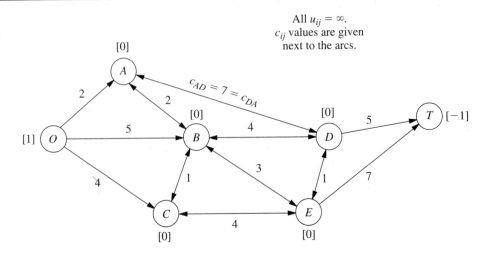

All $u_{ij} = \infty$.
c_{ij} values are given next to the arcs.

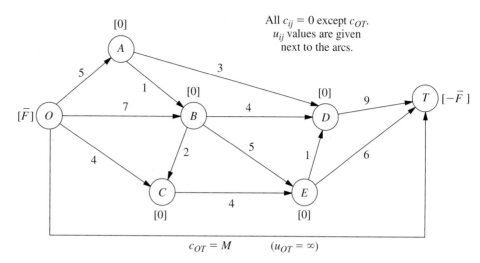

FIGURE 9.15
Formulation of the Seervada Park maximum flow problem as a minimum cost flow problem.

through the network, and then assign a supply and a demand of $\bar{F}$ to the supply node and the demand node, respectively. (Because all *other* nodes are transshipment nodes, they automatically have $b_i = 0$.) Third, add an arc going directly from the supply node to the demand node and assign it an arbitrarily large unit cost of $c_{ij} = M$ as well as an unlimited arc capacity ($u_{ij} = \infty$). Because of this positive unit cost for this arc and the zero unit cost for all the *other* arcs, the minimum cost flow problem will send the maximum feasible flow through the *other* arcs, which achieves the objective of the maximum flow problem.

Applying this formulation to the Seervada Park maximum flow problem shown in Fig. 9.6 yields the network given in Fig. 9.15, where the numbers given next to the original arcs are the arc capacities.

Final Comments. Except for the transshipment problem, each of these special cases has been the focus of a previous section in either this chapter or Chap. 8. When each was first presented, we talked about a special-purpose algorithm for solving it very efficiently. Therefore, it certainly is not necessary to reformulate these special cases to fit the format of the minimum cost flow problem in order to solve them. However, when a computer code is not readily available for the special-purpose algorithm, it is very reasonable to use the network simplex method instead. In fact, recent implementations of the network simplex method have become so powerful that it now provides an excellent alternative to the special-purpose algorithm.

The fact that these problems are special cases of the minimum cost flow problem is of interest for other reasons as well. One reason is that the underlying theory for the minimum cost flow problem and for the network simplex method provides a unifying theory for all these special cases. Another reason is that some of the many applications of the minimum cost flow problem include features of one or more of the special cases, so it is important to know how to reformulate these features into the broader framework of the general problem.

9.7   THE NETWORK SIMPLEX METHOD

The network simplex method is a highly streamlined version of the simplex method for solving minimum cost flow problems. As such, it goes through the same basic steps at each iteration—finding the entering basic variable, determining the leaving basic variable, and solving for the new BF solution—in order to move from the current BF solution to a better adjacent one. However, it executes these steps in ways that exploit the special network structure of the problem without ever needing a simplex tableau.

You may note some similarities between the network simplex method and the transportation simplex method presented in Sec. 8.2. In fact, both are streamlined versions of the simplex method that provide alternative algorithms for solving transportation problems in similar ways. The network simplex method extends these ideas to solving other types of minimum cost flow problems as well.

In this section, we provide a somewhat abbreviated description of the network simplex method that focuses just on the main concepts. We omit certain details needed for a full computer implementation, including how to construct an initial BF solution and how to perform certain calculations (such as for finding the entering basic variable) in the most efficient manner. These details are provided in various more specialized textbooks, such as Selected References 1, 2, 3, 5, and 8.

Incorporating the Upper Bound Technique

The first concept is to incorporate the upper bound technique described in Sec. 7.3 to deal efficiently with the arc capacity constraints $x_{ij} \leq u_{ij}$. Thus, rather than these constraints being treated as *functional* constraints, they are handled just as *nonnegativity* constraints are. Therefore, they are considered only when the leaving basic variable is determined. In particular, as the entering basic variable is increased from zero, the leaving basic variable is the *first* basic variable that reaches either its lower bound (0) or its upper bound (u_{ij}). A nonbasic variable at its upper bound $x_{ij} = u_{ij}$ is replaced by $x_{ij} = u_{ij} - y_{ij}$, so $y_{ij} = 0$ becomes the nonbasic variable. See Sec. 7.3 for further details.

In our current context, y_{ij} has an interesting network interpretation. Whenever y_{ij} becomes a basic variable with a strictly positive value ($\leq u_{ij}$), this value can be thought of as flow from node j to node i (so in the "wrong" direction through arc $i \rightarrow j$) that, in actuality, is *canceling* that amount of the previously assigned flow ($x_{ij} = u_{ij}$) from node i to node j. Thus, when $x_{ij} = u_{ij}$ is replaced by $x_{ij} = u_{ij} - y_{ij}$, we also replace the *real* arc $i \rightarrow j$ by the **reverse arc** $j \rightarrow i$, where this new arc has arc capacity u_{ij} (the maximum amount of the $x_{ij} = u_{ij}$ flow that can be canceled) and unit cost $- c_{ij}$ (since each unit of flow canceled saves c_{ij}). To reflect the flow of $x_{ij} = u_{ij}$ through the deleted arc, we shift this amount of net flow generated from node i to node j by *decreasing* b_i by u_{ij} and *increasing* b_j by u_{ij}. Later, if y_{ij} becomes the leaving basic variable by reaching its upper bound, then $y_{ij} = u_{ij}$ is replaced by $y_{ij} = u_{ij} - x_{ij}$ with $x_{ij} = 0$ as the new nonbasic variable, so the above process would be reversed (replace arc $j \rightarrow i$ by arc $i \rightarrow j$, etc.) to the original configuration.

To illustrate this process, consider the minimum cost flow problem shown in Fig. 9.12. While the network simplex method is generating a sequence of BF solutions, suppose that x_{AB} has become the leaving basic variable for some iteration by reaching its upper bound of 10. Consequently, $x_{AB} = 10$ is replaced by $x_{AB} = 10 - y_{AB}$, so $y_{AB} = 0$

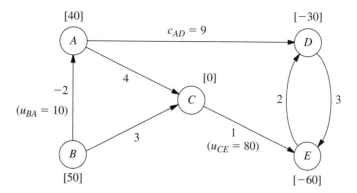

FIGURE 9.16
The adjusted network for the example when the upper-bound technique leads to replacing $x_{AB} = 10$ by $x_{AB} = 10 - y_{AB}$.

becomes the new nonbasic variable. At the same time, we replace arc $A \rightarrow B$ by arc $B \rightarrow A$ (with y_{AB} as its flow quantity), and we assign this new arc a capacity of 10 and a unit cost of -2. To take $x_{AB} = 10$ into account, we also decrease b_A from 50 to 40 and increase b_B from 40 to 50. The resulting adjusted network is shown in Fig. 9.16.

We shall soon illustrate the entire network simplex method with this same example, starting with $y_{AB} = 0$ ($x_{AB} = 10$) as a nonbasic variable and so using Fig. 9.16. A later iteration will show x_{CE} reaching its upper bound of 80 and so being replaced by $x_{CE} = 80 - y_{CE}$, and so on, and then the next iteration has y_{AB} reaching its upper bound of 10. You will see that all these operations are performed directly on the network, so we will not need to use the x_{ij} or y_{ij} labels for arc flows or even to keep track of which arcs are *real* arcs and which are *reverse* arcs (except when we record the final solution). Using the upper bound technique leaves the *node constraints* (flow out minus flow in = b_i) as the only functional constraints. Minimum cost flow problems tend to have far more arcs than nodes, so the resulting number of functional constraints generally is only a small fraction of what it would have been if the arc capacity constraints had been included. The computation time for the simplex method goes up relatively rapidly with the number of functional constraints, but only slowly with the number of variables (or the number of bounding constraints on these variables). Therefore, incorporating the upper bound technique here tends to provide a tremendous saving in computation time.

However, this technique is not needed for *uncapacitated* minimum cost flow problems (including all but the last special case considered in the preceding section), where there are no arc capacity constraints.

Correspondence between BF Solutions and Feasible Spanning Trees

The most important concept underlying the network simplex method is its network representation of *BF solutions*. Recall from Sec. 9.6 that with n nodes, every BF solution has $(n - 1)$ basic variables, where each basic variable x_{ij} represents the flow through arc $i \rightarrow j$. These $(n - 1)$ arcs are referred to as **basic arcs**. (Similarly, the arcs corresponding to the *nonbasic* variables $x_{ij} = 0$ or $y_{ij} = 0$ are called **nonbasic arcs.**)

A key property of basic arcs is that they never form undirected *cycles*. (This property prevents the resulting solution from being a weighted average of another pair of feasible solutions, which would violate one of the general properties of BF solutions.) However, *any* set of $n - 1$ arcs that contains no undirected cycles forms a *spanning tree*. Therefore, any complete set of $n - 1$ basic arcs forms a spanning tree.

Thus, BF solutions can be obtained by "solving" spanning trees, as summarized below. A **spanning tree solution** is obtained as follows:

1. For the arcs *not* in the spanning tree (the nonbasic arcs), set the corresponding variables (x_{ij} or y_{ij}) equal to zero.
2. For the arcs that are in the spanning tree (the basic arcs), solve for the corresponding variables (x_{ij} or y_{ij}) in the system of linear equations provided by the node constraints.

(The network simplex method actually solves for the new BF solution from the current one much more efficiently, without solving this system of equations from scratch.) Note that this solution process does not consider either the nonnegativity constraints or the arc capacity constraints for the basic variables, so the resulting spanning tree solution may or may not be feasible with respect to these constraints—which leads to our next definition.

> A **feasible spanning tree** is a spanning tree whose solution from the node constraints also satisfies all the other constraints ($0 \leq x_{ij} \leq u_{ij}$ or $0 \leq y_{ij} \leq u_{ij}$).

With these definitions, we now can summarize our key conclusion as follows:

> The **fundamental theorem for the network simplex method** says that basic solutions are *spanning tree solutions* (and conversely) and that BF solutions are solutions for *feasible spanning trees* (and conversely).

To begin illustrating the application of this fundamental theorem, consider the network shown in Fig. 9.16 that results from replacing $x_{AB} = 10$ by $x_{AB} = 10 - y_{AB}$ for our example in Fig. 9.12. One spanning tree for this network is the one shown in Fig. 9.3*e*, where the arcs are $A \rightarrow D$, $D \rightarrow E$, $C \rightarrow E$, and $B \rightarrow C$. With these as the *basic arcs*, the process of finding the spanning tree solution is shown below. On the left is the set of node constraints given in Sec. 9.6 after $10 - y_{AB}$ is substituted for x_{AB}, where the *basic* variables are shown in **boldface**. On the right, starting at the top and moving down, is the sequence of steps for setting or calculating the values of the variables.

$$
\begin{array}{lll}
& y_{AB} = 0,\ x_{AC} = 0,\ x_{ED} = 0 & \\
-y_{AB} + x_{AC} + \boldsymbol{x_{AD}} & = \ \ 40 & x_{AD} = 40. \\
y_{AB} \qquad\qquad + \boldsymbol{x_{BC}} & = \ \ 50 & x_{BC} = 50. \\
\quad - x_{AC} \ - \boldsymbol{x_{BC}} + \boldsymbol{x_{CE}} & = \ \ \ 0 & \text{so} \quad x_{CE} = 50. \\
\quad\quad - \boldsymbol{x_{AD}} \qquad + \boldsymbol{x_{DE}} - x_{ED} & = -30 & \text{so} \quad x_{DE} = 10. \\
\quad\quad\quad - \boldsymbol{x_{CE}} - \boldsymbol{x_{DE}} + x_{ED} & = -60 & \text{Redundant.}
\end{array}
$$

Since the values of all these basic variables satisfy the nonnegativity constraints and the one relevant arc capacity constraint ($x_{CE} \leq 80$), the spanning tree is a *feasible spanning tree,* so we have a *BF solution.*

We shall use this solution as the initial BF solution for demonstrating the network simplex method. Figure 9.17 shows its network representation, namely, the feasible spanning tree and its solution. Thus, the numbers given next to the arcs now represent *flows* (values of x_{ij}) rather than the unit costs c_{ij} previously given. (To help you distinguish, we shall always put parentheses around flows but not around costs.)

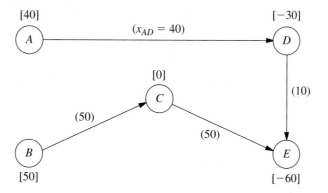

FIGURE 9.17
The initial feasible spanning tree and its solution for the example.

Selecting the Entering Basic Variable

To begin an iteration of the network simplex method, recall that the standard simplex method criterion for selecting the entering basic variable is to choose the nonbasic variable which, when increased from zero, will *improve Z at the fastest rate.* Now let us see how this is done without having a simplex tableau.

To illustrate, consider the nonbasic variable x_{AC} in our initial BF solution, i.e., the nonbasic arc $A \rightarrow C$. Increasing x_{AC} from zero to some value θ means that the arc $A \rightarrow C$ with flow θ must be added to the network shown in Fig. 9.17. Adding a nonbasic arc to a spanning tree *always* creates a unique undirected *cycle,* where the cycle in this case is seen in Fig. 9.18 to be *AC–CE–DE–AD.* Figure 9.18 also shows the effect of adding the flow θ to arc $A \rightarrow C$ on the other flows in the network. Specifically, the flow is thereby *increased* by θ for other arcs that have the *same* direction as $A \rightarrow C$ in the cycle (arc $C \rightarrow E$), whereas the *net* flow is *decreased* by θ for other arcs whose direction is *opposite* to $A \rightarrow C$ in the cycle (arcs $D \rightarrow E$ and $A \rightarrow D$). In the latter case, the new flow is, in effect, canceling a flow of θ in the opposite direction. Arcs not in the cycle (arc $B \rightarrow C$) are unaffected by the new flow. (Check these conclusions by noting the effect of the change in x_{AC} on the values of the other variables in the solution just derived for the initial feasible spanning tree.)

FIGURE 9.18
The effect on flows of adding arc $A \rightarrow C$ with flow θ to the initial feasible spanning tree.

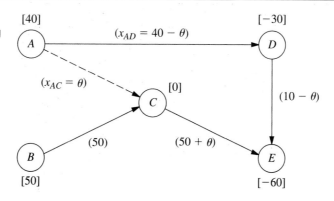

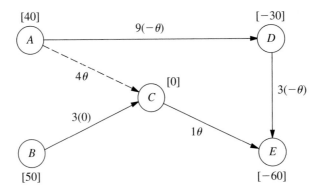

FIGURE 9.19
The incremental effect on costs of adding arc $A \rightarrow C$ with flow θ to the initial feasible spanning tree.

Now what is the incremental effect on Z (total flow cost) from adding the flow θ to arc $A \rightarrow C$? Figure 9.19 shows most of the answer by giving the unit cost times the change in the flow for each arc of Fig. 9.18. Therefore, the overall increment in Z is

$$\Delta Z = c_{AC}\theta + c_{CE}\theta + c_{DE}(-\theta) + c_{AD}(-\theta)$$
$$= 4\theta + \theta - 3\theta - 9\theta$$
$$= -7\theta.$$

Setting $\theta = 1$ then gives the *rate* of change of Z as x_{AC} is increased, namely,

$$\Delta Z = -7, \quad \text{when } \theta = 1.$$

Because the objective is to *minimize* Z, this large rate of decrease in Z by increasing x_{AC} is very desirable, so x_{AC} becomes a prime candidate to be the entering basic variable.

We now need to perform the same analysis for the other nonbasic variables before we make the final selection of the entering basic variable. The only other nonbasic variables are y_{AB} and x_{ED}, corresponding to the two other nonbasic arcs $B \rightarrow A$ and $E \rightarrow D$ in Fig. 9.16.

Figure 9.20 shows the incremental effect on costs of adding arc $B \rightarrow A$ with flow θ to the initial feasible spanning tree given in Fig. 9.17. Adding this arc creates the undi-

FIGURE 9.20
The incremental effect on costs of adding arc $B \rightarrow A$ with flow θ to the initial feasible spanning tree.

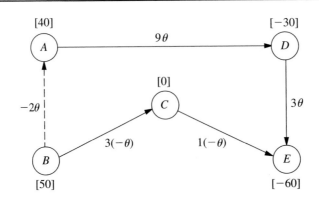

rected cycle BA–AD–DE–CE–BC, so the flow increases by θ for arcs $A \rightarrow D$ and $D \rightarrow E$ but decreases by θ for the two arcs in the opposite direction on this cycle, $C \rightarrow E$ and $B \rightarrow C$. These flow increments, θ and $-\theta$, are the multiplicands for the c_{ij} values in the figure. Therefore,

$$\Delta Z = -2\theta + 9\theta + 3\theta + 1(-\theta) + 3(-\theta) = 6\theta$$
$$= 6, \quad \text{when } \theta = 1.$$

The fact that Z *increases* rather than decreases when y_{AB} (flow through the reverse arc $B \rightarrow A$) is increased from zero rules out this variable as a candidate to be the entering basic variable. (Remember that increasing y_{AB} from zero really means decreasing x_{AB}, flow through the real arc $A \rightarrow B$, from its upper bound of 10.)

A similar result is obtained for the last nonbasic arc $E \rightarrow D$. Adding this arc with flow θ to the initial feasible spanning tree creates the undirected cycle ED–DE shown in Fig. 9.21, so the flow also increases by θ for arc $D \rightarrow E$, but no other arcs are affected. Therefore,

$$\Delta Z = 2\theta + 3\theta = 5\theta$$
$$= 5, \quad \text{when } \theta = 1,$$

so x_{ED} is ruled out as a candidate to be the entering basic variable.

To summarize,

$$\Delta Z = \begin{cases} -7, & \text{if } \Delta x_{AC} = 1 \\ 6, & \text{if } \Delta y_{AB} = 1 \\ 5, & \text{if } \Delta x_{ED} = 1 \end{cases}$$

so the negative value for x_{AC} implies that x_{AC} becomes the entering basic variable for the first iteration. If there had been more than one nonbasic variable with a *negative* value of ΔZ, then the one having the *largest* absolute value would have been chosen. (If there had been no nonbasic variables with a negative value of ΔZ, the current BF solution would have been optimal.)

Rather than identifying undirected cycles, etc., the network simplex method actually obtains these ΔZ values by an algebraic procedure that is considerably more efficient (especially for large networks). The procedure is analogous to that used by the transportation simplex method (see Sec. 8.2) to solve for u_i and v_j in order to obtain the value of

---

FIGURE 9.21
The incremental effect on costs of adding arc $E \rightarrow D$ with flow θ to the initial feasible spanning tree.

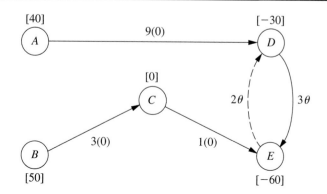

$c_{ij} - u_i - v_j$ for each nonbasic variable x_{ij}. We shall not describe this procedure further, so you should just use the undirected cycles method when you are doing problems at the end of the chapter.

Finding the Leaving Basic Variable and the Next BF Solution

After selection of the entering basic variable, only one more quick step is needed to simultaneously determine the leaving basic variable and solve for the next BF solution. For the first iteration of the example, the key is Fig. 9.18. Since x_{AC} is the entering basic variable, the flow θ through arc $A \rightarrow C$ is to be increased from zero as far as possible until one of the basic variables reaches *either* its lower bound (0) or its upper bound (u_{ij}). For those arcs whose flow *increases* with θ in Fig. 9.18 (arcs $A \rightarrow C$ and $C \rightarrow E$), only the *upper* bounds ($u_{AC} = \infty$ and $u_{CE} = 80$) need to be considered:

$$x_{AC} = \theta \leq \infty.$$
$$x_{CE} = 50 + \theta \leq 80, \qquad \text{so} \qquad \theta \leq 30.$$

For those arcs whose flow *decreases* with θ (arcs $D \rightarrow E$ and $A \rightarrow D$), only the *lower* bound of 0 needs to be considered:

$$x_{DE} = 10 - \theta \geq 0, \qquad \text{so} \qquad \theta \leq 10.$$
$$x_{AD} = 40 - \theta \geq 0, \qquad \text{so} \qquad \theta \leq 40.$$

Arcs whose flow is unchanged by θ (i.e., those not part of the undirected cycle), which is just arc $B \rightarrow C$ in Fig. 9.18, can be ignored since no bound will be reached as θ is increased.

For the five arcs in Fig. 9.18, the conclusion is that x_{DE} must be the leaving basic variable because it reaches a bound for the smallest value of θ (10). Setting $\theta = 10$ in this figure thereby yields the flows through the basic arcs in the next BF solution:

$$x_{AC} = \theta = 10,$$
$$x_{CE} = 50 + \theta = 60,$$
$$x_{AD} = 40 - \theta = 30,$$
$$x_{BC} = 50.$$

The corresponding feasible spanning tree is shown in Fig. 9.22.

If the leaving basic variable had reached its upper bound, then the adjustments discussed for the upper bound technique would have been needed at this point (as you will

FIGURE 9.22
The second feasible spanning tree and its solution for the example.

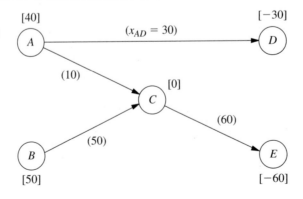

TABLE 9.4 Calculations for selecting the entering basic variable for iteration 2

Nonbasic Arc	Cycle Created	ΔZ When $\theta = 1$	
$B \rightarrow A$	BA–AC–BC	$-2 + 4 - 3 = -1$	
$D \rightarrow E$	DE–CE–AC–AD	$3 - 1 - 4 + 9 = 7$	
$E \rightarrow D$	ED–AD–AC–CE	$2 - 9 + 4 + 1 = -2$	← Minimum

see illustrated during the next two iterations). However, because it was the lower bound of 0 that was reached, nothing more needs to be done.

Completing the Example. For the two remaining iterations needed to reach the optimal solution, the primary focus will be on some features of the upper bound technique they illustrate. The pattern for finding the entering basic variable, the leaving basic variable, and the next BF solution will be very similar to that described for the first iteration, so we only summarize these steps briefly.

Iteration 2: Starting with the feasible spanning tree shown in Fig. 9.22 and referring to Fig. 9.16 for the unit costs c_{ij}, we arrive at the calculations for selecting the entering basic variable in Table 9.4. The second column identifies the unique undirected cycle that is created by adding the nonbasic arc in the first column to this spanning tree, and the third column shows the incremental effect on costs because of the changes in flows on this cycle caused by adding a flow of $\theta = 1$ to the nonbasic arc. Arc $E \rightarrow D$ has the largest (in absolute terms) negative value of ΔZ, so x_{ED} is the entering basic variable.

We now make the flow θ through arc $E \rightarrow D$ as large as possible, while satisfying the following flow bounds:

$$x_{ED} = \theta \leq u_{ED} = \infty, \qquad \text{so} \qquad \theta \leq \infty.$$
$$x_{AD} = 30 - \theta \geq 0, \qquad \text{so} \qquad \theta \leq 30.$$
$$x_{AC} = 10 + \theta \leq u_{AC} = \infty, \qquad \text{so} \qquad \theta \leq \infty.$$
$$x_{CE} = 60 + \theta \leq u_{CE} = 80, \qquad \text{so} \qquad \theta \leq 20. \qquad \leftarrow \text{Minimum}$$

Because x_{CE} imposes the smallest upper bound (20) on θ, x_{CE} becomes the leaving basic variable. Setting $\theta = 20$ in the above expressions for x_{ED}, x_{AD}, and x_{AC} then yields the flow through the basic arcs for the next BF solution (with $x_{BC} = 50$ unaffected by θ), as shown in Fig. 9.23.

FIGURE 9.23
The third feasible spanning tree and its solution for the example.

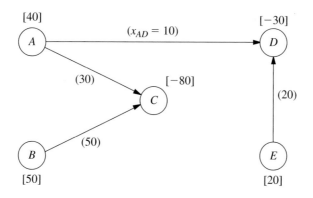

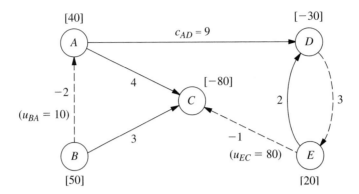

FIGURE 9.24
The adjusted network with
unit costs at the completion
of iteration 2.

What is of special interest here is that the leaving basic variable x_{CE} was obtained by the variable reaching its upper bound (80). Therefore, by using the upper bound technique, x_{CE} is replaced by $80 - y_{CE}$, where $y_{CE} = 0$ is the new nonbasic variable. At the same time, the original arc $C \rightarrow E$ with $c_{CE} = 1$ and $u_{CE} = 80$ is replaced by the reverse arc $E \rightarrow C$ with $c_{EC} = -1$ and $u_{EC} = 80$. The values of b_E and b_C also are adjusted by adding 80 to b_E and subtracting 80 from b_C. The resulting adjusted network is shown in Fig. 9.24, where the nonbasic arcs are shown as dashed lines and the numbers by all the arcs are unit costs.

Iteration 3: If Figs. 9.23 and 9.24 are used to initiate the next iteration, Table 9.5 shows the calculations that lead to selecting y_{AB} (reverse arc $B \rightarrow A$) as the entering basic variable. We then add as much flow θ through arc $B \rightarrow A$ as possible while satisfying the flow bounds below:

$$y_{AB} = \theta \le u_{BA} = 10, \qquad \text{so} \qquad \theta \le 10. \quad \leftarrow \text{Minimum}$$
$$x_{AC} = 30 + \theta \le u_{AC} = \infty, \qquad \text{so} \qquad \theta \le \infty.$$
$$x_{BC} = 50 - \theta \ge 0, \qquad \text{so} \qquad \theta \le 50.$$

The smallest upper bound (10) on θ is imposed by y_{AB}, so this variable becomes the leaving basic variable. Setting $\theta = 10$ in these expressions for x_{AC} and x_{BC} (along with the unchanged values of $x_{AC} = 10$ and $x_{ED} = 20$) then yields the next BF solution, as shown in Fig. 9.25.

As with iteration 2, the leaving basic variable (y_{AB}) was obtained here by the variable reaching its upper bound. In addition, there are two other points of special interest concerning this particular choice. One is that the *entering* basic variable y_{AB} also became

TABLE 9.5 Calculations for selecting the entering basic variable for iteration 3

Nonbasic Arc	Cycle Created	ΔZ When $\theta = 1$	
$B \rightarrow A$	BA–AC–BC	$-2 + 4 - 3 = -1$	$\leftarrow$ Minimum
$D \rightarrow E$	DE–ED	$3 + 2 = 5$	
$E \rightarrow C$	EC–AC–AD–ED	$-1 - 4 + 9 - 2 = 2$	

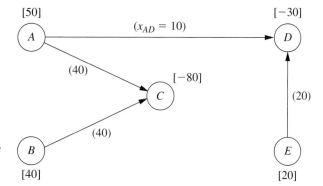

FIGURE 9.25
The fourth (and final) feasible spanning tree and its solution for the example.

the *leaving* basic variable on the same iteration! This event occurs occasionally with the upper bound technique whenever increasing the entering basic variable from zero causes *its* upper bound to be reached first before any of the other basic variables reach a bound.

The other interesting point is that the arc $B \rightarrow A$ that now needs to be replaced by a *reverse* arc $A \rightarrow B$ (because of the leaving basic variable reaching an upper bound) already is a reverse arc! This is no problem, because the reverse arc for a reverse arc is simply the original *real* arc. Therefore, the arc $B \rightarrow A$ (with $c_{BA} = -2$ and $u_{BA} = 10$) in Fig. 9.24 now is replaced by arc $A \rightarrow B$ (with $c_{AB} = 2$ and $u_{AB} = 10$), which is the arc between nodes A and B in the original network shown in Fig. 9.12, and a generated net flow of 10 is shifted from node B ($b_B = 50 \rightarrow 40$) to node A ($b_A = 40 \rightarrow 50$). Simultaneously, the variable $y_{AB} = 10$ is replaced by $10 - x_{AB}$, with $x_{AB} = 0$ as the new nonbasic variable. The resulting adjusted network is shown in Fig. 9.26.

Passing the Optimality Test: At this point, the algorithm would attempt to use Figs. 9.25 and 9.26 to find the next entering basic variable with the usual calculations shown in Table 9.6. However, *none* of the nonbasic arcs gives a *negative* value of ΔZ, so an improvement in Z *cannot* be achieved by introducing flow through any of them. This means that the current BF solution shown in Fig. 9.25 has *passed* the optimality test, so the algorithm stops.

To identify the flows through real arcs rather than reverse arcs for this optimal solution, the current adjusted network (Fig. 9.26) should be compared with the original network (Fig. 9.12). Note that each of the arcs has the same direction in the two networks with the one exception of the arc between nodes C and E. This means that the only re-

TABLE 9.6 Calculations for the optimality test at the end of iteration 3

Nonbasic Arc	Cycle Created	ΔZ When $\theta = 1$
$A \rightarrow B$	AB–BC–AC	$2 + 3 - 4 = 1$
$D \rightarrow E$	DE–EC–AC–AD	$3 - 1 - 4 + 9 = 7$
$E \rightarrow C$	EC–AC–AD–ED	$-1 - 4 + 9 - 2 = 2$

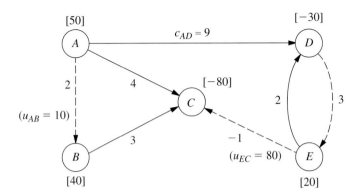

FIGURE 9.26
The adjusted network with
unit costs at the completion
of iteration 3.

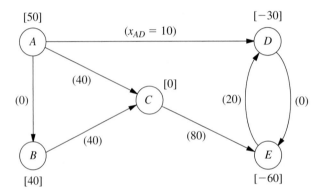

FIGURE 9.27
The optimal flow pattern in
the original network for the
Distribution Unlimited Co.
example.

verse arc in Fig. 9.26 is arc $E \rightarrow C$, where its flow is given by the variable y_{CE}. Therefore, calculate $x_{CE} = u_{CE} - y_{CE} = 80 - y_{CE}$. Arc $E \rightarrow C$ happens to be a nonbasic arc, so $y_{CE} = 0$ and $x_{CE} = 80$ is the flow through the real arc $C \rightarrow E$. All the other flows through real arcs are the flows given in Fig. 9.25. Therefore, the optimal solution is the one shown in Fig. 9.27.

Another complete example of applying the network simplex method is provided by the demonstration in the *Network Analysis Area* of your OR Tutor. Also included in your OR Courseware is an interactive routine for the network simplex method.

9.8   CONCLUSIONS

Networks of some type arise in a wide variety of contexts. Network representations are very useful for portraying the relationships and connections between the components of systems. Frequently, flow of some type must be sent through a network, so a decision needs to be made about the best way to do this. The kinds of network optimization models and algorithms introduced in this chapter provide a powerful tool for making such decisions.

The minimum cost flow problem plays a central role among these network optimization models, both because it is so broadly applicable and because it can be solved extremely efficiently by the network simplex method. Two of its special cases included in this chapter, the shortest-path problem and the maximum flow problem, also are basic network optimization models, as are additional special cases discussed in Chap. 8 (the transportation problem and the assignment problem).

Whereas all these models are concerned with optimizing the *operation* of an *existing* network, the minimum spanning tree problem is a prominent example of a model for optimizing the *design* of a *new* network.

This chapter has only scratched the surface of the current state of the art of network methodology. Because of their combinatorial nature, network problems often are extremely difficult to solve. However, great progress is being made in developing powerful modeling techniques and solution methodologies that are opening up new vistas for important applications. In fact, recent algorithmic advances are enabling us to solve successfully some complex network problems of enormous size.

SELECTED REFERENCES

1. Ahuja, R. K., T. L. Magnanti, and J. B. Orlin: *Network Flows: Theory, Algorithms, and Applications,* Prentice-Hall, Englewood Cliffs, NJ, 1993.
2. Ball, M., T. L. Magnanti, C. Monma, and G. L. Nemhauser: *Network Models,* Elsevier, New York, 1995.
3. Bazaraa, M. S., J. J. Jarvis, and H. D. Sherali: *Linear Programming and Network Flows,* 2d ed., Wiley, New York, 1990.
4. Dantzig, G. B., and M. N. Thapa: *Linear Programming 1: Introduction,* Springer, New York, 1997, chap. 9.
5. Glover, F., D. Klingman, and N. V. Phillips: *Network Models in Optimization and Their Applications in Practice,* Wiley, New York, 1992.
6. Hillier, F. S., M. S. Hillier, and G. J. Lieberman: *Introduction to Management Science: A Modeling and Case Studies Approach with Spreadsheets,* Irwin/McGraw-Hill, Burr Ridge, IL, 2000, chap. 7.
7. Magnanti, T. L., and R. T. Wong: "Network Design and Transportation Planning: Models and Algorithms," *Transportation Science,* **18:** 1–55, 1984.
8. Murty, K. G.: *Network Programming,* Prentice-Hall, Englewood Cliffs, NJ, 1992.

LEARNING AIDS FOR THIS CHAPTER IN YOUR OR COURSEWARE

A Demonstration Example in OR Tutor:

Network Simplex Method

An Interactive Routine:

Network Simplex Method—Interactive

An Excel Add-in:

Premium Solver

"Ch. 9—Network Opt Models" Files for Solving the Examples:

Excel File
LINGO/LINDO File
MPL/CPLEX File

See Appendix 1 for documentation of the software.

PROBLEMS

The symbols to the left of some of the problems (or their parts) have the following meaning:

D: The demonstration example listed above may be helpful.
I: We suggest that you use the interactive routine listed above (the printout records your work).
C: Use the computer with any of the software options available to you (or as instructed by your instructor) to solve the problem.

An asterisk on the problem number indicates that at least a partial answer is given in the back of the book.

9.2-1. Consider the following directed network.

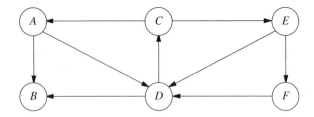

(a) Find a directed path from node A to node F, and then identify three other undirected paths from node A to node F.
(b) Find three directed cycles. Then identify an undirected cycle that includes every node.
(c) Identify a set of arcs that forms a spanning tree.
(d) Use the process illustrated in Fig. 9.3 to grow a tree one arc at a time until a spanning tree has been formed. Then repeat this process to obtain another spanning tree. [Do not duplicate the spanning tree identified in part (c).]

9.3-1. You need to take a trip by car to another town that you have never visited before. Therefore, you are studying a map to determine the shortest route to your destination. Depending on which route you choose, there are five other towns (call them A, B, C, D, E) that you might pass through on the way. The map

shows the mileage along each road that directly connects two towns without any intervening towns. These numbers are summarized in the following table, where a dash indicates that there is no road directly connecting these two towns without going through any other towns.

	Miles between Adjacent Towns					
Town	**A**	**B**	**C**	**D**	**E**	**Destination**
Origin	40	60	50	—	—	—
A		10	—	70	—	—
B			20	55	40	—
C				—	50	—
D					10	60
E						80

(a) Formulate this problem as a shortest-path problem by drawing a network where nodes represent towns, links represent roads, and numbers indicate the length of each link in miles.
(b) Use the algorithm described in Sec. 9.3 to solve this shortest-path problem.
C (c) Formulate and solve a spreadsheet model for this problem.
(d) If each number in the table represented your *cost* (in dollars) for driving your car from one town to the next, would the answer in part (b) or (c) now give your minimum cost route?
(e) If each number in the table represented your *time* (in minutes) for driving your car from one town to the next, would the answer in part (b) or (c) now give your minimum time route?

9.3-2. At a small but growing airport, the local airline company is purchasing a new tractor for a tractor-trailer train to bring luggage to and from the airplanes. A new mechanized luggage system will be installed in 3 years, so the tractor will not be needed after that. However, because it will receive heavy use, so that the running and maintenance costs will increase rapidly as the tractor ages, it may still be more economical to replace the tractor after 1 or 2 years. The following table gives the total net discounted cost associated with purchasing a tractor (purchase price minus trade-in allowance, plus running and maintenance costs) at the end of year i and trading it in at the end of year j (where year 0 is now).

			j	
		1	2	3
	0	$8,000	$18,000	$31,000
i	1		$10,000	$21,000
	2			$12,000

The problem is to determine at what times (if any) the tractor should be replaced to minimize the total cost for the tractors over 3 years. (Continue at the top of the next column.)

(a) Formulate this problem as a shortest-path problem.
(b) Use the algorithm described in Sec. 9.3 to solve this shortest-path problem.
c (c) Formulate and solve a spreadsheet model for this problem.

9.3-3.* Use the algorithm described in Sec. 9.3 to find the *shortest path* through each of the following networks, where the numbers represent actual distances between the corresponding nodes.

(a)

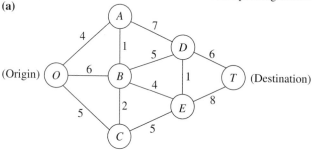

(b)

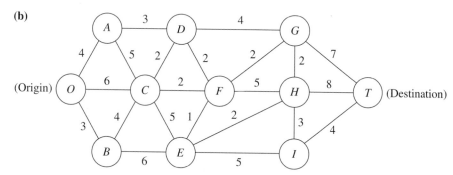

9.3-4. Formulate the shortest-path problem as a linear programming problem.

9.3-5. One of Speedy Airlines' flights is about to take off from Seattle for a nonstop flight to London. There is some flexibility in choosing the precise route to be taken, depending upon weather conditions. The following network depicts the possible routes under consideration, where SE and LN are Seattle and London, respectively, and the other nodes represent various intermediate locations. The winds along each arc greatly affect the flying time (and so the fuel consumption). Based on current meteorological reports, the flying times (in hours) for this particular flight are shown next to the arcs. Because the fuel consumed is so expensive, the management of Speedy Airlines has established a policy of choosing the route that minimizes the total flight time.

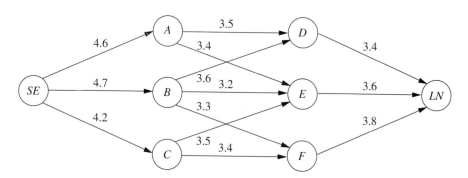

(a) What plays the role of "distances" in interpreting this problem to be a shortest-path problem?

(b) Use the algorithm described in Sec. 9.3 to solve this shortest-path problem.

c **(c)** Formulate and solve a spreadsheet model for this problem.

9.3-6. The Quick Company has learned that a competitor is planning to come out with a new kind of product with a great sales potential. Quick has been working on a similar product that had been scheduled to come to market in 20 months. However, research is nearly complete and Quick's management now wishes to rush the product out to meet the competition.

There are four nonoverlapping phases left to be accomplished, including the remaining research that currently is being conducted at a normal pace. However, each phase can instead be conducted at a priority or crash level to expedite completion, and these are the only levels that will be considered for the last three phases. The times required at these levels are given in the following table. (The times in parentheses at the normal level have been ruled out as too long.)

			Time	
Level	**Remaining Research**	**Development**	**Design of Manufacturing System**	**Initiate Production and Distribution**
Normal	5 months	(4 months)	(7 months)	(4 months)
Priority	4 months	3 months	5 months	2 months
Crash	2 months	2 months	3 months	1 month

Management has allocated $30 million for these four phases. The cost of each phase at the different levels under consideration is as follows:

			Cost	
Level	**Remaining Research**	**Development**	**Design of Manufacturing System**	**Initiate Production and Distribution**
Normal	$3 million	—	—	—
Priority	$6 million	$6 million	$9 million	$3 million
Crash	$9 million	$9 million	$12 million	$6 million

Management wishes to determine at which level to conduct each of the four phases to minimize the total time until the product can be marketed subject to the budget restriction of $30 million.

(a) Formulate this problem as a shortest-path problem.

(b) Use the algorithm described in Sec. 9.3 to solve this shortest-path problem.

9.4-1.* Reconsider the networks shown in Prob. 9.3-3. Use the algorithm described in Sec. 9.4 to find the *minimum spanning tree* for each of these networks.

9.4-2. The Wirehouse Lumber Company will soon begin logging eight groves of trees in the same general area. Therefore, it must develop a system of dirt roads that makes each grove accessible from every other grove. The distance (in miles) between every pair of groves is as follows:

			Distance between Pairs of Groves					
		1	**2**	**3**	**4**	**5**	**6**	**7**	**8**
	1	—	1.3	2.1	0.9	0.7	1.8	2.0	1.5
	2	1.3	—	0.9	1.8	1.2	2.6	2.3	1.1
	3	2.1	0.9	—	2.6	1.7	2.5	1.9	1.0
Grove	4	0.9	1.8	2.6	—	0.7	1.6	1.5	0.9
	5	0.7	1.2	1.7	0.7	—	0.9	1.1	0.8
	6	1.8	2.6	2.5	1.6	0.9	—	0.6	1.0
	7	2.0	2.3	1.9	1.5	1.1	0.6	—	0.5
	8	1.5	1.1	1.0	0.9	0.8	1.0	0.5	—

Management now wishes to determine between which pairs of groves the roads should be constructed to connect all groves with a minimum total length of road.

(a) Describe how this problem fits the network description of the minimum spanning tree problem.

(b) Use the algorithm described in Sec. 9.4 to solve the problem.

9.4-3. The Premiere Bank soon will be hooking up computer terminals at each of its branch offices to the computer at its main office using special phone lines with telecommunications devices. The phone line from a branch office need not be connected directly to the main office. It can be connected indirectly by being connected to another branch office that is connected (directly or indirectly) to the main office. The only requirement is that every branch office be connected by some route to the main office.

The charge for the special phone lines is $100 times the number of miles involved, where the distance (in miles) between every pair of offices is as follows:

			Distance between Pairs of Offices			
	Main	**B.1**	**B.2**	**B.3**	**B.4**	**B.5**
Main office	—	190	70	115	270	160
Branch 1	190	—	100	110	215	50
Branch 2	70	100	—	140	120	220
Branch 3	115	110	140	—	175	80
Branch 4	270	215	120	175	—	310
Branch 5	160	50	220	80	310	—

Management wishes to determine which pairs of offices should be directly connected by special phone lines in order to connect every branch office (directly or indirectly) to the main office at a minimum total cost.

(a) Describe how this problem fits the network description of the minimum spanning tree problem.

(b) Use the algorithm described in Sec. 9.4 to solve the problem.

9.5-1.* For networks (a) and (b), use the augmenting path algorithm described in Sec. 9.5 to find the flow pattern giving the *maximum flow* from the source to the sink, given that the arc capacity from node i to node j is the number nearest node i along the arc between these nodes.

(a)

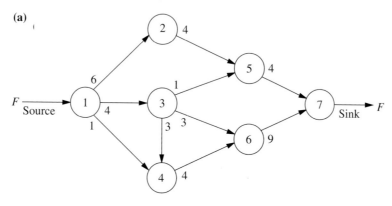

(b)

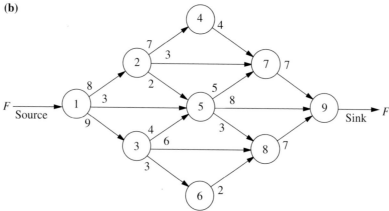

9.5-2. Formulate the maximum flow problem as a linear programming problem.

9.5-3. The diagram to the right depicts a system of aqueducts that originate at three rivers (nodes R1, R2, and R3) and terminate at a major city (node T), where the other nodes are junction points in the system.

Using units of thousands of acre feet, the following tables show the maximum amount of water that can be pumped through each aqueduct per day.

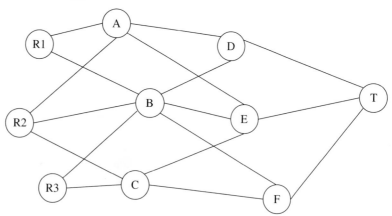

To From	A	B	C
R1	75	65	—
R2	40	50	60
R3	—	80	70

To From	D	E	F
A	60	45	—
B	70	55	45
C	—	70	90

To From	T
D	120
E	190
F	130

The city water manager wants to determine a flow plan that will maximize the flow of water to the city.

(a) Formulate this problem as a maximum flow problem by identifying a source, a sink, and the transshipment nodes, and then drawing the complete network that shows the capacity of each arc.

(b) Use the augmenting path algorithm described in Sec. 9.5 to solve this problem.

C **(c)** Formulate and solve a spreadsheet model for this problem.

9.5-4. The Texago Corporation has four oil fields, four refineries, and four distribution centers. A major strike involving the transportation industries now has sharply curtailed Texago's capacity to ship oil from the oil fields to the refineries and to ship petroleum products from the refineries to the distribution centers. Using units of thousands of barrels of crude oil (and its equivalent in refined products), the following tables show the maximum number of units that can be shipped per day from each oil field to each refinery, and from each refinery to each distribution center.

Oil Field	Refinery			
	New Orleans	Charleston	Seattle	St. Louis
Texas	11	7	2	8
California	5	4	8	7
Alaska	7	3	12	6
Middle East	8	9	4	15

Refinery	Distribution Center			
	Pittsburgh	Atlanta	Kansas City	San Francisco
New Orleans	5	9	6	4
Charleston	8	7	9	5
Seattle	4	6	7	8
St. Louis	12	11	9	7

The Texago management now wants to determine a plan for how many units to ship from each oil field to each refinery and from each refinery to each distribution center that will maximize the total number of units reaching the distribution centers.

(a) Draw a rough map that shows the location of Texago's oil fields, refineries, and distribution centers. Add arrows to show the flow of crude oil and then petroleum products through this distribution network.

(b) Redraw this distribution network by lining up all the nodes representing oil fields in one column, all the nodes representing refineries in a second column, and all the nodes representing distribution centers in a third column. Then add arcs to show the possible flow.

(c) Modify the network in part (b) as needed to formulate this problem as a maximum flow problem with a single source, a single sink, and a capacity for each arc.

(d) Use the augmenting path algorithm described in Sec. 9.5 to solve this maximum flow problem.

C **(e)** Formulate and solve a spreadsheet model for this problem.

9.5-5. One track of the Eura Railroad system runs from the major industrial city of Faireparc to the major port city of Portstown. This track is heavily used by both express passenger and freight trains. The passenger trains are carefully scheduled and have priority over the slow freight trains (this is a European railroad), so that the freight trains must pull over onto a siding whenever a passenger train is scheduled to pass them soon. It is now necessary to increase the freight service, so the problem is to schedule the freight trains so as to maximize the number that can be sent each day without interfering with the fixed schedule for passenger trains.

Consecutive freight trains must maintain a schedule differential of at least 0.1 hour, and this is the time unit used for scheduling them (so that the daily schedule indicates the status of each freight train at times 0.0, 0.1, 0.2, . . . , 23.9). There are S sidings between Faireparc and Portstown, where siding i is long enough to hold n_i freight trains ($i = 1, . . . , S$). It requires t_i time units (rounded up to an integer) for a freight train to travel from siding i to siding $i + 1$ (where t_0 is the time from the Faireparc station to siding 1 and t_s is the time from siding S to the Portstown station). A freight train is allowed to pass or leave siding i ($i = 0, 1, . . . , S$) at time j ($j = 0.0, 0.1, . . . , 23.9$) only if it would not be overtaken by a scheduled passenger train before reaching siding $i + 1$ (let $\delta_{ij} = 1$ if it would not be overtaken, and let $\delta_{ij} = 0$ if it would be). A freight train also is required to stop at a siding if there will not be room for it at all subsequent sidings that it would reach before being overtaken by a passenger train.

Formulate this problem as a maximum flow problem by identifying each node (including the supply node and the demand node) as well as each arc and its arc capacity for the network representation of the problem. (*Hint:* Use a different set of nodes for each of the 240 times.)

9.5-6. Consider the maximum flow problem shown next, where the source is node A, the sink is node F, and the arc capacities are the numbers shown next to these directed arcs.

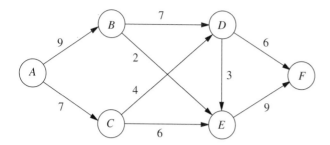

(a) Use the augmenting path algorithm described in Sec. 9.5 to solve this problem.

c **(b)** Formulate and solve a spreadsheet model for this problem.

9.6-1. Reconsider the maximum flow problem shown in Prob. 9.5-6. Formulate this problem as a minimum cost flow problem, including adding the arc $A \rightarrow F$. Use $\overline{F} = 20$.

9.6-2. A company will be producing the same new product at two different factories, and then the product must be shipped to two warehouses. Factory 1 can send an unlimited amount by rail to warehouse 1 only, whereas factory 2 can send an unlimited amount by rail to warehouse 2 only. However, independent truckers can be used to ship up to 50 units from each factory to a distribution center, from which up to 50 units can be shipped to each warehouse. The shipping cost per unit for each alternative is shown in the following table, along with the amounts to be produced at the factories and the amounts needed at the warehouses.

	Unit Shipping Cost			
		Warehouse		
To	**Distribution**			
From	**Center**	**1**	**2**	**Output**
Factory 1	3	7	—	80
Factory 2	4	—	9	70
Distribution center		2	4	
Allocation		60	90	

(a) Formulate the network representation of this problem as a minimum cost flow problem.

(b) Formulate the linear programming model for this problem.

9.6-3. Reconsider Prob. 9.3-1. Now formulate this problem as a minimum cost flow problem by showing the appropriate network representation.

9.6-4. The Makonsel Company is a fully integrated company that both produces goods and sells them at its retail outlets. After production, the goods are stored in the company's two warehouses until needed by the retail outlets. Trucks are used to transport the goods from the two plants to the warehouses, and then from the warehouses to the three retail outlets.

Using units of full truckloads, the following table shows each plant's monthly output, its shipping cost per truckload sent to each warehouse, and the maximum amount that it can ship per month to each warehouse.

To	**Unit Shipping Cost**		**Shipping Capacity**		
From	**Warehouse 1**	**Warehouse 2**	**Warehouse 1**	**Warehouse 2**	**Output**
Plant 1	$425	$560	125	150	200
Plant 2	$510	$600	175	200	300

For each retail outlet (RO), the next table shows its monthly demand, its shipping cost per truckload from each warehouse, and the maximum amount that can be shipped per month from each warehouse.

To	**Unit Shipping Cost**			**Shipping Capacity**		
From	**RO1**	**RO2**	**RO3**	**RO1**	**RO2**	**RO3**
Warehouse 1	$470	$505	$490	100	150	100
Warehouse 2	$390	$410	$440	125	150	75
Demand	150	200	150	150	200	150

Management now wants to determine a distribution plan (number of truckloads shipped per month from each plant to each warehouse and from each warehouse to each retail outlet) that will minimize the total shipping cost.

(a) Draw a network that depicts the company's distribution network. Identify the supply nodes, transshipment nodes, and demand nodes in this network.

(b) Formulate this problem as a minimum cost flow problem by inserting all the necessary data into this network.

c **(c)** Formulate and solve a spreadsheet model for this problem.

c **(d)** Use the computer to solve this problem without using Excel.

9.6-5. The Audiofile Company produces boomboxes. However, management has decided to subcontract out the production of the speakers needed for the boomboxes. Three vendors are available to supply the speakers. Their price for each shipment of 1,000 speakers is shown on the next page.

Vendor	Price
1	$22,500
2	$22,700
3	$22,300

In addition, each vendor would charge a shipping cost. Each shipment would go to one of the company's two warehouses. Each vendor has its own formula for calculating this shipping cost based on the mileage to the warehouse. These formulas and the mileage data are shown below.

Vendor	Charge per Shipment
1	$300 + 40¢/mile
2	$200 + 50¢/mile
3	$500 + 20¢/mile

Vendor	Warehouse 1	Warehouse 2
1	1,600 miles	400 miles
2	500 miles	600 miles
3	2,000 miles	1,000 miles

Whenever one of the company's two factories needs a shipment of speakers to assemble into the boomboxes, the company hires a trucker to bring the shipment in from one of the warehouses. The cost per shipment is given in the next column, along with the number of shipments needed per month at each factory.

	Unit Shipping Cost	
	Factory 1	Factory 2
Warehouse 1	$200	$700
Warehouse 2	$400	$500
Monthly demand	10	6

Each vendor is able to supply as many as 10 shipments per month. However, because of shipping limitations, each vendor is able to send a maximum of only 6 shipments per month to each warehouse. Similarly, each warehouse is able to send a maximum of only 6 shipments per month to each factory.

Management now wants to develop a plan for each month regarding how many shipments (if any) to order from each vendor, how many of those shipments should go to each warehouse, and then how many shipments each warehouse should send to each factory. The objective is to minimize the sum of the purchase costs (including the shipping charge) and the shipping costs from the warehouses to the factories.

(a) Draw a network that depicts the company's supply network. Identify the supply nodes, transshipment nodes, and demand nodes in this network.

(b) Formulate this problem as a minimum cost flow problem by inserting all the necessary data into this network. Also include a dummy demand node that receives (at zero cost) all the unused supply capacity at the vendors.

C (c) Formulate and solve a spreadsheet model for this problem.

C (d) Use the computer to solve this problem without using Excel.

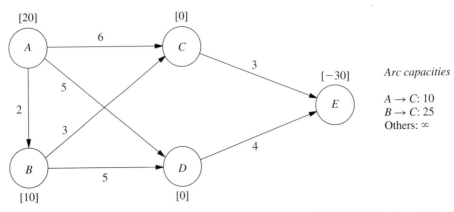

D **9.7-1.** Consider the minimum cost flow problem shown above, where the b_i values (net flows generated) are given by the nodes, the c_{ij} values (costs per unit flow) are given by the arcs, and the u_{ij} values (arc capacities) are given to the right of the network. Do the following work manually.

(a) Obtain an initial BF solution by solving the feasible spanning tree with basic arcs $A \rightarrow B$, $C \rightarrow E$, $D \rightarrow E$, and $C \rightarrow A$ (a reverse arc), where one of the nonbasic arcs ($C \rightarrow B$) also is a reverse arc. Show the resulting network (including b_i, c_{ij}, and u_{ij}) in the same format as the above one (except use dashed lines to draw the nonbasic arcs), and add the flows in parentheses next to the basic arcs.

(b) Use the optimality test to verify that this initial BF solution is optimal and that there are multiple optimal solutions. Apply one iteration of the network simplex method to find the other optimal BF solution, and then use these results to identify the other optimal solutions that are not BF solutions.

(c) Now consider the following BF solution.

Basic Arc	Flow	Nonbasic Arc
$A \to D$	20	$A \to B$
$B \to C$	10	$A \to C$
$C \to E$	10	$B \to D$
$D \to E$	20	

Starting from this BF solution, apply *one* iteration of the network simplex method. Identify the entering basic arc, the leaving basic arc, and the next BF solution, but do not proceed further.

9.7-2. Reconsider the minimum cost flow problem formulated in Prob. 9.6-1.

(a) Obtain an initial BF solution by solving the feasible spanning tree with basic arcs $A \to B$, $A \to C$, $A \to F$, $B \to D$, and $E \to F$, where two of the nonbasic arcs ($E \to C$ and $F \to D$) are *reverse* arcs.

D,I **(b)** Use the network simplex method yourself (without an automatic computer routine) to solve this problem.

9.7-3. Reconsider the minimum cost flow problem formulated in Prob. 9.6-2.

(a) Obtain an initial BF solution by solving the feasible spanning tree that corresponds to using just the two rail lines plus factory 1 shipping to warehouse 2 via the distribution center.

D,I **(b)** Use the network simplex method yourself (without an automatic computer routine) to solve this problem.

D,I **9.7-4.** Reconsider the minimum cost flow problem formulated in Prob. 9.6-3. Starting with the initial BF solution that corresponds to replacing the tractor every year, use the network simplex method yourself (without an automatic computer routine) to solve this problem.

D,I **9.7-5.** For the P & T Co. transportation problem given in Table 8.2, consider its network representation as a minimum cost flow problem presented in Fig. 8.2. Use the northwest corner rule to obtain an initial BF solution from Table 8.2. Then use the network simplex method yourself (without an automatic computer routine) to solve this problem (and verify the optimal solution given in Sec. 8.1).

9.7-6. Consider the Metro Water District transportation problem presented in Table 8.12.

(a) Formulate the network representation of this problem as a minimum cost flow problem. (*Hint:* Arcs where flow is prohibited should be deleted.)

D,I **(b)** Starting with the initial BF solution given in Table 8.19, use the network simplex method yourself (without an automatic computer routine) to solve this problem. Compare the sequence of BF solutions obtained with the sequence obtained by the transportation simplex method in Table 8.23.

D,I **9.7-7.** Consider the transportation problem having the following parameter table:

		Destination			
		1	**2**	**3**	**Supply**
Source	1	6	7	4	40
	2	5	8	6	60
Demand		30	40	30	

Formulate the network representation of this problem as a minimum cost flow problem. Use the northwest corner rule to obtain an initial BF solution. Then use the network simplex method yourself (without an automatic computer routine) to solve the problem.

D,I **9.7-8.** Consider the minimum cost flow problem shown below, where the b_i values are given by the nodes, the c_{ij} values are given by the arcs, and the *finite* u_{ij} values are given in parentheses by the arcs. Obtain an initial BF solution by solving the feasible spanning tree with basic arcs $A \to C$, $B \to A$, $C \to D$, and $C \to E$, where one of the nonbasic arcs ($D \to A$) is a *reverse* arc. Then use the network simplex method yourself (without an automatic computer routine) to solve this problem.

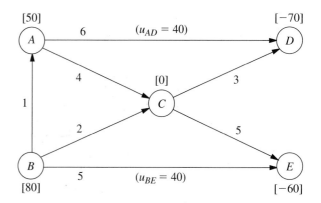

CASE 9.1 AIDING ALLIES

Commander Votachev steps into the cold October night and deeply inhales the smoke from his cigarette, savoring its warmth. He surveys the destruction surrounding him—shattered windows, burning buildings, torn roads—and smiles. His two years of work training revolutionaries east of the Ural Mountains has proved successful; his troops now occupy seven strategically important cities in the Russian Federation: Kazan, Perm, Yekaterinburg, Ufa, Samara, Saratov, and Orenburg. His siege is not yet over, however. He looks to the west. Given the political and economic confusion in the Russian Federation at this time, he knows that his troops will be able to conquer Saint Petersburg and Moscow shortly. Commander Votachev will then be able to rule with the wisdom and control exhibited by his communist predecessors Lenin and Stalin.

Across the Pacific Ocean, a meeting of the top security and foreign policy advisers of the United States is in progress at the White House. The President has recently been briefed about the communist revolution masterminded by Commander Votachev and is determining a plan of action. The President reflects upon a similar October long ago in 1917, and he fears the possibility of a new age of radical Communist rule accompanied by chaos, bloodshed, escalating tensions, and possibly nuclear war. He therefore decides that the United States needs to respond and to respond quickly. Moscow has requested assistance from the United States military, and the President plans to send troops and supplies immediately.

The President turns to General Lankletter and asks him to describe the preparations being taken in the United States to send the necessary troops and supplies to the Russian Federation.

General Lankletter informs the President that along with troops, weapons, ammunition, fuel, and supplies, aircraft, ships, and vehicles are being assembled at two port cities with airfields: Boston and Jacksonville. The aircraft and ships will transfer all troops and cargo across the Atlantic Ocean to the Eurasian continent. The general hands the President a list of the types of aircraft, ships, and vehicles being assembled along with a description of each type. The list is shown below.

Transportation Type	Name	Capacity	Speed
Aircraft	C-141 Starlifter	150 tons	400 miles per hour
Ship	Transport	240 tons	35 miles per hour
Vehicle	Palletized Load System Truck	16,000 kilograms	60 miles per hour

All aircraft, ships, and vehicles are able to carry both troops and cargo. Once an aircraft or ship arrives in Europe, it stays there to support the armed forces.

The President then turns to Tabitha Neal, who has been negotiating with the NATO countries for the last several hours to use their ports and airfields as stops to refuel and resupply before heading to the Russian Federation. She informs the President that the following ports and airfields in the NATO countries will be made available to the United States military.

Ports	Airfields
Napoli	London
Hamburg	Berlin
Rotterdam	Istanbul

The President stands and walks to the map of the world projected on a large screen in the middle of the room. He maps the progress of troops and cargo from the United States to three strategic cities in the Russian Federation that have not yet been seized by Commander Votachev. The three cities are Saint Petersburg, Moscow, and Rostov. He explains that the troops and cargo will be used both to defend the Russian cities and to launch a counterattack against Votachev to recapture the cities he currently occupies. (The map is shown at the end of the case.)

The President also explains that all Starlifters and transports leave Boston or Jacksonville. All transports that have traveled across the Atlantic must dock at one of the NATO ports to unload. Palletized load system trucks brought over in the transports will then carry all troops and materials unloaded from the ships at the NATO ports to the three strategic Russian cities not yet seized by Votachev. All Starlifters that have traveled across the Atlantic must land at one of the NATO airfields for refueling. The planes will then carry all troops and cargo from the NATO airfields to the three Russian cities.

(a) Draw a network showing the different routes troops and supplies may take to reach the Russian Federation from the United States.

(b) Moscow and Washington do not know when Commander Votachev will launch his next attack. Leaders from the two countries have therefore agreed that troops should reach each of the three strategic Russian cities as quickly as possible. The President has determined that the situation is so dire that cost is no object—as many Starlifters, transports, and trucks as are necessary will be used to transfer troops and cargo from the United States to Saint Petersburg, Moscow, and Rostov. Therefore, no limitations exist on the number of troops and amount of cargo that can be transferred between any cities.

The President has been given the following information about the length of the available routes between cities:

From	To	Length of route in kilometers
Boston	Berlin	7,250 km
Boston	Hamburg	8,250 km
Boston	Istanbul	8,300 km
Boston	London	6,200 km
Boston	Rotterdam	6,900 km
Boston	Napoli	7,950 km
Jacksonville	Berlin	9,200 km
Jacksonville	Hamburg	9,800 km
Jacksonville	Istanbul	10,100 km
Jacksonville	London	7,900 km
Jacksonville	Rotterdam	8,900 km
Jacksonville	Napoli	9,400 km

From	To	Length of route in kilometers
Berlin	Saint Petersburg	1,280 km
Hamburg	Saint Petersburg	1,880 km
Istanbul	Saint Petersburg	2,040 km
London	Saint Petersburg	1,980 km
Rotterdam	Saint Petersburg	2,200 km
Napoli	Saint Petersburg	2,970 km
Berlin	Moscow	1,600 km
Hamburg	Moscow	2,120 km
Istanbul	Moscow	1,700 km
London	Moscow	2,300 km
Rotterdam	Moscow	2,450 km
Napoli	Moscow	2,890 km
Berlin	Rostov	1,730 km
Hamburg	Rostov	2,470 km
Istanbul	Rostov	990 km
London	Rostov	2,860 km
Rotterdam	Rostov	2,760 km
Napoli	Rostov	2,800 km

Given the distance and the speed of the transportation used between each pair of cities, how can the President most quickly move troops from the United States to each of the three strategic Russian cities? Highlight the path(s) on the network. How long will it take troops and supplies to reach Saint Petersburg? Moscow? Rostov?

(c) The President encounters only one problem with his first plan: he has to sell the military deployment to Congress. Under the War Powers Act, the President is required to consult with Congress before introducing troops into hostilities or situations where hostilities will occur. If Congress does not give authorization to the President for such use of troops, the President must withdraw troops after 60 days. Congress also has the power to decrease the 60-day time period by passing a concurrent resolution.

The President knows that Congress will not authorize significant spending for another country's war, especially when voters have paid so much attention to decreasing the national debt. He therefore decides that he needs to find a way to get the needed troops and supplies to Saint Petersburg, Moscow, and Rostov at the minimum cost.

Each Russian city has contacted Washington to communicate the number of troops and supplies the city needs at a minimum for reinforcement. After analyzing the requests, General Lankletter has converted the requests from numbers of troops, gallons of gasoline, etc., to tons of cargo for easier planning. The requirements are listed below.

City	Requirements
Saint Petersburg	320,000 tons
Moscow	440,000 tons
Rostov	240,000 tons

Both in Boston and Jacksonville there are 500,000 tons of the necessary cargo available. When the United States decides to send a plane, ship, or truck between two cities, several costs occur—fuel costs, labor costs, maintenance costs, and appropriate port or airfield taxes and tariffs. These costs are listed below.

From	To	Cost
Boston	Berlin	$50,000 per Starlifter
Boston	Hamburg	$30,000 per transport
Boston	Istanbul	$55,000 per Starlifter
Boston	London	$45,000 per Starlifter
Boston	Rotterdam	$30,000 per transport
Boston	Napoli	$32,000 per transport
Jacksonville	Berlin	$57,000 per Starlifter
Jacksonville	Hamburg	$48,000 per transport
Jacksonville	Istanbul	$61,000 per Starlifter
Jacksonville	London	$49,000 per Starlifter
Jacksonville	Rotterdam	$44,000 per transport
Jacksonville	Napoli	$56,000 per transport
Berlin	Saint Petersburg	$24,000 per Starlifter
Hamburg	Saint Petersburg	$ 3,000 per truck
Istanbul	Saint Petersburg	$28,000 per Starlifter
London	Saint Petersburg	$22,000 per Starlifter
Rotterdam	Saint Petersburg	$ 3,000 per truck
Napoli	Saint Petersburg	$ 5,000 per truck
Berlin	Moscow	$22,000 per Starlifter
Hamburg	Moscow	$ 4,000 per truck
Istanbul	Moscow	$25,000 per Starlifter
London	Moscow	$19,000 per Starlifter
Rotterdam	Moscow	$ 5,000 per truck
Napoli	Moscow	$ 5,000 per truck
Berlin	Rostov	$23,000 per Starlifter
Hamburg	Rostov	$ 7,000 per truck
Istanbul	Rostov	$ 2,000 per Starlifter
London	Rostov	$ 4,000 per Starlifter
Rotterdam	Rostov	$ 8,000 per truck
Napoli	Rostov	$ 9,000 per truck

The President faces a number of restrictions when trying to satisfy the requirements. Early winter weather in northern Russia has brought a deep freeze with much snow. Therefore, General Lankletter is opposed to sending truck convoys in the area. He convinces the President to supply Saint Petersburg only through the air. Moreover, the truck routes into Rostov are quite limited, so that from each port at most 2,500 trucks can be sent to Rostov. The Ukrainian government is very sensitive about American airplanes flying through their air space. It restricts the U.S. military to at most 200 flights from Berlin to Rostov and to at most 200 flights from London to Rostov. (The U.S. military does not want to fly around the Ukraine and is thus restricted by the Ukrainian limitations.)

How does the President satisfy each Russian city's military requirements at minimum cost? Highlight the path to be used between the United States and Russian Federation on the network.

(d) Once the President releases the number of planes, ships, and trucks that will travel between the United States and the Russian Federation, Tabitha Neal contacts each of the American cities and NATO countries to indicate the number of planes to expect at the airfields, the number of ships to expect at the docks, and the number of trucks to expect traveling across the roads. Unfortunately, Tabitha learns that several additional restrictions exist which cannot be immediately eliminated. Because of airfield congestion and unalterable flight schedules, only a limited number of planes may be sent between any two cities. These plane limitations are given below.

From	To	Maximum
Boston	Berlin	300 airplanes
Boston	Istanbul	500 airplanes
Boston	London	500 airplanes
Jacksonville	Berlin	500 airplanes
Jacksonville	Istanbul	700 airplanes
Jacksonville	London	600 airplanes
Berlin	Saint Petersburg	500 airplanes
Istanbul	Saint Petersburg	0 airplanes
London	Saint Petersburg	1,000 airplanes
Berlin	Moscow	300 airplanes
Istanbul	Moscow	100 airplanes
London	Moscow	200 airplanes
Berlin	Rostov	0 airplanes
Istanbul	Rostov	900 airplanes
London	Rostov	100 airplanes

In addition, because some countries fear that citizens will become alarmed if too many military trucks travel the public highways, they object to a large number of trucks traveling through their countries. These objections mean that a limited number of trucks are able to travel between certain ports and Russian cities. These limitations are listed below.

From	To	Maximum
Rotterdam	Moscow	600 trucks
Rotterdam	Rostov	750 trucks
Hamburg	Moscow	700 trucks
Hamburg	Rostov	500 trucks
Napoli	Moscow	1,500 trucks
Napoli	Rostov	1,400 trucks

Tabitha learns that all shipping lanes have no capacity limits, owing to the American control of the Atlantic Ocean.

The President realizes that because of all the restrictions he will not be able to satisfy all the reinforcement requirements of the three Russian cities. He decides to disregard the cost issue and instead to maximize the total amount of cargo he can get to the Russian cities. How does the President maximize the total amount of cargo that reaches the Russian Federation? Highlight the path(s) used between the United States and the Russian Federation on the network.

(e) Even before all American troops and supplies had reached Saint Petersburg, Moscow, and Rostov, infighting among Commander Votachev's troops about whether to make the next attack against Saint Petersburg or against Moscow split the revolutionaries. Troops from Moscow easily overcame the vulnerable revolutionaries. Commander Votachev was imprisoned, and the next step became rebuilding the seven cities razed by his armies.

The President's top priority is to help the Russian government to reestablish communications between the seven Russian cities and Moscow at minimum cost. The price of installing communication lines between any two Russian cities varies given the cost of shipping wire to the area, the level of destruction in the area, and the roughness of the terrain. Luckily, a city is able to communicate with all others if it is connected only indirectly to every other city. Saint Petersburg and Rostov are already connected to Moscow, so if any of the seven cities is connected to Saint Petersburg or Rostov, it will also be connected to Moscow. The cost of replacing communication lines between two given cities for which this is possible is shown below.

Between	Cost to Reestablish Communication Lines
Saint Petersburg and Kazan	$210,000
Saint Petersburg and Perm	$185,000
Saint Petersburg and Ufa	$225,000
Moscow and Ufa	$310,000
Moscow and Samara	$195,000
Moscow and Orenburg	$440,000
Moscow and Saratov	$140,000
Rostov and Saratov	$200,000
Rostov and Orenburg	$120,000
Kazan and Perm	$150,000
Kazan and Ufa	$105,000
Kazan and Samara	$ 95,000
Perm and Yekaterinburg	$ 85,000
Perm and Ufa	$125,000
Yekaterinburg and Ufa	$125,000
Ufa and Samara	$100,000
Ufa and Orenburg	$ 75,000
Saratov and Samara	$100,000
Saratov and Orenburg	$ 95,000

Where should communication lines be installed to minimize the total cost of reestablishing communications between Moscow and all seven Russian cities?

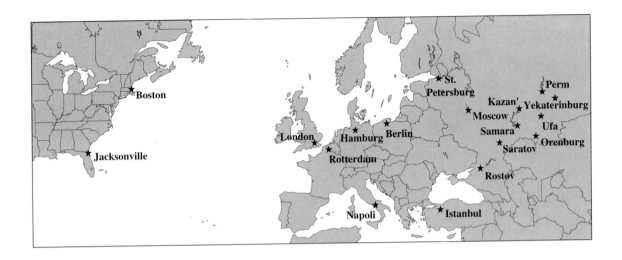

CASE 9.2   MONEY IN MOTION

Jake Nguyen runs a nervous hand through his once finely combed hair. He loosens his once perfectly knotted silk tie. And he rubs his sweaty hands across his once immaculately pressed trousers.

Today has certainly not been a good day.

Over the past few months, Jake had heard whispers circulating from Wall Street—whispers from the lips of investment bankers and stockbrokers famous for their outspokenness. They had whispered about a coming Japanese economic collapse—whispered because they had believed that publicly vocalizing their fears would hasten the collapse.

And today, their very fears have come true. Jake and his colleagues gather round a small television dedicated exclusively to the Bloomberg channel. Jake stares in disbelief as he listens to the horrors taking place in the Japanese market. And the Japanese market is taking the financial markets in all other East Asian countries with it on its tailspin. He goes numb. As manager of Asian foreign investment for Grant Hill Associates, a small West Coast investment boutique specializing in currency trading, Jake bears personal responsibility for any negative impacts of the collapse.

And Grant Hill Associates will experience negative impacts.

Jake had not heeded the whispered warnings of a Japanese collapse. Instead, he had greatly increased the stake Grant Hill Associates held in the Japanese market. Because the Japanese market had performed better than expected over the past year, Jake had increased investments in Japan from 2.5 million to 15 million dollars only 1 month ago. At that time, 1 dollar was worth 80 yen.

No longer. Jake realizes that today's devaluation of the yen means that 1 dollar is worth 125 yen. He will be able to liquidate these investments without any loss in yen, but now the dollar loss when converting back into U.S. currency would be huge. He takes a deep breath, closes his eyes, and mentally prepares himself for serious damage control.

Jake's meditation is interrupted by a booming voice calling for him from a large corner office. Grant Hill, the president of Grant Hill Associates, yells, "Nguyen, get the hell in here!"

Jake jumps and looks reluctantly toward the corner office hiding the furious Grant Hill. He smooths his hair, tightens his tie, and walks briskly into the office.

Grant Hill meets Jake's eyes upon his entrance and continues yelling, "I don't want one word out of you, Nguyen! No excuses; just fix this debacle! Get all of our money out of Japan! My gut tells me this is only the beginning! Get the money into safe U.S. bonds! NOW! And don't forget to get our cash positions out of Indonesia and Malaysia ASAP with it!"

Jake has enough common sense to say nothing. He nods his head, turns on his heel, and practically runs out of the office.

Safely back at his desk, Jake begins formulating a plan to move the investments out of Japan, Indonesia, and Malaysia. His experiences investing in foreign markets have taught him that when playing with millions of dollars, *how* he gets money out of a foreign market is almost as important as *when* he gets money out of the market. The banking partners of Grant Hill Associates charge different transaction fees for converting one currency into another one and wiring large sums of money around the globe.

And now, to make matters worse, the governments in East Asia have imposed very tight limits on the amount of money an individual or a company can exchange from the domestic currency into a particular foreign currency and withdraw it from the country. The goal of this dramatic measure is to reduce the outflow of foreign investments out of those countries to prevent a complete collapse of the economies in the region. Because of Grant Hill Associates' cash holdings of 10.5 billion Indonesian rupiahs and 28 million Malaysian ringgits, along with the holdings in yen, it is not clear how these holdings should be converted back into dollars.

Jake wants to find the most cost-effective method to convert these holdings into dollars. On his company's website he always can find on-the-minute exchange rates for most currencies in the world (Table 1).

The table states that, for example, 1 Japanese yen equals 0.008 U.S. dollars. By making a few phone calls he discovers the transaction costs his company must pay for large currency transactions during these critical times (Table 2).

Jake notes that exchanging one currency for another one results in the same transaction cost as a reverse conversion. Finally, Jake finds out the maximum amounts of domestic currencies his company is allowed to convert into other currencies in Japan, Indonesia, and Malaysia (Table 3).

(a) Formulate Jake's problem as a minimum cost flow problem, and draw the network for his problem. Identify the supply and demand nodes for the network.

(b) Which currency transactions must Jake perform in order to convert the investments from yen, rupiah, and ringgit into U.S. dollars to ensure that Grant Hill Associates has the maximum dollar amount after all transactions have occurred? How much money does Jake have to invest in U.S. bonds?

TABLE 1 Currency exchange rates

From \ To	Yen	Rupiah	Ringgit	U.S. Dollar	Canadian Dollar	Euro	Pound	Peso
Japanese yen	1	50	0.04	0.008	0.01	0.0064	0.0048	0.0768
Indonesian rupiah		1	0.0008	0.00016	0.0002	0.000128	0.000096	0.001536
Malaysian ringgit			1	0.2	0.25	0.16	0.12	1.92
U.S. dollar				1	1.25	0.8	0.6	9.6
Canadian dollar					1	0.64	0.48	7.68
European euro						1	0.75	12
English pound							1	16
Mexican peso								1

(c) The World Trade Organization forbids transaction limits because they promote protectionism. If no transaction limits exist, what method should Jake use to convert the Asian holdings from the respective currencies into dollars?

(d) In response to the World Trade Organization's mandate forbidding transaction limits, the Indonesian government introduces a new tax that leads to an increase of transaction costs for transaction of rupiah by 500 percent to protect their currency. Given these new transaction costs but no transaction limits, what currency transactions should Jake perform in order to convert the Asian holdings from the respective currencies into dollars?

TABLE 2 Transaction cost, percent

From \ To	Yen	Rupiah	Ringgit	U.S. Dollar	Canadian Dollar	Euro	Pound	Peso
Yen	—	0.5	0.5	0.4	0.4	0.4	0.25	0.5
Rupiah		—	0.7	0.5	0.3	0.3	0.75	0.75
Ringgit			—	0.7	0.7	0.4	0.45	0.5
U.S. dollar				—	0.05	0.1	0.1	0.1
Canadian dollar					—	0.2	0.1	0.1
Euro						—	0.05	0.5
Pound							—	0.5
Peso								—

TABLE 3 Transaction limits in equivalent of 1,000 dollars

To From	Yen	Rupiah	Ringgit	U.S. Dollar	Canadian Dollar	Euro	Pound	Peso
Yen	—	5,000	5,000	2,000	2,000	2,000	2,000	4,000
Rupiah	5,000	—	2,000	200	200	1,000	500	200
Ringgit	3,000	4,500	—	1,500	1,500	2,500	1,000	1,000

(e) Jake realizes that his analysis is incomplete because he has not included all aspects that might influence his planned currency exchanges. Describe other factors that Jake should examine before he makes his final decision.

10
Project Management with PERT/CPM

One of the most challenging jobs that any manager can take on is the management of a large-scale project that requires coordinating numerous activities throughout the organization. A myriad of details must be considered in planning how to coordinate all these activities, in developing a realistic schedule, and then in monitoring the progress of the project.

Fortunately, two closely related operations research techniques, **PERT** (program evaluation and review technique) and **CPM** (critical path method), are available to assist the project manager in carrying out these responsibilities. These techniques make heavy use of *networks* (as introduced in the preceding chapter) to help plan and display the coordination of all the activities. They also normally use a *software package* to deal with all the data needed to develop schedule information and then to monitor the progress of the project. *Project management software,* such as MS Project in your OR Courseware, now is widely available for these purposes.

PERT and CPM have been used for a variety of projects, including the following types.

1. Construction of a new plant
2. Research and development of a new product
3. NASA space exploration projects
4. Movie productions
5. Building a ship
6. Government-sponsored projects for developing a new weapons system
7. Relocation of a major facility
8. Maintenance of a nuclear reactor
9. Installation of a management information system
10. Conducting an advertising campaign

PERT and CPM were independently developed in the late 1950s. Ever since, they have been among the most widely used OR techniques.

The original versions of PERT and CPM had some important differences, as we will point out later in the chapter. However, they also had a great deal in common, and the two techniques have gradually merged further over the years. In fact, today's software packages often include all the important options from both original versions.

Consequently, practitioners now commonly use the two names interchangeably, or combine them into the single acronym PERT/CPM, as we often will do. We will make the distinction between them only when we are describing an option that was unique to one of the original versions.

The next section introduces a prototype example that will carry through the chapter to illustrate the various options for analyzing projects provided by PERT/CPM.

10.1 A PROTOTYPE EXAMPLE—THE RELIABLE CONSTRUCTION CO. PROJECT

The RELIABLE CONSTRUCTION COMPANY has just made the winning bid of $5.4 million to construct a new plant for a major manufacturer. The manufacturer needs the plant to go into operation within a year. Therefore, the contract incudes the following provisions:

- A penalty of $300,000 if Reliable has not completed construction by the deadline 47 weeks from now.
- To provide additional incentive for speedy construction, a *bonus* of $150,000 will be paid to Reliable if the plant is completed within 40 weeks.

Reliable is assigning its best construction manager, David Perty, to this project to help ensure that it stays on schedule. He looks forward to the challenge of bringing the project in on schedule, and perhaps even finishing early. However, since he is doubtful that it will be feasible to finish within 40 weeks without incurring excessive costs, he has decided to focus his initial planning on meeting the deadline of 47 weeks.

Mr. Perty will need to arrange for a number of crews to perform the various construction activities at different times. Table 10.1 shows his list of the various activities. The third column provides important additional information for coordinating the scheduling of the crews.

For any given activity, its **immediate predecessors** (as given in the third column of Table 10.1) are those activities that must be completed by no later than the starting time of the

TABLE 10.1 Activity list for the Reliable Construction Co. project

Activity	Activity Description	Immediate Predecessors	Estimated Duration
A	Excavate	—	2 weeks
B	Lay the foundation	A	4 weeks
C	Put up the rough wall	B	10 weeks
D	Put up the roof	C	6 weeks
E	Install the exterior plumbing	C	4 weeks
F	Install the interior plumbing	E	5 weeks
G	Put up the exterior siding	D	7 weeks
H	Do the exterior painting	E, G	9 weeks
I	Do the electrical work	C	7 weeks
J	Put up the wallboard	F, I	8 weeks
K	Install the flooring	J	4 weeks
L	Do the interior painting	J	5 weeks
M	Install the exterior fixtures	H	2 weeks
N	Install the interior fixtures	K, L	6 weeks

given activity. (Similarly, the given activity is called an **immediate successor** of each of its immediate predecessors.)

For example, the top entries in this column indicate that

1. Excavation does not need to wait for any other activities.
2. Excavation must be completed before starting to lay the foundation.
3. The foundation must be completely laid before starting to put up the rough wall, etc.

When a given activity has *more than one* immediate predecessor, all must be finished before the activity can begin.

In order to schedule the activities, Mr. Perty consults with each of the crew supervisors to develop an estimate of how long each activity should take when it is done in the normal way. These estimates are given in the rightmost column of Table 10.1.

Adding up these times gives a grand total of 79 weeks, which is far beyond the deadline for the project. Fortunately, some of the activities can be done in parallel, which substantially reduces the project completion time.

Given all the information in Table 10.1, Mr. Perty now wants to develop answers to the following questions.

1. How can the project be displayed graphically to better visualize the flow of the activities? (Section 10.2)
2. What is the total time required to complete the project if no delays occur? (Section 10.3)
3. When do the individual activities need to start and finish (at the latest) to meet this project completion time? (Section 10.3)
4. When can the individual activities start and finish (at the earliest) if no delays occur? (Section 10.3)
5. Which are the critical bottleneck activities where any delays must be avoided to prevent delaying project completion? (Section 10.3)
6. For the other activities, how much delay can be tolerated without delaying project completion? (Section 10.3)
7. Given the uncertainties in accurately estimating activity durations, what is the probability of completing the project by the deadline? (Section 10.4)
8. If extra money is spent to expedite the project, what is the least expensive way of attempting to meet the target completion time (40 weeks)? (Section 10.5)
9. How should ongoing costs be monitored to try to keep the project within budget? (Section 10.6)

Being a regular user of PERT/CPM, Mr. Perty knows that this technique will provide invaluable help in answering these questions (as you will see in the sections indicated in parentheses above).

10.2   USING A NETWORK TO VISUALLY DISPLAY A PROJECT

The preceding chapter describes how valuable *networks* can be to represent and help analyze many kinds of problems. In much the same way, networks play a key role in dealing with projects. They enable showing the relationships between the activities and placing everything into perspective. They then are used to help analyze the project and answer the kinds of questions raised at the end of the preceding section.

Project Networks

A network used to represent a project is called a **project network.** A project network consists of a number of *nodes* (typically shown as small circles or rectangles) and a number of *arcs* (shown as arrows) that lead from some node to another. (If you have not previously studied Chap. 9, where nodes and arcs are discussed extensively, just think of them as the names given to the small circles or rectangles and to the arrows in the network.)

As Table 10.1 indicates, three types of information are needed to describe a project.

1. Activity information: Break down the project into its individual *activities* (at the desired level of detail).
2. Precedence relationships: Identify the *immediate predecessor(s)* for each activity.
3. Time information: Estimate the *duration* of each activity.

The project network needs to convey all this information. Two alternative types of project networks are available for doing this.

One type is the **activity-on-arc (AOA)** project network, where each activity is represented by an *arc*. A node is used to separate an activity (an outgoing arc) from each of its immediate predecessors (an incoming arc). The sequencing of the arcs thereby shows the precedence relationships between the activities.

The second type is the **activity-on-node (AON)** project network, where each activity is represented by a *node*. The arcs then are used just to show the precedence relationships between the activities. In particular, the node for each activity with immediate predecessors has an arc coming in from each of these predecessors.

The original versions of PERT and CPM used AOA project networks, so this was the conventional type for some years. However, AON project networks have some important advantages over AOA project networks for conveying exactly the same information.

1. AON project networks are considerably easier to construct than AOA project networks.
2. AON project networks are easier to understand than AOA project networks for inexperienced users, including many managers.
3. AON project networks are easier to revise than AOA project networks when there are changes in the project.

For these reasons, AON project networks have become increasingly popular with practitioners. It appears somewhat likely that they will become the conventional type to use. Therefore, we now will focus solely on AON project networks, and will drop the adjective AON.

Figure 10.1 shows the project network for Reliable's project.[1] Referring also to the third column of Table 10.1, note how there is an arc leading to each activity from each of its immediate predecessors. Because activity *A* has no immediate predecessors, there is an arc leading from the start node to this activity. Similarly, since activities *M* and *N* have no immediate successors, arcs lead from these activities to the finish node. Therefore, the project network nicely displays at a glance all the precedence relationships be-

---

[1]Although project networks often are drawn from left to right, we go from top to bottom to better fit on the printed page.

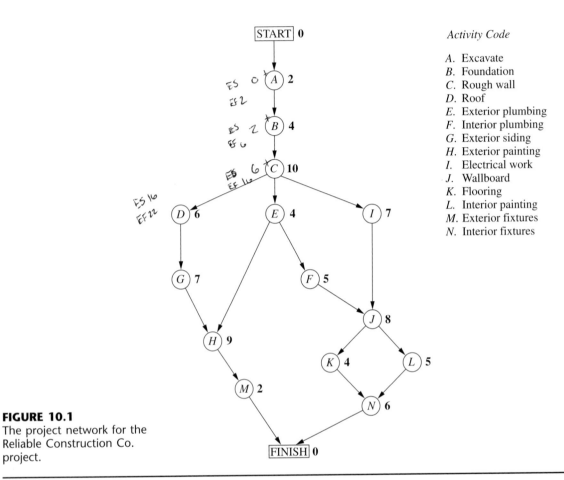

START 0

Activity Code

A. Excavate
B. Foundation
C. Rough wall
D. Roof
E. Exterior plumbing
F. Interior plumbing
G. Exterior siding
H. Exterior painting
I. Electrical work
J. Wallboard
K. Flooring
L. Interior painting
M. Exterior fixtures
N. Interior fixtures

ES 0 (A) 2
ES 2

ES 2 (B) 4
ES 6

ES 6 (C) 10
EF 16

ES 16   (D) 6   (E) 4   (I) 7
EF 22

(G) 7   (F) 5

(H) 9   (J) 8

(K) 4   (L) 5

(M) 2

(N) 6

FINISH 0

FIGURE 10.1
The project network for the
Reliable Construction Co.
project.

tween all the activities (plus the start and finish of the project). Based on the rightmost column of Table 10.1, the number next to the node for each activity then records the estimated duration (in weeks) of that activity.

In real applications, software commonly is used to construct the project network, etc. We next describe how MS Project (included in your OR Courseware) does this for Reliable's project.

Using Microsoft Project

The first step with Microsoft Project (commonly called MS Project) is to enter the information in the activity list (Table 10.1). Choose the View menu and then select its option called Table. From the resulting submenu, choose the option called Entry to bring up the table needed to enter the information. This table is displayed in Fig. 10.2 for Reliable's project. You enter the task (activity) names, the duration of each, a starting date for the first activity, and the immediate predecessors of each, as shown in the figure. The program automatically builds up the rest of the table (including the chart on the right) as you enter this information.

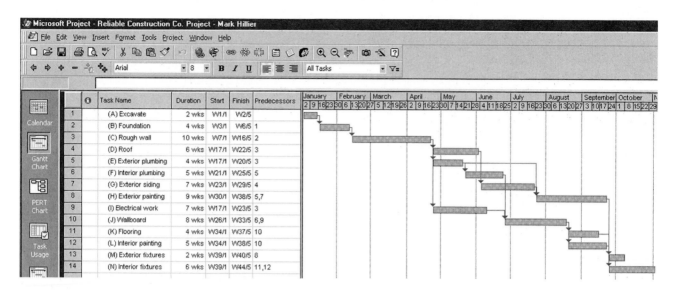

FIGURE 10.2
The spreadsheet used by MS Project for entering the activity list for the Reliable
Construction Co. project. On the right is a Gantt chart showing the project schedule.

The default duration is in units of days, but we have changed the units to weeks here. Such a change can be made by choosing Options under the Tools menu and then changing "Duration is entered in" under the Schedule options.

The default date format is a calendar date (e.g., 1/2/01). This can be changed by choosing Options from the Tools menu and then changing the "Date Format" option under the View options. We have chosen to count time from time 0. Thus, the start time for the first activity is given as W1/1, which is shorthand for Week 1, day 1. A 5-day work week is assumed. For example, since the duration of the first activity is 2 weeks, its finish time is given as W2/5 (Week 2, day 5).

The chart on the right is referred to as a **Gantt chart.** This kind of chart is a popular one in practice for displaying a project schedule, because the bars nicely show the scheduled start and finish times for the respective activities. (This figure assumes that the project begins at the beginning of a calendar year.) The arrows show the precedence relationships between the activities. For example, since both activities 5 and 7 are immediate predecessors of activity 8, there are arrows from both activities 5 and 7 leading to activity 8.

This project entry table can be returned to at any time by choosing Table:Entry in the View menu.

You can choose between various views with the view toolbar down the left side of the screen. The Gantt chart view is the default. The PERT chart view shows the project network. This view initially lines all the activity boxes up in a row, but they can be moved as desired by dragging the boxes with the mouse. Figure 10.3 shows this project network

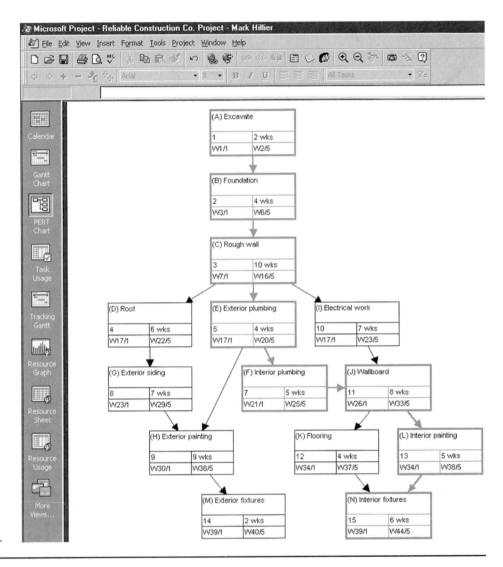

FIGURE 10.3
Reliable's project network as constructed with MS Project.

after placing the activity boxes in the same locations as the corresponding nodes in Fig. 10.1 (except no boxes are included now for the start and finish of the project). Note that each box provides considerable information about the activity. After giving its name, the second row shows the activity number and duration. The last row then gives the scheduled start and finish times.

MS Project also provides additional information of the types described in some of the subsequent sections. However, rather than continuing to display the form of the output in the upcoming sections, we will show it in the MS Project folder for this chapter in your OR Courseware. (Begin with this folder's document entitled "Instructions.")

10.3   SCHEDULING A PROJECT WITH PERT/CPM

At the end of Sec. 10.1, we mentioned that Mr. Perty, the project manager for the Reliable Construction Co. project, wants to use PERT/CPM to develop answers to a series of questions. His first question has been answered in the preceding section. Here are the five questions that will be answered in this section.

Question 2: What is the total time required to complete the project if no delays occur?

Question 3: When do the individual activities need to start and finish (at the latest) to meet this project completion time?

Question 4: When can the individual activities start and finish (at the earliest) if no delays occur?

Question 5: Which are the critical bottleneck activities where any delays must be avoided to prevent delaying project completion?

Question 6: For the other activities, how much delay can be tolerated without delaying project completion?

The project network in Fig. 10.1 enables answering all these questions by providing two crucial pieces of information, namely, the *order* in which certain activities must be performed and the (estimated) *duration* of each activity. We begin by focusing on Questions 2 and 5.

The Critical Path

How long should the project take? We noted earlier that summing the durations of all the activities gives a grand total of 79 weeks. However, this isn't the answer to the question because some of the activities can be performed (roughly) simultaneously.

What is relevant instead is the *length* of each *path* through the network.

A **path** through a project network is one of the routes following the arcs from the START node to the FINISH node. The **length** of a path is the *sum* of the (estimated) *durations* of the activities on the path.

The six paths through the project network in Fig. 10.1 are given in Table 10.2, along with the calculations of the lengths of these paths. The path lengths range from 31 weeks up to 44 weeks for the longest path (the fourth one in the table).

So given these path lengths, what should be the (estimated) **project duration** (the total time required for the project)? Let us reason it out.

Since the activities on any given path must be done one after another with no overlap, the project duration cannot be *shorter* than the path length. However, the project duration can be *longer* because some activity on the path with multiple immediate predecessors might have to wait longer for an immediate predecessor *not* on the path to finish than for the one on the path. For example, consider the second path in Table 10.2 and focus on activity *H*. This activity has two immediate predecessors, one (activity *G*) *not* on the path and one (activity *E*) that is. After activity *C* finishes, only 4 more weeks are required for activity *E* but 13 weeks will be needed for activity *D* and then activity *G* to finish. Therefore, the project duration must be considerably longer than the length of the second path in the table.

TABLE 10.2 The paths and path lengths through Reliable's project network

Path	Length	
START →A→B→C→D→G→H→M→ FINISH	2 + 4 + 10 + 6 + 7 + 9 + 2	= 40 weeks
START →A→B→C→E→H→M→ FINISH	2 + 4 + 10 + 4 + 9 + 2	= 31 weeks
START →A→B→C→E→F→J→K→N→ FINISH	2 + 4 + 10 + 4 + 5 + 8 + 4 + 6	= 43 weeks
START →A→B→C→E→F→J→L→N→ FINISH	2 + 4 + 10 + 4 + 5 + 8 + 5 + 6	= 44 weeks
START →A→B→C→I→J→K→N→ FINISH	2 + 4 + 10 + 7 + 8 + 4 + 6	= 41 weeks
START →A→B→C→I→J→L→N→ FINISH	2 + 4 + 10 + 7 + 8 + 5 + 6	= 42 weeks

However, the project duration will not be longer than one particular path. This is the *longest path* through the project network. The activities on this path can be performed sequentially without interruption. (Otherwise, this would not be the longest path.) Therefore, the time required to reach the FINISH node equals the length of this path. Furthermore, all the shorter paths will reach the FINISH node no later than this.

Here is the key conclusion.

The (estimated) *project duration* equals the *length of the longest path* through the project network. This longest path is called the **critical path.** (If more than one path tie for the longest, they all are critical paths.)

Thus, for the Reliable Construction Co. project, we have

Critical path: START →A→B→C→E→F→J→L→N→ FINISH
(Estimated) project duration = 44 weeks.

We now have answered Mr. Perty's Questions 2 and 5 given at the beginning of the section. If no delays occur, the total time required to complete the project should be about 44 weeks. Furthermore, the activities on this critical path are the critical bottleneck activities where any delays in their completion must be avoided to prevent delaying project completion. This is valuable information for Mr. Perty, since he now knows that he should focus most of his attention on keeping these particular activities on schedule in striving to keep the overall project on schedule. Furthermore, if he decides to reduce the duration of the project (remember that bonus for completion within 40 weeks), these are the main activities where changes should be made to reduce their durations.

For small project networks like Fig. 10.1, finding all the paths and determining the longest path is a convenient way to identify the critical path. However, this is not an efficient procedure for larger projects. PERT/CPM uses a considerably more efficient procedure instead.

Not only is this PERT/CPM procedure very efficient for larger projects, it also provides much more information than is available from finding all the paths. In particular, it answers *all five* of Mr. Perty's questions listed at the beginning of the section rather than just two. These answers provide the key information needed to schedule all the activities and then to evaluate the consequences should any activities slip behind schedule.

The components of this procedure are described in the remainder of this section.

Scheduling Individual Activities

The PERT/CPM scheduling procedure begins by addressing Question 4: When can the individual activities start and finish (at the earliest) if no delays occur? Having no delays means that (1) the *actual* duration of each activity turns out to be the same as its *estimated* duration and (2) each activity begins as soon as all its immediate predecessors are finished. The starting and finishing times of each activity if no delays occur anywhere in the project are called the **earliest start time** and the **earliest finish time** of the activity. These times are represented by the symbols

ES = earliest start time for a particular activity,
EF = earliest finish time for a particular activity,

where

EF = ES + (estimated) duration of the activity.

Rather than assigning calendar dates to these times, it is conventional instead to count the number of time periods (weeks for Reliable's project) from when the project started. Thus,

Starting time for project = 0.

Since activity *A* starts Reliable's project, we have

Activity *A:*   ES = 0,
            EF = 0 + duration (2 weeks)
               = 2,

where the duration (in weeks) of activity *A* is given in Fig. 10.1 as the boldfaced number next to this activity. Activity *B* can start as soon as activity *A* finishes, so

Activity *B:*   ES = EF for activity *A*
               = 2,
            EF = 2 + duration (4 weeks)
               = 6.

This calculation of ES for activity *B* illustrates our first rule for obtaining ES.

If an activity has only a *single* immediate predecessor, then

ES for the activity = EF for the immediate predecessor.

This rule (plus the calculation of each EF) immediately gives ES and EF for activity *C*, then for activities *D, E, I,* and then for activities *G, F* as well. Figure 10.4 shows ES and EF for each of these activities to the right of its node. For example,

Activity *G:*   ES = EF for activity *D*
               = 22,
            EF = 22 + duration (7 weeks)
               = 29,

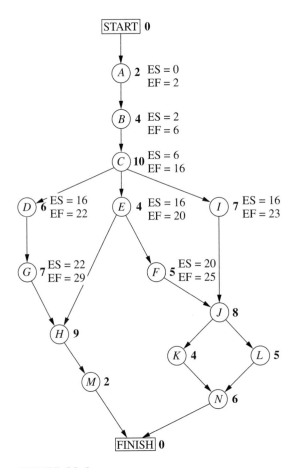

FIGURE 10.4
Earliest start time (ES) and earliest finish time (EF) values for the initial activities in Fig. 10.1 that have only a single immediate predecessor.

which means that this activity (putting up the exterior siding) should start 22 weeks and finish 29 weeks after the start of the project.

Now consider activity *H*, which has *two* immediate predecessors, activities *G* and *E*. Activity *H* must wait to start until *both* activities *G* and *E* are finished, which gives the following calculation.

Immediate predecessors of activity *H*:

> Activity *G* has EF = 29.
> Activity *E* has EF = 20.
> Larger EF = 29.

Therefore,

ES for activity *H* = larger EF above
                    = 29.

This calculation illustrates the general rule for obtaining the earliest start time for any activity.

Earliest Start Time Rule

The earliest start time of an activity is equal to the *largest* of the earliest finish times of its immediate predecessors. In symbols,

ES = largest EF of the immediate predecessors.

When the activity has only a single immediate predecessor, this rule becomes the same as the first rule given earlier. However, it also allows any larger number of immediate predecessors as well. Applying this rule to the rest of the activities in Fig. 10.4 (and calculating each EF from ES) yields the complete set of ES and EF values given in Fig. 10.5.

FIGURE 10.5
Earliest start time (ES) and earliest finish time (EF) values for all the activities (plus the START and FINISH nodes) of the Reliable Construction Co. project.

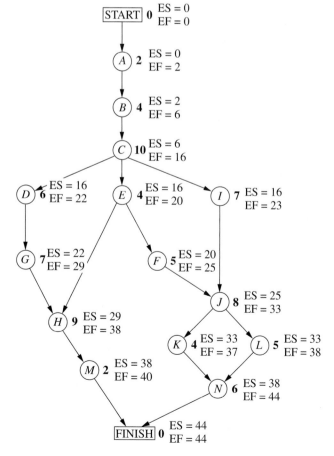

Note that Fig. 10.5 also includes ES and EF values for the START and FINISH nodes. The reason is that these nodes are conventionally treated as *dummy activities* that require no time. For the START node, ES=0=EF automatically. For the FINISH node, the earliest start time rule is used to calculate ES in the usual way, as illustrated below.

Immediate predecessors of the FINISH node:

Activity M has EF = 40.

Activity N has EF = 44.

Larger EF = 44.

Therefore,

ES for the FINISH node = larger EF above

= 44.

EF for the FINISH node = 44 + 0 = 44.

This last calculation indicates that the project should be completed in 44 weeks if everything stays on schedule according to the start and finish times for each activity given in Fig. 10.5. (This answers Question 2.) Mr. Perty now can use this schedule to inform the crew responsible for each activity as to when it should plan to start and finish its work.

This process of starting with the initial activities and working *forward* in time toward the final activities to calculate all the ES and EF values is referred to as making a **forward pass** through the network.

Keep in mind that the schedule obtained from this procedure assumes that the *actual* duration of each activity will turn out to be the same as its *estimated* duration. What happens if some activity takes longer than expected? Would this delay project completion? Perhaps, but not necessarily. It depends on which activity and the length of the delay.

The next part of the procedure focuses on determining how much later than indicated in Fig. 10.5 can an activity start or finish without delaying project completion.

> The **latest start time** for an activity is the latest possible time that it can start without delaying the completion of the project (so the FINISH node still is reached at its earliest finish time), assuming no subsequent delays in the project. The **latest finish time** has the corresponding definition with respect to finishing the activity.

In symbols,

LS = latest start time for a particular activity,

LF = latest finish time for a particular activity,

where

LS = LF − (estimated) duration of the activity.

To find LF, we have the following rule.

Latest Finish Time Rule

The latest finish time of an activity is equal to the *smallest* of the latest start times of its immediate successors. In symbols,

LF = smallest LS of the immediate successors.

Since an activity's immediate successors cannot start until the activity finishes, this rule is saying that the activity must finish in time to enable *all* its immediate successors to begin by their latest start times.

For example, consider activity *M* in Fig. 10.1. Its only immediate successor is the FINISH node. This node must be reached by time 44 in order to complete the project within 44 weeks, so we begin by assigning values to this node as follows.

FINISH node: LF = its EF = 44,
                        LS = 44 − 0 = 44.

Now we can apply the latest finish time rule to activity *M*.

Activity *M:*   LF = LS for the FINISH node
                        = 44,
                  LS = 44 − duration (2 weeks)
                        = 42.

(Since activity *M* is one of the activities that together complete the project, we also could have automatically set its LF equal to the earliest finish time of the FINISH node without applying the latest finish time rule.)

Since activity *M* is the only immediate successor of activity *H,* we now can apply the latest finish time rule to the latter activity.

Activity *H:*   LF = LS for activity *M*
                        = 42,
                  LS = 42 − duration (9 weeks)
                        = 33.

Note that the procedure being illustrated above is to start with the final activities and work *backward* in time toward the initial activities to calculate all the LF and LS values. Thus, in contrast to the *forward pass* used to find earliest start and finish times, we now are making a **backward pass** through the network.

Figure 10.6 shows the results of making a backward pass to its completion. For example, consider activity *C,* which has three immediate successors.

Immediate successors of activity *C:*

Activity *D* has LS = 20.
Activity *E* has LS = 16.
Activity *I* has LS = 18.
Smallest LS = 16.

Therefore,

LF for activity *C* = smallest LS above
                          = 16.

Mr. Perty now knows that the schedule given in Fig. 10.6 represents his "last chance schedule." Even if an activity starts and finishes as late as indicated in the figure, he still will be able to avoid delaying project completion beyond 44 weeks as long as there is no subsequent slippage in the schedule. However, to allow for unexpected delays, he would

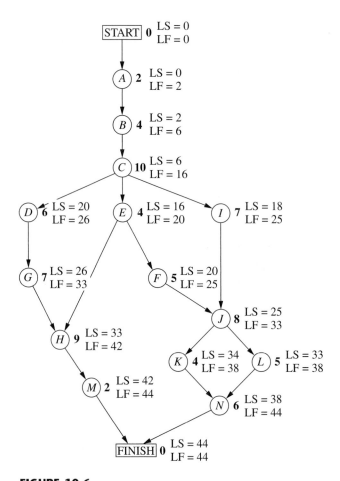

FIGURE 10.6
Latest start time (LS) and latest finish time (LF) for all the activities (plus the START and FINISH nodes) of the Reliable Construction Co. project.

prefer to stick instead to the *earliest time schedule* given in Fig. 10.5 whenever possible in order to provide some slack in parts of the schedule.

If the start and finish times in Fig. 10.6 for a particular activity are later than the corresponding earliest times in Fig. 10.5, then this activity has some slack in the schedule. The last part of the PERT/CPM procedure for scheduling a project is to identify this slack, and then to use this information to find the *critical path*. (This will answer both Questions 5 and 6.)

Identifying Slack in the Schedule

To identify slack, it is convenient to combine the latest times in Fig. 10.6 and the earliest times in Fig. 10.5 into a single figure. Using activity *M* as an example, this is done by displaying the information for each activity as follows.

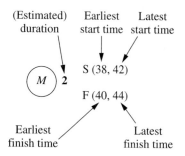

(Note that the S or F in front of each parentheses will remind you of whether these are Start times or Finish times.) Figure 10.7 displays this information for the entire project.

FIGURE 10.7
The complete project network showing ES and LS (in parentheses above the node) and EF and LF (in parentheses below the node) for each activity of the Reliable Construction Co. project. The darker arrows show the critical path through the project network.

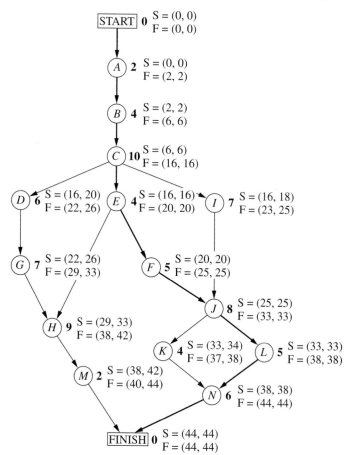

This figure makes it easy to see how much slack each activity has.

The **slack** for an activity is the difference between its latest finish time and its earliest finish time. In symbols,

$$\text{Slack} = \text{LF} - \text{EF}.$$

(Since LF − EF = LS − ES, either difference actually can be used to calculate slack.)

For example,

$$\text{Slack for activity } M = 44 - 40 = 4.$$

This indicates that activity M can be delayed up to 4 weeks beyond the earliest time schedule without delaying the completion of the project at 44 weeks. This makes sense, since the project is finished as soon as both activities M and N are completed and the earliest finish time for activity N (44) is 4 weeks later than for activity M (40). As long as activity N stays on schedule, the project still will finish at 44 weeks if any delays in starting activity M (perhaps due to preceding activities taking longer than expected) and in performing activity M do not cumulate more than 4 weeks.

Table 10.3 shows the slack for each of the activities. Note that some of the activities have *zero slack,* indicating that any delays in these activities will delay project completion. This is how PERT/CPM identifies the critical path(s).

> Each activity with *zero slack* is on a **critical path** through the project network such that any delay along this path will delay project completion.

Thus, the critical path is

$$\text{START} \rightarrow A \rightarrow B \rightarrow C \rightarrow E \rightarrow F \rightarrow J \rightarrow L \rightarrow N \rightarrow \text{FINISH},$$

TABLE 10.3 Slack for Reliable's activities

Activity	Slack (LF − EF)	On Critical Path?
A	0	Yes
B	0	Yes
C	0	Yes
D	4	No
E	0	Yes
F	0	Yes
G	4	No
H	4	No
I	2	No
J	0	Yes
K	1	No
L	0	Yes
M	4	No
N	0	Yes

just as we found by a different method at the beginning of the section. This path is high-lighted in Fig. 10.7 by the darker arrows. It is the activities on this path that Mr. Perty must monitor with special care to keep the project on schedule.

Review

Now let us review Mr. Perty's questions at the beginning of the section and see how all of them have been answered by the PERT/CPM scheduling procedure.

Question 2: What is the total time required to complete the project if no delays occur? This is the earliest finish time at the FINISH node (EF = 44 weeks), as given at the bottom of Figs. 10.5 and 10.7.

Question 3: When do the individual activities need to start and finish (at the latest) to meet this project completion time? These times are the latest start times (LS) and latest finish times (LF) given in Figs. 10.6 and 10.7. These times provide a "last chance schedule" to complete the project in 44 weeks if no further delays occur.

Question 4: When can the individual activities start and finish (at the earliest) if no delays occur? These times are the earliest start times (ES) and earliest finish times (EF) given in Figs. 10.5 and 10.7. These times usually are used to establish the initial schedule for the project. (Subsequent delays may force later adjustments in the schedule.)

Question 5: Which are the critical bottleneck activities where any delays must be avoided to prevent delaying project completion? These are the activities on the critical path shown by the darker arrows in Fig. 10.7. Mr. Perty needs to focus most of his attention on keeping these particular activities on schedule in striving to keep the overall project on schedule.

Question 6: For the other activities, how much delay can be tolerated without delaying project completion? These tolerable delays are the positive slacks given in the middle column of Table 10.3.

10.4 DEALING WITH UNCERTAIN ACTIVITY DURATIONS

Now we come to the next of Mr. Perty's questions posed at the end of Sec.10.1.

Question 7: Given the uncertainties in accurately estimating activity durations, what is the probability of completing the project by the deadline (47 weeks)?

Recall that Reliable will incur a large penalty ($300,000) if this deadline is missed. Therefore, Mr. Perty needs to know the probability of meeting the deadline. If this probability is not very high, he will need to consider taking costly measures (using overtime, etc.) to shorten the duration of some of the activities.

It is somewhat reassuring that the PERT/CPM scheduling procedure in the preceding section obtained an estimate of 44 weeks for the project duration. However, Mr. Perty understands very well that this estimate is based on the assumption that the *actual* duration of each activity will turn out to be the same as its *estimated* duration for at least the activities on the critical path. Since the company does not have much prior experience with this kind of project, there is considerable uncertainty about how much time actually will be needed for each activity. In reality, the duration of each activity is a *random variable* having some probability distribution.

The original version of PERT took this uncertainty into account by using three different types of estimates of the duration of an activity to obtain basic information about its probability distribution, as described below.

The PERT Three-Estimate Approach

The three estimates to be obtained for each activity are

Most likely estimate (m) = estimate of the most likely value of the duration,

Optimistic estimate (o) = estimate of the duration under the most favorable conditions,

Pessimistic estimate (p) = estimate of the duration under the most unfavorable conditions.

The intended location of these three estimates with respect to the probability distribution is shown in Fig. 10.8.

Thus, the optimistic and pessimistic estimates are meant to lie at the extremes of what is possible, whereas the most likely estimate provides the highest point of the probability distribution. PERT also assumes that the *form* of the probability distribution is a *beta distribution* (which has a shape like that in the figure) in order to calculate the *mean* (μ) and *variance* (σ^2) of the probability distribution. For most probability distributions such as the beta distribution, essentially the entire distribution lies inside the interval between ($\mu - 3\sigma$) and ($\mu + 3\sigma$). (For example, for a normal distribution, 99.73 percent of the distribution lies inside this interval.) Thus, the spread between the smallest and largest elapsed times in Fig. 10.8 is roughly 6σ. Therefore, an approximate formula for σ^2 is

$$\sigma^2 = \left(\frac{p - o}{6}\right)^2.$$

FIGURE 10.8
Model of the probability distribution of the duration of an activity for the PERT three-estimate approach: m = most likely estimate, o = optimistic estimate, and p = pessimistic estimate.

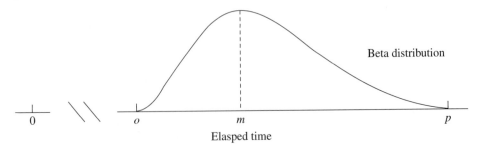

Similarly, an approximate formula for μ is

$$\mu = \frac{o + 4m + p}{6}.$$

Intuitively, this formula is placing most of the weight on the *most likely estimate* and then small equal weights on the other two estimates.

MS Project provides the option of calculating μ for each activity with this formula. Choosing Table:PA_PERT Entry under the View menu enables entering the three types of estimates for the respective activities (where the most likely estimate is labeled as the expected duration). Choosing Toolbars:PERT Analysis under the View menu then enables a toolbar that allows doing various types of analysis with these estimates. Using the "Calculate PERT" option on this toolbar recalculates "Duration" with the above formula to obtain μ. Another option is to show the Gantt charts based on each of the three kinds of estimates.

Mr. Perty now has contacted the supervisor of each crew that will be responsible for one of the activities to request that these three estimates be made of the duration of the activity. The responses are shown in the first four columns of Table 10.4.

The last two columns show the approximate mean and variance of the duration of each activity, as calculated from the above formulas. In this example, all the means happen to be the same as the estimated duration obtained in Table 10.1 of Sec. 10.1. Therefore, if all the activity durations were to equal their means, the duration of the project still would be 44 weeks, so 3 weeks before the deadline. (See Fig. 10.7 for the critical path requiring 44 weeks.)

However, this piece of information is not very reassuring to Mr. Perty. He knows that the durations fluctuate around their means. Consequently, it is inevitable that the duration of some activities will be larger than the mean, perhaps even nearly as large as the pessimistic estimate, which could greatly delay the project.

To check the *worst case scenario,* Mr. Perty reexamines the project network with the duration of each activity set equal to the *pessimistic estimate* (as given in the fourth column of Table 10.4). Table 10.5 shows the six paths through this network (as given previously in Table 10.2) and the length of each path using the pessimistic estimates. The fourth path, which was the critical path in Fig. 10.5, now has increased its length from 44 weeks to 69 weeks. However, the length of the first path, which originally was 40 weeks (as given in Table 10.2), now has increased all the way up to 70 weeks. Since this is the longest path, it is the critical path with pessimistic estimates, which would give a project duration of 70 weeks.

Given this dire (albeit unlikely) worst case scenario, Mr. Perty realizes that it is far from certain that the deadline of 47 weeks will be met. But what is the probability of doing so?

PERT/CPM makes three *simplifying approximations* to help calculate this probability.

Three Simplifying Approximations

To calculate the probability that *project duration* will be no more than 47 weeks, it is necessary to obtain the following information about the probability distribution of project duration.

TABLE 10.4 Expected value and variance of the duration of each activity for Reliable's project

Activity	Optimistic Estimate o	Most Likely Estimate m	Pessimistic Estimate p	Mean $\mu = \dfrac{o + 4m + p}{6}$	Variance $\sigma^2 = \left(\dfrac{p - o}{6}\right)^2$
A	1	2	3	2	$\dfrac{1}{9}$
B	2	$3\frac{1}{2}$	8	4	1
C	6	9	18	10	4
D	4	$5\frac{1}{2}$	10	6	1
E	1	$4\frac{1}{2}$	5	4	$\dfrac{4}{9}$
F	4	4	10	5	1
G	5	$6\frac{1}{2}$	11	7	1
H	5	8	17	9	4
I	3	$7\frac{1}{2}$	9	7	1
J	3	9	9	8	1
K	4	4	4	4	0
L	1	$5\frac{1}{2}$	7	5	1
M	1	2	3	2	$\dfrac{1}{9}$
N	5	$5\frac{1}{2}$	9	6	$\dfrac{4}{9}$

TABLE 10.5 The paths and path lengths through Reliable's project network when the duration of each activity equals its pessimistic estimate

Path	Length
START→A→B→C→D→G→H→M→FINISH	3 + 8 + 18 + 10 + 11 + 17 + 3 = 70 weeks
START→A→B→C→E→H→M→FINISH	3 + 8 + 18 + 5 + 17 + 3 = 54 weeks
START→A→B→C→E→F→J→K→N→FINISH	3 + 8 + 18 + 5 + 10 + 9 + 4 + 9 = 66 weeks
START→A→B→C→E→F→J→L→N→FINISH	3 + 8 + 18 + 5 + 10 + 9 + 7 + 9 = 69 weeks
START→A→B→C→I→J→K→N→FINISH	3 + 8 + 18 + 9 + 9 + 4 + 9 = 60 weeks
START→A→B→C→I→J→L→N→FINISH	3 + 8 + 18 + 9 + 9 + 7 + 9 = 63 weeks

Probability Distribution of Project Duration.

1. What is the *mean* (denoted by μ_p) of this distribution?

2. What is the *variance* (denoted by σ_p^2) of this distribution?

3. What is the *form* of this distribution?

Recall that project duration equals the *length* (total elapsed time) of the *longest path* through the project network. However, just about any of the six paths listed in Table 10.5

can turn out to be the longest path (and so the critical path), depending upon what the duration of each activity turns out to be between its optimistic and pessimistic estimates. Since dealing with all these paths would be complicated, PERT/CPM focuses on just the following path.

> The **mean critical path** is the path through the project network that would be the critical path if the duration of each activity equals its *mean*.

Reliable's mean critical path is

$$\text{START}\rightarrow A\rightarrow B\rightarrow C\rightarrow E\rightarrow F\rightarrow J\rightarrow L\rightarrow N\rightarrow\text{FINISH},$$

as highlighted in Fig. 10.7.

> **Simplifying Approximation 1:** Assume that the *mean critical path* will turn out to be the longest path through the project network. This is only a rough approximation, since the assumption occasionally does not hold in the usual case where some of the activity durations do not equal their means. Fortunately, when the assumption does not hold, the true longest path commonly is not much longer than the mean critical path (as illustrated in Table 10.5).

Although this approximation will enable us to calculate μ_p, we need one more approximation to obtain σ_p^2.

> **Simplifying Approximation 2:** Assume that the durations of the activities on the mean critical path are *statistically independent*. This assumption should hold if the activities are performed truly independently of each other. However, the assumption becomes only a rough approximation if the circumstances that cause the duration of one activity to deviate from its mean also tend to cause similar deviations for some other activities.

We now have a simple method for computing μ_p and σ_p^2.

> **Calculation of μ_p and σ_p^2:** Because of simplifying approximation 1, the *mean* of the probability distribution of project duration is approximately

> μ_p = sum of the *means* of the durations for the activities on the mean critical path.

Because of both simplifying approximations 1 and 2, the *variance* of the probability distribution of project duration is approximately

> σ_p^2 = sum of the variances of the durations for the activities on the mean critical path.

Since the means and variances of the durations for all the activities of Reliable's project already are given in Table 10.4, we only need to record these values for the activities on the mean critical path as shown in Table 10.6. Summing the second column and then summing the third column give

$$\mu_p = 44, \qquad \sigma_p^2 = 9.$$

TABLE 10.6 Calculation of μ_p and σ_p^2 for Reliable's project

Activities on Mean Critical Path	Mean	Variance
A	2	$\frac{1}{9}$
B	4	1
C	10	4
E	4	$\frac{4}{9}$
F	5	1
J	8	1
L	5	1
N	6	$\frac{4}{9}$
Project duration	$\mu_p = 44$	$\sigma_p^2 = 9$

Now we just need an approximation for the *form* of the probability distribution of project duration.

Simplifying Approximation 3: Assume that the form of the probability distribution of project duration is a *normal distribution,* as shown in Fig. 10.9. By using simplifying approximations 1 and 2, one version of the central limit theorem justifies this assumption as being a reasonable approximation if the number of activities on the mean critical path is not too small (say, at least 5). The approximation becomes better as this number of activities increases.

Now we are ready to determine (approximately) the probability of completing Reliable's project within 47 weeks.

FIGURE 10.9
The three simplifying approximations lead to the probability distribution of the duration of Reliable's project being approximated by the normal distribution shown here. The shaded area is the portion of the distribution that meets the deadline of 47 weeks.

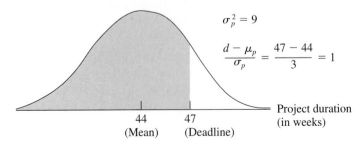

$$\sigma_p^2 = 9$$

$$\frac{d - \mu_p}{\sigma_p} = \frac{47 - 44}{3} = 1$$

44
(Mean)

47
(Deadline)

Project duration
(in weeks)

Approximating the Probability of Meeting the Deadline

Let

T = project duration (in weeks), which has (approximately) a normal distribution with mean $\mu_p = 44$ and variance $\sigma_p^2 = 9$,
d = deadline for the project = 47 weeks.

Since the standard deviation of T is $\sigma_p = 3$, the number of standard deviations by which d exceeds μ_p is

$$K_\alpha = \frac{d - \mu_p}{\sigma_p} = \frac{47 - 44}{3} = 1.$$

Therefore, using Table A5.1 in Appendix 5 for a *standard* normal distribution (a normal distribution with mean 0 and variance 1), the probability of meeting the deadline (given the three simplifying approximations) is

$$P(T \le d) = P(\text{standard normal} \le K_\alpha)$$
$$= 1 - P(\text{standard normal} > K_\alpha) = 1 - 0.1587 \approx 0.84.$$

Warning: This $P(T \le d)$ is only a rough approximation of the true probability of meeting the project deadline. Furthermore, because of simplifying approximation 1, it usually overstates the true probability somewhat. Therefore, the project manager should view $P(T \le d)$ as only providing rough guidance on the best odds of meeting the deadline without taking new costly measures to try to reduce the duration of some activities.

To assist you in carrying out this procedure for calculating $P(T \le d)$, we have provided an Excel template (labeled PERT) in this chapter's Excel file in your OR Courseware. Figure 10.10 illustrates the use of this template for Reliable's project. The data for the problem is entered in the light sections of the spreadsheet. After entering data, the results immediately appear in the dark sections. In particular, by entering the three time estimates for each activity, the spreadsheet will automatically calculate the corresponding estimates for the mean and variance. Next, by specifying the mean critical path (by entering * in column G for each activity on the mean critical path) and the deadline (in cell L10), the spreadsheet automatically calculates the mean and variance of the length of the mean critical path along with the probability that the project will be completed by the deadline. (If you are not sure which path is the mean critical path, the mean length of *any* path can be checked by entering a * for each activity on that path in column G. The path with the longest mean length then is the mean critical path.)

Realizing that $P(T \le d) = 0.84$ is probably an optimistic approximation, Mr. Perty is somewhat concerned that he may have perhaps only a 70 to 80 percent chance of meeting the deadline with the current plan. Therefore, rather than taking the significant chance of the company incurring the late penalty of $300,000, he decides to investigate what it would cost to reduce the project duration to about 40 weeks. If the *time-cost trade-off* for doing this is favorable, the company might then be able to earn the bonus of $150,000 for finishing within 40 weeks.

You will see this story unfold in the next section.

	A	B	C	D	E	F	G	H	I	J	K
1		**Template for PERT Three-Estimate Approach**									
2											
3				Time Estimates				On Mean			
4		Activity	o	m	p	μ	σ²	Critical Path		Mean Critical	
5		A	1	2	3	2	0.111	*		Path	
6		B	2	3.5	8	4	1	*			
7		C	6	9	18	10	4	*		μ =	44
8		D	4	5.5	10	6	1			σ² =	9
9		E	1	4.5	5	4	0.444	*			
10		F	4	4	10	5	1	*		P(T≤d) =	0.84134474
11		G	5	6.5	11	7	1			where	
12		H	5	8	17	9	4			d =	47
13		I	3	7.5	9	7	1				
14		J	3	9	9	8	1	*			
15		K	4	4	4	4	0				
16		L	1	5.5	7	5	1	*			
17		M	1	2	3	2	0.111				
18		N	5	5.5	9	6	0.444	*			
19											
20											
21			Data								
22			Results								

	F	G
5	=(C5+4*D5+E5)/6	=((E5-C5)/6)^2
6	=(C6+4*D6+E6)/6	=((E6-C6)/6)^2
7	=(C7+4*D7+E7)/6	=((E7-C7)/6)^2
8	=(C8+4*D8+E8)/6	=((E8-C8)/6)^2
9		:	:
10		:	:

	K
7	=SUMIF(H5:H18,"*",F5:F18)
8	=SUMIF(H5:H18,"*",G5:G18)
9	
10	=NORMDIST(K12,K7,SQRT(K8),1)

FIGURE 10.10
This PERT template in your OR Courseware enables efficient application of the PERT three-estimate approach, as illustrated here for Reliable's project.

10.5 CONSIDERING TIME-COST TRADE-OFFS

Mr. Perty now wants to investigate how much extra it would cost to reduce the expected project duration down to 40 weeks (the deadline for the company earning a bonus of $150,000 for early completion). Therefore, he is ready to address the next of his questions posed at the end of Sec. 10.1.

Question 8: If extra money is spent to expedite the project, what is the least expensive way of attempting to meet the target completion time (40 weeks)?

Mr. Perty remembers that CPM provides an excellent procedure for using *linear programming* to investigate such *time-cost trade-offs,* so he will use this approach again to address this question.

We begin with some background.

Time-Cost Trade-Offs for Individual Activities

The first key concept for this approach is that of *crashing.*

> **Crashing an activity** refers to taking special costly measures to reduce the duration of an activity below its normal value. These special measures might include using overtime, hiring additional temporary help, using special time-saving materials, obtaining special equipment, etc. **Crashing the project** refers to crashing a number of activities in order to reduce the duration of the project below its normal value.

The **CPM method of time-cost trade-offs** is concerned with determining how much (if any) to crash each of the activities in order to reduce the anticipated duration of the project to a desired value.

The data necessary for determining how much to crash a particular activity are given by the *time-cost graph* for the activity. Figure 10.11 shows a typical time-cost graph. Note the two key points on this graph labeled *Normal* and *Crash.*

> The **normal point** on the time-cost graph for an activity shows the time (duration) and cost of the activity when it is performed in the normal way. The **crash point** shows the time and cost when the activity is *fully crashed,* i.e., it is fully expedited with no cost spared to reduce its duration as much as possible. As an approximation, CPM assumes that these times and costs can be reliably predicted without significant uncertainty.

For most applications, it is assumed that *partially crashing* the activity at any level will give a combination of time and cost that will lie somewhere on the line segment between

FIGURE 10.11
A typical time-cost graph for an activity.

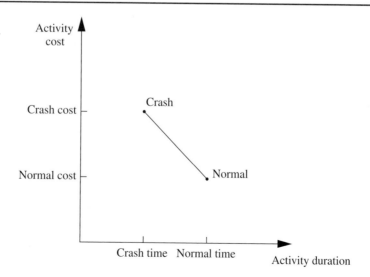

these two points. (For example, this assumption says that *half* of a full crash will give a point on this line segment that is midway between the normal and crash points.) This simplifying approximation reduces the necessary data gathering to estimating the time and cost for just two situations: *normal conditions* (to obtain the normal point) and a *full crash* (to obtain the crash point).

Using this approach, Mr. Perty has his staff and crew supervisors working on developing these data for each of the activities of Reliable's project. For example, the supervisor of the crew responsible for putting up the wallboard indicates that adding two temporary employees and using overtime would enable him to reduce the duration of this activity from 8 weeks to 6 weeks, which is the minimum possible. Mr. Perty's staff then estimates the cost of fully crashing the activity in this way as compared to following the normal 8-week schedule, as shown below.

Activity J (put up the wallboard):

Normal point: time = 8 weeks, cost = $430,000.
Crash point: time = 6 weeks, cost = $490,000.
Maximum reduction in time = $8 - 6 = 2$ weeks.

$$\text{Crash cost per week saved} = \frac{\$490,000 - \$430,000}{2}$$

$$= \$30,000.$$

Table 10.7 gives the corresponding data obtained for all the activities.

Which Activities Should Be Crashed?

Summing the *normal cost* and *crash cost* columns of Table 10.7 gives

Sum of normal costs = $4.55 million,
Sum of crash costs = $6.15 million.

TABLE 10.7 Time-cost trade-off data for the activities of Reliable's project

Activity	Time		Cost		Maximum Reduction in Time	Crash Cost per Week Saved
	Normal	Crash	Normal	Crash		
A	2 weeks	1 week	$180,000	$ 280,000	1 week	$100,000
B	4 weeks	2 weeks	$320,000	$ 420,000	2 weeks	$ 50,000
C	10 weeks	7 weeks	$620,000	$ 860,000	3 weeks	$ 80,000
D	6 weeks	4 weeks	$260,000	$ 340,000	2 weeks	$ 40,000
E	4 weeks	3 weeks	$410,000	$ 570,000	1 week	$160,000
F	5 weeks	3 weeks	$180,000	$ 260,000	2 weeks	$ 40,000
G	7 weeks	4 weeks	$900,000	$1,020,000	3 weeks	$ 40,000
H	9 weeks	6 weeks	$200,000	$ 380,000	3 weeks	$ 60,000
I	7 weeks	5 weeks	$210,000	$ 270,000	2 weeks	$ 30,000
J	8 weeks	6 weeks	$430,000	$ 490,000	2 weeks	$ 30,000
K	4 weeks	3 weeks	$160,000	$ 200,000	1 week	$ 40,000
L	5 weeks	3 weeks	$250,000	$ 350,000	2 weeks	$ 50,000
M	2 weeks	1 week	$100,000	$ 200,000	1 week	$100,000
N	6 weeks	3 weeks	$330,000	$ 510,000	3 weeks	$ 60,000

Recall that the company will be paid $5.4 million for doing this project. (This figure excludes the $150,000 bonus for finishing within 40 weeks and the $300,000 penalty for not finishing within 47 weeks.) This payment needs to cover some *overhead costs* in addition to the costs of the activities listed in the table, as well as provide a reasonable profit to the company. When developing the (winning) bid of $5.4 million, Reliable's management felt that this amount would provide a reasonable profit as long as the total cost of the activities could be held fairly close to the normal level of about $4.55 million. Mr. Perty understands very well that it is now his responsibility to keep the project as close to both budget and schedule as possible.

As found previously in Fig. 10.7, if all the activities are performed in the normal way, the anticipated duration of the project would be 44 weeks (if delays can be avoided). If *all* the activities were to be *fully crashed* instead, then a similar calculation would find that this duration would be reduced to only 28 weeks. But look at the prohibitive cost ($6.15 million) of doing this! Fully crashing all activities clearly is not an option that can be considered.

However, Mr. Perty still wants to investigate the possibility of partially or fully crashing just a few activities to reduce the anticipated duration of the project to 40 weeks.

The problem: What is the least expensive way of crashing some activities to reduce the (estimated) project duration to the specified level (40 weeks)?

One way of solving this problem is **marginal cost analysis,** which uses the last column of Table 10.7 (along with Fig. 10.7 in Sec. 10.3) to determine the least expensive way to reduce project duration 1 week at a time. The easiest way to conduct this kind of analysis is to set up a table like Table 10.8 that lists all the paths through the project network and the current length of each of these paths. To get started, this information can be copied directly from Table 10.2.

Since the fourth path listed in Table 10.8 has the longest length (44 weeks), the only way to reduce project duration by a week is to reduce the duration of the activities on this particular path by a week. Comparing the crash cost per week saved given in the last column of Table 10.7 for these activities, the smallest cost is $30,000 for activity *J*. (Note that activity *I* with this same cost is not on this path.) Therefore, the first change is to crash activity *J* enough to reduce its duration by a week.

This change results in reducing the length of each path that includes activity *J* (the third, fourth, fifth, and sixth paths in Table 10.8) by a week, as shown in the second row of Table 10.9. Because the fourth path still is the longest (43 weeks), the same process is repeated to find the least expensive activity to shorten on this path. This again is activity *J,* since the next-to-last column in Table 10.7 indicates that a maximum reduction of 2 weeks is allowed for this activity. This second reduction of a week for activity *J* leads to the third row of Table 10.9.

TABLE 10.8 The initial table for starting marginal cost analysis of Reliable's project

Activity to Crash	Crash Cost	Length of Path					
		ABCDGHM	**ABCEHM**	**ABCEFJKN**	**ABCEFJLN**	**ABCIJKN**	**ABCIJLN**
		40	31	43	44	41	42

TABLE 10.9 The final table for performing marginal cost analysis on Reliable's project

Activity to Crash	Crash Cost	Length of Path					
		ABCDGHM	ABCEHM	ABCEFJKN	ABCEFJLN	ABCIJKN	ABCIJLN
		40	31	43	44	41	42
J	$30,000	40	31	42	43	40	41
J	$30,000	40	31	41	42	39	40
F	$40,000	40	31	40	41	39	40
F	$40,000	40	31	39	40	39	40

At this point, the fourth path still is the longest (42 weeks), but activity J cannot be shortened any further. Among the other activities on this path, activity F now is the least expensive to shorten ($40,000 per week) according to the last column of Table 10.7. Therefore, this activity is shortened by a week to obtain the fourth row of Table 10.9, and then (because a maximum reduction of 2 weeks is allowed) is shortened by another week to obtain the last row of this table.

The longest path (a tie between the first, fourth, and sixth paths) now has the desired length of 40 weeks, so we don't need to do any more crashing. (If we did need to go further, the next step would require looking at the activities on all three paths to find the least expensive way of shortening all three paths by a week.) The total cost of crashing activities J and F to get down to this project duration of 40 weeks is calculated by adding the costs in the second column of Table 10.9—a total of $140,000. Figure 10.12 shows the resulting project network.

Since $140,000 is slightly less than the bonus of $150,000 for finishing within 40 weeks, it might appear that Mr. Perty should proceed with this solution. However, because of uncertainties about activity durations, he concludes that he probably should not crash the project at all. (We will discuss this further at the end of the section.)

Figure 10.12 shows that reducing the durations of activities F and J to their crash times has led to now having *three* critical paths through the network. The reason is that, as we found earlier from the last row of Table 10.9, the three paths tie for being the longest, each with a length of 40 weeks.

With larger networks, marginal cost analysis can become quite unwieldy. A more efficient procedure would be desirable for large projects.

For these reasons, the standard CPM procedure is to apply *linear programming* instead (commonly with a customized software package).

Using Linear Programming to Make Crashing Decisions

The problem of finding the least expensive way of crashing activities can be rephrased in a form more familiar to linear programming as follows.

Restatement of the problem: Let Z be the total cost of crashing activities. The problem then is to minimize Z, subject to the constraint that project duration must be less than or equal to the time desired by the project manager.

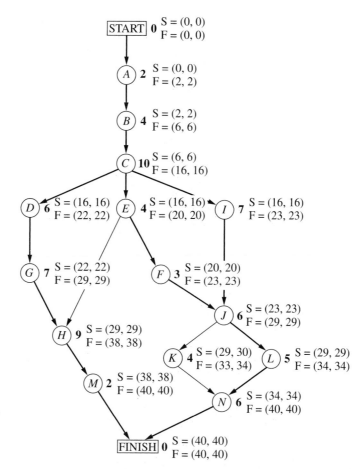

FIGURE 10.12
The project network if activities *J* and *F* are fully crashed (with all other activities normal) for Reliable's project. The darker arrows show the various critical paths through the project network.

The natural decision variables are

x_j = reduction in the duration of activity j due to crashing this activity,
    for $j = A, B \ldots, N$.

By using the last column of Table 10.7, the objective function to be minimized then is

$$Z = 100,000x_A + 50,000x_B + \cdots + 60,000x_N.$$

Each of the 14 decision variables on the right-hand side needs to be restricted to nonnegative values that do not exceed the maximum given in the next-to-last column of Table 10.7.

To impose the constraint that project duration must be less than or equal to the desired value (40 weeks), let

y_{FINISH} = project duration, i.e., the time at which the FINISH node in the project
    network is reached.

The constraint then is

$y_{\text{FINISH}} \leq 40.$

To help the linear programming model assign the appropriate value to y_{FINISH}, given the values of x_A, x_B, . . . , x_N, it is convenient to introduce into the model the following additional variables.

y_j = start time of activity j (for $j = B, C, \ldots, N$), given the values of x_A, x_B, . . . , x_N.

(No such variable is needed for activity A, since an activity that begins the project is automatically assigned a value of 0.) By treating the FINISH node as another activity (albeit one with zero duration), as we now will do, this definition of y_j for activity FINISH also fits the definition of y_{FINISH} given in the preceding paragraph.

The start time of each activity (including FINISH) is directly related to the start time and duration of each of its immediate predecessors as summarized below.

For each activity ($B, C, \ldots, N$, FINISH) and each of its immediate predecessors,
Start time of this activity $\geq$ (start time + duration) for this immediate predecessor.

Furthermore, by using the normal times from Table 10.7, the duration of each activity is given by the following formula:

Duration of activity j = its normal time $- x_j$,

To illustrate these relationships, consider activity F in the project network (Fig. 10.7 or 10.12).

Immediate predecessor of activity F:
Activity E, which has duration = $4 - x_E$.

Relationship between these activities:

$y_F \geq y_E + 4 - x_E$.

Thus, activity F cannot start until activity E starts and then completes its duration of $4 - x_E$.
Now consider activity J, which has two immediate predecessors.

Immediate predecessors of activity J:
Activity F, which has duration = $5 - x_F$.
Activity I, which has duration = $7 - x_I$.

Relationships between these activities:

$y_J \geq y_F + 5 - x_F$,
$y_J \geq y_I + 7 - x_I$.

These inequalities together say that activity j cannot start until both of its predecessors finish.

By including these relationships for all the activities as constraints, we obtain the complete linear programming model given below.

Minimize $Z = 100{,}000x_A + 50{,}000x_B + \cdots + 60{,}000x_N$,

subject to the following constraints:

1. Maximum reduction constraints:
   Using the next-to-last column of Table 10.7,

   $x_A \leq 1$, $x_B \leq 2$, . . . , $x_N \leq 3$.

2. Nonnegativity constraints:

$$x_A \geq 0, \, x_B \geq 0, \, \ldots, \, x_N \geq 0$$
$$y_B \geq 0, \, y_C \geq 0, \, \ldots, \, y_N \geq 0, \, y_{\text{FINISH}} \geq 0.$$

3. Start time constraints:

As described above the objective function, except for activity A (which starts the project), there is one such constraint for each activity with a single immediate predecessor (activities B, C, D, E, F, G, I, K, L, M) and two constraints for each activity with two immediate predecessors (activities H, J, N, FINISH), as listed below.

One immediate predecessor	Two immediate predecessors
$y_B \geq 0 + 2 - x_A$	$y_H \geq y_G + 7 - x_G$
$y_C \geq y_B + 4 - x_B$	$y_H \geq y_E + 4 - x_E$
$y_D \geq y_C + 10 - x_C$	$\vdots$
$\vdots$	$y_{\text{FINISH}} \geq y_M + 2 - x_M$
$y_M \geq y_H + 9 - x_H$	$y_{\text{FINISH}} \geq y_N + 6 - x_N$

4. Project duration constraint:

$$y_{\text{FINISH}} \leq 40.$$

Figure 10.13 shows how this problem can be formulated as a linear programming model on a spreadsheet. The decisions to be made are shown in the changing cells, I6:J19 and J21. Columns B to H correspond to the columns in Table 10.8. As the equations in the bottom half of the figure indicate, columns G and H are calculated in a straightforward way. The equations for column K express the fact that the finish time for each activity is its start time *plus* its normal time *minus* its time reduction due to crashing. The equation entered into the target cell (J22) adds all the normal costs plus the extra costs due to crashing to obtain the total cost.

The last set of constraints in the Solver dialogue box (J6:J19 $\leq$ G6:G19) specifies that the time reduction for each activity cannot exceed its maximum time reduction given in column G. The two preceding constraints (J21 $\geq$ K18 and J21 $\geq$ K19) indicate that the project cannot finish until each of the two immediate predecessors (activities M and N) finish. The constraint that J21 $\leq$ 40 is a key one that specifies that the project must finish within 40 weeks.

The constraints involving cells I7:I19 all are *start-time constraints* that specify that an activity cannot start until each of its immediate predecessors has finished. For example, the first constraint shown (I10 $\geq$ K8) says that activity E cannot start until activity C (its immediate predecessor) finishes. When an activity has more than one immediate predecessor, there is one such constraint for each of them. To illustrate, activity H has both activities E and G as immediate predecessors. Consequently, activity H has two start-time constraints, I13 $\geq$ K10 and I13 $\geq$ K12.

You may have noticed that the $\geq$ form of the *start-time constraints* allows a delay in starting an activity after all its immediate predecessors have finished. Although such a delay is feasible in the model, it cannot be optimal for any activity on a critical path, since this needless delay would increase the total cost (by necessitating additional crashing to meet the project duration constraint). Therefore, an optimal solution for the model will not have any such delays, except possibly for activities not on a critical path.

	A	B	C	D	E	F	G	H	I	J	K
1	Reliable Construction Co. Project Scheduling Problem with Time-Cost Trade-offs										
2											
3							Maximum	Crash Cost			
4			Time		Cost		Time	per Week	Start	Time	Finish
5		Activity	Normal	Crash	Normal	Crash	Reduction	saved	Time	Reduction	Time
6		A	2	1	$180000	$280000	1	$100000	0	0	2
7		B	4	2	$320000	$420000	2	$50000	2	0	6
8		C	10	7	$620000	$860000	3	$80000	6	0	16
9		D	6	4	$260000	$340000	2	$40000	16	0	22
10		E	4	3	$410000	$570000	1	$160000	16	0	20
11		F	5	3	$180000	$260000	2	$40000	20	2	23
12		G	7	4	$900000	$1020000	3	$40000	22	0	29
13		H	9	6	$200000	$380000	3	$60000	29	0	38
14		I	7	5	$210000	$270000	2	$30000	16	0	23
15		J	8	6	$430000	$490000	2	$30000	23	2	29
16		K	4	3	$160000	$200000	1	$40000	30	0	34
17		L	5	3	$250000	$350000	2	$50000	29	0	34
18		M	2	1	$100000	$200000	1	$100000	38	0	40
19		N	6	3	$330000	$510000	3	$60000	34	0	40
20											
21									Finish Time =	40	
22									Total Cost = $4,690,000		

Solver Parameters

Set Target Cell: $J$22

Equal To: ○ Max ● Min ○

By Changing Cells:

$I$6:$J$19,$J$21

Subject to the Constraints:

$I$10 >= $K$8	$I$19 >= $K$16
$I$11 >= $K$10	$I$19 >= $K$17
$I$12 >= $K$9	$I$6:$J$19 >= 0
$I$13 >= $K$10	$I$7 >= $K$6
$I$13 >= $K$12	$I$8 >= $K$7
$I$14 >= $K$8	$I$9 >= $K$8
$I$15 >= $K$11	$J$21 <= 40
$I$15 >= $K$14	$J$21 >= $K$18
$I$16 >= $K$15	$J$21 >= $K$19
$I$17 >= $K$15	$J$6:$J$19 <= $G$6:$G$19
$I$18 >= $K$13	

	G	H	K
6	=C6-D6	=(F6-E6)/G6	=I6+C6-J6
7	=C7-D7	=(F7-E7)/G7	=I7+C7-J7
8	=C8-D8	=(F8-E8)/G8	=I8+C8-J8
9	=C9-D9	=(F9-E9)/G9	=I9+C9-J9
10	=C10-D10	=(F10-E10)/G10	=I10+C10-J10
11	=C11-D11	=(F11-E11)/G11	=I11+C11-J11
12	=C12-D12	=(F12-E12)/G12	=I12+C12-J12
13	=C13-D13	=(F13-E13)/G13	=I13+C13-J13
14	=C14-D14	=(F14-E14)/G14	=I14+C14-J14
15	=C15-D15	=(F15-E15)/G15	=I15+C15-J15
16	=C16-D16	=(F16-E16)/G16	=I16+C16-J16
17	=C17-D17	=(F17-E17)/G17	=I17+C17-J17
18	=C18-D18	=(F18-E18)/G18	=I18+C18-J18
19	=C19-D19	=(F19-E19)/G19	=I19+C19-J19

	J
22	=SUM(E6:E19)+SUMPRODUCT(H6:H19,J6:J19)

Solver Options

☑ Assume Linear Model
☑ Assume Non-Negative

FIGURE 10.13

The spreadsheet displays the application of the CPM method of time-cost trade-offs to Reliable's project, where columns I and J show the optimal solution obtained by using the Excel Solver with the entries shown in the Solver dialogue box.

Columns I and J in Fig. 10.13 show the optimal solution obtained after having clicked on the Solve button. (Note that this solution involves one delay—activity K starts at 30 even though its only immediate predecessor, activity J, finishes at 29—but this doesn't matter since activity K is not on a critical path.) This solution corresponds to the one displayed in Fig. 10.12 that was obtained by marginal cost analysis.

Mr. Perty's Conclusions

Mr. Perty always keeps a sharp eye on the bottom line. Therefore, when his staff brings him the above plan for crashing the project to try to reduce its duration from about 44 weeks to about 40 weeks, he first looks at the estimated total cost of $4.69 million. Since the estimated total cost without any crashing is $4.55 million, the additional cost from the crashing would be about $140,000. This is $10,000 less than the bonus of $150,000 that the company would earn by finishing within 40 weeks.

However, Mr. Perty knows from long experience what we discussed in the preceding section, namely, that there is considerable uncertainty about how much time actually will be needed for each activity and so for the overall project. Recall that the PERT three-estimate approach led to having a *probability distribution* for project duration. Without crashing, this probability distribution has a *mean* of 44 weeks but such a large *variance* that there is even a substantial probability (roughly 0.2) of not even finishing within 47 weeks (which would trigger a penalty of $300,000). With the new crashing plan reducing the mean to 40 weeks, there is as much chance that the actual project duration will turn out to exceed 40 weeks as being within 40 weeks. Why spend an extra $140,000 to obtain a 50 percent chance of earning the bonus of $150,000?

> **Conclusion 1:** The plan for crashing the project only provides a probability of 0.5 of actually finishing the project within 40 weeks, so the extra cost of the plan ($140,000) is not justified. Therefore, Mr. Perty rejects any crashing at this stage.

Mr. Perty does note that the two activities that had been proposed for crashing (F and J) come about halfway through the project. Therefore, if the project is well ahead of schedule before reaching activity F, then implementing the crashing plan almost certainly would enable finishing the project within 40 weeks. Furthermore, Mr. Perty knows that it would be good for the company's reputation (as well as a feather in his own cap) to finish this early.

> **Conclusion 2:** The extra cost of the crashing plan can be justified if it almost certainly would earn the bonus of $150,000 for finishing the project within 40 weeks. Therefore, Mr. Perty will hold the plan in reserve to be implemented if the project is running well ahead of schedule before reaching activity F.

Mr. Perty is more concerned about the possibility that the project will run so far behind schedule that the penalty of $300,000 will be incurred for not finishing within 47 weeks. If this becomes likely without crashing, Mr. Perty sees that it probably can be avoided by crashing activity J (at a cost of $30,000 per week saved) and, if necessary, crashing activity F as well (at a cost of $40,000 per week saved). This will hold true as long as these activities remain on the critical path (as is likely) after the delays occurred.

> **Conclusion 3:** The extra cost of part or all of the crashing plan can be easily justified if it likely would make the difference in avoiding the penalty of $300,000

for not finishing the project within 47 weeks. Therefore, Mr. Perty will hold the crashing plan in reserve to be partially or wholly implemented if the project is running far behind schedule before reaching activity *F* or activity *J*.

In addition to carefully monitoring the schedule as the project evolves (and making a later decision about any crashing), Mr. Perty will be closely watching the costs to try to keep the project within budget. The next section describes how he plans to do this.

10.6 SCHEDULING AND CONTROLLING PROJECT COSTS

Any good project manager like Mr. Perty carefully plans and monitors both the *time* and *cost* aspects of the project. Both schedule and budget are important.

Sections 10.3 and 10.4 have described how PERT/CPM deals with the *time* aspect in developing a schedule and taking uncertainties in activity or project durations into account. Section 10.5 then placed an equal emphasis on time and cost by describing the CPM method of time-cost trade-offs.

Mr. Perty now is ready to turn his focus to *costs* by addressing the last of his questions posed at the end of Sec. 10.1.

Question 9: How should ongoing costs be monitored to try to keep the project within budget?

Mr. Perty recalls that the PERT/CPM technique known as PERT/Cost is specifically designed for this purpose.

> **PERT/Cost** is a systematic procedure (normally computerized) to help the project manager plan, schedule, and control project costs.

The PERT/Cost procedure begins with the hard work of developing an estimate of the cost of each activity when it is performed in the planned way (including any crashing). At this stage, Mr. Perty does not plan on any crashing, so the estimated costs of the activities in Reliable's project are given in the *normal cost* column of Table 10.7 in the preceding section. These costs then are displayed in the *project budget* shown in Table 10.10. This table also includes the estimated duration of each activity (as already given in Table 10.1 or in Figs. 10.1 to 10.7 or in the *normal time* column of Table 10.7). Dividing the cost of each activity by its duration gives the amount in the rightmost column of Table 10.10.

> **Assumption:** A common assumption when using PERT/Cost is that the costs of performing an activity are incurred at a constant rate throughout its duration. Mr. Perty is making this assumption, so the estimated cost during each week of an activity's duration is given by the rightmost column of Table 10.10.

When applying PERT/Cost to larger projects with numerous activities, it is common to combine each group of related activities into a "work package." Both the project budget and the schedule of project costs (described next) then are developed in terms of these work packages rather than the individual activities. Mr. Perty has chosen not to do this, since his project has only 14 activities.

TABLE 10.10 The project budget for Reliable's project

Activity	Estimated Duration	Estimated Cost	Cost per Week of Its Duration
A	2 weeks	$180,000	$ 90,000
B	4 weeks	$320,000	$ 80,000
C	10 weeks	$620,000	$ 62,000
D	6 weeks	$260,000	$ 43,333
E	4 weeks	$410,000	$102,500
F	5 weeks	$180,000	$ 36,000
G	7 weeks	$900,000	$128,571
H	9 weeks	$200,000	$ 22,222
I	7 weeks	$210,000	$ 30,000
J	8 weeks	$430,000	$ 53,750
K	4 weeks	$160,000	$ 40,000
L	5 weeks	$250,000	$ 50,000
M	2 weeks	$100,000	$ 50,000
N	6 weeks	$330,000	$ 55,000

Scheduling Project Costs

Mr. Perty needs to know how much money is required to cover project expenses week by week. PERT/Cost provides this information by using the rightmost column of Table 10.10 to develop a weekly schedule of expenses when the individual activities begin at their earliest start times. Then, to indicate how much flexibility is available for delaying expenses, PERT/Cost does the same thing when the individual activities begin at their latest start times instead.

To do this, this chapter's Excel file in your OR Courseware includes an Excel template (labeled PERT Cost) for generating a project's schedule of costs for up to 45 time periods. (MS Project generates basically the same information by choosing Table:Cost and then Reports under the View menu, and next choosing the Costs ... option and selecting the Cash Flow report.) Figure 10.14 shows this Excel template (including the equations entered into its output cells) for the beginning of Reliable's project, based on earliest start times (column B) as first obtained in Fig. 10.5, where columns B, C, and D come directly from Table 10.10. Figure 10.15 jumps ahead to show this same template for weeks 17 to 25. Since activities *D, E,* and *I* all have earliest start times of 16 (16 weeks after the commencement of the project), they all start in week 17, while activities *F* and *G* commence later during the period shown. Columns W through AE give the weekly cost (in dollars) of each of these activities, as obtained from column F (see Fig. 10.14), for the duration of the activity (given by column C). Row 22 shows the sum of the weekly activity costs for each week.

Row 23 of this template gives the total project cost from week 1 on up to the indicated week. For example, consider week 17. Prior to week 17, activities *A, B,* and *C* all have been completed but no other activities have begun, so the total cost for the first 16 weeks (from the third column of Table 10.10) is $180,000 + $320,000 + $620,000 = $1,120,000. Adding the weekly project cost for week 17 then gives $1,120,000 + $175,833 = $1,295,833.

	A	B	C	D	E	F	G	H	I
1		Template for PERT/Cost							
2									
3			Estimated						
4			Duration	Estimated	Start	Cost Per Week	Week	Week	...
5		Activity	(weeks)	Cost	Time	of Its Duration	1	2	
6		A	2	$180,000	0	$90,000	90000	90000	
7		B	4	$320,000	2	$80,000	0	0	
8		C	10	$620,000	6	$62,000	0	0	
9		D	6	$260,000	16	$43,333	0	0	...
10		E	4	$410,000	16	$102,500	0	0	
11		F	5	$180,000	20	$36,000	0	0	
12		G	7	$900,000	22	$128,571	0	0	
13		H	9	$200,000	29	$22,222	0	0	...
14		I	7	$210,000	16	$30,000	0	0	
15		J	8	$430,000	25	$53,750	0	0	
16		K	4	$160,000	33	$40,000	0	0	
17		L	5	$250,000	33	$50,000	0	0	...
18		M	2	$100,000	38	$50,000	0	0	
19		N	6	$330,000	38	$55,000	0	0	
20							0	0	
21									
22						Weekly Project Cost	90000	90000	...
23						Cumulative Project Cost	90000	180000	...
24									
25			Data						
26			Results						

	F	G	H	I
6	=D6/C6	=IF(AND(G5>E6,G5<=E6+C6),F6,0)	=IF(AND(H5>E6,H5<=E6+C6),F6,0)	
7	=D7/C7	=IF(AND(G5>E7,G5<=E7+C7),F7,0)	=IF(AND(H5>E7,H5<=E7+C7),F7,0)	
8	=D8/C8	=IF(AND(G5>E8,G5<=E8+C8),F8,0)	=IF(AND(H5>E8,H5<=E8+C8),F8,0)	
9	=D9/C9	=IF(AND(G5>E9,G5<=E9+C9),F9,0)	=IF(AND(H5>E9,H5<=E9+C9),F9,0)	...
10	:	:	:	
11	:	:	:	
21				
22	=SUM(G6:G20)		=SUM(H6:H20)	...
23	=G22		=G23+H22	...

FIGURE 10.14
This Excel template in your OR Courseware enables efficient application of the PERT/Cost procedure, as illustrated here for the beginning of Reliable's project when using earliest start times.

Thus, Fig. 10.15 (and its extension to earlier and later weeks) shows Mr. Perty just how much money he will need to cover each week's expenses, as well as the cumulative amount, assuming the project can stick to the earliest start time schedule.

Next, PERT/Cost uses the same procedure to develop the corresponding information when each activity begins at its *latest* start times instead. These latest start times were first obtained in Fig. 10.6 and are repeated here in column E of Fig. 10.16. The rest of this figure then is generated in the same way as for Fig. 10.15. For example, since activity *D* has a latest start time of 20 (versus an earliest start time of 16), its weekly cost of $43,333 now begins in week 21 rather than week 17. Similarly, activity *G* has a latest start time of 26, so it has no entries for the weeks considered in this figure.

Figure 10.16 (and its extension to earlier and later weeks) tells Mr. Perty what his weekly and cumulative expenses would be if he postpones each activity as long as possible without delaying project completion (assuming no unexpected delays occur). Comparing row 23 of Figs. 10.15 and 10.16 indicates that fairly substantial *temporary* savings

	Activity	Start Time	Week 17	Week 18	Week 19	Week 20	Week 21	Week 22	Week 23	Week 24	Week 25
1	Template for PERT/Cost										
6	A	0	0	0	0	0	0	0	0	0	0
7	B	2	0	0	0	0	0	0	0	0	0
8	C	6	0	0	0	0	0	0	0	0	0
9	D	16	43333.3	43333.3	43333.3	43333.3	43333.3	43333.3	0	0	0
10	E	16	102500	102500	102500	102500	0	0	0	0	0
11	F	20	0	0	0	0	36000	36000	36000	36000	36000
12	G	22	0	0	0	0	0	0	128571	128571	12857
13	H	29	0	0	0	0	0	0	0	0	0
14	I	16	30000	30000	30000	30000	30000	30000	30000	0	0
15	J	25	0	0	0	0	0	0	0	0	0
16	K	33	0	0	0	0	0	0	0	0	0
17	L	33	0	0	0	0	0	0	0	0	0
18	M	38	0	0	0	0	0	0	0	0	0
19	N	38	0	0	0	0	0	0	0	0	0
22	Weekly Project Cost=		175833	175833	175833	175833	109333	109333	194571	164571	16457
23	Cum. Project Cost=		1295833	1471667	1647500	1823333	1932667	2042000	2236571	2401143	256571

FIGURE 10.15
This spreadsheet extends the template in Fig. 10.14 to weeks 17 to 25.

can be achieved by such postponements, which is very helpful if the company is incurring cash shortages. (However, such postponements would only be used reluctantly since they would remove any latitude for avoiding a delay in the completion of the project if any activities incur unexpected delays.)

To better visualize the comparison between row 23 of Figs. 10.15 and 10.16, it is helpful to graph these two rows together over all 44 weeks of the project as shown in Fig. 10.17. Since the earliest start times and latest start times are the same for the first three activities (A, B, C), which encompass the first 16 weeks, the cumulative project cost is the same for the two kinds of start times over this period. After week 16, we obtain two distinct cost curves by plotting the values in row 23 of Figs. 10.15 and 10.16 (and their extensions to later weeks). Since sticking to either earliest start times or latest start times leads to project completion at the end of 44 weeks, the two cost curves come together again at that point with a total project cost of $4.55 million. The dots on either curve are the points at which the weekly project costs change.

Naturally, the start times and activity costs that lead to Fig. 10.17 are only estimates of what actually will transpire. However, the figure provides a *best forecast* of cumulative project costs week by week when following a work schedule based on either earliest or latest start times. If either of these work schedules is selected, this best forecast then becomes a *budget* to be followed as closely as possible. A budget in the shaded area be-

	A	B	E	W	X	Y	Z	AA	AB	AC	AD	AE
1	Template for PERT/Cost											
2												
3												
4			Start	Week	Week	Week	Week	Week	Week	Week	Week	Week
5		Activity	Time	17	18	19	20	21	22	23	24	25
6		A	0	0	0	0	0	0	0	0	0	0
7		B	2	0	0	0	0	0	0	0	0	0
8		C	6	0	0	0	0	0	0	0	0	0
9		D	20	0	0	0	0	43333.3	43333.3	43333.3	43333.3	43333.
10		E	16	102500	102500	102500	102500	0	0	0	0	0
11		F	20	0	0	0	0	36000	36000	36000	36000	3600C
12		G	26	0	0	0	0	0	0	0	0	0
13		H	33	0	0	0	0	0	0	0	0	0
14		I	18	0	0	30000	30000	30000	30000	30000	30000	3000C
15		J	25	0	0	0	0	0	0	0	0	0
16		K	34	0	0	0	0	0	0	0	0	0
17		L	33	0	0	0	0	0	0	0	0	0
18		M	42	0	0	0	0	0	0	0	0	0
19		N	38	0	0	0	0	0	0	0	0	0
20				0	0	0	0	0	0	0	0	0
21												
22	Weekly Project Cost=			102500	102500	132500	132500	109333	109333	109333	109333	10933
23	Cum. Project Cost=			1222500	1325000	1457500	1590000	1699333	1808667	1918000	2027333	213666

FIGURE 10.16
The application of the PERT/Cost procedure to weeks 17 to 25 of Reliable's project when using latest start times.

tween the two cost curves also can be obtained by selecting a work schedule that calls for beginning each activity somewhere between its earliest and latest start times. The only *feasible* budgets for scheduling project completion at the end of week 44 (without any crashing) lie in this shaded area or on one of the two cost curves.

Reliable Construction Co. has adequate funds to cover expenses until payments are received. Therefore, Mr. Perty has selected a work schedule based on earliest start times to provide the best chance for prompt completion. (He is still nervous about the significant probability of incurring the penalty of $300,000 for not finishing within 47 weeks.) Consequently, his budget is provided by the top cost curve in Fig. 10.17.

Controlling Project Costs

Once the project is under way, Mr. Perty will need to carefully monitor actual costs and take corrective action as needed to avoid serious cost overruns. One important way of monitoring costs is to compare actual costs to date with his budget provided by the top curve in Fig. 10.17.

However, since deviations from the planned work schedule may occur, this method of monitoring costs is not adequate by itself. For example, suppose that individual activ-

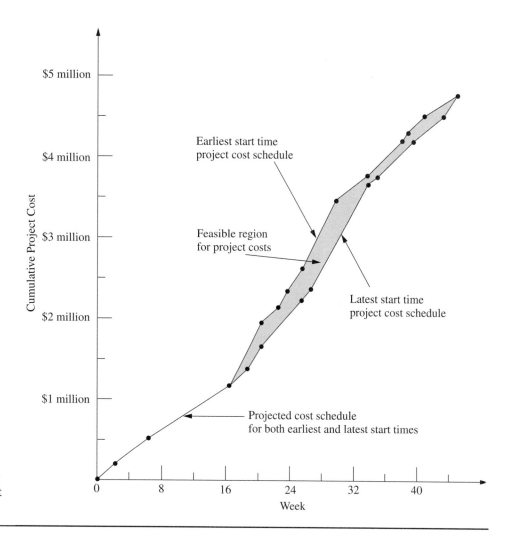

FIGURE 10.17
The schedule of cumulative project costs when all activities begin at their earliest start times (the top cost curve) or at their latest start times (the bottom cost curve).

ities have been costing more than budgeted, but delays have prevented some activities from beginning when scheduled. These delays might cause the total cost to date to be less than the budgeted cumulative project cost, thereby giving the illusion that project costs are well under control. Furthermore, regardless of whether the cost performance of the project as a whole seems satisfactory, Mr. Perty needs information about the cost performance of individual activities in order to identify trouble spots where corrective action is needed.

Therefore, PERT/Cost periodically generates a report that focuses on the cost performance of the individual activities. To illustrate, Table 10.11 shows the report that Mr. Perty received after the completion of week 22 (halfway through the project schedule). The first column lists the activities that have at least begun by this time. The next column gives the budgeted total cost of each activity (as given previously in the third column of Table 10.10). The third column indicates what percentage of the activity now has been

TABLE 10.11 PERT/Cost report after week 22 of Reliable's project

Activity	Budgeted Cost	Percent Completed	Value Completed	Actual Cost to Date	Cost Overrun to Date
A	$ 180,000	100%	$ 180,000	$ 200,000	$20,000
B	$ 320,000	100%	$ 320,000	$ 330,000	$10,000
C	$ 620,000	100%	$ 620,000	$ 600,000	−$20,000
D	$ 260,000	75%	$ 195,000	$ 200,000	$ 5,000
E	$ 410,000	100%	$ 410,000	$ 400,000	−$10,000
F	$ 180,000	25%	$ 45,000	$ 60,000	$15,000
I	$ 210,000	50%	$ 105,000	$ 130,000	$25,000
Total	$2,180,000		$1,875,000	$1,920,000	$45,000

completed. Multiplying the second and third columns then gives the fourth column, which thereby represents the budgeted value of the work completed on the activity.

The fourth column is the one that Mr. Perty wants to compare to the *actual cost* to date given in the fifth column. Subtracting the fourth column from the fifth gives the *cost overrun* to date of each activity, as shown in the rightmost column. (A negative number in the cost overrun column indicates a *cost underrun.*)

Mr. Perty pays special attention in the report to the activities that are not yet completed, since these are the ones that he can still affect. (He used earlier reports to monitor activities A, B, C, and E while they were under way, which led to meeting the total budget for these four activities.) Activity D is barely over budget (less than 3 percent), but Mr. Perty is very concerned about the large cost overruns to date for activities F and I. Therefore, he next will investigate these two activities and work with the supervisors involved to improve their cost performances.

Note in the bottom row of Table 10.11 that the cumulative project cost after week 22 is $1.92 million. This is considerably less than Mr. Perty's *budgeted* cumulative project cost of $2.042 million given in cell AB23 of Fig. 10.15. Without any further information, this comparison would suggest an excellent cost performance for the project so far. However, the real reason for being under budget is that the current activities all are behind schedule and so have not yet incurred some expenses that had been scheduled to occur earlier. Fortunately, the PERT/Cost report provides valuable additional information that paints a truer picture of cost performance to date. By focusing on individual activities rather than the overall project, the report identifies the current trouble spots (activities F and I) that require Mr. Perty's immediate attention. Thus, the report enables him to take corrective action while there is still time to reverse these cost overruns.

10.7 AN EVALUATION OF PERT/CPM

PERT/CPM has stood the test of time. Despite being more than 40 years old, it continues to be one of the most widely used OR techniques. It is a standard tool of project managers.

The Value of PERT/CPM

Much of the value of PERT/CPM derives from the basic framework it provides for planning a project. Recall its planning steps: (1) Identify the activities that are needed to carry out the project. (2) Estimate how much time will be needed for each activity. (3) Determine the activities that must immediately precede each activity. (4) Develop the project network that visually displays the relationships between the activities. The discipline of going through these steps forces the needed planning to be done.

The scheduling information generated by PERT/CPM also is vital to the project manager. When can each activity begin if there are no delays? How much delay in an activity can be tolerated without delaying project completion? What is the critical path of activities where no delay can be tolerated? What is the effect of uncertainty in activity times? What is the probability of meeting the project deadline under the current plan? PERT/CPM provides the answers.

PERT/CPM also assists the project manager in other ways. Schedule and budget are key concerns. The CPM method of time-cost trade-offs enables investigating ways of reducing the duration of the project at an additional cost. PERT/Cost provides a systematic procedure for planning, scheduling, and controlling project costs.

In many ways, PERT/CPM exemplifies the application of OR at its finest. Its modeling approach focuses on the key features of the problem (activities, precedence relationships, time, and cost) without getting mired down in unimportant details. The resulting model (a project network and an optional linear programming formulation) are easy to understand and apply. It addresses the issues that are important to management (planning, scheduling, dealing with uncertainty, time-cost trade-offs, and controlling costs). It assists the project manager in dealing with these issues in useful ways and in a timely manner.

Using the Computer

PERT/CPM continues to evolve to meet new needs. At its inception over 40 years ago, it was largely executed manually. The project network sometimes was spread out over the walls of the project manager. Recording changes in the plan became a major task. Communicating changes to crew supervisors and subcontractors was cumbersome. The computer has changed all of that.

For many years now, PERT/CPM has become highly computerized. There has been a remarkable growth in the number and power of software packages for PERT/CPM that run on personal computers or workstations. *Project management software* (for example, Microsoft Project) now is a standard tool for project managers. This has enabled applications to numerous projects that each involve many millions of dollars and perhaps even thousands of activities. Possible revisions in the project plan now can be investigated almost instantaneously. Actual changes and the resulting updates in the schedule, etc., are recorded virtually effortlessly. Communications to all parties involved through computer networks and telecommunication systems also have become quick and easy.

Nevertheless, PERT/CPM still is not a panacea. It has certain major deficiencies for some applications. We briefly describe each of these deficiencies below along with how it is being addressed through research on improvements or extensions to PERT/CPM.

Approximating the Means and Variances of Activity Durations

The PERT three-estimate approach described in Sec. 10.4 provides a straightforward procedure for approximating the mean and variance of the probability distribution of the duration of each activity. Recall that this approach involved obtaining a most likely estimate, an optimistic estimate, and a pessimistic estimate of the duration. Given these three estimates, simple formulas were given for approximating the mean and variance. The means and variances for the various activities then were used to estimate the probability of completing the project by a specified time.

Unfortunately, considerable subsequent research has shown that this approach tends to provide a pretty rough approximation of the mean and variance. Part of the difficulty lies in aiming the optimistic and pessimistic estimates at the *endpoints* of the probability distribution. These endpoints correspond to very rare events (the best and worst that could ever occur) that typically are outside the estimator's realm of experience. The accuracy and reliability of such estimates are not as good as for points that are not at the extremes of the probability distribution. For example, research has demonstrated that much better estimates can be obtained by aiming them at the 10 and 90 percent points of the probability distribution. The optimistic and pessimistic estimates then would be described in terms of having 1 chance in 10 of doing better or 1 chance in 10 of doing worse. The middle estimate also can be improved by aiming it at the 50 percent point (the median value) of the probability distribution.

Revising the definitions of the three estimates along these lines leads to considerably more complicated formulas for the mean and variance of the duration of an activity. However, this is no problem since the analysis is computerized anyway. The important consideration is that much better approximations of the mean and variance are obtained in this way.[1]

Approximating the Probability of Meeting the Deadline

Of all the assumptions and simplifying approximations made by PERT/CPM, one is particularly controversial. This is Simplifying Approximation 1 in Sec. 10.4, which assumes that the *mean critical path* will turn out to be the longest path through the project network. This approximation greatly simplifies the calculation of the approximate probability of completing the project by a specified deadline. Unfortunately, in reality, there usually is a significant chance, and sometimes a very substantial chance, that some other path or paths will turn out to be longer than the mean critical path. Consequently, the calculated probability of meeting the deadline usually overstates the true probability somewhat. PERT/CPM provides no information on the likely size of the error. (Research has found that the error often is modest, but can be very large.) Thus, the project manager who relies on the calculated probability can be badly misled.

Considerable research has been conducted to develop more accurate (albeit more complicated) analytical approximations of this probability. Of special interest are methods that provide both upper and lower bounds on the probability.[2]

Another alternative is to use the technique of simulation described in Chap. 22 to approximate this probability. This appears to be the most commonly used method in prac-

---

[1]For further information, see, for example, D. L. Keefer and W. A. Verdini, "Better Estimation of PERT Activity Time Parameters," *Management Science,* **39**: 1086–1091, Sept. 1993. Also see A. H.-L. Lau, H.-S. Lau, and Y. Zhang, "A Simple and Logical Alternative for Making PERT Time Estimates," *IIE Transactions,* **28**: 183–192, March 1996.

[2]See, for example, J. Kamburowski, "Bounding the Distribution of Project Duration in PERT Networks," *Operations Research Letters,* **12**: 17–22, July 1992.

tice (when any is used) to improve upon the PERT/CPM approximation. We describe in Sec. 22.6 how this would be done for the Reliable Construction Co. project.

Dealing with Overlapping Activities

Another key assumption of PERT/CPM is that an activity cannot begin until all its immediate predecessors are completely finished. Although this may appear to be a perfectly reasonable assumption, it too is sometimes only a rough approximation of reality.

For example, in the Reliable Construction Co. project, consider activity H (do the exterior painting) and its immediate predecessor, activity G (put up the exterior siding). Naturally, this painting cannot begin until the exterior siding is there on which to paint. However, it certainly is possible to begin painting on one wall while the exterior siding still is being put up to form the other walls. Thus, activity H actually can begin before activity G is completely finished. Although careful coordination is needed, this possibility to overlap activities can significantly reduce project duration below that predicted by PERT/CPM.

The **precedence diagramming method (PDM)** has been developed as an extension of PERT/CPM to deal with such overlapping activities.[1] PDM provides four options for the relationship between an activity and any one of its immediate predecessors.

Option 1: The activity cannot begin until the immediate predecessor has been in progress a certain amount of time.

Option 2: The activity cannot finish until a certain amount of time after the immediate predecessor has finished.

Option 3: The activity cannot finish until a certain amount of time after the immediate predecessor has started.

Option 4: The activity cannot begin until a certain amount of time after the immediate predecessor has finished. (Rather than overlapping the activities, note that this option creates a lag between them such as, for example, waiting for the paint to dry before beginning the activity that follows painting.)

Alternatively, the *certain amount of time* mentioned in each option also can be expressed as a certain percentage of the work content of the immediate predecessor.

After incorporating these options, PDM can be used much like PERT/CPM to determine earliest start times, latest start times, and the critical path and to investigate time-cost trade-offs, etc.

Although it adds considerable flexibility to PERT/CPM, PDM is neither as well known nor as widely used as PERT/CPM. This should gradually change.

Incorporating the Allocation of Resources to Activities

PERT/CPM assumes that each activity has available all the resources (money, personnel, equipment, etc.) needed to perform the activity in the normal way (or on a crashed basis). In actuality, many projects have only limited resources for which the activities must compete. A major challenge in planning the project then is to determine how the resources should be allocated to the activities.

---

[1]For an introduction to PDM, see pp. 136–144 in A. B. Badiru and P. S. Pulat, *Comprehensive Project Management: Integrating Optimization Models, Management Principles, and Computers,* Prentice-Hall, Englewood Cliffs, NJ, 1995.

Once the resources have been allocated, PERT/CPM can be applied in the usual way. However, it would be far better to combine the allocation of the resources with the kind of planning and scheduling done by PERT/CPM so as to strive simultaneously toward a desired objective. For example, a common objective is to allocate the resources so as to minimize the duration of the project.

Much research has been conducted (and is continuing) to develop the methodology for simultaneously allocating resources and scheduling the activities of a project. This subject is beyond the scope of this book, but considerable reading is available elsewhere.[1]

The Future

Despite its deficiencies, PERT/CPM undoubtedly will continue to be widely used for the foreseeable future. It provides the project manager with most of what he or she wants: structure, scheduling information, tools for controlling schedule (latest start times, slacks, the critical path, etc.) and controlling costs (PERT/Cost), as well as the flexibility to investigate time-cost trade-offs.

Even though some of the approximations involved with the PERT three-estimate approach are questionable, these inaccuracies ultimately may not be too important. Just the process of developing estimates of the duration of activities encourages effective interaction between the project manager and subordinates that leads to setting mutual goals for start times, activity durations, project duration, etc. Striving together toward these goals may make them self-fulfilling prophecies despite inaccuracies in the underlying mathematics that led to these goals.

Similarly, possibilities for a modest amount of overlapping of activities need not invalidate a schedule by PERT/CPM, despite its assumption that no overlapping can occur. Actually having a small amount of overlapping may just provide the slack needed to compensate for the "unexpected" delays that inevitably seem to slip into a schedule.

Even when needing to allocate resources to activities, just using common sense in this allocation and then applying PERT/CPM should be quite satisfactory for some projects.

Nevertheless, it is unfortunate that the kinds of improvements and extensions to PERT/CPM described in this section have not been incorporated much into practice to date. Old comfortable methods that have proved their value are not readily discarded, and it takes awhile to learn about and gain confidence in new, better methods. However, we anticipate that these improvements and extensions gradually will come into more widespread use as they prove their value as well. We also expect that the recent and current extensive research on techniques for project management and scheduling (much of it in Europe) will continue and will lead to further improvements in the future.

10.8   CONCLUSIONS

Ever since their inception in the late 1950s, PERT and CPM have been used extensively to assist project managers in planning, scheduling, and controlling their projects. Over time, these two techniques gradually have merged.

---

[1]See, for example, ibid., pp. 162–209. Also see L. Özdamar and G. Ulusay, "A Survey on the Resource-Constrained Project Scheduling Problem," *IIE Transactions,* **27:** 574–586, Oct. 1995.

The application of PERT/CPM begins by breaking the project down into its individual activities, identifying the immediate predecessors of each activity, and estimating the duration of each activity. A project network then is constructed to visually display all this information. The type of network that is becoming increasingly popular for this purpose is the activity-on-node (AON) project network, where each activity is represented by a node.

PERT/CPM generates a great deal of useful scheduling information for the project manager, including the earliest start time, the latest start time, and the slack for each activity. It also identifies the critical path of activities such that any delay along this path will delay project completion. Since the critical path is the longest path through the project network, its length determines the duration of the project, assuming all activities remain on schedule.

However, it is difficult for all activities to remain on schedule because there frequently is considerable uncertainty about what the duration of an activity will turn out to be. The PERT three-estimate approach addresses this situation by obtaining three different kinds of estimates (most likely, optimistic, and pessimistic) for the duration of each activity. This information is used to approximate the mean and variance of the probability distribution of this duration. It then is possible to approximate the probability that the project will be completed by the deadline.

The CPM method of time-cost trade-offs enables the project manager to investigate the effect on total cost of changing the estimated duration of the project to various alternative values. The data needed for this activity are the time and cost for each activity when it is done in the normal way and then when it is fully crashed (expedited). Either marginal cost analysis or linear programming can be used to determine how much (if any) to crash each activity in order to minimize the total cost of meeting any specified deadline for the project.

The PERT/CPM technique called PERT/Cost provides the project manager with a systematic procedure for planning, scheduling, and controlling project costs. It generates a complete schedule for what the project costs should be in each time period when activities begin at either their earliest start times or latest start times. It also generates periodic reports that evaluate the cost performance of the individual activities, including identifying those where cost overruns are occurring.

PERT/CPM does have some important deficiencies. These include questionable approximations made when estimating the mean and variance of activity durations as well as when estimating the probability that the project will be completed by the deadline. Another deficiency is that it does not allow an activity to begin until all its immediate predecessors are completely finished, even though some overlap is sometimes possible. In addition, PERT/CPM does not address the important issue of how to allocate limited resources to the various activities.

Nevertheless, PERT/CPM has stood the test of time in providing project managers with most of the help they want. Furthermore, much progress is being made in developing improvements and extensions to PERT/CPM (such as the precedence diagramming method for dealing with overlapping activities) that addresses these deficiencies.

SELECTED REFERENCES

1. Badiru, A. B., and P. S. Pulat: *Comprehensive Project Management: Integrating Optimization Models, Management Principles, and Computers,* Prentice-Hall, Englewood Cliffs, NJ, 1995.

2. Dreger, J. B.: *Project Management,* Van Nostrand Reinhold, New York, 1992.
3. Tavares, L. V.: *Advanced Models for Project Management,* Kluwer Academic Publishers, Boston, 1999.
4. Weglarz, J. (ed.): *PROJECT SCHEDULING: Advances in Modeling, Algorithms, and Applications,* Kluwer Academic Publishers, Boston, 1999.

(Also see the references cited in the footnotes in Sec. 10.7.)

LEARNING AIDS FOR THIS CHAPTER IN YOUR OR COURSEWARE

"Ch. 10—Project Management" Files:

Excel File
LINGO/LINDO File
MPL/CPLEX File

Excel Templates in Excel File:

Template for PERT Three-Estimate Approach (labeled PERT)
Template for PERT/Cost (labeled PERT Cost)

An Excel Add-in:

Premium Solver

Special Software:

MS Project

MS Project Folder:

Reliable's Schedule
Reliable's Three-Estimate Data
Reliable's Schedule of Costs Based on Earliest Start Times

See Appendix 1 for documentation of the software.

PROBLEMS

The symbols to the left of some of the problems (or their parts) have the following meaning:

P: Although this problem can be done by hand, another available option is to use MS Project. Your instructor may specify which option to use (or both).
T: The corresponding template listed above may be helpful.
C: Use the computer with any of the software options available to you (or as instructed by your instructor) to solve the problem.

An asterisk on the problem number indicates that at least a partial answer is given in the back of the book.

P **10.2-1.** Christine Phillips is in charge of planning and coordinating next spring's sales management training program for her company. Christine has listed the following activity information for this project:

Activity	Activity Description	Immediate Predecessors	Estimated Duration
A	Select location	—	2 weeks
B	Obtain speakers	—	3 weeks
C	Make speaker travel plans	A, B	2 weeks
D	Prepare and mail brochure	A, B	2 weeks
E	Take reservations	D	3 weeks

Construct the project network for this project.

P **10.2-2.*** Reconsider Prob. 10.2-1. Christine has done more detailed planning for this project and so now has the following expanded activity list:

Activity	Activity Description	Immediate Predecessors	Estimated Duration
A	Select location	—	2 weeks
B	Obtain keynote speaker	—	1 week
C	Obtain other speakers	B	2 weeks
D	Make travel plans for keynote speaker	A, B	2 weeks
E	Make travel plans for other speakers	A, C	3 weeks
F	Make food arrangements	A	2 weeks
G	Negotiate hotel rates	A	1 week
H	Prepare brochure	C, G	1 week
I	Mail brochure	H	1 week
J	Take reservations	I	3 weeks
K	Prepare handouts	C, F	4 weeks

Construct the new project network.

P **10.2-3.** Construct the project network for a project with the following activity list.

Activity	Immediate Predecessors	Estimated Duration
A	—	1 month
B	A	2 months
C	B	4 months
D	B	3 months
E	B	2 months
F	C	3 months
G	D, E	5 months
H	F	1 month
I	G, H	4 months
J	I	2 months
K	I	3 months
L	J	3 months
M	K	5 months
N	L	4 months

10.3-1. You and several friends are about to prepare a lasagna dinner. The tasks to be performed, their immediate predecessors, and their estimated durations are as follows:

Task	Task Description	Tasks that Must Precede	Time
A	Buy the mozzarella cheese*		30 minutes
B	Slice the mozzarella	A	5 minutes
C	Beat 2 eggs		2 minutes
D	Mix eggs and ricotta cheese	C	3 minutes
E	Cut up onions and mushrooms		7 minutes
F	Cook the tomato sauce	E	25 minutes
G	Boil large quantity of water		15 minutes
H	Boil the lasagna noodles	G	10 minutes
I	Drain the lasagna noodles	H	2 minutes
J	Assemble all the ingredients	I, F, D, B	10 minutes
K	Preheat the oven		15 minutes
L	Bake the lasagna	J, K	30 minutes

*There is none in the refrigerator.

P **(a)** Construct the project network for preparing this dinner.
(b) Find all the paths and path lengths through this project network. Which of these paths is a critical path?
(c) Find the earliest start time and earliest finish time for each activity.
(d) Find the latest start time and latest finish time for each activity.
(e) Find the slack for each activity. Which of the paths is a critical path?
(f) Because of a phone call, you were interrupted for 6 minutes when you should have been cutting the onions and mushrooms. By how much will the dinner be delayed? If you use your food processor, which reduces the cutting time from 7 to 2 minutes, will the dinner still be delayed?

10.3-2. Consider Christine Phillip's project involving planning and coordinating next spring's sales management training program for her company as described in Prob. 10.2-1. After constructing the project network, she now is ready for the following steps.
(a) Find all the paths and path lengths through this project network. Which of these paths is a critical path?
(b) Find the earliest times, latest times, and slack for each activity. Use this information to determine which of the paths is a critical path.
(c) It is now one week later, and Christine is ahead of schedule. She has already selected a location for the sales meeting, and all the other activities are right on schedule. Will this shorten the length of the project? Why or why not?

10.3-3. Refer to the activity list given in Prob. 10.2-2 as Christine Phillips does more detailed planning for next spring's sales management training program for her company. After constructing the project network (described in the back of the book as the answer for Prob. 10.2-2), she now is ready for the following steps.

(a) Find all the paths and path lengths through this project network. Which of these paths is a critical path?
(b) Find the earliest times, latest times, and slack for each activity. Use this information to determine which of the paths is a critical path.
(c) It is now one week later, and Christine is ahead of schedule. She has already selected a location for the sales meeting, and all the other activities are right on schedule. Will this shorten the length of the project? Why or why not?

10.3-4.* Ken Johnston, the data processing manager for Stanley Morgan Bank, is planning a project to install a new management information system. He now is ready to start the project, and wishes to finish in 20 weeks. After identifying the 14 separate activities needed to carry out this project, as well as their precedence relationships and estimated durations (in weeks), Ken has constructed the following project network:

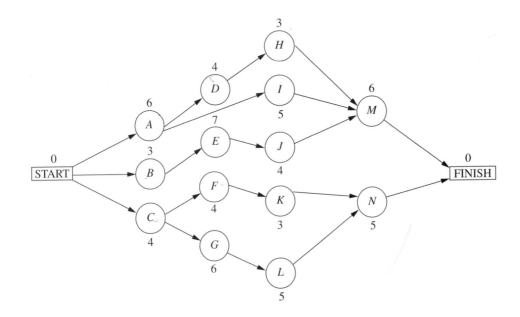

(a) Find all the paths and path lengths through this project network. Which of these paths is a critical path?
(b) Find the earliest times, latest times, and slack for each activity. Will Ken be able to meet his deadline if no delays occur?
(c) Use the information from part (b) to determine which of the paths is a critical path. What does this tell Ken about which activities he should focus most of his attention on for staying on schedule?
(d) Use the information from part (b) to determine what the duration of the project would be if the only delay is that activity I takes 2 extra weeks. What if the only delay is that activity H takes 2 extra weeks? What if the only delay is that activity J takes 2 extra weeks?

10.3-5. You are given the following information about a project consisting of six activities:

Activity	Immediate Predecessors	Estimated Duration
A	—	5 months
B	—	1 month
C	B	2 months
D	A, C	4 months
E	A	6 months
F	D, E	3 months

P (a) Construct the project network for this project.
(b) Find the earliest times, latest times, and slack for each activity. Which of the paths is a critical path?
(c) If all other activities take the estimated amount of time, what is the maximum duration of activity D without delaying the completion of the project?

10.3-6. Reconsider the Reliable Construction Co. project introduced in Sec. 10.1, including the complete project network obtained in Fig. 10.7 at the end of Sec. 10.3. Note that the estimated durations of the activities in this figure turn out to be the same as the mean durations given in Table 10.4 (Sec. 10.4) when using the PERT three-estimate approach.

Now suppose that the *pessimistic* estimates in Table 10.4 are used instead to provide the estimated durations in Fig. 10.7. Find the new earliest times, latest times, and slacks for all the activities in this project network. Also identify the critical path and the total estimated duration of the project. (Table 10.5 provides some clues.)

10.3-7.* Follow the instructions for Prob. 10.3-6 except use the *optimistic* estimates in Table 10.4 instead.

10.3-8. Follow the instructions for Prob. 10.3-6 except use the *crash times* given in Table 10.7 (Sec. 10.5) instead.

10.4-1.* Using the PERT three-estimate approach, the three estimates for one of the activities are as follows: optimistic estimate = 30 days, most likely estimate = 36 days, pessimistic estimate = 48 days. What are the resulting estimates of the mean and variance of the duration of the activity?

10.4-2. Alfred Lowenstein is the president of the research division for Better Health, Inc., a major pharmaceutical company. His most important project coming up is the development of a new drug to combat AIDS. He has identified 10 groups in his division which will need to carry out different phases of this research and development project. Referring to the work to be done by the respective groups as activities $A, B, \ldots, J$, the precedence relationships for when these groups need to do their work are shown in the following project network.

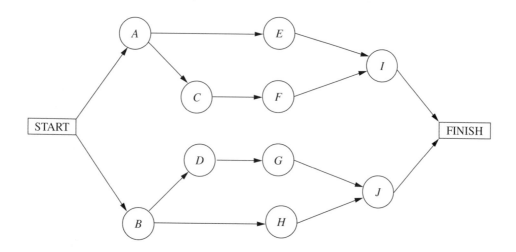

To beat the competition, Better Health's CEO has informed Alfred that he wants the drug ready within 22 months if possible.

Alfred knows very well that there is considerable uncertainty about how long each group will need to do its work. Using the PERT three-estimate approach, the manager of each group has provided a most likely estimate, an optimistic estimate, and a pessimistic estimate of the duration of that group's activity. Using PERT formulas, these estimates now have been converted into estimates of the mean and variance of the probability distribution of the duration of each group's activity, as given in the following table (after rounding to the nearest integer).

	Duration	
Activity	**Estimated Mean**	**Estimated Variance**
A	4 months	5 months
B	6 months	10 months
C	4 months	8 months
D	3 months	6 months
E	8 months	12 months
F	4 months	6 months
G	3 months	5 months
H	7 months	14 months
I	5 months	8 months
J	5 months	7 months

T (a) Find the mean critical path for this project.

T (b) Use this mean critical path to find the approximate probability that the project will be completed within 22 months.

T (c) Now consider the other three paths through this project network. For each of these paths, find the approximate probability that the path will be completed within 22 months.

(d) What should Alfred tell his CEO about the likelihood that the drug will be ready within 22 months?

T **10.4-3.** Reconsider Prob. 10.4-2. For each of the 10 activities, here are the three estimates that led to the estimates of the mean and variance of the duration of the activity (rounded to the nearest integer) given in the table for Prob. 10.4-2.

Activity	Optimistic Estimate	Most Likely Estimate	Pessimistic Estimate
A	1.5 months	2 months	15 months
B	2 months	3.5 months	21 months
C	1 month	1.5 months	18 months
D	0.5 month	1 month	15 months
E	3 months	5 months	24 months
F	1 month	2 months	16 months
G	0.5 month	1 month	14 months
H	2.5 months	3.5 months	25 months
I	1 month	3 months	18 months
J	2 months	3 months	18 months

(Note how the great uncertainty in the duration of these research activities causes each pessimistic estimate to be several times larger than either the optimistic estimate or the most likely estimate.)

Now use the Excel template in your OR Courseware (as depicted in Fig. 10.10) to help you carry out the instructions for Prob. 10.4-2. In particular, enter the three estimates for each activity, and the template immediately will display the estimates of the means and variances of the activity durations. After indicating each path of interest, the template also will display the approximate probability that the path will be completed within 22 months.

10.4-4. Bill Fredlund, president of Lincoln Log Construction, is considering placing a bid on a building project. Bill has determined that five tasks would need to be performed to carry out the proj-

ect. Using the PERT three-estimate approach, Bill has obtained the estimates in the table below for how long these tasks will take. Also shown are the precedence relationships for these tasks.

Task	Time Required			Immediate Predecessors
	Optimistic Estimate	Most Likely Estimate	Pessimistic Estimate	
A	3 weeks	4 weeks	5 weeks	—
B	2 weeks	2 weeks	2 weeks	A
C	3 weeks	5 weeks	6 weeks	B
D	1 week	3 weeks	5 weeks	A
E	2 weeks	3 weeks	5 weeks	B, D

There is a penalty of $500,000 if the project is not completed in 11 weeks. Therefore, Bill is very interested in how likely it is that his company could finish the project in time.

P (a) Construct the project network for this project.

T (b) Find the estimate of the mean and variance of the duration of each activity.

(c) Find the mean critical path.

T (d) Find the approximate probability of completing the project within 11 weeks.

(e) Bill has concluded that the bid he would need to make to have a realistic chance of winning the contract would earn Lincoln Log Construction a profit of about $250,000 if the project is completed within 11 weeks. However, because of the penalty for missing this deadline, his company would lose about $250,000 if the project takes more than 11 weeks. Therefore, he wants to place the bid only if he has at least a 50 percent chance of meeting the deadline. How would you advise him?

10.4-5.* Sharon Lowe, vice president for marketing for the Electronic Toys Company, is about to begin a project to design an advertising campaign for a new line of toys. She wants the project completed within 57 days in time to launch the advertising campaign at the beginning of the Christmas season.

Sharon has identified the six activities (labeled A, B, . . . , F) needed to execute this project. Considering the order in which these activities need to occur, she also has constructed the following project network.

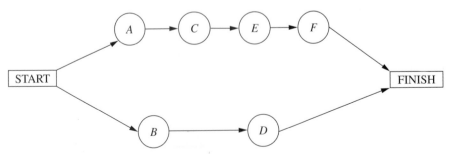

Using the PERT three-estimate approach, Sharon has obtained the following estimates of the duration of each activity.

Activity	Optimistic Estimate	Most Likely Estimate	Pessimistic Estimate
A	12 days	12 days	12 days
B	15 days	21 days	39 days
C	12 days	15 days	18 days
D	18 days	27 days	36 days
E	12 days	18 days	24 days
F	2 days	5 days	14 days

T **(a)** Find the estimate of the mean and variance of the duration of each activity.

(b) Find the mean critical path.

T **(c)** Use the mean critical path to find the approximate probability that the advertising campaign will be ready to launch within 57 days.

T **(d)** Now consider the other path through the project network. Find the approximate probability that this path will be completed within 57 days.

(e) Since these paths do not overlap, a better estimate of the probability that the project will finish within 57 days can be obtained as follows. The project will finish within 57 days if *both* paths are completed within 57 days. Therefore, the approximate probability that the project will finish within 57 days is the *product* of the probabilities found in parts (c) and (d). Perform this calculation. What does this answer say about the accuracy of the standard procedure used in part (c)?

10.4-6. The Lockhead Aircraft Co. is ready to begin a project to develop a new fighter airplane for the U.S. Air Force. The company's contract with the Department of Defense calls for project completion within 100 weeks, with penalties imposed for late delivery.

The project involves 10 activities (labeled A, B, . . . , J), where their precedence relationships are shown in the following project network.

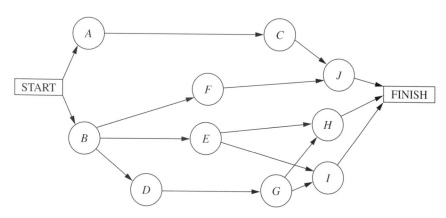

Using the PERT three-estimate approach, the usual three estimates of the duration of each activity have been obtained as given below.

Activity	Optimistic Estimate	Most Likely Estimate	Pessimistic Estimate
A	28 weeks	32 weeks	36 weeks
B	22 weeks	28 weeks	32 weeks
C	26 weeks	36 weeks	46 weeks
D	14 weeks	16 weeks	18 weeks
E	32 weeks	32 weeks	32 weeks
F	40 weeks	52 weeks	74 weeks
G	12 weeks	16 weeks	24 weeks
H	16 weeks	20 weeks	26 weeks
I	26 weeks	34 weeks	42 weeks
J	12 weeks	16 weeks	30 weeks

T **(a)** Find the estimate of the mean and variance of the duration of each activity.

(b) Find the mean critical path.

T **(c)** Find the approximate probability that the project will finish within 100 weeks.

(d) Is the approximate probability obtained in part (c) likely to be higher or lower than the true value?

10.4-7. Label each of the following statements about the PERT three-estimate approach as true or false, and then justify your answer by referring to specific statements (with page citations) in the chapter.

(a) Activity durations are assumed to be no larger than the optimistic estimate and no smaller than the pessimistic estimate.

(b) Activity durations are assumed to have a normal distribution.

(c) The mean critical path is assumed to always require the minimum elapsed time of any path through the project network.

10.5-1. The Tinker Construction Company is ready to begin a project that must be completed in 12 months. This project has four activities (*A, B, C, D*) with the project network shown below.

The project manager, Sean Murphy, has concluded that he cannot meet the deadline by performing all these activities in the normal way. Therefore, Sean has decided to use the CPM method of time-

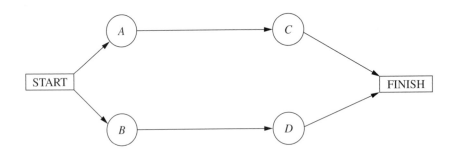

cost trade-offs to determine the most economical way of crashing the project to meet the deadline. He has gathered the following data for the four activities.

Activity	Normal Time	Crash Time	Normal Cost	Crash Cost
A	8 months	5 months	$25,000	$40,000
B	9 months	7 months	$20,000	$30,000
C	6 months	4 months	$16,000	$24,000
D	7 months	4 months	$27,000	$45,000

Use marginal cost analysis to solve the problem.

10.5-2. Reconsider the Tinker Construction Co. problem presented in Prob. 10.5-1. While in college, Sean Murphy took an OR course that devoted a month to linear programming, so Sean has decided to use linear programming to analyze this problem.

(a) Consider the upper path through the project network. Formulate a two-variable linear programming model for the problem of how to minimize the cost of performing this sequence of activities within 12 months. Use the graphical method to solve this model.

(b) Repeat part (*a*) for the lower path through the project network.

(c) Combine the models in parts (*a*) and (*b*) into a single complete linear programming model for the problem of how to minimize the cost of completing the project within 12 months. What must an optimal solution for this model be?

(d) Use the CPM linear programming formulation presented in Sec. 10.5 to formulate a complete model for this problem. [This model is a little larger than the one in part (*c*) because this method of formulation is applicable to more complicated project networks as well.]

C (e) Use Excel to solve this problem.

C (f) Use another software option to solve this problem.

C (g) Check the effect of changing the deadline by repeating part (*e*) or (*f*) with the deadline of 11 months and then with a deadline of 13 months.

10.5-3. Reconsider the Electronic Toys Co. problem presented in Prob. 10.4-5. Sharon Lowe is concerned that there is a significant chance that the vitally important deadline of 57 days will not be met. Therefore, to make it virtually certain that the deadline will be met, she has decided to crash the project, using the CPM method of time-cost trade-offs to determine how to do this in the most economical way.

Sharon now has gathered the data needed to apply this method, as given below.

Activity	Normal Time	Crash Time	Normal Cost	Crash Cost
A	12 days	9 days	$210,000	$270,000
B	23 days	18 days	$410,000	$460,000
C	15 days	12 days	$290,000	$320,000
D	27 days	21 days	$440,000	$500,000
E	18 days	14 days	$350,000	$410,000
F	6 days	4 days	$160,000	$210,000

The normal times are the estimates of the means obtained from the original data in Prob. 10.4-5. The mean critical path gives an estimate that the project will finish in 51 days. However, Sharon knows from the earlier analysis that some of the pessimistic estimates are far larger than the means, so the project duration might be considerably longer than 51 days. Therefore, to better ensure that the project will finish within 57 days, she has decided to require that the estimated project duration based on means (as used throughout the CPM analysis) must not exceed 47 days.

(a) Consider the lower path through the project network. Use marginal cost analysis to determine the most economical way of reducing the length of this path to 47 days.

(b) Repeat part (*a*) for the upper path through the project network. What is the total crashing cost for the optimal way of decreasing estimated project duration of 47 days?

C **(c)** Use Excel to solve the problem.

C **(d)** Use another software option to solve the problem.

10.5-4.* Good Homes Construction Company is about to begin the construction of a large new home. The company's President, Michael Dean, is currently planning the schedule for this project. Michael has identified the five major activities (labeled *A, B, . . . , E*) that will need to be performed according to the following project network.

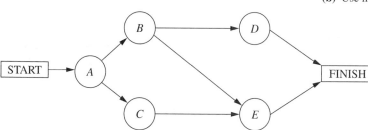

He also has gathered the following data about the normal point and crash point for each of these activities.

Activity	Normal Time	Crash Time	Normal Cost	Crash Cost
A	3 weeks	2 weeks	$54,000	$60,000
B	4 weeks	3 weeks	$62,000	$65,000
C	5 weeks	2 weeks	$66,000	$70,000
D	3 weeks	1 week	$40,000	$43,000
E	4 weeks	2 weeks	$75,000	$80,000

These costs reflect the company's direct costs for the material, equipment, and direct labor required to perform the activities. In addition, the company incurs indirect project costs such as supervision and other customary overhead costs, interest charges for capital tied up, and so forth. Michael estimates that these indirect costs run $5,000 per week. He wants to minimize the overall cost of the project. Therefore, to save some of these indirect costs, Michael concludes that he should shorten the project by doing some crashing to the extent that the crashing cost for each additional week saved is less than $5,000.

(a) To prepare for analyzing the effect of crashing, find the earliest times, latest times, and slack for each activity when they are done in the normal way. Also identify the corresponding critical path(s) and project duration.

(b) Use marginal cost analysis to determine which activities should be crashed and by how much to minimize the overall cost of the project. Under this plan, what is the duration and cost of each activity? How much money is saved by doing this crashing?

C **(c)** Now use the linear programming approach to do part (*b*) by shortening the deadline 1 week at a time from the project duration found in part (*a*).

10.5-5.* The 21st Century Studios is about to begin the production of its most important (and most expensive) movie of the year. The movie's producer, Dusty Hoffmer, has decided to use PERT/CPM to help plan and control this key project. He has identified the eight major activities (labeled *A, B, . . . , H*) required to produce the movie. Their precedence relationships are shown in the project network below.

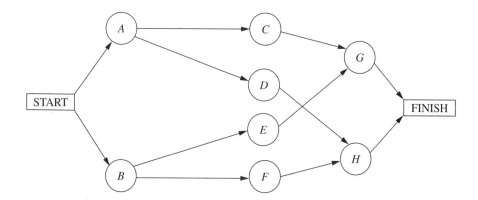

Dusty now has learned that another studio also will be coming out with a blockbuster movie during the middle of the upcoming summer, just when his movie was to be released. This would be very unfortunate timing. Therefore, he and the top management of 21st Century Studios have concluded that they must accelerate production of their movie and bring it out at the beginning of the summer (15 weeks from now) to establish it as THE movie of the year. Although this will require substantially increasing an already huge budget, management feels that this will pay off in much larger box office earnings both nationally and internationally.

Dusty now wants to determine the least costly way of meeting the new deadline 15 weeks hence. Using the CPM method of time-cost trade-offs, he has obtained the following data.

Activity	Normal Time	Crash Time	Normal Cost	Crash Cost
A	5 weeks	3 weeks	$20 million	$30 million
B	3 weeks	2 weeks	$10 million	$20 million
C	4 weeks	2 weeks	$16 million	$24 million
D	6 weeks	3 weeks	$25 million	$43 million
E	5 weeks	4 weeks	$22 million	$30 million
F	7 weeks	4 weeks	$30 million	$48 million
G	9 weeks	5 weeks	$25 million	$45 million
H	8 weeks	6 weeks	$30 million	$44 million

(a) Formulate a linear programming model for this problem.
C (b) Use Excel to solve the problem.
C (c) Use another software option to solve the problem.

10.5-6. Reconsider the Lockhead Aircraft Co. problem presented in Prob. 10.4-6 regarding a project to develop a new fighter airplane for the U.S. Air Force. Management is extremely concerned that current plans for this project have a substantial likelihood (roughly a probability of 0.5) of missing the deadline imposed in the Department of Defense contract to finish within 100 weeks. The company has a bad record of missing deadlines, and management is worried that doing so again would jeopardize obtaining future contracts for defense work. Furthermore, management would like to avoid the hefty penalties for missing the deadline in the current contract. Therefore, the decision has been made to crash the project, using the CPM method of time-cost trade-offs to determine how to do this in the most economical way. The data needed to apply this method are given next.

Activity	Normal Time	Crash Time	Normal Cost	Crash Cost
A	32 weeks	28 weeks	$160 million	$180 million
B	28 weeks	25 weeks	$125 million	$146 million
C	36 weeks	31 weeks	$170 million	$210 million
D	16 weeks	13 weeks	$ 60 million	$ 72 million
E	32 weeks	27 weeks	$135 million	$160 million
F	54 weeks	47 weeks	$215 million	$257 million
G	17 weeks	15 weeks	$ 90 million	$ 96 million
H	20 weeks	17 weeks	$120 million	$132 million
I	34 weeks	30 weeks	$190 million	$226 million
J	18 weeks	16 weeks	$ 80 million	$ 84 million

These normal times are the rounded estimates of the means obtained from the original data in Prob. 10.4-6. The corresponding mean critical path provides an estimate that the project will finish in 100 weeks. However, management understands well that the high variability of activity durations means that the actual duration of the project may be much longer. Therefore, the decision is made to require that the estimated project duration based on means (as used throughout the CPM analysis) must not exceed 92 weeks.
(a) Formulate a linear programming model for this problem.
C (b) Use Excel to solve the problem.
C (c) Use another software option to solve the problem.

10.6-1. Reconsider Prob. 10.5-4 involving the Good Homes Construction Co. project to construct a large new home. Michael Dean now has generated the plan for how to crash this project (as given as an answer in the back of the book). Since this plan causes all three paths through the project network to be critical paths, the earliest start time for each activity also is its latest start time.

Michael has decided to use PERT/Cost to schedule and control project costs.
(a) Find the earliest start time for each activity and the earliest finish time for the completion of the project.
(b) Construct a table like Table 10.10 to show the budget for this project.
(c) Construct a table like Fig. 10.15 (by hand) to show the schedule of costs based on earliest times for each of the 8 weeks of the project.
T (d) Now use the corresponding Excel template in your OR Courseware to do parts (b) and (c) on a single spreadsheet.
(e) After 4 weeks, activity A has been completed (with an actual cost of $65,000), and activity B has just now been completed (with an actual cost of $55,000), but activity C is just 33 percent completed (with an actual cost to date of $44,000). Construct a PERT/Cost report after week 4. Where should Michael concentrate his efforts to improve cost performances?

10.6-2.* The P-H Microchip Co. needs to undertake a major maintenance and renovation program to overhaul and modernize its facilities for wafer fabrication. This project involves six activities (labeled $A, B, \ldots, F$) with the precedence relationships shown in the following network.

The estimated durations and costs of these activities are shown below in the left column.

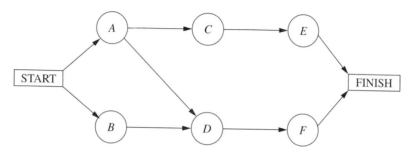

Activity	Estimated Duration	Estimated Cost
A	6 weeks	$420,000
B	2 weeks	$180,000
C	4 weeks	$540,000
D	5 weeks	$360,000
E	7 weeks	$590,000
F	9 weeks	$630,000

(a) Find the earliest times, latest times, and slack for each activity. What is the earliest finish time for the completion of the project?

T **(b)** Use the Excel template for PERT/Cost in your OR Courseware to display the budget and schedule of costs based on earliest start times for this project on a single spreadsheet.

T **(c)** Repeat part (b) except based on latest start times.

(d) Use these spreadsheets to draw a figure like Fig. 10.17 to show the schedule of cumulative project costs when all activities begin at their earliest start times or at their latest start times.

(e) After 4 weeks, activity B has been completed (with an actual cost of $200,000), activity A is 50 percent completed (with an actual cost to date of $200,000), and activity D is 50 percent completed (with an actual cost to date of $210,000). Construct a PERT/Cost report after week 4. Where should the project manager focus her attention to improve cost performances?

10.6-3. Reconsider Prob. 10.3-4 involving a project at Stanley Morgan Bank to install a new management information system. Ken Johnston already has obtained the earliest times, latest times, and slack for each activity (see a partial answer in the back of the book). He now is getting ready to use PERT/Cost to schedule and control the costs for this project. The estimated durations and costs of the various activities are given in the table on the right.

Activity	Estimated Duration	Estimated Cost
A	6 weeks	$180,000
B	3 weeks	$ 75,000
C	4 weeks	$120,000
D	4 weeks	$140,000
E	7 weeks	$175,000
F	4 weeks	$ 80,000
G	6 weeks	$210,000
H	3 weeks	$ 45,000
I	5 weeks	$125,000
J	4 weeks	$100,000
K	3 weeks	$ 60,000
L	5 weeks	$ 50,000
M	6 weeks	$ 90,000
N	5 weeks	$150,000

T **(a)** Use the Excel template for PERT/Cost in your OR Courseware to display the budget and schedule of costs based on earliest start times for this project on a single spreadsheet.

T **(b)** Repeat part (a) except based on latest start times.

(c) Use these spreadsheets to draw a figure like Fig. 10.17 to show the schedule of cumulative project costs when all activities begin at their earliest start times or at their latest start times.

(d) After 8 weeks, activities $A, B,$ and C have been completed with actual costs of $190,000, $70,000, and $150,000, respectively. Activities $D, E, F, G,$ and I are under way, with the percent completed being 40, 50, 60, 25, and 20 percent, respectively. Their actual costs to date are $70,000, $100,000, $45,000, $50,000, and $35,000, respectively. Construct a PERT/Cost report after week 8. Which activities should Ken Johnston investigate to try to improve their cost performances?

CASE 10.1   STEPS TO SUCCESS

Janet Richards fixes her eyes on those of her partner Gilbert Baker and says firmly, "All right. Let's do it."

And with those words, InterCat, a firm founded by Janet and Gilbert that specializes in the design and maintenance of Internet catalogs for small consumer businesses, will be going public. InterCat employs 30 individuals, with the majority of them computer programmers. Many of the employees have followed the high-technology market very closely and have decided that since high-technology firms are more understood and valued in the United States than in other countries, InterCat should issue its stock only in the United States. Five million shares of InterCat stock will comprise this new issue.

The task the company has ahead of itself is certainly daunting. Janet and Gilbert know that many steps have to be completed in the process of making an initial public offering. They also know that they need to complete the process within 28 weeks because they need the new capital fairly soon to ensure that InterCat has the resources to capture valuable new business from its competitors and continue growing. They also value a speedy initial public offering because they believe that the window of opportunity for obtaining a good stock price is presently wide open—the public is wild about shopping on the Internet, and few companies offering Web page design services have gone public.

Because the 28-week deadline is breathing down their necks, Janet and Gilbert decide to map the steps in the process of making an initial public offering. They list each major activity that needs to be completed, the activities that directly precede each activity, the time needed to complete each activity, and the cost of each activity. This list is shown below.

Activity	Preceding Activities	Time	Cost
Evaluate the prestige of each potential underwriter.		3 weeks	$ 8,000
Select a syndicate of underwriters.	Evaluate the prestige of each potential underwriter.	1.5 weeks	$ 4,500
Negotiate the commitment of each member of the syndicate.	Select a syndicate of underwriters.	2 weeks	$ 9,000
Negotiate the spread* for each member of the syndicate.	Select a syndicate of underwriters.	3 weeks	$12,000
Prepare the registration statement including the proposed financing and information about the firm's history, existing business, and plans for the future.	Negotiate both the commitment and spread for each member of the syndicate.	5 weeks	$50,000
Submit the registration statement to the Securities and Exchange Commission (SEC).	Prepare the registration statement.	1 week	$ 1,000

Activity	Preceding Activities	Time	Cost
Make presentations to institutional investors and develop the interest of potential buyers.	Submit the registration statement to the SEC.	6 weeks	$25,000
Distribute the preliminary prospectus affectionately termed the red herring.	Submit the registration statement to the SEC.	3 weeks	$15,000
Calculate the issue price.	Submit the registration statement to the SEC.	5 weeks	$12,000
Receive deficiency memorandum from the SEC.	Submit the registration statement to the SEC.	3 weeks	$ 0
Amend the registration statement and resubmit it to the SEC.	Receive deficiency memorandum from the SEC.	1 week	$ 6,000
Receive registration confirmation from the SEC.	Amend the registration statement and resubmit it to the SEC.	2 weeks	$ 0
Confirm that the new issue complies with the "blue sky" laws of each state.	Make presentations to institutional investors and develop the interest of potential buyers. Distribute the preliminary prospectus affectionately termed the red herring. Calculate the issue price. Receive registration confirmation from the SEC.	1 week	$ 5,000
Appoint a registrar.	Receive registration confirmation from the SEC.	3 weeks	$12,000
Appoint a transfer agent.	Receive registration confirmation from the SEC.	3.5 weeks	$13,000
Issue final prospectus that includes the final offer price and any amendments to all purchasers offered securities through the mail.	Confirm that the new issue complies with the "blue sky" laws of each state. Appoint a registrar and transfer agent.	4.5 weeks	$40,000
Phone interested buyers.	Confirm that the new issue complies with the "blue sky" laws of each state. Appoint a registrar and transfer agent.	4 weeks	$ 9,000

*The spread is the payment an underwriter receives for services.

Janet and Gilbert present the list of steps to the employees of InterCat. The head of the finance department, Leslie Grey, is fresh out of business school. She remembers the various project management tools she has learned in business school and suggests that Janet and Gilbert use PERT/CPM analysis to understand where their priorities should lie.

(a) Draw the project network for completing the initial public offering of InterCat stock. How long is the initial public offering process? What are the critical steps in the process?

(b) How would the change in the following activities affect the time to complete the initial public offering? Please evaluate each change independently.

(i) Some members of the syndicate are playing hardball. Therefore, the time it takes to negotiate the commitment of each member of the syndicate increases from 2 to 3 weeks.

(ii) The underwriters are truly math geniuses. Therefore, the time it takes to calculate the issue price decreases to 4 weeks.

(iii) Whoa! The SEC found many deficiencies in the initial registration statement. The underwriters must therefore spend 2.5 weeks amending the statement and resubmitting it to the SEC.

(iv) The new issue does not comply with the "blue sky" laws of a handful of states. The time it takes to edit the issue for each state to ensure compliance increases to 4 weeks.

(c) Janet and Gilbert hear through the grapevine that their most fierce competitor, Soft Sales, is also planning to go public. They fear that if InterCat does not complete its initial public offering before Soft Sales, the price investors are willing to pay for InterCat stock will drop, since investors will perceive Soft Sales to be a stronger, more organized company. Janet and Gilbert therefore decide that they want to complete the process of issuing new stock within 22 weeks. They think such a goal is possible if they throw more resources—workers and money—into some activities. They list the activities that can be shortened, the time the activity will take when it is fully shortened, and the cost of shortening the activity this much. They also conclude that partially shortening each activity listed below is possible and will give a time reduction and cost proportional to the amounts when fully shortening.

Activity	Time	Cost
Evaluate the prestige of each potential underwriter.	1.5 weeks	$14,000
Select a syndicate of underwriters.	0.5 week	$ 8,000
Prepare the registration statement including the proposed financing and information about the firm's history, existing business, and plans for the future.	4 weeks	$95,000
Make presentations to institutional investors and develop the interest of potential buyers.	4 weeks	$60,000
Distribute the preliminary prospectus affectionately termed the red herring.	2 weeks	$22,000
Calculate the issue price.	3.5 weeks	$31,000

Activity	Time	Cost
Amend the registration statement and resubmit it to the SEC.	0.5 week	$ 9,000
Confirm that the new issue complies with the "blue sky" laws of each state.	0.5 week	$ 8,300
Appoint a registrar.	1.5 weeks	$19,000
Appoint a transfer agent.	1.5 weeks	$21,000
Issue final prospectus that includes the final offer price and any amendments to all purchasers offered securities through the mail.	2 weeks	$99,000
Phone interested buyers.	1.5 weeks	$20,000

How can InterCat meet the new deadline set by Janet and Gilbert at minimum cost?

(d) Janet and Gilbert learn that the investment bankers are two-timing scoundrels! They are also serving as lead underwriters for the Soft Sales new issue! To keep the deal with InterCat, the bankers agree to let Janet and Gilbert in on a little secret. Soft Sales has been forced to delay its public issue because the company's records are disorganized and incomplete. Given this new information, Janet and Gilbert decide that they can be more lenient on the initial public offering timeframe. They want to complete the process of issuing new stock within 24 weeks instead of 22 weeks. Assume that the cost and time to complete the appointment of the registrar and transfer agent are the same as in part (c). How can InterCat meet this new deadline set by Janet and Gilbert at minimum cost?

CASE 10.2 "SCHOOL'S OUT FOREVER . . ."—Alice Cooper

Brent Bonnin begins his senior year of college filled with excitement and a twinge of fear. The excitement stems from his anticipation of being done with it all—professors, exams, problem sets, grades, group meetings, all-nighters. . . . The list could go on and on. The fear stems from the fact that he is graduating in December and has only 4 months to find a job.

Brent is a little unsure about how he should approach the job search. During his sophomore and junior years, he had certainly heard seniors talking about their strategies for finding the perfect job, and he knows that he should first visit the Campus Career Planning Center to devise a search plan.

On Sept. 1, the fist day of school, he walks through the doors of the Campus Career Planning Center and meets Elizabeth Merryweather, a recent graduate overflowing with energy and comforting smiles. Brent explains to Elizabeth that since he is graduating in December and plans to begin work in January, he wants to leave all of November and December open for interviews. Such a plan means that he has to have all his preliminary materials, such as cover letters and résumés, submitted to the companies where he wants to work by Oct. 31.

Elizabeth recognizes that Brent has to follow a very tight schedule, if he wants to meet his goal within the next 60 days. She suggests that the two of them sit down together and decide the major milestones that need to be completed in the job search process. Elizabeth and Brent list the 19 major milestones. For each of the 19 milestones, they identify the other milestones that must be accomplished directly before Brent can begin this next milestone. They also estimate the time needed to complete each milestone. The list is shown below.

Milestone	Milestones Directly Preceding Each Milestone	Time to Complete Each Milestone
A. Complete and submit an on-line registration form to the career center.	None.	2 days (This figure includes the time needed for the career center to process the registration form.)
B. Attend the career center orientation to learn about the resources available at the center and the campus recruiting process.	None.	5 days (This figure includes the time Brent must wait before the career center hosts an orientation.)
C. Write an initial résumé that includes all academic and career experiences.	None.	7 days
D. Search the Internet to find job opportunities available outside of campus recruiting.	None.	10 days
E. Attend the company presentations hosted during the fall to understand the cultures of companies and to meet with company representatives.	None.	25 days
F. Review the industry resources available at the career center to understand the career and growth opportunities available in each industry. Take career test to understand the career that provides the best fit with your skills and interests. Contact alumni listed in the career center directories to discuss the nature of a variety of jobs.	Complete and submit an on-line registration form to the career center. Attend the career center orientation.	7 days

Milestone	Milestones Directly Preceding Each Milestone	Time to Complete Each Milestone
G. Attend a mock interview hosted by the career center to practice interviewing and to learn effective interviewing styles.	Complete and submit an on-line registration form to the career center. Attend the career center orientation. Write the initial résumé.	4 days (This figure includes the time that elapses between the day that Brent signs up for the interview and the day that the interview takes place.)
H. Submit the initial résumé to the career center for review.	Complete and submit an on-line registration form to the career center. Attend the career center orientation. Write the initial résumé.	2 days (This figure includes the time the career center needs to review the résumé.)
I. Meet with a résumé expert to discuss improvements to the initial résumé.	Submit the initial résumé to the career center for review.	1 day
J. Revise the initial résumé.	Meet with a résumé expert to discuss improvements.	4 days
K. Attend the career fair to gather company literature, speak to company representatives, and submit résumés.	Revise the initial résumé.	1 day
L. Search campus job listings to identify the potential jobs that fit your qualifications and interests.	Review the industry resources, take the career test, and contact alumni.	5 days
M. Decide which jobs you will pursue given the job opportunities you found on the Internet, at the career fair, and through the campus job listings.	Search the Internet. Search the campus job listings. Attend the career fair.	3 days
N. Bid to obtain job interviews with companies that recruit through the campus career center and have open interview schedules.*	Decide which jobs you will pursue.	3 days

Milestone	Milestones Directly Preceding Each Milestone	Time to Complete Each Milestone
O. Write cover letters to seek jobs with companies that either do not recruit through the campus career center or recruit through the campus career center but have closed interview schedules.† Tailor each cover letter to the culture of each company.	Decide which jobs you will pursue. Attend company presentations.	10 days
P. Submit the cover letters to the career center for review.	Write the cover letters.	4 days (This figure includes the time the career center needs to review the cover letters.)
Q. Revise the cover letters.	Submit the cover letters to the career center for review.	4 days
R. For the companies that are not recruiting through the campus career center, mail the cover letter and résumé to the company's recruiting department.	Revise the cover letters.	6 days (This figure includes the time needed to print and package the application materials and the time needed for the materials to reach the companies.)
S. For the companies that recruit through the campus career center but that hold closed interview schedules, drop the cover letter and résumé at the career center.	Revise the cover letters	2 days (This figure includes the time needed to print and package the application materials).

*An open interview schedule occurs when the company does not select the candidates that it wants to interview. Any candidate may interview, but since the company has only a limited number of interview slots, interested candidates must bid points (out of their total allocation of points) for the interviews. The candidates with the highest bids win the interview slots.

†Closed interview schedules occur when a company requires candidates to submit their cover letters, résumés, and test scores so that the company is able to select the candidates it wants to interview.

In the evening after his meeting with Elizabeth, Brent meets with his buddies at the college coffeehouse to chat about their summer endeavors. Brent also tells his friends about the meeting he had earlier with Elizabeth. He describes the long to-do list he and Elizabeth developed and says that he is really worried about keeping track of all the major milestones and getting his job search organized. One of his friends reminds him of the cool OR class they all took together in the first semester of Brent's junior year, and how they had learned about some techniques to organize large projects. Brent remembers this class fondly, since he was able to use a number of the methods he studied in that class in his last summer job.

(a) Draw the project network for completing all milestones before the interview process. If everything stays on schedule, how long will it take Brent until he can start with the interviews? What are the critical steps in the process?

(b) Brent realizes that there is a lot of uncertainty in the times it will take him to complete some of the milestones. He expects to get really busy during his senior year, in particular since he is taking a demanding course load. Also, students sometimes have to wait quite a while before they get appointments with the counselors at the career center. In addition to the list estimating the most likely times that he and Elizabeth wrote down, he makes a list of optimistic and pessimistic estimates of how long the various milestones might take.

Milestone	Optimistic Estimate	Pessimistic Estimate
A	1 day	4 days
B	3 days	10 days
C	5 days	14 days
D	7 days	12 days
E	20 days	30 days
F	5 days	12 days
G	3 days	8 days
H	1 day	6 days
I	1 day	1 day
J	3 days	6 days
K	1 day	1 day
L	3 days	10 days
M	2 days	4 days
N	2 days	8 days
O	3 days	12 days
P	2 days	7 days
Q	3 days	9 days
R	4 days	10 days
S	1 day	3 days

How long will it take Brent to get done under the worst-case scenario? How long will it take if all his optimistic estimates are correct?

(c) Determine the mean critical path for Brent's job search process. What is the variance of the project duration?

(d) Give a rough estimate of the probability that Brent will be done within 60 days.

(e) Brent realizes that he has made a serious mistake in his calculations so far. He cannot schedule the career fair to fit his schedule. Brent read in the campus newspaper that the fair has been set 24 days from today on Sept. 25. Draw a revised project network that takes into account this complicating fact.

(f) What is the mean critical path for the new network? What is the probability that Brent will complete his project within 60 days?

11

Dynamic Programming

Dynamic programming is a useful mathematical technique for making a sequence of interrelated decisions. It provides a systematic procedure for determining the optimal combination of decisions.

In contrast to linear programming, there does not exist a standard mathematical formulation of "the" dynamic programming problem. Rather, dynamic programming is a general type of approach to problem solving, and the particular equations used must be developed to fit each situation. Therefore, a certain degree of ingenuity and insight into the general structure of dynamic programming problems is required to recognize when and how a problem can be solved by dynamic programming procedures. These abilities can best be developed by an exposure to a wide variety of dynamic programming applications and a study of the characteristics that are common to all these situations. A large number of illustrative examples are presented for this purpose.

11.1   A PROTOTYPE EXAMPLE FOR DYNAMIC PROGRAMMING

EXAMPLE 1   **The Stagecoach Problem**

The STAGECOACH PROBLEM is a problem specially constructed[1] to illustrate the features and to introduce the terminology of dynamic programming. It concerns a mythical fortune seeker in Missouri who decided to go west to join the gold rush in California during the mid-19th century. The journey would require traveling by stagecoach through unsettled country where there was serious danger of attack by marauders. Although his starting point and destination were fixed, he had considerable choice as to which states (or territories that subsequently became states) to travel through en route. The possible routes are shown in Fig. 11.1, where each state is represented by a circled letter and the direction of travel is always from left to right in the diagram. Thus, four stages (stagecoach runs) were required to travel from his point of embarkation in state *A* (Missouri) to his destination in state *J* (California).

This fortune seeker was a prudent man who was quite concerned about his safety. After some thought, he came up with a rather clever way of determining the safest route. Life

---

[1]This problem was developed by Professor Harvey M. Wagner while he was at Stanford University.

insurance policies were offered to stagecoach passengers. Because the cost of the policy for taking any given stagecoach run was based on a careful evaluation of the safety of that run, the safest route should be the one with the cheapest total life insurance policy.

The cost for the standard policy on the stagecoach run from state i to state j, which will be denoted by c_{ij}, is

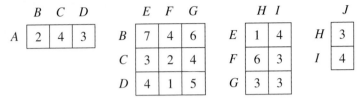

These costs are also shown in Fig. 11.1.

We shall now focus on the question of which route minimizes the total cost of the policy.

Solving the Problem

First note that the shortsighted approach of selecting the cheapest run offered by each successive stage need not yield an overall optimal decision. Following this strategy would give the route $A \rightarrow B \rightarrow F \rightarrow I \rightarrow J$, at a total cost of 13. However, sacrificing a little on one stage may permit greater savings thereafter. For example, $A \rightarrow D \rightarrow F$ is cheaper overall than $A \rightarrow B \rightarrow F$.

One possible approach to solving this problem is to use trial and error.[1] However, the number of possible routes is large (18), and having to calculate the total cost for each route is not an appealing task.

---

[1]This problem also can be formulated as a *shortest-path problem* (see Sec. 9.3), where *costs* here play the role of *distances* in the shortest-path problem. The algorithm presented in Sec. 9.3 actually uses the philosophy of dynamic programming. However, because the present problem has a fixed number of stages, the dynamic programming approach presented here is even better.

FIGURE 11.1
The road system and costs for the stagecoach problem.

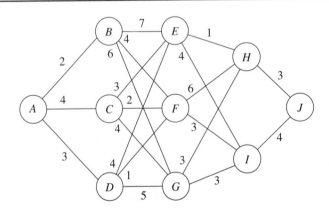

Fortunately, dynamic programming provides a solution with much less effort than exhaustive enumeration. (The computational savings are enormous for larger versions of this problem.) Dynamic programming starts with a small portion of the original problem and finds the optimal solution for this smaller problem. It then gradually enlarges the problem, finding the current optimal solution from the preceding one, until the original problem is solved in its entirety.

For the stagecoach problem, we start with the smaller problem where the fortune seeker has nearly completed his journey and has only one more stage (stagecoach run) to go. The obvious optimal solution for this smaller problem is to go from his current state (whatever it is) to his ultimate destination (state J). At each subsequent iteration, the problem is enlarged by increasing by 1 the number of stages left to go to complete the journey. For this enlarged problem, the optimal solution for where to go next from each possible state can be found relatively easily from the results obtained at the preceding iteration. The details involved in implementing this approach follow.

Formulation. Let the decision variables x_n ($n = 1, 2, 3, 4$) be the immediate destination on stage n (the nth stagecoach run to be taken). Thus, the route selected is $A \rightarrow x_1 \rightarrow x_2 \rightarrow x_3 \rightarrow x_4$, where $x_4 = J$.

Let $f_n(s, x_n)$ be the total cost of the best overall *policy* for the *remaining* stages, given that the fortune seeker is in state s, ready to start stage n, and selects x_n as the immediate destination. Given s and n, let x_n^* denote any value of x_n (not necessarily unique) that minimizes $f_n(s, x_n)$, and let $f_n^*(s)$ be the corresponding minimum value of $f_n(s, x_n)$. Thus,

$$f_n^*(s) = \min_{x_n} f_n(s, x_n) = f_n(s, x_n^*),$$

where

$$f_n(s, x_n) = \text{immediate cost (stage } n\text{)} + \text{minimum future cost (stages } n + 1 \text{ onward)}$$
$$= c_{sx_n} + f_{n+1}^*(x_n).$$

The value of c_{sx_n} is given by the preceding tables for c_{ij} by setting $i = s$ (the current state) and $j = x_n$ (the immediate destination). Because the ultimate destination (state J) is reached at the end of stage 4, $f_5^*(J) = 0$.

The objective is to find $f_1^*(A)$ and the corresponding route. Dynamic programming finds it by successively finding $f_4^*(s)$, $f_3^*(s)$, $f_2^*(s)$, for each of the possible states s and then using $f_2^*(s)$ to solve for $f_1^*(A)$.[1]

Solution Procedure. When the fortune seeker has only one more stage to go ($n = 4$), his route thereafter is determined entirely by his current state s (either H or I) and his final destination $x_4 = J$, so the route for this final stagecoach run is $s \rightarrow J$. Therefore, since $f_4^*(s) = f_4(s, J) = c_{s,J}$, the immediate solution to the $n = 4$ problem is

$n = 4$:	s	$f_4^*(s)$	x_4^*
	H	3	J
	I	4	J

[1] Because this procedure involves moving *backward* stage by stage, some writers also count n backward to denote the number of *remaining stages* to the destination. We use the more natural *forward counting* for greater simplicity.

When the fortune seeker has two more stages to go ($n = 3$), the solution procedure requires a few calculations. For example, suppose that the fortune seeker is in state F. Then, as depicted below, he must next go to either state H or I at an immediate cost of $c_{F,H} = 6$ or $c_{F,I} = 3$, respectively. If he chooses state H, the minimum additional cost after he reaches there is given in the preceding table as $f_4^*(H) = 3$, as shown above the H node in the diagram. Therefore, the total cost for this decision is $6 + 3 = 9$. If he chooses state I instead, the total cost is $3 + 4 = 7$, which is smaller. Therefore, the optimal choice is this latter one, $x_3^* = I$, because it gives the minimum cost $f_3^*(F) = 7$.

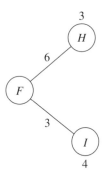

Similar calculations need to be made when you start from the other two possible states $s = E$ and $s = G$ with two stages to go. Try it, proceeding both graphically (Fig. 11.1) and algebraically [combining c_{ij} and $f_4^*(s)$ values], to verify the following complete results for the $n = 3$ problem.

		$f_3(s, x_3) = c_{sx_3} + f_4^*(x_3)$			
$n = 3$:	s	x_3		$f_3^*(s)$	x_3^*
		H	I		
	E	4	8	4	H
	F	9	7	7	I
	G	6	7	6	H

The solution for the second-stage problem ($n = 2$), where there are three stages to go, is obtained in a similar fashion. In this case, $f_2(s, x_2) = c_{sx_2} + f_3^*(x_2)$. For example, suppose that the fortune seeker is in state C, as depicted below.

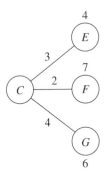

He must next go to state E, F, or G at an immediate cost of $c_{C,E} = 3$, $c_{C,F} = 2$, or $c_{C,G} = 4$, respectively. After getting there, the minimum additional cost for stage 3 to the end is given by the $n = 3$ table as $f_3^*(E) = 4$, $f_3^*(F) = 7$, or $f_3^*(G) = 6$, respectively, as shown above the E and F nodes and below the G node in the preceding diagram. The resulting calculations for the three alternatives are summarized below.

$$x_2 = E: \quad f_2(C, E) = c_{C,E} + f_3^*(E) = 3 + 4 = 7.$$
$$x_2 = F: \quad f_2(C, F) = c_{C,F} + f_3^*(F) = 2 + 7 = 9.$$
$$x_2 = G: \quad f_2(C, G) = c_{C,G} + f_3^*(G) = 4 + 6 = 10.$$

The minimum of these three numbers is 7, so the minimum total cost from state C to the end is $f_2^*(C) = 7$, and the immediate destination should be $x_2^* = E$.

Making similar calculations when you start from state B or D (try it) yields the following results for the $n = 2$ problem:

$n = 2$: s	$f_2(s, x_2) = c_{sx_2} + f_3^*(x_2)$			$f_2^*(s)$	x_2^*
	E	F	G		
B	11	11	12	11	E or F
C	7	9	10	7	E
D	8	8	11	8	E or F

In the first and third rows of this table, note that E and F tie as the minimizing value of x_2, so the immediate destination from either state B or D should be $x_2^* = E$ or F.

Moving to the first-stage problem ($n = 1$), with all four stages to go, we see that the calculations are similar to those just shown for the second-stage problem ($n = 2$), except now there is just *one* possible starting state $s = A$, as depicted below.

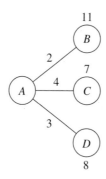

These calculations are summarized next for the three alternatives for the immediate destination:

$$x_1 = B: \quad f_1(A, B) = c_{A,B} + f_2^*(B) = 2 + 11 = 13.$$
$$x_1 = C: \quad f_1(A, C) = c_{A,C} + f_2^*(C) = 4 + 7 = 11.$$
$$x_1 = D: \quad f_1(A, D) = c_{A,D} + f_2^*(D) = 3 + 8 = 11.$$

Stage: 1   2   3   4

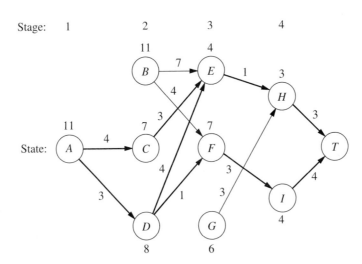

FIGURE 11.2
Graphical display of the dynamic programming solution of the stagecoach problem. Each arrow shows an optimal policy decision (the best immediate destination) from that state, where the number by the state is the resulting cost from there to the end. Following the boldface arrows from A to T gives the three optimal solutions (the three routes giving the minimum total cost of 11).

Since 11 is the minimum, $f_1^*(A) = 11$ and $x_1^* = C$ or D, as shown in the following table.

		$f_1(s, x_1) = c_{sx_1} + f_2^*(x_1)$				
$n = 1$:	s \\ x_1	B	C	D	$f_1^*(s)$	x_1^*
	A	13	11	11	11	C or D

An optimal solution for the entire problem can now be identified from the four tables. Results for the $n = 1$ problem indicate that the fortune seeker should go initially to either state C or state D. Suppose that he chooses $x_1^* = C$. For $n = 2$, the result for $s = C$ is $x_2^* = E$. This result leads to the $n = 3$ problem, which gives $x_3^* = H$ for $s = E$, and the $n = 4$ problem yields $x_4^* = J$ for $s = H$. Hence, one optimal route is $A \to C \to E \to H \to J$. Choosing $x_1^* = D$ leads to the other two optimal routes $A \to D \to E \to H \to J$ and $A \to D \to F \to I \to J$. They all yield a total cost of $f_1^*(A) = 11$.

These results of the dynamic programming analysis also are summarized in Fig. 11.2. Note how the two arrows for stage 1 come from the first and last columns of the $n = 1$ table and the resulting cost comes from the next-to-last column. Each of the other arrows (and the resulting cost) comes from one row in one of the other tables in just the same way.

You will see in the next section that the special terms describing the particular context of this problem—*stage, state,* and *policy*—actually are part of the general terminology of dynamic programming with an analogous interpretation in other contexts.

11.2   CHARACTERISTICS OF DYNAMIC PROGRAMMING PROBLEMS

The stagecoach problem is a literal prototype of dynamic programming problems. In fact, this example was purposely designed to provide a literal physical interpretation of the rather abstract structure of such problems. Therefore, one way to recognize a situation that can be formulated as a dynamic programming problem is to notice that its basic structure is analogous to the stagecoach problem.

These basic features that characterize dynamic programming problems are presented and discussed here.

1. The problem can be divided into **stages**, with a **policy decision** required at each stage.

   The stagecoach problem was literally divided into its four stages (stagecoaches) that correspond to the four legs of the journey. The policy decision at each stage was which life insurance policy to choose (i.e., which destination to select for the next stagecoach ride). Similarly, other dynamic programming problems require making a *sequence of interrelated decisions,* where each decision corresponds to one stage of the problem.

2. Each stage has a number of **states** associated with the beginning of that stage.

   The states associated with each stage in the stagecoach problem were the states (or territories) in which the fortune seeker could be located when embarking on that particular leg of the journey. In general, the states are the various *possible conditions* in which the system might be at that stage of the problem. The number of states may be either finite (as in the stagecoach problem) or infinite (as in some subsequent examples).

3. The effect of the policy decision at each stage is to *transform the current state to a state associated with the beginning of the next stage* (possibly according to a probability distribution).

   The fortune seeker's decision as to his next destination led him from his current state to the next state on his journey. This procedure suggests that dynamic programming problems can be interpreted in terms of the *networks* described in Chap. 9. Each *node* would correspond to a *state.* The network would consist of columns of nodes, with each *column* corresponding to a *stage,* so that the flow from a node can go only to a node in the next column to the right. The links from a node to nodes in the next column correspond to the possible policy decisions on which state to go to next. The value assigned to each link usually can be interpreted as the *immediate contribution* to the objective function from making that policy decision. In most cases, the objective corresponds to finding either the *shortest* or the *longest path* through the network.

4. The solution procedure is designed to find an **optimal policy** for the overall problem, i.e., a prescription of the optimal policy decision at each stage for *each* of the possible states.

   For the stagecoach problem, the solution procedure constructed a table for each stage (n) that prescribed the optimal decision (x_n^*) for *each* possible state (s). Thus, in addition to identifying three *optimal solutions* (optimal routes) for the overall problem, the results show the fortune seeker how he should proceed if he gets detoured to a state that is not on an optimal route. For any problem, dynamic programming provides this kind of *policy* prescription of what to do under every possible circumstance (which is why the actual decision made upon reaching a particular state at a given stage is referred to as a *policy* decision). Providing this additional information beyond simply specifying an optimal solution (optimal sequence of decisions) can be helpful in a variety of ways, including sensitivity analysis.

5. Given the current state, an *optimal policy for the remaining stages* is *independent* of the policy decisions adopted in *previous stages.* Therefore, the optimal immediate de-

cision depends on only the current state and not on how you got there. This is the **principle of optimality** for dynamic programming.

Given the state in which the fortune seeker is currently located, the optimal life insurance policy (and its associated route) from this point onward is independent of how he got there. For dynamic programming problems in general, knowledge of the current state of the system conveys all the information about its previous behavior necessary for determining the optimal policy henceforth. (This property is the *Markovian property,* discussed in Sec. 16.2.) Any problem lacking this property cannot be formulated as a dynamic programming problem.

6. The solution procedure begins by finding the *optimal policy for the last stage.*

The optimal policy for the last stage prescribes the optimal policy decision for *each* of the possible states at that stage. The solution of this one-stage problem is usually trivial, as it was for the stagecoach problem.

7. A **recursive relationship** that identifies the optimal policy for stage n, given the optimal policy for stage $n + 1$, is available.

For the stagecoach problem, this recursive relationship was

$$f_n^*(s) = \min_{x_n} \{c_{sx_n} + f_{n+1}^*(x_n)\}.$$

Therefore, finding the *optimal policy decision* when you start in state s at stage n requires finding the minimizing value of x_n. For this particular problem, the corresponding minimum cost is achieved by using this value of x_n and then following the optimal policy when you start in state x_n at stage $n + 1$.

The precise form of the recursive relationship differs somewhat among dynamic programming problems. However, notation analogous to that introduced in the preceding section will continue to be used here, as summarized below.

N = number of stages.

n = label for current stage ($n = 1, 2, \ldots, N$).

s_n = current *state* for stage n.

x_n = decision variable for stage n.

x_n^* = optimal value of x_n (given s_n).

$f_n(s_n, x_n)$ = contribution of stages $n, n + 1, \ldots, N$ to objective function if system starts in state s_n at stage n, immediate decision is x_n, and optimal decisions are made thereafter.

$$f_n^*(s_n) = f_n(s_n, x_n^*).$$

The recursive relationship will always be of the form

$$f_n^*(s_n) = \max_{x_n} \{f_n(s_n, x_n)\} \qquad \text{or} \qquad f_n^*(s_n) = \min_{x_n} \{f_n(s_n, x_n)\},$$

where $f_n(s_n, x_n)$ would be written in terms of s_n, x_n, $f_{n+1}^*(s_{n+1})$, and probably some measure of the immediate contribution of x_n to the objective function. It is the inclusion of $f_{n+1}^*(s_{n+1})$ on the right-hand side, so that $f_n^*(s_n)$ is defined in terms of $f_{n+1}^*(s_{n+1})$, that makes the expression for $f_n^*(s_n)$ a recursive relationship.

The recursive relationship keeps recurring as we move backward stage by stage. When the current stage number n is decreased by 1, the new $f_n^*(s_n)$ function is derived by using the $f^*_{n+1}(s_{n+1})$ function that was just derived during the preceding iteration, and then this process keeps repeating. This property is emphasized in the next (and final) characteristic of dynamic programming.

8. When we use this recursive relationship, the solution procedure starts at the end and moves *backward* stage by stage—each time finding the optimal policy for that stage—until it finds the optimal policy starting at the *initial* stage. This optimal policy immediately yields an optimal solution for the entire problem, namely, x^*_1 for the initial state s_1, then x^*_2 for the resulting state s_2, then x^*_3 for the resulting state s_3, and so forth to x^*_N for the resulting stage s_N.

This backward movement was demonstrated by the stagecoach problem, where the optimal policy was found successively beginning in each state at stages 4, 3, 2, and 1, respectively.[1] For all dynamic programming problems, a table such as the following would be obtained for each stage ($n = N, N - 1, \ldots, 1$).

s_n \ x_n	$f_n(s_n, x_n)$	$f^*_n(s_n)$	x^*_n

When this table is finally obtained for the initial stage ($n = 1$), the problem of interest is solved. Because the initial state is known, the initial decision is specified by x^*_1 in this table. The optimal value of the other decision variables is then specified by the other tables in turn according to the state of the system that results from the preceding decisions.

11.3 DETERMINISTIC DYNAMIC PROGRAMMING

This section further elaborates upon the dynamic programming approach to *deterministic* problems, where the *state* at the *next stage* is *completely determined* by the *state* and *policy decision* at the *current stage*. The *probabilistic* case, where there is a probability distribution for what the next state will be, is discussed in the next section.

Deterministic dynamic programming can be described diagrammatically as shown in Fig. 11.3. Thus, at stage n the process will be in some state s_n. Making policy decision x_n then moves the process to some state s_{n+1} at stage $n + 1$. The contribution *thereafter* to the objective function under an optimal policy has been previously calculated to be $f^*_{n+1}(s_{n+1})$. The policy decision x_n also makes some contribution to the objective function. Combining these two quantities in an appropriate way provides $f_n(s_n, x_n)$, the contribution of stages n onward to the objective function. Optimizing with respect to x_n then gives $f^*_n(s_n) = f_n(s_n, x^*_n)$. After x^*_n and $f^*_n(s_n)$ are found for each possible value of s_n, the solution procedure is ready to move back one stage.

One way of categorizing deterministic dynamic programming problems is by the *form of the objective function*. For example, the objective might be to minimize the sum of the contributions from the individual stages (as for the stagecoach problem), or to maximize

---

[1]Actually, for this problem the solution procedure can move *either* backward or forward. However, for many problems (especially when the stages correspond to *time periods*), the solution procedure *must* move backward.

FIGURE 11.3
The basic structure for
deterministic dynamic
programming.

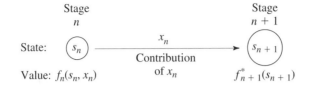

such a sum, or to minimize a product of such terms, and so on. Another categorization is in terms of the nature of the *set of states* for the respective stages. In particular, states s_n might be representable by a *discrete* state variable (as for the stagecoach problem) or by a *continuous* state variable, or perhaps a state *vector* (more than one variable) is required.

Several examples are presented to illustrate these various possibilities. More importantly, they illustrate that these apparently major differences are actually quite inconsequential (except in terms of computational difficulty) because the underlying basic structure shown in Fig. 11.3 always remains the same.

The first new example arises in a much different context from the stagecoach problem, but it has the same *mathematical formulation* except that the objective is to *maximize* rather than to minimize a sum.

EXAMPLE 2   **Distributing Medical Teams to Countries**

The WORLD HEALTH COUNCIL is devoted to improving health care in the underdeveloped countries of the world. It now has five medical teams available to allocate among three such countries to improve their medical care, health education, and training programs. Therefore, the council needs to determine how many teams (if any) to allocate to each of these countries to maximize the total effectiveness of the five teams. The teams must be kept intact, so the number allocated to each country must be an integer.

The measure of performance being used is *additional person-years of life.* (For a particular country, this measure equals the *increased life expectancy* in years times the country's population.) Table 11.1 gives the estimated additional person-years of life (in multiples of 1,000) for each country for each possible allocation of medical teams.

Which allocation maximizes the measure of performance?

TABLE 11.1 Data for the World Health Council problem

Medical Teams	Thousands of Additional Person-Years of Life		
	Country		
	1	2	3
0	0	0	0
1	45	20	50
2	70	45	70
3	90	75	80
4	105	110	100
5	120	150	130

Formulation. This problem requires making three *interrelated decisions,* namely, how many medical teams to allocate to each of the three countries. Therefore, even though there is no fixed sequence, these three countries can be considered as the three stages in a dynamic programming formulation. The decision variables x_n ($n = 1, 2, 3$) are the number of teams to allocate to stage (country) n.

The identification of the states may not be readily apparent. To determine the states, we ask questions such as the following. What is it that changes from one stage to the next? Given that the decisions have been made at the previous stages, how can the status of the situation at the current stage be described? What information about the current state of affairs is necessary to determine the optimal policy hereafter? On these bases, an appropriate choice for the "state of the system" is

s_n = number of medical teams still available for allocation to remaining countries
  $(n, \ldots , 3)$.

Thus, at stage 1 (country 1), where all three countries remain under consideration for allocations, $s_1 = 5$. However, at stage 2 or 3 (country 2 or 3), s_n is just 5 minus the number of teams allocated at preceding stages, so that the sequence of states is

$$s_1 = 5, \qquad s_2 = 5 - x_1, \qquad s_3 = s_2 - x_2.$$

With the dynamic programming procedure of solving backward stage by stage, when we are solving at stage 2 or 3, we shall not yet have solved for the allocations at the preceding stages. Therefore, we shall consider every possible state we could be in at stage 2 or 3, namely, $s_n = 0, 1, 2, 3, 4,$ or 5.

Figure 11.4 shows the states to be considered at each stage. The links (line segments) show the possible transitions in states from one stage to the next from making a feasible allocation of medical teams to the country involved. The numbers shown next to the links are the corresponding contributions to the measure of performance, where these numbers come from Table 11.1. From the perspective of this figure, the overall problem is to find the path from the initial state 5 (beginning stage 1) to the final state 0 (after stage 3) that maximizes the sum of the numbers along the path.

To state the overall problem mathematically, let $p_i(x_i)$ be the measure of performance from allocating x_i medical teams to country i, as given in Table 11.1. Thus, the objective is to choose x_1, x_2, x_3 so as to

$$\text{Maximize} \quad \sum_{i=1}^{3} p_i(x_i),$$

subject to

$$\sum_{i=1}^{3} x_i = 5,$$

and

x_i are nonnegative integers.

Using the notation presented in Sec. 11.2, we see that $f_n(s_n, x_n)$ is

$$f_n(s_n, x_n) = p_n(x_n) + \max \sum_{i=n+1}^{3} p_i(x_i),$$

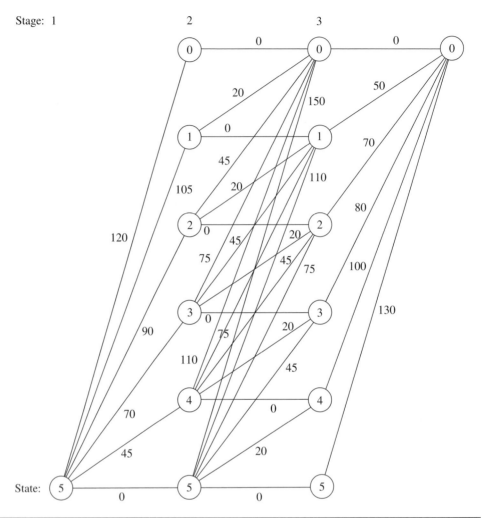

FIGURE 11.4
Graphical display of the World Health Council problem, showing the possible states at each stage, the possible transitions in states, and the corresponding contributions to the measure of performance.

where the maximum is taken over $x_{n+1}, \ldots, x_3$ such that

$$\sum_{i=n}^{3} x_i = s_n$$

and the x_i are nonnegative integers, for $n = 1, 2, 3$. In addition,

$$f_n^*(s_n) = \max_{x_n=0,1,\ldots,s_n} f_n(s_n, x_n)$$

Therefore,

$$f_n(s_n, x_n) = p_n(x_n) + f_{n+1}^*(s_n - x_n)$$

(with f_4^* defined to be zero). These basic relationships are summarized in Fig. 11.5.

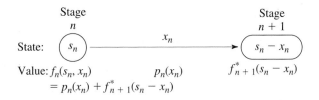

FIGURE 11.5
The basic structure for the
World Health Council
problem.

Consequently, the *recursive relationship* relating functions f_1^*, f_2^*, and f_3^* for this problem is

$$f_n^*(s_n) = \max_{x_n=0,1,\ldots,\,s_n} \{p_n(x_n) + f_{n+1}^*(s_n - x_n)\}, \qquad \text{for } n = 1, 2.$$

For the last stage ($n = 3$),

$$f_3^*(s_3) = \max_{x_3=0,1,\ldots,\,s_3} p_3(x_3).$$

The resulting dynamic programming calculations are given next.

Solution Procedure. Beginning with the last stage ($n = 3$), we note that the values of $p_3(x_3)$ are given in the last column of Table 11.1 and these values keep increasing as we move down the column. Therefore, with s_3 medical teams still available for allocation to country 3, the maximum of $p_3(x_3)$ is automatically achieved by allocating all s_3 teams; so $x_3^* = s_3$ and $f_3^*(s_3) = p_3(s_3)$, as shown in the following table.

$n = 3$:	s_3	$f_3^*(s_3)$	x_3^*
	0	0	0
	1	50	1
	2	70	2
	3	80	3
	4	100	4
	5	130	5

We now move backward to start from the next-to-last stage ($n = 2$). Here, finding x_2^* requires calculating and comparing $f_2(s_2, x_2)$ for the alternative values of x_2, namely, $x_2 = 0, 1, \ldots, s_2$. To illustrate, we depict this situation when $s_2 = 2$ graphically:

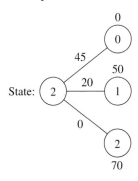

This diagram corresponds to Fig. 11.5 except that all three possible states at stage 3 are shown. Thus, if $x_2 = 0$, the resulting state at stage 3 will be $s_2 - x_2 = 2 - 0 = 2$, whereas $x_2 = 1$ leads to state 1 and $x_2 = 2$ leads to state 0. The corresponding values of $p_2(x_2)$ from the country 2 column of Table 11.1 are shown along the links, and the values of $f_3^*(s_2 - x_2)$ from the $n = 3$ table are given next to the stage 3 nodes. The required calculations for this case of $s_2 = 2$ are summarized below.

Formula: $f_2(2, x_2) = p_2(x_2) + f_3^*(2 - x_2)$.
$p_2(x_2)$ is given in the country 2 column of Table 11.1.
$f_3^*(2 - x_2)$ is given in the $n = 3$ table (bottom of preceding page).

$x_2 = 0$: $f_2(2, 0) = p_2(0) + f_3^*(2) = \;\;0 + 70 = 70$.
$x_2 = 1$: $f_2(2, 1) = p_2(1) + f_3^*(1) = 20 + 50 = 70$.
$x_2 = 2$: $f_2(2, 2) = p_2(2) + f_3^*(0) = 45 + \;\;\;0 = 45$.

Because the objective is *maximization*, $x_2^* = 0$ or 1 with $f_2^*(2) = 70$.

Proceeding in a similar way with the other possible values of s_2 (try it) yields the following table.

$n = 2$: s_2	x_2	$f_2(s_2, x_2) = p_2(x_2) + f_3^*(s_2 - x_2)$						$f_2^*(s_2)$	x_2^*
		0	**1**	**2**	**3**	**4**	**5**		
0		0						0	0
1		50	20					50	0
2		70	70	45				70	0 or 1
3		80	90	95	75			95	2
4		100	100	115	125	110		125	3
5		130	120	125	145	160	150	160	4

We now are ready to move backward to solve the original problem where we are starting from stage 1 ($n = 1$). In this case, the only state to be considered is the starting state of $s_1 = 5$, as depicted below.

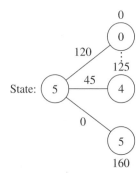

Since allocating x_1 medical teams to country 1 leads to a state of $5 - x_1$ at stage 2, a choice of $x_1 = 0$ leads to the bottom node on the right, $x = 1$ leads to the next node up, and so forth up to the top node with $x_1 = 5$. The corresponding $p_1(x_1)$ values from Table

11.1 are shown next to the links. The numbers next to the nodes are obtained from the $f_2^*(s_2)$ column of the $n = 2$ table. As with $n = 2$, the calculation needed for each alternative value of the decision variable involves adding the corresponding link value and node value, as summarized below.

Formula: $f_1(5, x_1) = p_1(x_1) + f_2^*(5 - x_1)$.
$p_1(x_1)$ is given in the country 1 column of Table 11.1.
$f_2^*(5 - x_1)$ is given in the $n = 2$ table.

$x_1 = 0$: $f_1(5, 0) = p_1(0) + f_2^*(5) = \quad 0 + 160 = 160$.
$x_1 = 1$: $f_1(5, 1) = p_1(1) + f_2^*(4) = \quad 45 + 125 = 170$.
$\vdots$
$x_1 = 5$: $f_1(5, 5) = p_1(5) + f_2^*(0) = 120 + \quad 0 = 120$.

The similar calculations for $x_1 = 2, 3, 4$ (try it) verify that $x_1^* = 1$ with $f_1^*(5) = 170$, as shown in the following table.

$n = 1$:	s_1 \ x_2	\multicolumn{6}{c}{$f_1(s_1, x_1) = p_1(x_1) + f_2^*(s_1 - x_1)$}	$f_1^*(s_1)$	x_1^*
		0	1	2	3	4	5		
	5	160	170	165	160	155	120	170	1

Thus, the optimal solution has $x_1^* = 1$, which makes $s_2 = 5 - 1 = 4$, so $x_2^* = 3$, which makes $s_3 = 4 - 3 = 1$, so $x_3^* = 1$. Since $f_1^*(5) = 170$, this (1, 3, 1) allocation of medical teams to the three countries will yield an estimated total of 170,000 additional person-years of life, which is at least 5,000 more than for any other allocation.

These results of the dynamic programming analysis also are summarized in Fig. 11.6.

A Prevalent Problem Type—The Distribution of Effort Problem

The preceding example illustrates a particularly common type of dynamic programming problem called the *distribution of effort problem*. For this type of problem, there is just one kind of *resource* that is to be allocated to a number of *activities*. The objective is to determine how to distribute the effort (the resource) among the activities most effectively. For the World Health Council example, the resource involved is the medical teams, and the three activities are the health care work in the three countries.

Assumptions. This interpretation of allocating resources to activities should ring a bell for you, because it is the typical interpretation for linear programming problems given at the beginning of Chap. 3. However, there also are some key differences between the distribution of effort problem and linear programming that help illuminate the general distinctions between dynamic programming and other areas of mathematical programming.

One key difference is that the distribution of effort problem involves only *one resource* (one functional constraint), whereas linear programming can deal with thousands of resources. (In principle, dynamic programming can handle slightly more than one resource, as we shall illustrate in Example 5 by solving the three-resource Wyndor Glass

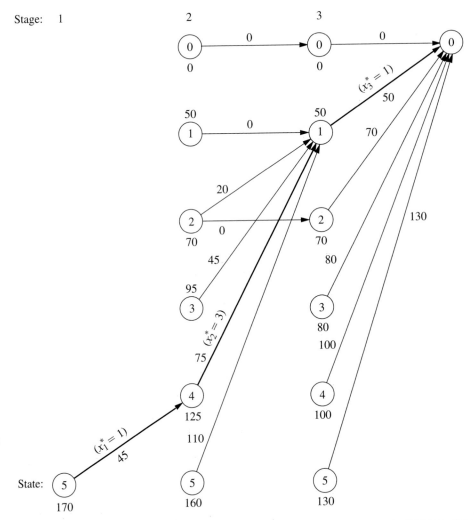

FIGURE 11.6
Graphical display of the dynamic programming solution of the World Health Council problem. An arrow from state s_n to state s_{n+1} indicates that an optimal policy decision from state s_n is to allocate $(s_n - s_{n+1})$ medical teams to country n. Allocating the medical teams in this way when following the boldfaced arrows from the initial state to the final state gives the optimal solution.

Co. problem, but it quickly becomes very inefficient when the number of resources is increased.)

On the other hand, the distribution of effort problem is far more general than linear programming in other ways. Consider the four assumptions of linear programming presented in Sec. 3.3: proportionality, additivity, divisibility, and certainty. *Proportionality* is routinely violated by nearly all dynamic programming problems, including distribution of effort problems (e.g., Table 11.1 violates proportionality). *Divisibility* also is often violated, as in Example 2, where the decision variables must be integers. In fact, dynamic programming calculations become more complex when divisibility does hold (as in Examples 4 and 5). Although we shall consider the distribution of effort problem only under the assumption of *certainty,* this is not necessary, and many other dynamic programming problems violate this assumption as well (as described in Sec. 11.4).

Of the four assumptions of linear programming, the *only* one needed by the distribution of effort problem (or other dynamic programming problems) is *additivity* (or its analog for functions involving a *product* of terms). This assumption is needed to satisfy the *principle of optimality* for dynamic programming (characteristic 5 in Sec. 11.2).

Formulation. Because they always involve allocating one kind of resource to a number of activities, distribution of effort problems always have the following dynamic programming formulation (where the ordering of the activities is arbitrary):

Stage n = activity n ($n = 1, 2, \ldots, N$).

x_n = amount of resource allocated to activity n.

State s_n = amount of resource still available for allocation to remaining activities ($n, \ldots, N$).

The reason for defining state s_n in this way is that the amount of the resource still available for allocation is precisely the information about the current state of affairs (entering stage n) that is needed for making the allocation decisions for the remaining activities.

When the system starts at stage n in state s_n, the choice of x_n results in the next state at stage $n + 1$ being $s_{n+1} = s_n - x_n$, as depicted below:[1]

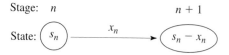

Note how the structure of this diagram corresponds to the one shown in Fig. 11.5 for the World Health Council example of a distribution of effort problem. What will differ from one such example to the next is the *rest* of what is shown in Fig. 11.5, namely, the relationship between $f_n(s_n, x_n)$ and $f_{n+1}^*(s_n - x_n)$, and then the resulting *recursive relationship* between the f_n^* and f_{n+1}^* functions. These relationships depend on the particular objective function for the overall problem.

The structure of the next example is similar to the one for the World Health Council because it, too, is a distribution of effort problem. However, its recursive relationship differs in that its objective is to minimize a product of terms for the respective stages.

At first glance, this example may appear *not* to be a deterministic dynamic programming problem because probabilities are involved. However, it does indeed fit our definition because the state at the next stage is completely determined by the state and policy decision at the current stage.

EXAMPLE 3   Distributing Scientists to Research Teams

A government space project is conducting research on a certain engineering problem that must be solved before people can fly safely to Mars. Three research teams are currently trying three different approaches for solving this problem. The estimate has been made that, under present circumstances, the probability that the respective teams—call them 1,

[1]This statement assumes that x_n and s_n are expressed in the same units. If it is more convenient to define x_n as some other quantity such that the amount of the resource allocated to activity n is $a_n x_n$, then $s_{n+1} = s_n - a_n x_n$.

2, and 3—will not succeed is 0.40, 0.60, and 0.80, respectively. Thus, the current probability that all three teams will fail is $(0.40)(0.60)(0.80) = 0.192$. Because the objective is to minimize the probability of failure, two more top scientists have been assigned to the project.

Table 11.2 gives the estimated probability that the respective teams will fail when 0, 1, or 2 additional scientists are added to that team. Only integer numbers of scientists are considered because each new scientist will need to devote full attention to one team. The problem is to determine how to allocate the two additional scientists to minimize the probability that all three teams will fail.

Formulation.   Because both Examples 2 and 3 are distribution of effort problems, their underlying structure is actually very similar. In this case, scientists replace medical teams as the kind of resource involved, and research teams replace countries as the activities. Therefore, instead of medical teams being allocated to countries, scientists are being allocated to research teams. The only basic difference between the two problems is in their objective functions.

With so few scientists and teams involved, this problem could be solved very easily by a process of exhaustive enumeration. However, the dynamic programming solution is presented for illustrative purposes.

In this case, stage n ($n = 1, 2, 3$) corresponds to research team n, and the state s_n is the number of new scientists *still available* for allocation to the remaining teams. The decision variables x_n ($n = 1, 2, 3$) are the number of additional scientists allocated to team n.

Let $p_i(x_i)$ denote the probability of failure for team i if it is assigned x_i additional scientists, as given by Table 11.2. If we let Π denote multiplication, the government's objective is to choose x_1, x_2, x_3 so as to

$$\text{Minimize} \quad \prod_{i=1}^{3} p_i(x_i) = p_1(x_1)p_2(x_2)p_3(x_3),$$

subject to

$$\sum_{i=1}^{3} x_i = 2$$

TABLE 11.2 Data for the Government Space Project problem

New Scientists	Probability of Failure Team		
	1	2	3
0	0.40	0.60	0.80
1	0.20	0.40	0.50
2	0.15	0.20	0.30

and

x_i are nonnegative integers.

Consequently, $f_n(s_n, x_n)$ for this problem is

$$f_n(s_n, x_n) = p_n(x_n) \cdot \min \prod_{i=n+1}^{3} p_i(x_i),$$

where the minimum is taken over $x_{n+1}, \ldots, x_3$ such that

$$\sum_{i=n}^{3} x_i = s_n$$

and

x_i are nonnegative integers,

for $n = 1, 2, 3$. Thus,

$$f_n^*(s_n) = \min_{x_n = 0,1, \ldots, s_n} f_n(s_n, x_n),$$

where

$$f_n(s_n, x_n) = p_n(x_n) \cdot f_{n+1}^*(s_n - x_n)$$

(with f_4^* defined to be 1). Figure 11.7 summarizes these basic relationships.

Thus, the *recursive relationship* relating the f_1^*, f_2^*, and f_3^* functions in this case is

$$f_n^*(s_n) = \min_{x_n = 0,1, \ldots, s_n} \{ p_n(x_n) \cdot f_{n+1}^*(s_n - x_n) \}, \quad \text{for } n = 1, 2,$$

and, when $n = 3$,

$$f_3^*(s_3) = \min_{x_3 = 0,1, \ldots, s_3} p_3(x_3).$$

Solution Procedure. The resulting dynamic programming calculations are as follows:

$n = 3$:	s_3	$f_3^*(s_3)$	x_3^*
	0	0.80	0
	1	0.50	1
	2	0.30	2

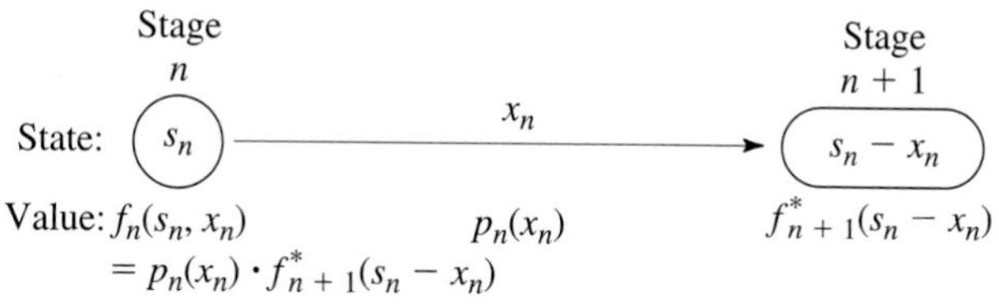

FIGURE 11.7
The basic structure for the government space project problem.

State: Stage n s_n $\xrightarrow{\quad x_n \quad}$ Stage $n + 1$ $s_n - x_n$

Value: $f_n(s_n, x_n)$ $p_n(x_n)$ $f_{n+1}^*(s_n - x_n)$
        $= p_n(x_n) \cdot f_{n+1}^*(s_n - x_n)$

$n = 2$: s_2	x_2	$f_2(s_2, x_2) = p_2(x_2) \cdot f_3^*(s_2 - x_2)$			$f_2^*(s_2)$	x_2^*
		0	**1**	**2**		
0		0.48			0.48	0
1		0.30	0.32		0.30	0
2		0.18	0.20	0.16	0.16	2

$n = 1$: s_1	x_1	$f_1(s_1, x_1) = p_1(x_1) \cdot f_2^*(s_1 - x_1)$			$f_1^*(s_1)$	x_1^*
		0	**1**	**2**		
2		0.064	0.060	0.072	0.060	1

Therefore, the optimal solution must have $x_1^* = 1$, which makes $s_2 = 2 - 1 = 1$, so that $x_2^* = 0$, which makes $s_3 = 1 - 0 = 1$, so that $x_3^* = 1$. Thus, teams 1 and 3 should each receive one additional scientist. The new probability that all three teams will fail would then be 0.060.

All the examples thus far have had a *discrete* state variable s_n at each stage. Furthermore, they all have been *reversible* in the sense that the solution procedure actually could have moved *either* backward or forward stage by stage. (The latter alternative amounts to renumbering the stages in reverse order and then applying the procedure in the standard way.) This reversibility is a general characteristic of distribution of effort problems such as Examples 2 and 3, since the activities (stages) can be ordered in any desired manner.

The next example is different in both respects. Rather than being restricted to integer values, its state variable s_n at stage n is a *continuous* variable that can take on *any* value over certain intervals. Since s_n now has an infinite number of values, it is no longer possible to consider each of its feasible values individually. Rather, the solution for $f_n^*(s_n)$ and x_n^* must be expressed as *functions* of s_n. Furthermore, this example is *not* reversible because its stages correspond to *time periods,* so the solution procedure *must* proceed backward.

EXAMPLE 4   Scheduling Employment Levels

The workload for the LOCAL JOB SHOP is subject to considerable seasonal fluctuation. However, machine operators are difficult to hire and costly to train, so the manager is reluctant to lay off workers during the slack seasons. He is likewise reluctant to maintain his peak season payroll when it is not required. Furthermore, he is definitely opposed to overtime work on a regular basis. Since all work is done to custom orders, it is not possible to build up inventories during slack seasons. Therefore, the manager is in a dilemma as to what his policy should be regarding employment levels.

The following estimates are given for the minimum employment requirements during the four seasons of the year for the foreseeable future:

Season	Spring	Summer	Autumn	Winter	Spring
Requirements	255	220	240	200	255

Employment will not be permitted to fall below these levels. Any employment above these levels is wasted at an approximate cost of $2,000 per person per season. It is estimated that the hiring and firing costs are such that the total cost of changing the level of employment from one season to the next is $200 times the square of the difference in employment levels. Fractional levels of employment are possible because of a few part-time employees, and the cost data also apply on a fractional basis.

Formulation. On the basis of the data available, it is not worthwhile to have the employment level go above the peak season requirements of 255. Therefore, spring employment should be at 255, and the problem is reduced to finding the employment level for the other three seasons.

For a dynamic programming formulation, the seasons should be the stages. There are actually an indefinite number of stages because the problem extends into the indefinite future. However, each year begins an identical cycle, and because spring employment is known, it is possible to consider only one cycle of four seasons ending with the spring season, as summarized below.

Stage 1 = summer,
Stage 2 = autumn,
Stage 3 = winter,
Stage 4 = spring.
x_n = employment level for stage n ($n = 1, 2, 3, 4$).
($x_4 = 255$.)

It is necessary that the spring season be the last stage because the optimal value of the decision variable for each state at the last stage must be either known or obtainable without considering other stages. For every other season, the solution for the optimal employment level must consider the effect on costs in the following season.

Let

r_n = minimum employment requirement for stage n,

where these requirements were given earlier as $r_1 = 220$, $r_2 = 240$, $r_3 = 200$, and $r_4 = 255$. Thus, the only feasible values for x_n are

$r_n \leq x_n \leq 255$.

Referring to the cost data given in the problem statement, we have

Cost for stage $n = 200(x_n - x_{n-1})^2 + 2,000(x_n - r_n)$.

Note that the cost at the current stage depends upon only the current decision x_n and the employment in the preceding season x_{n-1}. Thus, the preceding employment level is

TABLE 11.3 Data for the Local Job Shop problem

n	r_n	Feasible x_n	Possible $s_n = x_{n-1}$	Cost
1	220	$220 \leq x_1 \leq 255$	$s_1 = 255$	$200(x_1 - 255)^2 + 2,000(x_1 - 220)$
2	240	$240 \leq x_2 \leq 255$	$220 \leq s_2 \leq 255$	$200(x_2 - x_1)^2 + 2,000(x_2 - 240)$
3	200	$200 \leq x_3 \leq 255$	$240 \leq s_3 \leq 255$	$200(x_3 - x_2)^2 + 2,000(x_3 - 200)$
4	255	$x_4 = 255$	$200 \leq s_4 \leq 255$	$200(255 - x_3)^2$

all the information about the current state of affairs that we need to determine the optimal policy henceforth. Therefore, the state s_n for stage n is

State $s_n = x_{n-1}$.

When $n = 1$, $s_1 = x_0 = x_4 = 255$.

For your ease of reference while working through the problem, a summary of the data is given in Table 11.3 for each of the four stages.

The objective for the problem is to choose x_1, x_2, x_3 (with $x_0 = x_4 = 255$) so as to

$$\text{Minimize} \quad \sum_{i=1}^{4} [200(x_i - x_{i-1})^2 + 2,000(x_i - r_i)],$$

subject to

$$r_i \leq x_i \leq 255, \quad \text{for } i = 1, 2, 3, 4.$$

Thus, for stage n onward ($n = 1, 2, 3, 4$), since $s_n = x_{n-1}$

$$f_n(s_n, x_n) = 200(x_n - s_n)^2 + 2,000(x_n - r_n)$$

$$+ \min_{r_i \leq x_i \leq 255} \sum_{i=n+1}^{4} [200(x_i - x_{i-1})^2 + 2,000(x_i - r_i)],$$

where this summation equals zero when $n = 4$ (because it has no terms). Also,

$$f_n^*(s_n) = \min_{r_n \leq x_n \leq 255} f_n(s_n, x_n).$$

Hence,

$$f_n(s_n, x_n) = 200(x_n - s_n)^2 + 2,000(x_n - r_n) + f_{n+1}^*(x_n)$$

(with f_5^* defined to be zero because costs after stage 4 are irrelevant to the analysis). A summary of these basic relationships is given in Fig. 11.8.

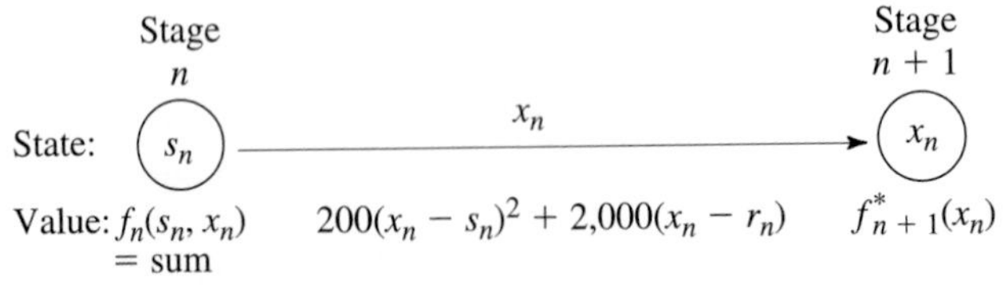

FIGURE 11.8
The basic structure for the Local Job Shop problem.

Stage n

State: s_n → x_n → Stage $n+1$: x_n

Value: $f_n(s_n, x_n)$ = sum $200(x_n - s_n)^2 + 2,000(x_n - r_n)$ $f_{n+1}^*(x_n)$

Consequently, the recursive relationship relating the f_n^* functions is

$$f_n^*(s_n) = \min_{r_n \leq x_n \leq 255} \{200(x_n - s_n)^2 + 2{,}000(x_n - r_n) + f_{n+1}^*(x_n)\}.$$

The dynamic programming approach uses this relationship to identify successively these functions—$f_4^*(s_4)$, $f_3^*(s_3)$, $f_2^*(s_2)$, $f_1^*(255)$—and the corresponding minimizing x_n.

Solution Procedure.   *Stage 4:* Beginning at the last stage ($n = 4$), we already know that $x_4^* = 255$, so the necessary results are

$n = 4$:	s_4	$f_4^*(s_4)$	x_4^*
	$200 \leq s_4 \leq 255$	$200(255 - s_4)^2$	255

Stage 3: For the problem consisting of just the last *two* stages ($n = 3$), the recursive relationship reduces to

$$f_3^*(s_3) = \min_{200 \leq x_3 \leq 255} \{200(x_3 - s_3)^2 + 2{,}000(x_3 - 200) + f_4^*(x_3)\}$$
$$= \min_{200 \leq x_3 \leq 255} \{200(x_3 - s_3)^2 + 2{,}000(x_3 - 200) + 200(255 - x_3)^2\},$$

where the possible values of s_3 are $240 \leq s_3 \leq 255$.

One way to solve for the value of x_3 that minimizes $f_3(s_3, x_3)$ for any particular value of s_3 is the graphical approach illustrated in Fig. 11.9.

FIGURE 11.9
Graphical solution for $f_3^*(s_3)$ for the Local Job Shop problem.

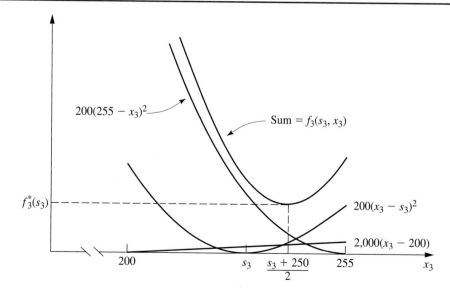

However, a faster way is to use *calculus*. We want to solve for the minimizing x_3 in terms of s_3 by considering s_3 to have some fixed (but unknown) value. Therefore, set the first (partial) derivative of $f_3(s_3, x_3)$ with respect to x_3 equal to zero:

$$\frac{\partial}{\partial x_3} f_3(s_3, x_3) = 400(x_3 - s_3) + 2{,}000 - 400(255 - x_3)$$
$$= 400(2x_3 - s_3 - 250)$$
$$= 0,$$

which yields

$$x_3^* = \frac{s_3 + 250}{2}.$$

Because the second derivative is positive, and because this solution lies in the feasible interval for x_3 ($200 \leq x_3 \leq 255$) for all possible s_3 ($240 \leq s_3 \leq 255$), it is indeed the desired minimum.

Note a key difference between the nature of this solution and those obtained for the preceding examples where there were only a few possible states to consider. We now have an *infinite* number of possible states ($240 \leq s_3 \leq 255$), so it is no longer feasible to solve separately for x_3^* for each possible value of s_3. Therefore, we instead have solved for x_3^* as a *function* of the unknown s_3.

Using

$$f_3^*(s_3) = f_3(s_3, x_3^*) = 200\left(\frac{s_3 + 250}{2} - s_3\right)^2 + 200\left(255 - \frac{s_3 + 250}{2}\right)^2$$
$$+ 2{,}000\left(\frac{s_3 + 250}{2} - 200\right)$$

and reducing this expression algebraically complete the required results for the third-stage problem, summarized as follows.

$n = 3$:	s_3	$f_3^*(s_3)$	x_3^*
	$240 \leq s_3 \leq 255$	$50(250 - s_3)^2 + 50(260 - s_3)^2 + 1{,}000(s_3 - 150)$	$\dfrac{s_3 + 250}{2}$

Stage 2: The second-stage ($n = 2$) and first-stage problems ($n = 1$) are solved in a similar fashion. Thus, for $n = 2$,

$$f_2(s_2, x_2) = 200(x_2 - s_2)^2 + 2{,}000(x_2 - r_2) + f_3^*(x_2)$$
$$= 200(x_2 - s_2)^2 + 2{,}000(x_2 - 240)$$
$$+ 50(250 - x_2)^2 + 50(260 - x_2)^2 + 1{,}000(x_2 - 150).$$

The possible values of s_2 are $220 \leq s_2 \leq 255$, and the feasible region for x_2 is $240 \leq x_2 \leq 255$. The problem is to find the minimizing value of x_2 in this region, so that

$$f_2^*(s_2) = \min_{240 \leq x_2 \leq 255} f_2(s_2, x_2).$$

Setting to zero the partial derivative with respect to x_2:

$$\frac{\partial}{\partial x_2} f_2(s_2, x_2) = 400(x_2 - s_2) + 2,000 - 100(250 - x_2) - 100(260 - x_2) + 1,000$$

$$= 200(3x_2 - 2s_2 - 240)$$

$$= 0$$

yields

$$x_2 = \frac{2s_2 + 240}{3}.$$

Because

$$\frac{\partial^2}{\partial x_2^2} f_2(s_2, x_2) = 600 > 0,$$

this value of x_2 is the desired minimizing value *if it is feasible* ($240 \leq x_2 \leq 255$). Over the possible s_2 values ($220 \leq s_2 \leq 255$), this solution actually is feasible only if $240 \leq s_2 \leq 255$.

Therefore, we still need to solve for the feasible value of x_2 that minimizes $f_2(s_2, x_2)$ when $220 \leq s_2 < 240$. The key to analyzing the behavior of $f_2(s_2, x_2)$ over the feasible region for x_2 again is the partial derivative of $f_2(s_2, x_2)$. When $s_2 < 240$,

$$\frac{\partial}{\partial x_2} f_2(s_2, x_2) > 0, \qquad \text{for } 240 \leq x_2 \leq 255,$$

so that $x_2 = 240$ is the desired minimizing value.

The next step is to plug these values of x_2 into $f_2(s_2, x_2)$ to obtain $f_2^*(s_2)$ for $s_2 \geq 240$ and $s_2 < 240$. This yields

$n = 2$:	s_2	$f_2^*(s_2)$	x_2^*
	$220 \leq s_2 \leq 240$	$200(240 - s_2)^2 + 115{,}000$	240
	$240 \leq s_2 \leq 255$	$\frac{200}{9} [(240 - s_2)^2 + (255 - s_2)^2 + (270 - s_2)^2] + 2{,}000(s_2 - 195)$	$\frac{2s_2 + 240}{3}$

Stage 1: For the first-stage problem ($n = 1$),

$$f_1(s_1, x_1) = 200(x_1 - s_1)^2 + 2,000(x_1 - r_1) + f_2^*(x_1).$$

Because $r_1 = 220$, the feasible region for x_1 is $220 \leq x_1 \leq 255$. The expression for $f_2^*(x_1)$ will differ in the two portions $220 \leq x_1 \leq 240$ and $240 \leq x_1 \leq 255$ of this region. Therefore,

$$f_1(s_1, x_1) = \begin{cases} 200(x_1 - s_1)^2 + 2,000(x_1 - 220) + 200(240 - x_1)^2 + 115,000, \\ \qquad\qquad\qquad\qquad\qquad\qquad\qquad\qquad \text{if } 220 \leq x_1 \leq 240 \\ 200(x_1 - s_1)^2 + 2,000(x_1 - 220) + \frac{200}{9} [(240 - x_1)^2 + (255 - x_1)^2 + (270 - x_1)^2] \\ \qquad + 2,000(x_1 - 195), \qquad\qquad\qquad\qquad\qquad\quad \text{if } 240 \leq x_1 \leq 255. \end{cases}$$

Considering first the case where $220 \leq x_1 \leq 240$, we have

$$\frac{\partial}{\partial x_1} f_1(s_1, x_1) = 400(x_1 - s_1) + 2{,}000 - 400(240 - x_1)$$

$$= 400(2x_1 - s_1 - 235).$$

It is known that $s_1 = 255$ (spring employment), so that

$$\frac{\partial}{\partial x_1} f_1(s_1, x_1) = 800(x_1 - 245) < 0$$

for all $x_1 \leq 240$. Therefore, $x_1 = 240$ is the minimizing value of $f_1(s_1, x_1)$ over the region $220 \leq x_1 \leq 240$.

When $240 \leq x_1 \leq 255$,

$$\frac{\partial}{\partial x_1} f_1(s_1, x_1) = 400(x_1 - s_1) + 2{,}000$$

$$- \frac{400}{9}[(240 - x_1) + (255 - x_1) + (270 - x_1)] + 2{,}000$$

$$= \frac{400}{3}(4x_1 - 3s_1 - 225).$$

Because

$$\frac{\partial^2}{\partial x_1^2} f_1(s_1, x_1) > 0 \qquad \text{for all } x_1,$$

set

$$\frac{\partial}{\partial x_1} f_1(s_1, x_1) = 0,$$

which yields

$$x_1 = \frac{3s_1 + 225}{4}.$$

Because $s_1 = 255$, it follows that $x_1 = 247.5$ minimizes $f_1(s_1, x_1)$ over the region $240 \leq x_1 \leq 255$.

Note that this region ($240 \leq x_1 \leq 255$) includes $x_1 = 240$, so that $f_1(s_1, 240) > f_1(s_1, 247.5)$. In the next-to-last paragraph, we found that $x_1 = 240$ minimizes $f_1(s_1, x_1)$ over the region $220 \leq x_1 \leq 240$. Consequently, we now can conclude that $x_1 = 247.5$ also minimizes $f_1(s_1, x_1)$ over the *entire* feasible region $220 \leq x_1 \leq 255$.

Our final calculation is to find $f_1^*(s_1)$ for $s_1 = 255$ by plugging $x_1 = 247.5$ into the expression for $f_1(255, x_1)$ that holds for $240 \leq x_1 \leq 255$. Hence,

$$f_1^*(255) = 200(247.5 - 255)^2 + 2{,}000(247.5 - 220)$$

$$+ \frac{200}{9}[2(250 - 247.5)^2 + (265 - 247.5)^2 + 30(742.5 - 575)]$$

$$= 185{,}000.$$

These results are summarized as follows:

$n = 1$:	s_1	$f_1^*(s_1)$	x_1^*
	255	185,000	247.5

Therefore, by tracing back through the tables for $n = 2$, $n = 3$, and $n = 4$, respectively, and setting $s_n = x_{n-1}^*$ each time, the resulting optimal solution is $x_1^* = 247.5$, $x_2^* = 245$, $x_3^* = 247.5$, $x_4^* = 255$, with a total estimated cost per cycle of $185,000.

To conclude our illustrations of deterministic dynamic programming, we give one example that requires *more than one* variable to describe the state at each stage.

EXAMPLE 5 Wyndor Glass Company Problem

Consider the following linear programming problem:

$$\text{Maximize} \quad Z = 3x_1 + 5x_2,$$

subject to

$$\begin{aligned} x_1 & \leq 4 \\ 2x_2 & \leq 12 \\ 3x_1 + 2x_2 & \leq 18 \end{aligned}$$

and

$$x_1 \geq 0, \qquad x_2 \geq 0.$$

(You might recognize this as being the model for the Wyndor Glass Co. problem—introduced in Sec. 3.1.) One way of solving small linear (or nonlinear) programming problems like this one is by dynamic programming, which is illustrated below.

Formulation. This problem requires making two interrelated decisions, namely, the level of activity 1, denoted by x_1, and the level of activity 2, denoted by x_2. Therefore, these two activities can be interpreted as the two stages in a dynamic programming formulation. Although they can be taken in either order, let stage n = activity n ($n = 1, 2$). Thus, x_n is the decision variable at stage n.

What are the states? In other words, given that the decision had been made at prior stages (if any), what information is needed about the current state of affairs before the decision can be made at stage n? Reflection might suggest that the required information is the *amount of slack* left in the functional constraints. Interpret the right-hand side of these constraints (4, 12, and 18) as the total available amount of resources 1, 2, and 3, respectively (as described in Sec. 3.1). Then state s_n can be defined as

State s_n = amount of respective resources still available for allocation to remaining activities.

(Note that the definition of the state is analogous to that for distribution of effort problems, including Examples 2 and 3, except that there are now three resources to be allocated instead of just one.) Thus,

$$s_n = (R_1, R_2, R_3),$$

where R_i is the amount of resource i remaining to be allocated ($i = 1, 2, 3$). Therefore,

$$s_1 = (4, 12, 18),$$
$$s_2 = (4 - x_1, 12, 18 - 3x_1).$$

However, when we begin by solving for stage 2, we do not yet know the value of x_1, and so we use $s_2 = (R_1, R_2, R_3)$ at that point.

Therefore, in contrast to the preceding examples, this problem has *three* state variables (i.e., a *state vector* with three components) at each stage rather than one. From a theoretical standpoint, this difference is not particularly serious. It only means that, instead of considering all possible values of the one state variable, we must consider all possible *combinations* of values of the several state variables. However, from the standpoint of computational efficiency, this difference tends to be a very serious complication. Because the number of combinations, in general, can be as large as the *product* of the number of possible values of the respective variables, the number of required calculations tends to "blow up" rapidly when additional state variables are introduced. This phenomenon has been given the apt name of the **curse of dimensionality**.

Each of the three state variables is *continuous*. Therefore, rather than consider each possible combination of values separately, we must use the approach introduced in Example 4 of solving for the required information as a *function* of the state of the system.

Despite these complications, this problem is small enough that it can still be solved without great difficulty. To solve it, we need to introduce the usual dynamic programming notation. Thus,

$$f_2(R_1, R_2, R_3, x_2) = \text{contribution of activity 2 to } Z \text{ if system starts in state}$$
$$(R_1, R_2, R_3) \text{ at stage 2 and decision is } x_2$$
$$= 5x_2,$$

$$f_1(4, 12, 18, x_1) = \text{contribution of activities 1 and 2 to } Z \text{ if system starts in state}$$
$$(4, 12, 18) \text{ at stage 1, immediate decision is } x_1, \text{ and then}$$
$$\text{optimal decision is made at stage 2,}$$
$$= 3x_1 + \max_{\substack{x_2 \leq 12 \\ 2x_2 \leq 18 - 3x_1 \\ x_2 \geq 0}} \{5x_2\}.$$

Similarly, for $n = 1, 2$,

$$f_n^*(R_1, R_2, R_3) = \max_{x_n} f_n(R_1, R_2, R_3, x_n),$$

where this maximum is taken over the feasible values of x_n. Consequently, using the relevant portions of the constraints of the problem gives

(1) $f_2^*(R_1, R_2, R_3) = \max_{\substack{2x_2 \leq R_2 \\ 2x_2 \leq R_3 \\ x_2 \geq 0}} \{5x_2\},$

(2) $f_1(4, 12, 18, x_1) = 3x_1 + f_2^*(4 - x_1, 12, 18 - 3x_1),$

(3) $f_1^*(4, 12, 18) = \max\limits_{\substack{x_1 \le 4 \\ 3x_1 \le 18 \\ x_1 \ge 0}} \{3x_1 + f_2^*(4 - x_1, 12, 18 - 3x_1)\}.$

Equation (1) will be used to solve the stage 2 problem. Equation (2) shows the basic dynamic programming structure for the overall problem, also depicted in Fig. 11.10. Equation (3) gives the *recursive relationship* between f_1^* and f_2^* that will be used to solve the stage 1 problem.

Solution Procedure.   *Stage 2:* To solve at the last stage ($n = 2$), Eq. (1) indicates that x_2^* must be the largest value of x_2 that *simultaneously* satisfies $2x_2 \le R_2$, $2x_2 \le R_3$, and $x_2 \ge 0$. Assuming that $R_2 \ge 0$ and $R_3 \ge 0$, so that feasible solutions exist, this largest value is the smaller of $R_2/2$ and $R_3/2$. Thus, the solution is

$n = 2$:	$(R_1,\ R_2,\ R_3)$	$f_2^*(R_1,\ R_2,\ R_3)$	x_2^*
	$R_2 \ge 0,\ R_3 \ge 0$	$5 \min\left\{\dfrac{R_2}{2}, \dfrac{R_3}{2}\right\}$	$\min\left\{\dfrac{R_2}{2}, \dfrac{R_3}{2}\right\}$

Stage 1: To solve the two-stage problem ($n = 1$), we plug the solution just obtained for $f_2^*(R_1, R_2, R_3)$ into Eq. (3). For stage 2,

$$(R_1, R_2, R_3) = (4 - x_1, 12, 18 - 3x_1),$$

so that

$$f_2^*(4 - x_1, 12, 18 - 3x_1) = 5 \min\left\{\frac{R_2}{2}, \frac{R_3}{2}\right\} = 5 \min\left\{\frac{12}{2}, \frac{18 - 3x_1}{2}\right\}$$

is the specific solution plugged into Eq. (3). After we combine its constraints on x_1, Eq. (3) then becomes

$$f_1{}^*(4, 12, 18) = \max\limits_{0 \le x_1 \le 4}\left\{3x_1 + 5 \min\left\{\frac{12}{2}, \frac{18 - 3x_1}{2}\right\}\right\}.$$

Over the feasible interval $0 \le x_1 \le 4$, notice that

$$\min\left\{\frac{12}{2}, \frac{18 - 3x_1}{2}\right\} = \begin{cases} 6 & \text{if } 0 \le x_1 \le 2 \\ 9 - \dfrac{3}{2}x_1 & \text{if } 2 \le x_1 \le 4, \end{cases}$$

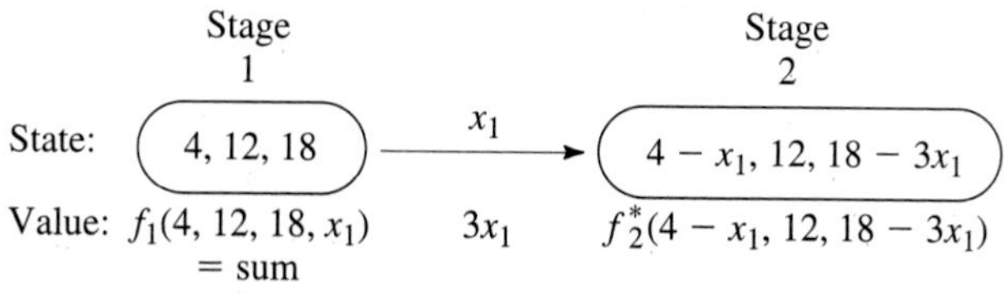

FIGURE 11.10
The basic structure for the Wyndor Glass Co. linear programming problem.

State: Stage 1 $\left(\ 4, 12, 18\ \right)$ $\xrightarrow{\ x_1\ }$ Stage 2 $\left(\ 4 - x_1, 12, 18 - 3x_1\ \right)$

Value: $f_1(4, 12, 18, x_1)$ $3x_1$ $f_2^*(4 - x_1, 12, 18 - 3x_1)$
= sum

so that

$$3x_1 + 5 \min\left\{\frac{12}{2}, \frac{18 - 3x_1}{2}\right\} = \begin{cases} 3x_1 + 30 & \text{if } 0 \le x_1 \le 2 \\ 45 - \dfrac{9}{2}x_1 & \text{if } 2 \le x_1 \le 4. \end{cases}$$

Because both

$$\max_{0 \le x_1 \le 2} \{3x_1 + 30\} \quad \text{and} \quad \max_{2 \le x_1 \le 4} \left\{45 - \frac{9}{2}x_1\right\}$$

achieve their maximum at $x_1 = 2$, it follows that $x_1^* = 2$ and that this maximum is 36, as given in the following table.

$n = 1$:	(R_1, R_2, R_3)	$f_1^*(R_1, R_2, R_3)$	x_1^*
	(4, 12, 18)	36	2

Because $x_1^* = 2$ leads to

$$R_1 = 4 - 2 = 2, \qquad R_2 = 12, \qquad R_3 = 18 - 3(2) = 12$$

for stage 2, the $n = 2$ table yields $x_2^* = 6$. Consequently, $x_1^* = 2$, $x_2^* = 6$ is the optimal solution for this problem (as originally found in Sec. 3.1), and the $n = 1$ table shows that the resulting value of Z is 36.

11.4   PROBABILISTIC DYNAMIC PROGRAMMING

Probabilistic dynamic programming differs from deterministic dynamic programming in that the state at the next stage is *not* completely determined by the state and policy decision at the current stage. Rather, there is a *probability distribution* for what the next state will be. However, this probability distribution still is completely determined by the state and policy decision at the current stage. The resulting basic structure for probabilistic dynamic programming is described diagrammatically in Fig. 11.11.

For the purposes of this diagram, we let S denote the number of possible states at stage $n + 1$ and label these states on the right side as 1, 2, . . . , S. The system goes to state i with probability p_i ($i = 1, 2, . . . , S$) given state s_n and decision x_n at stage n. If the system goes to state i, C_i is the contribution of stage n to the objective function.

When Fig. 11.11 is expanded to include all the possible states and decisions at all the stages, it is sometimes referred to as a **decision tree.** If the decision tree is not too large, it provides a useful way of summarizing the various possibilities.

Because of the probabilistic structure, the relationship between $f_n(s_n, x_n)$ and the $f_{n+1}^*(s_{n+1})$ necessarily is somewhat more complicated than that for deterministic dynamic programming. The precise form of this relationship will depend upon the form of the overall objective function.

To illustrate, suppose that the objective is to *minimize* the *expected sum* of the contributions from the individual stages. In this case, $f_n(s_n, x_n)$ represents the minimum ex-

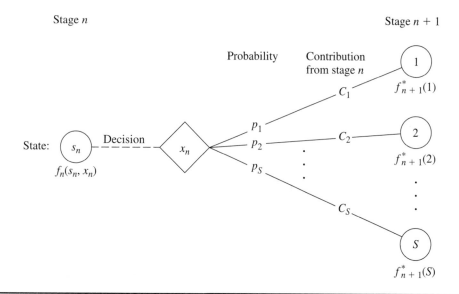

FIGURE 11.11
The basic structure for probabilistic dynamic programming.

pected sum from stage n onward, *given* that the state and policy decision at stage n are s_n and x_n, respectively. Consequently,

$$f_n(s_n, x_n) = \sum_{i=1}^{S} p_i[C_i + f_{n+1}^*(i)],$$

with

$$f_{n+1}^*(i) = \min_{x_{n+1}} f_{n+1}(i, x_{n+1}),$$

where this minimization is taken over the *feasible* values of x_{n+1}.

Example 6 has this same form. Example 7 will illustrate another form.

EXAMPLE 6   **Determining Reject Allowances**

The HIT-AND-MISS MANUFACTURING COMPANY has received an order to supply one item of a particular type. However, the customer has specified such stringent quality requirements that the manufacturer may have to produce more than one item to obtain an item that is acceptable. The number of *extra* items produced in a production run is called the *reject allowance*. Including a reject allowance is common practice when producing for a custom order, and it seems advisable in this case.

The manufacturer estimates that each item of this type that is produced will be *acceptable* with probability $\frac{1}{2}$ and *defective* (without possibility for rework) with probability $\frac{1}{2}$. Thus, the number of acceptable items produced in a lot of size L will have a *binomial distribution;* i.e., the probability of producing no acceptable items in such a lot is $\left(\frac{1}{2}\right)^L$.

Marginal production costs for this product are estimated to be $100 per item (even if defective), and excess items are worthless. In addition, a setup cost of $300 must be incurred whenever the production process is set up for this product, and a completely new setup at this same cost is required for each subsequent production run if a lengthy inspection procedure reveals that a completed lot has not yielded an acceptable item. The manufacturer has time to make no more than three production runs. If an acceptable item has not been obtained by the end of the third production run, the cost to the manufacturer in lost sales income and penalty costs will be $1,600.

The objective is to determine the policy regarding the lot size (1 + reject allowance) for the required production run(s) that minimizes total expected cost for the manufacturer.

Formulation.   A dynamic programming formulation for this problem is

Stage n = production run n (n = 1, 2, 3),
   x_n = lot size for stage n,
State s_n = number of acceptable items still needed (1 or 0) at beginning of stage n.

Thus, at stage 1, state $s_1 = 1$. If at least one acceptable item is obtained subsequently, the state changes to $s_n = 0$, after which no additional costs need to be incurred.

Because of the stated objective for the problem,

$f_n(s_n, x_n)$ = total expected cost for stages n, . . . , 3 if system starts in state s_n at stage n, immediate decision is x_n, and optimal decisions are made thereafter,

$$f_n^*(s_n) = \min_{x_n = 0, 1, \ldots} f_n(s_n, x_n),$$

where $f_n^*(0) = 0$. Using $100 as the unit of money, the contribution to cost from stage n is $[K(x_n) + x_n]$ regardless of the next state, where $K(x_n)$ is a function of x_n such that

$$K(x_n) = \begin{cases} 0, & \text{if } x_n = 0 \\ 3, & \text{if } x_n > 0. \end{cases}$$

Therefore, for $s_n = 1$,

$$f_n(1, x_n) = K(x_n) + x_n + \left(\frac{1}{2}\right)^{x_n} f_{n+1}^*(1) + \left[1 - \left(\frac{1}{2}\right)^{x_n}\right] f_{n+1}^*(0)$$

$$= K(x_n) + x_n + \left(\frac{1}{2}\right)^{x_n} f_{n+1}^*(1)$$

[where $f_4^*(1)$ is defined to be 16, the terminal cost if no acceptable items have been obtained]. A summary of these basic relationships is given in Fig. 11.12.

FIGURE 11.12
The basic structure for the Hit-and-Miss Manufacturing Co. problem.

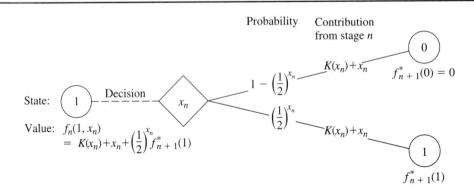

Consequently, the recursive relationship for the dynamic programming calculations is

$$f_n^*(1) = \min_{x_n=0, 1, \ldots} \left\{ K(x_n) + x_n + \left(\frac{1}{2}\right)^{x_n} f_{n+1}^*(1) \right\}$$

for $n = 1, 2, 3$.

Solution Procedure.   The calculations using this recursive relationship are summarized as follows.

$n = 3$:

s_3	x_3	$f_3(1, x_3) = K(x_3) + x_3 + 16\left(\frac{1}{2}\right)^{x_3}$						$f_3^*(s_3)$	x_3^*
		0	**1**	**2**	**3**	**4**	**5**		
0		0						0	0
1		16	12	9	8	8	$8\frac{1}{2}$	8	3 or 4

$n = 2$:

s_2	x_2	$f_2(1, x_2) = K(x_2) + x_2 + \left(\frac{1}{2}\right)^{x_2} f_3^*(1)$					$f_2^*(s_2)$	x_2^*
		0	**1**	**2**	**3**	**4**		
0		0					0	0
1		8	8	7	7	$7\frac{1}{2}$	7	2 or 3

$n = 1$:

s_1	x_1	$f_1(1, x_1) = K(x_1) + x_1 + \left(\frac{1}{2}\right)^{x_1} f_2^*(1)$					$f_1^*(s_1)$	x_1^*
		0	**1**	**2**	**3**	**4**		
1		7	$7\frac{1}{2}$	$6\frac{3}{4}$	$6\frac{7}{8}$	$7\frac{7}{16}$	$6\frac{3}{4}$	2

Thus, the optimal policy is to produce two items on the first production run; if none is acceptable, then produce either two or three items on the second production run; if none is acceptable, then produce either three or four items on the third production run. The total expected cost for this policy is $675.

EXAMPLE 7   Winning in Las Vegas

An enterprising young statistician believes that she has developed a system for winning a popular Las Vegas game. Her colleagues do not believe that her system works, so they have made a large bet with her that if she starts with three chips, she will not have at least five chips after three plays of the game. Each play of the game involves betting any desired number of available chips and then either winning or losing this number of chips. The statistician believes that her system will give her a probability of $\frac{2}{3}$ of winning a given play of the game.

Assuming the statistician is correct, we now use dynamic programming to determine her optimal policy regarding how many chips to bet (if any) at each of the three plays of the game. The decision at each play should take into account the results of earlier plays. The objective is to maximize the probability of winning her bet with her colleagues.

Formulation. The dynamic programming formulation for this problem is

Stage $n = n$th play of game ($n = 1, 2, 3$),
$\quad x_n =$ number of chips to bet at stage n,
State $s_n =$ number of chips in hand to begin stage n.

This definition of the state is chosen because it provides the needed information about the current situation for making an optimal decision on how many chips to bet next.

Because the objective is to maximize the probability that the statistician will win her bet, the objective function to be maximized at each stage must be the probability of finishing the three plays with at least five chips. (Note that the value of ending with more than five chips is just the same as ending with exactly five, since the bet is won either way.) Therefore,

$f_n(s_n, x_n) =$ probability of finishing three plays with at least five chips, given that the statistician starts stage n in state s_n, makes immediate decision x_n, and makes optimal decisions thereafter,

$$f_n^*(s_n) = \max_{x_n = 0, 1, \ldots, s_n} f_n(s_n, x_n).$$

The expression for $f_n(s_n, x_n)$ must reflect the fact that it may still be possible to accumulate five chips eventually even if the statistician should lose the next play. If she loses, the state at the next stage will be $s_n - x_n$, and the probability of finishing with at least five chips will then be $f_{n+1}^*(s_n - x_n)$. If she wins the next play instead, the state will become $s_n + x_n$, and the corresponding probability will be $f_{n+1}^*(s_n + x_n)$. Because the assumed probability of winning a given play is $\frac{2}{3}$, it now follows that

$$f_n(s_n, x_n) = \frac{1}{3} f_{n+1}^*(s_n - x_n) + \frac{2}{3} f_{n+1}^*(s_n + x_n)$$

[where $f_4^*(s_4)$ is defined to be 0 for $s_4 < 5$ and 1 for $s_4 \geq 5$]. Thus, there is no direct contribution to the objective function from stage n other than the effect of then being in the next state. These basic relationships are summarized in Fig. 11.13.

Therefore, the recursive relationship for this problem is

$$f_n^*(s_n) = \max_{x_n = 0, 1, \ldots, s_n} \left\{ \frac{1}{3} f_{n+1}^*(s_n - x_n) + \frac{2}{3} f_{n+1}^*(s_n + x_n) \right\},$$

for $n = 1, 2, 3$, with $f_4^*(s_4)$ as just defined.

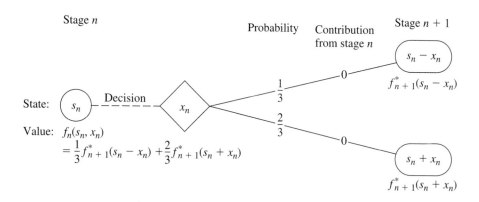

FIGURE 11.13
The basic structure for the Las Vegas problem.

Solution Procedure.   This recursive relationship leads to the following computational results.

$n = 3$:

s_3	$f_3^*(s_3)$	x_3^*
0	0	—
1	0	—
2	0	—
3	$\frac{2}{3}$	2 (or more)
4	$\frac{2}{3}$	1 (or more)
≥ 5	1	0 (or $\leq s_3 - 5$)

$n = 2$:

	$f_2(s_2, x_2) = \frac{1}{3}f_3^*(s_2 - x_2) + \frac{2}{3}f_3^*(s_2 + x_2)$						
s_2	x_2: 0	1	2	3	4	$f_2^*(s_2)$	x_2^*
0	0					0	—
1	0	0				0	—
2	0	$\frac{4}{9}$	$\frac{4}{9}$			$\frac{4}{9}$	1 or 2
3	$\frac{2}{3}$	$\frac{4}{9}$	$\frac{2}{3}$	$\frac{2}{3}$		$\frac{2}{3}$	0, 2, or 3
4	$\frac{2}{3}$	$\frac{8}{9}$	$\frac{2}{3}$	$\frac{2}{3}$	$\frac{2}{3}$	$\frac{8}{9}$	1
≥ 5	1					1	0 (or $\leq s_2 - 5$)

$n = 1$:

	$f_1(s_1, x_1) = \frac{1}{3}f_2^*(s_1 - x_1) + \frac{2}{3}f_2^*(s_1 + x_1)$					
s_1	x_1: 0	1	2	3	$f_1^*(s_1)$	x_1^*
3	$\frac{2}{3}$	$\frac{20}{27}$	$\frac{2}{3}$	$\frac{2}{3}$	$\frac{20}{27}$	1

Therefore, the optimal policy is

$$x_1^* = 1 \begin{cases} \text{if win,} \quad x_2^* = 1 \begin{cases} \text{if win,} \quad x_3^* = 0 \\ \text{if lose,} \quad x_3^* = 2 \text{ or } 3. \end{cases} \\ \text{if lose,} \quad x_2^* = 1 \text{ or } 2 \begin{cases} \text{if win,} \quad x_3^* = \begin{cases} 2 \text{ or } 3 & (\text{for } x_2^* = 1) \\ 1, 2, 3, \text{ or } 4 & (\text{for } x_2^* = 2) \end{cases} \\ \text{if lose,} \quad \text{bet is lost} \end{cases} \end{cases}$$

This policy gives the statistician a probability of $\frac{20}{27}$ of winning her bet with her colleagues.

11.5 CONCLUSIONS

Dynamic programming is a very useful technique for making a *sequence of interrelated decisions*. It requires formulating an appropriate *recursive relationship* for each individual problem. However, it provides a great computational savings over using exhaustive enumeration to find the best combination of decisions, especially for large problems. For example, if a problem has 10 stages with 10 states and 10 possible decisions at each stage, then exhaustive enumeration must consider up to 10 billion combinations, whereas dynamic programming need make no more than a thousand calculations (10 for each state at each stage).

This chapter has considered only dynamic programming with a *finite* number of stages. Chapter 21 is devoted to a general kind of model for probabilistic dynamic programming where the stages continue to recur indefinitely, namely, Markov decision processes.

SELECTED REFERENCES

1. Bertsekas, D. P.: *Dynamic Programming: Deterministic and Stochastic Models,* Prentice-Hall, Englewood Cliffs, NJ, 1987.
2. Denardo, E. V.: *Dynamic Programming Theory and Applications,* Prentice-Hall, Englewood Cliffs, NJ, 1982.
3. Howard, R. A.: "Dynamic Programming," *Management Science,* **12:** 317–345, 1966.
4. Smith, D. K.: *Dynamic Programming: A Practical Introduction,* Ellis Horwood, London, 1991.
5. Sniedovich, M.: *Dynamic Programming,* Marcel Dekker, New York, 1991.

LEARNING AIDS FOR THIS CHAPTER IN YOUR OR COURSEWARE

"Ch. 11—Dynamic Programming" LINGO File

PROBLEMS

An asterisk on the problem number indicates that at least a partial answer is given in the back of the book.

11.2-1. Consider the following network, where each number along a link represents the actual distance between the pair of nodes connected by that link. The objective is to find the shortest path from the origin to the destination.

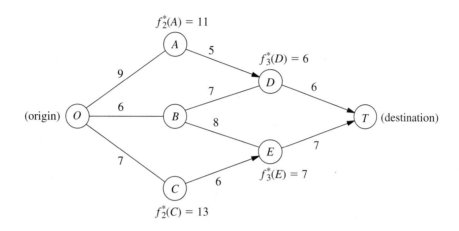

(a) What are the stages and states for the dynamic programming formulation of this problem?

(b) Use dynamic programming to solve this problem. However, instead of using the usual tables, show your work graphically (similar to Fig. 11.2). In particular, start with the given network, where the answers already are given for $f_n^*(s_n)$ for four of the nodes; then solve for and fill in $f_2^*(B)$ and $f_1^*(O)$. Draw an arrowhead that shows the optimal link to traverse out of each of the latter two nodes. Finally, identify the optimal path by following the arrows from node O onward to node T.

(c) Use dynamic programming to solve this problem by manually constructing the usual tables for $n = 3$, $n = 2$, and $n = 1$.

(d) Use the shortest-path algorithm presented in Sec. 9.3 to solve this problem. Compare and contrast this approach with the one in parts (b) and (c).

11.2-2. The sales manager for a publisher of college textbooks has six traveling salespeople to assign to three different regions of the country. She has decided that each region should be assigned at least one salesperson and that each individual salesperson should be restricted to one of the regions, but now she wants to determine how many salespeople should be assigned to the respective regions in order to maximize sales.

The following table gives the estimated increase in sales (in appropriate units) in each region if it were allocated various numbers of salespeople:

Salespersons	Region		
	1	**2**	**3**
1	35	21	28
2	48	42	41
3	70	56	63
4	89	70	75

(a) Use dynamic programming to solve this problem. Instead of using the usual tables, show your work graphically by constructing and filling in a network such as the one shown for Prob. 11.2-1. Proceed as in Prob. 11.2-1b by solving for $f_n^*(s_n)$ for each node (except the terminal node) and writing its value by the node. Draw an arrowhead to show the optimal link (or links in case of a tie) to take out of each node. Finally, identify the resulting optimal path (or paths) through the network and the corresponding optimal solution (or solutions).

(b) Use dynamic programming to solve this problem by constructing the usual tables for $n = 3$, $n = 2$, and $n = 1$.

11.2-3. Consider the following project network when applying PERT/CPM as described in Chap. 10, where the number over each node is the time required for the corresponding activity. Consider the problem of finding the *longest path* (the largest total time) through this network from start to finish, since the longest path is the critical path.

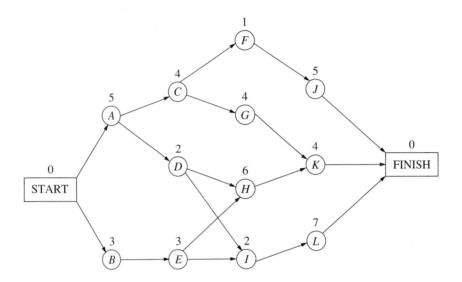

(a) What are the stages and states for the dynamic programming formulation of this problem?

(b) Use dynamic programming to solve this problem. However, instead of using the usual tables, show your work graphically. In particular, fill in the values of the various $f_n^*(s_n)$ under the corresponding nodes, and show the resulting optimal arc to traverse out of each node by drawing an arrowhead near the beginning of the arc. Then identify the optimal path (the longest path) by following these arrowheads from the Start node to the Finish node. If there is more than one optimal path, identify them all.

(c) Use dynamic programming to solve this problem by constructing the usual tables for $n = 4$, $n = 3$, $n = 2$, and $n = 1$.

11.2-4. Consider the following statements about solving dynamic programming problems. Label each statement as true or false, and then justify your answer by referring to specific statements (with page citations) in the chapter.

(a) The solution procedure uses a recursive relationship that enables solving for the optimal policy for stage $(n + 1)$ given the optimal policy for stage n.

(b) After completing the solution procedure, if a nonoptimal decision is made by mistake at some stage, the solution procedure will need to be reapplied to determine the new optimal decisions (given this nonoptimal decision) at the subsequent stages.

(c) Once an optimal policy has been found for the overall problem, the information needed to specify the optimal decision at a particular stage is the state at that stage and the decisions made at preceding stages.

11.3-1.* The owner of a chain of three grocery stores has purchased five crates of fresh strawberries. The estimated probability distribution of potential sales of the strawberries before spoilage differs among the three stores. Therefore, the owner wants to know how to allocate five crates to the three stores to maximize expected profit.

For administrative reasons, the owner does not wish to split crates between stores. However, he is willing to distribute no crates to any of his stores.

The following table gives the estimated expected profit at each store when it is allocated various numbers of crates:

	Store		
Crates	**1**	**2**	**3**
0	0	0	0
1	5	6	4
2	9	11	9
3	14	15	13
4	17	19	18
5	21	22	20

Use dynamic programming to determine how many of the five crates should be assigned to each of the three stores to maximize the total expected profit.

11.3-2. A college student has 7 days remaining before final examinations begin in her four courses, and she wants to allocate this study time as effectively as possible. She needs at least 1 day on each course, and she likes to concentrate on just one course each day, so she wants to allocate 1, 2, 3, or 4 days to each course. Having recently taken an OR course, she decides to use dynamic programming to make these allocations to maximize the total grade points to be obtained from the four courses. She estimates that the alternative allocations for each course would yield the number of grade points shown in the following table:

	Estimated Grade Points			
	Course			
Study Days	1	2	3	4
1	3	5	2	6
2	5	5	4	7
3	6	6	7	9
4	7	9	8	9

Solve this problem by dynamic programming.

11.3-3. A company is planning its advertising strategy for next year for its three major products. Since the three products are quite different, each advertising effort will focus on a single product. In units of millions of dollars, a total of 6 is available for advertising next year, where the advertising expenditure for each product must be an integer greater than or equal to 1. The vice-president for marketing has established the objective: Determine how much to spend on each product in order to maximize total sales. The following table gives the estimated increase in sales (in appropriate units) for the different advertising expenditures:

Advertising Expenditure	Product		
	1	2	3
1	7	4	6
2	10	8	9
3	14	11	13
4	17	14	15

Use dynamic programming to solve this problem.

11.3-4. A political campaign is entering its final stage, and polls indicate a very close election. One of the candidates has enough funds left to purchase TV time for a total of five prime-time commercials on TV stations located in four different areas. Based on polling information, an estimate has been made of the number of additional votes that can be won in the different broadcasting areas depending upon the number of commercials run. These estimates are given in the following table in thousands of votes:

Commercials	Area			
	1	2	3	4
0	0	0	0	0
1	4	6	5	3
2	7	8	9	7
3	9	10	11	12
4	12	11	10	14
5	15	12	9	16

Use dynamic programming to determine how the five commercials should be distributed among the four areas in order to maximize the estimated number of votes won.

11.3-5. A county chairwoman of a certain political party is making plans for an upcoming presidential election. She has received the services of six volunteer workers for precinct work, and she wants to assign them to four precincts in such a way as to maximize their effectiveness. She feels that it would be inefficient to assign a worker to more than one precinct, but she is willing to assign no workers to any one of the precincts if they can accomplish more in other precincts.

The following table gives the estimated increase in the number of votes for the party's candidate in each precinct if it were allocated various numbers of workers:

Workers	Precinct			
	1	2	3	4
0	0	0	0	0
1	4	7	5	6
2	9	11	10	11
3	15	16	15	14
4	18	18	18	16
5	22	20	21	17
6	24	21	22	18

This problem has several optimal solutions for how many of the six workers should be assigned to each of the four precincts to maximize the total estimated increase in the plurality of the party's candidate. Use dynamic programming to find all of them so the chairwoman can make the final selection based on other factors.

11.3-6. Use dynamic programming to solve the Northern Airplane Co. production scheduling problem presented in Sec. 8.1 (see Table 8.7). Assume that production quantities must be integer multiples of 5.

11.3-7. Reconsider the Build-Em-Fast Co. problem described in Prob. 8.1-9. Use dynamic programming to solve this problem.

11.3-8.* A company will soon be introducing a new product into a very competitive market and is currently planning its marketing strategy. The decision has been made to introduce the product in three phases. Phase 1 will feature making a special introductory offer of the product to the public at a greatly reduced price to attract first-time buyers. Phase 2 will involve an intensive advertising campaign to persuade these first-time buyers to continue purchasing the product at a regular price. It is known that another company will be introducing a new competitive product at about the time that phase 2 will end. Therefore, phase 3 will involve a follow-up advertising and promotion campaign to try to keep the regular purchasers from switching to the competitive product.

A total of $4 million has been budgeted for this marketing campaign. The problem now is to determine how to allocate this money most effectively to the three phases. Let m denote the initial share of the market (expressed as a percentage) attained in phase 1, f_2 the fraction of this market share that is retained in phase 2, and f_3 the fraction of the remaining market share that is retained in phase 3. Given the following data, use dynamic programming to determine how to allocate the $4 million to maximize the final share of the market for the new product, i.e., to maximize mf_2f_3.

(a) Assume that the money must be spent in integer multiples of $1 million in each phase, where the minimum permissible multiple is 1 for phase 1 and 0 for phases 2 and 3. The following table gives the estimated effect of expenditures in each phase:

Millions of Dollars Expended	Effect on Market Share		
	m	f_2	f_3
0	—	0.2	0.3
1	20	0.4	0.5
2	30	0.5	0.6
3	40	0.6	0.7
4	50	—	—

(b) Now assume that *any* amount within the total budget can be spent in each phase, where the estimated effect of spending an amount x_i (in units of *millions* of dollars) in phase i ($i = 1, 2, 3$) is

$$m = 10x_1 - x_1^2$$
$$f_2 = 0.40 + 0.10x_2$$
$$f_3 = 0.60 + 0.07x_3.$$

[*Hint:* After solving for the $f_2^*(s)$ and $f_3^*(s)$ functions analytically, solve for x_1^* graphically.]

11.3-9. The management of a company is considering three possible new products for next year's product line. A decision now needs to be made regarding which products to market and at what production levels.

Initiating the production of two of these products would require a substantial start-up cost, as shown in the first row of the table below. Once production is under way, the marginal net revenue from each unit produced is shown in the second row. The third row gives the percentage of the available production capacity that would be used for each unit produced.

	Product		
	1	**2**	**3**
Start-up cost	3	2	0
Marginal net revenue	2	3	1
Capacity used per unit, %	20	40	20

Only 3 units of product 1 could be sold, whereas all units that could be produced of the other two products could be sold. The objective is to determine the number of units of each product to produce in order to maximize the total profit (total net revenue minus start-up costs).

(a) Assuming that production quantities must be integers, use dynamic programming to solve this problem.
(b) Now consider the case where the divisibility assumption holds, so that the variables representing production quantities are treated as *continuous* variables. Assuming that proportionality holds for both net revenues and capacities used, use dynamic programming to solve this problem.

11.3-10. Consider an electronic system consisting of four components, each of which must work for the system to function. The reliability of the system can be improved by installing several parallel units in one or more of the components. The following table gives the probability that the respective components will function if they consist of one, two, or three parallel units:

Parallel Units	Probability of Functioning			
	Component 1	Component 2	Component 3	Component 4
1	0.5	0.6	0.7	0.5
2	0.6	0.7	0.8	0.7
3	0.8	0.8	0.9	0.9

The probability that the system will function is the product of the probabilities that the respective components will function.

The cost (in hundreds of dollars) of installing one, two, or three parallel units in the respective components is given by the following table:

Parallel Units	Cost			
	Component 1	Component 2	Component 3	Component 4
1	1	2	1	2
2	2	4	3	3
3	3	5	4	4

Because of budget limitations, a maximum of $1,000 can be expended.

Use dynamic programming to determine how many parallel units should be installed in each of the four components to maximize the probability that the system will function.

11.3-11. Consider the following integer nonlinear programming problem.

Maximize $Z = 3x_1^2 - x_1^3 + 5x_2^2 - x_2^3,$

subject to

$$x_1 + 2x_2 \le 4$$

and

$$x_1 \ge 0, \qquad x_2 \ge 0$$
$$x_1, x_2 \text{ are integers.}$$

Use dynamic programming to solve this problem.

11.3-12. Consider the following integer nonlinear programming problem.

Maximize $Z = 18x_1 - x_1^2 + 20x_2 + 10x_3,$

subject to

$$2x_1 + 4x_2 + 3x_3 \le 11$$

and

x_1, x_2, x_3 are nonnegative integers.

Use dynamic programming to solve this problem.

11.3-13. Consider the following integer nonlinear programming problem.

Maximize $Z = x_1 x_2^2 x_3^3,$

subject to

$$x_1 + 2x_2 + 3x_3 \le 10$$
$$x_1 \ge 1, \qquad x_2 \ge 1, \qquad x_3 \ge 1,$$

and

x_1, x_2, x_3 are integers.

Use dynamic programming to solve this problem.

11.3-14.* Consider the following nonlinear programming problem.

Maximize $Z = 36x_1 + 9x_1^2 - 6x_1^3 + 36x_2 - 3x_2^3,$

subject to

$$x_1 + x_2 \le 3$$

and

$$x_1 \ge 0, \qquad x_2 \ge 0.$$

Use dynamic programming to solve this problem.

11.3-15. Re-solve the Local Job Shop employment scheduling problem (Example 4) when the total cost of changing the level of employment from one season to the next is changed to $100 times the square of the difference in employment levels.

11.3-16. Consider the following nonlinear programming problem.

Maximize $Z = 2x_1^2 + 2x_2 + 4x_3 - x_3^2$

subject to

$$2x_1 + x_2 + x_3 \le 4$$

and

$$x_1 \ge 0, \qquad x_2 \ge 0, \qquad x_3 \ge 0.$$

Use dynamic programming to solve this problem.

11.3-17. Consider the following nonlinear programming problem.

Maximize $Z = 2x_1 + x_2^2,$

subject to

$$x_1^2 + x_2^2 \le 4$$

and

$$x_1 \ge 0, \qquad x_2 \ge 0.$$

Use dynamic programming to solve this problem.

11.3-18. Consider the following nonlinear programming problem.

$$\text{Minimize} \quad Z = x_1^4 + 2x_2^2$$

subject to

$$x_1^2 + x_2^2 \geq 2.$$

(There are no nonnegativity constraints.) Use dynamic programming to solve this problem.

11.3-19. Consider the following nonlinear programming problem.

$$\text{Maximize} \quad Z = x_1^2 x_2,$$

subject to

$$x_1^2 + x_2 \leq 2.$$

(There are no nonnegativity constraints.) Use dynamic programming to solve this problem.

11.3-20. Consider the following nonlinear programming problem.

$$\text{Maximize} \quad Z = x_1^3 + 4x_2^2 + 16x_3,$$

subject to

$$x_1 x_2 x_3 = 4$$

and

$$x_1 \geq 1, \qquad x_2 \geq 1, \qquad x_3 \geq 1.$$

(a) Solve by dynamic programming when, in addition to the given constraints, all three variables also are required to be integer.
(b) Use dynamic programming to solve the problem as given (continuous variables).

11.3-21. Consider the following nonlinear programming problem.

$$\text{Maximize} \quad Z = x_1(1 - x_2)x_3,$$

subject to

$$x_1 - x_2 + x_3 \leq 1$$

and

$$x_1 \geq 0, \qquad x_2 \geq 0, \qquad x_3 \geq 0.$$

Use dynamic programming to solve this problem.

11.3-22. Consider the following linear programming problem.

$$\text{Maximize} \quad Z = 15x_1 + 10x_2,$$

subject to

$$x_1 + 2x_2 \leq 6$$
$$3x_1 + x_2 \leq 8$$

and

$$x_1 \geq 0, \qquad x_2 \geq 0.$$

Use dynamic programming to solve this problem.

11.3-23. Consider the following nonlinear programming problem.

$$\text{Maximize} \quad Z = 5x_1 + x_2,$$

subject to

$$2x_1^2 + x_2 \leq 13$$
$$x_1^2 + x_2 \leq 9$$

and

$$x_1 \geq 0, \qquad x_2 \geq 0.$$

Use dynamic programming to solve this problem.

11.3-24. Consider the following "fixed-charge" problem.

$$\text{Maximize} \quad Z = 3x_1 + 7x_2 + 6f(x_3),$$

subject to

$$x_1 + 3x_2 + 2x_3 \leq 6$$
$$x_1 + x_2 \leq 5$$

and

$$x_1 \geq 0, \qquad x_2 \geq 0, \qquad x_3 \geq 0,$$

where

$$f(x_3) = \begin{cases} 0 & \text{if } x_3 = 0 \\ -1 + x_3 & \text{if } x_3 > 0. \end{cases}$$

Use dynamic programming to solve this problem.

11.4-1. A backgammon player will be playing three consecutive matches with friends tonight. For each match, he will have the opportunity to place an even bet that he will win; the amount bet can be *any* quantity of his choice between zero and the amount of money he still has left after the bets on the preceding matches. For each match, the probability is $\frac{1}{2}$ that he will win the match and thus win the amount bet, whereas the probability is $\frac{1}{2}$ that he will lose the match and thus lose the amount bet. He will begin with $75, and his goal is to have $100 at the end. (Because these are friendly matches, he does not want to end up with more than $100.) Therefore, he wants to find the optimal betting policy (including all ties) that maximizes the probability that he will have exactly $100 after the three matches.

Use dynamic programming to solve this problem.

11.4-2. Imagine that you have $5,000 to invest and that you will have an opportunity to invest that amount in either of two investments (*A* or *B*) at the beginning of each of the next 3 years. Both investments have uncertain returns. For investment *A* you will either lose your money entirely or (with higher probability) get back $10,000 (a profit of $5,000) at the end of the year. For investment *B* you will get back either just your $5,000 or (with low probability) $10,000 at the end of the year. The probabilities for these events are as follows:

Investment	Amount Returned ($)	Probability
A	0	0.3
	10,000	0.7
B	5,000	0.9
	10,000	0.1

You are allowed to make only (at most) *one* investment each year, and you can invest only $5,000 each time. (Any additional money accumulated is left idle.)

(a) Use dynamic programming to find the investment policy that maximizes the expected amount of money you will have after 3 years.

(b) Use dynamic programming to find the investment policy that maximizes the probability that you will have at least $10,000 after 3 years.

11.4-3.* Suppose that the situation for the Hit-and-Miss Manufacturing Co. problem (Example 6) has changed somewhat. After a more careful analysis, you now estimate that each item produced will be acceptable with probability $\frac{2}{3}$, rather than $\frac{1}{2}$, so that the probability of producing *zero* acceptable items in a lot of size *L* is $(\frac{1}{3})^L$. Furthermore, there now is only enough time available to make two production runs. Use dynamic programming to determine the new optimal policy for this problem.

11.4-4. Reconsider Example 7. Suppose that the bet is changed as follows: "Starting with two chips, she will not have at least five chips after five plays of the game." By referring to the previous computational results, make additional calculations to determine the new optimal policy for the enterprising young statistician.

11.4-5. The Profit & Gambit Co. has a major product that has been losing money recently because of declining sales. In fact, during the current quarter of the year, sales will be 4 million units below the break-even point. Because the marginal revenue for each unit sold exceeds the marginal cost by $5, this amounts to a loss of $20 million for the quarter. Therefore, management must take action quickly to rectify this situation. Two alternative courses of action are being considered. One is to abandon the product immediately, incurring a cost of $20 million for shutting down. The other alternative is to undertake an intensive advertising campaign to increase sales and then abandon the product (at the cost of $20 million) only if the campaign is not sufficiently successful. Tentative plans for this advertising campaign have been developed and analyzed. It would extend over the next three quarters (subject to early cancellation), and the cost would be $30 million in each of the three quarters. It is estimated that the increase in sales would be approximately 3 million units in the first quarter, another 2 million units in the second quarter, and another 1 million units in the third quarter. However, because of a number of unpredictable market variables, there is considerable uncertainty as to what impact the advertising actually would have; and careful analysis indicates that the estimates for each quarter could turn out to be off by as much as 2 million units in either direction. (To quantify this uncertainty, assume that the additional increases in sales in the three quarters are independent random variables having a uniform distribution with a range from 1 to 5 million, from 0 to 4 million, and from −1 to 3 million, respectively.) If the actual increases are too small, the advertising campaign can be discontinued and the product abandoned at the end of either of the next two quarters.

If the intensive advertising campaign were initiated and continued to its completion, it is estimated that the sales for some time thereafter would continue to be at about the same level as in the third (last) quarter of the campaign. Therefore, if the sales in that quarter still were below the break-even point, the product would be abandoned. Otherwise, it is estimated that the expected discounted profit thereafter would be $40 for each unit sold over the break-even point in the third quarter.

Use dynamic programming to determine the optimal policy maximizing the expected profit.

12

Integer Programming

In Chap. 3 you saw several examples of the numerous and diverse applications of linear programming. However, one key limitation that prevents many more applications is the assumption of divisibility (see Sec. 3.3), which requires that noninteger values be permissible for decision variables. In many practical problems, the decision variables actually make sense only if they have integer values. For example, it is often necessary to assign people, machines, and vehicles to activities in integer quantities. If requiring integer values is the only way in which a problem deviates from a linear programming formulation, then it is an *integer programming* (**IP**) problem. (The more complete name is *integer linear programming,* but the adjective *linear* normally is dropped except when this problem is contrasted with the more esoteric integer nonlinear programming problem, which is beyond the scope of this book.)

The mathematical model for integer programming is the linear programming model (see Sec. 3.2) with the one additional restriction that the variables must have integer values. If only *some* of the variables are required to have integer values (so the divisibility assumption holds for the rest), this model is referred to as **mixed integer programming (MIP).** When distinguishing the all-integer problem from this mixed case, we call the former *pure* integer programming.

For example, the Wyndor Glass Co. problem presented in Sec. 3.1 actually would have been an IP problem if the two decision variables x_1 and x_2 had represented the total number of units to be produced of products 1 and 2, respectively, instead of the production rates. Because both products (glass doors and wood-framed windows) necessarily come in whole units, x_1 and x_2 would have to be restricted to integer values.

Another example of an IP problem is provided by the prize-winning OR study done for the **San Francisco Police Department** that we introduced (and referenced) in Sec. 2.1. As indicated there, this study resulted in the development of a computerized system for optimally scheduling and deploying police patrol officers. The new system provided annual savings of $11 million, an annual $3 million increase in traffic citation revenues, and a 20 percent improvement in response times. The main decision variables in the mathematical model were the number of officers to schedule to go on duty at each of the shift start times. Since this number had to be an integer, these decision variables were restricted to having integer values.

There have been numerous such applications of integer programming that involve a direct extension of linear programming where the divisibility assumption must be dropped. However, another area of application may be of even greater importance, namely, problems involving a number of interrelated "yes-or-no decisions." In such decisions, the only two possible choices are *yes* and *no*. For example, should we undertake a particular fixed project? Should we make a particular fixed investment? Should we locate a facility in a particular site?

With just two choices, we can represent such decisions by decision variables that are restricted to just two values, say 0 and 1. Thus, the *j*th yes-or-no decision would be represented by, say, x_j such that

$$x_j = \begin{cases} 1 & \text{if decision } j \text{ is yes} \\ 0 & \text{if decision } j \text{ is no.} \end{cases}$$

Such variables are called **binary variables** (or 0–1 variables). Consequently, IP problems that contain only binary variables sometimes are called **binary integer programming (BIP)** problems (or 0–1 integer programming problems).

Section 12.1 presents a miniature version of a typical BIP problem and Sec. 12.2 surveys a variety of other BIP applications. Additional formulation possibilities with binary variables are discussed in Sec. 12.3, and Sec. 12.4 presents a series of formulation examples. The remaining sections then deal with ways to solve IP problems, including both BIP and MIP problems.

12.1 PROTOTYPE EXAMPLE

The CALIFORNIA MANUFACTURING COMPANY is considering expansion by building a new factory in either Los Angeles or San Francisco, or perhaps even in both cities. It also is considering building at most one new warehouse, but the choice of location is restricted to a city where a new factory is being built. The *net present value* (total profitability considering the time value of money) of each of these alternatives is shown in the fourth column of Table 12.1. The rightmost column gives the capital required (already included in the net present value) for the respective investments, where the total capital available is $10 million. The objective is to find the feasible combination of alternatives that maximizes the total net present value.

TABLE 12.1 Data for the California Manufacturing Co. example

Decision Number	Yes-or-No Question	Decision Variable	Net Present Value	Capital Required
1	Build factory in Los Angeles?	x_1	$9 million	$6 million
2	Build factory in San Francisco?	x_2	$5 million	$3 million
3	Build warehouse in Los Angeles?	x_3	$6 million	$5 million
4	Build warehouse in San Francisco?	x_4	$4 million	$2 million

Capital available: $10 million

The BIP Model

Although this problem is small enough that it can be solved very quickly by inspection (build factories in both cities but no warehouse), let us formulate the IP model for illustrative purposes. All the decision variables have the *binary* form

$$x_j = \begin{cases} 1 & \text{if decision } j \text{ is yes,} \\ 0 & \text{if decision } j \text{ is no,} \end{cases} \qquad (j = 1, 2, 3, 4).$$

Let

Z = total net present value of these decisions.

If the investment is made to build a particular facility (so that the corresponding decision variable has a value of 1), the estimated net present value from that investment is given in the fourth column of Table 12.1. If the investment is not made (so the decision variable equals 0), the net present value is 0. Therefore, using units of millions of dollars,

$$Z = 9x_1 + 5x_2 + 6x_3 + 4x_4.$$

The rightmost column of Table 12.1 indicates that the amount of capital expended on the four facilities cannot exceed \$10 million. Consequently, continuing to use units of millions of dollars, one constraint in the model is

$$6x_1 + 3x_2 + 5x_3 + 2x_4 \leq 10.$$

Because the last two decisions represent *mutually exclusive alternatives* (the company wants *at most* one new warehouse), we also need the constraint

$$x_3 + x_4 \leq 1.$$

Furthermore, decisions 3 and 4 are *contingent decisions,* because they are contingent on decisions 1 and 2, respectively (the company would consider building a warehouse in a city only if a new factory also were going there). Thus, in the case of decision 3, we require that $x_3 = 0$ if $x_1 = 0$. This restriction on x_3 (when $x_1 = 0$) is imposed by adding the constraint

$$x_3 \leq x_1.$$

Similarly, the requirement that $x_4 = 0$ if $x_2 = 0$ is imposed by adding the constraint

$$x_4 \leq x_2.$$

Therefore, after we rewrite these two constraints to bring all variables to the left-hand side, the complete BIP model is

$$\text{Maximize} \quad Z = 9x_1 + 5x_2 + 6x_3 + 4x_4,$$

subject to

$$
\begin{array}{rl}
6x_1 + 3x_2 + 5x_3 + 2x_4 & \leq 10 \\
x_3 + x_4 & \leq 1 \\
-x_1 \qquad\quad + x_3 \qquad\quad & \leq 0 \\
- x_2 \qquad\quad + x_4 & \leq 0 \\
x_j & \leq 1 \\
x_j & \geq 0
\end{array}
$$

and

x_j is integer,   for $j = 1, 2, 3, 4$.

Equivalently, the last three lines of this model can be replaced by the single restriction

x_j is binary,   for $j = 1, 2, 3, 4$.

Except for its small size, this example is typical of many real applications of integer programming where the basic decisions to be made are of the yes-or-no type. Like the second pair of decisions for this example, groups of yes-or-no decisions often constitute groups of **mutually exclusive alternatives** such that *only one* decision in the group can be yes. Each group requires a constraint that the sum of the corresponding binary variables must be equal to 1 (if *exactly one* decision in the group must be yes) or less than or equal to 1 (if *at most one* decision in the group can be yes). Occasionally, decisions of the yes-or-no type are **contingent decisions**, i.e., decisions that depend upon previous decisions. For example, one decision is said to be *contingent* on another decision if it is allowed to be yes *only if* the other is yes. This situation occurs when the contingent decision involves a follow-up action that would become irrelevant, or even impossible, if the other decision were no. The form that the resulting constraint takes always is that illustrated by the third and fourth constraints in the example.

Software Options for Solving Such Models

All the software packages featured in your OR Courseware (Excel, LINGO/LINDO, and MPL/CPLEX) include an algorithm for solving (pure or mixed) BIP models, as well as an algorithm for solving general (pure or mixed) IP models where variables need to be integer but not binary.

When using the Excel Solver, the procedure is basically the same as for linear programming. The one difference arises when you click on the "Add" button on the Solver dialogue box to add the constraints. In addition to the constraints that fit linear programming, you also need to add the integer constraints. In the case of integer variables that are not binary, this is accomplished in the Add Constraint dialogue box by choosing the range of integer-restricted variables on the left-hand side and then choosing "int" from the pop-up menu. In the case of binary variables, choose "bin" from the pop-up menu instead. (In earlier versions of Excel that do not include the "bin" option, choose "int" and then add ≥ 0 and ≤ 1 constraints on these binary variables.)

A LINGO model uses the function @BIN() to specify that the variable named inside the parentheses is a binary variable. For a *general* integer variable (one restricted to integer values but not just binary values), the function @GIN() is used in the same way. In either case, the function can be embedded inside an @FOR statement to impose this binary or integer constraint on an entire set of variables.

In a LINDO model, the binary or integer constraints are inserted after the END statement. A variable X is specified to be a general integer variable by entering GIN X. Alternatively, for any positive integer value of *n,* the statement GIN *n* specifies that the first *n* variables are general integer variables. Binary variables are handled in the same way except for substituting the word INTEGER for GIN.

For an MPL model, the keyword INTEGER is used to designate general integer variables, whereas BINARY is used for binary variables. In the variables section of an MPL model, all you need to do is add the appropriate adjective (INTEGER or BINARY) in front of the label VARIABLES to specify that the set of variables listed below the label is of that type. Alternatively, you can ignore this specification in the variables section and instead place the integer or binary constraints in the model section anywhere after the other constraints. In this case, the label over the set of variables becomes just INTEGER or BINARY.

The prime MPL solver CPLEX includes state-of-the-art algorithms for solving pure or mixed IP or BIP models. By selecting *MIP Strategy* from the *CPLEX Parameters* submenu in the *Options* menu, an experienced practitioner can even choose from a wide variety of options for exactly how to execute the algorithm to best fit the particular problem.

These instructions for how to use the various software packages become clearer when you see them applied to examples. The Excel, LINGO/LINDO, and MPL/CPLEX files for this chapter in your OR Courseware show how each of these software options would be applied to the prototype example introduced in this section, as well as to the subsequent IP examples.

The latter part of the chapter will focus on IP algorithms that are similar to those used in these software packages. Section 12.6 will use the prototype example to illustrate the application of the pure BIP algorithm presented there.

12.2 SOME BIP APPLICATIONS

Just as in the California Manufacturing Co. example, managers frequently must face *yes-or-no decisions*. Therefore, *binary integer programming* (BIP) is widely used to aid in these decisions.

We now will introduce various types of yes-or-no decisions. We also will mention some examples of actual applications where BIP was used to address these decisions.

Each of these applications is fully described in an article in the journal called *Interfaces*. In each case, we will mention the specific issue in which the article appears in case you want to read further.

Capital Budgeting with Fixed Investment Proposals

Linear programming sometimes is used to make capital budgeting decisions about how much to invest in various projects. However, as the California Manufacturing Co. example demonstrates, some capital budgeting decisions do not involve *how much* to invest, but rather, *whether* to invest a fixed amount. Specifically, the four decisions in the example were whether to invest the fixed amount of capital required to build a certain kind of facility (factory or warehouse) in a certain location (Los Angeles or San Francisco).

Management often must face decisions about whether to make fixed investments (those where the amount of capital required has been fixed in advance). Should we acquire a certain subsidiary being spun off by another company? Should we purchase a certain source of raw materials? Should we add a new production line to produce a certain input item ourselves rather than continuing to obtain it from a supplier?

In general, capital budgeting decisions about fixed investments are yes-or-no decisions of the following type.

Each yes-or-no decision:
Should we make a certain fixed investment?

$$\text{Its decision variable} = \begin{cases} 1 & \text{if yes} \\ 0 & \text{if no.} \end{cases}$$

The July–August 1990 issue of *Interfaces* describes how the *Turkish Petroleum Refineries Corporation* used BIP to analyze capital investments worth tens of millions of dollars to expand refinery capacity and conserve energy.

A rather different example that still falls somewhat into this category is described in the January–February 1997 issue of *Interfaces*. A major OR study was conducted for the *South African National Defense Force* to upgrade its capabilities with a smaller budget. The "investments" under consideration in this case were acquisition costs and ongoing expenses that would be required to provide specific types of military capabilities. A mixed BIP model was formulated to choose those specific capabilities that would maximize the overall effectiveness of the Defense Force while satisfying a budget constraint. The model had over 16,000 variables (including 256 binary variables) and over 5,000 functional constraints. The resulting optimization of the size and shape of the defense force provided savings of over $1.1 billion per year as well as vital nonmonetary benefits. The impact of this study won it the prestigious *first prize* among the 1996 Franz Edelman Awards for Management Science Achievement.

Site Selection

In this global economy, many corporations are opening up new plants in various parts of the world to take advantage of lower labor costs, etc. Before selecting a site for a new plant, many potential sites may need to be analyzed and compared. (The California Manufacturing Co. example had just two potential sites for each of two kinds of facilities.) Each of the potential sites involves a yes-or-no decision of the following type.

Each yes-or-no decision:
Should a certain site be selected for the location of a certain new facility?

Its decision variable $= \begin{cases} 1 & \text{if yes} \\ 0 & \text{if no.} \end{cases}$

In many cases, the objective is to select the sites so as to minimize the total cost of the new facilities that will provide the required output.

As described in the January–February 1990 issue of *Interfaces,* AT&T used a BIP model to help dozens of their customers select the sites for their telemarketing centers. The model minimizes labor, communications, and real estate costs while providing the desired level of coverage by the centers. In one year alone (1988), this approach enabled 46 AT&T customers to make their yes-or-no decisions on site locations swiftly and confidently, while committing to $375 million in annual network services and $31 million in equipment sales from AT&T.

We next describe an important type of problem for many corporations where site selection plays a key role.

Designing a Production and Distribution Network

Manufacturers today face great competitive pressure to get their products to market more quickly as well as to reduce their production and distribution costs. Therefore, any corporation that distributes its products over a wide geographical area (or even worldwide) must pay continuing attention to the design of its production and distribution network.

This design involves addressing the following kinds of yes-or-no decisions.

Should a certain plant remain open?
Should a certain site be selected for a new plant?
Should a certain distribution center remain open?
Should a certain site be selected for a new distribution center?

If each market area is to be served by a single distribution center, then we also have another kind of yes-or-no decision for each combination of a market area and a distribution center.

Should a certain distribution center be assigned to serve a certain market area?

For each of the yes-or-no decisions of any of these kinds,

$$\text{Its decision variable} = \begin{cases} 1 & \text{if yes} \\ 0 & \text{if no.} \end{cases}$$

Ault Foods Limited (July–August 1994 issue of *Interfaces*) used this approach to design its production and distribution center. Management considered 10 sites for plants, 13 sites for distribution centers, and 48 market areas. This application of BIP was credited with saving the company $200,000 per year.

Digital Equipment Corporation (January–February 1995 issue of *Interfaces*) provides another example of an application of this kind. At the time, this large multinational corporation was serving one-quarter million customer sites, with more than half of its $14 billion annual revenues coming from 81 countries outside the United States. Therefore, this application involved restructuring the corporation's entire *global supply chain,* consisting of its suppliers, plants, distribution centers, potential sites, and market areas all around the world. The restructuring generated annual cost reductions of $500 million in manufacturing and $300 million in logistics, as well as a reduction of over $400 million in required capital assets.

Dispatching Shipments

Once a production and distribution network has been designed and put into operation, daily operating decisions need to be made about how to send the shipments. Some of these decisions again are yes-or-no decisions.

For example, suppose that trucks are being used to transport the shipments and each truck typically makes deliveries to several customers during each trip. It then becomes necessary to select a route (sequence of customers) for each truck, so each candidate for a route leads to the following yes-or-no decision.

Should a certain route be selected for one of the trucks?

$$\text{Its decision variable} = \begin{cases} 1 & \text{if yes} \\ 0 & \text{if no.} \end{cases}$$

The objective would be to select the routes that would minimize the total cost of making all the deliveries.

Various complications also can be considered. For example, if different truck sizes are available, each candidate for selection would include both a certain route and a certain truck size. Similarly, if timing is an issue, a time period for the departure also can be specified as part of the yes-or-no decision. With both factors, each yes-or-no decision would have the form shown below.

Should all the following be selected simultaneously for a delivery run:

1. A certain route,
2. A certain size of truck, and
3. A certain time period for the departure?

$$\text{Its decision variable} = \begin{cases} 1 & \text{if yes} \\ 0 & \text{if no.} \end{cases}$$

Here are a few of the companies which use BIP to help make these kinds of decisions. A Michigan-based retail chain called *Quality Stores* (March–April 1987 issue of *Interfaces*) makes the routing decisions for its delivery trucks this way, thereby saving about $450,000 per year. *Air Products and Chemicals, Inc.* (December 1983 issue of *Interfaces*) saves approximately $2 million annually (about 8 percent of its prior distribution costs) by using this approach to produce its daily delivery schedules. The *Reynolds Metals Co.* (January–February 1991 issue of *Interfaces*) achieves savings of over $7 million annually with an automated dispatching system based partially on BIP for its freight shipments from over 200 plants, warehouses, and suppliers.

Scheduling Interrelated Activities

We all schedule interrelated activities in our everyday lives, even if it is just scheduling when to begin our various homework assignments. So too, managers must schedule various kinds of interrelated activities. When should we begin production for various new orders? When should we begin marketing various new products? When should we make various capital investments to expand our production capacity?

For any such activity, the decision about when to begin can be expressed in terms of a series of yes-or-no decisions, with one of these decisions for each of the possible time periods in which to begin, as shown below.

Should a certain activity begin in a certain time period?

$$\text{Its decision variable} = \begin{cases} 1 & \text{if yes} \\ 0 & \text{if no.} \end{cases}$$

Since a particular activity can begin in only one time period, the choice of the various time periods provides a group of *mutually exclusive alternatives,* so the decision variable for only one time period can have a value of 1.

For example, this approach was used to schedule the building of a series of office buildings on property adjacent to *Texas Stadium* (home of the Dallas Cowboys) over a 7-year planning horizon. In this case, the model had 49 binary decision variables, 7 for each office building corresponding to each of the 7 years in which its construction could begin. This application of BIP was credited with increasing the profit by $6.3 million. (See the October 1983 issue of *Interfaces*.)

A somewhat similar application on a vastly larger scale occurred in *China* recently (January–February 1995 issue of *Interfaces*). China was facing at least $240 billion in new investments over a 15-year horizon to meet the energy needs of its rapidly growing economy. Shortages of coal and electricity required developing new infrastructure for transporting coal and transmitting electricity, as well as building new dams and plants for generating thermal, hydro, and nuclear power. Therefore, the Chinese State Planning Commission and the World Bank collaborated in developing a huge mixed BIP model to guide the decisions on which projects to approve and when to undertake them over the 15-year planning period to minimize the total discounted cost. It is estimated that this OR application is saving China about $6.4 billion over the 15 years.

Scheduling Asset Divestitures

This next application actually is another example of the preceding one (scheduling interrelated activities). However, rather than dealing with such activities as constructing office buildings or investing in hydroelectric plants, the activities now are *selling* (divesting) *assets* to generate income. The assets can be either *financial* assets, such as stocks and bonds, or *physical* assets, such as real estate. Given a group of assets, the problem is to determine when to sell each one to maximize the net present value of total profit from these assets while generating the desired income stream.

In this case, each yes-or-no decision has the following form.

Should a certain asset be sold in a certain time period?

$$\text{Its decision variable} = \begin{cases} 1 & \text{if yes} \\ 0 & \text{if no.} \end{cases}$$

One company that deals with these kinds of yes-or-no decisions is *Homart Development Company* (January–February 1987 issue of *Interfaces*), which ranks among the largest commercial land developers in the United States. One of its most important strategic issues is scheduling divestiture of shopping malls and office buildings. At any particular time, well over 100 assets will be under consideration for divestiture over the next 10 years. Applying BIP to guide these decisions is credited with adding $40 million of profit from the divestiture plan.

Airline Applications

The airline industry is an especially heavy user of OR throughout its operations. For example, one large consulting firm called SABRE (spun off by American Airlines) employs several hundred OR professionals solely to focus on the problem of companies involved with transportation, including especially airlines. We will mention here just two of the applications which specifically use BIP.

One is the *fleet assignment problem.* Given several different types of airplanes available, the problem is to assign a specific type to each flight leg in the schedule so as to maximize the total profit from meeting the schedule. The basic trade-off is that if the airline uses an airplane that is too small on a particular flight leg, it will leave potential customers behind, while if it uses an airplane that is too large, it will suffer the greater expense of the larger airplane to fly empty seats.

For each combination of an airplane type and a flight leg, we have the following yes-or-no decision.

Should a certain type of airplane be assigned to a certain flight leg?

$$\text{Its decision variable} = \begin{cases} 1 & \text{if yes} \\ 0 & \text{if no.} \end{cases}$$

Delta Air Lines (January–February 1994 issue of *Interfaces*) flies over 2,500 domestic flight legs every day, using about 450 airplanes of 10 different types. They use a huge integer programming model (about 40,000 functional constraints, 20,000 binary variables, and 40,000 general integer variables) to solve their fleet assignment problem each time a change is needed. This application saves Delta approximately $100 million per year.

A fairly similar application is the *crew scheduling problem.* Here, rather than assigning airplane types to flight legs, we are instead assigning sequences of flight legs to crews of pilots and flight attendants. Thus, for each feasible sequence of flight legs that leaves from a crew base and returns to the same base, the following yes-or-no decision must be made.

Should a certain sequence of flight legs be assigned to a crew?

$$\text{Its decision variable} = \begin{cases} 1 & \text{if yes} \\ 0 & \text{if no.} \end{cases}$$

The objective is to minimize the total cost of providing crews that cover each flight leg in the schedule.

American Airlines (July–August 1989 and January–February 1991 issues of *Interfaces*) achieves annual savings of over $20 million by using BIP to solve its crew scheduling problem on a monthly basis.

A full-fledged formulation example of this type will be presented at the end of Sec. 12.4.

12.3 INNOVATIVE USES OF BINARY VARIABLES IN MODEL FORMULATION

You have just seen a number of examples where the *basic decisions* of the problem are of the *yes-or-no type,* so that *binary variables* are introduced to represent these decisions. We now will look at some other ways in which binary variables can be very useful. In particular, we will see that these variables sometimes enable us to take a problem whose natural formulation is intractable and *reformulate* it as a pure or mixed IP problem.

This kind of situation arises when the original formulation of the problem fits either an IP or a linear programming format *except* for minor disparities involving combinatorial relationships in the model. By expressing these combinatorial relationships in terms of questions that must be answered yes or no, *auxiliary* binary variables can be introduced to the model to represent these yes-or-no decisions. Introducing these variables reduces the problem to an MIP problem (or a *pure* IP problem if all the original variables also are required to have integer values).

Some cases that can be handled by this approach are discussed next, where the x_j denote the *original* variables of the problem (they may be either continuous or integer variables) and the y_i denote the *auxiliary* binary variables that are introduced for the reformulation.

Either-Or Constraints

Consider the important case where a choice can be made between two constraints, so that *only one* (either one) must hold (whereas the other one can hold but is not required to do so). For example, there may be a choice as to which of two resources to use for a certain purpose, so that it is necessary for only one of the two resource availability constraints to hold mathematically. To illustrate the approach to such situations, suppose that one of the requirements in the overall problem is that

Either $3x_1 + 2x_2 \leq 18$
or $x_1 + 4x_2 \leq 16,$

i.e., at least one of these two inequalities must hold but not necessarily both. This requirement must be reformulated to fit it into the linear programming format where *all* specified constraints must hold. Let M be a very large positive number. Then this requirement can be rewritten as

Either $3x_1 + 2x_2 \leq 18$
            $x_1 + 4x_2 \leq 16 + M$

or $3x_1 + 2x_2 \leq 18 + M$
            $x_1 + 4x_2 \leq 16.$

The key is that adding M to the right-hand side of such constraints has the effect of eliminating them, because they would be satisfied automatically by any solutions that satisfy the other constraints of the problem. (This formulation assumes that the set of feasible solutions for the overall problem is a bounded set and that M is large enough that it will not eliminate any feasible solutions.) This formulation is equivalent to the set of constraints

$3x_1 + 2x_2 \leq 18 + My$
$x_1 + 4x_2 \leq 16 + M(1 - y).$

Because the *auxiliary variable* y must be either 0 or 1, this formulation guarantees that one of the original constraints must hold while the other is, in effect, eliminated. This new set of constraints would then be appended to the other constraints in the overall model to give a pure or mixed IP problem (depending upon whether the x_j are integer or continuous variables).

This approach is related directly to our earlier discussion about expressing combinatorial relationships in terms of questions that must be answered yes or no. The combinatorial relationship involved concerns the combination of the *other* constraints of the model with the *first* of the two *alternative* constraints and then with the *second*. Which of these two combinations of constraints is *better* (in terms of the value of the objective function that then can be achieved)? To rephrase this question in yes-or-no terms, we ask two complementary questions:

1. Should $x_1 + 4x_2 \leq 16$ be selected as the constraint that must hold?
2. Should $3x_1 + 2x_2 \leq 18$ be selected as the constraint that must hold?

Because exactly one of these questions is to be answered affirmatively, we let the binary terms y and $1 - y$, respectively, represent these yes-or-no decisions. Thus, $y = 1$ if the answer is yes to the first question (and no to the second), whereas $1 - y = 1$ (that is, $y = 0$) if the answer is yes to the second question (and no to the first). Since $y + 1 - y = 1$ (one yes) automatically, there is no need to add another constraint to force these two decisions to be mutually exclusive. (If separate binary variables y_1 and y_2 had been used instead to represent these yes-or-no decisions, then an additional constraint $y_1 + y_2 = 1$ would have been needed to make them mutually exclusive.)

A formal presentation of this approach is given next for a more general case.

K out of N Constraints Must Hold

Consider the case where the overall model includes a set of N possible constraints such that only some K of these constraints *must* hold. (Assume that $K < N$.) Part of the optimization process is to choose the *combination* of K constraints that permits the objective function to reach its best possible value. The $N - K$ constraints *not* chosen are, in effect, eliminated from the problem, although feasible solutions might coincidentally still satisfy some of them.

This case is a direct generalization of the preceding case, which had $K = 1$ and $N = 2$. Denote the N possible constraints by

$$f_1(x_1, x_2, \ldots, x_n) \le d_1$$
$$f_2(x_1, x_2, \ldots, x_n) \le d_2$$
$$\vdots$$
$$f_N(x_1, x_2, \ldots, x_n) \le d_N.$$

Then, applying the same logic as for the preceding case, we find that an equivalent formulation of the requirement that some K of these constraints *must* hold is

$$f_1(x_1, x_2, \ldots, x_n) \le d_1 + My_1$$
$$f_2(x_1, x_2, \ldots, x_n) \le d_2 + My_2$$
$$\vdots$$
$$f_N(x_1, x_2, \ldots, x_n) \le d_N + My_N$$
$$\sum_{i=1}^{N} y_i = N - K,$$

and

$$y_i \text{ is binary}, \quad \text{for } i = 1, 2, \ldots, N,$$

where M is an extremely large positive number. For each binary variable y_i ($i = 1, 2, \ldots, N$), note that $y_i = 0$ makes $My_i = 0$, which reduces the new constraint i to the original constraint i. On the other hand, $y_i = 1$ makes $(d_i + My_i)$ so large that (again assuming a bounded feasible region) the new constraint i is automatically satisfied by any solution that satisfies the other new constraints, which has the effect of eliminating the original constraint i. Therefore, because the constraints on the y_i guarantee that K of these variables will equal 0 and those remaining will equal 1, K of the original constraints will be unchanged and the other $(N - K)$ original constraints will, in effect, be eliminated. The choice of *which* K constraints should be retained is made by applying the appropriate algorithm to the overall problem so it finds an optimal solution for *all* the variables simultaneously.

Functions with N Possible Values

Consider the situation where a given function is required to take on any one of N given values. Denote this requirement by

$$f(x_1, x_2, \ldots, x_n) = d_1 \quad \text{or} \quad d_2, \ldots, \quad \text{or} \quad d_N.$$

One special case is where this function is

$$f(x_1, x_2, \ldots, x_n) = \sum_{j=1}^{n} a_j x_j,$$

as on the left-hand side of a linear programming constraint. Another special case is where $f(x_1, x_2, \ldots, x_n) = x_j$ for a given value of j, so the requirement becomes that x_j must take on any one of N given values.

The equivalent IP formulation of this requirement is the following:

$$f(x_1, x_2, \ldots, x_n) = \sum_{i=1}^{N} d_i y_i$$

$$\sum_{i=1}^{N} y_i = 1$$

and

$$y_i \text{ is binary}, \quad \text{for } i = 1, 2, \ldots, N.$$

so this new set of constraints would replace this requirement in the statement of the overall problem. This set of constraints provides an *equivalent* formulation because exactly one y_i must equal 1 and the others must equal 0, so exactly one d_i is being chosen as the value of the function. In this case, there are N yes-or-no questions being asked, namely, should d_i be the value chosen ($i = 1, 2, \ldots, N$)? Because the y_i respectively represent these *yes-or-no decisions,* the second constraint makes them *mutually exclusive alternatives.*

To illustrate how this case can arise, reconsider the Wyndor Glass Co. problem presented in Sec. 3.1. Eighteen hours of production time per week in Plant 3 currently is unused and available for the two new products *or* for certain future products that will be ready for production soon. In order to leave any remaining capacity in usable blocks for these future products, management now wants to impose the restriction that the production time used by the two current new products be 6 *or* 12 *or* 18 hours per week. Thus, the third constraint of the original model ($3x_1 + 2x_2 \leq 18$) now becomes

$$3x_1 + 2x_2 = 6 \quad \text{or} \quad 12 \quad \text{or} \quad 18.$$

In the preceding notation, $N = 3$ with $d_1 = 6$, $d_2 = 12$, and $d_3 = 18$. Consequently, management's new requirement should be formulated as follows:

$$3x_1 + 2x_2 = 6y_1 + 12y_2 + 18y_3$$
$$y_1 + y_2 + y_3 = 1$$

and

$$y_1, y_2, y_3 \text{ are binary}.$$

The overall model for this new version of the problem then consists of the original model (see Sec. 3.1) plus this new set of constraints that replaces the original third constraint. This replacement yields a very tractable MIP formulation.

The Fixed-Charge Problem

It is quite common to incur a fixed charge or setup cost when undertaking an activity. For example, such a charge occurs when a production run to produce a batch of a particular product is undertaken and the required production facilities must be set up to initiate the run. In such cases, the total cost of the activity is the sum of a variable cost related to the level of the activity and the setup cost required to initiate the activity. Frequently the variable cost will be at least roughly proportional to the level of the activity. If this is the case, the *total cost* of the activity (say, activity j) can be represented by a function of the form

$$f_j(x_j) = \begin{cases} k_j + c_j x_j & \text{if } x_j > 0 \\ 0 & \text{if } x_j = 0, \end{cases}$$

where x_j denotes the level of activity j ($x_j \geq 0$), k_j denotes the setup cost, and c_j denotes the cost for each incremental unit. Were it not for the setup cost k_j, this cost structure would suggest the possibility of a *linear programming* formulation to determine the optimal levels of the competing activities. Fortunately, even with the k_j, MIP can still be used.

To formulate the overall model, suppose that there are n activities, each with the preceding cost structure (with $k_j \geq 0$ in every case and $k_j > 0$ for some $j = 1, 2, \ldots, n$), and that the problem is to

Minimize $Z = f_1(x_1) + f_2(x_2) + \cdots + f_n(x_n),$

subject to

given linear programming constraints.

To convert this problem to an MIP format, we begin by posing n questions that must be answered yes or no; namely, for each $j = 1, 2, \ldots, n$, should activity j be undertaken ($x_j > 0$)? Each of these *yes-or-no decisions* is then represented by an auxiliary *binary variable* y_j, so that

$$Z = \sum_{j=1}^{n} (c_j x_j + k_j y_j),$$

where

$$y_j = \begin{cases} 1 & \text{if } x_j > 0 \\ 0 & \text{if } x_j = 0. \end{cases}$$

Therefore, the y_j can be viewed as *contingent decisions* similar to (but not identical to) the type considered in Sec. 12.1. Let M be an extremely large positive number that exceeds the maximum feasible value of any x_j ($j = 1, 2, \ldots, n$). Then the constraints

$x_j \leq M y_j$ for $j = 1, 2, \ldots, n$

will ensure that $y_j = 1$ rather than 0 whenever $x_j > 0$. The one difficulty remaining is that these constraints leave y_j free to be either 0 or 1 when $x_j = 0$. Fortunately, this difficulty is automatically resolved because of the nature of the objective function. The case where $k_j = 0$ can be ignored because y_j can then be deleted from the formulation. So we consider the only other case, namely, where $k_j > 0$. When $x_j = 0$, so that the constraints permit a choice between $y_j = 0$ and $y_j = 1$, $y_j = 0$ must yield a smaller value of Z than $y_j = 1$. Therefore, because the objective is to minimize Z, an algorithm yielding an optimal solution would always choose $y_j = 0$ when $x_j = 0$.

To summarize, the MIP formulation of the fixed-charge problem is

$$\text{Minimize} \quad Z = \sum_{j=1}^{n} (c_j x_j + k_j y_j),$$

subject to

the original constraints, plus
$$x_j - M y_j \leq 0$$

and

$$y_j \text{ is binary}, \quad \text{for } j = 1, 2, \ldots, n.$$

If the x_j also had been restricted to be integer, then this would be a *pure* IP problem.

To illustrate this approach, look again at the Nori & Leets Co. air pollution problem described in Sec. 3.4. The first of the abatement methods considered—increasing the height of the smokestacks—actually would involve a substantial *fixed charge* to get ready for *any* increase in addition to a variable cost that would be roughly proportional to the amount of increase. After conversion to the equivalent annual costs used in the formulation, this fixed charge would be $2 million each for the blast furnaces and the open-hearth furnaces, whereas the variable costs are those identified in Table 3.14. Thus, in the preceding notation, $k_1 = 2$, $k_2 = 2$, $c_1 = 8$, and $c_2 = 10$, where the objective function is expressed in units of *millions* of dollars. Because the other abatement methods do not involve any fixed charges, $k_j = 0$ for $j = 3, 4, 5, 6$. Consequently, the new MIP formulation of this problem is

$$\text{Minimize} \quad Z = 8x_1 + 10x_2 + 7x_3 + 6x_4 + 11x_5 + 9x_6 + 2y_1 + 2y_2,$$

subject to

the constraints given in Sec. 3.4, plus
$$x_1 - M y_1 \leq 0,$$
$$x_2 - M y_2 \leq 0,$$

and

$$y_1, y_2 \text{ are binary}.$$

Binary Representation of General Integer Variables

Suppose that you have a pure IP problem where most of the variables are *binary* variables, but the presence of a few *general* integer variables prevents you from solving the problem by one of the very efficient BIP algorithms now available. A nice way to circumvent this difficulty is to use the *binary representation* for each of these general integer variables. Specifically, if the bounds on an integer variable x are

$$0 \leq x \leq u$$

and if N is defined as the integer such that

$$2^N \leq u < 2^{N+1},$$

then the **binary representation** of x is

$$x = \sum_{i=0}^{N} 2^i y_i,$$

where the y_i variables are (auxiliary) binary variables. Substituting this binary representation for each of the general integer variables (with a different set of auxiliary binary variables for each) thereby reduces the entire problem to a BIP model.

For example, suppose that an IP problem has just two general integer variables x_1 and x_2 along with many binary variables. Also suppose that the problem has nonnegativity constraints for both x_1 and x_2 and that the functional constraints include

$$
\begin{aligned}
x_1 &\leq 5 \\
2x_1 + 3x_2 &\leq 30.
\end{aligned}
$$

These constraints imply that $u = 5$ for x_1 and $u = 10$ for x_2, so the above definition of N gives $N = 2$ for x_1 (since $2^2 \leq 5 < 2^3$) and $N = 3$ for x_2 (since $2^3 \leq 10 < 2^4$). Therefore, the binary representations of these variables are

$$
\begin{aligned}
x_1 &= y_0 + 2y_1 + 4y_2 \\
x_2 &= y_3 + 2y_4 + 4y_5 + 8y_6.
\end{aligned}
$$

After we substitute these expressions for the respective variables throughout all the functional constraints and the objective function, the two functional constraints noted above become

$$
\begin{aligned}
y_0 + 2y_1 + 4y_2 &\leq 5 \\
2y_0 + 4y_1 + 8y_2 + 3y_3 + 6y_4 + 12y_5 + 24y_6 &\leq 30.
\end{aligned}
$$

Observe that each feasible value of x_1 corresponds to one of the feasible values of the vector (y_0, y_1, y_2), and similarly for x_2 and (y_3, y_4, y_5, y_6). For example, $x_1 = 3$ corresponds to $(y_0, y_1, y_2) = (1, 1, 0)$, and $x_2 = 5$ corresponds to $(y_3, y_4, y_5, y_6) = (1, 0, 1, 0)$.

For an IP problem where *all* the variables are (bounded) general integer variables, it is possible to use this same technique to reduce the problem to a BIP model. However, this is not advisable for most cases because of the explosion in the number of variables involved. Applying a good IP algorithm to the original IP model generally should be more efficient than applying a good BIP algorithm to the much larger BIP model.

In general terms, for *all* the formulation possibilities with auxiliary binary variables discussed in this section, we need to strike the same note of caution. This approach sometimes requires adding a relatively large number of such variables, which can make the model *computationally infeasible*. (Section 12.5 will provide some perspective on the sizes of IP problems that can be solved.)

12.4 SOME FORMULATION EXAMPLES

We now present a series of examples that illustrate a variety of formulation techniques with binary variables, including those discussed in the preceding sections. For the sake of clarity, these examples have been kept very small. In actual applications, these formulations typically would be just a small part of a vastly larger model.

EXAMPLE 1   **Making Choices When the Decision Variables Are Continuous.**

The Research and Development Division of the GOOD PRODUCTS COMPANY has developed three possible new products. However, to avoid undue diversification of the company's product line, management has imposed the following restriction.

> **Restriction 1:** From the three possible new products, *at most two* should be chosen to be produced.

Each of these products can be produced in either of two plants. For administrative reasons, management has imposed a second restriction in this regard.

> **Restriction 2:** Just one of the two plants should be chosen to be the sole producer of the new products.

The production cost per unit of each product would be essentially the same in the two plants. However, because of differences in their production facilities, the number of hours of production time needed per unit of each product might differ between the two plants. These data are given in Table 12.2, along with other relevant information, including marketing estimates of the number of units of each product that could be sold per week if it is produced. The objective is to choose the products, the plant, and the production rates of the chosen products so as to maximize total profit.

In some ways, this problem resembles a standard *product mix problem* such as the Wyndor Glass Co. example described in Sec. 3.1. In fact, if we changed the problem by dropping the two restrictions *and* by requiring each unit of a product to use the production hours given in Table 12.2 in *both plants* (so the two plants now perform different operations needed by the products), it would become just such a problem. In particular, if we let x_1, x_2, x_3 be the production rates of the respective products, the model then becomes

$$\text{Maximize} \quad Z = 5x_1 + 7x_2 + 3x_3,$$

subject to

$$3x_1 + 4x_2 + 2x_3 \leq 30$$
$$4x_1 + 6x_2 + 2x_3 \leq 40$$
$$x_1 \qquad\qquad \leq 7$$
$$\qquad x_2 \qquad \leq 5$$
$$\qquad\qquad x_3 \leq 9$$

TABLE 12.2 Data for Example 1 (the Good Products Co. problem)

	Production Time Used for Each Unit Produced			Production Time Available per Week
	Product 1	**Product 2**	**Product 3**	
Plant 1	3 hours	4 hours	2 hours	30 hours
Plant 2	4 hours	6 hours	2 hours	40 hours
Unit profit	5	7	3	(thousands of dollars)
Sales potential	7	5	9	(units per week)

and

$$x_1 \geq 0, \qquad x_2 \geq 0, \qquad x_3 \geq 0.$$

For the real problem, however, restriction 1 necessitates adding to the model the constraint

The number of strictly positive decision variables (x_1, x_2, x_3) must be ≤ 2.

This constraint does not fit into a linear or an integer programming format, so the key question is how to convert it to such a format so that a corresponding algorithm can be used to solve the overall model. If the decision variables were binary variables, then the constraint would be expressed in this format as $x_1 + x_2 + x_3 \leq 2$. However, with *continuous* decision variables, a more complicated approach involving the introduction of auxiliary binary variables is needed.

Requirement 2 necessitates replacing the first two functional constraints $(3x_1 + 4x_2 + 2x_3 \leq 30$ and $4x_1 + 6x_2 + 2x_3 \leq 40)$ by the restriction

Either	$3x_1 + 4x_2 + 2x_3 \leq 30$
Or	$4x_1 + 6x_2 + 2x_3 \leq 40$

must hold, where the choice of which constraint must hold corresponds to the choice of which plant will be used to produce the new products. We discussed in the preceding section how such an either-or constraint can be converted to a linear or an integer programming format, again with the help of an auxiliary binary variable.

Formulation with Auxiliary Binary Variables. To deal with requirement 1, we introduce three auxiliary binary variables (y_1, y_2, y_3) with the interpretation

$$y_j = \begin{cases} 1 & \text{if } x_j > 0 \text{ can hold (can produce product } j) \\ 0 & \text{if } x_j = 0 \text{ must hold (cannot produce product } j), \end{cases}$$

for $j = 1, 2, 3$. To enforce this interpretation in the model with the help of M (an extremely large positive number), we add the constraints

$$x_1 \leq My_1$$
$$x_2 \leq My_2$$
$$x_3 \leq My_3$$
$$y_1 + y_2 + y_3 \leq 2$$
$$y_j \text{ is binary}, \qquad \text{for } j = 1, 2, 3.$$

The either-or constraint and nonnegativity constraints give a *bounded* feasible region for the decision variables (so each $x_j \leq M$ throughout this region). Therefore, in each $x_j \leq My_j$ constraint, $y_j = 1$ allows any value of x_j in the feasible region, whereas $y_j = 0$ forces $x_j = 0$. (Conversely, $x_j > 0$ forces $y_j = 1$, whereas $x_j = 0$ allows either value of y_j.) Consequently, when the fourth constraint forces choosing at most two of the y_j to equal 1, this amounts to choosing at most two of the new products as the ones that can be produced.

To deal with requirement 2, we introduce another auxiliary binary variable y_4 with the interpretation

$$y_4 = \begin{cases} 1 & \text{if } 4x_1 + 6x_2 + 2x_3 \leq 40 \text{ must hold (choose Plant 2)} \\ 0 & \text{if } 3x_1 + 4x_2 + 2x_3 \leq 30 \text{ must hold (choose Plant 1).} \end{cases}$$

As discussed in Sec. 12.3, this interpretation is enforced by adding the constraints,

$$3x_1 + 4x_2 + 2x_3 \leq 30 + My_4$$
$$4x_1 + 6x_2 + 2x_3 \leq 40 + M(1 - y_4)$$

y_4 is binary.

Consequently, after we move all variables to the left-hand side of the constraints, the complete model is

Maximize $Z = 5x_1 + 7x_2 + 3x_3,$

subject to

$$x_1 \leq 7$$
$$x_2 \leq 5$$
$$x_3 \leq 9$$
$$x_1 - My_1 \leq 0$$
$$x_2 - My_2 \leq 0$$
$$x_3 - My_3 \leq 0$$
$$y_1 + y_2 + y_3 \leq 2$$
$$3x_1 + 4x_2 + 2x_3 - My_4 \leq 30$$
$$4x_1 + 6x_2 + 2x_3 + My_4 \leq 40 + M$$

and

$$x_1 \geq 0, \quad x_2 \geq 0, \quad x_3 \geq 0$$
$$y_j \text{ is binary,} \quad \text{for } j = 1, 2, 3, 4.$$

This now is an MIP model, with three variables (the x_j) not required to be integer and four binary variables, so an MIP algorithm can be used to solve the model. When this is done (after substituting a large numerical value for M),[1] the optimal solution is $y_1 = 1$, $y_2 = 0$, $y_3 = 1$, $y_4 = 1$, $x_1 = 5\frac{1}{2}$, $x_2 = 0$, and $x_3 = 9$; that is, choose products 1 and 3 to produce, choose Plant 2 for the production, and choose the production rates of $5\frac{1}{2}$ units per week for product 1 and 9 units per week for product 3. The resulting total profit is $54,500 per week.

EXAMPLE 2   Violating Proportionality.

The SUPERSUDS CORPORATION is developing its marketing plans for next year's new products. For three of these products, the decision has been made to purchase a total of five TV spots for commercials on national television networks. The problem we will focus on is how to allocate the five spots to these three products, with a maximum of three spots (and a minimum of zero) for each product.

---

[1]In practice, some care is taken to choose a value for M that definitely is large enough to avoid eliminating any feasible solutions, but as small as possible otherwise in order to avoid unduly enlarging the feasible region for the LP-relaxation (and to avoid numerical instability). For this example, a careful examination of the constraints reveals that the minimum feasible value of M is $M = 9$.

Table 12.3 shows the estimated impact of allocating zero, one, two, or three spots to each product. This impact is measured in terms of the *profit* (in units of millions of dollars) from the *additional sales* that would result from the spots, considering also the cost of producing the commercial and purchasing the spots. The objective is to allocate five spots to the products so as to maximize the total profit.

This small problem can be solved easily by dynamic programming (Chap. 10) or even by inspection. (The optimal solution is to allocate two spots to product 1, no spots to product 2, and three spots to product 3.) However, we will show two different BIP formulations for illustrative purposes. Such a formulation would become necessary if this small problem needed to be incorporated into a larger IP model involving the allocation of resources to marketing activities for all the corporation's new products.

One Formulation with Auxiliary Binary Variables. A natural formulation would be to let x_1, x_2, x_3 be the number of TV spots allocated to the respective products. The contribution of each x_j to the objective function then would be given by the corresponding column in Table 12.3. However, each of these columns violates the assumption of proportionality described in Sec. 3.3. Therefore, we cannot write a *linear* objective function in terms of these integer decision variables.

Now see what happens when we introduce an *auxiliary binary variable* y_{ij} for each positive integer value of $x_i = j$ ($j = 1, 2, 3$), where y_{ij} has the interpretation

$$y_{ij} = \begin{cases} 1 & \text{if } x_i = j \\ 0 & \text{otherwise.} \end{cases}$$

(For example, $y_{21} = 0$, $y_{22} = 0$, and $y_{23} = 1$ mean that $x_2 = 3$.) The resulting *linear* BIP model is

Maximize $\quad Z = y_{11} + 3y_{12} + 3y_{13} + 2y_{22} + 3y_{23} - y_{31} + 2y_{32} + 4y_{33}$,

subject to

$$y_{11} + y_{12} + y_{13} \leq 1$$
$$y_{21} + y_{22} + y_{23} \leq 1$$
$$y_{31} + y_{32} + y_{33} \leq 1$$
$$y_{11} + 2y_{12} + 3y_{13} + y_{21} + 2y_{22} + 3y_{23} + y_{31} + 2y_{32} + 3y_{33} = 5$$

TABLE 12.3 Data for Example 2 (the Supersuds Corp. problem)

Number of TV Spots	Profit		
	Product		
	1	2	3
0	0	0	0
1	1	0	-1
2	3	2	2
3	3	3	4

and

each y_{ij} is binary.

Note that the first three functional constraints ensure that each x_i will be assigned just one of its possible values. (Here $y_{i1} + y_{i2} + y_{i3} = 0$ corresponds to $x_i = 0$, which contributes nothing to the objective function.) The last functional constraint ensures that $x_1 + x_2 + x_3 = 5$. The *linear* objective function then gives the total profit according to Table 12.3.

Solving this BIP model gives an optimal solution of

$$
\begin{array}{llllll}
y_{11} = 0, & y_{12} = 1, & y_{13} = 0, & \text{so} & x_1 = 2 \\
y_{21} = 0, & y_{22} = 0, & y_{23} = 0, & \text{so} & x_2 = 0 \\
y_{31} = 0, & y_{32} = 0, & y_{33} = 1, & \text{so} & x_3 = 3.
\end{array}
$$

Another Formulation with Auxiliary Binary Variables.   We now redefine the above auxiliary binary variables y_{ij} as follows:

$$
y_{ij} = \begin{cases} 1 & \text{if } x_i \ge j \\ 0 & \text{otherwise.} \end{cases}
$$

Thus, the difference is that $y_{ij} = 1$ now if $x_i \ge j$ instead of $x_i = j$. Therefore,

$$
\begin{array}{lllll}
x_i = 0 & \Rightarrow & y_{i1} = 0, & y_{i2} = 0, & y_{i3} = 0, \\
x_i = 1 & \Rightarrow & y_{i1} = 1, & y_{i2} = 0, & y_{i3} = 0, \\
x_i = 2 & \Rightarrow & y_{i1} = 1, & y_{i2} = 1, & y_{i3} = 0, \\
x_i = 3 & \Rightarrow & y_{i1} = 1, & y_{i2} = 1, & y_{i3} = 1,
\end{array}
$$

so $x_i = y_{i1} + y_{i2} + y_{i3}$

for $i = 1, 2, 3$. Because allowing $y_{i2} = 1$ is contingent upon $y_{i1} = 1$ and allowing $y_{i3} = 1$ is contingent upon $y_{i2} = 1$, these definitions are enforced by adding the constraints

$$y_{i2} \le y_{i1} \quad \text{and} \quad y_{i3} \le y_{i2}, \quad \text{for } i = 1, 2, 3.$$

The new definition of the y_{ij} also changes the objective function, as illustrated in Fig. 12.1 for the product 1 portion of the objective function. Since y_{11}, y_{12}, y_{13} provide the successive increments (if any) in the value of x_1 (starting from a value of 0), the coefficients of y_{11}, y_{12}, y_{13} are given by the respective *increments* in the product 1 column of Table 12.3 ($1 - 0 = 1$, $3 - 1 = 2$, $3 - 3 = 0$). These *increments* are the *slopes* in Fig. 12.1, yielding $1y_{11} + 2y_{12} + 0y_{13}$ for the product 1 portion of the objective function. Note that applying this approach to all three products still must lead to a *linear* objective function.

After we bring all variables to the left-hand side of the constraints, the resulting complete BIP model is

Maximize $Z = y_{11} + 2y_{12} + 2y_{22} + y_{23} - y_{31} + 3y_{32} + 2y_{33}$,

subject to

$$
\begin{array}{l}
y_{12} - y_{11} \le 0 \\
y_{13} - y_{12} \le 0 \\
y_{22} - y_{21} \le 0 \\
y_{23} - y_{22} \le 0
\end{array}
$$

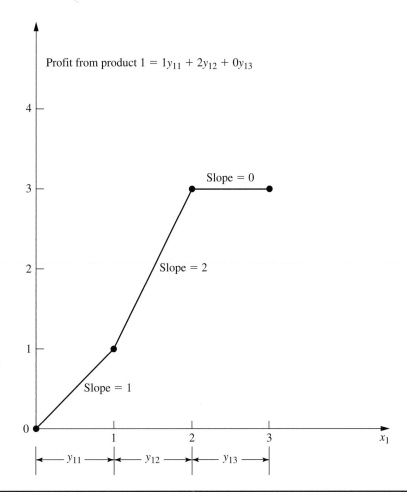

FIGURE 12.1
The profit from the additional sales of product 1 that would result from x_1 TV spots, where the slopes give the corresponding coefficients in the objective function for the second BIP formulation for Example 2 (the Supersuds Corp. problem).

Profit from product $1 = 1y_{11} + 2y_{12} + 0y_{13}$

Slope = 0

Slope = 2

Slope = 1

$$y_{32} - y_{31} \leq 0$$
$$y_{33} - y_{32} \leq 0$$
$$y_{11} + y_{12} + y_{13} + y_{21} + y_{22} + y_{23} + y_{31} + y_{32} + y_{33} = 5$$

and

each y_{ij} is binary.

Solving this BIP model gives an optimal solution of

$y_{11} = 1,$	$y_{12} = 1,$	$y_{13} = 0,$	so	$x_1 = 2$
$y_{21} = 0,$	$y_{22} = 0,$	$y_{23} = 0,$	so	$x_2 = 0$
$y_{31} = 1,$	$y_{32} = 1,$	$y_{33} = 1,$	so	$x_3 = 3.$

There is little to choose between this BIP model and the preceding one other than personal taste. They have the same number of binary variables (the prime consideration in determining computational effort for BIP problems). They also both have some *special structure* (constraints for *mutually exclusive alternatives* in the first model and constraints for *contingent decisions* in the second) that can lead to speedup. The second model does have more functional constraints than the first.

EXAMPLE 3 Covering All Characteristics.

SOUTHWESTERN AIRWAYS needs to assign its crews to cover all its upcoming flights. We will focus on the problem of assigning three crews based in San Francisco to the flights listed in the first column of Table 12.4. The other 12 columns show the 12 feasible sequences of flights for a crew. (The numbers in each column indicate the order of the flights.) Exactly three of the sequences need to be chosen (one per crew) in such a way that every flight is covered. (It is permissible to have more than one crew on a flight, where the extra crews would fly as passengers, but union contracts require that the extra crews would still need to be paid for their time as if they were working.) The cost of assigning a crew to a particular sequence of flights is given (in thousands of dollars) in the bottom row of the table. The objective is to minimize the total cost of the three crew assignments that cover all the flights.

Formulation with Binary Variables. With 12 feasible sequences of flights, we have 12 yes-or-no decisions:

Should sequence j be assigned to a crew? $\quad (j = 1, 2, \ldots, 12)$

Therefore, we use 12 binary variables to represent these respective decisions:

$$x_j = \begin{cases} 1 & \text{if sequence } j \text{ is assigned to a crew} \\ 0 & \text{otherwise.} \end{cases}$$

The most interesting part of this formulation is the nature of each constraint that ensures that a corresponding flight is covered. For example, consider the last flight in Table

TABLE 12.4 Data for Example 3 (the Southwestern Airways problem)

	Feasible Sequence of Flights											
Flight	**1**	**2**	**3**	**4**	**5**	**6**	**7**	**8**	**9**	**10**	**11**	**12**
1. San Francisco to Los Angeles	1			1			1			1		
2. San Francisco to Denver		1			1			1			1	
3. San Francisco to Seattle			1			1			1			1
4. Los Angeles to Chicago				2			2		3	2		3
5. Los Angeles to San Francisco	2					3				5	5	
6. Chicago to Denver				3	3				4			
7. Chicago to Seattle							3	3		3	3	4
8. Denver to San Francisco		2		4	4				5			
9. Denver to Chicago					2			2			2	
10. Seattle to San Francisco			2				4	4				5
11. Seattle to Los Angeles						2			2	4	4	2
Cost, $1,000's	2	3	4	6	7	5	7	8	9	9	8	9

12.4 [Seattle to Los Angeles (LA)]. Five sequences (namely, sequences 6, 9, 10, 11, and 12) include this flight. Therefore, at least one of these five sequences must be chosen. The resulting constraint is

$$x_6 + x_9 + x_{10} + x_{11} + x_{12} \geq 1.$$

Using similar constraints for the other 10 flights, the complete BIP model is

Minimize $\quad Z = 2x_1 + 3x_2 + 4x_3 + 6x_4 + 7x_5 + 5x_6 + 7x_7 + 8x_8 + 9x_9$
$$+ 9x_{10} + 8x_{11} + 9x_{12},$$

subject to

$$
\begin{array}{ll}
x_1 + x_4 + x_7 + x_{10} \geq 1 & \text{(SF to LA)} \\
x_2 + x_5 + x_8 + x_{11} \geq 1 & \text{(SF to Denver)} \\
x_3 + x_6 + x_9 + x_{12} \geq 1 & \text{(SF to Seattle)} \\
x_4 + x_7 + x_9 + x_{10} + x_{12} \geq 1 & \text{(LA to Chicago)} \\
x_1 + x_6 + x_{10} + x_{11} \geq 1 & \text{(LA to SF)} \\
x_4 + x_5 + x_9 \geq 1 & \text{(Chicago to Denver)} \\
x_7 + x_8 + x_{10} + x_{11} + x_{12} \geq 1 & \text{(Chicago to Seattle)} \\
x_2 + x_4 + x_5 + x_9 \geq 1 & \text{(Denver to SF)} \\
x_5 + x_8 + x_{11} \geq 1 & \text{(Denver to Chicago)} \\
x_3 + x_7 + x_8 + x_{12} \geq 1 & \text{(Seattle to SF)} \\
x_6 + x_9 + x_{10} + x_{11} + x_{12} \geq 1 & \text{(Seattle to LA)}
\end{array}
$$

$$\sum_{j=1}^{12} x_j = 3 \quad \text{(assign three crews)}$$

and

x_j is binary, $\quad$ for $j = 1, 2, \ldots, 12$.

One optimal solution for this BIP model is

$$
\begin{array}{ll}
x_3 = 1 & \text{(assign sequence 3 to a crew)} \\
x_4 = 1 & \text{(assign sequence 4 to a crew)} \\
x_{11} = 1 & \text{(assign sequence 11 to a crew)}
\end{array}
$$

and all other $x_j = 0$, for a total cost of $18,000. (Another optimal solution is $x_1 = 1$, $x_5 = 1$, $x_{12} = 1$, and all other $x_j = 0$.)

This example illustrates a broader class of problems called **set covering problems**.[1] Any set covering problem can be described in general terms as involving a number of potential *activities* (such as flight sequences) and *characteristics* (such as flights). Each activity possesses some but not all of the characteristics. The objective is to determine the least costly combination of activities that collectively possess (cover) each characteristic

---

[1]Strictly speaking, a set covering problem does not include any *other* functional constraints such as the last functional constraint in the above crew scheduling example. It also is sometimes assumed that every coefficient in the objective function being minimized equals *one,* and then the name *weighted set covering problem* is used when this assumption does not hold.

at least once. Thus, let S_i be the set of all activities that possess characteristic i. At least one member of the set S_i must be included among the chosen activities, so a constraint,

$$\sum_{j \in S_i} x_j \geq 1,$$

is included for each characteristic i.

A related class of problems, called **set partitioning problems,** changes each such constraint to

$$\sum_{j \in S_i} x_j = 1,$$

so now *exactly* one member of each set S_i must be included among the chosen activities. For the crew scheduling example, this means that each flight must be included *exactly* once among the chosen flight sequences, which rules out having extra crews (as passengers) on any flight.

12.5 SOME PERSPECTIVES ON SOLVING INTEGER PROGRAMMING PROBLEMS

It may seem that IP problems should be relatively easy to solve. After all, *linear programming* problems can be solved extremely efficiently, and the only difference is that IP problems have far fewer solutions to be considered. In fact, *pure* IP problems with a bounded feasible region are guaranteed to have just a *finite* number of feasible solutions.

Unfortunately, there are two fallacies in this line of reasoning. One is that having a finite number of feasible solutions ensures that the problem is readily solvable. Finite numbers can be astronomically large. For example, consider the simple case of BIP problems. With n variables, there are 2^n solutions to be considered (where some of these solutions can subsequently be discarded because they violate the functional constraints). Thus, each time n is increased by 1, the number of solutions is *doubled*. This pattern is referred to as the **exponential growth** of the difficulty of the problem. With $n = 10$, there are more than 1,000 solutions (1,024); with $n = 20$, there are more than 1,000,000; with $n = 30$, there are more than 1 billion; and so forth. Therefore, even the fastest computers are incapable of performing exhaustive enumeration (checking each solution for feasibility and, if it is feasible, calculating the value of the objective value) for BIP problems with more than a few dozen variables, let alone for *general* IP problems with the same number of integer variables. Sophisticated algorithms, such as those described in subsequent sections, can do somewhat better. In fact, Sec. 12.8 discusses how some algorithms have successfully solved certain *vastly* larger BIP problems. The best algorithms today are capable of solving *many* pure BIP problems with a few hundred variables and *some* considerably larger ones (including certain problems with several tens of thousands of variables). Nevertheless, because of *exponential growth,* even the best algorithms cannot be guaranteed to solve every relatively small problem (less than a hundred binary or integer variables). Depending on their characteristics, certain relatively small problems can be much more difficult to solve than some much larger ones.

The second fallacy is that removing some feasible solutions (the noninteger ones) from a linear programming problem will make it easier to solve. To the contrary, it is only because all these feasible solutions are there that the guarantee can be given (see Sec. 5.1) that there will be a corner-point feasible (CPF) solution [and so a corresponding basic feasible (BF) solution] that is optimal for the overall problem. *This* guarantee is the key to the remarkable efficiency of the simplex method. As a result, linear programming problems generally are *much* easier to solve than IP problems.

Consequently, most successful algorithms for integer programming incorporate the simplex method (or dual simplex method) as much as they can by relating portions of the IP problem under consideration to the corresponding linear programming problem (i.e., the same problem except that the integer restriction is deleted). For any given IP problem, this corresponding linear programming problem commonly is referred to as its **LP relaxation.** The algorithms presented in the next two sections illustrate how a sequence of LP relaxations for portions of an IP problem can be used to solve the overall IP problem effectively.

There is one special situation where solving an IP problem is no more difficult than solving its LP relaxation once by the simplex method, namely, when the optimal solution to the latter problem turns out to satisfy the integer restriction of the IP problem. When this situation occurs, this solution *must* be optimal for the IP problem as well, because it is the best solution among all the feasible solutions for the LP relaxation, which includes all the feasible solutions for the IP problem. Therefore, it is common for an IP algorithm to begin by applying the simplex method to the LP relaxation to check whether this fortuitous outcome has occurred.

Although it generally is quite fortuitous indeed for the optimal solution to the LP relaxation to be integer as well, there actually exist several *special types* of IP problems for which this outcome is *guaranteed.* You already have seen the most prominent of these special types in Chaps. 8 and 9, namely, the *minimum cost flow problem* (with integer parameters) and its special cases (including the *transportation problem,* the *assignment problem,* the *shortest-path problem,* and the *maximum flow problem*). This guarantee can be given for these types of problems because they possess a certain *special structure* (e.g., see Table 8.6) that ensures that every BF solution is integer, as stated in the integer solutions property given in Secs. 8.1 and 9.6. Consequently, these special types of IP problems can be treated as linear programming problems, because they can be solved completely by a streamlined version of the simplex method.

Although this much simplification is somewhat unusual, in practice IP problems frequently have *some* special structure that can be exploited to simplify the problem. (Examples 2 and 3 in the preceding section fit into this category, because of their *mutually exclusive alternatives* constraints or *contingent decisions* constraints or *set-covering* constraints.) Sometimes, very large versions of these problems can be solved successfully. Special-purpose algorithms designed specifically to exploit certain kinds of special structures are becoming increasingly important in integer programming.

Thus, the two primary determinants of *computational difficulty* for an IP problem are (1) the *number of integer variables* and (2) any *special structure* in the problem. This situation is in contrast to linear programming, where the number of (functional) constraints is much more important than the number of variables. In integer programming, the number of constraints is of *some* importance (especially if LP relaxations are being solved), but it is strictly secondary to the other two factors. In fact, there occasionally are cases where *increasing* the number of constraints *decreases* the computation time because the number of feasible solutions has been reduced. For MIP problems, it is the number of *in-*

teger variables rather than the *total* number of variables that is important, because the continuous variables have almost no effect on the computational effort.

Because IP problems are, in general, much more difficult to solve than linear programming problems, sometimes it is tempting to use the approximate procedure of simply applying the simplex method to the LP relaxation and then *rounding* the noninteger values to integers in the resulting solution. This approach may be adequate for some applications, especially if the values of the variables are quite large so that rounding creates relatively little error. However, you should beware of two pitfalls involved in this approach.

One pitfall is that an optimal linear programming solution is *not necessarily feasible* after it is rounded. Often it is difficult to see in which way the rounding should be done to retain feasibility. It may even be necessary to change the value of some variables by one or more units after rounding. To illustrate, consider the following problem:

$$\text{Maximize} \quad Z = x_2,$$

subject to

$$-x_1 + x_2 \leq \frac{1}{2}$$

$$x_1 + x_2 \leq 3\frac{1}{2}$$

and

$$x_1 \geq 0, \qquad x_2 \geq 0$$
$$x_1, x_2 \text{ are integers.}$$

As Fig. 12.2 shows, the optimal solution for the LP relaxation is $x_1 = 1\frac{1}{2}$, $x_2 = 2$, but it is impossible to round the noninteger variable x_1 to 1 or 2 (or any other integer) and retain feasibility. Feasibility can be retained only by also changing the integer value of x_2. It is easy to imagine how such difficulties can be compounded when there are tens or hundreds of constraints and variables.

Even if an optimal solution for the LP relaxation is rounded successfully, there remains another pitfall. There is no guarantee that this rounded solution will be the optimal integer solution. In fact, it may even be far from optimal in terms of the value of the objective function. This fact is illustrated by the following problem:

$$\text{Maximize} \quad Z = x_1 + 5x_2,$$

subject to

$$x_1 + 10x_2 \leq 20$$
$$x_1 \qquad \leq 2$$

and

$$x_1 \geq 0, \qquad x_2 \geq 0$$
$$x_1, x_2 \text{ are integers.}$$

Because there are only two decision variables, this problem can be depicted graphically as shown in Fig. 12.3. Either the graph or the simplex method may be used to find that

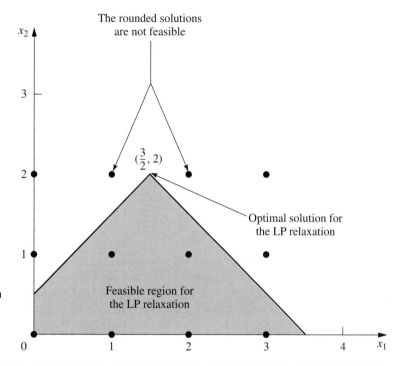

FIGURE 12.2
An example of an IP problem where the optimal solution for the LP relaxation cannot be rounded in any way that retains feasibility.

the optimal solution for the LP relaxation is $x_1 = 2$, $x_2 = \frac{9}{5}$, with $Z = 11$. If a graphical solution were not available (which would be the case with more decision variables), then the variable with the noninteger value $x_2 = \frac{9}{5}$ would normally be rounded in the feasible direction to $x_2 = 1$. The resulting integer solution is $x_1 = 2$, $x_2 = 1$, which yields $Z = 7$. Notice that this solution is far from the optimal solution $(x_1, x_2) = (0, 2)$, where $Z = 10$.

FIGURE 12.3
An example where rounding the optimal solution for the LP relaxation is far from optimal for the IP problem.

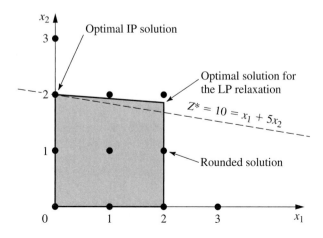

Because of these two pitfalls, a better approach for dealing with IP problems that are too large to be solved exactly is to use one of the available *heuristic algorithms*. These algorithms are extremely efficient for large problems, but they are not guaranteed to find an optimal solution. However, they do tend to be considerably more effective than the rounding approach just discussed in finding very good feasible solutions.

One of the particularly exciting developments in OR in recent years has been the rapid progress in developing very effective heuristic algorithms (commonly called *metaheuristics*) for various combinatorial problems such as IP problems. Three prominent types of metaheuristics are tabu search, simulated annealing, and genetic algorithms. All three use innovative concepts that guide a search procedure to move toward an optimal solution. *Tabu search* explores promising areas to hold good solutions by rapidly eliminating unpromising areas that are classified as tabu. *Simulated annealing* conducts the search by using the analog of a physical annealing process. The basic concept underlying the search with *genetic algorithms* is survival of the fittest through natural evolution. These sophisticated metaheuristics (described further in Selected Reference 8) can even be applied to integer *nonlinear* programming problems that have locally optimal solutions that may be far removed from a globally optimal solution.

Returning to integer *linear* programming, for IP problems that are small enough to be solved to optimality, a considerable number of algorithms now are available. However, no IP algorithm possesses computational efficiency that is even nearly comparable to the *simplex method* (except on special types of problems). Therefore, developing IP algorithms has continued to be an active area of research. Fortunately, some exciting algorithmic advances have been made within the last two decades, and additional progress can be anticipated during the coming years. These advances are discussed further in Sec. 12.8.

The most popular mode for IP algorithms is to use the *branch-and-bound technique* and related ideas to *implicitly enumerate* the feasible integer solutions, and we shall focus on this approach. The next section presents the branch-and-bound technique in a general context, and illustrates it with a basic branch-and-bound algorithm for BIP problems. Section 12.7 presents another algorithm of the same type for general MIP problems.

12.6 THE BRANCH-AND-BOUND TECHNIQUE AND ITS APPLICATION TO BINARY INTEGER PROGRAMMING

Because any bounded *pure* IP problem has only a finite number of feasible solutions, it is natural to consider using some kind of *enumeration procedure* for finding an optimal solution. Unfortunately, as we discussed in the preceding section, this finite number can be, and usually is, very large. Therefore, it is imperative that any enumeration procedure be cleverly structured so that only a tiny fraction of the feasible solutions actually need be examined. For example, dynamic programming (see Chap. 11) provides one such kind of procedure for many problems having a finite number of feasible solutions (although it is not particularly efficient for most IP problems). Another such approach is provided by the *branch-and-bound technique*. This technique and variations of it have been applied with some success to a variety of OR problems, but it is especially well known for its application to IP problems.

The basic concept underlying the branch-and-bound technique is to *divide and conquer*. Since the original "large" problem is too difficult to be solved directly, it is divided into smaller and smaller subproblems until these subproblems can be conquered. The dividing (*branching*) is done by partitioning the entire set of feasible solutions into smaller and smaller subsets. The conquering (*fathoming*) is done partially by *bounding* how good the best solution in the subset can be and then discarding the subset if its bound indicates that it cannot possibly contain an optimal solution for the original problem.

We shall now describe in turn these three basic steps—branching, bounding, and fathoming—and illustrate them by applying a branch-and-bound algorithm to the prototype example (the California Manufacturing Co. problem) presented in Sec. 12.1 and repeated here (with the constraints numbered for later reference).

$$\text{Maximize} \quad Z = 9x_1 + 5x_2 + 6x_3 + 4x_4,$$

subject to

$$
\begin{aligned}
(1) &\quad 6x_1 + 3x_2 + 5x_3 + 2x_4 \leq 10 \\
(2) &\quad \qquad\qquad\quad x_3 + x_4 \leq 1 \\
(3) &\quad -x_1 + \qquad\quad x_3 \qquad \leq 0 \\
(4) &\quad \qquad -x_2 \qquad\quad + x_4 \leq 0
\end{aligned}
$$

and

$$(5) \quad x_j \text{ is binary}, \quad \text{for } j = 1, 2, 3, 4.$$

Branching

When you are dealing with binary variables, the most straightforward way to partition the set of feasible solutions into subsets is to fix the value of one of the variables (say, x_1) at $x_1 = 0$ for one subset and at $x_1 = 1$ for the other subset. Doing this for the prototype example divides the whole problem into the two smaller subproblems shown below.

Subproblem 1:
Fix $x_1 = 0$ so the resulting subproblem is

$$\text{Maximize} \quad Z = 5x_2 + 6x_3 + 4x_4,$$

subject to

$$
\begin{aligned}
(1) &\quad 3x_2 + 5x_3 + 2x_4 \leq 10 \\
(2) &\quad \qquad\quad x_3 + x_4 \leq 1 \\
(3) &\quad \qquad\quad x_3 \qquad \leq 0 \\
(4) &\quad -x_2 \qquad + x_4 \leq 0 \\
(5) &\quad x_j \text{ is binary}, \quad \text{for } j = 2, 3, 4.
\end{aligned}
$$

Subproblem 2:
Fix $x_1 = 1$ so the resulting subproblem is

$$\text{Maximize} \quad Z = 9 + 5x_2 + 6x_3 + 4x_4,$$

subject to

$$
\begin{aligned}
(1) &\quad 3x_2 + 5x_3 + 2x_4 \leq 4 \\
(2) &\quad \qquad\quad x_3 + x_4 \leq 1 \\
(3) &\quad \qquad\quad x_3 \qquad \leq 1
\end{aligned}
$$

Variable: x_1

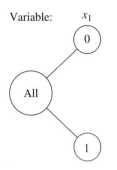

FIGURE 12.4
The solution tree created by
the branching for the first
iteration of the BIP branch-
and-bound algorithm for the
example in Sec. 12.1.

(4) $-x_2$ $+ \ x_4 \leq 0$
(5) x_j is binary,   for $j = 2, 3, 4$.

Figure 12.4 portrays this dividing (branching) into subproblems by a *tree* (defined in Sec. 9.2) with *branches* (arcs) from the *All* node (corresponding to the whole problem having *all* feasible solutions) to the two nodes corresponding to the two subproblems. This tree, which will continue "growing branches" iteration by iteration, is referred to as the **solution tree** (or **enumeration tree**) for the algorithm. The variable used to do this branching at any iteration by assigning values to the variable (as with x_1 above) is called the **branching variable.** (Sophisticated methods for selecting branching variables are an important part of some branch-and-bound algorithms but, for simplicity, we always select them in their natural order—$x_1, x_2, \ldots, x_n$—throughout this section.)

Later in the section you will see that one of these subproblems can be conquered (fathomed) immediately, whereas the other subproblem will need to be divided further into smaller subproblems by setting $x_2 = 0$ or $x_2 = 1$.

For other IP problems where the integer variables have more than two possible values, the branching can still be done by setting the branching variable at its respective individual values, thereby creating more than two new subproblems. However, a good alternate approach is to specify a *range* of values (for example, $x_j \leq 2$ or $x_j \geq 3$) for the branching variable for each new subproblem. This is the approach used for the algorithm presented in Sec. 12.7.

Bounding

For each of these subproblems, we now need to obtain a *bound* on how good its best feasible solution can be. The standard way of doing this is to quickly solve a simpler *relaxation* of the subproblem. In most cases, a **relaxation** of a problem is obtained simply by *deleting* ("relaxing") one set of constraints that had made the problem difficult to solve. For IP problems, the most troublesome constraints are those requiring the respective variables to be integer. Therefore, the most widely used relaxation is the *LP relaxation* that deletes this set of constraints.

To illustrate for the example, consider first the whole problem given in Sec. 12.1. Its LP relaxation is obtained by replacing the last line of the model (x_j is binary, for $j = 1$, 2, 3, 4) by the constraints that $x_j \leq 1$ and $x_j \geq 0$ for $j = 1, 2, 3, 4$. Using the simplex method to quickly solve this LP relaxation yields its optimal solution

$$(x_1, x_2, x_3, x_4) = \left(\frac{5}{6}, 1, 0, 1\right), \qquad \text{with } Z = 16\tfrac{1}{2}.$$

Therefore, $Z \leq 16\tfrac{1}{2}$ for all feasible solutions for the original BIP problem (since these solutions are a subset of the feasible solutions for the LP relaxation). In fact, as summarized below, this *bound* of $16\tfrac{1}{2}$ can be rounded down to 16, because all coefficients in the objective function are integer, so all integer solutions must have an integer value for Z.

Bound for whole problem: $Z \leq 16$.

Now let us obtain the bounds for the two subproblems in the same way. Their LP relaxations are obtained from the models in the preceding subsection by replacing the constraints that x_j is binary for $j = 2, 3, 4$ by the constraints $0 \leq x_j \leq 1$ for $j = 2, 3, 4$. Ap-

Variable: x_1

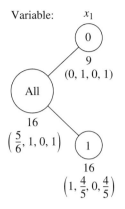

FIGURE 12.5
The results of bounding for the first iteration of the BIP branch-and-bound algorithm for the example in Sec. 12.1.

plying the simplex method then yields their optimal solutions (plus the fixed value of x_1) shown below.

LP relaxation of subproblem 1: $(x_1, x_2, x_3, x_4) = (0, 1, 0, 1)$ with $Z = 9$.

LP relaxation of subproblem 2: $(x_1, x_2, x_3, x_4) = \left(1, \frac{4}{5}, 0, \frac{4}{5}\right)$ with $Z = 16\frac{1}{5}$.

The resulting bounds for the subproblems then are

Bound for subproblem 1: $Z \leq 9$,
Bound for subproblem 2: $Z \leq 16$.

Figure 12.5 summarizes these results, where the numbers given just below the nodes are the bounds and below each bound is the optimal solution obtained for the LP relaxation.

Fathoming

A subproblem can be conquered (fathomed), and thereby dismissed from further consideration, in the three ways described below.

One way is illustrated by the results for subproblem 1 given by the $x_1 = 0$ node in Fig. 12.5. Note that the (unique) optimal solution for its LP relaxation, $(x_1, x_2, x_3, x_4) = (0, 1, 0, 1)$, is an *integer* solution. Therefore, this solution must also be the optimal solution for subproblem 1 itself. This solution should be stored as the first **incumbent** (the best feasible solution found so far) for the whole problem, along with its value of Z. This value is denoted by

$Z^* = $ value of Z for current incumbent,

so $Z^* = 9$ at this point. Since this solution has been stored, there is no reason to consider subproblem 1 any further by branching from the $x_1 = 0$ node, etc. Doing so could only lead to other feasible solutions that are inferior to the incumbent, and we have no interest in such solutions. Because it has been solved, we **fathom** (dismiss) subproblem 1 now.

The above results suggest a second key fathoming test. Since $Z^* = 9$, there is no reason to consider further any subproblem whose *bound* ≤ 9, since such a subproblem cannot have a feasible solution better than the *incumbent*. Stated more generally, a subproblem is fathomed whenever its

Bound $\leq Z^*$.

This outcome does not occur in the current iteration of the example because subproblem 2 has a bound of 16 that is larger than 9. However, it might occur later for **descendants** of this subproblem (new smaller subproblems created by branching on this subproblem, and then perhaps branching further through subsequent "generations"). Furthermore, as new incumbents with larger values of Z^* are found, it will become easier to *fathom* in this way.

The third way of fathoming is quite straightforward. If the simplex method finds that a subproblem's LP relaxation has *no feasible solutions,* then the subproblem itself must have *no feasible solutions,* so it can be dismissed (fathomed).

In all three cases, we are conducting our search for an optimal solution by retaining for further investigation only those subproblems that could possibly have a feasible solution better than the current incumbent.

Summary of Fathoming Tests.   A subproblem is *fathomed* (dismissed from further consideration) if

> *Test 1:* Its bound $\leq Z^*$,
>
> or
>
> *Test 2:* Its LP relaxation has no feasible solutions,
>
> or
>
> *Test 3:* The optimal solution for its LP relaxation is *integer.* (If this solution is better than the incumbent, it becomes the new incumbent, and test 1 is reapplied to all unfathomed subproblems with the new larger Z^*.)

Figure 12.6 summarizes the results of applying these three tests to subproblems 1 and 2 by showing the current *solution tree.* Only subproblem 1 has been fathomed, by test 3, as indicated by $F(3)$ next to the $x_1 = 0$ node. The resulting incumbent also is identified below this node.

The subsequent iterations will illustrate successful applications of all three tests. However, before continuing the example, we summarize the algorithm being applied to this BIP problem. (This algorithm assumes that all coefficients in the objective function are integer and that the ordering of the variables for branching is $x_1, x_2, \ldots, x_n$.)

Summary of the BIP Branch-and-Bound Algorithm.

> *Initialization:* Set $Z^* = -\infty$. Apply the bounding step, fathoming step, and optimality test described below to the whole problem. If not fathomed, classify this problem as the one remaining "subproblem" for performing the first full iteration below.

Steps for each iteration:

1. *Branching:* Among the *remaining* (unfathomed) subproblems, select the one that was created *most recently.* (Break ties according to which has the *larger bound.*) Branch from the node for this subproblem to create two new subproblems by fixing the next variable (the branching variable) at either 0 or 1.
2. *Bounding:* For each new subproblem, obtain its *bound* by applying the simplex method to its LP relaxation and rounding down the value of Z for the resulting optimal solution.
3. *Fathoming:* For each new subproblem, apply the three fathoming tests summarized above, and discard those subproblems that are fathomed by any of the tests.

FIGURE 12.6
The solution tree after the first iteration of the BIP branch-and-bound algorithm for the example in Sec. 12.1.

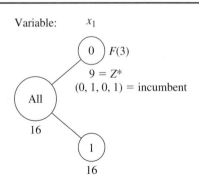

Variable: x_1

0) $F(3)$

$9 = Z^*$
$(0, 1, 0, 1) =$ incumbent

All

16

1

16

Optimality test: Stop when there are *no remaining* subproblems; the current *incumbent* is optimal.[1] Otherwise, return to perform another iteration.

The branching step for this algorithm warrants a comment as to why the subproblem to branch from is selected in this way. One option not used would have been always to select the remaining subproblem with the *best bound,* because this subproblem would be the most promising one to contain an optimal solution for the whole problem. The reason for instead selecting the *most recently created* subproblem is that *LP relaxations* are being solved in the bounding step. Rather than start the simplex method from scratch each time, each LP relaxation generally is solved by *reoptimization* in large-scale implementations of this algorithm. This reoptimization involves revising the final simplex tableau from the preceding LP relaxation as needed because of the few differences in the model (just as for sensitivity analysis) and then applying a few iterations of perhaps the dual simplex method. This reoptimization tends to be *much* faster than starting from scratch, *provided* the preceding and current models are closely related. The models will tend to be closely related under the branching rule used, but *not* when you are skipping around in the solution tree by selecting the subproblem with the best bound.

Completing the Example

The pattern for the remaining iterations will be quite similar to that for the first iteration described above except for the ways in which fathoming occurs. Therefore, we shall summarize the branching and bounding steps fairly briefly and then focus on the fathoming step.

Iteration 2. The only remaining subproblem corresponds to the $x_1 = 1$ node in Fig. 12.6, so we shall branch from this node to create the two new subproblems given below.

Subproblem 3:
Fix $x_1 = 1$, $x_2 = 0$ so the resulting subproblem is

$$\text{Maximize} \quad Z = 9 + 6x_3 + 4x_4,$$

subject to

$$
\begin{array}{lll}
(1) & 5x_3 + 2x_4 \leq 4 \\
(2) & x_3 + x_4 \leq 1 \\
(3) & x_3 \leq 1 \\
(4) & x_4 \leq 0 \\
(5) & x_j \text{ is binary,} & \text{for } j = 3, 4.
\end{array}
$$

Subproblem 4:
Fix $x_1 = 1$, $x_2 = 1$ so the resulting subproblem is

$$\text{Maximize} \quad Z = 14 + 6x_3 + 4x_4,$$

subject to

$$
\begin{array}{ll}
(1) & 5x_3 + 2x_4 \leq 1 \\
(2) & x_3 + x_4 \leq 1
\end{array}
$$

---

[1] If there is no incumbent, the conclusion is that the problem has no feasible solutions.

(3) x_3 ≤ 1
(4) $x_4 \leq 1$
(5) x_j is binary,   for $j = 3, 4$.

The LP relaxations of these subproblems are obtained by replacing the constraints x_j is binary for $j = 3, 4$ by the constraints $0 \leq x_j \leq 1$ for $j = 3, 4$. Their optimal solutions (plus the fixed values of x_1 and x_2) are

LP relaxation of subproblem 3: $(x_1, x_2, x_3, x_4) = \left(1, 0, \dfrac{4}{5}, 0\right)$ with $Z = 13\dfrac{4}{5}$,

LP relaxation of subproblem 4: $(x_1, x_2, x_3, x_4) = \left(1, 1, 0, \dfrac{1}{2}\right)$ with $Z = 16$.

The resulting bounds for the subproblems are

Bound for subproblem 3: $Z \leq 13$,
Bound for subproblem 4: $Z \leq 16$.

Note that both these bounds are larger than $Z^* = 9$, so fathoming test 1 fails in both cases. Test 2 also fails, since both LP relaxations have feasible solutions (as indicated by the existence of an optimal solution). Alas, test 3 fails as well, because both optimal solutions include variables with noninteger values.

Figure 12.7 shows the resulting solution tree at this point. The lack of an F to the right of either new node indicates that both remain unfathomed.

Iteration 3.   So far, the algorithm has created four subproblems. Subproblem 1 has been fathomed, and subproblem 2 has been replaced by (separated into) subproblems 3 and 4, but these last two remain under consideration. Because they were created simultaneously, but subproblem 4 ($x_1 = 1$, $x_2 = 1$) has the larger *bound* ($16 > 13$), the next branching is done from the $(x_1, x_2) = (1, 1)$ node in the solution tree, which creates the following new subproblems (where constraint 3 disappears because it does not contain x_4).

FIGURE 12.7
The solution tree after iteration 2 of the BIP branch-and-bound algorithm for the example in Sec. 12.1.

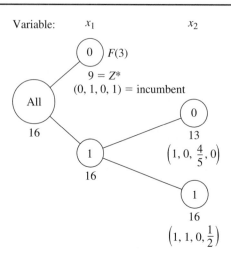

Subproblem 5:
Fix $x_1 = 1$, $x_2 = 1$, $x_3 = 0$ so the resulting subproblem is

$$\text{Maximize} \quad Z = 14 + 4x_4,$$

subject to

(1) $\qquad 2x_4 \leq 1$
(2), (4) $\qquad x_4 \leq 1 \qquad$ (twice)
(5) $\qquad x_4$ is binary.

Subproblem 6:
Fix $x_1 = 1$, $x_2 = 1$, $x_3 = 1$ so the resulting subproblem is

$$\text{Maximize} \quad Z = 20 + 4x_4,$$

subject to

(1) $\qquad 2x_4 \leq -4$
(2) $\qquad x_4 \leq 0$
(4) $\qquad x_4 \leq 1$
(5) $\qquad x_4$ is binary.

If we form their LP relaxations by replacing constraint 5 by

(5) $\qquad 0 \leq x_4 \leq 1$,

the following results are obtained:

LP relaxation of subproblem 5: $\qquad (x_1, x_2, x_3, x_4) = \left(1, 1, 0, \dfrac{1}{2}\right)$, with $Z = 16$.

LP relaxation of subproblem 6: $\qquad$ No feasible solutions.
Bound for subproblem 5: $\qquad Z \leq 16$.

Note how the combination of constraints 1 and 5 in the LP relaxation of subproblem 6 prevents any feasible solutions. Therefore, this subproblem is fathomed by test 2. However, subproblem 5 fails this test, as well as test 1 ($16 > 9$) and test 3 ($x_4 = \frac{1}{2}$ is not integer), so it remains under consideration.

We now have the solution tree shown in Fig. 12.8.

Iteration 4. The subproblems corresponding to nodes (1, 0) and (1, 1, 0) in Fig. 12.8 remain under consideration, but the latter node was created more recently, so it is selected for branching from next. Since the resulting branching variable x_4 is the *last* variable, fixing its value at either 0 or 1 actually creates a *single solution* rather than subproblems requiring fuller investigation. These single solutions are

$x_4 = 0$: $\quad (x_1, x_2, x_3, x_4) = (1, 1, 0, 0)$ is feasible, with $Z = 14$,
$x_4 = 1$: $\quad (x_1, x_2, x_3, x_4) = (1, 1, 0, 1)$ is infeasible.

Formally applying the fathoming tests, we see that the first solution passes test 3 and the second passes test 2. Furthermore, this feasible first solution is better than the incumbent ($14 > 9$), so it becomes the new incumbent, with $Z^* = 14$.

Because a new incumbent has been found, we now reapply fathoming test 1 with the new larger value of Z^* to the only remaining subproblem, the one at node (1, 0).

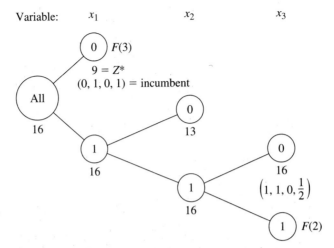

FIGURE 12.8
The solution tree after iteration 3 of the BIP branch-and-bound algorithm for the example in Sec. 12.1.

Subproblem 3:

Bound = $13 \leq Z^* = 14$.

Therefore, this subproblem now is fathomed.

We now have the solution tree shown in Fig. 12.9. Note that there are *no remaining* (unfathomed) subproblems. Consequently, the optimality test indicates that the current incumbent

$(x_1, x_2, x_3, x_4) = (1, 1, 0, 0)$

is optimal, so we are done.

FIGURE 12.9
The solution tree after the final (fourth) iteration of the BIP branch-and-bound algorithm for the example in Sec. 12.1.

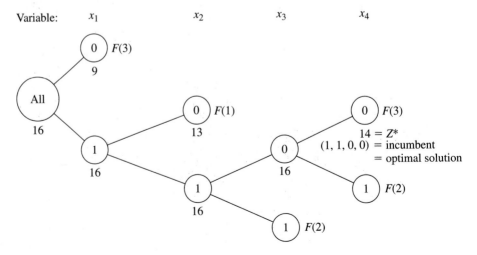

Your OR Tutor includes another example of applying this algorithm. Also included in the OR Courseware is an interactive routine for executing this algorithm. As usual, the Excel, LINGO/LINDO, and MPL/CPLEX files for this chapter in your OR Courseware show how the student version of these software packages is applied to the various examples in the chapter. The algorithms they use for BIP problems all are similar to the one described above.[1]

Other Options with the Branch-and-Bound Technique

This section has illustrated the branch-and-bound technique by describing a basic branch-and-bound algorithm for solving BIP problems. However, the general framework of the branch-and-bound technique provides a great deal of flexibility in how to design a specific algorithm for any given type of problem such as BIP. There are many options available, and constructing an efficient algorithm requires tailoring the specific design to fit the specific structure of the problem type.

Every branch-and-bound algorithm has the same three basic steps of *branching, bounding,* and *fathoming.* The flexibility lies in how these steps are performed.

Branching always involves *selecting* one remaining subproblem and *dividing* it into smaller subproblems. The flexibility here is found in the rules for selecting and dividing. Our BIP algorithm selected the *most recently created* subproblem, because this is very efficient for *reoptimizing* each LP relaxation from the preceding one. Selecting the subproblem with the *best bound* is the other most popular rule, because it tends to lead more quickly to better incumbents and so more fathoming. Combinations of the two rules also can be used. The *dividing* typically (but not always) is done by choosing a *branching variable* and assigning it either individual values (e.g., our BIP algorithm) or ranges of values (e.g., the algorithm in the next section). More sophisticated algorithms generally use a rule for strategically choosing a branching variable that should tend to lead to early fathoming.

Bounding usually is done by solving a *relaxation.* However, there are a variety of ways to form relaxations. For example, consider the **Lagrangian relaxation,** where the entire set of functional constraints $\mathbf{Ax} \leq \mathbf{b}$ (in matrix notation) is *deleted* (except possibly for any "convenient" constraints) and then the objective function

Maximize $Z = \mathbf{cx}$,

is replaced by

Maximize $Z_R = \mathbf{cx} - \boldsymbol{\lambda}(\mathbf{Ax} - \mathbf{b})$,

where the fixed vector $\boldsymbol{\lambda} \geq \mathbf{0}$. If $\mathbf{x}^*$ is an optimal solution for the original problem, its $Z \leq Z_R$, so solving the Lagrangian relaxation for the optimal value of Z_R provides a valid *bound.* If $\boldsymbol{\lambda}$ is chosen well, this bound tends to be a reasonably tight one (at least comparable to the bound from the LP relaxation). Without any functional constraints, this relaxation also can be solved extremely quickly. The drawbacks are that fathoming tests 2 and 3 (revised) are not as powerful as for the LP relaxation.

---

[1]In the professional version of LINGO, LINDO, and CPLEX, the BIP algorithm also uses a variety of sophisticated techniques along the lines described in Sec. 12.8.

In general terms, two features are sought in choosing a relaxation: it can be solved relatively quickly, and provides a relatively tight bound. Neither alone is adequate. The LP relaxation is popular because it provides an excellent trade-off between these two factors.

One option occasionally employed is to use a quickly solved relaxation and then, if fathoming is not achieved, to tighten the relaxation in some way to obtain a somewhat tighter bound.

Fathoming generally is done pretty much as described for the BIP algorithm. The three fathoming criteria can be stated in more general terms as follows.

Summary of Fathoming Criteria.   A subproblem is *fathomed* if an analysis of its *relaxation* reveals that

Criterion 1: Feasible solutions of the subproblem must have $Z \leq Z^*$, or
Criterion 2: The subproblem has no feasible solutions, or
Criterion 3: An optimal solution of the subproblem has been found.

Just as for the BIP algorithm, the first two criteria usually are applied by solving the relaxation to obtain a bound for the subproblem and then checking whether this bound is $\leq Z^*$ (test 1) or whether the relaxation has no feasible solutions (test 2). If the relaxation differs from the subproblem *only* by the deletion (or loosening) of some constraints, then the third criterion usually is applied by checking whether the optimal solution for the relaxation is *feasible* for the subproblem, in which case it must be *optimal* for the subproblem. For other relaxations (such as the Lagrangian relaxation), additional analysis is required to determine whether the optimal solution for the relaxation is also optimal for the subproblem.

If the original problem involves *minimization* rather than maximization, two options are available. One is to convert to maximization in the usual way (see Sec. 4.6). The other is to convert the branch-and-bound algorithm directly to minimization form, which requires changing the direction of the inequality for fathoming test 1 from

Is the subproblem's bound $\leq Z^*$?

to

Is the subproblem's bound $\geq Z^*$?

So far, we have described how to use the branch-and-bound technique to find only *one* optimal solution. However, in the case of ties for the optimal solution, it is sometimes desirable to identify *all* these optimal solutions so that the final choice among them can be made on the basis of intangible factors not incorporated into the mathematical model. To find them all, you need to make only a few slight alterations in the procedure. First, change the weak inequality for fathoming test 1 (Is the subproblem's bound $\leq Z^*$?) to a strict inequality (Is the subproblem's bound $< Z^*$?), so that fathoming will not occur if the subproblem can have a feasible solution *equal* to the incumbent. Second, if fathoming test 3 passes and the optimal solution for the subproblem has $Z = Z^*$, then store this solution as *another* (tied) incumbent. Third, if test 3 provides a new incumbent (tied or otherwise), then check whether the optimal solution obtained for the *relaxation* is *unique*. If it is not, then identify the other optimal solutions for the relaxation and check whether they are optimal for the subproblem as well, in which case they also become incumbents.

Finally, when the *optimality test* finds that there are *no remaining* (unfathomed) subsets, *all* the current *incumbents* will be the *optimal* solutions.

Finally, note that rather than find an optimal solution, the branch-and-bound technique can be used to find a *nearly optimal* solution, generally with much less computational effort. For some applications, a solution is "good enough" if its Z is "close enough" to the value of Z for an optimal solution (call it Z^{**}). *Close enough* can be defined in either of two ways as either

$$Z^{**} - K \leq Z \qquad \text{or} \qquad (1 - \alpha)Z^{**} \leq Z$$

for a specified (positive) constant K or α. For example, if the second definition is chosen and $\alpha = 0.05$, then the solution is required to be within 5 percent of optimal. Consequently, if it were known that the value of Z for the current incumbent (Z^*) satisfies either

$$Z^{**} - K \leq Z^* \qquad \text{or} \qquad (1 - \alpha)Z^{**} \leq Z^*$$

then the procedure could be terminated immediately by choosing the incumbent as the desired nearly optimal solution. Although the procedure does not actually identify an optimal solution and the corresponding Z^{**}, if this (unknown) solution is feasible (and so optimal) for the subproblem currently under investigation, then fathoming test 1 finds an upper bound such that

$$Z^{**} \leq \text{bound}$$

so that either

$$\text{Bound} - K \leq Z^* \qquad \text{or} \qquad (1 - \alpha)\text{bound} \leq Z^*$$

would imply that the corresponding inequality in the preceding sentence is satisfied. Even if this solution is not feasible for the current subproblem, a valid upper bound is still obtained for the value of Z for the subproblem's optimal solution. Thus, satisfying either of these last two inequalities is sufficient to fathom this subproblem because the incumbent must be "close enough" to the subproblem's optimal solution.

Therefore, to find a solution that is close enough to being optimal, only one change is needed in the usual branch-and-bound procedure. This change is to replace the usual fathoming test 1 for a subproblem

$$\text{Bound} \leq Z^* ?$$

by either

$$\text{Bound} - K \leq Z^* ?$$

or

$$(1 - \alpha)(\text{bound}) \leq Z^* ?$$

and then perform this test *after* test 3 (so that a feasible solution found with $Z > Z^*$ is still kept as the new incumbent). The reason this weaker test 1 suffices is that regardless of how close Z for the subproblem's (unknown) optimal solution is to the subproblem's bound, the incumbent is still close enough to this solution (if the new inequality holds) that the subproblem does not need to be considered further. When there are no remaining subproblems, the current incumbent will be the desired *nearly optimal* solution. However, it is much easier to fathom with this new fathoming test (in either form), so the algorithm should run much faster. For a large problem, this acceleration may make the difference between finishing with a solution guaranteed to be close to optimal and never terminating.

12.7   A BRANCH-AND-BOUND ALGORITHM FOR MIXED INTEGER PROGRAMMING

We shall now consider the general MIP problem, where *some* of the variables (say, I of them) are restricted to integer values (but not necessarily just 0 and 1) but the rest are ordinary continuous variables. For notational convenience, we shall order the variables so that the first I variables are the *integer-restricted* variables. Therefore, the general form of the problem being considered is

$$\text{Maximize} \quad Z = \sum_{j=1}^{n} c_j x_j,$$

subject to

$$\sum_{j=1}^{n} a_{ij} x_j \leq b_i, \quad \text{for } i = 1, 2, \ldots, m,$$

and

$$x_j \geq 0, \quad \text{for } j = 1, 2, \ldots, n,$$
$$x_j \text{ is integer}, \quad \text{for } j = 1, 2, \ldots, I; \ I \leq n.$$

(When $I = n$, this problem becomes the pure IP problem.)

We shall describe a basic branch-and-bound algorithm for solving this problem that, with a variety of refinements, has provided a standard approach to MIP. The structure of this algorithm was first developed by R. J. Dakin,[1] based on a pioneering branch-and-bound algorithm by A. H. Land and A. G. Doig.[2]

This algorithm is quite similar in structure to the BIP algorithm presented in the preceding section. Solving *LP relaxations* again provides the basis for both the *bounding* and *fathoming* steps. In fact, only four changes are needed in the BIP algorithm to deal with the generalizations from *binary* to *general* integer variables and from *pure* IP to *mixed* IP.

One change involves the choice of the *branching variable*. Before, the *next* variable in the natural ordering—$x_1, x_2, \ldots, x_n$—was chosen automatically. Now, the only variables considered are the *integer-restricted* variables that have a *noninteger* value in the optimal solution for the LP relaxation of the current subproblem. Our rule for choosing among these variables is to select the *first* one in the natural ordering. (Production codes generally use a more sophisticated rule.)

[1]R. J. Dakin, "A Tree Search Algorithm for Mixed Integer Programming Problems," *Computer Journal,* **8**(3): 250–255, 1965.

[2]A. H. Land and A. G. Doig, "An Automatic Method of Solving Discrete Programming Problems," *Econometrica,* **28**: 497–520, 1960.

The second change involves the values assigned to the branching variable for creating the new smaller subproblems. Before, the *binary* variable was fixed at 0 and 1, respectively, for the two new subproblems. Now, the *general* integer-restricted variable could have a very large number of possible integer values, and it would be inefficient to create *and* analyze *many* subproblems by fixing the variable at its individual integer values. Therefore, what is done instead is to create just *two* new subproblems (as before) by specifying two *ranges* of values for the variable.

To spell out how this is done, let x_j be the current branching variable, and let x_j^* be its (noninteger) value in the optimal solution for the LP relaxation of the current subproblem. Using square brackets to denote

$$[x_j^*] = \text{greatest integer} \leq x_j^*,$$

we have for the range of values for the two new subproblems

$$x_j \leq [x_j^*] \quad \text{and} \quad x_j \geq [x_j^*] + 1,$$

respectively. Each inequality becomes an *additional constraint* for that new subproblem. For example, if $x_j^* = 3\frac{1}{2}$, then

$$x_j \leq 3 \quad \text{and} \quad x_j \geq 4$$

are the respective additional constraints for the new subproblem.

When the two changes to the BIP algorithm described above are combined, an interesting phenomenon of a *recurring branching variable* can occur. To illustrate, as shown in Fig. 12.10, let $j = 1$ in the above example where $x_j^* = 3\frac{1}{2}$, and consider the new subproblem where $x_1 \leq 3$. When the LP relaxation of a descendant of this subproblem is solved, suppose that $x_1^* = 1\frac{1}{4}$. Then x_1 *recurs* as the branching variable, and the two new subproblems created have the additional constraint $x_1 \leq 1$ and $x_1 \geq 2$, respectively (as well as the previous additional constraint $x_1 \leq 3$). Later, when the LP relaxation for a descendant of, say, the $x_1 \leq 1$ subproblem is solved, suppose that $x_1^* = \frac{3}{4}$. Then x_1 *recurs* again as the branching variable, and the two new subproblems created have $x_1 = 0$ (be-

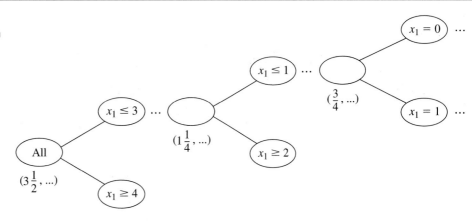

FIGURE 12.10
Illustration of the phenomenon of a *recurring branching variable,* where here x_1 becomes a branching variable three times because it has a noninteger value in the optimal solution for the LP relaxation at three nodes.

cause of the new $x_1 \leq 0$ constraint and the nonnegativity constraint on x_1) and $x_1 = 1$ (because of the new $x_1 \geq 1$ constraint and the previous $x_1 \leq 1$ constraint).

The third change involves the *bounding step*. Before, with a *pure* IP problem and integer coefficients in the objective function, the value of Z for the optimal solution for the subproblem's LP relaxation was *rounded down* to obtain the bound, because any feasible solution for the subproblem must have an *integer Z*. Now, with some of the variables *not* integer-restricted, the bound is the value of Z *without* rounding down.

The fourth (and final) change to the BIP algorithm to obtain our MIP algorithm involves fathoming test 3. Before, with a *pure* IP problem, the test was that the optimal solution for the subproblem's LP relaxation is *integer*, since this ensures that the solution is feasible, and therefore optimal, for the subproblem. Now, with a *mixed* IP problem, the test requires only that the *integer-restricted* variables be *integer* in the optimal solution for the subproblem's LP relaxation, because this suffices to ensure that the solution is feasible, and therefore optimal, for the subproblem.

Incorporating these four changes into the summary presented in the preceding section for the BIP algorithm yields the following summary for the new algorithm for MIP.

Summary of the MIP Branch-and-Bound Algorithm.

Initialization: Set $Z^* = -\infty$. Apply the bounding step, fathoming step, and optimality test described below to the whole problem. If not fathomed, classify this problem as the one remaining subproblem for performing the first full iteration below.

Steps for each iteration:

1. *Branching:* Among the *remaining* (unfathomed) subproblems, select the one that was created *most recently*. (Break ties according to which has the *larger bound*.) Among the *integer-restricted* variables that have a *noninteger* value in the optimal solution for the LP relaxation of the subproblem, choose the *first one* in the natural ordering of the variables to be the *branching variable*. Let x_j be this variable and x_j^* its value in this solution. Branch from the node for the subproblem to create two new subproblems by adding the respective constraints $x_j \leq [x_j^*]$ and $x_j \geq [x_j^*] + 1$.
2. *Bounding:* For each new subproblem, obtain its bound by applying the simplex method (or the dual simplex method when reoptimizing) to its LP relaxation and using the value of Z for the resulting optimal solution.
3. *Fathoming:* For each new subproblem, apply the three fathoming tests given below, and discard those subproblems that are fathomed by any of the tests.
   Test 1: Its bound $\leq Z^*$, where Z^* is the value of Z for the current *incumbent*.
   Test 2: Its LP relaxation has no feasible solutions.
   Test 3: The optimal solution for its LP relaxation has *integer* values for the *integer-restricted* variables. (If this solution is better than the incumbent, it becomes the new incumbent and test 1 is reapplied to all unfathomed subproblems with the new larger Z^*.)

Optimality test: Stop when there are no remaining subproblems; the current *incumbent* is optimal.[1] Otherwise, perform another iteration.

[1]If there is no incumbent, the conclusion is that the problem has no feasible solutions.

An MIP Example.   We will now illustrate this algorithm by applying it to the following MIP problem:

Maximize $Z = 4x_1 - 2x_2 + 7x_3 - x_4,$

subject to

$$
\begin{aligned}
x_1 \quad\quad\quad\ + 5x_3 \quad\quad\quad &\leq 10 \\
x_1 + x_2 - x_3 \quad\quad\quad &\leq 1 \\
6x_1 - 5x_2 \quad\quad\quad\quad\quad &\leq 0 \\
-x_1 \quad\quad\ + 2x_3 - 2x_4 &\leq 3
\end{aligned}
$$

and

$x_j \geq 0,$ for $j = 1, 2, 3, 4$
x_j is an integer,   for $j = 1, 2, 3$.

Note that the number of integer-restricted variables is $I = 3$, so x_4 is the only continuous variable.

Initialization.   After setting $Z^* = -\infty$, we form the LP relaxation of this problem by *deleting* the set of constraints that x_j is an integer for $j = 1, 2, 3$. Applying the simplex method to this LP relaxation yields its optimal solution below.

LP relaxation of whole problem: $(x_1, x_2, x_3, x_4) = \left(\dfrac{5}{4}, \dfrac{3}{2}, \dfrac{7}{4}, 0\right),$ with $Z = 14\dfrac{1}{4}$.

Because it has *feasible* solutions and this optimal solution has *noninteger* values for its integer-restricted variables, the whole problem is not fathomed, so the algorithm continues with the first full iteration below.

Iteration 1.   In this optimal solution for the LP relaxation, the *first* integer-restricted variable that has a noninteger value is $x_1 = \frac{5}{4}$, so x_1 becomes the branching variable. Branching from the *All* node (*all* feasible solutions) with this branching variable then creates the following two subproblems:

Subproblem 1:
Original problem plus additional constraint

$x_1 \leq 1.$

Subproblem 2:
Original problem plus additional constraint

$x_1 \geq 2.$

Deleting the set of integer constraints again and solving the resulting LP relaxations of these two subproblems yield the following results.

LP relaxation of subproblem 1: $(x_1, x_2, x_3, x_4) = \left(1, \dfrac{6}{5}, \dfrac{9}{5}, 0\right),$ with $Z = 14\dfrac{1}{5}$.

Bound for subproblem 1: $Z \leq 14\dfrac{1}{5}.$

LP relaxation of subproblem 2:   No feasible solutions.

This outcome for subproblem 2 means that it is fathomed by test 2. However, just as for the whole problem, subproblem 1 fails all fathoming tests.

These results are summarized in the solution tree shown in Fig. 12.11.

Iteration 2. With only one remaining subproblem, corresponding to the $x_1 \leq 1$ node in Fig. 12.11, the next branching is from this node. Examining its LP relaxation's optimal solution given below, we see that this node reveals that the *branching variable* is x_2, because $x_2 = \frac{6}{5}$ is the first integer-restricted variable that has a noninteger value. Adding one of the constraints $x_2 \leq 1$ or $x_2 \geq 2$ then creates the following two new subproblems.

Subproblem 3:
Original problem plus additional constraints

$$x_1 \leq 1, \qquad x_2 \leq 1.$$

Subproblem 4:
Original problem plus additional constraints

$$x_1 \leq 1, \qquad x_2 \geq 2.$$

Solving their LP relaxations gives the following results.

$$\text{LP relaxation of subproblem 3:} \quad (x_1, x_2, x_3, x_4) = \left(\frac{5}{6}, 1, \frac{11}{6}, 0\right), \qquad \text{with } Z = 14\frac{1}{6}.$$

$$\text{Bound for subproblem 3:} \qquad Z \leq 14\frac{1}{6}.$$

$$\text{LP relaxation of subproblem 4:} \quad (x_1, x_2, x_3, x_4) = \left(\frac{5}{6}, 2, \frac{11}{6}, 0\right), \qquad \text{with } Z = 12\frac{1}{6}.$$

$$\text{Bound for subproblem 4:} \qquad Z \leq 12\frac{1}{6}.$$

Because both solutions exist (feasible solutions) and have noninteger values for integer-restricted variables, neither subproblem is fathomed. (Test 1 still is not operational, since $Z^* = -\infty$ until the first incumbent is found.)

The solution tree at this point is given in Fig. 12.12.

Iteration 3. With two remaining subproblems (3 and 4) that were created simultaneously, the one with the larger bound (subproblem 3, with $14\frac{1}{6} > 12\frac{1}{6}$) is selected for the

FIGURES 12.11
The solution tree after the first iteration of the MIP branch-and-bound algorithm for the MIP example.

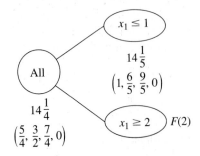

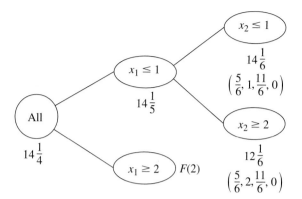

FIGURE 12.12
The solution tree after the second iteration of the MIP branch-and-bound algorithm for the MIP example.

next branching. Because $x_1 = \frac{5}{6}$ has a noninteger value in the optimal solution for this subproblem's LP relaxation, x_1 becomes the branching variable. (Note that x_1 now is a *recurring* branching variable, since it also was chosen at iteration 1.) This leads to the following new subproblems.

Subproblem 5:
Original problem plus additional constraints

$$x_1 \leq 1$$
$$x_2 \leq 1$$
$$x_1 \leq 0 \qquad (\text{so } x_1 = 0).$$

Subproblem 6:
Original problem plus additional constraints

$$x_1 \leq 1$$
$$x_2 \leq 1$$
$$x_1 \geq 1 \qquad (\text{so } x_1 = 1).$$

The results from solving their LP relaxations are given below.

$$\text{LP relaxation of subproblem 5:} \quad (x_1, x_2, x_3, x_4) = \left(0, 0, 2, \frac{1}{2}\right), \qquad \text{with } Z = 13\frac{1}{2}.$$

$$\text{Bound for subproblem 5:} \qquad Z \leq 13\frac{1}{2}.$$

LP relaxation of subproblem 6:   No feasible solutions.

Subproblem 6 is immediately fathomed by test 2. However, note that subproblem 5 also can be fathomed. Test 3 passes because the optimal solution for its LP relaxation has integer values ($x_1 = 0$, $x_2 = 0$, $x_3 = 2$) for all three integer-restricted variables. (It does not matter that $x_4 = \frac{1}{2}$, since x_4 is not integer-restricted.) This *feasible* solution for the original problem becomes our first incumbent:

$$\text{Incumbent} = \left(0, 0, 2, \frac{1}{2}\right) \qquad \text{with } Z^* = 13\frac{1}{2}.$$

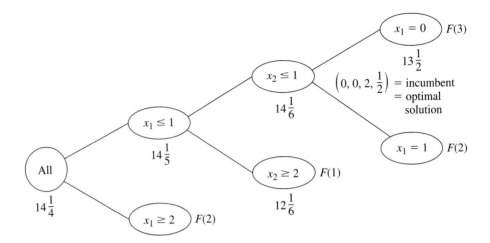

FIGURE 12.13
The solution tree after the final (third) iteration of the MIP branch-and-bound algorithm for the MIP example.

Using this Z^* to reapply fathoming test 1 to the only other subproblem (subproblem 4) is successful, because its bound $12\frac{1}{6} \leq Z^*$.

This iteration has succeeded in fathoming subproblems in all three possible ways. Furthermore, there now are no remaining subproblems, so the current incumbent is optimal.

$$\text{Optimal solution} = \left(0, 0, 2, \frac{1}{2}\right) \quad \text{with } Z = 13\frac{1}{2}.$$

These results are summarized by the final solution tree given in Fig. 12.13.

Another example of applying the MIP algorithm is presented in your OR Tutor. The OR Courseware also includes an interactive routine for executing this algorithm.

12.8   OTHER DEVELOPMENTS IN SOLVING BIP PROBLEMS

Integer programming has been an especially exciting area of OR since the mid-1980s because of the dramatic progress being made in its solution methodology.

Background

To place this progress into perspective, consider the historical background. One big breakthrough had come in the 1960s and early 1970s with the development and refinement of the branch-and-bound approach. But then the state of the art seemed to hit a plateau. Relatively small problems (well under 100 variables) could be solved very efficiently, but even a modest increase in problem size might cause an explosion in computation time beyond feasible limits. Little progress was being made in overcoming this exponential growth in computation time as the problem size was increased. Many important problems arising in practice could not be solved.

Then came the next breakthrough in the mid-1980s, as reported largely in four papers published in 1983, 1985, 1987, and 1991. (See Selected References 3, 6, 10, and 5.)

In the 1983 paper, Harlan Crowder, Ellis Johnson, and Manfred Padberg presented a new algorithmic approach to solving *pure* BIP problems that had successfully solved problems with no apparent special structure having up to 2,756 variables! This paper won the Lanchester Prize, awarded by the Operations Research Society of America for the most notable publication in operations research during 1983. In the 1985 paper, Ellis Johnson, Michael Kostreva, and Uwe Suhl further refined this algorithmic approach.

However, both of these papers were limited to *pure* BIP. For IP problems arising in practice, it is quite common for all the integer-restricted variables to be *binary*, but a large proportion of these problems are *mixed* BIP problems. What was critically needed was a way of extending this same kind of algorithmic approach to *mixed* BIP. This came in the 1987 paper by Tony Van Roy and Laurence Wolsey of Belgium. Once again, problems of *very* substantial size (up to nearly 1,000 binary variables and a larger number of continuous variables) were being solved successfully. And once again, this paper won a very prestigious award, the Orchard-Hays Prize given triannually by the Mathematical Programming Society.

In the 1991 paper, Karla Hoffman and Manfred Padberg followed up on the 1983 and 1985 papers by developing improved techniques for solving pure BIP problems. Using the name **branch-and-cut algorithm** for this algorithmic approach, they reported successfully solving problems with as many as 6,000 variables!

We do need to add one note of caution. This algorithmic approach cannot consistently solve *all* pure BIP problems with a few thousand variables, or even a few hundred variables. The very large pure BIP problems solved had *sparse* **A** matrices; i.e., the percentage of coefficients in the functional constraints that were *nonzeros* was quite small (perhaps less than 5 percent). In fact, the approach depends heavily upon this sparsity. (Fortunately, this kind of sparsity is typical in large practical problems.) Furthermore, there are other important factors besides sparsity and size that affect just how difficult a given IP problem will be to solve. IP formulations of fairly substantial size should still be approached with considerable caution.

On the other hand, each new algorithmic breakthrough in OR always generates a flurry of new research and development activity to try to refine the new approach further. We have seen substantial effort to develop sophisticated software packages for widespread use. For example, the kinds of IP techniques discussed above have been incorporated into the IP module of IBM's Optimization Subroutine Library (OSL). The developers of CPLEX have an ongoing project to maintain a fully state-of-the-art IP module. Theoretical research also continues.

Throughout the 1990s, we have seen further fruits of these intensified research and development activities in integer programming. Larger and larger problems are being solved. For example, at the end of that decade, CPLEX 6.5 successfully used a sophisticated branch-and-cut algorithm to solve a real-world problem with over 4,000 functional constraints and over 120,000 binary variables! MIP problems with thousands of general integer variables, along with numerous continuous variables and binary variables, also were being solved. (Selected Reference 2 provides details.)

Although it would be beyond the scope and level of this book to fully describe the algorithmic approach discussed above, we will now give a brief overview. (You are encouraged to read Selected References 2, 3, 5, 6, and 10 for further information.) This overview is limited to *pure* BIP, so *all* variables introduced later in this section are *binary* variables.

The approach mainly uses a combination of three kinds[1] of techniques: *automatic problem preprocessing,* the *generation of cutting planes,* and clever *branch-and-bound* techniques. You already are familiar with branch-and-bound techniques, and we will not elaborate further on the more advanced versions incorporated here. An introduction to the other two kinds of techniques is given below.

Automatic Problem Preprocessing for Pure BIP

Automatic problem preprocessing involves a "computer inspection" of the user-supplied formulation of the IP problem in order to spot reformulations that make the problem quicker to solve without eliminating any feasible solutions. These reformulations fall into three categories:

1. *Fixing variables:* Identify variables that can be fixed at one of their possible values (either 0 or 1) because the other value cannot possibly be part of a solution that is both feasible and optimal.
2. *Eliminating redundant constraints:* Identify and eliminate *redundant constraints* (constraints that automatically are satisfied by solutions that satisfy all the other constraints).
3. *Tightening constraints:* Tighten some constraints in a way that reduces the feasible region for the LP relaxation without eliminating any feasible solutions for the BIP problem.

These categories are described in turn.

Fixing Variables.   One general principle for fixing variables is the following.

> If one value of a variable cannot satisfy a certain constraint, even when the other variables equal their best values for trying to satisfy the constraint, then that variable should be fixed at its other value.

For example, *each* of the following $\leq$ constraints would enable us to fix x_1 at $x_1 = 0$, since $x_1 = 1$ with the best values of the other variables (0 with a nonnegative coefficient and 1 with a negative coefficient) would violate the constraint.

$$3x_1 \leq 2 \quad \Rightarrow \quad x_1 = 0, \quad \text{since} \quad 3(1) > 2.$$
$$3x_1 + x_2 \leq 2 \quad \Rightarrow \quad x_1 = 0, \quad \text{since} \quad 3(1) + 1(0) > 2.$$
$$5x_1 + x_2 - 2x_3 \leq 2 \quad \Rightarrow \quad x_1 = 0, \quad \text{since} \quad 5(1) + 1(0) - 2(1) > 2.$$

The general procedure for checking any $\leq$ constraint is to identify the variable with the *largest positive coefficient,* and if the *sum* of *that coefficient* and any *negative coefficients* exceeds the right-hand side, then that variable should be fixed at 0. (Once the variable has been fixed, the procedure can be repeated for the variable with the next largest positive coefficient, etc.)

An analogous procedure with $\geq$ constraints can enable us to fix a variable at 1 instead, as illustrated below three times.

$$3x_1 \geq 2 \quad \Rightarrow \quad x_1 = 1, \quad \text{since} \quad 3(0) < 2.$$
$$3x_1 + x_2 \geq 2 \quad \Rightarrow \quad x_1 = 1, \quad \text{since} \quad 3(0) + 1(1) < 2.$$
$$3x_1 + x_2 - 2x_3 \geq 2 \quad \Rightarrow \quad x_1 = 1, \quad \text{since} \quad 3(0) + 1(1) - 2(0) < 2.$$

---

[1]As discussed briefly in Sec. 12.4, still another technique that has played a significant role in the recent progress has been the use of *heuristics* for quickly finding good feasible solutions.

A $\geq$ constraint also can enable us to fix a variable at 0, as illustrated next.

$$x_1 + x_2 - 2x_3 \geq 1 \quad \Rightarrow \quad x_3 = 0, \quad \text{since} \quad 1(1) + 1(1) - 2(1) < 1.$$

The next example shows a $\geq$ constraint fixing one variable at 1 and another at 0.

$$3x_1 + x_2 - 3x_3 \geq 2 \quad \Rightarrow \quad x_1 = 1, \quad \text{since} \quad 3(0) + 1(1) - 3(0) < 2$$
$$\text{and} \quad \Rightarrow \quad x_3 = 0, \quad \text{since} \quad 3(1) + 1(1) - 3(1) < 2.$$

Similarly, a $\leq$ constraint with a *negative* right-hand side can result in either 0 or 1 becoming the fixed value of a variable. For example, both happen with the following constraint.

$$3x_1 - 2x_2 \leq -1 \quad \Rightarrow \quad x_1 = 0, \quad \text{since} \quad 3(1) - 2(1) > -1$$
$$\text{and} \quad \Rightarrow \quad x_2 = 1, \quad \text{since} \quad 3(0) - 2(0) > -1.$$

Fixing a variable from one constraint can sometimes generate a chain reaction of then being able to fix other variables from other constraints. For example, look at what happens with the following three constraints.

$$3x_1 + x_2 - 2x_3 \geq 2 \quad \Rightarrow \quad x_1 = 1 \quad \text{(as above)}.$$

Then

$$x_1 + x_4 + x_5 \leq 1 \quad \Rightarrow \quad x_4 = 0, \quad x_5 = 0.$$

Then

$$-x_5 + x_6 \leq 0 \quad \Rightarrow \quad x_6 = 0.$$

In some cases, it is possible to combine one or more *mutually exclusive alternatives* constraints with another constraint to fix a variable, as illustrated below,

$$\left.\begin{array}{r} 8x_1 - 4x_2 - 5x_3 + 3x_4 \leq 2 \\ x_2 + x_3 \leq 1 \end{array}\right\} \quad \Rightarrow \quad x_1 = 0,$$
$$\text{since} \quad 8(1) - \max\{4, 5\}(1) + 3(0) > 2.$$

There are additional techniques for fixing variables, including some involving optimality considerations, but we will not delve further into this topic.

Fixing variables can have a dramatic impact on reducing the size of a problem. One example is the problem with 2,756 variables reported in Selected Reference 3. A major factor in being able to solve this problem is that the algorithm succeeded in fixing 1,341 variables, thereby eliminating essentially half of the problem's variables from further consideration.

Eliminating Redundant Constraints. Here is one easy way to detect a redundant constraint.

If a functional constraint satisfies even the most challenging binary solution, then it has been made redundant by the binary constraints and can be eliminated from further consideration. For a $\leq$ constraint, the most challenging binary solution has variables equal to 1 when they have nonnegative coefficients and other variables equal to 0. (Reverse these values for a $\geq$ constraint.)

Some examples are given below.

$$3x_1 + 2x_2 \leq 6 \qquad \text{is redundant, since } 3(1) + 2(1) \leq 6.$$
$$3x_1 - 2x_2 \leq 3 \qquad \text{is redundant, since } 3(1) - 2(0) \leq 3.$$
$$3x_1 - 2x_2 \geq -3 \qquad \text{is redundant, since } 3(0) - 2(1) \geq -3.$$

In most cases where a constraint has been identified as redundant, it was not redundant in the original model but became so after fixing some variables. Of the 11 examples of fixing variables given above, *all* but the last one left a constraint that then was redundant.

Tightening Constraints.[1]   Consider the following problem.

Maximize $Z = 3x_1 + 2x_2,$

subject to

$$2x_1 + 3x_2 \leq 4$$

and

x_1, x_2 binary.

This BIP problem has just three feasible solutions—(0, 0), (1, 0), and (0, 1)—where the optimal solution is (1, 0) with $Z = 3$. The feasible region for the LP relaxation of this problem is shown in Fig. 12.14. The optimal solution for this LP relaxation is $(1, \frac{2}{3})$ with $Z = 4\frac{1}{3}$, which is not very close to the optimal solution for the BIP problem. A branch-and-bound algorithm would have some work to do to identify the optimal BIP solution.

---

[1]Also commonly called *coefficient reduction.*

FIGURE 12.14
The LP relaxation (including its feasible region and optimal solution) for the BIP example used to illustrate tightening a constraint.

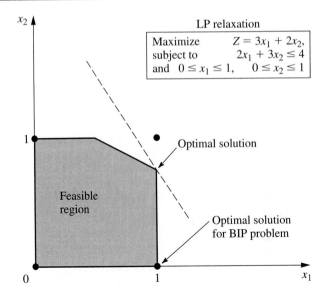

Now look what happens when the functional constraint $2x_1 + 3x_2 \leq 4$ is replaced by

$$x_1 + x_2 \leq 1.$$

The feasible solutions for the BIP problem remain exactly the same—(0, 0), (1, 0), and (0, 1)—so the optimal solution still is (1, 0). However, the feasible region for the LP relaxation has been greatly reduced, as shown in Fig. 12.15. In fact, this feasible region has been reduced so much that the optimal solution for the LP relaxation now is (1, 0), so the optimal solution for the BIP problem has been found without needing any additional work.

This is an example of tightening a constraint in a way that reduces the feasible region for the LP relaxation without eliminating any feasible solutions for the BIP problem. It was easy to do for this tiny two-variable problem that could be displayed graphically. However, with application of the same principles for tightening a constraint without eliminating any feasible BIP solutions, the following algebraic procedure can be used to do this for any $\leq$ constraint with any number of variables.

Procedure for Tightening a $\leq$ Constraint

Denote the constraint by $a_1x_1 + a_2x_2 + \cdots + a_nx_n \leq b$.

1. Calculate S = sum of the *positive* a_j.
2. Identify any $a_j \neq 0$ such that $S < b + |a_j|$.
    (*a*) If none, stop; the constraint cannot be tightened further.
    (*b*) If $a_j > 0$, go to step 3.
    (*c*) If $a_j < 0$, go to step 4.
3. ($a_j > 0$)   Calculate $\bar{a}_j = S - b$ and $\bar{b} = S - a_j$. Reset $a_j = \bar{a}_j$ and $b = \bar{b}$. Return to step 1.
4. ($a_j < 0$)   Increase a_j to $a_j = b - S$. Return to step 1.

FIGURE 12.15
The LP relaxation after tightening the constraint, $2x_1 + 3x_2 \leq 4$, to $x_1 + x_2 \leq 1$ for the example of Fig. 12.14.

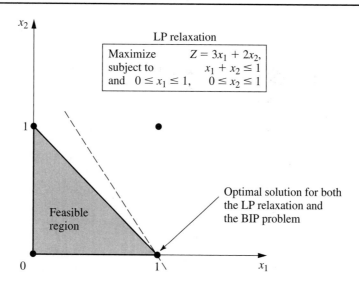

LP relaxation

Maximize $Z = 3x_1 + 2x_2,$
subject to $x_1 + x_2 \leq 1$
and $0 \leq x_1 \leq 1,$ $0 \leq x_2 \leq 1$

Feasible region

Optimal solution for both the LP relaxation and the BIP problem

Applying this procedure to the functional constraint in the above example flows as follows:

The constraint is $2x_1 + 3x_2 \leq 4$ ($a_1 = 2, a_2 = 3, b = 4$).

1. $S = 2 + 3 = 5$.
2. a_1 satisfies $S < b + |a_1|$, since $5 < 4 + 2$. Also a_2 satisfies $S < b + |a_2|$, since $5 < 4 + 3$. Choose a_1 arbitrarily.
3. $\bar{a}_1 = 5 - 4 = 1$ and $\bar{b} = 5 - 2 = 3$, so reset $a_1 = 1$ and $b = 3$. The new tighter constraint is

$$x_1 + 3x_2 \leq 3 \qquad (a_1 = 1, a_2 = 3, b = 3).$$

1. $S = 1 + 3 = 4$.
2. a_2 satisfies $S < b + |a_2|$, since $4 < 3 + 3$.
3. $\bar{a}_2 = 4 - 3 = 1$ and $\bar{b} = 4 - 3 = 1$, so reset $a_2 = 1$ and $b = 1$. The new tighter constraint is

$$x_1 + x_2 \leq 1 \qquad (a_1 = 1, a_2 = 1, b = 1).$$

1. $S = 1 + 1 = 2$.
2. No $a_j \neq 0$ satisfies $S < b + |a_j|$, so stop; $x_1 + x_2 \leq 1$ is the desired tightened constraint.

If the first execution of step 2 in the above example had chosen a_2 instead, then the first tighter constraint would have been $2x_1 + x_2 \leq 2$. The next series of steps again would have led to $x_1 + x_2 \leq 1$.

In the next example, the procedure tightens the constraint on the left to become the one on its right and then tightens further to become the second one on the right.

$$4x_1 - 3x_2 + x_3 + 2x_4 \leq 5 \quad \Rightarrow \quad 2x_1 - 3x_2 + x_3 + 2x_4 \leq 3$$
$$\Rightarrow \quad 2x_1 - 2x_2 + x_3 + 2x_4 \leq 3.$$

(Problem 12.8-5 asks you to apply the procedure to confirm these results.)

A constraint in $\geq$ form can be converted to $\leq$ form (by multiplying through both sides by -1) to apply this procedure directly.

Generating Cutting Planes for Pure BIP

A **cutting plane** (or **cut**) for any IP problem is a new functional constraint that reduces the feasible region for the LP relaxation without eliminating any feasible solutions for the IP problem. In fact, you have just seen one way of generating cutting planes for pure BIP problems, namely, apply the above procedure for tightening constraints. Thus, $x_1 + x_2 \leq 1$ is a cutting plane for the BIP problem considered in Fig. 12.14, which leads to the reduced feasible region for the LP relaxation shown in Fig. 12.15.

In addition to this procedure, a number of other techniques have been developed for generating cutting planes that will tend to accelerate how quickly a branch-and-bound algorithm can find an optimal solution for a pure BIP problem. We will focus on just one of these techniques.

To illustrate this technique, consider the California Manufacturing Co. pure BIP problem presented in Sec. 12.1 and used to illustrate the BIP branch-and-bound algorithm in

Sec. 12.6. The optimal solution for its LP relaxation is given in Fig. 12.5 as $(x_1, x_2, x_3, x_4) = (\frac{5}{6}, 1, 0, 1)$. One of the functional constraints is

$$6x_1 + 3x_2 + 5x_3 + 2x_4 \leq 10.$$

Now note that the binary constraints and this constraint together imply that

$$x_1 + x_2 + x_4 \leq 2.$$

This new constraint is a *cutting plane.* It eliminates part of the feasible region for the LP relaxation, including what had been the optimal solution, $(\frac{5}{6}, 1, 0, 1)$, but it does not eliminate any feasible *integer* solutions. Adding just this one cutting plane to the original model would improve the performance of the BIP branch-and-bound algorithm in Sec. 12.6 (see Fig. 12.9) in two ways. First, the optimal solution for the new (tighter) LP relaxation would be $(1, 1, \frac{1}{5}, 0)$, with $Z = 15\frac{1}{5}$, so the bounds for the *All* node, $x_1 = 1$ node, and $(x_1, x_2) = (1, 1)$ node now would be 15 instead of 16. Second, one less iteration would be needed because the optimal solution for the LP relaxation at the $(x_1, x_2, x_3) = (1, 1, 0)$ node now would be $(1, 1, 0, 0)$, which provides a new *incumbent* with $Z^* = 14$. Therefore, on the *third* iteration (see Fig. 12.8), this node would be fathomed by test 3, and the $(x_1, x_2) = (1, 0)$ node would be fathomed by test 1, thereby revealing that this incumbent is the optimal solution for the original BIP problem.

Here is the general procedure used to generate this cutting plane.

A Procedure for Generating Cutting Planes

1. Consider any functional constraint in $\leq$ form with only nonnegative coefficients.
2. Find a group of variables (called a **minimum cover** of the constraint) such that
   (*a*) The constraint is violated if every variable in the group equals 1 and all other variables equal 0.
   (*b*) But the constraint becomes satisfied if the value of *any one* of these variables is changed from 1 to 0.
3. By letting N denote the number of variables in the group, the resulting cutting plane has the form

Sum of variables in group $\leq N - 1$.

Applying this procedure to the constraint $6x_1 + 3x_2 + 5x_3 + 2x_4 \leq 10$, we see that the group of variables $\{x_1, x_2, x_4\}$ is a *minimal cover* because

   (*a*) $(1, 1, 0, 1)$ violates the constraint.
   (*b*) But the constraint becomes satisfied if the value of *any one* of these three variables is changed from 1 to 0.

Since $N = 3$ in this case, the resulting cutting plane is $x_1 + x_2 + x_4 \leq 2$.

This same constraint also has a second minimal cover $\{x_1, x_3\}$, since $(1, 0, 1, 0)$ violates the constraint but both $(0, 0, 1, 0)$ and $(1, 0, 0, 0)$ satisfy the constraint. Therefore, $x_1 + x_3 \leq 1$ is another valid cutting plane.

The new algorithmic approach presented in Selected References 3, 6, 10, 5, and 2 involves generating *many* cutting planes in a similar manner before then applying clever branch-and-bound techniques. The results of including the cutting planes can be quite dramatic in tightening the LP relaxations. For example, for the test problem with 2,756 binary variables considered in Selected Reference 3,326 cutting planes were generated. The result was that the *gap* between Z for the optimal solution for the LP relaxation of the whole BIP problem and Z for this problem's optimal solution was reduced by 98 percent. Similar results were obtained on about half of the problems considered in Selected Reference 3.

Ironically, the very first algorithms developed for integer programming, including Ralph Gomory's celebrated algorithm announced in 1958, were based on cutting planes (generated in a different way), but this approach proved to be unsatisfactory in practice (except for special classes of problems). However, these algorithms relied solely on cutting planes. We now know that judiciously *combining* cutting planes and branch-and-bound techniques (along with automatic problem preprocessing) provides a powerful algorithmic approach for solving large-scale BIP problems. This is one reason that the name *branch-and-cut algorithm* has been given to this new approach.

12.9 CONCLUSIONS

IP problems arise frequently because some or all of the decision variables must be restricted to integer values. There also are many applications involving yes-or-no decisions (including combinatorial relationships expressible in terms of such decisions) that can be represented by binary (0–1) variables. These factors have made integer programming one of the most widely used OR techniques.

IP problems are more difficult than they would be without the integer restriction, so the algorithms available for integer programming are generally much less efficient than the simplex method. The most important determinants of computation time are the *number of integer variables* and whether the problem has some *special structure* that can be exploited. For a fixed number of integer variables, BIP problems generally are much easier to solve than problems with general integer variables, but adding continuous variables (MIP) may not increase computation time substantially. For special types of BIP problems containing a special structure that can be exploited by a *special-purpose algorithm,* it may be possible to solve very large problems (thousands of binary variables) routinely. Other much smaller problems without such special structure may not be solvable.

Computer codes for IP algorithms now are commonly available in mathematical programming software packages. Traditionally, these algorithms usually have been based on the *branch-and-bound* technique and variations thereof.

A new era in IP solution methodology has now been ushered in by a series of landmark papers since the mid-1980s. The new *branch-and-cut* algorithmic approach involves combining automatic problem preprocessing, the generation of cutting planes, and clever branch-and-bound techniques. Research in this area is continuing, along with the development of sophisticated new software packages that incorporate these new techniques.

In recent years, there has been considerable investigation into the development of algorithms (including heuristic algorithms) for integer *nonlinear* programming, and this area continues to be a very active area of research.

SELECTED REFERENCES

1. Beasley, J. E. (ed).: *Advances in Linear and Integer Programming,* Oxford University Press, Oxford, England, 1996.
2. Bixby, R. E., M. Fenelon, Z. Gu, E. Rothberg, and R. Wunderling, "MIP: Theory and Practice Closing the Gap," *Proceedings of IFIP TC7 Conference, Cambridge 1999.*
3. Crowder, H., E. L. Johnson, and M. Padberg: "Solving Large-Scale Zero-One Linear Programming Problems," *Operations Research,* **31:** 803–834, 1983.
4. Hillier, F. S., M. S. Hillier, and G. J. Lieberman: *Introduction to Management Science: A Modeling and Case Studies Approach with Spreadsheets,* Irwin/McGraw-Hill, Burr Ridge, IL, 2000, chaps. 9, 10.
5. Hoffman, K. L., and M. Padberg: "Improving LP-Representations of Zero-One Linear Programs for Branch-and-Cut," *ORSA Journal on Computing,* **3:** 121–134, 1991.
6. Johnson, E. L., M. M. Kostreva, and U. H. Suhl: "Solving 0-1 Integer Programming Problems Arising from Large Scale Planning Models," *Operations Research,* **33:** 803–819, 1985.
7. Nemhauser, G. L., and L. A. Wolsey: *Integer and Combinatorial Optimization,* Wiley, New York, 1988.
8. Rayward-Smith, V. J., I. H. Osman, C. R. Reeves, and G. D. Smith (eds.): *Modern Heuristic Search Methods,* Wiley, New York, 1997.
9. Schriver, A.: *Theory of Linear and Integer Programming,* Wiley, New York, 1986.
10. Van Roy, T. J., and L. A. Wolsey: "Solving Mixed 0-1 Programs by Automatic Reformulation," *Operations Research,* **35:** 45–57, 1987.
11. Williams, H. P.: *Model Building in Mathematical Programming,* 3d ed., Wiley, New York, 1990.

LEARNING AIDS FOR THIS CHAPTER IN YOUR OR COURSEWARE

Demonstration Examples in OR Tutor:

Binary Integer Programming Branch-and-Bound Algorithm
Mixed Integer Programming Branch-and-Bound Algorithm

Interactive Routines:

Enter or Revise an Integer Programming Model
Solve Binary Integer Program Interactively
Solve Mixed Integer Program Interactively

An Excel Add-in:

Premium Solver

"Ch. 12—Integer Programming" Files for Solving the Examples:

Excel File
LINGO/LINDO File
MPL/CPLEX File

See Appendix 1 for documentation of the software.

PROBLEMS

The symbols to the left of some of the problems (or their parts) have the following meaning:

D: The corresponding demonstration example listed above may be helpful.

I: We suggest that you use the corresponding interactive routine listed above (the printout records your work).

C: Use the computer with any of the software options available to you (or as instructed by your instructor) to solve the problem.

An asterisk on the problem number indicates that at least a partial answer is given in the back of the book.

12.1-1. Reconsider the California Manufacturing Co. example presented in Sec. 12.1. The mayor of San Diego now has contacted the company's president to try to persuade him to build a factory and perhaps a warehouse in that city. With the tax incentives being offered the company, the president's staff estimates that the net present value of building a factory in San Diego would be $7 million and the amount of capital required to do this would be $4 million. The net present value of building a warehouse there would be $5 million and the capital required would be $3 million. (This option would be considered only if a factory also is being built there.)

The company president now wants the previous OR study revised to incorporate these new alternatives into the overall problem. The objective still is to find the feasible combination of investments that maximizes the total net present value, given that the amount of capital available for these investments is $10 million.

(a) Formulate a BIP model for this problem.
(b) Display this model on an Excel spreadsheet.
C (c) Use the computer to solve this model.

12.1-2* A young couple, Eve and Steven, want to divide their main household chores (marketing, cooking, dishwashing, and laundering) between them so that each has two tasks but the total time they spend on household duties is kept to a minimum. Their efficiencies on these tasks differ, where the time each would need to perform the task is given by the following table:

	Time Needed per Week			
	Marketing	**Cooking**	**Dishwashing**	**Laundry**
Eve	4.5 hours	7.8 hours	3.6 hours	2.9 hours
Steven	4.9 hours	7.2 hours	4.3 hours	3.1 hours

(a) Formulate a BIP model for this problem.
(b) Display this model on an Excel spreadsheet.
C (c) Use the computer to solve this model.

12.1-3. A real estate development firm, Peterson and Johnson, is considering five possible development projects. The following table shows the estimated long-run profit (net present value) that each project would generate, as well as the amount of investment required to undertake the project, in units of millions of dollars.

	Development Project				
	1	**2**	**3**	**4**	**5**
Estimated profit	1	1.8	1.6	0.8	1.4
Capital required	6	12	10	4	8

The owners of the firm, Dave Peterson and Ron Johnson, have raised $20 million of investment capital for these projects. Dave and Ron now want to select the combination of projects that will maximize their total estimated long-run profit (net present value) without investing more that $20 million.

(a) Formulate a BIP model for this problem.
(b) Display this model on an Excel spreadsheet.
C (c) Use the computer to solve this model.

12.1-4. The board of directors of General Wheels Co. is considering seven large capital investments. Each investment can be made only once. These investments differ in the estimated long-run profit (net present value) that they will generate as well as in the amount of capital required, as shown by the following table (in units of millions of dollars):

	Investment Opportunity						
	1	**2**	**3**	**4**	**5**	**6**	**7**
Estimated profit	17	10	15	19	7	13	9
Capital required	43	28	34	48	17	32	23

The total amount of capital available for these investments is $100 million. Investment opportunities 1 and 2 are mutually exclusive, and so are 3 and 4. Furthermore, neither 3 nor 4 can be undertaken unless one of the first two opportunities is undertaken. There are no such restrictions on investment opportunities 5, 6, and 7. The objective is to select the combination of capital investments that will maximize the total estimated long-run profit (net present value).

(a) Formulate a BIP model for this problem.
C (b) Use the computer to solve this model.

12.1-5. Reconsider Prob. 8.3-4, where a swim team coach needs to assign swimmers to the different legs of a 200-yard medley relay team. Formulate a BIP model for this problem. Identify the groups of mutually exclusive alternatives in this formulation.

12.1-6. Vincent Cardoza is the owner and manager of a machine shop that does custom order work. This Wednesday afternoon, he has received calls from two customers who would like to place rush orders. One is a trailer hitch company which would like some custom-made heavy-duty tow bars. The other is a mini-car-carrier company which needs some customized stabilizer bars. Both customers would like as many as possible by the end of the week (two working days). Since both products would require the use of the same two machines, Vincent needs to decide and inform the customers this afternoon about how many of each product he will agree to make over the next two days.

Each tow bar requires 3.2 hours on machine 1 and 2 hours on machine 2. Each stabilizer bar requires 2.4 hours on machine 1 and 3 hours on machine 2. Machine 1 will be available for 16 hours over the next two days and machine 2 will be available for 15 hours. The profit for each tow bar produced would be $130 and the profit for each stabilizer bar produced would be $150.

Vincent now wants to determine the mix of these production quantities that will maximize the total profit.
(a) Formulate an IP model for this problem.
(b) Use a graphical approach to solve this model.
C **(c)** Use the computer to solve the model.

12.1-7. Pawtucket University is planning to buy new copier machines for its library. Three members of its Operations Research Department are analyzing what to buy. They are considering two different models: Model A, a high-speed copier, and Model B, a lower-speed but less expensive copier. Model A can handle 20,000 copies a day, and costs $6,000. Model B can handle 10,000 copies a day, but costs only $4,000. They would like to have at least six copiers so that they can spread them throughout the library. They also would like to have at least one high-speed copier. Finally, the copiers need to be able to handle a capacity of at least 75,000 copies per day. The objective is to determine the mix of these two copiers which will handle all these requirements at minimum cost.
(a) Formulate an IP model for this problem.
(b) Use a graphical approach to solve this model.
C **(c)** Use the computer to solve the model.

12.1-8. Reconsider Prob. 8.2-23 involving a contractor (Susan Meyer) who needs to arrange for hauling gravel from two pits to three building sites.

Susan now needs to hire the trucks (and their drivers) to do the hauling. Each truck can only be used to haul gravel from a single pit to a single site. In addition to the hauling and gravel costs specified in Prob. 8.2-23, there now is a fixed cost of $50 associ-

ated with hiring each truck. A truck can haul 5 tons, but it is not required to go full. For each combination of pit and site, there are now two decisions to be made: the number of trucks to be used and the amount of gravel to be hauled.
(a) Formulate an MIP model for this problem.
C **(b)** Use the computer to solve this model.

12.2-1. Select one of the actual applications of BIP by a company or governmental agency mentioned in Sec. 12.2. Read the article describing the application in the referenced issue of *Interfaces*. Write a two-page summary of the application and its benefits.

12.2-2. Select three of the actual applications of BIP by a company or governmental agency mentioned in Sec. 12.2. Read the articles describing the applications in the referenced issues of *Interfaces*. For each one, write a one-page summary of the application and its benefits.

12.3-1.* The Research and Development Division of the Progressive Company has been developing four possible new product lines. Management must now make a decision as to which of these four products actually will be produced and at what levels. Therefore, an operations research study has been requested to find the most profitable product mix.

A substantial cost is associated with beginning the production of any product, as given in the first row of the following table. Management's objective is to find the product mix that maximizes the total profit (total net revenue minus start-up costs).

	Product			
	1	**2**	**3**	**4**
Start-up cost	$50,000	$40,000	$70,000	$60,000
Marginal revenue	$ 70	$ 60	$ 90	$ 80

Let the continuous decision variables x_1, x_2, x_3, and x_4 be the production levels of products 1, 2, 3, and 4, respectively. Management has imposed the following policy constraints on these variables:

1. No more than two of the products can be produced.
2. Either product 3 or 4 can be produced only if either product 1 or 2 is produced.
3. Either $5x_1 + 3x_2 + 6x_3 + 4x_4 \leq 6,000$
   or $4x_1 + 6x_2 + 3x_3 + 5x_4 \leq 6,000$.

(a) Introduce auxiliary binary variables to formulate a mixed BIP model for this problem.
C **(b)** Use the computer to solve this model.

12.3-2. Suppose that a mathematical model fits linear programming except for the restriction that $|x_1 - x_2| = 0$, or 3, or 6. Show how to reformulate this restriction to fit an MIP model.

12.3-3. Suppose that a mathematical model fits linear programming except for the restrictions that

1. At least one of the following two inequalities holds:

$$x_1 + x_2 + x_3 + x_4 \leq 4$$
$$3x_1 - x_2 - x_3 + x_4 \leq 3.$$

2. At least two of the following four inequalities holds:

$$5x_1 + 3x_2 + 3x_3 - x_4 \leq 10$$
$$2x_1 + 5x_2 - x_3 + 3x_4 \leq 10$$
$$-x_1 + 3x_2 + 5x_3 + 3x_4 \leq 10$$
$$3x_1 - x_2 + 3x_3 + 5x_4 \leq 10.$$

Show how to reformulate these restrictions to fit an MIP model.

12.3-4. The Toys-R-4-U Company has developed two new toys for possible inclusion in its product line for the upcoming Christmas season. Setting up the production facilities to begin production would cost $50,000 for toy 1 and $80,000 for toy 2. Once these costs are covered, the toys would generate a unit profit of $10 for toy 1 and $15 for toy 2.

The company has two factories that are capable of producing these toys. However, to avoid doubling the start-up costs, just one factory would be used, where the choice would be based on maximizing profit. For administrative reasons, the same factory would be used for both new toys if both are produced.

Toy 1 can be produced at the rate of 50 per hour in factory 1 and 40 per hour in factory 2. Toy 2 can be produced at the rate of 40 per hour in factory 1 and 25 per hour in factory 2. Factories 1 and 2, respectively, have 500 hours and 700 hours of production time available before Christmas that could be used to produce these toys.

It is not known whether these two toys would be continued after Christmas. Therefore, the problem is to determine how many units (if any) of each new toy should be produced before Christmas to maximize the total profit.

(a) Formulate an MIP model for this problem.

c **(b)** Use the computer to solve this model.

12.3-5.* Northeastern Airlines is considering the purchase of new long-, medium-, and short-range jet passenger airplanes. The purchase price would be $67 million for each long-range plane, $50 million for each medium-range plane, and $35 million for each short-range plane. The board of directors has authorized a maximum commitment of $1.5 billion for these purchases. Regardless of which airplanes are purchased, air travel of all distances is expected to be sufficiently large that these planes would be utilized at essentially maximum capacity. It is estimated that the net annual profit (after capital recovery costs are subtracted) would be $4.2 million per long-range plane, $3 million per medium-range plane, and $2.3 million per short-range plane.

It is predicted that enough trained pilots will be available to the company to crew 30 new airplanes. If only short-range planes were purchased, the maintenance facilities would be able to handle 40 new planes. However, each medium-range plane is equivalent to $1\frac{1}{3}$ short-range planes, and each long-range plane is equivalent to $1\frac{2}{3}$ short-range planes in terms of their use of the maintenance facilities.

The information given here was obtained by a preliminary analysis of the problem. A more detailed analysis will be conducted subsequently. However, using the preceding data as a first approximation, management wishes to know how many planes of each type should be purchased to maximize profit.

(a) Formulate an IP model for this problem.

c **(b)** Use the computer to solve this problem.

(c) Use a binary representation of the variables to reformulate the IP model in part (a) as a BIP problem.

c **(d)** Use the computer to solve the BIP model formulated in part (c). Then use this optimal solution to identify an optimal solution for the IP model formulated in part (a).

12.3-6. Consider the two-variable IP example discussed in Sec. 12.5 and illustrated in Fig. 12.3.

(a) Use a binary representation of the variables to reformulate this model as a BIP problem.

c **(b)** Use the computer to solve this BIP problem. Then use this optimal solution to identify an optimal solution for the original IP model.

12.3-7. The Fly-Right Airplane Company builds small jet airplanes to sell to corporations for the use of their executives. To meet the needs of these executives, the company's customers sometimes order a custom design of the airplanes being purchased. When this occurs, a substantial start-up cost is incurred to initiate the production of these airplanes.

Fly-Right has recently received purchase requests from three customers with short deadlines. However, because the company's production facilities already are almost completely tied up filling previous orders, it will not be able to accept all three orders. Therefore, a decision now needs to be made on the number of airplanes the company will agree to produce (if any) for each of the three customers.

The relevant data are given in the next table. The first row gives the start-up cost required to initiate the production of the airplanes for each customer. Once production is under way, the marginal net revenue (which is the purchase price minus the marginal production cost) from each airplane produced is shown in the second row. The third row gives the percentage of the available production capacity that would be used for each airplane produced. The last row indicates the maximum number of airplanes requested by each customer (but less will be accepted).

	Customer		
	1	**2**	**3**
Start-up cost	$3 million	$2 million	0
Marginal net revenue	$2 million	$3 million	$0.8 million
Capacity used per plane	20%	40%	20%
Maximum order	3 planes	2 planes	5 planes

Fly-Right now wants to determine how many airplanes to produce for each customer (if any) to maximize the company's total profit (total net revenue minus start-up costs).
(a) Formulate a model with both integer variables and binary variables for this problem.
C (b) Use the computer to solve this model.

12.4-1. Reconsider the Fly-Right Airplane Co. problem introduced in Prob. 12.3-7. A more detailed analysis of the various cost and revenue factors now has revealed that the potential profit from producing airplanes for each customer cannot be expressed simply in terms of a *start-up cost* and a fixed *marginal net revenue* per airplane produced. Instead, the profits are given by the following table.

Airplanes Produced	Profit from Customer		
	1	**2**	**3**
0	0	0	0
1	−$1 million	$1 million	$1 million
2	$2 million	$5 million	$3 million
3	$4 million		$5 million
4			$6 million
5			$7 million

(a) Formulate a BIP model for this problem that includes constraints for *mutually exclusive alternatives.*
C (b) Use the computer to solve the model formulated in part (a). Then use this optimal solution to identify the optimal number of airplanes to produce for each customer.
(c) Formulate another BIP model for this model that includes constraints for *contingent decisions.*
C (d) Repeat part (b) for the model formulated in part (c).

12.4-2. Reconsider the Wyndor Glass Co. problem presented in Sec. 3.1. Management now has decided that only one of the two

new products should be produced, and the choice is to be made on the basis of maximizing profit. Introduce *auxiliary binary variables* to formulate an MIP model for this new version of the problem.

12.4-3.* Reconsider Prob. 3.1-11, where the management of the Omega Manufacturing Company is considering devoting excess production capacity to one or more of three products. (See the Partial Answers to Selected Problems in the back of the book for additional information about this problem.) Management now has decided to add the restriction that no more than two of the three prospective products should be produced.
(a) Introduce *auxiliary binary variables* to formulate an MIP model for this new version of the problem.
C (b) Use the computer to solve this model.

12.4-4. Consider the following integer nonlinear programming problem.

$$\text{Maximize} \quad Z = 4x_1^2 - x_1^3 + 10x_2^2 - x_2^4,$$

subject to

$$x_1 + x_2 \le 3$$

and

$$x_1 \ge 0, \quad x_2 \ge 0$$
$$x_1 \text{ and } x_2 \text{ are integers.}$$

This problem can be reformulated in two different ways as an equivalent pure BIP problem (with a linear objective function) with six binary variables (y_{1j} and y_{2j} for $j = 1, 2, 3$), depending on the interpretation given the binary variables.
(a) Formulate a BIP model for this problem where the binary variables have the interpretation,

$$y_{ij} = \begin{cases} 1 & \text{if } x_i = j \\ 0 & \text{otherwise.} \end{cases}$$

C (b) Use the computer to solve the model formulated in part (a), and thereby identify an optimal solution for (x_1, x_2) for the original problem.
(c) Formulate a BIP model for this problem where the binary variables have the interpretation,

$$y_{ij} = \begin{cases} 1 & \text{if } x_i \ge j \\ 0 & \text{otherwise.} \end{cases}$$

C (d) Use the computer to solve the model formulated in part (c), and thereby identify an optimal solution for (x_1, x_2) for the original problem.

12.4-5. Consider the following discrete nonlinear programming problem.

$$\text{Maximize} \quad Z = 2x_1 - x_1^2 + 3x_2 - 3x_2^2,$$

subject to

$$x_1 + x_2 \leq 0.75$$

and

each variable is restricted to the values: $\frac{1}{2}, \frac{1}{3}, \frac{1}{4}, \frac{1}{5}$.

(Continue in the next column.)

(a) Reformulate this problem as a pure binary integer linear programming problem.

c (b) Use the computer to solve the model formulated in part (a), and thereby identify an optimal solution for (x_1, x_2) for the original problem.

12.4-6.* Consider the following special type of *shortest-path problem* (see Sec. 9.3) where the nodes are in columns and the only paths considered always move forward one column at a time.

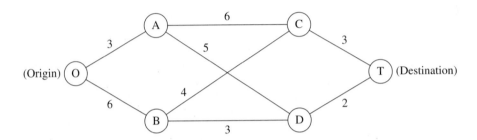

The numbers along the links represent distances, and the objective is to find the shortest path from the origin to the destination.

This problem also can be formulated as a BIP model involving both mutually exclusive alternatives and contingent decisions.

(a) Formulate this model. Identify the constraints that are for mutually exclusive alternatives and that are for contingent decisions.

c (b) Use the computer to solve this problem.

12.4-7. Consider the project network for a PERT-type system shown in Prob. 11.2-3. Formulate a BIP model for the problem of finding a *critical path* (i.e., a *longest path*) for this project network.

12.4-8. Speedy Delivery provides two-day delivery service of large parcels across the United States. Each morning at each collection center, the parcels that have arrived overnight are loaded onto several trucks for delivery throughout the area. Since the competitive battlefield in this business is speed of delivery, the parcels are divided among the trucks according to their geographical destinations to minimize the average time needed to make the deliveries.

On this particular morning, the dispatcher for the Blue River Valley Collection Center, Sharon Lofton, is hard at work. Her three drivers will be arriving in less than an hour to make the day's deliveries. There are nine parcels to be delivered, all at locations many miles apart. As usual, Sharon has loaded these locations into her computer. She is using her company's special software package, a decision support system called Dispatcher. The first thing Dispatcher does is use these locations to generate a considerable number of attractive possible routes for the individual delivery trucks. These routes are shown in the following table (where the numbers

in each column indicate the order of the deliveries), along with the estimated time required to traverse the route.

Delivery Location	Attractive Possible Route									
	1	**2**	**3**	**4**	**5**	**6**	**7**	**8**	**9**	**10**
A	1				1				1	
B		2		1		2			2	2
C			3	3			3		3	
D	2					1		1		
E			2	2		3				
F		1			2					
G	3						1	2		3
H			1		3					1
I		3		4			2			
Time (in hours)	6	4	7	5	4	6	5	3	7	6

Dispatcher is an interactive system that shows these routes to Sharon for her approval or modification. (For example, the computer may not know that flooding has made a particular route infeasible.) After Sharon approves these routes as attractive possibilities with reasonable time estimates, Dispatcher next formulates and solves a BIP model for selecting three routes that minimize their total time while including each delivery location on exactly one route. This morning, Sharon does approve all the routes.

(a) Formulate this BIP model.

c (b) Use the computer to solve this model.

12.4-9. An increasing number of Americans are moving to a warmer climate when they retire. To take advantage of this trend, Sunny Skies Unlimited is undertaking a major real estate development project. The project is to develop a completely new retirement community (to be called Pilgrim Haven) that will cover several square miles. One of the decisions to be made is where to locate the two fire stations that have been allocated to the community. For planning purposes, Pilgrim Haven has been divided into five tracts, with no more than one fire station to be located in any given tract. Each station is to respond to *all* the fires that occur in the tract in which it is located as well as in the other tracts that are assigned to this station. Thus, the decisions to be made consist of (1) the tracts to receive a fire station and (2) the assignment of each of the other tracts to one of the fire stations. The objective is to minimize the overall average of the *response times* to fires.

The following table gives the average response time to a fire in each tract (the columns) if that tract is served by a station in a given tract (the rows). The bottom row gives the forecasted average number of fires that will occur in each of the tracts per day.

Assigned Station Located in Tract	Response Times (in minutes) Fire in Tract				
	1	**2**	**3**	**4**	**5**
1	5	12	30	20	15
2	20	4	15	10	25
3	15	20	6	15	12
4	25	15	25	4	10
5	10	25	15	12	5
Average frequency of fires	2 per day	1 per day	3 per day	1 per day	3 per day

Formulate a BIP model for this problem. Identify any constraints that correspond to mutually exclusive alternatives or contingent decisions.

12.4-10. Reconsider Prob. 12.4-9. The management of Sunny Skies Unlimited now has decided that the decision on the locations of the fire stations should be based mainly on costs.

The cost of locating a fire station in a tract is $200,000 for tract 1, $250,000 for tract 2, $400,000 for tract 3, $300,000 for tract 4, and $500,000 for tract 5. Management's objective now is the following:

Determine which tracts should receive a station to minimize the total cost of stations while ensuring that each tract has at least one station close enough to respond to a fire in no more than 15 minutes (on the average).

In contrast to the original problem, note that the total number of fire stations is no longer fixed. Furthermore, if a tract without a station has more than one station within 15 minutes, it is no longer necessary to assign this tract to just one of these stations.

(a) Formulate a complete pure BIP model with 5 binary variables for this problem.
(b) Is this a *set covering problem?* Explain, and identify the relevant sets.
C **(c)** Use the computer to solve the model formulated in part (*a*).

12.4-11. Suppose that a state sends R persons to the U.S. House of Representatives. There are D counties in the state ($D > R$), and the state legislature wants to group these counties into R distinct electoral districts, each of which sends a delegate to Congress. The total population of the state is P, and the legislature wants to form districts whose population approximates $p = P/R$. Suppose that the appropriate legislative committee studying the electoral districting problem generates a long list of N *candidates* to be districts ($N > R$). Each of these candidates contains contiguous counties and a total population p_j ($j = 1, 2, \ldots, N$) that is acceptably close to p. Define $c_j = |p_j - p|$. Each county i ($i = 1, 2, \ldots, D$) is included in at least one candidate and typically will be included in a considerable number of candidates (in order to provide many feasible ways of selecting a set of R candidates that includes each county exactly once). Define

$$a_{ij} = \begin{cases} 1 & \text{if county } i \text{ is included in candidate } j \\ 0 & \text{if not.} \end{cases}$$

Given the values of the c_j and the a_{ij}, the objective is to select R of these N possible districts such that each county is contained in a single district and such that the largest of the associated c_j is as small as possible.

Formulate a BIP model for this problem.

12.4-12. A U.S. professor will be spending a short sabbatical leave at the University of Iceland. She wishes to bring all needed items with her on the airplane. After collecting the professional items that she must have, she finds that airline regulations on space and weight for checked luggage will severely limit the clothes she can take. (She plans to carry on a warm coat and then purchase a warm Icelandic sweater upon arriving in Iceland.) Clothes under consideration for checked luggage include 3 skirts, 3 slacks, 4 tops, and 3 dresses. The professor wants to maximize the number of outfits she will have in Iceland (including the special dress she will wear on the airplane). Each dress constitutes an outfit. Other outfits consist of a combination of a top and either a skirt or slacks. However, certain combinations are not fashionable and so will not qualify as an outfit.

In the following table, the combinations that will make an outfit are marked with an x.

		Top				
		1	**2**	**3**	**4**	**Icelandic Sweater**
	1	X	X			X
Skirt	2	X			X	
	3			X	X	X	X
	1	X		X		
Slacks	2	X	X		X	X
	3			X	X	X

The weight (in grams) and volume (in cubic centimeters) of each item are shown in the following table:

		Weight	**Volume**
	1	600	5,000
Skirt	2	450	3,500
	3	700	3,000
	1	600	3,500
Slacks	2	550	6,000
	3	500	4,000
	1	350	4,000
	2	300	3,500
Top	3	300	3,000
	4	450	5,000
	1	600	6,000
Dress	2	700	5,000
	3	800	4,000
Total allowed		4,000	32,000

Formulate a BIP model to choose which items of clothing to take. (*Hint:* After using binary decision variables to represent the individual items, you should introduce *auxiliary* binary variables to represent outfits involving combinations of items. Then use constraints and the objective function to ensure that these auxiliary variables have the correct values, given the values of the decision variables.)

12.5-1.* Consider the following IP problem.

Maximize $Z = 5x_1 + x_2$,

subject to

$$-x_1 + 2x_2 \leq 4$$
$$x_1 - x_2 \leq 1$$
$$4x_1 + x_2 \leq 12$$

and

$$x_1 \geq 0, \qquad x_2 \geq 0$$
x_1, x_2 are integers.

(a) Solve this problem graphically.
(b) Solve the LP relaxation graphically. Round this solution to the *nearest* integer solution and check whether it is feasible. Then enumerate *all* the rounded solutions by rounding this solution for the LP relaxation in *all* possible ways (i.e., by rounding each noninteger value both up and down). For each rounded solution, check for feasibility and, if feasible, calculate Z. Are any of these feasible rounded solutions optimal for the IP problem?

12.5-2. Follow the instructions of Prob. 12.5-1 for the following IP problem.

Maximize $Z = 220x_1 + 80x_2$,

subject to

$$5x_1 + 2x_2 \leq 16$$
$$2x_1 - x_2 \leq 4$$
$$-x_1 + 2x_2 \leq 4$$

and

$$x_1 \geq 0, \qquad x_2 \geq 0$$
x_1, x_2 are integers.

12.5-3. Follow the instructions of Prob. 12.5-1 for the following BIP problem.

Maximize $Z = 2x_1 + 5x_2$,

subject to

$$10x_1 + 30x_2 \leq 30$$
$$95x_1 - 30x_2 \leq 75$$

and

x_1, x_2 are binary.

12.5-4. Follow the instructions of Prob. 12.5-1 for the following BIP problem.

Maximize $Z = -5x_1 + 25x_2$,

subject to

$$-3x_1 + 30x_2 \leq 27$$
$$3x_1 + x_2 \leq 4$$

and

x_1, x_2 are binary.

12.5-5. Label each of the following statements as True or False, and then justify your answer by referring to specific statements (with page citations) in the chapter.

(a) Linear programming problems are generally much easier to solve than IP problems.

(b) For IP problems, the number of integer variables is generally more important in determining the computational difficulty than is the number of functional constraints.

(c) To solve an IP problem with an approximate procedure, one may apply the simplex method to the LP relaxation problem and then round each noninteger value to the nearest integer. The result will be a feasible but not necessarily optimal solution for the IP problem.

D,I **12.6-1.*** Use the BIP branch-and-bound algorithm presented in Sec. 12.6 to solve the following problem interactively.

$$\text{Maximize} \quad Z = 2x_1 - x_2 + 5x_3 - 3x_4 + 4x_5,$$

subject to

$$3x_1 - 2x_2 + 7x_3 - 5x_4 + 4x_5 \le 6$$
$$x_1 - x_2 + 2x_3 - 4x_4 + 2x_5 \le 0$$

and

$$x_j \text{ is binary,} \quad \text{for } j = 1, 2, \ldots, 5.$$

D,I **12.6-2.** Use the BIP branch-and-bound algorithm presented in Sec. 12.6 to solve the following problem interactively.

$$\text{Minimize} \quad Z = 5x_1 + 6x_2 + 7x_3 + 8x_4 + 9x_5,$$

subject to

$$3x_1 - x_2 + x_3 + x_4 - 2x_5 \ge 2$$
$$x_1 + 3x_2 - x_3 - 2x_4 + x_5 \ge 0$$
$$-x_1 - x_2 + 3x_3 + x_4 + x_5 \ge 1$$

and

$$x_j \text{ is binary,} \quad \text{for } j = 1, 2, \ldots, 5.$$

D,I **12.6-3.** Use the BIP branch-and-bound algorithm presented in Sec. 12.6 to solve the following problem interactively.

$$\text{Maximize} \quad Z = 5x_1 + 5x_2 + 8x_3 - 2x_4 - 4x_5,$$

subject to

$$-3x_1 + 6x_2 - 7x_3 + 9x_4 + 9x_5 \ge 10$$
$$x_1 + 2x_2 \qquad - x_4 - 3x_5 \le 0$$

and

$$x_j \text{ is binary,} \quad \text{for } j = 1, 2, \ldots, 5.$$

D,I **12.6-4.** Reconsider Prob. 12.3-6(*a*). Use the BIP branch-and-bound algorithm presented in Sec. 12.6 to solve this BIP model interactively.

D,I **12.6-5.** Reconsider Prob. 12.4-10(*a*). Use the BIP algorithm presented in Sec. 12.6 to solve this problem interactively.

12.6-6. Consider the following statements about any pure IP problem (in maximization form) and its LP relaxation. Label each of the statements as True or False, and then justify your answer.

(a) The feasible region for the LP relaxation is a subset of the feasible region for the IP problem.

(b) If an optimal solution for the LP relaxation is an integer solution, then the optimal value of the objective function is the same for both problems.

(c) If a noninteger solution is feasible for the LP relaxation, then the nearest integer solution (rounding each variable to the nearest integer) is a feasible solution for the IP problem.

12.6-7.* Consider the assignment problem with the following cost table:

		Task				
		1	**2**	**3**	**4**	**5**
	1	39	65	69	66	57
	2	64	84	24	92	22
Assignee	3	49	50	61	31	45
	4	48	45	55	23	50
	5	59	34	30	34	18

(a) Design a branch-and-bound algorithm for solving such assignment problems by specifying how the branching, bounding, and fathoming steps would be performed. (*Hint:* For the assignees not yet assigned for the current subproblem, form the relaxation by deleting the constraints that each of these assignees must perform exactly one task.)

(b) Use this algorithm to solve this problem.

12.6-8. Five jobs need to be done on a certain machine. However, the setup time for each job depends upon which job immediately preceded it, as shown by the following table:

		Setup Time				
		Job				
		1	**2**	**3**	**4**	**5**
	None	4	5	8	9	4
	1	—	7	12	10	9
Immediately	2	6	—	10	14	11
Preceding Job	3	10	11	—	12	10
	4	7	8	15	—	7
	5	12	9	8	16	—

The objective is to schedule the *sequence* of jobs that minimizes the sum of the resulting setup times.

(a) Design a branch-and-bound algorithm for sequencing problems of this type by specifying how the branch, bound, and fathoming steps would be performed.

(b) Use this algorithm to solve this problem.

12.6-9.* Consider the following *nonlinear* BIP problem.

$$\text{Maximize} \quad Z = 80x_1 + 60x_2 + 40x_3 + 20x_4 \\ - (7x_1 + 5x_2 + 3x_3 + 2x_4)^2,$$

subject to

$$x_j \text{ is binary}, \quad \text{for } j = 1, 2, 3, 4.$$

Given the value of the first k variables $x_1, \ldots, x_k$, where $k = 0$, 1, 2, or 3, an upper bound on the value of Z that can be achieved by the corresponding feasible solutions is

$$\sum_{j=1}^{k} c_j x_j - \left(\sum_{j=1}^{k} d_j x_j \right)^2$$

$$+ \sum_{j=k+1}^{4} \max \left\{ 0, c_j - \left[\left(\sum_{i=1}^{k} d_i x_i + d_j \right)^2 - \left(\sum_{i=1}^{k} d_i x_i \right)^2 \right] \right\},$$

where $c_1 = 80$, $c_2 = 60$, $c_3 = 40$, $c_4 = 20$, $d_1 = 7$, $d_2 = 5$, $d_3 = 3$, $d_4 = 2$. Use this bound to solve the problem by the branch-and-bound technique.

12.6-10. Consider the Lagrangian relaxation described near the end of Sec. 12.6.

(a) If **x** is a feasible solution for an MIP problem, show that **x** also must be a feasible solution for the corresponding Lagrangian relaxation.

(b) If **x*** is an optimal solution for an MIP problem, with an objective function value of Z, show that $Z \le Z_R^*$, where Z_R^* is the optimal objective function value for the corresponding Lagrangian relaxation.

12.7-1.* Consider the following IP problem.

$$\text{Maximize} \quad Z = -3x_1 + 5x_2,$$

subject to

$$5x_1 - 7x_2 \ge 3$$

and

$$x_j \le 3$$
$$x_j \ge 0$$
$$x_j \text{ is integer}, \quad \text{for } j = 1, 2.$$

(a) Solve this problem graphically.

(b) Use the MIP branch-and-bound algorithm presented in Sec. 12.7 to solve this problem by hand. For each subproblem, solve its LP relaxation *graphically*.

(c) Use the binary representation for integer variables to reformulate this problem as a BIP problem.

D,I (d) Use the BIP branch-and-bound algorithm presented in Sec. 12.6 to solve the problem as formulated in part (c) interactively.

12.7-2. Follow the instructions of Prob. 12.7-1 for the following IP model.

$$\text{Minimize} \quad Z = 2x_1 + 3x_2,$$

subject to

$$x_1 + x_2 \ge 3$$
$$x_1 + 3x_2 \ge 6$$

and

$$x_1 \ge 0, \qquad x_2 \ge 0$$
$$x_1, x_2 \text{ are integers}.$$

12.7-3. Reconsider the IP model of Prob. 12.5-1.

(a) Use the MIP branch-and-bound algorithm presented in Sec. 12.7 to solve this problem by hand. For each subproblem, solve its LP relaxation *graphically*.

D,I (b) Now use the interactive routine for this algorithm in your OR Courseware to solve this problem.

C (c) Check your answer by using an automatic routine to solve the problem.

12.7-4. Follow the instructions of Prob. 12.7-3 for the IP model of Prob. 12.5-2.

D,I **12.7-5.** Consider the IP example discussed in Sec. 12.5 and illustrated in Fig. 12.3. Use the MIP branch-and-bound algorithm presented in Sec. 12.7 to solve this problem interactively.

D,I **12.7-6.** Reconsider Prob. 12.3-5a. Use the MIP branch-and-bound algorithm presented in Sec. 12.7 to solve this IP problem interactively.

12.7-7. A machine shop makes two products. Each unit of the first product requires 3 hours on machine 1 and 2 hours on machine 2. Each unit of the second product requires 2 hours on machine 1 and 3 hours on machine 2. Machine 1 is available only 8 hours per day and machine 2 only 7 hours per day. The profit per unit sold is 16 for the first product and 10 for the second. The amount of each product produced per day must be an integral multiple of 0.25. The objective is to determine the mix of production quantities that will maximize profit.

(a) Formulate an IP model for this problem.

(b) Solve this model graphically.

(c) Use graphical analysis to apply the MIP branch-and-bound algorithm presented in Sec. 12.7 to solve this model.

D,I (d) Now use the interactive routine for this algorithm in your OR Courseware to solve this model.

C (e) Check your answers in parts (b), (c), and (d) by using an automatic routine to solve the model.

D,I 12.7-8. Use the MIP branch-and-bound algorithm presented in Sec. 12.7 to solve the following MIP problem interactively.

Maximize $\quad Z = 5x_1 + 4x_2 + 4x_3 + 2x_4,$

subject to

$$
\begin{aligned}
x_1 + 3x_2 + 2x_3 + x_4 &\le 10 \\
5x_1 + x_2 + 3x_3 + 2x_4 &\le 15 \\
x_1 + x_2 + x_3 + x_4 &\le 6
\end{aligned}
$$

and

$$
\begin{aligned}
x_j &\ge 0, &&\text{for } j = 1, 2, 3, 4 \\
x_j &\text{ is integer}, &&\text{for } j = 1, 2, 3.
\end{aligned}
$$

D,I 12.7-9. Use the MIP branch-and-bound algorithm presented in Sec. 12.7 to solve the following MIP problem interactively.

Maximize $\quad Z = 3x_1 + 4x_2 + 2x_3 + x_4 + 2x_5,$

subject to

$$
\begin{aligned}
2x_1 - x_2 + x_3 + x_4 + x_5 &\le 3 \\
-x_1 + 3x_2 + x_3 - x_4 - 2x_5 &\le 2 \\
2x_1 + x_2 - x_3 + x_4 + 3x_5 &\le 1
\end{aligned}
$$

and

$$
\begin{aligned}
x_j &\ge 0, &&\text{for } j = 1, 2, 3, 4, 5 \\
x_j &\text{ is binary}, &&\text{for } j = 1, 2, 3.
\end{aligned}
$$

D,I 12.7-10. Use the MIP branch-and-bound algorithm presented in Sec. 12.7 to solve the following MIP problem interactively.

Minimize $\quad Z = 5x_1 + x_2 + x_3 + 2x_4 + 3x_5,$

subject to

$$
\begin{aligned}
x_2 - 5x_3 + x_4 + 2x_5 &\ge -2 \\
5x_1 - x_2 + x_5 &\ge 7 \\
x_1 + x_2 + 6x_3 + x_4 &\ge 4
\end{aligned}
$$

and

$$
\begin{aligned}
x_j &\ge 0, &&\text{for } j = 1, 2, 3, 4, 5 \\
x_j &\text{ is integer}, &&\text{for } j = 1, 2, 3.
\end{aligned}
$$

12.7-11. Reconsider the discrete nonlinear programming problem given in Prob. 12.4-5.

(a) Use the following outline in designing the main features of a branch-and-bound algorithm for solving this problem (and similar problems) directly without reformulation.

  (i) Specify the tightest possible nonlinear programming relaxation that has only continuous variables and so can be solved efficiently by nonlinear programming techniques. (The next chapter will describe how such nonlinear programming problems can be solved efficiently.)

  (ii) Specify the fathoming tests.

  (iii) Specify a branching procedure that involves specifying two ranges of values for a single variable.

(b) Use the algorithm designed in part (a) to solve this problem by using an available software package to solve the *quadratic programming* relaxation at each iteration. (As described in Sec. 13.7, Excel, LINDO, LINGO, and MPL/CPLEX all are able to solve quadratic programming problems.)

12.8-1.* For each of the following constraints of pure BIP problems, use the constraint to fix as many variables as possible.
(a) $4x_1 + x_2 + 3x_3 + 2x_4 \le 2$
(b) $4x_1 - x_2 + 3x_3 + 2x_4 \le 2$
(c) $4x_1 - x_2 + 3x_3 + 2x_4 \ge 7$

12.8-2. For each of the following constraints of pure BIP problems, use the constraint to fix as many variables as possible.
(a) $20x_1 - 7x_2 + 5x_3 \le 10$
(b) $10x_1 - 7x_2 + 5x_3 \ge 10$
(c) $10x_1 - 7x_2 + 5x_3 \le -1$

12.8-3. Use the following set of constraints for the *same* pure BIP problem to fix as many variables as possible. Also identify the constraints which become redundant because of the fixed variables.

$$
\begin{aligned}
3x_3 - x_5 + x_7 &\le 1 \\
x_2 + x_4 + x_6 &\le 1 \\
x_1 - 2x_5 + 2x_6 &\ge 2 \\
x_1 + x_2 - x_4 &\le 0
\end{aligned}
$$

12.8-4. For each of the following constraints of pure BIP problems, identify which ones are made redundant by the binary constraints. Explain why each one is, or is not, redundant.
(a) $2x_1 + x_2 + 2x_3 \le 5$
(b) $3x_1 - 4x_2 + 5x_3 \le 5$
(c) $x_1 + x_2 + x_3 \ge 2$
(d) $3x_1 - x_2 - 2x_3 \ge -4$

12.8-5. In Sec. 12.8, at the end of the subsection on tightening constraints, we indicated that the constraint $4x_1 - 3x_2 + x_3 + 2x_4 \le 5$ can be tightened to $2x_1 - 3x_2 + x_3 + 2x_4 \le 3$ and then to $2x_1 - 2x_2 + x_3 + 2x_4 \le 3$. Apply the procedure for tightening constraints to confirm these results.

12.8-6. Apply the procedure for *tightening constraints* to the following constraint for a pure BIP problem.

$$3x_1 - 2x_2 + x_3 \le 3.$$

12.8-7. Apply the procedure for *tightening constraints* to the following constraint for a pure BIP problem.

$$x_1 - x_2 + 3x_3 + 4x_4 \ge 1.$$

12.8-8. Apply the procedure for *tightening constraints* to each of the following constraints for a pure BIP problem.
(a) $x_1 + 3x_2 - 4x_3 \leq 2$.
(b) $3x_1 - x_2 + 4x_3 \geq 1$.

12.8-9. In Sec. 12.8, a pure BIP example with the constraint, $2x_1 + 3x_2 \leq 4$, was used to illustrate the procedure for tightening constraints. Show that applying the procedure for generating cutting planes to this constraint yields the same new constraint, $x_1 + x_2 \leq 1$.

12.8-10. One of the constraints of a certain pure BIP problem is

$$x_1 + 3x_2 + 2x_3 + 4x_4 \leq 5.$$

Identify all the minimal covers for this constraint, and then give the corresponding cutting planes.

12.8-11. One of the constraints of a certain pure BIP problem is

$$3x_1 + 4x_2 + 2x_3 + 5x_4 \leq 7.$$

Identify all the minimal covers for this constraint, and then give the corresponding cutting planes.

12.8-12. Generate as many cutting planes as possible from the following constraint for a pure BIP problem.

$$3x_1 + 5x_2 + 4x_3 + 8x_4 \leq 10.$$

12.8-13. Generate as many cutting planes as possible from the following constraint for a pure BIP problem.

$$5x_1 + 3x_2 + 7x_3 + 4x_4 + 6x_5 \leq 9.$$

12.8-14. Consider the following BIP problem.

Maximize $Z = 2x_1 + 3x_2 + x_3 + 4x_4 + 3x_5$
$\qquad\qquad\quad + 2x_6 + 2x_7 + x_8 + 3x_9,$

subject to

$$3x_2 + x_4 + x_5 \geq 3$$
$$x_1 + x_2 \leq 1$$
$$x_2 + x_4 - x_5 - x_6 \leq -1$$
$$x_2 + 2x_6 + 3x_7 + x_8 + 2x_9 \geq 4$$
$$-x_3 + 2x_5 + x_6 + 2x_7 - 2x_8 + x_9 \leq 5$$

and

all x_j binary.

Develop the tightest possible formulation of this problem by using the techniques of automatic problem reprocessing (fixing variables, deleting redundant constraints, and tightening constraints). Then use this tightened formulation to determine an optimal solution by inspection.

CASE 12.1   CAPACITY CONCERNS

Bentley Hamilton throws the business section of the *New York Times* onto the conference room table and watches as his associates jolt upright in their overstuffed chairs.

Mr. Hamilton wants to make a point.

He throws the front page of the *Wall Street Journal* on top of the *New York Times* and watches as his associates widen their eyes once heavy with boredom.

Mr. Hamilton wants to make a big point.

He then throws the front page of the *Financial Times* on top of the newspaper pile and watches as his associates dab the fine beads of sweat off their brows.

Mr. Hamilton wants his point indelibly etched into his associates' minds.

"I have just presented you with three leading financial newspapers carrying today's top business story," Mr. Hamilton declares in a tight, angry voice. "My dear associates, our company is going to hell in a hand basket! Shall I read you the headlines? From the *New York Times*, 'CommuniCorp stock drops to lowest in 52 weeks.' From the *Wall Street Journal*, 'CommuniCorp loses 25 percent of the pager market in only one year.' Oh and my favorite, from the *Financial Times*, 'CommuniCorp cannot CommuniCate: CommuniCorp stock drops because of internal communications disarray.' How did our company fall into such dire straits?"

Mr. Hamilton throws a transparency showing a line sloping slightly upward onto the overhead projector. "This is a graph of our productivity over the last 12 months. As you can see from the graph, productivity in our pager production facility has increased steadily over the last year. Clearly, productivity is not the cause of our problem."

Mr. Hamilton throws a second transparency showing a line sloping steeply upward onto the overhead projector. "This is a graph of our missed or late orders over the last 12 months." Mr. Hamilton hears an audible gasp from his associates. "As you can see from the graph, our missed or late orders have increased steadily and significantly over the past 12 months. I think this trend explains why we have been losing market share, causing our stock to drop to its lowest level in 52 weeks. We have angered and lost the business of retailers, our customers who depend upon on-time deliveries to meet the demand of consumers."

"Why have we missed our delivery dates when our productivity level should have allowed us to fill all orders?" Mr. Hamilton asks. "I called several departments to ask this question."

"It turns out that we have been producing pagers for the hell of it!" Mr. Hamilton says in disbelief. "The marketing and sales departments do not communicate with the manufacturing department, so manufacturing executives do not know what pagers to produce to fill orders. The manufacturing executives want to keep the plant running, so they produce pagers regardless of whether the pagers have been ordered. Finished pagers are sent to the warehouse, but marketing and sales executives do not know the number and styles of pagers in the warehouse. They try to communicate with warehouse executives to determine if the pagers in inventory can fill the orders, but they rarely receive answers to their questions."

Mr. Hamilton pauses and looks directly at his associates. "Ladies and gentlemen, it seems to me that we have a serious internal communications problem. I intend to correct this problem immediately. I want to begin by installing a companywide computer network to ensure that all departments have access to critical documents and are able to easily communicate with each other through e-mail. Because this intranet will represent a large change from the current communications infrastructure, I expect some bugs in the system and some resistance from employees. I therefore want to phase in the installation of the intranet."

Mr. Hamilton passes the following timeline and requirements chart to his associates (IN = Intranet).

Month 1	Month 2	Month 3	Month 4	Month 5
IN Education	Install IN in Sales	Install IN in Manufacturing	Install IN in Warehouse	Install IN in Marketing

Department	Number of Employees
Sales	60
Manufacturing	200
Warehouse	30
Marketing	75

Mr. Hamilton proceeds to explain the timeline and requirements chart. "In the first month, I do not want to bring any department onto the intranet; I simply want to disseminate information about it and get buy-in from employees. In the second month, I want to bring the sales department onto the intranet since the sales department receives all critical information from customers. In the third month, I want to bring the manufacturing department onto the intranet. In the fourth month, I want to install the intranet at the warehouse, and in the fifth and final month, I want to bring the marketing department onto the intranet. The requirements chart under the timeline lists the number of employees requiring access to the intranet in each department."

Mr. Hamilton turns to Emily Jones, the head of Corporate Information Management. "I need your help in planning for the installation of the intranet. Specifically, the company needs to purchase servers for the internal network. Employees will connect to company servers and download information to their own desktop computers."

Mr. Hamilton passes Emily the following chart detailing the types of servers available, the number of employees each server supports, and the cost of each server.

Type of Server	Number of Employees Server Supports	Cost of Server
Standard Intel Pentium PC	Up to 30 employees	$ 2,500
Enhanced Intel Pentium PC	Up to 80 employees	$ 5,000
SGI Workstation	Up to 200 employees	$10,000
Sun Workstation	Up to 2,000 employees	$25,000

"Emily, I need you to decide what servers to purchase and when to purchase them to minimize cost and to ensure that the company possesses enough server capacity to follow the intranet implementation timeline," Mr. Hamilton says. "For example, you may decide to buy one large server during the first month to support all employees, or buy several small servers during the first month to support all employees, or buy one small server each month to support each new group of employees gaining access to the intranet."

"There are several factors that complicate your decision," Mr. Hamilton continues. "Two server manufacturers are willing to offer discounts to CommuniCorp. SGI is willing to give you a discount of 10 percent off each server purchased, but only if you purchase servers in the first or second month. Sun is willing to give you a 25 percent discount off all servers purchased in the first two months. You are also limited in the amount of money you can spend during the first month. CommuniCorp has already allocated much of the budget for the next two months, so you only have a total of $9,500 available to purchase servers in months 1 and 2. Finally, the Manufacturing Department requires at least one of the three more powerful servers. Have your decision on my desk at the end of the week."

(a) Emily first decides to evaluate the number and type of servers to purchase on a month-to-month basis. For each month, formulate an IP model to determine which servers Emily should purchase in that month to minimize costs in that month and support the new users. How many and which types of servers should she purchase in each month? How much is the total cost of the plan?

(b) Emily realizes that she could perhaps achieve savings if she bought a larger server in the initial months to support users in the final months. She therefore decides to evaluate the number and type of servers to purchase over the entire planning period. Formulate an IP model to determine which servers Emily should purchase in which months to minimize total cost and support all new users. How many and which types of servers should she purchase in each month? How much is the total cost of the plan?

(c) Why is the answer using the first method different from that using the second method?

(d) Are there other costs that Emily is not accounting for in her problem formulation? If so, what are they?

(e) What further concerns might the various departments of CommuniCorp have regarding the intranet?

CASE 12.2   ASSIGNING ART

It had been a dream come true for Ash Briggs, a struggling artist living in the San Francisco Bay Area. He had made a trip to the corner grocery store late one Friday afternoon to buy some milk, and on impulse, he had also purchased a California lottery ticket. One week later, he was a millionaire.

Ash did not want to squander his winnings on materialistic, trivial items. Instead he wanted to use his money to support his true passion: art. Ash knew all too well the difficulties of gaining recognition as an artist in this postindustrial, technological society where artistic appreciation is rare and financial support even rarer. He therefore decided to use the money to fund an exhibit of up-and-coming modern artists at the San Francisco Museum of Modern Art.

Ash approached the museum directors with his idea, and the directors became excited immediately after he informed them that he would fund the entire exhibit in addition to donating $1 million to the museum. Celeste McKenzie, a museum director, was assigned to work with Ash in planning the exhibit. The exhibit was slated to open one year from the time Ash met with the directors, and the exhibit pieces would remain on display for two months.

Ash began the project by combing the modern art community for potential artists and pieces. He presented the following list of artists, their pieces, and the price of displaying each piece[1] to Celeste.

Artist	Piece	Description of Piece	Price
Colin Zweibell	"Perfection"	A wire mesh sculpture of the human body	$300,000
	"Burden"	A wire mesh sculpture of a mule	$250,000
	"The Great Equalizer"	A wire mesh sculpture of a gun	$125,000
Rita Losky	"Chaos Reigns"	A series of computer-generated drawings	$400,000
	"Who Has Control?"	A computer-generated drawing intermeshed with lines of computer code	$500,000
	"Domestication"	A pen-and-ink drawing of a house	$400,000
	"Innocence"	A pen-and-ink drawing of a child	$550,000
Norm Marson	"Aging Earth"	A sculpture of trash covering a larger globe	$700,000
	"Wasted Resources"	A collage of various packaging materials	$575,000
Candy Tate	"Serenity"	An all blue watercolor painting	$200,000
	"Calm Before the Storm"	A painting with an all blue watercolor background and a black watercolor center	$225,000
Robert Bayer	"Void"	An all black oil painting	$150,000
	"Sun"	An all yellow oil painting	$150,000
David Lyman	"Storefront Window"	A photo-realistic painting of a jewelry store display window	$850,000
	"Harley"	A photo-realistic painting of a Harley-Davidson motorcycle	$750,000
Angie Oldman	"Consumerism"	A collage of magazine advertisements	$400,000
	"Reflection"	A mirror (considered a sculpture)	$175,000
	"Trojan Victory"	A wooden sculpture of a condom	$450,000

[1]The display price includes the cost of paying the artist for loaning the piece to the museum, transporting the piece to San Francisco, constructing the display for the piece, insuring the piece while it is on display, and transporting the piece back to its origin.

Artist	Piece	Description of Piece	Price
Rick Rawls	"Rick"	A photo-realistic self-portrait (painting)	$500,000
	"Rick II"	A cubist self-portrait (painting)	$500,000
	"Rick III"	An expressionist self-portrait (painting)	$500,000
Bill Reynolds	"Beyond"	A science fiction oil painting depicting Mars colonization	$650,000
	"Pioneers"	An oil painting of three astronauts aboard the space shuttle	$650,000
Bear Canton	"Wisdom"	A pen-and-ink drawing of an Apache chieftain	$250,000
	"Superior Powers"	A pen-and-ink drawing of a traditional Native American rain dance	$350,000
	"Living Land"	An oil painting of the Grand Canyon	$450,000
Helen Row	"Study of a Violin"	A cubist painting of a violin	$400,000
	"Study of a Fruit Bowl"	A cubist painting of a bowl of fruit	$400,000
Ziggy Lite	"My Namesake"	A collage of Ziggy cartoons	$300,000
	"Narcissism"	A collage of photographs of Ziggy Lite	$300,000
Ash Briggs	"All That Glitters"	A watercolor painting of the Golden Gate Bridge	$50,000*
	"The Rock"	A watercolor painting of Alcatraz	$ 50,000
	"Winding Road"	A watercolor painting of Lombard Street	$ 50,000
	"Dreams Come True"	A watercolor painting of the San Francisco Museum of Modern Art	$ 50,000

*Ash does not require personal compensation, and the cost for moving his pieces to the museum from his home in San Francisco is minimal. The cost of displaying his pieces therefore only includes the cost of constructing the display and insuring the pieces.

Ash possesses certain requirements for the exhibit. He believes the majority of Americans lack adequate knowledge of art and artistic styles, and he wants the exhibit to educate Americans. Ash wants visitors to become aware of the collage as an art form, but he believes collages require little talent. He therefore decides to include only one collage. Additionally, Ash wants viewers to compare the delicate lines in a three-dimensional wire mesh sculpture to the delicate lines in a two-dimensional computer-generated drawing. He therefore wants at least one wire mesh sculpture displayed if a computer-generated drawing is displayed. Alternatively, he wants at least one computer-generated drawing displayed if a wire mesh sculpture is displayed. Furthermore, Ash wants to expose viewers to all painting styles, but he wants to limit the number of paintings displayed to achieve a balance in the exhibit between paintings and other art forms. He therefore decides to include at least one photo-realistic painting, at least one cubist painting, at least one expressionist painting, at least one watercolor painting, and at least one oil painting. At the same time, he wants the number of paintings to be no greater than twice the number of other art forms.

Ash wants all his own paintings included in the exhibit since he is sponsoring the exhibit and since his paintings celebrate the San Francisco Bay Area, the home of the exhibit.

Ash possesses personal biases for and against some artists. Ash is currently having a steamy affair with Candy Tate, and he wants both of her paintings displayed. Ash counts both David Lyman and Rick Rawls as his best friends, and he does not want to play favorites among these two artists. He therefore decides to display as many pieces from David Lyman as from Rick Rawls and to display at least one piece from each of them. Although Ziggy Lite is very popular within art circles, Ash believes Ziggy makes a mockery of art. Ash will therefore only accept one display piece from Ziggy, if any at all.

Celeste also possesses her own agenda for the exhibit. As a museum director, she is interested in representing a diverse population of artists, appealing to a wide audience, and creating a politically correct exhibit. To advance feminism, she decides to include at least one piece from a female artist for every two pieces included from a male artist. To advance environmentalism, she decides to include either one or both of the pieces "Aging Earth" and "Wasted Resources." To advance Native American rights, she decides to include at least one piece by Bear Canton. To advance science, she decides to include at least one of the following pieces: "Chaos Reigns," "Who Has Control," "Beyond," and "Pioneers."

Celeste also understands that space is limited at the museum. The museum only has enough floor space for four sculptures and enough wall space for 20 paintings, collages, and drawings.

Finally, Celeste decides that if "Narcissism" is displayed, "Reflection" should also be displayed since "Reflection" also suggests narcissism.

Please explore the following questions independently except where otherwise indicated.

(a) Ash decides to allocate $4 million to fund the exhibit. Given the pieces available and the specific requirements from Ash and Celeste, formulate and solve a BIP model to maximize the number of pieces displayed in the exhibit without exceeding the budget. How many pieces are displayed? Which pieces are displayed?

(b) To ensure that the exhibit draws the attention of the public, Celeste decides that it must include at least 20 pieces. Formulate and solve a BIP model to minimize the cost of the exhibit while displaying at least 20 pieces and meeting the requirements set by Ash and Celeste. How much does the exhibit cost? Which pieces are displayed?

(c) An influential patron of Rita Losky's work who chairs the Museum Board of Directors learns that Celeste requires at least 20 pieces in the exhibit. He offers to pay the minimum amount required on top of Ash's $4 million to ensure that exactly 20 pieces are displayed in the exhibit and that all of Rita's pieces are displayed. How much does the patron have to pay? Which pieces are displayed?

CASE 12.3   STOCKING SETS

Daniel Holbrook, an expeditor at the local warehouse for Furniture City, sighed as he moved boxes and boxes of inventory to the side in order to reach the shelf where the particular item he needed was located. He dropped to his hands and knees and squinted at the inventory numbers lining the bottom row of the shelf. He did not find the number he needed. He worked his way up the shelf until he found the number matching the number on the order slip. Just his luck! The item was on the top row of the shelf! Daniel walked back through the warehouse to find a ladder, stumbling over boxes of inventory littering his path. When he finally climbed the ladder to reach the top shelf, his face crinkled in frustration. Not again! The item he needed was not in stock! All he saw above the inventory number was an empty space covered with dust!

Daniel trudged back through the warehouse to make the dreadful phone call. He dialed the number of Brenda Sims, the saleswoman on the kitchen showroom floor of Furniture City, and informed her that the particular light fixture the customer had requested was not in stock. He then asked her if she wanted him to look for the rest of the items in the kitchen set. Brenda told him that she would talk to the customer and call him back.

Brenda hung up the phone and frowned. Mr. Davidson, her customer, would not be happy. Ordering and receiving the correct light fixture from the regional warehouse would take at least two weeks.

Brenda then paused to reflect upon business during the last month and realized that over 80 percent of the orders for kitchen sets could not be filled because items needed to complete the sets were not in stock at the local warehouse. She also realized that Furniture City was losing customer goodwill and business because of stockouts. The furniture megastore was gaining a reputation for slow service and delayed deliveries, causing customers to turn to small competitors that sold furniture directly from the showroom floor.

Brenda decided to investigate the inventory situation at the local warehouse. She walked the short distance to the building next door and gasped when she stepped inside the warehouse. What she saw could only be described as chaos. Spaces allocated for some items were overflowing into the aisles of the warehouse while other spaces were completely bare. She walked over to one of the spaces overflowing with inventory to discover the item that was overstocked. She could not believe her eyes! The warehouse had at least 30 rolls of pea-green wallpaper! No customer had ordered pea-green wallpaper since 1973!

Brenda marched over to Daniel demanding an explanation. Daniel said that the warehouse had been in such a chaotic state since his arrival one year ago. He said the inventory problems occurred because management had a policy of stocking every furniture item on the showroom floor in the local warehouse. Management only replenished inventory every three months, and when inventory was replenished, management ordered every item regardless of if it had been sold. Daniel also said that he had tried to make management aware of the problems with overstocking unpopular items and understocking popular items, but that management would not listen to him because he was simply an expeditor.

Brenda understood that Furniture City required a new inventory policy. Not only was the megastore losing money by making customers unhappy with delivery delays, but it was also losing money by wasting warehouse space. By changing the inventory policy to stock only popular items and replenish them immediately when they are sold, Furniture City would ensure that the majority of customers receive their furniture immediately and that the valuable warehouse space was utilized effectively.

Brenda needed to sell her inventory policy to management. Using her extensive sales experience, she decided that the most effective sales strategy would be to use her kitchen department as a model for the new inventory policy. She would identify all kitchen sets comprising 85 percent of customers orders. Given the fixed amount of warehouse space allocated to the kitchen department, she would identify the items Furniture City should stock in order to satisfy the greatest number of customer orders. She would then calculate the revenue from satisfying customer orders under the new inventory policy, using the bottom line to persuade management to accept her policy.

Brenda analyzed her records over the past three years and determined that 20 kitchen sets were responsible for 85 percent of the customer orders. These 20 kitchen sets were composed of up to eight features in a variety of styles. Brenda listed each feature and its popular styles:

Floor Tile	Wallpaper	Light Fixtures	Cabinets
(T1) White textured tile	(W1) Plain ivory paper	(L1) One large rectangular frosted fixture	(C1) Light solid wood cabinets
(T2) Ivory textured tile	(W2) Ivory paper with dark brown pinstripes	(L2) Three small square frosted fixtures	(C2) Dark solid wood cabinets
(T3) White checkered tile with blue trim	(W3) Blue paper with marble texture	(L3) One large oval frosted fixture	(C3) Light wood cabinets with glass doors
(T4) White checkered tile with light yellow trim	(W4) Light yellow paper with marble texture	(L4) Three small frosted globe fixtures	(C4) Dark wood cabinets with glass doors

Countertops	Dishwashers	Sinks	Ranges
(O1) Plain light wood countertops	(D1) White energy-saving dishwasher	(S1) Sink with separate hot and cold water taps	(R1) White electric oven
(O2) Stained light wood countertops	(D2) Ivory energy-saving dishwasher	(S2) Divided sink with separate hot and cold water taps and garbage disposal	(R2) Ivory electric oven
(O3) White lacquer-coated countertops		(S3) Sink with one hot and cold water tap	(R3) White gas oven
(O4) Ivory lacquer-coated countertops		(S4) Divided sink with one hot and cold water tap and garbage disposal	(R4) Ivory gas oven

Brenda then created a table showing the 20 kitchen sets and the particular features composing each set. To simplify the table, she used the codes shown in parentheses above to represent the particular feature and style. The table is given below. For example, kitchen set 1 consists of floor tile T2, wallpaper W2, light fixture L4, cabinet C2, countertop O2, dishwasher D2, sink S2, and range R2. Notice that sets 14 through 20 do not contain dishwashers.

Brenda knew she had only a limited amount of warehouse space allocated to the kitchen department. The warehouse could hold 50 square feet of tile and 12 rolls of wallpaper in the inventory bins. The inventory shelves could hold two light fixtures, two cabinets, three countertops, and two sinks. Dishwashers and ranges are similar in size, so Furniture City stored them in similar locations. The warehouse floor could hold a total of four dishwashers and ranges.

Every kitchen set always includes exactly 20 square feet of tile and exactly five rolls of wallpaper. Therefore, 20 square feet of a particular style of tile and five rolls of a particular style of wallpaper are required for the styles to be in stock.

(a) Formulate and solve a BIP model to maximize the total number of kitchen sets (and thus the number of customer orders) Furniture City stocks in the local warehouse. Assume that when a customer orders a kitchen set, all the particular items composing that kitchen set are replenished at the local warehouse immediately.

(b) How many of each feature and style should Furniture City stock in the local warehouse? How many different kitchen sets are in stock?

(c) Furniture City decides to discontinue carrying nursery sets, and the warehouse space previously allocated to the nursery department is divided between the existing departments at Furniture City. The kitchen department receives enough additional space to allow it to stock both styles of dishwashers and three of the four styles of ranges. How does the optimal inventory policy for the kitchen department change with this additional warehouse space?

(d) Brenda convinces management that the kitchen department should serve as a testing ground for future inventory policies. To provide adequate space for testing, management decides to allocate all the space freed by the nursery department to the kitchen department. The extra

	T1	T2	T3	T4	W1	W2	W3	W4	L1	L2	L3	L4	C1	C2	C3	C4	O1	O2	O3	O4	D1	D2	S1	S2	S3	S4	R1	R2	R3	R4
Set 1		X				X						X	X	X						X	X	X	X	X		X		X	X	
Set 2	X				X		X					X	X		X					X	X	X		X		X		X	X	
Set 3			X				X	X		X			X				X			X	X			X	X				X	
Set 4		X					X		X		X				X				X	X	X						X			
Set 5				X				X		X			X		X			X			X		X	X			X			
Set 6	X				X				X			X	X		X		X				X	X			X				X	
Set 7	X						X					X	X		X		X			X	X			X	X		X			
Set 8	X				X					X	X	X	X				X		X		X	X			X	X		X		
Set 9	X				X				X		X		X		X			X			X	X	X					X		
Set 10	X				X				X				X		X	X		X	X		X				X	X			X	
Set 11		X			X				X		X		X		X		X				X		X						X	
Set 12	X					X		X	X				X	X	X			X			X				X	X		X		
Set 13			X	X			X				X	X			X		X		X		X		X				X		X	
Set 14				X			X					X			X		X		X		X		X					X		
Set 15		X			X		X		X		X		X		X	X	X		X					X	X		X		X	
Set 16		X			X		X		X		X		X		X				X		X		X				X		X	
Set 17	X				X		X		X		X		X		X		X				X			X		X			X	
Set 18	X				X		X		X		X		X	X		X				X	X		X			X	X			X
Set 19	X				X		X		X		X		X			X				X	X		X						X	
Set 20	X				X		X		X		X		X				X							X						X

space means that the kitchen department can store not only the dishwashers and ranges from part (c), but also all sinks, all countertops, three of the four light fixtures, and three of the four cabinets. How much does the additional space help?

(e) How would the inventory policy be affected if the items composing a kitchen set could not be replenished immediately? Under what conditions is the assumption of immediate replenishment nevertheless justified?

CASE 12.4   ASSIGNING STUDENTS TO SCHOOLS (REVISITED AGAIN)

Reconsider Case 4.3.

The Springfield School Board now has made the decision to prohibit the splitting of residential areas among multiple schools. Thus, each of the six areas must be assigned to a single school.

(a) Formulate a BIP model for this problem under the current policy of providing bussing for all middle school students who must travel more than approximately a mile.

(b) Referring to part (a) of Case 4.3, explain why that linear programming model and the BIP model just formulated are so different when they are dealing with nearly the same problem.

(c) Solve the BIP model formulated in part (a).

(d) Referring to part (c) of Case 4.3, determine how much the total bussing cost increases because of the decision to prohibit the splitting of residential areas among multiple schools.

(e, f, g, h) Repeat parts (e, f, g, h) of Case 4.3 under the new school board decision to prohibit splitting residential areas among multiple schools.

13

Nonlinear Programming

The fundamental role of linear programming in OR is accurately reflected by the fact that it is the focus of a *third* of this book. A key assumption of linear programming is that *all its functions* (objective function and constraint functions) are linear. Although this assumption essentially holds for numerous practical problems, it frequently does not hold. In fact, many economists have found that some degree of nonlinearity is the rule and not the exception in economic planning problems.[1] Therefore, it often is necessary to deal directly with nonlinear programming problems, so we turn our attention to this important area.

In one general form,[2] the *nonlinear programming problem* is to find $\mathbf{x} = (x_1, x_2, \ldots, x_n)$ so as to

Maximize $f(\mathbf{x})$,

subject to

$$g_i(\mathbf{x}) \leq b_i, \quad \text{for } i = 1, 2, \ldots, m,$$

and

$$\mathbf{x} \geq \mathbf{0},$$

where $f(\mathbf{x})$ and the $g_i(\mathbf{x})$ are given functions of the n decision variables.[3] No algorithm that will solve *every* specific problem fitting this format is available. However, substantial progress has been made for some important special cases of this problem by making various assumptions about these functions, and research is continuing very actively. This area is a large one, and we do not have the space to survey it completely. However, we do present a few sample applications and then introduce some of the basic ideas for solving certain important types of nonlinear programming problems.

Both Appendixes 2 and 3 provide useful background for this chapter, and we recommend that you review these appendixes as you study the next few sections.

[1] For example, see W. J. Baumol and R. C. Bushnell, "Error Produced by Linearization in Mathematical Programming," *Econometrica*, **35**: 447–471, 1967.

[2] The other *legitimate forms* correspond to those for *linear programming* listed in Sec. 3.2. Section 4.6 describes how to convert these other forms to the form given here.

[3] For simplicity, we assume throughout the chapter that *all* these functions either are *differentiable* everywhere or are *piecewise linear functions* (discussed in Secs. 13.1 and 13.8).

13.1 SAMPLE APPLICATIONS

The following examples illustrate a few of the many important types of problems to which nonlinear programming has been applied.

The Product-Mix Problem with Price Elasticity

In *product-mix* problems, such as the Wyndor Glass Co. problem of Sec. 3.1, the goal is to determine the optimal mix of production levels for a firm's products, given limitations on the resources needed to produce those products, in order to maximize the firm's total profit. In some cases, there is a fixed unit profit associated with each product, so the resulting objective function will be linear. However, in many product-mix problems, certain factors introduce *nonlinearities* into the objective function.

For example, a large manufacturer may encounter *price elasticity,* whereby the amount of a product that can be sold has an inverse relationship to the price charged. Thus, the *price-demand curve* for a typical product might look like the one shown in Fig. 13.1, where $p(x)$ is the price required in order to be able to sell x units. The firm's profit from producing and selling x units of the product then would be the sales revenue, $xp(x)$, minus the production and distribution costs. Therefore, if the unit cost for producing and distributing the product is fixed at c (see the dashed line in Fig. 13.1), the firm's profit from producing and selling x units is given by the nonlinear function

$$P(x) = xp(x) - cx,$$

as plotted in Fig. 13.2. If *each* of the firm's n products has a similar profit function, say, $P_j(x_j)$ for producing and selling x_j units of product j ($j = 1, 2, \ldots, n$), then the overall objective function is

$$f(\mathbf{x}) = \sum_{j=1}^{n} P_j(x_j),$$

a sum of nonlinear functions.

FIGURE 13.1
Price-demand curve.

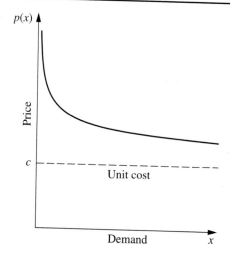

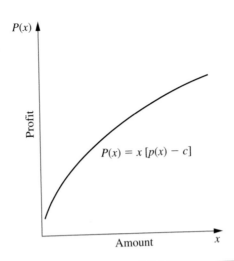

$$P(x) = x \, [p(x) - c]$$

FIGURE 13.2
Profit function.

Another reason that nonlinearities can arise in the objective function is the fact that the *marginal cost* of producing another unit of a given product varies with the production level. For example, the marginal cost may decrease when the production level is increased because of a *learning-curve effect* (more efficient production with more experience). On the other hand, it may increase instead, because special measures such as overtime or more expensive production facilities may be needed to increase production further.

Nonlinearities also may arise in the $g_i(\mathbf{x})$ constraint functions in a similar fashion. For example, if there is a budget constraint on total production cost, the cost function will be nonlinear if the marginal cost of production varies as just described. For constraints on the other kinds of resources, $g_i(\mathbf{x})$ will be nonlinear whenever the use of the corresponding resource is not strictly proportional to the production levels of the respective products.

The Transportation Problem with Volume Discounts on Shipping Costs

As illustrated by the P & T Company example in Sec. 8.1, a typical application of the transportation problem is to determine an optimal plan for shipping goods from various sources to various destinations, given supply and demand constraints, in order to minimize total shipping cost. It was assumed in Chap. 8 that the *cost per unit shipped* from a given source to a given destination is *fixed*, regardless of the amount shipped. In actuality, this cost may not be fixed. *Volume discounts* sometimes are available for large shipments, so that the *marginal cost* of shipping one more unit might follow a pattern like the one shown in Fig. 13.3. The resulting cost of shipping x units then is given by a *nonlinear* function $C(x)$, which is a *piecewise linear function* with slope equal to the marginal cost, like the one shown in Fig. 13.4. [The function in Fig. 13.4 consists of a line segment with slope 6.5 from (0, 0) to (0.6, 3.9), a second line segment with slope 5 from (0.6, 3.9) to (1.5, 8.4), a third line segment with slope 4 from (1.5, 8.4) to (2.7, 13.2), and

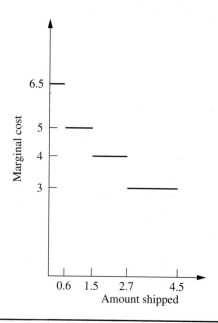

FIGURE 13.3
Marginal shipping cost.

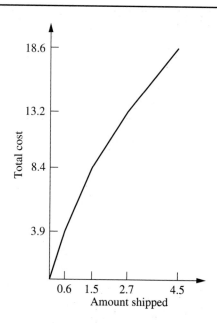

FIGURE 13.4
Shipping cost function.

a fourth line segment with slope 3 from (2.7, 13.2) to (4.5, 18.6).] Consequently, if *each* combination of source and destination has a similar shipping cost function, so that the cost of shipping x_{ij} units from source i ($i = 1, 2, \ldots, m$) to destination j ($j = 1, 2, \ldots, n$) is given by a nonlinear function $C_{ij}(x_{ij})$, then the overall objective function to be *minimized* is

$$f(\mathbf{x}) = \sum_{i=1}^{m} \sum_{j=1}^{n} C_{ij}(x_{ij}).$$

Even with this nonlinear objective function, the constraints normally are still the special linear constraints that fit the transportation problem model in Sec. 8.1.

Portfolio Selection with Risky Securities

It now is common practice for professional managers of large stock portfolios to use computer models based partially on nonlinear programming to guide them. Because investors are concerned about both the *expected return* (gain) and the *risk* associated with their investments, nonlinear programming is used to determine a portfolio that, under certain assumptions, provides an optimal trade-off between these two factors. This approach is based largely on path-breaking research done by Harry Markowitz and William Sharpe that helped them win the 1990 Nobel Prize in Economics.

A nonlinear programming model can be formulated for this problem as follows. Suppose that n stocks (securities) are being considered for inclusion in the portfolio, and let the decision variables x_j ($j = 1, 2, \ldots, n$) be the number of shares of stock j to be included. Let μ_j and σ_{jj} be the (estimated) *mean* and *variance*, respectively, of the return on each share of stock j, where σ_{jj} measures the risk of this stock. For $i = 1, 2, \ldots, n$ ($i \neq j$), let σ_{ij} be the *covariance* of the return on one share each of stock i and stock j. (Because it would be difficult to estimate all the σ_{ij} values, the usual approach is to make certain assumptions about market behavior that enable us to calculate σ_{ij} directly from σ_{ii} and σ_{jj}.) Then the expected value $R(\mathbf{x})$ and the variance $V(\mathbf{x})$ of the total return from the entire portfolio are

$$R(\mathbf{x}) = \sum_{j=1}^{n} \mu_j x_j$$

and

$$V(\mathbf{x}) = \sum_{i=1}^{n} \sum_{j=1}^{n} \sigma_{ij} x_i x_j,$$

where $V(\mathbf{x})$ measures the risk associated with the portfolio. One way to consider the trade-off between these two factors is to use $V(\mathbf{x})$ as the objective function to be minimized and then impose the constraint that $R(\mathbf{x})$ must be no smaller than the minimum acceptable expected return. The complete nonlinear programming model then would be

$$\text{Minimize} \quad V(\mathbf{x}) = \sum_{i=1}^{n} \sum_{j=1}^{n} \sigma_{ij} x_i x_j,$$

subject to

$$\sum_{j=1}^{n} \mu_j x_j \geq L$$

$$\sum_{j=1}^{n} P_j x_j \leq B$$

and

$$x_j \geq 0, \qquad \text{for } j = 1, 2, \ldots, n,$$

where L is the minimum acceptable expected return, P_j is the price for each share of stock j, and B is the amount of money budgeted for the portfolio.

One drawback of this formulation is that it is relatively difficult to choose an appropriate value for L for obtaining the best trade-off between $R(\mathbf{x})$ and $V(\mathbf{x})$. Therefore, rather than stopping with one choice of L, it is common to use a *parametric* (nonlinear) programming approach to generate the optimal solution as a function of L over a wide range of values of L. The next step is to examine the values of $R(\mathbf{x})$ and $V(\mathbf{x})$ for these solutions that are optimal for some value of L and then to choose the solution that seems to give the best trade-off between these two quantities. This procedure often is referred to as generating the solutions on the *efficient frontier* of the two-dimensional graph of $(R(\mathbf{x}), V(\mathbf{x}))$ points for feasible $\mathbf{x}$. The reason is that the $(R(\mathbf{x}), V(\mathbf{x}))$ point for an optimal $\mathbf{x}$ (for some L) lies on the *frontier* (boundary) of the feasible points. Furthermore, each optimal $\mathbf{x}$ is *efficient* in the sense that no other feasible solution is at least equally good with one measure (R or V) and strictly better with the other measure (smaller V or larger R).

13.2 GRAPHICAL ILLUSTRATION OF NONLINEAR PROGRAMMING PROBLEMS

When a nonlinear programming problem has just one or two variables, it can be represented graphically much like the Wyndor Glass Co. example for linear programming in Sec. 3.1. Because such a graphical representation gives considerable insight into the properties of optimal solutions for linear and nonlinear programming, let us look at a few examples. To highlight the difference between linear and nonlinear programming, we shall use some *nonlinear* variations of the Wyndor Glass Co. problem.

Figure 13.5 shows what happens to this problem if the only changes in the model shown in Sec. 3.1 are that both the second and the third functional constraints are replaced by the single nonlinear constraint $9x_1^2 + 5x_2^2 \leq 216$. Compare Fig. 13.5 with Fig. 3.3. The optimal solution still happens to be $(x_1, x_2) = (2, 6)$. Furthermore, it still lies on the boundary of the feasible region. However, it is *not* a corner-point feasible (CPF) solution. The optimal solution could have been a CPF solution with a different objective function (check $Z = 3x_1 + x_2$), but the fact that it need not be one means that we no longer have the tremendous simplification used in linear programming of limiting the search for an optimal solution to just the CPF solutions.

Now suppose that the linear constraints of Sec. 3.1 are kept unchanged, but the objective function is made nonlinear. For example, if

$$Z = 126x_1 - 9x_1^2 + 182x_2 - 13x_2^2,$$

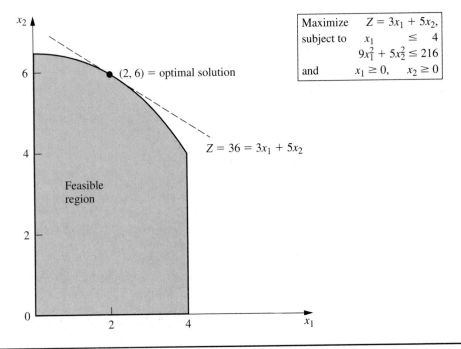

$$\text{Maximize} \quad Z = 3x_1 + 5x_2,$$
$$\text{subject to} \quad x_1 \leq 4$$
$$9x_1^2 + 5x_2^2 \leq 216$$
$$\text{and} \quad x_1 \geq 0, \quad x_2 \geq 0$$

(2, 6) = optimal solution

$Z = 36 = 3x_1 + 5x_2$

Feasible region

FIGURE 13.5
The Wyndor Glass Co. example with the nonlinear constraint $9x_1^2 + 5x_2^2 \leq 216$ replacing the original second and third functional constraints.

FIGURE 13.6
The Wyndor Glass Co. example with the original feasible region but with the nonlinear objective function $Z = 126x_1 - 9x_1^2 + 182x_2 - 13x_2^2$ replacing the original objective function.

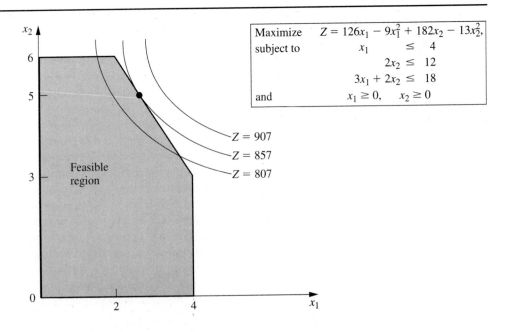

$$\text{Maximize} \quad Z = 126x_1 - 9x_1^2 + 182x_2 - 13x_2^2,$$
$$\text{subject to} \quad x_1 \leq 4$$
$$2x_2 \leq 12$$
$$3x_1 + 2x_2 \leq 18$$
$$\text{and} \quad x_1 \geq 0, \quad x_2 \geq 0$$

$Z = 907$
$Z = 857$
$Z = 807$

Feasible region

then the graphical representation in Fig. 13.6 indicates that the optimal solution is $x_1 = \frac{8}{3}$, $x_2 = 5$, which again lies on the boundary of the feasible region. (The value of Z for this optimal solution is $Z = 857$, so Fig. 13.6 depicts the fact that the locus of all points with $Z = 857$ intersects the feasible region at just this one point, whereas the locus of points with any larger Z does not intersect the feasible region at all.) On the other hand, if

$$Z = 54x_1 - 9x_1^2 + 78x_2 - 13x_2^2,$$

then Fig. 13.7 illustrates that the optimal solution turns out to be $(x_1, x_2) = (3, 3)$, which lies *inside* the boundary of the feasible region. (You can check that this solution is optimal by using calculus to derive it as the unconstrained global maximum; because it also satisfies the constraints, it must be optimal for the constrained problem.) Therefore, a gen-

FIGURE 13.7
The Wyndor Glass Co. example with the original feasible region but with another nonlinear objective function, $Z = 54x_1 - 9x_1^2 + 78x_2 - 13x_2^2$, replacing the original objective function.

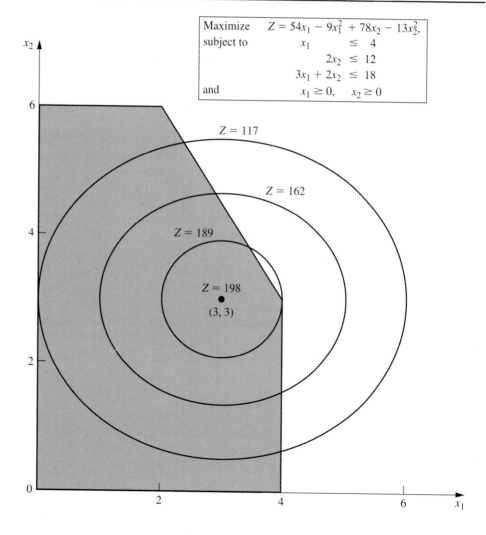

Maximize	$Z = 54x_1 - 9x_1^2 + 78x_2 - 13x_2^2,$		
subject to	x_1	$\leq$	4
	$2x_2$	$\leq$	12
	$3x_1 + 2x_2$	$\leq$	18
and	$x_1 \geq 0,$	$x_2 \geq 0$	

$Z = 117$

$Z = 162$

$Z = 189$

$Z = 198$

$(3, 3)$

eral algorithm for solving similar problems needs to consider *all* solutions in the feasible region, not just those on the boundary.

Another complication that arises in nonlinear programming is that a *local* maximum need not be a *global* maximum (the overall optimal solution). For example, consider the function of a single variable plotted in Fig. 13.8. Over the interval $0 \leq x \leq 5$, this function has three local maxima—$x = 0$, $x = 2$, and $x = 4$—but only one of these—$x = 4$—is a *global maximum.* (Similarly, there are local minima at $x = 1$, 3, and 5, but only $x = 5$ is a *global minimum.*)

Nonlinear programming algorithms generally are unable to distinguish between a local maximum and a global maximum (except by finding another *better* local maximum). Therefore, it becomes crucial to know the conditions under which any local maximum is *guaranteed* to be a global maximum over the feasible region. You may recall from calculus that when we maximize an ordinary (doubly differentiable) function of a single variable $f(x)$ without any constraints, this guarantee can be given when

$$\frac{d^2f}{dx^2} \leq 0 \qquad \text{for all } x.$$

Such a function that is always "curving downward" (or not curving at all) is called a **concave** function.[1] Similarly, if $\leq$ is replaced by $\geq$, so that the function is always "curving upward" (or not curving at all), it is called a **convex** function.[2] (Thus, a *linear* function is both concave and convex.) See Fig. 13.9 for examples. Then note that Fig. 13.8 illustrates a function that is neither concave nor convex because it alternates between curving upward and curving downward.

Functions of multiple variables also can be characterized as concave or convex if they always curve downward or curve upward. These intuitive definitions are restated in precise terms, along with further elaboration on these concepts, in Appendix 2. Appendix 2 also provides a convenient test for checking whether a function of two variables is concave, convex, or neither.

Here is a convenient way of checking this for a function of more than two variables when the function consists of a *sum* of smaller functions of just one or two variables each.

---

[1] Concave functions sometimes are referred to as *concave downward.*

[2] Convex functions sometimes are referred to as *concave upward.*

FIGURE 13.8
A function with several local maxima ($x = 0$, 2, 4), but only $x = 4$ is a global maximum.

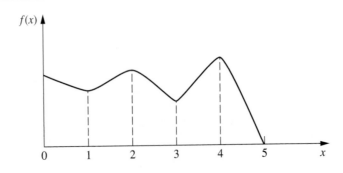

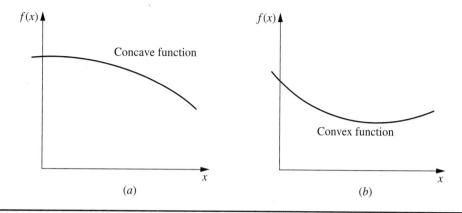

FIGURE 13.9
Examples of (*a*) a concave function and (*b*) a convex function.

If each smaller function is concave, then the overall function is concave. Similarly, the overall function is convex if each smaller function is convex.

To illustrate, consider the function

$$f(x_1, x_2, x_3) = 4x_1 - x_1^2 - (x_2 - x_3)^2$$
$$= [4x_1 - x_1^2] + [-(x_2 - x_3)^2],$$

which is the sum of the two smaller functions given in square brackets. The first smaller function $4x_1 - x_1^2$ is a function of the single variable x_1, so it can be found to be concave by noting that its second derivative is negative. The second smaller function $-(x_2 - x_3)^2$ is a function of just x_2 and x_3, so the test for functions of two variables given in Appendix 2 is applicable. In fact, Appendix 2 uses this particular function to illustrate the test and finds that the function is concave. Because both smaller functions are concave, the overall function $f(x_1, x_2, x_3)$ must be concave.

If a nonlinear programming problem has no constraints, the objective function being *concave* guarantees that a local maximum is a *global maximum.* (Similarly, the objective function being *convex* ensures that a local minimum is a *global minimum.*) If there are constraints, then one more condition will provide this guarantee, namely, that the *feasible region* is a **convex set.** As discussed in Appendix 2, a convex set is simply a set of points such that, for each pair of points in the collection, the entire line segment joining these two points is also in the collection. Thus, the feasible region for the original Wyndor Glass Co. problem (see Fig. 13.6 or 13.7) is a convex set. In fact, the feasible region for *any* linear programming problem is a convex set. Similarly, the feasible region in Fig. 13.5 is a convex set.

In general, the feasible region for a nonlinear programming problem is a convex set whenever all the $g_i(\mathbf{x})$ [for the constraints $g_i(\mathbf{x}) \leq b_i$] are convex functions. For the example of Fig. 13.5, both of its $g_i(\mathbf{x})$ are convex functions, since $g_1(\mathbf{x}) = x_1$ (a linear function is automatically both concave and convex) and $g_2(\mathbf{x}) = 9x_1^2 + 5x_2^2$ (both $9x_1^2$ and $5x_2^2$ are convex functions so their sum is a convex function). These two convex $g_i(\mathbf{x})$ lead to the feasible region of Fig. 13.5 being a convex set.

Now let's see what happens when just one of these $g_i(\mathbf{x})$ is a concave function instead. In particular, suppose that the only change made in the example of Fig. 13.5 is that its nonlinear constraint is replaced by $8x_1 - x_1^2 + 14x_2 - x_2^2 \leq 49$. Therefore, the new

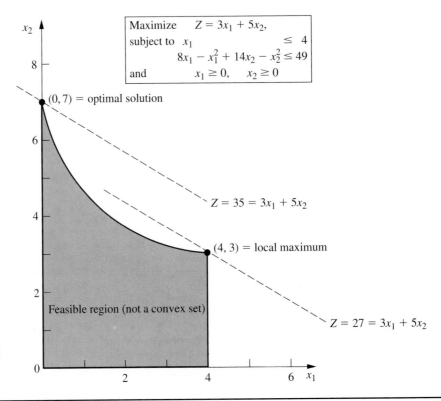

FIGURE 13.10
The Wyndor Glass Co. example with another nonlinear constraint, $8x_1 - x_1^2 + 14x_2 - x_2^2 \leq 49$, replacing the original second and third functional constraints.

$g_2(\mathbf{x}) = 8x_1 - x_1^2 + 14x_2 - x_2^2$, which is a concave function since both $8x_1 - x_1^2$ and $14x_2 - x_2^2$ are concave functions. The new feasible region shown in Fig. 13.10 is *not* a convex set. Why? Because this feasible region contains pairs of points, for example, $(0, 7)$ and $(4, 3)$, such that part of the line segment joining these two points is not in the feasible region. Consequently, we cannot guarantee that a local maximum is a global maximum. In fact, this example has two local maxima, $(0, 7)$ and $(4, 3)$, but only $(0, 7)$ is a global maximum.

Therefore, to guarantee that a local maximum is a global maximum for a nonlinear programming problem with constraints $g_i(\mathbf{x}) \leq b_i$ ($i = 1, 2, \ldots, m$) and $\mathbf{x} \geq \mathbf{0}$, the objective function $f(\mathbf{x})$ must be a *concave* function and each $g_i(\mathbf{x})$ must be a *convex* function. Such a problem is called a *convex programming problem,* which is one of the key types of nonlinear programming problems discussed in the next section.

13.3 TYPES OF NONLINEAR PROGRAMMING PROBLEMS

Nonlinear programming problems come in many different shapes and forms. Unlike the simplex method for linear programming, no single algorithm can solve all these different types of problems. Instead, algorithms have been developed for various individual *classes* (special types) of nonlinear programming problems. The most important classes are introduced briefly in this section. The subsequent sections then describe how some problems of these types can be solved.

Unconstrained Optimization

Unconstrained optimization problems have *no* constraints, so the objective is simply to

> Maximize $f(\mathbf{x})$

over *all* values of $\mathbf{x} = (x_1, x_2, \ldots, x_n)$. As reviewed in Appendix 3, the *necessary* condition that a particular solution $\mathbf{x} = \mathbf{x}^*$ be optimal when $f(\mathbf{x})$ is a differentiable function is

$$\frac{\partial f}{\partial x_j} = 0 \qquad \text{at } \mathbf{x} = \mathbf{x}^*, \text{ for } j = 1, 2, \ldots, n.$$

When $f(\mathbf{x})$ is a *concave* function, this condition also is *sufficient*, so then solving for $\mathbf{x}^*$ reduces to solving the system of n equations obtained by setting the n partial derivatives equal to zero. Unfortunately, for *nonlinear* functions $f(\mathbf{x})$, these equations often are going to be *nonlinear* as well, in which case you are unlikely to be able to solve analytically for their simultaneous solution. What then? Sections 13.4 and 13.5 describe *algorithmic search procedures* for finding $\mathbf{x}^*$, first for $n = 1$ and then for $n > 1$. These procedures also play an important role in solving many of the problem types described next, where there are constraints. The reason is that many algorithms for *constrained* problems are designed so that they can focus on an *unconstrained* version of the problem during a portion of each iteration.

When a variable x_j does have a nonnegativity constraint $x_j \geq 0$, the preceding necessary and (perhaps) sufficient condition changes slightly to

$$\frac{\partial f}{\partial x_j} \begin{cases} \leq 0 & \text{at } \mathbf{x} = \mathbf{x}^*, \quad \text{if } x_j^* = 0 \\ = 0 & \text{at } \mathbf{x} = \mathbf{x}^*, \quad \text{if } x_j^* > 0 \end{cases}$$

for each such j. This condition is illustrated in Fig. 13.11, where the optimal solution for a problem with a single variable is at $x = 0$ even though the derivative there is negative rather than zero. Because this example has a concave function to be maximized subject to a nonnegativity constraint, having the derivative less than or equal to 0 at $x = 0$ is both a necessary and sufficient condition for $x = 0$ to be optimal.

A problem that has some nonnegativity constraints but no functional constraints is one special case ($m = 0$) of the next class of problems.

Linearly Constrained Optimization

Linearly constrained optimization problems are characterized by constraints that completely fit linear programming, so that *all* the $g_i(\mathbf{x})$ constraint functions are linear, but the objective function $f(\mathbf{x})$ is nonlinear. The problem is considerably simplified by having just one nonlinear function to take into account, along with a linear programming feasible region. A number of special algorithms based upon *extending* the simplex method to consider the nonlinear objective function have been developed.

One important special case, which we consider next, is quadratic programming.

Quadratic Programming

Quadratic programming problems again have linear constraints, but now the objective function $f(\mathbf{x})$ must be *quadratic*. Thus, the only difference between such a problem and a linear programming problem is that some of the terms in the objective function involve the *square* of a variable or the *product* of two variables.

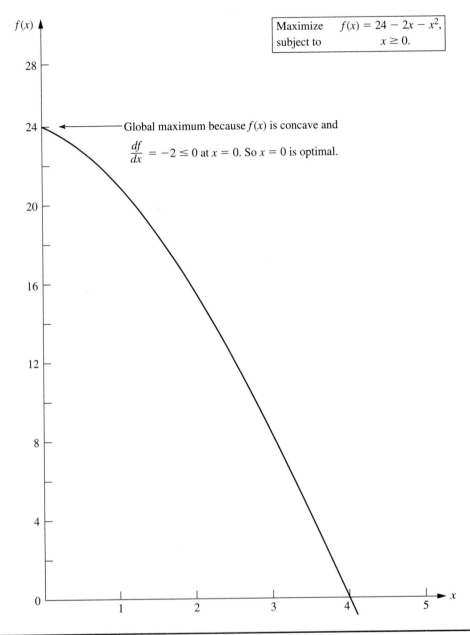

Maximize $f(x) = 24 - 2x - x^2,$
subject to $x \geq 0.$

Global maximum because $f(x)$ is concave and

$$\frac{df}{dx} = -2 \leq 0 \text{ at } x = 0. \text{ So } x = 0 \text{ is optimal.}$$

FIGURE 13.11
An example that illustrates
how an optimal solution can
lie at a point where a
derivative is negative instead
of zero, because that point
lies at the boundary of a
nonnegativity constraint.

Many algorithms have been developed for this case under the additional assumption that $f(\mathbf{x})$ is a concave function. Section 13.7 presents an algorithm that involves a direct extension of the simplex method.

Quadratic programming is very important, partially because such formulations arise naturally in many applications. For example, the problem of portfolio selection with risky securities described in Sec. 13.1 fits into this format. However, another major reason for its importance is that a common approach to solving general linearly constrained optimization problems is to solve a sequence of quadratic programming approximations.

Convex Programming

Convex programming covers a broad class of problems that actually encompasses as special cases all the preceding types when $f(\mathbf{x})$ is a concave function. The assumptions are that

1. $f(\mathbf{x})$ is a concave function.
2. Each $g_i(\mathbf{x})$ is a convex function.

As discussed at the end of Sec. 13.2, these assumptions are enough to ensure that a local maximum is a global maximum. You will see in Sec. 13.6 that the necessary and sufficient conditions for such an optimal solution are a natural generalization of the conditions just given for *unconstrained optimization* and its extension to include *nonnegativity constraints*. Section 13.9 then describes algorithmic approaches to solving convex programming problems.

Separable Programming

Separable programming is a special case of convex programming, where the one additional assumption is that

3. All the $f(\mathbf{x})$ and $g_i(\mathbf{x})$ functions are separable functions.

A **separable function** is a function where *each term* involves just a *single variable,* so that the function is separable into a sum of functions of individual variables. For example, if $f(\mathbf{x})$ is a separable function, it can be expressed as

$$f(\mathbf{x}) = \sum_{j=1}^{n} f_j(x_j),$$

where each $f_j(x_j)$ function includes only the terms involving just x_j. In the terminology of linear programming (see Sec. 3.3), separable programming problems satisfy the assumption of additivity but not the assumption of proportionality (for nonlinear functions).

To illustrate, the objective function considered in Fig. 13.6,

$$f(x_1, x_2) = 126x_1 - 9x_1^2 + 182x_2 - 13x_2^2$$

is a separable function because it can be expressed as

$$f(x_1, x_2) = f_1(x_1) + f_2(x_2)$$

where $f_1(x_1) = 126x_1 - 9x_1^2$ and $f_2(x_2) = 182x_2 - 13x_2^2$ are each a function of a single variable—x_1 and x_2, respectively. By the same reasoning, you can verify that the objective function considered in Fig. 13.7 also is a separable function.

It is important to distinguish separable programming problems from other convex programming problems, because any such problem can be closely approximated by a linear programming problem so that the extremely efficient simplex method can be used. This approach is described in Sec. 13.8. (For simplicity, we focus there on the *linearly constrained* case where the special approach is needed only on the objective function.)

Nonconvex Programming

Nonconvex programming encompasses all nonlinear programming problems that do not satisfy the assumptions of convex programming. Now, even if you are successful in finding a *local maximum,* there is no assurance that it also will be a *global maximum.* Therefore, there is no algorithm that will guarantee finding an optimal solution for all such problems. However, there do exist some algorithms that are relatively well suited for finding local maxima, especially when the forms of the nonlinear functions do not deviate too strongly from those assumed for convex programming. One such algorithm is presented in Sec. 13.10.

However, certain specific types of nonconvex programming problems can be solved without great difficulty by special methods. Two especially important such types are discussed briefly next.

Geometric Programming

When we apply nonlinear programming to engineering design problems, the objective function and the constraint functions frequently take the form

$$g(\mathbf{x}) = \sum_{i=1}^{N} c_i P_i(\mathbf{x}),$$

where

$$P_i(\mathbf{x}) = x_1^{a_{i1}} x_2^{a_{i2}} \cdots x_n^{a_{in}}, \qquad \text{for } i = 1, 2, \ldots, N.$$

In such cases, the c_i and a_{ij} typically represent physical constants, and the x_j are design variables. These functions generally are neither convex nor concave, so the techniques of convex programming cannot be applied directly to these *geometric programming* problems. However, there is one important case where the problem can be transformed to an equivalent convex programming problem. This case is where *all* the c_i coefficients in each function are strictly positive, so that the functions are *generalized positive polynomials*—(now called **posynomials**)—and the objective function is to be minimized. The equivalent convex programming problem with decision variables $y_1, y_2, \ldots, y_n$ is then obtained by setting

$$x_j = e^{y_j}, \qquad \text{for } j = 1, 2, \ldots, n$$

throughout the original model, so now a convex programming algorithm can be applied. Alternative solution procedures also have been developed for solving these *posynomial programming* problems, as well as for geometric programming problems of other types.[1]

Fractional Programming

Suppose that the objective function is in the form of a *fraction,* i.e., the ratio of two functions,

$$\text{Maximize} \quad f(\mathbf{x}) = \frac{f_1(\mathbf{x})}{f_2(\mathbf{x})}.$$

[1]R. J. Duffin, E. L. Peterson, and C. M. Zehner, *Geometric Programming,* Wiley, New York, 1967; C. Beightler and D. T. Phillips, *Applied Geometric Programming,* Wiley, New York, 1976.

Such *fractional programming* problems arise, e.g., when one is maximizing the ratio of output to person-hours expended (productivity), or profit to capital expended (rate of return), or expected value to standard deviation of some measure of performance for an investment portfolio (return/risk). Some special solution procedures[1] have been developed for certain forms of $f_1(\mathbf{x})$ and $f_2(\mathbf{x})$.

When it can be done, the most straightforward approach to solving a fractional programming problem is to transform it to an equivalent problem of a standard type for which effective solution procedures already are available. To illustrate, suppose that $f(\mathbf{x})$ is of the *linear fractional programming* form

$$f(\mathbf{x}) = \frac{\mathbf{c}\mathbf{x} + c_0}{\mathbf{d}\mathbf{x} + d_0},$$

where $\mathbf{c}$ and $\mathbf{d}$ are row vectors, $\mathbf{x}$ is a column vector, and c_0 and d_0 are scalars. Also assume that the constraint functions $g_i(\mathbf{x})$ are linear, so that the constraints in matrix form are $\mathbf{A}\mathbf{x} \leq \mathbf{b}$ and $\mathbf{x} \geq \mathbf{0}$.

Under mild additional assumptions, we can transform the problem to an equivalent *linear programming* problem by letting

$$\mathbf{y} = \frac{\mathbf{x}}{\mathbf{d}\mathbf{x} + d_0} \quad \text{and} \quad t = \frac{1}{\mathbf{d}\mathbf{x} + d_0},$$

so that $\mathbf{x} = \mathbf{y}/t$. This result yields

Maximize $\quad Z = \mathbf{c}\mathbf{y} + c_0 t,$

subject to

$$\mathbf{A}\mathbf{y} - \mathbf{b}t \leq \mathbf{0},$$
$$\mathbf{d}\mathbf{y} + d_0 t = 1,$$

and

$$\mathbf{y} \geq \mathbf{0}, \qquad t \geq 0,$$

which can be solved by the simplex method. More generally, the same kind of transformation can be used to convert a fractional programming problem with concave $f_1(\mathbf{x})$, convex $f_2(\mathbf{x})$, and convex $g_i(\mathbf{x})$ to an equivalent convex programming problem.

The Complementarity Problem

When we deal with quadratic programming in Sec. 13.7, you will see one example of how solving certain nonlinear programming problems can be reduced to solving the complementarity problem. Given variables $w_1, w_2, \ldots, w_p$ and $z_1, z_2, \ldots, z_p$, the **complementarity problem** is to find a *feasible* solution for the set of constraints

$$\mathbf{w} = F(\mathbf{z}), \qquad \mathbf{w} \geq \mathbf{0}, \qquad \mathbf{z} \geq \mathbf{0}$$

---

[1] The pioneering work on fractional programming was done by A. Charnes and W. W. Cooper, "'Programming with Linear Fractional Functionals," *Naval Research Logistics Quarterly,* **9:** 181–186, 1962. Also see S. Schaible, "A Survey of Fractional Programming," in S. Schaible and W. T. Ziemba (eds.), *Generalized Concavity in Optimization and Economics*, Academic Press, New York, 1981, pp. 417–440.

that also satisfies the **complementarity constraint**

$$\mathbf{w}^T\mathbf{z} = 0.$$

Here, $\mathbf{w}$ and $\mathbf{z}$ are column vectors, F is a given vector-valued function, and the superscript T denotes the transpose (see Appendix 4). The problem has no objective function, so technically it is not a full-fledged nonlinear programming problem. It is called the complementarity problem because of the complementary relationships that either

$$w_i = 0 \qquad \text{or} \qquad z_i = 0 \qquad \text{(or both)} \qquad \text{for each } i = 1, 2, \ldots, p.$$

An important special case is the **linear complementarity problem,** where

$$F(\mathbf{z}) = \mathbf{q} + \mathbf{Mz},$$

where $\mathbf{q}$ is a given column vector and $\mathbf{M}$ is a given $p \times p$ matrix. Efficient algorithms have been developed for solving this problem under suitable assumptions[1] about the properties of the matrix $\mathbf{M}$. One type involves pivoting from one basic feasible (BF) solution to the next, much like the simplex method for linear programming.

In addition to having applications in nonlinear programming, complementarity problems have applications in game theory, economic equilibrium problems, and engineering equilibrium problems.

13.4 ONE-VARIABLE UNCONSTRAINED OPTIMIZATION

We now begin discussing how to solve some of the types of problems just described by considering the simplest case—*unconstrained optimization* with just a single variable x ($n = 1$), where the differentiable function $f(x)$ to be maximized is *concave*.[2] Thus, the *necessary and sufficient condition* for a particular solution $x = x^*$ to be optimal (a global maximum) is

$$\frac{df}{dx} = 0 \qquad \text{at } x = x^*,$$

as depicted in Fig. 13.12. If this equation can be solved directly for x^*, you are done. However, if $f(x)$ is not a particularly simple function, so the derivative is not just a linear or quadratic function, you may not be able to solve the equation *analytically*. If not, the *one-dimensional search procedure* provides a straightforward way of solving the problem *numerically*.

The One-Dimensional Search Procedure

Like other search procedures in nonlinear programming, the *one-dimensional* search procedure finds a sequence of *trial solutions* that leads toward an optimal solution. At each iteration, you begin at the current trial solution to conduct a systematic search that culminates by identifying a new *improved* trial solution.

---

[1]See R. W. Cottle and G. B. Dantzig, "Complementary Pivot Theory of Mathematical Programming," *Linear Algebra and Its Applications,* **1:** 103–125, 1966; and R. W. Cottle, J.-S. Pang, and R. E. Stone, *The Linear Complementarity Problem,* Academic Press, Boston, 1992.

[2]See the beginning of Appendix 3 for a review of the corresponding case when $f(x)$ is not concave.

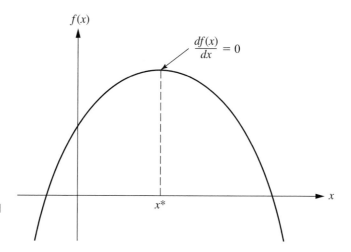

FIGURE 13.12
The one-variable unconstrained programming problem when the function is concave.

The idea behind the one-dimensional search procedure is a very intuitive one, namely, that whether the slope (derivative) is positive or negative at a trial solution definitely indicates whether improvement lies immediately to the right or left, respectively. Thus, if the derivative evaluated at a particular value of x is *positive,* then x^* must be larger than this x (see Fig. 13.12), so this x becomes a *lower bound* on the trial solutions that need to be considered thereafter. Conversely, if the derivative is *negative,* then x^* must be *smaller* than this x, so x would become an *upper bound.* Therefore, after both types of bounds have been identified, each new trial solution selected between the current bounds provides a new tighter bound of one type, thereby narrowing the search further. As long as a reasonable rule is used to select each trial solution in this way, the resulting *sequence* of trial solutions must *converge* to x^*. In practice, this means continuing the sequence until the distance between the bounds is sufficiently small that the next trial solution must be within a prespecified *error tolerance* of x^*.

This entire process is summarized next, given the notation

x' = current trial solution,

$\underline{x}$ = current lower bound on x^*,

$\bar{x}$ = current upper bound on x^*,

ϵ = error tolerance for x^*.

Although there are several reasonable rules for selecting each new trial solution, the one used in the following procedure is the **midpoint rule** (traditionally called the *Bolzano search plan*), which says simply to select the midpoint between the two current bounds.

Summary of the One-Dimensional Search Procedure.

Initialization: Select ϵ. Find an initial $\underline{x}$ and $\bar{x}$ by inspection (or by respectively finding any value of x at which the derivative is positive and then negative). Select an initial trial solution

$$x' = \frac{\underline{x} + \bar{x}}{2}.$$

Iteration:

1. Evaluate $\dfrac{df(x)}{dx}$ at $x = x'$.

2. If $\dfrac{df(x)}{dx} \geq 0$, reset $\underline{x} = x'$.

3. If $\dfrac{df(x)}{dx} \leq 0$, reset $\bar{x} = x'$.

4. Select a new $x' = \dfrac{\underline{x} + \bar{x}}{2}$.

Stopping rule: If $\bar{x} - \underline{x} \leq 2\epsilon$, so that the new x' must be within ϵ of x^*, stop. Otherwise, perform another iteration.

We shall now illustrate this procedure by applying it to the following example.

Example. Suppose that the function to be maximized is

$$f(x) = 12x - 3x^4 - 2x^6,$$

as plotted in Fig. 13.13. Its first two derivatives are

$$\frac{df(x)}{dx} = 12(1 - x^3 - x^5),$$

$$\frac{d^2f(x)}{dx^2} = -12(3x^2 + 5x^4).$$

FIGURE 13.13
Example for the one-dimensional search procedure.

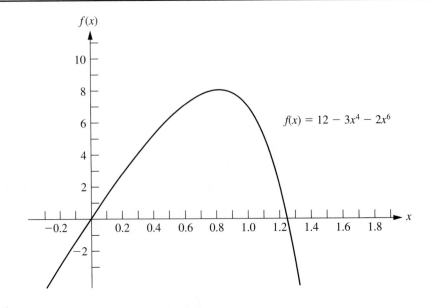

$f(x) = 12 - 3x^4 - 2x^6$

TABLE 13.1 Application of the one-dimensional search procedure to the example

Iteration	$\dfrac{df(x)}{dx}$	$\underline{x}$	$\bar{x}$	New x'	$f(x')$
0		0	2	1	7.0000
1	−12	0	1	0.5	5.7812
2	+10.12	0.5	1	0.75	7.6948
3	+4.09	0.75	1	0.875	7.8439
4	−2.19	0.75	0.875	0.8125	7.8672
5	+1.31	0.8125	0.875	0.84375	7.8829
6	−0.34	0.8125	0.84375	0.828125	7.8815
7	+0.51	0.828125	0.84375	0.8359375	7.8839
Stop					

Because the second derivative is nonpositive everywhere, $f(x)$ is a concave function, so the one-dimensional search procedure can be applied safely to find its global maximum (assuming a global maximum exists).

A quick inspection of this function (without even constructing its graph as shown in Fig. 13.13) indicates that $f(x)$ is positive for small positive values of x, but it is negative for $x < 0$ or $x > 2$. Therefore, $\underline{x} = 0$ and $\bar{x} = 2$ can be used as the initial bounds, with their midpoint, $x' = 1$, as the initial trial solution. Let $\epsilon = 0.01$ be the error tolerance for x^* in the stopping rule, so the final $(\bar{x} - \underline{x}) \leq 0.02$ with the final x' at the midpoint.

Applying the one-dimensional search procedure then yields the sequence of results shown in Table 13.1. [This table includes both the function and derivative values for your information, where the derivative is evaluated at the trial solution generated at the *preceding* iteration. However, note that the algorithm actually doesn't need to calculate $f(x')$ at all and that it only needs to calculate the derivative far enough to determine its sign.] The conclusion is that

$$x^* \approx 0.836,$$
$$0.828125 < x^* < 0.84375.$$

Your OR Courseware includes an interactive routine for executing the one-dimensional search procedure.

13.5 MULTIVARIABLE UNCONSTRAINED OPTIMIZATION

Now consider the problem of maximizing a *concave* function $f(\mathbf{x})$ of *multiple* variables $\mathbf{x} = (x_1, x_2, \ldots, x_n)$ when there are no constraints on the feasible values. Suppose again that the necessary and sufficient condition for optimality, given by the system of equations obtained by setting the respective partial derivatives equal to zero (see Sec. 13.3), cannot be solved analytically, so that a numerical search procedure must be used. How can the preceding one-dimensional search procedure be extended to this multidimensional problem?

In Sec. 13.4, the value of the ordinary derivative was used to select one of just two possible directions (increase x or decrease x) in which to move from the current trial solution to the next one. The goal was to reach a point eventually where this derivative is (essentially) 0. Now, there are *innumerable* possible directions in which to move; they correspond to the possible *proportional rates* at which the respective variables can be changed. The goal is to reach a point eventually where all the partial derivatives are (essentially) 0. Therefore, extending the one-dimensional search procedure requires using the values of the *partial* derivatives to select the specific direction in which to move. This selection involves using the gradient of the objective function, as described next.

Because the objective function $f(\mathbf{x})$ is assumed to be differentiable, it possesses a gradient, denoted by $\nabla f(\mathbf{x})$, at each point $\mathbf{x}$. In particular, the **gradient** at a specific point $\mathbf{x} = \mathbf{x}'$ is the *vector* whose elements are the respective *partial derivatives* evaluated at $\mathbf{x} = \mathbf{x}'$, so that

$$\nabla f(\mathbf{x}') = \left(\frac{\partial f}{\partial x_1}, \frac{\partial f}{\partial x_2}, \cdots, \frac{\partial f}{\partial x_n} \right) \qquad \text{at } \mathbf{x} = \mathbf{x}'.$$

The significance of the gradient is that the (infinitesimal) change in $\mathbf{x}$ that *maximizes* the rate at which $f(\mathbf{x})$ increases is the change that is *proportional* to $\nabla f(\mathbf{x})$. To express this idea geometrically, the "direction" of the gradient $\nabla f(\mathbf{x}')$ is interpreted as the *direction* of the directed line segment (arrow) from the origin $(0, 0, \ldots, 0)$ to the point $(\partial f/\partial x_1, \partial f/\partial x_2, \ldots, \partial f/\partial x_n)$, where $\partial f/\partial x_j$ is evaluated at $x_j = x_j'$. Therefore, it may be said that the rate at which $f(\mathbf{x})$ increases is maximized if (infinitesimal) changes in $\mathbf{x}$ are in the *direction* of the gradient $\nabla f(\mathbf{x})$. Because the objective is to find the feasible solution maximizing $f(\mathbf{x})$, it would seem expedient to attempt to move in the direction of the gradient as much as possible.

The Gradient Search Procedure

Because the current problem has no constraints, this interpretation of the gradient suggests that an efficient search procedure should keep moving in the direction of the gradient until it (essentially) reaches an optimal solution $\mathbf{x}^*$, where $\nabla f(\mathbf{x}^*) = \mathbf{0}$. However, normally it would not be practical to change $\mathbf{x}$ *continuously* in the direction of $\nabla f(\mathbf{x})$, because this series of changes would require continuously *reevaluating* the $\partial f/\partial x_j$ and changing the direction of the path. Therefore, a better approach is to keep moving in a *fixed* direction from the current trial solution, not stopping until $f(\mathbf{x})$ stops increasing. This stopping point would be the next trial solution, so the gradient then would be recalculated to determine the new direction in which to move. With this approach, each iteration involves changing the current trial solution $\mathbf{x}'$ as follows:

Reset $\mathbf{x}' = \mathbf{x}' + t^* \nabla f(\mathbf{x}')$,

where t^* is the positive value of t that *maximizes* $f(\mathbf{x}' + t \nabla f(\mathbf{x}'))$; that is,

$$f(\mathbf{x}' + t^* \nabla f(\mathbf{x}')) = \max_{t \geq 0} f(\mathbf{x}' + t \nabla f(\mathbf{x}')).$$

[Note that $f(\mathbf{x}' + t \nabla f(\mathbf{x}'))$ is simply $f(\mathbf{x})$ where

$$x_j = x_j' + t \left(\frac{\partial f}{\partial x_j} \right)_{\mathbf{x}=\mathbf{x}'}, \qquad \text{for } j = 1, 2, \ldots, n,$$

and that these expressions for the x_j involve only constants and t, so $f(\mathbf{x})$ becomes a function of just the single variable t.] The iterations of this gradient search procedure continue until $\nabla f(\mathbf{x}) = 0$ within a small tolerance ϵ, that is, until

$$\left| \frac{\partial f}{\partial x_j} \right| \leq \epsilon \qquad \text{for } j = 1, 2, \ldots, n. \text{[1]}$$

An analogy may help to clarify this procedure. Suppose that you need to climb to the top of a hill. You are nearsighted, so you cannot see the top of the hill in order to walk directly in that direction. However, when you stand still, you can see the ground around your feet well enough to determine the direction in which the hill is sloping upward most sharply. You are able to walk in a straight line. While walking, you also are able to tell when you stop climbing (zero slope in your direction). Assuming that the hill is *concave*, you now can use the *gradient search procedure* for climbing to the top efficiently. This problem is a *two-variable problem*, where (x_1, x_2) represents the coordinates (ignoring height) of your current location. The function $f(x_1, x_2)$ gives the height of the hill at (x_1, x_2). You start each iteration at your current location (current trial solution) by determining the direction [in the (x_1, x_2) coordinate system] in which the hill is sloping upward most sharply (the direction of the gradient) at this point. You then begin walking in this fixed direction and continue as long as you still are climbing. You eventually stop at a new trial location (solution) when the hill becomes level in your direction, at which point you prepare to do another iteration in another direction. You continue these iterations, following a zigzag path up the hill, until you reach a trial location where the slope is essentially zero in all directions. Under the assumption that the hill [$f(x_1, x_2)$] is concave, you must then be essentially at the top of the hill.

The most difficult part of the gradient search procedure usually is to find t^*, the value of t that maximizes f in the direction of the gradient, at each iteration. Because $\mathbf{x}$ and $\nabla f(\mathbf{x})$ have fixed values for the maximization, and because $f(\mathbf{x})$ is concave, this problem should be viewed as maximizing a *concave* function of a *single variable* t. Therefore, it can be solved by the one-dimensional search procedure of Sec. 13.4 (where the initial lower bound on t must be nonnegative because of the $t \geq 0$ constraint). Alternatively, if f is a simple function, it may be possible to obtain an analytical solution by setting the derivative with respect to t equal to zero and solving.

Summary of the Gradient Search Procedure.
Initialization: Select ϵ and any initial trial solution x'. Go first to the stopping rule.
Iteration:

1. Express $f(\mathbf{x}' + t \nabla f(\mathbf{x}'))$ as a function of t by setting

$$x_j = x_j' + t \left(\frac{\partial f}{\partial x_j} \right)_{\mathbf{x}=\mathbf{x}'}, \qquad \text{for } j = 1, 2, \ldots, n,$$

and then substituting these expressions into $f(\mathbf{x})$.

---

[1] This stopping rule generally will provide a solution $\mathbf{x}$ that is close to an optimal solution $\mathbf{x}^*$, with a value of $f(\mathbf{x})$ that is very close to $f(\mathbf{x}^*)$. However, this cannot be guaranteed, since it is possible that the function maintains a very small positive slope ($\leq \epsilon$) over a great distance from $\mathbf{x}$ to $\mathbf{x}^*$.

2. Use the one-dimensional search procedure (or calculus) to find $t = t^*$ that maximizes $f(\mathbf{x}' + t\,\nabla f(\mathbf{x}'))$ over $t \geq 0$.

3. Reset $\mathbf{x}' = \mathbf{x}' + t^*\,\nabla f(\mathbf{x}')$. Then go to the stopping rule.

Stopping rule: Evaluate $\nabla f(\mathbf{x}')$ at $\mathbf{x} = \mathbf{x}'$. Check if

$$\left| \frac{\partial f}{\partial x_j} \right| \leq \epsilon \qquad \text{for all } j = 1, 2, \ldots, n.$$

If so, stop with the current $\mathbf{x}'$ as the desired approximation of an optimal solution $\mathbf{x}^*$. Otherwise, perform another iteration.

Now let us illustrate this procedure.

Example.   Consider the following two-variable problem:

$$\text{Maximize} \qquad f(\mathbf{x}) = 2x_1 x_2 + 2x_2 - x_1^2 - 2x_2^2.$$

Thus,

$$\frac{\partial f}{\partial x_1} = 2x_2 - 2x_1,$$

$$\frac{\partial f}{\partial x_2} = 2x_1 + 2 - 4x_2.$$

We also can verify (see Appendix 2) that $f(\mathbf{x})$ is concave. To begin the gradient search procedure, suppose that $\mathbf{x} = (0, 0)$ is selected as the initial trial solution. Because the respective partial derivatives are 0 and 2 at this point, the gradient is

$$\nabla f(0, 0) = (0, 2).$$

Therefore, to begin the first iteration, set

$$x_1 = 0 + t(0) = 0,$$
$$x_2 = 0 + t(2) = 2t,$$

and then substitute these expressions into $f(\mathbf{x})$ to obtain

$$\begin{aligned} f(\mathbf{x}' + t\,\nabla f(\mathbf{x}')) &= f(0, 2t) \\ &= 2(0)(2t) + 2(2t) - 0^2 - 2(2t)^2 \\ &= 4t - 8t^2. \end{aligned}$$

Because

$$f(0, 2t^*) = \max_{t \geq 0} f(0, 2t) = \max_{t \geq 0} \{4t - 8t^2\}$$

and

$$\frac{d}{dt}(4t - 8t^2) = 4 - 16t = 0,$$

it follows that

$$t^* = \frac{1}{4},$$

so

Reset $\quad \mathbf{x}' = (0, 0) + \dfrac{1}{4}(0, 2) = \left(0, \dfrac{1}{2}\right).$

For this new trial solution, the gradient is

$$\nabla f\left(0, \dfrac{1}{2}\right) = (1, 0).$$

Thus, for the second iteration, set

$$\mathbf{x} = \left(0, \dfrac{1}{2}\right) + t(1, 0) = \left(t, \dfrac{1}{2}\right),$$

so

$$
\begin{aligned}
f(\mathbf{x}' + t\,\nabla f(\mathbf{x}')) &= f\left(0 + t, \dfrac{1}{2} + 0t\right) = f\left(t, \dfrac{1}{2}\right) \\
&= (2t)\left(\dfrac{1}{2}\right) + 2\left(\dfrac{1}{2}\right) - t^2 - 2\left(\dfrac{1}{2}\right)^2 \\
&= t - t^2 + \dfrac{1}{2}.
\end{aligned}
$$

Because

$$f\left(t^*, \dfrac{1}{2}\right) = \max_{t \geq 0} f\left(t, \dfrac{1}{2}\right) = \max_{t \geq 0}\left\{t - t^2 + \dfrac{1}{2}\right\}$$

and

$$\dfrac{d}{dt}\left(t - t^2 + \dfrac{1}{2}\right) = 1 - 2t = 0,$$

then

$$t^* = \dfrac{1}{2},$$

so

Reset $\quad \mathbf{x}' = \left(0, \dfrac{1}{2}\right) + \dfrac{1}{2}(1, 0) = \left(\dfrac{1}{2}, \dfrac{1}{2}\right).$

A nice way of organizing this work is to write out a table such as Table 13.2 which summarizes the preceding two iterations. At each iteration, the second column shows the current trial solution, and the rightmost column shows the eventual new trial solution, which then is carried down into the second column for the next iteration. The fourth column gives the expressions for the x_j in terms of t that need to be substituted into $f(\mathbf{x})$ to give the fifth column.

By continuing in this fashion, the subsequent trial solutions would be $(\frac{1}{2}, \frac{3}{4})$, $(\frac{3}{4}, \frac{3}{4})$, $(\frac{3}{4}, \frac{7}{8})$, $(\frac{7}{8}, \frac{7}{8})$, . . . , as shown in Fig. 13.14. Because these points are converging to $\mathbf{x}^* = (1, 1)$, this solution is the optimal solution, as verified by the fact that

$$\nabla f(1, 1) = (0, 0).$$

TABLE 13.2 Application of the gradient search procedure to the example

Iteration	$\mathbf{x}'$	$\nabla f(\mathbf{x}')$	$\mathbf{x}' + t\,\nabla f(\mathbf{x}')$	$f(\mathbf{x}' + t\,\nabla f(\mathbf{x}'))$	t^*	$\mathbf{x}' + t^*\,\nabla f(\mathbf{x}')$
1	$(0, 0)$	$(0, 2)$	$(0, 2t)$	$4t - 8t^2$	$\dfrac{1}{4}$	$\left(0, \dfrac{1}{2}\right)$
2	$\left(0, \dfrac{1}{2}\right)$	$(1, 0)$	$\left(t, \dfrac{1}{2}\right)$	$t - t^2 + \dfrac{1}{2}$	$\dfrac{1}{2}$	$\left(\dfrac{1}{2}, \dfrac{1}{2}\right)$

However, because this converging sequence of trial solutions never reaches its limit, the procedure actually will stop somewhere (depending on ϵ) slightly below $(1, 1)$ as its final approximation of $\mathbf{x}^*$.

As Fig. 13.14 suggests, the gradient search procedure zigzags to the optimal solution rather than moving in a straight line. Some modifications of the procedure have been developed that *accelerate* movement toward the optimal solution by taking this zigzag behavior into account.

If $f(\mathbf{x})$ were *not* a concave function, the gradient search procedure still would converge to a *local* maximum. The only change in the description of the procedure for this case is that t^* now would correspond to the *first local maximum* of $f(\mathbf{x}' + t\,\nabla f(\mathbf{x}'))$ as t is increased from 0.

If the objective were to *minimize* $f(\mathbf{x})$ instead, one change in the procedure would be to move in the *opposite* direction of the gradient at each iteration. In other words, the rule for obtaining the next point would be

Reset $\mathbf{x}' = \mathbf{x}' - t^*\,\nabla f(\mathbf{x}')$.

The only other change is that t^* now would be the nonnegative value of t that *minimizes* $f(\mathbf{x}' - t\,\nabla f(\mathbf{x}'))$; that is,

$$f(\mathbf{x}' - t^*\,\nabla f(\mathbf{x}')) = \min_{t \geq 0} f(\mathbf{x}' - t\,\nabla f(\mathbf{x}')).$$

FIGURE 13.14
Illustration of the gradient search procedure when $f(x_1, x_2) = 2x_1x_2 + 2x_2 - x_1^2 - 2x_2^2$.

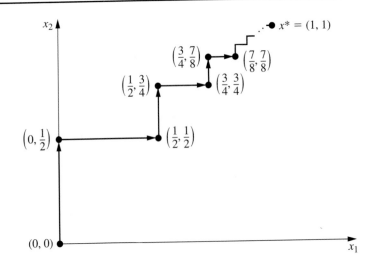

Another example of an application of the gradient search procedure is included in your OR Tutor. The OR Courseware includes both an interactive routine and an automatic routine for applying this algorithm.

13.6 THE KARUSH-KUHN-TUCKER (KKT) CONDITIONS FOR CONSTRAINED OPTIMIZATION

We now focus on the question of how to recognize an *optimal solution* for a nonlinear programming problem (with differentiable functions). What are the necessary and (perhaps) sufficient conditions that such a solution must satisfy?

In the preceding sections we already noted these conditions for *unconstrained optimization,* as summarized in the first two rows of Table 13.3. Early in Sec. 13.3 we also gave these conditions for the slight *extension* of unconstrained optimization where the *only* constraints are nonnegativity constraints. These conditions are shown in the third row of Table 13.3. As indicated in the last row of the table, the conditions for the general case are called the **Karush-Kuhn-Tucker conditions** (or **KKT conditions**), because they were derived independently by Karush[1] and by Kuhn and Tucker.[2] Their basic result is embodied in the following theorem.

Theorem.   Assume that $f(\mathbf{x})$, $g_1(\mathbf{x})$, $g_2(\mathbf{x})$, . . . , $g_m(\mathbf{x})$ are *differentiable* functions satisfying certain regularity conditions.[3] Then

$$\mathbf{x}^* = (x_1^*, x_2^*, \ldots, x_n^*)$$

[1]W. Karush, "Minima of Functions of Several Variables with Inequalities as Side Conditions," M.S. thesis, Department of Mathematics, University of Chicago, 1939.

[2]H. W. Kuhn and A. W. Tucker, "Nonlinear Programming," in Jerzy Neyman (ed.), *Proceedings of the Second Berkeley Symposium,* University of California Press, Berkeley, 1951, pp. 481–492.

[3]Ibid., p. 483.

TABLE 13.3 Necessary and sufficient conditions for optimality

Problem	Necessary Conditions for Optimality	Also Sufficient if:
One-variable unconstrained	$\dfrac{df}{dx} = 0$	$f(x)$ concave
Multivariable unconstrained	$\dfrac{\partial f}{\partial x_j} = 0 \quad (j = 1, 2, \ldots, n)$	$f(\mathbf{x})$ concave
Constrained, nonnegativity constraints only	$\dfrac{\partial f}{\partial x_j} = 0 \quad (j = 1, 2, \ldots, n)$ (or ≤ 0 if $x_j = 0$)	$f(\mathbf{x})$ concave
General constrained problem	Karush-Kuhn-Tucker conditions	$f(\mathbf{x})$ concave and $g_i(\mathbf{x})$ convex $(i = 1, 2, \ldots, m)$

can be an *optimal solution* for the nonlinear programming problem only if there exist m numbers $u_1, u_2, \ldots, u_m$ such that *all* the following *KKT conditions* are satisfied:

$$
\left.
\begin{aligned}
&\textbf{1.}\ \ \frac{\partial f}{\partial x_j} - \sum_{i=1}^{m} u_i \frac{\partial g_i}{\partial x_j} \leq 0 \\[2em]
&\textbf{2.}\ \ x_j^* \left(\frac{\partial f}{\partial x_j} - \sum_{i=1}^{m} u_i \frac{\partial g_i}{\partial x_j} \right) = 0
\end{aligned}
\right\} \quad \text{at } \mathbf{x} = \mathbf{x}^*, \text{ for } j = 1, 2, \ldots, n.
$$

$$
\left.
\begin{aligned}
&\textbf{3.}\ \ g_i(\mathbf{x}^*) - b_i \leq 0 \\
&\textbf{4.}\ \ u_i[g_i(\mathbf{x}^*) - b_i] = 0
\end{aligned}
\right\} \quad \text{for } i = 1, 2, \ldots, m.
$$

$$
\begin{aligned}
&\textbf{5.}\ \ x_j^* \geq 0, && \text{for } j = 1, 2, \ldots, n. \\
&\textbf{6.}\ \ u_i \geq 0, && \text{for } i = 1, 2, \ldots, m.
\end{aligned}
$$

Note that both conditions 2 and 4 require that the product of two quantities be zero. Therefore, each of these conditions really is saying that at least one of the two quantities must be zero. Consequently, condition 4 can be combined with condition 3 to express them in another equivalent form as

$$
(3, 4) \quad g_i(\mathbf{x}^*) - b_i = 0
$$
$$
(\text{or } \leq 0 \quad \text{if } u_i = 0), \quad \text{for } i = 1, 2, \ldots, m.
$$

Similarly, condition 2 can be combined with condition 1 as

$$
(1, 2) \quad \frac{\partial f}{\partial x_j} - \sum_{i=1}^{m} u_i \frac{\partial g_i}{\partial x_j} = 0
$$
$$
(\text{or } \leq 0 \quad \text{if } x_j^* = 0), \quad \text{for } j = 1, 2, \ldots, n.
$$

When $m = 0$ (no functional constraints), this summation drops out and the combined condition $(1, 2)$ reduces to the condition given in the third row of Table 13.3. Thus, for $m > 0$, each term in the summation modifies the $m = 0$ condition to incorporate the effect of the corresponding functional constraint.

In conditions 1, 2, 4, and 6, the u_i correspond to the *dual variables* of linear programming (we expand on this correspondence at the end of the section), and they have a comparable economic interpretation. However, the u_i actually arose in the mathematical derivation as *Lagrange multipliers* (discussed in Appendix 3). Conditions 3 and 5 do nothing more than ensure the feasibility of the solution. The other conditions eliminate most of the feasible solutions as possible candidates for an optimal solution.

However, note that satisfying these conditions does not guarantee that the solution is optimal. As summarized in the rightmost column of Table 13.3, certain additional *convexity* assumptions are needed to obtain this guarantee. These assumptions are spelled out in the following extension of the theorem.

Corollary. Assume that $f(\mathbf{x})$ is a *concave* function and that $g_1(\mathbf{x}), g_2(\mathbf{x}), \ldots, g_m(\mathbf{x})$ are *convex* functions (i.e., this problem is a convex programming problem), where all these functions satisfy the regularity conditions. Then $\mathbf{x}^* = (x_1^*, x_2^*, \ldots, x_n^*)$ is an *optimal solution* if and only if all the conditions of the theorem are satisfied.

Example. To illustrate the formulation and application of the *KKT conditions,* we consider the following two-variable nonlinear programming problem:

Maximize $\quad f(\mathbf{x}) = \ln(x_1 + 1) + x_2,$

subject to

$$2x_1 + x_2 \le 3$$

and

$$x_1 \ge 0, \qquad x_2 \ge 0,$$

where ln denotes the natural logarithm. Thus, $m = 1$ (one functional constraint) and $g_1(\mathbf{x}) = 2x_1 + x_2$, so $g_1(\mathbf{x})$ is convex. Furthermore, it can be easily verified (see Appendix 2) that $f(\mathbf{x})$ is concave. Hence, the corollary applies, so any solution that satisfies the KKT conditions will definitely be an optimal solution. Applying the formulas given in the theorem yields the following KKT conditions for this example:

1($j = 1$). $\quad \dfrac{1}{x_1 + 1} - 2u_1 \le 0.$

2($j = 1$). $\quad x_1 \left(\dfrac{1}{x_1 + 1} - 2u_1 \right) = 0.$

1($j = 2$). $\quad 1 - u_1 \le 0.$
2($j = 2$). $\quad x_2(1 - u_1) = 0.$
3. $\quad 2x_1 + x_2 - 3 \le 0.$
4. $\quad u_1(2x_1 + x_2 - 3) = 0.$
5. $\quad x_1 \ge 0, x_2 \ge 0.$
6. $\quad u_1 \ge 0.$

The steps in solving the KKT conditions for this particular example are outlined below.

1. $u_1 \ge 1$, from condition 1($j = 2$).
  $x_1 \ge 0$, from condition 5.
2. Therefore, $\dfrac{1}{x_1 + 1} - 2u_1 < 0.$
3. Therefore, $x_1 = 0$, from condition 2($j = 1$).
4. $u_1 \ne 0$ implies that $2x_1 + x_2 - 3 = 0$, from condition 4.
5. Steps 3 and 4 imply that $x_2 = 3$.
6. $x_2 \ne 0$ implies that $u_1 = 1$, from condition 2($j = 2$).
7. No conditions are violated by $x_1 = 0$, $x_2 = 3$, $u_1 = 1$.

Therefore, there exists a number $u_1 = 1$ such that $x_1 = 0$, $x_2 = 3$, and $u_1 = 1$ satisfy all the conditions. Consequently, $\mathbf{x}^* = (0, 3)$ is an optimal solution for this problem.

The particular progression of steps needed to solve the KKT conditions will differ from one problem to the next. When the logic is not apparent, it is sometimes helpful to consider separately the different cases where each x_j and u_i are specified to be either equal to or greater than 0 and then trying each case until one leads to a solution. In the example, there are eight such cases corresponding to the eight combinations of $x_1 = 0$ versus $x_1 > 0$, $x_2 = 0$ versus $x_2 > 0$, and $u_1 = 0$ versus $u_1 > 0$. Each case leads to a simpler statement and analysis of the conditions. To illustrate, consider first the case shown next, where $x_1 = 0$, $x_2 = 0$, and $u_1 = 0$.

KKT Conditions for the Case $x_1 = 0$, $x_2 = 0$, $u_1 = 0$

1($j = 1$). $\dfrac{1}{0 + 1} \leq 0.$ Contradiction.

1($j = 2$). $1 - 0 \leq 0.$ Contradiction.

3. $0 + 0 \leq 3.$

(All the other conditions are redundant.)

As listed below, the other three cases where $u_1 = 0$ also give immediate contradictions in a similar way, so no solution is available.

Case $x_1 = 0$, $x_2 > 0$, $u_1 = 0$ contradicts conditions 1($j = 1$), 1($j = 2$), and 2($j = 2$).
Case $x_1 > 0$, $x_2 = 0$, $u_1 = 0$ contradicts conditions 1($j = 1$), 2($j = 1$), and 1($j = 2$).
Case $x_1 > 0$, $x_2 > 0$, $u_1 = 0$ contradicts conditions 1($j = 1$), 2($j = 1$), 1($j = 2$), and 2($j = 2$).

The case $x_1 > 0$, $x_2 > 0$, $u_1 > 0$ enables one to delete these nonzero multipliers from conditions 2($j = 1$), 2($j = 2$), and 4, which then enables deletion of conditions 1($j = 1$), 1($j = 2$), and 3 as redundant, as summarized next.

KKT Conditions for the Case $x_1 > 0$, $x_2 > 0$, $u_1 > 0$

1($j = 1$). $\dfrac{1}{x_1 + 1} - 2u_1 = 0.$

2($j = 2$). $1 - u_1 = 0.$

4. $2x_1 + x_2 - 3 = 0.$

(All the other conditions are redundant.)

Therefore, $u_1 = 1$, so $x_1 = -\frac{1}{2}$, which contradicts $x_1 > 0$.

Now suppose that the case $x_1 = 0$, $x_2 > 0$, $u_1 > 0$ is tried next.

KKT Conditions for the Case $x_1 = 0$, $x_2 > 0$, $u_1 > 0$

1($j = 1$). $\dfrac{1}{0 + 1} - 2u_1 = 0.$

2($j = 2$). $1 - u_1 = 0.$

4. $0 + x_2 - 3 = 0.$

(All the other conditions are redundant.)

Therefore, $x_1 = 0$, $x_2 = 3$, $u_1 = 1$. Having found a solution, we know that no additional cases need be considered.

For problems more complicated than this example, it may be difficult, if not essentially impossible, to derive an optimal solution *directly* from the KKT conditions. Nevertheless, these conditions still provide valuable clues as to the identity of an optimal solution, and they also permit us to check whether a proposed solution may be optimal.

There also are many valuable *indirect* applications of the KKT conditions. One of these applications arises in the *duality theory* that has been developed for nonlinear programming to parallel the duality theory for linear programming presented in Chap. 6. In particular, for any given constrained maximization problem (call it the *primal problem*), the KKT conditions can be used to define a closely associated dual problem that is a constrained minimization problem. The variables in the dual problem[1] consist of both the Lagrange multipliers u_i ($i = 1, 2, \ldots, m$) and the primal variables x_j ($j = 1, 2, \ldots, n$). In the special case where the primal problem is a linear programming problem, the x_j variables drop out of the dual problem and it becomes the familiar dual problem of linear programming (where the u_i variables here correspond to the y_i variables in Chap. 6). When the primal problem is a convex programming problem, it is possible to establish relationships between the primal problem and the dual problem that are similar to those for linear programming. For example, the *strong duality property* of Sec. 6.1, which states that the optimal objective function values of the two problems are equal, also holds here. Furthermore, the values of the u_i variables in an optimal solution for the dual problem can again be interpreted as *shadow prices* (see Secs. 4.7 and 6.2); i.e., they give the rate at which the optimal objective function value for the primal problem could be increased by (slightly) increasing the right-hand side of the corresponding constraint. Because duality theory for nonlinear programming is a relatively advanced topic, the interested reader is referred elsewhere for further information.[2]

You will see another indirect application of the KKT conditions in the next section.

13.7 <u>QUADRATIC PROGRAMMING</u>

As indicated in Sec. 13.3, the quadratic programming problem differs from the linear programming problem only in that the objective function also includes x_j^2 and $x_i x_j$ ($i \neq j$) terms. Thus, if we use matrix notation like that introduced at the beginning of Sec. 5.2, the problem is to find $\mathbf{x}$ so as to

$$\text{Maximize} \quad f(\mathbf{x}) = \mathbf{c}\mathbf{x} - \frac{1}{2}\mathbf{x}^T\mathbf{Q}\mathbf{x},$$

subject to

$$\mathbf{A}\mathbf{x} \leq \mathbf{b} \quad \text{and} \quad \mathbf{x} \geq \mathbf{0},$$

where $\mathbf{c}$ is a row vector, $\mathbf{x}$ and $\mathbf{b}$ are column vectors, $\mathbf{Q}$ and $\mathbf{A}$ are matrices, and the superscript T denotes the transpose (see Appendix 4). The q_{ij} (elements of Q) are given constants such that $q_{ij} = q_{ji}$ (which is the reason for the factor of $\frac{1}{2}$ in the objective function). By performing the indicated vector and matrix multiplications, the objective function then is expressed in terms of these q_{ij}, the c_j (elements of $\mathbf{c}$), and the variables as follows:

$$f(\mathbf{x}) = \mathbf{c}\mathbf{x} - \frac{1}{2}\mathbf{x}^T\mathbf{Q}\mathbf{x} = \sum_{j=1}^{n} c_j x_j - \frac{1}{2}\sum_{i=1}^{n}\sum_{j=1}^{n} q_{ij}x_i x_j.$$

For each term where $i = j$ in this double summation, $x_i x_j = x_j^2$, so $-\frac{1}{2}q_{jj}$ is the coefficient of x_j^2. When $i \neq j$, then $-\frac{1}{2}(q_{ij}x_i x_j + q_{ji}x_j x_i) = -q_{ij}x_i x_j$, so $-q_{ij}$ is the total coefficient for the product of x_i and x_j.

---

[1]For details on this formulation, see O. T. Mangasarian, *Nonlinear Programming,* McGraw-Hill, New York, 1969, chap 8. For a unified survey of various approaches to duality in nonlinear programming, see A. M. Geoffrion, "Duality in Nonlinear Programming: A Simplified Applications-Oriented Development," *SIAM Review,* **13:** 1–37, 1971.
[2]Ibid.

To illustrate this notation, consider the following example of a quadratic programming problem.

$$\text{Maximize} \quad f(x_1, x_2) = 15x_1 + 30x_2 + 4x_1x_2 - 2x_1^2 - 4x_2^2,$$

subject to

$$x_1 + 2x_2 \leq 30$$

and

$$x_1 \geq 0, \qquad x_2 \geq 0.$$

In this case,

$$\mathbf{c} = [15 \quad 30], \qquad \mathbf{x} = \begin{bmatrix} x_1 \\ x_2 \end{bmatrix}, \qquad \mathbf{Q} = \begin{bmatrix} 4 & -4 \\ -4 & 8 \end{bmatrix},$$

$$\mathbf{A} = [1 \quad 2], \qquad \mathbf{b} = [30].$$

Note that

$$\mathbf{x}^T \mathbf{Q} \mathbf{x} = [x_1 \quad x_2] \begin{bmatrix} 4 & -4 \\ -4 & 8 \end{bmatrix} \begin{bmatrix} x_1 \\ x_2 \end{bmatrix}$$

$$= [(4x_1 - 4x_2) \quad (-4x_1 + 8x_2)] \begin{bmatrix} x_1 \\ x_2 \end{bmatrix}$$

$$= 4x_1^2 - 4x_2x_1 - 4x_1x_2 + 8x_2^2$$

$$= q_{11}x_1^2 + q_{21}x_2x_1 + q_{12}x_1x_2 + q_{22}x_2^2.$$

Multiplying through by $-\frac{1}{2}$ gives

$$-\frac{1}{2}\mathbf{x}^T\mathbf{Q}\mathbf{x} = -2x_1^2 + 4x_1x_2 - 4x_2^2,$$

which is the nonlinear portion of the objective function for this example. Since $q_{11} = 4$ and $q_{22} = 8$, the example illustrates that $-\frac{1}{2}q_{jj}$ is the coefficient of x_j^2 in the objective function. The fact that $q_{12} = q_{21} = -4$ illustrates that both $-q_{ij}$ and $-q_{ji}$ give the total coefficient of the product of x_i and x_j.

Several algorithms have been developed for the special case of the quadratic programming problem where the objective function is a *concave* function. (A way to verify that the objective function is concave is to verify the equivalent condition that

$$\mathbf{x}^T\mathbf{Q}\mathbf{x} \geq \mathbf{0}$$

for all $\mathbf{x}$, that is, $\mathbf{Q}$ is a *positive semidefinite* matrix.) We shall describe one[1] of these algorithms, the *modified simplex method*, that has been quite popular because it requires using only the simplex method with a slight modification. The key to this approach is to construct the KKT conditions from the preceding section and then to reexpress these conditions in a convenient form that closely resembles linear programming. Therefore, before describing the algorithm, we shall develop this convenient form.

---

[1]P. Wolfe, "The Simplex Method for Quadratic Programming," *Econometrics*, **27**: 382–398, 1959. This paper develops both a short form and a long form of the algorithm. We present a version of the *short form*, which assumes further that *either* $\mathbf{c} = \mathbf{0}$ *or* the objective function is *strictly* concave.

The KKT Conditions for Quadratic Programming

For concreteness, let us first consider the above example. Starting with the form given in the preceding section, its KKT conditions are the following.

1($j = 1$). $15 + 4x_2 - 4x_1 - u_1 \leq 0$.
2($j = 1$). $x_1(15 + 4x_2 - 4x_1 - u_1) = 0$.
1($j = 2$). $30 + 4x_1 - 8x_2 - 2u_1 \leq 0$.
2($j = 2$). $x_2(30 + 4x_1 - 8x_2 - 2u_1) = 0$.
3. $\quad\quad x_1 + 2x_2 - 30 \leq 0$.
4. $\quad\quad u_1(x_1 + 2x_2 - 30) = 0$.
5. $\quad\quad x_1 \geq 0, \quad\quad x_2 \geq 0$.
6. $\quad\quad u_1 \geq 0$.

To begin reexpressing these conditions in a more convenient form, we move the constants in conditions 1($j = 1$), 1($j = 2$), and 3 to the right-hand side and then introduce nonnegative *slack variables* (denoted by y_1, y_2, and v_1, respectively) to convert these inequalities to equations.

1($j = 1$). $-4x_1 + 4x_2 - u_1 + y_1 \quad\quad\quad\quad = -15$
1($j = 2$). $\quad 4x_1 - 8x_2 - 2u_1 \quad + y_2 \quad\quad = -30$
3. $\quad\quad\quad x_1 + 2x_2 \quad\quad\quad\quad + v_1 = \quad 30$

Note that condition 2($j = 1$) can now be reexpressed as simply requiring that either $x_1 = 0$ or $y_1 = 0$; that is,

2($j = 1$). $x_1 y_1 = 0$.

In just the same way, conditions 2($j = 2$) and 4 can be replaced by

2($j = 2$). $x_2 y_2 = 0$,
4. $\quad\quad u_1 v_1 = 0$.

For each of these three pairs—(x_1, y_1), (x_2, y_2), (u_1, v_1)—the two variables are called **complementary variables,** because only one of the two variables can be nonzero. These new forms of conditions 2($j = 1$), 2($j = 2$), and 4 can be combined into one constraint,

$$x_1 y_1 + x_2 y_2 + u_1 v_1 = 0,$$

called the **complementarity constraint.**

After multiplying through the equations for conditions 1($j = 1$) and 1($j = 2$) by -1 to obtain nonnegative right-hand sides, we now have the desired convenient form for the entire set of conditions shown here:

$$
\begin{aligned}
4x_1 - 4x_2 + u_1 - y_1 \quad\quad\quad\quad &= 15 \\
-4x_1 + 8x_2 + 2u_1 \quad - y_2 \quad\quad &= 30 \\
x_1 + 2x_2 \quad\quad\quad\quad + v_1 &= 30 \\
x_1 \geq 0, \quad x_2 \geq 0, \quad u_1 \geq 0, \quad y_1 \geq 0, \quad y_2 \geq 0, \quad v_1 &\geq 0 \\
x_1 y_1 + x_2 y_2 + u_1 v_1 &= 0
\end{aligned}
$$

This form is particularly convenient because, except for the complementarity constraint, these conditions are *linear programming constraints*.

For *any* quadratic programming problem, its KKT conditions can be reduced to this same convenient form containing just linear programming constraints plus one complementarity constraint. In matrix notation again, this general form is

$$Qx + A^T u - y = c^T,$$
$$Ax + v = b,$$
$$x \geq 0, \quad u \geq 0, \quad y \geq 0, \quad v \geq 0,$$
$$x^T y + u^T v = 0,$$

where the elements of the column vector **u** are the u_i of the preceding section and the elements of the column vectors **y** and **v** are slack variables.

Because the objective function of the original problem is assumed to be concave and because the constraint functions are linear and therefore convex, the corollary to the theorem of Sec. 13.6 applies. Thus, **x** is *optimal* if and only if there exist values of **y**, **u**, and **v** such that all four vectors together satisfy all these conditions. The original problem is thereby reduced to the equivalent problem of finding a *feasible solution* to these *constraints*.

It is of interest to note that this equivalent problem is one example of the *linear complementarity problem* introduced in Sec. 13.3 (see Prob. 13.3-6), and that a key constraint for the linear complementarity problem is its *complementarity constraint*.

The Modified Simplex Method

The *modified simplex method* exploits the key fact that, with the exception of the complementarity constraint, the KKT conditions in the convenient form obtained above are nothing more than linear programming constraints. Furthermore, the complementarity constraint simply implies that it is not permissible for *both* complementary variables of any pair to be (nondegenerate) basic variables (the only variables > 0) when (nondegenerate) BF solutions are considered. Therefore, the problem reduces to finding an initial BF solution to any linear programming problem that has these constraints, subject to this additional restriction on the identity of the basic variables. (This initial BF solution may be the only feasible solution in this case.)

As we discussed in Sec. 4.6, finding such an initial BF solution is relatively straightforward. In the simple case where $c^T \leq 0$ (unlikely) and $b \geq 0$, the initial basic variables are the elements of **y** and **v** (multiply through the first set of equations by -1), so that the desired solution is $x = 0$, $u = 0$, $y = -c^T$, $v = b$. Otherwise, you need to revise the problem by introducing an *artificial variable* into each of the equations where $c_j > 0$ (add the variable on the left) or $b_i < 0$ (subtract the variable on the left and then multiply through by -1) in order to use these artificial variables (call them z_1, z_2, and so on) as initial basic variables for the revised problem. (Note that this choice of initial basic variables satisfies the complementarity constraint, because as nonbasic variables $x = 0$ and $u = 0$ automatically.)

Next, use phase 1 of the *two-phase method* (see Sec. 4.6) to find a BF solution for the real problem; i.e., apply the simplex method (with one modification) to the following linear programming problem

Minimize $Z = \sum_j z_j,$

subject to the linear programming constraints obtained from the KKT conditions, but with these artificial variables included.

The one modification in the simplex method is the following change in the procedure for selecting an entering basic variable.

> **Restricted-Entry Rule:** When you are choosing an entering basic variable, exclude from consideration any nonbasic variable whose *complementary variable* already is a basic variable; the choice should be made from the other nonbasic variables according to the usual criterion for the simplex method.

This rule keeps the complementarity constraint satisfied throughout the course of the algorithm. When an optimal solution

$$\mathbf{x}^*, \mathbf{u}^*, \mathbf{y}^*, \mathbf{v}^*, z_1 = 0, \ldots, z_n = 0$$

is obtained for the phase 1 problem, $\mathbf{x}^*$ is the desired optimal solution for the original quadratic programming problem. Phase 2 of the two-phase method is not needed.

Example.   We shall now illustrate this approach on the example given at the beginning of the section. As can be verified from the results in Appendix 2 (see Prob. 13.7-1a), $f(x_1, x_2)$ is *strictly concave;* i.e.,

$$\mathbf{Q} = \begin{bmatrix} 4 & -4 \\ -4 & 8 \end{bmatrix}$$

is positive definite, so the algorithm can be applied.

The starting point for solving this example is its KKT conditions in the convenient form obtained earlier in the section. After the needed artificial variables are introduced, the linear programming problem to be addressed explicitly by the modified simplex method then is

Minimize $Z = z_1 + z_2,$

subject to

$$\begin{aligned}
4x_1 - 4x_2 + u_1 - y_1 \quad\quad\quad\;\; + z_1 \quad\quad\; &= 15 \\
-4x_1 + 8x_2 + 2u_1 \quad\quad\; - y_2 \quad\quad\quad\; + z_2 &= 30 \\
x_1 + 2x_2 \quad\quad\quad\quad\quad\quad\quad + v_1 \quad\quad\quad\quad &= 30
\end{aligned}$$

and

$$x_1 \geq 0, \quad x_2 \geq 0, \quad u_1 \geq 0, \quad y_1 \geq 0, \quad y_2 \geq 0, \quad v_1 \geq 0,$$
$$z_1 \geq 0, \quad z_2 \geq 0.$$

The additional complementarity constraint

$$x_1 y_1 + x_2 y_2 + u_1 v_1 = 0,$$

is not included explicitly, because the algorithm automatically enforces this constraint because of the *restricted-entry rule.* In particular, for each of the three pairs of complementary variables—(x_1, y_1), (x_2, y_2), (u_1, v_1)—whenever one of the two variables already is a basic variable, the other variable is *excluded* as a candidate for the entering basic variable. Remember that the only *nonzero* variables are basic variables. Because the initial set of basic variables for the linear programming problem—z_1, z_2, v_1—gives an initial BF solution that satisfies the complementarity constraint, there is no way that this constraint can be violated by any subsequent BF solution.

Table 13.4 shows the results of applying the modified simplex method to this problem. The first simplex tableau exhibits the initial system of equations *after* converting from minimizing Z to maximizing $-Z$ *and* algebraically eliminating the initial basic variables from Eq. (0), just as was done for the radiation therapy example in Sec. 4.6. The three iterations proceed just as for the regular simplex method, *except* for eliminating certain candidates for the entering basic variable because of the restricted-entry rule. In the first tableau, u_1 is eliminated as a candidate because its complementary variable (v_1) already is a basic variable (but x_2 would have been chosen anyway because $-4 < -3$). In the second tableau, both u_1 and y_2 are eliminated as candidates (because v_1 and x_2 are basic variables), so x_1 automatically is chosen as the only candidate with a negative coeffi-

TABLE 13.4 Application of the modified simplex method to the quadratic programming example

Iteration	Basic Variable	Eq.	Z	x_1	x_2	u_1	y_1	y_2	v_1	z_1	z_2	Right Side
0	Z	(0)	-1	0	-4	-3	1	1	0	0	0	-45
	z_1	(1)	0	4	-4	1	-1	0	0	1	0	15
	z_2	(2)	0	-4	8	2	0	-1	0	0	1	30
	v_1	(3)	0	1	2	0	0	0	1	0	0	30
1	Z	(0)	-1	-2	0	-2	1	$\frac{1}{2}$	0	0	$\frac{1}{2}$	-30
	z_1	(1)	0	2	0	2	-1	$-\frac{1}{2}$	0	1	$\frac{1}{2}$	30
	x_2	(2)	0	$-\frac{1}{2}$	1	$\frac{1}{4}$	0	$-\frac{1}{8}$	0	0	$\frac{1}{8}$	$3\frac{3}{4}$
	v_1	(3)	0	2	0	$-\frac{1}{2}$	0	$\frac{1}{4}$	1	0	$-\frac{1}{4}$	$22\frac{1}{2}$
2	Z	(0)	-1	0	0	$-\frac{5}{2}$	1	$\frac{3}{4}$	1	0	$\frac{1}{4}$	$-7\frac{1}{2}$
	z_1	(1)	0	0	0	$\frac{5}{2}$	-1	$-\frac{3}{4}$	-1	1	$\frac{3}{4}$	$7\frac{1}{2}$
	x_2	(2)	0	0	1	$\frac{1}{8}$	0	$-\frac{1}{16}$	$\frac{1}{4}$	0	$\frac{1}{16}$	$9\frac{3}{8}$
	x_1	(3)	0	1	0	$-\frac{1}{4}$	0	$\frac{1}{8}$	$\frac{1}{2}$	0	$-\frac{1}{8}$	$11\frac{1}{4}$
3	Z	(0)	-1	0	0	0	0	0	0	1	1	0
	u_1	(1)	0	0	0	1	$-\frac{2}{5}$	$-\frac{3}{10}$	$-\frac{2}{5}$	$\frac{2}{5}$	$\frac{3}{10}$	3
	x_2	(2)	0	0	1	0	$\frac{1}{20}$	$\frac{1}{40}$	$\frac{3}{10}$	$\frac{1}{20}$	$\frac{1}{40}$	9
	x_1	(3)	0	1	0	0	$-\frac{1}{10}$	$\frac{1}{20}$	$\frac{2}{5}$	$\frac{1}{10}$	$-\frac{1}{20}$	12

cient in row 0 (whereas the *regular* simplex method would have permitted choosing *either* x_1 or u_1 because they are tied for having the largest negative coefficient). In the third tableau, both y_1 and y_2 are eliminated (because x_1 and x_2 are basic variables). However, u_1 is *not* eliminated because v_1 no longer is a basic variable, so u_1 is chosen as the entering basic variable in the usual way.

The resulting optimal solution for this phase 1 problem is $x_1 = 12$, $x_2 = 9$, $u_1 = 3$, with the rest of the variables zero. (Problem 13.7-1c asks you to verify that this solution is optimal by showing that $x_1 = 12$, $x_2 = 9$, $u_1 = 3$ satisfy the KKT conditions for the original problem when they are written in the form given in Sec. 13.6.) Therefore, the optimal solution for the quadratic programming problem (which includes only the x_1 and x_2 variables) is $(x_1, x_2) = (12, 9)$.

Some Software Options

Your OR Tutor includes an interactive routine for the modified simplex method to help you learn this algorithm efficiently. In addition, Excel, LINGO, LINDO, and MPL/CPLEX all can solve quadratic programming problems.

The procedure for using Excel is almost the same as with linear programming. The one crucial difference is that the equation entered for the cell that contains the value of the objective function now needs to be a quadratic equation. To illustrate, consider again the example introduced at the beginning of the section, which has the objective function

$$f(x_1, x_2) = 15x_1 + 30x_2 + 4x_1x_2 - 2x_1^2 - 4x_2^2.$$

Suppose that the values of x_1 and x_2 are in cells B4 and C4 of the Excel spreadsheet, and that the value of the objective function is in cell F4. Then the equation for cell F4 needs to be

    F4 = 15*B4 + 30*C4 + 4*B4*C4 − 2*(B4^2) − 4*(C4^2),

where the symbol ^2 indicates an exponent of 2. Before solving the model, you should click on the Option button and make sure that the *Assume Linear Model* option is *not* selected (since this is not a *linear* programming model).

When using MPL/CPLEX, you should select the Quadratic Models option from the MPL Language option dialogue box and the Barrier method from the CPLEX Simplex options dialogue box. Otherwise, the procedure is the same as with linear programming except that the expression for the objective function now is a quadratic function. Thus, for the example, the objective function would be expressed as

    15x1 + 30x2 + 4x1*x2 − 2(x1^2) − 4(x2^2).

Nothing more needs to be done when calling CPLEX, since it will automatically recognize the model as being a quadratic programming problem.

This objective function would be expressed in this same way for a LINGO model. LINGO then will automatically call its nonlinear solver to solve the model. When using LINDO instead, the procedure is somewhat more involved, since it requires converting the model to an equivalent linear form in terms of the KKT conditions. The LINDO file for this chapter illustrates how this is done for the example.

In fact, the Excel, MPL/CPLEX, and LINGO/LINDO files for this chapter in your OR Courseware all demonstrate their procedures by showing the details for how these software packages set up and solve this example.

Some of these software packages also can be applied to more complicated kinds of nonlinear programming problems than quadratic programming. Although CPLEX cannot, the professional version of MPL does support some other solvers that can. The student version of MPL on the CD-ROM includes one such solver called CONOPT (a product of ARKI Consulting) that should be used instead of CPLEX after selecting Nonlinear Models for the Default Model Type entry in the MPL Language option dialogue box. Both Excel and LINGO include versatile nonlinear solvers. However, be aware that these solvers are not guaranteed to find an optimal solution for complicated problems, especially non-convex programming problems.

13.8   SEPARABLE PROGRAMMING

The preceding section showed how one class of nonlinear programming problems can be solved by an extension of the simplex method. We now consider another class, called *separable programming,* that actually can be solved by the simplex method itself, because any such problem can be approximated as closely as desired by a linear programming problem with a larger number of variables.

As indicated in Sec. 13.3, in separable programming it is assumed that the objective function $f(\mathbf{x})$ is concave, that each of the constraint functions $g_i(\mathbf{x})$ is convex, and that all these functions are separable functions (functions where each term involves just a single variable). However, to simplify the discussion, we focus here on the special case where the convex and separable $g_i(\mathbf{x})$ are, in fact, *linear functions,* just as for linear programming. Thus, only the objective function requires special treatment.

Under the preceding assumptions, the objective function can be expressed as a sum of concave functions of individual variables

$$f(\mathbf{x}) = \sum_{j=1}^{n} f_j(x_j),$$

so that each $f_j(x_j)$ has a shape[1] such as the one shown in Fig. 13.15 (either case) over the feasible range of values of x_j. Because $f(\mathbf{x})$ represents the measure of performance (say, profit) for all the activities together, $f_j(x_j)$ represents the *contribution to profit* from activity j when it is conducted at level x_j. The condition of $f(\mathbf{x})$ being separable simply implies additivity (see Sec. 3.3); i.e., there are no interactions between the activities (no cross-product terms) that affect total profit beyond their independent contributions. The assumption that each $f_j(x_j)$ is concave says that the *marginal profitability* (slope of the profit curve) either stays the same or decreases (*never* increases) as x_j is increased.

Concave profit curves occur quite frequently. For example, it may be possible to sell a limited amount of some product at a certain price, then a further amount at a lower price, and perhaps finally a further amount at a still lower price. Similarly, it may be necessary to purchase raw materials from increasingly expensive sources. In another common situ-

---

[1]$f(\mathbf{x})$ is concave if and only if *every* $f_j(x_j)$ is concave.

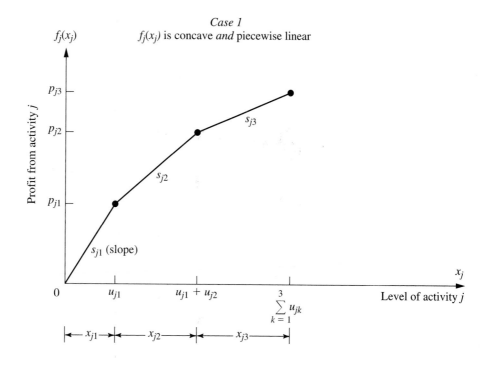

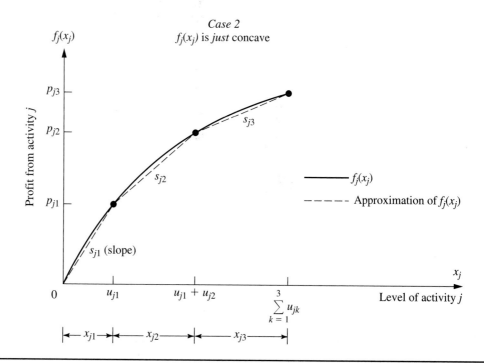

FIGURE 13.15
Shape of profit curves for
separable programming.

ation, a more expensive production process must be used (e.g., overtime rather than regular-time work) to increase the production rate beyond a certain point.

These kinds of situations can lead to either type of profit curve shown in Fig. 13.15. In case 1, the slope decreases only at certain *breakpoints,* so that $f_j(x_j)$ is a *piecewise linear function* (a sequence of connected line segments). For case 2, the slope may decrease continuously as x_j increases, so that $f_j(x_j)$ is a general concave function. Any such function can be approximated as closely as desired by a piecewise linear function, and this kind of approximation is used as needed for separable programming problems. (Figure 13.15 shows an approximating function that consists of just three line segments, but the approximation can be made even better just by introducing additional breakpoints.) This approximation is very convenient because a piecewise linear function of a single variable can be rewritten as a *linear function* of several variables, with one special restriction on the values of these variables, as described next.

Reformulation as a Linear Programming Problem

The key to rewriting a piecewise linear function as a linear function is to use a separate variable for each line segment. To illustrate, consider the piecewise linear function $f_j(x_j)$ shown in Fig. 13.15, case 1 (or the approximating piecewise linear function for case 2), which has three line segments over the feasible range of values of x_j. Introduce the three new variables x_{j1}, x_{j2}, and x_{j3} and set

$$x_j = x_{j1} + x_{j2} + x_{j3},$$

where

$$0 \leq x_{j1} \leq u_{j1}, \qquad 0 \leq x_{j2} \leq u_{j2}, \qquad 0 \leq x_{j3} \leq u_{j3}.$$

Then use the slopes s_{j1}, s_{j2}, and s_{j3} to rewrite $f_j(x_j)$ as

$$f_j(x_j) = s_{j1}x_{j1} + s_{j2}x_{j2} + s_{j3}x_{j3},$$

with the *special restriction* that

$$\begin{aligned} x_{j2} &= 0 \qquad \text{whenever} \qquad x_{j1} < u_{j1}, \\ x_{j3} &= 0 \qquad \text{whenever} \qquad x_{j2} < u_{j2}. \end{aligned}$$

To see why this special restriction is required, suppose that $x_j = 1$, where $u_{jk} > 1$ ($k = 1$, 2, 3), so that $f_j(1) = s_{j1}$. Note that

$$x_{j1} + x_{j2} + x_{j3} = 1$$

permits

$$\begin{aligned} x_{j1} &= 1, & x_{j2} &= 0, & x_{j3} &= 0 & \Rightarrow \quad f_j(1) &= s_{j1}, \\ x_{j1} &= 0, & x_{j2} &= 1, & x_{j3} &= 0 & \Rightarrow \quad f_j(1) &= s_{j2}, \\ x_{j1} &= 0, & x_{j2} &= 0, & x_{j3} &= 1 & \Rightarrow \quad f_j(1) &= s_{j3}, \end{aligned}$$

and so on, where

$$s_{j1} > s_{j2} > s_{j3}.$$

However, the special restriction permits only the first possibility, which is the only one giving the correct value for $f_j(1)$.

Unfortunately, the special restriction does not fit into the required format for linear programming constraints, so *some* piecewise linear functions cannot be rewritten in a linear programming format. However, *our* $f_j(x_j)$ are assumed to be concave, so $s_{j1} > s_{j2} > \cdots$, so that an algorithm for maximizing $f(\mathbf{x})$ *automatically* gives the highest priority to using x_{j1} when (in effect) increasing x_j from zero, the next highest priority to using x_{j2}, and so on, without even including the special restriction explicitly in the model. This observation leads to the following key property.

Key Property of Separable Programming. When $f(\mathbf{x})$ and the $g_i(\mathbf{x})$ satisfy the assumptions of separable programming, and when the resulting piecewise linear functions are rewritten as linear functions, deleting the *special restriction* gives a *linear programming model* whose optimal solution automatically satisfies the special restriction.

We shall elaborate further on the logic behind this key property later in this section in the context of a specific example. (Also see Prob. 13.8-8a.)

To write down the complete linear programming model in the above notation, let n_j be the number of line segments in $f_j(x_j)$ (or the piecewise linear function approximating it), so that

$$x_j = \sum_{k=1}^{n_j} x_{jk}$$

would be substituted throughout the original model and

$$f_j(x_j) = \sum_{k=1}^{n_j} s_{jk} x_{jk}$$

would be substituted[1] into the objective function for $j = 1, 2, \ldots, n$. The resulting model is

$$\text{Maximize} \qquad Z = \sum_{j=1}^{n} \left(\sum_{k=1}^{n_j} s_{jk} x_{jk} \right),$$

subject to

$$\sum_{j=1}^{n} a_{ij} \left(\sum_{k=1}^{n_j} x_{jk} \right) \le b_i, \qquad \text{for } i = 1, 2, \ldots, m$$

$$x_{jk} \le u_{jk}, \qquad \text{for } k = 1, 2, \ldots, n_j; j = 1, 2, \ldots, n$$

and

$$x_{jk} \ge 0, \qquad \text{for} \qquad k = 1, 2, \ldots, n_j; j = 1, 2, \ldots, n.$$

(The $\sum_{k=1}^{n_j} x_{jk} \ge 0$ constraints are deleted because they are ensured by the $x_{jk} \ge 0$ constraints.) If some original variable x_j has no upper bound, then $u_{jn_j} = \infty$, so the constraint involving this quantity will be deleted.

---

[1] If one or more of the $f_j(x_j)$ already are *linear* functions $f_j(x_j) = c_j x_j$, then $n_j = 1$ so neither of these substitutions will be made for j.

An efficient way of solving this model[1] is to use the streamlined version of the simplex method for dealing with upper bound constraints (described in Sec. 7.3). After obtaining an optimal solution for this model, you then would calculate

$$x_j = \sum_{k=1}^{n_j} x_{jk},$$

for $j = 1, 2, \ldots, n$ in order to identify an optimal solution for the original separable programming program (or its piecewise linear approximation).

Example.   The Wyndor Glass Co. (see Sec. 3.1) has received a special order for handcrafted goods to be made in Plants 1 and 2 throughout the next 4 months. Filling this order will require borrowing certain employees from the work crews for the regular products, so the remaining workers will need to work overtime to utilize the full production capacity of the plant's machinery and equipment for these regular products. In particular, for the two new regular products discussed in Sec. 3.1, overtime will be required to utilize the last 25 percent of the production capacity available in Plant 1 for product 1 and for the last 50 percent of the capacity available in Plant 2 for product 2. The additional cost of using overtime work will reduce the profit for each unit involved from $3 to $2 for product 1 and from $5 to $1 for product 2, giving the *profit curves* of Fig. 13.16, both of which fit the form for case 1 of Fig. 13.15.

---

[1]For a specialized algorithm for solving this model very efficiently, see R. Fourer, "A Specialized Algorithm for Piecewise-Linear Programming III: Computational Analysis and Applications," *Mathematical Programming,* **53:** 213–235, 1992. Also see A. M. Geoffrion, "Objective Function Approximations in Mathematical Programming," *Mathematical Programming,* **13:** 23–37, 1977.

FIGURE 13.16
Profit data during the next 4 months for the Wyndor Glass Co.

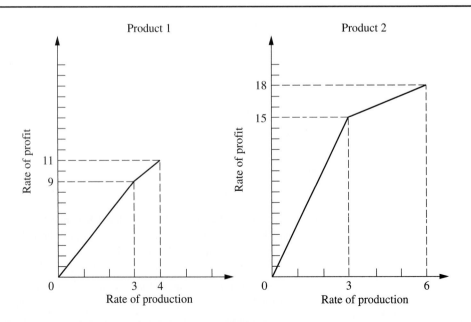

Management has decided to go ahead and use overtime work rather than hire additional workers during this temporary situation. However, it does insist that the work crew for each product be fully utilized on regular time before any overtime is used. Furthermore, it feels that the current production rates ($x_1 = 2$ for product 1 and $x_2 = 6$ for product 2) should be changed temporarily if this would improve overall profitability. Therefore, it has instructed the OR team to review products 1 and 2 again to determine the most profitable product mix during the next 4 months.

Formulation.   To refresh your memory, the linear programming model for the original Wyndor Glass Co. problem in Sec. 3.1 is

$$\text{Maximize} \quad Z = 3x_1 + 5x_2,$$

subject to

$$
\begin{aligned}
x_1 &\leq 4 \\
2x_2 &\leq 12 \\
3x_1 + 2x_2 &\leq 18
\end{aligned}
$$

and

$$x_1 \geq 0, \qquad x_2 \geq 0.$$

We now need to modify this model to fit the new situation described above. For this purpose, let the production rate for product 1 be $x_1 = x_{1R} + x_{1O}$, where x_{1R} is the production rate achieved on regular time and x_{1O} is the incremental production rate from using overtime. Define $x_2 = x_{2R} + x_{2O}$ in the same way for product 2. Thus, in the notation of the general linear programming model for separable programming given just before this example, $n = 2$, $n_1 = 2$, and $n_2 = 2$. Plugging the data given in Fig. 13.16 (including maximum rates of production on regular time and on overtime) into this general model gives the specific model for this application. In particular, the new linear programming problem is to determine the values of x_{1R}, x_{1O}, x_{2R}, and x_{2O} so as to

$$\text{Maximize} \quad Z = 3x_{1R} + 2x_{1O} + 5x_{2R} + x_{2O},$$

subject to

$$
\begin{aligned}
x_{1R} + x_{1O} &\leq 4 \\
2(x_{2R} + x_{2O}) &\leq 12 \\
3(x_{1R} + x_{1O}) + 2(x_{2R} + x_{2O}) &\leq 18 \\
x_{1R} \leq 3, \qquad x_{1O} \leq 1, \qquad x_{2R} \leq 3, \qquad x_{2O} &\leq 3
\end{aligned}
$$

and

$$x_{1R} \geq 0, \qquad x_{1O} \geq 0, \qquad x_{2R} \geq 0, \qquad x_{2O} \geq 0.$$

(Note that the upper bound constraints in the next-to-last row of the model make the first two functional constraints *redundant,* so these two functional constraints can be deleted.)

However, there is one important factor that is not taken into account explicitly in this formulation. Specifically, there is nothing in the model that requires all available regular time for a product to be fully utilized before any overtime is used for that product. In other words, it may be feasible to have $x_{1O} > 0$ even when $x_{1R} < 3$ and to have $x_{2O} > 0$

even when $x_{2R} < 3$. Such solutions would not, however, be acceptable to management. (Prohibiting such solutions is the *special restriction* discussed earlier in this section.)

Now we come to the *key property of separable programming*. Even though the model does not take this factor into account explicitly, the model does take it into account implicitly! Despite the model's having excess "feasible" solutions that actually are unacceptable, any *optimal* solution for the model is *guaranteed* to be a legitimate one that does not replace any available regular-time work with overtime work. (The reasoning here is analogous to that for the Big *M* method discussed in Sec. 4.6, where excess feasible but *nonoptimal* solutions also were allowed in the model as a matter of convenience.) Therefore, the simplex method can be safely applied to this model to find the most profitable acceptable product mix. The reasons are twofold. First, the two decision variables for each product *always* appear together as a *sum*, $x_{1R} + x_{1O}$ or $x_{2R} + x_{2O}$, in *each* functional constraint other than the upper bound constraints on individual variables. Therefore, it *always* is possible to convert an unacceptable feasible solution to an acceptable one having the same total production rates, $x_1 = x_{1R} + x_{1O}$ and $x_2 = x_{2R} + x_{2O}$, merely by replacing overtime production by regular-time production as much as possible. Second, overtime production is less profitable than regular-time production (i.e., the slope of each profit curve in Fig. 13.16 is a monotonic *decreasing* function of the rate of production), so converting an unacceptable feasible solution to an acceptable one in this way *must* increase the total rate of profit *Z*. Consequently, any feasible solution that uses overtime production for a product when regular-time production is still available *cannot* be optimal with respect to the model.

For example, consider the unacceptable feasible solution $x_{1R} = 1$, $x_{1O} = 1$, $x_{2R} = 1$, $x_{2O} = 3$, which yields a total rate of profit $Z = 13$. The acceptable way of achieving the same total production rates $x_1 = 2$ and $x_2 = 4$ is $x_{1R} = 2$, $x_{1O} = 0$, $x_{2R} = 3$, $x_{2O} = 1$. This latter solution is still feasible, but it also increases Z by $(3 - 2)(1) + (5 - 1)(2) = 9$ to a total rate of profit $Z = 22$.

Similarly, the optimal solution for this model turns out to be $x_{1R} = 3$, $x_{1O} = 1$, $x_{2R} = 3$, $x_{2O} = 0$, which is an acceptable feasible solution.

Extensions

Thus far we have focused on the special case of separable programming where the only nonlinear function is the objective function $f(\mathbf{x})$. Now consider briefly the general case where the constraint functions $g_i(\mathbf{x})$ need not be linear but are convex and separable, so that each $g_i(\mathbf{x})$ can be expressed as a sum of functions of individual variables

$$g_i(\mathbf{x}) = \sum_{j=1}^{n} g_{ij}(x_j),$$

where each $g_{ij}(x_j)$ is a *convex* function. Once again, each of these new functions may be approximated as closely as desired by a *piecewise linear* function (if it is not already in that form). The one new restriction is that for each variable x_j ($j = 1, 2, \ldots, n$), all the piecewise linear approximations of the functions of this variable $[f_j(x_j), g_{1j}(x_j), \ldots, g_{mj}(x_j)]$ must have the *same* breakpoints so that the same new variables $(x_{j1}, x_{j2}, \ldots, x_{jn_j})$ can be used for all these piecewise linear functions. This formulation leads to a linear programming model just like the one given for the special case except that for each i and j, the x_{jk} variables now have different coefficients in constraint i [where these coefficients are the corresponding slopes of the piecewise linear function approximating $g_{ij}(x_j)$]. Because the $g_{ij}(x_j)$ are required to be convex, essentially the same logic as before implies that the key property of separable programming still must hold. (See Prob. 13.8-8*b*.)

One drawback of approximating functions by piecewise linear functions as described in this section is that achieving a close approximation requires a large number of line segments (variables), whereas such a fine grid for the breakpoints is needed only in the immediate neighborhood of an optimal solution. Therefore, more sophisticated approaches that use a succession of *two-segment* piecewise linear functions have been developed[1] to obtain *successively closer approximations* within this immediate neighborhood. This kind of approach tends to be both faster and more accurate in closely approximating an optimal solution.

13.9 CONVEX PROGRAMMING

We already have discussed some special cases of convex programming in Secs. 13.4 and 13.5 (unconstrained problems), 13.7 (quadratic objective function with linear constraints), and 13.8 (separable functions). You also have seen some theory for the general case (necessary and sufficient conditions for optimality) in Sec. 13.6. In this section, we briefly discuss some types of approaches used to solve the general convex programming problem [where the objective function $f(\mathbf{x})$ to be maximized is concave and the $g_i(\mathbf{x})$ constraint functions are convex], and then we present one example of an algorithm for convex programming.

There is no single standard algorithm that always is used to solve convex programming problems. Many different algorithms have been developed, each with its own advantages and disadvantages, and research continues to be active in this area. Roughly speaking, most of these algorithms fall into one of the following three categories.

The first category is **gradient algorithms,** where the gradient search procedure of Sec. 13.5 is modified in some way to keep the search path from penetrating any constraint boundary. For example, one popular gradient method is the *generalized reduced gradient* (GRG) method.

The second category—**sequential unconstrained algorithms**—includes *penalty function* and *barrier function* methods. These algorithms convert the original constrained optimization problem to a sequence of *unconstrained optimization* problems whose optimal solutions converge to the optimal solution for the original problem. Each of these unconstrained optimization problems can be solved by the gradient search procedure of Sec. 13.5. This conversion is accomplished by incorporating the constraints into a penalty function (or barrier function) that is subtracted from the objective function in order to impose large penalties for violating constraints (or even being near constraint boundaries). You will see one example of this category of algorithms in the next section.

The third category—**sequential-approximation algorithms**—includes *linear approximation* and *quadratic approximation* methods. These algorithms replace the nonlinear objective function by a succession of linear or quadratic approximations. For linearly

---

[1]R. R. Meyer, "Two-Segment Separable Programming," *Management Science*, **25**: 385–395, 1979.

constrained optimization problems, these approximations allow repeated application of linear or quadratic programming algorithms. This work is accompanied by other analysis that yields a sequence of solutions that converges to an optimal solution for the original problem. Although these algorithms are particularly suitable for linearly constrained optimization problems, some also can be extended to problems with nonlinear constraint functions by the use of appropriate linear approximations.

As one example of a *sequential-approximation* algorithm, we present here the **Frank-Wolfe algorithm**[1] for the case of *linearly constrained* convex programming (so the constraints are $\mathbf{A}\mathbf{x} \leq \mathbf{b}$ and $\mathbf{x} \geq \mathbf{0}$ in matrix form). This procedure is particularly straightforward; it combines *linear* approximations of the objective function (enabling us to use the simplex method) with the one-dimensional search procedure of Sec. 13.4.

A Sequential Linear Approximation Algorithm (Frank-Wolfe)

Given a feasible trial solution $\mathbf{x}'$, the linear approximation used for the objective function $f(\mathbf{x})$ is the first-order Taylor series expansion of $f(\mathbf{x})$ around $\mathbf{x} = \mathbf{x}'$, namely,

$$f(\mathbf{x}') \approx f(\mathbf{x}') + \sum_{j=1}^{n} \frac{\partial f(\mathbf{x}')}{\partial x_j}(x_j - x_j') = f(\mathbf{x}') + \nabla f(\mathbf{x}')(\mathbf{x} - \mathbf{x}'),$$

where these partial derivatives are evaluated at $\mathbf{x} = \mathbf{x}'$. Because $f(\mathbf{x}')$ and $\nabla f(\mathbf{x}')\mathbf{x}'$ have fixed values, they can be dropped to give an equivalent linear objective function

$$g(\mathbf{x}) = \nabla f(\mathbf{x}')\mathbf{x} = \sum_{j=1}^{n} c_j x_j, \qquad \text{where } c_j = \frac{\partial f(\mathbf{x})}{\partial x_j} \qquad \text{at } \mathbf{x} = \mathbf{x}'.$$

The simplex method (or the graphical procedure if $n = 2$) then is applied to the resulting linear programming problem [maximize $g(\mathbf{x})$ subject to the original constraints, $\mathbf{A}\mathbf{x} \leq \mathbf{b}$ and $\mathbf{x} \geq \mathbf{0}$] to find *its* optimal solution x_{LP}. Note that the linear objective function necessarily increases steadily as one moves along the line segment from $\mathbf{x}'$ to $\mathbf{x}_{\text{LP}}$ (which is on the boundary of the feasible region). However, the linear approximation may not be a particularly close one for $\mathbf{x}$ far from $\mathbf{x}'$, so the *nonlinear* objective function may not continue to increase all the way from $\mathbf{x}'$ to $\mathbf{x}_{\text{LP}}$. Therefore, rather than just accepting $\mathbf{x}_{\text{LP}}$ as the next trial solution, we choose the point that maximizes the nonlinear objective function along this line segment. This point may be found by conducting the *one-dimensional search procedure* of Sec. 13.4, where the one variable for purposes of this search is the fraction t of the total distance from $\mathbf{x}'$ to $\mathbf{x}_{\text{LP}}$. This point then becomes the new trial solution for initiating the next iteration of the algorithm, as just described. The sequence of trial solutions generated by repeated iterations converges to an optimal solution for the original problem, so the algorithm stops as soon as the successive trial solutions are close enough together to have essentially reached this optimal solution.

---

[1] M. Frank and P. Wolfe, "An Algorithm for Quadratic Programming," *Naval Research Logistics Quarterly,* **3**: 95–110, 1956. Although originally designed for quadratic programming, this algorithm is easily adapted to the case of a general concave objective function considered here.

Summary of the Frank-Wolfe Algorithm.

Initialization: Find a feasible initial trial solution $\mathbf{x}^{(0)}$, for example, by applying linear programming procedures to find an initial BF solution. Set $k = 1$.

Iteration:

1. For $j = 1, 2, \ldots, n$, evaluate

$$\frac{\partial f(\mathbf{x})}{\partial x_j} \quad \text{at } \mathbf{x} = \mathbf{x}^{(k-1)}$$

and set c_j equal to this value.

2. Find an optimal solution $\mathbf{x}_{\text{LP}}^{(k)}$ for the following linear programming problem.

$$\text{Maximize} \qquad g(\mathbf{x}) = \sum_{j=1}^{n} c_j x_j,$$

subject to

$$\mathbf{Ax} \leq \mathbf{b} \qquad \text{and} \qquad \mathbf{x} \geq \mathbf{0}.$$

3. For the variable t ($0 \leq t \leq 1$), set

$$h(t) = f(\mathbf{x}) \qquad \text{for } \mathbf{x} = \mathbf{x}^{(k-1)} + t(\mathbf{x}_{\text{LP}}^{(k)} - \mathbf{x}^{(k-1)}),$$

so that $h(t)$ gives the value of $f(\mathbf{x})$ on the line segment between $\mathbf{x}^{(k-1)}$ (where $t = 0$) and $\mathbf{x}_{\text{LP}}^{(k)}$ (where $t = 1$). Use some procedure such as the one-dimensional search procedure (see Sec. 13.4) to maximize $h(t)$ over $0 \leq t \leq 1$, and set $\mathbf{x}^{(k)}$ equal to the corresponding $\mathbf{x}$. Go to the stopping rule.

Stopping rule: If $\mathbf{x}^{(k-1)}$ and $\mathbf{x}^{(k)}$ are sufficiently close, stop and use $\mathbf{x}^{(k)}$ (or some extrapolation of $\mathbf{x}^{(0)}, \mathbf{x}^{(1)}, \ldots, \mathbf{x}^{(k-1)}, \mathbf{x}^{(k)}$) as your estimate of an optimal solution. Otherwise, reset $k = k + 1$ and perform another iteration.

Now let us illustrate this procedure.

Example. Consider the following linearly constrained convex programming problem:

$$\text{Maximize} \qquad f(\mathbf{x}) = 5x_1 - x_1^2 + 8x_2 - 2x_2^2,$$

subject to

$$3x_1 + 2x_2 \leq 6$$

and

$$x_1 \geq 0, \qquad x_2 \geq 0.$$

Note that

$$\frac{\partial f}{\partial x_1} = 5 - 2x_1, \qquad \frac{\partial f}{\partial x_2} = 8 - 4x_2,$$

so that the *unconstrained* maximum $\mathbf{x} = (\frac{5}{2}, 2)$ violates the functional constraint. Thus, more work is needed to find the *constrained* maximum.

Because $\mathbf{x} = (0, 0)$ is clearly feasible (and corresponds to the initial BF solution for the linear programming constraints), let us choose it as the initial trial solution $\mathbf{x}^{(0)}$ for the Frank-Wolfe algorithm. Plugging $x_1 = 0$ and $x_2 = 0$ into the expressions for the partial derivatives gives $c_1 = 5$ and $c_2 = 8$, so that $g(\mathbf{x}) = 5x_1 + 8x_2$ is the initial linear approximation of the objective function. Graphically, solving this linear programming problem (see Fig. 13.17*a*) yields $\mathbf{x}_{LP}^{(1)} = (0, 3)$. For step 3 of the first iteration, the points on the line segment between $(0, 0)$ and $(0, 3)$ shown in Fig. 13.17*a* are expressed by

$$(x_1, x_2) = (0, 0) + t[(0, 3) - (0, 0)] \qquad \text{for } 0 \le t \le 1$$
$$= (0, 3t)$$

as shown in the sixth column of Table 13.5. This expression then gives

$$h(t) = f(0, 3t) = 8(3t) - 2(3t)^2$$
$$= 24t - 18t^2,$$

so that the value $t = t^*$ that maximizes $h(t)$ over $0 \le t \le 1$ may be obtained in this case by setting

$$\frac{dh(t)}{dt} = 24 - 36t = 0,$$

so that $t^* = \frac{2}{3}$. This result yields the next trial solution

$$\mathbf{x}^{(1)} = (0, 0) + \frac{2}{3}[(0, 3) - (0, 0)]$$

$$= (0, 2),$$

which completes the first iteration.

FIGURE 13.17
Illustration of the Frank-Wolfe algorithm.

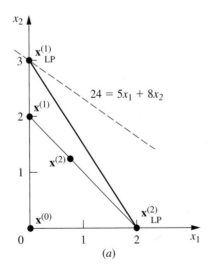

(*a*)

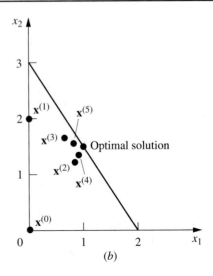

(*b*)

TABLE 13.5 Application of the Frank-Wolfe algorithm to the example

k	$x^{(k-1)}$	c_1	c_2	$x_{LP}^{(k)}$	x for $h(t)$	$h(t)$	t^*	$x^{(k)}$
1	(0, 0)	5	8	(0, 3)	(0, 3t)	$24t - 18t^2$	$\frac{2}{3}$	(0, 2)
2	(0, 2)	5	0	(2, 0)	(2t, 2 − 2t)	$8 + 10t - 12t^2$	$\frac{5}{12}$	$\left(\frac{5}{6}, \frac{7}{6}\right)$

To sketch the calculations that lead to the results in the second row of Table 13.5, note that $x^{(1)} = (0, 2)$ gives

$$c_1 = 5 - 2(0) = 5,$$
$$c_2 = 8 - 4(2) = 0.$$

For the objective function $g(x) = 5x_1$, graphically solving the problem over the feasible region in Fig. 13.17a gives $x_{LP}^{(2)} = (2, 0)$. Therefore, the expression for the line segment between $x^{(1)}$ and $x_{LP}^{(2)}$ (see Fig. 13.17a) is

$$x = (0, 2) + t[(2, 0) - (0, 2)]$$
$$= (2t, 2 - 2t),$$

so that

$$h(t) = f(2t, 2 - 2t)$$
$$= 5(2t) - (2t)^2 + 8(2 - 2t) - 2(2 - 2t)^2$$
$$= 8 + 10t - 12t^2.$$

Setting

$$\frac{dh(t)}{dt} = 10 - 24t = 0$$

yields $t^* = \frac{5}{12}$. Hence,

$$x^{(2)} = (0, 2) + \frac{5}{12}[(2, 0) - (0, 2)]$$

$$= \left(\frac{5}{6}, \frac{7}{6}\right).$$

You can see in Fig. 13.17b how the trial solutions keep alternating between two trajectories that appear to intersect at approximately the point $x = (1, \frac{3}{2})$. This point is, in fact, the optimal solution, as can be verified by applying the KKT conditions from Sec. 13.6.

This example illustrates a common feature of the Frank-Wolfe algorithm, namely, that the trial solutions alternate between two (or more) trajectories. When they alternate in this way, we can extrapolate the trajectories to their approximate point of intersection to estimate an optimal solution. This estimate tends to be better than using the last trial solution generated. The reason is that the trial solutions tend to converge rather slowly toward an optimal solution, so the last trial solution may still be quite far from optimal.

In conclusion, we emphasize that the Frank-Wolfe algorithm is just one example of sequential-approximation algorithms. Many of these algorithms use *quadratic* instead of *linear* approximations at each iteration because quadratic approximations provide a considerably closer fit to the original problem and thus enable the sequence of solutions to converge considerably more rapidly toward an optimal solution than was the case in Fig. 13.17*b*. For this reason, even though sequential linear approximation methods such as the Frank-Wolfe algorithm are relatively straightforward to use, *sequential quadratic approximation methods*[1] now are generally preferred in actual applications. Popular among these are the *quasi-Newton* (or *variable metric*) methods, which compute a quadratic approximation to the curvature of a nonlinear function without explicitly calculating second (partial) derivatives. (For linearly constrained optimization problems, this nonlinear function is just the objective function; whereas with nonlinear constraints, it is the Lagrangian function described in Appendix 3.) Some quasi-Newton algorithms do not even explicitly form and solve an approximating quadratic programming problem at each iteration, but instead incorporate some of the basic ingredients of *gradient algorithms*.

For further information about convex programming algorithms, see Selected References 4 and 6.

Some Software Options

Another example illustrating the application of the Frank-Wolfe algorithm is provided in your OR Tutor. The OR Courseware also includes an interactive routine for this algorithm.

As indicated at the end of Sec. 13.7, both Excel and LINGO can solve convex programming problems, but LINDO and CPLEX cannot except for the special case of quadratic programming (which includes the example in this section). Details for this example are given in the Excel and LINGO/LINDO files for this chapter in your OR Courseware. The professional version of MPL supports a large number of solvers, including some that can handle convex programming. One of these, called CONOPT, is included with the student version of MPL that is on the CD-ROM. The convex programming examples that are formulated in this chapter's MPL file have been solved with this solver after selecting Nonlinear Models for the Default Model Type entry in the MPL Language option dialogue box.

13.10 NONCONVEX PROGRAMMING

The assumptions of convex programming are very convenient ones, because they ensure that any *local maximum* also is a *global maximum*. Unfortunately, the nonlinear programming problems that arise in practice frequently only come fairly close to satisfying these assumptions, but they have some relatively minor disparities. What kind of approach can be used to deal with such *nonconvex programming* problems?

A common approach is to apply an algorithmic *search procedure* that will stop when it finds a *local maximum* and then to restart it a number of times from a variety of initial trial solutions in order to find as many distinct local maxima as possible. The best of these

---

[1]For a survey of these methods, see M. J. D. Powell, "Variable Metric Methods for Constrained Optimization," in A. Bachem, M. Grotschel, and B. Korte (eds.), *Mathematical Programming: The State of the Art,* Springer-Verlag, Berlin, 1983, pp. 288–311.

local maxima is then chosen for implementation. Normally, the search procedure is one that has been designed to find a global maximum when all the assumptions of convex programming hold, but it also can operate to find a local maximum when they do not.

One such search procedure that has been widely used since its development in the 1960s is the *sequential unconstrained minimization technique* (or *SUMT* for short).[1] There actually are two main versions of SUMT, one of which is an *exterior-point* algorithm that deals with *infeasible* solutions while using a *penalty function* to force convergence to the feasible region. We shall describe the other version, which is an *interior-point* algorithm that deals directly with *feasible* solutions while using a *barrier function* to force staying inside the feasible region. Although SUMT was originally presented as a minimization technique, we shall convert it to a maximization technique in order to be consistent with the rest of the chapter. Therefore, we continue to assume that the problem is in the form given at the beginning of the chapter and that all the functions are differentiable.

Sequential Unconstrained Minimization Technique (SUMT)

As the name implies, SUMT replaces the original problem by a *sequence* of *unconstrained* optimization problems whose solutions *converge* to a solution (local maximum) of the original problem. This approach is very attractive because unconstrained optimization problems are much easier to solve (see the gradient search procedure in Sec. 13.5) than those with constraints. Each of the unconstrained problems in this sequence involves choosing a (successively smaller) strictly positive value of a scalar r and then solving for $\mathbf{x}$ so as to

Maximize $\quad P(\mathbf{x}; r) = f(\mathbf{x}) - rB(\mathbf{x}).$

Here $B(\mathbf{x})$ is a **barrier function** that has the following properties (for $\mathbf{x}$ that are feasible for the original problem):

1. $B(\mathbf{x})$ is *small* when $\mathbf{x}$ is *far* from the boundary of the feasible region.
2. $B(\mathbf{x})$ is *large* when $\mathbf{x}$ is *close* to the boundary of the feasible region.
3. $B(\mathbf{x}) \to \infty$ as the distance from the (nearest) boundary of the feasible region $\to 0$.

Thus, by starting the search procedure with a *feasible* initial trial solution and then attempting to increase $P(\mathbf{x}; r)$, $B(\mathbf{x})$ provides a *barrier* that prevents the search from ever crossing (or even reaching) the boundary of the feasible region for the original problem.

The most common choice of $B(\mathbf{x})$ is

$$B(\mathbf{x}) = \sum_{i=1}^{m} \frac{1}{b_i - g_i(\mathbf{x})} + \sum_{j=1}^{n} \frac{1}{x_j}.$$

For feasible values of $\mathbf{x}$, note that the denominator of each term is proportional to the distance of $\mathbf{x}$ from the constraint boundary for the corresponding functional or nonnegativity constraint. Consequently, *each term is a boundary repulsion term* that has all the preceding three properties with respect to this particular constraint boundary. Another attractive feature of this $B(\mathbf{x})$ is that when all the assumptions of *convex programming* are satisfied, $P(\mathbf{x}; r)$ is a *concave* function.

---

[1]See Selected Reference 3.

Because $B(\mathbf{x})$ keeps the search away from the boundary of the feasible region, you probably are asking the very legitimate question: What happens if the desired solution lies there? This concern is the reason that SUMT involves solving a *sequence* of these unconstrained optimization problems for successively smaller values of r approaching zero (where the final trial solution from each one becomes the initial trial solution for the next). For example, each new r might be obtained from the preceding one by multiplying by a constant θ $(0 < \theta < 1)$, where a typical value is $\theta = 0.01$. As r approaches 0, $P(\mathbf{x}; r)$ approaches $f(\mathbf{x})$, so the corresponding local maximum of $P(\mathbf{x}; r)$ converges to a local maximum of the original problem. Therefore, it is necessary to solve only enough unconstrained optimization problems to permit extrapolating their solutions to this limiting solution.

How many are enough to permit this extrapolation? When the original problem satisfies the assumptions of convex programming, useful information is available to guide us in this decision. In particular, if $\bar{x}$ is a global maximizer of $P(\mathbf{x}; r)$, then

$$f(\bar{\mathbf{x}}) \leq f(\mathbf{x}^*) \leq f(\bar{\mathbf{x}}) + rB(\bar{\mathbf{x}}),$$

where $\mathbf{x}^*$ is the (unknown) *optimal* solution for the original problem. Thus, $rB(\bar{\mathbf{x}})$ is the *maximum error* (in the value of the objective function) that can result by using $\bar{\mathbf{x}}$ to approximate $\mathbf{x}^*$, and extrapolating beyond $\bar{\mathbf{x}}$ to increase $f(\mathbf{x})$ further decreases this error. If an *error tolerance* is established in advance, then you can stop as soon as $rB(\bar{\mathbf{x}})$ is less than this quantity.

Unfortunately, no such guarantee for the maximum error can be given for nonconvex programming problems. However, $rB(\bar{\mathbf{x}})$ still is *likely* to exceed the actual error when $\bar{\mathbf{x}}$ and $\mathbf{x}^*$ now are corresponding *local maxima* of $P(\mathbf{x}; r)$ and the original problem, respectively.

Summary of SUMT.

Initialization: Identify a *feasible* initial trial solution $\mathbf{x}^{(0)}$ that is not on the boundary of the feasible region. Set $k = 1$ and choose appropriate strictly positive values for the initial r and for $\theta < 1$ (say, $r = 1$ and $\theta = 0.01$).[1]

Iteration: Starting from $\mathbf{x}^{(k-1)}$, apply the gradient search procedure described in Sec. 13.5 (or some similar method) to find a local maximum $\mathbf{x}^{(k)}$ of

$$P(\mathbf{x}; r) = f(\mathbf{x}) - r \left[\sum_{i=1}^{m} \frac{1}{b_i - g_i(\mathbf{x})} + \sum_{j=1}^{n} \frac{1}{x_j} \right].$$

Stopping rule: If the change from $\mathbf{x}^{(k-1)}$ to $\mathbf{x}^{(k)}$ is negligible, stop and use $\mathbf{x}^{(k)}$ (or an extrapolation of $\mathbf{x}^{(0)}, \mathbf{x}^{(1)}, \ldots, \mathbf{x}^{(k-1)}, \mathbf{x}^{(k)}$) as your estimate of a *local maximum* of the original problem. Otherwise, reset $k = k + 1$ and $r = \theta r$ and perform another iteration.

When the assumptions of convex programming are not satisfied, this algorithm should be repeated a number of times by starting from a variety of feasible initial trial solutions. The best of the *local maxima* thereby obtained for the original problem should be used as the best available approximation of a *global maximum.*

---

[1] A reasonable criterion for choosing the initial r is one that makes $rB(\mathbf{x})$ about the same order of magnitude as $f(\mathbf{x})$ for feasible solutions $\mathbf{x}$ that are not particularly close to the boundary.

Finally, note that SUMT also can be extended to accommodate *equality* constraints $g_i(\mathbf{x}) = b_i$. One standard way is as follows. For each equality constraint,

$$\frac{-[b_i - g_i(\mathbf{x})]^2}{\sqrt{r}} \qquad \text{replaces} \qquad \frac{-r}{b_i - g_i(\mathbf{x})}$$

in the expression for $P(\mathbf{x}; r)$ given under "Summary of SUMT," and then the same procedure is used. The numerator $-[b_i - g_i(\mathbf{x})]^2$ imposes a large penalty for deviating substantially from satisfying the equality constraint, and then the denominator tremendously increases this penalty as r is decreased to a tiny amount, thereby forcing the sequence of trial solutions to converge toward a point that satisfies the constraint.

SUMT has been widely used because of its simplicity and versatility. However, numerical analysts have found that it is relatively prone to *numerical instability*, so considerable caution is advised. For further information on this issue as well as similar analyses for alternative algorithms, see Selected Reference 4.

Example. To illustrate SUMT, consider the following two-variable problem:

Maximize $\quad f(\mathbf{x}) = x_1 x_2,$

subject to

$$x_1^2 + x_2 \le 3$$

and

$$x_1 \ge 0, \qquad x_2 \ge 0.$$

Even though $g_1(\mathbf{x}) = x_1^2 + x_2$ is convex (because each term is convex), this problem is a *nonconvex* programming problem because $f(\mathbf{x}) = x_1 x_2$ is *not* concave (see Appendix 2).

For the initialization, $(x_1, x_2) = (1, 1)$ is one obvious feasible solution that is not on the boundary of the feasible region, so we can set $\mathbf{x}^{(0)} = (1, 1)$. Reasonable choices for r and θ are $r = 1$ and $\theta = 0.01$.

For each iteration,

$$P(\mathbf{x}; r) = x_1 x_2 - r \left(\frac{1}{3 - x_1^2 - x_2} + \frac{1}{x_1} + \frac{1}{x_2} \right).$$

With $r = 1$, applying the gradient search procedure starting from $(1, 1)$ to maximize this expression eventually leads to $\mathbf{x}^{(1)} = (0.90, 1.36)$. Resetting $r = 0.01$ and restarting the gradient search procedure from $(0.90, 1.36)$ then lead to $\mathbf{x}^{(2)} = (0.983, 1.933)$. One more iteration with $r = 0.01(0.01) = 0.0001$ leads from $\mathbf{x}^{(2)}$ to $\mathbf{x}^{(3)} = (0.998, 1.994)$. This sequence of points, summarized in Table 13.6, quite clearly is converging to $(1, 2)$. Applying the KKT conditions to this solution verifies that it does indeed satisfy the necessary condition for optimality. Graphical analysis demonstrates that $(x_1, x_2) = (1, 2)$ is, in fact, a global maximum (see Prob. 13.10-4*b*).

For this problem, there are no local maxima other than $(x_1, x_2) = (1, 2)$, so reapplying SUMT from various feasible initial trial solutions always leads to this same solution.[1]

---

[1] The technical reason is that $f(\mathbf{x})$ is a (strictly) *quasiconcave* function that shares the property of concave functions that a local maximum always is a global maximum. For further information, see M. Avriel, W. E. Diewert, S. Schaible, and I. Zang, *Generalized Concavity,* Plenum, New York, 1985.

TABLE 13.6 Illustration of SUMT

k	r	$x_1^{(k)}$	$x_2^{(k)}$
0		1	1
1	1	0.90	1.36
2	10^{-2}	0.983	1.933
3	10^{-4}	0.998	1.994
		↓	↓
		1	2

Your OR Tutor includes another example illustrating the application of SUMT. The OR Courseware includes an automatic routine for executing SUMT.

13.11 CONCLUSIONS

Practical optimization problems frequently involve *nonlinear* behavior that must be taken into account. It is sometimes possible to *reformulate* these nonlinearities to fit into a linear programming format, as can be done for *separable programming* problems. However, it is frequently necessary to use a *nonlinear programming* formulation.

In contrast to the case of the simplex method for linear programming, there is no efficient all-purpose algorithm that can be used to solve all nonlinear programming problems. In fact, some of these problems cannot be solved in a very satisfactory manner by any method. However, considerable progress has been made for some important classes of problems, including *quadratic programming, convex programming,* and certain special types of *nonconvex programming.* A variety of algorithms that frequently perform well are available for these cases. Some of these algorithms incorporate highly efficient procedures for *unconstrained optimization* for a portion of each iteration, and some use a succession of linear or quadratic approximations to the original problem.

There has been a strong emphasis in recent years on developing high-quality, reliable *software packages* for general use in applying the best of these algorithms. (See Selected Reference 7 for a comprehensive survey of the available software packages for nonlinear programming.) For example, several powerful software packages such as MINOS have been developed in the Systems Optimization Laboratory at Stanford University. These packages are widely used elsewhere for solving many of the types of problems discussed in this chapter (as well as linear programming problems). The steady improvements being made in both algorithmic techniques and software now are bringing some rather large problems into the range of computational feasibility.

Research in nonlinear programming remains very active.

SELECTED REFERENCES

1. Bazaraa, M. S., H. D. Sherali, and C. M. Shetty: *Nonlinear Programming: Theory and Algorithms,* 2d ed., Wiley, New York, 1993.
2. Bertsekas, D. P.: *Nonlinear Programming,* Athena Scientific, Belmont, MA, 1995.

3. Fiacco, A. V., and G. P. McCormick: *Nonlinear Programming: Sequential Unconstrained Minimization Techniques,* Classics in Applied Mathematics 4, Society for Industrial and Applied Mathematics, Philadelphia, 1990. (Reprint of a classic book published in 1968.)

4. Gill, P. E., W. Murray, and M. H. Wright: *Practical Optimization,* Academic Press, London, 1981.

5. Horst, R., and P. M. Pardalos (eds.): *Handbook of Global Optimization,* Kluwer Academic Publishers, Boston, 1995.

6. Murray, W., "Algorithms for Large Nonlinear Programming Problems," pp. 172–185 in J. R. Birge and K. G. Murty (eds.), *Mathematical Programming: State of the Art 1994,* 15th International Symposium on Mathematical Programming, University of Michigan, Ann Arbor, MI, 1994.

7. Nash, S. G.: "Software Survey: NLP," *OR/MS Today,* April 1995, pp. 60–71.

8. Nemhauser, G. L., A. H. G. Rinnooy Kan, and M. J. Todd (eds.): *Optimization,* Handbooks in Operations Research and Management Science, Volume 1, North-Holland, Amsterdam, 1989.

9. Nesterov, Y., and A. Nemirovskii: *Interior-Point Polynomial Algorithms in Convex Programming,* Studies in Applied Mathematics 13, Society for Industrial and Applied Mathematics, Philadelphia, 1993.

10. Nocedal, J.: "Recent Advances in Large-Scale Nonlinear Optimization," pp. 208–219 in J. R. Birge and K. G. Murty (eds.), *Mathematical Programming: State of the Art 1994,* 15th International Symposium on Mathematical Programming, University of Michigan, Ann Arbor, MI, 1994.

LEARNING AIDS FOR THIS CHAPTER IN YOUR OR COURSEWARE

Demonstration Examples in OR Tutor:

Gradient Search Procedure
Frank-Wolfe Algorithm
Sequential Unconstrained Minimization Technique—SUMT

Interactive Routines:

Interactive One-Dimensional Search Procedure
Interactive Gradient Search Procedure
Interactive Modified Simplex Method
Interactive Frank-Wolfe Algorithm

Automatic Routines:

Automatic Gradient Search Procedure
Sequential Unconstrained Minimization Technique—SUMT

An Excel Add-in:

Premium Solver

"Ch. 13—Nonlinear Programming" Files for Solving the Examples:

Excel File
LINGO/LINDO File
MPL/CPLEX/CONOPT File

See Appendix 1 for documentation of the software.

PROBLEMS

The symbols to the left of some of the problems (or their parts) have the following meaning:

D: The corresponding demonstration example listed above may be helpful.

I: We suggest that you use the corresponding interactive routine listed above (the printout records your work).

C: Use the computer with any of the software options available to you (or as instructed by your instructor) to solve the problem.

An asterisk on the problem number indicates that at least a partial answer is given in the back of the book.

13.1-1. Consider the *product mix* problem described in Prob. 3.1-11. Suppose that this manufacturing firm actually encounters *price elasticity* in selling the three products, so that the profits would be different from those stated in Chap. 3. In particular, suppose that the unit costs for producing products 1, 2, and 3 are $25, $10, and $15, respectively, and that the prices required (in dollars) in order to be able to sell x_1, x_2, and x_3 units are $(35 + 100x_1^{-\frac{1}{3}})$, $(15 + 40x_2^{-\frac{1}{4}})$, and $(20 + 50x_3^{-\frac{1}{2}})$, respectively.

Formulate a nonlinear programming model for the problem of determining how many units of each product the firm should produce to maximize profit.

13.1-2. For the P & T Co. problem described in Sec. 8.1, suppose that there is a 10 percent discount in the shipping cost for all truckloads *beyond* the first 40 for each combination of cannery and warehouse. Draw figures like Figs. 13.3 and 13.4, showing the marginal cost and total cost for shipments of truckloads of peas from cannery 1 to warehouse 1. Then describe the overall nonlinear programming model for this problem.

13.1-3. A stockbroker, Richard Smith, has just received a call from his most important client, Ann Hardy. Ann has $50,000 to invest, and wants to use it to purchase two stocks. Stock 1 is a solid blue-chip security with a respectable growth potential and little risk involved. Stock 2 is much more speculative. It is being touted in two investment newsletters as having outstanding growth potential, but also is considered very risky. Ann would like a large return on her investment, but also has considerable aversion to risk. Therefore, she has instructed Richard to analyze what mix of investments in the two stocks would be appropriate for her.

Ann is used to talking in units of thousands of dollars and 1,000-share blocks of stocks. Using these units, the price per block is 20 for stock 1 and 30 for stock 2. After doing some research, Richard has made the following estimates. The expected return per block is 5 for stock 1 and 10 for stock 2. The variance of the return on each block is 4 for stock 1 and 100 for stock 2. The covariance of the return on one block each of the two stocks is 5.

Without yet assigning a specific numerical value to the minimum acceptable expected return, formulate a nonlinear programming model for this problem.

13.2-1. Reconsider Prob. 13.1-1. Verify that this problem is a convex programming problem.

13.2-2. Reconsider Prob. 13.1-3. Show that the model formulated is a convex programming problem by using the test in Appendix 2 to show that the objective function being minimized is convex.

13.2-3. Consider the variation of the Wyndor Glass Co. example represented in Fig. 13.5, where the second and third functional constraints of the original problem (see Sec. 3.1) have been replaced by $9x_1^2 + 5x_2^2 \leq 216$. Demonstrate that $(x_1, x_2) = (2, 6)$ with $Z = 36$ is indeed optimal by showing that the objective function line $36 = 3x_1 + 5x_2$ is *tangent* to this constraint boundary at $(2, 6)$. (*Hint:* Express x_2 in terms of x_1 on this boundary, and then differentiate this expression with respect to x_1 to find the slope of the boundary.)

13.2-4. Consider the variation of the Wyndor Glass Co. problem represented in Fig. 13.6, where the original objective function (see Sec. 3.1) has been replaced by $Z = 126x_1 - 9x_1^2 + 182x_2 - 13x_2^2$. Demonstrate that $(x_1, x_2) = (\frac{8}{3}, 5)$ with $Z = 857$ is indeed optimal by showing that the ellipse $857 = 126x_1 - 9x_1^2 + 182x_2 - 13x_2^2$ is *tangent* to the constraint boundary $3x_1 + 2x_2 = 18$ at $(\frac{8}{3}, 5)$. (*Hint:* Solve for x_2 in terms of x_1 for the ellipse, and then differentiate this expression with respect to x_1 to find the slope of the ellipse.)

13.2-5. Consider the following function:

$$f(x) = 48x - 60x^2 + x^3.$$

(a) Use the first and second derivatives to find the local maxima and local minima of $f(x)$.

(b) Use the first and second derivatives to show that $f(x)$ has neither a global maximum nor a global minimum because it is unbounded in both directions.

13.2-6. For each of the following functions, show whether it is convex, concave, or neither.
(a) $f(x) = 10x - x^2$
(b) $f(x) = x^4 + 6x^2 + 12x$
(c) $f(x) = 2x^3 - 3x^2$
(d) $f(x) = x^4 + x^2$
(e) $f(x) = x^3 + x^4$

13.2-7.* For each of the following functions, use the test given in Appendix 2 to determine whether it is convex, concave, or neither.

(a) $f(\mathbf{x}) = x_1 x_2 - x_1^2 - x_2^2$
(b) $f(\mathbf{x}) = 3x_1 + 2x_1^2 + 4x_2 + x_2^2 - 2x_1 x_2$
(c) $f(\mathbf{x}) = x_1^2 + 3x_1 x_2 + 2x_2^2$
(d) $f(\mathbf{x}) = 20x_1 + 10x_2$
(e) $f(\mathbf{x}) = x_1 x_2$

13.2-8. Consider the following function:

$$f(\mathbf{x}) = 5x_1 + 2x_2^2 + x_3^2 - 3x_3 x_4 + 4x_4^2 + 2x_5^4 + x_5^2 + 3x_5 x_6 + 6x_6^2 + 3x_6 x_7 + x_7^2.$$

Show that $f(\mathbf{x})$ is convex by expressing it as a sum of functions of one or two variables and then showing (see Appendix 2) that all these functions are convex.

13.2-9. Consider the following nonlinear programming problem:

Maximize $f(\mathbf{x}) = x_1 + x_2$,

subject to

$$x_1^2 + x_2^2 \le 1$$

and

$$x_1 \ge 0, \qquad x_2 \ge 0.$$

(a) Verify that this is a convex programming problem.
(b) Solve this problem graphically.

13.2-10. Consider the following nonlinear programming problem:

Minimize $Z = x_1^4 + 2x_2^2$,

subject to

$$x_1^2 + x_2^2 \ge 2.$$
(No nonnegativity constraints.)

(a) Use geometric analysis to determine whether the feasible region is a convex set.
(b) Now use algebra and calculus to determine whether the feasible region is a convex set.

13.3-1. Reconsider Prob. 13.1-2. Show that this problem is a nonconvex programming problem.

13.3-2. Consider the following constrained optimization problem:

Maximize $f(x) = -6x + 3x^2 - 2x^3$,

subject to

$$x \ge 0.$$

Use just the first and second derivatives of $f(x)$ to derive an optimal solution.

13.3-3. Consider the following nonlinear programming problem:

Minimize $Z = x_1^4 + 2x_1^2 + 2x_1 x_2 + 4x_2^2$,

subject to

$$2x_1 + x_2 \ge 10$$
$$x_1 + 2x_2 \ge 10$$

and

$$x_1 \ge 0, \qquad x_2 \ge 0.$$

(a) Of the special types of nonlinear programming problems described in Sec. 13.3, to which type or types can this particular problem be fitted? Justify your answer.
(b) Now suppose that the problem is changed slightly by replacing the nonnegativity constraints by $x_1 \ge 1$ and $x_2 \ge 1$. Convert this new problem to an equivalent problem that has just two functional constraints, two variables, and two nonnegativity constraints.

13.3-4. Consider the following geometric programming problem:

Minimize $f(\mathbf{x}) = 2x_1^{-2}x_2^{-1} + x_2^{-2}$,

subject to

$$4x_1 x_2 + x_1^2 x_2^2 \le 12$$

and

$$x_1 \ge 0, \qquad x_2 \ge 0.$$

(a) Transform this problem to an equivalent convex programming problem.
(b) Use the test given in Appendix 2 to verify that the model formulated in part (a) is indeed a convex programming problem.

13.3-5. Consider the following linear fractional programming problem:

Maximize $f(\mathbf{x}) = \dfrac{10x_1 + 20x_2 + 10}{3x_1 + 4x_2 + 20}$,

subject to

$$x_1 + 3x_2 \le 50$$
$$3x_1 + 2x_2 \le 80$$

and

$$x_1 \ge 0, \qquad x_2 \ge 0.$$

(a) Transform this problem to an equivalent linear programming problem.
C **(b)** Use the computer to solve the model formulated in part (a). What is the resulting optimal solution for the original problem?

13.3-6. Consider the expressions in matrix notation given in Sec. 13.7 for the general form of the KKT conditions for the quadratic programming problem. Show that the problem of finding a feasible solution for these conditions is a linear complementarity problem, as introduced in Sec. 13.3, by identifying **w**, **z**, **q**, and **M** in terms of the vectors and matrices in Sec. 13.7.

I **13.4-1.*** Use the one-dimensional search procedure to interactively solve (approximately) the following problem:

Maximize $f(x) = x^3 + 2x - 2x^2 - 0.25x^4$.

Use an error tolerance $\epsilon = 0.04$ and initial bounds $\underline{x} = 0, \bar{x} = 2.4$.

I **13.4-2.** Use the one-dimensional search procedure with an error tolerance $\epsilon = 0.04$ and with the following initial bounds to interactively solve (approximately) each of the following problems.
(a) Maximize $f(x) = 6x - x^2$, with $\underline{x} = 0, \bar{x} = 4.8$.
(b) Minimize $f(x) = 6x + 7x^2 + 4x^3 + x^4$, with $\underline{x} = -4, \bar{x} = 1$.

I **13.4-3.** Use the one-dimensional search procedure to interactively solve (approximately) the following problem:

Maximize $f(x) = 48x^5 + 42x^3 + 3.5x - 16x^6$
                    $- 61x^4 - 16.5x^2$.

Use an error tolerance $\epsilon = 0.08$ and initial bounds $\underline{x} = -1, \bar{x} = 4$.

I **13.4-4.** Use the one-dimensional search procedure to interactively solve (approximately) the following problem:

Maximize $f(x) = x^3 + 30x - x^6 - 2x^4 - 3x^2$.

Use an error tolerance $\epsilon = 0.07$ and find appropriate initial bounds by inspection.

13.4-5. Consider the following convex programming problem:

Minimize $Z = x^4 + x^2 - 4x$,

subject to

$x \leq 2$ and $x \geq 0$.

(a) Use one simple calculation *just* to check whether the optimal solution lies in the interval $0 \leq x \leq 1$ or the interval $1 \leq x \leq 2$. (Do *not* actually solve for the optimal solution in order to determine in which interval it must lie.) Explain your logic.
I (b) Use the one-dimensional search procedure with initial bounds $\underline{x} = 0, \bar{x} = 2$ and with an error tolerance $\epsilon = 0.02$ to interactively solve (approximately) this problem.

13.4-6. Consider the problem of maximizing a differentiable function $f(x)$ of a single unconstrained variable x. Let $\underline{x}_0$ and $\bar{x}_0$, respectively, be a valid lower bound and upper bound on the same global maximum (if one exists). Prove the following general properties of the one-dimensional search procedure (as presented in Sec. 13.4) for attempting to solve such a problem.

(a) Given $\underline{x}_0$, $\bar{x}_0$, and $\epsilon = 0$, the sequence of trial solutions selected by the *midpoint rule* must *converge* to a limiting solution. [*Hint:* First show that $\lim_{n \to \infty}(\bar{x}_n - \underline{x}_n) = 0$, where $\bar{x}_n$ and $\underline{x}_n$ are the upper and lower bounds identified at iteration n.]
(b) If $f(x)$ is concave [so that $df(x)/dx$ is a monotone decreasing function of x], then the limiting solution in part (a) must be a global maximum.
(c) If $f(x)$ is not concave everywhere, but would be concave if its domain were restricted to the interval between $\underline{x}_0$ and $\bar{x}_0$, then the limiting solution in part (a) must be a global maximum.
(d) If $f(x)$ is not concave even over the interval between $\underline{x}_0$ and $\bar{x}_0$, then the limiting solution in part (a) need not be a global maximum. (Prove this by graphically constructing a counterexample.)
(e) If $df(x)/dx < 0$ for all x, then no $\underline{x}_0$ exists. If $df(x)/dx > 0$ for all x, then no $\bar{x}_0$ exists. In either case, $f(x)$ does not possess a global maximum.
(f) If $f(x)$ is concave and $\lim_{x \to \infty} f(x)/dx < 0$, then no $\underline{x}_0$ exists. If $f(x)$ is concave and $\lim_{x \to \infty} df(x)/dx > 0$, then no $\bar{x}_0$ exists. In either case, $f(x)$ does not possess a global maximum.

I **13.4-7.** Consider the following linearly constrained convex programming problem:

Maximize $f(\mathbf{x}) = 32x_1 + 50x_2 - 10x_2^2 + x_2^3 - x_1^4 - x_2^4$,

subject to

$3x_1 + x_2 \leq 11$
$2x_1 + 5x_2 \leq 16$

and

$x_1 \geq 0, \qquad x_2 \geq 0$.

Ignore the constraints and solve the resulting two *one-variable unconstrained optimization* problems. Use calculus to solve the problem involving x_1 and use the *one-dimensional search procedure* with $\epsilon = 0.001$ and initial bounds 0 and 4 to solve the problem involving x_2. Show that the resulting solution for (x_1, x_2) satisfies all of the constraints, so it is actually optimal for the original problem.

13.5-1. Consider the following unconstrained optimization problem:

Maximize $f(\mathbf{x}) = 2x_1x_2 + x_2 - x_1^2 - 2x_2^2$.

D,I (a) Starting from the initial trial solution $(x_1, x_2) = (1, 1)$, interactively apply the gradient search procedure with $\epsilon = 0.25$ to obtain an approximate solution.
(b) Solve the system of linear equations obtained by setting $\nabla f(\mathbf{x}) = \mathbf{0}$ to obtain the exact solution.
(c) Referring to Fig 13.14 as a sample for a similar problem, draw the path of trial solutions you obtained in part (a). Then show

the apparent *continuation* of this path with your best guess for the next three trial solutions [based on the pattern in part (*a*) and in Fig. 13.14]. Also show the exact solution from part (*b*) toward which this sequence of trial solutions is converging.

C **(d)** Apply the automatic routine for the gradient search procedure (with $\epsilon = 0.01$) in your OR Courseware to this problem.

13.5-2. Repeat the four parts of Prob. 13.5-1 (except with $\epsilon = 0.5$) for the following unconstrained optimization problem:

$$\text{Maximize} \quad f(\mathbf{x}) = 2x_1x_2 - 2x_1^2 - x_2^2.$$

D,I,C **13.5-3.** Starting from the initial trial solution $(x_1, x_2) = (1, 1)$, interactively apply two iterations of the gradient search procedure to begin solving the following problem, and then apply the automatic routine for this procedure (with $\epsilon = 0.01$).

$$\text{Maximize} \quad f(\mathbf{x}) = 4x_1x_2 - 2x_1^2 - 3x_2^2.$$

Then solve $\nabla f(\mathbf{x}) = \mathbf{0}$ directly to obtain the exact solution.

D,I,C **13.5-4.*** Starting from the initial trial solution $(x_1, x_2) = (0, 0)$, interactively apply the gradient search procedure with $\epsilon = 0.3$ to obtain an approximate solution for the following problem, and then apply the automatic routine for this procedure (with $\epsilon = 0.01$).

$$\text{Maximize} \quad f(\mathbf{x}) = 8x_1 - x_1^2 - 12x_2 - 2x_2^2 + 2x_1x_2.$$

Then solve $\nabla f(\mathbf{x}) = \mathbf{0}$ directly to obtain the exact solution.

D,I,C **13.5-5.** Starting from the initial trial solution $(x_1, x_2) = (0, 0)$, interactively apply two iterations of the gradient search procedure to begin solving the following problem, and then apply the automatic routine for this procedure (with $\epsilon = 0.01$).

$$\text{Maximize} \quad f(\mathbf{x}) = 6x_1 + 2x_1x_2 - 2x_2 - 2x_1^2 - x_2^2.$$

Then solve $\nabla f(\mathbf{x}) = \mathbf{0}$ directly to obtain the exact solution.

13.5-6. Starting from the initial trial solution $(x_1, x_2) = (0, 0)$, apply *one* iteration of the gradient search procedure to the following problem by hand:

$$\text{Maximize} \quad f(\mathbf{x}) = 4x_1 + 2x_2 + x_1^2 - x_1^4 - 2x_1x_2 - x_2^2.$$

To complete this iteration, approximately solve for t^* by manually applying *two* iterations of the one-dimensional search procedure with initial bounds $\underline{t} = 0$, $\bar{t} = 1$.

13.5-7. Consider the following unconstrained optimization problem:

$$\text{Maximize} \quad f(\mathbf{x}) = 3x_1x_2 + 3x_2x_3 - x_1^2 - 6x_2^2 - x_3^2.$$

(a) Describe how solving this problem can be reduced to solving a *two-variable* unconstrained optimization problem.

D,I **(b)** Starting from the initial trial solution $(x_1, x_2, x_3) = (1, 1, 1)$, interactively apply the gradient search procedure with

$\epsilon = 0.05$ to solve (approximately) the two-variable problem identified in part (*a*).

C **(c)** Repeat part (*b*) with the automatic routine for this procedure (with $\epsilon = 0.005$).

D,I,C **13.5-8.*** Starting from the initial trial solution $(x_1, x_2) = (0, 0)$, interactively apply the *gradient search procedure* with $\epsilon = 1$ to solve (approximately) each of the following problems, and then apply the automatic routine for this procedure (with $\epsilon = 0.01$).

(a) Maximize $\quad f(\mathbf{x}) = x_1x_2 + 3x_2 - x_1^2 - x_2^2.$
(b) Minimize $\quad f(\mathbf{x}) = x_1^2x_2^2 + 2x_1^2 + 2x_2^2 - 4x_1 + 4x_2.$

13.6-1. Reconsider the one-variable convex programming model given in Prob. 13.4-5. Use the KKT conditions to derive an optimal solution for this model.

13.6-2. Reconsider Prob. 13.2-9. Use the KKT conditions to check whether $(x_1, x_2) = (1/\sqrt{2}, 1/\sqrt{2})$ is optimal.

13.6-3.* Reconsider the model given in Prob. 13.3-3. What are the KKT conditions for this model? Use these conditions to determine whether $(x_1, x_2) = (0, 10)$ can be optimal.

13.6-4. Consider the following convex programming problem:

$$\text{Maximize} \quad f(\mathbf{x}) = 24x_1 - x_1^2 + 10x_2 - x_2^2,$$

subject to

$$x_1 \le 8,$$
$$x_2 \le 7,$$

and

$$x_1 \ge 0, \qquad x_2 \ge 0.$$

(a) Use the KKT conditions for this problem to derive an optimal solution.

(b) Decompose this problem into two separate constrained optimization problems involving just x_1 and just x_2, respectively. For each of these two problems, plot the objective function over the feasible region in order to *demonstrate* that the value of x_1 or x_2 derived in part (*a*) is indeed optimal. Then *prove* that this value is optimal by using just the first and second derivatives of the objective function and the constraints for the respective problems.

13.6-5. Consider the following linearly constrained optimization problem:

$$\text{Maximize} \quad f(\mathbf{x}) = \ln(1 + x_1 + x_2),$$

subject to

$$x_1 + 2x_2 \le 5$$

and

$$x_1 \ge 0, \qquad x_2 \ge 0,$$

where ln denotes the natural logarithm.

(a) Verify that this problem is a convex programming problem.

(b) Use the KKT conditions to derive an optimal solution.

(c) Use intuitive reasoning to demonstrate that the solution obtained in part (*b*) is indeed optimal. [*Hint:* Note that $\ln(1 + x_1 + x_2)$ is a monotonic strictly increasing function of $1 + x_1 + x_2$.]

13.6-6. Consider the following linearly constrained optimization problem:

Maximize $f(\mathbf{x}) = \ln(x_1 + 1) - x_2^2,$

subject to

$$x_1 + 2x_2 \le 3$$

and

$$x_1 \ge 0, \qquad x_2 \ge 0,$$

where ln denotes the natural logarithm,

(a) Verify that this problem is a convex programming problem.

(b) Use the KKT conditions to derive an optimal solution.

(c) Use intuitive reasoning to demonstrate that the solution obtained in part (*b*) is indeed optimal.

13.6-7. Consider the following convex programming problem:

Maximize $f(\mathbf{x}) = 10x_1 - 2x_1^2 - x_1^3 + 8x_2 - x_2^2,$

subject to

$$x_1 + x_2 \le 2$$

and

$$x_1 \ge 0, \qquad x_2 \ge 0.$$

(a) Use the KKT conditions to demonstrate that $(x_1, x_2) = (1, 1)$ is *not* an optimal solution.

(b) Use the KKT conditions to derive an optimal solution.

13.6-8.* Consider the nonlinear programming problem given in Prob. 11.3-14. Determine whether $(x_1, x_2) = (1, 2)$ can be optimal by applying the KKT conditions.

13.6-9. Consider the following nonlinear programming problem:

Maximize $f(\mathbf{x}) = \dfrac{x_1}{x_2 + 1},$

subject to

$$x_1 - x_2 \le 2$$

and

$$x_1 \ge 0, \qquad x_2 \ge 0.$$

(a) Use the KKT conditions to demonstrate that $(x_1, x_2) = (4, 2)$ is *not* optimal.

(b) Derive a solution that does satisfy the KKT conditions.

(c) Show that this problem is *not* a convex programming problem.

(d) Despite the conclusion in part (*c*), use *intuitive* reasoning to show that the solution obtained in part (*b*) is, in fact, optimal. [The theoretical reason is that $f(\mathbf{x})$ is *pseudo-concave.*]

(e) Use the fact that this problem is a linear fractional programming problem to transform it into an equivalent linear programming problem. Solve the latter problem and thereby identify the optimal solution for the original problem. (*Hint:* Use the equality constraint in the linear programming problem to substitute one of the variables out of the model, and then solve the model graphically.)

13.6-10.* Use the KKT conditions to derive an optimal solution for each of the following problems.

(a)   Maximize $f(\mathbf{x}) = x_1 + 2x_2 - x_2^3,$

subject to

$$x_1 + x_2 \le 1$$

and

$$x_1 \ge 0, \qquad x_2 \ge 0.$$

(b)   Maximize $f(\mathbf{x}) = 20x_1 + 10x_2,$

subject to

$$x_1^2 + \quad x_2^2 \le 1$$
$$x_1 + 2x_2 \le 2$$

and

$$x_1 \ge 0, \qquad x_2 \ge 0.$$

13.6-11. Reconsider the nonlinear programming model given in Prob. 11.3-16.

(a) Use the KKT conditions to determine whether $(x_1, x_2, x_3) = (1, 1, 1)$ can be optimal.

(b) If a specific solution satisfies the KKT conditions for this problem, can you draw the definite conclusion that this solution is optimal? Why?

13.6-12. What are the KKT conditions for nonlinear programming problems of the following form?

Minimize $f(\mathbf{x}),$

subject to

$$g_i(\mathbf{x}) \ge b_i, \qquad \text{for } i = 1, 2, \ldots, m$$

and

$$\mathbf{x} \geq \mathbf{0}.$$

(*Hint:* Convert this form to our standard form assumed in this chapter by using the techniques presented in Sec. 4.6 and then applying the KKT conditions as given in Sec. 13.6.)

13.6-13. Consider the following nonlinear programming problem:

Minimize $Z = 2x_1^2 + x_2^2,$

subject to

$$x_1 + x_2 = 10$$

and

$$x_1 \geq 0, \qquad x_2 \geq 0.$$

(a) Of the special types of nonlinear programming problems described in Sec. 13.3, to which type or types can this particular problem be fitted? Justify your answer. (*Hint:* First convert this problem to an equivalent nonlinear programming problem that fits the form given in the second paragraph of the chapter, with $m = 2$ and $n = 2.$)
(b) Obtain the KKT conditions for this problem.
(c) Use the KKT conditions to derive an optimal solution.

13.6-14. Consider the following linearly constrained programming problem:

Minimize $f(\mathbf{x}) = x_1^3 + 4x_2^2 + 16x_3,$

subject to

$$x_1 + x_2 + x_3 = 5$$

and

$$x_1 \geq 1, \qquad x_2 \geq 1, \qquad x_3 \geq 1.$$

(a) Convert this problem to an equivalent nonlinear programming problem that fits the form given at the beginning of the chapter (second paragraph), with $m = 2$ and $n = 3.$
(b) Use the form obtained in part (*a*) to construct the KKT conditions for this problem.
(c) Use the KKT conditions to check whether $(x_1, x_2, x_3) = (2, 1, 2)$ is optimal.

13.6-15. Consider the following linearly constrained convex programming problem:

Minimize $Z = x_1^2 - 6x_1 + x_2^3 - 3x_2,$

subject to

$$x_1 + x_2 \leq 1$$

and

$$x_1 \geq 0, \qquad x_2 \geq 0.$$

(a) Obtain the KKT conditions for this problem.
(b) Use the KKT conditions to check whether $(x_1, x_2) = (\frac{1}{2}, \frac{1}{2})$ is an optimal solution.
(c) Use the KKT conditions to derive an optimal solution.

13.6-16. Consider the following linearly constrained convex programming problem:

Maximize $f(\mathbf{x}) = 8x_1 - x_1^2 + 2x_2 + x_3,$

subject to

$$x_1 + 3x_2 + 2x_3 \leq 12$$

and

$$x_1 \geq 0, \qquad x_2 \geq 0, \qquad x_3 \geq 0.$$

(a) Use the KKT conditions to demonstrate that $(x_1, x_2, x_3) = (2, 2, 2)$ is *not* an optimal solution.
(b) Use the KKT conditions to derive an optimal solution. (*Hint:* Do some preliminary intuitive analysis to determine the most promising case regarding which variables are nonzero and which are zero.)

13.6-17. Use the KKT conditions to determine whether $(x_1, x_2, x_3) = (1, 1, 1)$ can be optimal for the following problem:

Minimize $Z = 2x_1 + x_2^3 + x_3^2,$

subject to

$$x_1^2 + 2x_2^2 + x_3^2 \geq 4$$

and

$$x_1 \geq 0, \qquad x_2 \geq 0, \qquad x_3 \geq 0.$$

13.6-18. Reconsider the model given in Prob. 13.2-10. What are the KKT conditions for this problem? Use these conditions to determine whether $(x_1, x_2) = (1, 1)$ can be optimal.

13.6-19. Reconsider the linearly constrained convex programming model given in Prob. 13.4-7. Use the KKT conditions to determine whether $(x_1, x_2) = (2, 2)$ can be optimal.

13.7-1. Consider the quadratic programming example presented in Sec. 13.7.
(a) Use the test given in Appendix 2 to show that the objective function is *strictly concave*.
(b) Verify that the objective function is strictly concave by demonstrating that $\mathbf{Q}$ is a *positive definite* matrix; that is, $\mathbf{x}^T\mathbf{Q}\mathbf{x} > 0$ for all $\mathbf{x} \neq \mathbf{0}$. (*Hint:* Reduce $\mathbf{x}^T\mathbf{Q}\mathbf{x}$ to a sum of squares.)
(c) Show that $x_1 = 12$, $x_2 = 9$, and $u_1 = 3$ satisfy the KKT conditions when they are written in the form given in Sec. 13.6.

13.7-2.* Consider the following quadratic programming problem:

$$\text{Maximize} \quad f(\mathbf{x}) = 8x_1 - x_1^2 + 4x_2 - x_2^2,$$

subject to

$$x_1 + x_2 \le 2$$

and

$$x_1 \ge 0, \quad x_2 \ge 0.$$

(a) Use the KKT conditions to derive an optimal solution.

(b) Now suppose that this problem is to be solved by the modified simplex method. Formulate the linear programming problem that is to be addressed explicitly, and then identify the additional complementarity constraint that is enforced automatically by the algorithm.

I **(c)** Apply the modified simplex method to the problem as formulated in part (b).

C **(d)** Use the computer to solve the quadratic programming problem directly.

13.7-3. Consider the following quadratic programming problem:

$$\text{Maximize} \quad f(\mathbf{x}) = 20x_1 - 20x_1^2 + 50x_2 - 5x_2^2 + 18x_1x_2,$$

subject to

$$\begin{aligned} x_1 + x_2 &\le 6 \\ x_1 + 4x_2 &\le 18 \end{aligned}$$

and

$$x_1 \ge 0, \quad x_2 \ge 0.$$

Suppose that this problem is to be solved by the modified simplex method.

(a) Formulate the linear programming problem that is to be addressed explicitly, and then identify the additional complementarity constraint that is enforced automatically by the algorithm.

I **(b)** Apply the modified simplex method to the problem as formulated in part (a).

13.7-4. Consider the following quadratic programming problem.

$$\text{Maximize} \quad f(\mathbf{x}) = 2x_1 + 3x_2 - x_1^2 - x_2^2,$$

subject to

$$x_1 + x_2 \le 2$$

and

$$x_1 \ge 0, \quad x_2 \ge 0.$$

(a) Use the KKT conditions to derive an optimal solution directly.

(b) Now suppose that this problem is to be solved by the modified simplex method. Formulate the linear programming problem that is to be addressed explicitly, and then identify the additional complementarity constraint that is enforced automatically by the algorithm.

(c) Without applying the modified simplex method, show that the solution derived in part (a) is indeed optimal ($Z = 0$) for the equivalent problem formulated in part (b).

I **(d)** Apply the modified simplex method to the problem as formulated in part (b).

C **(e)** Use the computer to solve the quadratic programming problem directly.

13.7-5. Reconsider the first quadratic programming variation of the Wyndor Glass Co. problem presented in Sec. 13.2 (see Fig. 13.6). Analyze this problem by following the instructions of parts (a), (b), and (c) of Prob. 13.7-4.

C **13.7-6.** Reconsider Prob. 13.1-3 and its quadratic programming model.

(a) Display this model [including the values of $R(\mathbf{x})$ and $V(\mathbf{x})$] on an Excel spreadsheet.

(b) Solve this model for four cases: minimum acceptable expected return = 13, 14, 15, 16.

(c) For typical probability distributions (with mean μ and variance σ^2) of the total return from the entire portfolio, the probability is fairly high (about 0.8 or 0.9) that the return will exceed $\mu - \sigma$, and the probability is extremely high (often close to 0.999) that the return will exceed $\mu - 3\sigma$. Calculate $\mu - \sigma$ and $\mu - 3\sigma$ for the four portfolios obtained in part (b). Which portfolio will give the highest μ among those that also give $\mu - \sigma \ge 0$?

13.7-7. Jim Matthews, Vice President for Marketing of the J. R. Nickel Company, is planning advertising campaigns for two unrelated products. These two campaigns need to use some of the same resources. Therefore, Jim knows that his decisions on the levels of the two campaigns need to be made jointly after considering these resource constraints. In particular, letting x_1 and x_2 denote the levels of campaigns 1 and 2, respectively, these constraints are $4x_1 + x_2 \le 20$ and $x_1 + 4x_2 \le 20$.

In facing these decisions, Jim is well aware that there is a point of diminishing returns when raising the level of an advertising campaign too far. At that point, the cost of additional advertising becomes larger than the increase in net revenue (excluding advertising costs) generated by the advertising. After careful analysis, he and his staff estimate that the net profit from the first product (including advertising costs) when conducting the first campaign at level x_1 would be $3x_1 - (x_1 - 1)^2$ in millions of dollars. The corresponding estimate for the second product is $3x_2 - (x_2 - 2)^2$.

This analysis led to the following quadratic programming model for determining the levels of the two advertising campaigns:

$$\text{Maximize} \quad Z = 3x_1 - (x_1 - 1)^2 + 3x_2 - (x_2 - 2)^2,$$

subject to

$$4x_1 + x_2 \le 20$$
$$x_1 + 4x_2 \le 20$$

and

$$x_1 \ge 0, \qquad x_2 \ge 0.$$

(a) Obtain the KKT conditions for this problem in the form given in Sec. 13.6.

(b) You are given the information that the optimal solution does *not* lie on the boundary of the feasible region. Use this information to derive the optimal solution from the KKT conditions.

(c) Now suppose that this problem is to be solved by the modified simplex method. Formulate the linear programming problem that is to be addressed explicitly, and then identify the additional complementarity constraint that is enforced automatically by the algorithm.

(d) Apply the modified simplex method to the problem as formulated in part (c).

C **(e)** Use the computer to solve the quadratic programming problem directly.

13.8-1. Reconsider the quadratic programming model given in Prob. 13.7-7.

(a) Use the separable programming formulation presented in Sec. 13.8 to formulate an approximate linear programming model for this problem. Use $x_1, x_2 = 0, 2.5, 5$ as the breakpoints of the piecewise linear functions.

C **(b)** Use the computer to solve the model formulated in part (a). Then reexpress this solution in terms of the *original* variables of the problem.

C **(c)** To improve the approximation, now use $x_1, x_2 = 0, 1, 2, 3, 4, 5$ as the breakpoints of the piecewise linear functions and repeat parts (a) and (b).

13.8-2. The MFG Corporation is planning to produce and market three different products. Let x_1, x_2, and x_3 denote the number of units of the three respective products to be produced. The preliminary estimates of their potential profitability are as follows.

For the first 15 units produced of Product 1, the unit profit would be approximately $360. The unit profit would be only $30 for any additional units of Product 1. For the first 20 units produced of Product 2, the unit profit is estimated at $240. The unit profit would be $120 for each of the next 20 units and $90 for any additional units. For the first 10 units of Product 3, the unit profit would be $450. The unit profit would be $300 for each of the next 5 units and $180 for any additional units.

Certain limitations on the use of needed resources impose the following constraints on the production of the three products:

$$x_1 + x_2 + x_3 \le 60$$
$$3x_1 + 2x_2 \qquad \le 200$$
$$x_1 \qquad + 2x_3 \le 70.$$

Management wants to know what values of x_1, x_2 and x_3 should be chosen to maximize the total profit.

(a) Plot the profit graph for each of the three products.

(b) Use separable programming to formulate a linear programming model for this problem.

C **(c)** Solve the model. What is the resulting recommendation to management about the values of x_1, x_2, and x_3 to use?

(d) Now suppose that there is an additional constraint that the profit from products 1 and 2 must total at least $9,000. Use the technique presented in the "Extensions" subsection of Sec. 13.8 to add this constraint to the model formulated in part (b).

C **(e)** Repeat part (c) for the model formulated in part (d).

13.8-3.* The Dorwyn Company has two new products that will compete with the two new products for the Wyndor Glass Co. (described in Sec. 3.1). Using units of hundreds of dollars for the objective function, the linear programming model shown below has been formulated to determine the most profitable product mix.

Maximize $\quad Z = 4x_1 + 6x_2,$

subject to

$$x_1 + 3x_2 \le 8$$
$$5x_1 + 2x_2 \le 14$$

and

$$x_1 \ge 0, \qquad x_2 \ge 0.$$

However, because of the strong competition from Wyndor, Dorwyn management now realizes that the company will need to make a strong marketing effort to generate substantial sales of these products. In particular, it is estimated that achieving a production and sales rate of x_1 units of Product 1 per week will require weekly marketing costs of x_1^3 hundred dollars. The corresponding marketing costs for Product 2 are estimated to be $2x_2^2$ hundred dollars. Thus, the objective function in the model should be $Z = 4x_1 + 6x_2 - x_1^3 - 2x_2^2$.

Dorwyn management now would like to use the revised model to determine the most profitable product mix.

(a) Verify that $(x_1, x_2) = (2/\sqrt{3}, \frac{3}{2})$ is an optimal solution by applying the KKT conditions.

(b) Construct tables to show the profit data for each product when the production rate is 0, 1, 2, 3.

(c) Draw a figure like Fig. 13.15b that plots the weekly profit points for each product when the production rate is 0, 1, 2, 3. Connect the pairs of consecutive points with (dashed) line segments.

(d) Use separable programming based on this figure to formulate an approximate linear programming model for this problem.

C **(e)** Solve the model. What does this say to Dorwyn management about which product mix to use?

13.8-4. Reconsider the production scheduling problem of the Build-Em-Fast Company described in Prob. 8.1-9. The special restriction for such a situation is that overtime should not be used in any particular period unless regular time in that period is completely used up. Explain why the logic of separable programming implies that this restriction will be satisfied automatically by any optimal solution for the transportation problem formulation of the problem.

13.8-5. The B. J. Jensen Company specializes in the production of power saws and power drills for home use. Sales are relatively stable throughout the year except for a jump upward during the Christmas season. Since the production work requires considerable work and experience, the company maintains a stable employment level and then uses overtime to increase production in November. The workers also welcome this opportunity to earn extra money for the holidays.

B. J. Jensen, Jr., the current president of the company, is overseeing the production plans being made for the upcoming November. He has obtained the following data.

	Maximum Monthly Production*		Profit per Unit Produced	
	Regular Time	Overtime	Regular Time	Overtime
Power saws	3,000	2,000	$150	$50
Power drills	5,000	3,000	$100	$75

*Assuming adequate supplies of materials from the company's vendors.

However, Mr. Jensen now has learned that, in addition to the limited number of labor hours available, two other factors will limit the production levels that can be achieved this November. One is that the company's vendor for power supply units will only be able to provide 10,000 of these units for November (2,000 more than his usual monthly shipment). Each power saw and each power drill requires one of these units. Second, the vendor who supplies a key part for the gear assemblies will only be able to provide 15,000 for November (4,000 more than for other months). Each power saw requires two of these parts and each power drill requires one.

Mr. Jensen now wants to determine how many power saws and how many power drills to produce in November to maximize the company's total profit.

(a) Draw the profit graph for each of these two products.

(b) Use separable programming to formulate a linear programming model for this problem.

C **(c)** Solve the model. What does this say about how many power saws and how many power drills to produce in November?

13.8-6. Reconsider the linearly constrained convex programming model given in Prob. 13.4-7.

(a) Use the separable programming technique presented in Sec. 13.8 to formulate an approximate linear programming model for this problem. Use $x_1 = 0, 1, 2, 3$ and $x_2 = 0, 1, 2, 3$ as the breakpoints of the piecewise linear functions.

C **(b)** Use the simplex method to solve the model formulated in part (a). Then reexpress this solution in terms of the *original* variables of the problem.

13.8-7. Suppose that the separable programming technique has been applied to a certain problem (the "original problem") to convert it to the following equivalent linear programming problem:

$$\text{Maximize} \quad Z = 5x_{11} + 4x_{12} + 2x_{13} + 4x_{21} + x_{22},$$

subject to

$$3x_{11} + 3x_{12} + 3x_{13} + 2x_{21} + 2x_{22} \le 25$$
$$2x_{11} + 2x_{12} + 2x_{13} - x_{21} - x_{22} \le 10$$

and

$$0 \le x_{11} \le 2 \qquad 0 \le x_{21} \le 3$$
$$0 \le x_{12} \le 3 \qquad 0 \le x_{22} \le 1.$$
$$0 \le x_{13}$$

What was the mathematical model for the original problem? (You may define the objective function either algebraically or graphically, but express the constraints algebraically.)

13.8-8. For each of the following cases, *prove* that the key property of separable programming given in Sec. 13.8 must hold. (*Hint:* Assume that there exists an optimal solution that violates this property, and then contradict this assumption by showing that there exists a better feasible solution.)

(a) The special case of separable programming where all the $g_i(\mathbf{x})$ are linear functions.

(b) The general case of separable programming where all the functions are nonlinear functions of the designated form. [*Hint:* Think of the functional constraints as constraints on resources, where $g_{ij}(x_j)$ represents the amount of resource i used by running activity j at level x_j, and then use what the convexity assumption implies about the slopes of the approximating piecewise linear function.]

13.8-9. The MFG Company produces a certain subassembly in each of two separate plants. These subassemblies are then brought to a third nearby plant where they are used in the production of a certain product. The peak season of demand for this product is approaching, so to maintain the production rate within a desired range, it is necessary to use temporarily some overtime in making the subassemblies. The cost per subassembly on regular time (RT) and on overtime (OT) is shown in the following table for both plants, along with the maximum number of subassemblies that can be produced on RT and on OT each day.

	Unit Cost		Capacity	
	RT	OT	RT	OT
Plant 1	$15	$25	2,000	1,000
Plant 2	$16	$24	1,000	500

Let x_1 and x_2 denote the total number of subassemblies produced per day at plants 1 and 2, respectively. The objective is to maximize $Z = x_1 + x_2$, subject to the constraint that the total daily cost not exceed $60,000. Note that the mathematical programming formulation of this problem (with x_1 and x_2 as decision variables) has the same form as the main case of the separable programming model described in Sec. 13.8, except that the separable functions appear in a constraint function rather than the objective function. However, the same approach can be used to reformulate the problem as a linear programming model where it is feasible to use OT even when the RT capacity at that plant is not fully used.

(a) Formulate this linear programming model.

(b) Explain why the logic of separable programming also applies here to guarantee that an optimal solution for the model formulated in part (a) never uses OT unless the RT capacity at that plant has been fully used.

13.8-10. Consider the following nonlinear programming problem (first considered in Prob. 11.3-23).

Maximize $\quad Z = 5x_1 + x_2,$

subject to

$$2x_1^2 + x_2 \leq 13$$
$$x_1^2 + x_2 \leq 9$$

and

$$x_1 \geq 0, \qquad x_2 \geq 0.$$

(a) Show that this problem is a convex programming problem.

(b) Use the separable programming technique discussed at the end of Sec. 13.8 to formulate an approximate linear programming model for this problem. Use the integers as the breakpoints of the piecewise linear function.

C **(c)** Use the computer to solve the model formulated in part (b). Then reexpress this solution in terms of the *original* variables of the problem.

13.8-11. Consider the following convex programming problem:

Maximize $\quad Z = 32x_1 - x_1^4 + 4x_2 - x_2^2,$

subject to

$$x_1^2 + x_2^2 \leq 9$$

and

$$x_1 \geq 0, \qquad x_2 \geq 0.$$

(a) Apply the separable programming technique discussed at the end of Sec. 13.8, with $x_1 = 0, 1, 2, 3$ and $x_2 = 0, 1, 2, 3$ as the breakpoint of the piecewise linear functions, to formulate an approximate linear programming model for this problem.

C **(b)** Use the computer to solve the model formulated in part (a). Then reexpress this solution in terms of the *original* variables of the problem.

(c) Use the KKT conditions to determine whether the solution for the original variables obtained in part (b) actually is optimal for the original problem (not the approximate model).

13.8-12. Reconsider the integer nonlinear programming model given in Prob. 11.3-11.

(a) Show that the objective function is not concave.

(b) Formulate an equivalent *pure binary* integer *linear* programming model for this problem as follows. Apply the separable programming technique with the feasible integers as the breakpoints of the piecewise linear functions, so that the auxiliary variables are binary variables. Then add some linear programming constraints on these binary variables to enforce the *special restriction* of separable programming. (Note that the *key property* of separable programming does not hold for this problem because the objective function is not concave.)

C **(c)** Use the computer to solve this problem as formulated in part (b). Then reexpress this solution in terms of the *original* variables of the problem.

D,I **13.9-1.*** Reconsider the linearly constrained convex programming model given in Prob. 13.6-5. Starting from the initial trial solution $(x_1, x_2) = (1, 1)$, use one iteration of the Frank-Wolfe algorithm to obtain exactly the same solution you found in part (b) of Prob. 13.6-5, and then use a second iteration to verify that it is an optimal solution (because it is replicated exactly). Explain why exactly the same results would be obtained on these two iterations with any other initial trial solution.

D,I **13.9-2.** Reconsider the linearly constrained convex programming model given in Prob. 13.6-6. Starting from the initial trial solution $(x_1, x_2) = (0, 0)$, use one iteration of the Frank-Wolfe algorithm to obtain exactly the same solution you found in part (b) of Prob. 13.6-6, and then use a second iteration to verify that it is an optimal solution (because it is replicated exactly).

D,I **13.9-3.** Reconsider the linearly constrained convex programming model given in Prob. 13.6-15. Starting from the initial trial solution $(x_1, x_2) = (0, 0)$, use one iteration of the Frank-Wolfe algorithm to obtain exactly the same solution you found in part (c) of Prob. 13.6-15, and then use a second iteration to verify that it is an optimal solution (because it is replicated exactly). Explain why exactly the same results would be obtained on these two iterations with any other trial solution.

D,I **13.9-4.** Reconsider the linearly constrained convex programming model given in Prob. 13.6-16. Starting from the initial trial solution $(x_1, x_2, x_3) = (0, 0, 0)$, apply two iterations of the Frank-Wolfe algorithm.

D,I **13.9-5.** Consider the quadratic programming example presented in Sec. 13.7. Starting from the initial trial solution $(x_1, x_2) = (5, 5)$, apply seven iterations of the Frank-Wolfe algorithm.

13.9-6. Reconsider the quadratic programming model given in Prob. 13.7-4.
D,I **(a)** Starting from the initial trial solution $(x_1, x_2) = (0, 0)$, use the Frank-Wolfe algorithm (six iterations) to solve the problem (approximately).
(b) Show graphically how the sequence of trial solutions obtained in part (a) can be extrapolated to obtain a closer approximation of an optimal solution. What is your resulting estimate of this solution?

D,I **13.9-7.** Reconsider the first quadratic programming variation of the Wyndor Glass Co. problem presented in Sec. 13.2 (see Fig. 13.6). Starting from the initial trial solution $(x_1, x_2) = (0, 0)$, use three iterations of the Frank-Wolfe algorithm to obtain and verify the optimal solution.

D,I **13.9-8.** Reconsider the linearly constrained convex programming model given in Prob. 13.4-7. Starting from the initial trial solution $(x_1, x_2) = (0, 0)$, use the Frank-Wolfe algorithm (four iterations) to solve this model (approximately).

D,I **13.9-9.** Consider the following linearly constrained convex programming problem:

Maximize $f(\mathbf{x}) = 3x_1x_2 + 40x_1 + 30x_2 - 4x_1^2 - x_1^4$
$\qquad\qquad\qquad - 3x_2^2 - x_2^4$,

subject to

$4x_1 + 3x_2 \leq 12$
$x_1 + 2x_2 \leq 4$

and

$x_1 \geq 0, \qquad x_2 \geq 0.$

Starting from the initial trial solution $(x_1, x_2) = (0, 0)$, apply two iterations of the Frank-Wolfe algorithm.

D,I **13.9-10.*** Consider the following linearly constrained convex programming problem:

Maximize $f(\mathbf{x}) = 3x_1 + 4x_2 - x_1^3 - x_2^2$,

subject to

$x_1 + x_2 \leq 1$

and

$x_1 \geq 0, \qquad x_2 \geq 0.$

(a) Starting from the initial trial solution $(x_1, x_2) = (\frac{1}{4}, \frac{1}{4})$, apply three iterations of the Frank-Wolfe algorithm.
(b) Use the KKT conditions to check whether the solution obtained in part (a) is, in fact, optimal.

13.9-11. Consider the following linearly constrained convex programming problem:

Maximize $f(\mathbf{x}) = 4x_1 - x_1^4 + 2x_2 - x_2^2$,

subject to

$4x_1 + 2x_2 \leq 5$

and

$x_1 \geq 0, \qquad x_2 \geq 0.$

(a) Starting from the initial trial solution $(x_1, x_2) = (\frac{1}{2}, \frac{1}{2})$, apply four iterations of the Frank-Wolfe algorithm.
(b) Show graphically how the sequence of trial solutions obtained in part (a) can be extrapolated to obtain a closer approximation of an optimal solution. What is your resulting estimate of this solution?
(c) Use the KKT conditions to check whether the solution you obtained in part (b) is, in fact, optimal. If not, use these conditions to derive the exact optimal solution.

13.10-1. Reconsider the linearly constrained convex programming model given in Prob. 13.9-10.
(a) If SUMT were to be applied to this problem, what would be the unconstrained function $P(\mathbf{x}; r)$ to be maximized at each iteration?
(b) Setting $r = 1$ and using $(\frac{1}{4}, \frac{1}{4})$ as the initial trial solution, manually apply one iteration of the gradient search procedure (except stop before solving for t^*) to begin maximizing the function $P(\mathbf{x}; r)$ you obtained in part (a).
D,C **(c)** Beginning with the same initial trial solution as in part (b), use the automatic routine in your OR Courseware to apply SUMT to this problem with $r = 1, 10^{-2}, 10^{-4}$.
(d) Compare the final solution obtained in part (c) to the true optimal solution for Prob. 13.9-10 given in the back of the book. What is the percentage error in x_1, in x_2, and in $f(\mathbf{x})$?

13.10-2. Reconsider the linearly constrained convex programming model given in Prob. 13.9-11. Follow the instructions of parts (a), (b), and (c) of Prob. 13.10-1 for this model, except use $(x_1, x_2) = (\frac{1}{2}, \frac{1}{2})$ as the initial trial solution and use $r = 1, 10^{-2}, 10^{-4}, 10^{-6}$.

13.10-3. Reconsider the model given in Prob. 13.3-3.
(a) If SUMT were to be applied directly to this problem, what would be the unconstrained function $P(\mathbf{x}; r)$ to be *minimized* at each iteration?
(b) Setting $r = 100$ and using $(x_1, x_2) = (5, 5)$ as the initial trial solution, manually apply one iteration of the gradient search procedure (except stop before solving for t^*) to begin minimizing the function $P(\mathbf{x}; r)$ you obtained in part (a).
D,C **(c)** Beginning with the same initial trial solution as in part (b), use the automatic routine in your OR Courseware to apply SUMT to this problem with $r = 100, 1, 10^{-2}, 10^{-4}$. (*Hint:* The computer routine assumes that the problem has been converted to *maximization* form with the functional constraints in $\leq$ form.)

13.10-4. Consider the example for applying SUMT given in Sec. 13.10.
(a) Show that $(x_1, x_2) = (1, 2)$ satisfies the KKT conditions.
(b) Display the feasible region graphically, and then plot the locus of points $x_1 x_2 = 2$ to demonstrate that $(x_1, x_2) = (1, 2)$ with $f(1, 2) = 2$ is, in fact, a *global maximum*.

13.10-5.* Consider the following convex programming problem:

Maximize $\quad f(\mathbf{x}) = -2x_1 - (x_2 - 3)^2,$

subject to

$\quad x_1 \geq 3 \quad$ and $\quad x_2 \geq 3.$

(a) If SUMT were applied to this problem, what would be the unconstrained function $P(\mathbf{x}; r)$ to be maximized at each iteration?
(b) Derive the maximizing solution of $P(\mathbf{x}; r)$ analytically, and then give this solution for $r = 1, 10^{-2}, 10^{-4}, 10^{-6}$.
D,C **(c)** Beginning with the initial trial solution $(x_1, x_2) = (4, 4)$, use the automatic routine in your OR Courseware to apply SUMT to this problem with $r = 1, 10^{-2}, 10^{-4}, 10^{-6}$.

13.10-6. Use SUMT to solve the following convex programming problem:

Minimize $\quad f(\mathbf{x}) = \dfrac{(x_1 + 1)^3}{3} + x_2,$

subject to

$\quad x_1 \geq 1 \quad$ and $\quad x_2 \geq 0.$

(a) If SUMT were applied directly to this problem, what would be the unconstrained function $P(\mathbf{x}; r)$ to be minimized at each iteration?

(b) Derive the minimizing solution of $P(\mathbf{x}; r)$ analytically, and then give this solution for $r = 1, 10^{-2}, 10^{-4}, 10^{-6}$.
D,C **(c)** Beginning with the initial trial solution $(x_1, x_2) = (2, 1)$, use the automatic routine in your OR Courseware to apply SUMT to this problem (in maximization form) with $r = 1, 10^{-2}, 10^{-4}, 10^{-6}$.

D,C **13.10-7.** Consider the following convex programming problem:

Maximize $\quad f(\mathbf{x}) = x_1 x_2 - x_1 - x_1^2 - x_2 - x_2^2,$

subject to

$\quad x_2 \geq 0.$

Beginning with the initial trial solution $(x_1, x_2) = (1, 1)$, use the automatic routine in your OR Courseware to apply SUMT to this problem with $r = 1, 10^{-2}, 10^{-4}$.

D,C **13.10-8.** Reconsider the quadratic programming model given in Prob. 13.7-4. Beginning with the initial trial solution $(x_1, x_2) = (\frac{1}{2}, \frac{1}{2})$, use the automatic routine in your OR Courseware to apply SUMT to this model with $r = 1, 10^{-2}, 10^{-4}, 10^{-6}$.

D,C **13.10-9.** Reconsider the first quadratic programming variation of the Wyndor Glass Co. problem presented in Sec. 13.2 (see Fig. 13.6). Beginning with the initial trial solution $(x_1, x_2) = (2, 3)$, use the automatic routine in your OR Courseware to apply SUMT to this problem with $r = 10^2, 1, 10^{-2}, 10^{-4}$.

13.10-10. Consider the following nonconvex programming problem:

Maximize $\quad f(x) = 1,000x - 400x^2 + 40x^3 - x^4,$

subject to

$\quad x^2 + x \leq 500$

and

$\quad x \geq 0.$

(a) Identify the feasible values for x. Obtain general expressions for the first three derivatives of $f(x)$. Use this information to help you draw a rough sketch of $f(x)$ over the feasible region for x. Without calculating their values, mark the points on your graph that correspond to *local* maxima and minima.
I **(b)** Use the one-dimensional search procedure with $\epsilon = 0.05$ to find each of the local maxima. Use your sketch from part (a) to identify appropriate initial bounds for each of these searches. Which of the local maxima is a global maximum?
D,C **(c)** Use the automatic routine in your OR Courseware to apply SUMT to this problem with $r = 10^3, 10^2, 10, 1$ to find each of the local maxima. Use $x = 3$ and $x = 15$ as the initial trial solutions for these searches. Which of the local maxima is a global maximum?

13.10-11. Consider the following nonconvex programming problem:

$$\text{Maximize} \quad f(\mathbf{x}) = 3x_1x_2 - 2x_1^2 - x_2^2,$$

subject to

$$x_1^2 + 2x_2^2 \leq 4$$
$$2x_1 - x_2 \leq 3$$
$$x_1x_2^2 + x_1^2x_2 = 2$$

and

$$x_1 \geq 0, \qquad x_2 \geq 0.$$

(a) If SUMT were to be applied to this problem, what would be the unconstrained function $P(\mathbf{x}; r)$ to be maximized at each iteration?

D,C **(b)** Starting from the initial trial solution $(x_1, x_2) = (1, 1)$, use the automatic routine in your OR Courseware to apply SUMT to this problem with $r = 1, 10^{-2}, 10^{-4}$.

13.10-12. Reconsider the convex programming model with an equality constraint given in Prob. 13.6-14.

(a) If SUMT were to be applied to this model, what would be the unconstrained function $P(\mathbf{x}; r)$ to be *minimized* at each iteration?

D,C **(b)** Starting from the initial trial solution $(x_1, x_2, x_3) = (\frac{3}{2}, \frac{3}{2}, 2)$, use the automatic routine in your OR Courseware to apply SUMT to this model with $r = 10^{-2}, 10^{-4}, 10^{-6}, 10^{-8}$.

13.10-13. Consider the following nonconvex programming problem.

$$\text{Minimize} \quad f(\mathbf{x}) = \sin 3x_1 + \cos 3x_2 + \sin(x_1 + x_2),$$

subject to

$$x_1^2 - 10x_2 \geq -1$$
$$10x_1 + x_2^2 \leq 100$$

and

$$x_1 \geq 0, \qquad x_2 \geq 0.$$

(a) If SUMT were applied to this problem, what would be the unconstrained function $P(\mathbf{x}; r)$ to be minimized at each iteration?

(b) Describe how SUMT should be applied to attempt to obtain a global minimum. (Do not actually solve.)

13.11-1. Consider the following problem:

$$\text{Maximize} \quad Z = 4x_1 - x_1^2 + 10x_2 - x_2^2,$$

subject to

$$x_1^2 + 4x_2^2 \leq 16$$

and

$$x_1 \geq 0, \qquad x_2 \geq 0.$$

(a) Is this a convex programming problem? Answer yes or no, and then justify your answer.

(b) Can the modified simplex method be used to solve this problem? Answer yes or no, and then justify your answer (but do not actually solve.)

(c) Can the Frank-Wolfe algorithm be used to solve this problem? Answer yes or no, and then justify your answer (but do not actually solve.)

(d) What are the KKT conditions for this problem? Use these conditions to determine whether $(x_1, x_2) = (1, 1)$ can be optimal.

(e) Use the separable programming technique to formulate an *approximate* linear programming model for this problem. Use the feasible integers as the breakpoints for each piecewise linear function.

C **(f)** Use the simplex method to solve the problem as formulated in part (e).

(g) Give the function $P(\mathbf{x}; r)$ to be maximized at each iteration when applying SUMT to this problem. (Do not actually solve.)

D,C **(h)** Use SUMT (the automatic routine in your OR Courseware) to solve the problem as formulated in part (g). Begin with the initial trial solution $(x_1, x_2) = (2, 1)$ and use $r = 1, 10^{-2}, 10^{-4}, 10^{-6}$.

CASE 13.1 SAVVY STOCK SELECTION

Ever since the day she took her first economics class in high school, Lydia wondered about the financial practices of her parents. They worked very hard to earn enough money to live a comfortable middle-class life, but they never made their money work for them. They simply deposited their hard-earned paychecks in savings accounts earning a nominal amount of interest. (Fortunately, there always was enough money when it came time to pay her college bills.) She promised herself that when she became an adult, she would not follow the same financially conservative practices as her parents.

And Lydia kept this promise. Every morning while getting ready for work, she watches the CNN financial reports. She plays investment games on the World Wide Web, finding portfolios that maximize her return while minimizing her risk. She reads the *Wall Street Journal* and *Financial Times* with a thirst she cannot quench.

Lydia also reads the investment advice columns of the financial magazines, and she has noticed that on average, the advice of the investment advisers turns out to be very good. Therefore, she decides to follow the advice given in the latest issue of one of the magazines. In his monthly column the editor Jonathan Taylor recommends three stocks that he believes will rise far above market average. In addition, the well-known mutual fund guru Donna Carter advocates the purchase of three more stocks that she thinks will outperform the market over the next year.

BIGBELL (ticker symbol on the stock exchange: BB), one of the nation's largest telecommunications companies, trades at a price-earnings ratio well below market average. Huge investments over the last 8 months have depressed earnings considerably. However, with their new cutting edge technology, the company is expected to significantly raise their profit margins. Taylor predicts that the stock will rise from its current price of $60 per share to $72 per share within the next year.

LOTSOFPLACE (LOP) is one of the leading hard drive manufacturers in the world. The industry recently underwent major consolidation, as fierce price wars over the last few years were followed by many competitors going bankrupt or being bought by LOTSOFPLACE and its competitors. Due to reduced competition in the hard drive market, revenues and earnings are expected to rise considerably over the next year. Taylor predicts a one-year increase of 42 percent in the stock of LOTSOFPLACE from the current price of $127 per share.

INTERNETLIFE (ILI) has survived the many ups and downs of Internet companies. With the next Internet frenzy just around the corner, Taylor expects a doubling of this company's stock price from $4 to $8 within a year.

HEALTHTOMORROW (HEAL) is a leading biotechnology company that is about to get approval for several new drugs from the Food and Drug Administration, which will help earnings to grow 20 percent over the next few years. In particular a new drug to significantly reduce the risk of heart attacks is supposed to reap huge profits. Also, due to several new great-tasting medications for children, the company has been able to build an excellent image in the media. This public relations coup will surely have positive effects for the sale of its over-the-counter medications. Carter is convinced that the stock will rise from $50 to $75 per share within a year.

QUICKY (QUI) is a fast-food chain which has been vastly expanding its network of restaurants all over the United States. Carter has followed this company closely since it went public some 15 years ago when it had only a few dozen restaurants on the west coast of the United States. Since then the company has expanded, and it now has restaurants in every state. Due to its emphasis on healthy foods, it is capturing a growing market share. Carter believes that the stock will continue to perform well above market average for an increase of 46 percent in one year from its current stock price of $150.

AUTOMOBILE ALLIANCE (AUA) is a leading car manufacturer from the Detroit area that just recently introduced two new models. These models show very strong initial sales, and therefore the company's stock is predicted to rise from $20 to $26 over the next year.

On the World Wide Web Lydia found data about the risk involved in the stocks of these companies. The historical variances of return of the six stocks and their covariances are shown below.

Company	BB	LOP	ILI	HEAL	QUI	AUA
Variance	0.032	0.1	0.333	0.125	0.065	0.08

Covariances	LOP	ILI	HEAL	QUI	AUA
BB	0.005	0.03	−0.031	−0.027	0.01
LOP		0.085	−0.07	−0.05	0.02
ILI			−0.11	−0.02	0.042
HEAL				0.05	−0.06
QUI					−0.02

(a) At first, Lydia wants to ignore the risk of all the investments. Given this strategy, what is her optimal investment portfolio; that is, what fraction of her money should she invest in each of the six different stocks? What is the total risk of her portfolio?

(b) Lydia decides that she doesn't want to invest more than 40 percent in any individual stock. While still ignoring risk, what is her new optimal investment portfolio? What is the total risk of her new portfolio?

(c) Now Lydia wants to take into account the risk of her investment opportunities. Identify one of the model types described in this chapter that is applicable to her problem, and then formulate a model of this kind to be used in the following parts.

(d) What fractions of her money should Lydia put into the various stocks if she decides to maximize the expected return minus beta times the risk of her investment for beta = 0.25?

(e) Lydia recently received a bonus at work, $15,000 after taxes, that she wishes to invest. For the investment policy in part (d), how much money does she invest in the various stocks? How many shares of each stock does she buy?

(f) How does the solution in part (e) change if beta = 0.5? If beta = 1? If beta = 2?

(g) Give an intuitive explanation for the change in the expected return and the risk in part (f) as beta changes.

(h) Lydia wants to ensure that she receives an expected return of at least 35 percent. She wants to reach this goal at minimum risk. What investment portfolio allows her to do that?

(i) What is the minimum risk Lydia can achieve if she wants an expected return of at least 25 percent? Of at least 40 percent?

(j) Do you see any problems or disadvantages with Lydia's approach to her investment strategy?

CASE 13.2   INTERNATIONAL INVESTMENTS

Charles Rosen relaxes in a plush, overstuffed recliner by the fire, enjoying the final vestiges of his week-long winter vacation. As a financial analyst working for a large investment firm in Germany, Charles has very few occasions to enjoy these private moments, since he is generally catching red-eye flights around the world to evaluate various investment opportunities. Charles pats the loyal golden retriever lying at his feet and takes a swig of brandy, enjoying the warmth of the liquid. He sighs and realizes that he must begin attending to his own financial matters while he still has the time during the holiday. He opens a folder placed conspicuously on the top of a large stack of papers. The folder contains information about an investment Charles made when he graduated from college four years ago. . . .

Charles remembers his graduation day fondly. He obtained a degree in business administration and was full of investment ideas that were born while he had been day-dreaming in his numerous finance classes. Charles maintained a well-paying job throughout college, and he was able to save a large portion of the college fund that his parents had invested for him.

Upon graduation, Charles decided that he should transfer the college funds to a more lucrative investment opportunity. Since he had signed to work in Germany, he evaluated investment opportunities in that country. Ultimately, he decided to invest 30,000 German marks (DM) in so-called B-Bonds that would mature in 7 years. Charles purchased the bonds just 4 years ago last week (in early January of what will be called the "first year" in this discussion). He considered the bonds an excellent investment opportunity, since they offered high interest rates (see Table I) that would rise over the subsequent 7 years and because he could sell the bonds whenever he wanted after the first year. He calculated the amount that he would be paid if he sold bonds originally worth DM 100 on the last day of any of the 7 years (see Table II). The amount paid included the principal plus the interest. For example, if he sold bonds originally worth DM 100 on December 31 of the sixth year, he would be paid DM 163.51 (the principal is DM 100, and the interest is DM 63.51).

Charles did not sell any of the bonds during the first four years. Last year, however, the German federal government introduced a capital gains tax on interest income. The German government designated that the first DM 6,100 a single individual earns in interest per year would be tax-free. Any interest income beyond DM 6,100 would

TABLE 1 Interest rates over the 7 years

Year	Interest Rate	Annual Percentage Yield
1	7.50%	7.50%
2	8.50%	8.00%
3	8.50%	8.17%
4	8.75%	8.31%
5	9.00%	8.45%
6	9.00%	8.54%
7	9.00%	8.61%

TABLE II Total return on 100 DM

Year	DM
1	107.50
2	116.64
3	126.55
4	137.62
5	150.01
6	163.51
7	178.23

be taxed at a rate of 30 percent. For example, if Charles earned interest income of DM 10,100, he would be required to pay 30 percent of DM 4,000 (DM 10,100 − DM 6,100) in taxes, or DM 1,200. His after-tax income would therefore be DM 8,900.

Because of the new tax implemented last year, Charles has decided to reevaluate the investment. He knows that the new tax affects his potential return on the B-Bonds, but he also knows that most likely a strategy exists for maximizing his return on the bonds. He might be able to decrease the tax he has to pay on interest income by selling portions of his bonds in different years. Charles considers his strategy viable because the government requires investors to pay taxes on interest income only when they sell their B-Bonds. For example, if Charles were to sell one-third of his B-Bonds on December 31 of the sixth year, he would have to pay taxes on the interest income of DM 251 (DM 6,351 − DM 6,100).

Charles asks himself several questions. Should he keep all the bonds until the end of the seventh year? If so, he would earn 0.7823 times DM 30,000 in interest income, but he would have to pay very substantial taxes for that year. Considering these tax payments, Charles wonders if he should sell a portion of the bonds at the end of this year (the fifth year) and at the end of next year.

If Charles sells his bonds, his alternative investment opportunities are limited. He could purchase a certificate of deposit (CD) paying 4.0 percent interest, so he investigates this alternative. He meets with an investment adviser from the local branch of a bank, and the adviser tells him to keep the B-Bonds until the end of the seventh year. She argues that even if he had to pay 30 percent in taxes on the 9.00 percent rate of interest the B-Bonds would be paying in their last year (see Table I), this strategy would still result in a net rate of 6.30 percent interest, which is much better than the 4.0 percent interest he could obtain on a CD.

Charles concludes that he would make all his transactions on December 31, regardless of the year. Also, since he intends to attend business school in the United States in the fall of the seventh year and plans to pay his tuition for his second, third, and fourth semester with his investment, he does not plan to keep his money in Germany beyond December 31 of the seventh year.

(For the first three parts, assume that if Charles sells a portion of his bonds, he will put the money under his mattress earning zero percent interest. For the subsequent parts, assume that he could invest the proceeds of the bonds in the certificate of deposit.)

(a) Identify one of the model types described in this chapter that is applicable to this problem, and then formulate a model of this kind to be used in the following parts.

(b) What is the optimal investment strategy for Charles?

(c) What is fundamentally wrong with the advice Charles got from the investment adviser at the bank?

(d) Now that Charles is considering investment in the certificate of deposit, what is his optimal investment strategy?

(e) What would his optimal investment strategy for the fifth, sixth, and seventh years have been if he had originally invested DM 50,000?

(f) Charles and his fiancée have been planning to get married after his first year in business school. However, Charles learns that for married couples, the tax-free amount of interest earnings each year is DM 12,200. How much money could Charles save on his DM 30,000 investment by getting married this year (the fifth year for his investment)?

(g) Due to a recession in Germany, interest rates are low and are expected to remain low. However, since the American economy is booming, interest rates are expected to rise in the United States. A rise in interest rates would lead to a rise of the dollar in comparison to the mark. Analysts at Charles' investment bank expect the dollar to remain at the current exchange rate of DM 1.50 per dollar for the fifth year and then to rise to DM 1.80 per dollar by the end of the seventh year. Therefore, Charles is considering investing at the beginning of the sixth year in a 2-year American municipal bond paying 3.6 percent tax-exempt interest to help pay tuition. How much money should he plan to convert into dollars by selling B-Bonds for this investment?

14

Game Theory

Life is full of conflict and competition. Numerous examples involving adversaries in conflict include parlor games, military battles, political campaigns, advertising and marketing campaigns by competing business firms, and so forth. A basic feature in many of these situations is that the final outcome depends primarily upon the combination of strategies selected by the adversaries. Game theory is a mathematical theory that deals with the general features of competitive situations like these in a formal, abstract way. It places particular emphasis on the decision-making processes of the adversaries.

As briefly surveyed in Sec. 14.6, research on game theory continues to delve into rather complicated types of competitive situations. However, the focus in this chapter is on the simplest case, called **two-person, zero-sum games.** As the name implies, these games involve only two adversaries or *players* (who may be armies, teams, firms, and so on). They are called *zero-sum* games because one player wins whatever the other one loses, so that the sum of their net winnings is zero.

Section 14.1 introduces the basic model for two-person, zero-sum games, and the next four sections describe and illustrate different approaches to solving such games. The chapter concludes by mentioning some other kinds of competitive situations that are dealt with by other branches of game theory.

14.1 THE FORMULATION OF TWO-PERSON, ZERO-SUM GAMES

To illustrate the basic characteristics of two-person, zero-sum games, consider the game called *odds and evens*. This game consists simply of each player simultaneously showing either one finger or two fingers. If the number of fingers matches, so that the total number for both players is even, then the player taking evens (say, player 1) wins the bet (say, $1) from the player taking odds (player 2). If the number does not match, player 1 pays $1 to player 2. Thus, each player has two *strategies:* to show either one finger or two fingers. The resulting payoff to player 1 in dollars is shown in the *payoff table* given in Table 14.1.

In general, a two-person game is characterized by

1. The strategies of player 1
2. The strategies of player 2
3. The payoff table

TABLE 14.1 Payoff table for the odds and evens game

Strategy	Player 2	
	1	2
Player 1 1	1	−1
2	−1	1

Before the game begins, each player knows the strategies she or he has available, the ones the opponent has available, and the payoff table. The actual play of the game consists of each player simultaneously choosing a strategy without knowing the opponent's choice.

A strategy may involve only a simple action, such as showing a certain number of fingers in the odds and evens game. On the other hand, in more complicated games involving a series of moves, a **strategy** is a predetermined rule that specifies completely how one intends to respond to each possible circumstance at each stage of the game. For example, a strategy for one side in chess would indicate how to make the next move for *every* possible position on the board, so the total number of possible strategies would be astronomical. Applications of game theory normally involve far less complicated competitive situations than chess does, but the strategies involved can be fairly complex.

The **payoff table** shows the gain (positive or negative) for player 1 that would result from each combination of strategies for the two players. It is given only for player 1 because the table for player 2 is just the negative of this one, due to the zero-sum nature of the game.

The entries in the payoff table may be in any units desired, such as dollars, provided that they accurately represent the *utility* to player 1 of the corresponding outcome. However, utility is not necessarily proportional to the amount of money (or any other commodity) when large quantities are involved. For example, $2 million (after taxes) is probably worth much less than twice as much as $1 million to a poor person. In other words, given the choice between (1) a 50 percent chance of receiving $2 million rather than nothing and (2) being sure of getting $1 million, a poor person probably would much prefer the latter. On the other hand, the outcome corresponding to an entry of 2 in a payoff table should be "worth twice as much" to player 1 as the outcome corresponding to an entry of 1. Thus, given the choice, he or she should be indifferent between a 50 percent chance of receiving the former outcome (rather than nothing) and definitely receiving the latter outcome instead.[1]

A primary objective of game theory is the development of *rational criteria* for selecting a strategy. Two key assumptions are made:

1. *Both* players are *rational.*
2. *Both* players choose their strategies solely to *promote their own welfare* (no compassion for the opponent).

---

[1] See Sec. 15.5 for a further discussion of the concept of utility.

Game theory contrasts with *decision analysis* (see Chap. 15), where the assumption is that the decision maker is playing a game with a passive opponent—nature—which chooses its strategies in some random fashion.

We shall develop the standard game theory criteria for choosing strategies by means of illustrative examples. In particular, the next section presents a prototype example that illustrates the formulation of a two-person, zero-sum game and its solution in some simple situations. A more complicated variation of this game is then carried into Sec. 14.3 to develop a more general criterion. Sections 14.4 and 14.5 describe a graphical procedure and a linear programming formulation for solving such games.

14.2 SOLVING SIMPLE GAMES—A PROTOTYPE EXAMPLE

Two politicians are running against each other for the U.S. Senate. Campaign plans must now be made for the final 2 days, which are expected to be crucial because of the closeness of the race. Therefore, both politicians want to spend these days campaigning in two key cities, Bigtown and Megalopolis. To avoid wasting campaign time, they plan to travel at night and spend either 1 full day in each city or 2 full days in just one of the cities. However, since the necessary arrangements must be made in advance, neither politician will learn his (or her)[1] opponent's campaign schedule until after he has finalized his own. Therefore, each politician has asked his campaign manager in each of these cities to assess what the impact would be (in terms of votes won or lost) from the various possible combinations of days spent there by himself and by his opponent. He then wishes to use this information to choose his best strategy on how to use these 2 days.

Formulation as a Two-Person, Zero-Sum Game

To formulate this problem as a two-person, zero-sum game, we must identify the two *players* (obviously the two politicians), the *strategies* for each player, and the *payoff table.*

As the problem has been stated, each player has the following three strategies:

Strategy 1 = spend 1 day in each city.
Strategy 2 = spend both days in Bigtown.
Strategy 3 = spend both days in Megalopolis.

By contrast, the strategies would be more complicated in a different situation where each politician learns where his opponent will spend the first day before he finalizes his own plans for his second day. In that case, a typical strategy would be: Spend the first day in Bigtown; if the opponent also spends the first day in Bigtown, then spend the second day in Bigtown; however, if the opponent spends the first day in Megalopolis, then spend the second day in Megalopolis. There would be eight such strategies, one for each combination of the two first-day choices, the opponent's two first-day choices, and the two second-day choices.

Each entry in the payoff table for player 1 represents the *utility* to player 1 (or the negative utility to player 2) of the outcome resulting from the corresponding strategies used by the two players. From the politician's viewpoint, the objective is to *win votes,*

---

[1] We use only *his* or only *her* in some examples and problems for ease of reading: we do not mean to imply that only men or only women are engaged in the various activities.

TABLE 14.2 Form of the payoff table for politician 1 for the political campaign problem

		Total Net Votes Won by Politician 1 (in Units of 1,000 Votes)		
			Politician 2	
Strategy		1	2	3
Politician 1	1			
	2			
	3			

and each additional vote (before he learns the outcome of the election) is of equal value to him. Therefore, the appropriate entries for the payoff table for politician 1 are the *total net votes won* from the opponent (i.e., the sum of the net vote changes in the two cities) resulting from these 2 days of campaigning. Using units of 1,000 votes, this formulation is summarized in Table 14.2. Game theory assumes that both players are using the same formulation (including the same payoffs for player 1) for choosing their strategies.

However, we should also point out that this payoff table would *not* be appropriate if additional information were available to the politicians. In particular, assume that they know exactly how the populace is planning to vote 2 days before the election, so that each politician knows exactly how many net votes (positive or negative) he needs to switch in his favor during the last 2 days of campaigning to win the election. Consequently, the only significance of the data prescribed by Table 14.2 would be to indicate which politician would win the election with each combination of strategies. Because the ultimate goal is to win the election and because the size of the plurality is relatively inconsequential, the utility entries in the table then should be some positive constant (say, $+1$) when politician 1 wins and -1 when he loses. Even if only a *probability* of winning can be determined for each combination of strategies, the appropriate entries would be the probability of winning minus the probability of losing because they then would represent *expected* utilities. However, sufficiently accurate data to make such determinations usually are not available, so this example uses the thousands of total net votes won by politician 1 as the entries in the payoff table.

Using the form given in Table 14.2, we give three alternative sets of data for the payoff table to illustrate how to solve three different kinds of games.

Variation 1 of the Example

Given that Table 14.3 is the payoff table for player 1 (politician 1), which strategy should each player select?

This situation is a rather special one, where the answer can be obtained just by applying the concept of **dominated strategies** to rule out a succession of inferior strategies until only one choice remains.

TABLE 14.3 Payoff table for player 1 for variation 1 of the political campaign problem

		Player 2		
Strategy		**1**	**2**	**3**
	1	1	2	4
Player 1	2	1	0	5
	3	0	1	−1

A strategy is **dominated** by a second strategy if the second strategy is *always at least as good* (and sometimes better) regardless of what the opponent does. A dominated strategy can be eliminated immediately from further consideration.

At the outset, Table 14.3 includes no dominated strategies for player 2. However, for player 1, strategy 3 is dominated by strategy 1 because the latter has larger payoffs ($1 > 0, 2 > 1, 4 > -1$) regardless of what player 2 does. Eliminating strategy 3 from further consideration yields the following reduced payoff table:

	1	2	3
1	1	2	4
2	1	0	5

Because both players are assumed to be rational, player 2 also can deduce that player 1 has only these two strategies remaining under consideration. Therefore, player 2 now *does* have a dominated strategy—strategy 3, which is dominated by both strategies 1 and 2 because they always have smaller losses for player 2 (payoffs to player 1) in this reduced payoff table (for strategy 1: $1 < 4$, $1 < 5$; for strategy 2: $2 < 4$, $0 < 5$). Eliminating this strategy yields

	1	2
1	1	2
2	1	0

At this point, strategy 2 for player 1 becomes dominated by strategy 1 because the latter is better in column 2 ($2 > 0$) and equally good in column 1 ($1 = 1$). Eliminating the dominated strategy leads to

	1	2
1	1	2

Strategy 2 for player 2 now is dominated by strategy 1 ($1 < 2$), so strategy 2 should be eliminated.

Consequently, both players should select their strategy 1. Player 1 then will receive a payoff of 1 from player 2 (that is, politician 1 will gain 1,000 votes from politician 2).

In general, the payoff to player 1 when both players play optimally is referred to as the **value of the game.** A game that has a value of 0 is said to be a **fair game.** Since this particular game has a value of 1, it is *not* a fair game.

The concept of a dominated strategy is a very useful one for reducing the size of the payoff table that needs to be considered and, in unusual cases like this one, actually identifying the optimal solution for the game. However, most games require another approach to at least finish solving, as illustrated by the next two variations of the example.

Variation 2 of the Example

Now suppose that the current data give Table 14.4 as the payoff table for player 1 (politician 1). This game does not have dominated strategies, so it is not obvious what the players should do. What line of reasoning does game theory say they should use?

Consider player 1. By selecting strategy 1, he could win 6 or could lose as much as 3. However, because player 2 is rational and thus will seek a strategy that will protect himself from large payoffs to player 1, it seems likely that player 1 would incur a loss by playing strategy 1. Similarly, by selecting strategy 3, player 1 could win 5, but more probably his rational opponent would avoid this loss and instead administer a loss to player 1 which could be as large as 4. On the other hand, if player 1 selects strategy 2, he is guaranteed not to lose anything and he could even win something. Therefore, because it provides the *best guarantee* (a payoff of 0), strategy 2 seems to be a "rational" choice for player 1 against his rational opponent. (This line of reasoning assumes that both players are averse to risking larger losses than necessary, in contrast to those individuals who enjoy gambling for a large payoff against long odds.)

Now consider player 2. He could lose as much as 5 or 6 by using strategy 1 or 3, but is guaranteed at least breaking even with strategy 2. Therefore, by the same reasoning of seeking the best guarantee against a rational opponent, his apparent choice is strategy 2.

If both players choose their strategy 2, the result is that both break even. Thus, in this case, neither player improves upon his best guarantee, but both also are forcing the opponent into the same position. Even when the opponent deduces a player's strategy, the opponent cannot exploit this information to improve his position. Stalemate.

TABLE 14.4 Payoff table for player 1 for variation 2 of the political campaign problem

Strategy		Player 2 1	2	3	Minimum
	1	−3	−2	6	−3
Player 1	2	2	0	2	0 ← Maximin value
	3	5	−2	−4	−4
	Maximum:	5	0	6	

↑
Minimax value

The end product of this line of reasoning is that each player should play in such a way as to *minimize his maximum losses* whenever the resulting choice of strategy cannot be exploited by the opponent to then improve his position. This so-called **minimax criterion** is a standard criterion proposed by game theory for selecting a strategy. In effect, this criterion says to select a strategy that would be best even if the selection were being announced to the opponent before the opponent chooses a strategy. In terms of the payoff table, it implies that *player 1* should select the strategy whose *minimum payoff* is *largest*, whereas *player 2* should choose the one whose *maximum payoff to player 1* is the *smallest*. This criterion is illustrated in Table 14.4, where strategy 2 is identified as the *maximin strategy* for player 1 and strategy 2 is the *minimax strategy* for player 2. The resulting payoff of 0 is the value of the game, so this is a fair game.

Notice the interesting fact that the same entry in this payoff table yields both the maximin and minimax values. The reason is that this entry is both the minimum in its row and the maximum of its column. The position of any such entry is called a **saddle point.**

The fact that this game possesses a saddle point was actually crucial in determining how it should be played. Because of the saddle point, neither player can take advantage of the opponent's strategy to improve his own position. In particular, when player 2 predicts or learns that player 1 is using strategy 2, player 2 would incur a loss instead of breaking even if he were to change from his original plan of using his strategy 2. Similarly, player 1 would only worsen his position if he were to change his plan. Thus, neither player has any motive to consider changing strategies, either to take advantage of his opponent or to prevent the opponent from taking advantage of him. Therefore, since this is a **stable solution** (also called an *equilibrium solution*), players 1 and 2 should exclusively use their maximin and minimax strategies, respectively.

As the next variation illustrates, some games do not possess a saddle point, in which case a more complicated analysis is required.

Variation 3 of the Example

Late developments in the campaign result in the final payoff table for player 1 (politician 1) given by Table 14.5. How should this game be played?

Suppose that both players attempt to apply the minimax criterion in the same way as in variation 2. Player 1 can guarantee that he will lose no more than 2 by playing strategy 1. Similarly, player 2 can guarantee that he will lose no more than 2 by playing strategy 3.

TABLE 14.5 Payoff table for player 1 for variation 3 of the political campaign problem

		Player 2			
Strategy		**1**	**2**	**3**	**Minimum**
	1	0	−2	2	−2 ← Maximin value
Player 1	2	5	4	−3	−3
	3	2	3	−4	−4
	Maximum:	5	4	2	
				↑	
				Minimax value	

However, notice that the maximin value (-2) and the minimax value (2) do not coincide in this case. The result is that there is *no saddle point*.

What are the resulting consequences if both players plan to use the strategies just derived? It can be seen that player 1 would win 2 from player 2, which would make player 2 unhappy. Because player 2 is rational and can therefore foresee this outcome, he would then conclude that he can do much better, actually winning 2 rather than losing 2, by playing strategy 2 instead. Because player 1 is also rational, he would anticipate this switch and conclude that he can improve considerably, from -2 to 4, by changing to strategy 2. Realizing this, player 2 would then consider switching back to strategy 3 to convert a loss of 4 to a gain of 3. This possibility of a switch would cause player 1 to consider again using strategy 1, after which the whole cycle would start over again. Therefore, even though this game is being played only once, *any* tentative choice of a strategy leaves that player with a motive to consider changing strategies, either to take advantage of his opponent or to prevent the opponent from taking advantage of him.

In short, the originally suggested solution (player 1 to play strategy 1 and player 2 to play strategy 3) is an **unstable solution,** so it is necessary to develop a more satisfactory solution. But what kind of solution should it be?

The key fact seems to be that whenever one player's strategy is predictable, the opponent can take advantage of this information to improve his position. Therefore, an essential feature of a rational plan for playing a game such as this one is that neither player should be able to deduce which strategy the other will use. Hence, in this case, rather than applying some known criterion for determining a single strategy that will definitely be used, it is necessary to choose among alternative acceptable strategies on some kind of random basis. By doing this, neither player knows in advance which of his own strategies will be used, let alone what his opponent will do.

This suggests, in very general terms, the kind of approach that is required for games lacking a saddle point. In the next section we discuss the approach more fully. Given this foundation, the following two sections will develop procedures for finding an optimal way of playing such games. This particular variation of the political campaign problem will continue to be used to illustrate these ideas as they are developed.

14.3 GAMES WITH MIXED STRATEGIES

Whenever a game does not possess a saddle point, game theory advises each player to assign a probability distribution over her set of strategies. To express this mathematically, let

x_i = probability that player 1 will use strategy i ($i = 1, 2, \ldots, m$),
y_j = probability that player 2 will use strategy j ($j = 1, 2, \ldots, n$),

where m and n are the respective numbers of available strategies. Thus, player 1 would specify her plan for playing the game by assigning values to $x_1, x_2, \ldots, x_m$. Because these values are probabilities, they would need to be nonnegative and add to 1. Similarly, the plan for player 2 would be described by the values she assigns to her decision variables $y_1, y_2, \ldots, y_n$. These plans $(x_1, x_2, \ldots, x_m)$ and $(y_1, y_2, \ldots, y_n)$ are usually referred to as **mixed strategies,** and the original strategies are then called **pure strategies.**

When the game is actually played, it is necessary for each player to use one of her pure strategies. However, this pure strategy would be chosen by using some random device to obtain a random observation from the probability distribution specified by the mixed strategy, where this observation would indicate which particular pure strategy to use.

To illustrate, suppose that players 1 and 2 in variation 3 of the political campaign problem (see Table 14.5) select the mixed strategies $(x_1, x_2, x_3) = (\frac{1}{2}, \frac{1}{2}, 0)$ and $(y_1, y_2, y_3) = (0, \frac{1}{2}, \frac{1}{2})$, respectively. This selection would say that player 1 is giving an equal chance (probability of $\frac{1}{2}$) of choosing either (pure) strategy 1 or 2, but he is discarding strategy 3 entirely. Similarly, player 2 is randomly choosing between his last two pure strategies. To play the game, each player could then flip a coin to determine which of his two acceptable pure strategies he will actually use.

Although no completely satisfactory measure of performance is available for evaluating mixed strategies, a very useful one is the *expected payoff*. By applying the probability theory definition of expected value, this quantity is

$$\text{Expected payoff for player 1} = \sum_{i=1}^{m} \sum_{j=1}^{n} p_{ij} x_i y_j,$$

where p_{ij} is the payoff if player 1 uses pure strategy i and player 2 uses pure strategy j. In the example of mixed strategies just given, there are four possible payoffs $(-2, 2, 4, -3)$, each occurring with a probability of $\frac{1}{4}$, so the expected payoff is $\frac{1}{4}(-2 + 2 + 4 - 3) = \frac{1}{4}$. Thus, this measure of performance does not disclose anything about the risks involved in playing the game, but it does indicate what the average payoff will tend to be if the game is played many times.

By using this measure, game theory extends the concept of the minimax criterion to games that lack a saddle point and thus need mixed strategies. In this context, the **minimax criterion** says that a given player should select the mixed strategy that *minimizes* the *maximum expected loss* to himself. Equivalently, when we focus on payoffs (player 1) rather than losses (player 2), this criterion says to *maximin* instead, i.e., *maximize* the *minimum expected payoff* to the player. By the *minimum expected payoff* we mean the smallest possible expected payoff that can result from any mixed strategy with which the opponent can counter. Thus, the mixed strategy for player 1 that is *optimal* according to this criterion is the one that provides the *guarantee* (minimum expected payoff) that is *best* (maximal). (The value of this best guarantee is the *maximin value,* denoted by $\underline{v}$.) Similarly, the *optimal* strategy for player 2 is the one that provides the *best guarantee,* where *best* now means *minimal* and *guarantee* refers to the *maximum expected loss* that can be administered by any of the opponent's mixed strategies. (This best guarantee is the *minimax value,* denoted by $\bar{v}$.)

Recall that when only pure strategies were used, games not having a saddle point turned out to be *unstable* (no stable solutions). The reason was essentially that $\underline{v} < \bar{v}$, so that the players would want to change their strategies to improve their positions. Similarly, for games with mixed strategies, it is necessary that $\underline{v} = \bar{v}$ for the optimal solution to be *stable.* Fortunately, according to the minimax theorem of game theory, this condition always holds for such games.

Minimax theorem: If mixed strategies are allowed, the pair of mixed strategies that is optimal according to the minimax criterion provides a *stable solution* with $\underline{v} = \bar{v} = v$ (the value of the game), so that neither player can do better by unilaterally changing her or his strategy.

One proof of this theorem is included in Sec. 14.5.

Although the concept of mixed strategies becomes quite intuitive if the game is played *repeatedly,* it requires some interpretation when the game is to be played just *once.* In this case, using a mixed strategy still involves selecting and using *one* pure strategy (randomly selected from the specified probability distribution), so it might seem more sensible to ignore this randomization process and just choose the one "best" pure strategy to be used. However, we have already illustrated for variation 3 in the preceding section that a player must *not* allow the opponent to deduce what his strategy will be (i.e., the solution procedure under the rules of game theory must not *definitely* identify which pure strategy will be used when the game is unstable). Furthermore, even if the opponent is able to use only his knowledge of the tendencies of the first player to deduce probabilities (for the pure strategy chosen) that are different from those for the optimal mixed strategy, then the opponent still can take advantage of this knowledge to reduce the expected payoff to the first player. Therefore, the only way to guarantee attaining the optimal expected payoff v is to randomly select the pure strategy to be used from the probability distribution for the optimal mixed strategy. (Valid statistical procedures for making such a random selection are discussed in Sec. 22.4.)

Now we need to show how to find the optimal mixed strategy for each player. There are several methods of doing this. One is a graphical procedure that may be used whenever one of the players has only two (undominated) pure strategies; this approach is described in the next section. When larger games are involved, the usual method is to transform the problem to a linear programming problem that then can be solved by the simplex method on a computer; Sec. 14.5 discusses this approach.

14.4 GRAPHICAL SOLUTION PROCEDURE

Consider any game with mixed strategies such that, after dominated strategies are eliminated, one of the players has only two pure strategies. To be specific, let this player be player 1. Because her mixed strategies are (x_1, x_2) and $x_2 = 1 - x_1$, it is necessary for her to solve only for the optimal value of x_1. However, it is straightforward to plot the expected payoff as a function of x_1 for each of her opponent's pure strategies. This graph can then be used to identify the point that maximizes the minimum expected payoff. The opponent's minimax mixed strategy can also be identified from the graph.

To illustrate this procedure, consider variation 3 of the political campaign problem (see Table 14.5). Notice that the third pure strategy for player 1 is dominated by her second, so the payoff table can be reduced to the form given in Table 14.6. Therefore, for

TABLE 14.6 Reduced payoff table for player 1 for variation 3 of the political campaign problem

		Probability		Player 2		
				y_1	y_2	y_3
	Probability	Pure Strategy		1	2	3
Player 1	x_1	1		0	-2	2
	$1 - x_1$	2		5	4	-3

each of the pure strategies available to player 2, the expected payoff for player 1 will be

(y_1, y_2, y_3)	Expected Payoff
$(1, 0, 0)$	$0x_1 + 5(1 - x_1) = 5 - 5x_1$
$(0, 1, 0)$	$-2x_1 + 4(1 - x_1) = 4 - 6x_1$
$(0, 0, 1)$	$2x_1 - 3(1 - x_1) = -3 + 5x_1$

Now plot these expected-payoff lines on a graph, as shown in Fig. 14.1. For any given values of x_1 and (y_1, y_2, y_3), the expected payoff will be the appropriate weighted average of the corresponding points on these three lines. In particular,

Expected payoff for player 1 $= y_1(5 - 5x_1) + y_2(4 - 6x_1) + y_3(-3 + 5x_1)$.

Remember that player 2 wants to minimize this expected payoff for player 1. Given x_1, player 2 can minimize this expected payoff by choosing the pure strategy that corresponds to the "bottom" line for that x_1 in Fig. 14.1 (either $-3 + 5x_1$ or $4 - 6x_1$, but never $5 - 5x_1$). According to the minimax (or maximin) criterion, player 1 wants to maximize this minimum expected payoff. Consequently, player 1 should select the value of x_1 where the bottom line peaks, i.e., where the $(-3 + 5x_1)$ and $(4 - 6x_1)$ lines intersect, which yields an expected payoff of

$$\underline{v} = \overline{v} = \max_{0 \leq x_1 \leq 1} \{\min\{-3 + 5x_1, 4 - 6x_1\}\}.$$

To solve algebraically for this optimal value of x_1 at the intersection of the two lines $-3 + 5x_1$ and $4 - 6x_1$, we set

$$-3 + 5x_1 = 4 - 6x_1,$$

FIGURE 14.1
Graphical procedure for solving games

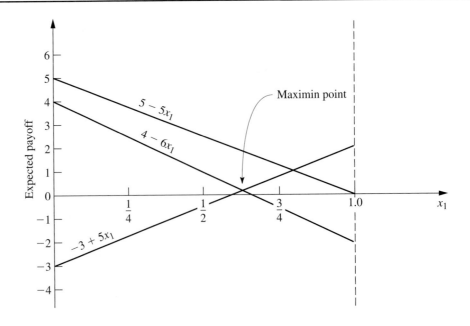

which yields $x_1 = \frac{7}{11}$. Thus, $(x_1, x_2) = (\frac{7}{11}, \frac{4}{11})$ is the *optimal mixed strategy* for player 1, and

$$\underline{v} = v = -3 + 5\left(\frac{7}{11}\right) = \frac{2}{11}$$

is the value of the game.

To find the corresponding optimal mixed strategy for player 2, we now reason as follows. According to the definition of the minimax value $\bar{v}$ and the minimax theorem, the expected payoff resulting from the optimal strategy $(y_1, y_2, y_3) = (y_1^*, y_2^*, y_3^*)$ will satisfy the condition

$$y_1^*(5 - 5x_1) + y_2^*(4 - 6x_1) + y_3^*(-3 + 5x_1) \leq \bar{v} = v = \frac{2}{11}$$

for all values of x_1 $(0 \leq x_1 \leq 1)$. Furthermore, when player 1 is playing optimally (that is, $x_1 = \frac{7}{11}$), this inequality will be an equality (by the minimax theorem), so that

$$\frac{20}{11}y_1^* + \frac{2}{11}y_2^* + \frac{2}{11}y_3^* = v = \frac{2}{11}.$$

Because (y_1, y_2, y_3) is a probability distribution, it is also known that

$$y_1^* + y_2^* + y_3^* = 1.$$

Therefore, $y_1^* = 0$ because $y_1^* > 0$ would violate the next-to-last equation; i.e., the expected payoff on the graph at $x_1 = \frac{7}{11}$ would be above the maximin point. (In general, any line that does not pass through the maximin point must be given a zero weight to avoid increasing the expected payoff above this point.)

Hence,

$$y_2^* (4 - 6x_1) + y_3^* (-3 + 5x_1) \begin{cases} \leq \dfrac{2}{11} & \text{for } 0 \leq x_1 \leq 1, \\[2ex] = \dfrac{2}{11} & \text{for } x_1 = \dfrac{7}{11}. \end{cases}$$

But y_2^* and y_3^* are numbers, so the left-hand side is the equation of a straight line, which is a fixed weighted average of the two "bottom" lines on the graph. Because the ordinate of this line must equal $\frac{2}{11}$ at $x_1 = \frac{7}{11}$, and because it must never exceed $\frac{2}{11}$, the line necessarily is horizontal. (This conclusion is always true unless the optimal value of x_1 is either 0 or 1, in which case player 2 also should use a single pure strategy.) Therefore,

$$y_2^*(4 - 6x_1) + y_3^*(-3 + 5x_1) = \frac{2}{11}, \qquad \text{for } 0 \leq x_1 \leq 1.$$

Hence, to solve for y_2^* and y_3^*, select two values of x_1 (say, 0 and 1), and solve the resulting two simultaneous equations. Thus,

$$4y_2^* - 3y_3^* = \frac{2}{11},$$

$$-2y_2^* + 2y_3^* = \frac{2}{11},$$

which has a simultaneous solution of $y_2^* = \frac{5}{11}$ and $y_3^* = \frac{6}{11}$. Therefore, the *optimal mixed strategy* for player 2 is $(y_1, y_2, y_3) = (0, \frac{5}{11}, \frac{6}{11})$.

If, in another problem, there should happen to be more than two lines passing through the maximin point, so that more than two of the y_j^* values can be greater than zero, this condition would imply that there are many ties for the optimal mixed strategy for player 2. One such strategy can then be identified by setting all but two of these y_j^* values equal to zero and solving for the remaining two in the manner just described. For the remaining two, the associated lines must have positive slope in one case and negative slope in the other.

Although this graphical procedure has been illustrated for only one particular problem, essentially the same reasoning can be used to solve any game with mixed strategies that has only two undominated pure strategies for one of the players.

14.5 SOLVING BY LINEAR PROGRAMMING

Any game with mixed strategies can be solved by transforming the problem to a linear programming problem. As you will see, this transformation requires little more than applying the minimax theorem and using the definitions of the maximin value $\underline{v}$ and minimax value $\bar{v}$.

First, consider how to find the optimal mixed strategy for player 1. As indicated in Sec. 14.3,

$$\text{Expected payoff for player 1} = \sum_{i=1}^{m} \sum_{j=1}^{n} p_{ij} x_i y_j$$

and the strategy $(x_1, x_2, \ldots, x_m)$ is optimal if

$$\sum_{i=1}^{m} \sum_{j=1}^{n} p_{ij} x_i y_j \geq \underline{v} = v$$

for all opposing strategies $(y_1, y_2, \ldots, y_n)$. Thus, this inequality will need to hold, e.g., for each of the pure strategies of player 2, that is, for each of the strategies $(y_1, y_2, \ldots, y_n)$ where one $y_j = 1$ and the rest equal 0. Substituting these values into the inequality yields

$$\sum_{i=1}^{m} p_{ij} x_i \geq v \qquad \text{for } j = 1, 2, \ldots, n,$$

so that the inequality *implies* this set of n inequalities. Furthermore, this set of n inequalities *implies* the original inequality (rewritten)

$$\sum_{j=1}^{n} y_j \left(\sum_{i=1}^{m} p_{ij} x_i \right) \geq \sum_{j=1}^{n} y_j v = v,$$

since

$$\sum_{j=1}^{n} y_j = 1.$$

Because the implication goes in both directions, it follows that imposing this set of n linear inequalities is *equivalent* to requiring the original inequality to hold for all strategies

$(y_1, y_2, \ldots, y_n)$. But these n inequalities are legitimate linear programming constraints, as are the additional constraints

$$x_1 + x_2 + \cdots + x_m = 1$$
$$x_i \geq 0, \qquad \text{for } i = 1, 2, \ldots, m$$

that are required to ensure that the x_i are probabilities. Therefore, any solution $(x_1, x_2, \ldots, x_m)$ that satisfies this entire set of linear programming constraints is the desired optimal mixed strategy.

Consequently, the problem of finding an optimal mixed strategy has been reduced to finding a feasible solution for a linear programming problem, which can be done as described in Chap. 4. The two remaining difficulties are that (1) v is unknown and (2) the linear programming problem has no objective function. Fortunately, both these difficulties can be resolved at one stroke by replacing the unknown constant v by the variable x_{m+1} and then *maximizing* x_{m+1}, so that x_{m+1} automatically will equal v (by definition) at the *optimal* solution for the linear programming problem!

To summarize, player 1 would find his optimal mixed strategy by using the simplex method to solve the linear programming problem:

Maximize $\quad x_{m+1}$,

subject to

$$p_{11}x_1 + p_{21}x_2 + \cdots + p_{m1}x_m - x_{m+1} \geq 0$$
$$p_{12}x_1 + p_{22}x_2 + \cdots + p_{m2}x_m - x_{m+1} \geq 0$$
$$\cdots\cdots\cdots\cdots\cdots\cdots\cdots\cdots\cdots\cdots\cdots\cdots\cdots$$
$$p_{1n}x_1 + p_{2n}x_2 + \cdots + p_{mn}x_m - x_{m+1} \geq 0$$
$$x_1 + x_2 + \cdots + x_m = 1$$

and

$$x_i \geq 0, \qquad \text{for } i = 1, 2, \ldots, m.$$

Note that x_{m+1} is not restricted to be nonnegative, whereas the simplex method can be applied only after *all* the variables have nonnegativity constraints. However, this matter can be easily rectified, as will be discussed shortly.

Now consider player 2. He could find his optimal mixed strategy by rewriting the payoff table as the payoff to himself rather than to player 1 and then by proceeding exactly as just described. However, it is enlightening to summarize his formulation in terms of the original payoff table. By proceeding in a way that is completely analogous to that just described, player 2 would conclude that his optimal mixed strategy is given by an optimal solution to the linear programming problem:

Minimize $\quad y_{n+1}$,

subject to

$$p_{11}y_1 + p_{12}y_2 + \cdots + p_{1n}y_n - y_{n+1} \leq 0$$
$$p_{21}y_1 + p_{22}y_2 + \cdots + p_{2n}y_n - y_{n+1} \leq 0$$
$$\cdots\cdots\cdots\cdots\cdots\cdots\cdots\cdots\cdots\cdots\cdots\cdots\cdots$$
$$p_{m1}y_1 + p_{m2}y_2 + \cdots + p_{mn}y_n - y_{n+1} \leq 0$$
$$y_1 + y_2 + \cdots + y_n = 1$$

and

$$y_j \geq 0, \quad \text{for } j = 1, 2, \ldots, n.$$

It is easy to show (see Prob. 14.5-5 and its hint) that this linear programming problem and the one given for player 1 are *dual* to each other in the sense described in Secs. 6.1 and 6.4. This fact has several important implications. One implication is that the optimal mixed strategies for both players can be found by solving only one of the linear programming problems because the optimal dual solution is an automatic by-product of the simplex method calculations to find the optimal primal solution. A second implication is that this brings all *duality theory* (described in Chap. 6) to bear upon the interpretation and analysis of games.

A related implication is that this provides a simple proof of the minimax theorem. Let x_{m+1}^* and y_{n+1}^* denote the value of x_{m+1} and y_{n+1} in the optimal solution of the respective linear programming problems. It is known from the *strong duality property* given in Sec. 6.1 that $-x_{m+1}^* = -y_{n+1}^*$, so that $x_{m+1}^* = y_{n+1}^*$. However, it is evident from the definition of $\underline{v}$ and $\bar{v}$ that $\underline{v} = x_{m+1}^*$ and $\bar{v} = y_{n+1}^*$, so it follows that $\underline{v} = \bar{v}$, as claimed by the minimax theorem.

One remaining loose end needs to be tied up, namely, what to do about x_{m+1} and y_{n+1} being unrestricted in sign in the linear programming formulations. If it is clear that $v \geq 0$ so that the optimal values of x_{m+1} and y_{n+1} are nonnegative, then it is safe to introduce nonnegativity constraints for these variables for the purpose of applying the simplex method. However, if $v < 0$, then an adjustment needs to be made. One possibility is to use the approach described in Sec. 4.6 for replacing a variable without a nonnegativity constraint by the difference of two nonnegative variables. Another is to reverse players 1 and 2 so that the payoff table would be rewritten as the payoff to the original player 2, which would make the corresponding value of v positive. A third, and the most commonly used, procedure is to add a sufficiently large fixed constant to all the entries in the payoff table that the new value of the game will be positive. (For example, setting this constant equal to the absolute value of the largest negative entry will suffice.) Because this same constant is added to every entry, this adjustment cannot alter the optimal mixed strategies in any way, so they can now be obtained in the usual manner. The indicated value of the game would be increased by the amount of the constant, but this value can be readjusted after the solution has been obtained.

To illustrate this linear programming approach, consider again variation 3 of the political campaign problem after dominated strategy 3 for player 1 is eliminated (see Table 14.6). Because there are some negative entries in the reduced payoff table, it is unclear at the outset whether the *value* of the game v is *nonnegative* (it turns out to be). For the moment, let us assume that $v \geq 0$ and proceed without making any of the adjustments discussed in the preceding paragraph.

To write out the linear programming model for player 1 for this example, note that p_{ij} in the general model is the entry in row i and column j of Table 14.6, for $i = 1, 2$ and $j = 1, 2, 3$. The resulting model is

> Maximize $\quad x_3,$

subject to

$$5x_2 - x_3 \geq 0$$
$$-2x_1 + 4x_2 - x_3 \geq 0$$

$$2x_1 - 3x_2 - x_3 \geq 0$$
$$x_1 + x_2 \qquad = 1$$

and

$$x_1 \geq 0, \qquad x_2 \geq 0.$$

Applying the simplex method to this linear programming problem (after adding the constraint $x_3 \geq 0$) yields $x_1^* = \frac{7}{11}, x_2^* = \frac{4}{11}, x_3^* = \frac{2}{11}$ as the optimal solution. (See Probs. 14.5-7 and 14.5-8.) Consequently, just as was found by the graphical procedure in the preceding section, the optimal mixed strategy for player 1 according to the minimax criterion is $(x_1, x_2) = (\frac{7}{11}, \frac{4}{11})$, and the value of the game is $v = x_3^* = \frac{2}{11}$. The simplex method also yields the optimal solution for the dual (given next) of this problem, namely, $y_1^* = 0, y_2^* = \frac{5}{11}, y_3^* = \frac{6}{11}, y_4^* = \frac{2}{11}$, so the optimal mixed strategy for player 2 is $(y_1, y_2, y_3) = (0, \frac{5}{11}, \frac{6}{11})$.

The dual of the preceding problem is just the linear programming model for player 2 (the one with variables $y_1, y_2, \ldots, y_n, y_{n+1}$) shown earlier in this section. (See Prob. 14.5-6.) By plugging in the values of p_{ij} from Table 14.6, this model is

Minimize $\qquad y_4$,

subject to

$$- 2y_2 + 2y_3 - y_4 \leq 0$$
$$5y_1 + 4y_2 - 3y_3 - y_4 \leq 0$$
$$y_1 + y_2 + y_3 \qquad = 1$$

and

$$y_1 \geq 0, \qquad y_2 \geq 0, \qquad y_3 \geq 0.$$

Applying the simplex method directly to this model (after adding the constraint $y_4 \geq 0$) yields the optimal solution: $y_1^* = 0, y_2^* = \frac{5}{11}, y_3^* = \frac{6}{11}, y_4^* = \frac{2}{11}$ (as well as the optimal dual solution $x_1^* = \frac{7}{11}, x_2^* = \frac{4}{11}, x_3^* = \frac{2}{11}$). Thus, the optimal mixed strategy for player 2 is $(y_1, y_2, y_3) = (0, \frac{5}{11}, \frac{6}{11})$, and the value of the game is again seen to be $v = y_4^* = \frac{2}{11}$.

Because we already had found the optimal mixed strategy for player 2 while dealing with the first model, we did not have to solve the second one. In general, you always can find optimal mixed strategies for *both* players by choosing just one of the models (either one) and then using the simplex method to solve for both an optimal solution and an optimal dual solution.

When the simplex method was applied to both of these linear programming models, a nonnegativity constraint was added that assumed that $v \geq 0$. If this assumption were violated, both models would have no feasible solutions, so the simplex method would stop quickly with this message. To avoid this risk, we could have added a positive constant, say, 3 (the absolute value of the largest negative entry), to all the entries in Table 14.6. This then would increase by 3 all the coefficients of x_1, x_2, y_1, y_2, and y_3 in the inequality constraints of the two models. (See Prob. 14.5-1.)

14.6 EXTENSIONS

Although this chapter has considered only two-person, zero-sum games with a finite number of pure strategies, game theory extends far beyond this kind of game. In fact, extensive research has been done on a number of more complicated types of games, including the ones summarized in this section.

The simplest generalization is to the *two-person, constant-sum game*. In this case, the sum of the payoffs to the two players is a fixed constant (positive or negative) regardless of which combination of strategies is selected. The only difference from a two-person, zero-sum game is that, in the latter case, the constant must be zero. A nonzero constant may arise instead because, in addition to one player winning whatever the other one loses, the two players may share some reward (if the constant is positive) or some cost (if the constant is negative) for participating in the game. Adding this fixed constant does nothing to affect which strategies should be chosen. Therefore, the analysis for determining optimal strategies is exactly the same as described in this chapter for two-person, zero-sum games.

A more complicated extension is to the *n-person game*, where more than two players may participate in the game. This generalization is particularly important because, in many kinds of competitive situations, frequently more than two competitors are involved. This may occur, e.g., in competition among business firms, in international diplomacy, and so forth. Unfortunately, the existing theory for such games is less satisfactory than it is for two-person games.

Another generalization is the *nonzero-sum game*, where the sum of the payoffs to the players need not be 0 (or any other fixed constant). This case reflects the fact that many competitive situations include noncompetitive aspects that contribute to the mutual advantage or mutual disadvantage of the players. For example, the advertising strategies of competing companies can affect not only how they will split the market but also the total size of the market for their competing products. However, in contrast to a constant-sum game, the size of the mutual gain (or loss) for the players depends on the combination of strategies chosen.

Because mutual gain is possible, nonzero-sum games are further classified in terms of the degree to which the players are permitted to cooperate. At one extreme is the *noncooperative game*, where there is no preplay communication between the players. At the other extreme is the *cooperative game*, where preplay discussions and binding agreements are permitted. For example, competitive situations involving trade regulations between countries, or collective bargaining between labor and management, might be formulated as cooperative games. When there are more than two players, cooperative games also allow some of or all the players to form coalitions.

Still another extension is to the class of *infinite games*, where the players have an infinite number of pure strategies available to them. These games are designed for the kind of situation where the strategy to be selected can be represented by a *continuous* decision variable. For example, this decision variable might be the time at which to take a certain action, or the proportion of one's resources to allocate to a certain activity, in a competitive situation.

However, the analysis required in these extensions beyond the two-person, zero-sum, finite game is relatively complex and will not be pursued further here.

14.7   CONCLUSIONS

The general problem of how to make decisions in a competitive environment is a very common and important one. The fundamental contribution of game theory is that it provides a basic conceptual framework for formulating and analyzing such problems in simple situations. However, there is a considerable gap between what the theory can handle and the complexity of most competitive situations arising in practice. Therefore, the conceptual tools of game theory usually play just a supplementary role in dealing with these situations.

Because of the importance of the general problem, research is continuing with some success to extend the theory to more complex situations.

SELECTED REFERENCES

1. Aumann, R. J., and S. Hart (eds.): *Handbook of Game Theory: With Application to Economics,* vols. 1, 2, and 3, North-Holland, Amsterdam, 1992, 1994, 1995.
2. Binmore, K.: *Fun and Games: A Text on Game Theory,* Heath, Lexington, MA, 1992.
3. Fudenberg, D., and J. Tirole: *Game Theory,* MIT Press, Cambridge, MA, 1991.
4. Meyerson, R. B.: *Game Theory: Analysis of Conflict,* Harvard University Press, Cambridge, MA, 1991.
5. Owen, G.: *Game Theory,* 3d ed., Academic Press, San Diego, 1995.
6. Parthasarathy, T., B. Dutta, and A. Sen (eds.): *Game Theoretical Applications to Economics and Operations Research,* Kluwer Academic Publishers, Boston, 1997.
7. Shubik, M.: *Game Theory in the Social Sciences,* vols. 1 (1982) and 2 (1987), MIT Press, Cambridge, MA.

LEARNING AIDS IN YOUR OR COURSEWARE FOR THIS CHAPTER

"Ch. 14—Game Theory" Files for Solving the Examples:

Excel File
LINGO/LINDO File
MPL/CPLEX File

See Appendix 1 for documentation of the software.

PROBLEMS

The symbol to the left of some of the problems (or their parts) has the following meaning.

C: Use the computer with any of the software options available to you (or as instructed by your instructor) to solve the problem.

An asterisk on the problem number indicates that at least a partial answer is given in the back of the book.

14.1-1. The labor union and management of a particular company have been negotiating a new labor contract. However, negotiations have now come to an impasse, with management making a "final" offer of a wage increase of $1.10 per hour and the union making a "final" demand of a $1.60 per hour increase.

Therefore, both sides have agreed to let an impartial arbitrator set the wage increase somewhere between $1.10 and $1.60 per hour (inclusively).

The arbitrator has asked each side to submit to her a confidential proposal for a fair and economically reasonable wage increase (rounded to the nearest dime). From past experience, both sides know that this arbitrator normally accepts the proposal of the side that gives the most from its final figure. If neither side changes its final figure, or if they both give in the same amount, then the arbitrator normally compromises halfway between ($1.35 in this case). Each side now needs to determine what wage increase to propose for its own maximum advantage.

Formulate this problem as a two-person, zero-sum game.

14.1-2. Two manufacturers currently are competing for sales in two different but equally profitable product lines. In both cases the sales volume for manufacturer 2 is three times as large as that for manufacturer 1. Because of a recent technological breakthrough, both manufacturers will be making a major improvement in both products. However, they are uncertain as to what development and marketing strategy to follow.

If both product improvements are developed simultaneously, either manufacturer can have them ready for sale in 12 months. Another alternative is to have a "crash program" to develop only one product first to try to get it marketed ahead of the competition. By doing this, manufacturer 2 could have one product ready for sale in 9 months, whereas manufacturer 1 would require 10 months (because of previous commitments for its production facilities). For either manufacturer, the second product could then be ready for sale in an additional 9 months.

For either product line, if both manufacturers market their improved models simultaneously, it is estimated that manufacturer 1 would increase its share of the total future sales of this product by 8 percent of the total (from 25 to 33 percent). Similarly, manufacturer 1 would increase its share by 20, 30, and 40 percent of the total if it marketed the product sooner than manufacturer 2 by 2, 6, and 8 months, respectively. On the other hand, manufacturer 1 would lose 4, 10, 12, and 14 percent of the total if manufacturer 2 marketed it sooner by 1, 3, 7, and 10 months, respectively.

Formulate this problem as a two-person, zero-sum game, and then determine which strategy the respective manufacturers should use according to the minimax criterion.

14.1-3. Consider the following parlor game to be played between two players. Each player begins with three chips: one red, one white, and one blue. Each chip can be used only once.

To begin, each player selects one of her chips and places it on the table, concealed. Both players then uncover the chips and determine the payoff to the winning player. In particular, if both players play the same kind of chip, it is a draw; otherwise, the following table indicates the winner and how much she receives from the other player. Next, each player selects one of her two remaining chips and repeats the procedure, resulting in another payoff according to the following table. Finally, each player plays her one remaining chip, resulting in the third and final payoff.

Winning Chip	Payoff ($)
Red beats white	50
White beats blue	40
Blue beats red	30
Matching colors	0

Formulate this problem as a two-person, zero-sum game by identifying the form of the strategies and payoffs.

14.2-1. Reconsider Prob. 14.1-1.
(a) Use the concept of dominated strategies to determine the best strategy for each side.
(b) Without eliminating dominated strategies, use the minimax criterion to determine the best strategy for each side.

14.2-2.* For each of the following payoff tables, determine the optimal strategy for each player by successively eliminating dominated strategies. (Indicate the order in which you eliminated strategies.)

(a)

Strategy		Player 2 1	Player 2 2	Player 2 3
	1	−3	1	2
Player 1	2	1	2	1
	3	1	0	−2

(b)

Strategy		Player 2 1	Player 2 2	Player 2 3
	1	1	2	0
Player 1	2	2	−3	−2
	3	0	3	−1

14.2-3. Consider the game having the following payoff table.

Strategy		Player 2 1	Player 2 2	Player 2 3	Player 2 4
	1	2	−3	−1	1
Player 1	2	−1	1	−2	2
	3	−1	2	−1	3

Determine the optimal strategy for each player by successively eliminating dominated strategies. Give a list of the dominated strategies (and the corresponding dominating strategies) in the order in which you were able to eliminate them.

14.2-4. Find the saddle point for the game having the following payoff table.

Strategy		Player 2 1	Player 2 2	Player 2 3
	1	1	−1	1
Player 1	2	−2	0	3
	3	3	1	2

Use the minimax criterion to find the best strategy for each player. Does this game have a saddle point? Is it a stable game?

14.2-5. Find the saddle point for the game having the following payoff table.

		Player 2			
Strategy		**1**	**2**	**3**	**4**
	1	3	−3	−2	−4
Player 1	2	−4	−2	−1	1
	3	1	−1	2	0

Use the minimax criterion to find the best strategy for each player. Does this game have a saddle point? Is it a stable game?

14.2-6. Two companies share the bulk of the market for a particular kind of product. Each is now planning its new marketing plans for the next year in an attempt to wrest some sales away from the other company. (The total sales for the product are relatively fixed, so one company can increase its sales only by winning them away from the other.) Each company is considering three possibilities: (1) better packaging of the product, (2) increased advertising, and (3) a slight reduction in price. The costs of the three alternatives are quite comparable and sufficiently large that each company will select just one. The estimated effect of each combination of alternatives on the *increased percentage of the sales* for company 1 is as follows:

		Player 2		
Strategy		**1**	**2**	**3**
	1	2	3	1
Player 1	2	1	4	0
	3	3	−2	−1

Each company must make its selection before learning the decision of the other company.
(a) Without eliminating dominated strategies, use the minimax (or maximin) criterion to determine the best strategy for each company.
(b) Now identify and eliminate dominated strategies as far as possible. Make a list of the dominated strategies, showing the order in which you were able to eliminate them. Then show the resulting reduced payoff table with no remaining dominated strategies.

14.2-7.* Two politicians soon will be starting their campaigns against each other for a certain political office. Each must now select the main issue she will emphasize as the theme of her campaign. Each has three advantageous issues from which to choose, but the relative effectiveness of each one would depend upon the issue chosen by the opponent. In particular, the estimated increase in the vote for politician 1 (expressed as a percentage of the total vote) resulting from each combination of issues is as follows:

		Issue for Politician 2		
		1	**2**	**3**
Issue for	1	7	−1	3
Politician 1	2	1	0	2
	3	−5	−3	−1

However, because considerable staff work is required to research and formulate the issue chosen, each politician must make her own choice before learning the opponent's choice. Which issue should she choose?

For each of the situations described here, formulate this problem as a two-person, zero-sum game, and then determine which issue should be chosen by each politician according to the specified criterion.
(a) The current preferences of the voters are very uncertain, so each additional percent of votes won by one of the politicians has the same value to her. Use the minimax criterion.
(b) A reliable poll has found that the percentage of the voters currently preferring politician 1 (before the issues have been raised) lies between 45 and 50 percent. (Assume a uniform distribution over this range.) Use the concept of dominated strategies, beginning with the strategies for politician 1.
(c) Suppose that the percentage described in part (*b*) actually were 45 percent. Should politician 1 use the minimax criterion? Explain. Which issue would you recommend? Why?

14.2-8. Briefly describe what you feel are the advantages and disadvantages of the minimax criterion.

14.3-1. Consider the following parlor game between two players. It begins when a referee flips a coin, notes whether it comes up heads or tails, and then shows this result to player 1 only. Player 1 may then (1) pass and thereby pay $5 to player 2 or (2) bet. If player 1 passes, the game is terminated. However, if he bets, the game continues, in which case player 2 may then either (1) pass and thereby pay $5 to player 1 or (2) call. If player 2 calls, the referee then shows him the coin; if it came up heads, player 2 pays $10 to player 1; if it came up tails, player 2 receives $10 from player 1.

(a) Give the pure strategies for each player. (*Hint:* Player 1 will have four pure strategies, each one specifying how he would respond to each of the two results the referee can show him; player 2 will have two pure strategies, each one specifying how he will respond if player 1 bets.)

(b) Develop the payoff table for this game, using expected values for the entries when necessary. Then identify and eliminate any dominated strategies.

(c) Show that none of the entries in the resulting payoff table are a saddle point. Then explain why any fixed choice of a pure strategy for each of the two players must be an unstable solution, so mixed strategies should be used instead.

(d) Write an expression for the expected payoff in terms of the probabilities of the two players using their respective pure strategies. Then show what this expression reduces to for the following three cases: (i) Player 2 definitely uses his first strategy, (ii) player 2 definitely uses his second strategy, (iii) player 2 assigns equal probabilities to using his two strategies.

14.4-1. Reconsider Prob. 14.3-1. Use the graphical procedure described in Sec. 14.4 to determine the optimal mixed strategy for each player according to the minimax criterion. Also give the corresponding value of the game.

14.4-2. Consider the game having the following payoff table.

		Player 2	
Strategy		**1**	**2**
Player 1	1	3	−2
	2	−1	2

Use the graphical procedure described in Sec. 14.4 to determine the value of the game and the optimal mixed strategy for each player according to the minimax criterion. Check your answer for player 2 by constructing *his* payoff table and applying the graphical procedure directly to this table.

14.4-3.* For each of the following payoff tables, use the graphical procedure described in Sec. 14.4 to determine the value of the game and the optimal mixed strategy for each player according to the minimax criterion.

(a)

		Player 2		
Strategy		**1**	**2**	**3**
Player 1	1	4	3	1
	2	0	1	2

(b)

		Player 2		
Strategy		**1**	**2**	**3**
Player 1	1	1	−1	3
	2	0	4	1
	3	3	−2	5
	4	−3	6	−2

14.4-4. The A. J. Swim Team soon will have an important swim meet with the G. N. Swim Team. Each team has a star swimmer (John and Mark, respectively) who can swim very well in the 100-yard butterfly, backstroke, and breaststroke events. However, the rules prevent them from being used in more than two of these events. Therefore, their coaches now need to decide how to use them to maximum advantage.

Each team will enter three swimmers per event (the maximum allowed). For each event, the following table gives the best time previously achieved by John and Mark as well as the best time for each of the other swimmers who will definitely enter that event. (Whichever event John or Mark does not swim, his team's third entry for that event will be slower than the two shown in the table.)

	A. J. Swim Team			G. N. Swim Team		
	Entry			**Entry**		
	1	**2**	**John**	**Mark**	**1**	**2**
Butterfly stroke	1:01.6	59.1	57.5	58.4	1:03.2	59.8
Backstroke	1:06.8	1:05.6	1:03.3	1:02.6	1:04.9	1:04.1
Breaststroke	1:13.9	1:12.5	1:04.7	1:06.1	1:15.3	1:11.8

The points awarded are 5 points for first place, 3 points for second place, 1 point for third place, and none for lower places. Both coaches believe that all swimmers will essentially equal their best times in this meet. Thus, John and Mark each will definitely be entered in two of these three events.

(a) The coaches must submit all their entries before the meet without knowing the entries for the other team, and no changes are permitted later. The outcome of the meet is very uncertain, so each additional point has equal value for the coaches. Formulate this problem as a two-person, zero-sum game. Eliminate dominated strategies, and then use the graphical procedure described in Sec. 14.4 to find the optimal mixed strategy for each team according to the minimax criterion.

(b) The situation and assignment are the same as in part (*a*), except that both coaches now believe that the A. J. team will win the swim meet if it can win 13 or more points in these three events, but will lose with less than 13 points. [Compare the resulting optimal mixed strategies with those obtained in part (a).]

(c) Now suppose that the coaches submit their entries during the meet one event at a time. When submitting his entries for an event, the coach does not know who will be swimming that event for the other team, but he does know who has swum in *preceding* events. The three key events just discussed are swum in the order listed in the table. Once again, the A. J. team needs 13 points in these events to win the swim meet. Formulate this problem as a two-person, zero-sum game. Then use the concept of dominated strategies to determine the best strategy for the G. N. team that actually "guarantees" it will win under the assumptions being made.

(d) The situation is the same as in part (c). However, now assume that the coach for the G. N. team does not know about game theory and so may, in fact, choose any of his available strategies that have Mark swimming two events. Use the concept of dominated strategies to determine the best strategies from which the coach for the A. J. team should choose. If this coach knows that the other coach has a tendency to enter Mark in the butterfly and the backstroke more often than in the breaststroke, which strategy should she choose?

14.5-1. Refer to the last paragraph of Sec. 14.5. Suppose that 3 were added to all the entries of Table 14.6 to ensure that the corresponding linear programming models for both players have feasible solutions with $x_3 \geq 0$ and $y_4 \geq 0$. Write out these two models. Based on the information given in Sec. 14.5, what are the optimal solutions for these two models? What is the relationship between x_3^* and y_4^*? What is the relationship between the *value* of the original game v and the values of x_3^* and y_4^*?

14.5-2.* Consider the game having the following payoff table.

Strategy		Player 2			
		1	2	3	4
Player 1	1	5	0	3	1
	2	2	4	3	2
	3	3	2	0	4

(a) Use the approach described in Sec. 14.5 to formulate the problem of finding optimal mixed strategies according to the minimax criterion as a linear programming problem.

C (b) Use the simplex method to find these optimal mixed strategies.

14.5-3. Follow the instructions of Prob. 14.5-2 for the game having the following payoff table.

Strategy		Player 2		
		1	2	3
Player 1	1	4	2	-3
	2	-1	0	3
	3	2	3	-2

14.5-4. Follow the instructions of Prob. 14.5-2 for the game having the following payoff table.

Strategy		Player 2				
		1	2	3	4	5
Player 1	1	1	-3	2	-2	1
	2	2	3	0	3	-2
	3	0	4	-1	-3	2
	4	-4	0	-2	2	-1

14.5-5. Section 14.5 presents a general linear programming formulation for finding an optimal mixed strategy for player 1 and for player 2. Using Table 6.14, show that the linear programming problem given for player 2 is the dual of the problem given for player 1. (*Hint:* Remember that a dual variable with a nonpositivity constraint $y_i' \leq 0$ can be replaced by $y_i = -y_i'$ with a nonnegativity constraint $y_i \geq 0$.)

14.5-6. Consider the linear programming models for players 1 and 2 given near the end of Sec. 14.5 for variation 3 of the political campaign problem (see Table 14.6). Follow the instructions of Prob. 14.5-5 for these two models.

14.5-7. Consider variation 3 of the political campaign problem (see Table 14.6). Refer to the resulting linear programming model for player 1 given near the end of Sec. 14.5. Ignoring the objective function variable x_3, plot the *feasible region* for x_1 and x_2 graphically (as described in Sec. 3.1). (*Hint:* This feasible region consists of a single line segment.) Next, write an algebraic expression for the maximizing value of x_3 for any point in this feasible region. Finally, use this expression to demonstrate that the optimal solution must, in fact, be the one given in Sec. 14.5.

C **14.5-8.** Consider the linear programming model for player 1 given near the end of Sec. 14.5 for variation 3 of the political campaign problem (see Table 14.6). Verify the optimal mixed strategies for both players given in Sec. 14.5 by applying an automatic routine for the simplex method to this model to find both its optimal solution and its optimal dual solution.

14.5-9. Consider the general $m \times n$, two-person, zero-sum game. Let p_{ij} denote the payoff to player 1 if he plays his strategy i $(i = 1, \ldots, m)$ and player 2 plays her strategy j $(j = 1, \ldots, n)$. Strategy 1 (say) for player 1 is said to be *weakly dominated* by strategy 2 (say) if $p_{1j} \leq p_{2j}$ for $j = 1, \ldots, n$ and $p_{1j} = p_{2j}$ for one or more values of j.

(a) Assume that the payoff table possesses one or more saddle points, so that the players have corresponding optimal pure strategies under the minimax criterion. Prove that eliminating *weakly dominated* strategies from the payoff table cannot eliminate all these saddle points and cannot produce any new ones.

(b) Assume that the payoff table does not possess any saddle points, so that the optimal strategies under the minimax criterion are mixed strategies. Prove that eliminating weakly dominated pure strategies from the payoff table cannot eliminate all optimal mixed strategies and cannot produce any new ones.

15

Decision Analysis

The previous chapters have focused mainly on decision making when the consequences of alternative decisions are known with a reasonable degree of certainty. This decision-making environment enabled formulating helpful mathematical models (linear programming, integer programming, nonlinear programming, etc.) with objective functions that specify the estimated consequences of any combination of decisions. Although these consequences usually cannot be predicted with complete certainty, they could at least be estimated with enough accuracy to justify using such models (along with sensitivity analysis, etc.).

However, decisions often must be made in environments that are much more fraught with uncertainty. Here are a few examples.

1. A manufacturer introducing a new product into the marketplace. What will be the reaction of potential customers? How much should be produced? Should the product be test marketed in a small region before deciding upon full distribution? How much advertising is needed to launch the product successfully?
2. A financial firm investing in securities. Which are the market sectors and individual securities with the best prospects? Where is the economy headed? How about interest rates? How should these factors affect the investment decisions?
3. A government contractor bidding on a new contract. What will be the actual costs of the project? Which other companies might be bidding? What are their likely bids?
4. An agricultural firm selecting the mix of crops and livestock for the upcoming season. What will be the weather conditions? Where are prices headed? What will costs be?
5. An oil company deciding whether to drill for oil in a particular location. How likely is oil there? How much? How deep will they need to drill? Should geologists investigate the site further before drilling?

These are the kinds of decision making in the face of great uncertainty that *decision analysis* is designed to address. Decision analysis provides a framework and methodology for rational decision making when the outcomes are uncertain.

The preceding chapter describes how game theory also can be used for certain kinds of decision making in the face of uncertainty. There are some similarities in the approaches used by game theory and decision analysis. However, there also are differences because they are designed for different kinds of applications. We will describe these similarities and differences in Sec. 15.2.

Frequently, one question to be addressed with decision analysis is whether to make the needed decision immediately or to first do some *testing* (at some expense) to reduce the level of uncertainty about the outcome of the decision. For example, the testing might be field testing of a proposed new product to test consumer reaction before making a decision on whether to proceed with full-scale production and marketing of the product. This testing is referred to as performing *experimentation*. Therefore, decision analysis divides decision making between the cases of *without experimentation* and *with experimentation*.

The first section introduces a prototype example that will be carried throughout the chapter for illustrative purposes. Sections 15.2 and 15.3 then present the basic principles of *decision making without experimentation* and *decision making with experimentation*. We next describe *decision trees,* a useful tool for depicting and analyzing the decision process when a series of decisions needs to be made. Section 15.5 introduces *utility theory,* which provides a way of calibrating the possible outcomes of the decision to reflect the true value of these outcomes to the decision maker. We then conclude the chapter by discussing the practical application of decision analysis and summarizing a variety of applications that have been very beneficial to the organizations involved.

15.1   A PROTOTYPE EXAMPLE

The GOFERBROKE COMPANY owns a tract of land that may contain oil. A consulting geologist has reported to management that she believes there is 1 chance in 4 of oil.

Because of this prospect, another oil company has offered to purchase the land for $90,000. However, Goferbroke is considering holding the land in order to drill for oil itself. The cost of drilling is $100,000. If oil is found, the resulting expected revenue will be $800,000, so the company's expected profit (after deducting the cost of drilling) will be $700,000. A loss of $100,000 (the drilling cost) will be incurred if the land is dry (no oil).

Table 15.1 summarizes these data. Section 15.2 discusses how to approach the decision of whether to drill or sell based just on these data. (We will refer to this as the *first* Goferbroke Co. problem.)

However, before deciding whether to drill or sell, another option is to conduct a detailed seismic survey of the land to obtain a better estimate of the probability of finding oil. Section 15.3 discusses this case of *decision making with experimentation,* at which point the necessary additional data will be provided.

This company is operating without much capital, so a loss of $100,000 would be quite serious. In Sec. 15.5, we describe how to refine the evaluation of the consequences of the various possible outcomes.

TABLE 15.1 Prospective profits for the Goferbroke Company

Alternative	Status of Land	Payoff	
		Oil	Dry
Drill for oil		$700,000	−$100,000
Sell the land		$ 90,000	$ 90,000
Chance of status		1 in 4	3 in 4

15.2 DECISION MAKING WITHOUT EXPERIMENTATION

Before seeking a solution to the first Goferbroke Co. problem, we will formulate a general framework for decision making.

In general terms, the decision maker must choose an **action** from a set of possible actions. The set contains all the *feasible alternatives* under consideration for how to proceed with the problem of concern.

This choice of an action must be made in the face of uncertainty, because the outcome will be affected by random factors that are outside the control of the decision maker. These random factors determine what situation will be found at the time that the action is executed. Each of these possible situations is referred to as a possible **state of nature.**

For each combination of an action and a state of nature, the decision maker knows what the resulting payoff would be. The **payoff** is a quantitative measure of the value to the decision maker of the consequences of the outcome. For example, the payoff frequently is represented by the *net monetary gain* (profit), although other measures also can be used (as described in Sec. 15.5). If the consequences of the outcome do not become completely certain even when the state of nature is given, then the payoff becomes an *expected value* (in the statistical sense) of the measure of the consequences. A **payoff table** commonly is used to provide the payoff for each combination of an action and a state of nature.

If you previously studied game theory (Chap. 14), we should point out an interesting analogy between this decision analysis framework and the two-person, zero-sum games described in Chap. 14. The *decision maker* and *nature* can be viewed as the *two players* of such a game. The *alternative actions* and the possible *states of nature* can then be viewed as the available *strategies* for these respective players, where each combination of strategies results in some *payoff* to player 1 (the decision maker). From this viewpoint, the decision analysis framework can be summarized as follows:

1. The *decision maker* needs to choose one of the *alternative actions.*
2. *Nature* then would choose one of the possible *states of nature.*
3. Each combination of an action and state of nature would result in a *payoff,* which is given as one of the entries in a *payoff table.*
4. This payoff table should be used to find an *optimal action* for the decision maker according to an appropriate criterion.

Soon we will present three possibilities for this criterion, where the first one (the maximin payoff criterion) comes from game theory.

However, this analogy to two-person, zero-sum games breaks down in one important respect. In game theory, *both* players are assumed to be *rational* and choosing their strategies to *promote their own welfare.* This description still fits the decision maker, but certainly not nature. By contrast, nature now is a passive player that chooses its strategies (states of nature) in some random fashion. This change means that the game theory criterion for how to choose an optimal strategy (action) will not appeal to many decision makers in the current context.

One additional element needs to be added to the decision analysis framework. The decision maker generally will have some information that should be taken into account about the relative likelihood of the possible states of nature. Such information can usually be translated to a probability distribution, acting as though the state of nature is a random variable, in which case this distribution is referred to as a **prior distribution.** Prior distributions are often subjective in that they may depend upon the experience or intuition of an individual. The probabilities for the respective states of nature provided by the prior distribution are called **prior probabilities.**

Formulation of the Prototype Example in This Framework

As indicated in Table 15.1, the Goferbroke Co. has two possible actions under consideration: drill for oil or sell the land. The possible states of nature are that the land contains oil and that it does not, as designated in the column headings of Table 15.1 by *oil* and *dry.* Since the consulting geologist has estimated that there is 1 chance in 4 of oil (and so 3 chances in 4 of no oil), the prior probabilities of the two states of nature are 0.25 and 0.75, respectively. Therefore, with the payoff in units of thousands of dollars of profit, the payoff table can be obtained directly from Table 15.1, as shown in Table 15.2.

We will use this payoff table next to find the optimal action according to each of the three criteria described below. In each case, we will employ an Excel template provided in this chapter's Excel file for the criterion. These templates expedite entering a payoff table in a spreadsheet format and then applying the criteria.

The Maximin Payoff Criterion

If the decision maker's problem were to be viewed as a *game against nature,* then game theory would say to choose the action according to the *minimax criterion* (as described in Sec. 14.2). From the viewpoint of player 1 (the decision maker), this criterion is more aptly named the *maximin payoff criterion,* as summarized below.

> **Maximin payoff criterion:** For each possible action, find the *minimum payoff* over all possible states of nature. Next, find the *maximum* of these minimum payoffs. Choose the action whose minimum payoff gives this maximum.

The Excel template displayed in Fig. 15.1 shows the application of this criterion to the prototype example. Thus, since the minimum payoff for selling (90) is larger than that for drilling (-100), the former alternative (sell the land) will be chosen as the action to take.

The rationale for this criterion is that it provides the *best guarantee* of the payoff that will be obtained. Regardless of what the true state of nature turns out to be for the example, the payoff from selling the land cannot be less than 90, which provides the best available guarantee. Thus, this criterion takes the pessimistic viewpoint that, regardless of

TABLE 15.2 Payoff table for the decision analysis formulation of the Goferbroke Co. problem

Alternative	State of Nature	
	Oil	Dry
1. Drill for oil	700	−100
2. Sell the land	90	90
Prior probability	0.25	0.75

	A	B	C	D	E	F	G	H	I
1		Maximin Payoff Criterion for the Goferbroke Co. Problem							
2									
3				State of Nature				Minimum	
4		Alternative	Oil	Dry				in Row	
5		Drill	700	-100				-100	
6		Sell	90	90				90	Maximin
7									
8									
9									

	H	I
5	=MIN(C5:G5)	=IF(H5=MAX($H$5:$H$9),"Maximin","")
6	=MIN(C6:G6)	=IF(H6=MAX($H$5:$H$9),"Maximin","")
7	=MIN(C7:G7)	=IF(H7=MAX($H$5:$H$9),"Maximin","")
8	=MIN(C8:G8)	=IF(H8=MAX($H$5:$H$9),"Maximin","")
9	=MIN(C9:G9)	=IF(H9=MAX($H$5:$H$9),"Maximin","")

FIGURE 15.1
The application of the Excel template for the *maximin payoff criterion* to the first Goferbroke Co. problem.

which action is selected, the worst state of nature for that action is likely to occur, so we should choose the action which provides the best payoff with its worst state of nature.

This rationale is quite valid when one is competing against a rational and malevolent opponent. However, this criterion is not often used in games against nature because it is an extremely conservative criterion in this context. In effect, it assumes that nature is a conscious opponent that wants to inflict as much damage as possible on the decision maker. Nature is not a malevolent opponent, and the decision maker does not need to focus solely on the worst possible payoff from each action. This is especially true when the worst possible payoff from an action comes from a relatively unlikely state of nature.

Thus, this criterion normally is of interest only to a very cautious decision maker.

The Maximum Likelihood Criterion

The next criterion focuses on the *most likely* state of nature, as summarized below.

> **Maximum likelihood criterion:** Identify the most likely state of nature (the one with the largest prior probability). For this state of nature, find the action with the maximum payoff. Choose this action.

Applying this criterion to the example, Fig. 15.2 indicates that the *Dry* state has the largest prior probability. In the Dry column, the sell alternative has the maximum payoff, so the choice is to sell the land.

The appeal of this criterion is that the most important state of nature is the most likely one, so the action chosen is the best one for this particularly important state of nature. Basing the decision on the assumption that this state of nature will occur tends to give a better chance of a favorable outcome than assuming any other state of nature. Furthermore, the criterion does not rely on questionable subjective estimates of the probabilities of the respective states of nature other than identifying the most likely state.

	A	B	C	D	E	F	G	H
1	**Maximum Likelihood Criterion for the Goferbroke Co. Problem**							
2								
3				State of Nature				
4		Alternative	Oil	Dry				
5		Drill	700	-100				
6		Sell	90	90				Maximum
7								
8								
9								
10		Prior Probability	0.25	0.75				
11			Maximum					

FIGURE 15.2
The application of the Excel template for the *maximum likelihood criterion* to the first Goferbroke Co. problem.

The major drawback of the criterion is that it completely ignores much relevant information. No state of nature is considered other than the most likely one. In a problem with many possible states of nature, the probability of the most likely one may be quite small, so focusing on just this one state of nature is quite unwarranted. Even in the example, where the prior probability of the *Dry* state is 0.75, this criterion ignores the extremely attractive payoff of 700 if the company drills and finds oil. In effect, the criterion does not permit gambling on a low-probability big payoff, no matter how attractive the gamble may be.

Bayes' Decision Rule[1]

Our third criterion, and the one commonly chosen, is *Bayes' decision rule*, described below.

Bayes' decision rule: Using the best available estimates of the probabilities of the respective states of nature (currently the prior probabilities), calculate the expected value of the payoff for each of the possible actions. Choose the action with the maximum expected payoff.

For the prototype example, these expected payoffs are calculated directly from Table 15.2 as follows:

$$E[\text{Payoff (drill)}] = 0.25(700) + 0.75(-100)$$
$$= 100.$$
$$E[\text{Payoff (sell)}] = 0.25(90) + 0.75(90)$$
$$= 90.$$

Since 100 is larger than 90, the alternative action selected is to drill for oil.

Note that this choice contrasts with the selection of the sell alternative under each of the two preceding criteria.

---

[1]The origin of this name is that this criterion is often credited to the Reverend Thomas Bayes, a nonconforming 18th-century English minister who won renown as a philosopher and mathematician. (The same basic idea has even longer roots in the field of economics.) This decision rule also is sometimes called the *expected monetary value* (*EMF*) criterion, although this is a misnomer for those cases where the measure of the payoff is something other than monetary value (as in Sec. 15.5).

	A	B	C	D	E	F	G	H	I
1		Bayes' Decision Rule for the Goferbroke Co. Problem							
2									
3					State of Nature			Expected	
4		Alternative	Oil	Dry				Payoff	
5		Drill	700	-100				100	Maximum
6		Sell	90	90				90	
7									
8									
9									
10		Prior Probability	0.25	0.75					

	H	I
5	=SUMPRODUCT(C5:G5,C10:G10)	=IF(H5=MAX($H$5:$H$9),"Maximum","")
6	=SUMPRODUCT(C6:G6,C10:G10)	=IF(H6=MAX($H$5:$H$9),"Maximum","")
7	=SUMPRODUCT(C7:G7,C10:G10)	=IF(H7=MAX($H$5:$H$9),"Maximum","")
8	=SUMPRODUCT(C8:G8,C10:G10)	=IF(H8=MAX($H$5:$H$9),"Maximum","")
9	=SUMPRODUCT(C9:G9,C10:G10)	=IF(H9=MAX($H$5:$H$9),"Maximum","")

FIGURE 15.3
The application of the Excel template for *Bayes' decision rule* to the first Goferbroke Co. problem.

Figure 15.3 shows the application of the Excel template for Bayes' decision rule to this problem. The word *Maximum* in cell I5 signifies that the drill alternative in row 5 should be chosen because it has the maximum expected payoff.

The big advantage of Bayes' decision rule is that it incorporates all the available information, including all the payoffs and the best available estimates of the probabilities of the respective states of nature.

It is sometimes argued that these estimates of the probabilities necessarily are largely subjective and so are too shaky to be trusted. There is no accurate way of predicting the future, including a future state of nature, even in probability terms. This argument has some validity. The reasonableness of the estimates of the probabilities should be assessed in each individual situation.

Nevertheless, under many circumstances, past experience and current evidence enable one to develop reasonable estimates of the probabilities. Using this information should provide better grounds for a sound decision than ignoring it. Furthermore, experimentation frequently can be conducted to improve these estimates, as described in the next section. Therefore, we will be using only Bayes' decision rule throughout the remainder of the chapter.

To assess the effect of possible inaccuracies in the prior probabilities, it often is helpful to conduct sensitivity analysis, as described below.

Sensitivity Analysis with Bayes' Decision Rule

Sensitivity analysis commonly is used with various applications of operations research to study the effect if some of the numbers included in the mathematical model are not correct. In this case, the mathematical model is represented by the payoff table shown in Fig. 15.3. The numbers in this table that are most questionable are the prior probabilities in cells C10 and D10. We will focus the sensitivity analysis on these numbers, although a similar approach could be applied to the payoffs given in the table.

The sum of the two prior probabilities must equal 1, so increasing one of these probabilities automatically decreases the other one by the same amount, and vice versa. Goferbroke's management feels that the true chances of having oil on the tract of land are likely to lie somewhere between 15 and 35 percent. In other words, the true prior probability of having oil is likely to be in the range from 0.15 to 0.35, so the corresponding prior probability of the land being dry would range from 0.85 to 0.65.

Sensitivity analysis begins by reapplying Bayes' decision rule twice, once when the prior probability of oil is at the lower end of this range (0.15) and next when it is at the upper end (0.35). Figure 15.4 shows the results from doing this. When the prior probability of oil is only 0.15, the decision swings over to selling the land by a wide margin (an expected payoff of 90 versus only 20 for drilling). However, when this probability is 0.35, the decision is to drill by a wide margin (expected payoff = 180 versus only 90 for selling). Thus, the decision is very *sensitive* to the prior probability of oil. This sensitivity analysis has revealed that it is important to do more, if possible, to pin down just what the true value of the probability of oil is.

Letting

p = prior probability of oil,

the expected payoff from drilling for any p is

$$E[\text{Payoff (drill)}] = 700p - 100(1 - p)$$
$$= 800p - 100.$$

FIGURE 15.4
Performing sensitivity analysis by trying alternative values of the prior probability of oil.

	A	B	C	D	E	F	G	H	I
1	Bayes' Decision Rule for the Goferbroke Co. Problem								
2									
3				State of Nature				Expected	
4		Alternative	Oil	Dry				Payoff	
5		Drill	700	-100				20	
6		Sell	90	90				90	Maximum
7									
8									
9									
10		Prior Probability	0.15	0.85					

	A	B	C	D	E	F	G	H	I
1	Bayes' Decision Rule for the Goferbroke Co. Problem								
2									
3				State of Nature				Expected	
4		Alternative	Oil	Dry				Payoff	
5		Drill	700	-100				180	Maximum
6		Sell	90	90				90	
7									
8									
9									
10		Prior Probability	0.35	0.65					

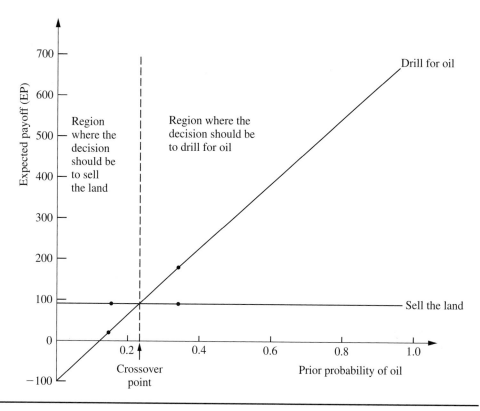

FIGURE 15.5
Graphical display of how the expected payoff for each alternative action changes when the prior probability of oil changes for the first Goferbroke Co. problem.

The slanting line in Fig. 15.5 shows the plot of this expected payoff versus p, which is just the line passing through the two points given by cells C10 and H5 in the two spreadsheets in Fig. 15.4. Since the payoff from selling the land would be 90 for any p, the flat line in Fig. 15.5 gives $E[\text{Payoff (sell)}]$ versus p.

The point in Fig. 15.5 where the two lines intersect is the **crossover point** where the decision shifts from one alternative (sell the land) to the other (drill for oil) as the prior probability increases. To find this point, we set

$$E[\text{Payoff (drill)}] = E[\text{Payoff (sell)}]$$
$$800p - 100 = 90$$
$$p = \frac{190}{800} = 0.2375$$

Conclusion: Should sell the land if $p < 0.2375$.
Should drill for oil if $p > 0.2375$.

For other problems that have more than two alternative actions, the same kind of analysis can be applied. The main difference is that there now would be more than two lines (one per alternative) in the graphical display corresponding to Fig. 15.5. However, the top line for any particular value of the prior probability still indicates which alternative should be chosen. With more than two lines, there might be more than one crossover point where the decision shifts from one alternative to another.

For a problem with more than two possible states of nature, the most straightforward approach is to focus the sensitivity analysis on only two states at a time as described above. This again would involve investigating what happens when the prior probability of one state increases as the prior probability of the other state decreases by the same amount, holding fixed the prior probabilities of the remaining states. This procedure then can be repeated for as many other pairs of states as desired.

Practitioners sometimes use software to assist them in performing this kind of sensitivity analysis, including generating the graphs. For example, an Excel add-in in your OR Courseware called SensIt is designed specifically for conducting sensitivity analysis with probabilistic models such as when applying Bayes' decision rule. Complete documentation for SensIt is included on your CD-ROM.

Because the decision the Goferbroke Co. should make depends so critically on the true probability of oil, serious consideration should be given to conducting a seismic survey to estimate this probability more closely. We will explore this option in the next two sections.

15.3   DECISION MAKING WITH EXPERIMENTATION

Frequently, additional testing (experimentation) can be done to improve the preliminary estimates of the probabilities of the respective states of nature provided by the prior probabilities. These improved estimates are called **posterior probabilities.**

We first update the Goferbroke Co. example to incorporate experimentation, then describe how to derive the posterior probabilities, and finally discuss how to decide whether it is worthwhile to conduct experimentation.

Continuing the Prototype Example

As mentioned at the end of Sec. 15.1, an available option before making a decision is to conduct a detailed seismic survey of the land to obtain a better estimate of the probability of oil. The cost is $30,000.

A seismic survey obtains seismic soundings that indicate whether the geological structure is favorable to the presence of oil. We will divide the possible findings of the survey into the following two categories:

USS: Unfavorable seismic soundings; oil is fairly unlikely.
FSS: Favorable seismic soundings; oil is fairly likely.

Based on past experience, if there is oil, then the probability of unfavorable seismic soundings is

$$P(\text{USS} \mid \text{State} = \text{Oil}) = 0.4, \qquad \text{so} \qquad P(\text{FSS} \mid \text{State} = \text{Oil}) = 1 - 0.4 = 0.6.$$

Similarly, if there is no oil (i.e., the true state of nature is *Dry*), then the probability of unfavorable seismic soundings is estimated to be

$$P(\text{USS} \mid \text{State} = \text{Dry}) = 0.8, \qquad \text{so} \qquad P(\text{FSS} \mid \text{State} = \text{Dry}) = 1 - 0.8 = 0.2.$$

We soon will use these data to find the posterior probabilities of the respective states of nature *given* the seismic soundings.

Posterior Probabilities

Proceeding now in general terms, we let

n = number of possible states of nature;

$P(\text{State} = \text{state } i)$ = prior probability that true state of nature is state i, for $i = 1, 2, \ldots, n$;

Finding = finding from experimentation (a random variable);

Finding j = one possible value of finding;

$P(\text{State} = \text{state } i \mid \text{Finding} = \text{finding } j)$ = posterior probability that true state of nature is state i, given that Finding = finding j, for $i = 1, 2, \ldots, n$.

The question currently being addressed is the following:

Given $P(\text{State} = \text{state } i)$ and $P(\text{Finding} = \text{finding } j \mid \text{State} = \text{state } i)$, for $i = 1, 2, \ldots, n$, what is $P(\text{State} = \text{state } i \mid \text{Finding} = \text{finding } j)$?

This question is answered by combining the following standard formulas of probability theory:

$$P(\text{State} = \text{state } i \mid \text{Finding} = \text{finding } j) = \frac{P(\text{State} = \text{state } i, \text{Finding} = \text{finding } j)}{P(\text{Finding} = \text{finding } j)}$$

$$P(\text{Finding} = \text{finding } j) = \sum_{k=1}^{n} P(\text{State} = \text{state } k, \text{Finding} = \text{finding } j)$$

$$P(\text{State} = \text{state } i, \text{Finding} = \text{finding } j) = P(\text{Finding} = \text{finding } j \mid \text{State} = \text{state } i) P(\text{State} = \text{state } i).$$

Therefore, for each $i = 1, 2, \ldots, n$, the desired formula for the corresponding posterior probability is

$$P(\text{State} = \text{state } i \mid \text{Finding} = \text{finding } j) =$$
$$\frac{P(\text{Finding} = \text{finding } j \mid \text{State} = \text{state } i) P(\text{State} = \text{state } i)}{\sum_{k=1}^{n} P(\text{Finding} = \text{finding } j \mid \text{State} = \text{state } k) P(\text{State} = \text{state } k)}$$

(This formula often is referred to as **Bayes' theorem** because it was developed by Thomas Bayes, the same 18th-century mathematician who is credited with developing Bayes' decision rule.)

Now let us return to the prototype example and apply this formula. If the finding of the seismic survey is unfavorable seismic soundings (USS), then the posterior probabilities are

$$P(\text{State} = \text{Oil} \mid \text{Finding} = \text{USS}) = \frac{0.4(0.25)}{0.4(0.25) + 0.8(0.75)} = \frac{1}{7},$$

$$P(\text{State} = \text{Dry} \mid \text{Finding} = \text{USS}) = 1 - \frac{1}{7} = \frac{6}{7}.$$

Similarly, if the seismic survey gives favorable seismic soundings (FSS), then

$$P(\text{State} = \text{Oil} \mid \text{Finding} = \text{FSS}) = \frac{0.6(0.25)}{0.6(0.25) + 0.2(0.75)} = \frac{1}{2},$$

$$P(\text{State} = \text{Dry} \mid \text{Finding} = \text{FSS}) = 1 - \frac{1}{2} = \frac{1}{2}.$$

The **probability tree diagram** in Fig. 15.6 shows a nice way of organizing these calculations in an intuitive manner. The prior probabilities in the first column and the conditional probabilities in the second column are part of the input data for the problem. Multiplying each probability in the first column by a probability in the second column gives the corresponding joint probability in the third column. Each joint probability then becomes the numerator in the calculation of the corresponding posterior probability in the fourth column. Cumulating the joint probabilities with the same finding (as shown at the bottom of the figure) provides the denominator for each posterior probability with this finding.

Your OR Courseware also includes an Excel template for computing these posterior probabilities, as shown in Fig. 15.7.

After these computations have been completed, Bayes' decision rule can be applied just as before, with the posterior probabilities now replacing the prior probabilities. Again,

FIGURE 15.6
Probability tree diagram for the full Goferbroke Co. problem showing all the probabilities leading to the calculation of each posterior probability of the state of nature given the finding of the seismic survey.

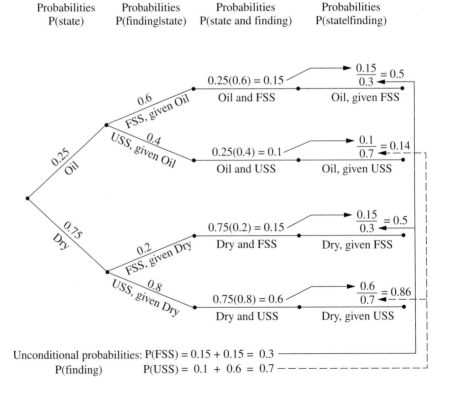

	A	B	C	D	E	F	G	H
1	**Posterior Probabilities**							
2								
3		Data:			P(Finding I State)			
4		State of	Prior		Finding			
5		Nature	Probability	FSS	USS			
6		Oil	0.25	0.6	0.4			
7		Dry	0.75	0.2	0.8			
8								
9								
10								
11								
12		Posterior			P(State I Finding)			
13		Probabilities:			State of Nature			
14		Finding	P(Finding)	Oil	Dry			
15		FSS	0.3	0.5	0.5			
16		USS	0.7	0.1429	0.8571			
17								
18								
19								

FIGURE 15.7
This *posterior probabilities* template in your OR Courseware enables efficient calculation of posterior probabilities, as illustrated here for the full Goferbroke Co. problem.

	B	C	D
14	Finding	P(Finding)	=B6
15	=D5	=SUMPRODUCT(C6:C10,D6:D10)	=C6*D6/SUMPRODUCT(C6:C10,D6:D10)
16	=E5	=SUMPRODUCT(C6:C10,E6:E10)	=C6*E6/SUMPRODUCT(C6:C10,E6:E10)
17	=F5	=SUMPRODUCT(C6:C10,F6:F10)	=C6*F6/SUMPRODUCT(C6:C10,F6:F10)
18	=G5	=SUMPRODUCT(C6:C10,G6:G10)	=C6*G6/SUMPRODUCT(C6:C10,G6:G10)
19	=H5	=SUMPRODUCT(C6:C10,H6:H10)	=C6*H6/SUMPRODUCT(C6:C10,H6:H10)

by using the payoffs (in units of thousands of dollars) from Table 15.2 and subtracting the cost of the experimentation, we obtain the results shown below.

Expected payoffs if finding is unfavorable seismic soundings (USS):

$$E[\text{Payoff (drill} \mid \text{Finding} = \text{USS})] = \frac{1}{7}(700) + \frac{6}{7}(-100) - 30$$
$$= -15.7.$$

$$E[\text{Payoff (sell} \mid \text{Finding} = \text{USS})] = \frac{1}{7}(90) + \frac{6}{7}(90) - 30$$
$$= 60.$$

Expected payoffs if finding is favorable seismic soundings (FSS):

$$E[\text{Payoff (drill} \mid \text{Finding} = \text{FSS})] = \frac{1}{2}(700) + \frac{1}{2}(-100) - 30$$
$$= 270.$$

TABLE 15.3 The optimal policy with experimentation, under Bayes' decision rule, for the Goferbroke Co. problem

Finding from Seismic Survey	Optimal Action	Expected Payoff Excluding Cost of Survey	Expected Payoff Including Cost of Survey
USS	Sell the land	90	60
FSS	Drill for oil	300	270

$$E[\text{Payoff (sell} \mid \text{Finding = FSS)]} = \frac{1}{2}(90) + \frac{1}{2}(90) - 30$$
$$= 60.$$

Since the objective is to maximize the expected payoff, these results yield the optimal policy shown in Table 15.3.

However, what this analysis does not answer is whether it is worth spending $30,000 to conduct the experimentation (the seismic survey). Perhaps it would be better to forgo this major expense and just use the optimal solution without experimentation (drill for oil, with an expected payoff of $100,000). We address this issue next.

The Value of Experimentation

Before performing any experiment, we should determine its potential value. We present two complementary methods of evaluating its potential value.

The first method assumes (unrealistically) that the experiment will remove *all* uncertainty about what the true state of nature is, and then this method makes a very quick calculation of what the resulting *improvement in the expected payoff* would be (ignoring the cost of the experiment). This quantity, called the *expected value of perfect information,* provides an *upper bound* on the potential value of the experiment. Therefore, if this upper bound is less than the cost of the experiment, the experiment definitely should be forgone.

However, if this upper bound exceeds the cost of the experiment, then the second (slower) method should be used next. This method calculates the *actual* improvement in the expected payoff (ignoring the cost of the experiment) that would result from performing the experiment. Comparing this improvement with the cost indicates whether the experiment should be performed.

Expected Value of Perfect Information. Suppose now that the experiment could definitely identify what the true state of nature is, thereby providing "perfect" information. Whichever state of nature is identified, you naturally choose the action with the maximum payoff for that state. We do not know in advance which state of nature will be identified, so a calculation of the expected payoff with perfect information (ignoring the cost of the experiment) requires weighting the maximum payoff for each state of nature by the prior probability of that state of nature.

Figure 15.8 shows the Excel template in your OR Courseware that can be used to organize and perform this calculation. Using the equation given for cell F13,

Expected payoff with perfect information = 0.25(700) + 0.75(90)
= 242.5.

	A	B	C	D	E	F	G
1		**Expected Payoff with Perfect Information for Goferbroke**					
2							
3				State of Nature			
4		Alternative	Oil	Dry			
5		Drill	700	-100			
6		Sell	90	90			
7							
8							
9							
10		Prior Probability	0.25	0.75			
11		Maximum Payoff	700	90			
12							
13		Expected Payoff with Perfect Information =		242.5			

FIGURE 15.8
This Excel template for obtaining the expected payoff with perfect information is applied here to the first Goferbroke Co. problem.

	C	D	E	F	G
11	=MAX(C5:C9)	=MAX(D5:D9)	=MAX(E5:E9)	=MAX(F5:F9)	=MAX(G5:G9)

	F
13	=SUMPRODUCT(C10:G10,C11:G11)

Thus, if the Goferbroke Co. could learn before choosing its action whether the land contains oil, the expected payoff as of now (before acquiring this information) would be $242,500 (excluding the cost of the experiment generating the information.)

To evaluate whether the experiment should be conducted, we now use this quantity to calculate the expected value of perfect information.

The **expected value of perfect information,** abbreviated **EVPI,** is calculated as

EVPI = expected payoff with perfect information − expected payoff without experimentation.[1]

Thus, since experimentation usually cannot provide perfect information, EVPI provides an upper bound on the expected value of experimentation.

For the prototype example, we found in Sec. 15.2 that the expected payoff without experimentation (under Bayes' decision rule) is 100. Therefore,

EVPI = 242.5 − 100 = 142.5.

Since 142.5 far exceeds 30, the cost of experimentation (a seismic survey), it may be worthwhile to proceed with the seismic survey. To find out for sure, we now go to the second method of evaluating the potential benefit of experimentation.

[1]The *value of perfect information* is a random variable equal to the payoff with perfect information *minus* the payoff without experimentation. EVPI is the expected value of this random variable.

Expected Value of Experimentation.   Rather than just obtain an upper bound on the *expected increase in payoff* (excluding the cost of the experiment) due to performing experimentation, we now will do somewhat more work to calculate this expected increase directly. This quantity is called the *expected value of experimentation.*

Calculating this quantity requires first computing the expected payoff with experimentation (excluding the cost of the experiment). Obtaining this latter quantity requires doing all the work described earlier to find all the posterior probabilities, the resulting optimal policy with experimentation, and the corresponding expected payoff (excluding the cost of the experiment) for each possible finding from the experiment. Then each of these expected payoffs needs to be weighted by the probability of the corresponding finding, that is,

$$\text{Expected payoff with experimentation} = \sum_j P(\text{Finding} = \text{finding } j) \\ E[\text{payoff} \mid \text{Finding} = \text{finding } j],$$

where the summation is taken over all possible values of *j*.

For the prototype example, we have already done all the work to obtain the terms on the right side of this equation. The values of $P(\text{Finding} = \text{finding } j)$ for the two possible findings from the seismic survey—unfavorable (USS) and favorable (FSS)—were calculated at the bottom of the probability tree diagram in Fig. 15.6 as

$$P(\text{USS}) = 0.7, \qquad P(\text{FSS}) = 0.3.$$

For the optimal policy with experimentation, the corresponding expected payoff (excluding the cost of the seismic survey) for each finding was obtained in the third column of Table 15.3 as

$$E(\text{Payoff} \mid \text{Finding} = \text{USS}) = 90,$$
$$E(\text{Payoff} \mid \text{Finding} = \text{FSS}) = 270.$$

With these numbers,

$$\text{Expected payoff with experimentation} = 0.7(90) + 0.3(300) \\ = 153.$$

Now we are ready to calculate the expected value of experimentation.

The **expected value of experimentation,** abbreviated **EVE,** is calculated as

EVE = expected payoff with experimentation − expected payoff without experimentation.

Thus, EVE identifies the potential value of experimentation.

For the Goferbroke Co.,

$$\text{EVE} = 153 - 100 = 53.$$

Since this value exceeds 30, the cost of conducting a detailed seismic survey (in units of thousands of dollars), this experimentation should be done.

15.4 DECISION TREES

Decision trees provide a useful way of *visually displaying* the problem and then *organizing the computational work* already described in the preceding two sections. These trees are especially helpful when a *sequence of decisions* must be made.

Constructing the Decision Tree

The prototype example involves a sequence of two decisions:

1. Should a seismic survey be conducted before an action is chosen?
2. Which action (drill for oil or sell the land) should be chosen?

The corresponding decision tree (before adding numbers and performing computations) is displayed in Fig. 15.9.

The nodes of the decision tree are referred to as **forks,** and the arcs are called **branches.**

> A **decision fork,** represented by a square, indicates that a decision needs to be made at that point in the process. A **chance fork,** represented by a circle, indicates that a random event occurs at that point.

Thus, in Fig. 15.9, the first decision is represented by decision fork *a*. Fork *b* is a chance fork representing the random event of the outcome of the seismic survey. The two branches emanating from fork *b* represent the two possible outcomes of the survey. Next

FIGURE 15.9
The decision tree (before including any numbers) for the full Goferbroke Co. problem.

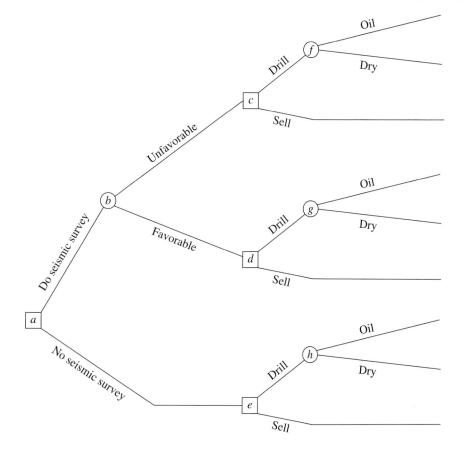

comes the second decision (forks *c, d,* and *e*) with its two possible choices. If the decision is to drill for oil, then we come to another chance fork (forks *f, g,* and *h*), where its two branches correspond to the two possible states of nature.

Note that the path followed from fork *a* to reach any terminal branch (except the bottom one) is determined both by the decisions made and by random events that are outside the control of the decision maker. This is characteristic of problems addressed by decision analysis.

The next step in constructing the decision tree is to insert numbers into the tree as shown in Fig. 15.10. The numbers under or over the branches that are *not* in parentheses are the cash flows (in thousands of dollars) that occur at those branches. For each path through the tree from node *a* to a terminal branch, these same numbers then are added to obtain the resulting total payoff shown in boldface to the right of that branch. The last set of numbers is the probabilities of random events. In particular, since each branch emanating from a chance fork represents a possible random event, the probability of this event occurring from this fork has been inserted in parentheses along this branch. From chance

FIGURE 15.10
The decision tree in Fig. 15.9 after adding both the probabilities of random events and the payoffs.

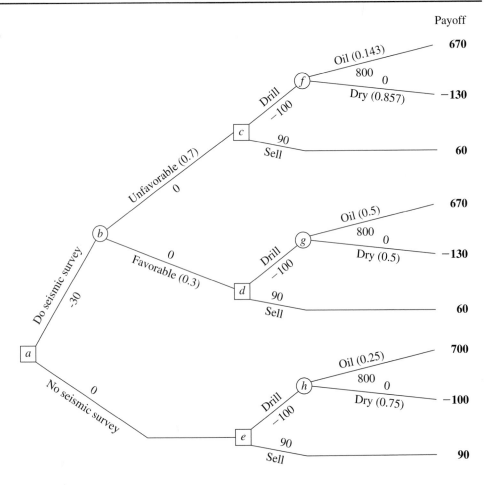

fork *h,* the probabilities are the *prior probabilities* of these states of nature, since no seismic survey has been conducted to obtain more information in this case. However, chance forks *f* and *g* lead out of a decision to do the seismic survey (and then to drill). Therefore, the probabilities from these chance forks are the *posterior probabilities* of the states of nature, given the finding from the seismic survey, where these numbers are given in Figs. 15.6 and 15.7. Finally, we have the two branches emanating from chance fork *b.* The numbers here are the probabilities of these findings from the seismic survey, Favorable (FSS) or Unfavorable (USS), as given underneath the probability tree diagram in Fig. 15.6 or in cells C15:C16 of Fig. 15.7.

Performing the Analysis

Having constructed the decision tree, including its numbers, we now are ready to analyze the problem by using the following procedure.

1. Start at the right side of the decision tree and move left one column at a time. For each column, perform either step 2 or step 3 depending upon whether the forks in that column are chance forks or decision forks.
2. For each chance fork, calculate its *expected payoff* by multiplying the expected payoff of each branch (shown in boldface to the right of the branch) by the probability of that branch and then summing these products. Record this expected payoff for each decision fork in boldface next to the fork, and designate this quantity as also being the expected payoff for the branch leading to this fork.
3. For each decision fork, compare the expected payoffs of its branches and choose the alternative whose branch has the largest expected payoff. In each case, record the choice on the decision tree by inserting a double dash as a barrier through each rejected branch.

To begin the procedure, consider the rightmost column of forks, namely, chance forks *f, g,* and *h.* Applying step 2, their expected payoffs (EP) are calculated as

$$EP = \frac{1}{7}(670) + \frac{6}{7}(-130) = -15.7, \qquad \text{for fork } f,$$

$$EP = \frac{1}{2}(670) + \frac{1}{2}(-130) = 270, \qquad \text{for fork } g,$$

$$EP = \frac{1}{4}(700) + \frac{3}{4}(-100) = 100, \qquad \text{for fork } h.$$

These expected payoffs then are placed above these forks, as shown in Fig. 15.11.

Next, we move one column to the left, which consists of decision forks *c, d,* and *e.* The expected payoff for a branch that leads to a chance fork now is recorded in boldface over that chance fork. Therefore, step 3 can be applied as follows.

Fork *c:*   Drill alternative has EP = −15.7.
            Sell alternative has EP = 60.
60 > −15.7, so choose the Sell alternative.

Fork *d:*   Drill alternative has EP = 270.
            Sell alternative has EP = 60.
270 > 60, so choose the Drill alternative.

Payoff

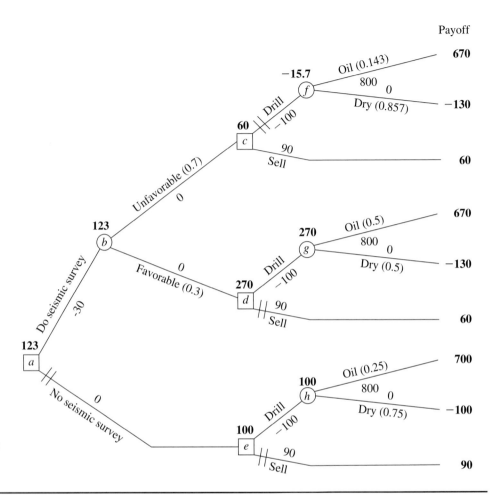

FIGURE 15.11
The final decision tree that records the analysis for the full Goferbroke Co. problem when using monetary payoffs.

Fork *e:*   Drill alternative has EP = 100.
             Sell alternative has EP = 90.
100 > 90, so choose the Drill alternative.

The expected payoff for each chosen alternative now would be recorded in boldface over its decision node, as already shown in Fig. 15.11. The chosen alternative also is indicated by inserting a double dash as a barrier through each rejected branch.

Next, moving one more column to the left brings us to fork *b*. Since this is a chance fork, step 2 of the procedure needs to be applied. The expected payoff for each of its branches is recorded over the following decision fork. Therefore, the expected payoff is

$$EP = 0.7(60) + 0.3(270) = 123, \qquad \text{for fork } b,$$

as recorded over this fork in Fig. 15.11.

Finally, we move left to fork *a,* a decision fork. Applying step 3 yields

Fork *a:*   Do seismic survey has EP = 123.
             No seismic survey has EP = 100.
123 > 100, so choose Do seismic survey.

This expected payoff of 123 now would be recorded over the fork, and a double dash inserted to indicate the rejected branch, as already shown in Fig. 15.11.

This procedure has moved from right to left for analysis purposes. However, having completed the decision tree in this way, the decision maker now can read the tree from left to right to see the actual progression of events. The double dashes have closed off the undesirable paths. Therefore, given the payoffs for the final outcomes shown on the right side, *Bayes' decision rule* says to follow only the open paths from left to right to achieve the largest possible expected payoff.

Following the open paths from left to right in Fig. 15.11 yields the following optimal policy, according to Bayes' decision rule.

Optimal policy:
Do the seismic survey.
If the result is unfavorable, sell the land.
If the result is favorable, drill for oil.
The expected payoff (including the cost of the seismic survey) is 123 ($123,000).

This (unique) optimal solution naturally is the same as that obtained in the preceding section without the benefit of a decision tree. (See the optimal policy with experimentation given in Table 15.3 and the conclusion at the end of Sec. 15.3 that experimentation is worthwhile.)

For any decision tree, this **backward induction procedure** always will lead to the *optimal policy* (or policies) after the probabilities are computed for the branches emanating from a chance fork.

Helpful Software

Practitioners sometimes use special software to help construct and analyze decision trees. This software often is in the form of an Excel add-in. One popular add-in of this type is *TreePlan,* which is shareware developed by Professor Michael Middleton. The academic version of TreePlan is included in your OR Courseware, along with Professor Middleton's companion shareware SensIt mentioned at the end of Sec. 15.2.

It is straightforward to use TreePlan to quickly construct a decision tree equivalent to the one in Fig. 15.11, as well as much larger ones. In the process, TreePlan also will automatically solve the decision tree. The Excel file for this chapter includes the TreePlan decision trees for three versions of the Goferbroke Co. problem. Complete documentation for TreePlan also is included on the CD-ROM.

To construct a decision tree with TreePlan, go to its Tools menu and choose *Decision Tree,* which brings up the "TreePlan . . . New" dialogue box shown in Fig. 15.12. Clicking on New Tree then adds a tree to the spreadsheet that initially consists of a single (square) decision fork with two branches. Clicking just to the right of a terminal fork

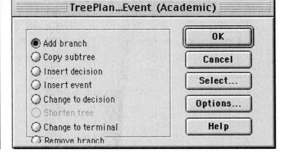

FIGURE 15.12
The dialogue boxes used by TreePlan for constructing a decision tree.

(displayed by a vertical hash mark at the end of a branch) and then choosing Decision Tree from the Tools menu brings up the "TreePlan . . . Terminal" dialogue box (see Fig. 15.12), which enables you to change the terminal fork into either a decision fork or a chance fork with the desired number of branches (between 1 and 5). (TreePlan refers to decision forks as *decision nodes* and to chance forks as *event nodes*.) At any time, you also can click on any existing decision fork (a square) or chance fork (circle) and choose Decision Tree from the Tools menu to bring up the corresponding dialogue box— "TreePlan . . . Decision" or "TreePlan . . . Event"—to make any of the modifications listed in Fig. 15.12 at that fork. To complete the decision tree, the names, cash flows, and probabilities for the various branches are typed directly into the spreadsheet. TreePlan then automatically adds the cash flows to obtain the total cash flows (payoffs) to be shown at the right of each end branch.

15.5 UTILITY THEORY

Thus far, when applying Bayes' decision rule, we have assumed that the expected payoff in *monetary terms* is the appropriate measure of the consequences of taking an action. However, in many situations this assumption is inappropriate.

For example, suppose that an individual is offered the choice of (1) accepting a 50:50 chance of winning $100,000 or nothing or (2) receiving $40,000 with certainty. Many people would prefer the $40,000 even though the expected payoff on the 50:50 chance of winning $100,000 is $50,000. A company may be unwilling to invest a large sum of money in a new product even when the expected profit is substantial if there is a risk of losing its investment and thereby becoming bankrupt. People buy insurance even though it is a poor investment from the viewpoint of the expected payoff.

Do these examples invalidate Bayes' decision rule? Fortunately, the answer is no, because there is a way of transforming *monetary values* to an appropriate scale that reflects the decision maker's preferences. This scale is called the *utility function for money*.

Utility Functions for Money

Figure 15.13 shows a typical utility function $u(M)$ for money M. It indicates that an individual having this utility function would value obtaining $30,000 twice as much as $10,000 and would value obtaining $100,000 twice as much as $30,000. This reflects the fact that

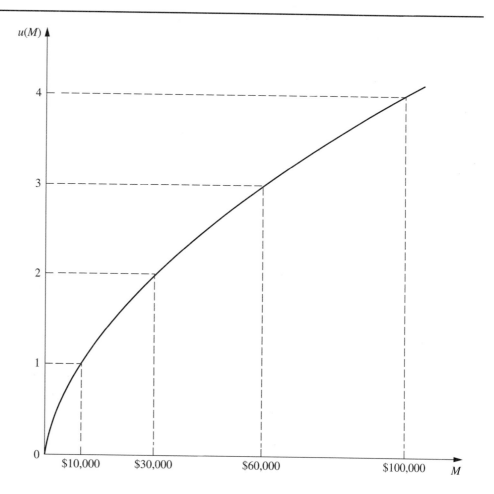

FIGURE 15.13
A typical utility function for money, where $u(M)$ is the utility of obtaining an amount of money M.

the person's highest-priority needs would be met by the first $10,000. Having this decreasing slope of the function as the amount of money increases is referred to as having a **decreasing marginal utility for money.** Such an individual is referred to as being **risk-averse.**

However, not all individuals have a decreasing marginal utility for money. Some people are **risk seekers** instead of *risk-averse,* and they go through life looking for the "big score." The slope of their utility function *increases* as the amount of money increases, so they have an **increasing marginal utility for money.**

The intermediate case is that of a **risk-neutral** individual, who prizes money at its face value. Such an individual's utility for money is simply proportional to the amount of money involved. Although some people appear to be risk-neutral when only small amounts of money are involved, it is unusual to be truly risk-neutral with very large amounts.

It also is possible to exhibit a mixture of these kinds of behavior. For example, an individual might be essentially risk-neutral with small amounts of money, then become a risk seeker with moderate amounts, and then turn risk-averse with large amounts. In addition, one's attitude toward risk can shift over time depending upon circumstances.

An individual's attitude toward risk also may be different when dealing with one's personal finances than when making decisions on behalf of an organization. For example, managers of a business firm need to consider the company's circumstances and the collective philosophy of top management in determining the appropriate attitude toward risk when making managerial decisions.

The fact that different people have different utility functions for money has an important implication for decision making in the face of uncertainty.

> When a *utility function for money* is incorporated into a decision analysis approach to a problem, this utility function must be constructed to fit the preferences and values of the decision maker involved. (The decision maker can be either a single individual or a group of people.)

The key to constructing the utility function for money to fit the decision maker is the following fundamental property of utility functions.

> **Fundamental Property:** Under the assumptions of utility theory, the decision maker's *utility function for money* has the property that the decision maker is *indifferent* between two alternative courses of action if the two alternatives have the *same expected utility.*

To illustrate, suppose that the decision maker has the utility function shown in Fig. 15.13. Further suppose that the decision maker is offered the following opportunity.

> **Offer:** An opportunity to obtain either $100,000 (utility = 4) with probability p or nothing (utility = 0) with probability $(1 - p)$.

Thus,

$E(\text{utility}) = 4p,$ for this offer.

Therefore, for *each* of the following three pairs of alternatives, the decision maker is indifferent between the first and second alternatives:

1. The offer with $p = 0.25$ [$E(\text{utility}) = 1$] or definitely obtaining $10,000 (utility = 1)
2. The offer with $p = 0.5$ [$E(\text{utility}) = 2$] or definitely obtaining $30,000 (utility = 2)
3. The offer with $p = 0.75$ [$E(\text{utility}) = 3$] or definitely obtaining $60,000 (utility = 3)

This example also illustrates one way in which the decision maker's utility function for money can be constructed in the first place. The decision maker would be made the same hypothetical offer to obtain either a large amount of money (for example, $100,000) with probability p or nothing. Then, for each of a few smaller amounts of money (for example, $10,000, $30,000, and $60,000), the decision maker would be asked to choose a value of p that would make him or her *indifferent* between the offer and definitely obtaining that amount of money. The utility of the smaller amount of money then is p times the utility of the large amount.

The *scale* of the utility function (e.g., utility = 1 for $10,000) is irrelevant. It is only the *relative values* of the utilities that matter. All the utilities can be multiplied by any positive constant without affecting which alternative course of action will have the largest expected utility.

Now we are ready to summarize the basic role of utility functions in decision analysis.

> When the decision maker's utility function for money is used to measure the relative worth of the various possible monetary outcomes, *Bayes' decision rule* replaces monetary payoffs by the corresponding utilities. Therefore, the optimal action (or series of actions) is the one which *maximizes the expected utility.*

Only utility functions *for money* have been discussed here. However, we should mention that utility functions can sometimes still be constructed when some of or all the important consequences of the alternative courses of action are *not* monetary. (For example, the consequences of a doctor's decision alternatives in treating a patient involve the future health of the patient.) Nevertheless, under these circumstances, it is important to incorporate such value judgments into the decision process. This is not necessarily easy, since it may require making value judgments about the relative desirability of rather intangible consequences. Nevertheless, under these circumstances, it is important to incorporate such value judgments into the decision process.

Applying Utility Theory to the Goferbroke Co. Problem

At the end of Sec. 15.1, we mentioned that the Goferbroke Co. was operating without much capital, so a loss of $100,000 would be quite serious. The (primary) owner of the company already has gone heavily into debt to keep going. The worst-case scenario would be to come up with $30,000 for a seismic survey and then still lose $100,000 by drilling when there is no oil. This scenario would not bankrupt the company at this point, but definitely would leave it in a precarious financial position.

On the other hand, striking oil is an exciting prospect, since earning $700,000 finally would put the company on a fairly solid financial footing.

To apply the owner's (decision maker's) *utility function for money* to the problem as described in Secs. 15.1 and 15.3, it is necessary to identify the utilities for all the possible monetary payoffs. In units of thousands of dollars, these possible payoffs and the corresponding utilities are given in Table 15.4. We now will discuss how these utilities were obtained.

As a starting point in constructing the utility function, it is natural to let the utility of *zero* money be zero, so $u(0) = 0$. An appropriate next step is to consider the worst scenario and best scenario and then to address the following question.

TABLE 15.4 Utilities for the Goferbroke Co. problem

Monetary Payoff	Utility
−130	−150
−100	−105
60	60
90	90
670	580
700	600

Suppose you have only the following two alternatives. Alternative 1 is to do nothing (payoff and utility = 0). Alternative 2 is to have a probability p of a payoff of 700 and a probability $1 − p$ of a payoff of −130 (loss of 130). What value of p makes you *indifferent* between two alternatives?

The decision maker's choice: $p = \dfrac{1}{5}$.

If we continue to let $u(M)$ denote the utility of a monetary payoff of M, this choice of p implies that

$$\frac{4}{5}u(-130) + \frac{1}{5}u(700) = 0 \qquad \text{(utility of alternative 1).}$$

The value of either $u(-130)$ or $u(700)$ can be set arbitrarily (provided only that the first is negative and the second positive) to establish the scale of the utility function. By choosing $u(-130) = -150$ (a convenient choice since it will make $u(M)$ approximately equal to M when M is in the vicinity of 0), this equation then yields $u(700) = 600$.

To identify $u(-100)$, a choice of p is made that makes the decision maker indifferent between a payoff of −130 with probability p or definitely incurring a payoff of −100. The choice is $p = 0.7$, so

$$u(-100) = p\, u(-130) = 0.7(-150) = -105.$$

To obtain $u(90)$, a value of p is selected that makes the decision maker indifferent between a payoff of 700 with probability p or definitely obtaining a payoff of 90. The value chosen is $p = 0.15$, so

$$u(90) = p\, u(700) = 0.15(600) = 90.$$

At this point, a smooth curve was drawn through $u(-130)$, $u(-100)$, $u(90)$, and $u(700)$ to obtain the decision maker's *utility function for money* shown in Fig. 15.14. The values on this curve at $M = 60$ and $M = 670$ provide the corresponding utilities, $u(60) = 60$ and $u(670) = 580$, which completes the list of utilities given in the right column of Table 15.4. For contrast, the dashed line drawn at 45° in Fig. 15.14 shows the monetary value M of the amount of money M. This dashed line has provided the values of the payoffs used exclusively in the preceding sections. Note how $u(M)$ essentially equals M for small values

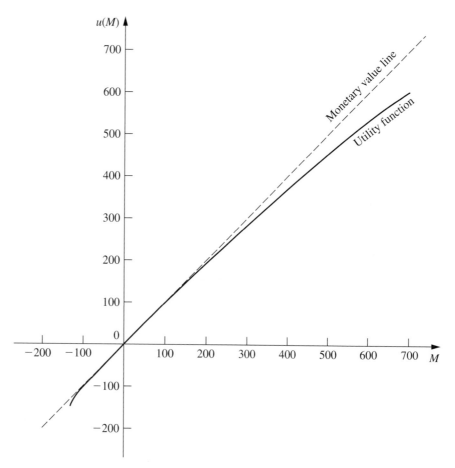

FIGURE 15.14
The utility function for money of the owner of the Goferbroke Co.

(positive or negative) of M, and then how $u(M)$ gradually falls off M for larger values of M. This is typical for a moderately risk-averse individual.

By nature, the owner of the Goferbroke Co. is inclined to be a risk seeker. However, the difficult financial circumstances of his company, which he badly wants to keep solvent, have forced him to adopt a moderately risk-averse stance in addressing his current decisions.

Another Approach for Estimating $u(M)$

The above procedure for constructing $u(M)$ asks the decision maker to repeatedly make a difficult decision about which probability would make him or her indifferent between two alternatives. Many individuals would be uncomfortable with making this kind of decision. Therefore, an alternative approach is sometimes used instead to estimate the utility function for money.

This approach is to assume that the utility function has a certain mathematical form, and then adjust this form to fit the decision maker's attitude toward risk as closely as possible. For example, one particularly popular form to assume (because of its relative simplicity) is the **exponential utility function,**

$$u(M) = R\left(1 - e^{-\frac{M}{R}}\right),$$

where R is the decision maker's *risk tolerance*. This utility function has a decreasing marginal utility for money, so it is designed to fit a *risk-averse* individual. A great aversion to risk corresponds to a small value of R (which would cause the utility function curve to bend sharply), whereas a small aversion to risk corresponds to a large value of R (which gives a much more gradual bend in the curve).

Since the owner of the Goferbroke Co. has a relatively small aversion to risk, the utility function curve in Fig. 15.14 bends quite slowly. The value of R that would give the utilities of $u(670) = 580$ and $u(700) = 600$ is approximately $R = 2,250$. On the other hand, the owner becomes much more risk-averse when large losses can occur, since this now would threaten bankruptcy, so the value of R that would give the utility of $u(-130) = -150$ is only about $R = 465$.

Unfortunately, it is not possible to use two different values of R for the same utility function. A drawback of the exponential utility function is that it assumes a constant aversion to risk (a fixed value of R), regardless of how much (or how little) money the decision maker currently has. This doesn't fit the Goferbroke Co. situation, since the current shortage of money makes the owner much more concerned than usual about incurring a large loss.

In other situations where the consequences of the potential losses are not as severe, assuming an exponential utility function may provide a reasonable approximation. In such a case, here is an easy (slightly approximate) way of estimating the appropriate value of R. The decision maker would be asked to choose the number R that would make him (or her) indifferent between the following two alternatives.

A_1: A 50-50 gamble where he would gain R dollars with probability 0.5 and lose $\frac{R}{2}$ dollars with probability 0.5.

A_2: Neither gain nor lose anything.

TreePlan includes the option of using the exponential utility function. All you need to do is click on the Options button in the TreePlan dialogue box and then select "Use Exponential Utility Function." TreePlan uses a different form for the exponential utility function that requires specifying the values of three constants (by choosing Define Name under the Insert menu and entering the values). By choosing the value of R for all three of these constants, this utility function becomes the same as the exponential utility function described above.

Using a Decision Tree to Analyze the Goferbroke Co. Problem with Utilities

Now that the utility function for money of the owner of the Goferbroke Co. has been obtained in Table 15.4 (and Fig. 15.14), this information can be used with a decision tree as summarized next.

The procedure for using a decision tree to analyze the problem now is *identical* to that described in the preceding section *except* for substituting utilities for monetary payoffs. Therefore, the value obtained to evaluate each fork of the tree now is the *expected utility* there rather than the expected (monetary) payoff. Consequently, the optimal decisions selected by Bayes' decision rule maximize the expected utility for the overall problem.

Thus, our final decision tree shown in Fig. 15.15 closely resembles the one in Fig. 15.11 given in the preceding section. The forks and branches are exactly the same, as are the probabilities for the branches emanating from the chance forks. For informational purposes, the total monetary payoffs still are given to the right of the terminal branches (but we no longer bother to show the individual monetary payoffs next to any of the branches). However, we now have added the utilities on the right side. It is these numbers that have been used to compute the expected utilities given next to all the forks.

These expected utilities lead to the same decisions at forks *a*, *c*, and *d* as in Fig. 15.11, but the decision at fork *e* now switches to *sell* instead of *drill*. However, the backward induction procedure still leaves fork *e* on a *closed* path. Therefore, the overall optimal policy remains the same as given at the end of Sec. 15.4 (do the seismic survey; sell if the result is unfavorable; drill if the result is favorable).

FIGURE 15.15
The final decision tree for the full Goferbroke Co. problem, using the owner's utility function for money to maximize expected utility.

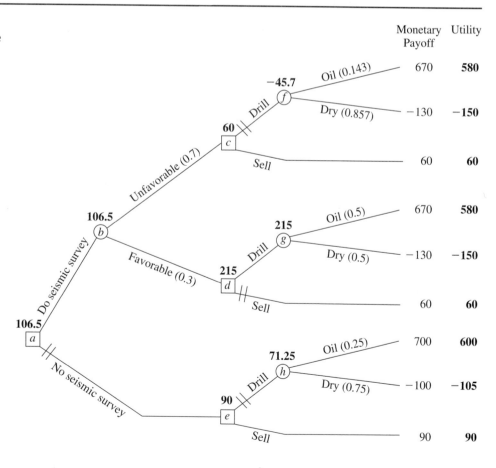

The approach used in the preceding sections of maximizing the expected monetary payoff amounts to assuming that the decision maker is risk-neutral, so that $u(M) = M$. By using utility theory, the optimal solution now reflects the decision maker's attitude about risk. Because the owner of the Goferbroke Co. adopted only a moderately risk-averse stance, the optimal policy did not change from before. For a somewhat more risk-averse owner, the optimal solution would switch to the more conservative approach of immediately selling the land (no seismic survey). (See Prob. 15.5-1.)

The current owner is to be commended for incorporating utility theory into a decision analysis approach to his problem. Utility theory helps to provide a rational approach to decision making in the face of uncertainty. However, many decision makers are not sufficiently comfortable with the relatively abstract notion of utilities, or with working with probabilities to construct a utility function, to be willing to use this approach. Consequently, utility theory is not yet used very widely in practice.

15.6   THE PRACTICAL APPLICATION OF DECISION ANALYSIS

In one sense, this chapter's prototype example (the Goferbroke Co. problem) is a very typical application of decision analysis. Like other applications, management needed to make some decisions (Do a seismic survey? Drill for oil or sell the land?) in the face of great uncertainty. The decisions were difficult because their payoffs were so unpredictable. The outcome depended on factors that were outside management's control (does the land contain oil or is it dry?). Therefore, management needed a framework and methodology for rational decision making in this uncertain environment. These are the usual characteristics of applications of decision analysis.

However, in other ways, the Goferbroke problem is not such a typical application. It was oversimplified to include only two possible states of nature (Oil and Dry), whereas there actually would be a considerable number of distinct possibilities. For example, the actual state might be dry, a small amount of oil, a moderate amount, a large amount, and a huge amount, plus different possibilities concerning the depth of the oil and soil conditions that impact the cost of drilling to reach the oil. Management also was considering only two alternatives for each of two decisions. Real applications commonly involve more decisions, more alternatives to be considered for each one, and many possible states of nature.

When dealing with larger problems, the decision tree can explode in size, with perhaps many thousand terminal branches. In this case, it clearly would not be feasible to construct the tree by hand, including computing posterior probabilities, and calculating the expected payoffs (or utilities) for the various forks, and then identifying the optimal decisions. Fortunately, some excellent software packages (mainly for personal computers) are available specifically for doing this work. Furthermore, special algebraic techniques are being developed and incorporated into the computer solvers for dealing with ever larger problems.[1]

Sensitivity analysis also can become unwieldy on large problems. Although it normally is supported by the computer software, the amount of data generated can easily overwhelm

[1]For example, see C. W. Kirkwood, "An Algebraic Approach to Formulating and Solving Large Models for Sequential Decisions under Uncertainty," *Management Science,* **39:** 900–913, July 1993.

an analyst or decision maker. Therefore, some graphical techniques, such as *tornado diagrams,* have been developed to organize the data in a readily understandable way.[1]

Other kinds of graphical techniques also are available to complement the decision tree in representing and solving decision analysis problems. One that has become quite popular is called the *influence diagram,* and researchers continue to develop others as well.[2]

Many strategic business decisions are made collectively by several members of management. One technique for group decision making is called *decision conferencing.* This is a process where the group comes together for discussions in a decision conference with the help of an analyst and a group facilitator. The facilitator works directly with the group to help it structure and focus discussions, think creatively about the problem, bring assumptions to the surface, and address the full range of issues involved. The analyst uses decision analysis to assist the group in exploring the implications of the various decision alternatives. With the assistance of a computerized group decision support system, the analyst builds and solves models on the spot, and then performs sensitivity analysis to respond to what-if questions from the group.[3]

Applications of decision analysis commonly involve a partnership between the managerial decision maker (whether an individual or a group) and an analyst (whether an individual or a team) with training in OR. Some companies do not have a staff member who is qualified to serve as the analyst. Therefore, a considerable number of management consulting firms specializing in decision analysis have been formed to fill this role. (For example, a few large ones are located in Silicon Valley next to Stanford University, with names such as Applied Decision Analysis and the Strategic Decisions Group.)

Decision analysis is widely used around the world. For proprietary reasons (among others), companies usually do not publish articles in professional journals to describe their applications of OR techniques, including decision analysis. Fortunately, such articles do filter out once in awhile, with some of them appearing in the journal called *Interfaces.* The articles about decision analysis provide valuable insights about the practical application of this technique in practice.

Table 15.5 briefly summarizes the nature of some of the applications of decision analysis that have appeared in *Interfaces.* The rightmost column identifies the specific issue of the journal for each application. Note in the other columns the wide diversity of organizations and applications (with public utilities as the heaviest users). For each specific application, think about how uncertainties in the situation make decision analysis a natural technique to use.

---

[1] For further information, see T. G. Eschenbach, "Spiderplots versus Tornado Diagrams for Sensitivity Analysis," *Interfaces,* **22:** 40–46, Nov.–Dec. 1992.

[2] For example, see P. P. Schnoy, "A Comparison of Graphical Techniques for Decision Analysis," *European Journal of Operational Research,* **78:** 1–21, Oct. 13, 1994. Also see Z. Covaliu and R. M. Oliver, "Representation and Solution of Decision Problems Using Sequential Decision Diagrams," *Management Science,* **41:** 1860–1881, Dec., 1995, as well as Chaps. 4 and 9 in K. T. Marshall and R. M. Oliver, *Decision Making and Forecasting,* McGraw-Hill, New York, 1995.

[3] For further information, see the two articles on decision conferencing in the November–December 1992 issue of *Interfaces,* where one describes an application in Australia and the other summarizes the experience of 26 decision conferences in Hungary.

TABLE 15.5 Some applications of decision analysis

Organization	Nature of Application	Issue of *Interfaces*
Amoco Oil Co.	Used utilities to evaluate strategies for marketing its products through full-facility service stations.	Dec., 1982
Ohio Edison Co.	Evaluated and selected particulate emission control equipment for a coal-fired power plant.	Feb., 1983
New England Electric System	Determined an appropriate bid for the salvage rights to a grounded ship.	March–April, 1984
National Weather Service	Developed a plan for responding to flood forecasts and warnings.	May–June, 1984
National Forest Administrations	Planned prescribed fires to improve forest and rangeland ecosystems.	Sept.–Oct., 1984
Tomco Oil Corp.	Chose between two site locations for drilling an oil well, with 74 states of nature.	March–April, 1986
Personal decision	Used decision criteria without probabilities to choose between adjustable-rate and fixed-rate mortgages.	May–June, 1986
U.S. Postal Service	Chose between six alternatives for a postal automation program, saving $200 million.	March–April, 1987; Jan.–Feb., 1988
Santa Clara University	Evaluated whether to implement a drug-testing program for their intercollegiate athletes.	May–June, 1990
Independent Living Center (Australia)	A decision conference developed a strategic plan for reorganizing the center.	Nov.–Dec., 1992
DuPont Corp.	Many applications to strategic planning; one added $175 million in value.	Nov.–Dec., 1992
British Columbia Hydro and Power Authority	Elicited a utility function for clarifying value trade-offs for many strategic issues.	Nov.–Dec., 1992
U.S. Department of Defense	Improved the decision process for the acquisition of weapon systems.	Nov.–Dec., 1992
Electric utility industry	Considered health and environmental risks in dealing with utility-generated solid wastes and air emissions.	Nov.–Dec., 1992
An anonymous international bank	Developed a contingency-planning program against fire and power failure for all services.	Nov.–Dec., 1992
General Motors	More than 40 major decision analysis projects over 5 years.	Nov.–Dec., 1992
Southern Company (electric utility)	Evaluated alternative preventive maintenance programs for motor vehicle and construction equipment fleets.	May–June, 1993

Organization	Nature of Application	Issue of *Interfaces*
ICI Americas	Selected research and development projects with little data available for assessing them.	Nov.–Dec., 1993
Federal National Mortgage Association	Used utilities to select the composition of a portfolio of home mortgage assets.	May–June, 1994
Oglethorpe Power Corp.	Evaluated whether to invest in a major transmission system and how to finance it.	March–April, 1995
Phillips Petroleum Co.	Evaluated oil exploration opportunities with a consistent risk-taking policy.	Nov.–Dec., 1995
Energy Electric System	Evaluated schedules for preventive maintenance for electrical generator units.	July–Aug., 1996

If you would like to do more reading about the practical application of decision analysis, a good place to begin would be the November–December 1992 issue of *Interfaces*. This is a special issue devoted entirely to decision analysis and the related area of risk analysis. It includes many interesting articles, including descriptions of basic methods, sensitivity analysis, and decision conferencing. Also included are several of the articles on applications that are listed in Table 15.5.

15.7   CONCLUSIONS

Decision analysis has become an important technique for decision making in the face of uncertainty. It is characterized by enumerating all the available courses of action, identifying the payoffs for all possible outcomes, and quantifying the subjective probabilities for all the possible random events. When these data are available, decision analysis becomes a powerful tool for determining an optimal course of action.

One option that can be readily incorporated into the analysis is to perform experimentation to obtain better estimates of the probabilities of the possible states of nature. Decision trees are a useful visual tool for analyzing this option or any series of decisions.

Utility theory provides a way of incorporating the decision maker's attitude toward risk into the analysis.

Good software (including TreePlan and SensIt in your OR Courseware) is becoming widely available for performing decision analysis.

SELECTED REFERENCES

1. Clemen, R. T.: *Making Hard Decisions: An Introduction to Decision Analysis,* 2d ed., Duxbury Press, Belmont, CA, 1996.
2. Edwards, W. (ed.): *Utility Theories: Measurements and Applications,* Kluwer Academic Publishers, Boston, 1992.
3. Fishburn, P. C.: "Foundations of Decision Analysis: Along the Way," *Management Science,* **35:** 387–405, 1989.

4. Fishburn, P. C.: *Nonlinear Preference and Utility Theory,* The Johns Hopkins Press, Baltimore, MD, 1988.

5. Hillier, F. S., M. S. Hillier, and G. J. Lieberman: *Introduction to Management Science: A Modeling and Case Studies Approach with Spreadsheets,* Irwin/McGraw-Hill, Burr Ridge, IL, 2000, chap. 10.

6. Marshall, K. T., and R. M. Oliver: *Decision Making and Forecasting,* McGraw-Hill, New York, 1995.

LEARNING AIDS FOR THIS CHAPTER IN YOUR OR COURSEWARE

"Ch. 15—Decision Analysis" Excel File:

TreePlan Decision Trees for Goferbroke Problems (3)
Template for Maximin Payoff Criterion
Template for Maximum Likelihood Criterion
Template for Bayes' Decision Rule
Decision Analysis Spreadsheets for Goferbroke Problems (2)
Template for Expected Payoff with Perfect Information
Template for Posterior Probabilities

Excel Add-Ins:

TreePlan (academic version)
SensIt (academic version)

PROBLEMS

The symbols to the left of some of the problems (or their parts) have the following meaning:

T: The corresponding Excel template listed above can be helpful.
A: The corresponding Excel add-in listed above can be used.

An asterisk on the problem number indicates that at least a partial answer is given in the back of the book.

15.2-1.* Silicon Dynamics has developed a new computer chip that will enable it to begin producing and marketing a personal computer if it so desires. Alternatively, it can sell the rights to the computer chip for $15 million. If the company chooses to build computers, the profitability of the venture depends upon the company's ability to market the computer during the first year. It has sufficient access to retail outlets that it can guarantee sales of 10,000 computers. On the other hand, if this computer catches on, the company can sell 100,000 machines. For analysis purposes, these two levels of sales are taken to be the two possible outcomes of marketing the computer, but it is unclear what their prior probabilities are. The cost of setting up the assembly line is $6 million. The difference between the selling price and the variable cost of each computer is $600.

(a) Develop a decision analysis formulation of this problem by identifying the alternative actions, the states of nature, and the payoff table.

(b) Develop a graph that plots the expected payoff for each of the alternative actions versus the prior probability of selling 10,000 computers.

(c) Referring to the graph developed in part (b), use algebra to solve for the *crossover point*. Explain the significance of this point.

A (d) Develop a graph that plots the expected payoff (when using Bayes' decision rule) versus the prior probability of selling 10,000 computers.

T (e) Assuming the prior probabilities of the two levels of sales are both 0.5, which alternative action should be chosen?

15.2-2. Jean Clark is the manager of the Midtown Saveway Grocery Store. She now needs to replenish her supply of strawberries. Her regular supplier can provide as many cases as she wants. However, because these strawberries already are very ripe, she will need to sell them tomorrow and then discard any that remain unsold. Jean estimates that she will be able to sell 10, 11, 12, or 13 cases tomorrow. She can purchase the strawberries for $3 per case and sell them for $8 per case. Jean now needs to decide how many cases to purchase.

Jean has checked the store's records on daily sales of strawberries. On this basis, she estimates that the prior probabilities are 0.2, 0.4, 0.3, and 0.1 for being able to sell 10, 11, 12, and 13 cases of strawberries tomorrow.

(a) Develop a decision analysis formulation of this problem by identifying the alternative actions, the states of nature, and the payoff table.

T (b) How many cases of strawberries should Jean purchase if she uses the maximin payoff criterion?

T (c) How many cases should be purchased according to the maximum likelihood criterion?

T (d) How many cases should be purchased according to Bayes' decision rule?

T (e) Jean thinks she has the prior probabilities just about right for selling 10 cases and selling 13 cases, but is uncertain about how to split the prior probabilities for 11 cases and 12 cases. Reapply Bayes' decision rule when the prior probabilities of 11 and 12 cases are (i) 0.2 and 0.5, (ii) 0.3 and 0.4, and (iii) 0.5 and 0.2.

T **15.2-3.*** Warren Buffy is an enormously wealthy investor who has built his fortune through his legendary investing acumen. He currently has been offered three major investments and he would like to choose one. The first one is a *conservative investment* that would perform very well in an improving economy and only suffer a small loss in a worsening economy. The second is a *speculative investment* that would perform extremely well in an improving economy but would do very badly in a worsening economy. The third is a *countercyclical investment* that would lose some money in an improving economy but would perform well in a worsening economy.

Warren believes that there are three possible scenarios over the lives of these potential investments: (1) an improving economy, (2) a stable economy, and (3) a worsening economy. He is pessimistic about where the economy is headed, and so has assigned prior probabilities of 0.1, 0.5, and 0.4, respectively, to these three scenarios. He also estimates that his profits under these respective scenarios are those given by the following table:

	Improving Economy	Stable Economy	Worsening Economy
Conservative investment	$30 million	$ 5 million	−$10 million
Speculative investment	$40 million	$10 million	−$30 million
Countercyclical investment	−$10 million	0	$15 million
Prior probability	0.1	0.5	0.4

Which investment should Warren make under each of the following criteria?

(a) Maximin payoff criterion.

(b) Maximum likelihood criterion.

(c) Bayes' decision rule.

15.2-4. Reconsider Prob. 15.2-3. Warren Buffy decides that Bayes' decision rule is his most reliable decision criterion. He believes that 0.1 is just about right as the prior probability of an improving economy, but is quite uncertain about how to split the remaining probabilities between a stable economy and a worsening economy. Therefore, he now wishes to do sensitivity analysis with respect to these latter two prior probabilities.

T (a) Reapply Bayes' decision rule when the prior probability of a stable economy is 0.3 and the prior probability of a worsening economy is 0.6.

T (b) Reapply Bayes' decision rule when the prior probability of a stable economy is 0.7 and the prior probability of a worsening economy is 0.2.

(c) Graph the expected profit for each of the three investment alternatives versus the prior probability of a stable economy (with the prior probability of an improving economy fixed at 0.1). Use this graph to identify the crossover points where the decision shifts from one investment to another.

(d) Use algebra to solve for the crossover points identified in part (c).

A (e) Develop a graph that plots the expected profit (when using Bayes' decision rule) versus the prior probability of a stable economy.

15.2-5.* Consider a decision analysis problem whose payoffs (in units of thousands of dollars) are given by the following payoff table:

	State of Nature	
Alternative	S_1	S_2
A_1	80	25
A_2	30	50
A_3	60	40
Prior probability	0.4	0.6

T (a) Which alternative should be chosen under the maximin payoff criterion?

T (b) Which alternative should be chosen under the maximum likelihood criterion?

T (c) Which alternative should be chosen under Bayes' decision rule?

A **(d)** Using Bayes' decision rule, do sensitivity analysis graphically with respect to the prior probabilities to determine the crossover points where the decision shifts from one alternative to another.

(e) Use algebra to solve for the crossover points identified in part (d).

15.2-6. You are given the following payoff table (in units of thousands of dollars) for a decision analysis problem:

	State of Nature		
Alternative	S_1	S_2	S_3
A_1	220	170	110
A_2	200	180	150
Prior probability	0.6	0.3	0.1

T **(a)** Which alternative should be chosen under the maximin payoff criterion?

T **(b)** Which alternative should be chosen under the maximum likelihood criterion?

T **(c)** Which alternative should be chosen under Bayes' decision rule?

(d) Using Bayes' decision rule, do sensitivity analysis graphically with respect to the prior probabilities of states S_1 and S_2 (without changing the prior probability of state S_3) to determine the crossover point where the decision shifts from one alternative to the other. Then use algebra to calculate this crossover point.

(e) Repeat part (d) for the prior probabilities of states S_1 and S_3.

(f) Repeat part (d) for the prior probabilities of states S_2 and S_3.

(g) If you feel that the true probabilities of the states of nature are within 10 percent of the given prior probabilities, which alternative would you choose?

15.2-7. Dwight Moody is the manager of a large farm with 1,000 acres of arable land. For greater efficiency, Dwight always devotes the farm to growing one crop at a time. He now needs to make a decision on which one of four crops to grow during the upcoming growing season. For each of these crops, Dwight has obtained the following estimates of crop yields and net incomes per bushel under various weather conditions.

	Expected Yield, Bushels/Acre			
Weather	Crop 1	Crop 2	Crop 3	Crop 4
Dry	20	15	30	40
Moderate	35	20	25	40
Damp	40	30	25	40
Net income per bushel	$1.00	$1.50	$1.00	$0.50

After referring to historical meteorological records, Dwight also estimated the following prior probabilities for the weather during the growing season:

Dry	0.3
Moderate	0.5
Damp	0.2

(a) Develop a decision analysis formulation of this problem by identifying the alternative actions, the states of nature, and the payoff table.

T **(b)** Use Bayes' decision rule to determine which crop to grow.

T **(c)** Using Bayes' decision rule, do sensitivity analysis with respect to the prior probabilities of moderate weather and damp weather (without changing the prior probability of dry weather) by re-solving when the prior probability of moderate weather is 0.2, 0.3, 0.4, and 0.6.

T **15.2-8.*** A new type of airplane is to be purchased by the Air Force, and the number of spare engines to be ordered must be determined. The Air Force must order these spare engines in batches of five, and it can choose among only 15, 20, or 25 spares. The supplier of these engines has two plants, and the Air Force must make its decision prior to knowing which plant will be used. However, the Air Force knows from past experience that two-thirds of all types of airplane engines are produced in Plant A, and only one-third are produced in Plant B. The Air Force also knows that the number of spare engines required when production takes place at Plant A is approximated by a Poisson distribution with mean $\theta = 21$, whereas the number of spare engines required when production takes place at Plant B is approximated by a Poisson distribution with mean $\theta = 24$. The cost of a spare engine purchased now is $400,000, whereas the cost of a spare engine purchased at a later date is $900,000. Spares must always be supplied if they are demanded, and unused engines will be scrapped when the airplanes become obsolete. Holding costs and interest are to be neglected. From these data, the total costs (negative payoffs) have been computed as follows:

	State of Nature	
Alternative	$\theta = 21$	$\theta = 24$
Order 15	1.155×10^7	1.414×10^7
Order 20	1.012×10^7	1.207×10^7
Order 25	1.047×10^7	1.135×10^7

Determine the optimal action under Bayes' decision rule.

15.2-9. An individual makes decisions according to Bayes' decision rule. For her current problem, she has constructed the following payoff table, and she now wishes to maximize the expected payoff.

Alternative	State of Nature		
	θ_1	θ_2	θ_3
a_1	$2x$	60	10
a_2	25	40	90
a_3	35	$3x$	30
Prior probability	0.4	0.2	0.4

The value of x currently is 50, but there is an opportunity to increase x by spending some money now.

What is the maximum amount that should be spent to increase x to 75?

15.3-1.* Reconsider Prob. 15.2-1. Management of Silicon Dynamics now is considering doing full-fledged market research at a cost of $1 million to predict which of the two levels of demand is likely to occur. Previous experience indicates that such market research is correct two-thirds of the time.
T **(a)** Find EVPI for this problem.
(b) Does the answer in part (*a*) indicate that it might be worthwhile to perform this market research?
(c) Develop a probability tree diagram to obtain the posterior probabilities of the two levels of demand for each of the two possible outcomes of the market research.
T **(d)** Use the corresponding Excel template to check your answers in part (*c*).
(d) Find EVE. Is it worthwhile to perform the market research?

15.3-2. You are given the following payoff table (in units of thousands of dollars) for a decision analysis problem:

Alternative	State of Nature		
	S_1	S_2	S_3
A_1	4	0	0
A_2	0	2	0
A_3	3	0	1
Prior probability	0.2	0.5	0.3

T **(a)** According to Bayes' decision rule, which alternative should be chosen?
T **(b)** Find EVPI.

(c) You are given the opportunity to spend $1,000 to obtain more information about which state of nature is likely to occur. Given your answer to part (*b*), might it be worthwhile to spend this money?

15.3-3.* Betsy Pitzer makes decisions according to Bayes' decision rule. For her current problem, Betsy has constructed the following payoff table (in units of dollars):

Alternative	State of Nature		
	S_1	S_2	S_3
A_1	50	100	-100
A_2	0	10	-10
A_3	20	40	-40
Prior probability	0.5	0.3	0.2

T **(a)** Which alternative should Betsy choose?
T **(b)** Find EVPI.
(c) What is the most that Betsy should consider paying to obtain more information about which state of nature will occur?

15.3-4. Using Bayes' decision rule, consider the decision analysis problem having the following payoff table (in units of thousands of dollars):

Alternative	State of Nature		
	S_1	S_2	S_3
A_1	-100	10	100
A_2	-10	20	50
A_3	10	10	60
Prior probability	0.2	0.3	0.5

T **(a)** Which alternative should be chosen? What is the resulting expected payoff?
(b) You are offered the opportunity to obtain information which will tell you with certainty whether the first state of nature S_1 will occur. What is the maximum amount you should pay for the information? Assuming you will obtain the information, how should this information be used to choose an alternative? What is the resulting expected payoff (excluding the payment)?
(c) Now repeat part (*b*) if the information offered concerns S_2 instead of S_1.
(d) Now repeat part (*b*) if the information offered concerns S_3 instead of S_1.

T **(e)** Now suppose that the opportunity is offered to provide information which will tell you with certainty which state of nature will occur (perfect information). What is the maximum amount you should pay for the information? Assuming you will obtain the information, how should this information be used to choose an alternative? What is the resulting expected payoff (excluding the payment)?

(f) If you have the opportunity to do some testing that will give you partial additional information (not perfect information) about the state of nature, what is the maximum amount you should consider paying for this information?

15.3-5. Reconsider the Goferbroke Co. prototype example, including its analysis in Sec. 15.3. With the help of a consulting geologist, some historical data have been obtained that provide more precise information on the likelihood of obtaining favorable seismic soundings on similar tracts of land. Specifically, when the land contains oil, favorable seismic soundings are obtained 80 percent of the time. This percentage changes to 40 percent when the land is dry.

(a) Revise Fig. 15.6 to find the new posterior probabilities.

T **(b)** Use the corresponding Excel template to check your answers in part (a).

(c) What is the resulting optimal policy?

15.3-6. You are given the following payoff table (in units of dollars):

	State of Nature	
Alternative	S_1	S_2
A_1	400	−100
A_2	0	100
Prior probability	0.4	0.6

You have the option of paying $100 to have research done to better predict which state of nature will occur. When the true state of nature is S_1, the research will accurately predict S_1 60 percent of the time (but will inaccurately predict S_2 40 percent of the time). When the true state of nature is S_2, the research will accurately predict S_2 80 percent of the time (but will inaccurately predict S_1 20 percent of the time).

T **(a)** Given that the research is not done, use Bayes' decision rule to determine which decision alternative should be chosen.

T **(b)** Find EVPI. Does this answer indicate that it might be worthwhile to do the research?

(c) Given that the research is done, find the joint probability of each of the following pairs of outcomes: (i) the state of nature is S_1 and the research predicts S_1, (ii) the state of nature is S_1 and the research predicts S_2, (iii) the state of nature is S_2 and

the research predicts S_1, and (iv) the state of nature is S_2 and the research predicts S_2.

(d) Find the unconditional probability that the research predicts S_1. Also find the unconditional probability that the research predicts S_2.

(e) Given that the research is done, use your answers in parts (c) and (d) to determine the posterior probabilities of the states of nature for each of the two possible predictions of the research.

T **(f)** Use the corresponding Excel template to obtain the answers for part (e).

T **(g)** Given that the research predicts S_1, use Bayes' decision rule to determine which decision alternative should be chosen and the resulting expected payoff.

T **(h)** Repeat part (g) when the research predicts S_2.

T **(i)** Given that research is done, what is the expected payoff when using Bayes' decision rule?

(j) Use the preceding results to determine the optimal policy regarding whether to do the research and the choice of the decision alternative.

15.3-7. You are given the opportunity to guess whether a coin is fair or two-headed, where the prior probabilities are 0.5 for each of these possibilities. If you are correct, you win $5; otherwise, you lose $5. You are also given the option of seeing a demonstration flip of the coin before making your guess. You wish to use Bayes' decision rule to maximize expected profit.

(a) Develop a decision analysis formulation of this problem by identifying the alternative actions, states of nature, and payoff table.

T **(b)** What is the optimal action, given that you decline the option of seeing a demonstration flip?

T **(c)** Find EVPI.

(d) Use the procedure presented in Sec. 15.3 to calculate the posterior distribution if the demonstration flip is a tail. Do the same if the flip is a head.

T **(e)** Use the corresponding Excel template to confirm your results in part (d).

(f) Determine your optimal policy.

(g) Now suppose that you must pay to see the demonstration flip. What is the most that you should be willing to pay?

T **15.3-8.*** Reconsider Prob. 15.2-8. Suppose now that the Air Force knows that a similar type of engine was produced for an earlier version of the type of airplane currently under consideration. The order size for this earlier version was the same as for the current type. Furthermore, the probability distribution of the number of spare engines required, given the plant where production takes place, is believed to be the same for this earlier airplane model and the current one. The engine for the current order will be produced in the same plant as the previous model, although the Air Force does not know which of the two plants this is. The Air Force does have access to the data on the number of spares actually required for the older version, but the supplier has not revealed the production location.

(a) How much money is it worthwhile to pay for perfect information on which plant will produce these engines?

(b) Assume that the cost of the data on the old airplane model is free and that 30 spares were required. You are given that the probability of 30 spares, given a Poisson distribution with mean θ, is 0.013 for $\theta = 21$ and 0.036 for $\theta = 24$. Find the optimal action under Bayes' decision rule.

15.3-9.* Vincent Cuomo is the credit manager for the Fine Fabrics Mill. He is currently faced with the question of whether to extend $100,000 credit to a potential new customer, a dress manufacturer. Vincent has three categories for the credit-worthiness of a company: poor risk, average risk, and good risk, but he does not know which category fits this potential customer. Experience indicates that 20 percent of companies similar to this dress manufacturer are poor risks, 50 percent are average risks, and 30 percent are good risks. If credit is extended, the expected profit for poor risks is $-\$15,000$, for average risks $\$10,000$, and for good risks $\$20,000$. If credit is not extended, the dress manufacturer will turn to another mill. Vincent is able to consult a credit-rating organization for a fee of $5,000 per company evaluated. For companies whose actual credit record with the mill turns out to fall into each of the three categories, the following table shows the percentages that were given each of the three possible credit evaluations by the credit-rating organization.

Credit Evaluation	Actual Credit Record		
	Poor	Average	Good
Poor	50%	40%	20%
Average	40%	50%	40%
Good	10%	10%	40%

(a) Develop a decision analysis formulation of this problem by identifying the alternative actions, the states of nature, and the payoff table when the credit-rating organization is not used.

T (b) Assuming the credit-rating organization is not used, use Bayes' decision rule to determine which decision alternative should be chosen.

T (c) Find EVPI. Does this answer indicate that consideration should be given to using the credit-rating organization?

(d) Assume now that the credit-rating organization is used. Develop a probability tree diagram to find the posterior probabilities of the respective states of nature for each of the three possible credit evaluations of this potential customer.

T (e) Use the corresponding Excel template to obtain the answers for part (d).

(f) Determine Vincent's optimal policy.

15.3-10. An athletic league does drug testing of its athletes, 10 percent of whom use drugs. This test, however, is only 95 percent reliable. That is, a drug user will test positive with probability 0.95 and negative with probability 0.05, and a nonuser will test negative with probability 0.95 and positive with probability 0.05.

Develop a probability tree diagram to determine the posterior probability of each of the following outcomes of testing an athlete.

(a) The athlete is a drug user, given that the test is positive.

(b) The athlete is not a drug user, given that the test is positive.

(c) The athlete is a drug user, given that the test is negative.

(d) The athlete is not a drug user, given that the test is negative.

T (e) Use the corresponding Excel template to check your answers in the preceding parts.

15.3-11. Management of the Telemore Company is considering developing and marketing a new product. It is estimated to be twice as likely that the product would prove to be successful as unsuccessful. It it were successful, the expected profit would be $1,500,000. If unsuccessful, the expected loss would be $1,800,000. A marketing survey can be conducted at a cost of $300,000 to predict whether the product would be successful. Past experience with such surveys indicates that successful products have been predicted to be successful 80 percent of the time, whereas unsuccessful products have been predicted to be unsuccessful 70 percent of the time.

(a) Develop a decision analysis formulation of this problem by identifying the alternative actions, the states of nature, and the payoff table when the market survey is not conducted.

T (b) Assuming the market survey is not conducted, use Bayes' decision rule to determine which decision alternative should be chosen.

T (c) Find EVPI. Does this answer indicate that consideration should be given to conducting the market survey?

T (d) Assume now that the market survey is conducted. Find the posterior probabilities of the respective states of nature for each of the two possible predictions from the market survey.

(e) Find the optimal policy regarding whether to conduct the market survey and whether to develop and market the new product.

15.3-12. The Hit-and-Miss Manufacturing Company produces items that have a probability p of being defective. These items are produced in lots of 150. Past experience indicates that p for an entire lot is either 0.05 or 0.25. Furthermore, in 80 percent of the lots produced, p equals 0.05 (so p equals 0.25 in 20 percent of the lots). These items are then used in an assembly, and ultimately their quality is determined before the final assembly leaves the plant. Initially the company can *either* screen each item in a lot at a cost of

$10 per item and replace defective items *or* use the items directly without screening. If the latter action is chosen, the cost of rework is ultimately $100 per defective item. Because screening requires scheduling of inspectors and equipment, the decision to screen or not screen must be made 2 days before the screening is to take place. However, one item can be taken from the lot and sent to a laboratory for inspection, and its quality (defective or nondefective) can be reported before the screen/no screen decision must be made. The cost of this initial inspection is $125.

(a) Develop a decision analysis formulation of this problem by identifying the alternative actions, the states of nature, and the payoff table if the single item is not inspected in advance.

T (b) Assuming the single item is not inspected in advance, use Bayes' decision rule to determine which decision alternative should be chosen.

T (c) Find EVPI. Does this answer indicate that consideration should be given to inspecting the single item in advance?

T (d) Assume now that the single item is inspected in advance. Find the posterior probabilities of the respective states of nature for each of the two possible outcomes of this inspection.

(e) Find EVE. Is inspecting the single item worthwhile?

(f) Determine the optimal policy.

T **15.3-13.*** Consider two weighted coins. Coin 1 has a probability of 0.3 of turning up heads, and coin 2 has a probability of 0.6 of turning up heads. A coin is tossed once; the probability that coin 1 is tossed is 0.6, and the probability that coin 2 is tossed is 0.4. The decision maker uses Bayes' decision rule to decide which coin is tossed. The payoff table is as follows:

Alternative	State of Nature	
	Coin 1 Tossed	Coin 2 Tossed
Say coin 1 tossed	0	−1
Say coin 2 tossed	−1	0
Prior probability	0.6	0.4

(a) What is the optimal action before the coin is tossed?

(b) What is the optimal action after the coin is tossed if the outcome is heads? If it is tails?

15.3-14. A new type of photographic film has been developed. It is packaged in sets of five sheets, where each sheet provides an instantaneous snapshot. Because this process is new, the manufacturer has attached an additional sheet to the package, so that the store may test one sheet before it sells the package of five. In promoting the film, the manufacturer offers to refund the entire purchase price of the film if one of the five is defective. This refund

must be paid by the camera store, and the selling price has been fixed at $2 if this guarantee is to be valid. The camera store may sell the film for $1 if the preceding guarantee is replaced by one that pays $0.20 for each defective sheet. The cost of the film to the camera store is $0.40, and the film is not returnable. The store may choose any one of three actions:

1. Scrap the film.
2. Sell the film for $2.
3. Sell the film for $1.

(a) If the six states of nature correspond to 0, 1, 2, 3, 4, and 5 defective sheets in the package, complete the following payoff table:

Alternative	State of Nature					
	0	1	2	3	4	5
1	−0.40					
2	1.60		−0.40			
3	0.60	0.40		0.00		

T (b) The store has accumulated the following information on sales of 60 such packages:

Quality of Attached Sheet	Defectives in Package					
	0	1	2	3	4	5
Good	10	8	6	4	2	0
Bad	0	2	4	6	8	10
Total	10	10	10	10	10	10

These data indicate that each state of nature is equally likely, so that this prior distribution can be assumed. What is the optimal action under Bayes' decision rule (before the attached sheet is tested) for a package of film?

(c) Now assume that the attached sheet is tested. Use a probability tree diagram to find the posterior probabilities of the state of nature for each of the two possible outcomes of this testing.

T (d) What is the optimal expected payoff for a package of film if the attached sheet is tested? What is the optimal action if the sheet is good? If it is bad?

15.3-15. There are two biased coins with probabilities of landing heads of 0.8 and 0.4, respectively. One coin is chosen at random (each with probability $\frac{1}{2}$) to be tossed twice. You are to receive $100 if you correctly predict how many heads will occur in two tosses.

T (a) Using Bayes' decision rule, what is the optimal prediction, and what is the corresponding expected payoff?

T (b) Suppose now that you may observe a practice toss of the chosen coin before predicting. Use the corresponding Excel template to find the posterior probabilities for which coin is being tossed.

T (c) Determine your optimal prediction after observing the practice toss. What is the resulting expected payoff?

(d) Find EVE for observing the practice toss. If you must pay $30 to observe the practice toss, what is your optimal policy?

15.4-1.* Reconsider Prob. 15.3-1. The management of Silicon Dynamics now wants to see a decision tree displaying the entire problem.

(a) Construct and solve this decision tree by hand.

A (b) Use TreePlan to construct and solve this decision tree.

15.4-2. You are given the decision tree to the right, where the numbers in parentheses are probabilities and the numbers on the far right are payoffs at these terminal points.

(a) Analyze this decision tree to obtain the optimal policy.

A (b) Use TreePlan to construct and solve the same decision tree.

15.4-3. You are given the decision tree below, with the probabilities at chance forks shown in parentheses and with the payoffs at terminal points shown on the right. Analyze this decision tree to obtain the optimal policy.

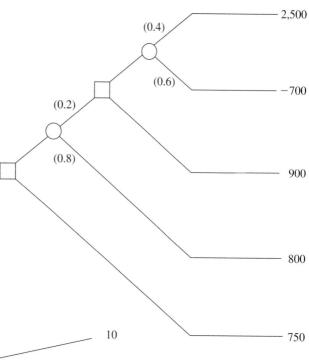

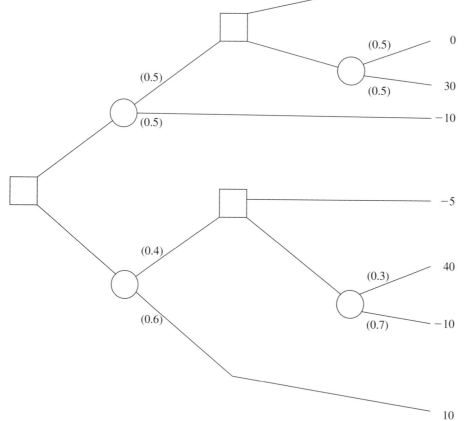

15.4-4.* The Athletic Department of Leland University is considering whether to hold an extensive campaign next year to raise funds for a new athletic field. The response to the campaign depends heavily upon the success of the football team this fall. In the past, the football team has had winning seasons 60 percent of the time. If the football team has a winning season (W) this fall, then many of the alumnae and alumni will contribute and the campaign will raise $3 million. If the team has a losing season (L), few will contribute and the campaign will lose $2 million. If no campaign is undertaken, no costs are incurred. On September 1, just before the football season begins, the Athletic Department needs to make its decision about whether to hold the campaign next year.

(a) Develop a decision analysis formulation of this problem by identifying the alternative actions, the states of nature, and the payoff table.

T (b) According to Bayes' decision rule, should the campaign be undertaken?

T (c) What is EVPI?

(d) A famous football guru, William Walsh, has offered his services to help evaluate whether the team will have a winning season. For $100,000, he will carefully evaluate the team throughout spring practice and then throughout preseason workouts. William then will provide his prediction on September 1 regarding what kind of season, W or L, the team will have. In similar situations in the past when evaluating teams that have winning seasons 50 percent of the time, his predictions have been correct 75 percent of the time. Considering that this team has more of a winning tradition, if William predicts a winning season, what is the posterior probability that the team actually will have a winning season? What is the posterior probability of a losing season? If Williams predicts a losing season instead, what is the posterior probability of a winning season? Of a losing season? Show how these answers are obtained from a probability tree diagram.

T (e) Use the corresponding Excel template to obtain the answers requested in part (d).

(f) Draw the decision tree for this entire problem by hand. Analyze this decision tree to determine the optimal policy regarding whether to hire William and whether to undertake the campaign.

A (g) Use TreePlan to construct and solve this decision tree.

15.4-5. The comptroller of the Macrosoft Corporation has $100 million of excess funds to invest. She has been instructed to invest the entire amount for 1 year in either stocks or bonds (but not both) and then to reinvest the entire fund in either stocks or bonds (but not both) for 1 year more. The objective is to maximize the expected monetary value of the fund at the end of the second year.

The annual rates of return on these investments depend on the economic environment, as shown in the following table:

Economic Environment	Rate of Return	
	Stocks	Bonds
Growth	20%	5%
Recession	−10%	10%
Depression	−50%	20%

The probabilities of growth, recession, and depression for the first year are 0.7, 0.3, and 0, respectively. If growth occurs in the first year, these probabilities remain the same for the second year. However, if a recession occurs in the first year, these probabilities change to 0.2, 0.7, and 0.1, respectively, for the second year.

(a) Construct the decision tree for this problem by hand.

(b) Analyze the decision tree to identify the optimal policy.

A (c) Use TreePlan to construct and solve the decision tree.

15.4-6. On Monday, a certain stock closed at $10 per share. On Tuesday, you expect the stock to close at $9, $10, or $11 per share, with respective probabilities 0.3, 0.3, and 0.4. On Wednesday, you expect the stock to close 10 percent lower, unchanged, or 10 percent higher than Tuesday's close, with the following probabilities:

Today's Close	10% Lower	Unchanged	10% Higher
$ 9	0.4	0.3	0.3
$10	0.2	0.2	0.6
$11	0.1	0.2	0.7

On Tuesday, you are directed to buy 100 shares of the stock before Thursday. All purchases are made at the end of the day, at the known closing price for that day, so your only options are to buy at the end of Tuesday or at the end of Wednesday. You wish to determine the optimal strategy for whether to buy on Tuesday or defer the purchase until Wednesday, given the Tuesday closing price, to minimize the expected purchase price.

(a) Develop and evaluate a decision tree by hand for determining the optimal strategy.

A (b) Use TreePlan to construct and solve the decision tree.

15.4-7. Use the scenario given in Prob. 15.3-7.

(a) Draw and properly label the decision tree. Include all the payoffs but not the probabilities.

T (b) Find the probabilities for the branches emanating from the chance forks.

(c) Apply the backward induction procedure, and identify the resulting optimal policy.

A **15.4-8.** Jose Morales manages a large outdoor fruit stand in one of the less affluent neighborhoods of San Jose, California. To replenish his supply, Jose buys boxes of fruit early each morning from a grower south of San Jose. About 90 percent of the boxes of fruit turn out to be of satisfactory quality, but the other 10 percent are unsatisfactory. A satisfactory box contains 80 percent excellent fruit and will earn $200 profit for Jose. An unsatisfactory box contains 30 percent excellent fruit and will produce a loss of $1,000. Before Jose decides to accept a box, he is given the opportunity to sample one piece of fruit to test whether it is excellent. Based on that sample, he then has the option of rejecting the box without paying for it. Jose wonders (1) whether he should continue buying from this grower, (2) if so, whether it is worthwhile sampling just one piece of fruit from a box, and (3) if so, whether he should be accepting or rejecting the box based on the outcome of this sampling.

Use TreePlan (and the Excel template for posterior probabilities) to construct and solve the decision tree for this problem.

15.4-9. Use the scenario given in Prob. 15.3-9.
(a) Draw and properly label the decision tree. Include all the payoffs but not the probabilities.
T **(b)** Find the probabilities for the branches emanating from the chance forks.
(c) Apply the backward induction procedure, and identify the resulting optimal policy.

15.4-10.* The Morton Ward Company is considering the introduction of a new product that is believed to have a 50-50 chance of being successful. One option is to try out the product in a test market, at a cost of $5 million, before making the introduction decision. Past experience shows that ultimately successful products are approved in the test market 80 percent of the time, whereas ultimately unsuccessful products are approved in the test market only 25 percent of the time. If the product is successful, the net profit to the company will be $40 million; if unsuccessful, the net loss will be $15 million.
T **(a)** Discarding the option of trying out the product in a test market, develop a decision analysis formulation of the problem by identifying the alternative actions, states of nature, and payoff table. Then apply Bayes' decision rule to determine the optimal decision alternative.
T **(b)** Find EVPI.
A **(c)** Now including the option of trying out the product in a test market, use TreePlan (and the Excel template for posterior probabilities) to construct and solve the decision tree for this problem.
A **(d)** There is some uncertainty in the stated profit and loss figures ($40 million and $15 million). Either could vary from its base by as much as 25 percent in either direction. Use SensIt to generate a graph for each that plots the expected payoff over this range of variability.

15.4-11. Use the scenario given in Prob. 15.3.-11.
(a) Draw and properly label the decision tree. Include all the payoffs but not the probabilities.
T **(b)** Find the probabilities for the branches emanating from the chance forks.
(c) Apply the backward induction procedure, and identify the resulting optimal policy.

15.4-12. Use the scenario given in Prob. 15.3-12.
(a) Draw and properly label the decision tree. Include all the payoffs but not the probabilities.
T **(b)** Find the probabilities for the branches emanating from the chance forks.
(c) Apply the backward induction procedure, and identify the resulting optimal policy.

15.4-13. Use the scenario given in Prob. 15.3-13.
(a) Draw and properly label the decision tree. Include all the payoffs but not the probabilities.
T **(b)** Find the probabilities for the branches emanating from the chance forks.
(c) Apply the backward induction procedure, and identify the resulting optimal policy.

15.4-14. Chelsea Bush is an emerging candidate for her party's nomination for President of the United States. She now is considering whether to run in the high-stakes Super Tuesday primaries. If she enters the Super Tuesday (S.T.) primaries, she and her advisers believe that she will either do well (finish first or second) or do poorly (finish third or worse) with probabilities 0.4 and 0.6, respectively. Doing well on Super Tuesday will net the candidate's campaign approximately $16 million in new contributions, whereas a poor showing will mean a loss of $10 million after numerous TV ads are paid for. Alternatively, she may choose not to run at all on Super Tuesday and incur no costs.

Chelsea's advisers realize that her chances of success on Super Tuesday may be affected by the outcome of the smaller New Hampshire (N.H.) primary occurring 3 weeks before Super Tuesday. Political analysts feel that the results of New Hampshire's primary are correct two-thirds of the time in predicting the results of the Super Tuesday primaries. Among Chelsea's advisers is a decision analysis expert who uses this information to calculate the following probabilities:

$$P\{\text{Chelsea does well in S.T. primaries, given she does well in N.H.}\} = \frac{4}{7}$$

$$P\{\text{Chelsea does well in S.T. primaries, given she does poorly in N.H.}\} = \frac{1}{4}$$

$$P\{\text{Chelsea does well in N.H. primary}\} = \frac{7}{15}$$

The cost of entering and campaigning in the New Hampshire primary is estimated to be $1.6 million.

Chelsea feels that her chance of winning the nomination depends largely on having substantial funds available after the Super Tuesday primaries to carry on a vigorous campaign the rest of the way. Therefore, she wants to choose the strategy (whether to run in the New Hampshire primary and then whether to run in the Super Tuesday primaries) that will maximize her expected funds after these primaries.

(a) Construct and solve the decision tree for this problem.

A (b) There is some uncertainty in the estimates of a gain of $16 million or a loss of $10 million depending on the showing on Super Tuesday. Either amount could differ from this estimate by as much as 25 percent in either direction. Develop a graph for each amount that plots the expected payoff over this range of variability.

A **15.4-15.** The executive search being conducted for Western Bank by Headhunters Inc. may finally be bearing fruit. The position to be filled is a key one—Vice President for Information Processing—because this person will have responsibility for developing a state-of-the-art management information system that will link together Western's many branch banks. However, Headhunters feels they have found just the right person, Matthew Fenton, who has an excellent record in a similar position for a midsized bank in New York.

After a round of interviews, Western's president believes that Matthew has a probability of 0.7 of designing the management information system successfully. If Matthew is successful, the company will realize a profit of $2 million (net of Matthew's salary, training, recruiting costs, and expenses). If he is not successful, the company will realize a net loss of $400,000.

For an additional fee of $20,000, Headhunters will provide a detailed investigative process (including an extensive background check, a battery of academic and psychological tests, etc.) that will further pinpoint Matthew's potential for success. This process has been found to be 90 percent reliable; i.e., a candidate who would successfully design the management information system will pass the test with probability 0.9, and a candidate who would not successfully design the system will fail the test with probability 0.9.

Western's top management needs to decide whether to hire Matthew and whether to have Headhunters conduct the detailed investigative process before making this decision.

(a) Construct the decision tree for this problem.

T (b) Find the probabilities for the branches emanating from the chance nodes.

(c) Analyze the decision tree to identify the optimal policy.

(d) Now suppose that the Headhunters' fee for administering its detailed investigative process is negotiable. What is the maximum amount that Western Bank should pay?

15.5-1. Reconsider the Goferbroke Co. prototype example, including the application of utilities in Sec. 15.5. The owner now has decided that, given the company's precarious financial situation, he needs to take a much more risk-averse approach to the problem. Therefore, he has revised the utilities given in Table 15.4 as follows: $u(-130) = -200$, $u(-100) = -130$, $u(60) = 60$, $u(90) = 90$, $u(670) = 440$, and $u(700) = 450$.

(a) Analyze the revised decision tree corresponding to Fig. 15.15 by hand to obtain the new optimal policy.

A (b) Use TreePlan to construct and solve this revised decision tree.

15.5-2.* You live in an area that has a possibility of incurring a massive earthquake, so you are considering buying earthquake insurance on your home at an annual cost of $180. The probability of an earthquake damaging your home during 1 year is 0.001. If this happens, you estimate that the cost of the damage (fully covered by earthquake insurance) will be $160,000. Your total assets (including your home) are worth $250,000.

T (a) Apply Bayes' decision rule to determine which alternative (take the insurance or not) maximizes your expected assets after 1 year.

(b) You now have constructed a utility function that measures how much you value having total assets worth x dollars ($x \geq 0$). This utility function is $u(x) = \sqrt{x}$. Compare the utility of reducing your total assets next year by the cost of the earthquake insurance with the expected utility next year of not taking the earthquake insurance. Should you take the insurance?

15.5-3. For your graduation present from college, your parents are offering you your choice of two alternatives The first alternative is to give you a money gift of $19,000. The second alternative is to make an investment in your name. This investment will quickly have the following two possible outcomes:

Outcome	Probability
Receive $10,000	0.3
Receive $30,000	0.7

Your utility for receiving M thousand dollars is given by the utility function $u(M) = \sqrt{M + 6}$. Which choice should you make to maximize expected utility?

15.5-4.* Reconsider Prob. 15.5-3. You now are uncertain about what your true utility function for receiving money is, so you are in the process of constructing this utility function. So far, you have found that $u(19) = 16.7$ and $u(30) = 20$ are the utility of receiving $19,000 and $30,000, respectively. You also have concluded that you are indifferent between the two alternatives offered to you by your parents. Use this information to find $u(10)$.

15.5-5. You wish to construct your personal utility function $u(M)$ for receiving M thousand dollars. After setting $u(0) = 0$, you next set $u(1) = 1$ as your utility for receiving \$1,000. You next want to find $u(10)$ and then $u(5)$.

(a) You offer yourself the following two hypothetical alternatives:

A_1: Obtain \$10,000 with probability p.
Obtain 0 with probability $(1 - p)$.
A_2: Definitely obtain \$1,000.

You then ask yourself the question: What value of p makes you indifferent between these two alternatives? Your answer is $p = 0.125$. Find $u(10)$.

(b) You next repeat part (a) except for changing the second alternative to definitely receiving \$5,000. The value of p that makes you indifferent between these two alternatives now is $p = 0.5625$. Find $u(5)$.

(c) Repeat parts (a) and (b), but now use *your* personal choices for p.

15.5-6. You are given the following payoff table:

	State of Nature	
Alternative	S_1	S_2
A_1	25	36
A_2	100	0
A_3	0	49
Prior probability	p	$1 - p$

(a) Assume that your utility function for the payoffs is $u(x) = \sqrt{x}$. Plot the expected utility of each alternative action versus the value of p on the same graph. For each alternative action, find the range of values of p over which this alternative maximizes the expected utility.

A **(b)** Now assume that your utility function is the exponential utility function with a risk tolerance of $R = 5$. Use TreePlan to construct and solve the resulting decision tree in turn for $p = 0.25$, $p = 0.5$, and $p = 0.75$.

15.5-7. Dr. Switzer has a seriously ill patient but has had trouble diagnosing the specific cause of the illness. The doctor now has narrowed the cause down to two alternatives: disease A or disease B. Based on the evidence so far, she feels that the two alternatives are equally likely.

Beyond the testing already done, there is no test available to determine if the cause is disease B. One test is available for disease A, but it has two major problems. First, it is very expensive. Second, it is somewhat unreliable, giving an accurate result only 80 percent of the time. Thus, it will give a positive result (indicat-

ing disease A) for only 80 percent of patients who have disease A, whereas it will give a positive result for 20 percent of patients who actually have disease B instead.

Disease B is a very serious disease with no known treatment. It is sometimes fatal, and those who survive remain in poor health with a poor quality of life thereafter. The prognosis is similar for victims of disease A if it is left untreated. However, there is a fairly expensive treatment available that eliminates the danger for those with disease A, and it may return them to good health. Unfortunately, it is a relatively radical treatment that always leads to death if the patient actually has disease B instead.

The probability distribution for the prognosis for this patient is given for each case in the following table, where the column headings (after the first one) indicate the disease for the patient.

	Outcome Probabilities			
	No Treatment		Receive Treatment for Disease A	
Outcome	**A**	**B**	**A**	**B**
Die	0.2	0.5	0	1.0
Survive with poor health	0.8	0.5	0.5	0
Return to good health	0	0	0.5	0

The patient has assigned the following utilities to the possible outcomes:

Outcome	Utility
Die	0
Survive with poor health	10
Return to good health	30

In addition, these utilities should be incremented by -2 if the patient incurs the cost of the test for disease A and by -1 if the patient (or the patient's estate) incurs the cost of the treatment for disease A.

Use decision analysis with a complete decision tree to determine if the patient should undergo the test for disease A and then how to proceed (receive the treatment for disease A?) to maximize the patient's expected utility.

15.5-8. Consider the following decision tree, where the probabilities for each chance fork are shown in parentheses.

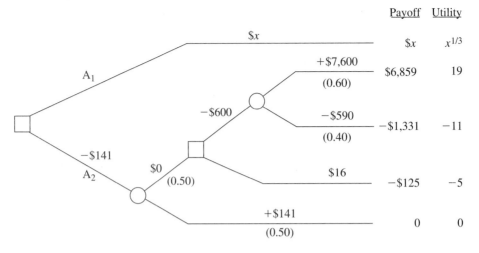

Payoff	Utility
$x	$x^{1/3}$
$6,859	19
−$1,331	−11
−$125	−5
0	0

The dollar amount given next to each branch is the cash flow generated along that branch, where these intermediate cash flows add up to the total net cash flow shown to the right of each terminal branch. (The unknown amount for the top branch is represented by the variable x.) The decision maker has a utility function $u(y) = y^{\frac{1}{3}}$ where y is the total net cash flow after a terminal branch. The resulting utilities for the various terminal branches are shown to the right of the decision tree.

Use these utilities to analyze the decision tree. Then determine the value of x for which the decision maker is indifferent between alternative actions A_1 and A_2.

15.5-9. You want to choose between actions A_1 and A_2 in the following decision tree, but you are uncertain about the value of the probability p, so you need to perform sensitivity analysis of p as well.

Payoff

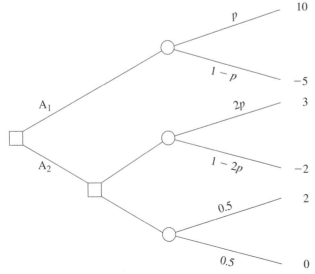

Your utility function for money (the payoff received) is

$$u(M) = \begin{cases} M^2 & \text{if } M \geq 0 \\ M & \text{if } M < 0. \end{cases}$$

(a) For $p = 0.25$, determine which action is optimal in the sense that it maximizes the expected utility of the payoff.
(b) Determine the range of values of the probability p ($0 \leq p \leq 0.5$) for which this same action remains optimal.

15.6-1. Select one of the applications of decision analysis listed in Table 15.5. Read the article describing the application in the indicated issue of *Interfaces*. Write a two-page summary of the application and the benefits it provided.

15.6-2. Select three of the applications of decision analysis listed in Table 15.5. Read the articles describing the applications in the indicated issues of *Interfaces*. For each one, write a one-page summary of the application and the benefits it provided.

CASE 15.1   BRAINY BUSINESS

While El Niño is pouring its rain on northern California, Charlotte Rothstein, CEO, major shareholder and founder of Cerebrosoft, sits in her office, contemplating the decision she faces regarding her company's newest proposed product, Brainet. This has been a particularly difficult decision. Brainet might catch on and sell very well. However, Charlotte is concerned about the risk involved. In this competitive market, marketing Brainet also could lead to substantial losses. Should she go ahead anyway and start the marketing campaign? Or just abandon the product? Or perhaps buy additional marketing research information from a local market research company before deciding whether to launch the product? She has to make a decision very soon and so, as she slowly drinks from her glass of high protein-power multivitamin juice, she reflects on the events of the past few years.

Cerebrosoft was founded by Charlotte and two friends after they had graduated from business school. The company is located in the heart of Silicon Valley. Charlotte and her friends managed to make money in their second year in business and continued to do so every year since. Cerebrosoft was one of the first companies to sell software over the World Wide Web and to develop PC-based software tools for the multimedia sector. Two of the products generate 80 percent of the company's revenues: Audiatur and Videatur. Each product has sold more than 100,000 units during the past year. Business is done over the Web: customers can download a trial version of the software, test it, and if they are satisfied with what they see, they can purchase the product (by using a password that enables them to disable the time counter in the trial version). Both products are priced at $75.95 and are exclusively sold over the Web.

Although the World Wide Web is a network of computers of different types, running different kinds of software, a standardized protocol between the computers enables them to communicate. Users can "surf" the Web and visit computers many thousand miles away, accessing information available at the site. Users can also make files available on the Web, and this is how Cerebrosoft generates its sales. Selling software over the Web eliminates many of the traditional cost factors of consumer products: packaging, storage, distribution, sales force, etc. Instead, potential customers can download a trial version, take a look at it (that is, use the product) before its trial period expires, and then decide whether to buy it. Furthermore, Cerebrosoft can always make the most recent files available to the customer, avoiding the problem of having outdated software in the distribution pipeline.

Charlotte is interrupted in her thoughts by the arrival of Jeannie Korn. Jeannie is in charge of marketing for on-line products and Brainet has had her particular attention from the beginning. She is more than ready to provide the advice that Charlotte has requested. "Charlotte, I think we should really go ahead with Brainet. The software engineers have convinced me that the current version is robust and we want to be on the market with this as soon as possible! From the data for our product launches during the past two years we can get a rather reliable estimate of how the market will respond to the new product, don't you think? And look!" She pulls out some presentation slides. "During that time period we launched 12 new products altogether and 4 of them sold more than 30,000 units during the first 6 months alone! Even better: the last two we launched even sold more than 40,000 copies during the first two quarters!" Charlotte knows these numbers as well as Jeannie does. After all, two of these launches have been products she herself helped to develop. But she feels uneasy about this particular product launch. The company has grown rapidly during the past three years and its financial capabilities are already rather stretched. A poor product launch for Brainet would cost the company a lot of money, something that isn't available right now due to the investments Cerebrosoft has recently made.

Later in the afternoon, Charlotte meets with Reggie Ruffin, a jack-of-all-trades and the production manager. Reggie has a solid track record in his field and Charlotte wants his opinion on the Brainet project.

"Well, Charlotte, quite frankly I think that there are three main factors that are relevant to the success of this project: competition, units sold, and cost—ah, and of course our pricing. Have you decided on the price yet?"

"I am still considering which of the three strategies would be most beneficial to us. Selling for $50.00 and trying to maximize revenues—or selling for $30.00 and trying to maximize market share. Of course, there is still your third alternative; we could sell for $40.00 and try to do both."

At this point Reggie focuses on the sheet of paper in front of him. "And I still believe that the $40.00 alternative is the best one. Concerning the costs, I checked the records; basically we have to amortize the development costs we incurred for Brainet. So far we have spent $800,000 and we expect to spend another $50,000 per year for support and shipping the CDs to those who want a hardcopy on top of their downloaded software." Reggie next hands a report to Charlotte. "Here we have some data on the industry. I just received that yesterday, hot off the press. Let's see what we can learn about the industry here." He shows Charlotte some of the highlights. Reggie then agrees to compile the most relevant information contained in the report and have it ready for Charlotte the following morning. It takes him long into the night to gather the data from the pages of the report, but in the end he produces three tables, one for each of the three alternative pricing strategies. Each table shows the corresponding probability of various amounts of sales given the level of competition (high, medium, or low) that develops from other companies.

The next morning Charlotte is sipping from another power drink. Jeannie and Reggie will be in her office any moment now and, with their help, she will have to decide what to do with Brainet. Should they launch the product? If so, at what price?

TABLE 1 Probability distribution of unit sales, given a high price ($50)

	Level of Competition		
Sales	High	Medium	Low
50,000 units	0.2	0.25	0.3
30,000 units	0.25	0.3	0.35
20,000 units	0.55	0.45	0.35

TABLE 2 Probability distribution of unit sales, given a medium price ($40)

Sales	Level of Competition		
	High	**Medium**	**Low**
50,000 units	0.25	0.30	0.40
30,000 units	0.35	0.40	0.50
20,000 units	0.40	0.30	0.10

TABLE 3 Probability distribution of unit sales, given a low price ($30)

Sales	Level of Competition		
	High	**Medium**	**Low**
50,000 units	0.35	0.40	0.50
30,000 units	0.40	0.50	0.45
20,000 units	0.25	0.10	0.05

When Jeannie and Reggie enter the office, Jeannie immediately bursts out: "Guys, I just spoke to our marketing research company. They say that they could do a study for us about the competitive situation for the introduction of Brainet and deliver the results within a week."

"How much do they want for the study?"

"I knew you'd ask that, Reggie. They want $10,000 and I think it's a fair deal."

At this point Charlotte steps into the conversation. "Do we have any data on the quality of the work of this marketing research company?"

"Yes, I do have some reports here. After analyzing them, I have come to the conclusion that the marketing research company is not very good in predicting the competitive environment for medium or low pricing. Therefore, we should not ask them to do the study for us if we decide on one of these two pricing strategies. However, in the case of high pricing, they do quite well: given that the competition turned out to be high, they predicted it correctly 80 percent of the time, while 15 percent of the time they predicted medium competition in that setting. Given that the competition turned out to be medium, they predicted high competition 15 percent of the time and medium competition 80 percent of the time. Finally, for the case of low competition, the numbers were 90 percent of the time a correct prediction, 7 percent of the time a 'medium' prediction and 3 percent of the time a 'high' prediction."

Charlotte feels that all these numbers are too much for her. "Don't we have a simple estimate of how the market will react?"

"Some prior probabilities, you mean? Sure, from our past experience, the likelihood of facing high competition is 20 percent, whereas it is 70 percent for medium competition and 10 percent for low competition," Jeannie has her numbers always ready when needed.

All that is left to do now is to sit down and make sense of all this. . . .

(a) For the initial analysis, ignore the opportunity of obtaining more information by hiring the marketing research company. Identify the alternative actions and the states of nature. Construct the payoff table. Then formulate the decision problem in a decision tree. Clearly distinguish between decision and chance forks and include all the relevant data.

(b) What is Charlotte's decision if she uses the maximum likelihood criterion? The maximin payoff criterion?

(c) What is Charlotte's decision if she uses Bayes' decision rule?

(d) Now consider the possibility of doing the market research. Develop the corresponding decision tree. Calculate the relevant probabilities and analyze the decision tree. Should Cerebrosoft pay the $10,000 for the marketing research? What is the overall optimal policy?

CASE 15.2   SMART STEERING SUPPORT

On a sunny May morning, Marc Binton, CEO of Bay Area Automobile Gadgets (BAAG), enters the conference room on the 40th floor of the Gates building in San Francisco, where BAAG's offices are located. The other executive officers of the company have already gathered. The meeting has only one item on its agenda: planning a research and development project to develop a new driver support system (DSS). Brian Huang, Manager of Research and Development, is walking around nervously. He has to inform the group about the R&D strategy he has developed for the DSS. Marc has identified DSS as the strategic new product for the company. Julie Aker, Vice President of Marketing, will speak after Brian. She will give detailed information about the target segment, expected sales, and marketing costs associated with the introduction of the DSS.

BAAG builds electronic nonaudio equipment for luxury cars. Founded by a group of Stanford graduates, the company sold its first product—a car routing system relying on a technology called global positioning satellites (GPS)—a few years ago. Such routing systems help drivers to find directions to their desired destinations using satellites to determine the exact position of the car. To keep up with technology and to meet the wishes of their customers, the company has added a number of new features to its router during the last few years. The DSS will be a completely new product, incorporating recent developments in GPS as well as voice recognition and display technologies. Marc strongly supports this product, as it will give BAAG a competitive advantage over its Asian and European competitors.

Driver support systems have been a field of intense research for more than a decade. These systems provide the driver with a wide range of information, such as directions, road conditions, traffic updates, etc. The information exchange can take place verbally or via projection of text onto the windscreen. Other features help the driver avoid obstacles that have been identified by cars ahead on the road (these cars transmit the information to the following vehicles). Marc wants to incorporate all these features and other technologies into one support system that would then be sold to BAAG's customers in the automobile industry.

After all the attendees have taken their seats, Brian starts his presentation: "Marc asked me to inform you about our efforts with the driver support system, particularly the road scanning device. We have reached a stage where we basically have to make a go or no-go decision concerning the research for this device, which, as you all know by now, is a key feature in the DSS. We have already integrated the other devices, such as the PGS-based positioning and direction system. The question we have to deal with is whether to fund basic research into the road scanning device. If this research were successful, we then would have to decide if we want to develop a product based on these results—or if we just want to sell the technology without developing a product. If we do decide to develop the product ourselves, there is a chance that the product development process might not be successful. In that case, we could still sell the technology. In the case of successful product development, we would have to decide whether to market the product. If we decide not to market the developed product, we could at least sell the product concept that was the result of our successful research and development efforts. Doing so would earn more than just selling the technology prematurely. If, on the other hand, we decide to market the driver support system, then we are faced with the uncertainty of how the product will be received by our customers."

"You completely lost me." snipes Marc.

Max, Julie's assistant, just shakes his head and murmurs, "those techno-nerds. . . ."

Brian starts to explain: "Sorry for the confusion. Let's just go through it again, step by step."

"Good idea—and perhaps make smaller steps!" Julie obviously dislikes Brian's style of presentation.

"OK, the first decision we are facing is whether to invest in research for the road scanning device."

"How much would that cost us?" asks Marc.

"Our estimated budget for this is $300,000. Once we invest that money, the outcome of the research effort is somewhat uncertain. Our engineers assess the probability of successful research at 80 percent."

"That's a pretty optimistic success rate, don't you think?" Julie remarks sarcastically. She still remembers the disaster with Brian's last project, the fingerprint-based car security system. After spending half a million dollars, the development engineers concluded that it would be impossible to produce the security system at an attractive price.

Brian senses Julie's hostility and shoots back: "In engineering we are quite accustomed to these success rates—something we can't say about marketing. . . ."

"What would be the next step?" intervenes Marc.

"Hm, sorry. If the research is not successful, then we can only sell the DSS in its current form."

"The profit estimate for that scenario is $2 million," Julie throws in.

"If, however, the research effort is successful, then we will have to make another decision, namely, whether to go on to the development stage."

"If we wouldn't want to develop a product at that point, would that mean that we would have to sell the DSS as it is now?" asks Max.

"Yes, Max. Except that additionally we would earn some $200,000 from selling our research results to GM. Their research division is very interested in our work and they have offered me that money for our findings."

"Ah, now that's good news," remarks Julie.

Brian continues, "If, however, after successfully completing the research stage, we decide to develop a new product then we'll have to spend another $800,000 for that task, at a chance of 35 percent of not being successful."

"So you are telling us we'll have to spend $800,000 for a ticket in a lottery where we have a 35 percent chance of not winning anything?" asks Julie.

"Julie, don't focus on the losses, but on the potential gains! The chance of winning in this lottery, as you call it, is 65 percent. I believe that that's much more than with a normal lottery ticket," says Marc.

"Thanks, Marc," says Brian. "Once we invest that money in development, we have two possible outcomes: either we will be successful in developing the road scanning device or we won't. If we fail, then once again we'll sell the DSS in its current form and cash in the $200,000 from GM for the research results. If the development process is successful, then we have to decide whether to market the new product."

"Why wouldn't we want to market it after successfully developing it?" asks Marc.

"That's a good question. Basically what I mean is that we could decide not to sell the product ourselves but instead give the right to sell it to somebody else, to GM, for example. They would pay us $1 million for it."

"I like those numbers!" remarks Julie.

"Once we decide to build the product and market it, we will face the market uncertainties and I'm sure that Julie has those numbers ready for us. Thanks."

At this point, Brian sits down and Julie comes forward to give her presentation. Immediately some colorful slides are projected on the wall behind her as Max operates the computer.

"Thanks, Brian. Well, here's the data we have been able to gather from some marketing research. The acceptance of our new product in the market can be high, medium, or low," Julie is pointing to some figures projected on the wall behind her. "Our estimates indicate that high acceptance would result in profits of $8.0 million, and that medium acceptance would give us $4.0 million. In the unfortunate case of a poor reception by our customers, we still expect $2.2 million in profit. I should mention that these profits do not include the additional costs of marketing or R&D expenses."

"So, you are saying that in the worst case we'll make barely more money than with the current product?" asks Brian.

"Yes, that's what I am saying."

"What budget would you need for the marketing of our DSS with the road scanner?" asks Marc.

"For that we would need an additional $200,000 on top of what has already been included in the profit estimates," Julie replies.

"What are the chances of ending up with a high, medium, or low acceptance of the new DSS?" asks Brian.

"We can see those numbers at the bottom of the slide," says Julie, while she is turning toward the projection behind her. There is a 30 percent chance of high market acceptance and a 20 percent chance of low market acceptance.

At this point, Marc moves in his seat and asks: "Given all these numbers and bits of information, what are you suggesting that we do?"

(a) Organize the available data on cost and profit estimates in a table.
(b) Formulate the problem in a decision tree. Clearly distinguish between decision and chance forks.
(c) Calculate the expected payoffs for each fork in the decision tree.
(d) What is BAAG's optimal policy according to Bayes' decision rule?
(e) What would be the expected value of perfect information on the outcome of the research effort?
(f) What would be the expected value of perfect information on the outcome of the development effort?
(g) Marc is a risk-averse decision maker. In a number of interviews, his utility function for money was assessed to be

$$u(M) = \frac{1 - e^{-\frac{M}{12}}}{1 - e^{-\frac{1}{12}}},$$

where M is the company's net profit in units of hundreds of thousands of dollars (e.g., $M = 8$ would imply a net profit of $800,000). Using Marc's utility function, calculate the utility for each terminal branch of the decision tree.
(h) Determine the expected utilities for all forks in the decision tree.
(i) Based on Marc's utility function, what is BAAG's optimal policy?
(j) Based on Marc's utility function, what would be the expected value of perfect information on the outcome of the research effort?
(k) Based on Marc's utility function, what would be the expected value of perfect information on the outcome of the development effort?

16

Markov Chains

The preceding chapter focused on decision making in the face of uncertainty about *one* future event (learning the true state of nature). However, some decisions need to take into account uncertainty about *many* future events. We now begin laying the groundwork for decision making in this broader context.

In particular, this chapter presents probability models for processes that *evolve over time* in a probabilistic manner. Such processes are called *stochastic processes*. After briefly introducing general stochastic processes in the first section, the remainder of the chapter focuses on a special kind called a *Markov chain*. Markov chains have the special property that probabilities involving how the process will evolve in the future depend only on the present state of the process, and so are independent of events in the past. Many processes fit this description, so Markov chains provide an especially important kind of probability model.

16.1 STOCHASTIC PROCESSES

A **stochastic process** is defined to be an indexed collection of random variables $\{X_t\}$, where the index t runs through a given set T. Often T is taken to be the set of non-negative integers, and X_t represents a measurable characteristic of interest at time t. For example, X_t might represent the inventory level of a particular product at the end of week t.

Stochastic processes are of interest for describing the behavior of a system operating over some period of time. A stochastic process often has the following structure.

> The current status of the system can fall into any one of $M + 1$ mutually exclusive categories called **states.** For notational convenience, these states are labeled 0, 1, . . . , M. The random variable X_t represents the *state of the system* at time t, so its only possible values are 0, 1, . . . , M. The system is observed at particular points of time, labeled $t = 0, 1, 2, \ldots$. Thus, the stochastic process $\{X_t\} = \{X_0, X_1, X_2, \ldots\}$ provides a mathematical representation of how the status of the physical system evolves over time.

This kind of process is referred to as being a *discrete time* stochastic process with a *finite state space*. Except for Sec. 16.8, this will be the only kind of stochastic process considered in this chapter. (Section 16.8 describes a certain *continuous time* stochastic process.)

An Inventory Example

Consider the following inventory problem. A camera store stocks a particular model camera that can be ordered weekly. Let $D_1, D_2, \ldots$ represent the *demand* for this camera (the number of units that would be sold if the inventory is not depleted) during the first week, second week, $\ldots$, respectively. It is assumed that the D_i are independent and identically distributed random variables having a *Poisson distribution* with a mean of 1. Let X_0 represent the number of cameras on hand at the outset, X_1 the number of cameras on hand at the end of week 1, X_2 the number of cameras on hand at the end of week 2, and so on. Assume that $X_0 = 3$. On Saturday night the store places an order that is delivered in time for the next opening of the store on Monday. The store uses the following order policy: If there are no cameras in stock, the store orders 3 cameras. However, if there are any cameras in stock, no order is placed. Sales are lost when demand exceeds the inventory on hand. Thus, $\{X_t\}$ for $t = 0, 1, \ldots$ is a stochastic process of the form just described. The possible states of the process are the integers 0, 1, 2, 3, representing the possible number of cameras on hand at the end of the week. The random variables X_t are dependent and may be evaluated iteratively by the expression

$$X_{t+1} = \begin{cases} \max\{3 - D_{t+1}, 0\} & \text{if } X_t = 0 \\ \max\{X_t - D_{t+1}, 0\} & \text{if } X_t \geq 1, \end{cases}$$

for $t = 0, 1, 2, \ldots$.

This example is used for illustrative purposes throughout many of the following sections. Section 16.2 further defines the particular type of stochastic process considered in this chapter.

16.2 MARKOV CHAINS

Assumptions regarding the joint distribution of $X_0, X_1, \ldots$ are necessary to obtain analytical results. One assumption that leads to analytical tractability is that the stochastic process is a Markov chain, which has the following key property:

A stochastic process $\{X_t\}$ is said to have the **Markovian property** if $P\{X_{t+1} = j \mid X_0 = k_0, X_1 = k_1, \ldots, X_{t-1} = k_{t-1}, X_t = i\} = P\{X_{t+1} = j \mid X_t = i\}$, for $t = 0, 1, \ldots$ and every sequence $i, j, k_0, k_1, \ldots, k_{t-1}$.

In words, this Markovian property says that the conditional probability of any future "event," given any past "event" and the present state $X_t = i$, is *independent* of the past event and depends only upon the present state.

A stochastic process $\{X_t\}$ $(t = 0, 1, \ldots)$ is a **Markov chain** if it has the *Markovian property*.

The conditional probabilities $P\{X_{t+1} = j \mid X_t = i\}$ for a Markov chain are called (one-step) **transition probabilities.** If, for each i and j,

$$P\{X_{t+1} = j \mid X_t = i\} = P\{X_1 = j \mid X_0 = i\}, \qquad \text{for all } t = 1, 2, \ldots,$$

then the (one-step) transition probabilities are said to be *stationary.* Thus, having **stationary transition probabilities** implies that the transition probabilities do not change over time. The existence of stationary (one-step) transition probabilities also implies that, for each i, j, and n ($n = 0, 1, 2, \ldots$),

$$P\{X_{t+n} = j \mid X_t = i\} = P\{X_n = j \mid X_0 = i\}$$

for all $t = 0, 1, \ldots$. These conditional probabilities are called **n-step transition probabilities.**

To simplify notation with stationary transition probabilities, let

$$p_{ij} = P\{X_{t+1} = j \mid X_t = i\},$$
$$p_{ij}^{(n)} = P\{X_{t+n} = j \mid X_t = i\}.$$

Thus, the n-step transition probability $p_{ij}^{(n)}$ is just the conditional probability that the system will be in state j after exactly n steps (time units), given that it starts in state i at any time t. When $n = 1$, note that $p_{ij}^{(1)} = p_{ij}$.[1]

Because the $p_{ij}^{(n)}$ are conditional probabilities, they must be nonnegative, and since the process must make a transition into some state, they must satisfy the properties

$$p_{ij}^{(n)} \geq 0, \qquad \text{for all } i \text{ and } j; n = 0, 1, 2, \ldots,$$

and

$$\sum_{j=0}^{M} p_{ij}^{(n)} = 1 \qquad \text{for all } i; n = 0, 1, 2, \ldots.$$

A convenient way of showing all the n-step transition probabilities is the matrix form

$$
\mathbf{P}^{(n)} =
\begin{array}{c|cccc}
\text{State} & 0 & 1 & \cdots & M \\
\hline
0 & p_{00}^{(n)} & p_{01}^{(n)} & \cdots & p_{0M}^{(n)} \\
1 & p_{10}^{(n)} & p_{11}^{(n)} & \cdots & p_{1M}^{(n)} \\
\vdots & & \cdots\cdots\cdots & & \\
M & p_{M0}^{(n)} & p_{M1}^{(n)} & \cdots & p_{MM}^{(n)}
\end{array}
\quad, \qquad \text{for } n = 0, 1, 2, \ldots
$$

or, equivalently, the *n-step transition matrix*

$$
\mathbf{P}^{(n)} =
\begin{array}{cc}
 & \begin{array}{cccc} \text{State} \quad 0 & 1 & \cdots & M \end{array} \\
\begin{array}{c} 0 \\ 1 \\ \vdots \\ M \end{array} &
\left[\begin{array}{cccc}
p_{00}^{(n)} & p_{01}^{(n)} & \cdots & p_{0M}^{(n)} \\
p_{10}^{(n)} & p_{11}^{(n)} & \cdots & p_{1M}^{(n)} \\
\cdots & \cdots & \cdots & \cdots \\
p_{M0}^{(n)} & p_{M1}^{(n)} & \cdots & p_{MM}^{(n)}
\end{array} \right]
\end{array}
$$

Note that the transition probability in a particular row and column is for the transition *from* the row state *to* the column state. When $n = 1$, we drop the superscript n and simply refer to this as the *transition matrix*.

---

[1] For $n = 0$, $p_{ij}^{(0)}$ is just $P\{X_0 = j \mid X_0 = i\}$ and hence is 1 when $i = j$ and is 0 when $i \neq j$.

The Markov chains to be considered in this chapter have the following properties:

1. A finite number of states.
2. Stationary transition probabilities.

We also will assume that we know the initial probabilities $P\{X_0 = i\}$ for all i.

Formulating the Inventory Example as a Markov Chain

Returning to the inventory example developed in the preceding section, recall that X_t is the number of cameras in stock at the end of week t (before ordering any more), where X_t represents the *state of the system* at time t. Given that the current state is $X_t = i$, the expression at the end of Sec. 16.1 indicates that X_{t+1} depends only on D_{t+1} (the demand in week $t + 1$) and X_t. Since X_{t+1} is independent of any past history of the inventory system, the stochastic process $\{X_t\}$ ($t = 0, 1, \ldots$) has the *Markovian property* and so is a Markov chain.

Now consider how to obtain the (one-step) transition probabilities, i.e., the elements of the (one-step) *transition matrix*

$$
\mathbf{P} = \begin{array}{c} \\ 0 \\ 1 \\ 2 \\ 3 \end{array}
\begin{array}{cccc} \text{State} \quad 0 \quad\ \ 1 \quad\ \ 2 \quad\ \ 3 \end{array}
\begin{bmatrix}
p_{00} & p_{01} & p_{02} & p_{03} \\
p_{10} & p_{11} & p_{12} & p_{13} \\
p_{20} & p_{21} & p_{22} & p_{23} \\
p_{30} & p_{31} & p_{32} & p_{33}
\end{bmatrix}
$$

given that D_{t+1} has a Poisson distribution with a mean of 1. Thus,

$$
P\{D_{t+1} = n\} = \frac{(1)^n e^{-1}}{n!}, \qquad \text{for } n = 0, 1, \ldots,
$$

so

$$
\begin{aligned}
P\{D_{t+1} = 0\} &= e^{-1} = 0.368, \\
P\{D_{t+1} = 1\} &= e^{-1} = 0.368,
\end{aligned}
$$

$$
P\{D_{t+1} = 2\} = \frac{1}{2}e^{-1} = 0.184,
$$

$$
P\{D_{t+1} \geq 3\} = 1 - P\{D_{t+1} \leq 2\} = 1 - (0.368 + 0.368 + 0.184) = 0.080.
$$

For the first row of $\mathbf{P}$, we are dealing with a transition from state $X_t = 0$ to some state X_{t+1}. As indicated at the end of Sec. 16.1,

$$
X_{t+1} = \max\{3 - D_{t+1}, 0\} \qquad \text{if } X_t = 0.
$$

Therefore, for the transition to $X_{t+1} = 3$ or $X_{t+1} = 2$ or $X_{t+1} = 1$,

$$
\begin{aligned}
p_{03} &= P\{D_{t+1} = 0\} = 0.368, \\
p_{02} &= P\{D_{t+1} = 1\} = 0.368, \\
p_{01} &= P\{D_{t+1} = 2\} = 0.184.
\end{aligned}
$$

A transition from $X_t = 0$ to $X_{t+1} = 0$ implies that the demand for cameras in week $t + 1$ is 3 or more after 3 cameras are added to the depleted inventory at the beginning of the week, so

$$p_{00} = P\{D_{t+1} \geq 3\} = 0.080.$$

For the other rows of **P**, the formula at the end of Sec. 16.1 for the next state is

$$X_{t+1} = \max \{X_t - D_{t+1}, 0\} \qquad \text{if } X_{t+1} \geq 1.$$

This implies that $X_{t+1} \leq X_t$, so $p_{12} = 0$, $p_{13} = 0$, and $p_{23} = 0$. For the other transitions,

$$p_{11} = P\{D_{t+1} = 0\} = 0.368,$$
$$p_{10} = P\{D_{t+1} \geq 1) = 1 - P\{D_{t+1} = 0\} = 0.632,$$
$$p_{22} = P\{D_{t+1} = 0\} = 0.368,$$
$$p_{21} = P\{D_{t+1} = 1\} = 0.368,$$
$$p_{20} = P\{D_{t+1} \geq 2\} = 1 - P\{D_{t+1} \leq 1\} = 1 - (0.368 + 0.368) = 0.264.$$

For the last row of **P**, week $t + 1$ begins with 3 cameras in inventory, so the calculations for the transition probabilities are exactly the same as for the first row. Consequently, the complete transition matrix is

$$
\mathbf{P} = \begin{array}{c} \text{State} \\ 0 \\ 1 \\ 2 \\ 3 \end{array}
\begin{array}{cccc}
0 & 1 & 2 & 3 \\
\left[\begin{array}{cccc}
0.080 & 0.184 & 0.368 & 0.368 \\
0.632 & 0.368 & 0 & 0 \\
0.264 & 0.368 & 0.368 & 0 \\
0.080 & 0.184 & 0.368 & 0.368
\end{array}\right]
\end{array}
$$

The information given by this transition matrix can also be depicted graphically with the state transition diagram in Fig. 16.1. The four possible states for the number of cameras on hand at the end of a week are represented by the four nodes (circles) in the diagram. The

FIGURE 16.1
State transition diagram for the inventory example for a camera store.

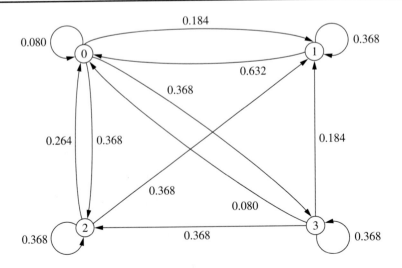

arrows show the possible transitions from one state to another, or sometimes from a state back to itself, when the camera store goes from the end of one week to the end of the next week. The number next to each arrow gives the probability of that particular transition occurring next when the camera store is in the state at the base of the arrow.

Additional Examples of Markov Chains

A Stock Example.   Consider the following model for the value of a stock. At the end of a given day, the price is recorded. If the stock has gone up, the probability that it will go up tomorrow is 0.7. If the stock has gone down, the probability that it will go up tomorrow is only 0.5. This is a Markov chain, where state 0 represents the stock's going up and state 1 represents the stock's going down. The transition matrix is given by

$$\mathbf{P} = \begin{array}{c} \\ 0 \\ 1 \end{array} \begin{array}{cc} \text{State} \quad 0 \quad\;\; 1 \\ \begin{bmatrix} 0.7 & 0.3 \\ 0.5 & 0.5 \end{bmatrix} \end{array}$$

A Second Stock Example.   Suppose now that the stock market model is changed so that the stock's going up tomorrow depends upon whether it increased today *and* yesterday. In particular, if the stock has increased for the past two days, it will increase tomorrow with probability 0.9. If the stock increased today but decreased yesterday, then it will increase tomorrow with probability 0.6. If the stock decreased today but increased yesterday, then it will increase tomorrow with probability 0.5. Finally, if the stock decreased for the past two days, then it will increase tomorrow with probability 0.3. If we define the state as representing whether the stock goes up or down today, the system is no longer a Markov chain. However, we can transform the system to a Markov chain by defining the states as follows:[1]

State 0: The stock increased both today and yesterday.
State 1: The stock increased today and decreased yesterday.
State 2: The stock decreased today and increased yesterday.
State 3: The stock decreased both today and yesterday.

This leads to a four-state Markov chain with the following transition matrix:

$$\mathbf{P} = \begin{array}{c} \\ 0 \\ 1 \\ 2 \\ 3 \end{array} \begin{array}{c} \text{State} \quad 0 \quad\; 1 \quad\; 2 \quad\; 3 \\ \begin{bmatrix} 0.9 & 0 & 0.1 & 0 \\ 0.6 & 0 & 0.4 & 0 \\ 0 & 0.5 & 0 & 0.5 \\ 0 & 0.3 & 0 & 0.7 \end{bmatrix} \end{array}$$

A Gambling Example.   Another example involves gambling. Suppose that a player has \$1 and with each play of the game wins \$1 with probability $p > 0$ or loses \$1 with probability $1 - p$. The game ends when the player either accumulates \$3 or goes broke.

---

[1]This example demonstrates that Markov chains are able to incorporate arbitrary amounts of history, but at the cost of significantly increasing the number of states.

This game is a Markov chain with the states representing the player's current holding of money, that is, 0, \$1, \$2, or \$3, and with the transition matrix given by

$$
\mathbf{P} = \begin{array}{c} \text{State} \\ 0 \\ 1 \\ 2 \\ 3 \end{array}
\begin{array}{cccc}
0 & 1 & 2 & 3 \\
\left[\begin{array}{cccc}
1 & 0 & 0 & 0 \\
1-p & 0 & p & 0 \\
0 & 1-p & 0 & p \\
0 & 0 & 0 & 1
\end{array}\right]
\end{array}
$$

Note that in both the inventory and gambling examples, the numeric labeling of the states that the process reaches coincides with the physical expression of the system—i.e., actual inventory levels and the player's holding of money, respectively—whereas the numeric labeling of the states in the stock examples has no physical significance.

16.3   CHAPMAN-KOLMOGOROV EQUATIONS

Section 16.2 introduced the n-step transition probability $p_{ij}^{(n)}$. The following *Chapman-Kolmogorov equations* provide a method for computing these n-step transition probabilities:

$$
p_{ij}^{(n)} = \sum_{k=0}^{M} p_{ik}^{(m)} p_{kj}^{(n-m)}, \qquad
\begin{array}{l}
\text{for all } i = 0, 1, \ldots, M, \\
\qquad\qquad j = 0, 1, \ldots, M, \\
\text{and any } m = 1, 2, \ldots, n-1, \\
\qquad\qquad n = m+1, m+2, \ldots.^{1}
\end{array}
$$

These equations point out that in going from state i to state j in n steps, the process will be in some state k after exactly m (less than n) states. Thus, $p_{ik}^{(m)} \, p_{kj}^{(n-m)}$ is just the conditional probability that, given a starting point of state i, the process goes to state k after m steps and then to state j in $n-m$ steps. Therefore, summing these conditional probabilities over all possible k must yield $p_{ij}^{(n)}$. The special cases of $m=1$ and $m=n-1$ lead to the expressions

$$
p_{ij}^{(n)} = \sum_{k=0}^{M} p_{ik} p_{kj}^{(n-1)}
$$

and

$$
p_{ij}^{(n)} = \sum_{k=0}^{M} p_{ik}^{(n-1)} p_{kj},
$$

for all states i and j. These expressions enable the n-step transition probabilities to be obtained from the one-step transition probabilities recursively. This recursive relationship is best explained in matrix notation (see Appendix 4). For $n=2$, these expressions become

$$
p_{ij}^{(2)} = \sum_{k=0}^{M} p_{ik} p_{kj}, \qquad \text{for all states } i \text{ and } j,
$$

---

[1] These equations also hold in a trivial sense when $m=0$ or $m=n$, but $m=1, 2, \ldots, n-1$ are the only interesting cases.

where the $p_{ij}^{(2)}$ are the elements of a matrix $\mathbf{P}^{(2)}$. Also note that these elements are obtained by multiplying the matrix of one-step transition probabilities by itself; i.e.,

$$\mathbf{P}^{(2)} = \mathbf{P} \cdot \mathbf{P} = \mathbf{P}^2.$$

In the same manner, the above expressions for $p_{ij}^{(n)}$ when $m = 1$ and $m = n - 1$ indicate that the matrix of n-step transition probabilities is

$$\begin{aligned}\mathbf{P}^{(n)} &= \mathbf{P}\mathbf{P}^{(n-1)} = \mathbf{P}^{(n-1)}\mathbf{P}\\&= \mathbf{P}\mathbf{P}^{n-1} = \mathbf{P}^{n-1}\mathbf{P}\\&= \mathbf{P}^n.\end{aligned}$$

Thus, the n-step transition probability matrix $\mathbf{P}^n$ can be obtained by computing the nth power of the one-step transition matrix $\mathbf{P}$.

n-Step Transition Matrices for the Inventory Example

Returning to the inventory example, its one-step transition matrix $\mathbf{P}$ obtained in Sec. 16.2 can now be used to calculate the two-step transition matrix $\mathbf{P}^{(2)}$ as follows:

$$\mathbf{P}^{(2)} = \mathbf{P}^2 = \begin{bmatrix} 0.080 & 0.184 & 0.368 & 0.368 \\ 0.632 & 0.368 & 0 & 0 \\ 0.264 & 0.368 & 0.368 & 0 \\ 0.080 & 0.184 & 0.368 & 0.368 \end{bmatrix} \begin{bmatrix} 0.080 & 0.184 & 0.368 & 0.368 \\ 0.632 & 0.368 & 0 & 0 \\ 0.264 & 0.368 & 0.368 & 0 \\ 0.080 & 0.184 & 0.368 & 0.368 \end{bmatrix}$$

$$= \begin{bmatrix} 0.249 & 0.286 & 0.300 & 0.165 \\ 0.283 & 0.252 & 0.233 & 0.233 \\ 0.351 & 0.319 & 0.233 & 0.097 \\ 0.249 & 0.286 & 0.300 & 0.165 \end{bmatrix}.$$

For example, given that there is one camera left in stock at the end of a week, the probability is 0.283 that there will be no cameras in stock 2 weeks later, that is, $p_{10}^{(2)} = 0.283$. Similarly, given that there are two cameras left in stock at the end of a week, the probability is 0.097 that there will be three cameras in stock 2 weeks later, that is, $p_{23}^{(2)} = 0.097$.

The four-step transition matrix can also be obtained as follows:

$$\mathbf{P}^{(4)} = \mathbf{P}^4 = \mathbf{P}^{(2)} \cdot \mathbf{P}^{(2)}$$

$$= \begin{bmatrix} 0.249 & 0.286 & 0.300 & 0.165 \\ 0.283 & 0.252 & 0.233 & 0.233 \\ 0.351 & 0.319 & 0.233 & 0.097 \\ 0.249 & 0.286 & 0.300 & 0.165 \end{bmatrix} \begin{bmatrix} 0.249 & 0.286 & 0.300 & 0.165 \\ 0.283 & 0.252 & 0.233 & 0.233 \\ 0.351 & 0.319 & 0.233 & 0.097 \\ 0.249 & 0.286 & 0.300 & 0.165 \end{bmatrix}$$

$$= \begin{bmatrix} 0.289 & 0.286 & 0.261 & 0.164 \\ 0.282 & 0.285 & 0.268 & 0.166 \\ 0.284 & 0.283 & 0.263 & 0.171 \\ 0.289 & 0.286 & 0.261 & 0.164 \end{bmatrix}.$$

For example, given that there is one camera left in stock at the end of a week, the probability is 0.282 that there will be no cameras in stock 4 weeks later, that is, $p_{10}^{(4)} = 0.282$.

Similarly, given that there are two cameras left in stock at the end of a week, the probability is 0.171 there will be three cameras in stock 4 weeks later, that is, $p_{23}^{(4)} = 0.171$.

Your OR Courseware includes a routine for calculating $\mathbf{P}^{(n)} = \mathbf{P}^n$ for any positive integer $n \le 99$.

Unconditional State Probabilities

Recall that one- or n-step transition probabilities are *conditional* probabilities; for example, $P\{X_n = j \mid X_0 = i\} = p_{ij}^{(n)}$. If the *unconditional* probability $P\{X_n = j\}$ is desired, it is necessary to specify the probability distribution of the initial state, namely, $P\{X_0 = i\}$ for $i = 0, 1, \ldots, M$. Then

$$P\{X_n = j\} = P\{X_0 = 0\}\, p_{0j}^{(n)} + P\{X_0 = 1\}p_{1j}^{(n)} + \cdots + P\{X_0 = M\}p_{Mj}^{(n)}.$$

In the inventory example, it was assumed that initially there were 3 units in stock, that is, $X_0 = 3$. Thus, $P\{X_0 = 0\} = P\{X_0 = 1\} = P\{X_0 = 2\} = 0$ and $P\{X_0 = 3\} = 1$. Hence, the (unconditional) probability that there will be three cameras in stock 2 weeks after the inventory system began is $P\{X_2 = 3\} = (1)p_{33}^{(2)} = 0.165$.

16.4   CLASSIFICATION OF STATES OF A MARKOV CHAIN

It is evident that the transition probabilities associated with the states play an important role in the study of Markov chains. To further describe the properties of Markov chains, it is necessary to present some concepts and definitions concerning these states.

State j is said to be **accessible** from state i if $p_{ij}^{(n)} > 0$ for some $n \ge 0$. (Recall that $p_{ij}^{(n)}$ is just the conditional probability of being in state j after n steps, starting in state i.) Thus, state j being accessible from state i means that it is possible for the system to enter state j eventually when it starts from state i. In the inventory example, $p_{ij}^{(2)} > 0$ for all i and j, so every state is accessible from every other state. In general, a sufficient condition for *all* states to be accessible is that there exists a value of n for which $p_{ij}^{(n)} > 0$ for all i and j.

In the gambling example given at the end of Sec. 16.2, state 2 is not accessible from state 3. This can be deduced from the context of the game (once the player reaches state 3, the player never leaves this state), which implies that $p_{32}^{(n)} = 0$ for all $n \ge 0$. However, even though state 2 is *not* accessible from state 3, state 3 *is* accessible from state 2 since, for $n = 1$, the transition matrix given at the end of Sec. 16.2 indicates that $p_{23} = p > 0$.

If state j is accessible from state i and state i is accessible from state j, then states i and j are said to **communicate**. In the inventory example, all states communicate. In the gambling example, states 2 and 3 do not. In general,

1. Any state communicates with itself (because $p_{ii}^{(0)} = P\{X_0 = i \mid X_0 = i\} = 1$).
2. If state i communicates with state j, then state j communicates with state i.
3. If state i communicates with state j and state j communicates with state k, then state i communicates with state k.

Properties 1 and 2 follow from the definition of states communicating, whereas property 3 follows from the Chapman-Kolmogorov equations.

As a result of these three properties of communication, the states may be partitioned into one or more separate **classes** such that those states that communicate with each other are in the same class. (A class may consist of a single state). If there is only one class, i.e., all the states communicate, the Markov chain is said to be **irreducible.** In the inventory example, the Markov chain is irreducible. In the first stock example in Sec. 16.2, the Markov chain is irreducible. The gambling example contains three classes. State 0 forms a class, state 3 forms a class, and states 1 and 2 form a class.

Recurrent States and Transient States

It is often useful to talk about whether a process entering a state will ever return to this state. Here is one possibility.

> A state is said to be a **transient** state if, upon entering this state, the process *may never return* to this state again. Therefore, state i is transient if and only if there exists a state j ($j \neq i$) that is accessible from state i but not vice versa, that is, state i is not accessible from state j.

Thus, if state i is transient and the process visits this state, there is a positive probability (perhaps even a probability of 1) that the process will later move to state j and so will never return to state i. Consequently, a transient state will be visited only a finite number of times.

When starting in state i, another possibility is that the process *definitely* will return to this state.

> A state is said to be a **recurrent** state if, upon entering this state, the process *definitely will return* to this state again. Therefore, a state is recurrent if and only if it is not transient.

Since a recurrent state definitely will be revisited after each visit, it will be visited infinitely often if the process continues forever.

If the process enters a certain state and then stays in this state at the next step, this is considered a *return* to this state. Hence, the following kind of state is a special type of recurrent state.

> A state is said to be an **absorbing** state if, upon entering this state, the process *never will leave* this state again. Therefore, state i is an absorbing state if and only if $p_{ii} = 1$.

We will discuss absorbing states further in Sec. 16.7.

Recurrence is a class property. That is, all states in a class are either recurrent or transient. Furthermore, in a finite-state Markov chain, not all states can be transient. Therefore, all states in an irreducible finite-state Markov chain are recurrent. Indeed, one can identify an irreducible finite-state Markov chain (and therefore conclude that all states are recurrent) by showing that all states of the process communicate. It has already been pointed out that a sufficient condition for *all* states to be accessible (and therefore communicate with each other) is that there exists a value of n for which $p_{ij}^{(n)} > 0$ for all i and j. Thus, all states in the inventory example are recurrent, since $p_{ij}^{(2)}$ is positive for all i and j. Similarly, the first stock example contains only recurrent states, since p_{ij} is positive for all i and j. By calculating $p_{ij}^{(2)}$ for all i and j in the second stock example in Sec. 16.2, it follows that all states are recurrent since $p_{ij}^{(2)} > 0$.

As another example, suppose that a Markov chain has the following transition matrix:

$$\mathbf{P} = \begin{array}{c} \\ 0 \\ 1 \\ 2 \\ 3 \\ 4 \end{array} \begin{array}{c} \text{State} \\ \\ \end{array} \begin{array}{ccccc} 0 & 1 & 2 & 3 & 4 \\ \begin{bmatrix} \frac{1}{4} & \frac{3}{4} & 0 & 0 & 0 \\ \frac{1}{2} & \frac{1}{2} & 0 & 0 & 0 \\ 0 & 0 & 1 & 0 & 0 \\ 0 & 0 & \frac{1}{3} & \frac{2}{3} & 0 \\ 1 & 0 & 0 & 0 & 0 \end{bmatrix} \end{array}$$

Note that state 2 is an absorbing state (and hence a recurrent state) because if the process enters state 2 (row 3 of the matrix), it will never leave. State 3 is a transient state because if the process is in state 3, there is a positive probability that it will never return. The probability is $\frac{1}{3}$ that the process will go from state 3 to state 2 on the first step. Once the process is in state 2, it remains in state 2. State 4 also is a transient state because if the process starts in state 4, it immediately leaves and can never return. States 0 and 1 are recurrent states. To see this, observe from $\mathbf{P}$ that if the process starts in either of these states, it can never leave these two states. Furthermore, whenever the process moves from one of these states to the other one, it always will return to the original state eventually.

Periodicity Properties

Another useful property of Markov chains is *periodicities*. The **period** of state i is defined to be the integer t $(t > 1)$ such that $p_{ii}^{(n)} = 0$ for all values of n other than $t, 2t, 3t, \ldots$ and t is the largest integer with this property. In the gambling example (end of Section 16.2), starting in state 1, it is possible for the process to enter state 1 only at times $2, 4, \ldots$, so state 1 has period 2. The reason is that the player can break even (be neither winning nor losing) only at times $2, 4, \ldots$, which can be verified by calculating $p_{11}^{(n)}$ for all n and noting that $p_{11}^{(n)} = 0$ for n odd.

If there are two consecutive numbers s and $s + 1$ such that the process can be in state i at times s and $s + 1$, the state is said to have period 1 and is called an **aperiodic** state.

Just as recurrence is a class property, it can be shown that periodicity is a class property. That is, if state i in a class has period t, the all states in that class have period t. In the gambling example, state 2 also has period 2 because it is in the same class as state 1 and we noted above that state 1 has period 2.

In a finite-state Markov chain, recurrent states that are aperiodic are called **ergodic** states. A Markov chain is said to be *ergodic* if all its states are ergodic states.

16.5   LONG-RUN PROPERTIES OF MARKOV CHAINS

Steady-State Probabilities

In Sec. 16.3 the four-step transition matrix for the inventory example was obtained. It will now be instructive to examine the eight-step transition probabilities given by the matrix

$$\mathbf{P}^{(8)} = \mathbf{P}^8 = \mathbf{P}^4 \cdot \mathbf{P}^4 = \begin{array}{c} \\ 0 \\ 1 \\ 2 \\ 3 \end{array} \begin{array}{c} \text{State} \\ \\ \end{array} \begin{array}{cccc} 0 & 1 & 2 & 3 \\ \begin{bmatrix} 0.286 & 0.285 & 0.264 & 0.166 \\ 0.286 & 0.285 & 0.264 & 0.166 \\ 0.286 & 0.285 & 0.264 & 0.166 \\ 0.286 & 0.285 & 0.264 & 0.166 \end{bmatrix} \end{array}.$$

Notice the rather remarkable fact that each of the four rows has identical entries. This implies that the probability of being in state j after 8 weeks is essentially independent of the initial level of inventory. In other words, it appears that there is a limiting probability that the system will be in each state j after a large number of transitions, and that this probability is independent of the initial state. These properties of the long-run behavior of finite-state Markov chains do, in fact, hold under relatively general conditions, as summarized below.

For any irreducible ergodic Markov chain, $\lim_{n \to \infty} p_{ij}^{(n)}$ exists and is independent of i. Furthermore,

$$\lim_{n \to \infty} p_{ij}^{(n)} = \pi_j > 0,$$

where the π_j uniquely satisfy the following **steady-state equations**

$$\pi_j = \sum_{i=0}^{M} \pi_i p_{ij}, \qquad \text{for } j = 0, 1, \ldots, M,$$

$$\sum_{j=0}^{M} \pi_j = 1.$$

The π_j are called the **steady-state probabilities** of the Markov chain. The term *steady-state* probability means that the probability of finding the process in a certain state, say j, after a large number of transitions tends to the value π_j, independent of the probability distribution of the initial state. It is important to note that the steady-state probability does *not* imply that the process settles down into one state. On the contrary, the process continues to make transitions from state to state, and at any step n the transition probability from state i to state j is still p_{ij}.

The π_j can also be interpreted as *stationary probabilities* (not to be confused with stationary transition probabilities) in the following sense. If the *initial* probability of being in state j is given by π_j (that is, $P\{X_0 = j\} = \pi_j$) for all j, then the probability of finding the process in state j at time $n = 1, 2, \ldots$ is also given by π_j (that is, $P\{X_n = j\} = \pi_j$).

Note that the steady-state equations consist of $M + 2$ equations in $M + 1$ unknowns. Because it has a unique solution, at least one equation must be redundant and can, therefore, be deleted. It cannot be the equation

$$\sum_{j=0}^{M} \pi_j = 1,$$

because $\pi_j = 0$ for all j will satisfy the other $M + 1$ equations. Furthermore, the solutions to the other $M + 1$ steady-state equations have a unique solution up to a multiplicative constant, and it is the final equation that forces the solution to be a probability distribution.

Returning to the inventory example, we see that the steady-state equations can be expressed as

$$\begin{aligned}
\pi_0 &= \pi_0 p_{00} + \pi_1 p_{10} + \pi_2 p_{20} + \pi_3 p_{30}, \\
\pi_1 &= \pi_0 p_{01} + \pi_1 p_{11} + \pi_2 p_{21} + \pi_3 p_{31}, \\
\pi_2 &= \pi_0 p_{02} + \pi_1 p_{12} + \pi_2 p_{22} + \pi_3 p_{32}, \\
\pi_3 &= \pi_0 p_{03} + \pi_1 p_{13} + \pi_2 p_{23} + \pi_3 p_{33}, \\
1 &= \pi_0 \quad + \pi_1 \quad + \pi_2 \quad + \pi_3.
\end{aligned}$$

Substituting values for p_{ij} into these equations leads to the equations

$$\begin{aligned}
\pi_0 &= 0.080\pi_0 + 0.632\pi_1 + 0.264\pi_2 + 0.080\pi_3, \\
\pi_1 &= 0.184\pi_0 + 0.368\pi_1 + 0.368\pi_2 + 0.184\pi_3, \\
\pi_2 &= 0.368\pi_0 \qquad\quad + 0.368\pi_2 + 0.368\pi_3, \\
\pi_3 &= 0.368\pi_0 \qquad\qquad\qquad\quad + 0.368\pi_3, \\
1 &= \quad \pi_0 + \quad \pi_1 + \quad \pi_2 + \quad \pi_3.
\end{aligned}$$

Solving the last four equations simultaneously provides the solution

$$\pi_0 = 0.286, \qquad \pi_1 = 0.285, \qquad \pi_2 = 0.263, \qquad \pi_3 = 0.166,$$

which is essentially the result that appears in matrix $\mathbf{P}^{(8)}$. Thus, after many weeks the probability of finding zero, one, two, and three cameras in stock tends to 0.286, 0.285, 0.263, and 0.166, respectively.

Your OR Courseware includes a routine for solving the steady-state equations to obtain the steady-state probabilities.

There are other important results concerning steady-state probabilities. In particular, if i and j are recurrent states belonging to different classes, then

$$p_{ij}^{(n)} = 0, \qquad \text{for all } n.$$

This result follows from the definition of a class.

Similarly, if j is a transient state, then

$$\lim_{n \to \infty} p_{ij}^{(n)} = 0, \qquad \text{for all } i.$$

Thus, the probability of finding the process in a transient state after a large number of transitions tends to zero.

Expected Average Cost per Unit Time

The preceding subsection dealt with finite-state Markov chains whose states were ergodic (recurrent and aperiodic). If the requirement that the states be aperiodic is relaxed, then the limit

$$\lim_{n \to \infty} p_{ij}^{(n)}$$

may not exist. To illustrate this point, consider the two-state transition matrix

$$\mathbf{P} = \begin{matrix} & \text{State} & 0 & 1 \\ & 0 & \\ & 1 & \end{matrix} \begin{bmatrix} 0 & 1 \\ 1 & 0 \end{bmatrix}.$$

If the process starts in state 0 at time 0, it will be in state 0 at times 2, 4, 6, . . . and in state 1 at times 1, 3, 5, ... Thus, $p_{00}^{(n)} = 1$ if n is even and $p_{00}^{(n)} = 0$ if n is odd, so that

$$\lim_{n \to \infty} p_{00}^{(n)}$$

does not exist. However, the following limit always exists for an irreducible (finite-state) Markov chain:

$$\lim_{n \to \infty} \left(\frac{1}{n} \sum_{k=1}^{n} p_{ij}^{(k)} \right) = \pi_j,$$

where the π_j satisfy the steady-state equations given in the preceding subsection.

This result is important in computing the *long-run average cost per unit time* associated with a Markov chain. Suppose that a cost (or other penalty function) $C(X_t)$ is incurred when the process is in state X_t at time t, for $t = 0, 1, 2, \ldots$. Note that $C(X_t)$ is a random variable that takes on any one of the values $C(0), C(1), \ldots, C(M)$ and that the function $C(\cdot)$ is independent of t. The expected average cost incurred over the first n periods is given by

$$E\left[\frac{1}{n} \sum_{t=1}^{n} C(X_t) \right].$$

By using the result that

$$\lim_{n \to \infty} \left(\frac{1}{n} \sum_{k=1}^{n} p_{ij}^{(k)} \right) = \pi_j,$$

it can be shown that the (long-run) *expected average cost per unit time* is given by

$$\lim_{n \to \infty} E\left[\frac{1}{n} \sum_{t=1}^{n} C(X_t) \right] = \sum_{j=0}^{M} \pi_j C(j).$$

To illustrate, consider the inventory example introduced in Sec. 16.1, where the solution for the π_j was obtained in the preceding subsection. Suppose the camera store finds that a storage charge is being allocated for each camera remaining on the shelf at the end of the week. The cost is charged as follows:

$$C(x_t) = \begin{cases} 0 & \text{if} & x_t = 0 \\ 2 & \text{if} & x_t = 1 \\ 8 & \text{if} & x_t = 2 \\ 18 & \text{if} & x_t = 3 \end{cases}$$

The long-run expected average storage cost per week can then be obtained from the preceding equation, i.e.,

$$\lim_{n \to \infty} E\left[\frac{1}{n} \sum_{t=1}^{n} C(X_t) \right] = 0.286(0) + 0.285(2) + 0.263(8) + 0.166(18) = 5.662.$$

Note that an alternative measure to the (long-run) expected average cost per unit time is the (long-run) *actual average cost per unit time*. It can be shown that this latter measure is given by

$$\lim_{n \to \infty} \left[\frac{1}{n} \sum_{t=1}^{n} C(X_t) \right] = \sum_{j=0}^{M} \pi_j C(j)$$

for essentially all paths of the process. Thus, either measure leads to the same result. These results can also be used to interpret the meaning of the π_j. To do so, let

$$C(X_t) = \begin{cases} 1 & \text{if } X_t = j \\ 0 & \text{if } X_t \neq j. \end{cases}$$

The (long-run) expected fraction of times the system is in state j is then given by

$$\lim_{n \to \infty} E\left[\frac{1}{n} \sum_{t=1}^{n} C(X_t)\right] = \lim_{n \to \infty} E(\text{fraction of times system is in state } j) = \pi_j.$$

Similarly, π_j can also be interpreted as the (long-run) actual fraction of times that the system is in state j.

Expected Average Cost per Unit Time for Complex Cost Functions

In the preceding subsection, the cost function was based solely on the state that the process is in at time t. In many important problems encountered in practice, the cost may also depend upon some other random variable.

For example, in the inventory example of Sec. 16.1, suppose that the costs to be considered are the ordering cost and the penalty cost for unsatisfied demand (storage costs are so small they will be ignored). It is reasonable to assume that the number of cameras ordered to arrive at the beginning of week t depends only upon the state of the process X_{t-1} (the number of cameras in stock) when the order is placed at the end of week $t - 1$. However, the cost of unsatisfied demand in week t will also depend upon the demand D_t. Therefore, the total cost (ordering cost plus cost of unsatisfied demand) for week t is a function of X_{t-1} and D_t, that is, $C(X_{t-1}, D_t)$.

Under the assumptions of this example, it can be shown that the (long-run) *expected average cost per unit time* is given by

$$\lim_{n \to \infty} E\left[\frac{1}{n} \sum_{t=1}^{n} C(X_{t-1}, D_t)\right] = \sum_{j=0}^{M} k(j)\, \pi_j,$$

where

$$k(j) = E[C(j, D_t)],$$

and where this latter (conditional) expectation is taken with respect to the probability distribution of the random variable D_t, given the state j. Similarly, the (long-run) actual average cost per unit time is given by

$$\lim_{n \to \infty} \left[\frac{1}{n} \sum_{t=1}^{n} C(X_{t-1}, D_t)\right] = \sum_{j=0}^{M} k(j)\pi_j.$$

Now let us assign numerical values to the two components of $C(X_{t-1}, D_t)$ in this example, namely, the ordering cost and the penalty cost for unsatisfied demand. If $z > 0$ cameras are ordered, the cost incurred is $(10 + 25z)$ dollars. If no cameras are ordered, no ordering cost is incurred. For each unit of unsatisfied demand (lost sales), there is a penalty of \$50. Therefore, given the ordering policy described in Sec. 16.1, the cost in week t is given by

$$C(X_{t-1}, D_t) = \begin{cases} 10 + (25)(3) + 50 \max\{D_t - 3, 0\} & \text{if } X_{t-1} = 0 \\ 50 \max\{D_t - X_{t-1}, 0\} & \text{if } X_{t-1} \geq 1, \end{cases}$$

for $t = 1, 2, \ldots$. Hence,

$$C(0, D_t) = 85 + 50 \max\{D_t - 3, 0\},$$

so that

$$\begin{aligned} k(0) &= E[C(0, D_t)] = 85 + 50E(\max\{D_t - 3, 0\}) \\ &= 85 + 50[P_D(4) + 2P_D(5) + 3P_D(6) + \cdots], \end{aligned}$$

where $P_D(i)$ is the probability that the demand equals i, as given by a Poisson distribution with a mean of 1, so that $P_D(i)$ becomes negligible for i larger than about 6. Since $P_D(4) = 0.015$, $P_D(5) = 0.003$, and $P_D(6) = 0.001$, we obtain $k(0) = 86.2$. Also using $P_D(2) = 0.184$ and $P_D(3) = 0.061$, similar calculations lead to the results

$$\begin{aligned} k(1) &= E[C(1, D_t)] = 50E(\max\{D_t - 1, 0\}) \\ &= 50[P_D(2) + 2P_D(3) + 3P_D(4) + \cdots] \\ &= 18.4, \end{aligned}$$

$$\begin{aligned} k(2) &= E[C(2, D_t)] = 50E(\max\{D_t - 2, 0\}) \\ &= 50[P_D(3) + 2P_D(4) + 3P_D(5) + \cdots] \\ &= 5.2, \end{aligned}$$

and

$$\begin{aligned} k(3) &= E[C(3, D_t)] = 50E(\max\{D_t - 3, 0\}) \\ &= 50[P_D(4) + 2P_D(5) + 3P_D(6) + \cdots] \\ &= 1.2. \end{aligned}$$

Thus, the (long-run) expected average cost per week is given by

$$\sum_{j=0}^{3} k(j)\pi_j = 86.2(0.286) + 18.4(0.285) + 5.2(0.263) + 1.2(0.166) = \$31.46.$$

This is the cost associated with the particular ordering policy described in Sec. 16.1. The cost of other ordering policies can be evaluated in a similar way to identify the policy that minimizes the expected average cost per week.

The results of this subsection were presented only in terms of the inventory example. However, the (nonnumerical) results still hold for other problems as long as the following conditions are satisfied:

1. $\{X_t\}$ is an irreducible (finite-state) Markov chain.
2. Associated with this Markov chain is a sequence of random variables $\{D_t\}$ which are independent and identically distributed.
3. For a fixed $m = 0, \pm 1, \pm 2, \ldots$, a cost $C(X_t, D_{t+m})$ is incurred at time t, for $t = 0, 1, 2, \ldots$.
4. The sequence $X_0, X_1, X_2, \ldots, X_t$ must be independent of D_{t+m}.

In particular, if these conditions are satisfied, then

$$\lim_{n\to\infty} E\left[\frac{1}{n}\sum_{t=1}^{n} C(X_t, D_{t+m})\right] = \sum_{j=0}^{M} k(j)\pi_j,$$

where

$$k(j) = E[C(j, D_{t+m})],$$

and where this latter conditional expectation is taken with respect to the probability distribution of the random variable D_t, given the state j. Furthermore,

$$\lim_{n\to\infty} \left[\frac{1}{n}\sum_{t=1}^{n} C(X_t, D_{t+m})\right] = \sum_{j=0}^{M} k(j)\pi_j$$

for essentially all paths of the process.

16.6   FIRST PASSAGE TIMES

Section 16.3 dealt with finding n-step transition probabilities from state i to state j. It is often desirable to also make probability statements about the number of transitions made by the process in going from state i to state j *for the first time*. This length of time is called the **first passage time** in going from state i to state j. When $j = i$, this first passage time is just the number of transitions until the process returns to the initial state i. In this case, the first passage time is called the **recurrence time** for state i.

To illustrate these definitions, reconsider the inventory example introduced in Sec. 16.1, where X_t is the number of cameras on hand at the end of week t, where we start with $X_0 = 3$. Suppose that it turns out that

$$X_0 = 3, \quad X_1 = 2, \quad X_2 = 1, \quad X_3 = 0, \quad X_4 = 3, \quad X_5 = 1.$$

In this case, the first passage time in going from state 3 to state 1 is 2 weeks, the first passage time in going from state 3 to state 0 is 3 weeks, and the recurrence time for state 3 is 4 weeks.

In general, the first passage times are random variables. The probability distributions associated with them depend upon the transition probabilities of the process. In particular, let $f_{ij}^{(n)}$ denote the probability that the first passage time from state i to j is equal to n. For $n > 1$, this first passage time is n if the first transition is from state i to some state k ($k \neq j$) and then the first passage time from state k to state j is $n - 1$. Therefore, these probabilities satisfy the following recursive relationships:

$$f_{ij}^{(1)} = p_{ij}^{(1)} = p_{ij},$$

$$f_{ij}^{(2)} = \sum_{k\neq j} p_{ik}f_{kj}^{(1)},$$

$$f_{ij}^{(n)} = \sum_{k\neq j} p_{ik}f_{kj}^{(n-1)}.$$

Thus, the probability of a first passage time from state i to state j in n steps can be computed recursively from the one-step transition probabilities.

In the inventory example, the probability distribution of the first passage time in going from state 3 to state 0 is obtained from these recursive relationships as follows:

$$f_{30}^{(1)} = p_{30} = 0.080,$$
$$f_{30}^{(2)} = p_{31}f_{10}^{(1)} + p_{32}f_{20}^{(1)} + p_{33}f_{30}^{(1)}$$
$$= 0.184(0.632) + 0.368(0.264) + 0.368(0.080) = 0.243,$$
$$\vdots$$

where the p_{3k} and $f_{k0}^{(1)} = p_{k0}$ are obtained from the (one-step) transition matrix given in Sec. 16.2.

For fixed i and j, the $f_{ij}^{(n)}$ are nonnegative numbers such that

$$\sum_{n=1}^{\infty} f_{ij}^{(n)} \leq 1.$$

Unfortunately, this sum may be strictly less than 1, which implies that a process initially in state i may never reach state j. When the sum does equal 1, $f_{ij}^{(n)}$ (for $n = 1, 2, \ldots$) can be considered as a probability distribution for the random variable, the first passage time.

Although obtaining $f_{ij}^{(n)}$ for all n may be tedious, it is relatively simple to obtain the expected first passage time from state i to state j. Denote this expectation by μ_{ij}, which is defined by

$$\mu_{ij} = \begin{cases} \infty & \text{if } \sum_{n=1}^{\infty} f_{ij}^{(n)} < 1 \\ \sum_{n=1}^{\infty} n f_{ij}^{(n)} & \text{if } \sum_{n=1}^{\infty} f_{ij}^{(n)} = 1. \end{cases}$$

Whenever

$$\sum_{n=1}^{\infty} f_{ij}^{(n)} = 1,$$

μ_{ij} uniquely satisfies the equation

$$\mu_{ij} = 1 + \sum_{k \neq j} p_{ik} \mu_{kj}.$$

This equation recognizes that the first transition from state i can be to either state j or to some other state k. If it is to state j, the first passage time is 1. Given that the first transition is to some state k ($k \neq j$) instead, which occurs with probability p_{ik}, the conditional expected first passage time from state i to state j is $1 + \mu_{kj}$. Combining these facts, and summing over all the possibilities for the first transition, leads directly to this equation.

For the inventory example, these equations for the μ_{ij} can be used to compute the expected time until the cameras are out of stock, given that the process is started when three cameras are available. This expected time is just the expected first passage time μ_{30}. Since all the states are recurrent, the system of equations leads to the expressions

$$\mu_{30} = 1 + p_{31}\mu_{10} + p_{32}\mu_{20} + p_{33}\mu_{30},$$
$$\mu_{20} = 1 + p_{21}\mu_{10} + p_{22}\mu_{20} + p_{23}\mu_{30},$$
$$\mu_{10} = 1 + p_{11}\mu_{10} + p_{12}\mu_{20} + p_{13}\mu_{30},$$

or

$$\mu_{30} = 1 + 0.184\mu_{10} + 0.368\mu_{20} + 0.368\mu_{30},$$
$$\mu_{20} = 1 + 0.368\mu_{10} + 0.368\mu_{20},$$
$$\mu_{10} = 1 + 0.368\mu_{10}.$$

The simultaneous solution to this system of equations is

$$\mu_{10} = 1.58 \text{ weeks},$$
$$\mu_{20} = 2.51 \text{ weeks},$$
$$\mu_{30} = 3.50 \text{ weeks},$$

so that the expected time until the cameras are out of stock is 3.50 weeks. Thus, in making these calculations for μ_{30}, we also obtain μ_{20} and μ_{10}.

For the case of μ_{ij} where $j = i$, μ_{ii} is the expected number of transitions until the process returns to the initial state i, and so is called the **expected recurrence time** for state i. After obtaining the steady-state probabilities ($\pi_0, \pi_1, \ldots, \pi_M$) as described in the preceding section, these expected recurrence times can be calculated immediately as

$$\mu_{ii} = \frac{1}{\pi_i}, \qquad \text{for } i = 0, 1, \ldots, M.$$

Thus, for the inventory example, where $\pi_0 = 0.286$, $\pi_1 = 0.285$, $\pi_2 = 0.263$, and $\pi_3 = 0.166$, the corresponding expected recurrence times are

$$\mu_{00} = \frac{1}{\pi_0} = 3.50 \text{ weeks}, \qquad \mu_{22} = \frac{1}{\pi_2} = 3.80 \text{ weeks},$$

$$\mu_{11} = \frac{1}{\pi_1} = 3.51 \text{ weeks}, \qquad \mu_{33} = \frac{1}{\pi_3} = 6.02 \text{ weeks}.$$

16.7   ABSORBING STATES

It was pointed out in Sec. 16.4 that a state k is called an *absorbing state* if $p_{kk} = 1$, so that once the chain visits k it remains there forever. If k is an absorbing state, and the process starts in state i, the probability of *ever* going to state k is called the **probability of absorption** into state k, given that the system started in state i. This probability is denoted by f_{ik}.

When there are two or more absorbing states in a Markov chain, and it is evident that the process will be absorbed into one of these states, it is desirable to find these probabilities of absorption. These probabilities can be obtained by solving a system of linear equations that considers all the possibilities for the first transition and then, given the first transition, considers the conditional probability of absorption into state k. In particular, if the state k is an absorbing state, then the set of absorption probabilities f_{ik} satisfies the system of equations

$$f_{ik} = \sum_{j=0}^{M} p_{ij} f_{jk}, \qquad \text{for } i = 0, 1, \ldots, M,$$

subject to the conditions

$$f_{kk} = 1,$$
$$f_{ik} = 0, \qquad \text{if state } i \text{ is recurrent and } i \neq k.$$

Absorption probabilities are important in random walks. A **random walk** is a Markov chain with the property that if the system is in a state i, then in a single transition the system either remains at i or moves to one of the two states immediately adjacent to i. For example, a random walk often is used as a model for situations involving gambling.

To illustrate, consider a gambling example similar to that presented in Sec. 16.2. However, suppose now that two players (A and B), each having \$2, agree to keep playing the game and betting \$1 at a time until one player is broke. The probability of A winning a single bet is $\frac{1}{3}$, so B wins the bet with probability $\frac{2}{3}$. The number of dollars that player A has before each bet (0, 1, 2, 3, or 4) provides the states of a Markov chain with transition matrix

$$
\mathbf{P} = \begin{array}{c} \text{State} \\ 0 \\ 1 \\ 2 \\ 3 \\ 4 \end{array}
\begin{array}{ccccc}
0 & 1 & 2 & 3 & 4
\end{array}
\left[
\begin{array}{ccccc}
1 & 0 & 0 & 0 & 0 \\
\frac{2}{3} & 0 & \frac{1}{3} & 0 & 0 \\
0 & \frac{2}{3} & 0 & \frac{1}{3} & 0 \\
0 & 0 & \frac{2}{3} & 0 & \frac{1}{3} \\
0 & 0 & 0 & 0 & 1
\end{array}
\right].
$$

Starting from state 2, the probability of absorption into state 0 (A losing all her money) can be obtained from the preceding system of equations as $f_{20} = \frac{1}{5}$, and the probability of A winning \$4 (B going broke) is given by $f_{24} = \frac{4}{5}$.

There are many other situations where absorbing states play an important role. Consider a department store that classifies the balance of a customer's bill as fully paid (state 0), 1 to 30 days in arrears (state 1), 31 to 60 days in arrears (state 2), or bad debt (state 3). The accounts are checked *monthly* to determine the state of each customer. In general, credit is not extended and customers are expected to pay their bills within 30 days. Occasionally, customers pay only portions of their bill. If this occurs when the balance is within 30 days in arrears (state 1), the store views the customer as remaining in state 1. If this occurs when the balance is between 31 and 60 days in arrears, the store views the customer as moving to state 1 (1 to 30 days in arrears). Customers that are more than 60 days in arrears are put into the bad-debt category (state 3), and then bills are sent to a collection agency. After examining data over the past several years on the month by month progression of individual customers from state to state, the store has developed the following transition matrix:[1]

---

[1]Customers who are fully paid (in state 0) and then subsequently fall into arrears on new purchases are viewed as "new" customers who start in state 1.

State \ State	0: Fully Paid	1: 1 to 30 Days in Arrears	2: 31 to 60 Days in Arrears	3: Bad Debt
0: fully paid	1	0	0	0
1: 1 to 30 days in arrears	0.7	0.2	0.1	0
2: 31 to 60 days in arrears	0.5	0.1	0.2	0.2
3: bad debt	0	0	0	1

Although each customer ends up in state 0 or 3, the store is interested in determining the probability that a customer will end up as a bad debt given that the account belongs to the 1 to 30 days in arrears state, and similarly, given that the account belongs to the 31 to 60 days in arrears state.

To obtain this information, the set of equations presented at the beginning of this section must be solved to obtain f_{13} and f_{23}. By substituting, the following two equations are obtained:

$$f_{13} = p_{10}f_{03} + p_{11}f_{13} + p_{12}f_{23} + p_{13}f_{33},$$
$$f_{23} = p_{20}f_{03} + p_{21}f_{13} + p_{22}f_{23} + p_{23}f_{33}.$$

Noting that $f_{03} = 0$ and $f_{33} = 1$, we now have two equations in two unknowns, namely,

$$(1 - p_{11})f_{13} = p_{13} + p_{12}f_{23},$$
$$(1 - p_{22})f_{23} = p_{23} + p_{21}f_{13}.$$

Substituting the values from the transition matrix leads to

$$0.8f_{13} = 0.1f_{23},$$
$$0.8f_{23} = 0.2 + 0.1f_{13},$$

and the solution is

$$f_{13} = 0.032,$$
$$f_{23} = 0.254.$$

Thus, approximately 3 percent of the customers whose accounts are 1 to 30 days in arrears end up as bad debts, whereas about 25 percent of the customers whose accounts are 31 to 60 days in arrears end up as bad debts.

16.8 CONTINUOUS TIME MARKOV CHAINS

In all the previous sections, we assumed that the time parameter t was discrete (that is, $t = 0, 1, 2, \ldots$). Such an assumption is suitable for many problems, but there are certain cases (such as for some queueing models considered in the next chapter) where a continuous time parameter (call it t') is required, because the evolution of the process is being observed *continuously* over time. The definition of a Markov chain given in Sec. 16.2 also extends to such continuous processes. This section focuses on describing these "continuous time Markov chains" and their properties.

Formulation

As before, we label the possible **states** of the system as $0, 1, \ldots, M$. Starting at time 0 and letting the time parameter t' run continuously for $t' \geq 0$, we let the random variable $X(t')$ be the state of the system at time t'. Thus, $X(t')$ will take on one of its possible $(M + 1)$ values over some interval, $0 \leq t' < t_1$, then will jump to another value over the next interval, $t_1 \leq t' < t_2$, etc., where these transit points $(t_1, t_2, \ldots)$ are random points in time (*not* necessarily integer).

Now consider the three points in time (1) $t' = r$ (where $r \geq 0$), (2) $t' = s$ (where $s > r$), and (3) $t' = s + t$ (where $t > 0$), interpreted as follows:

$t' = r$ is a past time,
$t' = s$ is the current time,
$t' = s + t$ is t time units into the future.

Therefore, the state of the system now has been observed at times $t' = s$ and $t' = r$. Label these states as

$$X(s) = i \quad \text{and} \quad X(r) = x(r).$$

Given this information, it now would be natural to seek the probability distribution of the state of the system at time $t' = s + t$. In other words, what is

$$P\{X(s + t) = j \mid X(s) = i \text{ and } X(r) = x(r)\}, \quad \text{for } j = 0, 1, \ldots, M?$$

Deriving this conditional probability often is very difficult. However, this task is considerably simplified if the stochastic process involved possesses the following key property.

A continuous time stochastic process $\{X(t'); t' \geq 0\}$ has the **Markovian property** if

$$P\{X(t + s) = j \mid X(s) = i \text{ and } X(r) = x(r)\} = P\{X(t + s) = j \mid X(s) = i\},$$

for all $i, j = 0, 1, \ldots, M$ and for all $r \geq 0$, $s > r$, and $t > 0$.

Note that $P\{X(t + s) = j \mid X(s) = i\}$ is a **transition probability**, just like the transition probabilities for discrete time Markov chains considered in the preceding sections, where the only difference is that t now need not be an integer.

If the transition probabilities are independent of s, so that

$$P\{X(t + s) = j \mid X(s) = i\} = P\{X(t) = j \mid X(0) = i\}$$

for all $s > 0$, they are called **stationary transition probabilities.**

To simplify notation, we shall denote these stationary transition probabilities by

$$p_{ij}(t) = P\{X(t) = j \mid X(0) = i\},$$

where $p_{ij}(t)$ is referred to as the **continuous time transition probability function.** We assume that

$$\lim_{t \to 0} p_{ij}(t) = \begin{cases} 1 & \text{if } i = j \\ 0 & \text{if } i \neq j. \end{cases}$$

Now we are ready to define the continuous time Markov chains to be considered in this section.

A continuous time stochastic process $\{X(t'); t' \geq 0\}$ is a **continuous time Markov chain** if it has the *Markovian property.*

We shall restrict our consideration to continuous time Markov chains with the following properties:

1. A finite number of states.
2. Stationary transition probabilities.

Some Key Random Variables

In the analysis of continuous time Markov chains, one key set of random variables is the following.

Each time the process enters state i, the amount of time it spends in that state before moving to a different state is a random variable T_i, where $i = 0, 1, \ldots, M$.

Suppose that the process enters state i at time $t' = s$. Then, for any fixed amount of time $t > 0$, note that $T_i > t$ if and only if $X(t') = i$ for all t' over the interval $s \leq t' \leq s + t$. Therefore, the Markovian property (with stationary transition probabilities) implies that

$$P\{T_i > t + s \mid T_i > s\} = P\{T_i > t\}.$$

This is a rather unusual property for a probability distribution to possess. It says that the probability distribution of the *remaining* time until the process transits out of a given state always is the same, regardless of how much time the process has already spent in that state. In effect, the random variable is memoryless; the process forgets its history. There is only one (continuous) probability distribution that possesses this property—the *exponential distribution*. The exponential distribution has a single parameter, call it q, where the mean is $1/q$ and the cumulative distribution function is

$$P\{T_i \leq t\} = 1 - e^{-qt}, \qquad \text{for } t \geq 0.$$

(We shall describe the properties of the exponential distribution in detail in Sec. 17.4.)

This result leads to an equivalent way of describing a continuous time Markov chain:

1. The random variable T_i has an exponential distribution with a mean of $1/q_i$.
2. When leaving state i, the process moves to a state j with probability p_{ij}, where the p_{ij} satisfy the conditions

   $$p_{ij} = 0 \qquad \text{for all } i,$$

   and

   $$\sum_{j=0}^{M} p_{ij} = 1 \qquad \text{for all } i.$$

3. The next state visited after state i is independent of the time spent in state i.

Just as the one-step transition probabilities played a major role in describing discrete time Markov chains, the analogous role for a continuous time Markov chain is played by the transition intensities.

The **transition intensities** are

$$q_i = -\frac{d}{dt}p_{ii}(0) = \lim_{t \to 0} \frac{1 - p_{ii}(t)}{t}, \qquad \text{for } i = 0, 1, 2, \ldots, M,$$

and

$$q_{ij} = \frac{d}{dt}p_{ij}(0) = \lim_{t \to 0} \frac{p_{ij}(t)}{t} = q_i p_{ij}, \qquad \text{for all } j \neq i,$$

where $p_{ij}(t)$ is the *continuous time transition probability function* introduced at the beginning of the section and p_{ij} is the probability described in property 2 of the preceding paragraph. Furthermore, q_i as defined here turns out to still be the parameter of the exponential distribution for T_i as well (see property 1 of the preceding paragraph).

The intuitive interpretation of the q_i and q_{ij} is that they are *transition rates*. In particular, q_i is the *transition rate out of state i* in the sense that q_i is the expected number of times that the process leaves state i per unit of time spent in state i. (Thus, q_i is the reciprocal of the expected time that the process spends in state i per visit to state i; that is, $q_i = 1/E[T_i]$.) Similarly, q_{ij} is the *transition rate from state i to state j* in the sense that q_{ij} is the expected number of times that the process transits from state i to state j per unit of time spent in state i. Thus,

$$q_i = \sum_{j \neq i} q_{ij}.$$

Just as q_i is the parameter of the exponential distribution for T_i, each q_{ij} is the parameter of an exponential distribution for a related random variable described below.

> Each time the process enters state i, the amount of time it will spend in state i before a transition to state j occurs (if a transition to some other state does not occur first) is a random variable T_{ij}, where $i, j = 0, 1, \ldots, M$ and $j \neq i$. The T_{ij} are independent random variables, where each T_{ij} has an *exponential distribution* with parameter q_{ij}, so $E[T_{ij}] = 1/q_{ij}$. The time spent in state i until a transition occurs (T_i) is the *minimum* (over $j \neq i$) of the T_{ij}. When the transition occurs, the probability that it is to state j is $p_{ij} = q_{ij}/q_i$.

Steady-State Probabilities

Just as the transition probabilities for a discrete time Markov chain satisfy the Chapman-Kolmogorov equations, the continuous time transition probability function also satisfies these equations. Therefore, for any states i and j and nonnegative numbers t and s ($0 \leq s \leq t$),

$$p_{ij}(t) = \sum_{k=1}^{M} p_{ik}(s)p_{kj}(t - s).$$

A pair of states i and j are said to *communicate* if there are times t_1 and t_2 such that $p_{ij}(t_1) > 0$ and $p_{ji}(t_2) > 0$. All states that communicate are said to form a *class*. If all states form a single class, i.e., if the Markov chain is *irreducible* (hereafter assumed), then

$$p_{ij}(t) > 0, \qquad \text{for all } t > 0 \text{ and all states } i \text{ and } j.$$

Furthermore,

$$\lim_{t \to \infty} p_{ij}(t) = \pi_j$$

always exists and is independent of the initial state of the Markov chain, for $j = 0, 1, \ldots,$ M. These limiting probabilities are commonly referred to as the **steady-state probabilities** (or *stationary probabilities*) of the Markov chain.

The π_j satisfy the equations

$$\pi_j = \sum_{i=0}^{M} \pi_i p_{ij}(t), \qquad \text{for } j = 0, 1, \ldots, M \text{ and every } t \geq 0.$$

However, the following **steady-state equations** provide a more useful system of equations for solving for the steady-state probabilities:

$$\pi_j q_j = \sum_{i \neq j} \pi_i q_{ij}, \qquad \text{for } j = 0, 1, \ldots, M.$$

and

$$\sum_{j=0}^{M} \pi_j = 1.$$

The steady-state equation for state j has an intuitive interpretation. The left-hand side $(\pi_j q_j)$ is the *rate* at which the process *leaves* state j, since π_j is the (steady-state) probability that the process is in state j and q_j is the transition rate out of state j given that the process is in state j. Similarly, each term on the right-hand side $(\pi_i q_{ij})$ is the *rate* at which the process *enters* state j from state i, since q_{ij} is the transition rate from state i to state j given that the process is in state i. By summing over all $i \neq j$, the entire right-hand side then gives the rate at which the process enters state j from any other state. The overall equation thereby states that the rate at which the process leaves state j must equal the rate at which the process enters state j. Thus, this equation is analogous to the conservation of flow equations encountered in many engineering and science courses.

Because each of the first $M + 1$ *steady-state equations* requires that two rates be *in balance* (equal), these equations sometimes are called the **balance equations.**

Example.   A certain shop has two identical machines that are operated continuously except when they are broken down. Because they break down fairly frequently, the top-priority assignment for a full-time maintenance person is to repair them whenever needed.

The time required to repair a machine has an exponential distribution with a mean of $\frac{1}{2}$ day. Once the repair of a machine is completed, the time until the next breakdown of that machine has an exponential distribution with a mean of 1 day. These distributions are independent.

Define the random variable $X(t')$ as

$X(t') =$ number of machines broken down at time t',

so the possible values of $X(t')$ are 0, 1, 2. Therefore, by letting the time parameter t' run continuously from time 0, the continuous time stochastic process $\{X(t'); t' \geq 0\}$ gives the evolution of the number of machines broken down.

Because both the repair time and the time until a breakdown have exponential distributions, $\{X(t'); t' \geq 0\}$ is a *continuous time Markov chain*[1] with states 0, 1, 2. Consequently, we can use the steady-state equations given in the preceding subsection to find the steady-state probability distribution of the number of machines broken down. To do this, we need to determine all the *transition rates*, i.e., the q_i and q_{ij} for $i, j = 0, 1, 2$.

The state (number of machines broken down) increases by 1 when a breakdown occurs and decreases by 1 when a repair occurs. Since both breakdowns and repairs occur one at a time, $q_{02} = 0$ and $q_{20} = 0$. The expected repair time is $\frac{1}{2}$ day, so the rate at which repairs are completed (when any machines are broken down) is 2 per day, which implies that $q_{21} = 2$ and $q_{10} = 2$. Similarly, the expected time until a particular operational machine breaks down is 1 day, so the rate at which it breaks down (when operational) is 1

---

[1] Proving this fact requires the use of two properties of the exponential distribution discussed in Sec. 17.4 (*lack of memory* and *the minimum of exponentials is exponential*), since these properties imply that the T_{ij} random variables introduced earlier do indeed have exponential distributions.

FIGURE 16.2
Rate diagram for the
example of a continuous
time Markov chain.

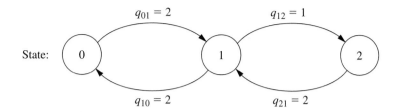

per day, which implies that $q_{12} = 1$. During times when both machines are operational, breakdowns occur at the rate of $1 + 1 = 2$ per day, so $q_{01} = 2$.

These transition rates are summarized in the rate diagram shown in Fig. 16.2. These rates now can be used to calculate the *total transition rate* out of each state.

$$q_0 = q_{01} = 2.$$
$$q_1 = q_{10} + q_{12} = 3.$$
$$q_2 = q_{21} = 2.$$

Plugging all the rates into the steady-state equations given in the preceding subsection then yields

Balance equation for state 0:	$2\pi_0 = 2\pi_1$
Balance equation for state 1:	$3\pi_1 = 2\pi_0 + 2\pi_2$
Balance equation for state 2:	$2\pi_2 = \pi_1$
Probabilities sum to 1:	$\pi_0 + \pi_1 + \pi_2 = 1$

Any one of the balance equations (say, the second) can be deleted as redundant, and the simultaneous solution of the remaining equations gives the steady-state distribution as

$$(\pi_0, \pi_1, \pi_2) = \left(\frac{2}{5}, \frac{2}{5}, \frac{1}{5}\right).$$

Thus, in the long run, both machines will be broken down simultaneously 20 percent of the time, and one machine will be broken down another 40 percent of the time.

The next chapter (on queueing theory) features many more examples of continuous time Markov chains. In fact, most of the basic models of queueing theory fall into this category. The current example actually fits one of these models (the finite calling population variation of the *M/M/s* model included in Sec. 17.6).

SELECTED REFERENCES

1. Heyman, D., and M. Sobel: *Stochastic Models in Operations Research,* vol. 1, McGraw-Hill, New York, 1982.
2. Kao, E. P. C.: *An Introduction to Stochastic Processes,* Duxbury Press, Belmont, CA, 1997.
3. Resnick, S. I.: *Adventures in Stochastic Processes,* Birkhäuser, Boston, 1992.
4. Ross, S.: *Stochastic Processes,* 2d ed., Wiley, New York, 1995.

5. Stewart, W. J. (ed.): *Numerical Solution of Markov Chains,* Marcel Dekker, New York, 1991.

6. Taylor, H., and S. Karlin: *An Introduction to Stochastic Modeling,* revised edition, Academic Press, San Diego, 1993.

7. Tijms, H. C.: *Stochastic Models: An Algorithmic Approach,* Wiley, New York, 1994.

LEARNING AIDS FOR THIS CHAPTER IN YOUR OR COURSEWARE

Automatic Routines in OR Courseware:

Enter Transition Matrix
Chapman-Kolmogorov Equations
Steady-State Probabilities

See Appendix 1 for documentation of the software.

PROBLEMS

The symbol to the left of some of the problems (or their parts) has the following meaning.

C: Use the computer with the corresponding automatic routines listed above (or other equivalent routines) to solve the problem.

An asterisk on the problem number indicates that at least a partial answer is given in the back of the book.

16.2-1. Assume that the probability of rain tomorrow is 0.5 if it is raining today, and assume that the probability of its being clear (no rain) tomorrow is 0.9 if it is clear today. Also assume that these probabilities do not change if information is also provided about the weather before today.

(a) Explain why the stated assumptions imply that the *Markovian property* holds for the evolution of the weather.

(b) Formulate the evolution of the weather as a Markov chain by defining its states and giving its (one-step) transition matrix.

16.2-2. Consider the second version of the stock market model presented as an example in Sec. 16.2. Whether the stock goes up tomorrow depends upon whether it increased today *and* yesterday. If the stock increased today and yesterday, it will increase tomorrow with probability α_1. If the stock increased today and decreased yesterday, it will increase tomorrow with probability α_2. If the stock decreased today and increased yesterday, it will increase tomorrow with probability α_3. Finally, if the stock decreased today and yesterday, it will increase tomorrow with probability α_4.

(a) Construct the (one-step) transition matrix of the Markov chain.

(b) Explain why the states used for this Markov chain cause the mathematical definition of the Markovian property to hold even though what happens in the future (tomorrow) depends upon what happened in the past (yesterday) as well as the present (today).

16.2-3. Reconsider Prob. 16.2-2. Suppose now that whether or not the stock goes up tomorrow depends upon whether it increased today, yesterday, *and* the day before yesterday. Can this problem be formulated as a Markov chain? If so, what are the possible states? Explain why these states give the process the *Markovian property* whereas the states in Prob. 16.2-2 do not.

16.3-1. Reconsider Prob. 16.2-1.

C **(a)** Use the routine *Chapman-Kolmogorov Equations* in your OR Courseware to find the *n*-step transition matrix $\mathbf{P}^{(n)}$ for $n = 2, 5, 10, 20$.

(b) The probability that it will rain today is 0.5. Use the results from part (*a*) to determine the probability that it will rain *n* days from now, for $n = 2, 5, 10, 20$.

C **(c)** Use the routine *Steady-State Probabilities* in your OR Courseware to determine the steady-state probabilities of the state of the weather. Describe how the probabilities in the *n*-step transition matrices obtained in part (*a*) compare to these steady-state probabilities as *n* grows large.

16.3-2. Suppose that a communications network transmits binary digits, 0 or 1, where each digit is transmitted 10 times in succession. During each transmission, the probability is 0.99 that the digit

entered will be transmitted accurately. In other words, the probability is 0.01 that the digit being transmitted will be recorded with the opposite value at the end of the transmission. For each transmission after the first one, the digit entered for transmission is the one that was recorded at the end of the preceding transmission. If X_0 denotes the binary digit entering the system, X_1 the binary digit recorded after the first transmission, X_2 the binary digit recorded after the second transmission, . . . , then $\{X_n\}$ is a Markov chain.
(a) Construct the (one-step) transition matrix.
C (b) Use your OR Courseware to find the 10-step transition matrix $\mathbf{P}^{(10)}$. Use this result to identify the probability that a digit entering the network will be recorded accurately after the last transmission.
C (c) Suppose that the network is redesigned to improve the probability that a single transmission will be accurate from 0.99 to 0.999. Repeat part (b) to find the new probability that a digit entering the network will be recorded accurately after the last transmission.

16.3-3.* A particle moves on a circle through points that have been marked 0, 1, 2, 3, 4 (in a clockwise order). The particle starts at point 0. At each step it has probability 0.5 of moving one point clockwise (0 follows 4) and 0.5 of moving one point counterclockwise. Let X_n $(n \geq 0)$ denote its location on the circle after step n. $\{X_n\}$ is a Markov chain.
(a) Construct the (one-step) transition matrix.
C (b) Use your OR Courseware to determine the n-step transition matrix $\mathbf{P}^{(n)}$ for $n = 5, 10, 20, 40, 80$.
C (c) Use your OR Courseware to determine the steady-state probabilities of the state of the Markov chain. Describe how the probabilities in the n-step transition matrices obtained in part (b) compare to these steady-state probabilities as n grows large.

16.4-1.* Given the following (one-step) transition matrices of a Markov chain, determine the classes of the Markov chain and whether they are recurrent.

(a) $\mathbf{P} =$

State	0	1	2	3
0	0	0	$\frac{1}{3}$	$\frac{2}{3}$
1	1	0	0	0
2	0	1	0	0
3	0	1	0	0

(b) $\mathbf{P} =$

State	0	1	2	3
0	1	0	0	0
1	1	$\frac{1}{2}$	$\frac{1}{2}$	0
2	0	$\frac{1}{2}$	$\frac{1}{2}$	0
3	$\frac{1}{2}$	0	0	$\frac{1}{2}$

16.4-2. Given each of the following (one-step) transition matrices of a Markov chain, determine the classes of the Markov chain and whether they are recurrent.

(a) $\mathbf{P} =$

State	0	1	2	3
0	0	$\frac{1}{3}$	$\frac{1}{3}$	$\frac{1}{3}$
1	$\frac{1}{3}$	0	$\frac{1}{3}$	$\frac{1}{3}$
2	$\frac{1}{3}$	$\frac{1}{3}$	0	$\frac{1}{3}$
3	$\frac{1}{3}$	$\frac{1}{3}$	$\frac{1}{3}$	0

(b) $\mathbf{P} =$

State	0	1	2
0	0	0	1
1	$\frac{1}{2}$	$\frac{1}{2}$	0
2	0	1	0

16.4-3. Given the following (one-step) transition matrix of a Markov chain, determine the classes of the Markov chain and whether they are recurrent.

$\mathbf{P} =$

State	0	1	2	3	4
0	$\frac{1}{4}$	$\frac{3}{4}$	0	0	0
1	$\frac{3}{4}$	$\frac{1}{4}$	0	0	0
2	$\frac{1}{3}$	$\frac{1}{3}$	$\frac{1}{3}$	0	0
3	0	0	0	$\frac{3}{4}$	$\frac{1}{4}$
4	0	0	0	$\frac{1}{4}$	$\frac{3}{4}$

16.4-4. Determine the period of each of the states in the Markov chain that has the following (one-step) transition matrix.

$\mathbf{P} =$

State	0	1	2	3	4	5
0	0	0	0	$\frac{2}{3}$	0	$\frac{1}{3}$
1	0	0	1	0	0	0
2	1	0	0	0	0	0
3	0	$\frac{1}{4}$	0	0	$\frac{3}{4}$	0
4	0	0	1	0	0	0
5	0	$\frac{1}{2}$	0	0	$\frac{1}{2}$	0

16.4-5. Consider the Markov chain that has the following (one-step) transition matrix.

$\mathbf{P} =$

State	0	1	2	3	4
0	0	$\frac{4}{5}$	0	$\frac{1}{5}$	0
1	$\frac{1}{4}$	0	$\frac{1}{2}$	$\frac{1}{4}$	0
2	0	$\frac{1}{2}$	0	$\frac{1}{10}$	$\frac{2}{5}$
3	0	0	0	1	0
4	$\frac{1}{3}$	0	$\frac{1}{3}$	$\frac{1}{3}$	0

(a) Determine the classes of this Markov chain and, for each class, determine whether it is recurrent or transient.

(b) For each of the classes identified in part (b), determine the period of the states in that class.

16.5-1. Reconsider Prob. 16.2-1. Suppose now that the given probabilities, 0.5 and 0.9, are replaced by arbitrary values, α and β, respectively. Solve for the *steady-state probabilities* of the state of the weather in terms of α and β.

16.5-2. A transition matrix $\mathbf{P}$ is said to be doubly stochastic if the sum over each column equals 1; that is,

$$\sum_{i=0}^{M} p_{ij} = 1, \quad \text{for all } j.$$

If such a chain is irreducible, aperiodic, and consists of $M + 1$ states, show that

$$\pi_j = \frac{1}{M+1}, \quad \text{for } j = 0, 1, \ldots, M.$$

16.5-3. Reconsider Prob. 16.3-3. Use the results given in Prob. 16.5-2 to find the steady-state probabilities for this Markov chain. Then find what happens to these steady-state probabilities if, at each step, the probability of moving one point clockwise changes to 0.9 and the probability of moving one point counterclockwise changes to 0.1.

C **16.5-4.** The leading brewery on the West Coast (labeled A) has hired an OR analyst to analyze its market position. It is particularly concerned about its major competitor (labeled B). The analyst believes that brand switching can be modeled as a Markov chain using three states, with states A and B representing customers drinking beer produced from the aforementioned breweries and state C representing all other brands. Data are taken monthly, and the analyst has constructed the following (one-step) transition matrix from past data.

	A	B	C
A	0.7	0.2	0.1
B	0.2	0.75	0.05
C	0.1	0.1	0.8

What are the steady-state market shares for the two major breweries?

16.5-5. Consider the following blood inventory problem facing a hospital. There is need for a rare blood type, namely, type AB, Rh negative blood. The demand D (in pints) over any 3-day period is given by

$$P\{D = 0\} = 0.4, \quad P\{D = 1\} = 0.3,$$
$$P\{D = 2\} = 0.2, \quad \text{and} \quad P\{D = 3\} = 0.1.$$

Note that the expected demand is 1 pint, since $E(D) = 0.3(1) + 0.2(2) + 0.1(3) = 1$. Suppose that there are 3 days between deliver-

ies. The hospital proposes a policy of receiving 1 pint at each delivery and using the oldest blood first. If more blood is required than is on hand, an expensive emergency delivery is made. Blood is discarded if it is still on the shelf after 21 days. Denote the state of the system as the number of pints on hand just after a delivery. Thus, because of the discarding policy, the largest possible state is 7.
(a) Construct the (one-step) transition matrix for this Markov chain.
C **(b)** Find the steady-state probabilities of the state of the Markov chain.
(c) Use the results from part (b) to find the steady-state probability that a pint of blood will need to be discarded during a 3-day period. (*Hint*: Because the oldest blood is used first, a pint reaches 21 days only if the state was 7 and then $D = 0$.)
(d) Use the results from part (b) to find the steady-state probability that an emergency delivery will be needed during the 3-day period between regular deliveries.

16.5-6. A soap company specializes in a luxury type of bath soap. The sales of this soap fluctuate between two levels—"Low" and "High"—depending upon two factors: (1) whether they advertise, and (2) the advertising and marketing of new products being done by competitors. The second factor is out of the company's control, but it is trying to determine what its own advertising policy should be. For example, the marketing manager's proposal is to advertise when sales are low but not to advertise when sales are high. Advertising in any quarter of a year has its primary impact on sales in the *following* quarter. Therefore, at the beginning of each quarter, the needed information is available to forecast accurately whether sales will be low or high that quarter and to decide whether to advertise that quarter.

The cost of advertising is $1 million for each quarter of a year in which it is done. When advertising is done during a quarter, the probability of having high sales the next quarter is $\frac{1}{2}$ or $\frac{3}{4}$, depending upon whether the current quarter's sales are low or high. These probabilities go down to $\frac{1}{4}$ or $\frac{1}{2}$ when advertising is not done during the current quarter. The company's quarterly profits (excluding advertising costs) are $4 million when sales are high but only $2 million when sales are low. (Hereafter, use units of millions of dollars.)
(a) Construct the (one-step) transition matrix for each of the following advertising strategies: (i) never advertise, (ii) always advertise, (iii) follow the marketing manager's proposal.
(b) Determine the steady-state probabilities manually for each of the three cases in part (a).
(c) Find the long-run expected average profit (including a deduction for advertising costs) per quarter for each of the three advertising strategies in part (a). Which of these strategies is best according to this measure of performance?

C **16.5-7.** In the last subsection of Sec. 16.5, the (long-run) expected average cost per week (based on just ordering costs and unsatisfied demand costs) is calculated for the inventory example of Sec. 16.1. Suppose now that the ordering policy is changed to the following. Whenever the number of cameras on hand at the end of the week is 0 or 1, an order is placed that will bring this number up to 3. Otherwise, no order is placed.

Recalculate the (long-run) expected average cost per week under this new inventory policy.

16.5-8.* Consider the inventory example introduced in Sec. 16.1, but with the following change in the ordering policy. If the number of cameras on hand at the end of each week is 0 or 1, two additional cameras will be ordered. Otherwise, no ordering will take place. Assume that the storage costs are the same as given in the second subsection of Sec. 16.5.

C **(a)** Find the steady-state probabilities of the state of this Markov chain.

(b) Find the long-run expected average storage cost per week.

16.5-9. Consider the following inventory policy for a certain product. If the demand during a period exceeds the number of items available, this unsatisfied demand is backlogged; i.e., it is filled when the next order is received. Let Z_n ($n = 0, 1, \ldots$) denote the amount of inventory on hand minus the number of units backlogged before ordering at the end of period n ($Z_0 = 0$). If Z_n is zero or positive, no orders are backlogged. If Z_n is negative, then $-Z_n$ represents the number of backlogged units and no inventory is on hand. At the end of period n, if $Z_n < 1$, an order is placed for $2m$ units, where m is the smallest integer such that $Z_n + 2m \geq 1$. Orders are filled immediately.

Let $D_1, D_2, \ldots$, be the demand for a product in periods 1, 2, ..., respectively. Assume that the D_n are independent and identically distributed random variables taking on the values, 0, 1, 2, 3, 4, each with probability $\frac{1}{5}$. Let X_n denote the amount of stock on hand *after* ordering at the end of period n (where $X_0 = 2$), so that

$$X_n = \begin{cases} X_{n-1} - D_n + 2m & \text{if } X_{n-1} - D_n < 1 \\ X_{n-1} - D_n & \text{if } X_{n-1} - D_n \geq 1 \end{cases} \quad (n = 1, 2, \ldots),$$

when $\{X_n\}$ ($n = 0, 1, \ldots$) is a Markov chain. It has only two states, 1 and 2, because the only time that ordering will take place is when $Z_n = 0, -1, -2,$ or -3, in which case 2, 2, 4, and 4 units are ordered, respectively, leaving $X_n = 2, 1, 2, 1$, respectively.

(a) Construct the (one-step) transition matrix.

(b) Use the steady-state equations to solve manually for the steady-state probabilities.

(c) Now use the result given in Prob. 16.5-2 to find the steady-state probabilities.

(d) Suppose that the ordering cost is given by $(2 + 2m)$ if an order is placed and zero otherwise. The holding cost per period is Z_n if $Z_n \geq 0$ and zero otherwise. The shortage cost per period is $-4Z_n$ if $Z_n < 0$ and zero otherwise. Find the (long-run) expected average cost per unit time.

16.5-10. An important unit consists of two components placed in parallel. The unit performs satisfactorily if one of the two components is operating. Therefore, only one component is operated at a time, but both components are kept operational (capable of being operated) as often as possible by repairing them as needed. An operating component breaks down in a given period with probability 0.2. When this occurs, the parallel component takes over, if it is operational, at the beginning of the next period. Only one component can be repaired at a time. The repair of a component starts at the beginning of the first available period and is completed at the end of the next period. Let X_t be a vector consisting of two elements U and V, where U represents the number of components that are operational at the end of period t and V represents the number of periods of repair that have been completed on components that are not yet operational. Thus, $V = 0$ if $U = 2$ or if $U = 1$ and the repair of the nonoperational component is just getting under way. Because a repair takes two periods, $V = 1$ if $U = 0$ (since then one nonoperational component is waiting to begin repair while the other one is entering its second period of repair) or if $U = 1$ and the nonoperational component is entering its second period of repair. Therefore, the state space consists of the four states (2, 0), (1, 0), (0, 1), and (1, 1). Denote these four states by 0, 1, 2, 3, respectively. $\{X_t\}$ ($t = 0, 1, \ldots$) is a Markov chain (assume that $X_0 = 0$) with the (one-step) transition matrix

$$\mathbf{P} = \begin{array}{c} \text{State} \\ 0 \\ 1 \\ 2 \\ 3 \end{array} \begin{array}{cccc} 0 & 1 & 2 & 3 \\ \begin{bmatrix} 0.8 & 0.2 & 0 & 0 \\ 0 & 0 & 0.2 & 0.8 \\ 0 & 1 & 0 & 0 \\ 0.8 & 0.2 & 0 & 0 \end{bmatrix} \end{array}.$$

C **(a)** What is the probability that the unit will be inoperable (because both components are down) after n periods, for $n = 2, 5, 10, 20$?

C **(b)** What are the steady-state probabilities of the state of this Markov chain?

(c) If it costs \$30,000 per period when the unit is inoperable (both components down) and zero otherwise, what is the (long-run) expected average cost per period?

16.6-1. A computer is inspected at the end of every hour. It is found to be either working (up) or failed (down). If the computer is found to be up, the probability of its remaining up for the next hour is 0.90. If it is down, the computer is repaired, which may require more than 1 hour. Whenever the computer is down (regardless of how long it has been down), the probability of its still being down 1 hour later is 0.35.

(a) Construct the (one-step) transition matrix for this Markov chain.

(b) Use the approach described in Sec. 16.6 to find the μ_{ij} (the expected first passage time from state i to state j) for all i and j.

16.6-2. A manufacturer has a machine that, when operational at the beginning of a day, has a probability of 0.1 of breaking down sometime during the day. When this happens, the repair is done the next day and completed at the end of that day.

(a) Formulate the evolution of the status of the machine as a Markov chain by identifying three possible states at the end of each day, and then constructing the (one-step) transition matrix.

(b) Use the approach described in Sec. 16.6 to find the μ_{ij} (the expected first passage time from state i to state j) for all i and j. Use these results to identify the expected number of full days that the machine will remain operational before the next breakdown after a repair is completed.

(c) Now suppose that the machine already has gone 20 full days without a breakdown since the last repair was completed. How does the expected number of full days *hereafter* that the machine will remain operational before the next breakdown compare with the corresponding result from part (*b*) when the repair had just been completed? Explain.

16.6-3. Reconsider Prob. 16.6-2. Now suppose that the manufacturer keeps a spare machine that only is used when the primary machine is being repaired. During a repair day, the spare machine has a probability of 0.1 of breaking down, in which case it is repaired the next day. Denote the state of the system by (x, y), where x and y, respectively, take on the values 1 or 0 depending upon whether the primary machine (x) and the spare machine (y) are operational (value of 1) or not operational (value of 0) at the end of the day. [*Hint:* Note that $(0, 0)$ is not a possible state.]

(a) Construct the (one-step) transition matrix for this Markov chain.

(b) Find the *expected recurrence time* for the state $(1, 0)$.

16.6-4. Consider the inventory example presented in Sec. 16.1 except that demand now has the following probability distribution:

$$P\{D = 0\} = \frac{1}{4}, \qquad P\{D = 2\} = \frac{1}{4},$$

$$P\{D = 1\} = \frac{1}{2}, \qquad P\{D \geq 3\} = 0.$$

The ordering policy now is changed to ordering just 2 cameras at the end of the week if none are in stock. As before, no order is placed if there are any cameras in stock. Assume that there is one camera in stock at the time (the end of a week) the policy is instituted.

(a) Construct the (one-step) transition matrix.

C (b) Find the probability distribution of the state of this Markov chain n weeks after the new inventory policy is instituted, for $n = 2, 5, 10$.

(c) Find the μ_{ij} (the expected first passage time from state i to state j) for all i and j.

C (d) Find the steady-state probabilities of the state of this Markov chain.

(e) Assuming that the store pays a storage cost for each camera remaining on the shelf at the end of the week according to the function $C(0) = 0$, $C(1) = \$2$, and $C(2) = \$8$, find the long-run expected average storage cost per week.

16.6-5. A production process contains a machine that deteriorates rapidly in both quality and output under heavy usage, so that it is inspected at the end of each day. Immediately after inspection, the condition of the machine is noted and classified into one of four possible states:

State	Condition
0	Good as new
1	Operable—minimum deterioration
2	Operable—major deterioration
3	Inoperable and replaced by a good-as-new machine

The process can be modeled as a Markov chain with its (one-step) transition matrix **P** given by

State	0	1	2	3
0	0	$\frac{7}{8}$	$\frac{1}{16}$	$\frac{1}{16}$
1	0	$\frac{3}{4}$	$\frac{1}{8}$	$\frac{1}{8}$
2	0	0	$\frac{1}{2}$	$\frac{1}{2}$
3	1	0	0	0

C (a) Find the steady-state probabilities.

(b) If the costs of being in states 0, 1, 2, 3, are 0, $\$1,000$, $\$3,000$, and $\$6,000$, respectively, what is the long-run expected average cost per day?

(c) Find the *expected recurrence time* for state 0 (i.e., the expected length of time a machine can be used before it must be replaced).

16.7-1. Consider the following gambler's ruin problem. A gambler bets $\$1$ on each play of a game. Each time, he has a probability p of winning and probability $q = 1 - p$ of losing the dollar bet. He will continue to play until he goes broke or nets a fortune of T dollars. Let X_n denote the number of dollars possessed by the gambler after the nth play of the game. Then

$$X_{n+1} = \begin{cases} X_n + 1 & \text{with probability } p \\ X_n - 1 & \text{with probability } q = 1 - p \end{cases} \quad \text{for } 0 < X_n < T,$$

$$X_{n+1} = X_n, \qquad\qquad\qquad\qquad\qquad\qquad\qquad \text{for } X_n = 0 \text{ or } T.$$

$\{X_n\}$ is a Markov chain. The gambler starts with X_0 dollars, where X_0 is a positive integer less than T.

(a) Construct the (one-step) transition matrix of the Markov chain.

(b) Find the classes of the Markov chain.

(c) Let $T = 3$ and $p = 0.3$. Using the notation of Sec. 16.7, find $f_{10}, f_{1T}, f_{20}, f_{2T}$.

(d) Let $T = 3$ and $p = 0.7$. Find $f_{10}, f_{1T}, f_{20}, f_{2T}$.

16.7-2. A video cassette recorder manufacturer is so certain of its quality control that it is offering a complete replacement warranty if a recorder fails within 2 years. Based upon compiled data, the company has noted that only 1 percent of its recorders fail during the first year, whereas 5 percent of the recorders that survive the first year will fail during the second year. The warranty does not cover replacement recorders.

(a) Formulate the evolution of the status of a recorder as a Markov chain whose states include two absorption states that involve needing to honor the warranty or having the recorder survive the warranty period. Then construct the (one-step) transition matrix.

(b) Use the approach described in Sec. 16.7 to find the probability that the manufacturer will have to honor the warranty.

16.8-1. Reconsider the example presented at the end of Sec. 16.8. Suppose now that a third machine, identical to the first two, has been added to the shop. The one maintenance person still must maintain all the machines.

(a) Develop the *rate diagram* for this Markov chain.

(b) Construct the *steady-state equations.*

(c) Solve these equations for the *steady-state probabilities.*

16.8-2. The state of a particular continuous time Markov chain is defined as the number of jobs currently at a certain work center, where a maximum of three jobs are allowed. Jobs arrive individually. Whenever fewer than three jobs are present, the time until the next arrival has an exponential distribution with a mean of $\frac{1}{2}$ day. Jobs are processed at the work center one at a time and then leave immediately. Processing times have an exponential distribution with a mean of $\frac{1}{4}$ day.

(a) Construct the *rate diagram* for this Markov chain.

(b) Write the *steady-state equations.*

(c) Solve these equations for the *steady-state probabilities.*

17

Queueing Theory

Queues (waiting lines) are a part of everyday life. We all wait in queues to buy a movie ticket, make a bank deposit, pay for groceries, mail a package, obtain food in a cafeteria, start a ride in an amusement park, etc. We have become accustomed to considerable amounts of waiting, but still get annoyed by unusually long waits.

However, having to wait is not just a petty personal annoyance. The amount of time that a nation's populace wastes by waiting in queues is a major factor in both the quality of life there and the efficiency of the nation's economy. For example, before its dissolution, the U.S.S.R. was notorious for the tremendously long queues that its citizens frequently had to endure just to purchase basic necessities. Even in the United States today, it has been estimated that Americans spend 37,000,000,000 hours per year waiting in queues. If this time could be spent productively instead, it would amount to nearly 20 million person-years of useful work each year!

Even this staggering figure does not tell the whole story of the impact of causing excessive waiting. Great inefficiencies also occur because of other kinds of waiting than people standing in line. For example, making *machines* wait to be repaired may result in lost production. *Vehicles* (including ships and trucks) that need to wait to be unloaded may delay subsequent shipments. *Airplanes* waiting to take off or land may disrupt later travel schedules. Delays in *telecommunication* transmissions due to saturated lines may cause data glitches. Causing *manufacturing jobs* to wait to be performed may disrupt subsequent production. Delaying *service jobs* beyond their due dates may result in lost future business.

Queueing theory is the study of waiting in all these various guises. It uses *queueing models* to represent the various types of *queueing systems* (systems that involve queues of some kind) that arise in practice. Formulas for each model indicate how the corresponding queueing system should perform, including the average amount of waiting that will occur, under a variety of circumstances.

Therefore, these queueing models are very helpful for determining how to operate a queueing system in the most effective way. Providing too much service capacity to operate the system involves excessive costs. But not providing enough service capacity results in excessive waiting and all its unfortunate consequences. The models enable finding an appropriate balance between the cost of service and the amount of waiting.

After some general discussion, this chapter presents most of the more elementary queueing models and their basic results. Chapter 18 discusses how the information provided by queueing theory can be used to design queueing systems that minimize the total cost of service and waiting.

17.1 PROTOTYPE EXAMPLE

The emergency room of COUNTY HOSPITAL provides quick medical care for emergency cases brought to the hospital by ambulance or private automobile. At any hour there is always one doctor on duty in the emergency room. However, because of a growing tendency for emergency cases to use these facilities rather than go to a private physician, the hospital has been experiencing a continuing increase in the number of emergency room visits each year. As a result, it has become quite common for patients arriving during peak usage hours (the early evening) to have to wait until it is their turn to be treated by the doctor. Therefore, a proposal has been made that a second doctor should be assigned to the emergency room during these hours, so that two emergency cases can be treated simultaneously. The hospital's management engineer has been assigned to study this question.[1]

The management engineer began by gathering the relevant historical data and then projecting these data into the next year. Recognizing that the emergency room is a queueing system, she applied several alternative queueing theory models to predict the waiting characteristics of the system with one doctor and with two doctors, as you will see in the latter sections of this chapter (see Tables 17.2, 17.3, and 17.4).

17.2 BASIC STRUCTURE OF QUEUEING MODELS

The Basic Queueing Process

The basic process assumed by most queueing models is the following. *Customers* requiring service are generated over time by an *input source*. These customers enter the *queueing system* and join a *queue*. At certain times, a member of the queue is selected for service by some rule known as the *queue discipline*. The required service is then performed for the customer by the *service mechanism,* after which the customer leaves the queueing system. This process is depicted in Fig. 17.1.

Many alternative assumptions can be made about the various elements of the queueing process; they are discussed next.

Input Source (Calling Population)

One characteristic of the input source is its size. The *size* is the total number of customers that might require service from time to time, i.e., the total number of distinct potential customers. This population from which arrivals come is referred to as the **calling population.** The size may be assumed to be either *infinite* or *finite* (so that the input source also is said to be either *unlimited* or *limited*). Because the calculations are far easier for the infinite case, this assumption often is made even when the actual size is some rela-

---

[1]For one actual case study of this kind, see W. Blaker Bolling, "Queueing Model of a Hospital Emergency Room," *Industrial Engineering,* September 1972, pp. 26–31.

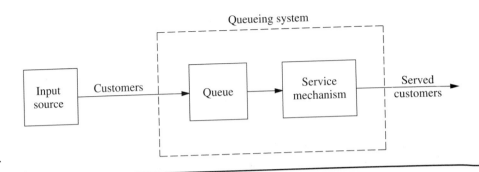

FIGURE 17.1
The basic queueing process.

tively large finite number; and it should be taken to be the implicit assumption for any queueing model that does not state otherwise. The finite case is more difficult analytically because the number of customers in the queueing system affects the number of potential customers outside the system at any time. However, the finite assumption must be made if the rate at which the input source generates new customers is significantly affected by the number of customers in the queueing system.

The statistical pattern by which customers are generated over time must also be specified. The common assumption is that they are generated according to a *Poisson process;* i.e., the number of customers generated until any specific time has a Poisson distribution. As we discuss in Sec. 17.4, this case is the one where arrivals to the queueing system occur randomly but at a certain fixed mean rate, regardless of how many customers already are there (so the *size* of the input source is *infinite*). An equivalent assumption is that the probability distribution of the time between consecutive arrivals is an *exponential* distribution. (The properties of this distribution are described in Sec. 17.4.) The time between consecutive arrivals is referred to as the **interarrival time.**

Any unusual assumptions about the behavior of arriving customers must also be specified. One example is *balking,* where the customer refuses to enter the system and is lost if the queue is too long.

Queue

The queue is where customers wait *before* being served. A queue is characterized by the maximum permissible number of customers that it can contain. Queues are called *infinite* or *finite,* according to whether this number is infinite or finite. The assumption of an *infinite queue* is the standard one for most queueing models, even for situations where there actually is a (relatively large) finite upper bound on the permissible number of customers, because dealing with such an upper bound would be a complicating factor in the analysis. However, for queueing systems where this upper bound is small enough that it actually would be reached with some frequency, it becomes necessary to assume a *finite queue.*

Queue Discipline

The queue discipline refers to the order in which members of the queue are selected for service. For example, it may be first-come-first-served, random, according to some priority procedure, or some other order. First-come-first-served usually is assumed by queueing models, unless it is stated otherwise.

Service Mechanism

The service mechanism consists of one or more *service facilities,* each of which contains one or more *parallel service channels,* called **servers.** If there is more than one service facility, the customer may receive service from a sequence of these (*service channels in series*). At a given facility, the customer enters one of the parallel service channels and is completely serviced by that server. A queueing model must specify the arrangement of the facilities and the number of servers (parallel channels) at each one. Most elementary models assume one service facility with either one server or a finite number of servers.

The time elapsed from the commencement of service to its completion for a customer at a service facility is referred to as the **service time** (or *holding time*). A model of a particular queueing system must specify the probability distribution of service times for each server (and possibly for different types of customers), although it is common to assume the *same* distribution for all servers (all models in this chapter make this assumption). The service-time distribution that is most frequently assumed in practice (largely because it is far more tractable than any other) is the *exponential* distribution discussed in Sec. 17.4, and most of our models will be of this type. Other important service-time distributions are the *degenerate* distribution (constant service time) and the *Erlang* (gamma) distribution, as illustrated by models in Sec. 17.7.

An Elementary Queueing Process

As we have already suggested, queueing theory has been applied to many different types of waiting-line situations. However, the most prevalent type of situation is the following: A single waiting line (which may be empty at times) forms in the front of a single service facility, within which are stationed one or more servers. Each customer generated by an input source is serviced by one of the servers, perhaps after some waiting in the queue (waiting line). The queueing system involved is depicted in Fig. 17.2.

FIGURE 17.2
An elementary queueing system (each customer is indicated by a C and each server by an S).

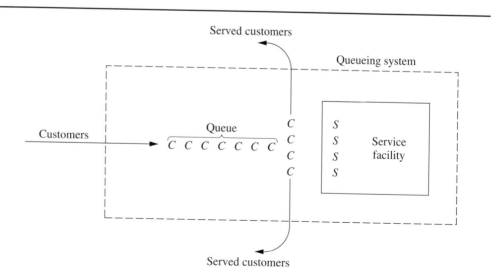

Notice that the queueing process in the illustrative example of Sec. 17.1 is of this type. The input source generates customers in the form of emergency cases requiring medical care. The emergency room is the service facility, and the doctors are the servers.

A server need not be a single individual; it may be a group of persons, e.g., a repair crew that combines forces to perform simultaneously the required service for a customer. Furthermore, servers need not even be people. In many cases, a server can instead be a machine, a vehicle, an electronic device, etc. By the same token, the customers in the waiting line need not be people. For example, they may be items waiting for a certain operation by a given type of machine, or they may be cars waiting in front of a tollbooth.

It is not necessary that there actually be a physical waiting line forming in front of a physical structure that constitutes the service facility. The members of the queue may instead be scattered throughout an area, waiting for a server to come to them, e.g., machines waiting to be repaired. The server or group of servers assigned to a given area constitutes the service facility for that area. Queueing theory still gives the average number waiting, the average waiting time, and so on, because it is irrelevant whether the customers wait together in a group. The only essential requirement for queueing theory to be applicable is that changes in the number of customers waiting for a given service occur just as though the physical situation described in Fig. 17.2 (or a legitimate counterpart) prevailed.

Except for Sec. 17.9, all the queueing models discussed in this chapter are of the elementary type depicted in Fig. 17.2. Many of these models further assume that all *interarrival times* are independent and identically distributed and that all *service times* are independent and identically distributed. Such models conventionally are labeled as follows:

Distribution of service times

$$-/-/- \quad \text{Number of servers}$$

Distribution of interarrival times,

where M = exponential distribution (Markovian), as described in Sec. 17.4,

D = degenerate distribution (constant times), as discussed in Sec. 17.7,

E_k = Erlang distribution (shape parameter = k), as described in Sec. 17.7,

G = general distribution (any arbitrary distribution allowed),[1] as discussed in Sec. 17.7.

For example, the *M/M/s* model discussed in Sec. 17.6 assumes that both interarrival times and service times have an exponential distribution and that the number of servers is s (any positive integer). The *M/G/1* model discussed again in Sec. 17.7 assumes that interarrival times have an exponential distribution, but it places no restriction on what the distribution of service times must be, whereas the number of servers is restricted to be exactly 1. Various other models that fit this labeling scheme also are introduced in Sec. 17.7.

---

[1] When we refer to interarrival times, it is conventional to replace the symbol G by GI = general independent distribution.

Terminology and Notation

Unless otherwise noted, the following standard terminology and notation will be used:

State of system = number of customers in queueing system.

Queue length = number of customers waiting for service to begin

= state of system *minus* number of customers being served.

$N(t)$ = number of customers in queueing system at time t ($t \geq 0$).

$P_n(t)$ = probability of exactly n customers in queueing system at time t, given number at time 0.

s = number of servers (parallel service channels) in queueing system.

λ_n = mean arrival rate (expected number of arrivals per unit time) of new customers when n customers are in system.

μ_n = mean service rate for overall system (expected number of customers completing service per unit time) when n customers are in system. *Note:* μ_n represents *combined* rate at which all *busy* servers (those serving customers) achieve service completions.

λ, μ, ρ = see following paragraph.

When λ_n is a constant for all n, this constant is denoted by λ. When the mean service rate *per busy server* is a constant for all $n \geq 1$, this constant is denoted by μ. (In this case, $\mu_n = s\mu$ when $n \geq s$, that is, when all s servers are busy.) Under these circumstances, $1/\lambda$ and $1/\mu$ are the *expected interarrival time* and the *expected service time,* respectively. Also, $\rho = \lambda/(s\mu)$ is the **utilization factor** for the service facility, i.e., the expected fraction of time the individual servers are busy, because $\lambda/(s\mu)$ represents the fraction of the system's service capacity ($s\mu$) that is being *utilized* on the average by arriving customers (λ).

Certain notation also is required to describe *steady-state* results. When a queueing system has recently begun operation, the state of the system (number of customers in the system) will be greatly affected by the initial state and by the time that has since elapsed. The system is said to be in a **transient condition.** However, after sufficient time has elapsed, the state of the system becomes essentially independent of the initial state and the elapsed time (except under unusual circumstances).[1] The system has now essentially reached a **steady-state condition,** where the probability distribution of the state of the system remains the same (the *steady-state* or *stationary* distribution) over time. Queueing theory has tended to focus largely on the steady-state condition, partially because the transient case is more difficult analytically. (Some transient results exist, but they are generally beyond the technical scope of this book.) The following notation assumes that the system is in a *steady-state condition:*

P_n = probability of exactly n customers in queueing system.

L = expected number of customers in queueing system = $\sum_{n=0}^{\infty} nP_n$.

---

[1] When λ and μ are defined, these unusual circumstances are that $\rho \geq 1$, in which case the state of the system tends to grow continually larger as time goes on.

L_q = expected queue length (excludes customers being served) = $\sum_{n=s}^{\infty} (n - s)P_n$.

$\mathcal{W}$ = waiting time in system (includes service time) for each individual customer.

$W = E(\mathcal{W})$.

$\mathcal{W}_q$ = waiting time in queue (excludes service time) for each individual customer.

$W_q = E(\mathcal{W}_q)$.

Relationships between *L*, *W*, *L_q*, and *W_q*

Assume that λ_n is a constant λ for all n. It has been proved that in a steady-state queueing process,

$$L = \lambda W.$$

(Because John D. C. Little[1] provided the first rigorous proof, this equation sometimes is referred to as **Little's formula.**) Furthermore, the same proof also shows that

$$L_q = \lambda W_q.$$

If the λ_n are not equal, then λ can be replaced in these equations by $\bar{\lambda}$, the *average* arrival rate over the long run. (We shall show later how $\bar{\lambda}$ can be determined for some basic cases.)

Now assume that the mean service time is a constant, $1/\mu$ for all $n \geq 1$. It then follows that

$$W = W_q + \frac{1}{\mu}.$$

These relationships are extremely important because they enable all four of the fundamental quantities—L, W, L_q, and W_q—to be immediately determined as soon as one is found analytically. This situation is fortunate because some of these quantities often are much easier to find than others when a queueing model is solved from basic principles.

17.3   EXAMPLES OF REAL QUEUEING SYSTEMS

Our description of queueing systems in the preceding section may appear relatively abstract and applicable to only rather special practical situations. On the contrary, queueing systems are surprisingly prevalent in a wide variety of contexts. To broaden your horizons on the applicability of queueing theory, we shall briefly mention various examples of real queueing systems.

One important class of queueing systems that we all encounter in our daily lives is **commercial service systems,** where outside customers receive service from commercial organizations. Many of these involve person-to-person service at a fixed location, such as a barber shop (the barbers are the servers), bank teller service, checkout stands at a grocery store, and a cafeteria line (service channels in series). However, many others do not,

[1] J. D. C. Little, "A Proof for the Queueing Formula: $L = \lambda W$," *Operations Research,* **9**(3): 383–387, 1961; also see S. Stidham, Jr., "A Last Word on $L = \lambda W$," *Operations Research,* **22**(2): 417–421, 1974.

such as home appliance repairs (the server travels to the customers), a vending machine (the server is a machine), and a gas station (the cars are the customers).

Another important class is **transportation service systems.** For some of these systems the vehicles are the customers, such as cars waiting at a tollbooth or traffic light (the server), a truck or ship waiting to be loaded or unloaded by a crew (the server), and airplanes waiting to land or take off from a runway (the server). (An unusual example of this kind is a parking lot, where the cars are the customers and the parking spaces are the servers, but there is no queue because arriving customers go elsewhere to park if the lot is full.) In other cases, the vehicles, such as taxicabs, fire trucks, and elevators, are the servers.

In recent years, queueing theory probably has been applied most to **internal service systems,** where the customers receiving service are *internal* to the organization. Examples include materials-handling systems, where materials-handling units (the servers) move loads (the customers); maintenance systems, where maintenance crews (the servers) repair machines (the customers); and inspection stations, where quality control inspectors (the servers) inspect items (the customers). Employee facilities and departments servicing employees also fit into this category. In addition, machines can be viewed as servers whose customers are the jobs being processed. A related example is a computer laboratory, where each computer is viewed as the server.

There is now growing recognition that queueing theory also is applicable to **social service systems.** For example, a judicial system is a queueing network, where the courts are service facilities, the judges (or panels of judges) are the servers, and the cases waiting to be tried are the customers. A legislative system is a similar queueing network, where the customers are the bills waiting to be processed. Various health-care systems also are queueing systems. You already have seen one example in Sec. 17.1 (a hospital emergency room), but you can also view ambulances, x-ray machines, and hospital beds as servers in their own queueing systems. Similarly, families waiting for low- and moderate-income housing, or other social services, can be viewed as customers in a queueing system.

Although these are four broad classes of queueing systems, they still do not exhaust the list. In fact, queueing theory first began early in this century with applications to telephone engineering (the founder of queueing theory, A. K. Erlang, was an employee of the Danish Telephone Company in Copenhagen), and telephone engineering still is an important application. Furthermore, we all have our own personal queues—homework assignments, books to be read, and so forth. However, these examples are sufficient to suggest that queueing systems do indeed pervade many areas of society.

17.4 THE ROLE OF THE EXPONENTIAL DISTRIBUTION

The operating characteristics of queueing systems are determined largely by two statistical properties, namely, the probability distribution of *interarrival times* (see "Input Source" in Sec. 17.2) and the probability distribution of *service times* (see "Service Mechanism" in Sec. 17.2). For real queueing systems, these distributions can take on almost any form. (The only restriction is that negative values cannot occur.) However, to formulate a queueing theory *model* as a representation of the real system, it is necessary to specify the assumed form of each of these distributions. To be useful, the assumed form should be *sufficiently realistic* that the model provides *reasonable predictions* while, at the same time, being *sufficiently simple* that the model is *mathematically tractable*. Based on these considerations, the most important probability distribution in queueing theory is the *exponential distribution*.

Suppose that a random variable T represents either interarrival or service times. (We shall refer to the occurrences marking the end of these times—arrivals or service completions—as *events*.) This random variable is said to have an *exponential distribution with parameter α* if its probability density function is

$$f_T(t) = \begin{cases} \alpha e^{-\alpha t} & \text{for } t \geq 0 \\ 0 & \text{for } t < 0, \end{cases}$$

as shown in Fig. 17.3. In this case, the cumulative probabilities are

$$P\{T \leq t\} = 1 - e^{-\alpha t}$$
$$P\{T > t\} = e^{-\alpha t} \qquad (t \geq 0),$$

and the expected value and variance of T are, respectively,

$$E(T) = \frac{1}{\alpha},$$

$$\text{var}(T) = \frac{1}{\alpha^2}.$$

What are the implications of assuming that T has an exponential distribution for a queueing model? To explore this question, let us examine six key properties of the exponential distribution.

Property 1: $f_T(t)$ is a strictly *decreasing* function of t ($t \geq 0$).

One consequence of Property 1 is that

$$P\{0 \leq T \leq \Delta t\} > P\{t \leq T \leq t + \Delta t\}$$

for any strictly positive values of Δt and t. [This consequence follows from the fact that these probabilities are the area under the $f_T(t)$ curve over the indicated interval of length Δt, and the average height of the curve is less for the second probability than for the first.]

FIGURE 17.3
Probability density function for the exponential distribution.

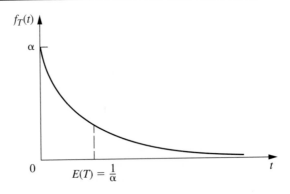

Therefore, it is not only possible but also relatively likely that T will take on a small value near zero. In fact,

$$P\left\{0 \le T \le \frac{1}{2}\frac{1}{\alpha}\right\} = 0.393$$

whereas

$$P\left\{\frac{1}{2}\frac{1}{\alpha} \le T \le \frac{3}{2}\frac{1}{\alpha}\right\} = 0.383,$$

so that the value T takes on is more likely to be "small" [i.e., less than half of $E(T)$] than "near" its expected value [i.e., no further away than half of $E(T)$], even though the second interval is twice as wide as the first.

Is this really a reasonable property for T in a queueing model? If T represents *service times,* the answer depends upon the general nature of the service involved, as discussed next.

If the service required is essentially identical for each customer, with the server always performing the same sequence of service operations, then the actual service times tend to be near the expected service time. Small deviations from the mean may occur, but usually because of only minor variations in the efficiency of the server. A small service time far below the mean is essentially impossible, because a certain minimum time is needed to perform the required service operations even when the server is working at top speed. The exponential distribution clearly does not provide a close approximation to the service-time distribution for this type of situation.

On the other hand, consider the type of situation where the specific tasks required of the server differ among customers. The broad nature of the service may be the same, but the specific type and amount of service differ. For example, this is the case in the County Hospital emergency room problem discussed in Sec. 17.1. The doctors encounter a wide variety of medical problems. In most cases, they can provide the required treatment rather quickly, but an occasional patient requires extensive care. Similarly, bank tellers and grocery store checkout clerks are other servers of this general type, where the required service is often brief but must occasionally be extensive. An exponential service-time distribution would seem quite plausible for this type of service situation.

If T represents *interarrival times,* Property 1 rules out situations where potential customers approaching the queueing system tend to postpone their entry if they see another customer entering ahead of them. On the other hand, it is entirely consistent with the common phenomenon of arrivals occurring "randomly," described by subsequent properties. Thus, when arrival times are plotted on a time line, they sometimes have the appearance of being clustered with occasional large gaps separating clusters, because of the substantial probability of small interarrival times and the small probability of large interarrival times, but such an irregular pattern is all part of true randomness.

Property 2: Lack of memory.

This property can be stated mathematically as

$$P\{T > t + \Delta t \mid T > \Delta t\} = P\{T > t\}$$

for any positive quantities t and Δt. In other words, the probability distribution of the *remaining* time until the event (arrival or service completion) occurs always is the same, regardless of how much time (Δt) already has passed. In effect, the process "forgets" its history. This surprising phenomenon occurs with the exponential distribution because

$$P\{T > t + \Delta t \,|\, T > \Delta t\} = \frac{P\{T > \Delta t, \, T > t + \Delta t\}}{P\{T > \Delta t\}}$$

$$= \frac{P\{T > t + \Delta t\}}{P\{T > \Delta t\}}$$

$$= \frac{e^{-\alpha(t + \Delta t)}}{e^{-\alpha \Delta t}}$$

$$= e^{-\alpha t}$$

$$= P\{T > t\}.$$

For *interarrival times*, this property describes the common situation where the time until the next arrival is completely uninfluenced by when the last arrival occurred. For *service times*, the property is more difficult to interpret. We should not expect it to hold in a situation where the server must perform the same fixed sequence of operations for each customer, because then a long elapsed service should imply that probably little remains to be done. However, in the type of situation where the required service operations differ among customers, the mathematical statement of the property may be quite realistic. For this case, if considerable service has already elapsed for a customer, the only implication may be that this particular customer requires more extensive service than most.

Property 3: The *minimum* of several independent exponential random variables has an exponential distribution.

To state this property mathematically, let $T_1, T_2, \ldots, T_n$ be *independent* exponential random variables with parameters $\alpha_1, \alpha_2, \ldots, \alpha_n$, respectively. Also let U be the random variable that takes on the value equal to the *minimum* of the values actually taken on by $T_1, T_2, \ldots, T_n$; that is,

$U = \min \{T_1, T_2, \ldots, T_n\}.$

Thus, if T_i represents the time until a particular kind of event occurs, then U represents the time until the *first* of the n different events occurs. Now note that for any $t \geq 0$,

$$P\{U > t\} = P\{T_1 > t, T_2 > t, \ldots, T_n > t\}$$
$$= P\{T_1 > t\}P\{T_2 > t\} \cdots P\{T_n > t\}$$
$$= e^{-\alpha_1 t}e^{-\alpha_2 t} \cdots e^{\alpha_n t}$$
$$= \exp\left(-\sum_{i=1}^{n} \alpha_i t\right),$$

so that U indeed has an exponential distribution with parameter

$$\alpha = \sum_{i=1}^{n} \alpha_i.$$

This property has some implications for interarrival times in queueing models. In particular, suppose that there are several (n) *different* types of customers, but the interarrival times for *each* type (type i) have an exponential distribution with parameter α_i ($i = 1$, $2, \ldots, n$). By Property 2, the *remaining* time from any specified instant until the next arrival of a customer of type i has this same distribution. Therefore, let T_i be this remaining time, measured from the instant a customer of *any* type arrives. Property 3 then tells us that U, the interarrival times for the queueing system as a whole, has an exponential distribution with parameter α defined by the last equation. As a result, you can choose to ignore the distinction between customers and still have exponential interarrival times for the queueing model.

However, the implications are even more important for *service times* in multiple-server queueing models than for interarrival times. For example, consider the situation where all the servers have the same exponential service-time distribution with parameter μ. For this case, let n be the number of servers *currently* providing service, and let T_i be the *remaining* service time for server i ($i = 1, 2, \ldots, n$), which also has an exponential distribution with parameter $\alpha_i = \mu$. It then follows that U, the time until the *next* service completion from any of these servers, has an exponential distribution with parameter $\alpha = n\mu$. In effect, the queueing system *currently* is performing just like a *single*-server system where service times have an exponential distribution with parameter $n\mu$. We shall make frequent use of this implication for analyzing multiple-server models later in the chapter.

When using this property, it sometimes is useful to also determine the probabilities for *which* of the exponential random variables will turn out to be the one which has the minimum value. For example, you might want to find the probability that a particular server j will finish serving a customer first among n busy exponential servers. It is fairly straightforward (see Prob. 17.4-10) to show that this probability is proportional to the parameter α_j. In particular, the probability that T_j will turn out to be the smallest of the n random variables is

$$P\{T_j = U\} = \alpha_j \Big/ \sum_{i=1}^{n} \alpha_i, \qquad \text{for } j = 1, 2, \ldots, n.$$

Property 4: Relationship to the Poisson distribution.

Suppose that the *time* between consecutive occurrences of some particular kind of event (e.g., arrivals or service completions by a continuously busy server) has an exponential distribution with parameter α. Property 4 then has to do with the resulting implication about the probability distribution of the *number* of times this kind of event occurs over a specified time. In particular, let $X(t)$ be the number of occurrences by time t ($t \geq 0$), where time 0 designates the instant at which the count begins. The implication is that

$$P\{X(t) = n\} = \frac{(\alpha t)^n e^{-\alpha t}}{n!}, \qquad \text{for } n = 0, 1, 2, \ldots;$$

that is, $X(t)$ has a Poisson distribution with parameter αt. For example, with $n = 0$,

$$P\{X(t) = 0\} = e^{-\alpha t},$$

which is just the probability from the exponential distribution that the *first* event occurs after time t. The mean of this Poisson distribution is

$$E\{X(t)\} = \alpha t,$$

so that the expected number of events *per unit time* is α. Thus, α is said to be the *mean rate* at which the events occur. When the events are counted on a continuing basis, the counting process $\{X(t); t \geq 0\}$ is said to be a **Poisson process** with parameter α (the mean rate).

This property provides useful information about *service completions* when service times have an exponential distribution with parameter μ. We obtain this information by defining $X(t)$ as the number of service completions achieved by a *continuously busy* server in elapsed time t, where $\alpha = \mu$. For *multiple*-server queueing models, $X(t)$ can also be defined as the number of service completions achieved by n continuously busy servers in elapsed time t, where $\alpha = n\mu$.

The property is particularly useful for describing the probabilistic behavior of *arrivals* when interarrival times have an exponential distribution with parameter λ. In this case, $X(t)$ is the *number* of arrivals in elapsed time t, where $\alpha = \lambda$ is the *mean arrival rate*. Therefore, arrivals occur according to a **Poisson input process** with parameter λ. Such queueing models also are described as assuming a *Poisson input*.

Arrivals sometimes are said to occur *randomly*, meaning that they occur in accordance with a Poisson input process. One intuitive interpretation of this phenomenon is that every time period of fixed length has the *same* chance of having an arrival regardless of when the preceding arrival occurred, as suggested by the following property.

Property 5: For all positive values of t, $P\{T \leq t + \Delta t \mid T > t\} \approx \alpha \, \Delta t$, for small Δt.

Continuing to interpret T as the time from the last event of a certain type (arrival or service completion) until the next such event, we suppose that a time t already has elapsed without the event's occurring. We know from Property 2 that the probability that the event will occur within the next time interval of fixed length Δt is a *constant* (identified in the next paragraph), regardless of how large or small t is. Property 5 goes further to say that when the value of Δt is small, this constant probability can be approximated very closely by $\alpha \, \Delta t$. Furthermore, when considering different small values of Δt, this probability is essentially *proportional* to Δt, with proportionality factor α. In fact, α is the *mean rate* at which the events occur (see Property 4), so that the *expected number* of events in the interval of length Δt is *exactly* $\alpha \, \Delta t$. The only reason that the probability of an event's occurring differs slightly from this value is the possibility that *more than one* event will occur, which has negligible probability when Δt is small.

To see why Property 5 holds mathematically, note that the constant value of our probability (for a fixed value of $\Delta t > 0$) is just

$$P\{T \leq t + \Delta t \mid T > t\} = P\{T \leq \Delta t\}$$
$$= 1 - e^{-\alpha \, \Delta t},$$

for any $t \geq 0$. Therefore, because the series expansion of e^x for any exponent x is

$$e^x = 1 + x + \sum_{n=2}^{\infty} \frac{x^n}{n!},$$

it follows that

$$P\{T \leq t + \Delta t \mid T > t\} = 1 - 1 + \alpha \, \Delta t - \sum_{n=2}^{\infty} \frac{(-\alpha \, \Delta t)^n}{n!}$$

$$\approx \alpha \, \Delta t, \qquad \text{for small } \Delta t,^1$$

because the summation terms become relatively negligible for sufficiently small values of $\alpha \, \Delta t$.

Because T can represent either interarrival or service times in queueing models, this property provides a convenient approximation of the probability that the event of interest occurs in the next small interval (Δt) of time. An analysis based on this approximation also can be made exact by taking appropriate limits as $\Delta t \to 0$.

Property 6: Unaffected by aggregation or disaggregation.

This property is relevant primarily for verifying that the *input process* is *Poisson*. Therefore, we shall describe it in these terms, although it also applies directly to the exponential distribution (exponential interarrival times) because of Property 4.

We first consider the aggregation (combining) of several Poisson input processes into one overall input process. In particular, suppose that there are several (n) *different* types of customers, where the customers of each type (type i) arrive according to a *Poisson input process* with parameter λ_i ($i = 1, 2, \ldots, n$). Assuming that these are *independent* Poisson processes, the property says that the *aggregate* input process (arrival of all customers without regard to type) also must be Poisson, with parameter (arrival rate) $\lambda = \lambda_1 + \lambda_2 + \cdots + \lambda_n$. In other words, having a Poisson process is *unaffected by aggregation.*

This part of the property follows directly from Properties 3 and 4. The latter property implies that the interarrival times for customers of type i have an exponential distribution with parameter λ_i. For this identical situation, we already discussed for Property 3 that it implies that the interarrival times for all customers also must have an exponential distribution, with parameter $\lambda = \lambda_1 + \lambda_2 + \cdots + \lambda_n$. Using Property 4 again then implies that the aggregate input process is Poisson.

The second part of Property 6 ("unaffected by disaggregation") refers to the reverse case, where the *aggregate* input process (the one obtained by combining the input processes for several customer types) is known to be Poisson with parameter λ, but the question now concerns the nature of the *disaggregated* input processes (the individual input processes for the individual customer types). Assuming that each arriving customer has a *fixed* probability p_i of being of type i ($i = 1, 2, \ldots, n$), with

$$\lambda_i = p_i \lambda \qquad \text{and} \qquad \sum_{i=1}^{n} p_i = 1,$$

---

[1]More precisely,

$$\lim_{\Delta t \to 0} \frac{P\{T \leq t + \Delta t \mid T > t\}}{\Delta t} = \alpha.$$

the property says that the input process for customers of type i also must be Poisson with parameter λ_i. In other words, having a Poisson process is *unaffected by disaggregation*.

As one example of the usefulness of this second part of the property, consider the following situation. Indistinguishable customers arrive according to a Poisson process with parameter λ. Each arriving customer has a fixed probability p of *balking* (leaving without entering the queueing system), so the probability of entering the system is $1 - p$. Thus, there are two types of customers—those who balk and those who enter the system. The property says that each type arrives according to a Poisson process, with parameters $p\lambda$ and $(1 - p)\lambda$, respectively. Therefore, by using the latter Poisson process, queueing models that assume a Poisson input process can still be used to analyze the performance of the queueing system for those customers who enter the system.

17.5   THE BIRTH-AND-DEATH PROCESS

Most elementary queueing models assume that the inputs (arriving customers) and outputs (leaving customers) of the queueing system occur according to the *birth-and-death process*. This important process in probability theory has applications in various areas. However, in the context of queueing theory, the term **birth** refers to the *arrival* of a new customer into the queueing system, and **death** refers to the *departure* of a served customer. The *state* of the system at time t $(t \geq 0)$, denoted by $N(t)$, is the number of customers in the queueing system at time t. The birth-and-death process describes *probabilistically* how $N(t)$ changes as t increases. Broadly speaking, it says that *individual* births and deaths occur *randomly*, where their mean occurrence rates depend only upon the current state of the system. More precisely, the assumptions of the birth-and-death process are the following:

Assumption 1.   Given $N(t) = n$, the current probability distribution of the *remaining* time until the next *birth* (arrival) is *exponential* with parameter λ_n $(n = 0, 1, 2, \ldots)$.

Assumption 2.   Given $N(t) = n$, the current probability distribution of the *remaining* time until the next *death* (service completion) is *exponential* with parameter μ_n $(n = 1, 2, \ldots)$.

Assumption 3.   The random variable of assumption 1 (the remaining time until the next *birth*) and the random variable of assumption 2 (the remaining time until the next *death*) are mutually independent. The next transition in the state of the process is either

$$n \rightarrow n + 1 \quad \text{(a single birth)}$$

or

$$n \rightarrow n - 1 \quad \text{(a single death)},$$

depending on whether the former or latter random variable is smaller.

Because of these assumptions, the birth-and-death process is a special type of *continuous time Markov chain*. (See Sec. 16.8 for a description of continuous time Markov chains and their properties, including an introduction to the general procedure for finding steady-state probabilities that will be applied in the remainder of this section.) Queueing models that can be represented by a continuous time Markov chain are far more tractable analytically than any other.

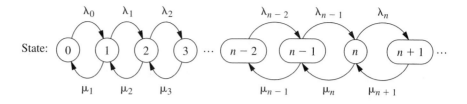

FIGURE 17.4
Rate diagram for the birth-and-death process.

Because Property 4 for the exponential distribution (see Sec. 17.4) implies that the λ_n and μ_n are mean rates, we can summarize these assumptions by the rate diagram shown in Fig. 17.4. The arrows in this diagram show the only possible *transitions* in the state of the system (as specified by assumption 3), and the entry for each arrow gives the mean rate for that transition (as specified by assumptions 1 and 2) when the system is in the state at the base of the arrow.

Except for a few special cases, analysis of the birth-and-death process is very difficult when the system is in a *transient* condition. Some results about the probability distribution of $N(t)$ have been obtained,[1] but they are too complicated to be of much practical use. On the other hand, it is relatively straightforward to derive this distribution *after* the system has reached a *steady-state* condition (assuming that this condition can be reached). This derivation can be done directly from the rate diagram, as outlined next.

Consider any particular state of the system n ($n = 0, 1, 2, \ldots$). Starting at time 0, suppose that a count is made of the number of times that the process enters this state and the number of times it leaves this state, as denoted below:

$E_n(t)$ = number of times that process enters state n by time t.

$L_n(t)$ = number of times that process leaves state n by time t.

Because the two types of events (entering and leaving) must alternate, these two numbers must always either be equal or differ by just 1; that is,

$$\left| E_n(t) - L_n(t) \right| \leq 1.$$

Dividing through both sides by t and then letting $t \to \infty$ gives

$$\left| \frac{E_n(t)}{t} - \frac{L_n(t)}{t} \right| \leq \frac{1}{t}, \qquad \text{so} \qquad \lim_{t \to \infty} \left| \frac{E_n(t)}{t} - \frac{L_n(t)}{t} \right| = 0.$$

Dividing $E_n(t)$ and $L_n(t)$ by t gives the *actual rate* (number of events per unit time) at which these two kinds of events have occurred, and letting $t \to \infty$ then gives the *mean rate* (expected number of events per unit time):

$$\lim_{t \to \infty} \frac{E_n(t)}{t} = \text{mean rate at which process enters state } n.$$

$$\lim_{t \to \infty} \frac{L_n(t)}{t} = \text{mean rate at which process leaves state } n.$$

These results yield the following key principle:

[1] S. Karlin and J. McGregor, "Many Server Queueing Processes with Poisson Input and Exponential Service Times," *Pacific Journal of Mathematics*, **8:** 87–118, 1958.

Rate In = Rate Out Principle.   For any state of the system n ($n = 0, 1, 2, \ldots$), mean entering rate = mean leaving rate.

The equation expressing this principle is called the **balance equation** for state n. After constructing the balance equations for all the states in terms of the *unknown* P_n probabilities, we can solve this system of equations (plus an equation stating that the probabilities must sum to 1) to find these probabilities.

To illustrate a balance equation, consider state 0. The process enter this state *only* from state 1. Thus, the steady-state probability of being in state 1 (P_1) represents the proportion of time that it would be *possible* for the process to enter state 0. Given that the process is in state 1, the mean rate of entering state 0 is μ_1. (In other words, for each cumulative unit of time that the process spends in state 1, the expected number of times that it would leave state 1 to enter state 0 is μ_1.) From any *other* state, this mean rate is 0. Therefore, the overall mean rate at which the process leaves its current state to enter state 0 (the *mean entering rate*) is

$$\mu_1 P_1 + 0(1 - P_1) = \mu_1 P_1.$$

By the same reasoning, the *mean leaving rate* must be $\lambda_0 P_0$, so the balance equation for state 0 is

$$\mu_1 P_1 = \lambda_0 P_0.$$

For every other state there are two possible transitions both into and out of the state. Therefore, each side of the balance equations for these states represents the *sum* of the mean rates for the two transitions involved. Otherwise, the reasoning is just the same as for state 0. These balance equations are summarized in Table 17.1.

Notice that the first balance equation contains two variables for which to solve (P_0 and P_1), the first two equations contain three variables (P_0, P_1, and P_2), and so on, so that there always is one "extra" variable. Therefore, the procedure in solving these equations is to solve in terms of one of the variables, the most convenient one being P_0. Thus, the first equation is used to solve for P_1 in terms of P_0; this result and the second equation are then used to solve for P_2 in terms of P_0; and so forth. At the end, the requirement that the sum of all the probabilities equal 1 can be used to evaluate P_0.

TABLE 17.1 Balance equations for the birth-and-death process

State	Rate In = Rate Out
0	$\mu_1 P_1 = \lambda_0 P_0$
1	$\lambda_0 P_0 + \mu_2 P_2 = (\lambda_1 + \mu_1) P_1$
2	$\lambda_1 P_1 + \mu_3 P_3 = (\lambda_2 + \mu_2) P_2$
$\vdots$	$\vdots$
$n - 1$	$\lambda_{n-2} P_{n-2} + \mu_n P_n = (\lambda_{n-1} + \mu_{n-1}) P_{n-1}$
n	$\lambda_{n-1} P_{n-1} + \mu_{n+1} P_{n+1} = (\lambda_n + \mu_n) P_n$
$\vdots$	$\vdots$

Applying this procedure yields the following results:

State:

0: $\quad P_1 \;=\; \dfrac{\lambda_0}{\mu_1} P_0$

1: $\quad P_2 \;=\; \dfrac{\lambda_1}{\mu_2} P_1 + \dfrac{1}{\mu_2}(\mu_1 P_1 - \lambda_0 P_0) \qquad\qquad = \dfrac{\lambda_1}{\mu_2} P_1 \quad = \dfrac{\lambda_1 \lambda_0}{\mu_2 \mu_1} P_0$

2: $\quad P_3 \;=\; \dfrac{\lambda_2}{\mu_3} P_2 + \dfrac{1}{\mu_3}(\mu_2 P_2 - \lambda_1 P_1) \qquad\qquad = \dfrac{\lambda_2}{\mu_3} P_2 \quad = \dfrac{\lambda_2 \lambda_1 \lambda_0}{\mu_3 \mu_2 \mu_1} P_0$

$\quad\vdots \qquad\qquad \vdots$

$n-1:$ $\quad P_n \;=\; \dfrac{\lambda_{n-1}}{\mu_n} P_{n-1} + \dfrac{1}{\mu_n}(\mu_{n-1}P_{n-1} - \lambda_{n-2}P_{n-2}) = \dfrac{\lambda_{n-1}}{\mu_n} P_{n-1} = \dfrac{\lambda_{n-1}\lambda_{n-2}\cdots\lambda_0}{\mu_n \mu_{n-1} \cdots \mu_1} P_0$

$n:$ $\quad P_{n+1} = \dfrac{\lambda_n}{\mu_{n+1}} P_n + \dfrac{1}{\mu_{n+1}}(\mu_n P_n - \lambda_{n-1}P_{n-1}) \quad = \dfrac{\lambda_n}{\mu_{n+1}} P_n \quad = \dfrac{\lambda_n \lambda_{n-1} \cdots \lambda_0}{\mu_{n+1}\mu_n \cdots \mu_1} P_0$

$\quad\vdots \qquad\qquad \vdots$

To simplify notation, let

$$C_n = \frac{\lambda_{n-1}\lambda_{n-2}\cdots\lambda_0}{\mu_n \mu_{n-1}\cdots \mu_1}, \qquad \text{for } n = 1, 2, \ldots,$$

and then define $C_n = 1$ for $n = 0$. Thus, the steady-state probabilities are

$$P_n = C_n P_0, \qquad \text{for } n = 0, 1, 2, \ldots .$$

The requirement that

$$\sum_{n=0}^{\infty} P_n = 1$$

implies that

$$\left(\sum_{n=0}^{\infty} C_n \right) P_0 = 1,$$

so that

$$P_0 = \left(\sum_{n=0}^{\infty} C_n \right)^{-1}.$$

When a queueing model is based on the birth-and-death process, so the state of the system n represents the number of customers in the queueing system, the key measures of performance for the queueing system (L, L_q, W, and W_q) can be obtained immediately after calculating the P_n from the above formulas. The definitions of L and L_q given in Sec. 17.2 specify that

$$L = \sum_{n=0}^{\infty} nP_n, \qquad L_q = \sum_{n=s}^{\infty} (n - s)P_n.$$

Furthermore, the relationships given at the end of Sec. 17.2 yield

$$W = \frac{L}{\bar{\lambda}}, \qquad W_q = \frac{L_q}{\bar{\lambda}},$$

where $\bar{\lambda}$ is the *average* arrival rate over the long run. Because λ_n is the mean arrival rate while the system is in state n ($n = 0, 1, 2, \ldots$) and P_n is the proportion of time that the system is in this state,

$$\bar{\lambda} = \sum_{n=0}^{\infty} \lambda_n P_n.$$

Several of the expressions just given involve summations with an infinite number of terms. Fortunately, these summations have analytic solutions for a number of interesting special cases,[1] as seen in the next section. Otherwise, they can be approximated by summing a finite number of terms on a computer.

These steady-state results have been derived under the assumption that the λ_n and μ_n parameters have values such that the process actually can *reach* a steady-state condition. This assumption *always* holds if $\lambda_n = 0$ for some value of n greater than the initial state, so that only a finite number of states (those less than this n) are possible. It also *always* holds when λ and μ are defined (see "Terminology and Notation" in Sec. 17.2) and $\rho = \lambda/(s\mu) < 1$. It does *not* hold if $\sum_{n=1}^{\infty} C_n = \infty$.

The following section describes several queueing models that are special cases of the birth-and-death process. Therefore, the general steady-state results just given in boxes will be used over and over again to obtain the specific steady-state results for these models.

17.6   QUEUEING MODELS BASED ON THE BIRTH-AND-DEATH PROCESS

Because each of the mean rates $\lambda_0, \lambda_1, \ldots$ and $\mu_1, \mu_2, \ldots$ for the birth-and-death process can be assigned any nonnegative value, we have great flexibility in modeling a queueing system. Probably the most widely used models in queueing theory are based directly upon

---

[1]These solutions are based on the following known results for the sum of any geometric series:

$$\sum_{n=0}^{N} x^n = \frac{1 - x^{N+1}}{1 - x}, \qquad \text{for any } x \neq 1,$$

$$\sum_{n=0}^{\infty} x^n = \frac{1}{1 - x}, \qquad \text{if } |x| < 1.$$

this process. Because of assumptions 1 and 2 (and Property 4 for the exponential distribution), these models are said to have a **Poisson input** and **exponential service times.** The models differ only in their assumptions about how the λ_n and μ_n change with n. We present four of these models in this section for four important types of queueing systems.

The *M/M/s* Model

As described in Sec. 17.2, the *M/M/s* model assumes that all *interarrival times* are independently and identically distributed according to an exponential distribution (i.e., the input process is Poisson), that all *service times* are independent and identically distributed according to another exponential distribution, and that the number of servers is s (any positive integer). Consequently, this model is just the special case of the birth-and-death process where the queueing system's *mean arrival rate* and *mean service rate per busy server* are constant (λ and μ, respectively) regardless of the state of the system. When the system has just a *single server* ($s = 1$), the implication is that the parameters for the birth-and-death process are $\lambda_n = \lambda$ ($n = 0, 1, 2, \ldots$) and $\mu_n = \mu$ ($n = 1, 2, \ldots$). The resulting rate diagram is shown in Fig. 17.5a.

However, when the system has *multiple servers* ($s > 1$), the μ_n cannot be expressed this simply. Keep in mind that μ_n represents the mean service rate for the *overall* queueing system (i.e., the mean rate at which service completions occur, so that customers leave the system) when there are n customers currently in the system. As mentioned for Property 4 of the exponential distribution (see Sec. 17.4), when the mean service rate per busy server is μ, the overall mean service rate for n busy servers must be $n\mu$. Therefore, $\mu_n = n\mu$ when $n \leq s$, whereas $\mu_n = s\mu$ when $n \geq s$ so that all s servers are busy. The rate diagram for this case is shown in Fig. 17.5b.

When the maximum mean service rate $s\mu$ exceeds the mean arrival rate λ, that is, when

$$\rho = \frac{\lambda}{s\mu} < 1,$$

FIGURE 17.5
Rate diagrams for the *M/M/s* model.

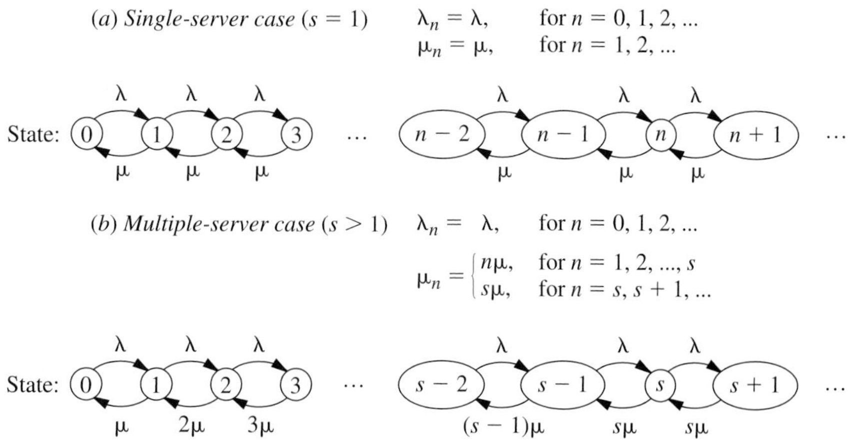

(a) *Single-server case* ($s = 1$) $\lambda_n = \lambda$,   for $n = 0, 1, 2, \ldots$
                                         $\mu_n = \mu$,   for $n = 1, 2, \ldots$

(b) *Multiple-server case* ($s > 1$) $\lambda_n = \lambda$,   for $n = 0, 1, 2, \ldots$

$$\mu_n = \begin{cases} n\mu, & \text{for } n = 1, 2, \ldots, s \\ s\mu, & \text{for } n = s, s+1, \ldots \end{cases}$$

a queueing system fitting this model will eventually reach a steady-state condition. In this situation, the steady-state results derived in Sec. 17.5 for the general birth-and-death process are directly applicable. However, these results simplify considerably for this model and yield closed-form expressions for P_n, L, L_q, and so forth, as shown next.

Results for the Single-Server Case (M/M/1).   For $s = 1$, the C_n factors for the birth-and-death process reduce to

$$C_n = \left(\frac{\lambda}{\mu}\right)^n = \rho^n, \qquad \text{for } n = 0, 1, 2, \ldots$$

Therefore,

$$P_n = \rho^n P_0, \qquad \text{for } n = 0, 1, 2, \ldots,$$

where

$$P_0 = \left(\sum_{n=0}^{\infty} \rho^n\right)^{-1}$$

$$= \left(\frac{1}{1 - \rho}\right)^{-1}$$

$$= 1 - \rho.$$

Thus,

$$P_n = (1 - \rho)\rho^n, \qquad \text{for } n = 0, 1, 2, \ldots.$$

Consequently,

$$L = \sum_{n=0}^{\infty} n(1 - \rho)\rho^n$$

$$= (1 - \rho)\rho \sum_{n=0}^{\infty} \frac{d}{d\rho}(\rho^n)$$

$$= (1 - \rho)\rho \frac{d}{d\rho}\left(\sum_{n=0}^{\infty} \rho^n\right)$$

$$= (1 - \rho)\rho \frac{d}{d\rho}\left(\frac{1}{1 - \rho}\right)$$

$$= \frac{\rho}{1 - \rho} = \frac{\lambda}{\mu - \lambda}.$$

Similarly,

$$L_q = \sum_{n=1}^{\infty} (n - 1)P_n$$

$$= L - 1(1 - P_0)$$

$$= \frac{\lambda^2}{\mu(\mu - \lambda)}.$$

When $\lambda \geq \mu$, so that the mean arrival rate exceeds the mean service rate, the preceding solution "blows up" (because the summation for computing P_0 diverges). For this case, the queue would "explode" and grow without bound. If the queueing system begins operation with no customers present, the server might succeed in keeping up with arriving customers over a short period of time, but this is impossible in the long run. (Even when $\lambda = \mu$, the *expected* number of customers in the queueing system slowly grows without bound over time because, even though a temporary return to no customers present always is possible, the probabilities of huge numbers of customers present become increasingly significant over time.)

Assuming again that $\lambda < \mu$, we now can derive the probability distribution of the *waiting time in the system* (so *including* service time) $\mathcal{W}$ for a random arrival when the queue discipline is first-come-first-served. If this arrival finds n customers already in the system, then the arrival will have to wait through $n + 1$ exponential service times, including his or her own. (For the customer currently being served, recall the lack-of-memory property for the exponential distribution discussed in Sec. 17.4.) Therefore, let $T_1, T_2, \ldots$ be independent service-time random variables having an exponential distribution with parameter μ, and let

$$S_{n+1} = T_1 + T_2 + \cdots + T_{n+1}, \qquad \text{for } n = 0, 1, 2, \ldots,$$

so that S_{n+1} represents the *conditional* waiting time given n customers already in the system. As discussed in Sec. 17.7, S_{n+1} is known to have an *Erlang distribution*.[1] Because the probability that the random arrival will find n customers in the system is P_n, it follows that

$$P\{\mathcal{W} > t\} = \sum_{n=0}^{\infty} P_n P\{S_{n+1} > t\},$$

which reduces after considerable manipulation (see Prob. 17.6-17) to

$$P\{\mathcal{W} > t\} = e^{-\mu(1-\rho)t}, \qquad \text{for } t \geq 0.$$

The surprising conclusion is that $\mathcal{W}$ has an *exponential* distribution with parameter $\mu(1 - \rho)$. Therefore,

$$W = E(\mathcal{W}) = \frac{1}{\mu(1 - \rho)}$$

$$= \frac{1}{\mu - \lambda}.$$

These results *include* service time in the waiting time. In some contexts (e.g., the County Hospital emergency room problem), the more relevant waiting time is just until service begins. Thus, consider the *waiting time in the queue* (so *excluding* service time) $\mathcal{W}_q$ for a random arrival when the queue discipline is first-come-first-served. If this arrival finds no customers already in the system, then the arrival is served immediately, so that

$$P\{\mathcal{W}_q = 0\} = P_0 = 1 - \rho.$$

---

[1] Outside queueing theory, this distribution is known as the *gamma distribution*.

If this arrival finds $n > 0$ customers already there instead, then the arrival has to wait through n exponential service times until his or her own service begins, so that

$$P\{\mathcal{W}_q > t\} = \sum_{n=1}^{\infty} P_n P\{S_n > t\}$$

$$= \sum_{n=1}^{\infty} (1 - \rho)\rho^n P\{S_n > t\}$$

$$= \rho \sum_{n=0}^{\infty} P_n P\{S_{n+1} > t\}$$

$$= \rho P\{\mathcal{W} > t\}$$

$$= \rho e^{-\mu(1-\rho)t}, \qquad \text{for } t \geq 0.$$

Note that Wq does not quite have an exponential distribution, because $P\{\mathcal{W}_q = 0\} > 0$. However, the *conditional* distribution of $\mathcal{W}_q$, given that $\mathcal{W}_q > 0$, does have an exponential distribution with parameter $\mu(1 - \rho)$, just as $\mathcal{W}$ does, because

$$P\{\mathcal{W}_q > t \,|\, \mathcal{W}_q > 0\} = \frac{P\{\mathcal{W}_q > t\}}{P\{\mathcal{W}_q > 0\}} = e^{-\mu(1-\rho)t}, \qquad \text{for } t \geq 0.$$

By deriving the mean of the (unconditional) distribution of $\mathcal{W}_q$ (or applying either $L_q = \lambda W_q$ or $W_q = W - 1/\mu$),

$$W_q = E(\mathcal{W}_q) = \frac{\lambda}{\mu(\mu - \lambda)}.$$

Results for the Multiple-Server Case ($s > 1$).   When $s > 1$, the C_n factors become

$$C_n = \begin{cases} \dfrac{(\lambda/\mu)^n}{n!} & \text{for } n = 1, 2, \ldots, s \\[2ex] \dfrac{(\lambda/\mu)^s}{s!}\left(\dfrac{\lambda}{s\mu}\right)^{n-s} = \dfrac{(\lambda/\mu)^n}{s!\,s^{n-s}} & \text{for } n = s, s+1, \ldots. \end{cases}$$

Consequently, if $\lambda < s\mu$ [so that $\rho = \lambda/(s\mu) < 1$], then

$$P_0 = 1 \bigg/ \left[1 + \sum_{n=1}^{s-1} \frac{(\lambda/\mu)^n}{n!} + \frac{(\lambda/\mu)^s}{s!} \sum_{n=s}^{\infty} \left(\frac{\lambda}{s\mu}\right)^{n-s} \right]$$

$$= 1 \bigg/ \left[\sum_{n=0}^{s-1} \frac{(\lambda/\mu)^n}{n!} + \frac{(\lambda/\mu)^s}{s!} \frac{1}{1 - \lambda/(s\mu)} \right],$$

where the $n = 0$ term in the last summation yields the correct value of 1 because of the convention that $n! = 1$ when $n = 0$. These C_n factors also give

$$P_n = \begin{cases} \dfrac{(\lambda/\mu)^n}{n!} P_0 & \text{if } 0 \leq n \leq s \\[2ex] \dfrac{(\lambda/\mu)^n}{s!\,s^{n-s}} P_0 & \text{if } n \geq s. \end{cases}$$

Furthermore,

$$L_q = \sum_{n=s}^{\infty} (n - s)P_n$$

$$= \sum_{j=0}^{\infty} jP_{s+j}$$

$$= \sum_{j=0}^{\infty} j \frac{(\lambda/\mu)^s}{s!} \rho^j P_0$$

$$= P_0 \frac{(\lambda/\mu)^s}{s!} \rho \sum_{j=0}^{\infty} \frac{d}{d\rho} (\rho^j)$$

$$= P_0 \frac{(\lambda/\mu)^s}{s!} \rho \frac{d}{d\rho} \left(\sum_{j=0}^{\infty} \rho^j \right)$$

$$= P_0 \frac{(\lambda/\mu)^s}{s!} \rho \frac{d}{d\rho} \left(\frac{1}{1 - \rho} \right)$$

$$= \frac{P_0 (\lambda/\mu)^s \rho}{s!(1 - \rho)^2};$$

$$W_q = \frac{L_q}{\lambda};$$

$$W = W_q + \frac{1}{\mu};$$

$$L = \lambda \left(W_q + \frac{1}{\mu} \right) = L_q + \frac{\lambda}{\mu}.$$

Figures 17.6 and 17.7 show how P_0 and L change with ρ for various values of s.

The single-server method for finding the probability distribution of waiting times also can be extended to the multiple-server case. This yields[1] (for $t \geq 0$)

$$P\{\mathcal{W} > t\} = e^{-\mu t} \left[1 + \frac{P_0(\lambda/\mu)^s}{s!(1 - \rho)} \left(\frac{1 - e^{-\mu t(s-1-\lambda/\mu)}}{s - 1 - \lambda/\mu} \right) \right]$$

and

$$P\{\mathcal{W}_q > t\} = (1 - P\{\mathcal{W}_q = 0\})e^{-s\mu(1-\rho)t},$$

where

$$P\{\mathcal{W}_q = 0\} = \sum_{n=0}^{s-1} P_n.$$

The above formulas for the various measures of performance (including the P_n) are relatively imposing for hand calculations. However, this chapter's Excel file in your OR

---

[1] When $s - 1 - \lambda/\mu = 0$, $(1 - e^{-\mu t(s-1-\lambda/\mu)})/(s - 1 - \lambda/\mu)$ should be replaced by μt.

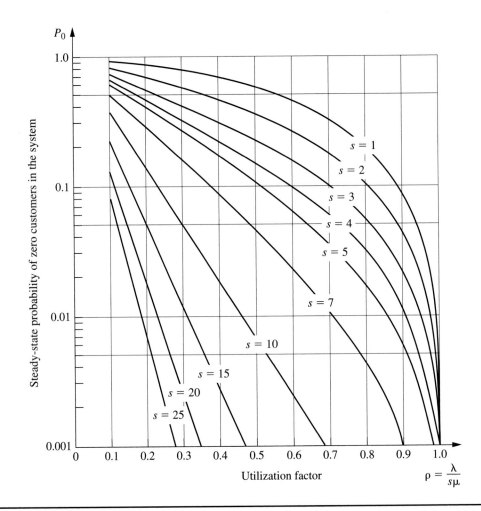

P_0

Steady-state probability of zero customers in the system

$s = 1$
$s = 2$
$s = 3$
$s = 4$
$s = 5$
$s = 7$
$s = 10$
$s = 15$
$s = 20$
$s = 25$

Utilization factor

$\rho = \dfrac{\lambda}{s\mu}$

FIGURE 17.6
Values of P_0 for the *M/M/s*
model (Sec. 17.6).

Courseware includes an Excel template that performs all these calculations simultaneously for any values of t, s, λ, and μ you want, provided that $\lambda < s\mu$.

If $\lambda \geq s\mu$, so that the mean arrival rate exceeds the maximum mean service rate, then the queue grows without bound, so the preceding steady-state solutions are not applicable.

The County Hospital Example with the *M/M/s* Model.   For the County Hospital emergency room problem (see Sec. 17.1), the management engineer has concluded that the emergency cases arrive pretty much at random (a *Poisson input process*), so that interarrival times have an exponential distribution. She also has concluded that the time spent by a doctor treating the cases approximately follows an *exponential distribution*. Therefore, she has chosen the *M/M/s* model for a preliminary study of this queueing system.

By projecting the available data for the early evening shift into next year, she estimates that patients will arrive at an *average* rate of 1 every $\frac{1}{2}$ hour. A doctor re-

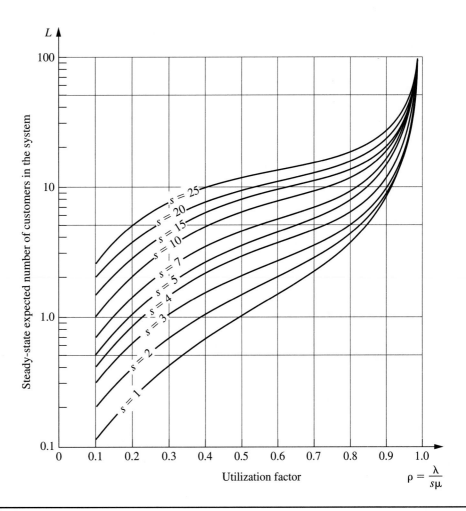

FIGURE 17.7
Values for L for the $M/M/s$ model (Sec. 17.6).

quires an average of 20 minutes to treat each patient. Thus, with one hour as the unit of time,

$$\frac{1}{\lambda} = \frac{1}{2} \text{ hour per customer}$$

and

$$\frac{1}{\mu} = \frac{1}{3} \text{ hour per customer,}$$

so that

$$\lambda = 2 \text{ customers per hour}$$

and

$$\mu = 3 \text{ customers per hour.}$$

The two alternatives being considered are to continue having just one doctor during this shift ($s = 1$) or to add a second doctor ($s = 2$). In both cases,

$$\rho = \frac{\lambda}{s\mu} < 1,$$

so that the system should approach a steady-state condition. (Actually, because λ is somewhat different during other shifts, the system will never truly reach a steady-state condition, but the management engineer feels that steady-state results will provide a good approximation.) Therefore, the preceding equations are used to obtain the results shown in Table 17.2.

On the basis of these results, she tentatively concluded that a single doctor would be inadequate next year for providing the relatively prompt treatment needed in a hospital emergency room. You will see later how she checked this conclusion by applying two other queueing models that provide better representations of the real queueing system in some ways.

TABLE 17.2 Steady-state results from the $M/M/s$ model for the County Hospital problem

	$s = 1$	$s = 2$
ρ	$\frac{2}{3}$	$\frac{1}{3}$
P_0	$\frac{1}{3}$	$\frac{1}{2}$
P_1	$\frac{2}{9}$	$\frac{1}{3}$
P_n for $n \geq 2$	$\frac{1}{3}\left(\frac{2}{3}\right)^n$	$\left(\frac{1}{3}\right)^n$
L_q	$\frac{4}{3}$	$\frac{1}{12}$
L	2	$\frac{3}{4}$
W_q	$\frac{2}{3}$ hour	$\frac{1}{24}$ hour
W	1 hour	$\frac{3}{8}$ hour
$P\{W_q > 0\}$	0.667	0.167
$P\left\{W_q > \frac{1}{2}\right\}$	0.404	0.022
$P\{W_q > 1\}$	0.245	0.003
$P\{W_q > t\}$	$\frac{2}{3}e^{-t}$	$\frac{1}{6}e^{-4t}$
$P\{W > t\}$	e^{-t}	$\frac{1}{2}e^{-3t}(3 - e^{-t})$

The Finite Queue Variation of the *M/M/s* Model
(Called the *M/M/s/K* Model)

We mentioned in the discussion of queues in Sec. 17.2 that queueing systems sometimes have a *finite queue;* i.e., the number of customers in the system is not permitted to exceed some specified number (denoted by K) so the queue capacity is $K - s$. Any customer that arrives while the queue is "full" is refused entry into the system and so leaves forever. From the viewpoint of the birth-and-death process, the mean input rate into the system becomes zero at these times. Therefore, the one modification needed in the *M/M/s* model to introduce a finite queue is to change the λ_n parameters to

$$\lambda_n = \begin{cases} \lambda & \text{for } n = 0, 1, 2, \ldots, K - 1 \\ 0 & \text{for } n \geq K. \end{cases}$$

Because $\lambda_n = 0$ for some values of n, a queueing system that fits this model always will eventually reach a steady-state condition, even when $\rho = \lambda/s\mu \geq 1$.

This model commonly is labeled *M/M/s/K*, where the presence of the fourth symbol distinguishes it from the *M/M/s* model. The single difference in the formulation of these two models is that K is finite for the *M/M/s/K* model and $K = \infty$ for the *M/M/s* model.

The usual physical interpretation for the *M/M/s/K* model is that there is only *limited waiting room* that will accommodate a maximum of K customers in the system. For example, for the County Hospital emergency room problem, this system actually would have a finite queue if there were only K cots for the patients and if the policy were to send arriving patients to another hospital whenever there were no empty cots.

Another possible interpretation is that arriving customers will leave and "take their business elsewhere" whenever they find too many customers (K) ahead of them in the system because they are not willing to incur a long wait. This balking phenomenon is quite common in commercial service systems. However, there are other models available (e.g., see Prob. 17.5-5) that fit this interpretation even better.

The rate diagram for this model is identical to that shown in Fig. 17.5 for the *M/M/s* model, *except* that it stops with state K.

Results for the Single-Server Case (*M/M/1/K*). For this case,

$$C_n = \begin{cases} \left(\dfrac{\lambda}{\mu}\right)^n = \rho^n & \text{for } n = 0, 1, 2, \ldots, K \\ 0 & \text{for } n > K. \end{cases}$$

Therefore, for $\rho \neq 1$,[1]

$$P_0 = \frac{1}{\sum_{n=0}^{K} (\lambda/\mu)^n}$$

$$= 1 \Big/ \left[\frac{1 - (\lambda/\mu)^{K+1}}{1 - \lambda/\mu} \right]$$

$$= \frac{1 - \rho}{1 - \rho^{K+1}},$$

---

[1]If $\rho = 1$, then $P_n = 1/(K + 1)$ for $n = 0, 1, 2, \ldots, K$, so that $L = K/2$.

so that

$$P_n = \frac{1 - \rho}{1 - \rho^{K+1}} \rho^n, \qquad \text{for } n = 0, 1, 2, \ldots, K.$$

Hence,

$$
\begin{aligned}
L &= \sum_{n=0}^{K} nP_n \\
&= \frac{1 - \rho}{1 - \rho^{K+1}} \rho \sum_{n=0}^{K} \frac{d}{d\rho}(\rho^n) \\
&= \frac{1 - \rho}{1 - \rho^{K+1}} \rho \frac{d}{d\rho}\left(\sum_{n=0}^{K} \rho^n\right) \\
&= \frac{1 - \rho}{1 - \rho^{K+1}} \rho \frac{d}{d\rho}\left(\frac{1 - \rho^{K+1}}{1 - \rho}\right) \\
&= \rho \frac{-(K+1)\rho^K + K\rho^{K+1} + 1}{(1 - \rho^{K+1})(1 - \rho)} \\
&= \frac{\rho}{1 - \rho} - \frac{(K+1)\rho^{K+1}}{1 - \rho^{K+1}}.
\end{aligned}
$$

As usual (when $s = 1$),

$$L_q = L - (1 - P_0).$$

Notice that the preceding results do not require that $\lambda < \mu$ (i.e., that $\rho < 1$).

When $\rho < 1$, it can be verified that the second term in the final expression for L converges to 0 as $K \to \infty$, so that *all* the preceding results do indeed converge to the corresponding results given earlier for the $M/M/1$ model.

The waiting-time distributions can be derived by using the same reasoning as for the $M/M/1$ model (see Prob. 17.6-31). However, no simple expressions are obtained in this case, so computer calculations are required. Fortunately, even though $L \neq \lambda W$ and $L_q \neq \lambda W_q$ for the current model because the λ_n are not equal for all n (see the end of Sec. 17.2), the *expected* waiting times for customers entering the system still can be obtained directly from the expressions given at the end of Sec. 17.5:

$$W = \frac{L}{\bar{\lambda}}, \qquad W_q = \frac{L_q}{\bar{\lambda}},$$

where

$$
\begin{aligned}
\bar{\lambda} &= \sum_{n=0}^{\infty} \lambda_n P_n \\
&= \sum_{n=0}^{K-1} \lambda P_n \\
&= \lambda(1 - P_K).
\end{aligned}
$$

Results for the Multiple-Server Case ($s > 1$). Because this model does not allow more than K customers in the system, K is the maximum number of servers that could ever be used. Therefore, assume that $s \leq K$. In this case, C_n becomes

$$
C_n = \begin{cases} \dfrac{(\lambda/\mu)^n}{n!} & \text{for } n = 0, 1, 2, \ldots, s \\[2ex] \dfrac{(\lambda/\mu)^s}{s!}\left(\dfrac{\lambda}{s\mu}\right)^{n-s} = \dfrac{(\lambda/\mu)^n}{s!\,s^{n-s}} & \text{for } n = s, s+1, \ldots, K \\[2ex] 0 & \text{for } n > K. \end{cases}
$$

Hence,

$$
P_n = \begin{cases} \dfrac{(\lambda/\mu)^n}{n!}P_0 & \text{for } n = 1, 2, \ldots, s \\[2ex] \dfrac{(\lambda/\mu)^n}{s!\,s^{n-s}}P_0 & \text{for } n = s, s+1, \ldots, K \\[2ex] 0 & \text{for } n > K, \end{cases}
$$

where

$$
P_0 = 1 \bigg/ \left[\sum_{n=0}^{s} \frac{(\lambda/\mu)^n}{n!} + \frac{(\lambda/\mu)^s}{s!} \sum_{n=s+1}^{K} \left(\frac{\lambda}{s\mu}\right)^{n-s} \right].
$$

Adapting the derivation of L_q for the $M/M/s$ model to this case (see Prob. 17.6-28) yields

$$
L_q = \frac{P_0(\lambda/\mu)^s \rho}{s!(1-\rho)^2}\,[1 - \rho^{K-s} - (K-s)\rho^{K-s}(1-\rho)],
$$

where $\rho = \lambda/(s\mu)$.[1] It can then be shown (see Prob. 17.2-5) that

$$
L = \sum_{n=0}^{s-1} nP_n + L_q + s\left(1 - \sum_{n=0}^{s-1} P_n\right).
$$

And W and W_q are obtained from these quantities just as shown for the single-server case.

This chapter's Excel file includes an Excel template for calculating the above measures of performance (including the P_n) for this model.

One interesting special case of this model is where $K = s$ so the queue capacity is $K - s = 0$. In this case, customers who arrive when all servers are busy will leave immediately and be lost to the system. This would occur, for example, in a telephone network with s trunk lines so callers get a busy signal and hang up when all the trunk lines are busy. This kind of system (a "queueing system" with no queue) is referred to as *Erlang's loss system* because it was first studied in the early 20th century by A. K. Erlang, a Danish telephone engineer who is considered the founder of queueing theory.

---

[1]If $\rho = 1$, it is necessary to apply L'Hôpital's rule twice to this expression for L_q. Otherwise, all these multiple-server results hold for all $\rho > 0$. The reason that this queueing system can reach a steady-state condition even when $\rho \geq 1$ is that $\lambda_n = 0$ for $n \geq K$, so that the number of customers in the system cannot continue to grow indefinitely.

The Finite Calling Population Variation of the *M/M/s* Model

Now assume that the only deviation from the *M/M/s* model is that (as defined in Sec. 17.2) the *input source* is *limited;* i.e., the size of the *calling population* is *finite.* For this case, let N denote the size of the calling population. Thus, when the number of customers in the queueing system is n ($n = 0, 1, 2, \ldots, N$), there are only $N - n$ *potential* customers remaining in the input source.

The most important application of this model has been to the machine repair problem, where one or more maintenance people are assigned the responsibility of maintaining in operational order a certain group of N machines by repairing each one that breaks down. (The example given at the end of Sec. 16.8 illustrates this application when the general procedures for solving any *continuous time Markov chain* are used rather than the specific formulas available for the birth-and-death process.) The maintenance people are considered to be individual servers in the queueing system if they work individually on different machines, whereas the entire crew is considered to be a single server if crew members work together on each machine. The machines constitute the calling population. Each one is considered to be a customer in the queueing system when it is down waiting to be repaired, whereas it is outside the queueing system while it is operational.

Note that each member of the calling population alternates between being *inside* and *outside* the queueing system. Therefore, the analog of the *M/M/s* model that fits this situation assumes that *each* member's *outside time* (i.e., the elapsed time from leaving the system until returning for the next time) has an *exponential distribution* with parameter λ. When n of the members are *inside,* and so $N - n$ members are *outside,* the current probability distribution of the *remaining* time until the next arrival to the queueing system is the distribution of the *minimum* of the *remaining outside times* for the latter $N - n$ members. Properties 2 and 3 for the exponential distribution imply that this distribution must be exponential with parameter $\lambda_n = (N - n)\lambda$. Hence, this model is just the special case of the birth-and-death process that has the rate diagram shown in Fig. 17.8.

FIGURE 17.8
Rate diagrams for the finite calling population variation of the *M/M/s* model.

(*a*) *Single-server case* ($s = 1$)

$$\lambda_n = \begin{cases} (N-n)\lambda, & \text{for } n = 0, 1, 2, \ldots, N \\ 0, & \text{for } n \geq N \end{cases}$$

$$\mu_n = \mu, \quad \text{for } n = 1, 2, \ldots$$

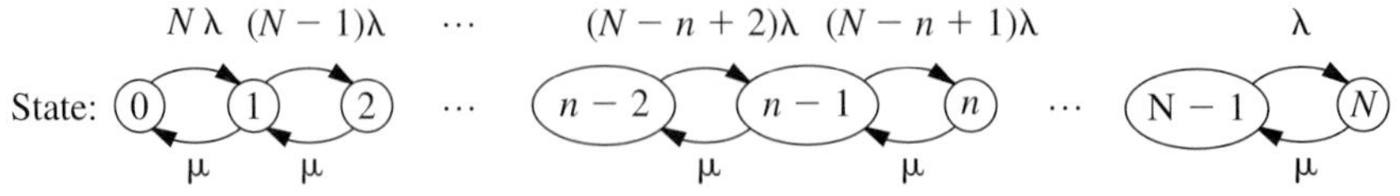

(*b*) *Multiple-server case* ($s > 1$)

$$\lambda_n = \begin{cases} (N-n)\lambda, & \text{for } n = 0, 1, 2, \ldots, N \\ 0, & \text{for } n \geq N \end{cases}$$

$$\mu_n = \begin{cases} n\mu, & \text{for } n = 1, 2, \ldots, s \\ s\mu, & \text{for } n = s, s+1, \ldots \end{cases}$$

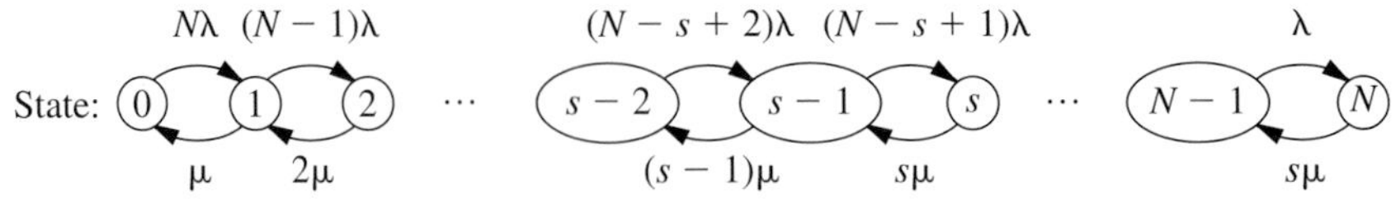

Because $\lambda_n = 0$ for $n = N$, any queueing system that fits this model will eventually reach a steady-state condition. The available steady-state results are summarized as follows:

Results for the Single-Server Case ($s = 1$). When $s = 1$, the C_n factors in Sec. 17.5 reduce to

$$C_n = \begin{cases} N(N-1)\cdots(N-n+1)\left(\dfrac{\lambda}{\mu}\right)^n = \dfrac{N!}{(N-n)!}\left(\dfrac{\lambda}{\mu}\right)^n & \text{for } n \leq N \\ 0 & \text{for } n > N, \end{cases}$$

for this model. Therefore,

$$P_0 = 1 \bigg/ \sum_{n=0}^{N} \left[\frac{N!}{(N-n)!}\left(\frac{\lambda}{\mu}\right)^n \right];$$

$$P_n = \frac{N!}{(N-n)!}\left(\frac{\lambda}{\mu}\right)^n P_0, \qquad \text{if } n = 1, 2, \ldots, N;$$

$$L_q = \sum_{n=1}^{N} (n-1)P_n,$$

which can be reduced to

$$L_q = N - \frac{\lambda + \mu}{\lambda}(1 - P_0);$$

$$L = \sum_{n=0}^{N} nP_n = L_q + 1 - P_0$$

$$= N - \frac{\mu}{\lambda}(1 - P_0).$$

Finally,

$$W = \frac{L}{\bar{\lambda}} \qquad \text{and} \qquad W_q = \frac{L_q}{\bar{\lambda}},$$

where

$$\bar{\lambda} = \sum_{n=0}^{\infty} \lambda_n P_n = \sum_{n=0}^{N} (N-n)\lambda P_n = \lambda(N - L).$$

Results for the Multiple-Server Case ($s > 1$). For $N \geq s > 1$,

$$C_n = \begin{cases} \dfrac{N!}{(N-n)!\,n!}\left(\dfrac{\lambda}{\mu}\right)^n & \text{for } n = 0, 1, 2, \ldots, s \\ \dfrac{N!}{(N-n)!\,s!\,s^{n-s}}\left(\dfrac{\lambda}{\mu}\right)^n & \text{for } n = s, s+1, \ldots, N \\ 0 & \text{for } n > N. \end{cases}$$

Hence,

$$
P_n = \begin{cases}
\dfrac{N!}{(N-n)!\,n!}\left(\dfrac{\lambda}{\mu}\right)^n P_0 & \text{if } 0 \le n \le s \\[3ex]
\dfrac{N!}{(N-n)!\,s!\,s^{n-s}}\left(\dfrac{\lambda}{\mu}\right)^n P_0 & \text{if } s \le n \le N \\[3ex]
0 & \text{if } n > N,
\end{cases}
$$

where

$$
P_0 = 1 \bigg/ \left[\sum_{n=0}^{s-1} \frac{N!}{(N-n)!\,n!}\left(\frac{\lambda}{\mu}\right)^n + \sum_{n=s}^{N} \frac{N!}{(N-n)!\,s!\,s^{n-s}}\left(\frac{\lambda}{\mu}\right)^n \right].
$$

Finally,

$$
L_q = \sum_{n=s}^{N} (n-s)P_n
$$

and

$$
L = \sum_{n=0}^{s-1} nP_n + L_q + s\left(1 - \sum_{n=0}^{s-1} P_n\right),
$$

which then yield W and W_q by the same equations as in the single-server case.

This chapter's Excel file includes an Excel template for performing all the above calculations.

Extensive tables of computational results also are available[1] for this model for both the single-server and multiple-server cases.

For both cases, it has been shown[2] that the preceding formulas for P_n and P_0 (and so for L_q, L, W, and W_q) *also* hold for a generalization of this model. In particular, we can *drop* the assumption that the times spent *outside* the queueing system by the members of the calling population have an *exponential distribution,* even though this takes the model outside the realm of the birth-and-death process. As long as these times are identically distributed with mean $1/\lambda$ (and the assumption of exponential service times still holds), these outside times can have *any* probability distribution!

A Model with State-Dependent Service Rate and/or Arrival Rate

All the models thus far have assumed that the mean service rate is always a constant, regardless of how many customers are in the system. Unfortunately, this rate often is not a constant in real queueing systems, particularly when the servers are people. When there is a large backlog of work (i.e., a long queue), it is quite likely that such servers will tend to work faster than they do when the backlog is small or nonexistent. This increase in the service rate may result merely because the servers increase their efforts when they are under the pressure of a long queue. However, it may also result partly because the quality of the service is compromised or because assistance is obtained on certain service phases.

---

[1] L. G. Peck and R. N. Hazelwood, *Finite Queueing Tables,* Wiley, New York, 1958.

[2] B. D. Bunday and R. E. Scraton, "The G/M/r Machine Interference Model," *European Journal of Operational Research,* **4:** 399–402, 1980.

Given that the mean service rate does increase as the queue size increases, it is desirable to develop a theoretical model that seems to describe the pattern by which it increases. This model not only should be a reasonable approximation of the actual pattern but also should be simple enough to be practical for implementation. One such model is formulated next. (You have the flexibility to formulate many similar models within the framework of the birth-and-death process.) We then show how the same results apply when the arrival rate is affected by the queue size in an analogous way.

Formulation for the Single-Server Case ($s = 1$).   Let

$$\mu_n = n^c \mu_1, \qquad \text{for } n = 1, 2, \ldots,$$

where $n =$ number of customers in system,

$\quad \mu_n =$ mean service rate when n customers are in system,

$\quad 1/\mu_1 =$ expected "normal" service time—expected time to service customer when that customer is only one in system,

$\quad c =$ pressure coefficient—positive constant that indicates degree to which service rate of system is affected by system state.

Thus, by selecting $c = 1$, for example, we hypothesize that the mean service rate is directly proportional to n; $c = \frac{1}{2}$ implies that the mean service rate is proportional to the square root of n; and so on. The preceding queueing models in this section have implicitly assumed that $c = 0$.

Now assume additionally that the queueing system has a Poisson input with $\lambda_n = \lambda$ (for $n = 0, 1, 2, \ldots$) and exponential service times with μ_n as just given. This case is now a special case of the birth-and-death process, where

$$C_n = \frac{(\lambda/\mu_1)^n}{(n!)^c}, \qquad \text{for } n = 0, 1, 2, \ldots.$$

Thus, all the steady-state results given in Sec. 17.5 are applicable to this model. (A steady-state condition always can be reached when $c > 0$.) Unfortunately, analytical expressions are not available for the summations involved. However, nearly exact values of P_0 and L have been tabulated[1] for various values of c and λ/μ_1 by summing a finite number of terms on a computer. A small portion of these results also is shown in Figs. 17.9 and 17.10.

A queueing system may react to a long queue by decreasing the arrival rate instead of increasing the service rate. (The arrival rate may be decreased, e.g., by diverting some of the customers requiring service to another service facility.) The corresponding model for describing mean arrival rates for this case lets

$$\lambda_n = (n + 1)^{-b} \lambda_0, \qquad \text{for } n = 0, 1, 2, \ldots,$$

where b is a constant whose interpretation is analogous to that for c. The C_n values for the birth-and-death process with these λ_n (and with $\mu_n = \mu$ for $n = 1, 2, \ldots$) are *identical* to those just shown (replacing λ by λ_0) for the state-dependent service rate model when $c = b$ and $\lambda/\mu_1 = \lambda_0/\mu$, so the steady-state results also are the same.

---

[1] R. W. Conway and W. L. Maxwell, "A Queueing Model with State Dependent Service Rate," *Journal of Industrial Engineering,* **12:** 132–136, 1961.

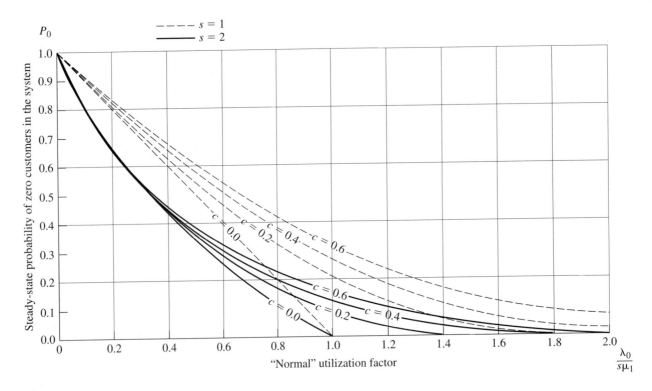

FIGURE 17.9
Values of P_0 for the state-dependent model (Sec. 17.6).

A more general model that combines these two patterns can also be used when both the mean arrival rates and the mean service rates are state-dependent. Thus, let

$$\mu_n = n^a \mu_1 \qquad \text{for } n = 1, 2, \ldots$$

and

$$\lambda_n = (n + 1)^{-b} \lambda_0 \qquad \text{for } n = 0, 1, 2, \ldots.$$

Once again, the C_n values for the birth-and-death process with these parameters are identical to those shown for the state-dependent service rate model when $c = a + b$ and $\lambda/\mu_1 = \lambda_0/\mu_1$, so the tabulated steady-state results actually are applicable to this general model.

Formulation for the Multiple-Server Case ($s > 1$).   To generalize this combined model further to the multiple-server case, it seems natural to have the μ_n and λ_n vary with the number of customers *per server* (n/s) in essentially the same way that they vary with n for the single-server case. Thus, let

$$\mu_n = \begin{cases} n\mu_1 & \text{if } n \leq s \\ \left(\dfrac{n}{s}\right)^a s\mu_1 & \text{if } n \geq s \end{cases}$$

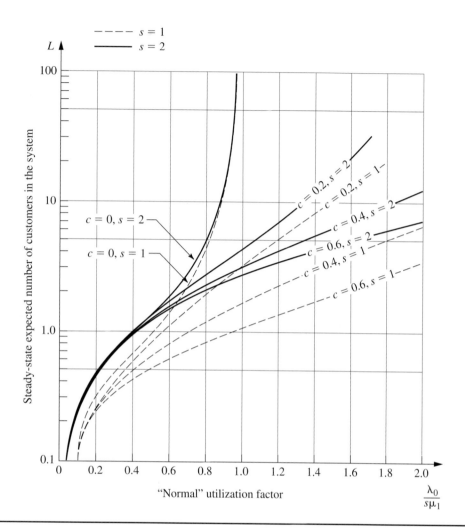

FIGURE 17.10
Values of L for the state-dependent model (Sec. 17.6).

and

$$\lambda_n = \begin{cases} \lambda_0 & \text{if } n \leq s - 1 \\ \left(\dfrac{s}{n+1}\right)^b \lambda_0 & \text{if } n \geq s - 1. \end{cases}$$

Therefore, the birth-and-death process with these parameters has

$$C_n = \begin{cases} \dfrac{(\lambda_0/\mu_1)^n}{n!} & \text{for } n = 0, 1, 2, \ldots, s \\[2ex] \dfrac{(\lambda_0/\mu_1)^n}{s!\,(n!/s!)^c\, s^{(1-c)(n-s)}} & \text{for } n = s, s+1, \ldots, \end{cases}$$

where $c = a + b$.

Computational results for P_0, L_q, and L have been tabulated[1] for various values of c, λ_0/μ_1, and s. Some of these results also are given in Figs. 17.9 and 17.10.

The County Hospital Example with State-Dependent Service Rates. After gathering additional data for the County Hospital emergency room, the management engineer found that the time a doctor spends with a patient tends to decrease as the number of patients waiting increases. Part of the explanation is simply that the doctor works faster, but the main reason is that more of the treatment is turned over to a nurse for completion. The pattern of the μ_n (the mean rate at which a doctor treats patients while there are a total of n patients to be treated in the emergency room) seems to fit reasonably the state-dependent service rate model presented here. Therefore, the management engineer has decided to apply this model.

The new data indicate that the average time a doctor spends treating a patient is 24 minutes if no other patients are waiting, whereas this average becomes 12 minutes when each doctor has six patients (so five are waiting their turn). Thus, with a single doctor on duty,

$$\mu_1 = 2\frac{1}{2} \text{ customers per hour,}$$

$$\mu_6 = 5 \text{ customers per hour.}$$

Therefore, the pressure coefficient c (or a in the general model) must satisfy the relationship

$$\mu_6 = 6^c\mu_1, \qquad \text{so} \qquad 6^c = 2.$$

Using logarithms to solve for c yields $c = 0.4$. Because $\lambda = 2$ from before, this solution for c completes the specification of parameter values for this model.

To compare the two alternatives of having one doctor ($s = 1$) or two doctors ($s = 2$) on duty, the management engineer developed the various measures of performance shown in Table 17.3. The values of P_0, L, and (for $s = 2$) L_q were obtained directly from the tabulated results for this model. (Except for this L_q, you can approximate the same values from Figs. 17.9 and 17.10.) These values were then used to calculate

$$P_1 = C_1 P_0,$$
$$L_q = L - (1 - P_0), \qquad \text{if } s = 1,$$
$$L_q = L - P_1 - 2(1 - P_0 - P_1), \qquad \text{if } s = 2,$$
$$W_q = \frac{L_q}{\lambda}, \qquad W = \frac{L}{\lambda},$$

$$P\{\mathcal{W}_q > 0\} = 1 - \sum_{n=0}^{s-1} P_n.$$

The fact that some of the results in Table 17.3 do not deviate substantially from those in Table 17.2 reinforces the tentative conclusion that a single doctor will be inadequate next year.

---

[1] F. S. Hillier, R. W. Conway, and W. L. Maxwell, "A Multiple Server Queueing Model with State Dependent Service Rate," *Journal of Industrial Engineering,* **15:** 153–157, 1964.

TABLE 17.3 Steady-state results from the state-dependent service rate model for the County Hospital problem

	$s = 1$	$s = 2$
$\dfrac{\lambda}{s\mu_1}$	0.8	0.4
$\dfrac{\lambda}{s\mu_{6s}}$	0.4	0.2
P_0	0.367	0.440
P_1	0.294	0.352
L_q	0.618	0.095
L	1.251	0.864
W_q	0.309 hour	0.048 hour
W	0.626 hour	0.432 hour
$P\{W_q > 0\}$	0.633	0.208

17.7 QUEUEING MODELS INVOLVING NONEXPONENTIAL DISTRIBUTIONS

Because all the queueing theory models in the preceding section (except for one generalization) are based on the birth-and-death process, both their interarrival and service times are required to have *exponential* distributions. As discussed in Sec. 17.4, this type of probability distribution has many convenient properties for queueing theory, but it provides a reasonable fit for only certain kinds of queueing systems. In particular, the assumption of exponential interarrival times implies that arrivals occur randomly (a Poisson input process), which is a reasonable approximation in many situations but *not* when the arrivals are carefully scheduled or regulated. Furthermore, the actual service-time distribution frequently deviates greatly from the exponential form, particularly when the service requirements of the customers are quite similar. Therefore, it is important to have available other queueing models that use alternative distributions.

Unfortunately, the mathematical analysis of queueing models with nonexponential distributions is much more difficult. However, it has been possible to obtain some useful results for a few such models. This analysis is beyond the level of this book, but in this section we shall summarize the models and describe their results.

The *M/G/*1 Model

As introduced in Sec. 17.2, the *M/G/*1 model assumes that the queueing system has a *single server* and a *Poisson input process* (exponential interarrival times) with a *fixed* mean arrival rate λ. As usual, it is assumed that the customers have *independent* service times with the *same* probability distribution. However, no restrictions are imposed on what this service-time distribution can be. In fact, it is only necessary to know (or estimate) the mean $1/\mu$ and variance σ^2 of this distribution.

Any such queueing system can eventually reach a steady-state condition if $\rho = \lambda/\mu < 1$. The readily available steady-state results[1] for this general model are the following:

$$P_0 = 1 - \rho,$$

$$L_q = \frac{\lambda^2\sigma^2 + \rho^2}{2(1 - \rho)},$$

$$L = \rho + L_q,$$

$$W_q = \frac{L_q}{\lambda},$$

$$W = W_q + \frac{1}{\mu}.$$

Considering the complexity involved in analyzing a model that permits *any* service-time distribution, it is remarkable that such a simple formula can be obtained for L_q. This formula is one of the most important results in queueing theory because of its ease of use and the prevalence of *M/G/*1 queueing systems in practice. This equation for L_q (or its counterpart for W_q) commonly is referred to as the **Pollaczek-Khintchine formula,** named after two pioneers in the development of queueing theory who derived the formula independently in the early 1930s.

For any fixed expected service time $1/\mu$, notice that L_q, L, W_q, and W all increase as σ^2 is increased. This result is important because it indicates that the consistency of the server has a major bearing on the performance of the service facility—not just the server's average speed. This key point is illustrated in the next subsection.

When the service-time distribution is exponential, $\sigma^2 = 1/\mu^2$, and the preceding results will reduce to the corresponding results for the *M/M/*1 model given at the beginning of Sec. 17.6.

The complete flexibility in the service-time distribution provided by this model is extremely useful, so it is unfortunate that efforts to derive similar results for the multiple-server case have been unsuccessful. However, some multiple-server results have been obtained for the important special cases described by the following two models. (Excel templates are available in this chapter's Excel file for performing the calculations for both the *M/G/*1 model and the two models considered below when $s = 1$.)

The *M/D/s* Model

When the service consists of essentially the same routine task to be performed for all customers, there tends to be little variation in the service time required. The *M/D/s* model often provides a reasonable representation for this kind of situation, because it assumes that all service times actually equal some fixed *constant* (the *degenerate* service-time distribution) and that we have a *Poisson* input process with a fixed mean arrival rate λ.

---

[1]A recursion formula also is available for calculating the probability distribution of the number of customers in the system; see A. Hordijk and H. C. Tijms, "A Simple Proof of the Equivalence of the Limiting Distribution of the Continuous-Time and the Embedded Process of the Queue Size in the *M/G/*1 Queue," *Statistica Neerlandica,* **36:** 97–100, 1976.

When there is just a single server, the $M/D/1$ model is just the special case of the $M/G/1$ model where $\sigma^2 = 0$, so that the *Pollaczek-Khintchine formula* reduces to

$$L_q = \frac{\rho^2}{2(1 - \rho)},$$

where L, W_q, and W are obtained from L_q as just shown. Notice that these L_q and W_q are exactly *half* as large as those for the exponential service-time case of Sec. 17.6 (the $M/M/1$ model), where $\sigma^2 = 1/\mu^2$, so decreasing σ^2 can *greatly* improve the measures of performance of a queueing system.

For the multiple-server version of this model ($M/D/s$), a complicated method is available[1] for deriving the steady-state probability distribution of the number of customers in the system and its mean [assuming $\rho = \lambda/(s\mu) < 1$]. These results have been tabulated for numerous cases,[2] and the means (L) also are given graphically in Fig. 17.11.

The $M/E_k/s$ Model

The $M/D/s$ model assumes *zero* variation in the service times ($\sigma = 0$), whereas the *exponential* service-time distribution assumes a very large variation ($\sigma = 1/\mu$). Between these two rather extreme cases lies a long middle ground ($0 < \sigma < 1/\mu$), where most *actual* service-time distributions fall. Another kind of theoretical service-time distribution that fills this middle ground is the **Erlang distribution** (named after the founder of queueing theory).

The probability density function for the Erlang distribution is

$$f(t) = \frac{(\mu k)^k}{(k - 1)!}\, t^{k-1} e^{-k\mu t}, \qquad \text{for } t \geq 0,$$

where μ and k are strictly positive parameters of the distribution and k is further restricted to be integer. (Except for this integer restriction and the definition of the parameters, this distribution is *identical* to the *gamma distribution*.) Its mean and standard deviation are

$$\text{Mean} = \frac{1}{\mu}$$

and

$$\text{Standard deviation} = \frac{1}{\sqrt{k}}\frac{1}{\mu}.$$

Thus, k is the parameter that specifies the degree of variability of the service times relative to the mean. It usually is referred to as the *shape parameter.*

The Erlang distribution is a very important distribution in queueing theory for two reasons. To describe the first one, suppose that $T_1, T_2, \ldots, T_k$ are k independent random variables with an identical exponential distribution whose mean is $1/(k\mu)$. Then their sum

$$T = T_1 + T_2 + \cdots + T_k$$

---

[1]See N. U. Prabhu: *Queues and Inventories,* Wiley, New York, 1965, pp. 32–34; also see pp. 286–288 in Selected Reference 3.

[2]F. S. Hillier and O. S. Yu, with D. Avis, L. Fossett, F. Lo, and M. Reiman, *Queueing Tables and Graphs,* Elsevier North-Holland, New York, 1981.

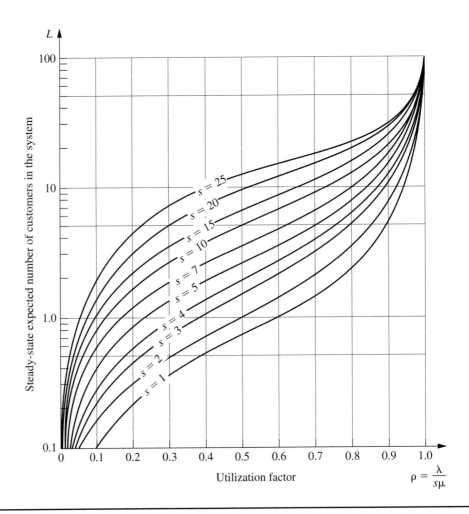

FIGURE 17.11
Values of L for the $M/D/s$
model (Sec. 17.7).

has an *Erlang* distribution with parameters μ and k. The discussion of the exponential distribution in Sec. 17.4 suggested that the time required to perform certain kinds of tasks might well have an exponential distribution. However, the total service required by a customer may involve the server's performing not just one specific task but a sequence of k tasks. If the respective tasks have an identical exponential distribution for their duration, the total service time will have an Erlang distribution. This will be the case, e.g., if the server must perform the *same* exponential task k times for each customer.

The Erlang distribution also is very useful because it is a large (two-parameter) family of distributions permitting only nonnegative values. Hence, empirical service-time distributions can usually be reasonably approximated by an Erlang distribution. In fact, both the *exponential* and the *degenerate* (constant) distributions are special cases of the Erlang distribution, with $k = 1$ and $k = \infty$, respectively. Intermediate values of k provide intermediate distributions with mean $= 1/\mu$, mode $= (k - 1)/(k\mu)$, and variance $= 1/(k\mu^2)$, as

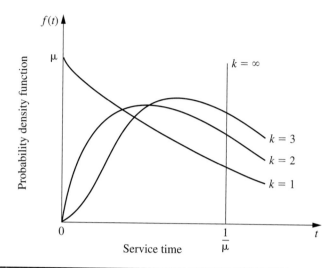

FIGURE 17.12
A family of Erlang distributions with constant mean $1/\mu$.

suggested by Fig. 17.12. Therefore, after estimating the mean and variance of an empirical service-time distribution, these formulas for the mean and variance can be used to choose the integer value of k that matches the estimates most closely.

Now consider the $M/E_k/1$ model, which is just the special case of the $M/G/1$ model where service times have an Erlang distribution with shape parameter $= k$. Applying the Pollaczek-Khintchine formula with $\sigma^2 = 1/(k\mu^2)$ (and the accompanying results given for $M/G/1$) yields

$$L_q = \frac{\lambda^2/(k\mu^2) + \rho^2}{2(1 - \rho)} = \frac{1 + k}{2k} \frac{\lambda^2}{\mu(\mu - \lambda)},$$

$$W_q = \frac{1 + k}{2k} \frac{\lambda}{\mu(\mu - \lambda)},$$

$$W = W_q + \frac{1}{\mu},$$

$$L = \lambda W.$$

With multiple servers ($M/E_k/s$), the relationship of the Erlang distribution to the exponential distribution just described can be exploited to formulate a *modified* birth-and-death process (continuous time Markov chain) in terms of individual exponential service phases (k per customer) rather than complete customers. However, it has not been possible to derive a general steady-state solution [when $\rho = \lambda/(s\mu) < 1$] for the probability distribution of the number of customers in the system as we did in Sec. 17.5. Instead, advanced theory is required to solve individual cases numerically. Once again, these results have been obtained and tabulated for numerous cases.[1] The means (L) also are given graphically in Fig. 17.13 for some cases where $s = 2$.

[1]Ibid.

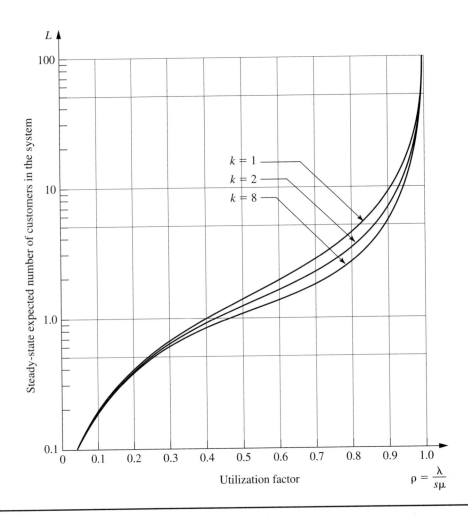

FIGURE 17.13
Values of L for the $M/E_k/2$ model (Sec. 17.7).

In the figure: L (vertical axis), Steady-state expected number of customers in the system; curves labeled $k = 1$, $k = 2$, $k = 8$; Utilization factor (horizontal axis); $\rho = \dfrac{\lambda}{s\mu}$

Models without a Poisson Input

All the queueing models presented thus far have assumed a Poisson input process (exponential interarrival times). However, this assumption is violated if the arrivals are scheduled or regulated in some way that prevents them from occurring randomly, in which case another model is needed.

As long as the service times have an exponential distribution with a fixed parameter, three such models are readily available. These models are obtained by merely *reversing* the assumed distributions of the *interarrival* and *service times* in the preceding three models. Thus, the first new model (*GI/M/s*) imposes no restriction on what the *interarrival time* distribution can be. In this case, there are some steady-state results available[1] (particularly in regard to waiting-time distributions) for both the single-server and multiple-

---

[1]For example, see pp. 248–260 of Selected Reference 3.

server versions of the model, but these results are not nearly as convenient as the simple expressions given for the $M/G/1$ model. The second new model ($D/M/s$) assumes that all interarrival times equal some fixed *constant,* which would represent a queueing system where arrivals are *scheduled* at regular intervals. The third new model ($E_k/M/s$) assumes an *Erlang* interarrival time distribution, which provides a middle ground between *regularly scheduled* (constant) and *completely random* (exponential) arrivals. Extensive computational results have been tabulated[1] for these latter two models, including the values of L given graphically in Figs. 17.14 and 17.15.

If neither the interarrival times nor the service times for a queueing system have an exponential distribution, then there are three additional queueing models for which com-

---

[1]Hillier and Yu, op. cit.

FIGURE 17.14
Values of L for the $D/M/s$ model (Sec. 17.7).

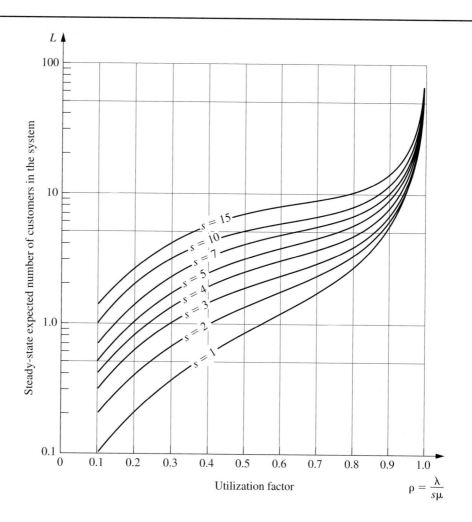

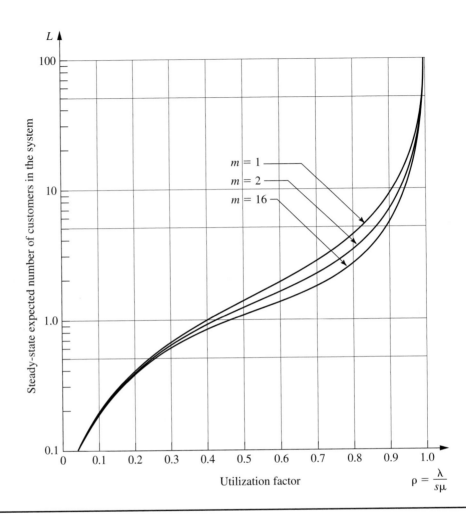

FIGURE 17.15
Values of L for the $E_k/M/2$
model (Sec. 17.7).

putational results also are available.[1] One of these models ($E_m/E_k/s$) assumes an Erlang distribution for both these times. The other two models ($E_k/D/s$ and $D/E_k/s$) assume that one of these times has an Erlang distribution and the other time equals some fixed constant.

Other Models

Although you have seen in this section a large number of queueing models that involve nonexponential distributions, we have far from exhausted the list. For example, another distribution that occasionally is used for either interarrival times or service times is the **hyperexponential distribution.** The key characteristic of this distribution is that even though only nonnegative values are allowed, its standard deviation σ actually is larger than its mean $1/\mu$. This characteristic is in contrast to the Erlang distribution, where $\sigma < 1/\mu$ in every

---

[1]Ibid.

case except $k = 1$ (exponential distribution), which has $\sigma = 1/\mu$. To illustrate a typical situation where $\sigma > 1/\mu$ can occur, we suppose that the service involved in the queueing system is the repair of some kind of machine or vehicle. If many of the repairs turn out to be routine (small service times) but occasional repairs require an extensive overhaul (very large service times), then the standard deviation of service times will tend to be quite large relative to the mean, in which case the hyperexponential distribution may be used to represent the service-time distribution. Specifically, this distribution would assume that there are fixed probabilities, p and $(1 - p)$, for which kind of repair will occur, that the time required for each kind has an exponential distribution, but that the parameters for these two exponential distributions are different. (In general, the hyperexponential distribution is such a composite of two or more exponential distributions.)

Another family of distributions coming into general use consists of **phase-type distributions** (some of which also are called *generalized Erlangian distributions*). These distributions are obtained by breaking down the total time into a number of phases, each having an exponential distribution, where the parameters of these exponential distributions may be different and the phases may be either in series or in parallel (or both). A group of phases being *in parallel* means that the process randomly selects *one* of the phases to go through each time according to specified probabilities. This approach is, in fact, how the hyperexponential distribution is derived, so this distribution is a special case of the phase-type distributions. Another special case is the Erlang distribution, which has the restrictions that all its k phases are in series and that these phases have the *same* parameter for their exponential distributions. Removing these restrictions means that phase-type distributions in general can provide considerably more flexibility than the Erlang distribution in fitting the actual distribution of interarrival times or service times observed in a real queueing system. This flexibility is especially valuable when using the actual distribution directly in the model is not analytically tractable, and the ratio of the *mean* to the *standard deviation* for the actual distribution does not closely match the available ratios ($\sqrt{k}$ for $k = 1, 2, \ldots$) for the Erlang distribution.

Since they are built up from combinations of exponential distributions, queueing models using phase-type distributions still can be represented by a *continuous time Markov chain*. This Markov chain generally will have an infinite number of states, so solving for the steady-state distribution of the state of the system requires solving an infinite system of linear equations that has a relatively complicated structure. Solving such a system is far from a routine thing, but recent theoretical advances have enabled us to solve these queueing models numerically in some cases. An extensive tabulation of these results for models with various phase-type distributions (including the hyperexponential distribution) is available.[1]

17.8 PRIORITY-DISCIPLINE QUEUEING MODELS

In priority-discipline queueing models, the queue discipline is based on a *priority system*. Thus, the order in which members of the queue are selected for service is based on their assigned priorities.

---

[1]L. P. Seelen, H. C. Tijms, and M. H. Van Hoorn, *Tables for Multi-Server Queues*, North-Holland, Amsterdam, 1985.

Many real queueing systems fit these priority-discipline models much more closely than other available models. Rush jobs are taken ahead of other jobs, and important customers may be given precedence over others. Therefore, the use of priority-discipline models often provides a very welcome refinement over the more usual queueing models.

We present two basic priority-discipline models here. Since both models make the same assumptions, except for the nature of the priorities, we first describe the models together and then summarize their results separately.

The Models

Both models assume that there are *N priority classes* (class 1 has the highest priority and class *N* has the lowest) and that whenever a server becomes free to begin serving a new customer from the queue, the one customer selected is that member of the *highest* priority class represented in the queue who has waited longest. In other words, customers are selected to begin service in the order of their priority classes, but on a first-come-first-served basis within each priority class. A *Poisson* input process and *exponential* service times are assumed for each priority class. Except for one special case considered later, the models also make the somewhat restrictive assumption that the expected service time is the *same* for all priority classes. However, the models do permit the mean arrival rate to differ among priority classes.

The distinction between the two models is whether the priorities are *nonpreemptive* or *preemptive*. With **nonpreemptive priorities,** a customer being served cannot be ejected back into the queue (preempted) if a higher-priority customer enters the queueing system. Therefore, once a server has begun serving a customer, the service must be completed without interruption. The first model assumes nonpreemptive priorities.

With **preemptive priorities,** the lowest-priority customer being served is *preempted* (ejected back into the queue) whenever a higher-priority customer enters the queueing system. A server is thereby freed to begin serving the new arrival immediately. (When a server does succeed in *finishing* a service, the next customer to begin receiving service is selected just as described at the beginning of this subsection, so a preempted customer normally will get back into service again and, after enough tries, will eventually finish.) Because of the lack-of-memory property of the exponential distribution (see Sec. 17.4), we do not need to worry about defining the point at which service begins when a preempted customer returns to service; the distribution of the *remaining* service time *always* is the same. (For any other service-time distribution, it becomes important to distinguish between *preemptive-resume* systems, where service for a preempted customer resumes at the point of interruption, and *preemptive-repeat* systems, where service must start at the beginning again.) The second model assumes preemptive priorities.

For both models, if the distinction between customers in different priority classes were ignored, Property 6 for the exponential distribution (see Sec. 17.4) implies that *all* customers would arrive according to a Poisson input process. Furthermore, all customers have the *same* exponential distribution for service times. Consequently, the two models actually are identical to the *M/M/s* model studied in Sec. 17.6 *except* for the order in which customers are served. Therefore, when we count just the *total* number of customers in the system, the steady-state distribution for the *M/M/s* model also applies to both models. Consequently, the formulas for L and L_q also carry over, as do the expected waiting-time results (by Little's formula) W and W_q, for a randomly selected customer. What changes is the *distribution* of waiting times, which was derived in Sec. 17.6 under the assumption of a first-come-first-served queue discipline. With a priority discipline, this distribution has a much larger *variance,* because the waiting times of customers in the highest priority classes tend to be much smaller than those under a first-come-first-served discipline, whereas the waiting times in the lowest priority classes tend to be much larger. By the same token, the breakdown of the total number of customers in the system tends to be disproportionately weighted toward the lower-priority classes. But this condition is just the reason for imposing priorities on the queueing system in the first place. We want to *improve* the *measures of performance* for each of the higher-priority classes at the expense of performance for the lower-priority classes. To determine how much improvement is being made, we need to obtain such measures as *expected waiting time in the system* and *expected number of customers in the system* for the individual priority classes. Expressions for these measures are given next for the two models in turn.

Results for the Nonpreemptive Priorities Model

Let W_k be the steady-state expected waiting time in the system (including service time) for a member of priority class k. Then

$$W_k = \frac{1}{AB_{k-1}B_k} + \frac{1}{\mu}, \qquad \text{for } k = 1, 2, \dots, N,$$

where

$$A = s! \frac{s\mu - \lambda}{r^s} \sum_{j=0}^{s-1} \frac{r^j}{j!} + s\mu,$$

$$B_0 = 1,$$

$$B_k = 1 - \frac{\sum_{i=1}^{k} \lambda_i}{s\mu},$$

s = number of servers,

μ = mean service rate per busy server,

λ_i = mean arrival rate for priority class i,

$$\lambda = \sum_{i=1}^{N} \lambda_i,$$

$$r = \frac{\lambda}{\mu}.$$

(This result assumes that

$$\sum_{i=1}^{k} \lambda_i < s\mu,$$

so that priority class k can reach a steady-state condition.) *Little's formula* still applies to individual priority classes, so L_k, the steady-state expected number of members of priority class k in the queueing system (including those being served), is

$$L_k = \lambda_k W_k, \qquad \text{for } k = 1, 2, \dots, N.$$

To determine the expected waiting time in the queue (excluding service time) for priority class k, merely subtract $1/\mu$ from W_k; the corresponding expected queue length is again obtained by multiplying by λ_k. For the special case where $s = 1$, the expression for A reduces to $A = \mu^2/\lambda$.

An Excel template is provided in your OR Courseware for performing the above calculations.

A Single-Server Variation of the Nonpreemptive Priorities Model

The above assumption that the expected service time $1/\mu$ is the same for all priority classes is a fairly restrictive one. In practice, this assumption sometimes is violated because of differences in the service requirements for the different priority classes.

Fortunately, for the special case of a single server, it is possible to allow different expected service times and still obtain useful results. Let $1/\mu_k$ denote the mean of the exponential service-time distribution for priority class k, so

$$\mu_k = \text{mean service rate for priority class } k, \qquad \text{for } k = 1, 2, \ldots, N.$$

Then the steady-state expected waiting time in the system for a member of priority class k is

$$W_k = \frac{a_k}{b_{k-1}b_k} + \frac{1}{\mu_k}, \qquad \text{for } k = 1, 2, \ldots, N,$$

$$\text{where} \qquad a_k = \sum_{i=1}^{k} \frac{\lambda_i}{\mu_i^2},$$

$$b_0 = 1,$$

$$b_k = 1 - \sum_{i=1}^{k} \frac{\lambda_i}{\mu_i}.$$

This result holds as long as

$$\sum_{i=1}^{k} \frac{\lambda_i}{\mu_i} < 1,$$

which enables priority class k to reach a steady-state condition. Little's formula can be used as described above to obtain the other main measures of performance for each priority class.

Results for the Preemptive Priorities Model

For the preemptive priorities model, we need to reinstate the assumption that the expected service time is the same for all priority classes. Using the same notation as for the original nonpreemptive priorities model, having the preemption changes the *total* expected waiting time in the system (including the total service time) to

$$W_k = \frac{1/\mu}{B_{k-1}B_k}, \qquad \text{for } k = 1, 2, \ldots, N,$$

for the *single-server* case ($s = 1$). When $s > 1$, W_k can be calculated by an iterative procedure that will be illustrated soon by the County Hospital example. The L_k continue to satisfy the relationship

$$L_k = \lambda_k W_k, \qquad \text{for } k = 1, 2, \ldots, N.$$

The corresponding results for the queue (excluding customers in service) also can be obtained from W_k and L_k as just described for the case of nonpreemptive priorities. Because of the lack-of-memory property of the exponential distribution (see Sec. 17.4), preemptions do not affect the service process (occurrence of service completions) in any way. The expected total service time for any customer still is $1/\mu$.

This chapter's Excel file includes an Excel template for calculating the above measures of performance for the single-server case.

The County Hospital Example with Priorities

For the County Hospital emergency room problem, the management engineer has noticed that the patients are not treated on a first-come-first-served basis. Rather, the admitting nurse seems to divide the patients into roughly three categories: (1) *critical* cases, where prompt treatment is vital for survival; (2) *serious* cases, where early treatment is important to prevent further deterioration; and (3) *stable* cases, where treatment can be delayed without adverse medical consequences. Patients are then treated in this order of priority, where those in the same category are normally taken on a first-come-first-served basis. A doctor will interrupt treatment of a patient if a new case in a higher-priority category arrives. Approximately 10 percent of the patients fall into the first category, 30 percent into the second, and 60 percent into the third. Because the more serious cases will be sent to the hospital for further care after receiving emergency treatment, the average treatment time by a doctor in the emergency room actually does not differ greatly among these categories.

The management engineer has decided to use a priority-discipline queueing model as a reasonable representation of this queueing system, where the three categories of patients constitute the three priority classes in the model. Because treatment is interrupted by the arrival of a higher-priority case, the *preemptive priorities model* is the appropriate one. Given the previously available data ($\mu = 3$ and $\lambda = 2$), the preceding percentages yield $\lambda_1 = 0.2$, $\lambda_2 = 0.6$, and $\lambda_3 = 1.2$. Table 17.4 gives the resulting expected waiting times in the queue (so *excluding* treatment time) for the respective priority classes[1] when there is one ($s = 1$) or two ($s = 2$) doctors on duty. (The corresponding results for the nonpreemptive priorities model also are given in Table 17.4 to show the effect of preempting.)

Deriving the Preemptive Priority Results. These preemptive priority results for $s = 2$ were obtained as follows. Because the waiting times for priority class 1 customers are completely unaffected by the presence of customers in the lower-priority classes, W_1 will be the same for any other values of λ_2 and λ_3, including $\lambda_2 = 0$ and $\lambda_3 = 0$. There-

---

[1]Note that these expected times can no longer be interpreted as the expected time before treatment begins when $k > 1$, because treatment may be interrupted at least once, causing additional waiting time before service is completed.

TABLE 17.4 Steady-state results from the priority-discipline models for the County Hospital problem

	Preemptive Priorities		Nonpreemptive Priorities	
	s = 1	s = 2	s = 1	s = 2
A	—	—	4.5	36
B_1	0.933	—	0.933	0.967
B_2	0.733	—	0.733	0.867
B_3	0.333	—	0.333	0.667
$W_1 - \dfrac{1}{\mu}$	0.024 hour	0.00037 hour	0.238 hour	0.029 hour
$W_2 - \dfrac{1}{\mu}$	0.154 hour	0.00793 hour	0.325 hour	0.033 hour
$W_3 - \dfrac{1}{\mu}$	1.033 hours	0.06542 hour	0.889 hour	0.048 hour

fore, W_1 must equal W for the corresponding *one-class* model (the *M/M/s* model in Sec. 17.6) with $s = 2$, $\mu = 3$, and $\lambda = \lambda_1 = 0.2$, which yields

$$W_1 = W = 0.33370 \text{ hour}, \qquad \text{for } \lambda = 0.2$$

so

$$W_1 - \frac{1}{\mu} = 0.33370 - 0.33333 = 0.00037 \text{ hour.}$$

Now consider the first two priority classes. Again note that customers in these classes are completely unaffected by lower-priority classes (just priority class 3 in this case), which can therefore be ignored in the analysis. Let $\overline{W}_{1-2}$ be the expected waiting time in the system (so including service time) of a *random arrival* in *either* of these two classes, so the probability is $\lambda_1/(\lambda_1 + \lambda_2) = \frac{1}{4}$ that this arrival is in class 1 and $\lambda_2/(\lambda_1 + \lambda_2) = \frac{3}{4}$ that it is in class 2. Therefore,

$$\overline{W}_{1-2} = \frac{1}{4}W_1 + \frac{3}{4}W_2.$$

Furthermore, because the *expected* waiting time is the same for *any* queue discipline, $\overline{W}_{1-2}$ must also equal W for the *M/M/s* model in Sec. 17.6, with $s = 2$, $\mu = 3$, and $\lambda = \lambda_1 + \lambda_2 = 0.8$, which yields

$$\overline{W}_{1-2} = W = 0.33937 \text{ hour}, \qquad \text{for } \lambda = 0.8.$$

Combining these facts gives

$$W_2 = \frac{4}{3}\left[0.33937 - \frac{1}{4}(0.33370)\right] = 0.34126 \text{ hour.}$$

$$\left(W_2 - \frac{1}{\mu} = 0.00793 \text{ hour.}\right)$$

Finally, let $\overline{W}_{1-3}$ be the expected waiting time in the system (so including service time) for a *random arrival* in *any* of the three priority classes, so the probabilities are 0.1, 0.3, and 0.6 that it is in classes 1, 2, and 3, respectively. Therefore,

$$\overline{W}_{1-3} = 0.1W_1 + 0.3W_2 + 0.6W_3.$$

Furthermore, $\overline{W}_{1-3}$ must also equal W for the *M/M/s* model in Sec. 17.6, with $s = 2$, $\mu = 3$, and $\lambda = \lambda_1 + \lambda_2 + \lambda_3 = 2$, so that (from Table 17.2)

$$\overline{W}_{1-3} = W = 0.375 \text{ hour}, \qquad \text{for } \lambda = 2.$$

Consequently,

$$W_3 = \frac{1}{0.6} [0.375 - 0.1(0.33370) - 0.3(0.34126)]$$

$$= 0.39875 \text{ hour}.$$

$$\left(W_3 - \frac{1}{\mu} = 0.06542 \text{ hour.} \right)$$

The corresponding W_q results for the *M/M/s* model in Sec. 17.6 also could have been used in exactly the same way to derive the $W_k - 1/\mu$ quantities directly.

Conclusions. When $s = 1$, the $W_k - 1/\mu$ values in Table 17.4 for the preemptive priorities case indicate that providing just a single doctor would cause critical cases to wait about $1\frac{1}{2}$ minutes (0.024 hour) on the average, serious cases to wait more than 9 minutes, and stable cases to wait more than 1 hour. (Contrast these results with the average wait of $W_q = \frac{2}{3}$ hour for all patients that was obtained in Table 17.2 under the first-come-first-served queue discipline.) However, these values represent *statistical expectations,* so some patients have to wait considerably longer than the average for their priority class. This wait would not be tolerable for the critical and serious cases, where a few minutes can be vital. By contrast, the $s = 2$ results in Table 17.4 (preemptive priorities case) indicate that adding a second doctor would virtually eliminate waiting for all but the stable cases. Therefore, the management engineer recommended that there be two doctors on duty in the emergency room during the early evening hours next year. The board of directors for County Hospital adopted this recommendation and simultaneously raised the charge for using the emergency room!

17.9 QUEUEING NETWORKS

Thus far we have considered only queueing systems that have a *single* service facility with one or more servers. However, queueing systems encountered in OR studies are sometimes actually *queueing networks,* i.e., networks of service facilities where customers must receive service at some of or all these facilities. For example, orders being processed through a job shop must be routed through a sequence of machine groups (service facilities). It is therefore necessary to study the entire network to obtain such information as the expected total waiting time, expected number of customers in the entire system, and so forth.

Because of the importance of queueing networks, research into this area has been very active. However, this is a difficult area, so we limit ourselves to a brief introduction.

One result is of such fundamental importance for queueing networks that this finding and its implications warrant special attention here. This fundamental result is the following *equivalence property* for the *input process* of arriving customers and the *output process* of departing customers for certain queueing systems.

> **Equivalence property:** Assume that a service facility with s servers and an infinite queue has a Poisson input with parameter λ and the same exponential service-time distribution with parameter μ for each server (the *M/M/s* model), where $s\mu > \lambda$. Then the steady-state *output* of this service facility is also a Poisson process[1] with parameter λ.

Notice that this property makes no assumption about the type of queue discipline used. Whether it is first-come-first-served, random, or even a priority discipline as in Sec. 17.8, the served customers will leave the service facility according to a Poisson process. The crucial implication of this fact for queueing networks is that if these customers must then go to another service facility for further service, this second facility *also* will have a Poisson input. With an exponential service-time distribution, the equivalence property will hold for this facility as well, which can then provide a Poisson input for a third facility, etc. We discuss the consequences for two basic kinds of networks next.

Infinite Queues in Series

Suppose that customers must all receive service at a *series* of m service facilities in a fixed sequence. Assume that each facility has an infinite queue (no limitation on the number of customers allowed in the queue), so that the series of facilities form a system of *infinite queues in series*. Assume further that the customers arrive at the first facility according to a Poisson process with parameter λ and that each facility i ($i = 1, 2, \ldots, m$) has an exponential service-time distribution with parameter μ_i for its s_i servers, where $s_i\mu_i > \lambda$. It then follows from the equivalence property that (under steady-state conditions) each service facility has a Poisson input with parameter λ. Therefore, the elementary *M/M/s* model of Sec. 17.6 (or its priority-discipline counterparts in Sec. 17.8) can be used to analyze each service facility independently of the others!

Being able to use the *M/M/s* model to obtain all measures of performance for each facility independently, rather than analyzing interactions between facilities, is a tremendous simplification. For example, the probability of having n customers at a given facility is given by the formula for P_n in Sec. 17.6 for the *M/M/s* model. The *joint probability* of n_1 customers at facility 1, n_2 customers at facility 2, $\ldots$, then, is the *product* of the individual probabilities obtained in this simple way. In particular, this joint probability can be expressed as

$$P\{(N_1, N_2, \ldots, N_m) = (n_1, n_2, \ldots, n_m)\} = P_{n_1}P_{n_2}\cdots P_{n_m}.$$

(This simple form for the solution is called the **product form solution.**) Similarly, the expected total waiting time and the expected number of customers in the entire system can be obtained by merely summing the corresponding quantities obtained at the respective facilities.

---

[1] For a proof, see P. J. Burke: "The Output of a Queueing System," *Operations Research,* **4**(6): 699–704, 1956.

Unfortunately, the equivalence property and its implications do not hold for the case of *finite* queues discussed in Sec. 17.6. This case is actually quite important in practice, because there is often a definite limitation on the queue length in front of service facilities in networks. For example, only a small amount of buffer storage space is typically provided in front of each facility (station) in a production-line system. For such systems of finite queues in series, no simple product form solution is available. The facilities must be analyzed jointly instead, and only limited results have been obtained.

Jackson Networks

Systems of infinite queues in series are not the only queueing networks where the *M/M/s* model can be used to analyze each service facility independently of the others. Another prominent kind of network with this property (a product form solution) is the *Jackson network,* named after the individual who first characterized the network and showed that this property holds.[1]

The characteristics of a Jackson network are the same as assumed above for the system of infinite queues in series, except now the customers visit the facilities in different orders (and may not visit them all). For each facility, its arriving customers come from *both* outside the system (according to a Poisson process) and the other facilities. These characteristics are summarized below.

A **Jackson network** is a system of m service facilities where facility i ($i = 1, 2, \ldots, m$) has

1. An infinite queue
2. Customers arriving from outside the system according to a Poisson input process with parameter a_i
3. s_i servers with an exponential service-time distribution with parameter μ_i.

A customer leaving facility i is routed next to facility j ($j = 1, 2, \ldots, m$) with probability p_{ij} or departs the system with probability

$$q_i = 1 - \sum_{j=1}^{m} p_{ij}.$$

Any such network has the following key property.

Under steady-state conditions, each facility j ($j = 1, 2, \ldots, m$) in a Jackson network behaves as if it were an *independent M/M/s* queueing system with arrival rate

$$\lambda_j = a_j + \sum_{i=1}^{m} \lambda_i p_{ij},$$

where $s_j \mu_j > \lambda_j$.

This key property cannot be *proved* directly from the equivalence property this time (the reasoning would become circular), but its *intuitive underpinning* is still provided by the latter property. The intuitive viewpoint (not quite technically correct) is that, for each facility i, its input processes from the various sources (outside and other facilities) are *independent Poisson processes,* so the *aggregate* input process is Poisson with parameter λ_i (Prop-

---

[1] See J. R. Jackson, "Jobshop-Like Queueing Systems," *Management Science,* **10**(1): 131–142, 1963.

erty 6 in Sec. 17.4). The equivalence property then says that the *aggregate output* process for facility i must be Poisson with parameter λ_i. By disaggregating this output process (Property 6 again), the process for customers going from facility i to facility j must be Poisson with parameter $\lambda_i p_{ij}$. This process becomes one of the Poisson *input* processes for facility j, thereby helping to maintain the series of Poisson processes in the overall system.

The equation given for obtaining λ_j is based on the fact that λ_i is the *departure rate* as well as the arrival rate for all customers using facility i. Because p_{ij} is the proportion of customers departing from facility i who go next to facility j, the rate at which customers from facility i arrive at facility j is $\lambda_i p_{ij}$. Summing this product over all i, and then adding this sum to a_j, gives the *total arrival rate* to facility j from all sources.

To calculate λ_j from this equation requires knowing the λ_i for $i \neq j$, but these λ_i also are unknowns given by the corresponding equations. Therefore, the procedure is to solve *simultaneously* for $\lambda_1, \lambda_2, \ldots, \lambda_m$ by obtaining the simultaneous solution of the entire system of linear equations for λ_j for $j = 1, 2, \ldots, m$. Your OR Courseware includes an Excel template for solving for the λ_j in this way.

To illustrate these calculations, consider a Jackson network with three service facilities that have the parameters shown in Table 17.5. Plugging into the formula for λ_j for $j = 1, 2, 3$, we obtain

$$\begin{aligned}
\lambda_1 &= 1 && + 0.1\lambda_2 + 0.4\lambda_3 \\
\lambda_2 &= 4 + 0.6\lambda_1 && + 0.4\lambda_3 \\
\lambda_3 &= 3 + 0.3\lambda_1 + 0.3\lambda_2.
\end{aligned}$$

(Reason through each equation to see why it gives the total arrival rate to the corresponding facility.) The simultaneous solution for this system is

$$\lambda_1 = 5, \qquad \lambda_2 = 10, \qquad \lambda_3 = 7\frac{1}{2}.$$

Given this simultaneous solution, each of the three service facilities now can be analyzed *independently* by using the formulas for the *M/M/s* model given in Sec. 17.6. For example, to obtain the distribution of the number of customers $N_i = n_i$ at facility i, note that

$$\rho_i = \frac{\lambda_i}{s_i \mu_i} = \begin{cases} \dfrac{1}{2} & \text{for } i = 1 \\[2mm] \dfrac{1}{2} & \text{for } i = 2 \\[2mm] \dfrac{3}{4} & \text{for } i = 3. \end{cases}$$

TABLE 17.5 Data for the example of a Jackson network

Facility j	s_j	μ_j	a_j	p_{ij} $i = 1$	$i = 2$	$i = 3$
$j = 1$	1	10	1	0	0.1	0.4
$j = 2$	2	10	4	0.6	0	0.4
$j = 3$	1	10	3	0.3	0.3	0

Plugging these values (and the parameters in Table 17.5) into the formula for P_n gives

$$P_{n_1} = \frac{1}{2}\left(\frac{1}{2}\right)^{n_1} \qquad \text{for facility 1,}$$

$$P_{n_2} = \begin{cases} \dfrac{1}{3} & \text{for } n_2 = 0 \\[2mm] \dfrac{1}{3} & \text{for } n_2 = 1 \qquad \text{for facility 2,} \\[2mm] \dfrac{1}{3}\left(\dfrac{1}{2}\right)^{n_2-1} & \text{for } n_2 \geq 2 \end{cases}$$

$$P_{n_3} = \frac{1}{4}\left(\frac{3}{4}\right)^{n_3} \qquad \text{for facility 3.}$$

The *joint probability* of (n_1, n_2, n_3) then is given simply by the product form solution

$$P\{(N_1, N_2, N_3) = (n_1, n_2, n_3)\} = P_{n_1}P_{n_2}P_{n_3}.$$

In a similar manner, the expected number of customers L_i at facility i can be calculated from Sec. 17.6 as

$$L_1 = 1, \qquad L_2 = \frac{4}{3}, \qquad L_3 = 3.$$

The expected *total* number of customers in the entire system then is

$$L = L_1 + L_2 + L_3 = 5\frac{1}{3}.$$

Obtaining W, the expected *total* waiting time in the system (including service times) for a customer, is a little trickier. You cannot simply add the expected waiting times at the respective facilities, because a customer does not necessarily visit each facility exactly once. However, Little's formula can still be used, where the system arrival rate λ is the sum of the arrival rates *from outside* to the facilities, $\lambda = a_1 + a_2 + a_3 = 8$. Thus,

$$W = \frac{L}{a_1 + a_2 + a_3} = \frac{2}{3}.$$

In conclusion, we should point out that there do exist other (more complicated) kinds of queueing networks where the individual service facilities can be analyzed independently from the others. In fact, finding queueing networks with a product form solution has been the Holy Grail for research on queueing networks. Two sources of additional information are Selected References 6 and 7.

17.10 CONCLUSIONS

Queueing systems are prevalent throughout society. The adequacy of these systems can have an important effect on the quality of life and productivity.

Queueing theory studies queueing systems by formulating mathematical models of their operation and then using these models to derive measures of performance. This analysis provides vital information for effectively designing queueing systems that achieve an appropriate balance between the cost of providing a service and the cost associated with waiting for that service.

This chapter presented the most basic models of queueing theory for which particularly useful results are available. However, many other interesting models could be considered if space permitted. In fact, several thousand research papers formulating and/or analyzing queueing models have already appeared in the technical literature, and many more are being published each year!

The *exponential distribution* plays a fundamental role in queueing theory for representing the distribution of interarrival and service times, because this assumption enables us to represent the queueing system as a *continuous time Markov chain.* For the same reason, *phase-type distributions* such as the *Erlang distribution,* where the total time is broken down into individual phases having an exponential distribution, are very useful. Useful analytical results have been obtained for only a relatively few queueing models making other assumptions.

Priority-discipline queueing models are useful for the common situation where some categories of customers are given priority over others for receiving service.

In another common situation, customers must receive service at several different service facilities. Models for queueing networks are gaining widespread use for such situations. This is an area of especially active ongoing research.

When no tractable model that provides a reasonable representation of the queueing system under study is available, a common approach is to obtain relevant performance data by developing a computer program for simulating the operation of the system. This technique is discussed in Chap. 22.

Chapter 18 describes how queueing theory can be used to help design effective queueing systems.

SELECTED REFERENCES

1. Cooper, R. B.: *Introduction to Queueing Theory,* 2d ed., Elsevier North-Holland, New York, 1981. (Also distributed by the George Washington University Continuing Engineering Education Program, Washington, DC.)
2. Cooper, R. B.: "Queueing Theory," Chap. 10 in D. P. Heyman and M. J. Soble (eds.), *Stochastic Models,* North Holland, Amsterdam and New York, 1990. (This survey paper also is distributed by the George Washington University Continuing Engineering Education Program, Washington, DC.)
3. Gross, D., and C. M. Harris: *Fundamentals of Queueing Theory,* 3d ed., Wiley, New York, 1998.
4. Kleinrock, L.: *Queueing Systems, Vol. I: Theory,* Wiley, New York, 1975.
5. Prabhu, N. U.: *Foundations of Queueing Theory,* Kluwer Academic Publishers, Boston, 1997.
6. van Dijk, N. M.: *Queueing Networks and Product Forms: A Systems Approach,* Wiley, New York, 1993.
7. Walrand, J.: *An Introduction to Queueing Networks,* Prentice-Hall, Englewood Cliffs, NJ, 1988.
8. Wolff, R. W.: *Stochastic Modeling and the Theory of Queues,* Prentice-Hall, Englewood Cliffs, NJ, 1989.

LEARNING AIDS FOR THIS CHAPTER IN YOUR OR COURSEWARE

"Ch. 17—Queueing Theory" Excel File:

Template for *M/M/s* Model
Template for Finite Queue Variation of *M/M/s* Model

Template for Finite Calling Population Variation of $M/M/s$ Model
Template for $M/G/1$ Model
Template for $M/D/1$ Model
Template for $M/E_k/1$ Model
Template for Nonpreemptive Priorities Model
Template for Preemptive Priorities Model
Template for a Jackson Network

"Ch. 17—Queueing Theory" LINGO File for Selected Examples

See Appendix 1 for documentation of the software.

PROBLEMS[1]

To the left of each of the following problems (or their parts), we have inserted a T whenever one of the templates listed above can be helpful. An asterisk on the problem number indicates that at least a partial answer is given in the back of the book.

17.2-1.* Consider a typical barber shop. Demonstrate that it is a queueing system by describing its components.

17.2-2.* Newell and Jeff are the two barbers in a barber shop they own and operate. They provide two chairs for customers who are waiting to begin a haircut, so the number of customers in the shop varies between 0 and 4. For $n = 0, 1, 2, 3, 4$, the probability P_n that exactly n customers are in the shop is $P_0 = \frac{1}{16}$, $P_1 = \frac{4}{16}$, $P_2 = \frac{6}{16}$, $P_3 = \frac{4}{16}$, $P_4 = \frac{1}{16}$.
(a) Calculate L. How would you describe the meaning of L to Newell and Jeff?
(b) For each of the possible values of the number of customers in the queueing system, specify how many customers are in the queue. Then calculate L_q. How would you describe the meaning of L_q to Newell and Jeff?
(c) Determine the expected number of customers being served.
(d) Given that an average of 4 customers per hour arrive and stay to receive a haircut, determine W and W_q. Describe these two quantities in terms meaningful to Newell and Jeff.
(e) Given that Newell and Jeff are equally fast in giving haircuts, what is the average duration of a haircut?

17.2-3. Mom-and-Pop's Grocery Store has a small adjacent parking lot with three parking spaces reserved for the store's customers. During store hours, cars enter the lot and use one of the spaces at a mean rate of 2 per hour. For $n = 0, 1, 2, 3$, the probability P_n that exactly n spaces currently are being used is $P_0 = 0.2$, $P_1 = 0.3$, $P_2 = 0.3$, $P_3 = 0.2$.

$\lambda = 2/hr$

(a) Describe how this parking lot can be interpreted as being a queueing system. In particular, identify the customers and the servers. What is the service being provided? What constitutes a service time? What is the queue capacity?
(b) Determine the basic measures of performance—L, L_q, W, and W_q—for this queueing system.
(c) Use the results from part (b) to determine the average length of time that a car remains in a parking space.

17.2-4. For each of the following statements about the queue in a queueing system, label the statement as true or false and then justify your answer by referring to a specific statement in the chapter.
(a) The queue is where customers wait in the queueing system until their service is completed.
(b) Queueing models conventionally assume that the queue can hold only a limited number of customers.
(c) The most common queue discipline is first-come-first-served.

17.2-5. Midtown Bank always has two tellers on duty. Customers arrive to receive service from a teller at a mean rate of 40 per hour. A teller requires an average of 2 minutes to serve a customer. When both tellers are busy, an arriving customer joins a single line to wait for service. Experience has shown that customers wait in line an average of 1 minute before service begins.
(a) Describe why this is a queueing system.
(b) Determine the basic measures of performance—W_q, W, L_q, and L—for this queueing system. (*Hint:* We don't know the probability distributions of interarrival times and service times for this queueing system, so you will need to use the relationships between these measures of performance to help answer the question.)

---

[1]See also the end of Chap. 18 for problems involving the application of queueing theory.

17.2-6. Explain why the utilization factor ρ for the server in a single-server queueing system must equal $1 - P_0$, where P_0 is the probability of having 0 customers in the system.

17.2-7. You are given two queueing systems, Q_1 and Q_2. The mean arrival rate, the mean service rate per busy server, and the steady-state expected number of customers for Q_2 are twice the corresponding values for Q_1. Let W_i = the steady-state expected waiting time in the system for Q_i, for $i = 1$, 2. Determine W_2/W_1.

17.2-8. Consider a single-server queueing system with *any* service-time distribution and *any* distribution of interarrival times (the *GI/G/1* model). Use only basic definitions and the relationships given in Sec. 17.2 to verify the following general relationships:
(a) $L = L_q + (1 - P_0)$.
(b) $L = L_q + \rho$.
(c) $P_0 = 1 - \rho$.

17.2-9. Show that

$$L = \sum_{n=0}^{s-1} nP_n + L_q + s\left(1 - \sum_{n=0}^{s-1} P_n\right)$$

by using the statistical definitions of L and L_q in terms of the P_n.

17.3-1. Identify the customers and the servers in the queueing system in each of the following situations:
(a) The checkout stand in a grocery store.
(b) A fire station.
(c) The toll booth for a bridge.
(d) A bicycle repair shop.
(e) A shipping dock.
(f) A group of semiautomatic machines assigned to one operator.
(g) The materials-handling equipment in a factory area.
(h) A plumbing shop.
(i) A job shop producing custom orders.
(j) A secretarial typing pool.

17.4-1. Suppose that a queueing system has two servers, an exponential interarrival time distribution with a mean of 2 hours, and an exponential service-time distribution with a mean of 2 hours for each server. Furthermore, a customer has just arrived at 12:00 noon.
(a) What is the probability that the next arrival will come (i) before 1:00 P.M., (ii) between 1:00 and 2:00 P.M., and (iii) after 2:00 P.M.?
(b) Suppose that no additional customers arrive before 1:00 P.M. Now what is the probability that the next arrival will come between 1:00 and 2:00 P.M.?
(c) What is the probability that the number of arrivals between 1:00 and 2:00 P.M. will be (i) 0, (ii) 1, and (iii) 2 or more?
(d) Suppose that both servers are serving customers at 1:00 P.M. What is the probability that *neither* customer will have service

completed (i) before 2:00 P.M., (ii) before 1:10 P.M., and (iii) before 1:01 P.M.?

17.4-2.* The jobs to be performed on a particular machine arrive according to a *Poisson* input process with a mean rate of two per hour. Suppose that the machine breaks down and will require 1 hour to be repaired. What is the probability that the number of new jobs that will arrive during this time is (a) 0, (b) 2, and (c) 5 or more?

17.4-3. The time required by a mechanic to repair a machine has an exponential distribution with a mean of 4 hours. However, a special tool would reduce this mean to 2 hours. If the mechanic repairs a machine in less than 2 hours, he is paid \$100; otherwise, he is paid \$80. Determine the mechanic's expected increase in pay per machine repaired if he uses the special tool.

17.4-4. A three-server queueing system has a controlled arrival process that provides customers in time to keep the servers continuously busy. Service times have an exponential distribution with mean 0.5.

You observe the queueing system starting up with all three servers beginning service at time $t = 0$. You then note that the first completion occurs at time $t = 1$. Given this information, determine the expected amount of time after $t = 1$ until the next service completion occurs.

17.4-5. A queueing system has three servers with expected service times of 20 minutes, 15 minutes, and 10 minutes. The service times have an exponential distribution. Each server has been busy with a current customer for 5 minutes. Determine the expected remaining time until the next service completion.

17.4-6. Consider a queueing system with two types of customers. Type 1 customers arrive according to a Poisson process with a mean rate of 5 per hour. Type 2 customers also arrive according to a Poisson process with a mean rate of 5 per hour. The system has two servers, both of which serve both types of customers. For both types, service times have an exponential distribution with a mean of 10 minutes. Service is provided on a first-come-first-served basis.
(a) What is the probability distribution (including its mean) of the time between consecutive arrivals of customers of any type?
(b) When a particular type 2 customer arrives, she finds two type 1 customers there in the process of being served but no other customers in the system. What is the probability distribution (including its mean) of this type 2 customer's waiting time in the queue?

17.4-7. Consider a two-server queueing system where all service times are independent and identically distributed according to an exponential distribution with a mean of 10 minutes. When a particular customer arrives, he finds that both servers are busy and no one is waiting in the queue.

(a) What is the probability distribution (including its mean and standard deviation) of this customer's waiting time in the queue?

(b) Determine the expected value and standard deviation of this customer's waiting time in the system.

(c) Suppose that this customer still is waiting in the queue 5 minutes after its arrival. Given this information, how does this change the expected value and the standard deviation of this customer's total waiting time in the system from the answers obtained in part (b)?

17.4-8. A queueing system has two servers whose service times are independent random variables with an exponential distribution with a mean of 15 minutes. Customer X arrives when both servers are idle. Five minutes later, customer Y arrives and customer X still is being served. Another 10 minutes later, customer Z arrives and both customers X and Y still are being served. No other customers arrived during this 15-minute interval.

(a) What is the probability that customer X will complete service before customer Y?

(b) What is the probability that customer Z will complete service before customer X?

(c) What is the probability that customer Z will complete service before customer Y?

(d) Determine the cumulative distribution function of the waiting time in the system for customer X. Also determine the mean and standard deviation.

(e) Repeat part (d) for customer Y.

(f) Determine the expected value and standard deviation of the waiting time in the system for customer Z.

(g) Determine the probability of exactly 2 more customers arriving during the next 15-minute interval.

17.4-9. For each of the following statements regarding service times modeled by the exponential distribution, label the statement as true or false and then justify your answer by referring to specific statements (with page citations) in the chapter.

(a) The expected value and variance of the service times are always equal.

(b) The exponential distribution always provides a good approximation of the actual service-time distribution when each customer requires the same service operations.

(c) At an s-server facility, $s > 1$, with exactly s customers already in the system, a new arrival would have an expected waiting time before entering service of $1/\mu$ time units, where μ is the mean service rate for each busy server.

17.4-10. As for Property 3 of the exponential distribution, let $T_1, T_2, \ldots, T_n$ be independent exponential random variables with parameters $\alpha_1, \alpha_2, \ldots, \alpha_n$, respectively, and let $U = \min\{T_1, T_2, \ldots, T_n\}$. Show that the probability that a particu-

lar random variable T_j will turn out to be smallest of the n random variables is

$$P\{T_j = U\} = \alpha_j \Big/ \sum_{i=1}^{n} \alpha_i, \qquad \text{for } j = 1, 2, \ldots, n.$$

(*Hint*: $P\{T_j = U\} = \int_0^\infty P\{T_i > T_j \text{ for all } i \neq j \,|\, T_j = t\}\alpha_j e^{-\alpha_j t} dt$.)

17.5-1. Consider the birth-and-death process with all $\mu_n = 2$ ($n = 1, 2, \ldots$), $\lambda_0 = 3$, $\lambda_1 = 2$, $\lambda_2 = 1$, and $\lambda_n = 0$ for $n = 3, 4, \ldots$.

(a) Display the rate diagram.

(b) Calculate P_0, P_1, P_2, P_3, and P_n for $n = 4, 5, \ldots$.

(c) Calculate L, L_q, W, and W_q.

17.5-2. Consider a birth-and-death process with just three attainable states (0, 1, and 2), for which the steady-state probabilities are P_0, P_1, and P_2, respectively. The birth-and-death rates are summarized in the following table:

State	Birth Rate	Death Rate
0	1	—
1	1	2
2	0	2

(a) Construct the rate diagram for this birth-and-death process.

(b) Develop the balance equations.

(c) Solve these equations to find P_0, P_1, and P_2.

(d) Use the general formulas for the birth-and-death process to calculate P_0, P_1, and P_2. Also calculate L, L_q, W, and W_q.

17.5-3. Consider the birth-and-death process with the following mean rates. The birth rates are $\lambda_0 = 2$, $\lambda_1 = 3$, $\lambda_2 = 2$, $\lambda_3 = 1$, and $\lambda_n = 0$ for $n > 3$. The death rates are $\mu_1 = 3$, $\mu_2 = 4$, $\mu_3 = 1$, and $\mu_n = 2$ for $n > 4$.

(a) Construct the rate diagram for this birth-and-death process.

(b) Develop the balance equations.

(c) Solve these equations to find the steady-state probability distribution P_0, P_1, ...

(d) Use the general formulas for the birth-and-death process to calculate P_0, P_1, ... Also calculate L, L_q, W, and W_q.

17.5-4. Consider the birth-and-death process with all $\lambda_n = 2$ ($n = 0, 1, \ldots$), $\mu_1 = 2$, and $\mu_n = 4$ for $n = 2, 3, \ldots$.

(a) Display the rate diagram.

(b) Calculate P_0 and P_1. Then give a general expression for P_n in terms of P_0 for $n = 2, 3, \ldots$.

(c) Consider a queueing system with two servers that fits this process. What is the mean arrival rate for this queueing system? What is the mean service rate for each server when it is busy serving customers?

17.5-5.* A service station has one gasoline pump. Cars wanting gasoline arrive according to a Poisson process at a mean rate of 15 per hour. However, if the pump already is being used, these potential customers may *balk* (drive on to another service station). In particular, if there are n cars already at the service station, the probability that an arriving potential customer will balk is $n/3$ for $n = 1, 2, 3$. The time required to service a car has an exponential distribution with a mean of 4 minutes.

(a) Construct the rate diagram for this queueing system.

(b) Develop the balance equations.

(c) Solve these equations to find the steady-state probability distribution of the number of cars at the station. Verify that this solution is the same as that given by the general solution for the birth-and-death process.

(d) Find the expected waiting time (including service) for those cars that stay.

17.5-6. A maintenance person has the job of keeping two machines in working order. The amount of time that a machine works before breaking down has an exponential distribution with a mean of 10 hours. The time then spent by the maintenance person to repair the machine has an exponential distribution with a mean of 8 hours.

(a) Show that this process fits the birth-and-death process by defining the states, specifying the values of the λ_n and μ_n, and then constructing the rate diagram.

(b) Calculate the P_n.

(c) Calculate L, L_q, W, and W_q.

(d) Determine the proportion of time that the maintenance person is busy.

(e) Determine the proportion of time that any given machine is working.

(f) Refer to the nearly identical example of a *continuous time Markov chain* given at the end of Sec. 16.8. Describe the relationship between continuous time Markov chains and the birth-and-death process that enables both to be applied to this same problem.

17.5-7. Consider a single-server queueing system where interarrival times have an exponential distribution with parameter λ and service times have an exponential distribution with parameter μ. In addition, customers *renege* (leave the queueing system without being served) if their waiting time in the queue grows too large. In particular, assume that the time each customer is willing to wait in the queue before reneging has an exponential distribution with a mean of $1/\theta$.

(a) Construct the rate diagram for this queueing system.

(b) Develop the balance equations.

17.5-8. Consider a single-server queueing system where some potential customers *balk* (refuse to enter the system) and some customers who enter the system later get impatient and *renege* (leave without being served). Potential customers arrive according to a Poisson process with a mean rate of 4 per hour. An arriving potential customer who finds n customers already there will balk with the following probabilities:

$$P\{\text{balk} \mid n \text{ already there}\} = \begin{cases} 0, & \text{if } n = 0, \\ \dfrac{1}{2}, & \text{if } n = 1, \\ \dfrac{3}{4}, & \text{if } n = 2, \\ 1, & \text{if } n = 3. \end{cases}$$

Service times have an exponential distribution with a mean of 1 hour.

A customer already in service never reneges, but the customers in the queue may renege. In particular, the remaining time that the customer at the front of the queue is willing to wait in the queue before reneging has an exponential distribution with a mean of 1 hour. For a customer in the second position in the queue, the time that she or he is willing to wait in this position before reneging has an exponential distribution with a mean of $\frac{1}{2}$ hour.

(a) Construct the rate diagram for this queueing system.

(b) Obtain the steady-state distribution of the number of customers in the system.

(c) Find the expected fraction of arriving potential customers who are lost due to balking.

(d) Find L_q and L.

17.5-9.* A certain small grocery store has a single checkout stand with a full-time cashier. Customers arrive at the stand "randomly" (i.e., a Poisson input process) at a mean rate of 30 per hour. When there is only one customer at the stand, she is processed by the cashier alone, with an expected service time of 1.5 minutes. However, the stock boy has been given standard instructions that whenever there is more than one customer at the stand, he is to help the cashier by bagging the groceries. This help reduces the expected time required to process a customer to 1 minute. In both cases, the service-time distribution is exponential.

(a) Construct the rate diagram for this queueing system.

(b) What is the steady-state probability distribution of the number of customers at the checkout stand?

(c) Derive L for this system. (*Hint*: Refer to the derivation of L for the $M/M/1$ model at the beginning of Sec. 17.6.) Use this information to determine L_q, W, and W_q.

17.5-10. A department has one word-processing operator. Documents produced in the department are delivered for word processing according to a Poisson process with an expected interarrival time of 20 minutes. When the operator has just one document to process, the expected processing time is 15 minutes. When she has more than one document, then editing assistance that is available reduces the expected processing time for each document to 10 minutes. In both cases, the processing times have an exponential distribution.

(a) Construct the rate diagram for this queueing system.

(b) Find the steady-state distribution of the number of documents that the operator has received but not yet completed.

(c) Derive L for this system. (*Hint:* Refer to the derivation of L for the $M/M/1$ model at the beginning of Sec. 17.6.) Use this information to determine L_q, W, and W_q.

17.5-11. Consider a self-service model in which the customer is also the server. Note that this corresponds to having an infinite number of servers available. Customers arrive according to a Poisson process with parameter λ, and service times have an exponential distribution with parameter μ.

(a) Find L_q and W_q.

(b) Construct the rate diagram for this queueing system.

(c) Use the balance equations to find the expression for P_n in terms of P_0.

(d) Find P_0.

(e) Find L and W.

17.5-12. Customers arrive at a queueing system according to a Poisson process with a mean arrival rate of 2 customers per minute. The service time has an exponential distribution with a mean of 1 minute. An unlimited number of servers are available as needed so customers never wait for service to begin. Calculate the steady-state probability that exactly 1 customer is in the system.

17.5-13. Suppose that a single-server queueing system fits all the assumptions of the birth-and-death process *except* that customers always arrive in *pairs*. The mean arrival rate is 2 pairs per hour (4 customers per hour) and the mean service rate (when the server is busy) is 5 customers per hour.

(a) Construct the rate diagram for this queueing system.

(b) Develop the balance equations.

(c) For comparison purposes, display the rate diagram for the corresponding queueing system that completely fits the birth-and-death process, i.e., where customers arrive *individually* at a mean rate of 4 per hour.

17.5-14. The Copy Shop is open 5 days per week for copying materials that are brought to the shop. It has three identical copying machines that are run by employees of the shop. Only two operators are kept on duty to run the machines, so the third machine is a spare that is used only when one of the other machines breaks down. When a machine is being used, the time until it breaks down has an exponential distribution with a mean of 2 weeks. If one machine breaks down while the other two are operational, a service representative is called in to repair it, in which case the total time from the breakdown until the repair is completed has an exponential distribution with a mean of 0.2 week. However, if a second machine breaks down before the first one has been repaired, the third machine is shut off while the two operators work together to repair this second machine quickly, in which case its repair time has an exponential distribution with a mean of only $\frac{1}{15}$ week. If the service representative finishes repairing the first machine before the two operators complete the repair of the second, the operators go back to running the two operational machines while the representative finishes the second repair, in which case the remaining repair time has an exponential distribituion with a mean of 0.2 week.

(a) Letting the state of the system be the number of machines not working, construct the rate diagram for this queueing system.

(b) Find the steady-state distribution of the number of machines not working.

(c) What is the expected number of operators available for copying?

17.5-15. Consider a single-server queueing system with a finite queue that can hold a maximum of 2 customers *excluding* any being served. The server can provide *batch service* to 2 customers simultaneously, where the service time has an exponential distribution with a mean of 1 unit of time regardless of the number being served. Whenever the queue is not full, customers arrive individually according to a Poisson process at a mean rate of 1 per unit of time.

(a) Assume that the server *must* serve 2 customers simultaneously. Thus, if the server is idle when only 1 customer is in the system, the server must wait for another arrival before beginning service. Formulate the queueing model as a continuous time Markov chain by defining the states and then constructing the rate diagram. Give the balance equations, but do not solve further.

(b) Now assume that the batch size for a service is 2 only if 2 customers are in the queue when the server finishes the preceding service. Thus, if the server is idle when only 1 customer is in the system, the server must serve this single customer, and any subsequent arrivals must wait in the queue until service is completed for this customer. Formulate the resulting queueing model as a continuous time Markov chain by defining the states and then constructing the rate diagram. Give the balance equations, but do not solve further.

17.5-16. Consider a queueing system that has two classes of customers, two clerks providing service, and *no queue*. Potential customers from each class arrive according to a Poisson process, with a mean arrival rate of 10 customers per hour for class 1 and 5 customers per hour for class 2, but these arrivals are lost to the system if they cannot immediately enter service.

Each customer of class 1 that enters the system will receive service from either one of the clerks that is free, where the service times have an exponential distribution with a mean of 5 minutes.

Each customer of class 2 that enters the system requires the *simultaneous use of both clerks* (the two clerks work together as a single server), where the service times have an exponential distribution with a mean of 5 minutes. Thus, an arriving customer of this kind would be lost to the system unless both clerks are free to begin service immediately.

(a) Formulate the queueing model as a continuous time Markov chain by defining the states and constructing the rate diagram.
(b) Now describe how the formulation in part (a) can be fitted into the format of the birth-and-death process.
(c) Use the results for the birth-and-death process to calculate the steady-state joint distribution of the number of customers of each class in the system.
(d) For each of the two classes of customers, what is the expected fraction of arrivals who are unable to enter the system?

17.6-1.* The 4M Company has a single turret lathe as a key work center on its factory floor. Jobs arrive at this work center according to a Poisson process at a mean rate of 2 per day. The processing time to perform each job has an exponential distribution with a mean of $\frac{1}{4}$ day. Because the jobs are bulky, those not being worked on are currently being stored in a room some distance from the machine. However, to save time in fetching the jobs, the production manager is proposing to add enough in-process storage space next to the turret lathe to accommodate 3 jobs in addition to the one being processed. (Excess jobs will continue to be stored temporarily in the distant room.) Under this proposal, what proportion of the time will this storage space next to the turret lathe be adequate to accommodate all waiting jobs?

(a) Use available formulas to calculate your answer.
T (b) Use the corresponding Excel template to obtain the probabilities needed to answer the question.

17.6-2. Customers arrive at a single-server queueing system according to a Poisson process at a mean rate of 10 per hour. If the server works continuously, the number of customers that can be served in an hour has a Poisson distribution with a mean of 15. Determine the proportion of time during which no one is waiting to be served.

17.6-3. Consider the $M/M/1$ model, with $\lambda < \mu$.
(a) Determine the steady-state probability that a customer's actual waiting time in the system is longer than the expected waiting time in the system, i.e., $P\{\mathcal{W} > W\}$.
(b) Determine the steady-state probability that a customer's actual waiting time in the queue is longer than the expected waiting time in the queue, i.e., $P\{\mathcal{W}_q > W_q\}$.

17.6-4. Verify the following relationships for an $M/M/1$ queueing system:

$$\lambda = \frac{(1 - P_0)^2}{W_q P_0}, \qquad \mu = \frac{1 - P_0}{W_q P_0}.$$

17.6-5. It is necessary to determine how much in-process storage space to allocate to a particular work center in a new factory. Jobs arrive at this work center according to a Poisson process with a mean rate of 3 per hour, and the time required to perform the necessary work has an exponential distribution with a mean of 0.25 hour. Whenever the waiting jobs require more in-process storage space than has been allocated, the excess jobs are stored temporarily in a less convenient location. If each job requires 1 square foot of floor space while it is in in-process storage at the work center, how much space must be provided to accommodate all waiting jobs (a) 50 percent of the time, (b) 90 percent of the time, and (c) 99 percent of the time? Derive an analytical expression to answer these three questions. *Hint:* The sum of a geometric series is

$$\sum_{n=0}^{N} x^n = \frac{1 - x^{N+1}}{1 - x}.$$

17.6-6. Consider the following statements about an $M/M/1$ queueing system and its utilization factor ρ. Label each of the statements as true or false, and then justify your answer.
(a) The probability that a customer has to wait before service begins is proportional to ρ.
(b) The expected number of customers in the system is proportional to ρ.
(c) If ρ has been increased from $\rho = 0.9$ to $\rho = 0.99$, the effect of any further increase in ρ on L, L_q, W, and W_q will be relatively small as long as $\rho < 1$.

17.6-7. Customers arrive at a single-server queueing system in accordance with a Poisson process with an expected interarrival time of 25 minutes. Service times have an exponential distribution with a mean of 30 minutes.

Label each of the following statements about this system as true or false, and then justify your answer.
(a) The server definitely will be busy forever after the first customer arrives.
(b) The queue will grow without bound.
(c) If a second server with the same service-time distribution is added, the system can reach a steady-state condition.

17.6-8. For each of the following statements about an $M/M/1$ queueing system, label the statement as true or false and then justify your answer by referring to specific statements (with page citations) in the chapter.
(a) The waiting time in the system has an exponential distribution.
(b) The waiting time in the queue has an exponential distribution.
(c) The conditional waiting time in the system, given the number of customers already in the system, has an Erlang (gamma) distribution.

17.6-9. The Friendly Neighbor Grocery Store has a single check-out stand with a full-time cashier. Customers arrive randomly at the stand at a mean rate of 30 per hour. The service-time distribution is exponential, with a mean of 1.5 minutes. This situation has resulted in occasional long lines and complaints from customers. Therefore, because there is no room for a second checkout stand, the manager is considering the alternative of hiring another person to help the cashier by bagging the groceries. This help would reduce the expected time required to process a customer to 1 minute, but the distribution still would be exponential.

The manager would like to have the percentage of time that there are more than two customers at the checkout stand down below 25 percent. She also would like to have no more than 5 percent of the customers needing to wait at least 5 minutes before beginning service, or at least 7 minutes before finishing service.

(a) Use the formulas for the $M/M/1$ model to calculate L, W, W_q, L_q, P_0, P_1, and P_2 for the current mode of operation. What is the probability of having more than two customers at the checkout stand?

T (b) Use the Excel template for this model to check your answers in part (a). Also find the probability that the waiting time before beginning service exceeds 5 minutes, and the probability that the waiting time before finishing service exceeds 7 minutes.

(c) Repeat part (a) for the alternative being considered by the manager.

(d) Repeat part (b) for this alternative.

(e) Which approach should the manager use to satisfy her criteria as closely as possible?

T **17.6-10.** The Centerville International Airport has two runways, one used exclusively for takeoffs and the other exclusively for landings. Airplanes arrive in the Centerville air space to request landing instructions according to a Poisson process at a mean rate of 10 per hour. The time required for an airplane to land after receiving clearance to do so has an exponential distribution with a mean of 3 minutes, and this process must be completed before giving clearance to do so to another airplane. Airplanes awaiting clearance must circle the airport.

The Federal Aviation Administration has a number of criteria regarding the safe level of congestion of airplanes waiting to land. These criteria depend on a number of factors regarding the airport involved, such as the number of runways available for landing. For Centerville, the criteria are (1) the average number of airplanes waiting to receive clearance to land should not exceed 1, (2) 95 percent of the time, the actual number of airplanes waiting to receive clearance to land should not exceed 4, (3) for 99 percent of the airplanes, the amount of time spent circling the airport before receiving clearance to land should not exceed 30 minutes (since exceeding this amount of time often would require rerouting the

plane to another airport for an emergency landing before its fuel runs out).

(a) Evaluate how well these criteria are currently being satisfied.

(b) A major airline is considering adding this airport as one of its hubs. This would increase the mean arrival rate to 15 airplanes per hour. Evaluate how well the above criteria would be satisfied if this happens.

(c) To attract additional business [including the major airline mentioned in part (b)], airport management is considering adding a second runway for landings. It is estimated that this eventually would increase the mean arrival rate to 25 airplanes per hour. Evaluate how well the above criteria would be satisfied if this happens.

T **17.6-11.** The Security & Trust Bank employs 4 tellers to serve its customers. Customers arrive according to a Poisson process at a mean rate of 2 per minute. However, business is growing and management projects that the mean arrival rate will be 3 per minute a year from now. The transaction time between the teller and customer has an exponential distribution with a mean of 1 minute.

Management has established the following guidelines for a satisfactory level of service to customers. The average number of customers waiting in line to begin service should not exceed 1. At least 95 percent of the time, the number of customers waiting in line should not exceed 5. For at least 95 percent of the customers, the time spent in line waiting to begin service should not exceed 5 minutes.

(a) Use the $M/M/s$ model to determine how well these guidelines are currently being satisfied.

(b) Evaluate how well the guidelines will be satisfied a year from now if no change is made in the number of tellers.

(c) Determine how many tellers will be needed a year from now to completely satisfy these guidelines.

17.6-12. Consider the $M/M/s$ model.

T (a) Suppose there is one server and the expected service time is exactly 1 minute. Compare L for the cases where the mean arrival rate is 0.5, 0.9, and 0.99 customers per minute, respectively. Do the same for L_q, W, W_q, and $P\{\mathcal{W} > 5\}$. What conclusions do you draw about the impact of increasing the utilization factor ρ from small values (e.g., $\rho = 0.5$) to fairly large values (e.g., $\rho = 0.9$) and then to even larger values very close to 1 (e.g., $\rho = 0.99$)?

(b) Now suppose there are two servers and the expected service time is exactly 2 minutes. Follow the instructions for part (a).

T **17.6-13.** Consider the $M/M/s$ model with a mean arrival rate of 10 customers per hour and an expected service time of 5 minutes. Use the Excel template for this model to obtain and print out the various measures of performance (with $t = 10$ and $t = 0$, respectively, for the two waiting time probabilities) when the number of servers is 1, 2, 3, 4, and 5. Then, for each of the following possible criteria for a satisfactory level of service (where the unit of time is 1 minute), use the printed results to determine how many servers are needed to satisfy this criterion.

(a) $L_q \le 0.25$

(b) $L \le 0.9$

(c) $W_q \le 0.1$

(d) $W \le 6$

(e) $P\{W_q > 0\} \le 0.01$

(f) $P\{W > 10\} \le 0.2$

(g) $\sum_{n=0}^{s} P_n \ge 0.95$

17.6-14. Airplanes arrive for takeoff at the runway of an airport according to a Poisson process at a mean rate of 20 per hour. The time required for an airplane to take off has an exponential distribution with a mean of 2 minutes, and this process must be completed before the next airplane can begin to take off.

Because a brief thunderstorm has just begun, all airplanes which have not commenced takeoff have just been grounded temporarily. However, airplanes continue to arrive at the runway during the thunderstorm to await its end.

Assuming steady-state operation before the thunderstorm, determine the expected number of airplanes that will be waiting to take off at the end of the thunderstorm if it lasts 30 minutes.

17.6-15. A gas station with only one gas pump employs the following policy: If a customer has to wait, the price is $1 per gallon; if she does not have to wait, the price is $1.20 per gallon. Customers arrive according to a Poisson process with a mean rate of 15 per hour. Service times at the pump have an exponential distribution with a mean of 3 minutes. Arriving customers always wait until they can eventually buy gasoline. Determine the expected price of gasoline per gallon.

17.6-16. You are given an $M/M/1$ queueing system with mean arrival rate λ and mean service rate μ. An arriving customer receives n dollars if n customers are already in the system. Determine the expected cost in dollars per customer.

17.6-17. Section 17.6 gives the following equations for the $M/M/1$ model:

(1) $P\{W > t\} = \sum_{n=0}^{\infty} P_n P\{S_{n+1} > t\}.$

(2) $P\{W > t\} = e^{-\mu(1-\rho)t}.$

Show that Eq. (1) reduces algebraically to Eq. (2). (*Hint:* Use differentiation, algebra, and integration.)

17.6-18. Derive W_q directly for the following cases by developing and reducing an expression analogous to Eq. (1) in Prob. 17.6-17.

(*Hint:* Use the *conditional* expected waiting time in the queue given that a random arrival finds n customers already in the system.)

(a) The $M/M/1$ model

(b) The $M/M/s$ model

т **17.6-19.** Consider an $M/M/2$ queueing system with $\lambda = 4$ and $\mu = 3$. Determine the mean rate at which service completions occur during the periods when no customers are waiting in the queue.

т **17.6-20.** You are given an $M/M/2$ queueing system with $\lambda = 4$ per hour and $\mu = 6$ per hour. Determine the probability that an arriving customer will wait more than 30 minutes in the queue, given that at least 2 customers are already in the system.

17.6-21.* In the Blue Chip Life Insurance Company, the deposit and withdrawal functions associated with a certain investment product are separated between two clerks, Clara and Clarence. Deposit slips arrive randomly (a Poisson process) at Clara's desk at a mean rate of 16 per hour. Withdrawal slips arrive randomly (a Poisson process) at Clarence's desk at a mean rate of 14 per hour. The time required to process either transaction has an exponential distribution with a mean of 3 minutes. To reduce the expected waiting time in the system for both deposit slips and withdrawal slips, the actuarial department has made the following recommendations: (1) Train each clerk to handle both deposits and withdrawals, and (2) put both deposit and withdrawal slips into a single queue that is accessed by both clerks.

(a) Determine the expected waiting time in the system under current procedures for each type of slip. Then combine these results to calculate the expected waiting time in the system for a random arrival of either type of slip.

т (b) If the recommendations are adopted, determine the expected waiting time in the system for arriving slips.

т (c) Now suppose that adopting the recommendations would result in a slight increase in the expected processing time. Use the Excel template for the $M/M/s$ model to determine by trial and error the expected processing time (within 0.001 hour) that would cause the expected waiting time in the system for a random arrival to be essentially the same under current procedures and under the recommendations.

17.6-22. People's Software Company has just set up a call center to provide technical assistance on its new software package. Two technical representatives are taking the calls, where the time required by either representative to answer a customer's questions has an exponential distribution with a mean of 8 minutes. Calls are arriving according to a Poisson process at a mean rate of 10 per hour.

By next year, the mean arrival rate of calls is expected to decline to 5 per hour, so the plan is to reduce the number of technical representatives to one then.

T **(a)** Assuming that μ will continue to be 7.5 calls per hour for next year's queueing system, determine L, L_q, W, and W_q for both the current system and next year's system. For each of these four measures of performance, which system yields the smaller value?

(b) Now assume that μ will be adjustable when the number of technical representatives is reduced to one. Solve algebraically for the value of μ that would yield the same value of W as for the current system.

(c) Repeat part (b) with W_q instead of W.

17.6-23. You are given an $M/M/1$ queueing system in which the expected waiting time and expected number in the system are 120 minutes and 8 customers, respectively. Determine the probability that a customer's service time exceeds 20 minutes.

17.6-24. Consider a generalization of the $M/M/1$ model where the server needs to "warm up" at the beginning of a busy period, and so serves the first customer of a busy period at a slower rate than other customers. In particular, if an arriving customer finds the server idle, the customer experiences a service time that has an exponential distribution with parameter μ_1. However, if an arriving customer finds the server busy, that customer joins the queue and subsequently experiences a service time that has an exponential distribution with parameter μ_2, where $\mu_1 < \mu_2$. Customers arrive according to a Poisson process with mean rate λ.

(a) Formulate this model as a continuous time Markov chain by defining the states and constructing the rate diagram accordingly.

(b) Develop the balance equations.

(c) Suppose that numerical values are specified for μ_1, μ_2, and λ, and that $\lambda < \mu_2$ (so that a steady-state distribution exists). Since this model has an infinite number of states, the steady-state distribution is the simultaneous solution of an infinite number of balance equations (plus the equation specifying that the sum of the probabilities equals 1). Suppose that you are unable to obtain this solution analytically, so you wish to use a computer to solve the model numerically. Considering that it is impossible to solve an infinite number of equations numerically, briefly describe what still can be done with these equations to obtain an approximation of the steady-state distribution. Under what circumstances will this approximation be essentially exact?

(d) Given that the steady-state distribution has been obtained, give explicit expressions for calculating L, L_q, W, and W_q.

(e) Given this steady-state distribution, develop an expression for $P\{W > t\}$ that is analogous to Eq. (1) in Prob. 17.6-17.

17.6-25. For each of the following models, write the balance equations and show that they are satisfied by the solution given in Sec. 17.6 for the steady-state distribution of the number of customers in the system.

(a) The $M/M/1$ model.

(b) The finite queue variation of the $M/M/1$ model, with $K = 2$.

(c) The finite calling population variation of the $M/M/1$ model, with $N = 2$.

T **17.6-26.** Consider a telephone system with three lines. Calls arrive according to a Poisson process at a mean rate of 6 per hour. The duration of each call has an exponential distribution with a mean of 15 minutes. If all lines are busy, calls will be put on hold until a line becomes available.

(a) Print out the measures of performance provided by the Excel template for this queueing system (with $t = 1$ hour and $t = 0$, respectively, for the two waiting time probabilities).

(b) Use the printed result giving $P\{W_q > 0\}$ to identify the steady-state probability that a call will be answered immediately (not put on hold). Then verify this probability by using the printed results for the P_n.

(c) Use the printed results to identify the steady-state probability distribution of the number of calls on hold.

(d) Print out the new measures of performance if arriving calls are lost whenever all lines are busy. Use these results to identify the steady-state probability that an arriving call is lost.

17.6-27. Reconsider the specific birth-and-death process described in Prob. 17.5-1.

(a) Identify a queueing model (and its parameter values) in Sec. 17.6 that fits this process.

T **(b)** Use the corresponding Excel template to obtain the answers for parts (b) and (c) of Prob. 17.5-1.

17.6-28. The reservation office for Central Airlines has two agents answering incoming phone calls for flight reservations. In addition, one caller can be put on hold until one of the agents is available to take the call. If all three phone lines (both agent lines and the hold line) are busy, a potential customer gets a busy signal, in which case the call may go to another airline. The calls and attempted calls occur randomly (i.e., according to a Poisson process) at a mean rate of 15 per hour. The length of a telephone conversation has an exponential distribution with a mean of 4 minutes.

(a) Construct the rate diagram for this queueing system.

T **(b)** Find the steady-state probability that

    (i) A caller will get to talk to an agent immediately,

    (ii) The caller will be put on hold, and

    (iii) The caller will get a busy signal.

17.6-29.* Janet is planning to open a small car-wash operation, and she must decide how much space to provide for waiting cars. Janet estimates that customers would arrive randomly (i.e., a Poisson input process) with a mean rate of 1 every 4 minutes, unless the waiting area is full, in which case the arriving customers would take their cars elsewhere. The time that can be attributed to washing one car has an exponential distribution with a mean of 3 minutes. Compare the expected fraction of potential customers that will be *lost* because of inadequate waiting space if (*a*) 0 spaces (not including the car being washed), (*b*) 2 spaces, and (*c*) 4 spaces were provided.

17.6-30. Consider the finite queue variation of the *M/M/s* model. Derive the expression for L_q given in Sec. 17.6 for this model.

17.6-31. For the finite queue variation of the *M/M/*1 model, develop an expression analogous to Eq. (1) in Prob. 17.6-17 for the following probabilities:
(**a**) $P\{\mathcal{W} > t\}$.
(**b**) $P\{\mathcal{W}_q > t\}$.
[*Hint:* Arrivals can occur only when the system is not full, so the probability that a random arrival finds *n* customers already there is $P_n/(1 - P_K)$.]

17.6-32. At the Forrester Manufacturing Company, one repair technician has been assigned the responsibility of maintaining three machines. For each machine, the probability distribution of the running time before a breakdown is exponential, with a mean of 9 hours. The repair time also has an exponential distribution, with a mean of 2 hours.
(**a**) Which queueing model fits this queueing system?
T (**b**) Use this queueing model to find the probability distribution of the number of machines not running, and the mean of this distribution.
(**c**) Use this mean to calculate the expected time between a machine breakdown and the completion of the repair of that machine.
(**d**) What is the expected fraction of time that the repair technician will be busy?
T (**e**) As a crude approximation, assume that the calling population is infinite and that machine breakdowns occur randomly at a mean rate of 3 every 9 hours. Compare the result from part (*b*) with that obtained by making this approximation while using (i) the *M/M/s* model and (ii) the finite queue variation of the *M/M/s* model with *K* = 3.
T (**f**) Repeat part (*b*) when a second repair technician is made available to repair a second machine whenever more than one of these three machines require repair.

T **17.6-33.*** The Dolomite Corporation is making plans for a new factory. One department has been allocated 12 semiautomatic machines. A small number (yet to be determined) of operators will be hired to provide the machines the needed occasional servicing (loading, unloading, adjusting, setup, and so on). A decision now needs to be made on how to organize the operators to do this. Alternative 1 is to assign each operator to her own machines. Alternative 2 is to pool the operators so that any idle operator can take the next machine needing servicing. Alternative 3 is to combine

the operators into a single crew that will work together on any machine needing servicing.

The running time (time between completing service and the machine's requiring service again) of each machine is expected to have an exponential distribution, with a mean of 150 minutes. The service time is assumed to have an exponential distribution, with a mean of 15 minutes (for Alternatives 1 and 2) or 15 minutes divided by the number of operators in the crew (for Alternative 3). For the department to achieve the required production rate, the machines must be running at least 89 percent of the time on average.
(**a**) For Alternative 1, what is the maximum number of machines that can be assigned to an operator while still achieving the required production rate? What is the resulting utilization of each operator?
(**b**) For Alternative 2, what is the minimum number of operators needed to achieve the required production rate? What is the resulting utilization of the operators?
(**c**) For Alternative 3, what is the minimum size of the crew needed to achieve the required production rate? What is the resulting utilization of the crew?

17.6-34. A shop contains three identical machines that are subject to a failure of a certain kind. Therefore, a maintenance system is provided to perform the maintenance operation (recharging) required by a failed machine. The time required by each operation has an exponential distribution with a mean of 30 minutes. However, with probability $\frac{1}{3}$, the operation must be performed a second time (with the same distribution of time) in order to bring the failed machine back to a satisfactory operational state. The maintenance system works on only one failed machine at a time, performing all the operations (one or two) required by that machine, on a first-come-first-served basis. After a machine is repaired, the time until its next failure has an exponential distribution with a mean of 3 hours.
(**a**) How should the states of the system be defined in order to formulate this queueing system as a continuous time Markov chain? (*Hint:* Given that a first operation is being performed on a failed machine, completing this operation *successfully* and completing it *unsuccessfully* are two separate events of interest. Then use Property 6 regarding disaggregation for the exponential distribution.)
(**b**) Construct the corresponding rate diagram.
(**c**) Develop the balance equations.

17.6-35. Consider a single-server queueing system. It has been observed that (1) this server seems to speed up as the number of customers in the system increases and (2) the pattern of acceleration seems to fit the state-dependent model presented at the end of Sec. 17.6. Furthermore, it is estimated that the expected service time is 8 minutes when there is only 1 customer in the system. Determine the pressure coefficient *c* for this model for the following cases:

(a) The expected service time is estimated to be 4 minutes when there are 4 customers in the system.

(b) The expected service time is estimated to be 5 minutes when there are 4 customers in the system.

T **17.6-36.** For the state-dependent model presented at the end of Sec. 17.6, show the effect of the *pressure coefficient c* by using Fig. 17.10 to construct a table giving the ratio (expressed as a decimal number) of L for this model to L for the corresponding $M/M/s$ model (i.e., with $c = 0$). Tabulate these ratios for $\lambda_0/s\mu_1 = 0.5, 0.9, 0.99$ when $c = 0.2, 0.4, 0.6$, and $s = 1, 2$.

17.7-1.* Consider the $M/G/1$ model.

(a) Compare the expected waiting time in the queue if the service-time distribution is (i) exponential, (ii) constant, (iii) Erlang with the amount of variation (i.e., the standard deviation) halfway between the constant and exponential cases.

(b) What is the effect on the expected waiting time in the queue and on the expected queue length if both λ and μ are doubled and the scale of the service-time distribution is changed accordingly?

17.2-2. Consider the $M/G/1$ model with $\lambda = 0.2$ and $\mu = 0.25$.

T **(a)** Use the Excel template for this model (or hand calculations) to find the main measures of performance—L, L_q, W, W_q—for each of the following values of σ: 4, 3, 2, 1, 0.

(b) What is the ratio of L_q with $\sigma = 4$ to L_q with $\sigma = 0$? What does this say about the importance of reducing the variability of the service times?

(c) Calculate the reduction in L_q when σ is reduced from 4 to 3, from 3 to 2, from 2 to 1, and from 1 to 0. Which is the largest reduction? Which is the smallest?

(d) Use trial and error with the template to see approximately how much μ would need to be increased with $\sigma = 4$ to achieve the same L_q as with $\mu = 0.25$ and $\sigma = 0$.

17.7-3. Consider the following statements about an $M/G/1$ queueing system, where σ^2 is the variance of service times. Label each statement as true or false, and then justify your answer.

(a) Increasing σ^2 (with fixed λ and μ) will increase L_q and L, but will not change W_q and W.

(b) When choosing between a tortoise (small μ and σ^2) and a hare (large μ and σ^2) to be the server, the tortoise always wins by providing a smaller L_q.

(c) With λ and μ fixed, the value of L_q with an exponential service-time distribution is twice as large as with constant service times.

(d) Among all possible service-time distributions (with λ and μ fixed), the exponential distribution yields the largest value of L_q.

17.7-4. Marsha operates an expresso stand. Customers arrive according to a Poisson process at a mean rate of 30 per hour. The

time needed by Marsha to serve a customer has an exponential distribution with a mean of 75 seconds.

(a) Use the $M/G/1$ model to find L, L_q, W, and W_q.

(b) Suppose Marsha is replaced by an expresso vending machine that requires exactly 75 seconds for each customer to operate. Find L, L_q, W, and W_q.

(c) What is the ratio of L_q in part (b) to L_q in part (a)?

T **(d)** Use trial and error with the Excel template for the $M/G/1$ model to see approximately how much Marsha would need to reduce her expected service time to achieve the same L_q as with the expresso vending machine.

17.7-5. Antonio runs a shoe repair store by himself. Customers arrive to bring a pair of shoes to be repaired according to a Poisson process at a mean rate of 1 per hour. The time Antonio requires to repair each individual shoe has an exponential distribution with a mean of 15 minutes.

(a) Consider the formulation of this queueing system where the individual shoes (not pairs of shoes) are considered to be the customers. For this formulation, construct the rate diagram and develop the balance equations, but do not solve further.

(b) Now consider the formulation of this queueing system where the pairs of shoes are considered to be the customers. Identify the specific queueing model that fits this formulation.

(c) Calculate the expected number of pairs of shoes in the shop.

(d) Calculate the expected amount of time from when a customer drops off a pair of shoes until they are repaired and ready to be picked up.

T **(e)** Use the corresponding Excel template to check your answers in parts (c) and (d).

17.7-6.* The maintenance base for Friendly Skies Airline has facilities for overhauling only one airplane engine at a time. Therefore, to return the airplanes to use as soon as possible, the policy has been to stagger the overhauling of the four engines of each airplane. In other words, only one engine is overhauled each time an airplane comes into the shop. Under this policy, airplanes have arrived according to a Poisson process at a mean rate of 1 per day. The time required for an engine overhaul (once work has begun) has an exponential distribution with a mean of $\frac{1}{2}$ day.

A proposal has been made to change the policy so that all four engines are overhauled consecutively each time an airplane comes into the shop. Although this would quadruple the expected service time, each plane would need to come to the maintenance base only one-fourth as often.

Management now needs to decide whether to continue the status quo or adopt the proposal. The objective is to minimize the average amount of flying time lost by the entire fleet per day due to engine overhauls.

(a) Compare the two alternatives with respect to the average amount of flying time lost by an airplane each time it comes to the maintenance base.

(b) Compare the two alternatives with respect to the average number of airplanes losing flying time due to being at the maintenance base.

(c) Which of these two comparisons is the appropriate one for making management's decision? Explain.

17.7-7. Reconsider Prob. 17.7-6. Management has adopted the proposal but now wants further analysis conducted of this new queueing system.

(a) How should the state of the system be defined in order to formulate the queueing model as a continuous time Markov chain?

(b) Construct the corresponding rate diagram.

17.7-8. Consider a queueing system with a Poisson input, where the server must perform two distinguishable tasks in sequence for each customer, so the total service time is the sum of the two task times (which are statistically independent).

(a) Suppose that the first task time has an exponential distribution with a mean of 3 minutes and that the second task time has an Erlang distribution with a mean of 9 minutes and with the shape parameter $k = 3$. Which queueing theory model should be used to represent this system?

(b) Suppose that part (a) is modified so that the first task time also has an Erlang distribution with the shape parameter $k = 3$ (but with the mean still equal to 3 minutes). Which queueing theory model should be used to represent this system?

17.7-9. The McAllister Company factory currently has *two* tool cribs, each with a *single* clerk, in its manufacturing area. One tool crib handles only the tools for the heavy machinery; the second one handles all other tools. However, for each crib the mechanics arrive to obtain tools at a mean rate of 24 per hour, and the expected service time is 2 minutes.

Because of complaints that the mechanics coming to the tool crib have to wait too long, it has been proposed that the two tool cribs be combined so that either clerk can handle either kind of tool as the demand arises. It is believed that the mean arrival rate to the combined two-clerk tool crib would double to 48 per hour and that the expected service time would continue to be 2 minutes. However, information is not available on the *form* of the probability distributions for interarrival and service times, so it is not clear which queueing model would be most appropriate.

Compare the status quo and the proposal with respect to the total expected number of mechanics at the tool crib(s) and the expected waiting time (including service) for each mechanic. Do this by tabulating these data for the four queueing models considered in Figs. 17.7, 17.11, 17.13, and 17.14 (use $k = 2$ when an Erlang distribution is appropriate).

17.7-10.* Consider a single-server queueing system with a Poisson input, Erlang service times, and a finite queue. In particular, suppose that $k = 2$, the mean arrival rate is 2 customers per hour, the expected service time is 0.25 hour, and the maximum permissible number of customers in the system is 2. This system can be formulated as a continuous time Markov chain by dividing each service time into two consecutive phases, each having an exponential distribution with a mean of 0.125 hour, and then defining the state of the system as (n, p), where n is the number of customers in the system $(n = 0, 1, 2)$, and p indicates the phase of the customer being served $(p = 0, 1, 2,$ where $p = 0$ means that no customer is being served).

(a) Construct the corresponding rate diagram. Write the balance equations, and then use these equations to solve for the steady-state distribution of the state of this Markov chain.

(b) Use the steady-state distribution obtained in part (a) to identify the steady-state distribution of the number of customers in the system (P_0, P_1, P_2) and the steady-state expected number of customers in the system (L).

(c) Compare the results from part (b) with the corresponding results when the service-time distribution is exponential.

17.7-11. Consider the $E_2/M/1$ model with $\lambda = 4$ and $\mu = 5$. This model can be formulated as a continuous time Markov chain by dividing each interarrival time into two consecutive phases, each having an exponential distribution with a mean of $1/(2\lambda) = 0.125$, and then defining the state of the system as (n, p), where n is the number of customers in the system $(n = 0, 1, 2, \ldots)$ and p indicates the phase of the *next* arrival (not yet in the system) $(p = 1, 2)$.

Construct the corresponding rate diagram (but do not solve further).

17.7-12. A company has one repair technician to keep a large group of machines in running order. Treating this group as an infinite calling population, individual breakdowns occur according to a Poisson process at a mean rate of 1 per hour. For each breakdown, the probability is 0.9 that only a minor repair is needed, in which case the repair time has an exponential distribution with a mean of $\frac{1}{2}$ hour. Otherwise, a major repair is needed, in which case the repair time has an exponential distribution with a mean of 5 hours. Because both of these *conditional* distributions are exponential, the *unconditional* (combined) distribution of repair times is *hyperexponential*.

(a) Compute the mean and standard deviation of this hyperexponential distribution. [*Hint:* Use the general relationships from probability theory that, for any random variable X and any pair of mutually exclusive events E_1 and E_2, $E(X) = E(X | E_1)P(E_1) + E(X | E_2)P(E_2)$ and $\text{var}(X) = E(X^2) - E(X)^2$.] Compare this standard deviation with that for an exponential distribution having this mean.

(b) What are P_0, L_q, L, W_q, and W for this queueing system?

(c) What is the conditional value of W, given that the machine involved requires major repair? A minor repair? What is the division of L between machines requiring the two types of repairs? (*Hint:* Little's formula still applies for the individual categories of machines.)

(d) How should the states of the system be defined in order to formulate this queueing system as a continuous time Markov chain? (*Hint:* Consider what additional information must be given, besides the number of machines down, for the conditional distribution of the time remaining until the next event of each kind to be exponential.)

(e) Construct the corresponding rate diagram.

17.7-13. Consider the finite queue variation of the $M/G/1$ model, where K is the maximum number of customers allowed in the system. For $n = 1, 2, \ldots$, let the random variable X_n be the number of customers in the system at the moment t_n when the nth customer has just finished being served. (Do not count the departing customer.) The times $\{t_1, t_2, \ldots\}$ are called *regeneration points*. Furthermore, $\{X_n\}$ ($n = 1, 2, \ldots$) is a discrete time Markov chain and is known as an *embedded Markov chain*. Embedded Markov chains are useful for studying the properties of continuous time stochastic processes such as for an $M/G/1$ model.

Now consider the particular special case where $K = 4$, the service time of successive customers is a fixed constant, say, 10 minutes, and the mean arrival rate is 1 every 50 minutes. Therefore, $\{X_n\}$ is an embedded Markov chain with states 0, 1, 2, 3. (Because there are never more than 4 customers in the system, there can never be more than 3 in the system at a regeneration point.) Because the system is observed at successive departures, X_n can never decrease by more than 1. Furthermore, the probabilities of transitions that result in increases in X_n are obtained directly from the Poisson distribution.

(a) Find the one-step transition matrix for the embedded Markov chain. (*Hint:* In obtaining the transition probability from state 3 to state 3, use the probability of 1 or more arrivals rather than just 1 arrival, and similarly for other transitions to state 3.)

(b) Use the corresponding routine in the Markov chains area of your OR Courseware to find the steady-state probabilities for the number of customers in the system at regeneration points.

(c) Compute the expected number of customers in the system at regeneration points, and compare it to the value of L for the $M/D/1$ model (with $K = \infty$) in Sec. 17.7.

17.8-1.* Southeast Airlines is a small commuter airline serving primarily the state of Florida. Their ticket counter at the Orlando airport is staffed by a single ticket agent. There are two separate lines—one for first-class passengers and one for coach-class passengers. When the ticket agent is ready for another customer, the next first-class passenger is served if there are any in line. If not, the next coach-class passenger is served. Service times have an ex-

ponential distribution with a mean of 3 minutes for both types of customers. During the 12 hours per day that the ticket counter is open, passengers arrive randomly at a mean rate of 2 per hour for first-class passengers and 10 per hour for coach-class passengers.

(a) What kind of queueing model fits this queueing system?

T **(b)** Find the main measures of performance—L, L_q, W, and W_q— for both first-class passengers and coach-class passengers.

(c) What is the expected waiting time before service begins for first-class customers as a fraction of this waiting time for coach-class customers?

(d) Determine the average number of hours per day that the ticket agent is busy.

T **17.8-2.** Consider the model with nonpreemptive priorities presented in Sec. 17.8. Suppose there are two priority classes, with $\lambda_1 = 4$ and $\lambda_2 = 4$. In designing this queueing system, you are offered the choice between the following alternatives: (1) one fast server ($\mu = 10$) and (2) two slow servers ($\mu = 5$).

Compare these alternatives with the usual four mean measures of performance (W, L, W_q, L_q) for the individual priority classes (W_1, W_2, L_1, L_2, and so forth). Which alternative is preferred if your primary concern is expected waiting time in the *system* for priority class 1 (W_1)? Which is preferred if your primary concern is expected waiting time in the *queue* for priority class 1?

17.8-3. Consider the single-server variation of the nonpreemptive priorities model presented in Sec. 17.8. Suppose there are three priority classes, with $\lambda_1 = 1$, $\lambda_2 = 1$, and $\lambda_3 = 1$. The expected service times for priority classes 1, 2, and 3 are 0.4, 0.3, and 0.2, respectively, so $\mu_1 = 2.5$, $\mu_2 = 3\frac{1}{3}$, and $\mu_3 = 5$.

(a) Calculate W_1, W_2, and W_3.

(b) Repeat part (*a*) when using the approximation of applying the general model for nonpreemptive priorities presented in Sec. 17.8 instead. Since this general model assumes that the expected service time is the same for all priority classes, use an expected service time of 0.3 so $\mu = 3\frac{1}{3}$. Compare the results with those obtained in part (*a*) and evaluate how good an approximation is provided by making this assumption.

T **17.8-4.*** A particular work center in a job shop can be represented as a single-server queueing system, where jobs arrive according to a Poisson process, with a mean rate of 8 per day. Although the arriving jobs are of three distinct types, the time required to perform any of these jobs has the same exponential distribution, with a mean of 0.1 working day. The practice has been to work on arriving jobs on a first-come-first-served basis. However, it is important that jobs of type 1 not wait very long, whereas the wait is only moderately important for jobs of type 2 and is relatively unimportant for jobs of type 3. These three types arrive with a mean rate of 2, 4, and 2 per day, respectively. Because all three types have experienced rather long delays on average, it has been proposed that the jobs be selected according to an appropriate priority discipline instead.

Compare the expected waiting time (including service) for each of the three types of jobs if the queue discipline is (a) first-come-first-served, (b) nonpreemptive priority, and (c) preemptive priority.

T **17.8-5.** Reconsider the *County Hospital* emergency room problem as analyzed in Sec. 17.8. Suppose that the definitions of the three categories of patients are tightened somewhat in order to move marginal cases into a lower category. Consequently, only 5 percent of the patients will qualify as critical cases, 20 percent as serious cases, and 75 percent as stable cases. Develop a table showing the data presented in Table 17.4 for this revised problem.

17.8-6. Reconsider the queueing system described in Prob. 17.4-6. Suppose now that type 1 customers are more important than type 2 customers. If the queue discipline were changed from first-come-first-served to a priority system with type 1 customers being given nonpreemptive priority over type 2 customers, would this increase, decrease, or keep unchanged the expected total number of customers in the system?
(a) Determine the answer without any calculations, and then present the reasoning that led to your conclusion.
T (b) Verify your conclusion in part (a) by finding the expected total number of customers in the system under each of these two queue disciplines.

17.8-7. Consider the queueing model with a preemptive priority queue discipline presented in Sec. 17.8. Suppose that $s = 1$, $N = 2$, and $(\lambda_1 + \lambda_2) < \mu$; and let P_{ij} be the steady-state probability that there are i members of the higher-priority class and j members of the lower-priority class in the queueing system ($i = 0, 1, 2, \ldots$; $j = 0, 1, 2, \ldots$). Use a method analogous to that presented in Sec. 17.5 to derive a system of linear equations whose simultaneous solution is the P_{ij}. Do not actually obtain this solution.

17.9-1. Consider a queueing system with two servers, where the customers arrive from two different sources. From source 1, the customers always arrive 2 at a time, where the time between consecutive arrivals of pairs of customers has an exponential distribution with a mean of 20 minutes. Source 2 is itself a two-server queueing system, which has a Poisson input process with a mean rate of 7 customers per hour, and the service time from each of these two servers has an exponential distribution with a mean of 15 minutes. When a customer completes service at source 2, he or she immediately enters the queueing system under consideration for another type of service. In the latter queueing system, the queue discipline is preemptive priority where customers from source 1 always have preemptive priority over customers from source 2. However, service times are independent and identically distributed

for both types of customers according to an exponential distribution with a mean of 6 minutes.
(a) First focus on the problem of deriving the steady-state distribution of *only* the number of source 1 customers in the queueing system under consideration. Using a continuous time Markov chain formulation, define the states and construct the rate diagram for most efficiently deriving this distribution (but do not actually derive it).
(b) Now focus on the problem of deriving the steady-state distribution of the *total* number of customers of both types in the queueing system under consideration. Using a continuous time Markov chain formulation, define the states and construct the rate diagram for most efficiently deriving this distribution (but do not actually derive it).
(c) Now focus on the problem of deriving the steady-state *joint* distribution of the number of customers of each type in the queueing system under consideration. Using a continuous time Markov chain formulation, define the states and construct the rate diagram for deriving this distribution (but do not actually derive it).

17.9-2. Consider a system of two infinite queues in series, where each of the two service facilities has a single server. All service times are independent and have an exponential distribution, with a mean of 3 minutes at facility 1 and 4 minutes at facility 2. Facility 1 has a Poisson input process with a mean rate of 10 per hour.
(a) Find the steady-state distribution of the number of customers at facility 1 and then at facility 2. Then show the product form solution for the *joint* distribution of the number at the respective facilities.
(b) What is the probability that both servers are idle?
(c) Find the expected *total* number of customers in the system and the expected *total* waiting time (including service times) for a customer.

17.9-3. Under the assumptions specified in Sec. 17.9 for a system of infinite queues in series, this kind of queueing network actually is a special case of a Jackson network. Demonstrate that this is true by describing this system as a Jackson network, including specifying the values of the a_j and the p_{ij}, given λ for this system.

17.9-4. Consider a Jackson network with three service facilities having the parameter values shown below.

Facility j	s_j	μ_j	a_j	p_{ij}		
				$i = 1$	$i = 2$	$i = 3$
$j = 1$	1	40	10	0	0.3	0.4
$j = 2$	1	50	15	0.5	0	0.5
$j = 3$	1	30	3	0.3	0.2	0

T **(a)** Find the total arrival rate at each of the facilities.

(b) Find the steady-state distribution of the number of customers at facility 1, facility 2, and facility 3. Then show the product form solution for the joint distribution of the number at the respective facilities.

(c) What is the probability that all the facilities have empty queues (no customers waiting to begin service)?

(d) Find the expected total number of customers in the system.

(e) Find the expected total waiting time (including service times) for a customer.

CASE 17.1   REDUCING IN-PROCESS INVENTORY

Jim Wells, vice-president for manufacturing of the Northern Airplane Company, is exasperated. His walk through the company's most important plant this morning has left him in a foul mood. However, he now can vent his temper at Jerry Carstairs, the plant's production manager, who has just been summoned to Jim's office.

"Jerry, I just got back from walking through the plant, and I am very upset." "What is the problem, Jim?" "Well, you know how much I have been emphasizing the need to cut down on our in-process inventory." "Yes, we've been working hard on that," responds Jerry. "Well, not hard enough!" Jim raises his voice even higher. "Do you know what I found by the presses?" "No." "Five metal sheets still waiting to be formed into wing sections. And then, right next door at the inspection station, 13 wing sections! The inspector was inspecting one of them, but the other 12 were just sitting there. You know we have a couple hundred thousand dollars tied up in each of those wing sections. So between the presses and the inspection station, we have a few million bucks worth of terribly expensive metal just sitting there. We can't have that!"

The chagrined Jerry Carstairs tries to respond. "Yes, Jim, I am well aware that that inspection station is a bottleneck. It usually isn't nearly as bad as you found it this morning, but it is a bottleneck. Much less so for the presses. You really caught us on a bad morning." "I sure hope so," retorts Jim, "but you need to prevent anything nearly this bad happening even occasionally. What do you propose to do about it?" Jerry now brightens noticeably in his response. "Well actually, I've already been working on this problem. I have a couple proposals on the table and I have asked an operations research analyst on my staff to analyze these proposals and report back with recommendations." "Great," responds Jim, "glad to see you are on top of the problem. Give this your highest priority and report back to me as soon as possible." "Will do," promises Jerry.

Here is the problem that Jerry and his OR analyst are addressing. Each of 10 identical presses is being used to form wing sections out of large sheets of specially processed metal. The sheets arrive randomly to the group of presses at a mean rate of 7 per hour. The time required by a press to form a wing section out of a metal sheet has an exponential distribution with a mean of 1 hour. When finished, the wing sections arrive randomly at an inspection station at the same mean rate as the metal sheets arrived at the presses (7 per hour). A single inspector has the full-time job of inspecting these wing sections to make sure they meet specifications. Each inspection takes her $7\frac{1}{2}$ minutes, so she can inspect 8 wing sections per hour. This inspection rate has resulted in a substantial average amount of in-process inventory at the inspection station (i.e., the average number of wing sheets waiting to complete inspection is fairly large), in addition to that already found at the group of machines.

The cost of this in-process inventory is estimated to be $8 per hour for each metal sheet at the presses or each wing section at the inspection station. Therefore, Jerry Carstairs has made two alternative proposals to reduce the average level of in-process inventory.

Proposal 1 is to use slightly less power for the presses (which would increase their average time to form a wing section to 1.2 hours), so that the inspector can keep up with their output better. This also would reduce the cost of the power for running each machine from $7.00 to $6.50 per hour. (By contrast, increasing to maximum power would increase this cost to $7.50 per hour while decreasing the average time to form a wing section to 0.8 hour.)

Proposal 2 is to substitute a certain younger inspector for this task. He is somewhat faster (albeit with some variability in his inspection times because of less experience), so he should keep up better. (His inspection time would have an Erlang distribution with a mean of 7.2 minutes and a shape parameter $k = 2$.) This inspector is in a job classification that calls for a total compensation (including benefits) of $19 per hour, whereas the current inspector is in a lower job classification where the compensation is $17 per hour. (The inspection times for each of these inspectors are typical of those in the same job classification.)

You are the OR analyst on Jerry Carstair's staff who has been asked to analyze this problem. He wants you to "use the latest OR techniques to see how much each proposal would cut down on in-process inventory and then make your recommendations."

(a) To provide a basis of comparison, begin by evaluating the status quo. Determine the expected amount of in-process inventory at the presses and at the inspection station. Then calculate the expected total cost per hour when considering all of the following: the cost of the in-process inventory, the cost of the power for runnng the presses, and the cost of the inspector.

(b) What would be the effect of proposal 1? Why? Make specific comparisons to the results from part (a). Explain this outcome to Jerry Carstairs.

(c) Determine the effect of proposal 2. Make specific comparisons to the results from part (a). Explain this outcome to Jerry Carstairs.

(d) Make your recommendations for reducing the average level of in-process inventory at the inspection station and at the group of machines. Be specific in your recommendations, and support them with quantitative analysis like that done in part (a). Make specific comparisons to the results from part (a), and cite the improvements that your recommendations would yield.

18

The Application of Queueing Theory

Queueing theory has enjoyed a prominent place among the modern analytical techniques of OR. However, the emphasis thus far has been on developing a descriptive mathematical theory. Thus, queueing theory is not directly concerned with achieving the goal of OR: optimal decision making. Rather, it develops information on the behavior of queueing systems. This theory provides part of the information needed to conduct an OR study attempting to find the best design for a queueing system.

This chapter discusses the *application* of queueing theory in the broader context of an overall OR study. It begins by introducing three examples that will be used for illustration throughout the chapter. Section 18.2 discusses the basic considerations for decision making in this context. The following two sections then develop decision models for the *optimal* design of queueing systems. The chapter concludes with a survey of some award-winning applications of queueing theory.

18.1 EXAMPLES

Example 1—How Many Repairers?

SIMULATION, INC., a small company that makes gidgets for analog computers, has 10 gidget-making machines. However, because these machines break down and require repair frequently, the company has only enough operators to operate eight machines at a time, so two machines are available on a standby basis for use while other machines are down. Thus, eight machines are always operating whenever no more than two machines are waiting to be repaired, but the number of operating machines is reduced by 1 for each additional machine waiting to be repaired.

The time until any given operating machine breaks down has an exponential distribution, with a mean of 20 days. (A machine that is idle on a standby basis cannot break down.) The time required to repair a machine also has an exponential distribution, with a mean of 2 days. Until now the company has had just one repairer to repair these machines, which has frequently resulted in reduced productivity because fewer than eight machines are operating. Therefore, the company is considering hiring a second repairer, so that two machines can be repaired simultaneously.

Thus, the queueing system to be studied has the repairers as its servers and the machines requiring repair as its customers, where the problem is to choose between having one or two servers. (Notice the analogy between this problem and the County Hospital emergency room problem described in Sec. 17.1.) With one slight exception, this system fits the *finite calling population variation* of the $M/M/s$ model presented in Sec. 17.6, where $N = 10$ machines, $\lambda = \frac{1}{20}$ customer per day (for each operating machine), and $\mu = \frac{1}{2}$ customer per day. The exception is that the λ_0 and λ_1 parameters of the birth-and-death process are changed from $\lambda_0 = 10\lambda$ and $\lambda_1 = 9\lambda$ to $\lambda_0 = 8\lambda$ and $\lambda_1 = 8\lambda$. (All the other parameters are the same as those given in Sec. 17.6.) Therefore, the C_n factors for calculating the P_n probabilities change accordingly (see Sec. 17.5).

Each repairer costs the company approximately $280 per day. However, the estimated *lost profit* from having fewer than eight machines operating to produce gidgets is $400 per day for each machine down. (The company can sell the full output from eight operating machines, but not much more.)

The analysis of this problem will be pursued in Secs. 18.3 and 18.4.

Example 2—Which Computer?

EMERALD UNIVERSITY is making plans to lease a supercomputer to be used for scientific research by the faculty and students. Two models are being considered: one from the MBI Corporation and the other from the CRAB Company. The MBI computer costs more but is somewhat faster than the CRAB computer. In particular, if a sequence of typical jobs were run continuously for one 24-hour day, the number completed would have a Poisson distribution with a mean of 30 and 25 for the MBI and the CRAB computers, respectively. It is estimated that an average of 20 jobs will be submitted per day and that the time from one submission to the next will have an exponential distribution with a mean of 0.05 day. The leasing cost per day would be $5,000 for the MBI computer and $3,750 for the CRAB computer.

Thus, the queueing system of concern has the computer as its (single) server and the jobs to be run as its customers. Furthermore, this system fits the $M/M/1$ model presented at the beginning of Sec. 17.6. With 1 day as the unit of time, $\lambda = 20$ customers per day, and $\mu = 30$ and 25 customers per day with the MBI and the CRAB computers, respectively. You will see in Secs. 18.3 and 18.4 how the decision was made between the two computers.

Example 3—How Many Tool Cribs?

The MECHANICAL COMPANY is designing a new plant. This plant will need to include one or more tool cribs in the factory area to store tools required by the shop mechanics. The tools will be handed out by clerks as the mechanics arrive and request them and will be returned to the clerks when they are no longer needed. In existing plants, there have been frequent complaints from supervisors that their mechanics have had to waste too much time traveling to tool cribs and waiting to be served, so it appears that there should be *more* tool cribs and *more* clerks in the new plant. On the other hand, management is exerting pressure to reduce overhead in the new plant, and this reduction would lead to *fewer* tool cribs and *fewer* clerks. To resolve these conflicting pressures, an OR study is to be conducted to determine just how many tool cribs and clerks the new plant should have.

Each tool crib constitutes a queueing system, with the clerks as its servers and the mechanics as its customers. Based on previous experience, it is estimated that the time required by a tool crib clerk to service a mechanic has an exponential distribution, with a mean of $\frac{1}{2}$ minute. Judging from the anticipated number of mechanics in the entire factory area, it is also predicted that they would require this service randomly but at a mean rate of 2 mechanics per minute. Therefore, it was decided to use the *M/M/s* model of Sec. 17.6 to represent each queueing system. With 1 hour as the unit of time, $\mu = 120$. If only one tool crib were to be provided, λ also would be 120. With more than one tool crib, this mean arrival rate would be divided among the different queueing systems.

The total cost to the company of each tool crib clerk is about $20 per hour. The capital recovery costs, upkeep costs, and so forth associated with each tool crib provided are estimated to be $16 per working hour. While a mechanic is busy, the value to the company of his or her output averages about $48 per hour.

Sections 18.3 and 18.4 include discussions of how this (and additional) information was used to make the required decisions.

18.2 DECISION MAKING

Queueing-type situations that require decision making arise in a wide variety of contexts. For this reason, it is not possible to present a meaningful decision-making procedure that is applicable to all these situations. Instead, this section attempts to give a broad conceptual picture of a typical approach.

Designing a queueing system typically involves making one or a combination of the following decisions:

1. Number of servers at a service facility
2. Efficiency of the servers
3. Number of service facilities.

When such problems are formulated in terms of a queueing model, the corresponding decision variables usually are s (number of servers at each facility), μ (mean service rate per busy server), and λ (mean arrival rate at each facility). The *number of service facilities* is directly related to λ because, assuming a uniform workload among the facilities, λ equals the total mean arrival rate to all facilities divided by the number of facilities.

Refer to Sec. 18.1 and note how the three examples there respectively illustrate situations involving these three decisions. In particular, the decision facing Simulation, Inc., is *how many repairers* (servers) to provide. The problem for Emerald University is *how fast a computer* (server) is needed. The problem facing Mechanical Company is *how many tool cribs* (service facilities) to install as well as *how many clerks* (servers) to provide at each facility.

The first kind of decision is particularly common in practice. However, the other two also arise frequently, particularly for the internal service systems described in Sec. 17.3. One example illustrating a decision on the efficiency of the servers is the selection of the type of materials-handling equipment (the servers) to purchase to transport certain kinds of loads (the customers). Another such example is the determination of the size of a maintenance crew (where the entire crew is one server). Other decisions concern the number of service facilities, such as copy centers, computer facilities, tool cribs, storage areas, and so on, to distribute throughout an area.

All the specific decisions discussed here involve the general question of the *appropriate level of service* to provide in a queueing system. As mentioned at the beginning of Chap. 17, decisions regarding the amount of service capacity to provide usually are based primarily on two considerations: (1) the cost incurred by providing the service, as shown in Fig. 18.1, and (2) the amount of waiting for that service, as suggested in Fig. 18.2. Figure 18.2 can be obtained by using the appropriate waiting-time equation from queueing theory.

These two considerations create conflicting pressures on the decision maker. The objective of reducing service costs recommends a minimal level of service. On the other hand, long waiting times are undesirable, which recommends a high level of service. Therefore, it is necessary to strive for some type of compromise. To assist in finding this compromise, Figs. 18.1 and 18.2 may be combined, as shown in Fig. 18.3. The problem is thereby reduced to selecting the point on the curve of Fig. 18.3 that gives the best balance between the average delay in being serviced and the cost of providing that service. Reference to Figs. 18.1 and 18.2 indicates the corresponding level of service.

FIGURE 18.1
Service cost as a function of service level.

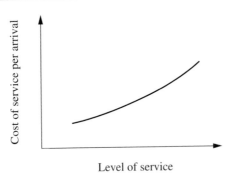

FIGURE 18.2
Expected waiting time as a function of service level.

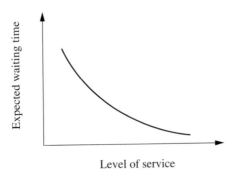

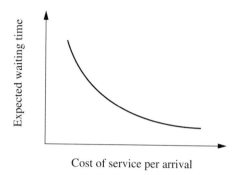

FIGURE 18.3
Relationship between average delay and service cost.

Obtaining the proper balance between delays and service costs requires answers to such questions as, How much expenditure on service is equivalent (in its detrimental impact) to a customer's being delayed 1 unit of time? Thus, to compare service costs and waiting times, it is necessary to adopt (explicitly or implicitly) a common measure of their impact. The natural choice for this common measure is cost, which then requires estimation of the cost of waiting.

Because of the diversity of waiting-line situations, no single process for estimating the cost of waiting is generally applicable. However, we shall discuss the basic considerations involved for several types of situations.

One broad category is where the customers are *external* to the organization providing the service; i.e., they are *outsiders* bringing their business to the organization. Consider first the case of *profit-making* organizations (typified by the commercial service systems described in Sec. 17.3). From the viewpoint of the decision maker, the cost of waiting probably consists primarily of the *lost profit* from *lost business*. This loss of business may occur immediately (because the customer grows impatient and leaves) or in the future (because the customer is sufficiently irritated that he or she does not come again). This kind of cost is quite difficult to estimate, and it may be necessary to revert to other criteria, such as a tolerable probability distribution of waiting times. When the customer is not a human being, but a job being performed on order, there may be more readily identifiable costs incurred, such as those caused by idle in-process inventories or increased expediting and administrative effort.

Now consider the type of situation where service is provided on a *nonprofit* basis to customers *external* to the organization (typical of social service systems and some transportation service systems described in Sec. 17.3). In this case, the cost of waiting usually is a *social cost* of some kind. Thus, it is necessary to evaluate the consequences of the waiting for the individuals involved and/or for society as a whole and to try to impute a monetary value to avoiding these consequences. Once again, this kind of cost is quite difficult to estimate, and it may be necessary to revert to other criteria.

A situation may be more amenable to estimating waiting costs if the customers are *internal* to the organization providing the service (as for the internal service systems discussed in Sec. 17.3). For example, the customers may be machines (as in Example 1) or employees (as in Example 3) of a firm. Therefore, it may be possible to identify directly some of or all the costs associated with the idleness of these customers. Typically, what

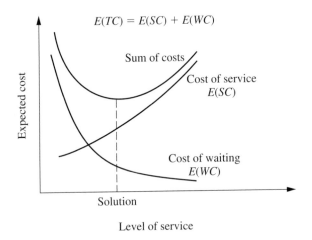

FIGURE 18.4
Conceptual solution procedure for many waiting-line problems.

is being wasted by this idleness is *productive output,* in which case the waiting cost becomes the *lost profit* from *all lost productivity.*

Given that the *cost of waiting* has been evaluated explicitly, the remainder of the analysis is conceptually straightforward. The objective is to determine the level of service that minimizes the total of the expected cost of service and the expected cost of waiting for that service. This concept is depicted in Fig. 18.4, where WC denotes *waiting cost,* SC denotes *service cost,* and TC denotes *total cost.* Thus, the mathematical statement of the objective is to

Minimize $E(TC) = E(SC) + E(WC)$.

The next two sections are concerned with the application of this concept to various types of problems. Thus, Sec. 18.3 describes how $E(WC)$ can be expressed mathematically. Section 18.4 then focuses on $E(SC)$ to formulate the overall objective function $E(TC)$ for several basic design problems (including some with multiple decision variables, so that the level-of-service axis in Fig. 18.4 then requires more than one dimension).

18.3 FORMULATION OF WAITING-COST FUNCTIONS

To express $E(WC)$ mathematically, we must first formulate a *waiting-cost function* that describes how the actual waiting cost being incurred varies with the current behavior of the queueing system. The form of this function depends on the context of the individual problem. However, most situations can be represented by one of the two basic forms described next.

The $g(N)$ Form

Consider first the situation discussed in the preceding section where the queueing system *customers* are *internal* to the organization providing the service, and so the primary cost of waiting may be the *lost profit from lost productivity.* The *rate* at which productive output is lost sometimes is essentially *proportional* to the number of customers in the queueing system. However, in many cases there is not enough productive work available to keep all the members of the calling population continuously busy. Therefore, little productive output may be lost by having just a few members idle, waiting for service in the queueing system, whereas the loss may increase greatly if a few more members are made idle because they require service. Consequently, the primary property of the queueing system that determines the *current rate* at which waiting costs are being incurred is N, the number of customers in the system. Thus, the form of the waiting-cost function for this kind of situation is that illustrated in Fig. 18.5, namely, a function of N. We shall denote this form by $g(N)$.

The $g(N)$ function is constructed for a particular situation by estimating $g(n)$, the waiting-cost rate incurred when $N = n$, for $n = 1, 2, \ldots$, where $g(0) = 0$. After computing the P_n probabilities for a given design of the queueing system, we can calculate

$$E(\text{WC}) = E(g(N)).$$

Because N is a random variable, this calculation is made by using the expression for the expected value of a *function* of a *discrete* random variable

$$E(\text{WC}) = \sum_{n=0}^{\infty} g(n)P_n.$$

The Linear Case.   For the special case where $g(N)$ is a *linear function* (i.e., when the waiting cost is proportional to N), then

$$g(N) = C_w N,$$

where C_w is the cost of waiting per unit time for each customer. In this case, $E(\text{WC})$ reduces to

$$E(\text{WC}) = C_w \sum_{n=0}^{\infty} n P_n = C_w L.$$

FIGURE 18.5
The waiting-cost function as a function of N.

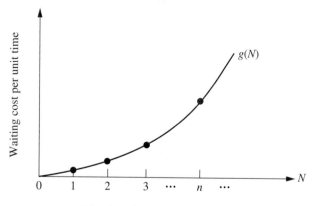

Number of customers in the system

Example 1—How Many Repairers?   For Example 1 of Sec. 18.1, Simulation, Inc., has two standby widget-making machines, so there is no lost productivity as long as the number of customers (machines requiring repair) in the system does not exceed 2. However, for each *additional* customer (up to the maximum of 10 total), the estimated lost profit is $400 per day. Therefore,

$$g(n) = \begin{cases} 0 & \text{for } n = 0, 1, 2 \\ 400(n-2) & \text{for } n = 3, 4, \ldots, 10, \end{cases}$$

as shown in Table 18.1. Consequently, after calculating the P_n probabilities as described in Sec. 18.1, $E(\text{WC})$ is calculated by summing the rightmost column of Table 18.1 for each of the two cases of interest, namely, having one repairer ($s = 1$) or two repairers ($s = 2$).

The $h(\mathcal{W})$ Form

Now consider the cases discussed in Sec. 18.2 where the queueing system *customers* are *external* to the organization providing the service. Three major types of queueing systems described in Sec. 17.3—commercial service systems, transportation service systems, and social service systems—typically fall into this category. In the case of commercial service systems, the primary cost of waiting may be the lost profit from lost future business. For transportation service systems and social systems, the primary cost of waiting may be in the form of a social cost. However, for either type of cost, its magnitude tends to be affected greatly by the size of the waiting times experienced by the customers. Thus, the primary property of the queueing system that determines the waiting cost currently being incurred is $\mathcal{W}$, the waiting time in the system for the *individual* customers. Consequently, the form of the waiting-cost function for this kind of situation is that illustrated in Fig. 18.6, namely, a function of $\mathcal{W}$. We shall denote this form by $h(\mathcal{W})$.

Note that the example of a $h(\mathcal{W})$ function shown in Fig. 18.6 is a nonlinear function where the slope keeps increasing as $\mathcal{W}$ increases. Although $h(\mathcal{W})$ sometimes is a simple linear function instead, it is fairly common to have this kind of nonlinear function. An in-

TABLE 18.1 Calculation of $E(\text{WC})$ for Example 1

$N = n$	$g(n)$	$s = 1$		$s = 2$	
		P_n	$g(n)P_n$	P_n	$g(n)P_n$
0	0	0.271	0	0.433	0
1	0	0.217	0	0.346	0
2	0	0.173	0	0.139	0
3	400	0.139	56	0.055	24
4	800	0.097	78	0.019	16
5	1,200	0.058	70	0.006	8
6	1,600	0.029	46	0.001	0
7	2,000	0.012	24	3×10^{-4}	0
8	2,400	0.003	7	4×10^{-5}	0
9	2,800	7×10^{-4}	0	4×10^{-6}	0
10	3,200	7×10^{-5}	0	2×10^{-7}	0
$E(\text{WC})$			\$281 per day		\$48 per day

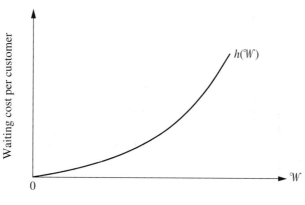

FIGURE 18.6
The waiting-cost function as a function of $\mathcal{W}$.

creasing slope reflects a situation where the *marginal cost* of extending the waiting time keeps increasing. A customer may not mind a "normal" wait of reasonable length, in which case there may be virtually no negative consequences for the organization providing the service in terms of lost profit from lost future business, a social cost, etc. However, if the wait extends even further, the customer may become increasingly exasperated, perhaps even missing deadlines. In such a situation, the negative consequences to the organization may rapidly become relatively severe.

One way of constructing the $h(\mathcal{W})$ function is to estimate $h(w)$ (the waiting cost incurred when a customer's waiting time $\mathcal{W} = w$) for several values of w and then to fit a polynomial to these points. The expectation of this function of a continuous random variable is then defined as

$$E(h(\mathcal{W})) = \int_0^\infty h(w)f_W(w)\,dw,$$

where $f_W(w)$ is the probability density function of $\mathcal{W}$. However, because $E(h(\mathcal{W}))$ is the expected waiting cost *per customer* and $E(\text{WC})$ is the expected waiting cost *per unit time,* these two quantities are not equal in this case. To relate them, it is necessary to multiply $E(h(\mathcal{W}))$ by the expected *number of customers per unit time* entering the queueing system. In particular, if the mean arrival rate is a constant λ, then

$$E(\text{WC}) = \lambda E(h(\mathcal{W})) = \lambda \int_0^\infty h(w)f_W(w)\,dw.$$

Example 2—Which Computer?   Because the faculty and students of Emerald University would experience different turnaround times with the two computers under consideration (see Sec. 18.1), the choice between the computers required an evaluation of the consequences of making them wait for their jobs to be run. Therefore, several leading scientists on the faculty were asked to evaluate these consequences.

The scientists agreed that one major consequence is a *delay in getting research done.* Little effective progress can be made while one is awaiting the results from a computer run. The scientists estimated that it would be worth $500 to reduce this delay by a day. Therefore, this component of waiting cost was estimated to be $500 per day, that is, $500\mathcal{W}$, where $\mathcal{W}$ is expressed in days.

The scientists also pointed out that a second major consequence of waiting is a *break in the continuity of the research.* Although a short delay (a fraction of a day) causes little problem in this regard, a longer delay causes significant wasted time in having to gear up to resume the research. The scientists estimated that this wasted time would be roughly proportional to the *square* of the delay time. Dollar figures of $100 and $400 were then imputed to the value of being able to avoid this consequence entirely rather than having a wait of $\frac{1}{2}$ day and 1 day, respectively. Therefore, this component of the waiting cost was estimated to be $400\mathcal{W}^2$.

This analysis yields

$$h(\mathcal{W}) = 500\mathcal{W} + 400\mathcal{W}^2.$$

Because

$$f_W(w) = \mu(1 - \rho)e^{-\mu(1-\rho)w}$$

for the *M/M/*1 model (see Sec. 17.6) fitting this single-server queueing system,

$$E(h(\mathcal{W})) = \int_0^\infty (500w + 400w^2)\mu(1 - \rho)e^{-\mu(1-\rho)w}\,dw,$$

where $\rho = \lambda/\mu$ for a single-server system. Since $\mu(1 - \rho) = (\mu - \lambda)$, the values of μ and λ presented in Sec. 18.1 give

$$\mu(1 - \rho) = \begin{cases} 10 & \text{for MBI computer} \\ 5 & \text{for CRAB computer.} \end{cases}$$

Evaluating the integral for these two cases yields

$$E(h(\mathcal{W})) = \begin{cases} 58 & \text{for MBI computer} \\ 132 & \text{for CRAB computer.} \end{cases}$$

The result represents the expected waiting cost (in dollars) for each person arriving with a job to be run. Because $\lambda = 20$, the total expected waiting cost per day becomes

$$E(\text{WC}) = \begin{cases} \$1,160 \text{ per day} & \text{for MBI computer} \\ \$2,640 \text{ per day} & \text{for CRAB computer.} \end{cases}$$

The Linear Case.   Before turning to the next example, consider now the special case where $h(\mathcal{W})$ is a linear function,

$$h(\mathcal{W}) = C_w\mathcal{W},$$

where C_w is the cost of waiting per unit time for each customer. In this case, $E(\text{WC})$ reduces to

$$E(\text{WC}) = \lambda E(C_w\mathcal{W}) = C_w(\lambda W) = C_w L.$$

Note that this result is identical to the result when $g(N)$ is a linear function. Consequently, when the total waiting cost incurred by the queueing system is simply *proportional* to the total waiting time, it does not matter whether the $g(N)$ or the $h(\mathcal{W})$ form is used for the waiting-cost function.

Example 3—How Many Tool Cribs? As indicated in Sec. 18.1, the value to the Mechanical Company of a busy mechanic's output averages about \$48 per hour. Thus, $C_w = 48$. Consequently, for each tool crib the expected waiting cost per hour is

$$E(\text{WC}) = 48L,$$

where L represents the expected number of mechanics waiting (or being served) at the tool crib.

18.4 DECISION MODELS

We mentioned in Sec. 18.2 that three common decision variables in designing queueing systems are s (number of servers), μ (mean service rate for each server), and λ (mean arrival rate at each service facility). We shall now formulate models for making some of these decisions.

Model 1—Unknown *s*

Model 1 is designed for the case where both μ and λ are fixed at a particular service facility, but where a decision must be made on the number of servers to have on duty at the facility.

Formulation of Model 1.

Definition: C_s = marginal cost of a server per unit time.
Given: μ, λ, C_s.
To find: s.
Objective: Minimize $E(\text{TC}) = C_s s + E(\text{WC})$.

Because only a few alternative values of s normally need to be considered, the usual way of solving this model is to calculate $E(\text{TC})$ for these values of s and select the minimizing one. For the linear case where $E(\text{WC}) = C_w L$, an Excel template has been provided in your OR Courseware for performing these calculations when the queueing system fits the $M/M/s$ queueing model. However, as long as the queueing model is tractable, it often is not very difficult to perform these calculations yourself for other cases, as illustrated by the following example.

Example 1—How Many Repairers? For Example 1 of Sec. 18.1, each repairer (server) costs Simulation, Inc., approximately \$280 per day. Thus, with 1 day as the unit of time, $C_s = 280$. Using the values of $E(\text{WC})$ calculated in Table 18.1 then yields the results shown in Table 18.2, which indicate that the company should continue having just one repairer.

Model 2—Unknown μ and *s*

Model 2 is designed for the case where both the efficiency of service, measured by μ, and the number of servers s at a service facility need to be selected.

TABLE 18.2 Calculation of $E(TC)$ in dollars per day for Example 1

s	$C_s s$	$E(WC)$	$E(TC)$
1	$280	$281	$561 per day ← minimum
2	$560	$ 48	$608 per day
≥3	≥$840	≥$ 0	≥$840 per day

Alternative values of μ may be available because there is a choice on the *quality* of the servers. For example, when the servers will be materials-handling units, the quality of the units to be purchased affects their service rate for moving loads.

Another possibility is that the *speed* of the servers can be adjusted mechanically. For example, the speed of machines frequently can be adjusted by changing the amount of power consumed, which also changes the cost of operation.

Still another type of example is the selection of the number of crews (the servers) and the size of each crew (which determines μ) for jointly performing a certain task. The task might be maintenance work, or loading and unloading operations, or inspection work, or setup of machines, and so forth.

In many cases, only a few alternative values of μ are available, e.g., the efficiency of the alternative types of materials-handling equipment or the efficiency of the alternative crew sizes.

Formulation of Model 2.

Definitions: $f(\mu)$ = marginal cost of server per unit time when mean service rate is μ.

A = set of feasible values of μ.

Given: $\lambda, f(\mu), A$.

To find: μ, s.

Objective: Minimize $E(TC) = f(\mu)s + E(WC)$,   subject to $\mu \in A$.

Example 2—Which Computer?   As indicated in Sec. 18.1, $\mu = 30$ for the MBI computer and $\mu = 25$ for the CRAB computer, where 1 day is the unit of time. These computers are the only two being considered by Emerald University, so

$$A = \{25, 30\}.$$

Because the leasing cost per day is $3,750 for the CRAB computer ($\mu = 25$) and $5,000 for the MBI computer ($\mu = 30$),

$$f(\mu) = \begin{cases} 3,750 & \text{for } \mu = 25 \\ 5,000 & \text{for } \mu = 30. \end{cases}$$

The supercomputer chosen will be the only one available to the faculty and students, so the number of servers (supercomputers) for this queueing system is restricted to $s = 1$. Hence,

$$E(TC) = f(\mu) + E(WC),$$

where $E(WC)$ is given in Sec. 18.3 for the two alternatives. Thus,

$$E(TC) = \begin{cases} 3{,}750 + 2{,}640 = \$6{,}390 \text{ per day} & \text{for CRAB computer} \\ 5{,}000 + 1{,}160 = \$6{,}160 \text{ per day} & \text{for MBI computer.} \end{cases}$$

Consequently, the decision was made to lease the MBI supercomputer.

The Application of Model 2 to Other Situations. This example illustrates a case where the number of feasible values of μ is *finite* but the value of s is fixed. If s were not fixed, a two-stage approach could be used to solve such a problem. First, for each individual value of μ, set $C_s = f(\mu)$, and solve for the value of s that minimizes $E(TC)$ for model 1. Second, compare these minimum $E(TC)$ for the alternative values of μ, and select the one giving the overall minimum.

When the number of feasible values of μ is *infinite* (such as when the speed of a machine or piece of equipment is set mechanically within some feasible interval), another two-stage approach sometimes can be used to solve the problem. First, for each individual value of s, *analytically* solve for the value of μ that minimizes $E(TC)$. [This approach requires setting to zero the derivative of $E(TC)$ with respect to μ and then solving this equation for μ, which can be done only when analytical expressions are available for both $f(\mu)$ and $E(WC)$.] Second, compare these minimum $E(TC)$ for the alternative values of s, and select the one giving the overall minimum.

This analytical approach frequently is relatively straightforward for the case of $s = 1$ (see Prob. 18.4-17). However, because far fewer and less convenient analytical results are available for multiple-server versions of queueing models, this approach is either difficult (requiring computer calculations with numerical methods to solve the equation for μ) or completely impossible when $s > 1$. Therefore, a more practical approach is to consider only a relatively small number of representative values of μ and to use available tabulated results for the appropriate queueing model to obtain (or approximate) $E(TC)$ for these μ values.

A Special Result with Model 2. Fortunately, under certain fairly common circumstances described next, $s = 1$ (and its minimizing value of μ) *must* yield the overall minimum $E(TC)$ for model 2, so $s > 1$ cases need not be considered at all.

> **Optimality of a Single Server.** Under certain conditions, $s = 1$ necessarily is *optimal* for model 2.
>
> The primary conditions[1] are that
>
> 1. The value of μ minimizing $E(TC)$ for $s = 1$ is feasible.
> 2. Function $f(\mu)$ is either *linear* or *concave* (as defined in Appendix 2).

In effect, this optimality result indicates that it is better to concentrate service capacity into one fast server rather than dispersing it among several slow servers. Condition 2 says that this concentrating of a given amount of service capacity can be done without increasing the cost of service. Condition 1 says that it must be possible to make μ sufficiently large that a single server can be used to full advantage.

---

[1]There also are minor restrictions on the queueing model and the waiting-cost function. However, any of the constant service-rate queueing models presented in Chap. 17 for $s \geq 1$ are allowed. If the $g(N)$ form is used for the waiting-cost function, it can be any *increasing* function. If the $h(\mathcal{W})$ form is used, it can be any linear function or any convex function (as defined in Appendix 2), which fits most cases of interest.

TABLE 18.3 Comparison of service efficiency for Model 2 solutions

N = n	Mean Rate of Service Completions
	$(s, \mu) = (s^*, \mu^*)$ versus $(s, \mu) = (1, s^*\mu^*)$
$n = 0$	$0 = 0$
$n = 1, 2, \ldots, s^* - 1$	$n\mu^* < s^*\mu^*$
$n \geq s^*$	$s^*\mu^* = s^*\mu^*$

To understand why this result holds, consider any other solution to model 2, $(s, \mu) = (s^*, \mu^*)$, where $s^* > 1$. The service capacity of this system (as measured by the mean rate of service completions when all servers are working) is $s^*\mu^*$. We shall now compare this solution with the corresponding single-server solution $(s, \mu) = (1, s^*\mu^*)$ having the *same* service capacity. In particular, Table 18.3 compares the mean rate at which service completions occur for each given number of customers in the system $N = n$. This table shows that the service efficiency of the (s^*, μ^*) solution sometimes is worse but never is better than for the $(1, s^*\mu^*)$ solution because it can use the full service capacity only when there are at least s^* customers in the system, whereas the single-server solution uses the full capacity whenever there are *any* customers in the system. Because this lower service efficiency can only increase waiting in the system, $E(WC)$ must be larger for (s^*, μ^*) than for $(1, s^*\mu^*)$. Furthermore, the expected service cost must be at least as large because condition 2 [and $f(0) = 0$] implies that

$$f(\mu^*)s \geq f(s^*\mu^*).$$

Therefore, $E(TC)$ is larger for (s^*, μ^*) than $(1, s^*\mu^*)$. Finally, note that condition 1 implies that there is a feasible solution with $s = 1$ that is at least as good as $(1, s^*\mu^*)$. The conclusion is that *any* $s > 1$ solution *cannot* be optimal for model 2, so $s = 1$ must be optimal.[1]

This result is still of some use even when one or both conditions fail to hold. If μ cannot be made sufficiently large to permit a single server, it still suggests that a *few* fast servers should be preferred to many slow ones. If condition 2 does not hold, we still know that $E(WC)$ is minimized by concentrating any given amount of service capacity into a single server, so the best $s = 1$ solution must be at least nearly optimal unless it causes a *substantial* increase in service cost.

Model 3—Unknown λ and s

Model 3 is designed especially for the case where it is necessary to select both the *number of service facilities* and the *number of servers s* at each facility. In the typical situation, a population (such as the employees in an industrial building) must be provided with a certain service, so a decision must be made as to what proportion of the population (and therefore what value of λ) should be assigned to each service facility. Examples of such facilities include employee facilities (drinking fountains, vending machines, and rest-

[1]For a rigorous proof of this result, see S. Stidham, Jr., "On the Optimality of Single-Server Queueing Systems," *Operations Research,* **18**: 708–732, 1970.

rooms), storage facilities, and reproduction equipment facilities. It may sometimes be clear that only a single server should be provided at each facility (e.g., one drinking fountain or one copy machine), but s often is also a decision variable.

To simplify our presentation, we shall require in model 3 that λ and s be the same for all service facilities. However, it should be recognized that a slight improvement in the indicated solution might be achieved by permitting minor deviations in these parameters at individual facilities. This should be investigated as part of the detailed analysis that generally follows the application of the mathematical model.

Formulation of Model 3.

Definitions: C_s = marginal cost of server per unit time.
C_f = fixed cost of service per service facility per unit time.
λ_p = mean arrival rate for entire calling population.
n = number of service facilities = λ_p/λ.

Given: μ, C_s, C_f, λ_p.
To find: λ, s.
Objective: Minimize $E(\text{TC})$, subject to $\lambda = \lambda_p/n$, where $n = 1, 2, \ldots$.

Finding $E(\text{TC})$. It might appear at first glance that the appropriate expression for the expected total cost per unit time of all the facilities should be

$$E(\text{TC}) \overset{?}{=} n[(C_f + C_s s) + E(\text{WC})],$$

where $E(\text{WC})$ here represents the expected waiting cost per unit time for *each* facility. However, if this expression actually were valid, it would imply that $n = 1$ *necessarily* is optimal for model 3. The reasoning is completely analogous to that for the optimality of a single-server result for model 2; namely, any solution $(n, s) = (n^*, s^*)$ with $n^* > 1$ has higher service costs than the $(n, s) = (1, n^*s^*)$ solution, and it *also* has a higher expected waiting cost because it sometimes makes less effective use of the available service capacity. In particular, it sometimes has idle servers at one facility while customers are waiting at another facility, so the mean rate of service completions would be less than if the customers had access to *all* the servers at one common facility.

Because there are many situations where it obviously would *not* be optimal to have just one service facility (e.g., the number of restrooms in a 50-story building), something must be wrong with this expression. Its deficiency is that it considers only the cost of service and the cost of waiting *at the service facilities* while totally ignoring the cost of the time wasted in *traveling* to and from the facilities. Because travel time would be prohibitive with only one service facility for a large population, enough separate facilities must be distributed throughout the calling population to hold travel time down to a reasonable level.

Thus, letting the random variable T be the round-trip travel time for a customer coming to and going back from one of the service facilities, we see that the total time lost by the customer actually is $\mathcal{W} + T$. (Recall from Chap. 17 that $\mathcal{W}$ is the waiting time in the queueing system *after* the customer arrives.) Therefore, a customer's *total* cost for time lost should be based on $\mathcal{W} + T$ rather than just $\mathcal{W}$. To simplify the analysis, let us separate this total cost into the sum of the waiting-time cost based on $\mathcal{W}$ (or N) and the travel-time cost based on T. We shall also assume that the travel-time cost is proportional to T, where C_t is the cost of each unit of travel time for each customer. For ease of presentation, suppose that the probability distribution of T is the same for each service facility, so that $C_t E(T)$ is the *expected travel cost* for each arrival at any of the service facilities. The resulting expression for $E(\text{TC})$ is

$$E(\text{TC}) = n[(C_f + C_s s) + E(\text{WC}) + \lambda C_t E(T)]$$

because λ is the expected number of arrivals *per unit time* at each facility. Consequently, by evaluating (or estimating) $E(T)$ for each case of interest, model 3 can be solved by calculating $E(\text{TC})$ for various values of s for each n and then selecting the solution giving the overall minimum.

Example 3—How Many Tool Cribs?   For the new plant being designed for the Mechanical Company (see Sec. 18.1), the layout of the portion of the factory area where the mechanics will work is shown in Fig. 18.7. The three possible locations for tool cribs are identified as locations 1, 2, and 3, where access to these locations will be provided by a system of orthogonal aisles parallel to the sides of the indicated area. The coordinates are given in units of feet.

The three basic alternatives being considered are these:

Alternative 1: Have one tool crib—use location 2.
Alternative 2: Have two tool cribs—use locations 1 and 3.
Alternative 3: Have three tool cribs—use locations 1, 2, and 3.

FIGURE 18.7
Layout for Example 3.

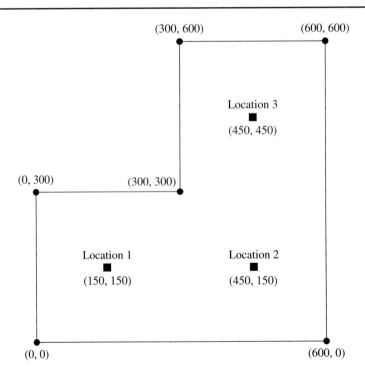

TABLE 18.4 Calculation of $E(TC)$, in dollars per hour for Example 3

n	λ	s	L	$E(T)$	$C_f + C_s s$	$E(WC)$	$\lambda C_t E(T)$	$E(TC)$
1	120	1	∞	0.04	$36	∞	$230.40	∞
1	120	2	1.333	0.04	$56	$64.00	$230.40	$350.40
1	120	3	1.044	0.04	$76	$50.11	$230.40	$356.51
2	60	1	1.000	0.0278	$36	$48.00	$ 80.00	$328.00
2	60	2	0.534	0.0278	$56	$25.63	$ 80.00	$323.26
3	40	1	0.500	0.02	$36	$24.00	$ 38.40	$295.20
3	40	2	0.344	0.02	$56	$16.51	$ 38.40	$332.73

The mechanics will be distributed quite uniformly throughout the area shown, and each mechanic will be assigned to the *nearest* tool crib. It is estimated that the mechanics will walk to and from a tool crib at an average speed of slightly less than 3 miles per hour. Based on this information and an estimate of the average distance traveled on each trip to and from the tool crib, $E(T)$ is estimated to be 0.04, 0.0278, and 0.02 hour for alternatives 1, 2, and 3, respectively. [A supplement to this chapter on the CD-ROM discusses the evaluation of travel time and also spells out how these particular values of $E(T)$ were obtained for this example.]

The stage now is set for using model 3 to choose from these alternatives. Most of the data required for this model are given in Sec. 18.1, namely,

$$\mu = 120 \text{ per hour}, \qquad C_f = \$16 \text{ per hour},$$
$$C_s = \$20 \text{ per hour},$$
$$\lambda_p = 120 \text{ per hour}, \qquad C_t = \$48 \text{ per hour},$$

where the *M/M/s* model given in Sec. 17.6 is used to calculate L and so on. In addition, the end of Sec. 18.3 gives $E(WC) = 48L$ in dollars per hour. Therefore,

$$E(TC) = n\left[(16 + 20s) + 48L + \frac{120}{n} 48E(T)\right].$$

The resulting calculation of $E(TC)$ for various s values for each n is given in Table 18.4, which indicates that the *overall minimum* $E(TC)$ of $295.20 per hour is obtained by having three tool cribs (so $\lambda = 40$ for each), with one clerk at each tool crib.

18.5 SOME AWARD-WINNING APPLICATIONS OF QUEUEING THEORY

The prestigious *Franz Edelman Awards for Management Science Achievement* are awarded annually by the Institute of Operations Research and Management Sciences (INFORMS) for the year's best applications of OR. A rather substantial number of these awards have been given for innovative applications of queueing theory. We briefly describe some of these applications in this section.

One of the early first-prize winners (described in the November 1975 issue, Part 2, of *Interfaces*) was the *Xerox Corporation.* The company had recently introduced a major new duplicating system that was proving to be particularly valuable for its owners. Consequently, these customers were demanding that Xerox's tech reps reduce the waiting times to repair the machines. An OR team then applied queueing theory to study how to best meet the new service requirements. This resulted in replacing the previous one-person tech rep territories by larger three-person tech rep territories. This change had the dramatic effect of both substantially reducing the average waiting times of the customers and increasing the utilization of the tech reps by over 50 percent.

In Sec. 3.5, we described an award-winning application by *United Airlines* (January 1986 issue of *Interfaces*) that resulted in annual savings of over $6 million. This application involved scheduling the work assignments of United's 4,000 reservations sales representatives and support personnel at its 11 reservations offices and the 1,000 customer service agents at its 10 largest airports. After determining how many employees are needed at each location during each half hour of the week, we discussed how linear programming was applied to design the work schedules for all the employees to meet these service requirements most efficiently. However, we never mentioned how these service requirements on the number of employees needed each half hour were determined.

We now are in a position to point out that these service requirements were determined by applying *queueing theory.* Each specific location (e.g., the check-in counters at an airport) constitutes a queueing system with the employees as the servers. After forecasting the mean arrival rate during each half hour of the week, queueing models are used to find the minimum number of servers that will provide satisfactory measures of performance for the queueing system.

L.L. Bean, Inc., the large telemarketer and mail-order catalog house, relied mainly on queueing theory for its award-winning study of how to allocate its telecommunications resources. (The article describing this study is in the January 1991 issue of *Interfaces,* and other articles giving additional information are in the November 1989 and March–April 1993 issues of this journal.) The telephone calls coming in to its call center to place orders are the customers in a large queueing system, with the telephone agents as the servers. The key questions being asked during the study were the following.

1. How many telephone trunk lines should be provided for incoming calls to the call center?
2. How many telephone agents should be scheduled at various times?
3. How many hold positions should be provided for customers waiting for a telephone agent? (Note that the limited number of hold positions causes the system to have a finite queue.)

For each interesting combination of these three quantities, queueing models provide the measures of performance of the queueing system. Given these measures, the OR team carefully assessed the cost of lost sales due to making some customers either incur a busy signal or be placed on hold too long. By adding the cost of the telemarketing resources, the team then was able to find the combination of the three quantities that minimizes the expected total cost. This resulted in cost savings of $9 to $10 million per year.

New York City has a long-standing tradition of using OR techniques in planning and operating many of its complex urban service systems. Starting in the late 1960s, award-winning studies involving queueing theory have been conducted for its Fire Department and its Police Department. (Fires and police emergencies are the customers in these respective queueing systems.) Subsequently, major OR studies (including several more involving queueing theory) have been conducted for its Department of Sanitation, Department of Transportation, Department of Health and Hospitals, Department of Environmental Protection, Office of Management and Budget, and Department of Probation. Because of the success of these studies, many of these departments now have their own in-house OR groups.

The award-winning study in New York City that we will describe here involves its arrest-to-arraignment system. This system consists of the process from when individuals are arrested until they are arraigned (the first court appearance before an arraignment judge, who determines whether there was probable cause for the arrest). Before the study, the city's arrestees (the customers in a queueing system) were in custody waiting to be arraigned for an average of 40 hours (occasionally more than 70 hours). These waiting times were considered excessive, because the arrestees were being held in crowded, noisy conditions that were emotionally stressful, unhealthy, and often physically dangerous. Therefore, a 2-year OR study was conducted to overhaul the system. Both queueing theory and simulation (the subject of Chap. 22) were used. This led to sweeping operational and policy changes that simultaneously reduced average waiting times until arraignment to 24 hours or less and provided annual savings of $9.5 million. (See the January 1993 issue of *Interfaces* for details.)

The first prize in the 1993 competition was won by *AT&T* for a study that (like the preceding one) also combined the use of queueing theory and simulation (January–February 1994 issue of *Interfaces*). The queueing models are of both AT&T's telecommunication network and the call center environment for the typical business customers of AT&T that have such a center. The purpose of the study was to develop a user-friendly PC-based system that AT&T's business customers can use to guide them in how to design or redesign their call centers. Since call centers comprise one of the United States' fastest-growing industries, this system had been used about 2,000 times by AT&T's business customers by 1992. This resulted in more than $750 million in annual profit for these customers.

KeyCorp is one of the largest bank holding companies in the United States, with more than 1,300 branches and over 6,000 tellers. This company's award-winning OR study (January 1996 issue of *Interfaces*) focused on using queueing theory to improve the performance of each branch's queueing system where the tellers serve the customers. This resulted in developing a companywide service excellence management system (SEMS). A key part of SEMS is a performance capture system that collects data on a continuous basis for each discrete component of each teller transaction in a completely automated process. This system enables SEMS to measure branch activities and generate reports on customer waiting times, teller proficiency, and productivity levels. These reports help managers schedule tellers to better match customer arrivals. They also identify opportunities for enhancing the productivity and service provided by the tellers by redesigning the service process and providing performance standards. These efforts led to a huge 53 percent reduction in the average service times, a dramatic improvement in customer waiting times, and a major increase in the level of customer satisfaction. At the same time, SEMS is expected to reduce personnel expenses by $98 million over 5 years.

There have been many other award-winning applications of queueing theory, as well as numerous additional articles describing other successful applications. However, the several examples presented in this section hopefully have given you a feeling for the kinds of applications that are occurring and for the impact they sometimes have.

18.6 CONCLUSIONS

This chapter has discussed the application of queueing theory for *designing* queueing systems. Every individual problem has its own special characteristics, so no standard procedure can be prescribed to fit every situation. Therefore, the emphasis has been on introducing fundamental considerations and approaches that can be adapted to most cases. We have focused on three particularly common decision variables (s, μ, and λ) as a vehicle for introducing and illustrating these concepts. However, there are many other possible decision variables (e.g., the size of a waiting room for a queueing system) and many more complicated situations (e.g., designing a *priority* queueing system) that can also be analyzed in a similar way.

Another useful area for the application of queueing theory is the development of policies for *controlling* queueing systems, e.g., for *dynamically* adjusting the number of servers or the service rate to compensate for changes in the number of customers in the system. Research is being conducted in this area.

Queueing theory has proved to be a very useful tool, and we anticipate that its use will continue to grow as recognition of the many guises of queueing systems grows.

SELECTED REFERENCES

1. Allen, A. O.: *Probability, Statistics, and Queueing Theory with Computer Science Applications,* 2d ed., Academic Press, New York, 1990, chaps. 5–6.
2. Hall, R. W.: *Queueing Methods: For Services and Manufacturing,* Prentice-Hall, Englewood Cliffs, NJ, 1991.
3. Hillier, F. S., M. S. Hillier, and G. J. Lieberman: *Introduction to Management Science: A Modeling and Case Studies Approach with Spreadsheets,* Irwin/McGraw-Hill, Burr Ridge, IL, 2000, chap. 14.
4. Kleinrock, L.: *Queueing Systems, vol. II: Computer Applications,* Wiley, New York, 1976.
5. Lee, A. M.: *Applied Queueing Theory,* St. Martin's Press, New York, 1966.
6. Newell, G. F.: *Applications of Queueing Theory,* 2d ed., Chapman and Hall, London, 1982.
7. Papadopoulos, H. T., C. Heavey, and J. Browne: *Queueing Theory in Manufacturing Systems Analysis and Design,* Chapman and Hall, London, 1993.

LEARNING AIDS FOR THIS CHAPTER IN YOUR OR COURSEWARE

"Ch. 18—Application of QT" Excel File:

Same templates as listed at the end of Chap. 17, plus
Template for *M/M/s* Economic Analysis of Number of Servers

Supplement to This Chapter:

The Evaluation of Travel Time (appears on the book's website, www.mhhe.com/hillier).

See Appendix 1 for documentation of the software.

PROBLEMS

To the left of each of the following problems (or their parts), we have inserted a T whenever one of the templates for this chapter (and the preceding chapter) can be useful. An asterisk on the problem number indicates that at least a partial answer is given in the back of the book.

18.2-1. For each kind of queueing system listed in Prob. 17.3-1, briefly describe the nature of the *cost of service* and the *cost of waiting* that would need to be considered in designing the system.

18.3-1.* Suppose that a queueing system fits the $M/M/1$ model described in Sec. 17.6, with $\lambda = 2$ and $\mu = 4$. Evaluate the expected waiting cost per unit time $E(\text{WC})$ for this system when its waiting-cost function has the form
(a) $g(N) = 10N + 2N^2$.
(b) $h(\mathcal{W}) = 25\mathcal{W} + \mathcal{W}^3$.

18.3-2. Follow the instructions of Prob. 18.3-1 for the following waiting-cost functions.

(a) $g(N) = \begin{cases} 10N & \text{for } N = 0, 1, 2 \\ 6N^2 & \text{for } N = 3, 4, 5 \\ N^3 & \text{for } N > 5. \end{cases}$

(b) $h(\mathcal{W}) = \begin{cases} \mathcal{W} & \text{for } 0 \le \mathcal{W} \le 1 \\ \mathcal{W}^2 & \text{for } \mathcal{W} \ge 1. \end{cases}$

T **18.4-1.** Section 18.3 indicates that a linear waiting-cost function yields $E(\text{WC}) = C_w L$, where C_w is the cost of waiting per unit time for each customer. In this case, the objective for decision model 1 in Sec. 18.4 is to minimize $E(\text{TC}) = C_s s + C_w L$. The purpose of this problem is to enable you to explore the effect that the relative sizes of C_s and C_w have on the optimal number of servers.

Suppose that the queueing system under consideration fits the $M/M/s$ model with $\lambda = 8$ customers per hour and $\mu = 10$ customers per hour. Use the Excel template in your OR Courseware for economic analysis with the $M/M/s$ model to find the optimal number of servers for each of the following cases.
(a) $C_s = \$100$ and $C_w = \$10$.
(b) $C_s = \$100$ and $C_w = \$100$.
(c) $C_s = \$10$ and $C_w = \$100$.

T **18.4-2.*** Jim McDonald, manager of the fast-food hamburger restaurant McBurger, realizes that providing fast service is a key to the success of the restaurant. Customers who have to wait very long are likely to go to one of the other fast-food restaurants in town next time. He estimates that each minute a customer has to wait in line before completing service costs him an average of 30 cents in lost future business. Therefore, he wants to be sure that enough cash registers always are open to keep waiting to a mini-

mum. Each cash register is operated by a part-time employee who obtains the food ordered by each customer and collects the payment. The total cost for each such employee is $9 per hour.

During lunch time, customers arrive according to a Poisson process at a mean rate of 66 per hour. The time needed to serve a customer is estimated to have an exponential distribution with a mean of 2 minutes.

Determine how many cash registers Jim should have open during lunch time to minimize his expected total cost per hour.

T **18.4-3.** The Garrett-Tompkins Company provides three copy machines in its copying room for the use of its employees. However, due to recent complaints about considerable time being wasted waiting for a copier to become free, management is considering adding one or more additional copy machines.

During the 2,000 working hours per year, employees arrive at the copying room according to a Poisson process at a mean rate of 30 per hour. The time each employee needs with a copy machine is believed to have an exponential distribution with a mean of 5 minutes. The lost productivity due to an employee spending time in the copying room is estimated to cost the company an average of $25 per hour. Each copy machine is leased for $3,000 per year.

Determine how many copy machines the company should have to minimize its expected total cost per hour.

18.4-4. A certain queueing system has a Poisson input, with a mean arrival rate of 4 customers per hour. The service-time distribution is exponential, with a mean of 0.2 hour. The marginal cost of providing each server is $20 per hour, where it is estimated that the cost that is incurred by having each customer *idle* (i.e., in the queueing system) is $120 per hour for the first customer and $180 per hour for each additional customer. Determine the number of servers that should be assigned to the system to minimize the expected total cost per hour. [*Hint:* Express $E(\text{WC})$ in terms of L, P_0, and ρ, and then use Figs. 17.6 and 17.7.]

18.4-5.* Reconsider Prob. 17.6-9. The total compensation for the new employee would be $8 per hour, which is just half that for the cashier. It is estimated that the grocery store incurs lost profit due to lost future business of $0.08 for each minute that each customer has to wait (including service time). The manager now wants to determine on an expected total cost basis whether it would be worthwhile to hire the new person.
(a) Which decision model presented in Sec. 18.4 applies to this problem? Why?
(b) Use this model to determine whether to continue the status quo or to adopt the proposal.

18.4-6. Customers arrive at a fast-food restaurant with one server according to a Poisson process at a mean rate of 30 per hour. The server has just resigned, and the two candidates for the replacement are X (fast but expensive) and Y (slow but inexpensive). Both candidates would have an exponential distribution for service times, with X having a mean of 1.2 minutes and Y having a mean of 1.5 minutes. Restaurant revenue per month is given by $\$6,000/W$, where W is the expected waiting time (in minutes) of a customer in the system.

Determine the upper bound on the difference in their monthly compensations that would justify hiring X rather than Y.

18.4-7. Jerry Jansen, Materials Handling Manager at the Casper-Edison Corporation's new factory, needs to make a purchasing decision. He needs to choose between two types of materials-handling equipment, a small tractor-trailer train and a heavy-duty forklift truck, for transporting heavy goods between certain producing centers in the factory. Calls for the materials-handling unit to move a load occur according to a Poisson process at a mean rate of 4 per hour. The total time required to move a load has an exponential distribution, where the expected time would be 12 minutes for the tractor-trailer train and 9 minutes for the forklift truck. The total equivalent uniform hourly cost (capital recovery cost plus operating cost) would be $50 for the tractor-trailer train and $150 for the forklift truck. The estimated cost of idle goods (waiting to be moved or in transit) because of increased in-process inventory is $20 per load per hour.

Jerry also has established certain criteria that he would like the materials-handling unit to satisfy in order to keep production flowing on schedule as much as possible. He would like to average no more than half an hour for completing the move of a load after receiving the call requesting the move. He also would like the time for completing the move to be no more than 1 hour 80 percent of the time. Finally, he would like to have no more than three loads waiting to start their move at least 80 percent of the time.

T **(a)** Obtain the various measures of performance if the tractor-trailer train were to be chosen. Evaluate how well these measures meet the above criteria.

T **(b)** Repeat part (a) if the forklift truck were to be chosen.

(c) Compare the two alternatives in terms of their expected total cost per hour (including the cost of idle goods).

(d) Which alternative do you think Jerry should choose?

18.4-8. The Southern Railroad Company has been subcontracting for the painting of its railroad cars as needed. However, management has decided that the company can save money by doing this work itself. A decision now needs to be made to choose between two alternative ways of doing this.

Alternative 1 is to provide two paint shops, where painting is done by hand (one car at a time in each shop), for a total hourly cost of $70. The painting time for a car would be 6 hours. Alter-

native 2 is to provide one spray shop involving an hourly cost of $100. In this case, the painting time for a car (again done one at a time) would be 3 hours. For both alternatives, the cars arrive according to a Poisson process with a mean rate of 1 every 5 hours. The cost of idle time per car is $100 per hour.

(a) Use Fig. 17.11 to estimate L, L_q, W, and W_q for Alternative 1.

(b) Find these same measures of performance for Alternative 2.

(c) Determine and compare the expected total cost per hour for these alternatives.

18.4-9. An airline maintenance base wants to make a change in its overhaul operation. The present situation is that only one airplane can be repaired at a time, and the expected repair time is 36 hours, whereas the expected time between arrivals is 45 hours. This situation has led to frequent and prolonged delays in repairing incoming planes, even though the base operates continuously. The average cost of an idle plane to the airline is $3,000 per hour. It is estimated that each plane goes into the maintenance shop 5 times per year. It is believed that the input process for the base is essentially Poisson and that the probability distribution of repair times is Erlang, with shape parameter $k = 2$.

Alternative A is to provide a duplicate maintenance shop, so that two planes can be repaired simultaneously. The cost, amortized over 5 years, is $400,000 per year for each of the airline's airplanes.

Alternative B is to replace the present maintenance equipment by the most efficient (and expensive) equipment available, thereby reducing the expected repair time to 18 hours. The cost, amortized over 5 years, is $550,000 per year for each airplane.

Which alternative should the airline choose?

18.4-10.* The production of tractors at the Jim Buck Company involves producing several subassemblies and then using an assembly line to assemble the subassemblies and other parts into finished tractors. Approximately three tractors per day are produced in this way. An in-process inspection station is used to inspect the subassemblies before they enter the assembly line. At present there are two inspectors at the station, and they work together to inspect each subassembly. The inspection time has an exponential distribution, with a mean of 15 minutes. The cost of providing this inspection system is $40 per hour.

A proposal has been made to streamline the inspection procedure so that it can be handled by only one inspector. This inspector would begin by visually inspecting the exterior of the subassembly, and she would then use new efficient equipment to complete the inspection. Although this process with just one inspector would slightly increase the mean of the distribution of inspection times from 15 minutes to 16 minutes, it also would reduce the variance of this distribution to only 40 percent of its current value.

The subassemblies arrive at the inspection station according to a Poisson process at a mean rate of 3 per hour. The cost of having the subassemblies wait at the inspection station (thereby increasing in-process inventory and possibly disrupting subsequent production) is estimated to be $20 per hour for each subassembly.

Management now needs to make a decision about whether to continue the status quo or adopt the proposal.

T **(a)** Find the main measures of performance—L, L_q, W, W_q—for the current queueing system.

(b) Repeat part (a) for the proposed queueing system.

(c) What conclusions can you draw about what management should do from the results in parts (a) and (b)?

(d) Determine and compare the expected total cost per hour for the status quo and the proposal.

18.4-11. The car rental company, Try Harder, has been subcontracting for the maintenance of its cars in St. Louis. However, due to long delays in getting its cars back, the company has decided to open its own maintenance shop to do this work more quickly. This shop will operate 42 hours per week.

Alternative 1 is to hire two mechanics (at a cost of $1,500 per week each), so that two cars can be worked on at a time. The time required by a mechanic to service a car has an Erlang distribution, with a mean of 5 hours and a shape parameter of $k = 8$.

Alternative 2 is to hire just one mechanic (for $1,500 per week) but to provide some additional special equipment (at a capitalized cost of $1,250 per week) to speed up the work. In this case, the maintenance work on each car is done in two stages, where the time required for each stage has an Erlang distribution with the shape parameter $k = 4$, where the mean is 2 hours for the first stage and 1 hour for the second stage.

For both alternatives, the cars arrive according to a Poisson process at a mean rate of 0.3 car per hour (during work hours). The company estimates that its net lost revenue due to having its cars unavailable for rental is $150 per week per car.

(a) Use Fig. 17.13 to estimate L, L_q, W, and W_q for alternative 1.

(b) Find these same measures of performance for alternative 2.

(c) Determine and compare the expected total cost per week for these alternatives.

18.4-12. A certain small car-wash business is currently being analyzed to see if costs can be reduced. Customers arrive according to a Poisson process at a mean rate of 15 per hour, and only one car can be washed at a time. At present the time required to wash a car has an exponential distribution, with a mean of 4 minutes. It also has been noticed that if there are already 4 cars waiting (including the one being washed), then any additional arriving customers leave and take their business elsewhere. The lost incremental profit from each such lost customer is $6.

Two proposals have been made. Proposal 1 is to add certain equipment, at a capitalized cost of $6 per hour, which would reduce the expected washing time to 3 minutes. In addition, each arriving customer would be given a guarantee that if she had to wait

longer than $\frac{1}{2}$ hour (according to a time slip she receives upon arrival) before her car is ready, then she receives a free car wash (at a marginal cost of $4 for the company). This guarantee would be well posted and advertised, so it is believed that no arriving customers would be lost.

Proposal 2 is to obtain the most advanced equipment available, at an increased cost of $20 per hour, and each car would be sent through two cycles of the process in succession. The time required for a cycle has an exponential distribution, with a mean of 1 minute, so total expected washing time would be 2 minutes. Because of the increased speed and effectiveness, it is believed that essentially no arriving customers would be lost.

The owner also feels that because of the loss of customer goodwill (and consequent lost future business) when customers have to wait, a cost of $0.20 for each minute that a customer has to wait before her car wash begins should be included in the analysis of all alternatives.

Evaluate the expected total cost per hour E(TC) of the status quo, proposal 1, and proposal 2 to determine which one should be chosen.

18.4-13.* The Seabuck and Roper Company has a large warehouse in southern California to store its inventory of goods until they are needed by the company's many furniture stores in that area. A single crew with four members is used to unload and/or load each truck that arrives at the loading dock of the warehouse. Management currently is downsizing to cut costs, so a decision needs to be made about the future size of this crew.

Trucks arrive at the loading dock according to a Poisson process at a mean rate of 1 per hour. The time required by a crew to unload and/or load a truck has an exponential distribution (regardless of crew size). The mean of this distribution with the four-member crew is 15 minutes. If the size of the crew were to be changed, it is estimated that the mean service rate of the crew (now $\mu = 4$ customers per hour) would be proportional to its size.

The cost of providing each member of the crew is $20 per hour. The cost that is attributable to having a truck not in use (i.e., a truck standing at the loading dock) is estimated to be $30 per hour.

(a) Identify the customers and servers for this queueing system. How many servers does it currently have?

T **(b)** Use the appropriate Excel template to find the various measures of performance for this queueing system with four members on the crew. (Set $t = 1$ hour in the Excel template for the waiting-time probabilities.)

T **(c)** Repeat (b) with three members.

T **(d)** Repeat part (b) with two members.

(e) Should a one-member crew also be considered? Explain.

(f) Given the previous results, which crew size do you think management should choose?

(g) Use the cost figures to determine which crew size would minimize the expected total cost per hour.

(h) Assume now that the mean service rate of the crew is proportional to the square root of its size. What should the size be to minimize expected total cost per hour?

18.4-14. Trucks arrive at a warehouse according to a Poisson process with a mean rate of 4 per hour. Only one truck can be loaded at a time. The time required to load a truck has an exponential distribution with a mean of $10/n$ minutes, where n is the number of loaders ($n = 1, 2, 3, \ldots$). The costs are (i) $18 per hour for each loader and (ii) $20 per hour for each truck being loaded or waiting in line to be loaded. Determine the number of loaders that minimizes the expected hourly cost.

18.4-15. A company's machines break down according to a Poisson process at a mean rate of 3 per hour. Nonproductive time on any machine costs the company $60 per hour. The company employs a maintenance person who repairs machines at a mean rate of μ machines per hour (when continuously busy) if the company pays that person a wage of 5μ per hour. The repair time has an exponential distribution.

Determine the hourly wage that minimizes the company's total expected cost.

18.4-16. Jake's Machine Shop contains a grinder for sharpening the machine cutting tools. A decision must now be made on the speed at which to set the grinder.

The grinding time required by a machine operator to sharpen the cutting tool has an exponential distribution, where the mean $1/\mu$ can be set at 0.5 minute, 1 minute, or 1.5 minutes, depending upon the speed of the grinder. The running and maintenance costs go up rapidly with the speed of the grinder, so the estimated cost per minute is $1.60 for providing a mean of 0.5 minute, $0.40 for a mean of 1.0 minute, and $0.20 for a mean of 1.5 minutes.

The machine operators arrive randomly to sharpen their tools at a mean rate of 1 every 2 minutes. The estimated cost of an operator being away from his or her machine to the grinder is $0.80 per minute.

T **(a)** Obtain the various measures of performance for this queueing system for each of the three alternative speeds for the grinder. (Set $t = 5$ minutes in the Excel template for the waiting time probabilities.)

(b) Use the cost figures to determine which grinder speed minimizes the expected total cost per minute.

18.4-17. Consider the special case of model 2 where (1) any $\mu > \lambda/s$ is feasible and (2) both $f(\mu)$ and the waiting-cost function are linear functions, so that

$$E(\text{TC}) = C_r s\mu + C_w L,$$

where C_r is the marginal cost per unit time for each unit of a server's mean service rate and C_w is the cost of waiting per unit time for each customer. The optimal solution is $s = 1$ (by the optimality of a single-server result), and

$$\mu = \lambda + \sqrt{\frac{\lambda C_w}{C_r}}$$

for any queueing system fitting the $M/M/1$ model presented in Sec. 17.6.

Show that this μ is indeed optimal for the $M/M/1$ model.

18.4-18. Greg is making plans to open a new fast-food restaurant soon. He is estimating that customers will arrive randomly (a Poisson process) at a mean rate of 150 per hour during the busiest times of the day. He is planning to have three employees directly serving the customers. He now needs to make a decision about how to organize these employees.

Option 1 is to have three cash registers with one employee at each to take the orders and get the food and drinks. In this case, it is estimated that the average time to serve each customer would be 1 minute, and the distribution of service times is assumed to be exponential.

Option 2 is to have one cash register with the three employees working together to serve each customer. One would take the order, a second would get the food, and the third would get the drinks. Greg estimates that this would reduce the average time to serve each customer down to 20 seconds, with the same assumption of exponential service times.

Greg wants to choose the option that would provide the best service to his customers. However, since Option 1 has three cash registers, both options would serve the customers at a mean rate of 3 per minute when everybody is busy serving customers, so it is not clear which option is better.

T **(a)** Use the main measures of performance—L, L_q, W, W_q—to compare the two options.

(b) Explain why these comparisons make sense intuitively.

(c) Which measure do you think would be most important to Greg's customers? Why? Which option is better with respect to this measure?

18.4-19. Consider a harbor with a single dock for unloading ships. The ships arrive according to a Poisson process at a mean rate of λ ships per week, and the service-time distribution is exponential with a mean rate of μ unloadings per week. Assume that harbor facilities are owned by the shipping company, so that the objective is to balance the cost associated with idle ships with the cost of running the dock. The shipping company has no control over the arrival rate λ (that is, λ is fixed); however, by changing the size of the unloading crew, and so on, the shipping company can adjust the value of μ as desired.

Suppose that the expected cost per unit time of running the unloading dock is $D\mu$. The waiting cost for each idle ship is some constant (C) times the *square* of the total waiting time (including loading time). The shipping company wishes to adjust μ so that the expected total cost (including the waiting cost for idle ships) per unit time is minimized. Derive this optimal value of μ in terms of D and C.

18.4-20. Consider a queueing system with two types of customers. Type 1 customers arrive according to a Poisson process with a mean rate of 5 per hour. Type 2 customers also arrive according to a Poisson process with a mean rate of 5 per hour. The system has two servers, and both serve both types of customers. For types 1 and 2, service times have an exponential distribution with a mean of 10 minutes. Service is provided on a first-come-first-served basis.

Management now wants you to compare this system's design of having both servers serve both types of customers with the alternative design of having one server serve just type 1 customers and the other server serve just type 2 customers. Assume that this alternative design would not change the probability distribution of service times.

(a) Without doing any calculations, indicate which design would give a smaller expected total number of customers in the system. What result are you using to draw this conclusion?

T **(b)** Verify your conclusion in part (a) by finding the expected total number of customers in the system under the original design and then under the alternative design.

18.4-21. Reconsider Prob. 17.6-33.

(a) Formulate part (a) to fit as closely as possible a special case of one of the decision models presented in Sec. 18.4. (Do not solve.)

(b) Describe Alternatives 2 and 3 in queueing theory terms, including their relationship (if any) to the decision models presented in Sec. 18.4. Briefly indicate why, in comparison with Alternative 1, each of these other alternatives might decrease the total number of operators (thereby increasing their utilization) needed to achieve the required production rate. Also point out any dangers that might prevent this decrease.

18.4-22. George is planning to open a drive-through photo-developing booth with a single service window that will be open approximately 200 hours per month in a busy commercial area. Space for a drive-through lane is available for a rental of $200 per month per car length. George needs to decide how many car lengths of space to provide for his customers.

Excluding this rental cost for the drive-through lane, George believes that he will average a profit of $4 per customer served (nothing for a drop-off of film and $8 when the photographs are picked up). He also estimates that customers will arrive randomly (a Poisson process) at a mean rate of 20 per hour, although those

who find the drive-through lane full will be forced to leave. Half of the customers who find the drive-through lane full wanted to drop off film and the other half wanted to pick up their photographs. The half who wanted to drop off film will take their business elsewhere instead. The other half of the customers who find the drive-through lane full will not be lost because they will keep trying later until they get in and pick up their photographs. George assumes that the time required to serve a customer will have an exponential distribution with a mean of 2 minutes.

T **(a)** Find L and the mean rate at which customers are lost when the number of car lengths of space provided is 2, 3, 4, and 5.

(b) Calculate W from L for the cases considered in part (a).

(c) Use the results from part (a) to calculate the decrease in the mean rate at which customers are lost when the number of car lengths of space provided is increased from 2 to 3, from 3 to 4, and from 4 to 5. Then calculate the increase in expected profit per hour (excluding space rental costs) for each of these three cases.

(d) Compare the increases in expected profit found in part (c) with the cost per hour of renting each car length of space. What conclusion do you draw about the number of car lengths of space that George should provide?

18.4-23. Consider a factory whose floor area is a square with 600 feet on each side. Suppose that one service facility of a certain kind is provided in the center of the factory. The employees are distributed uniformly throughout the factory, and they walk to and from the facility at an average speed of 3 miles per hour along a system of orthogonal aisles.

Find the expected travel time $E(T)$ per arrival.

18.4-24. A certain large shop doing light fabrication work uses a single central storage facility (dispatch station) for material in-process storage. The typical procedure is that each employee personally delivers his finished work (by hand, tote box, or hand cart) and receives new work and materials at the facility. Although this procedure worked well in earlier years when the shop was smaller, it appears that it may now be advisable to divide the shop into two semi-independent parts, with a separate storage facility for each one. You have been assigned the job of comparing the use of two facilities and of one facility from a cost standpoint.

The factory has the shape of a rectangle 150 by 100 yards. Thus, by letting 1 yard be the unit of distance, the (x, y) coordinates of the corners are (0, 0), (150, 0), (150, 100), and (0, 100). With this coordinate system, the existing facility is located at (50, 50), and the location available for the second facility is (100, 50).

Each facility would be operated by a single clerk. The time required by a clerk to service a caller has an exponential distribution, with a mean of 2 minutes. Employees arrive at the present facility according to a Poisson input process at a mean rate of 24 per hour. The employees are rather uniformly distributed throughout the shop, and if the second facility were installed, each employee would normally use the nearer of the two facilities. Employees walk at an average speed of about 5,000 yards per hour. All aisles are parallel to the outer walls of the shop. The net cost of providing each facility is estimated to be about $20 per hour, plus $15 per hour for the clerk. The estimated total cost of an employee being idled by traveling or waiting at the facility is $25 per hour.

Given the preceding cost factors, which alternative minimizes the expected total cost?

18.4-25.* Consider the formulation of the County Hospital emergency room problem as a preemptive priority queueing system, as presented in Sec. 17.8. Suppose that the following inputted costs are assigned to making patients wait (*excluding* treatment time): $10 per hour for stable cases, $1,000 per hour for serious cases, and $100,000 per hour for critical cases. The cost associated with having an additional doctor on duty would be $40 per hour. Referring to Table 17.4, determine on an expected-total-cost basis whether there should be one or two doctors on duty.

T **18.4-26.** The Becker Company factory has been experiencing long delays in jobs going through the turret lathe department because of inadequate capacity. The head of this department contends that five machines are required, as opposed to the three machines now in place. However, because of pressure from management to hold down capital expenditures, only one additional machine will be authorized unless there is solid evidence that a second one is necessary.

This shop does three kinds of jobs, namely, government jobs, commercial jobs, and standard products. Whenever a turret lathe operator finishes a job, he starts a government job if one is waiting; if not, he starts a commercial job if any are waiting; if not, he starts on a standard product if any are waiting. Jobs of the same type are taken on a first-come-first-served basis.

Although much overtime work is required currently, management wants the turret lathe department to operate on an 8-hour, 5-day-per-week basis. The probability distribution of the time required by a turret lathe operator for a job appears to be approximately exponential, with a mean of 10 hours. Jobs come into the shop randomly (a Poisson process) at a mean rate of 6 per week for governments jobs, 4 per week for commercial jobs, and 2 per week for standard products. (These figures are expected to remain the same for the indefinite future.)

Management feels that the average waiting time before work begins in the turret lathe department should not exceed 0.25 (working) day for government jobs, 0.5 day for commercial jobs, and 2 days for standard products.

(a) Determine how many additional turret lathes need to be obtained to satisfy these management guidelines.
(b) It is worth about $750, $450, and $150 to avoid a delay of 1 additional (working) day in a government, commercial, and standard job, respectively. The incremental capitalized cost of providing each turret lathe (including the operator and so on) is estimated to be $250 per working day. Determine the number of additional turret lathes that should be obtained to minimize the expected total cost.

CASE 18.1   QUEUEING QUANDARY[1]

Never dull. That is how you would describe your job at the centralized records and benefits administration center for Cutting Edge, a large company manufacturing computers and computer peripherals. Since opening the facility six months ago, you and Mark Lawrence, the Director of Human Resources, have endured one long roller coaster ride. Receiving the go-ahead from corporate headquarters to establish the centralized records and benefits administration center was definitely an up. Getting caught in the crossfire of angry customers (all employees of Cutting Edge) because of demand overload for the records and benefits call center was definitely a down. Accurately forecasting the demand for the call center provided another up.

And today you are faced with another down. Mark approaches your desk with a not altogether attractive frown on his face.

[1]The scenario in this case is a sequel, a few months later, to the scenario introduced in Case 20.1. However, this case can be considered completely independently of Case 20.1.

He begins complaining immediately, "I just don't understand. The forecasting job you did for us two months ago really allowed us to understand the weekly demand for the center, but we still have not been able to get a grasp on the staffing problem. We used both historical data and your forecasts to calculate the average weekly demand for the call center. We transformed this average weekly demand into average hourly demand by dividing the weekly demand by the number of hours in the workweek. We then staffed the center to meet this average hourly demand by taking into account the average number of calls a representative is able to handle per hour.

But something is horribly wrong. Operational data records show that over thirty percent of the customers wait over four minutes for a representative to answer the call! Customers are still sending me numerous complaints, and executives from corporate headquarters are still breathing down my neck! I need help!"

You calm Mark down and explain to him that you think you know the problem: the number of calls received in a certain hour can be much greater (or much less) than the average because of the stochastic nature of the demand. In addition, the number of calls a representative is able to handle per hour can be much less (or much greater) than the average depending upon the types of calls received.

You then tell him to have no fear, you have the problem under control. You have been reading about the successful application of queueing theory to the operation of call centers, and you decide that the queueing models you learned in school will help you determine the appropriate staffing level.

(a) You ask Mark to describe the demand and service rate. He tells you that calls are randomly received by the call center and that the center receives an average of 70 calls per hour. The computer system installed to answer and hold the calls is so advanced that its capacity far exceeds the demand. Because the nature of a call is random, the time required to process a call is random, where the time frequently is small but occasionally can be much longer. On average, however, representatives can handle 6 calls per hour. Which queueing model seems appropriate for this situation? Given that slightly more than 35 percent of customers wait over 4 minutes before a representative answers the call, use this model to estimate how many representatives Mark currently employs.

(b) Mark tells you that he will not be satisfied unless 95 percent of the customers wait only 1 minute or less for a representative to answer the call. Given this customer service level and the average arrival rates and service rates from part (a), how many representatives should Mark employ?

(c) Each representative receives an annual salary of $30,000, and Mark tells you that he simply does not have the resources available to hire the number of representatives required to achieve the customer service level desired in part (b). He asks you to perform sensitivity analysis. How many representatives would he need to employ to ensure that 80 percent of customers wait 1 minute or less? How many would he need to employ to ensure that 95 percent of customers wait 90 seconds or less? How would you recommend Mark choose a customer service level? Would the decision criteria be different if Mark's call center were to serve external customers (not connected to the company) instead of internal customers (employees)?

(d) Mark tells you that he is not happy with the number of representatives required to achieve a high customer service level. He therefore wants to explore alternatives to simply hiring additional representatives. The alternative he considers is instituting a training program that will teach representatives to more efficiently use computer tools to answer calls. He believes that this alternative will increase the average number of calls a representative is able to handle per hour from 6 calls to 8 calls. The training program will cost $2,500 per employee per year since employees' knowledge will have to be updated yearly. How many representatives will Mark have to employ and train to achieve the customer service level desired in part (b)? Do you prefer this alternative to simply hiring additional representatives? Why or why not?

(e) Mark realizes that queueing theory helps him only so much in determining the number of representatives needed. He realizes that the queueing models will not provide accurate answers if the inputs used in the models are inaccurate. What inputs do you think need reevaluation? How would you go about estimating these inputs?

19

Inventory Theory

"Sorry, we're out of that item." How often have you heard that during shopping trips? In many of these cases, what you have encountered are stores that aren't doing a very good job of managing their *inventories* (stocks of goods being held for future use or sale). They aren't placing orders to replenish inventories soon enough to avoid shortages. These stores could benefit from the kinds of techniques of scientific inventory management that are described in this chapter.

It isn't just retail stores that must manage inventories. In fact, inventories pervade the business world. Maintaining inventories is necessary for any company dealing with physical products, including manufacturers, wholesalers, and retailers. For example, manufacturers need inventories of the materials required to make their products. They also need inventories of the finished products awaiting shipment. Similarly, both wholesalers and retailers need to maintain inventories of goods to be available for purchase by customers.

The total value of all inventory—including finished goods, partially finished goods, and raw materials—in the United States is more than a *trillion* dollars. This is more than $4,000 each for every man, woman, and child in the country.

The costs associated with storing ("carrying") inventory are also very large, perhaps a quarter of the value of the inventory. Therefore, the costs being incurred for the storage of inventory in the United States run into the hundreds of billions of dollars annually. Reducing storage costs by avoiding unnecessarily large inventories can enhance any firm's competitiveness.

Some Japanese companies were pioneers in introducing the *just-in-time inventory system*—a system that emphasizes planning and scheduling so that the needed materials arrive "just-in-time" for their use. Huge savings are thereby achieved by reducing inventory levels to a bare minimum.

Many companies in other parts of the world also have been revamping the way in which they manage their inventories. The application of operations research techniques in this area (sometimes called *scientific inventory management*) is providing a powerful tool for gaining a competitive edge.

How do companies use operations research to improve their **inventory policy** for when and how much to replenish their inventory? They use **scientific inventory management** comprising the following steps:

1. Formulate a *mathematical model* describing the behavior of the inventory system.
2. Seek an *optimal* inventory policy with respect to this model.
3. Use a computerized *information processing system* to maintain a record of the current inventory levels.
4. Using this record of current inventory levels, apply the optimal inventory policy to signal when and how much to replenish inventory.

The mathematical inventory models used with this approach can be divided into two broad categories—deterministic models and stochastic models—according to the *predictability of demand* involved. The **demand** for a product in inventory is the number of units that will need to be withdrawn from inventory for some use (e.g., sales) during a specific period. If the demand in future periods can be forecast with considerable precision, it is reasonable to use an inventory policy that assumes that all forecasts will always be completely accurate. This is the case of *known demand* where a *deterministic* inventory model would be used. However, when demand cannot be predicted very well, it becomes necessary to use a *stochastic* inventory model where the demand in any period is a random variable rather than a known constant.

There are several basic considerations involved in determining an inventory policy that must be reflected in the mathematical inventory model. These are illustrated in the examples presented in the first section and then are described in general terms in Sec. 19.2. Section 19.3 develops and analyzes deterministic inventory models for situations where the inventory level is under continuous review. Section 19.4 does the same for situations where the planning is being done for a series of periods rather than continuously. The following three sections present stochastic models, first under continuous review, then for a single period, and finally for a series of periods. The chapter concludes with a discussion of how scientific inventory management is being used in practice to deal with very large inventory systems, as illustrated by case studies at IBM and Hewlett-Packard.

19.1   EXAMPLES

We present two examples in rather different contexts (a manufacturer and a wholesaler) where an inventory policy needs to be developed.

EXAMPLE 1   Manufacturing Speakers for TV Sets

A television manufacturing company produces its own speakers, which are used in the production of its television sets. The television sets are assembled on a continuous production line at a rate of 8,000 per month, with one speaker needed per set. The speakers are produced in batches because they do not warrant setting up a continuous production line, and relatively large quantities can be produced in a short time. Therefore, the speakers are placed into inventory until they are needed for assembly into television sets on the production line. The company is interested in determining when to produce a batch of speakers and how many speakers to produce in each batch. Several costs must be considered:

1. Each time a batch is produced, a **setup cost** of $12,000 is incurred. This cost includes the cost of "tooling up," administrative costs, record keeping, and so forth. Note that the existence of this cost argues for producing speakers in large batches.
2. The **unit production cost** of a single speaker (excluding the setup cost) is $10, independent of the batch size produced. (In general, however, the unit production cost need not be constant and may decrease with batch size.)
3. The production of speakers in large batches leads to a large inventory. The estimated **holding cost** of keeping a speaker in stock is $0.30 per month. This cost includes the cost of capital tied up in inventory. Since the money invested in inventory cannot be used in other productive ways, this cost of capital consists of the lost return (referred to as the *opportunity cost*) because alternative uses of the money must be forgone. Other components of the holding cost include the cost of leasing the storage space, the cost of insurance against loss of inventory by fire, theft, or vandalism, taxes based on the value of the inventory, and the cost of personnel who oversee and protect the inventory.
4. Company policy prohibits deliberately planning for shortages of any of its components. However, a shortage of speakers occasionally crops up, and it has been estimated that each speaker that is not available when required costs $1.10 per month. This **shortage cost** includes the extra cost of installing speakers after the television set is fully assembled otherwise, the interest lost because of the delay in receiving sales revenue, the cost of extra record keeping, and so forth.

We will develop the inventory policy for this example with the help of the first inventory model presented in Sec. 19.3.

EXAMPLE 2   Wholesale Distribution of Bicycles

A wholesale distributor of bicycles is having trouble with shortages of a popular model (a small, one-speed girl's bicycle) and is currently reviewing the inventory policy for this model. The distributor purchases this model bicycle from the manufacturer monthly and then supplies it to various bicycle shops in the western United States in response to purchase orders. What the total demand from bicycle shops will be in any given month is quite uncertain. Therefore, the question is, How many bicycles should be ordered from the manufacturer for any given month, given the stock level leading into that month?

The distributor has analyzed her costs and has determined that the following are important:

1. The **ordering cost**, i.e., the cost of placing an order plus the cost of the bicycles being purchased, has two components: The administrative cost involved in placing an order is estimated as $200, and the actual cost of each bicycle is $35 for this wholesaler.
2. The *holding cost,* i.e., the cost of maintaining an inventory, is $1 per bicycle remaining at the end of the month. This cost represents the costs of capital tied up, warehouse space, insurance, taxes, and so on.
3. The *shortage cost* is the cost of not having a bicycle on hand when needed. This particular model is easily reordered from the manufacturer, and stores usually accept a

delay in delivery. Still, although shortages are permissible, the distributor feels that she incurs a loss, which she estimates to be $15 per bicycle per month of shortage. This estimated cost takes into account the possible loss of future sales because of the loss of customer goodwill. Other components of this cost include lost interest on delayed sales revenue, and additional administrative costs associated with shortages. If some stores were to cancel orders because of delays, the lost revenues from these lost sales would need to be included in the shortage cost. Fortunately, such cancellations normally do not occur for this model.

We will return to this example again in Sec. 19.6.

These examples illustrate that there are two possibilities for how a firm *replenishes inventory,* depending on the situation. One possibility is that the firm *produces* the needed units itself (like the television manufacturer producing speakers). The other is that the firm *orders* the units from a supplier (like the bicycle distributor ordering bicycles from the manufacturer). Inventory models do not need to distinguish between these two ways of replenishing inventory, so we will use such terms as *producing* and *ordering* interchangeably.

Both examples deal with one specific product (speakers for a certain kind of television set or a certain bicycle model). In most inventory models, just one product is being considered at a time. Except in Sec. 19.8, all the inventory models presented in this chapter assume a single product.

Both examples indicate that there exists a trade-off between the costs involved. The next section discusses the basic cost components of inventory models for determining the optimal trade-off between these costs.

19.2   COMPONENTS OF INVENTORY MODELS

Because inventory policies affect profitability, the choice among policies depends upon their relative profitability. As already seen in Examples 1 and 2, some of the costs that determine this profitability are (1) the ordering costs, (2) holding costs, and (3) shortage costs. Other relevant factors include (4) revenues, (5) salvage costs, and (6) discount rates. These six factors are described in turn below.

The **cost of ordering** an amount z (either through *purchasing* or *producing this amount*) can be represented by a function $c(z)$. The simplest form of this function is one that is directly proportional to the amount ordered, that is, $c \cdot z$, where c represents the unit price paid. Another common assumption is that $c(z)$ is composed of two parts: a term that is directly proportional to the amount ordered and a term that is a constant K for z positive and is 0 for $z = 0$. For this case,

$$c(z) = \text{cost of ordering } z \text{ units}$$
$$= \begin{cases} 0 & \text{if } z = 0 \\ K + cz & \text{if } z > 0, \end{cases}$$

where K = setup cost and c = unit cost.

The constant K includes the administrative cost of ordering or, when producing, the costs involved in setting up to start a production run.

There are other assumptions that can be made about the cost of ordering, but this chapter is restricted to the cases just described.

In Example 1, the speakers are produced and the setup cost for a production run is $12,000. Furthermore, each speaker costs $10, so that the *production* cost when ordering a production run of z speakers is given by

$$c(z) = 12,000 + 10z, \qquad \text{for } z > 0.$$

In Example 2, the distributor orders bicycles from the manufacturer and the *ordering* cost is given by

$$c(z) = 200 + 35z, \qquad \text{for } z > 0.$$

The **holding cost** (sometimes called the *storage cost*) represents all the costs associated with the storage of the inventory until it is sold or used. Included are the cost of capital tied up, space, insurance, protection, and taxes attributed to storage. The holding cost can be assessed either continuously or on a period-by-period basis. In the latter case, the cost may be a function of the maximum quantity held during a period, the average amount held, or the quantity in inventory at the end of the period. The last viewpoint is usually taken in this chapter.

In the bicycle example, the holding cost is $1 per bicycle remaining at the end of the month. In the TV speakers example, the holding cost is assessed continuously as $0.30 per speaker in inventory per month, so the average holding cost per month is $0.30 times the average number of speakers in inventory.

The **shortage cost** (sometimes called the *unsatisfied demand cost*) is incurred when the amount of the commodity required (demand) exceeds the available stock. This cost depends upon which of the following two cases applies.

In one case, called **backlogging,** the excess demand is not lost, but instead is held until it can be satisfied when the next normal delivery replenishes the inventory. For a firm incurring a temporary shortage in supplying its customers (as for the bicycle example), the shortage cost then can be interpreted as the loss of customers' goodwill and the subsequent reluctance to do business with the firm, the cost of delayed revenue, and the extra administrative costs. For a manufacturer incurring a temporary shortage in materials needed for production (such as a shortage of speakers for assembly into television sets), the shortage cost becomes the cost associated with delaying the completion of the production process.

In the second case, called **no backlogging,** if any excess of demand over available stock occurs, the firm cannot wait for the next normal delivery to meet the excess demand. Either (1) the excess demand is met by a priority shipment, or (2) it is not met at all because the orders are canceled. For situation 1, the shortage cost can be viewed as the cost of the priority shipment. For situation 2, the shortage cost is the loss of current revenue from not meeting the demand plus the cost of losing future business because of lost goodwill.

Revenue may or may not be included in the model. If both the price and the demand for the product are established by the market and so are outside the control of the company, the revenue from sales (assuming demand is met) is independent of the firm's inventory policy and may be neglected. However, if revenue is neglected in the model, the *loss in revenue* must then be included in the shortage cost whenever the firm cannot meet the demand and the sale is lost. Furthermore, even in the case where demand is backlogged, the cost of the delay in revenue must also be included in the shortage cost. With these interpretations, revenue will not be considered explicitly in the remainder of this chapter.

The **salvage value** of an item is the value of a leftover item when no further inventory is desired. The salvage value represents the disposal value of the item to the firm, perhaps through a discounted sale. The negative of the salvage value is called the **salvage cost.** If there is a cost associated with the disposal of an item, the salvage cost may be positive. We assume hereafter that any salvage cost is incorporated into the *holding cost*.

Finally, the **discount rate** takes into account the time value of money. When a firm ties up capital in inventory, the firm is prevented from using this money for alternative purposes. For example, it could invest this money in secure investments, say, government bonds, and have a return on investment 1 year hence of, say, 7 percent. Thus, $1 invested today would be worth $1.07 in year 1, or alternatively, a $1 profit 1 year hence is equivalent to $\alpha = \$1/\$1.07$ today. The quantity α is known as the **discount factor.** Thus, in adding up the total profit from an inventory policy, the profit or costs 1 year hence should be multiplied by α; in 2 years hence by α^2; and so on. (Units of time other than 1 year also can be used.) The total profit calculated in this way normally is referred to as the *net present value.*

In problems having short time horizons, α may be assumed to be 1 (and thereby neglected) because the current value of $1 delivered during this short time horizon does not change very much. However, in problems having long time horizons, the discount factor must be included.

In using quantitative techniques to seek optimal inventory policies, we use the criterion of minimizing the total (expected) discounted cost. Under the assumptions that the price and demand for the product are not under the control of the company and that the lost or delayed revenue is included in the shortage penalty cost, minimizing cost is equivalent to maximizing net income. Another useful criterion is to keep the inventory policy simple, i.e., keep the rule for indicating *when to order* and *how much to order* both understandable and easy to implement. Most of the policies considered in this chapter possess this property.

As mentioned at the beginning of the chapter, inventory models are usually classified as either *deterministic* or *stochastic* according to whether the demand for a period is known or is a random variable having a known probability distribution. The production of batches of speakers in Example 1 of Sec. 19.1 illustrates deterministic demand because the speakers are used in television assemblies at a fixed rate of 8,000 per month. The bicycle shops' purchases of bicycles from the wholesale distributor in Example 2 of Sec. 19.1 illustrates random demand because the total monthly demand varies from month to month according to some probability distribution. Another component of an inventory model is the **lead time,** which is the amount of time between the placement of an order to replenish inventory (through either purchasing or producing) and the receipt of the goods into inventory. If the lead time always is the same (a *fixed* lead time), then the replenishment can be scheduled just when desired. Most models in this chapter assume that each replenishment occurs just when desired, either because the delivery is nearly instantaneous or because it is known when the replenishment will be needed and there is a fixed lead time.

Another classification refers to whether the current inventory level is being monitored continuously or periodically. In **continuous review,** an order is placed as soon as the stock level falls down to the prescribed reorder point. In **periodic review,** the inventory level is checked at discrete intervals, e.g., at the end of each week, and ordering decisions are made only at these times even if the inventory level dips below the reorder point between the preceding and current review times. (In practice, a periodic review policy can be used to approximate a continuous review policy by making the time interval sufficiently small.)

19.3 DETERMINISTIC CONTINUOUS-REVIEW MODELS

The most common inventory situation faced by manufacturers, retailers, and wholesalers is that stock levels are depleted over time and then are replenished by the arrival of a batch of new units. A simple model representing this situation is the following **economic order quantity model** or, for short, the **EOQ model.** (It sometimes is also referred to as the *economic lot-size model.*)

Units of the product under consideration are assumed to be withdrawn from inventory continuously at a *known constant rate,* denoted by a; that is, the demand is a units per unit time. It is further assumed that inventory is replenished when needed by ordering (through either purchasing or producing) a batch of fixed size (Q units), where all Q units arrive simultaneously at the desired time. For the *basic EOQ model* to be presented first, the only costs to be considered are

K = setup cost for ordering one batch,

c = unit cost for producing or purchasing each unit,

h = holding cost per unit per unit of time held in inventory.

The objective is to determine when and by how much to replenish inventory so as to minimize the sum of these costs per unit time.

We assume *continuous review,* so that inventory can be replenished whenever the inventory level drops sufficiently low. We shall first assume that shortages are not allowed (but later we will relax this assumption). With the fixed demand rate, shortages can be avoided by replenishing inventory each time the inventory level drops to zero, and this also will minimize the holding cost. Figure 19.1 depicts the resulting pattern of inventory levels over time when we start at time 0 by ordering a batch of Q units in order to increase the initial inventory level from 0 to Q and then repeat this process each time the inventory level drops back down to 0.

FIGURE 19.1
Diagram of inventory level as a function of time for the basic EOQ model.

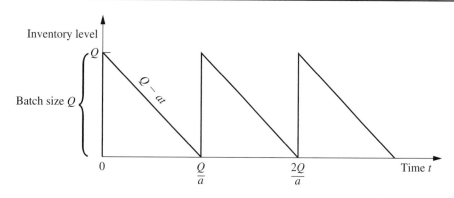

Example 1 in Sec. 19.1 (manufacturing speakers for TV sets) fits this model and will be used to illustrate the following discussion.

The Basic EOQ Model

To summarize, in addition to the costs specified above, the basic EOQ model makes the following assumptions.

Assumptions (Basic EOQ Model).

1. A known constant demand rate of a units per unit time.
2. The order quantity (Q) to replenish inventory arrives all at once just when desired, namely, when the inventory level drops to 0.
3. Planned shortages are not allowed.

In regard to assumption 2, there usually is a lag between when an order is placed and when it arrives in inventory. As indicated in Sec. 19.2, the amount of time between the placement of an order and its receipt is referred to as the *lead time*. The inventory level at which the order is placed is called the **reorder point.** To satisfy assumption 2, this reorder point needs to be set at the *product* of the demand rate and the lead time. Thus, assumption 2 is implicitly assuming a *constant* lead time.

The time between consecutive replenishments of inventory (the vertical line segments in Fig. 19.1) is referred to as a *cycle*. For the speaker example, a cycle can be viewed as the time between production runs. Thus, if 24,000 speakers are produced in each production run and are used at the rate of 8,000 per month, then the cycle length is $24,000/8,000 = 3$ months. In general, the cycle length is Q/a.

The total cost per unit time T is obtained from the following components.

Production or ordering cost per cycle $= K + cQ$.

The average inventory level during a cycle is $(Q + 0)/2 = Q/2$ units, and the corresponding cost is $hQ/2$ per unit time. Because the cycle length is Q/a,

$$\text{Holding cost per cycle} = \frac{hQ^2}{2a}.$$

Therefore,

$$\text{Total cost per cycle} = K + cQ + \frac{hQ^2}{2a},$$

so the total cost per unit time is

$$T = \frac{K + cQ + hQ^2/(2a)}{Q/a} = \frac{aK}{Q} + ac + \frac{hQ}{2}.$$

The value of Q, say Q^*, that minimizes T is found by setting the first derivative to zero (and noting that the second derivative is positive).

$$\frac{dT}{dQ} = -\frac{aK}{Q^2} + \frac{h}{2} = 0,$$

so that

$$Q^* = \sqrt{\frac{2aK}{h}},$$

which is the well-known *EOQ formula.*[1] (It also is sometimes referred to as the *square root formula.*) The corresponding *cycle time,* say t^*, is

$$t^* = \frac{Q^*}{a} = \sqrt{\frac{2K}{ah}}.$$

It is interesting to observe that Q^* and t^* change in intuitively plausible ways when a change is made in K, h, or a. As the setup cost K increases, both Q^* and t^* increase (fewer setups). When the unit holding cost h increases, both Q^* and t^* decrease (smaller inventory levels). As the demand rate a increases, Q^* increases (larger batches) but t^* decreases (more frequent setups).

These formulas for Q^* and t^* will now be applied to the speaker example. The appropriate parameter values from Sec. 19.1 are

$$K = 12{,}000, \qquad h = 0.30, \qquad a = 8{,}000,$$

so that

$$Q^* = \sqrt{\frac{(2)(8{,}000)(12{,}000)}{0.30}} = 25{,}298$$

and

$$t^* = \frac{25{,}298}{8{,}000} = 3.2 \text{ months.}$$

Hence, the optimal solution is to set up the production facilities to produce speakers once every 3.2 months and to produce 25,298 speakers each time. (The total cost curve is rather flat near this optimal value, so any similar production run that might be more convenient, say 24,000 speakers every 3 months, would be nearly optimal.)

The EOQ Model with Planned Shortages

One of the banes of any inventory manager is the occurrence of an inventory shortage (sometimes referred to as a *stockout*)—demand that cannot be met currently because the inventory is depleted. This causes a variety of headaches, including dealing with unhappy customers and having extra record keeping to arrange for filling the demand later (*backorders*) when the inventory can be replenished. By assuming that planned shortages are not allowed, the basic EOQ model presented above satisfies the common desire of managers to avoid shortages as much as possible. (Nevertheless, unplanned shortages can still occur if the demand rate and deliveries do not stay on schedule.)

---

[1]An interesting historical account of this model and formula, including a reprint of a 1913 paper that started it all, is given by D. Erlenkotter, "Ford Whitman Harris and the Economic Order Quantity Model," *Operations Research,* **38**: 937–950, 1990.

However, there are situations where permitting limited planned shortages makes sense from a managerial perspective. The most important requirement is that the customers generally are able and willing to accept a reasonable delay in filling their orders if need be. If so, the costs of incurring shortages described in Secs. 19.1 and 19.2 (including lost future business) should not be exorbitant. If the cost of holding inventory is high relative to these shortage costs, then lowering the average inventory level by permitting occasional brief shortages may be a sound business decision.

The **EOQ model with planned shortages** addresses this kind of situation by replacing only the third assumption of the basic EOQ model by the following new assumption.

> Planned shortages now are allowed. When a shortage occurs, the affected customers will wait for the product to become available again. Their backorders are filled immediately when the order quantity arrives to replenish inventory.

Under these assumptions, the pattern of inventory levels over time has the appearance shown in Fig. 19.2. The saw-toothed appearance is the same as in Fig. 19.1. However, now the inventory levels extend down to negative values that reflect the number of units of the product that are backordered.

Let

$$p = \text{shortage cost per unit short per unit of time short,}$$

$$S = \text{inventory level just after a batch of } Q \text{ units is added to inventory,}$$

$$Q - S = \text{shortage in inventory just before a batch of } Q \text{ units is added.}$$

The total cost per unit time now is obtained from the following components.

Production or ordering cost per cycle $= K + cQ$.

During each cycle, the inventory level is positive for a time S/a. The average inventory level *during this time* is $(S + 0)/2 = S/2$ units, and the corresponding cost is $hS/2$ per unit time. Hence,

$$\text{Holding cost per cycle} = \frac{hS}{2} \frac{S}{a} = \frac{hS^2}{2a}.$$

Similarly, shortages occur for a time $(Q - S)/a$. The average amount of shortages *during this time* is $(0 + Q - S)/2 = (Q - S)/2$ units, and the corresponding cost is $p(Q - S)/2$ per unit time. Hence,

$$\text{Shortage cost per cycle} = \frac{p(Q - S)}{2} \frac{Q - S}{a} = \frac{p(Q - S)^2}{2a}.$$

FIGURE 19.2
Diagram of inventory level as a function of time for the EOQ model with planned shortages.

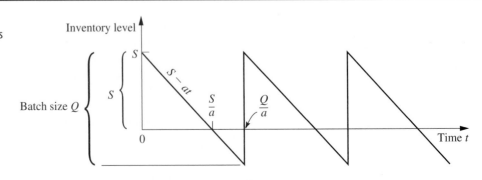

Therefore,

$$\text{Total cost per cycle} = K + cQ + \frac{hS^2}{2a} + \frac{p(Q-S)^2}{2a},$$

and the *total cost per unit time* is

$$T = \frac{K + cQ + hS^2/(2a) + p(Q-S)^2/(2a)}{Q/a}$$

$$= \frac{aK}{Q} + ac + \frac{hS^2}{2Q} + \frac{p(Q-S)^2}{2Q}.$$

In this model, there are two decision variables (S and Q), so the optimal values (S^* and Q^*) are found by setting the partial derivatives $\partial T/\partial S$ and $\partial T/\partial Q$ equal to zero. Thus,

$$\frac{\partial T}{\partial S} = \frac{hS}{Q} - \frac{p(Q-S)}{Q} = 0.$$

$$\frac{\partial T}{\partial Q} = -\frac{aK}{Q^2} - \frac{hS^2}{2Q^2} + \frac{p(Q-S)}{Q} - \frac{p(Q-S)^2}{2Q^2} = 0.$$

Solving these equations simultaneously leads to

$$S^* = \sqrt{\frac{2aK}{h}} \sqrt{\frac{p}{p+h}}, \qquad Q^* = \sqrt{\frac{2aK}{h}} \sqrt{\frac{p+h}{p}}.$$

The optimal cycle length t^* is given by

$$t^* = \frac{Q^*}{a} = \sqrt{\frac{2K}{ah}} \sqrt{\frac{p+h}{p}}.$$

The maximum shortage is

$$Q^* - S^* = \sqrt{\frac{2aK}{p}} \sqrt{\frac{h}{p+h}}.$$

In addition, from Fig. 19.2, the fraction of time that no shortage exists is given by

$$\frac{S^*/a}{Q^*/a} = \frac{p}{p+h},$$

which is independent of K.

When either p or h is made much larger than the other, the above quantities behave in intuitive ways. In particular, when $p \to \infty$ with h constant (so shortage costs dominate holding costs), $Q^* - S^* \to 0$ whereas both Q^* and t^* converge to their values for the basic EOQ model. Even though the current model permits shortages, $p \to \infty$ implies that having them is not worthwhile.

On the other hand, when $h \to \infty$ with p constant (so holding costs dominate shortage costs), $S^* \to 0$. Thus, having $h \to \infty$ makes it uneconomical to have positive inventory levels, so each new batch of Q^* units goes no further than removing the current shortage in inventory.

If planned shortages are permitted in the speaker example, the *shortage cost* is estimated in Sec. 19.1 as

$$p = 1.10.$$

As before,

$$K = 12{,}000, \qquad h = 0.30, \qquad a = 8{,}000,$$

so now

$$S^* = \sqrt{\frac{(2)(8{,}000)(12{,}000)}{0.30}} \sqrt{\frac{1.1}{1.1 + 0.3}} = 22{,}424,$$

$$Q^* = \sqrt{\frac{(2)(8{,}000)(12{,}000)}{0.30}} \sqrt{\frac{1.1 + 0.3}{1.1}} = 28{,}540,$$

and

$$t^* = \frac{28{,}540}{8{,}000} = 3.6 \text{ months.}$$

Hence, the production facilities are to be set up every 3.6 months to produce 28,540 speakers. The maximum shortage is 6,116 speakers. Note that Q^* and t^* are not very different from the no-shortage case. The reason is that p is much larger than h.

The EOQ Model with Quantity Discounts

When specifying their cost components, the preceding models have assumed that the unit cost of an item is the same regardless of the quantity in the batch. In fact, this assumption resulted in the optimal solutions being independent of this unit cost. The *EOQ model with quantity discounts* replaces this assumption by the following new assumption.

> The unit cost of an item now depends on the quantity in the batch. In particular, an incentive is provided to place a large order by replacing the unit cost for a small quantity by a smaller unit cost for every item in a larger batch, and perhaps by even smaller unit costs for even larger batches.

Otherwise, the assumptions are the same as for the basic EOQ model.

To illustrate this model, consider the TV speakers example introduced in Sec. 19.1. Suppose now that the unit cost for *every* speaker is $c_1 = \$11$ if less than 10,000 speakers are produced, $c_2 = \$10$ if production falls between 10,000 and 80,000 speakers, and $c_3 = \$9.50$ if production exceeds 80,000 speakers. What is the optimal policy? The solution to this specific problem will reveal the general method.

From the results for the basic EOQ model, the total cost per unit time T_j if the unit cost is c_j is given by

$$T_j = \frac{aK}{Q} + ac_j + \frac{hQ}{2}, \qquad \text{for } j = 1, 2, 3.$$

(This expression assumes that h is independent of the unit cost of the items, but a common small refinement would be to make h proportional to the unit cost to reflect the fact that the cost of capital tied up in inventory varies in this way.) A plot of T_j versus Q is shown in Fig. 19.3 for each j, where the solid part of each curve extends over the feasible range of values of Q for that discount category.

For each curve, the value of Q that minimizes T_j is found just as for the basic EOQ model. For $K = 12{,}000$, $h = 0.30$, and $a = 8{,}000$, this value is

$$\sqrt{\frac{(2)(8{,}000)(12{,}000)}{0.30}} = 25{,}298.$$

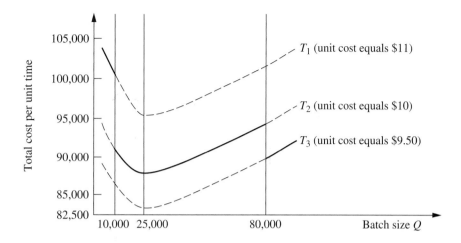

FIGURE 19.3
Total cost per unit time for the speaker example with quantity discounts.

(If h were not independent of the unit cost of the items, then the minimizing value of Q would be slightly different for the different curves.) This minimizing value of Q is a feasible value for the cost function T_2. For any fixed Q, $T_2 < T_1$, so T_1 can be eliminated from further consideration. However, T_3 cannot be immediately discarded. Its minimum feasible value (which occurs at $Q = 80,000$) must be compared to T_2 evaluated at 25,298 (which is \$87,589). Because T_3 evaluated at 80,000 equals \$89,200, it is better to produce in quantities of 25,298, so this quantity is the optimal value for this set of quantity discounts.

If the quantity discount led to a unit cost of \$9 (instead of \$9.50) when production exceeded 80,000, then T_3 evaluated at 80,000 would equal 85,200, and the optimal production quantity would become 80,000.

Although this analysis concerned a specific problem, the same approach is applicable to any similar problem. Here is a summary of the general procedure.

1. For each available unit cost c_j, use the EOQ formula for the EOQ model to calculate its optimal order quantity Q_j^*.
2. For each c_j where Q_j^* is within the feasible range of order quantities for c_j, calculate the corresponding total cost per unit time T_j.
3. For each c_j where Q_j^* is not within this feasible range, determine the order quantity Q_j that is at the endpoint of this feasible range that is closest to Q_j^*. Calculate the total cost per unit time T_j for Q_j and c_j.
4. Compare the T_j obtained for all the c_j and choose the minimum T_j. Then choose the order quantity Q_j obtained in step 2 or 3 that gives this minimum T_j.

A similar analysis can be used for other types of quantity discounts, such as incremental quantity discounts where a cost c_0 is incurred for the first q_0 units, c_1 for the next q_1 units, and so on.

Some Useful Excel Templates

For your convenience, we have included five Excel templates for the EOQ models in this chapter's Excel file on the CD-ROM. Two of these templates are for the basic EOQ model. In both cases, you enter basic data (a, K, and h), as well as the lead time for the deliveries and the number of working days per year for the firm. The template then calculates the firm's total annual expenditures for setups and for holding costs, as well as the sum of these two costs (the *total variable cost*). It also calculates the *reorder point*—the inventory level at which the order needs to be placed to replenish inventory so the replenishment will arrive when the inventory level drops to 0. One template (the *Solver version*) enables you to enter any order quantity you want and then see what the annual costs and reorder point would be. This version also enables you to use the Excel Solver to solve for the optimal order quantity. The second template (the *analytical version*) uses the EOQ formula to obtain the optimal order quantity.

The corresponding pair of templates also is provided for the EOQ model with planned shortages. After entering the data (including the unit shortage cost p), each of these templates will obtain the various annual costs (including the annual shortage cost). With the Solver version, you can either enter trial values of the order quantity Q and maximum shortage $Q - S$ or solve for the optimal values, whereas the analytical version uses the formulas for Q^* and $Q^* - S^*$ to obtain the optimal values. The corresponding maximum inventory level S^* also is included in the results.

The final template is an analytical version for the EOQ model with quantity discounts. This template includes the refinement that the unit holding cost h is proportional to the unit cost c, so

$$h = Ic,$$

where the proportionality factor I is referred to as the *inventory holding cost rate*. Thus, the data entered includes I along with a and K. You also need to enter the number of discount categories (where the lowest-quantity category with no discount counts as one of these), as well as the unit price and range of order quantities for each of the categories. The template then finds the feasible order quantity that minimizes the total annual cost for each category, and also shows the individual annual costs (including the annual purchase cost) that would result. Using this information, the template identifies the overall optimal order quantity and the resulting total annual cost.

All these templates can be helpful for calculating a lot of information quickly after entering the basic data for the problem. However, perhaps a more important use is for performing sensitivity analysis on these data. You can immediately see how the results would change for any specific change in the data by entering the new data values in the spreadsheet. Doing this repeatedly for a variety of changes in the data is a convenient way to perform sensitivity analysis.

Observations about EOQ Models

1. If it is assumed that the unit cost of an item is constant throughout time independent of the batch size (as with the first two EOQ models), the unit cost does not appear in the optimal solution for the batch size. This result occurs because no matter what inventory policy is used, the same number of units is required per unit time, so this cost per unit time is fixed.
2. The analysis of the EOQ models assumed that the batch size Q is constant from cycle to cycle. The resulting *optimal* batch size Q^* actually minimizes the total cost per unit time for any cycle, so the analysis shows that this constant batch size should be used from cycle to cycle even if a constant batch size is not assumed.

3. The optimal inventory level at which inventory should be replenished can never be greater than zero under these models. Waiting until the inventory level drops to zero (or less than zero when planned shortages are permitted) reduces both holding costs and the frequency of incurring the setup cost K. However, if the assumptions of *a known constant demand rate* and *the order quantity will arrive just when desired* (because of a constant lead time) are not completely satisfied, it may become prudent to plan to have some "safety stock" left when the inventory is scheduled to be replenished. This is accomplished by increasing the reorder point above that implied by the model.

4. The basic assumptions of the EOQ models are rather demanding ones. They seldom are satisfied completely in practice. For example, even when a constant demand rate is planned (as with the production line in the TV speakers example in Sec. 19.1), interruptions and variations in the demand rate still are likely to occur. It also is very difficult to satisfy the assumption that the order quantity to replenish inventory arrives just when desired. Although the schedule may call for a constant lead time, variations in the actual lead times often will occur. Fortunately, the EOQ models have been found to be robust in the sense that they generally still provide nearly optimal results even when their assumptions are only rough approximations of reality. This is a key reason why these models are so widely used in practice. However, in those cases where the assumptions are significantly violated, it is important to do some preliminary analysis to evaluate the adequacy of an EOQ model before it is used. This preliminary analysis should focus on calculating the total cost per unit time provided by the model for various order quantities and then assessing how this cost curve would change under more realistic assumptions.

A Broader Perspective of the Speaker Example

Example 2 (wholesale distribution of bicycles) introduced in Sec. 19.1 focused on managing the inventory of one model of bicycle. The demand for this product is generated by the wholesaler's customers (various retailers) who purchase these bicycles to replenish their inventories according to their own schedules. The wholesaler has no control over this demand. Because this model is sold separately from other models, its demand does not even depend on the demand for any of the company's other products. Such demand is referred to as **independent demand.**

The situation is different for the speaker example introduced in Sec. 19.1. Here, the product under consideration—television speakers—is just one component being assembled into the company's final product—television sets. Consequently, the demand for the speakers depends on the demand for the television set. The pattern of this demand for the speakers is determined internally by the production schedule that the company establishes for the television sets by adjusting the production rate for the production line producing the sets. Such demand is referred to as **dependent demand.**

The television manufacturing company produces a considerable number of products— various parts and subassemblies—that become components of the television sets. Like the speakers, these various products also are **dependent-demand products.**

Because of the dependencies and interrelationships involved, managing the inventories of dependent-demand products can be considerably more complicated than for independent-demand products. A popular technique for assisting in this task is **material re-**

quirements planning, abbreviated as **MRP.** MRP is a computer-based system for planning, scheduling, and controlling the production of all the components of a final product. The system begins by "exploding" the product by breaking it down into all its subassemblies and then into all its individual component parts. A production schedule is then developed, using the demand and lead time for each component to determine the demand and lead time for the subsequent component in the process. In addition to a *master production schedule* for the final product, a *bill of materials* provides detailed information about all its components. Inventory status records give the current inventory levels, number of units on order, etc., for all the components. When more units of a component need to be ordered, the MRP system automatically generates either a purchase order to the vendor or a work order to the internal department that produces the component.

When the basic EOQ model was used to calculate the optimal production lot size for the speaker example, a very large quantity (25,298 speakers) was obtained. This enables having relatively infrequent setups to initiate production runs (only once every 3.2 months). However, it also causes large average inventory levels (12,649 speakers), which leads to a large total holding cost per year of over $45,000.

The basic reason for this large cost is the high setup cost of $K = \$12,000$ for each production run. The setup cost is so sizable because the production facilities need to be set up again from scratch each time. Consequently, even with less than four production runs per year, the annual setup cost is over $45,000, just like the annual holding costs.

Rather than continuing to tolerate a $12,000 setup cost each time in the future, another option for the company is to seek ways to reduce this setup cost. One possibility is to develop methods for quickly transferring machines from one use to another. Another is to dedicate a group of production facilities to the production of speakers so they would remain set up between production runs in preparation for beginning another run whenever needed.

Suppose the setup cost could be drastically reduced from $12,000 all the way down to $K = \$120$. This would reduce the optimal production lot size from 25,298 speakers down to $Q^* = 2,530$ speakers, so a new production run lasting only a brief time would be initiated more than 3 times per month. This also would reduce both the annual setup cost and the annual holding cost from over $45,000 down to only slightly over $4,500 each. By having such frequent (but inexpensive) production runs, the speakers would be produced essentially *just in time* for their assembly into television sets.

Just in time actually is a well-developed philosophy for managing inventories. A **just-in-time (JIT)** inventory system places great emphasis on reducing inventory levels to a bare minimum, and so providing the items just in time as they are needed. This philosophy was first developed in Japan, beginning with the Toyota Company in the late 1950s, and is given part of the credit for the remarkable gains in Japanese productivity through much of the late 20th century. The philosophy also has become popular in other parts of the world, including the United States, in more recent years.

Although the just-in-time philosophy sometimes is misinterpreted as being incompatible with using an EOQ model (since the latter gives a large order quantity when the setup cost is large), they actually are complementary. A JIT inventory system focuses on finding ways to greatly reduce the setup costs so that the optimal order quantity will be small. Such a system also seeks ways to reduce the lead time for the delivery of an order, since this reduces the uncertainty about the number of units that will be needed when the delivery occurs. Another emphasis is on improving preventive maintenance so that the required production facilities will be available to produce the units when they are needed. Still another emphasis is on improving the production process to guarantee good quality. Providing just the right number of units just in time does not provide any leeway for including defective units.

In more general terms, the focus of the just-in-time philosophy is on *avoiding waste* wherever it might occur in the production process. One form of waste is unnecessary inventory. Others are unnecessarily large setup costs, unnecessarily long lead times, production facilities that are not operational when they are needed, and defective items. Minimizing these forms of waste is a key component of superior inventory management.

19.4 A DETERMINISTIC PERIODIC-REVIEW MODEL

The preceding section explored the basic EOQ model and some of its variations. The results were dependent upon the assumption of a constant demand rate. When this assumption is relaxed, i.e., when the amounts that need to be withdrawn from inventory are allowed to vary from period to period, the *EOQ formula* no longer ensures a minimum-cost solution.

Consider the following periodic-review model. Planning is to be done for the next n periods regarding how much (if any) to produce or order to replenish inventory at the beginning of each of the periods. (The order to replenish inventory can involve either *purchasing* the units or *producing* them, but the latter case is far more common with applications of this model, so we mainly will use the terminology of *producing* the units.) The demands for the respective periods are *known* (but *not* the same in every period) and are denoted by

r_i = demand in period i,   for $i = 1, 2, \ldots, n$.

These demands must be met on time. There is no stock on hand initially, but there is still time for a delivery at the beginning of period 1.

The costs included in this model are similar to those for the basic EOQ model:

K = setup cost for producing or purchasing any units to replenish inventory at beginning of period,

c = unit cost for producing or purchasing each unit,

h = holding cost for each unit left in inventory at end of period.

Note that this holding cost h is assessed only on inventory left at the end of a period. There also are holding costs for units that are in inventory for a portion of the period before being withdrawn to satisfy demand. However, these are *fixed* costs that are independent of the inventory policy and so are not relevant to the analysis. Only the *variable* costs that are affected by which inventory policy is chosen, such as the extra holding costs that are incurred by carrying inventory over from one period to the next, are relevant for selecting the inventory policy.

By the same reasoning, the unit cost c is an irrelevant fixed cost because, over all the time periods, all inventory policies produce the same number of units at the same cost. Therefore, c will be dropped from the analysis hereafter.

The objective is to minimize the total cost over the n periods. This is accomplished by ignoring the fixed costs and minimizing the total variable cost over the n periods, as illustrated by the following example.

Example.   An airplane manufacturer specializes in producing small airplanes. It has just received an order from a major corporation for 10 customized executive jet airplanes for the use of the corporation's upper management. The order calls for three of the airplanes to be delivered (and paid for) during the upcoming winter months (period 1), two more to be delivered during the spring (period 2), three more during the summer (period 3), and the final two during the fall (period 4).

Setting up the production facilities to meet the corporation's specifications for these airplanes requires a setup cost of $2 million. The manufacturer has the capacity to produce all 10 airplanes within a couple of months, when the winter season will be under way. However, this would necessitate holding seven of the airplanes in inventory, at a cost of $200,000 per airplane per period, until their scheduled delivery times. To reduce or eliminate these substantial holding costs, it may be worthwhile to produce a smaller number of these airplanes now and then to repeat the setup (again incurring the cost of $2 million) in some or all of the subsequent periods to produce additional small numbers. Management would like to determine the least costly production schedule for filling this order.

Thus, using the notation of the model, the demands for this particular airplane during the four upcoming periods (seasons) are

$$r_1 = 3, \qquad r_2 = 2, \qquad r_3 = 3, \qquad r_4 = 2.$$

Using units of millions of dollars, the relevant costs are

$$K = 2, \qquad h = 0.2.$$

The problem is to determine how many airplanes to produce (if any) during the beginning of each of the four periods in order to minimize the total variable cost.

The high setup cost K gives a strong incentive not to produce airplanes every period and preferably just once. However, the significant holding cost h makes it undesirable to carry a large inventory by producing the entire demand for all four periods (10 airplanes) at the beginning. Perhaps the best approach would be an intermediate strategy where airplanes are produced more than once but less than four times. For example, one such feasible solution (but not an optimal one) is depicted in Fig. 19.4, which shows the evolution of the inventory level over the next year that results from producing three airplanes at the beginning of the first period, six airplanes at the beginning of the second period, and one airplane at the beginning of the fourth period. The dots give the inventory levels after any production at the beginning of the four periods.

How can the optimal production schedule be found? For this model in general, production (or purchasing) is automatic in period 1, but a decision on whether to produce must be made for each of the other $n - 1$ periods. Therefore, one approach to solving this model is to enumerate, for each of the 2^{n-1} combinations of production decisions, the possible quantities that can be produced in each period where production is to occur. This approach is rather cumbersome, even for moderate-sized n, so a more efficient method is desirable. Such a method is described next in general terms, and then we will return to

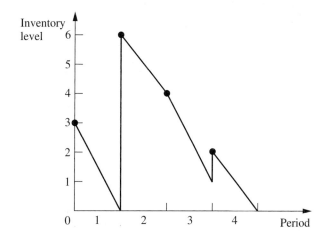

FIGURE 19.4
The inventory levels that result from one sample production schedule for the airplane example.

finding the optimal production schedule for the example. Although the general method can be used when either producing or purchasing to replenish inventory, we now will only use the terminology of producing for definiteness.

An Algorithm

The key to developing an efficient algorithm for finding an *optimal inventory policy* (or equivalently, an *optimal production schedule*) for the above model is the following insight into the nature of an optimal policy.

> An optimal policy (production schedule) produces *only* when the inventory level is *zero.*

To illustrate why this result is true, consider the policy shown in Fig. 19.4 for the example. (Call it policy *A*.) Policy *A* violates the above characterization of an optimal policy because production occurs at the beginning of period 4 when the inventory level is *greater than zero* (namely, one airplane). However, this policy can easily be adjusted to satisfy the above characterization by simply producing one less airplane in period 2 and one more airplane in period 4. This adjusted policy (call it *B*) is shown by the dashed line in Fig. 19.5 wherever *B* differs from *A* (the solid line). Now note that policy *B must* have less total cost than policy *A*. The setup costs (and the production costs) for both policies are the same. However, the holding cost is smaller for *B* than for *A* because *B* has less inventory than *A* in periods 2 and 3 (and the same inventory in the other periods). Therefore, *B* is better than *A*, so *A* cannot be optimal.

This characterization of optimal policies can be used to identify policies that are not optimal. In addition, because it implies that the only choices for the amount produced at the beginning of the ith period are 0, r_i, $r_i + r_{i+1}$, . . . , or $r_i + r_{i+1} + \cdots + r_n$, it can be exploited to obtain an efficient algorithm that is related to the *deterministic dynamic programming* approach described in Sec. 11.3.

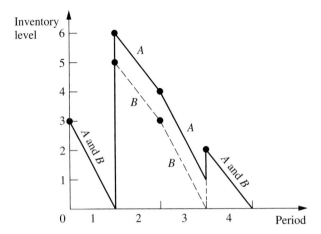

FIGURE 19.5
Comparison of two inventory policies (production schedules) for the airplane example.

In particular, define

C_i = total variable cost of an optimal policy for periods $i, i + 1, \ldots, n$ when period i starts with zero inventory (before producing), for $i = 1, 2, \ldots, n$.

By using the dynamic programming approach of solving *backward* period by period, these C_i values can be found by first finding C_n, then finding C_{n-1}, and so on. Thus, after C_n, $C_{n-1}, \ldots, C_{i+1}$ are found, then C_i can be found from the *recursive relationship*

$$C_i = \min_{j=i,\, i+1,\, \ldots,\, n} \{C_{j+1} + K + h[r_{i+1} + 2r_{i+2} + 3r_{i+3} + \cdots + (j - i)r_j]\},$$

where j can be viewed as an index that denotes the (end of the) period when the inventory reaches a zero level for the first time after production at the beginning of period i. In the time interval from period i through period j, the term with coefficient h represents the total *holding cost* over this interval. When $j = n$, the term $C_{n+1} = 0$. The *minimizing value* of j indicates that if the inventory level does indeed drop to zero upon entering period i, then the production in period i should cover all demand from period i through this period j.

The algorithm for solving the model consists basically of solving for $C_n, C_{n-1}, \ldots,$ C_1 in turn. For $i = 1$, the minimizing value of j then indicates that the production in period 1 should cover the demand through period j, so the second production will be in period $j + 1$. For $i = j + 1$, the new minimizing value of j identifies the time interval covered by the second production, and so forth to the end. We will illustrate this approach with the example.

The application of this algorithm is much quicker than the full dynamic programming approach.[1] As in dynamic programming, $C_n, C_{n-1}, \ldots, C_2$ must be found before C_1 is obtained. However, the number of calculations is much smaller, and the number of possible production quantities is greatly reduced.

---

[1]The full dynamic programming approach is useful, however, for solving *generalizations* of the model (e.g., *nonlinear* production cost and holding cost functions) where the above algorithm is no longer applicable. (See Probs. 19.4-3 and 19.4-4 for examples where dynamic programming would be used to deal with generalizations of the model.)

Application of the Algorithm to the Example

Returning to the airplane example, first we consider the case of finding C_4, the cost of the optimal policy from the beginning of period 4 to the end of the planning horizon:

$$C_4 = C_5 + 2 = 0 + 2 = 2.$$

To find C_3, we must consider two cases, namely, the first time after period 3 when the inventory reaches a zero level occurs at (1) the end of the third period or (2) the end of the fourth period. In the recursive relationship for C_3, these two cases correspond to (1) $j = 3$ and (2) $j = 4$. Denote the corresponding costs (the right-hand side of the recursive relationship with this j) by $C_3^{(3)}$ and $C_3^{(4)}$, respectively. The policy associated with $C_3^{(3)}$ calls for producing only for period 3 and then following the optimal policy for period 4, whereas the policy associated with $C_3^{(4)}$ calls for producing for periods 3 and 4. The cost C_3 is then the minimum of $C_3^{(3)}$ and $C_3^{(4)}$. These cases are reflected by the policies given in Fig. 19.6.

$$C_3^{(3)} = C_4 + 2 = 2 + 2 = 4.$$
$$C_3^{(4)} = C_5 + 2 + 0.2(2) = 0 + 2 + 0.4 = 2.4.$$
$$C_3 = \min\{4, 2.4\} = 2.4.$$

Therefore, if the inventory level drops to zero upon entering period 3 (so production should occur then), the production in period 3 should cover the demand for both periods 3 and 4.

To find C_2, we must consider three cases, namely, the first time after period 2 when the inventory reaches a zero level occurs at (1) the end of the second period, (2) the end of the third period, or (3) the end of the fourth period. In the recursive relationship for C_2, these cases correspond to (1) $j = 2$, (2) $j = 3$, and (3) $j = 4$, where the corresponding costs are $C_2^{(2)}$, $C_2^{(3)}$, and $C_2^{(4)}$, respectively. The cost C_2 is then the minimum of $C_2^{(2)}$, $C_2^{(3)}$, and $C_2^{(4)}$.

$$C_2^{(2)} = C_3 + 2 = 2.4 + 2 = 4.4.$$
$$C_2^{(3)} = C_4 + 2 + 0.2(3) = 2 + 2 + 0.6 = 4.6.$$
$$C_2^{(4)} = C_5 + 2 + 0.2[3 + 2(2)] = 0 + 2 + 1.4 = 3.4.$$
$$C_2 = \min\{4.4, 4.6, 3.4\} = 3.4.$$

FIGURE 19.6
Alternative production schedules when production is required at the beginning of period 3 for the airplane example.

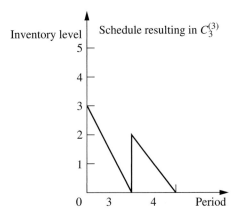

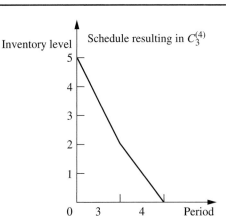

Consequently, if production occurs in period 2 (because the inventory level drops to zero), this production should cover the demand for all the remaining periods.

Finally, to find C_1, we must consider four cases, namely, the first time after period 1 when the inventory reaches zero occurs at the end of (1) the first period, (2) the second period, (3) the third period, or (4) the fourth period. These cases correspond to $j = 1, 2, 3, 4$ and to the costs $C_1^{(1)}$, $C_1^{(2)}$, $C_1^{(3)}$, $C_1^{(4)}$, respectively. The cost C_1 is then the minimum of $C_1^{(1)}$, $C_1^{(2)}$, $C_1^{(3)}$, and $C_1^{(4)}$.

$$C_1^{(1)} = C_2 + 2 = 3.4 + 2 = 5.4.$$
$$C_1^{(2)} = C_3 + 2 + 0.2(2) = 2.4 + 2 + 0.4 = 4.8.$$
$$C_1^{(3)} = C_4 + 2 + 0.2[2 + 2(3)] = 2 + 2 + 1.6 = 5.6.$$
$$C_1^{(4)} = C_5 + 2 + 0.2[2 + 2(3) + 3(2)] = 0 + 2 + 2.8 = 4.8.$$
$$C_1 = \min\{5.4, 4.8, 5.6, 4.8\} = 4.8.$$

Note that $C_1^{(2)}$ and $C_1^{(4)}$ tie as the minimum, giving C_1. This means that the policies corresponding to $C_1^{(2)}$ and $C_1^{(4)}$ tie as being the optimal policies. The $C_1^{(4)}$ policy says to produce enough in period 1 to cover the demand for all four periods. The $C_1^{(2)}$ policy covers only the demand through period 2. Since the latter policy has the inventory level drop to zero at the end of period 2, the C_3 result is used next, namely, produce enough in period 3 to cover the demand for periods 3 and 4. The resulting production schedules are summarized below.

Optimal Production Schedules.

1. Produce 10 airplanes in period 1.

Total variable cost = \$4.8 million.

2. Produce 5 airplanes in period 1 and 5 airplanes in period 3.

Total variable cost = \$4.8 million.

19.5 A STOCHASTIC CONTINUOUS-REVIEW MODEL

We now turn to *stochastic* inventory models, which are designed for analyzing inventory systems where there is considerable uncertainty about future demands. In this section, we consider a *continuous-review* inventory system. Thus, the inventory level is being monitored on a continuous basis so that a new order can be placed as soon as the inventory level drops to the reorder point.

The traditional method of implementing a *continuous-review* inventory system was to use a **two-bin system.** All the units for a particular product would be held in two bins. The capacity of one bin would equal the reorder point. The units would first be withdrawn from the other bin. Therefore, the emptying of this second bin would trigger placing a new order. During the lead time until this order is received, units would then be withdrawn from the first bin.

In more recent years, two-bin systems have been largely replaced by **computerized inventory systems.** Each addition to inventory and each sale causing a withdrawal are recorded electronically, so that the current inventory level always is in the computer. (For example, the modern scanning devices at retail store checkout stands may both itemize your purchases and record the sales of stable products for purposes of adjusting the current inventory levels.) Therefore, the computer will trigger a new order as soon as the inventory level has dropped to the reorder point. Several excellent software packages are available from software companies for implementing such a system.

Because of the extensive use of computers for modern inventory management, continuous-review inventory systems have become increasingly prevalent for products that are sufficiently important to warrant a formal inventory policy.

A continuous-review inventory system for a particular product normally will be based on two critical numbers:

R = reorder point.
Q = order quantity.

For a manufacturer managing its finished products inventory, the order will be for a *production run* of size Q. For a wholesaler or retailer (or a manufacturer replenishing its raw materials inventory from a supplier), the order will be a *purchase order* for Q units of the product.

An inventory policy based on these two critical numbers is a simple one.

Inventory policy: Whenever the inventory level of the product drops to R units, place an order for Q more units to replenish the inventory.

Such a policy is often called a *reorder-point, order-quantity policy,* or **(R, Q) policy** for short. [Consequently, the overall model might be referred to as the (R, Q) model. Other variations of these names, such as (Q, R) policy, (Q, R) model, etc., also are sometimes used.]

After summarizing the model's assumptions, we will outline how R and Q can be determined.

The Assumptions of the Model

1. Each application involves a single product.
2. The inventory level is under *continuous review,* so its current value always is known.
3. An (R, Q) policy is to be used, so the only decisions to be made are to choose R and Q.
4. There is a *lead time* between when the order is placed and when the order quantity is received. This lead time can be either fixed or variable.
5. The *demand* for withdrawing units from inventory to sell them (or for any other purpose) during this lead time is uncertain. However, the probability distribution of demand is known (or at least estimated).
6. If a stockout occurs before the order is received, the excess demand is *backlogged,* so that the backorders are filled once the order arrives.
7. A fixed *setup cost* (denoted by K) is incurred each time an order is placed.
8. Except for this setup cost, the cost of the order is proportional to the order quantity Q.
9. A certain holding cost (denoted by h) is incurred for each unit in inventory per unit time.
10. When a stockout occurs, a certain shortage cost (denoted by p) is incurred for each unit backordered per unit time until the backorder is filled.

This model is closely related to the *EOQ model with planned shortages* presented in Sec. 19.3. In fact, all these assumptions also are consistent with that model, with the one key exception of assumption 5. Rather than having uncertain demand, that model assumed *known demand* with a fixed rate.

Because of the close relationship between these two models, their results should be fairly similar. The main difference is that, because of the uncertain demand for the current model, some safety stock needs to be added when setting the reorder point to provide some cushion for having well-above-average demand during the lead time. Otherwise, the trade-offs between the various cost factors are basically the same, so the order quantities from the two models should be similar.

Choosing the Order Quantity Q

The most straightforward approach to choosing Q for the current model is to simply use the formula given in Sec. 19.3 for the EOQ model with planned shortages. This formula is

$$Q = \sqrt{\frac{2AK}{h}} \sqrt{\frac{p + h}{p}},$$

where A now is the *average* demand per unit time, and where K, h, and p are defined in assumptions 7, 9, and 10, respectively.

This Q will be only an approximation of the optimal order quantity for the current model. However, no formula is available for the exact value of the optimal order quantity, so an approximation is needed. Fortunately, the approximation given above is a fairly good one.[1]

Choosing the Reorder Point R

A common approach to choosing the reorder point R is to base it on management's desired level of service to customers. Thus, the starting point is to obtain a managerial decision on service level. (Problem 19.5-3 analyzes the factors involved in this managerial decision.)

Service level can be defined in a number of different ways in this context, as outlined below.

Alternative Measures of Service Level.

1. The probability that a stockout will not occur between the time an order is placed and the order quantity is received.
2. The average number of stockouts per year.
3. The average percentage of annual demand that can be satisfied immediately (no stockout).
4. The average delay in filling backorders when a stockout occurs.
5. The overall average delay in filling orders (where the delay without a stockout is 0).

Measures 1 and 2 are closely related. For example, suppose that the order quantity Q has been set at 10 percent of the annual demand, so an average of 10 orders are placed

---

[1]For further information about the quality of this approximation, see S. Axsäter, "Using the Deterministic EOQ Formula in Stochastic Inventory Control," *Management Science,* **42:** 830–834, 1996. Also see Y.-S. Zheng, "On Properties of Stochastic Systems," *Management Science,* **38:** 87–103, 1992.

per year. If the probability is 0.2 that a stockout *will* occur during the lead time until an order is received, then the average number of stockouts per year would be $10(0.2) = 2$.

Measures 2 and 3 also are related. For example, suppose an average of 2 stockouts occur per year and the average length of a stockout is 9 days. Since $2(9) = 18$ days of stockout per year are essentially 5 percent of the year, the average percentage of annual demand that can be satisfied immediately would be 95 percent.

In addition, measures 3, 4, and 5 are related. For example, suppose that the average percentage of annual demand that can be satisfied immediately is 95 percent and the average delay in filling backorders when a stockout occurs is 5 days. Since only 5 percent of the customers incur this delay, the overall average delay in filling orders then would be $0.05(5) = 0.25$ day per order.

A managerial decision needs to be made on the desired value of at least one of these measures of service level. After selecting one of these measures on which to focus primary attention, it is useful to explore the implications of several alternative values of this measure on some of the other measures before choosing the best alternative.

Measure 1 probably is the most convenient one to use as the primary measure, so we now will focus on this case. We will denote the desired level of service under this measure by L, so

L = management's desired probability that a stockout will not occur between the time an order quantity is placed and the order quantity is received.

Using measure 1 involves working with the estimated probability distribution of the following random variable.

D = demand during the lead time in filling an order.

For example, with a uniform distribution, the formula for choosing the reorder point R is a simple one.

If the probability distribution of D is a *uniform distribution* over the interval from a to b, set

$$R = a + L(b - a),$$

because then

$$P(D \leq R) = L.$$

Since the mean of this distribution is

$$E(D) = \frac{a + b}{2},$$

the amount of **safety stock** (the expected inventory level *just* before the order quantity is received) provided by the reorder point R is

$$\text{Safety stock} = R - E(D) = a + L(b - a) - \frac{a + b}{2}$$

$$= \left(L - \frac{1}{2}\right)(b - a).$$

When the demand distribution is something other than a uniform distribution, the procedure for choosing R is similar.

General Procedure for Choosing R under Service Level Measure 1.

1. Choose L.
2. Solve for R such that

$$P(D \leq R) = L.$$

For example, suppose that D has a normal distribution with mean μ and variance σ^2, as shown in Fig. 19.7. Given the value of L, the table for the normal distribution given in Appendix 5 then can be used to determine the value of R. In particular, you just need to find the value of K_{1-L} in this table and then plug into the following formula to find R.

$$R = \mu + K_{1-L}\sigma.$$

The resulting amount of safety stock is

$$\text{Safety stock} = R - \mu = K_{1-L}\sigma.$$

To illustrate, if $L = 0.75$, then $K_{1-L} = 0.675$, so

$$R = \mu + 0.675\sigma,$$

as shown in Fig. 19.7. This provides

$$\text{Safety stock} = 0.675\sigma.$$

Your OR Courseware also includes an Excel template that will calculate both the order quantity Q and the reorder point R for you. You need to enter the average demand per unit time (A), the costs (K, h, and p), and the service level based on measure 1. You also indicate whether the probability distribution of the demand during the lead time is a uniform distribution or a normal distribution. For a uniform distribution, you specify the interval over which the distribution extends by entering the lower endpoint and upper endpoint of this interval. For a normal distribution, you instead enter the mean μ and standard deviation σ of the distribution. After you provide all this information, the template immediately calculates Q and R and displays these results on the right side.

FIGURE 19.7
Calculation of the reorder point R for the stochastic continuous-review model when $L = 0.75$ and the probability distribution of the demand over the lead time is a normal distribution with mean μ and standard deviation σ.

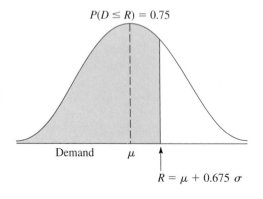

An Example. Consider once again Example 1 (manufacturing speakers for TV sets) presented in Sec. 19.1. Recall that the setup cost to produce the speakers is $K = \$12,000$, the unit holding cost is $h = \$0.30$ per speaker per month, and the unit shortage cost is $p = \$1.10$ per speaker per month.

Originally, there was a fixed demand rate of 8,000 speakers per month to be assembled into television sets being produced on a production line at this fixed rate. However, sales of the TV sets have been quite variable, so the inventory level of finished sets has fluctuated widely. To reduce inventory holding costs for finished sets, management has decided to adjust the production rate for the sets on a daily basis to better match the output with the incoming orders.

Consequently, the demand for the speakers now is quite variable. There is a *lead time* of 1 month between ordering a production run to produce speakers and having speakers ready for assembly into television sets. The demand for speakers during this lead time is a random variable D that has a normal distribution with a mean of 8,000 and a standard deviation of 2,000. To minimize the risk of disrupting the production line producing the TV sets, management has decided that the safety stock for speakers should be large enough to avoid a stockout during this lead time 95 percent of the time.

To apply the model, the order quantity for each production run of speakers should be

$$Q = \sqrt{\frac{2AK}{h}} \sqrt{\frac{p + h}{p}} = \sqrt{\frac{2(8,000)(12,000)}{0.30}} \sqrt{\frac{1.1 + 0.3}{1.1}} = 28,540.$$

This is the same order quantity that was found by the EOQ model with planned shortages in Sec. 19.3 for the previous version of this example where there was a *constant* (rather than average) demand rate of 8,000 speakers per month and planned shortages were allowed. However, the key difference from before is that safety stock now needs to be provided to counteract the variable demand. Management has chosen a service level of $L = 0.95$, so the normal table in Appendix 5 gives $K_{1-L} = 1.645$. Therefore, the reorder point should be

$$R = \mu + K_{1-L}\sigma = 8,000 + 1.645(2,000) = 11,290.$$

The resulting amount of safety stock is

$$\text{Safety stock} = R - \mu = 3,290.$$

19.6 A STOCHASTIC SINGLE-PERIOD MODEL FOR PERISHABLE PRODUCTS

When choosing the inventory model to use for a particular product, a distinction should be made between two types of products. One type is a **stable product,** which will remain sellable indefinitely so there is no deadline for disposing of its inventory. This is the kind of product considered in the preceding sections (as well as the next section). The other type, by contrast, is a **perishable product,** which can be carried in inventory for only a very limited period of time before it can no longer be sold. This is the kind of product for which the single-period model (and its variations) presented in this section is designed. In particular, the single period in the model is the very limited period before the product can no longer be sold.

One example of a perishable product is a daily newspaper being sold at a newsstand. A particular day's newspaper can be carried in inventory for only a single day before it becomes outdated and needs to be replaced by the next day's newspaper. When the demand for the newspaper is a random variable (as assumed in this section), the owner of the newsstand needs to choose a daily order quantity that provides an appropriate trade-off between the potential cost of overordering (the wasted expense of ordering more newspapers than can be sold) and the potential cost of underordering (the lost profit from ordering fewer newspapers than can be sold). This section's model enables solving for the daily order quantity that would maximize the expected profit.

Because the general problem being analyzed fits this example so well, the problem has traditionally been called the **newsboy problem.**[1] However, it has always been recognized that the model being used is just as applicable to other perishable products as to newspapers. In fact, most of the applications have been to perishable products other than newspapers, including the examples of perishable products listed below.

Some Types of Perishable Products

As you read through the list below of various types of perishable products, think about how the inventory management of such products is analogous to a newsstand dealing with a daily newspaper since these products also cannot be sold after a single time period. All that may differ is that the length of this time period may be a week, a month, or even several months rather than just one day.

1. Periodicals, such as newspapers and magazines.
2. Flowers being sold by a florist.
3. The makings of fresh food to be prepared in a restaurant.
4. Produce, including fresh fruits and vegetables, to be sold in a grocery store.
5. Christmas trees.
6. Seasonal clothing, such as winter coats, where any goods remaining at the end of the season must be sold at highly discounted prices to clear space for the next season.
7. Seasonal greeting cards.
8. Fashion goods that will be out of style soon.
9. New cars at the end of a model year.
10. Any product that will be obsolete soon.
11. Vital spare parts that must be produced during the last production run of a certain model of a product (e.g., an airplane) for use as needed throughout the lengthy field life of that model.
12. Reservations provided by an airline for a particular flight. Reservations provided in excess of the number of seats available (overbooking) can be viewed as the inventory of a perishable product (they cannot be sold after the flight has occurred), where the demand then is the number of no-shows. With this interpretation, the cost of underordering (too little overbooking) would be the lost profit from empty seats and the cost of overordering (too much overbooking) would be the cost of compensating bumped customers.

---

[1]Recently, some writers have been substituting the name *newsvendor problem.* Other names include the *single-period probabilistic model* and *single-period stochastic model.*

This last type is a particularly interesting one because major airlines (and various other companies involved with transporting passengers) now are making extensive use of this section's model to analyze how much overbooking to do. For example, an article in the January–February 1992 issue of *Interfaces* describes how *American Airlines* is dealing with overbooking in this way. In addition, the article describes how the company is also using operations research to address some related issues (such as the fare structure). These particular OR applications (commonly called *revenue management*) are credited with increasing American Airline's annual revenues by over $500 million. The total impact on annual profits throughout the passenger transportation industry would run into the billions of dollars.

When managing the inventory of these various types of perishable products, it is occasionally necessary to deal with some considerations beyond those that will be discussed in this section. Extensive research has been conducted to extend the model to encompass these considerations, and considerable progress has been made. Further information is available in the footnoted references.[1]

An Example

Refer back to Example 2 in Sec. 19.1, which involves the wholesale distribution of a particular bicycle model (a small one-speed girl's bicycle). There now has been a new development. The manufacturer has just informed the distributor that this model is being discontinued. To help clear out its stock, the manufacturer is offering the distributor the opportunity to make one final purchase at very favorable terms, namely, a *unit cost* of only $20 per bicycle. With these special arrangements, the distributor also would incur *no setup cost* to place this order.

The distributor feels that this offer provides an ideal opportunity to make one final round of sales to its customers (bicycle shops) for the upcoming Christmas season for a reduced price of only $45 per bicycle, thereby making a profit of $25 per bicycle. This will need to be a one-time sale only because this model soon will be replaced by a new model that will make it obsolete. Therefore, any bicycles not sold during this sale will become almost worthless. However, the distributor believes that she will be able to dispose of any remaining bicycles after Christmas by selling them for the nominal price of $10 each (the *salvage value*), thereby recovering half of her purchase cost. Considering this loss if she orders more than she can sell, as well as the lost profit if she orders fewer than can be sold, the distributor needs to decide what order quantity to submit to the manufacturer.

Another relevant expense is the cost of maintaining unsold bicycles in inventory until they can be disposed of after Christmas. Combining the cost of capital tied up in inventory and other storage costs, this inventory cost is estimated to be $1 per bicycle remaining in inventory after Christmas. Thus, considering the salvage value of $10 as well, the *unit holding cost* is −$9 per bicycle left in inventory at the end.

Two remaining cost components still require discussion, the shortage cost and the revenue. If the demand exceeds the supply, those customers who fail to purchase a bicy-

---

[1]See H.-S. Lau and A. H.-L. Lau, "The Newsstand Problem: A Capacitated Multiple Product Single-Period Inventory Problem," *European Journal of Operational Research,* **94:** 29–42, Oct. 11, 1996, and its references. Also see pp. 610–628 in E. L. Porteus, "Stochastic Inventory Theory," in D. P. Heyman and M. J. Sobel (eds.), *Stochastic Models,* North Holland, Amsterdam, 1990.

cle may bear some ill will, thereby resulting in a "cost" to the distributor. This cost is the per-item quantification of the loss of goodwill times the unsatisfied demand whenever a shortage occurs. The distributor considers this cost to be negligible.

If we adopt the criterion of maximizing profit, we must include revenue in the model. Indeed, the total profit is equal to total revenue minus the costs incurred (the ordering, holding, and shortage costs). Assuming no initial inventory, this profit for the distributor is

$$\text{Profit} = \$45 \times \text{number sold by distributor}$$
$$- \$20 \times \text{number purchased by distributor}$$
$$+ \$9 \times \text{number unsold and so disposed of for salvage value.}$$

Let

$$y = \text{number purchased by distributor}$$

and

$$D = \text{demand by bicycle shops (a random variable),}$$

so that

$$\min\{D, y\} = \text{number sold,}$$
$$\max\{0, y - D\} = \text{number unsold.}$$

Then

$$\text{Profit} = 45 \min\{D, y\} - 20y + 9 \max\{0, y - D\}.$$

The first term also can be written as

$$45 \min\{D, y\} = 45D - 45 \max\{0, D - y\}.$$

The term $45 \max\{0, D - y\}$ represents the *lost revenue from unsatisfied demand*. This lost revenue, plus any cost of the loss of customer goodwill due to unsatisfied demand (assumed negligible in this example), will be interpreted as the *shortage cost* throughout this section.

Now note that $45D$ is independent of the inventory policy (the value of y chosen) and so can be deleted from the objective function, which leaves

$$\text{Relevant profit} = -45 \max\{0, D - y\} - 20y + 9 \max\{0, y - D\}$$

to be maximized. All the terms on the right are the *negative* of *costs*, where these costs are the *shortage cost*, the *ordering cost*, and the *holding cost* (which has a negative value here), respectively. Rather than *maximizing* the *negative* of *total cost*, we instead will do the equivalent of *minimizing*

$$\text{Total cost} = 45 \max\{0, D - y\} + 20y - 9 \max\{0, y - D\}.$$

More precisely, since total cost is a random variable (because D is a random variable), the objective adopted for the model is to *minimize the expected total cost*.

In the discussion about the interpretation of the shortage cost, we assumed that the unsatisfied demand was lost (no backlogging). If the unsatisfied demand could be met by a priority shipment, similar reasoning applies. The revenue component of net income would become the sales price of a bicycle ($45) times the demand *minus* the unit cost of the priority shipment times the unsatisfied demand whenever a shortage occurs. If our wholesale distributor could be forced to meet the unsatisfied demand by purchasing bicycles from the manufacturer for $35 each plus an air freight charge of, say, $2 each, then the appropriate shortage cost would be $37 per bicycle. (If there were any costs associated with loss of goodwill, these also would be added to this amount.)

The distributor does not know what the demand for these bicycles will be; i.e., demand D is a random variable. However, an optimal inventory policy can be obtained if information about the probability distribution of D is available. Let

$$P_D(d) = P\{D = d\}.$$

It will be assumed that $P_D(d)$ is known for all values of d.

We now are in a position to summarize the model in general terms.

The Assumptions of the Model

1. Each application involves a single perishable product.
2. Each application involves a single time period because the product cannot be sold later.
3. However, it will be possible to dispose of any units of the product remaining at the end of the period, perhaps even receiving a *salvage value* for the units.
4. There is no initial inventory on hand.
5. The only decision to be made is the value of y, the number of units to order (either through purchasing or producing) so they can be placed into inventory at the beginning of the period.
6. The *demand* for withdrawing units from inventory to sell them (or for any other purpose) during the period is a random variable D. However, the probability distribution of D is known (or at least estimated).
7. After deleting the revenue if the demand were satisfied (since this is independent of the decision y), the objective becomes to minimize the expected total cost, where the cost components are

c = unit cost for purchasing or producing each unit,

h = holding cost per unit remaining at end of period (includes storage cost minus salvage value),

p = shortage cost per unit of unsatisfied demand (includes lost revenue and cost of loss of customer goodwill).

Analysis of the Model

The decision on the value of y, the amount of inventory to acquire, depends heavily on the probability distribution of demand D. More than the expected demand may be desirable, but probably less than the maximum possible demand. A trade-off is needed between (1) the risk of being short and thereby incurring shortage costs and (2) the risk of having an excess and thereby incurring wasted costs of ordering and holding excess units. This is accomplished by minimizing the expected value (in the statistical sense) of the sum of these costs.

The amount sold is given by

$$\min\{D, y\} = \begin{cases} D & \text{if } D < y \\ y & \text{if } D \geq y. \end{cases}$$

Hence, the cost incurred if the demand is D and y is stocked is given by

$$C(D, y) = cy + p \max\{0, D - y\} + h \max\{0, y - D\}.$$

Because the demand is a random variable [with probability distribution $P_D(d)$], this cost is also a random variable. The expected cost is then given by $C(y)$, where

$$C(y) = E[C(D, y)] = \sum_{d=0}^{\infty} (cy + p \max\{0, d - y\} + h \max\{0, y - d\})P_D(d)$$

$$= cy + \sum_{d=y}^{\infty} p(d - y)P_D(d) + \sum_{d=0}^{y-1} h(y - d)P_D(d).$$

The function $C(y)$ depends upon the probability distribution of D. Frequently, a representation of this probability distribution is difficult to find, particularly when the demand ranges over a large number of possible values. Hence, this *discrete random variable* is often approximated by a *continuous random variable*. Furthermore, when demand ranges over a large number of possible values, this approximation will generally yield a nearly exact value of the optimal amount of inventory to stock. In addition, when discrete demand is used, the resulting expressions may become slightly more difficult to solve analytically. Therefore, unless otherwise stated, *continuous demand* is assumed throughout the remainder of this chapter.

For this continuous random variable D, let

$$\varphi_D(\xi) = \text{probability density function of } D$$

and

$$\Phi(a) = \text{cumulative distribution function (CDF) of } D,$$

so

$$\Phi(a) = \int_0^a \varphi_D(\xi)\, d\xi.$$

When choosing an order quantity y, the CDF $\Phi(y)$ becomes the probability that a shortage will *not* occur before the period ends. As in the preceding section, this probability is referred to as the **service level** being provided by the order quantity. The corresponding expected cost $C(y)$ is expressed as

$$C(y) = E[C(D, y)] = \int_0^{\infty} C(\xi, y)\varphi_D(\xi)\, d\xi$$

$$= \int_0^{\infty} (cy + p \max\{0, \xi - y\} + h \max\{0, y - \xi\})\varphi_D(\xi)\, d\xi$$

$$= cy + \int_y^{\infty} p(\xi - y)\varphi_D(\xi)\, d\xi + \int_0^y h(y - \xi)\varphi_D(\xi)\, d\xi$$

$$= cy + L(y),$$

where $L(y)$ is often called the *expected shortage plus holding cost.* It then becomes necessary to find the value of y, say y^0, which minimizes $C(y)$. First we give the answer, and then we will show the derivation a little later.

The optimal quantity to order y^0 is that value which satisfies

$$\Phi(y^0) = \frac{p - c}{p + h}.$$

Thus, $\Phi(y^0)$ is the *optimal service level* and the corresponding order quantity y^0 can be obtained either by solving this equation algebraically or by plotting the CDF and then identifying y^0 graphically. To interpret the right-hand side of this equation, the numerator can be viewed as

$p - c =$ unit cost of underordering
$\quad\quad\quad\;= $ decrease in profit that results from failing to order a unit that could have been sold during the period.

Similarly,

$c + h =$ unit cost of overordering
$\quad\quad\quad\;=$ decrease in profit that results from ordering a unit that could not be sold during the period.

Therefore, denoting the unit cost of underordering and of overordering by C_{under} and C_{over}, respectively, this equation is specifying that

$$\text{Optimal service level} = \frac{C_{under}}{C_{under} + C_{over}}.$$

When the demand has either a uniform or an exponential distribution, an Excel template is available in your OR Courseware for calculating y^0.

If D is assumed to be a discrete random variable having the CDF

$$F_D(b) = \sum_{d=0}^{b} P_D(d),$$

a similar result for the optimal order quantity is obtained. In particular, the optimal quantity to order y^0 is the smallest integer such that

$$F_D(y^0) \geq \frac{p - c}{p + h}.$$

Application to the Example

Returning to the bicycle example described at the beginning of this section, we assume that the demand has an exponential distribution with a mean of 10,000, so that its probability density function is

$$\varphi_D(\xi) = \begin{cases} \dfrac{1}{10,000} e^{-\xi/10,000} & \text{if } \xi \geq 0 \\ 0 & \text{otherwise} \end{cases}$$

and the CDF is

$$\Phi(a) = \int_0^a \frac{1}{10,000} e^{-\xi/10,000} \, d\xi = 1 - e^{-a/10,000}.$$

From the data given,

$$c = 20, \qquad p = 45, \qquad h = -9.$$

Consequently, the optimal quantity to order y^0 is that value which satisfies

$$1 - e^{-y^0/10,000} = \frac{45 - 20}{45 - 9} = 0.69444.$$

By using the natural logarithm (denoted by ln), this equation can be solved as follows:

$$e^{-y^0/10,000} = 0.30556,$$
$$\ln e^{-y^0/10,000} = \ln 0.30556,$$

$$\frac{-y_0}{10,000} = -1.1856,$$
$$y^0 = 11,856.$$

Therefore, the distributor should stock 11,856 bicycles in the Christmas season. Note that this number is slightly more than the expected demand of 10,000.

Whenever the demand is exponential with expectation λ, then y^0 can be obtained from the relation

$$y^0 = -\lambda \ln \frac{c + h}{p + h}.$$

The Model with Initial Stock Level

In the above model we assume that there is no initial inventory. As a slight variation, suppose now that the distributor begins with 500 bicycles on hand. How does this stock influence the optimal inventory policy?

In general terms, suppose that the initial stock level is given by x, and the decision to be made is the value of y, the inventory level *after replenishment* by ordering (or producing) additional units. Thus, $y - x$ is to be ordered, so that

Amount available (y) = initial stock (x) + amount ordered ($y - x$).

The cost equation presented earlier remains identical except for the term that was previously cy. This term now becomes $c(y - x)$, so that minimizing the expected cost is given by

$$\min_{y \geq x} \left[c(y - x) + \int_y^\infty p(\xi - y)\varphi_D(\xi) \, d\xi + \int_0^y h(y - \xi)\varphi_D(\xi) \, d\xi \right].$$

The constraint $y \geq x$ must be added because the inventory level y after replenishing cannot be less than the initial inventory level x.

The optimal inventory policy is the following:

If $\quad x \begin{cases} < y^0 & \text{order } y^0 - x \text{ to bring inventory level up to } y^0 \\ \geq y^0 & \text{do not order,} \end{cases}$

where y^0 satisfies

$$\Phi(y^0) = \frac{p-c}{p+h}.$$

Thus, in the bicycle example, if there are 500 bicycles on hand, the optimal policy is to bring the inventory level up to 11,856 bicycles (which implies ordering 11,356 additional bicycles). On the other hand, if there were 12,000 bicycles already on hand, the optimal policy would be not to order.

Derivation of the Optimal Policy.[1]   We start by assuming that the initial stock level is zero.

For any positive constants c_1 and c_2, define $g(\xi, y)$ as

$$g(\xi, y) = \begin{cases} c_1(y - \xi) & \text{if } y > \xi \\ c_2(\xi - y) & \text{if } y \leq \xi, \end{cases}$$

and let

$$G(y) = \int_0^{\infty} g(\xi, y)\varphi_D(\xi) \, d\xi + cy,$$

where $c > 0$. Then $G(y)$ is minimized at $y = y^0$, where y^0 is the solution to

$$\Phi(y^0) = \frac{c_2 - c}{c_2 + c_1}.$$

To see why this value of y^0 minimizes $G(y)$, note that, by definition,

$$G(y) = c_1 \int_0^y (y - \xi)\varphi_D(\xi) \, d\xi + c_2 \int_y^{\infty} (\xi - y)\varphi_D(\xi) \, d\xi + cy.$$

Taking the derivative (see the end of Appendix 3) and setting it equal to zero lead to

$$\frac{dG(y)}{dy} = c_1 \int_0^y \varphi_D(\xi) \, d\xi - c_2 \int_y^{\infty} \varphi_D(\xi) \, d\xi + c = 0.$$

This expression implies that

$$c_1\Phi(y^0) - c_2[1 - \Phi(y^0)] + c = 0,$$

because

$$\int_0^{\infty} \varphi_D(\xi) \, d\xi = 1.$$

Solving this expression results in

$$\Phi(y^0) = \frac{c_2 - c}{c_2 + c_1}.$$

---

[1]This subsection may be omitted by the less mathematically inclined reader.

The solution of this equation minimizes $G(y)$ because

$$\frac{d^2G(y)}{dy^2} = (c_1 + c_2)\varphi_D(y) \geq 0$$

for all y.

To apply this result, it is sufficient to show that

$$C(y) = cy + \int_y^\infty p(\xi - y)\varphi_D(\xi)\,d\xi + \int_0^y h(y - \xi)\varphi_D(\xi)\,d\xi$$

has the form of $G(y)$. Clearly, $c_1 = h$, $c_2 = p$, and $c = c$, so that the optimal quantity to order y^0 is that value which satisfies

$$\Phi(y^0) = \frac{p - c}{p + h}.$$

To derive the results for the case where the initial stock level is $x > 0$, recall that it is necessary to solve the relationship

$$\min_{y \geq x} \left\{ -cx + \left[\int_y^\infty p(\xi - y)\varphi_D(\xi)\,d\xi + \int_0^y h(y - \xi)\varphi_D(\xi)\,d\xi + cy \right] \right\}.$$

Note that the expression in brackets has the form of $G(y)$, with $c_1 = h$, $c_2 = p$, and $c = c$. Hence, the cost function to be minimized can be written as

$$\min_{y \geq x} \{ -cx + G(y) \}.$$

It is clear that $-cx$ is a constant, so that it is sufficient to find the y that satisfies the expression

$$\min_{y \geq x} G(y).$$

Therefore, the value of y^0 that minimizes $G(y)$ satisfies

$$\Phi(y^0) = \frac{p - c}{p + h}.$$

Furthermore, $G(y)$ must be a convex function, because

$$\frac{d^2G(y)}{dy^2} \geq 0.$$

Also,

$$\lim_{y \to 0} \frac{dG(y)}{dy} = c - p,$$

which is negative,[1] and

$$\lim_{y \to \infty} \frac{dG(y)}{dy} = h + c,$$

---

[1] If $c - p$ is nonnegative, $G(y)$ will be a monotone increasing function. This implies that the item should not be stocked, that is, $y^0 = 0$.

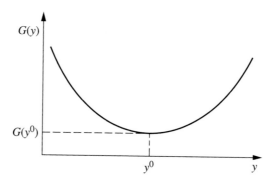

FIGURE 19.8
Graph of $G(y)$ for the stochastic single-period model.

which is positive. Hence, $G(y)$ must be as shown in Fig. 19.8. Thus, the optimal policy must be given by the following:

If $x < y^0$, order $y^0 - x$ to bring the inventory level up to y^0, because y^0 can be achieved together with the minimum value $G(y^0)$. If $x \geq y^0$, do not order because any $G(y)$ with $y > x$ must exceed $G(x)$.

A similar argument can be constructed for obtaining optimal policies for the following model with nonlinear costs.

Model with Nonlinear Costs.   Similar results for these models can be obtained for other than linear holding and shortage costs. Denote the holding cost by

$$h[y - D] \quad \text{if } y \geq D,$$
$$0 \quad\quad\quad \text{if } y < D,$$

where $h[\cdot]$ is a mathematical function, not necessarily linear.
   Similarly, the shortage cost can be denoted by

$$p[D - y] \quad \text{if } D \geq y,$$
$$0 \quad\quad\quad \text{if } D < y,$$

where $p[\cdot]$ is also a function, not necessarily linear.
   Thus, the total expected cost is given by

$$c(y - x) + \int_y^\infty p[\xi - y]\varphi_D(\xi)\, d\xi + \int_0^y h[y - \xi]\varphi_D(\xi)\, d\xi,$$

where x is the amount on hand.
   If $L(y)$ is defined as the *expected shortage plus holding cost,* i.e.,

$$L(y) = \int_y^\infty p[\xi - y]\varphi_D(\xi)\, d\xi + \int_0^y h[y - \xi]\varphi_D(\xi)\, d\xi,$$

then the total expected cost can be written as

$$c(y - x) + L(y).$$

The optimal policy is obtained by minimizing this expression, subject to the constraint that $y \geq x$, that is,

$$\min_{y \geq x} \{c(y - x) + L(y)\}.$$

If $L(y)$ is strictly convex[1] [a sufficient condition being that the shortage and holding costs each are convex and $\varphi_D(\xi) > 0$], then the optimal policy is the following:

$$\text{If} \quad x \begin{cases} < y^0 & \text{order } y^0 - x \text{ to bring inventory level up to } y^0 \\ \geq y^0 & \text{do not order,} \end{cases}$$

where y^0 is the value of y that satisfies the expression

$$\frac{dL(y)}{dy} + c = 0.$$

A Single-Period Model with a Setup Cost

In discussing the bicycle example previously in this section, we assumed that there was no setup cost incurred in ordering the bicycles for the Christmas season. Suppose now that the cost of placing this special order is $800, so this cost should be included in the analysis of the model. In fact, inclusion of the setup cost generally causes major changes in the results.

In general, the setup cost will be denoted by K. To begin, the shortage and holding costs will each be assumed to be linear. Their resulting effect is then given by $L(y)$, where

$$L(y) = p\int_y^\infty (\xi - y)\varphi_D(\xi)\, d\xi + h\int_0^y (y - \xi)\varphi_D(\xi)\, d\xi.$$

Thus, the total expected cost incurred by bringing the inventory level up to y is given by

$$K + c(y - x) + L(y) \qquad \text{if } y > x,$$
$$L(x) \qquad\qquad\qquad\quad \text{if } y = x.$$

Note that $cy + L(y)$ is the same expected cost considered earlier when the setup cost was omitted. If $cy + L(y)$ is drawn as a function of y, it will appear as shown in Fig. 19.9.[2] Define S as the value of y that minimizes $cy + L(y)$, and define s as the smallest value of y for which $cs + L(s) = K + cS + L(S)$. From Fig. 19.9, it can be seen that

$$\text{If} \quad x > S, \quad \text{then} \quad K + cy + L(y) > cx + L(x), \quad \text{for all } y > x,$$

so that

$$K + c(y - x) + L(y) > L(x).$$

The left-hand side of the last inequality represents the expected total cost of ordering $y - x$ to bring the inventory level up to y, and the right-hand side of this inequality

---

[1]See Appendix 2 for the definition of a strictly convex function.
[2]In the derivation of the optimal policy for the single-period model with no setup cost, $cy + L(y)$ was denoted by $G(y)$ and was rigorously shown to be a convex function of the form plotted in Fig. 19.9.

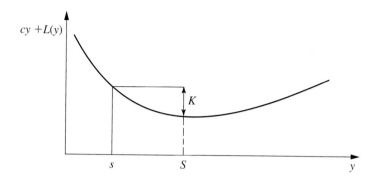

FIGURE 19.9
Graph of $cy + L(y)$ for the stochastic single-period model with a setup cost.

represents the expected total cost if no ordering occurs. Hence, the optimal policy indicates that if $x > S$, do not order.

If $s \leq x \leq S$, it can also be seen from Fig. 19.9 that

$$K + cy + L(y) \geq cx + L(x), \qquad \text{for all } y > x,$$

so that

$$K + c(y - x) + L(y) \geq L(x).$$

Again, no ordering is less expensive than ordering.

Finally, if $x < s$, it follows from Fig. 19.9 that

$$\min_{y \geq x} \{K + cy + L(y)\} = K + cS + L(S) < cx + L(x),$$

or

$$\min_{y \geq x} \{K + c(y - x) + L(y)\} = K + c(S - x) + L(S) < L(x),$$

so that it pays to order. The minimum cost is incurred by bringing the inventory level up to S.

The optimal inventory policy is the following:

If $x \begin{cases} < s & \text{order } S - x \text{ to bring inventory level up to } S \\ \geq s & \text{do not order.} \end{cases}$

The value of S is obtained from

$$\Phi(S) = \frac{p - c}{p + h},$$

and s is the smallest value that satisfies the expression

$$cs + L(s) = K + cS + L(S).$$

When the demand has either a uniform or an exponential distribution, an Excel template is available in your OR Courseware for calculating s and S.

This kind of policy is referred to as an **(s, S) policy.** It has had extensive use in industry.

Example.   Referring to the bicycle example, we found earlier that

$$y^0 = S = 11,856.$$

If $K = 800$, $c = 20$, $p = 45$, and $h = -9$, then s is obtained from

$$20s + 45\int_s^\infty (\xi - s)\frac{1}{10,000}\, e^{-\xi/10,000}\, d\xi - 9\int_0^s (s - \xi)\frac{1}{10,000}e^{-\xi/10,000}\, d\xi$$

$$= 800 + 20(11,856) + 45\int_{11,856}^\infty (\xi - 11,856)\frac{1}{10,000}e^{-\xi/10,000}\, d\xi$$

$$-9\int_0^{11,856} (11,856 - \xi)\frac{1}{10,000}e^{-\xi/10,000}\, d\xi,$$

which leads to

$$s = 10,674.$$

Hence, the optimal policy calls for bringing the inventory level up to $S = 11,856$ bicycles if the amount on hand is less than $s = 10,674$. Otherwise, no order is placed.

Solution When the Demand Distribution Is Exponential.   Now consider the special case where the distribution of demand D is exponential, i.e.,

$$\varphi_D(\xi) = \alpha e^{-\alpha\xi}, \qquad \text{for } \xi \geq 0.$$

From the no-setup-cost results,

$$1 - e^{-\alpha S} = \frac{p - c}{p + h},$$

so

$$S = \frac{1}{\alpha} \ln \frac{h + p}{h + c}.$$

For any y,

$$cy + L(y) = cy + h\int_0^y (y - \xi)\alpha e^{-\alpha\xi}\, d\xi + p\int_y^\infty (\xi - y)\alpha e^{-\alpha\xi}\, d\xi$$

$$= (c + h)y + \frac{1}{\alpha}(h + p)e^{-\alpha y} - \frac{h}{\alpha}.$$

Evaluating $cy + L(y)$ at the points $y = s$ and $y = S$ leads to

$$(c + h)s + \frac{1}{\alpha}(h + p)e^{-\alpha s} - \frac{h}{\alpha} = K + (c + h)S + \frac{1}{\alpha}(h + p)e^{-\alpha S} - \frac{h}{\alpha},$$

or

$$(c + h)s + \frac{1}{\alpha}(h + p)e^{-\alpha s} = K + (c + h)S + \frac{1}{\alpha}(c + h).$$

Although this last equation does not have a closed-form solution, it can be solved numerically quite easily. An approximate analytical solution can be obtained as follows. By letting

$$\Delta = S - s,$$

the last equation yields

$$e^{\alpha\Delta} = \frac{\alpha K}{c + h} + \alpha\Delta + 1.$$

If $\alpha\Delta$ is close to zero, $e^{\alpha\Delta}$ can be expanded into a Taylor series around zero. If the terms beyond the quadratic term are neglected, the result becomes

$$1 + \alpha\Delta + \frac{\alpha^2\Delta^2}{2} \cong \frac{\alpha K}{c + h} + \alpha\Delta + 1,$$

so that

$$\Delta = \sqrt{\frac{2K}{\alpha(c + h)}}.$$

Using this approximation in the bicycle example results in

$$\Delta = \sqrt{\frac{(2)(10,000)(800)}{20 - 9}} = 1,206,$$

which is quite close to the exact value of $\Delta = 1,182$.

Model with Nonlinear Costs. These results can be extended to the case where the expected shortage plus holding cost $L(y)$ is a *strictly convex* function. This extension results in a strictly convex $cy + L(y)$, similar to Fig. 19.9.

For this model, the optimal inventory policy has the following form:

$$\text{If} \quad x \begin{cases} < s & \text{order } S - x \text{ to bring inventory level up to } S \\ \geq s & \text{do not order,} \end{cases}$$

where S is the value of y that satisfies

$$c + \frac{dL(y)}{dy} = 0$$

and s is the smallest value that satisfies the expression

$$cs + L(s) = K + cS + L(S).$$

19.7 STOCHASTIC PERIODIC-REVIEW MODELS

The preceding section presented a stochastic single-period model that is designed for dealing with *perishable* products. We now return to considering *stable* products that will remain sellable indefinitely, as in the first five sections of the chapter. We again assume that the demand is uncertain so that a stochastic model is needed. However, in contrast to the continuous-review inventory system considered in Sec. 19.5, we now assume that the system is only being monitored periodically. At the end of each period, when the current inventory level is determined, a decision is made on how much to order (if any) to replenish inventory for the next period. Each of these decisions takes into account the planning for multiple periods into the future.

We begin with the simplest case where the planning is only being done for the next two periods and no setup cost is incurred when placing an order to replenish inventory.

A Stochastic Two-Period Model with No Setup Cost

One option with a stochastic periodic-review inventory system is to plan ahead only one period at a time, using the stochastic single-period model from the preceding section to make the ordering decision each time. However, this approach would only provide a relatively crude approximation. If the probability distribution of demand in each period can be forecasted multiple periods into the future, better decisions can be made by coordinating the plans for all these periods than by planning ahead just one period at a time. This can be quite difficult for many periods, but is considerably less difficult when considering only two periods at a time.

Even for a planning horizon of two periods, using the optimal one-period solution twice is not generally the optimal policy for the two-period problem. Smaller costs can usually be achieved by viewing the problem from a two-period viewpoint and then using the methods of probabilistic dynamic programming introduced in Sec. 11.4 to obtain the best inventory policy.

Assumptions.   Except for having two periods, the assumptions for this model are basically the same as for the one-period model presented in the preceding section, as summarized below.

1. Each application involves a single stable product.
2. Planning is being done for two periods, where unsatisfied demand in period 1 is backlogged to be met in period 2, but there is no backlogging of unsatisfied demand in period 2.
3. The demands D_1 and D_2 for periods 1 and 2 are *independent and identically distributed* random variables. Their common probability distribution has probability density function $\phi_D(\xi)$ and cumulative distribution function $\Phi(\xi)$.
4. The initial inventory level (before replenishing) at the beginning of period 1 is x_1 ($x_1 \geq 0$).
5. The decisions to be made are y_1 and y_2, the inventory levels to reach by replenishing (if needed) at the beginning of period 1 and period 2, respectively.
6. The objective is to *minimize the expected total cost for both periods,* where the cost components for each period are

    > c = unit cost for purchasing or producing each unit,
    >
    > h = holding cost per unit remaining at end of each period,
    >
    > p = shortage cost per unit of unsatisfied demand at end of each period.

For simplicity, we are assuming that the demand distributions for the two periods are the same and that the values of the above cost components also are the same for the two periods. In many applications, there will be differences between the periods that should be incorporated into the analysis. For example, because of assumption 2, the value of p

may well be different for the two periods. Such extensions of the model can be incorporated into the dynamic programming analysis presented below, but we will not delve into these extensions.

Analysis. To begin the analysis, let

y_i^0 = optimal value of y_i,   for $i = 1, 2$,

$C_1(x_1)$ = expected total cost for both periods when following an optimal policy given that x_1 is initial inventory level (before replenishing) at beginning of period 1,

$C_2(x_2)$ = expected total cost for just period 2 when following an optimal policy given that x_2 is inventory level (before replenishing) at beginning of period 2.

To use the dynamic programming approach, we begin by solving for $C_2(x_2)$ and y_2^0, where there is just one period to go. Then we will use these results to find $C_1(x_1)$ and y_1^0.

From the results for the single-period model, y_2^0 is found by solving the equation

$$\Phi(y_2^0) = \frac{p - c}{p + h}.$$

Given x_2, the resulting optimal policy then is the following:

If $x_2 \begin{cases} < y_2^0 \\ \geq y_2^0 \end{cases}$ $\begin{array}{l} \text{order } y_2^0 - x_2 \text{ to bring inventory level up to } y_2^0 \\ \text{do not order.} \end{array}$

The cost of this optimal policy can be expressed as

$$C_2(x_2) = \begin{cases} L(x_2) & \text{if } x_2 \geq y_2^0 \\ c(y_2^0 - x_2) + L(y_2^0) & \text{if } x_2 < y_2^0, \end{cases}$$

where $L(z)$ is the expected shortage plus holding cost for a single period when the inventory level (after replenishing) is z. Now $L(z)$ can be expressed as

$$L(z) = \int_z^\infty p(\xi - z)\varphi_D(\xi)\,d\xi + \int_0^z h(z - \xi)\varphi_D(\xi)\,d\xi.$$

When both periods 1 and 2 are considered, the costs incurred consist of the ordering cost $c(y_1 - x_1)$, the expected shortage plus holding cost $L(y_1)$, and the costs associated with following an optimal policy during the second period. Thus, the expected cost of following the optimal policy for two periods is given by

$$C_1(x_1) = \min_{y_1 \geq x_1} \{c(y_1 - x_1) + L(y_1) + E[C_2(x_2)]\},$$

where $E[C_2(x_2)]$ is obtained as follows. Note that

$$x_2 = y_1 - D_1,$$

so x_2 is a random variable when beginning period 1. Thus,

$$C_2(x_2) = C_2(y_1 - D_1) = \begin{cases} L(y_1 - D_1) & \text{if } y_1 - D_1 \geq y_2^0 \\ c(y_2^0 - y_1 + D_1) + L(y_2^0) & \text{if } y_1 - D_1 < y_2^0. \end{cases}$$

Hence, $C_2(x_2)$ is a random variable, and its expected value is given by

$$E[C_2(x_2)] = \int_0^\infty C_2(y_1 - \xi)\varphi_D(\xi)\,d\xi$$

$$= \int_0^{y_1 - y_2^0} L(y_1 - \xi)\varphi_D(\xi)\,d\xi$$

$$+ \int_{y_1 - y_2^0}^\infty [c(y_2^0 - y_1 + \xi) + L(y_2^0)]\varphi_D(\xi)\,d\xi.$$

Therefore,

$$C_1(x_1) = \min_{y_1 \geq x_1} \left\{ c(y_1 - x_1) + L(y_1) + \int_0^{y_1 - y_2^0} L(y_1 - \xi)\varphi_D(\xi)\,d\xi \right.$$

$$\left. + \int_{y_1 - y_2^0}^\infty [(y_2^0 - y_1 + \xi) + L(y_2^0)]\varphi_D(\xi)\,d\xi \right\}.$$

It can be shown that $C_1(x_1)$ has a unique minimum and that the optimal value of y_1, denoted by y_1^0, satisfies the equation

$$-p + (p + h)\Phi(y_1^0) + (c - p)\Phi(y_1^0 - y_2^0)$$

$$+ (p + h)\int_0^{y_1^0 - y_2^0} \Phi(y_1^0 - \xi)\varphi_D(\xi)\,d\xi = 0.$$

The resulting optimal policy for period 1 then is the following:

If x_1 $\begin{cases} < y_1^0 & \text{order } y_1^0 - x_1 \text{ to bring inventory level up to } y_1^0 \\ \geq y_1^0 & \text{do not order.} \end{cases}$

The procedure for finding y_1^0 reduces to a simpler result for certain demand distributions. We summarize two such cases next.

Suppose that the demand in each period has a *uniform distribution* over the range 0 to t, that is,

$$\varphi_D(\xi) = \begin{cases} \dfrac{1}{t} & \text{if } 0 \leq \xi \leq t \\ 0 & \text{otherwise.} \end{cases}$$

Then y_1^0 can be obtained from the expression

$$y_1^0 = \sqrt{(y_2^0)^2 + \frac{2t(c - p)}{p + h}y_2^0 + \frac{t^2[2p(p + h) + (h + c)^2]}{(p + h)^2}} - \frac{t(h + c)}{p + h}.$$

Now suppose that the demand in each period has an *exponential distribution*, i.e.,

$$\phi(\xi) = \alpha e^{-\alpha\xi}, \qquad \text{for } \xi \geq 0.$$

Then y_1^0 satisfies the relationship

$$(h + c)e^{-\alpha(y_1^0 - y_2^0)} + (p + h)e^{-\alpha y_1^0} + \alpha(p + h)(y_1^0 - y_2^0)e^{-\alpha y_1^0} = 2h + c.$$

An alternative way of finding y_1^0 is to let z^0 denote $\alpha(y_1^0 - y_2^0)$. Then z^0 satisfies the relationship

$$e^{-z^0}[(h + c) + (p + h)e^{-\alpha y_2^0} + z^0(p + h)e^{-\alpha y_2^0}] = 2h + c,$$

and

$$y_1^0 = \frac{1}{\alpha} z^0 + y_2^0.$$

When the demand has either a uniform or an exponential distribution, an Excel template is available in your OR Courseware for calculating y_1^0 and y_2^0.

Example. Consider a two-period problem where

$$c = 10, \qquad h = 10, \qquad p = 15,$$

and where the probability density function of the demand in each period is given by

$$\varphi_D(\xi) = \begin{cases} \dfrac{1}{10} & \text{if } 0 \le \xi \le 10 \\ 0 & \text{otherwise,} \end{cases}$$

so that the cumulative distribution function of demand is

$$\Phi(\xi) = \begin{cases} 0 & \text{if } \xi < 0 \\ \dfrac{\xi}{10} & \text{if } 0 \le \xi \le 10 \\ 1 & \text{if } \xi > 10. \end{cases}$$

We find y_2^0 from the equation

$$\Phi(y_2^0) = \frac{p - c}{p + h} = \frac{15 - 10}{15 + 10} = \frac{1}{5},$$

so that

$$y_2^0 = 2.$$

To find y_1^0, we plug into the expression given for y_1^0 for the case of a *uniform* demand distribution, and we obtain

$$y_1^0 = \sqrt{2^2 + \frac{2(10)(10 - 15)}{15 + 10}(2) + 10^2 \frac{2(15)(15 + 10) + (10 + 10)^2}{(15 + 10)^2}}$$

$$- \frac{10(10 + 10)}{15 + 10}$$

$$= \sqrt{4 - 8 + 184} - 8 = 13.42 - 8 = 5.42.$$

Substituting $y_1^0 = 5$ and $y_1^0 = 6$ into $C_1(x_1)$ leads to a smaller value with $y_1^0 = 5$. Thus, the optimal policy can be described as follows:

If $x_1 < 5$,   order $5 - x_1$ to bring inventory level up to 5.
If $x_1 \geq 5$,   do not order in period 1.
If $x_2 < 2$,   order $2 - x_2$ to bring inventory level up to 2.
If $x_2 \geq 2$,   do not order in period 2.

Since unsatisfied demand in period 1 is backlogged to be met in period 2, $x_2 = 5 - D$ can turn out to be either positive or negative.

Stochastic Multiperiod Models—An Overview

The two-period model can be extended to several periods or to an infinite number of periods. This section presents a summary of multiperiod results that have practical importance.

Multiperiod Model with No Setup Cost.   Consider the direct extension of the above two-period model to n periods ($n > 2$) with the identical assumptions. The only difference is that a *discount factor* α (described in Sec. 19.2), with $0 < \alpha < 1$, now will be used in calculating the expected total cost for n periods. The problem still is to find the critical numbers $y_1^0, y_2^0, \ldots, y_n^0$ that describe the optimal inventory policy. As in the two-period model, these values are difficult to obtain numerically, but it can be shown[1] that the optimal policy has the following form.

For each period i ($i = 1, 2, \ldots, n$), with x_i as the inventory level entering that period (before replenishing), do the following

If $x_i \begin{cases} < y_i^0 & \text{order } y_i^0 - x_i \text{ to bring inventory level up to } y_i^0 \\ \geq y_i^0 & \text{do not order in period } i. \end{cases}$

Furthermore,

$$y_n^0 \leq y_{n-1}^0 \leq \cdots \leq y_2^0 \leq y_1^0.$$

For the *infinite-period* case (where $n = \infty$), all these critical numbers $y_1^0, y_2^0, \ldots$ are *equal*. Let y^0 denote this constant value. It can be shown that y^0 satisfies the equation

$$\Phi(y^0) = \frac{p - c(1 - \alpha)}{p + h}.$$

When the demand has either a uniform or an exponential distribution, an Excel template is available in your OR Courseware for calculating y^0.

A Variation of the Multiperiod Inventory Model with No Setup Cost.   These results for the infinite-period case (all the critical numbers equal the same value y^0 and y^0 satisfies the above equation) also apply when n is finite if two new assumptions are

---

[1]See Theorem 4 in R. Bellman, I. Glicksberg, and O. Gross, "On the Optimal Inventory Equation," *Management Science*, **2:** 83–104, 1955. Also see p. 163 in K. J. Arrow, S. Karlin, and H. Scarf (eds.), *Studies in the Mathematical Theory of Inventory and Production*, Stanford University Press, Stanford, CA, 1958.

made about what happens at the end of the last period. One new assumption is that each unit left over at the end of the final period can be salvaged with a return of the initial purchase cost c. Similarly, if there is a shortage at this time, assume that the shortage is met by an emergency shipment with the same unit purchase cost c.

Example. Consider again the bicycle example as it was introduced in Example 2 of Sec. 19.1. The cost estimates given there imply that

$$c = 35, \qquad h = 1, \qquad p = 15.$$

Suppose now that the distributor places an order with the manufacturer for various bicycle models on the first working day of each month. Because of this routine, she is willing to assume that the marginal setup cost is zero for including an order for the bicycle model under consideration. The appropriate discount factor is $\alpha = 0.995$. From past history, the distribution of demand can be approximated by a uniform distribution with the probability density function

$$\varphi_D(\xi) = \begin{cases} \dfrac{1}{800} & \text{if } 0 \le \xi \le 800 \\ 0 & \text{otherwise,} \end{cases}$$

so the cumulative distribution function over this interval is

$$\Phi(\xi) = \frac{1}{800}\xi, \qquad \text{if } 0 \le \xi \le 800.$$

The distributor expects to stock this model indefinitely, so the *infinite-period model with no setup cost* is appropriate.

For this model, the critical number y^0 for every period satisfies the equation

$$\Phi(y^0) = \frac{p - c(1 - \alpha)}{p + h},$$

so

$$\frac{y^0}{800} = \frac{15 - 35(1 - 0.995)}{15 + 1} = 0.9266,$$

which yields $y^0 = 741$. Thus, if the number of bicycles on hand x at the first of each month is fewer than 741, the optimal policy calls for bringing the inventory level up to 741 (ordering $741 - x$ bicycles). Otherwise, no order is placed.

Multiperiod Model with Setup Cost. The introduction of a fixed setup cost K that is incurred when ordering (whether through purchasing or producing) often adds more realism to the model. For the *single-period model with a setup cost* described in Sec. 19.6, we found that an (s, S) policy is optimal, so that the two critical numbers s and S indicate *when* to order (namely, if the inventory level is less than s) and *how much* to order (bring the inventory level up to S). Now with multiple periods, an (s, S) policy again is optimal, but the value of each critical number may be different in different periods. Let

s_i and S_i denote these critical numbers for period i, and again let x_i be the inventory level (before replenishing) at the beginning of period i.

> The optimal policy is to do the following at the beginning of each period i ($i = 1$, $2, \ldots, n$):
>
> If $x_i \begin{cases} < s_i \\ \geq s_i \end{cases}$ $\begin{array}{l} \text{order } S_i - x_i \text{ to bring inventory level up to } S_i \\ \text{do not order.} \end{array}$

Unfortunately, computing exact values of the s_i and S_i is extremely difficult.

A Multiperiod Model with Batch Orders and No Setup Cost.

In the preceding models, *any quantity* could be ordered (or produced) at the beginning of each period. However, in some applications, the product may come in a standard batch size, e.g., a case or a truckload. Let Q be the number of units in each batch. In our next model we assume that the number of units ordered must be a *nonnegative integer multiple* of Q.

This model makes the same assumptions about what happens at the end of the last period as the variation of the multiperiod model with no setup cost presented earlier. Thus, we assume that each unit left over at the end of the final period can be salvaged with a return of the initial purchase cost c. Similarly, if there is a shortage at this time, we assume that the shortage is met by an emergency shipment with the same unit purchase cost c.

Otherwise, the assumptions are the same as for our standard multiperiod model with no setup cost.

The optimal policy for this model is known as a **(k, Q) policy** because it uses a critical number k and the quantity Q as described below.

> If at the beginning of a period the inventory level (before replenishing) is less than k, an order should be placed for the smallest integer multiple of Q that will bring the inventory level up to at least k (and probably higher). Otherwise, an order should not be placed. The same critical number k is used in each period.

The critical number k is chosen as follows. Plot the function

$$G(y) = (1 - \alpha)cy + h \int_0^y (y - \xi)\varphi_D(\xi) \, d\xi + p \int_y^\infty (\xi - y)\varphi_D(\xi) \, d\xi,$$

as shown in Fig. 19.10. This function necessarily has the convex shape shown in the figure. As before, the minimizing value y^0 satisfies the equation

$$\Phi(y^0) = \frac{p - c(1 - \alpha)}{p + h}.$$

As shown in this figure, if a "ruler" of length Q is placed horizontally into the "valley," k is that value of the abscissa to the left of y^0 where the ruler intersects the valley. If the inventory level lies in R_1, then Q is ordered; if it lies in R_2, then $2Q$ is ordered; and so on. However, if the inventory level is at least k, then no order should be placed.

These results hold regardless of whether the number of periods n is finite or infinite.

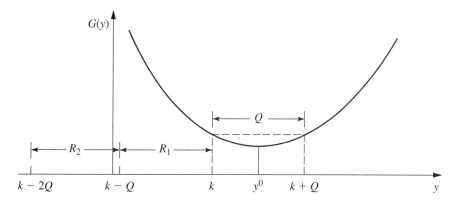

FIGURE 19.10
Plot of the $G(y)$ function for the stochastic multiperiod model with batch orders and no setup cost.

19.8   LARGER INVENTORY SYSTEMS IN PRACTICE

All the inventory models presented in this chapter have been concerned with the management of the inventory of a single product at a single geographical location. Such models provide the basic building blocks of scientific inventory management.

Multiproduct Inventory Systems

However, it is important to recognize that many inventory systems must deal simultaneously with many products, sometimes even hundreds or thousands of products. Furthermore, the inventory of each product often is dispersed geographically, perhaps even globally.

With multiple products, it commonly is possible to apply the appropriate single-product model to each of the products individually. However, companies may not bother to do this for the less important products because of the costs involved in regularly monitoring the inventory level to implement such a model. One popular approach in practice is the **ABC control method.** This involves dividing the products into three groups called the *A* group, *B* group, and *C* group. The products in the *A* group are the particularly important ones that are to be carefully monitored according to a formal inventory model. Products in the *C* group are the least important, so they are only monitored informally on a very occasional basis. Group *B* products receive an intermediate treatment.

It occasionally is not appropriate to apply a single-product inventory model because of interactions between the products. Various interactions are possible. Perhaps similar products can be substituted for each other as needed. For a manufacturer, perhaps its products must compete for production time when ordering production runs. For a wholesaler or retailer, perhaps its setup cost for ordering a product can be reduced by placing a joint order for a number of products simultaneously. Perhaps there also are joint budget limitations involving all the products. Perhaps the products need to compete for limited storage space.

It is common in practice to have a little bit of such interactions between products and still apply a single-product inventory model as a reasonable approximation. However, when an interaction is playing a major role, further analysis is needed. Some research has been conducted already to develop *multiproduct inventory models* to deal with some of these interactions.

Multiechelon Inventory Systems

Our growing global economy has caused a dramatic shift in inventory management entering the 21st century. Now, as never before, the inventory of many manufacturers is scattered throughout the world. Even the inventory of an individual product may be dispersed globally.

This inventory may be stored initially at the point or points of manufacture (one *echelon* of the inventory system), then at national or regional warehouses (a second echelon), then at field distribution centers (a third echelon), etc. Such a system with multiple echelons of inventory is referred to as a **multiechelon inventory system.** In the case of a fully integrated corporation that both manufactures its products and sells them at the retail level, its echelons will extend all the way down to its retail outlets.

Some coordination is needed between the inventories of any particular product at the different echelons. Since the inventory at each echelon (except the top one) is replenished from the next higher echelon, the inventory level currently needed at the higher echelon is affected by how soon replenishment will be needed at the various locations for the lower echelon.

Considerable research (with roots tracing back to the middle of the 20th century) is being conducted to develop multiechelon inventory models.

Now let us see how one major corporation has been managing one of its multiechelon inventory systems.

Multiechelon Inventory Management at IBM[1]

IBM has roughly 1,000 products in service. Therefore, it employs over 15,000 customer engineers who are trained to repair and maintain all the installed computer systems sold or leased by IBM throughout the United States.

To support this effort, IBM maintains a huge multiechelon inventory system of spare parts. This system controls over 200,000 part numbers, with the total inventory valued in the *billions of dollars*. Millions of parts transactions are processed annually.

The echelons of this system start with the manufacture of the parts, then national or regional warehouses, then field distribution centers, then parts stations, and finally many thousand outside locations (including customer stock locations and the car trunks or tool chests of the company's customer engineers).

To coordinate and control all these inventories at the different echelons, a huge computerized system called *Optimizer* was developed. Optimizer consists of four major modules. A forecasting system module contains a few programs for estimating the failure rates of individual types of parts. A data delivery system module consists of approximately 100 programs that process over 15 gigabytes of data to provide the needed input into Optimizer. A decision system module then optimizes control of the inventories on a weekly basis. The fourth module includes six programs that integrate Optimizer into IBM's Parts Inventory Management System (PIMS). PIMS is a sophisticated information and control system that contains millions of lines of code.

Optimizer tracks the inventory level for each part number at all stocking locations (except at the outside locations, where only parts costing more than a certain threshold

[1]M. Cohen, P. V. Kamesam, P. Kleindorfer, H. Lee, and A. Tekerian, "Optimizer: IBM's Multi-Echelon Inventory Systems for Managing Service Logistics," *Interfaces,* **20:** 65–82, Jan.–Feb., 1990.

are tracked). An (R, Q) type of inventory policy is used for each part at each location and echelon in the system.

Careful planning was required to *implement* such a complex system after it had been designed. Three factors proved to be especially important in achieving a successful implementation. The first was the inclusion of a *user team* (consisting of operational managers) as advisers to the project team throughout the study. By the time of the implementation phase, these operational managers had a strong sense of ownership and so had become ardent supporters for installing Optimizer in their functional areas. A second success factor was a very extensive *user acceptance test* whereby users could identify problem areas that needed rectifying prior to full implementation. The third key was that the new system was phased in gradually, with careful testing at each phase, so the major bugs would be eliminated before the system went live nationally.

This new multiechelon inventory system proved to be extremely successful. It provided savings of about $20 million per year through improved operational efficiency. It also gave even larger annual savings in holding costs (including the cost of capital tied up in inventory) by reducing the value of IBM's inventories by over $250 million. Despite this large reduction in inventories, the improved inventory management still enabled providing better service to IBM's customers. Specifically, the new system yielded a 10 percent improvement in the parts availability at the lower echelons (where the customers are affected) while maintaining the parts availability levels at the higher echelons.

Supply Chain Management

Another key concept that has emerged in this global economy is that of supply chain management. This concept pushes the management of a multiechelon inventory system one step further by also considering what needs to happen to bring a product into the inventory system in the first place. However, as with inventory management, a main purpose still is to win the competitive battle against other companies in bringing the product to the customers as promptly as possible.

A **supply chain** is a network of facilities that procure raw materials, transform them into intermediate goods and then final products, and finally deliver the products to customers through a distribution system that includes a (probably multiechelon) inventory system. Thus, it spans procurement, manufacturing, and distribution, with effective inventory management as one key element. To fill orders efficiently, it is necessary to understand the linkages and interrelationships of all the key elements of the supply chain. Therefore, integrated management of the supply chain has become a key success factor for some of today's leading companies.

We summarize below the experience of one of the companies that have led the way in making supply chain management part of their corporate culture.

Supply Chain Management at Hewlett-Packard[1]

Hewlett-Packard (HP) is one of today's leading high-technology companies. Its scope is truly global. Nearly half of its employees are outside the United States. In 1993, it had

---

[1]H. L. Lee and C. Billington, "The Evolution of Supply-Chain-Management Models and Practices at Hewlett-Packard," *Interfaces,* **25:** 42–63, Sept.–Oct., 1995.

manufacturing or research and development sites in 16 countries, as well as sales and service offices in 110 countries. Its total number of catalog products exceeded 22,000.

Late in the 1980s, HP faced inventories mounting into the billions of dollars and alarming customer dissatisfaction with its order fulfillment process. Management was very concerned, since order fulfillment was becoming a major battlefield in the high-technology industries. Recognizing the need for OR models to support top management decision making, HP formed a group known as Strategic Planning and Modeling (SPaM) in 1988. Management charged the group with developing and introducing innovations in OR and industrial engineering.

In 1989, SPaM began bringing supply chain management concepts into HP. HP's supply chain includes manufacturing integrated circuits, board assembly, final assembly, and delivery to customers on a global basis. With such diverse and complex products, grappling with supply chain issues can be very challenging. Variabilities and uncertainties are prevalent all along the chain. Suppliers can be late in their shipments, or the incoming materials may be flawed. The production process may break down, or the production yield may be imperfect. Finally, product demands also are highly uncertain.

Much of SPaM's initial focus was on inventory modeling. This effort led to the development of HP's *Worldwide Inventory Network Optimizer (WINO)*. Like IBM's Optimizer described earlier in this section, WINO manages a multiechelon inventory system. However, rather than dealing just with inventories of finished products, WINO also considers the inventories of incoming goods and departing goods at each site along the supply chain.

WINO uses a discrete-review inventory model to determine the reorder point and order quantities for each of these inventories. By introducing more frequent reviews of inventories, better balancing of related inventories, elimination of redundant safety stocks, etc., inventory reductions of 10 to 30 percent typically were obtained.

WINO was even extended to include the inventory systems of some key dealers. This enabled reducing the inventories of finished products at both HP's distribution centers and the dealers while maintaining the same service target for the customers.

SPaM's initial focus on inventory modeling soon broadened to dealing with distribution strategy issues. For example, its realignment of the distribution network in Europe reduced the total distribution cost there by $18 million per year.

SPaM's work also evolved into other functional areas, including design and engineering, finance, and marketing.

The importance of supply chain management now is recognized throughout HP. Several key divisions have formalized such positions as supply chain project managers, supply chain analysts, and supply chain coordinators. These individuals work closely with SPaM to ensure that supply chain models are used effectively and to identify new problems that feed SPaM's research and development effort.

The work of SPaM in applying OR to integrate supply chain management into HP has paid tremendous dividends. SPaM has often identified cost savings of $10 million to $40 million per year from just a single project. Therefore, total cost savings now run into the hundreds of millions of dollars annually. There have been key intangible benefits as well, including enhancing HP's reputation as a progressive company that can be counted on by its customers to fill their orders promptly.

19.9 CONCLUSIONS

We have introduced only rather basic kinds of inventory models here, but they serve the purpose of introducing the general nature of inventory models. Furthermore, they are sufficiently accurate representations of many actual inventory situations that they frequently are useful in practice. For example, the EOQ models have been particularly widely used. These models are sometimes modified to include some type of stochastic demand, such as the stochastic continuous-review model does. The stochastic single-period model is a very convenient one for perishable products. The stochastic multiperiod models have been important in characterizing the types of policies to follow, for example, (s, S) policies, even though the optimal values of s and S may be difficult to obtain.

Nevertheless, many inventory situations possess complications that are not taken into account by the models in this chapter, e.g., interactions between products or multiple echelons of a supply system. More complex models have been formulated in an attempt to fit such situations, but it is difficult to achieve both adequate realism and sufficient tractability to be useful in practice. The development of useful models for supply chain management currently is a particularly active area of research.

Continued growth is occurring in the computerization of inventory data processing, along with an accompanying growth in scientific inventory management.

SELECTED REFERENCES

1. Axsäter, S.: *Inventory Control,* Kluwer Academic Publishers, Boston, 2000.
2. Hillier, F. S., M. S. Hillier, and G. J. Lieberman: *Introduction to Management Science, A Modeling and Case Studies Approach with Spreadsheets,* Irwin/McGraw-Hill, Burr Ridge, IL, 2000, chaps. 11–12.
3. Liu, B., and A. O. Esogbue: *Decision Criteria and Optimal Inventory Processes,* Kluwer Academic Publishers, Boston, 1999.
4. Nahmias, S.: "Perishable Inventory Theory: A Review," *Operations Research,* **30:** 680–708, 1982.
5. Nahmias, S.: *Production and Operations Analysis,* 3d ed., Irwin/McGraw-Hill, Burr Ridge, IL, 1997.
6. Sherbrooke, C. C.: *Optimal Inventory Modeling of Systems: Multi-Echelon Techniques,* Wiley, New York, 1992.
7. Silver, E., D. Pyke, and R. Peterson: *Inventory Management and Production Planning and Scheduling,* 3d ed., Wiley, New York, 1998.
8. Tayur, S., R. Ganeshan, and M. Magazine (eds.): *Quantitative Models for Supply Chain Management,* Kluwer Academic Publishers, Boston, 1998.

LEARNING AIDS FOR THIS CHAPTER IN YOUR OR COURSEWARE

"Ch. 19—Inventory Theory" Excel File:

Templates for the Basic EOQ Model (a Solver Version and an Analytical Version)
Templates for the EOQ Model with Planned Shortages (a Solver Version and an Analytical Version)
Template for the EOQ Model with Quantity Discounts (Analytical Version Only)

Template for the Stochastic Continuous-Review Model
Template for the Stochastic Single-Period Model for Perishable Products, No Setup Cost
Template for the Stochastic Single-Period Model for Perishable Products, with Setup Cost
Template for the Stochastic Two-Period Model, No Setup Cost
Template for the Stochastic Infinite-Period Model, No Setup Cost

"Ch. 19—Inventory Theory" LINGO File for Selected Examples

PROBLEMS

To the left of each of the following problems (or their parts), we have inserted a T whenever one of the templates listed above can be useful. An asterisk on the problem number indicates that at least a partial answer is given in the back of the book.

T **19.3-1.*** Suppose that the demand for a product is 30 units per month and the items are withdrawn at a constant rate. The setup cost each time a production run is undertaken to replenish inventory is $15. The production cost is $1 per item, and the inventory holding cost is $0.30 per item per month.

(a) Assuming shortages are not allowed, determine how often to make a production run and what size it should be.

(b) If shortages are allowed but cost $3 per item per month, determine how often to make a production run and what size it should be.

T **19.3-2.** The demand for a product is 600 units per week, and the items are withdrawn at a constant rate. The setup cost for placing an order to replenish inventory is $25. The unit cost of each item is $3, and the inventory holding cost is $0.05 per item per week.

(a) Assuming shortages are not allowed, determine how often to order and what size the order should be.

(b) If shortages are allowed but cost $2 per item per week, determine how often to order and what size the order should be.

19.3-3.* Tim Madsen is the purchasing agent for Computer Center, a large discount computer store. He has recently added the hottest new computer, the Power model, to the store's stock of goods. Sales of this model now are running at about 13 per week. Tim purchases these customers directly from the manufacturer at a unit cost of $3,000, where each shipment takes half a week to arrive.

Tim routinely uses the basic EOQ model to determine the store's inventory policy for each of its more important products. For this purpose, he estimates that the annual cost of holding items in inventory is 20 percent of their purchase cost. He also estimates that the administrative cost associated with placing each order is $75.

T **(a)** Tim currently is using the policy of ordering 5 Power model computers at a time, where each order is timed to have the shipment arrive just about when the inventory of these computers is being depleted. Use the Solver version of the Excel template for the basic EOQ model to determine the various annual costs being incurred with this policy.

T **(b)** Use this same spreadsheet to generate a table that shows how these costs would change if the order quantity were changed to the following values: 5, 7, 9, . . . , 25.

T **(c)** Use the Solver to find the optimal order quantity.

T **(d)** Now use the analytical version of the Excel template for the basic EOQ model (which applies the EOQ formula directly) to find the optimal quantity. Compare the results (including the various costs) with those obtained in part (c).

(e) Verify your answer for the optimal order quantity obtained in part (d) by applying the EOQ formula by hand.

(f) With the optimal order quantity obtained above, how frequently will orders need to be placed on the average? What should the approximate inventory level be when each order is placed?

(g) How much does the optimal inventory policy reduce the total variable inventory cost per year (holding costs plus administrative costs for placing orders) for Power model computers from that for the policy described in part (a)? What is the percentage reduction?

19.3-4. The Blue Cab Company is the primary taxi company in the city of Maintown. It uses gasoline at the rate of 8,500 gallons per month. Because this is such a major cost, the company has made a special arrangement with the Amicable Petroleum Company to purchase a huge quantity of gasoline at a reduced price of $1.05 per gallon every few months. The cost of arranging for each order, including placing the gasoline into storage, is $1,000. The cost of holding the gasoline in storage is estimated to be $0.01 per gallon per month.

T **(a)** Use the Solver version of the Excel template for the basic EOQ model to determine the costs that would be incurred annually if the gasoline were to be ordered monthly.

T **(b)** Use this same spreadsheet to generate a table that shows how these costs would change if the number of months between orders were to be changed to the following values: 1, 2, 3, . . . , 10.

T **(c)** Use the Solver to find the optimal order quantity.

T **(d)** Now use the analytical version of the Excel template for the basic EOQ model to find the optimal order quantity. Compare the results (including the various costs) with those obtained in part (c).

(e) Verify your answer for the optimal order quantity obtained in part (d) by applying the EOQ formula by hand.

T **19.3-5.** Computronics is a manufacturer of calculators, currently producing 200 per week. One component for every calculator is a liquid crystal display (LCD), which the company purchases from Displays, Inc. (DI) for $1 per LCD. Computronics management wants to avoid any shortage of LCDs, since this would disrupt production, so DI guarantees a delivery time of $\frac{1}{2}$ week on each order. The placement of each order is estimated to require 1 hour of clerical time, with a direct cost of $15 per hour plus overhead costs of another $5 per hour. A rough estimate has been made that the annual cost of capital tied up in Computronics' inventory is 15 percent of the value (measured by purchase cost) of the inventory. Other costs associated with storing and protecting the LCDs in inventory amount to 5 cents per LCD per year.

(a) What should the order quantity and reorder point be for the LCDs? What is the corresponding total variable inventory cost per year (holding costs plus administrative costs for placing orders)?

(b) Suppose the true annual cost of capital tied up in Computronics' inventory actually is 10 percent of the value of the inventory. Then what should the order quantity be? What is the difference between this order quantity and the one obtained in part (a)? What would the total variable inventory cost per year (TVC) be? How much more would TVC be if the order quantity obtained in part (a) still were used here because of the incorrect estimate of the cost of capital tied up in inventory?

(c) Repeat part (b) if the true annual cost of capital tied up in Computronics' inventory actually is 20 percent of the value of the inventory.

(d) Perform sensitivity analysis systematically on the unit holding cost by generating a table that shows what the optimal order quantity would be if the true annual cost of capital tied up in Computronics' inventory were each of the following percentages of the value of the inventory: 10, 12, 14, 16, 18, 20.

(e) Assuming that the rough estimate of 15 percent is correct for the cost of capital, perform sensitivity analysis on the setup cost by generating a table that shows what the optimal order quantity would be if the true number of hours of clerical time required to place each order were each of the following: 0.5, 0.75, 1, 1.25, 1.5.

(f) Perform sensitivity analysis simultaneously on the unit holding cost and the setup cost by generating a table that shows the optimal order quantity for the various combinations of values considered in parts (d) and (e).

19.3-6. For the basic EOQ model, use the square root formula to determine how Q^* would change for each of the following changes in the costs or the demand rate. (Unless otherwise noted, consider each change by itself.)

(a) The setup cost is reduced to 25 percent of its original value.

(b) The annual demand rate becomes four times as large as its original value.

(c) Both changes in parts (a) and (b).

(d) The unit holding cost is reduced to 25 percent of its original value.

(e) Both changes in parts (a) and (d).

19.3-7.* Kris Lee, the owner and manager of the Quality Hardware Store, is reassessing his inventory policy for hammers. He sells an average of 50 hammers per month, so he has been placing an order to purchase 50 hammers from a wholesaler at a cost of $20 per hammer at the end of each month. However, Kris does all the ordering for the store himself and finds that this is taking a great deal of his time. He estimates that the value of his time spent in placing each order for hammers is $75.

(a) What would the unit holding cost for hammers need to be for Kris' current inventory policy to be optimal according to the basic EOQ model? What is this unit holding cost as a percentage of the unit acquisition cost?

T **(b)** What is the optimal order quantity if the unit holding cost actually is 20 percent of the unit acquisition cost? What is the corresponding value of TVC = total variable inventory cost per year (holding costs plus the administrative costs for placing orders)? What is TVC for the current inventory policy?

T **(c)** If the wholesaler typically delivers an order of hammers in 5 working days (out of 25 working days in an average month), what should the reorder point be (according to the basic EOQ model)?

(d) Kris doesn't like to incur inventory shortages of important items. Therefore, he has decided to add a safety stock of 5 hammers to safeguard against late deliveries and larger-than-usual sales. What is his new reorder point? How much does this safety stock add to TVC?

19.3-8. Cindy Stewart and Misty Whitworth graduated from business school together. They now are inventory managers for competing wholesale distributors, making use of the scientific inventory management techniques they learned in school. Both of them are purchasing 85-horsepower speedboat engines for their inventories from the same manufacturer. Cindy has found that the setup cost for initiating each order is $200 and the unit holding cost is $400.

Cindy has learned that Misty is ordering 10 engines each time. Cindy assumes that Misty is using the basic EOQ model and has the same setup cost and unit holding cost as Cindy. Show how Cindy can use this information to deduce what the annual demand rate must be for Misty's company for these engines.

19.3-9.* Consider Example 1 (manufacturing speakers for TV sets) introduced in Sec. 19.1 and used in Sec. 19.3 to illustrate the EOQ models. Use the EOQ model with planned shortages to solve this example when the unit shortage cost is changed to $5 per speaker short per month.

19.3-10. Speedy Wheels is a wholesale distributor of bicycles. Its Inventory Manager, Ricky Sapolo, is currently reviewing the inventory policy for one popular model that is selling at the rate of 250 per month. The administrative cost for placing an order for this model from the manufacturer is $200 and the purchase price is $70 per bicycle. The annual cost of the capital tied up in inventory is 20 percent of the value (based on purchase price) of these bicycles. The additional cost of storing the bicycles—including leasing warehouse space, insurance, taxes, and so on—is $6 per bicycle per year.

T (a) Use the basic EOQ model to determine the optimal order quantity and the total variable inventory cost per year.

T (b) Speedy Wheel's customers (retail outlets) generally do not object to short delays in having their orders filled. Therefore, management has agreed to a new policy of having small planned shortages occasionally to reduce the variable inventory cost. After consultations with management, Ricky estimates that the annual shortage cost (including lost future business) would be $30 times the average number of bicycles short throughout the year. Use the EOQ model with planned shortages to determine the new optimal inventory policy.

T **19.3-11.** Reconsider Prob. 19.3-3. Because of the popularity of the Power model computer, Tim Madsen has found that customers are willing to purchase a computer even when none are currently in stock as long as they can be assured that their order will be filled in a reasonable period of time. Therefore, Tim has decided to switch from the basic EOQ model to the EOQ model with planned shortages, using a shortage cost of $200 per computer short per year.

(a) Use the Solver version of the Excel template for the EOQ model with planned shortages (with constraints added in the Solver dialogue box that C10:C11 = integer) to find the new optimal inventory policy and its total variable inventory cost per year (TVC). What is the reduction in the value of TVC found for Prob. 19.3-3 (and given in the back of the book) when planned shortages were not allowed?

(b) Use this same spreadsheet to generate a table that shows how TVC and its components would change if the maximum shortage were kept the same as found in part (a) but the order quantity were changed to the following values: 15, 17, 19, ..., 35.

(c) Use this same spreadsheet to generate a table that shows how TVC and its components would change if the order quantity were kept the same as found in part (a) but the maximum shortage were changed to the following values: 10, 12, 14, ..., 30.

19.3-12. You have been hired as an operations research consultant by a company to reevaluate the inventory policy for one of its products. The company currently uses the basic EOQ model. Under this model, the optimal order quantity for this product is 1,000 units, so the maximum inventory level also is 1,000 units and the maximum shortage is 0.

You have decided to recommend that the company switch to using the EOQ model with planned shortages instead after determining how large the unit shortage cost (p) is compared to the unit holding cost (h). Prepare a table for management that shows what the optimal order quantity, maximum inventory level, and maximum shortage would be under this model for each of the following ratios of p to h: $\frac{1}{3}$, 1, 2, 3, 5, 10.

19.3-13. Consider the EOQ model with planned shortages, as presented in Sec. 19.3. Suppose, however, that the constraint $S/Q = 0.8$ is added to the model. Derive the expression for the optimal value of Q.

19.3-14. In the basic EOQ model, suppose the stock is replenished uniformly (rather than instantaneously) at the rate of b items per unit time until the order quantity Q is fulfilled. Withdrawals from the inventory are made at the rate of a items per unit time, where $a < b$. Replenishments and withdrawals of the inventory are made simultaneously. For example, if Q is 60, b is 3 per day, and a is 2 per day, then 3 units of stock arrive each day for days 1 to 20, 31 to 50, and so on, whereas units are withdrawn at the rate of 2 per day every day. The diagram of inventory level versus time is given below for this example.

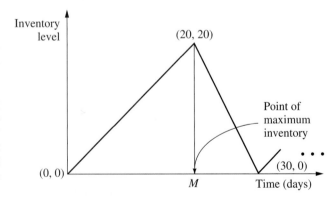

(a) Find the total cost per unit time in terms of the setup cost K, production quantity Q, unit cost c, holding cost h, withdrawal rate a, and replenishment rate b.

(b) Determine the economic order quantity Q^*.

19.3-15.* MBI is a manufacturer of personal computers. All its personal computers use a 3.5-inch high-density floppy disk drive which it purchases from Ynos. MBI operates its factory 52 weeks per year, which requires assembling 100 of these floppy disk drives into computers per week. MBI's annual holding cost rate is 20 percent of the value (based on purchase cost) of the inventory. Regardless of order size, the administrative cost of placing an order with Ynos has been estimated to be $50. A quantity discount is offered by Ynos for large orders as shown below, where the price for each category applies to *every* disk drive purchased.

Discount Category	Quantity Purchased	Price (per Disk Drive)
1	1 to 99	$100
2	100 to 499	$ 95
3	500 or more	$ 90

T (a) Determine the optimal order quantity according to the EOQ model with quantity discounts. What is the resulting total cost per year?
(b) With this order quantity, how many orders need to be placed per year? What is the time interval between orders?

19.3-16. The Gilbreth family drinks a case of Royal Cola every day, 365 days a year. Fortunately, a local distributor offers quantity discounts for large orders as shown in the table below, where the price for each category applies to *every* case purchased. Considering the cost of gasoline, Mr. Gilbreth estimates it costs him about $5 to go pick up an order of Royal Cola. Mr. Gilbreth also is an investor in the stock market, where he has been earning a 20 percent average annual return. He considers the return lost by buying the Royal Cola instead of stock to be the only holding cost for the Royal Cola.

Discount Category	Quantity Purchased	Price (per Case)
1	1 to 49	$4.00
2	50 to 99	$3.90
3	100 or more	$3.80

T (a) Determine the optimal order quantity according to the EOQ model with quantity discounts. What is the resulting total cost per year?
(b) With this order quantity, how many orders need to be placed per year? What is the time interval between orders?

19.3-17. Kenichi Kaneko is the manager of a production department which uses 400 boxes of rivets per year. To hold down his inventory level, Kenichi has been ordering only 50 boxes each time. However, the supplier of rivets now is offering a discount for

higher-quantity orders according to the following price schedule, where the price for each category applies to *every* box purchased.

Discount Category	Quantity	Price (per Box)
1	1 to 99	$8.50
2	100 to 999	$8.00
3	1,000 or more	$7.50

The company uses an annual holding cost rate of 20 percent of the price of the item. The total cost associated with placing an order is $80 per order.

Kenichi has decided to use the EOQ model with quantity discounts to determine his optimal inventory policy for rivets.

(a) For each discount category, write an expression for the total cost per year (TC) as a function of the order quantity Q.
T (b) For each discount category, use the EOQ formula for the basic EOQ model to calculate the value of Q (feasible or infeasible) that gives the minimum value of TC. (You may use the analytical version of the Excel template for the basic EOQ model to perform this calculation if you wish.)
(c) For each discount category, use the results from parts (a) and (b) to determine the *feasible* value of Q that gives the *feasible* minimum value of TC and to calculate this value of TC.
(d) Draw rough hand curves of TC versus Q for each of the discount categories. Use the same format as in Fig. 19.3 (a solid curve where feasible and a dashed curve where infeasible). Show the points found in parts (b) and (c). However, you don't need to perform any additional calculations to make the curves particularly accurate at other points.
(e) Use the results from parts (c) and (d) to determine the optimal order quantity and the corresponding value of TC.
T (f) Use the Excel template for the EOQ model with quantity discounts to check your answers in parts (b), (c), and (e).
(g) For discount category 2, the value of Q that minimizes TC turns out to be feasible. Explain why learning this fact would allow you to rule out discount category 1 as a candidate for providing the optimal order quantity without even performing the calculations for this category that were done in parts (b) and (c).
(h) Given the optimal order quantity from parts (e) and (f), how many orders need to be placed per year? What is the time interval between orders?

19.3-18. Sarah operates a concession stand at a downtown location throughout the year. One of her most popular items is circus peanuts, selling about 200 bags per month.

Sarah purchases the circus peanuts from Peter's Peanut Shop. She has been purchasing 100 bags at a time. However, to encourage larger purchases, Peter now is offering her discounts for larger order sizes according to the following price schedule, where the price for each category applies to *every* bag purchased.

Discount Category	Order Quantity	Price (per Bag)
1	1 to 199	$1.00
2	200 to 499	$0.95
3	500 or more	$0.90

Sarah wants to use the EOQ model with quantity discounts to determine what her order quantity should be. For this purpose, she estimates an annual holding cost rate of 17 percent of the value (based on purchase price) of the peanuts. She also estimates a setup cost of $4 for placing each order.

Follow the instructions of Prob. 19.3-17 to analyze Sarah's problem.

19.4-1. Suppose that production planning is to be done for the next 5 months, where the respective demands are $r_1 = 2$, $r_2 = 4$, $r_3 = 2$, $r_4 = 2$, and $r_5 = 3$. The setup cost is $4,000, the unit production cost is $1,000, and the unit holding cost is $300. Use the deterministic periodic-review model to determine the optimal production schedule that satisfies the monthly requirements.

19.4-2. Reconsider the example used to illustrate the deterministic periodic-review model in Sec. 19.4. Solve this problem when the demands are increased by 1 airplane in each period.

19.4-3. Reconsider the example used to illustrate the deterministic periodic-review model in Sec. 19.4. Suppose that the following single change is made in the example. The cost of producing each airplane now varies from period to period. In particular, in addition to the setup cost of $2 million, the cost of producing airplanes in either period 1 or period 3 is $1.4 million per airplane, whereas it is only $1 million per airplane in either period 2 or period 4.

Use dynamic programming to determine how many airplanes (if any) should be produced in each of the four periods to minimize the total cost.

19.4-4.* Consider a situation where a particular product is produced and placed in in-process inventory until it is needed in a subsequent production process. The number of units required in each of the next 3 months, the setup cost, and the regular-time unit production cost (in units of thousands of dollars) that would be incurred in each month are as follows:

Month	Requirement	Setup Cost	Regular-Time Unit Cost
1	1	5	8
2	3	10	10
3	2	5	9

There currently is 1 unit in inventory, and we want to have 2 units in inventory at the end of 3 months. A maximum of 3 units can be produced on regular-time production in each month, although 1 additional unit can be produced on overtime at a cost that is 2 larger than the regular-time unit production cost. The holding cost is 2 per unit for each extra month that it is stored.

Use dynamic programming to determine how many units should be produced in each month to minimize the total cost.

19.4-5. Consider a situation where a particular product is produced and placed in in-process inventory until it is needed in a subsequent production process. No units currently are in inventory, but three units will be needed in the coming month and an additional four units will be needed in the following month. The unit production cost is the same in either month. The setup cost to produce in either month is $5,000. The holding cost for each unit left in inventory at the end of a month is $300.

Determine the optimal schedule that satisfies the monthly requirements by using the algorithm presented in Sec. 19.4.

19.5-1. Henry Edsel is the owner of Honest Henry's, the largest car dealership in its part of the country. His most popular car model is the Triton, so his largest costs are those associated with ordering these cars from the factory and maintaining an inventory of Tritons on the lot. Therefore, Henry has asked his general manager, Ruby Willis, who once took a course in operations research, to use this background to develop a cost-effective policy for when to place these orders for Tritons and how many to order each time.

Ruby decides to use the stochastic continuous-review model presented in Sec. 19.5 to determine an (R, Q) policy. After some investigation, she estimates that the administrative cost for placing each order is $1,500 (a lot of paperwork is needed for ordering cars), the holding cost for each car is $3,000 per year (15 percent of the agency's purchase price of $20,000), and the shortage cost per car short is $1,000 per year (an estimated probability of $\frac{1}{3}$ of losing a car sale and its profit of about $3,000). After considering both the seriousness of incurring shortages and the high holding cost, Ruby and Henry agree to use a 75 percent service level (a probability of 0.75 of not incurring a shortage between the time an order is placed and the delivery of the cars ordered). Based on previous experience, they also estimate that the Tritons sell at a relatively uniform rate of about 900 per year.

After an order is placed, the cars are delivered in about two-thirds of a month. Ruby's best estimate of the probability distribution of demand during the lead time before a delivery arrives is a normal distribution with a mean of 50 and a standard deviation of 15.

(a) Solve by hand for the order quantity.

(b) Use a table for the normal distribution (Appendix 5) to solve for the reorder point.

T **(c)** Use the Excel template for this model in your OR Courseware to check your answers in parts (a) and (b).

(d) Given your previous answers, how much safety stock does this inventory policy provide?

(e) This policy can lead to placing a new order before the delivery from the preceding order arrives. Indicate when this would happen.

19.5-2. One of the largest selling items in J.C. Ward's Department Store is a new model of refrigerator that is highly energy-efficient. About 40 of these refrigerators are being sold per month. It takes about a week for the store to obtain more refrigerators from a wholesaler. The demand during this time has a uniform distribution between 5 and 15. The administrative cost of placing each order is $40. For each refrigerator, the holding cost per month is $8 and the shortage cost per month is estimated to be $1.

The store's inventory manager has decided to use the stochastic continuous-review model presented in Sec. 19.5, with a service level (measure 1) of 0.8, to determine an (R, Q) policy.

(a) Solve by hand for R and Q.

T **(b)** Use the corresponding Excel template to check your answer in part (a).

(c) What will be the average number of stockouts per year with this inventory policy?

19.5-3. When using the stochastic continuous-review model presented in Sec. 19.5, a difficult managerial judgment decision needs to be made on the level of service to provide to customers. The purpose of this problem is to enable you to explore the trade-off involved in making this decision.

Assume that the measure of service level being used is $L =$ probability that a stockout will not occur during the lead time. Since management generally places a high priority on providing excellent service to customers, the temptation is to assign a very high value to L. However, this would result in providing a very large amount of safety stock, which runs counter to management's desire to eliminate unnecessary inventory. (Remember the *just-in-time philosophy* discussed in Sec. 19.3 that is heavily influencing managerial thinking today.) What is the best trade-off between providing good service and eliminating unnecessary inventory?

Assume that the probability distribution of demand during the lead time is a normal distribution with mean μ and standard deviation σ. Then the reorder point R is $R = \mu + K_{1-L}\sigma$, where K_{1-L}

is obtained from Appendix 5. The amount of safety stock provided by this reorder point is $K_{1-L}\sigma$. Thus, if h denotes the holding cost for each unit held in inventory per year, the *average annual holding cost for safety stock* (denoted by C) is $C = hK_{1-L}\sigma$.

(a) Construct a table with five columns. The first column is the service level L, with values 0.5, 0.75, 0.9, 0.95, 0.99, and 0.999. The next four columns give C for four cases. Case 1 is $h = \$1$ and $\sigma = 1$. Case 2 is $h = \$100$ and $\sigma = 1$. Case 3 is $h = \$1$ and $\sigma = 100$. Case 4 is $h = \$100$ and $\sigma = 100$.

(b) Construct a second table that is based on the table obtained in part (a). The new table has five rows and the same five columns as the first table. Each entry in the new table is obtained by subtracting the corresponding entry in the first table from the entry in the next row of the first table. For example, the entries in the first column of the new table are $0.75 - 0.5 = 0.25$, $0.9 - 0.75 = 0.15$, $0.95 - 0.9 = 0.05$, $0.99 - 0.95 = 0.04$, and $0.999 - 0.99 = 0.009$. Since these entries represent increases in the service level L, each entry in the next four columns represents the increase in C that would result from increasing L by the amount shown in the first column.

(c) Based on these two tables, what advice would you give a manager who needs to make a decision on the value of L to use?

19.5-4. The preceding problem describes the factors involved in making a managerial decision on the service level L to use. It also points out that for any given values of L, h (the unit holding cost per year), and σ (the standard deviation when the demand during the lead time has a normal distribution), the average annual holding cost for the safety stock would turn out to be $C = hK_{1-L}\sigma$, where C denotes this holding cost and K_{1-L} is given in Appendix 5. Thus, the amount of variability in the demand, as measured by σ, has a major impact on this holding cost C.

The value of σ is substantially affected by the duration of the lead time. In particular, σ increases as the lead time increases. The purpose of this problem is to enable you to explore this relationship further.

To make this more concrete, suppose that the inventory system under consideration currently has the following values: $L = 0.9$, $h = \$100$, and $\sigma = 100$ with a lead time of 4 days. However, the vendor being used to replenish inventory is proposing a change in the delivery schedule that would change your lead time. You want to determine how this would change σ and C.

We assume for this inventory system (as is commonly the case) that the demands on separate days are statistically independent. In this case, the relationship between σ and the lead time is given by the formula

$$\sigma = \sqrt{d}\sigma_1,$$

where $d =$ number of days in the lead time,

$\sigma_1 =$ standard deviation if $d = 1$.

(a) Calculate C for the current inventory system.

(b) Determine σ_1. Then find how C would change if the lead time were reduced from 4 days to 1 day.

(c) How would C change if the lead time were doubled, from 4 days to 8 days?

(d) How long would the lead time need to be in order for C to double from its current value with a lead time of 4 days?

19.5-5. What is the effect on the amount of safety stock provided by the stochastic continuous-review model presented in Sec. 19.5 when the following change is made in the inventory system. (Consider each change independently.)

(a) The lead time is reduced to 0 (instantaneous delivery).

(b) The service level (measure 1) is decreased.

(c) The unit shortage cost is doubled.

(d) The mean of the probability distribution of demand during the lead time is increased (with no other change to the distribution).

(e) The probability distribution of demand during the lead time is a uniform distribution from a to b, but now $(b - a)$ has been doubled.

(f) The probability distribution of demand during the lead time is a normal distribution with mean μ and standard deviation σ, but now σ has been doubled.

19.5-6.* Jed Walker is the manager of Have a Cow, a hamburger restaurant in the downtown area. Jed has been purchasing all the restaurant's beef from Ground Chuck (a local supplier) but is considering switching to Chuck Wagon (a national warehouse) because its prices are lower.

Weekly demand for beef averages 500 pounds, with some variability from week to week. Jed estimates that the *annual* holding cost is 30 cents per pound of beef. When he runs out of beef, Jed is forced to buy from the grocery store next door. The high purchase cost and the hassle involved are estimated to cost him about $3 per pound of beef short. To help avoid shortages, Jed has decided to keep enough safety stock to prevent a shortage before the delivery arrives during 95 percent of the order cycles. Placing an order only requires sending a simple fax, so the administrative cost is negligible.

Have a Cow's contract with Ground Chuck is as follows: The purchase price is $1.49 per pound. A fixed cost of $25 per order is added for shipping and handling. The shipment is guaranteed to arrive within 2 days. Jed estimates that the demand for beef during this lead time has a uniform distribution from 50 to 150 pounds.

The Chuck Wagon is proposing the following terms: The beef will be priced at $1.35 per pound. The Chuck Wagon ships via refrigerated truck, and so charges additional shipping costs of $200 per order plus $0.10 per pound. The shipment time will be roughly a week, but is guaranteed not to exceed 10 days. Jed estimates that

the probability distribution of demand during this lead time will be a normal distribution with a mean of 500 pounds and a standard deviation of 200 pounds.

T **(a)** Use the stochastic continuous-review model presented in Sec. 19.5 to obtain an (R, Q) policy for Have a Cow for each of the two alternatives of which supplier to use.

(b) Show how the reorder point is calculated for each of these two policies.

(c) Determine and compare the amount of safety stock provided by the two policies obtained in part (a).

(d) Determine and compare the average annual holding cost under these two policies.

(e) Determine and compare the average annual acquisition cost (combining purchase price and shipping cost) under these two policies.

(f) Since shortages are very infrequent, the only important costs for comparing the two suppliers are those obtained in parts (d) and (e). Add these costs for each supplier. Which supplier should be selected?

(g) Jed likes to use the beef (which he keeps in a freezer) within a month of receiving it. How would this influence his choice of supplier?

19.5-7. Micro-Apple is a manufacturer of personal computers. It currently manufactures a single model—the MacinDOS—on an assembly line at a steady rate of 500 per week. MicroApple orders the floppy disk drives for the MacinDOS (1 per computer) from an outside supplier at a cost of $30 each. Additional administrative costs for placing an order total $30. The annual holding cost is $6 per drive. If MicroApple stocks out of floppy disk drives, production is halted, costing $100 per drive short. Because of the seriousness of stockouts, management wants to keep enough safety stock to prevent a shortage before the delivery arrives during 99 percent of the order cycles.

The supplier now is offering two shipping options. With option 1, the lead time would have a normal distribution with a mean of 0.5 week and a standard deviation of 0.1 week. For each order, the shipping cost charged to MicroApple would be $100 plus $3 per drive. With option 2, the lead time would have a uniform distribution from 1.0 week to 2.0 weeks. For each order, the shipping cost charged to MicroApple would be $20 plus $2 per drive.

T **(a)** Use the stochastic continuous-review model presented in Sec. 19.5 to obtain an (R, Q) policy under each of these two shipping options.

(b) Show how the reorder point is calculated for each of these two policies.

(c) Determine and compare the amount of safety stock provided by these two policies.

(d) Determine and compare the average annual holding cost under these two policies.

(e) Determine and compare the average annual acquisition cost (combining purchase price and shipping cost) under these two policies.

(f) Since shortages are very infrequent (and very small when they do occur), the only important costs for comparing the two shipping options are those obtained in parts (d) and (e). Add these costs for each option. Which option should be selected?

T **19.6-1.** A newspaper stand purchases newspapers for $0.36 and sells them for $0.50. The shortage cost is $0.50 per newspaper (because the dealer buys papers at retail price to satisfy shortages). The holding cost is $0.002 per newspaper left at the end of the day. The demand distribution is a uniform distribution between 200 and 300. Find the optimal number of papers to buy.

19.6-2. Freddie the newsboy runs a newstand. Because of a nearby financial services office, one of the newspapers he sells is the daily *Financial Journal*. He purchases copies of this newspaper from its distributor at the beginning of each day for $1.50 per copy, sells it for $2.50 each, and then receives a refund of $0.50 from the distributor the next morning for each unsold copy. The number of requests for this newspaper range from 15 to 18 copies per day. Freddie estimates that there are 15 requests on 40 percent of the days, 16 requests on 20 percent of the days, 17 requests on 30 percent of the days, and 18 requests on the remaining days.

(a) Use Bayes' decision rule presented in Sec. 15.2 to determine what Freddie's new order quantity should be to maximize his expected daily profit.

(b) Apply Bayes' decision rule again, but this time with the criterion of minimizing Freddie's expected daily cost of underordering or overordering.

(c) Use the stochastic single-period model for perishable products to determine Freddie's optimal order quantity.

(d) Draw the cumulative distribution function of demand and then show graphically how the model in part (c) finds the optimal order quantity.

19.6-3. Jennifer's Donut House serves a large variety of doughnuts, one of which is a blueberry-filled, chocolate-covered, supersized doughnut supreme with sprinkles. This is an extra large doughnut that is meant to be shared by a whole family. Since the dough requires so long to rise, preparation of these doughnuts begins at 4:00 in the morning, so a decision on how many to prepare must be made long before learning how many will be needed. The cost of the ingredients and labor required to prepare each of these doughnuts is $1. Their sale price is $3 each. Any not sold that day are sold to a local discount grocery store for $0.50. Over the last several weeks, the number of these doughnuts sold for $3 each day has been tracked. These data are summarized next.

Number Sold	Percentage of Days
0	10%
1	15%
2	20%
3	30%
4	15%
5	10%

(a) What is the unit cost of underordering? The unit cost of overordering?

(b) Use Bayes' decision rule presented in Sec. 15.2 to determine how many of these doughnuts should be prepared each day to minimize the average daily cost of underordering or overordering.

(c) After plotting the cumulative distribution function of demand, apply the stochastic single-period model for perishable products graphically to determine how many of these doughnuts to prepare each day.

(d) Given the answer in part (c), what will be the probability of running short of these doughnuts on any given day?

(e) Some families make a special trip to the Donut House just to buy this special doughnut. Therefore, Jennifer thinks that the cost when they run short might be greater than just the lost profit. In particular, there may be a cost for lost customer goodwill each time a customer orders this doughnut but none are available. How high would this cost have to be before they should prepare one more of these doughnuts each day than was found in part (c)?

19.6-4.* Swanson's Bakery is well known for producing the best fresh bread in the city, so the sales are very substantial. The daily demand for its fresh bread has a uniform distribution between 300 and 600 loaves. The bread is baked in the early morning, before the bakery opens for business, at a cost of $2 per loaf. It then is sold that day for $3 per loaf. Any bread not sold on the day it is baked is relabeled as day-old bread and sold subsequently at a discount price of $1.50 per loaf.

(a) Apply the stochastic single-period model for perishable products to determine the optimal service level.

(b) Apply this model graphically to determine the optimal number of loaves to bake each morning.

(c) With such a wide range of possible values in the demand distribution, it is difficult to draw the graph in part (b) carefully enough to determine the exact value of the optimal number of loaves. Use algebra to calculate this exact value.

(d) Given your answer in part (a), what is the probability of incurring a shortage of fresh bread on any given day?

(e) Because the bakery's bread is so popular, its customers are quite disappointed when a shortage occurs. The owner of the bakery, Ken Swanson, places high priority on keeping his customers satisfied, so he doesn't like having shortages. He feels that the analysis also should consider the loss of customer goodwill due to shortages. Since this loss of goodwill can have a negative effect on future sales, he estimates that a cost of $1.50 per loaf should be assessed each time a customer cannot purchase fresh bread because of a shortage. Determine the new optimal number of loaves to bake each day with this change. What is the new probability of incurring a shortage of fresh bread on any given day?

19.6-5. Reconsider Prob. 19.6-4. The bakery owner, Ken Swanson, now wants you to conduct a financial analysis of various inventory policies. You are to begin with the policy obtained in the first four parts of Prob. 19.6-4 (ignoring any cost for the loss of customer goodwill). As given with the answers in the back of the book, this policy is to bake 500 loaves of bread each morning, which gives a probability of incurring a shortage of $\frac{1}{3}$.

(a) For any day that a shortage *does* occur, calculate the revenue from selling fresh bread.

(b) For those days where shortages do *not* occur, use the probability distribution of demand to determine the expected number of loaves of fresh bread sold. Use this number to calculate the expected daily revenue from selling fresh bread on those days.

(c) Combine your results from parts (a) and (b) to calculate the expected daily revenue from selling fresh bread when considering *all* days.

(d) Calculate the expected daily revenue from selling day-old bread.

(e) Use the results in parts (c) and (d) to calculate the expected total daily revenue and then the expected daily profit (excluding overhead).

(f) Now consider the inventory policy of baking 600 loaves each morning, so that shortages never occur. Calculate the expected daily profit (excluding overhead) from this policy.

(g) Consider the inventory policy found in part (e) of Prob. 19.6-4. As implied by the answers in the back of the book, this policy is to bake 550 loaves each morning, which gives a probability of incurring a shortage of $\frac{1}{6}$. Since this policy is midway between the policy considered here in parts (a) to (e) and the one considered in part (f), its expected daily profit (excluding overhead and the cost of the loss of customer goodwill) also is midway between the expected daily profit for those two policies. Use this fact to determine its expected daily profit.

(h) Now consider the cost of the loss of customer goodwill for the inventory policy analyzed in part (g). Calculate the expected daily cost of the loss of customer goodwill and then the expected daily profit when considering this cost.

(i) Repeat part (h) for the inventory policy considered in parts (a) to (e).

19.6-6. Reconsider Prob. 19.6-4. The bakery owner, Ken Swanson, now has developed a new plan to decrease the size of shortages. The bread will be baked twice a day, once before the bakery opens (as before) and the other during the day after it becomes clearer what the demand for that day will be. The first baking will produce 300 loaves to cover the minimum demand for the day. The size of the second baking will be based on an estimate of the remaining demand for the day. This remaining demand is assumed to have a uniform distribution from a to b, where the values of a and b are chosen each day based on the sales so far. It is anticipated that $(b - a)$ typically will be approximately 75, as opposed to the range of 300 for the distribution of demand in Prob. 19.6-4.

(a) Ignoring any cost of the loss of customer goodwill [as in parts (a) to (d) of Prob. 19.6-4], write a formula for how many loaves should be produced in the second baking in terms of a and b.

(b) What is the probability of still incurring a shortage of fresh bread on any given day? How should this answer compare to the corresponding probability in Prob. 19.6-4?

(c) When $b - a = 75$, what is the maximum size of a shortage that can occur? What is the maximum number of loaves of fresh bread that will not be sold? How do these answers compare to the corresponding numbers for the situation in Prob. 19.6-4 where only one (early morning) baking occurs per day?

(d) Now consider just the cost of underordering and the cost of overordering. Given your answers in part (c), how should the expected total daily cost of underordering and overordering for this new plan compare with that for the situation in Prob. 19.6-4? What does this say in general about the value of obtaining as much information as possible about what the demand will be before placing the final order for a perishable product?

(e) Repeat parts (a), (b), and (c) when including the cost of the loss of customer goodwill as in part (e) of Prob. 19.6-4.

19.6-7. Suppose that the demand D for a spare airplane part has an exponential distribution with mean 50, that is,

$$\varphi_D(\xi) = \begin{cases} \dfrac{1}{50}e^{-\xi/50} & \text{for } \xi \geq 0 \\ 0 & \text{otherwise.} \end{cases}$$

This airplane will be obsolete in 1 year, so all production of the spare part is to take place at present. The production costs now are $1,000 per item—that is, $c = 1,000$—but they become $10,000 per item if they must be supplied at later dates—that is, $p = 10,000$. The holding costs, charged on the excess after the end of the period, are $300 per item.

T (a) Determine the optimal number of spare parts to produce.

(b) Suppose that the manufacturer has 23 parts already in inventory (from a similar, but now obsolete airplane). Determine the optimal inventory policy.

(c) Suppose that p cannot be determined now, but the manufacturer wishes to order a quantity so that the probability of a shortage equals 0.1. How many units should be ordered?

(d) If the manufacturer were following an optimal policy that resulted in ordering the quantity found in part (c), what is the implied value of p?

19.6-8.* A college student, Stan Ford, recently took a course in operations research. He now enjoys applying what he learned to optimize his personal decisions. He is analyzing one such decision currently, namely, how much money (if any) to take out of his savings account to buy $100 traveler's checks before leaving on a short vacation trip to Europe next summer.

Stan already has used the money he had in his checking account to buy traveler's checks worth $1,200, but this may not be enough. In fact, he has estimated the probability distribution of what he will need as shown in the following table:

Amount needed ($)	1,000	1,100	1,200	1,300	1,400	1,500	1,600	1,700
Probability	0.05	0.10	0.15	0.25	0.20	0.10	0.10	0.05

If he turns out to have less than he needs, then he will have to leave Europe 1 day early for every $100 short. Because he places a value of $150 on each day in Europe, each day lost would thereby represent a net loss of $50 to him. However, every $100 traveler's check costs an extra $1. Furthermore, each such check left over at the end of the trip (which would be redeposited in the savings account) represents a loss of $2 in interest that could have been earned in the savings account during the trip, so he does not want to purchase too many.

(a) Describe how this problem can be interpreted to be an inventory problem with uncertain demand for a perishable product. Also identify the unit cost of underordering and the unit cost of overordering.

(b) Use Bayes' decision rule presented in Sec. 15.2 to determine how many additional $100 travelers' checks Stan should purchase to minimize his expected cost of underordering or overordering.

(c) Use the stochastic single-period model for perishable products and the table of probabilities to make Stan's decision.

(d) Draw a graph of the CDF of demand to show the application of the model in part (c) graphically.

19.6-9. Reconsider Prob. 19.5-1 involving Henry Edsel's car dealership. The current model year is almost over, but the Tritons are selling so well that the current inventory will be depleted before the end-of-year demand can be satisfied. Fortunately, there still is time to place one more order with the factory to replenish the inventory of Tritons just about when the current supply will be gone.

The general manager, Ruby Willis, now needs to decide how many Tritons to order from the factory. Each one costs $20,000. She then is able to sell them at an average price of $23,000, provided they are sold before the end of the model year. However, any of these Tritons left at the end of the model year would then need to be sold at a special sale price of $19,500. Furthermore, Ruby estimates that the extra cost of the capital tied up by holding these cars such an unusually long time would be $500 per car, so the net revenue would be only $19,000. Since she would lose $1,000 on each of these cars left at the end of the model year, Ruby concludes that she needs to be cautious to avoid ordering too many cars, but she also wants to avoid running out of cars to sell before the end of the model year if possible. Therefore, she decides to use the stochastic single-period model for perishable products to select the order quantity. To do this, she estimates that the number of Tritons being ordered now that could be sold before the end of the model year has a normal distribution with a mean of 50 and a standard deviation of 15.

(a) Determine the optimal service level.

(b) Determine the number of Tritons that Ruby should order from the factory.

19.6-10. The management of Quality Airlines has decided to base its overbooking policy on the stochastic single-period model for perishable products, since this will maximize expected profit. This policy now needs to be applied to a new flight from Seattle to Atlanta. The airplane has 125 seats available for a fare of $250. However, since there commonly are a few no-shows, the airline should accept a few more than 125 reservations. On those occasions when more than 125 people arrive to take the flight, the airline will find volunteers who are willing to be put on a later flight in return for being given a certificate worth $150 toward any future travel on this airline.

Based on previous experience with similar flights, it is estimated that the relative frequency of the number of no-shows will be as shown below.

Number of No-Shows	Relative Frequency
0	5%
1	10%
2	15%
3	15%
4	15%
5	15%
6	10%
7	10%
8	5%

(a) When interpreting this problem as an inventory problem, what are the units of a perishable product being placed into inventory?

(b) Identify the unit cost of underordering and the unit cost of overordering.

(c) Use the model with these costs to determine how many overbooked reservations to accept.

(d) Draw a graph of the CDF of demand to show the application of the model graphically.

19.6-11. The campus bookstore must decide how many textbooks to order for a course that will be offered only once. The number of students who will take the course is a random variable D, whose distribution can be approximated by a (continuous) uniform distribution on the interval [40, 60]. After the quarter starts, the value of D becomes known. If D exceeds the number of books available, the known shortfall is made up by placing a rush order at a cost of $14 plus $2 per book over the normal ordering cost. If D is less than the stock on hand, the extra books are returned for their original ordering cost less $1 each. What is the order quantity that minimizes the expected cost?

19.6-12. Consider the following inventory model, which is a single-period model with known density of demand $\varphi_D(\xi) = e^{-\xi}$ for $\xi \geq 0$ and $\varphi_D(\xi) = 0$ elsewhere. There are two costs connected with the model. The first is the purchase cost, given by $c(y - x)$. The second is a cost p that is incurred once if there is *any* unsatisfied demand (independent of the amount of unsatisfied demand).

(a) If x units are available and goods are ordered to bring the inventory level up to y (if $x < y$), write the expression for the expected loss and describe completely the optimal policy.

(b) If a fixed cost K is also incurred whenever an order is placed, describe the optimal policy.

T **19.6-13.** Find the optimal ordering policy for the stochastic single-period model with a setup cost where the demand has the probability density function

$$\varphi_D(\xi) = \begin{cases} \dfrac{1}{20} & \text{for } 0 \leq \xi \leq 20 \\ 0 & \text{otherwise,} \end{cases}$$

and the costs are

Holding cost = $1 per item,

Shortage cost = $3 per item,

Setup cost = $1.50,

Production cost = $2 per item.

Show your work, and then check your answer by using the corresponding Excel template in your OR Courseware.

T **19.6-14.** Using the approximation for finding the optimal policy for the stochastic single-period model with a setup cost when demand has an exponential distribution, find this policy when

$$\varphi_D(\xi) = \begin{cases} \dfrac{1}{25} e^{-\xi/25} & \text{for } \xi \geq 0 \\ 0 & \text{otherwise,} \end{cases}$$

and the costs are

Holding cost = 40 cents per item,

Shortage cost = $1.50 per item,

Purchase price = $1 per item,

Setup cost = $10.

Show your work, and then check your answer by using the corresponding Excel template in your OR Courseware.

T **19.7-1.** Consider the following inventory situation. Demands in different periods are independent but with a common probability density function given by

$$\varphi_D(\xi) = \begin{cases} \dfrac{e^{-\xi/25}}{25} & \text{for } \xi \geq 0 \\ 0 & \text{otherwise.} \end{cases}$$

Orders may be placed at the start of each period without setup cost at a unit cost of $c = 10$. There are a holding cost of 6 per unit remaining in stock at the end of each period and a shortage cost of 15 per unit of unsatisfied demand at the end of each period (with backlogging except for the final period).

(a) Find the optimal one-period policy.

(b) Find the optimal two-period policy.

T **19.7-2.** Consider the following inventory situation. Demands in different periods are independent but with a common probability density function $\phi_D(\xi) = \frac{1}{50}$ for $0 \leq \xi \leq 50$. Orders may be placed at the start of each period without setup cost at a unit cost of $c = 10$. There are a holding cost of 8 per unit remaining in stock at the end of each period and a penalty cost of 15 per unit of unsatisfied demand at the end of each period (with backlogging except for the final period).

(a) Find the optimal one-period policy.

(b) Find the optimal two-period policy.

T **19.7-3.*** Find the optimal inventory policy for the following two-period model by using a discount factor of $\alpha = 0.9$. The demand D has the probability density function

$$\varphi_D(\xi) = \begin{cases} \dfrac{1}{25} e^{-\xi/25} & \text{for } \xi \geq 0 \\ 0 & \text{otherwise,} \end{cases}$$

and the costs are

Holding cost = $0.25 per item,

Shortage cost = $2 per item,

Purchase price = $1 per item.

Stock left over at the end of the final period is salvaged for $1 per item, and shortages remaining at this time are met by purchasing the needed items at $1 per item.

T **19.7-4.** Solve Prob. 19.7-3 for a two-period model, assuming no salvage value, no backlogging at the end of the second period, and no discounting.

T **19.7-5.** Solve Prob. 19.7-3 for an infinite-period model.

T **19.7-6.** Determine the optimal inventory policy when the goods are to be ordered at the end of every month from now on. The cost of bringing the inventory level up to y when x already is available is given by $2(y - x)$. Similarly, the cost of having the monthly demand D exceed y is given by $5(D - y)$. The probability density function for D is given by $\phi_D(\xi) = e^{-\xi}$. The holding cost when y exceeds D is given by $y - D$. A monthly discount factor of 0.95 is used.

T **19.7-7.** Solve the inventory problem given in Prob. 19.7-6, but assume that the policy is to be used for only 1 year (a 12-period model). Shortages are backlogged each month, except that any shortages remaining at the end of the year are made up by purchasing similar items at a unit cost of $2. Any remaining inventory at the end of the year can be sold at a unit price of $2.

T **19.7-8.** A supplier of high-fidelity receiver kits is interested in using an optimal inventory policy. The distribution of demand per month is uniform between 2,000 and 3,000 kits. The supplier's cost for each kit is $150. The holding cost is estimated to be $2 per kit remaining at the end of a month, and the shortage cost is $30 per kit of unsatisfied demand at the end of a month. Using a monthly discount factor of $\alpha = 0.99$, find the optimal inventory policy for this infinite-period problem.

T **19.7-9.** The weekly demand for a certain type of electronic calculator is estimated to be

$$\varphi_D(\xi) = \begin{cases} \dfrac{1}{1,000}e^{-\xi/1,000} & \text{for } \xi \geq 0 \\ 0 & \text{otherwise.} \end{cases}$$

The unit cost of these calculators is $80. The holding cost is $0.70 per calculator remaining at the end of a week. The shortage cost is $2 per calculator of unsatisfied demand at the end of a week. Using a weekly discount factor of $\alpha = 0.998$, find the optimal inventory policy for this infinite-period problem.

19.7-10.* Consider a one-period model where the only two costs are the holding cost, given by

$$h(y - D) = \frac{3}{10}(y - D), \qquad \text{for } y \geq D,$$

and the shortage cost, given by

$$p(D - y) = 2.5(D - y), \qquad \text{for } D \geq y.$$

The probability density function for demand is given by

$$\varphi_D(\xi) = \begin{cases} \dfrac{e^{-\xi/25}}{25} & \text{for } \xi \geq 0 \\ 0 & \text{otherwise.} \end{cases}$$

If you order, you must order an *integer* number of *batches* of 100 units each, and this quantity is delivered immediately. Let $G(y)$ denote the total expected cost when there are y units available for the period (after ordering).

(a) Write the expression for $G(y)$.
(b) What is the optimal ordering policy?

19.7-11. Find the optimal (k, Q) policy for Prob. 19.7-10 for an infinite-period model with a discount factor of $\alpha = 0.90$.

19.7-12. For the infinite-period model with no setup cost, show that the value of y^0 that satisfies

$$\Phi(y^0) = \frac{p - c(1 - \alpha)}{p + h}$$

is equivalent to the value of y that satisfies

$$\frac{dL(y)}{dy} + c(1 - \alpha) = 0,$$

where $L(y)$, the expected shortage plus holding cost, is given by

$$L(y) = \int_y^\infty p(\xi - y)\varphi_D(\xi)\, d\xi + \int_0^y h(y - \xi)\varphi_D(\xi)\, d\xi.$$

CASE 19.1   BRUSHING UP ON INVENTORY CONTROL

Robert Gates rounds the corner of the street and smiles when he sees his wife pruning rose bushes in their front yard. He slowly pulls his car into the driveway, turns off the engine, and falls into his wife's open arms.

"How was your day?" she asks.

"Great! The drugstore business could not be better!" Robert replies, "Except for the traffic coming home from work! That traffic can drive a sane man crazy! I am so tense right now. I think I will go inside and make myself a relaxing martini."

Robert enters the house and walks directly into the kitchen. He sees the mail on the kitchen counter and begins flipping through the various bills and advertisements until he comes across the new issue of *OR/MS Today*. He prepares his drink, grabs the magazine, treads into the living room, and settles comfortably into his recliner. He has all that he wants—except for one thing. He sees the remote control lying on the top of the television. He sets his drink and magazine on the coffee table and reaches for the remote control. Now, with the remote control in one hand, the magazine in the other, and the drink on the table near him, Robert is finally the master of his domain.

Robert turns on the television and flips the channels until he finds the local news. He then opens the magazine and begins reading an article about scientific inventory management. Occasionally he glances at the television to learn the latest in business, weather, and sports.

As Robert delves deeper into the article, he becomes distracted by a commercial on television about toothbrushes. His pulse quickens slightly in fear because the commercial for Totalee toothbrushes reminds him of the dentist. The commerical concludes that the customer should buy a Totalee toothbrush because the toothbrush is Totalee revolutionary and Totalee effective. It certainly is effective; it is the most popular toothbrush on the market!

At that moment, with the inventory article and the toothbrush commercial fresh in his mind, Robert experiences a flash of brilliance. He knows how to control the inventory of Totalee toothbrushes at Nightingale Drugstore!

As the inventory control manager at Nightingale Drugstore, Robert has been experiencing problems keeping Totalee toothbrushes in stock. He has discovered that customers are very loyal to the Totalee brand name since Totalee holds a patent on the toothbrush endorsed by 9 out of 10 dentists. Customers are willing to wait for the toothbrushes to arrive at Nightingale Drugstore since the drugstore sells the toothbrushes for 20 percent less than other local stores. This demand for the toothbrushes at Nightingale means that the drugstore is often out of Totalee toothbrushes. The store is able to receive a shipment of toothbrushes several hours after an order is placed to the Totalee regional warehouse because the warehouse is only 20 miles away from the store. Nevertheless, the current inventory situation causes problems because numerous emergency orders cost the store unnecessary time and paperwork and because customers become disgruntled when they must return to the store later in the day.

Robert now knows a way to prevent the inventory problems through scientific inventory management! He grabs his coat and car keys and rushes out of the house.

As he runs to the car, his wife yells, "Honey, where are you going?"

"I'm sorry, darling," Robert yells back. "I have just discovered a way to control the inventory of a critical item at the drugstore. I am really excited because I am able to apply my industrial engineering degree to my job! I need to get the data from the store and work out the new inventory policy! I will be back before dinner!"

Because rush hour traffic has dissipated, the drive to the drugstore takes Robert no time at all. He unlocks the darkened store and heads directly to his office where he rummages through file cabinets to find demand and cost data for Totalee toothbrushes over the past year.

Aha! Just as he suspected! The demand data for the toothbrushes is almost constant across the months. Whether in winter or summer, customers have teeth to brush, and they need toothbrushes. Since a toothbrush will wear out after a few months of use, customers will always return to buy another toothbrush. The demand data shows that Nightingale Drugstore customers purchase an average of 250 Totalee toothbrushes per month (30 days).

After examining the demand data, Robert investigates the cost data. Because Nightingale Drugstore is such a good customer, Totalee charges its lowest wholesale price of only $1.25 per toothbrush. Robert spends about 20 minutes to place each order with Totalee. His salary and benefits add up to $18.75 per hour. The annual holding cost for the inventory is 12 percent of the capital tied up in the inventory of Totalee toothbrushes.

(a) Robert decides to create an inventory policy that normally fulfills all demand since he believes that stock-outs are just not worth the hassle of calming customers or the risk of losing future business. He therefore does not allow any planned shortages. Since Nightingale Drugstore receives an order several hours after it is placed, Robert makes the simplifying assumption that delivery is instantaneous. What is the optimal inventory policy under these conditions? How many Totalee toothbrushes should Robert order each time and how frequently? What is the total variable inventory cost per year with this policy?

(b) Totalee has been experiencing financial problems because the company has lost money trying to branch into producing other personal hygiene products, such as hairbrushes and dental floss. The company has therefore decided to close the warehouse located 20 miles from Nightingale Drugstore. The drugstore must now place orders with a warehouse located 350 miles away and must wait 6 days after it places an order to receive the shipment. Given this new lead time, how many Totalee toothbrushes should Robert order each time, and when should he order?

(c) Robert begins to wonder whether he would save money if he allows planned shortages to occur. Customers would wait to buy the toothbrushes from Nightingale since they have high brand loyalty and since Nightingale sells the toothbrushes for less. Even though customers would wait to purchase the Totalee toothbrush from Nightingale, they would become unhappy with the prospect of having to return to the store again for the product. Robert decides that he needs to place a dollar value on the negative ramifications from shortages. He knows that an employee would have to calm each disgruntled customer and track down the delivery date for a new shipment of Totalee toothbrushes. Robert also believes that customers would become upset with the inconvenience of shopping at Nightingale and would perhaps begin looking for another store providing better service. He estimates the costs of dealing with disgruntled customers and losing customer goodwill and future sales as $1.50 per unit short per year. Given the 6-day lead time and the shortage allowance, how many Totalee toothbrushes should Robert order each time, and when should he order? What is the maximum shortage under this optimal inventory policy? What is the total variable inventory cost per year?

(d) Robert realizes that his estimate for the shortage cost is simply that—an estimate. He realizes that employees sometimes must spend several minutes with each customer who wishes to purchase a toothbrush when none is currently available. In addition, he realizes that the cost of losing customer goodwill and future sales could vary within a wide range. He estimates that the cost of dealing with disgruntled customers and losing customer goodwill and future sales could range from 85 cents to $25 per unit short per year. What effect would changing the estimate of the unit shortage cost have on the inventory policy and total variable inventory cost per year found in part (c)?

(e) Closing warehouses has not improved Totalee's bottom line significantly, so the company has decided to institute a discount policy to encourage more sales. Totalee will charge $1.25 per toothbrush for any order of up to 500 toothbrushes, $1.15 per toothbrush for orders of more than 500 but less than 1000 toothbrushes, and $1 per toothbrush for orders of 1000 toothbrushes or more. Robert still assumes a 6-day lead time, but he does not want planned shortages to occur. Under the new discount policy, how many Totalee toothbrushes should Robert order each time, and when should he order? What is the total inventory cost (including purchase costs) per year?

CASE 19.2   TNT: TACKLING NEWSBOY'S TEACHINGS

Howie Rogers sits in an isolated booth at his favorite coffee shop completely immersed in the classified ads of the local newspaper. He is searching for his next get-rich-quick venture. As he meticulously reviews each ad, he absent-mindedly sips his lemonade and wonders how he will be able to exploit each opportunity to his advantage.

He is becoming quite disillusioned with his chosen vocation of being an entrepreneur looking for high-flying ventures. These past few years have not dealt him a lucky hand. Every project he has embarked upon has ended in utter disaster, and he is slowly coming to the realization that he just might have to find a real job.

He reads the date at the top of the newspaper. June 18. Ohhhh. No need to look for a real job until the end of the summer.

Each advertisement Howie reviews registers as only a minor blip on his radar screen until the word Corvette jumps out at him. He narrows his eyes and reads:

WIN A NEW CORVETTE AND EARN CASH AT THE SAME TIME! Fourth of July is fast approaching, and we need YOU to sell firecrackers. Call 1-800-555-3426 to establish a firecracker stand in your neighborhood. Earn fast money AND win the car of your dreams!

Well, certainly not a business that will make him a millionaire, but a worthwhile endeavor nonetheless! Howie tears the advertisement out of the newspaper and heads to the payphone in the back.

A brief—but informative—conversation reveals the details of the operation. Leisure Limited, a large wholesaler that distributes holiday products—Christmas decorations, Easter decorations, firecrackers, etc.—to small independents for resale, is recruiting entrepreneurs to run local firecracker stands for the Fourth of July. The wholesaler is offering to rent wooden shacks to entrepreneurs who will purchase firecrackers from Leisure Limited and will subsequently resell the firecrackers in these shacks on the side of the road to local customers for a higher price. The entrepreneurs will sell firecrackers until the Fourth of July, but after the holiday, customers will no longer want to purchase firecrackers until New Year's Eve. Therefore, the entrepreneurs will return any firecrackers not sold by the Fourth of July while keeping the revenues from all firecrackers sold. Leisure Limited will refund only part of the cost of the returned firecrackers, however, since returned firecrackers must be restocked and since they lose their explosiveness with age. And the Corvette? The individual who sells the greatest number of Leisure Limited firecrackers in the state will win a new Corvette.

Before Howie hangs up the phone, the Leisure Limited representative reveals one hitch—once an entrepreneur places an order for firecrackers, 7 days are required for the delivery of the firecrackers. Howie realizes that he better get started quickly so that he will be able to sell firecrackers during the week preceding the Fourth of July when most of the demand occurs.

People could call Howie many things, but "pokey" they could not. Howie springs to action by reserving a wooden shack and scheduling a delivery 7 days hence. He then places another quarter in the payphone to order firecracker sets, but as he starts dialing the phone, he realizes that he has no idea how many sets he should order.

How should he solve this problem? If he orders too few firecracker sets, he will not have time to place and receive another order before the holiday and will therefore lose valuable sales (not to mention the chance to win the Corvette). If he orders too many firecracker sets, he will simply throw away money since he will not obtain a full refund for the cost of the surplus sets.

Quite a dilemma! He hangs up the phone and bangs his head against the hard concrete wall. After several bangs, he stands up straight with a thought. Of course! His sister would help him. She had graduated from college several years ago with an industrial engineering degree, and he is sure that she will agree to help him.

Howie calls Talia, his sister, at her work and explains his problem. Once she hears the problem, she is confident that she will be able to tell Howie how many sets he should order. Her dedicated operations research teacher in college had taught her well. Talia asks Howie to give her the number for Leisure Limited, and she would then have the answer for him the next day.

Talia calls Leisure Limited and asks to speak to the manager on duty. Buddy Williams, the manager, takes her call, and Talia explains to him that she wants to run a firecracker stand. To decide the number of firecracker sets she should order, however, she needs some information from him. She persuades Buddy that he should not hesitate to give her the information since a more informed order is better for Leisure Limited—the wholesaler will not lose too many sales and will not have to deal with too many returns.

Talia receives the following information from Buddy. Entrepreneurs purchase firecracker sets from Leisure Limited at a cost of $3.00 per set. Entrepreneurs are able to sell the firecracker sets for any price that they deem reasonable. In addition to the wholesale price of the firecracker sets, entrepreneurs also have to pay administrative and delivery fees for each order they place. These fees average approximately $20.00 per order. After the Fourth of July, Leisure Limited returns only half of the wholesale cost for each firecracker set returned. To return the unsold firecracker sets, entrepreneurs also have to pay shipping costs that average $0.50 per firecracker set.

Finally, Talia asks about the demand for firecracker sets. Buddy is not able to give her very specific information, but he is able to give her general information about last year's sales. Data compiled from last year's stand sales throughout the state indicate that stands sold between 120 and 420 firecracker sets. The stands operated any time between June 20 and July 4 and sold the firecracker sets for an average of $5.00 per set.

Talia thanks Buddy, hangs up the phone, and begins making assumptions to help her overcome the lack of specific data. Even though Howie will operate his stand only during the week preceding the Fourth of July, she decides to use the demands quoted by Buddy for simplicity. She assumes that the demand follows a uniform distribution. She decides to use the average of $5.00 for the unit sale price.

(a) How many firecracker sets should Howie purchase from Leisure Limited to maximize his expected profit?

(b) How would Howie's order quantity change if Leisure Limited refunds 75 percent of the wholesale price for returned firecracker sets? How would it change if Leisure Limited refunds 25 percent of the wholesale price for returned firecracker sets?

(c) Howie is not happy with selling the firecracker sets for $5.00 per set. He needs to make some serious dough! Suppose Howie wants to sell the firecracker sets for $6.00 per set instead. What factors would Talia have to take into account when recalculating the optimal order quantity?

(d) What do you think of Talia's strategy for estimating demand?

CASE 19.3   JETTISONING SURPLUS STOCK

Scarlett Windermere cautiously approaches the expansive gray factory building and experiences a mixture of fear and excitement. The first day of a new consulting assignment always leaves her fighting conflicting emotions. She takes a deep breath, clutches her briefcase, and marches into the small, stuffy reception area of American Aerospace.

"Scarlett Windermere here to see Bryan Zimmerman," she says to the bored security guard behind the reception desk.

The security guard eyes Scarlett suspiciously and says, "Ya don't belong here, do ya? Of course ya don't. Then ya gotta fill out this paperwork for a temporary security pass."

As Scarlett completes the necessary paperwork, Bryan exits through the heavy door leading to the factory floor and enters the reception area. His eyes roam the reception area and rest upon Scarlett. He approaches Scarlett booming, "So you must be the inventory expert—Scarlett Windermere. So glad to finally meet you face to face! They already got you pouring out your life story, huh? Well, there will be enough time for that. Right now, let's get you back to the factory floor to help me solve my inventory problem!"

And with that, Bryan stuffs a pair of safety glasses in Scarlett's right hand, stuffs the incomplete security forms in her left hand, and hustles her through the heavy security door.

As Scarlett walks through the security door, she feels as though she has entered another world. Machines twice the size of humans line the aisles as far as the eye can see. These monsters make high-pitched squeals or low, horrifying rumbles as they cut and grind metal. Surrounding these machines are shelves piled with metal pieces.

As Bryan leads Scarlett down the aisles of the factory, he yells to her over the machines, "As you well know from the proposal stage of this project, this factory produces the stationary parts for the military jet engines American Aerospace sells. Most people think the aerospace industry is real high-tech. Well, not this factory. This factory is as dirty as they come. Jet engines are made out of a lot of solid metal parts, and this factory cuts, grinds, and welds those parts."

"This factory produces over 200 different stationary parts for jet engines. Each jet engine model requires different parts. And each part requires different raw materials. Hence, the factory's current inventory problem."

"We hold all kinds of raw materials—from rivets to steel sheets—here on the factory floor, and we currently mismanage our raw materials inventory. We order enough raw materials to produce a year's worth of some stationary parts, but only enough raw materials to produce a week's worth of others. We waste a ton of money stocking raw materials that are not needed and lose a ton of money dealing with late deliveries of orders. We need you to tell us how to control the inventory—how many raw materials we need to stock for each part, how often we need to order additional raw materials, and how many we should order."

As she walks down the aisle, Scarlett studies the shelves and shelves of inventory. She has quite a mission to accomplish in this factory!

Bryan continues, "Let me tell you how we receive orders for this factory. Whenever the American Aerospace sales department gets an order for a particular jet engine, the order is transferred to its assembly plant here on the site. The assembly plant then submits an order to this factory here for the stationary parts required to assemble the engine. Unfortunately, because this factory is frequently running out of raw materials, it takes us an average of a month between the time we receive an order and the time we deliver the finished order to the assembly plant. The finished order includes all the stationary parts needed to assemble that particular jet engine. BUT—and that's a big but—the delivery time really depends upon which stationary parts are included in the order."

Scarlett interrupts Bryan and says, "Then I guess now would be as good a time as any to start collecting the details of the orders and solving your inventory problem!"

Bryan smiles and says, "That's the attitude I like to see—chomping at the bit to solve the problem! Well, I'll show you to your computer. We just had another consulting firm complete a data warehouse started by American Aerospace three years ago, so you can access any of the data you need right from your desktop!" And with a flurry, Bryan heads back down the aisle.

Scarlett realizes that the inventory system is quite complicated. She remembers a golden rule from her consulting firm: break down a complex system into simple parts. She therefore decides to analyze the control of inventory for each stationary part independently. But with 200 different stationary parts, where should she begin?

She remembers that when the assembly plant receives an order for a particular jet engine, it places an order with the factory for the stationary parts required to assemble the engine. The factory delivers an order to the assembly plant when all stationary parts for that order have been completed. The stationary part that takes the longest to complete in a given order therefore determines the delivery date of the order.

Scarlett decides to begin her analysis with the most time-intensive stationary part required to assemble the most popular jet engine. She types a command into the computer to determine the most popular jet engine. She learns that the MX332 has received the largest number of orders over the past year. She types another command to generate the following printout of the monthly orders for the MX332.

Month	Number of MX332 ordered
June	25
July	31
August	18
September	22
October	40
November	19
December	38
January	21
February	25
March	36
April	34
May	28
June	27

She enters the monthly order quantities for the MX332 into a computerized statistical program to estimate the underlying distribution. She learns that the orders roughly follow a normal distribution. It appears to Scarlett that the number of orders in a particular month does not depend on the number of orders in the previous or following months.

(a) What is the sample mean and sample variance of the set of monthly orders for the MX332?

Scarlett next researches the most time-intensive stationary part required to assemble the MX332. She types a command into the computer to generate a list of parts required to assemble the MX332. She then types a command to list the average delivery time for each part. She learns that part 10003487 typically requires the longest time to complete, and that this part is only used for the MX332. She investigates the pattern for the part further and learns that over the past year, part 10003487 has taken an average of one month to complete once an order is placed. She also learns that the factory can produce the part almost immediately if all the necessary raw materials for the production process are on hand. So the completion time actually depends on how long it takes to obtain these raw materials from the supplier. On those unusual occasions when all the raw materials already are available in inventory, the completion time for the part is essentially zero. But typically the completion time is $1\frac{1}{2}$ months.

Scarlett performs further analysis on the computer and learns that each MX332 jet engine requires two parts numbered 10003487. Each part 10003487 accepts one solid steel part molded into a cylindrical shape as its main raw material input. The data show that several times the delivery of all the stationary parts for the MX332 to the assembly plant got delayed for up to $1\frac{1}{2}$ months only because a part 10003487 was not completed. And why wasn't it completed? The factory had run out of those steel parts and had to wait for another shipment from its supplier! It takes the supplier $1\frac{1}{2}$ months to produce and deliver the steel parts after receiving an order from the factory. Once an order of steel parts arrives, the factory quickly sets up and executes a production run to use all the steel parts for producing parts 10003487. Apparently the production problems in the factory are mainly due to the inventory management for those unassuming steel parts. And that inventory management appears to be completely out of whack. The only good news is that there is no significant administrative cost associated with placing an order for the steel parts with the supplier.

After Scarlett has finished her work on the computer, she heads to Bryan's office to obtain the financials needed to complete her analysis. A short meeting with Bryan yields the following financial information.

Setup cost for a production run to produce part 10003487	$5,800
Holding cost for machine part 10003487	$750 per part per year
Shortage cost for part 10003487 (includes outsourcing cost, cost of production delay, and cost of the loss of future orders)	$3,250 per part per year
Desired probability that a shortage for machine part 10003487 will not occur between the time an order for the steel parts is placed and the time the order is delivered	0.85

Now Scarlett has all of the information necessary to perform her inventory analysis for part 10003487!

(b) What is the inventory policy that American Aerospace should implement for part 10003487?
(c) What are the average annual holding costs and setup costs associated with this inventory policy?

(d) How do the average annual holding costs and setup costs change if the desired probability that a shortage will not occur between the time an order is placed and the time the order is delivered is increased to 0.95?

(e) Do you think Scarlett's independent analysis of each stationary part could generate inaccurate inventory policies? Why or why not?

(f) Scarlett knows that the aerospace industry is very cyclical—the industry experiences several years of high sales, several years of mediocre sales, and several years of low sales. How would you recommend incorporating this fact into the analysis?

20

Forecasting

How much will the economy grow over the next year? Where is the stock market headed? What about interest rates? How will consumer tastes be changing? What will be the hot new products?

Forecasters have answers to all these questions. Unfortunately, these answers will more than likely be wrong. Nobody can accurately predict the future every time.

Nevertheless, the future success of any business depends heavily on how savvy its management is in spotting trends and developing appropriate strategies. The leaders of the best companies often seem to have a sixth sense for when to change direction to stay a step ahead of the competition. These companies seldom get into trouble by badly misestimating what the demand will be for their products. Many other companies do. The ability to forecast well makes the difference.

The preceding chapter has presented a considerable number of models for the management of inventories. All these models are based on a forecast of future demand for a product, or at least a probability distribution for that demand. Therefore, the missing ingredient for successfully implementing these inventory models is an approach for forecasting demand.

Fortunately, when historical sales data are available, some proven **statistical forecasting methods** have been developed for using these data to forecast future demand. Such a method assumes that historical trends will continue, so management then needs to make any adjustments to reflect current changes in the marketplace.

Several **judgmental forecasting methods** that solely use expert judgment also are available. These methods are especially valuable when little or no historical sales data are available or when major changes in the marketplace make these data unreliable for forecasting purposes.

Forecasting product demand is just one important application of the various forecasting methods. A variety of applications are surveyed in the first section. The second section outlines the main judgmental forecasting methods. Section 20.3 then describes *time series,* which form the basis for the statistical forecasting methods presented in the subsequent five sections. Section 20.9 turns to another important type of statistical forecasting method, *regression analysis,* where the variable to be forecasted is expressed as a mathematical function of one or more other variables whose values will be known at the time of the forecast. The chapter then concludes by surveying forecasting practices in U.S. corporations.

20.1 SOME APPLICATIONS OF FORECASTING

We now will discuss some main areas in which forecasting is widely used. In each case, we will illustrate this use by mentioning one or more actual applications that have been described in published articles. A summary table at the end of the section will tell you where these articles can be found in case you want to read further.

Sales Forecasting

Any company engaged in selling goods needs to forecast the demand for those goods. Manufacturers need to know how much to produce. Wholesalers and retailers need to know how much to stock. Substantially underestimating demand is likely to lead to many lost sales, unhappy customers, and perhaps allowing the competition to gain the upper hand in the marketplace. On the other hand, significantly overestimating demand also is very costly due to (1) excessive inventory costs, (2) forced price reductions, (3) unneeded production or storage capacity, and (4) lost opportunities to market more profitable goods. Successful marketing and production managers understand very well the importance of obtaining good sales forecasts.

The *Merit Brass Company* is a family-owned company that supplies several thousand products to the pipe, valve, and fittings industry. In 1990, Merit Brass embarked on a modernization program that emphasized installing OR methodologies in statistical sales forecasting and finished-goods inventory management (two activities that go hand in glove). This program led to major improvements in customer service (as measured by product availability) while simultaneously achieving substantial cost reductions.

A major Spanish electric utility, *Hidroeléctrica Español*, has developed and implemented a hierarchy of OR models to assist in managing its system of reservoirs used for generating hydroelectric power. All these models are driven by forecasts of both energy demand (this company's sales) and reservoir inflows. A sophisticated statistical forecasting method is used to forecast energy demand on both a short-term and long-term basis. A hydrological forecasting model generates the forecasts of reservoir inflows.

Airline companies now depend heavily on the high fares paid by business people traveling on short notice while providing discount fares to others to help fill the seats. The decision on how to allocate seats to the different fare classes is a crucial one for maximizing revenue. *American Airlines,* for example, uses statistical forecasting of the demand at each fare to make this decision.

Forecasting the Need for Spare Parts

Although effective sales forecasting is a key for virtually any company, some organizations must rely on other types of forecasts as well. A prime example involves forecasts of the need for spare parts.

Many companies need to maintain an inventory of spare parts to enable them to quickly repair either their own equipment or their products sold or leased to customers. In some cases, this inventory is huge. For example, IBM's spare-parts inventory described in Sec. 19.8 is valued in the billions of dollars and includes many thousand different parts.

Just as for a finished-goods inventory ready for sale, effective management of a spare-parts inventory depends upon obtaining a reliable forecast of the demand for that inventory. Although the types of costs incurred by misestimating demand are somewhat different, the consequences may be no less severe for spare parts. For example, the consequence for an airline not having a spare part available on location when needed to continue flying an airplane probably is at least one canceled flight.

To support its operation of several hundred aircraft, *American Airlines* maintains an extensive inventory of spare parts. Included are over 5,000 different types of rotatable parts (e.g., landing gear and wing flaps) with an average value of $5,000 per item. When a rotatable part on an airplane is found to be defective, it is immediately replaced by a corresponding part in inventory so the airplane can depart. However, the replaced part then is repaired and placed back into inventory for subsequent use as a replacement part.

American Airlines uses a PC-based forecasting system called the Rotatables Allocation and Planning System (RAPS) to forecast demand for the rotatable parts and to help allocate these parts to the various airports. The statistical forecast uses an 18-month history of parts usage and flying hours for the fleet, and then projects ahead based on planned flying hours.

Forecasting Production Yields

The yield of a production process refers to the percentage of the completed items that meet quality standards (perhaps after rework) and so do not need to be discarded. Particularly with high-technology products, the yield frequently is well under 100 percent.

If the forecast for the production yield is somewhat under 100 percent, the size of the production run probably should be somewhat larger than the order quantity to provide a good chance of fulfilling the order with acceptable items. (The difference between the run size and the order quantity is referred to as the *reject allowance*.) If an expensive setup is required for each production run, or if there is only time for one production run, the reject allowance may need to be quite large. However, an overly large value should be avoided to prevent excessive production costs.

Obtaining a reliable forecast of production yield is essential for choosing an appropriate value of the reject allowance.

This was the case for the *Albuquerque Microelectronics Operation,* a dedicated production source for radiation-hardened microchips. The first phase in the production of its microchips, the wafer fabrication process, was continuing to provide erratic production yields. For a given product, the yield typically would be quite small (0 to 40 percent) for the first several lots and then would gradually increase to a higher range (35 to 75 percent) for later lots. Therefore, a statistical forecasting method that considered this increasing trend was used to forecast the production yield.

Forecasting Economic Trends

With the possible exception of sales forecasting, the most extensive forecasting effort is devoted to forecasting economic trends on a regional, national, or even international level. How much will the nation's gross domestic product grow next quarter? Next year? What is the forecast for the rate of inflation? The unemployment rate? The balance of trade?

Statistical models to forecast economic trends (commonly called *econometric models*) have been developed in a number of governmental agencies, university research centers, large corporations, and consulting firms, both in the United States and elsewhere.

Using historical data to project ahead, these econometric models typically consider a very large number of factors that help drive the economy. Some models include hundreds of variables and equations. However, except for their size and scope, these models resemble some of the statistical forecasting methods used by businesses for sales forecasting, etc.

These econometric models can be very influential in determining governmental policies. For example, the forecasts provided by the U.S. Congressional Budget Office strongly guide Congress in developing the federal budgets. These forecasts also help businesses in assessing the general economic outlook.

As an example on a smaller scale, the *U.S. Department of Labor* contracted with a consulting firm to develop the *unemployment insurance econometric forecasting model* (UIEFM). The model is now in use by state employment security agencies around the nation. By projecting such fundamental economic factors as unemployment rates, wage levels, the size of the labor force covered by unemployment insurance, etc., UIEFM forecasts how much the state will need to pay in unemployment insurance. By projecting tax inflows into the state's unemployment insurance trust fund, UIEFM also forecasts trust fund balances over a 10-year period. Therefore, UIEFM has proved to be invaluable in managing state unemployment insurance systems and in guiding related legislative policies.

Forecasting Staffing Needs

One of the major trends in the American economy is a shifting emphasis from manufacturing to services. More and more of our manufactured goods are being produced outside the country (where labor is cheaper) and then imported. At the same time, an increasing number of American business firms are specializing in providing a service of some kind (e.g., travel, tourism, entertainment, legal aid, health services, financial, educational, design, maintenance, etc.). For such a company, forecasting "sales" becomes forecasting the demand for services, which then translates into forecasting staffing needs to provide those services.

For example, one of the fastest-growing service industries in the United States today is call centers. A call center receives telephone calls from the general public requesting a particular type of service. Depending on the center, the service might be providing technical assistance over the phone, or making a travel reservation, or filling a telephone order for goods, or booking services to be performed later, etc. There now are more than 350,000 call centers in the United States, with over $25 billion invested to date and an annual growth rate of 20 percent.

As with any service organization, an erroneous forecast of staffing requirements for a call center has serious consequences. Providing too few agents to answer the telephone leads to unhappy customers, lost calls, and perhaps lost business. Too many agents cause excessive personnel costs.

Section 3.5 described a major OR study that involved personnel scheduling at *United Airlines*. With over 4,000 reservations sales representatives and support personnel at its 11 reservations offices, and about 1,000 customer service agents at its 10 largest airports, a computerized planning system was developed to design the work schedules for these employees. Although several other OR techniques (including linear programming) were incorporated into this system, statistical forecasting of staffing requirements also was a key ingredient. This system provided annual savings of over $6 million as well as improved customer service and reduced support staff requirements.

TABLE 20.1 Some applications of statistical forecasting methods

Organization	Quantity Being Forecasted	Issue of *Interfaces*
Merit Brass Co.	Sales of finished goods	Jan.–Feb. 1993
Hidroeléctrica Español	Energy demand	Jan.–Feb. 1990
American Airlines	Demand for different fare classes	Jan.–Feb. 1992
American Airlines	Need for spare parts to repair airplanes	July–Aug. 1989
Albuquerque Microelectronics	Production yield in wafer fabrication	March–April 1994
U.S. Department of Labor	Unemployment insurance payments	March–April 1988
United Airlines	Demand at reservations offices and airports	Jan.–Feb. 1986
L.L. Bean	Staffing needs at call center	Nov.–Dec. 1995

L.L. Bean is a major retailer of high-quality outdoor goods and apparel. Over 70 percent of its total sales volume is generated through orders taken at the company's call center. Two 800 numbers are provided, one for placing orders and the second for making inquiries or reporting problems. Each of the company's agents is trained to answer just one of the 800 numbers. Therefore, separate statistical forecasting models were developed to forecast staffing requirements for the two 800 numbers on a weekly basis. The improved precision of these models is estimated to have saved L.L. Bean $300,000 annually through enhanced scheduling efficiency.

Other

Table 20.1 summarizes the actual applications of statistical forecasting methods presented in this section. The last column cites the issue of *Interfaces* which includes the article that describes each application in detail.

All five categories of forecasting applications discussed in this section use the types of forecasting methods presented in the subsequent sections. There also are other important categories (including forecasting weather, the stock market, and prospects for new products before market testing) that use specialized techniques that are not discussed here.

20.2 JUDGMENTAL FORECASTING METHODS

Judgmental forecasting methods are, by their very nature, subjective, and they may involve such qualities as intuition, expert opinion, and experience. They generally lead to forecasts that are based upon qualitative criteria.

These methods may be used when no data are available for employing a statistical forecasting method. However, even when good data are available, some decision makers prefer a judgmental method instead of a formal statistical method. In many other cases, a combination of the two may be used.

Here is a brief overview of the main judgmental forecasting methods.

1. **Manager's opinion:** This is the most informal of the methods, because it simply involves a single manager using his or her best judgment to make the forecast. In some cases, some data may be available to help make this judgment. In others, the manager may be drawing solely on experience and an intimate knowledge of the current conditions that drive the forecasted quantity.

2. **Jury of executive opinion:** This method is similar to the first one, except now it involves a small group of high-level managers who pool their best judgment to collectively make the forecast. This method may be used for more critical forecasts for which several executives share responsibility and can provide different types of expertise.

3. **Sales force composite:** This method is often used for sales forecasting when a company employs a sales force to help generate sales. It is a *bottom-up approach* whereby each salesperson provides an estimate of what sales will be in his or her region. These estimates then are sent up through the corporate chain of command, with managerial review at each level, to be aggregated into a corporate sales forecast.

4. **Consumer market survey:** This method goes even further than the preceding one in adopting a *grass-roots approach* to sales forecasting. It involves surveying customers and potential customers regarding their future purchasing plans and how they would respond to various new features in products. This input is particularly helpful for designing new products and then in developing the initial forecasts of their sales. It also is helpful for planning a marketing campaign.

5. **Delphi method:** This method employs a panel of experts in different locations who independently fill out a series of questionnaires. However, the results from each questionnaire are provided with the next one, so each expert then can evaluate this group information in adjusting his or her responses next time. The goal is to reach a relatively narrow spread of conclusions from most of the experts. The decision makers then assess this input from the panel of experts to develop the forecast. This involved process normally is used only at the highest levels of a corporation or government to develop long-range forecasts of broad trends.

The decision on whether to use one of these judgmental forecasting methods should be based on an assessment of whether the individuals who would execute the method have the background needed to make an informed judgment. Another factor is whether the expertise of these individuals or the availability of relevant historical data (or a combination of both) appears to provide a better basis for obtaining a reliable forecast.

The next seven sections discuss statistical forecasting methods based on relevant historical data.

20.3 TIME SERIES

Most statistical forecasting methods are based on using historical data from a *time series*.

A **time series** is a series of observations over time of some quantity of interest (a random variable). Thus, if X_i is the random variable of interest at time i, and if observations are taken at times[1] $i = 1, 2, \ldots, t$, then the observed values $\{X_1 = x_1, X_2 = x_2, \ldots, X_t = x_t\}$ are a time series.

For example, the recent monthly sales figures for a product comprises a time series, as illustrated in Fig. 20.1.

Because a time series is a description of the past, a logical procedure for forecasting the future is to make use of these historical data. If the past data are indicative of what

---

[1]These times of observation sometimes are actually time periods (months, years, etc.), so we often will refer to the times as periods.

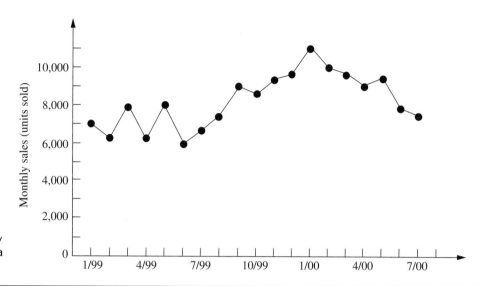

FIGURE 20.1
The evolution of the monthly sales of a product illustrates a time series.

we can expect in the future, we can postulate an underlying mathematical model that is representative of the process. The model can then be used to generate forecasts.

In most realistic situations, we do not have complete knowledge of the exact form of the model that generates the time series, so an approximate model must be chosen. Frequently, the choice is made by observing the pattern of the time series. Several typical time series patterns are shown in Fig. 20.2. Figure 20.2*a* displays a typical time series if the generating process were represented by a **constant level** superimposed with random fluctuations. Figure 20.2*b* displays a typical time series if the generating process were represented by a **linear trend** superimposed with random fluctuations. Finally, Fig. 20.2*c* shows a time series that might be observed if the generating process were represented by a constant level superimposed with a **seasonal effect** together with random fluctuations. There are many other plausible representations, but these three are particularly useful in practice and so are considered in this chapter.

FIGURE 20.2
Typical time series patterns, with random fluctuations around (*a*) a constant level, (*b*) a linear trend, and (*c*) a constant level plus seasonal effects.

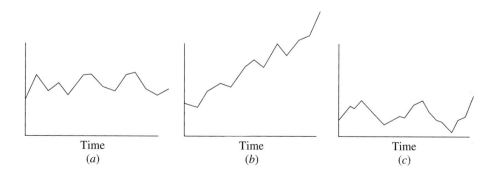

Once the form of the model is chosen, a mathematical representation of the generating process of the time series can be given. For example, suppose that the generating process is identified as a **constant-level model** superimposed with random fluctuations, as illustrated in Fig. 20.2a. Such a representation can be given by

$$X_i = A + e_i, \qquad \text{for } i = 1, 2, \ldots,$$

where X_i is the random variable observed at time i, A is the constant level of the model, and e_i is the random error occurring at time i (assumed to have expected value equal to zero and constant variance). Let

F_{t+1} = forecast of the values of the time series at time $t + 1$, given the observed values, $X_1 = x_1, X_2 = x_2, \ldots, X_t = x_t$.

Because of the random error e_{t+1}, it is impossible for F_{t+1} to predict the value $X_{t+1} = x_{t+1}$ precisely, but the goal is to have F_{t+1} estimate the constant level $A = E(X_{t+1})$ as closely as possible. It is reasonable to expect that F_{t+1} will be a function of at least some of the observed values of the time series.

20.4 FORECASTING METHODS FOR A CONSTANT-LEVEL MODEL

We now present four alternative forecasting methods for the constant-level model introduced in the preceding paragraph. This model, like any other, is only intended to be an idealized representation of the actual situation. For the real time series, at least small shifts in the value of A may be occurring occasionally. Each of the following methods reflects a different assessment of how recently (if at all) a significant shift may have occurred.

Last-Value Forecasting Method

By interpreting t as the *current time*, the last-value forecasting procedure uses the value of the time series observed at time t (x_t) as the forecast at time $t + 1$. Therefore,

$$F_{t+1} = x_t.$$

For example, if x_t represents the sales of a particular product in the quarter just ended, this procedure uses these sales as the forecast of the sales for the next quarter.

This forecasting procedure has the disadvantage of being imprecise; i.e., its variance is large because it is based upon a sample of size 1. It is worth considering only if (1) the underlying assumption about the constant-level model is "shaky" and the process is changing so rapidly that anything before time t is almost irrelevant or misleading or (2) the assumption that the random error e_t has constant variance is unreasonable and the variance at time t actually is much smaller than at previous times.

The last-value forecasting method sometimes is called the **naive method,** because statisticians consider it naive to use just a *sample size of one* when additional relevant data are available. However, when conditions are changing rapidly, it may be that the last value is the only relevant data point for forecasting the next value under current conditions. Therefore, decision makers who are anything but naive do occasionally use this method under such circumstances.

Averaging Forecasting Method

This method goes to the other extreme. Rather than using just a sample size of one, this method uses *all* the data points in the time series and simply *averages* these points. Thus, the forecast of what the next data point will turn out to be is

$$F_{t+1} = \sum_{i=1}^{t} \frac{x_i}{t}.$$

This estimate is an excellent one if the process is entirely stable, i.e., if the assumptions about the underlying model are correct. However, frequently there exists skepticism about the persistence of the underlying model over an extended time. Conditions inevitably change eventually. Because of a natural reluctance to use very old data, this procedure generally is limited to young processes.

Moving-Average Forecasting Method

Rather than using very old data that may no longer be relevant, this method averages the data for only the last n periods as the forecast for the next period, i.e.,

$$F_{t+1} = \sum_{i=t-n+1}^{t} \frac{x_i}{n}.$$

Note that this forecast is easily updated from period to period. All that is needed each time is to lop off the first observation and add the last one.

The *moving-average* estimator combines the advantages of the *last value* and *averaging* estimators in that it uses only recent history *and* it uses multiple observations. A disadvantage of this method is that it places as much weight on x_{t-n+1} as on x_t. Intuitively, one would expect a good method to place more weight on the most recent observation than on older observations that may be less representative of current conditions. Our next method does just this.

Exponential Smoothing Forecasting Method

This method uses the formula

$$F_{t+1} = \alpha x_t + (1 - \alpha)F_t,$$

where α $(0 < \alpha < 1)$ is called the **smoothing constant.** (The choice of α is discussed later.) Thus, the forecast is just a weighted sum of the last observation x_t and the preceding forecast F_t for the period just ended. Because of this recursive relationship between F_{t+1} and F_t, alternatively F_{t+1} can be expressed as

$$F_{t+1} = \alpha x_t + \alpha(1 - \alpha)x_{t-1} + \alpha(1 - \alpha)^2 x_{t-2} + \cdots.$$

In this form, it becomes evident that exponential smoothing gives the most weight to x_t and decreasing weights to earlier observations. Furthermore, the first form reveals that the forecast is simple to calculate because the data prior to period t need not be retained; all that is required is x_t and the previous forecast F_t.

Another alternative form for the exponential smoothing technique is given by

$$F_{t+1} = F_t + \alpha(x_t - F_t),$$

which gives a heuristic justification for this method. In particular, the forecast of the time series at time $t + 1$ is just the preceding forecast at time t plus the *product* of the forecasting error at time t and a discount factor α. This alternative form is often simpler to use.

A measure of effectiveness of exponential smoothing can be obtained under the assumption that the process is completely stable, so that $X_1, X_2, \ldots$ are independent, identically distributed random variables with variance σ^2. It then follows that (for large t)

$$\text{var}[F_{t+1}] \approx \frac{\alpha\sigma^2}{2 - \alpha} = \frac{\sigma^2}{(2 - \alpha)/\alpha},$$

so that the variance is statistically equivalent to a moving average with $(2 - \alpha)/\alpha$ observations. For example, if α is chosen equal to 0.1, then $(2 - \alpha)/\alpha = 19$. Thus, in terms of its variance, the exponential smoothing method with this value of α is *equivalent* to the moving-average method that uses 19 observations. However, if a change in the process does occur (e.g., if the mean starts increasing), exponential smoothing will react more quickly with better tracking of the change than the moving-average method.

An important drawback of exponential smoothing is that it lags behind a continuing trend; i.e., if the constant-level model is incorrect and the mean is increasing steadily, then the forecast will be several periods behind. However, the procedure can be easily adjusted for trend (and even seasonally adjusted).

Another disadvantage of exponential smoothing is that it is difficult to choose an appropriate smoothing constant α. Exponential smoothing can be viewed as a statistical filter that inputs raw data from a stochastic process and outputs smoothed estimates of a mean that varies with time. If α is chosen to be small, response to change is slow, with resultant smooth estimators. On the other hand, if α is chosen to be large, response to change is fast, with resultant large variability in the output. Hence, there is a need to compromise, depending upon the degree of stability of the process. It has been suggested that α should not exceed 0.3 and that a reasonable choice for α is approximately 0.1. This value can be increased temporarily if a change in the process is expected or when one is just starting the forecasting. At the start, a reasonable approach is to choose the forecast for period 2 according to

$$F_2 = \alpha x_1 + (1 - \alpha)(\text{initial estimate}),$$

where some initial estimate of the constant level A must be obtained. If past data are available, such an estimate may be the average of these data.

Your OR Courseware includes a pair of Excel templates for each of the four forecasting methods presented in this section. In each use, one template (*without seasonality*) applies the method just as described here. The second template (*with seasonality*) also incorporates into the method the seasonal factors discussed in the next section.

20.5   INCORPORATING SEASONAL EFFECTS INTO FORECASTING METHODS

It is fairly common for a time series to have a *seasonal pattern* with higher values at certain times of the year than others. For example, this occurs for the sales of a product that is a popular choice for Christmas gifts. Such a time series violates the basic assumption of a *constant-level model,* so the forecasting methods presented in the preceding section should not be applied directly.

Fortunately, it is relatively straightforward to make *seasonal adjustments* in such a time series so that these forecasting methods based on a constant-level model can still be applied. We will illustrate the procedure with the following example.

Example.   The COMPUTER CLUB WAREHOUSE (commonly referred to as CCW) sells various computer products at bargain prices by taking telephone orders directly from customers at its call center. Figure 20.3 shows the average number of calls received per day in each of the four quarters of the past three years. Note how the call volume jumps up sharply in each Quarter 4 because of Christmas sales. There also is a tendency for the call volume to be a little higher in Quarter 3 than in Quarter 1 or 2 because of back-to-school sales.

To quantify these seasonal effects, the second column of Table 20.2 shows the average daily call volume for each quarter over the past three years. Underneath this column, the *overall average* over all four quarters is calculated to be 7,529. Dividing the average for each quarter by this overall average gives the *seasonal factor* shown in the third column.

In general, the **seasonal factor** for any period of a year (a quarter, a month, etc.) measures how that period compares to the overall average for an entire year. Specifically, using historical data, the seasonal factor is calculated to be

$$\text{Seasonal factor} = \frac{\text{average for the period}}{\text{overall average}}.$$

Your OR Courseware includes an Excel template for calculating these seasonal factors.

FIGURE 20.3
The average number of calls received per day at the CCW call center in each of the four quarters of the past three years.

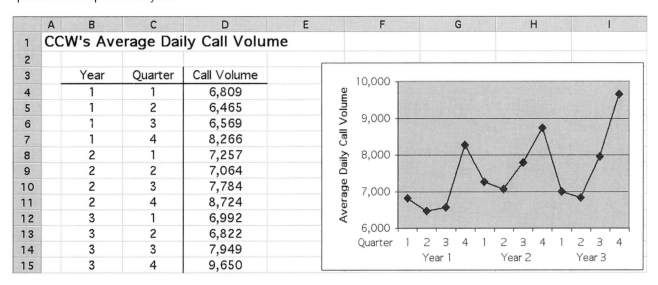

	A	B	C	D	E	F	G	H	I
1	CCW's Average Daily Call Volume								
2									
3		Year	Quarter	Call Volume					
4		1	1	6,809					
5		1	2	6,465					
6		1	3	6,569					
7		1	4	8,266					
8		2	1	7,257					
9		2	2	7,064					
10		2	3	7,784					
11		2	4	8,724					
12		3	1	6,992					
13		3	2	6,822					
14		3	3	7,949					
15		3	4	9,650					

TABLE 20.2 Calculation of the seasonal factors for the CCW problem

Quarter	Three-Year Average	Seasonal Factor
1	7,019	$\frac{7,019}{7,529} = 0.93$
2	6,784	$\frac{6,784}{7,529} = 0.90$
3	7,434	$\frac{7,434}{7,529} = 0.99$
4	8,880	$\frac{8,880}{7,529} = 1.18$

Total = 30,117

Average = $\frac{30,117}{4}$ = 7,529.

The Seasonally Adjusted Time Series

It is much easier to analyze a time series and detect new trends if the data are first adjusted to remove the effect of seasonal patterns. To remove the seasonal effects from the time series shown in Fig. 20.3, each of these average daily call volumes needs to be divided by the corresponding seasonal factor given in Table 20.2. Thus, the formula is

$$\text{Seasonally adjusted call volume} = \frac{\text{actual call volume}}{\text{seasonal factor}}.$$

Applying this formula to all 12 call volumes in Fig. 20.3 gives the seasonally adjusted call volumes shown in column F of the spreadsheet in Fig. 20.4.

In effect, these seasonally adjusted call volumes show what the call volumes would have been if the calls that occur because of the time of the year (Christmas shopping, back-to-school shopping, etc.) had been spread evenly throughout the year instead. Compare the plots in Figs. 20.4 and 20.3. After considering the smaller vertical scale in Fig. 20.4, note how much less fluctuation this figure has than Fig. 20.3 because of removing seasonal effects. However, this figure still is far from completely flat because fluctuations in call volume occur for other reasons beside just seasonal effects. For example, hot new products attract a flurry of calls. A jump also occurs just after the mailing of a catalog. Some random fluctuations occur without any apparent explanation. Figure 20.4 enables seeing and analyzing these fluctuations in sales volumes that are not caused by seasonal effects.

The General Procedure

After seasonally adjusting a time series, any of the forecasting methods presented in the preceding section (or the next section) can then be applied. Here is an outline of the general procedure.

1. Use the following formula to seasonally adjust each value in the time series:

$$\text{Seasonally adjusted value} = \frac{\text{actual value}}{\text{seasonal factor}}.$$

	A	B	C	D	E	F
1	Seasonally Adjusted Time Series for CCW					
2						
3				Seasonal	Actual	Seasonally Adjusted
4		Year	Quarter	Factor	Call Volume	Call Volume
5		1	1	0.93	6809	7322
6		1	2	0.90	6465	7183
7		1	3	0.99	6569	6635
8		1	4	1.18	8266	7005
9		2	1	0.93	7257	7803
10		2	2	0.90	7064	7849
11		2	3	0.99	7784	7863
12		2	4	1.18	8724	7393
13		3	1	0.93	6992	7518
14		3	2	0.90	6822	7580
15		3	3	0.99	7949	8029
16		3	4	1.18	9650	8178

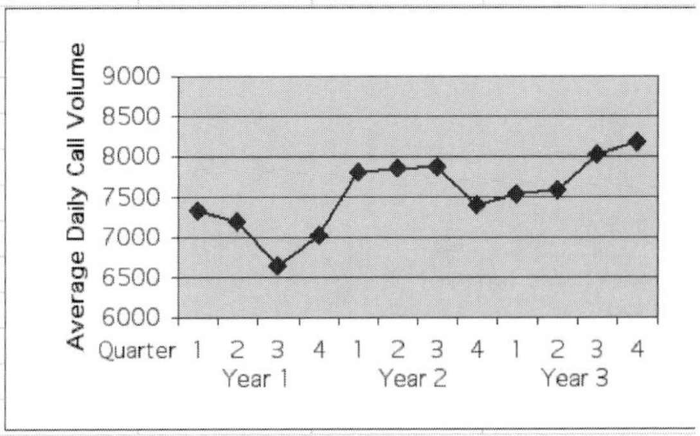

	F
5	=E5/D5
6	=E6/D6
7	=E7/D7
8	=E8/D8
9	:
10	:

FIGURE 20.4
The seasonally adjusted time series for the CCW problem obtained by dividing each actual average daily call volume in Fig. 20.3 by the corresponding seasonal factor obtained in Table 20.2.

2. Select a time series forecasting method.
3. Apply this method to the seasonally adjusted time series to obtain a forecast of the next *seasonally adjusted* value (or values).
4. Multiply this forecast by the corresponding seasonal factor to obtain a forecast of the next *actual* value (without seasonal adjustment).

As mentioned at the end of the preceding section, an Excel template that incorporates seasonal effects is available in your OR Courseware for each of the forecasting methods to assist you with combining the method with this procedure.

20.6 AN EXPONENTIAL SMOOTHING METHOD FOR A LINEAR TREND MODEL

Recall that the constant-level model introduced in Sec. 20.3 assumes that the sequence of random variables $\{X_1, X_2, \ldots, X_t\}$ generating the time series has a constant expected value denoted by A, where the goal of the forecast F_{t+1} is to estimate A as closely as possible. However, as was illustrated in Fig. 20.2*b*, some time series violate this assumption by having a continuing trend where the expected values of successive random variables keep changing in the same direction. Therefore, a forecasting method based on the constant-level model (perhaps after adjusting for seasonal effects) would do a poor job of forecasting for such a time series because it would be continually lagging behind the trend. We now turn to another model that is designed for this kind of time series.

Suppose that the generating process of the observed time series can be represented by a *linear trend* superimposed with *random fluctuations,* as illustrated in Fig. 20.2*b.* Denote the slope of the linear trend by *B,* where the slope is called the **trend factor.** The model is represented by

$$X_i = A + Bi + e_i, \qquad \text{for } i = 1, 2, \ldots,$$

where X_i is the random variable that is observed at time i, A is a constant, B is the trend factor, and e_i is the random error occurring at time i (assumed to have expected value equal to zero and constant variance).

For a real time series represented by this model, the assumptions may not be completely satisfied. It is common to have at least small shifts in the values of A and B occasionally. It is important to detect these shifts relatively quickly and reflect them in the forecasts. Therefore, practitioners generally prefer a forecasting method that places substantial weight on recent observations and little if any weight on old observations. The exponential smoothing method presented next is designed to provide this kind of approach.

Adapting Exponential Smoothing to This Model

The exponential smoothing method introduced in Sec. 20.4 can be adapted to include the trend factor incorporated into this model. This is done by also using exponential smoothing to estimate this trend factor.

Let

$T_{t+1} =$ exponential smoothing estimate of the trend factor B at time $t + 1$, given the observed values, $X_1 = x_1, X_2 = x_2, \ldots, X_t = x_t$.

Given T_{t+1}, the forecast of the value of the time series at time $t + 1$ (F_{t+1}) is obtained simply by adding T_{t+1} to the formula for F_{t+1} given in Sec. 20.4, so

$$F_{t+1} = \alpha x_t + (1 - \alpha)F_t + T_{t+1}.$$

To motivate the procedure for obtaining T_{t+1}, note that the model assumes that

$$B = E(X_{i+1}) - E(X_i), \qquad \text{for } i = 1, 2, \ldots.$$

Thus, the standard statistical estimator of B would be the *average* of the observed differences, $x_2 - x_1, x_3 - x_2, \ldots, x_t - x_{t-1}$. However, the exponential smoothing approach recognizes that the parameters of the stochastic process generating the time series (including A and B) may actually be gradually shifting over time so that the most recent observations are the most reliable ones for estimating the current parameters. Let

$L_{t+1} =$ latest trend at time $t + 1$ based on the last two values (x_t and x_{t-1}) and the last two forecasts (F_t and F_{t-1}).

The exponential smoothing formula used for L_{t+1} is

$$L_{t+1} = \alpha(x_t - x_{t-1}) + (1 - \alpha)(F_t - F_{t-1}).$$

Then T_{t+1} is calculated as

$$T_{t+1} = \beta L_{t+1} + (1 - \beta)T_t,$$

where β is the **trend smoothing constant** which, like α, must be between 0 and 1. Calculating L_{t+1} and T_{t+1} in order then permits calculating F_{t+1} with the formula given in the preceding paragraph.

Getting started with this forecasting method requires making two initial estimates about the status of the time series just prior to beginning forecasting. These initial estimates are

x_0 = initial estimate of the *expected value* of the time series (A) if the conditions just prior to beginning forecasting were to remain unchanged without any trend;

T_1 = initial estimate of the *trend* of the time series (B) just prior to beginning forecasting.

The resulting forecasts for the first two periods are

$$F_1 = x_0 + T_1,$$
$$L_2 = \alpha(x_1 - x_0) + (1 - \alpha)(F_1 - x_0),$$
$$T_2 = \beta L_2 + (1 - \beta)T_1,$$
$$F_2 = \alpha x_1 + (1 - \alpha)F_1 + T_2.$$

The above formulas for L_{t+1}, T_{t+1}, and F_{t+1} then are used directly to obtain subsequent forecasts.

Since the calculations involved with this method are relatively involved, a computer commonly is used to implement the method. Your OR Courseware includes two Excel templates (one without seasonal adjustments and one with) for this method.

Application of the Method to the CCW Example

Reconsider the example involving the Computer Club Warehouse (CCW) that was introduced in the preceding section. Figure 20.3 shows the time series for this example (representing the average daily call volume quarterly for 3 years) and then Fig. 20.4 gives the seasonally adjusted time series based on the seasonal factors calculated in Table 20.2. We now will assume that these seasonal factors were determined *prior* to these three years of data and that the company then was using *exponential smoothing with trend* to forecast the average daily call volume quarter by quarter over the 3 years based on these data. CCW management has chosen the following initial estimates and smoothing constants:

$$x_0 = 7,500, \qquad T_1 = 0, \qquad \alpha = 0.3, \qquad \beta = 0.3.$$

Working with the seasonally adjusted call volumes given in Fig. 20.4, these initial estimates lead to the following seasonally adjusted forecasts.

Y1, Q1: $F_1 = 7,500 + 0 = 7,500.$
Y1, Q2: $L_2 = 0.3(7,322 - 7,500) + 0.7(7,500 - 7,500) = -53.4.$
$T_2 = 0.3(-53.4) + 0.7(0) = -16.$
$F_2 = 0.3(7,322) + 0.7(7,500) - 16 = 7,431.$

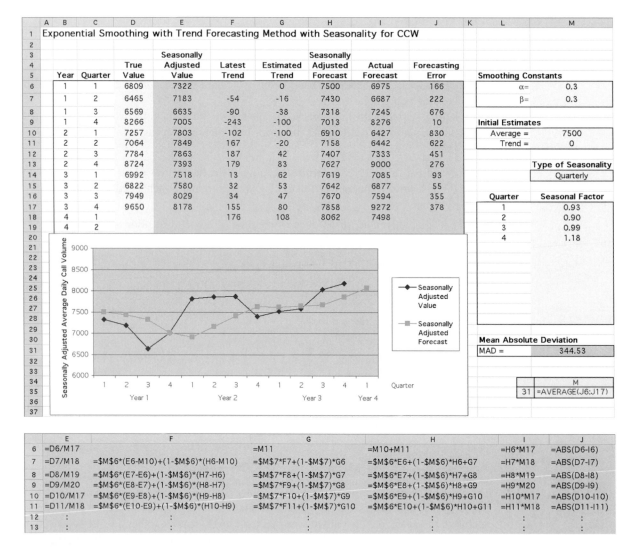

FIGURE 20.5
The Excel template in your OR Courseware for the exponential smoothing with trend method with seasonal adjustments is applied here to the CCW problem.

Y1, Q3: $L_3 = 0.3(7,183 - 7,322) + 0.7(7,431 - 7,500) = -90.$
            $T_3 = 0.3(-90) + 0.7(-16) = -38.2.$
            $F_3 = 0.3(7,183) + 0.7(7,431) - 38.2 = 7,318.$
            $\vdots$

The Excel template in Fig. 20.5 shows the results from these calculations for all 12 quarters over the 3 years, as well as for the upcoming quarter. The middle of the figure shows the plots of all the seasonally adjusted call volumes and seasonally adjusted forecasts. Note how each trend up or down in the call volumes causes the forecasts to gradually trend in the same direction, but then the trend in the forecasts takes a couple of quarters to turn around when the trend in call volumes suddenly reverses direction. Each number in column I is calculated by multiplying the seasonally adjusted forecast in column H by the corresponding seasonal factor in column M to obtain the forecast of the actual value (not seasonally adjusted) for the average daily call volume. Column J then shows the resulting *forecasting errors* (the absolute value of the difference between columns D and I).

Forecasting More Than One Time Period Ahead

We have focused thus far on forecasting what will happen in the *next* time period (the next quarter in the case of CCW). However, decision makers sometimes need to forecast further into the future. How can the various forecasting methods be adapted to do this?

In the case of the methods for a constant-level model presented in Sec. 20.4, the forecast for the next period F_{t+1} also is the best available forecast for subsequent periods as well. However, when there is a *trend* in the data, as we are assuming in this section, it is important to take this trend into account for long-range forecasts. *Exponential smoothing with trend* provides a straightforward way of doing this. In particular, after determining the *estimated trend* T_{t+1}, this method's forecast for n time periods into the future is

$$F_{t+n} = \alpha x_t + (1 - \alpha)F_t + nT_{t+1}.$$

20.7 FORECASTING ERRORS

Several forecasting methods now have been presented. How does one choose the appropriate method for any particular application? Identifying the underlying model that best fits the time series (constant-level, linear trend, etc., perhaps in combination with seasonal effects) is an important first step. Assessing how *stable* the parameters of the model are, and so how much reliance can be placed on older data for forecasting, also helps to narrow down the selection of the method. However, the final choice between two or three methods may still not be clear. Some measure of performance is needed.

The goal is to generate forecasts that are as accurate as possible, so it is natural to base a measure of performance on the *forecasting errors.*

> The **forecasting error** (also called the *residual*) for any period t is the absolute value of the deviation of the forecast for period t (F_t) from what then turns out to be the observed value of the time series for period t (x_t). Thus, letting E_t denote this error,
>
> $$E_t = |x_t - F_t|.$$

For example, column J of the spreadsheet in Fig. 20.5 gives the forecasting errors when applying *exponential smoothing with trend* to the CCW example.

Given the forecasting errors for n time periods ($t = 1, 2, \ldots , n$), two popular measures of performance are available. One, called the **mean absolute deviation (MAD)** is simply the average of the errors, so

$$\text{MAD} = \frac{\sum_{t=1}^{n} E_t}{n}.$$

This is the measure shown in cell M31 of Fig. 20.5. (Most of the Excel templates for this chapter use this measure.) The other measure, called the **mean square error (MSE),** instead averages the *square* of the forecasting errors, so

$$\text{MSE} = \frac{\sum_{t=1}^{n} E_t^2}{n}.$$

The advantages of MAD are its ease of calculation and its straightforward interpretation. However, the advantage of MSE is that it imposes a relatively large penalty for a large forecasting error that can have serious consequences for the organization while almost ignoring inconsequentially small forecasting errors. In practice, managers often prefer to use MAD, whereas statisticians generally prefer MSE.

Either measure of performance might be used in two different ways. One is to compare alternative forecasting methods in order to choose one with which to begin forecasting. This is done by applying the methods *retrospectively* to the time series in the past (assuming such data exist). This is a very useful approach as long as the future behavior of the time series is expected to resemble its past behavior. Similarly, this retrospective testing can be used to help select the parameters for a particular forecasting method, e.g., the smoothing constant(s) for exponential smoothing. Second, after the real forecasting begins with some method, one of the measures of performance (or possibly both) normally would be calculated periodically to monitor how well the method is performing. If the performance is disappointing, the same measure of performance can be calculated for alternative forecasting methods to see if any of them would have performed better.

20.8   BOX-JENKINS METHOD

In practice, a forecasting method often is chosen without adequately checking whether the underlying model is an appropriate one for the application. The beauty of the **Box-Jenkins method** is that it carefully coordinates the model and the procedure. (Practitioners often use this name for the method because it was developed by G.E.P. Box and G.M. Jenkins. An alternative name is the *ARIMA method,* which is an acronym for autoregressive integrated moving average.) This method employs a systematic approach to identifying an appropriate model, chosen from a rich class of models. The historical data are used to test the validity of the model. The model also generates an appropriate forecasting procedure.

To accomplish all this, the Box-Jenkins method requires a great amount of past data (a minimum of 50 time periods), so it is used only for major applications. It also is a sophisticated and complex technique, so we will provide only a conceptual overview of the method. (See Selected References 2 and 6 for further details.)

The Box-Jenkins method is iterative in nature. First, a model is chosen. To choose this model, we must compute autocorrelations and partial autocorrelations and examine their patterns. An *autocorrelation* measures the correlation between time series values separated by a fixed number of periods. This fixed number of periods is called the *lag*. Therefore, the autocorrelation for a lag of two periods measures the correlation between every other observation; i.e., it is the correlation between the original time series and the same series moved forward two periods. The *partial autocorrelation* is a conditional autocorrelation between the original time series and the same series moved forward a fixed number of periods, holding the effect of the other lagged times fixed. Good estimates of both the autocorrelations and the partial autocorrelations for all lags can be obtained by using a computer to calculate the *sample* autocorrelations and the *sample* partial autocorrelations. (These are "good" estimates because we are assuming large amounts of data.)

From the autocorrelations and the partial autocorrelations, we can identify the functional form of one or more possible models because a rich class of models is characterized by these quantities. Next we must estimate the parameters associated with the model by using the historical data. Then we can compute the residuals (the forecasting errors when the forecasting is done retrospectively with the historical data) and examine their behavior. Similarly, we can examine the behavior of the estimated parameters. If both the residuals and the estimated parameters behave as expected under the presumed model, the model appears to be validated. If they do not, then the model should be modified and the procedure repeated until a model is validated. At this point, we can obtain an actual forecast for the next period.

For example, suppose that the sample autocorrelations and the sample partial autocorrelations have the patterns shown in Fig. 20.6. The sample autocorrelations appear to decrease exponentially as a function of the time lags, while the same partial autocorrelations have spikes at the first and second time lags followed by values that seem to be of negligible magnitude. This behavior is characteristic of the functional form

$$X_t = B_0 + B_1 X_{t-1} + B_2 X_{t-2} + e_t.$$

Assuming this functional form, we use the time series data to estimate B_0, B_1, and B_2. Denote these estimates by b_0, b_1, and b_2, respectively. Together with the time series data, we then obtain the residuals

$$x_t - (b_0 + b_1 x_{t-1} + b_2 x_{t-2}).$$

FIGURE 20.6
Plot of sample autocorrelation and partial autocorrelation versus time lags.

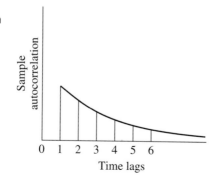

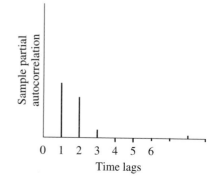

If the assumed functional form is adequate, the residuals and the estimated parameters should behave in a predictable manner. In particular, the sample residuals should behave approximately as independent, normally distributed random variables, each having mean 0 and variance σ^2 (assuming that e_t, the random error at time period t, has mean 0 and variance σ^2). The estimated parameters should be uncorrelated and significantly different from zero. Statistical tests are available for this diagnostic checking.

The Box-Jenkins procedure appears to be a complex one, and it is. Fortunately, computer software is available. The programs calculate the sample autocorrelations and the sample partial autocorrelations necessary for identifying the form of the model. They also estimate the parameters of the model and do the diagnostic checking. These programs, however, cannot accurately identify one or more models that are compatible with the autocorrelations and the partial autocorrelations. Expert human judgment is required. This expertise can be acquired, but it is beyond the scope of this text. Although the Box-Jenkins method is complicated, the resulting forecasts are extremely accurate and, when the time horizon is short, better than most other forecasting methods. Furthermore, the procedure produces a measure of the forecasting error.

20.9 CAUSAL FORECASTING WITH LINEAR REGRESSION

In the preceding six sections, we have focused on *time series forecasting methods,* i.e., methods that forecast the next value in a time series based on its previous values. We now turn to another type of approach to forecasting.

Causal Forecasting

In some cases, the variable to be forecasted has a rather direct relationship with one or more other variables whose values will be known at the time of the forecast. If so, it would make sense to base the forecast on this relationship. This kind of approach is called *causal forecasting.*

> **Causal forecasting** obtains a forecast of the quantity of interest (the *dependent variable*) by relating it directly to one or more other quantities (the *independent* variables) that drive the quantity of interest.

Table 20.3 shows some examples of the kinds of situations where causal forecasting sometimes is used. In each of the first three cases, the indicated dependent variable can be expected to go up or down rather directly with the independent variable(s) listed in the rightmost column. The last case also applies when some quantity of interest (e.g., sales

TABLE 20.3 Possible examples of causal forecasting

Type of Forecasting	Possible Dependent Variable	Possible Independent Variables
Sales	Sales of a product	Amount of advertising
Spare parts	Demand for spare parts	Usage of equipment
Economic trends	Gross domestic product	Various economic factors
Any quantity	This same quantity	Time

of a product) tends to follow a steady trend upward (or downward) with the passage of time (the independent variable that drives the quantity of interest).

As one specific example, Sec. 20.1 includes a description of American Airline's elaborate system for forecasting its need for expensive spare parts (its "rotatable" parts) to continue operating its fleet of several hundred airplanes. This system uses causal forecasting, where the demand for spare parts is the dependent variable and the number of flying hours is the independent variable. This makes sense because the demand for spare parts should be roughly proportional to the number of flying hours for the fleet.

Linear Regression

We will focus on the type of causal forecasting where the mathematical relationship between the dependent variable and the independent variable(s) is assumed to be a linear one (plus some random fluctuations). The analysis in this case is referred to as *linear regression.*

To illustrate the linear regression approach, suppose that a publisher of textbooks is concerned about the initial press run for her books. She sells books both through bookstores and through mail orders. This latter method uses an extensive advertising campaign on line, as well as through publishing media and direct mail. The advertising campaign is conducted prior to the publication of the book. The sales manager has noted that there is a rather interesting linear relationship between the number of mail orders and the number sold through bookstores during the first year. He suggests that this relationship be exploited to determine the initial press run for subsequent books.

Thus, if the number of mail order sales for a book is denoted by X and the number of bookstore sales by Y, then the random variables X and Y exhibit a *degree of association.* However there is *no functional relationship* between these two random variables; i.e., given the number of mail order sales, one does not expect to determine *exactly* the number of bookstore sales. For any given number of mail order sales, there is a range of possible bookstore sales, and vice versa.

What, then, is meant by the statement, "The sales manager has noted that there is a rather interesting linear relationship between the number of mail orders and the number sold through bookstores during the first year"? Such a statement implies that the *expected value* of the number of bookstore sales is linear with respect to the number of mail order sales, i.e.,

$$E[Y\,|\,X = x] = A + Bx.$$

Thus, if the number of mail order sales is x for many different books, the average number of corresponding bookstore sales would tend to be approximately $A + Bx$. This relationship between X and Y is referred to as a **degree of association model.**

As already suggested in Table 20.3, other examples of this degree of association model can easily be found. A college admissions officer may be interested in the relationship between a student's performance on the college entrance examination and subsequent performance in college. An engineer may be interested in the relationship between tensile strength and hardness of a material. An economist may wish to predict a measure of inflation as a function of the cost of living index, and so on.

The degree of association model is not the only model of interest. In some cases, there exists a **functional relationship** between two variables that may be linked linearly.

In a forecasting context, one of the two variables is time, while the other is the variable of interest. In Sec. 20.6, such an example was mentioned in the context of the generating process of the time series being represented by a linear trend superimposed with random fluctuations, i.e.,

$$X_t = A + Bt + e_t,$$

where A is a constant, B is the slope, and e_t is the random error, assumed to have expected value equal to zero and constant variance. (The symbol X_t can also be read as X given t or as $X \mid t$.) It follows that

$$E(X_t) = A + Bt.$$

Note that both the degree of association model and the *exact functional relationship* model lead to the same linear relationship, and their subsequent treatment is almost identical. Hence, the publishing example will be explored further to illustrate how to treat both kinds of models, although the special structure of the model

$$E(X_t) = A + Bt,$$

with t taking on integer values starting with 1, leads to certain simplified expressions. In the standard notation of regression analysis, X represents the **independent variable** and Y represents the **dependent variable** of interest. Consequently, the notational expression for this special time series model now becomes

$$Y_t = A + Bt + e_t.$$

Method of Least Squares

Suppose that bookstore sales and mail order sales are given for 15 books. These data appear in Table 20.4, and the resulting plot is given in Fig. 20.7.

TABLE 20.4 Data for the mail-order and bookstore sales example

Mail-Order Sales	Bookstore Sales
1,310	4,360
1,313	4,590
1,320	4,520
1,322	4,770
1,338	4,760
1,340	5,070
1,347	5,230
1,355	5,080
1,360	5,550
1,364	5,390
1,373	5,670
1,376	5,490
1,384	5,810
1,395	6,060
1,400	5,940

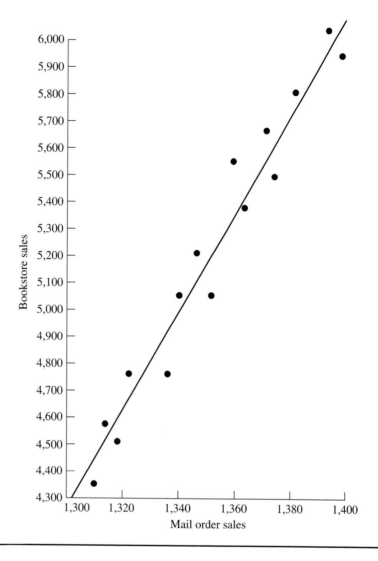

FIGURE 20.7
Plot of mail order sales
versus bookstore sales from
Table 20.3.

It is evident that the points in Fig. 20.7 do not lie on a straight line. Hence, it is not clear where the line should be drawn to show the linear relationship. Suppose that an arbitrary line, given by the expression $\tilde{y} = a + bx$, is drawn through the data. A measure of how well this line fits the data can be obtained by computing the *sum of squares* of the vertical deviations of the actual points from the fitted line. Thus, let y_i represent the bookstore sales of the ith book and x_i the corresponding mail order sales. Denote by $\tilde{y}_i$ the point on the fitted line corresponding to the mail order sales of x_i. The proposed measure of fit is then given by

$$Q = (y_1 - \tilde{y}_1)^2 + (y_2 - \tilde{y}_2)^2 + \cdots + (y_{15} - \tilde{y}_{15})^2 = \sum_{i=1}^{15} (y_i - \tilde{y}_i)^2.$$

The usual method for identifying the "best" fitted line is the **method of least squares**. This method chooses that line $a + bx$ that makes Q a minimum. Thus, a and b are obtained simply by setting the partial derivatives of Q with respect to a and b equal to zero and solving the resulting equations. This method yields the solution

$$b = \frac{\sum_{i=1}^{n}(x_i - \bar{x})(y_i - \bar{y})}{\sum_{i=1}^{n}(x_i - \bar{x})^2} = \frac{\sum_{i=1}^{n} x_i y_i - \left(\sum_{i=1}^{n} x_i \sum_{i=1}^{n} y_i\right)\Big/ n}{\sum_{i=1}^{n} x_i^2 - \left(\sum_{i=1}^{n} x_i\right)^2 \Big/ n}$$

and

$$a = \bar{y} - b\bar{x},$$

where

$$\bar{x} = \sum_{i=1}^{n} \frac{x_i}{n}$$

and

$$\bar{y} = \sum_{i=1}^{n} \frac{y_i}{n}.$$

(Note that $\bar{y}$ is not the same as $\tilde{y} = a + bx$ discussed in the preceding paragraph.)

For the publishing example, the data in Table 20.4 and Fig. 20.7 yield

$$\bar{x} = 1,353.1,$$
$$\bar{y} = 5,219.3,$$

$$\sum_{i=1}^{15}(x_i - \bar{x})(y_i - \bar{y}) = 214,543.9,$$

$$\sum_{i=1}^{15}(x_i - \bar{x})^2 = 11,966,$$

$$a = -19,041.9,$$
$$b = 17.930.$$

Hence, the least-squares estimate of bookstore sales $\tilde{y}$ with mail order sales x is given by

$$\tilde{y} = -19,041.9 + 17.930x,$$

and this is the line drawn in Fig. 20.7. Such a line is referred to as a **regression line.**

An Excel template called Linear Regression is available in your OR Courseware for calculating a regression line in this way.

This regression line is useful for forecasting purposes. For a given value of x, the corresponding value of y represents the forecast.

The decision maker may be interested in some measure of uncertainty that is associated with this forecast. This measure is easily obtained provided that certain assumptions can be made. Therefore, for the remainder of this section, it is assumed that

1. A random sample of n pairs (x_1, Y_1), (x_2, Y_2), . . . , (x_n, Y_n) is to be taken.
2. The Y_i are normally distributed with mean $A + Bx_i$ and variance σ^2 (independent of i).

The assumption that Y_i is normally distributed is not a critical assumption in determining the uncertainty in the forecast, but the assumption of constant variance is crucial. Furthermore, an estimate of this variance is required.

An unbiased estimate of σ^2 is given by $s^2_{y\,|\,x}$, where

$$s^2_{y\,|\,x} = \sum_{i=1}^{n} \frac{(y_i - \tilde{y}_i)^2}{n - 2}.$$

Confidence Interval Estimation of $E(Y\,|\,x = x^*)$

A very important reason for obtaining the linear relationship between two variables is to use the line for future decision making. From the regression line, it is possible to estimate $E(Y\,|\,x)$ by a *point* estimate (the forecast) and a *confidence interval* estimate (a measure of forecast uncertainty).

For example, the publisher might want to use this approach to estimate the expected number of bookstore sales corresponding to mail order sales of, say, 1,400, by both a point estimate and a confidence interval estimate for forecasting purposes.

A point estimate of $E(Y\,|\,x = x^*)$ is given by

$$\tilde{y}^* = a + bx^*,$$

where x^* denotes the given value of the independent variable and $\tilde{y}^*$ is the corresponding point estimate.

The endpoints of a $(100)(1 - \alpha)$ percent confidence interval for $E(Y\,|\,x = x^*)$ are given by

$$a + bx^* - t_{\alpha/2;n-2}s_{y\,|\,x}\sqrt{\frac{1}{n} + \frac{(x^* - \bar{x})^2}{\displaystyle\sum_{i=1}^{n}(x_i - \bar{x})^2}}$$

and

$$a + bx^* + t_{\alpha/2;n-2}s_{y\,|\,x}\sqrt{\frac{1}{n} + \frac{(x^* - \bar{x})^2}{\displaystyle\sum_{i=1}^{n}(x_i - \bar{x})^2}},$$

where $s^2_{y\,|\,x}$ is the estimate of σ^2, and $t_{\alpha/2;n-2}$ is the $100\alpha/2$ percentage point of the t distribution with $n - 2$ degrees of freedom (see Table A5.2 of Appendix 5). Note that the interval is narrowest where $x^* = \bar{x}$, and it becomes wider as x^* departs from the mean.

In the publishing example with $x^* = 1,400$, $s^2_{y\,|\,x}$ is computed from the data in Table 20.4 to be 17,030, so $s_{y\,|\,x} = 130.5$. If a 95 percent confidence interval is required, Table A5.2 gives $t_{0.025;13} = 2.160$. The earlier calculation of a and b yields

$$a + bx^* = -19,041.9 + 17.930(1,400) = 6,060$$

as the point estimate of $E(Y|1,400)$, that is, the forecast. Consequentially, the confidence limits corresponding to mail order sales of 1,400 are

$$\text{Lower confidence limit} = 6,060 - 2.160(130.5)\sqrt{\frac{1}{15} + \frac{46.9^2}{11,966}}$$

$$= 5,919,$$

$$\text{Upper confidence limit} = 6,060 + 2.160(130.5)\sqrt{\frac{1}{15} + \frac{46.9^2}{11,966}}$$

$$= 6,201.$$

The fact that the confidence interval was obtained at a data point ($x = 1,400$) is purely coincidental.

The Excel template for linear regression in your OR Courseware does most of the computational work involved in calculating these confidence limits. In addition to computing a and b (the regression line), it calculates $s_{y\,|\,x}^2$, $\bar{x}$, and $\sum_{i=1}^{n}(x_i - \bar{x})^2$.

Predictions

The confidence interval statement for the expected number of bookstore sales corresponding to mail order sales of 1,400 may be useful for budgeting purposes, but it is not too useful for making decisions about the *actual* press run. Instead of obtaining bounds on the *expected* number of bookstore sales, this kind of decision requires bounds on what the *actual* bookstore sales will be, i.e., a **prediction interval** on the value that the random variable (bookstore sales) takes on. This measure is a *different* measure of forecast uncertainty.

The two endpoints of a prediction interval are given by the expressions

$$a + bx_+ - t_{\alpha/2;n-2}s_{y\,|\,x}\sqrt{1 + \frac{1}{n} + \frac{(x_+ - \bar{x})^2}{\sum_{i=1}^{n}(x_i - \bar{x})^2}}$$

and

$$a + bx_+ + t_{\alpha/2;n-2}s_{y\,|\,x}\sqrt{1 + \frac{1}{n} + \frac{(x_+ - \bar{x})^2}{\sum_{i=1}^{n}(x_i - \bar{x})^2}}$$

For any given value of x (denoted here by x_+), the probability is $1 - \alpha$ that the value of the future Y_+ associated with x_+ will fall in this interval.

Thus, in the publishing example, if x_+ is 1,400, then the corresponding 95 percent prediction interval for the number of bookstore sales is given by $6,060 \pm 315$, which is naturally wider than the confidence interval for the expected number of bookstore sales, $6,060 \pm 141$.

This method of finding a prediction interval works fine if it is only being done once. However, it is not feasible to use the same data to find multiple prediction intervals with various values of x_+ in this way and then specify a probability that *all* these predictions will be correct. For example, suppose that the publisher wants prediction intervals for several different books. For each individual book, she still is able to use these expressions to find the prediction interval and then make the prediction that the bookstore sales will be within this interval, where the probability is $1 - \alpha$ that the prediction will be correct. However, what she cannot do is specify a probability that *all* these predictions will be correct. The reason is that these predictions are all based upon the same statistical data, so the predictions are not statistically independent. *If* the predictions were independent and if k future bookstore sales were being predicted, with each prediction being made with probability $1 - \alpha$, then the probability would be $(1 - \alpha)^k$ that *all* k predictions of future bookstore sales will be correct. Unfortunately, the predictions are *not* independent, so the actual probability cannot be calculated, and $(1 - \alpha)^k$ does not even provide a reasonable approximation.

This difficulty can be overcome by using **simultaneous tolerance intervals.** Using this technique, the publisher can take the mail order sales of any book, find an interval (based on the previously determined linear regression line) that will contain the actual bookstore sales with probability at least $1 - \alpha$, and repeat this for any number of books having the same or different mail order sales. Furthermore, the probability is P that *all* these predictions will be correct. An alternative interpretation is as follows. If every publisher followed this procedure, each using his or her own linear regression line, then $100P$ percent of the publishers (on average) would find that at least $100(1 - \alpha)$ percent of their bookstore sales fell into the predicted intervals. The expression for the endpoints of each such tolerance interval is given by

$$a + bx_+ - c^{**}s_{y|x}\sqrt{\frac{1}{n} + \frac{(x_+ - \bar{x})^2}{\sum\limits_{i=1}^{n}(x_i - \bar{x})^2}}$$

and

$$a + bx_+ + c^{**}s_{y|x}\sqrt{\frac{1}{n} + \frac{(x_+ - \bar{x})^2}{\sum\limits_{i=1}^{n}(x_i - \bar{x})^2}},$$

where c^{**} is given in Table 20.5.

Thus, the publisher can predict that the bookstore sales corresponding to known mail order sales will fall in these tolerance intervals. Such statements can be made for as many books as the publisher desires. Furthermore, the probability is P that at least $100(1 - \alpha)$ percent of bookstore sales corresponding to mail order sales will fall in these intervals. If P is chosen as 0.90 and $\alpha = 0.05$, the appropriate value of c^{**} is 11.625. Hence, the number of bookstore sales corresponding to mail order sales of 1,400 books is predicted to fall in the interval $6,060 \pm 759$. If another book had mail order sales of 1,353, the bookstore sales are predicted to fall in the interval $5,258 \pm 390$, and so on. At least 95 percent of the bookstore sales will fall into their predicted intervals, and these statements are made with confidence 0.90.

To summarize, we now have described three *measures of forecast uncertainty.* The first (in the preceding subsection) is a *confidence interval* on the *expected value* of the random variable Y (for example, bookstore sales) given the observed value x of the independent variable X (for example, mail order sales). The second is a *prediction interval* on

TABLE 20.5 Values of c^{**}

n	$\alpha = 0.50$	$\alpha = 0.25$	$\alpha = 0.10$	$\alpha = 0.05$	$\alpha = 0.01$	$\alpha = 0.001$
			$P = 0.90$			
4	7.471	10.160	13.069	14.953	18.663	23.003
6	5.380	7.453	9.698	11.150	14.014	17.363
8	5.037	7.082	9.292	10.722	13.543	16.837
10	4.983	7.093	9.366	10.836	13.733	17.118
12	5.023	7.221	9.586	11.112	14.121	17.634
14	5.101	7.394	9.857	11.447	14.577	18.232
16	5.197	7.586	10.150	11.803	15.057	18.856
18	5.300	7.786	10.449	12.165	15.542	19.484
20	5.408	7.987	10.747	12.526	16.023	20.140
			$P = 0.95$			
4	10.756	14.597	18.751	21.445	26.760	32.982
6	6.652	9.166	11.899	13.669	17.167	21.266
8	5.933	8.281	10.831	12.484	·15.750	19.568
10	5.728	8.080	10.632	12.286	15.553	19.369
12	5.684	8.093	10.701	12.391	15.724	19.619
14	5.711	8.194	10.880	12.617	16.045	20.050
16	5.771	8.337	11.107	12.898	16.431	20.559
18	5.848	8.499	11.357	13.204	16.845	21.097
20	5.937	8.672	11.619	13.521	17.272	21.652
			$P = 0.99$			
4	24.466	33.019	42.398	48.620	60.500	74.642
6	10.444	14.285	18.483	21.215	26.606	32.920
8	8.290	11.453	14.918	17.166	21.652	26.860
10	7.567	10.539	13.796	15.911	20.097	24.997
12	7.258	10.182	13.383	15.479	19.579	24.403
14	7.127	10.063	13.267	15.355	19.485	24.316
16	7.079	10.055	13.306	15.410	19.582	24.467
18	7.074	10.111	13.404	15.552	19.794	24.746
20	7.108	10.198	13.566	15.745	20.065	25.122

Source: Reprinted by permission from G. J. Lieberman and R. G. Miller, "Simultaneous Tolerance Intervals in Regression," *Biometrika*, **50**(1 and 2): 164, 1963.

the *actual value* that Y will take on, given x. The third is *simultaneous tolerance intervals* on a *succession* of *actual values* that Y will take on given a succession of observed values of X.

20.10 FORECASTING IN PRACTICE

You now have seen the major forecasting methods used in practice. We conclude with a brief look at how widely the various methods are used.

To begin, consider the actual forecasting applications discussed in Sec. 20.1 and summarized in Table 20.1 there. Most of this table is repeated here in Table 20.6, but the right-

TABLE 20.6 The forecasting methods used in the actual applications presented in Section 20.1

Organization	Quantity Being Forecasted	Forecasting Model
Merit Brass Co.	Sales of finished goods	Exponential smoothing
Hidroeléctrica Español	Energy demand	ARIMA (Box-Jenkins), etc.
American Airlines	Demand for different fare classes	Exponential smoothing
American Airlines	Need for spare parts to repair airplanes	Linear regression
Albuquerque Microelectronics	Production yield in wafer fabrication	Exponential smoothing with a linear trend
U.S. Department of Labor	Unemployment insurance payments	Linear regression
United Airlines	Demand at reservation offices and airports	ARIMA (Box-Jenkins)
L.L. Bean	Staffing needs at call center	ARIMA (Box-Jenkins)

most column now identifies which forecasting method was used in each application. Not surprisingly, these major forecasting projects chose one of the more sophisticated statistical forecasting methods. (The most sophisticated is the ARIMA method, commonly called the Box-Jenkins method, that is described in Sec. 20.8.)

Every company needs to do at least some forecasting, but their methods often are not as sophisticated as with these major projects. Some insight into their general approach was provided by a survey conducted a few years ago[1] of sales forecasting practices at 500 U.S. corporations.

This survey indicates that, generally speaking, judgmental forecasting methods are somewhat more widely used than statistical methods. The main reasons given for using judgmental methods were accuracy and difficulty in obtaining the data required for statistical methods. Comments also were made that upper management is not familiar with quantitative techniques, that judgmental methods create a sense of ownership, and that these methods add a commonsense element to the forecast.

Among the judgmental methods, the most popular is a jury of executive opinion. This is especially true for companywide or industry sales forecasts but also holds true by a small margin over manager's opinion when forecasting sales of individual products or families of products.

Statistical forecasting methods also are fairly widely used, especially in companies with high sales. Compared to earlier surveys, familiarity with such methods is increasing. However, many survey respondents cited better data availability as the improvement they most wanted to see in their organizations. The availability of good data is crucial for the use of these methods.

The survey indicates that the moving-average method and linear regression are the most widely used statistical forecasting methods. The moving-average method is more popular for short- and medium-range forecasts (less than a year), as well as for forecasting sales of individual products and families of products. Linear regression is more popular for longer-range forecasts and for forecasting either companywide or industry sales. Both exponential smoothing and the last-value method also receive considerable use. However, the highest dissatisfaction is with the last-value method, and its popularity is decreasing compared to earlier surveys.

When statistical forecasting methods are used, it is fairly common to also use judgmental methods to adjust the forecasts.

[1]N. R. Sanders and K. B. Manrodt, "Forecasting Practices in U.S. Corporations: Survey Results," *Interfaces*, **24:** 92–100, March–April 1994.

As managers become more familiar with statistical methods, and more used to using the computer to compile data and implement OR techniques, we anticipate a continuing increase in the usage of statistical forecasting methods. However, there always will be an important role for judgmental methods, both alone and in combination with statistical methods.

20.11   CONCLUSIONS

The future success of any business depends heavily on the ability of its management to forecast well. Judgmental forecasting methods often play an important role in this process. However, the ability to forecast well is greatly enhanced if historical data are available to help guide the development of a statistical forecasting method. By studying these data, an appropriate model can be structured. A forecasting method that behaves well under the model should be selected. This method may require choosing one or more parameters— e.g., the smoothing constant α in exponential smoothing—and the historical data may prove useful in making this choice. After forecasting begins, the performance should be monitored carefully to assess whether modifications should be made in the method.

SELECTED REFERENCES

1. Armstrong, J. E. (ed.): *Handbook of Forecasting Principles,* Kluwer Academic Publishers, Boston, 2001.
2. Box, G. E. P., and G. M. Jenkins: *Time Series Analysis, Forecasting and Control,* Holden-Day, San Francisco, 1976.
3. Bunn, D., and G. Wright: "Interaction of Judgmental and Statistical Methods: Issues and Analysis," *Management Science,* **37:** 501–518, 1991.
4. Gardner, E. S., Jr.: "Exponential Smoothing: The State of the Art," *Journal of Forecasting,* **4:** 1–38, 1985.
5. Hillier, F. S., M. S. Hillier, and G. J. Lieberman: *Introduction to Management Science: A Modeling and Case Studies Approach with Spreadsheets,* Irwin/McGraw-Hill, Burr Ridge, IL, 2000, chap. 13.
6. Hoff, J. C.: *A Practical Guide to Box-Jenkins Forecasting,* Lifetime Learning Publications, Belmont, CA, 1983.
7. Marshall, K. T., and R. M. Oliver: *Decision Making and Forecasting,* McGraw-Hill, New York, 1995.
8. Sanders, N. R., and K. B. Manrodt: "Forecasting Practices in U.S. Corporations: Survey Results," *Interfaces,* **24**(2): 92–100, March–April 1994.
9. Rust, R. T., D. Simester, R. J. Brodie, and V. Nilikant: "Model Selection Criteria: An Investigation of Relative Accuracy, Posterior Probabilities, and Combinations of Criteria," *Management Science,* **41:** 322–333, 1995.
10. Yurkiewicz, J.: "Forecasting Software Survey," *OR/MS Today,* Dec. 1996, pp. 70–75.

LEARNING AIDS FOR THIS CHAPTER IN YOUR OR COURSEWARE

"Ch. 20—Forecasting" Excel File:

Template for *Seasonal Factors*
Templates for *Last-Value* Method (with and without Seasonality)

Templates for *Averaging* Method (with and without Seasonality)
Templates for *Moving-Average* Method (with and without Seasonality)
Templates for *Exponential Smoothing* Method (with and without Seasonality)
Templates for *Exponential Smoothing with Trend* (with and without Seasonality)
Template for *Linear Regression*

"Ch. 20—Forecasting" LINGO File for Selected Examples

PROBLEMS

To the left of each of the following problems (or their parts), we have inserted a T whenever the corresponding template listed above can be helpful. An asterisk on the problem number indicates that at least a partial answer is given in the back of the book.

20.1-1. Select one of the applications of statistical forecasting methods listed in Table 20.1. Read the article describing the application in the indicated issue of *Interfaces*. Write a two-page summary of the application and the benefits it provided.

20.1-2. Select three of the applications of statistical forecasting methods listed in Table 20.1. Read the articles describing the applications in the indicated issues of *Interfaces*. For each one, write a one-page summary of the application and the benefits it provided.

20.4-1.* The Hammaker Company's newest product has had the following sales during its first five months: 5 17 29 41 39. The sales manager now wants a forecast of sales in the next month. (Use hand calculations rather than an Excel template.)
(a) Use the last-value method.
(b) Use the averaging method.
(c) Use the moving-average method with the 3 most recent months.
(d) Given the sales pattern so far, do any of these methods seem inappropriate for obtaining the forecast? Why?

20.4-2. Sales of stoves have been going well for the Good-Value Department Store. These sales for the past five months have been 15 18 12 17 13. Use the following methods to obtain a forecast of sales for the next month. (Use hand calculations rather than an Excel template.)
(a) The last-value method.
(b) The averaging method.
(c) The moving-average method with 3 months.
(d) If you feel that the conditions affecting sales next month will be the same as in the last five months, which of these methods do you prefer for obtaining the forecast? Why?

20.4-3.* You are using the moving-average forecasting method based upon the last four observations. When making the forecast for the last period, the oldest of the four observations was 1,945 and the forecast was 2,083. The true value for the last period then turned out to be 1,977. What is your new forecast for the next period?

20.4-4. You are using the moving-average forecasting method based upon sales in the last three months to forecast sales for the next month. When making the forecast for last month, sales for the third month before were 805. The forecast for last month was 782 and then the actual sales turned out to be 793. What is your new forecast for next month?

20.4-5. After graduating from college with a degree in mathematical statistics, Ann Preston has been hired by the Monty Ward Company to apply statistical methods for forecasting the company's sales. For one of the company's products, the moving-average method based upon sales in the 10 most recent months already is being used. Ann's first task is to update last month's forecast to obtain the forecast for next month. She learns that the forecast for last month was 1,551 and that the actual sales then turned out to be 1,532. She also learns that the sales for the tenth month before last month was 1,632. What is Ann's forecast for next month?

20.4-6. The J.J. Bone Company uses exponential smoothing to forecast the average daily call volume at its call center. The forecast for last month was 782, and then the actual value turned out to be 792. Obtain the forecast for next month for each of the following values of the smoothing constant: $\alpha = 0.1, 0.3, 0.5$.

20.4-7.* You are using exponential smoothing to obtain monthly forecasts of the sales of a certain product. The forecast for last month was 2,083, and then the actual sales turned out to be 1,973. Obtain the forecast for next month for each of the following values of the smoothing constant: $\alpha = 0.1, 0.3, 0.5$.

20.4-8. If α is set equal to 0 or 1 in the exponential smoothing expression, what happens to the forecast?

20.4-9. A company uses exponential smoothing with $\alpha = \frac{1}{2}$ to forecast demand for a product. For each month, the company keeps a record of the forecast demand (made at the end of the preceding month) and the actual demand. Some of the records have been lost; the remaining data appear in the table below.

	January	February	March	April	May	June
Forecast			400	380	390	380
Actual	400		360	—	—	

(a) Using only data in the table for March, April, May, and June, determine the actual demands in April and May.
(b) Suppose now that a clerical error is discovered; the actual demand in January was 432, not 400, as shown in the table. Using only the actual demands going back to January (even though the February actual demand is unknown), give the corrected forecast for June.

20.5-1. Figure 20.3 shows CCW's average daily call volume for each quarter of the past three years, and column F of Fig. 20.4 gives the seasonally adjusted call volumes. Management now wonders what these seasonally adjusted call volumes would have been if the company had started using seasonal factors two years ago rather than applying them retrospectively now. (Use hand calculations rather than an Excel template.)
(a) Use only the call volumes in Year 1 to determine the seasonal factors for Year 2 (so that the "average" call volume for each quarter is just the actual call volume for that quarter in Year 1).
(b) Use these seasonal factors to determine the seasonally adjusted call volumes for Year 2.
(c) Use the call volumes in Year 1 and 2 to determine the seasonal factors for Year 3.
(d) Use the seasonal factors obtained in part (c) to determine the seasonally adjusted call volumes for Year 3.

20.5-2. Even when the economy is holding steady, the unemployment rate tends to fluctuate because of seasonal effects. For example, unemployment generally goes up in Quarter 3 (summer) as students (including new graduates) enter the labor market. The unemployment rate then tends to go down in Quarter 4 (fall) as students return to school and temporary help is hired for the Christmas season. Therefore, using seasonal factors to obtain a seasonally adjusted unemployment rate is helpful for painting a truer picture of economic trends.
    Over the past 10 years, one state's average unemployment rates (not seasonally adjusted) in Quarters 1, 2, 3, and 4 have been 6.2 percent, 6.0 percent, 7.5 percent, and 5.5 percent, respectively. The overall average has been 6.3 percent. (Use hand calculations below rather than an Excel template.)
(a) Determine the seasonal factors for the four quarters.

(b) Over the next year, the unemployment rates (not seasonally adjusted) for the four quarters turn out to be 7.8 percent, 7.4 percent, 8.7 percent, and 6.1 percent. Determine the seasonally adjusted unemployment rates for the four quarters. What does this progression of rates suggest about whether the state's economy is improving?

20.5-3. Ralph Billett is the manager of a real estate agency. He now wishes to develop a forecast of the number of houses that will be sold by the agency over the next year.
    The agency's quarter-by-quarter sales figures over the last three years are shown below.

Quarter	Year 1	Year 2	Year 3
1	23	19	21
2	22	21	26
3	31	27	32
4	26	24	28

(Use hand calculations below rather than an Excel template.)
(a) Determine the seasonal factors for the four quarters.
(b) After considering seasonal effects, use the last-value method to forecast sales in Quarter 1 of next year.
(c) Assuming that each of the quarterly forecasts is correct, what would the last-value method forecast as the sales in each of the four quarters next year?
(d) Based on his assessment of the current state of the housing market, Ralph's best judgment is that the agency will sell 100 houses next year. Given this forecast for the year, what is the quarter-by-quarter forecast according to the seasonal factors?

20.5-4. A manufacturer sells a certain product in batches of 100 to wholesalers. The following table shows the quarterly sales figure for this product over the last several years.

Quarter of 1996	Sales	Quarter of 1997	Sales	Quarter of 1998	Sales	Quarter of 1999	Sales	Quarter of 2000	Sales
1	6,900	1	8,200	1	9,400	1	11,400	1	8,800
2	6,700	2	7,000	2	9,200	2	10,000	2	7,600
3	7,900	3	7,300	3	9,800	3	9,400	3	7,500
4	7,100	4	7,500	4	9,900	4	8,400	4	—

The company incorporates seasonal effects into its forecasting of future sales. It then uses exponential smoothing (with seasonality) with a smoothing constant of $\alpha = 0.1$ to make these forecasts. When starting the forecasting, it uses the average sales over the past four quarters to make the initial estimate of the seasonally adjusted constant level A for the underlying constant-level model.

T **(a)** Suppose that the forecasting started at the beginning of 1997. Use the data for 1996 to determine the seasonal factors and then determine the forecast of sales for each quarter of 1997.

T **(b)** Suppose that the forecasting started at the beginning of 1998. Use the data for both 1996 and 1997 to determine the seasonal factors and then determine the forecast of sales for each quarter of 1998.

T **(c)** Suppose that the forecasting started at the beginning of 2000. Use the data for 1996 through 1999 to determine the seasonal factors and then determine the forecast of sales for each quarter of 2000.

(d) Under the assumptions of the constant-level model, the forecast obtained for any period of one year also provides the best available forecast at that time for the same period in any subsequent year. Use the results from parts (a), (b), and (c) to record the forecast of sales for Quarter 4 of 2000 when entering Quarter 4 of 1997, 1998, and 2000, respectively.

(e) Evaluate whether it is important to incorporate seasonal effects into the forecasting procedure for this particular product.

(f) Evaluate how well the constant-level assumption of the constant-level model (after incorporating seasonal effects) appears to hold for this particular product.

20.6-1. Look ahead at the scenario described in Prob. 20.7-3. Notice the steady trend upward in the number of applications over the past three years—from 4,600 to 5,300 to 6,000. Suppose now that the admissions office of Ivy College had been able to foresee this kind of trend and so had decided to use exponential smoothing with trend to do the forecasting. Suppose also that the initial estimates just over three years ago had been *expected value* = 3,900 and *trend* = 700. Then, with any values of the smoothing constants, the forecasts obtained by this forecasting method would have been exactly correct for all three years.

Illustrate this fact by doing the calculations to obtain these forecasts when the smoothing constant is $\alpha = 0.25$ and the trend smoothing constant is $\beta = 0.25$. (Use hand calculations rather than an Excel template.)

20.6-2.* Exponential smoothing with trend, with a smoothing constant of $\alpha = 0.2$ and a trend smoothing constant of $\beta = 0.3$, is being used to forecast values in a time series. At this point, the last two values have been 535 and then 550. The last two forecasts have been 530 and then 540. The last estimate of the trend factor has been 10. Use this information to forecast the next value in the time series. (Use hand calculations rather than an Excel template.)

20.6-3. The Healthwise Company produces a variety of exercise equipment. Healthwise management is very pleased with the increasing sales of its newest model of exercise bicycle. The sales during the last two months have been 4,655 and then 4,935.

Management has been using exponential smoothing with trend, with a smoothing constant of $\alpha = 0.1$ and a trend smooth-

ing constant of $\beta = 0.2$, to forecast sales for the next month each time. The forecasts for the last two months were 4,720 and then 4,975. The last estimate of the trend factor was 240.

Calculate the forecast of sales for next month. (Use hand calculations rather than an Excel template.)

T **20.6-4.*** The Pentel Microchip Company has started production of its new microchip. The first phase in this production is the wafer fabrication process. Because of the great difficulty in fabricating acceptable wafers, many of these tiny wafers must be rejected because they are defective. Therefore, management places great emphasis on continually improving the wafer fabrication process to increase its *production yield* (the percentage of wafers fabricated in the current lot that are of acceptable quality for producing microchips).

So far, the production yields of the respective lots have been 15, 21, 24, 32, 37, 41, 40, 47, 51, 53 percent. Use exponential smoothing with trend to forecast the production yield of the next lot. Begin with initial estimates of 10 percent for the expected value and 5 percent for the trend. Use smoothing constants of $\alpha = 0.2$ and $\beta = 0.2$.

20.7-1.* You have been forecasting sales the last four quarters. These forecasts and the true values that subsequently were obtained are shown below.

Quarter	Forecast	True Value
1	327	345
2	332	317
3	328	336
4	330	311

(a) Calculate MAD.
(b) Calculate MSE.

20.7-2. Sharon Johnson, sales manager for the Alvarez-Baines Company, is trying to choose between two methods for forecasting sales that she has been using during the past five months. During these months, the two methods obtained the forecasts shown below for the company's most important product, where the subsequent actual sales are shown on the right.

Month	Forecast Method 1	Forecast Method 2	Actual Sales
1	5,324	5,208	5,582
2	5,405	5,377	4,906
3	5,195	5,462	5,755
4	5,511	5,414	6,320
5	5,762	5,549	5,153

(a) Calculate and compare MAD for these two forecasting methods.

(b) Calculate and compare MSE for these two forecasting methods.

(c) Sharon is uncomfortable with choosing between these two methods based on such limited data, but she also does not want to delay further before making her choice. She does have similar sales data for the three years prior to using these forecasting methods the past five months. How can these older data be used to further help her evaluate the two methods and choose one?

20.7-3. Three years ago, the admissions office for Ivy College began using exponential smoothing with a smoothing constant of 0.25 to forecast the number of applications for admission each year. Based on previous experience, this process was begun with an initial estimate of 5,000 applications. The actual number of applications then turned out to be 4,600 in the first year. Thanks to new favorable ratings in national surveys, this number grew to 5,300 in the second year and 6,000 last year. (Use hand calculations below rather than an Excel template.)

(a) Determine the forecasts that were made for each of the past three years.

(b) Calculate MAD for these three years.

(c) Calculate MSE for these three years.

(d) Determine the forecast for next year.

20.7-4.* Ben Swanson, owner and manager of Swanson's Department Store, has decided to use statistical forecasting to get a better handle on the demand for his major products. However, Ben now needs to decide which forecasting method is most appropriate for each category of product. One category is major household appliances, such as washing machines, which have a relatively stable sales level. Monthly sales of washing machines last year are shown below.

Month	Sales	Month	Sales	Month	Sales
January	23	May	22	September	21
February	24	June	27	October	29
March	22	July	20	November	23
April	28	August	26	December	28

(a) Considering that the sales level is relatively stable, which of the most basic forecasting methods—the last-value method or the averaging method or the moving-average method—do you feel would be most appropriate for forecasting future sales? Why?

T **(b)** Use the last-value method retrospectively to determine what the forecasts would have been for the last 11 months of last year. What is MAD?

T **(c)** Use the averaging method retrospectively to determine what the forecasts would have been for the last 11 months of last year. What is MAD?

T **(d)** Use the moving-average method with $n = 3$ retrospectively to determine what the forecasts would have been for the last 9 months of last year. What is MAD?

(e) Use their MAD values to compare the three methods.

(f) Do you feel comfortable in drawing a definitive conclusion about which of the three forecasting methods should be the most accurate in the future based on these 12 months of data?

T **20.7-5.** Reconsider Prob. 20.7-4. Ben Swanson now has decided to use the exponential smoothing method to forecast future sales of washing machines, but he needs to decide on which smoothing constant to use. Using an initial estimate of 24, apply this method retrospectively to the 12 months of last year with $\alpha = 0.1, 0.2, 0.3, 0.4,$ and 0.5.

(a) Compare MAD for these five values of the smoothing constant α.

(b) Calculate and compare MSE for these five values of α.

20.7-6. Management of the Jackson Manufacturing Corporation wishes to choose a statistical forecasting method for forecasting total sales for the corporation. Total sales (in millions of dollars) for each month of last year are shown below.

Month	Sales	Month	Sales	Month	Sales
January	126	May	153	September	147
February	137	June	154	October	151
March	142	July	148	November	159
April	150	August	145	December	166

(a) Note how the sales level is shifting significantly from month to month—first trending upward and then dipping down before resuming an upward trend. Assuming that similar patterns would continue in the future, evaluate how well you feel each of the five forecasting methods introduced in Secs. 20.4 and 20.6 would perform in forecasting future sales.

T **(b)** Apply the last-value method, the averaging method, and the moving-average method (with $n = 3$) retrospectively to last year's sales and compare their MAD values.

T **(c)** Using an initial estimate of 120, apply the exponential smoothing method retrospectively to last year's sales with $\alpha = 0.1, 0.2, 0.3, 0.4,$ and 0.5. Compare MAD for these five values of the smoothing constant α.

T **(d)** Using initial estimates of 120 for the expected value and 10 for the trend, apply exponential smoothing with trend retrospectively to last year's sales. Use all combinations of the smoothing constants where $\alpha = 0.1$ or 0.3 or 0.5 and $\beta = 0.1$ or 0.3 or 0.5. Compare MAD for these nine combinations.

(e) Which one of the above forecasting methods would you recommend that management use? Using this method, what is the forecast of total sales for January of the new year?

T **20.7-7.** Choosing an appropriate value of the smoothing constant α is a key decision when applying the exponential smoothing method. When relevant historical data exist, one approach to making this decision is to apply the method retrospectively to these data with different values of α and then choose the value of α that gives the smallest MAD. Use this approach for choosing α with each of the following time series representing monthly sales. In each case, use an initial estimate of 50 and compare $\alpha = 0.1, 0.2, 0.3, 0.4$, and 0.5.
(a) 51 48 52 49 53 49 48 51 50 49
(b) 52 50 53 51 52 48 52 53 49 52
(c) 50 52 51 55 53 56 52 55 54 53

T **20.7-8.** The choice of the smoothing constants α and β has a considerable effect on the accuracy of the forecasts obtained by using exponential smoothing with trend. For each of the following time series, set $\alpha = 0.2$ and then compare MAD obtained with $\beta = 0.1, 0.2, 0.3, 0.4$, and 0.5. Begin with initial estimates of 50 for the expected value and 2 for the trend.
(a) 52 55 55 58 59 63 64 66 67 72 73 74
(b) 52 55 59 61 66 69 71 72 73 74 73 74
(c) 52 53 51 50 48 47 49 52 57 62 69 74

20.7-9. The Andes Mining Company mines and ships copper ore. The company's sales manager, Juanita Valdes, has been using the moving-average method based on the last three years of sales to forecast the demand for the next year. However, she has become dissatisfied with the inaccurate forecasts being provided by this method.

Here are the annual demands (in tons of copper ore) over the past 10 years: 382 405 398 421 426 415 443 451 446 464
(a) Explain why this pattern of demands inevitably led to significant inaccuracies in the moving-average forecasts.
T **(b)** Determine the moving-average forecasts for the past 7 years. What is MAD? What is the forecast for next year?
T **(c)** Determine what the forecasts would have been for the past 10 years if the exponential smoothing method had been used instead with an initial estimate of 380 and a smoothing constant of $\alpha = 0.5$. What is MAD? What is the forecast for next year?
T **(d)** Determine what the forecasts would have been for the past 10 years if exponential smoothing with trend had been used instead. Use initial estimates of 370 for the expected value and 10 for the trend, with smoothing constants $\alpha = 0.25$ and $\beta = 0.25$.
(e) Based on the MAD values, which of these three methods do you recommend using hereafter?

20.7-10. The Centerville Water Department provides water for the entire town and outlying areas. The number of acre-feet of water consumed in each of the four seasons of the three preceding years is shown below.

Season	Year 1	Year 2	Year 3
Winter	25	27	24
Spring	47	46	49
Summer	68	72	70
Fall	42	39	44

T **(a)** Determine the seasonal factors for the four seasons.
T **(b)** After considering seasonal effects, use the last-value method to forecast water consumption next winter.
(c) Assuming that each of the forecasts for the next three seasons is correct, what would the last-value method forecast as the water consumption in each of the four seasons next year?
T **(d)** After considering seasonal effects, use the averaging method to forecast water consumption next winter.
T **(e)** After considering seasonal effects, use the moving-average method based on four seasons to forecast water consumption next winter.
T **(f)** After considering seasonal effects, use the exponential smoothing method with an initial estimate of 46 and a smoothing constant of $\alpha = 0.1$ to forecast water consumption next winter.
T **(g)** Compare the MAD values of these four forecasting methods when they are applied retrospectively to the last three years.
T **(h)** Calculate and compare the MSE values of these four forecasting methods when they are applied retrospectively to the last three years.

20.7-11. Reconsider Prob. 20.5-3. Ralph Billett realizes that the last-value method is considered to be the naive forecasting method, so he wonders whether he should be using another method. Therefore, he has decided to use the available Excel templates that consider seasonal effects to apply various statistical forecasting methods retrospectively to the past three years of data and compare their MAD values.
T **(a)** Determine the seasonal factors for the four quarters.
T **(b)** Apply the last-value method.
T **(c)** Apply the averaging method.
T **(d)** Apply the moving-average method based on the four most recent quarters of data.
T **(e)** Apply the exponential smoothing method with an initial estimate of 25 and a smoothing constant of $\alpha = 0.25$.
T **(f)** Apply exponential smoothing with trend with smoothing constants of $\alpha = 0.25$ and $\beta = 0.25$. Use initial estimates of 25 for the expected value and 0 for the trend.

T **(g)** Compare the MAD values for these methods. Use the one with the smallest MAD to forecast sales in Quarter 1 of next year.

(h) Use the forecast in part (g) and the seasonal factors to make long-range forecasts now of the sales in the remaining quarters of next year.

T **20.7-12.** Transcontinental Airlines maintains a computerized forecasting system to forecast the number of customers in each fare class who will fly on each flight in order to allocate the available reservations to fare classes properly. For example, consider *economy-class customers* flying in midweek on the noon flight from New York to Los Angeles. The following table shows the average number of such passengers during each month of the year just completed. The table also shows the seasonal factor that has been assigned to each month based on historical data.

Month	Average Number	Seasonal Factor	Month	Average Number	Seasonal Factor
January	68	0.90	July	94	1.17
February	71	0.88	August	96	1.15
March	66	0.91	September	80	0.97
April	72	0.93	October	73	0.91
May	77	0.96	November	84	1.05
June	85	1.09	December	89	1.08

(a) After considering seasonal effects, compare the MAD values for the last-value method, the averaging method, the moving-average method (based on the most recent three months), and the exponential smoothing method (with an initial estimate of 80 and a smoothing constant of $\alpha = 0.2$) when they are applied retrospectively to the past year.

(b) Use the forecasting method with the smallest MAD value to forecast the average number of these passengers flying in January of the new year.

20.7-13. Reconsider Prob. 20.7-12. The economy is beginning to boom so the management of Transcontinental Airlines is predicting that the number of people flying will steadily increase this year over the relatively flat (seasonally adjusted) level of last year. Since the forecasting methods considered in Prob. 20.7-12 are relatively slow in adjusting to such a trend, consideration is being given to switching to exponential smoothing with trend.

Subsequently, as the year goes on, management's prediction proves to be true. The following table shows the average number of the passengers under consideration in each month of the new year.

Month	Average Number	Month	Average Number	Month	Average Number
January	75	May	85	September	94
February	76	June	99	October	90
March	81	July	107	November	106
April	84	August	108	December	110

T **(a)** Repeat part (a) of Prob. 20.7-12 for the two years of data.

T **(b)** After considering seasonal effects, apply exponential smoothing with trend to just the new year. Use initial estimates of 80 for the expected value and 2 for the trend, along with smoothing constants of $\alpha = 0.2$ and $\beta = 0.2$. Compare MAD for this method to the MAD values obtained in part (a).

T **(c)** Repeat part (b) when exponential smoothing with trend is begun at the beginning of the first year and then applied to both years, just like the other forecasting methods in part (a). Use the same initial estimates and smoothing constants except change the initial estimate of trend to 0.

(d) Based on these results, which forecasting method would you recommend that Transcontinental Airlines use hereafter?

20.7-14. Quality Bikes is a wholesale firm that specializes in the distribution of bicycles. In the past, the company has maintained ample inventories of bicycles to enable filling orders immediately, so informal rough forecasts of demand were sufficient to make the decisions on when to replenish inventory. However, the company's new president, Marcia Salgo, intends to run a tighter ship. Scientific inventory management is to be used to reduce inventory levels and minimize total variable inventory costs. At the same time, Marcia has ordered the development of a computerized forecasting system based on statistical forecasting that considers seasonal effects. The system is to generate three sets of forecasts—one based on the moving-average method, a second based on the exponential smoothing method, and a third based on exponential smoothing with trend. The average of these three forecasts for each month is to be used for inventory management purposes.

The following table gives the available data on monthly sales of 10-speed bicycles over the past three years. The last column also shows monthly sales this year, which is the first year of operation of the new forecasting system.

Month	Past Sales			Current Sales This Year
	Year 1	Year 2	Year 3	
January	352	317	338	364
February	329	331	346	343
March	365	344	383	391
April	358	386	404	437

Month	Past Sales			Current Sales This Year
	Year 1	Year 2	Year 3	
May	412	423	431	458
June	446	472	459	494
July	420	415	433	468
August	471	492	518	555
September	355	340	309	387
October	312	301	335	364
November	567	629	594	662
December	533	505	527	581

T (a) Determine the seasonal factors for the 12 months based on past sales.

T (b) After considering seasonal effects, apply the moving-average method based on the most recent three months to forecast monthly sales this year.

T (c) After considering seasonal effects, apply the exponential smoothing method to forecast monthly sales this year. Use an initial estimate of 420 and a smoothing constant of $\alpha = 0.2$.

T (d) After considering seasonal effects, apply exponential smoothing with trend to forecast monthly sales this year. Use initial estimates of 420 for the expected value and 0 for the trend, along with smoothing constants of $\alpha = 0.2$ and $\beta = 0.2$.

(e) Compare the MAD values obtained in parts (b), (c), and (d).

(f) Calculate the combined forecast for each month by averaging the forecasts for that month obtained in parts (b), (c), and (d). Then calculate the MAD for these combined forecasts.

(g) Based on these results, what is your recommendation for how to do the forecasts next year?

20.7-15. Reconsider the sales data for a certain product given in Prob. 20.5-4. The company's management now has decided to discontinue incorporating seasonal effects into its forecasting procedure for this product because there does not appear to be a substantial seasonal pattern. Management also is concerned that exponential smoothing may not be the best forecasting method for this product and so has decided to test and compare several forecasting methods. Each method is to be applied retrospectively to the given data and then its MSE is to be calculated. The method with the smallest value of MSE will be chosen to begin forecasting.

Apply this retrospective test and calculate MSE for each of the following methods. (Also obtain the forecast for the upcoming quarter with each method.)

T (a) The *moving-average* method based on the last four quarters, so start with a forecast for the fifth quarter.

T (b) The *exponential smoothing* method with $\alpha = 0.1$. Start with a forecast for the third quarter by using the sales for the sec-

ond quarter as the latest observation and the sales for the first quarter as the initial estimate.

T (c) The *exponential smoothing method* with $\alpha = 0.3$. Start as described in part (b).

T (d) The *exponential smoothing with trend* method with $\alpha = 0.3$ and $\beta = 0.3$. Start with a forecast for the third quarter by using the sales for the second quarter as the initial estimate of the *expected value* of the time series (A) and the difference (sales for second quarter *minus* sales for first quarter) as the initial estimate of the *trend* of the time series (B).

(e) Compare MSE for these methods. Which one has the smallest value of MSE?

20.7-16. Follow the instructions of Prob. 20.7-15 for a product with the following sales history.

Quarter	Sales	Quarter	Sales	Quarter	Sales
1	546	5	647	9	736
2	528	6	594	10	724
3	530	7	665	11	813
4	508	8	630	12	—

20.9-1.* Long a market leader in the production of heavy machinery, the Spellman Corporation recently has been enjoying a steady increase in the sales of its new lathe. The sales over the past 10 months are shown below.

Month	Sales	Month	Sales
1	430	6	514
2	446	7	532
3	464	8	548
4	480	9	570
5	498	10	591

Because of this steady increase, management has decided to use *causal forecasting,* with the month as the independent variable and sales as the dependent variable, to forecast sales in the coming months.

(a) Plot these data on a two-dimensional graph with the month on the horizontal axis and sales on the vertical axis.

T (b) Find the formula for the linear regression line that fits these data.

(c) Plot this line on the graph constructed in part (a).

(d) Use this line to forecast sales in month 11.

(e) Use this line to forecast sales in month 20.

(f) What does the formula for the linear regression line indicate is roughly the average growth in sales per month?

20.9-2. Reconsider Probs. 20.7-3 and 20.6-1. Since the number of applications for admission submitted to Ivy College has been increasing at a steady rate, causal forecasting can be used to forecast the number of applications in future years by letting the year be the independent variable and the number of applications be the dependent variable.

(a) Plot the data for Years 1, 2, and 3 on a two-dimensional graph with the year on the horizontal axis and the number of applications on the vertical axis.

(b) Since the three points in this graph line up in a straight line, this straight line is the linear regression line. Draw this line.

T **(c)** Find the formula for this linear regression line.

(d) Use this line to forecast the number of applications for each of the next five years (Years 4 through 8).

(e) As these next years go on, conditions change for the worse at Ivy College. The favorable ratings in the national surveys that had propelled the growth in applications turn unfavorable. Consequently, the number of applications turn out to be 6,300 in Year 4 and 6,200 in Year 5, followed by sizable drops to 5,600 in Year 6 and 5,200 in Year 7. Does it still make sense to use the forecast for Year 8 obtained in part (*d*)? Explain.

T **(f)** Plot the data for all seven years. Find the formula for the linear regression line based on all these data and plot this line. Use this formula to forecast the number of applications for Year 8. Does the linear regression line provide a close fit to the data? Given this answer, do you have much confidence in the forecast it provides for Year 8? Does it make sense to continue to use a linear regression line when changing conditions cause a large shift in the underlying trend in the data?

T **(g)** Apply exponential smoothing with trend to all seven years of data to forecast the number of applications in Year 8. Use initial estimates of 3,900 for the expected value and 700 for the trend, along with smoothing constants of $\alpha = 0.5$ and $\beta = 0.5$. When the underlying trend in the data stays the same, causal forecasting provides the best possible linear regression line (according to the method of least squares) for making forecasts. However, when changing conditions cause a shift in the underlying trend, what advantage does exponential smoothing with trend have over causal forecasting?

20.9-3. Reconsider Prob. 20.7-9. Despite some fluctuations from year to year, note that there has been a basic trend upward in the annual demand for copper ore over the past 10 years. Therefore, by projecting this trend forward, causal forecasting can be used to forecast demands in future years by letting the year be the independent variable and the demand be the dependent variable.

(a) Plot the data for the past 10 years (Years 1 through 10) on a two-dimensional graph with the year on the horizontal axis and the demand on the vertical axis.

T **(b)** Find the formula for the linear regression line that fits these data.

(c) Plot this line on the graph constructed in part (*a*).

(d) Use this line to forecast demand next year (Year 11).

(e) Use this line to forecast demand in Year 15.

(f) What does the formula for the linear regression line indicate is roughly the average growth in demand per year?

20.9-4. Luxury Cruise Lines has a fleet of ships that travel to Alaska repeatedly every summer (and elsewhere during other times of the year). A considerable amount of advertising is done each winter to help generate enough passenger business for that summer. With the coming of a new winter, a decision needs to be made about how much advertising to do this year.

The following table shows the amount of advertising (in thousands of dollars) and the resulting sales (in thousands of passengers booked for a cruise) for each of the past five years.

Amount of advertising ($1,000s)	225	400	350	275	450
Sales (thousands of passengers)	16	21	20	17	23

(a) To use causal forecasting to forecast sales for a given amount of advertising, what needs to be the dependent variable and the independent variable?

(b) Plot the data on a graph.

T **(c)** Find the formula for the linear regression line that fits these data. Then plot this line on the graph constructed in part (*b*).

(d) Forecast the sales that would be attained by expending $300,000 on advertising.

(e) Estimate the amount of advertising that would need to be done to attain a booking of 22,000 passengers.

(f) According to the linear regression line, about how much increase in sales can be attained on the average per $1,000 increase in the amount of advertising?

20.9-5. To support its large fleet, North American Airlines maintains an extensive inventory of spare parts, including wing flaps. The number of wing flaps needed in inventory to replace damaged wing flaps each month depends partially on the number of flying hours for the fleet that month, since increased usage increases the chances of damage.

The following table shows both the number of replacement wing flaps needed and the number of thousands of flying hours for the entire fleet for each of several recent months.

Thousands of flying hours	162	149	185	171	138	154
Number of wing flaps needed	12	9	13	14	10	11

(a) Identify the dependent variable and the independent variable for doing causal forecasting of the number of wing flaps needed for a given number of flying hours.

(b) Plot the data on a graph.

T **(c)** Find the formula for the linear regression line.

(d) Plot this line on the graph constructed in part (b).

(e) Forecast the average number of wing flaps needed in a month in which 150,000 flying hours are planned.

(f) Repeat part (e) for 200,000 flying hours.

T **20.9-6.** Joe Barnes is the owner of Standing Tall, one of the major roofing companies in town. Much of the company's business comes from building roofs on new houses. Joe has learned that general contractors constructing new houses typically will subcontract the roofing work about 2 months after construction begins. Therefore, to help him develop long-range schedules for his work crews, Joe has decided to use county records on the number of housing construction permits issued each month to forecast the number of roofing jobs on new houses he will have 2 months later.

Joe has now gathered the following data for each month over the past year, where the second column gives the number of housing construction permits issued in that month and the third column shows the number of roofing jobs on new houses that were subcontracted out to Standing Tall in that month.

Month	Permits	Jobs	Month	Permits	Jobs
January	323	19	July	446	34
February	359	17	August	407	37
March	396	24	September	374	33
April	421	23	October	343	30
May	457	28	November	311	27
June	472	32	December	277	22

Use a causal forecasting approach to develop a forecasting procedure for Joe to use hereafter.

20.9-7. The following data relate road width x and accident frequency y. Road width (in feet) was treated as the independent variable, and values y of the random variable Y, in accidents per 10^8 vehicle miles, were observed.

Number of Observations = 7		x	y
$\sum_{i=1}^{7} x_i = 354$	$\sum_{i=1}^{7} y_i = 481$	26	92
		30	85
		44	78
$\sum_{i=1}^{7} x_i^2 = 19,956$	$\sum_{i=1}^{7} y_i^2 = 35,451$	50	81
		62	54
$\sum_{i=1}^{7} x_i y_i = 22,200$		68	51
		74	40

Assume that Y is normally distributed with mean $A + Bx$ and constant variance for all x and that the sample is random. Interpolate if necessary.

(a) Fit a least-squares line to the data, and forecast the accident frequency when the road width is 55 feet.

(b) Construct a 95 percent prediction interval for Y_+, a future observation of Y, corresponding to $x_+ = 55$ feet.

(c) Suppose that two future observations on Y, both corresponding to $x_+ = 55$ feet, are to be made. Construct prediction intervals for both of these observations so that the probability is *at least* 95 percent that *both* future values of Y will fall into them simultaneously. [*Hint:* If k predictions are to be made, such as given in part (d), each with probability $1 - \alpha$, then the probability is *at least* $1 - k\alpha$ that all k future observations will fall into their respective intervals.]

(d) Construct a simultaneous tolerance interval for the future value of Y corresponding to $x_+ = 55$ feet with $P = 0.90$ and $1 - \alpha = 0.95$.

T **20.9-8.** The following data are observations y_i on a dependent random variable Y taken at various levels of an independent variable x. [It is assumed that $E(Y_i | x_i) = A + Bx_i$, and the Y_i are independent normal random variables with mean 0 and variance σ^2.]

x_i	0	2	4	6	8
y_i	0	4	7	13	16

(a) Estimate the linear relationship by the method of least squares, and forecast the value of Y when $x = 10$.

(b) Find a 95 percent confidence interval for the expected value of Y at $x^* = 10$.

(c) Find a 95 percent prediction interval for a future observation to be taken at $x_+ = 10$.

(d) For $x_+ = 10$, $P = 0.90$, and $1 - \alpha = 0.95$, find a simultaneous tolerance interval for the future value of Y_+. Interpolate if necessary.

T **20.9-9.** If a particle is dropped at time $t = 0$, physical theory indicates that the relationship between the distance traveled r and the time elapsed t is $r = gt^k$ for some positive constants g and k. A transformation to linearity can be obtained by taking logarithms:

$$\log r = \log g + k \log t.$$

By letting $y = \log r$, $A = \log g$, and $x = \log t$, this relation becomes $y = A + kx$. Due to random error in measurement, however, it can be stated only that $E(Y | x) = A + kx$. Assume that Y is normally distributed with mean $A + kx$ and variance σ^2.

A physicist who wishes to estimate k and g performs the following experiment: At time 0 the particle is dropped. At time t the distance r is measured. He performs this experiment five times, obtaining the following data (where all logarithms are to base 10).

$y = \log r$	$x = \log t$
-3.95	-2.0
-2.12	-1.0
0.08	0.0
2.20	$+1.0$
3.87	$+2.0$

(a) Obtain least-squares estimates for k and $\log g$, and forecast the distance traveled when $\log t = +3.0$.

(b) Starting with a forecast for $\log r$ when $\log t = 0$, use the exponential smoothing method with an initial estimate of $\log r = -3.95$ and $\alpha = 0.1$, that is,

$$\text{Forecast of } \log r \text{ (when } \log t = 0) = 0.1(-2.12) \\ + 0.9(-3.95),$$

to forecast each $\log r$ for all integer $\log t$ through $\log t = +3.0$.

(c) Repeat part (b), except adjust the exponential smoothing method to incorporate a trend factor into the underlying model as described in Sec. 20.6. Use an initial estimate of trend equal to the slope found in part (a). Let $\beta = 0.1$.

20.9-10. Suppose that the relation between Y and x is given by

$$E(Y \mid x) = Bx,$$

where Y is assumed to be normally distributed with mean Bx and *known* variance σ^2. Also n independent pairs of observations are taken and are denoted by $x_1, y_1; x_2, y_2; \ldots; x_n, y_n$. Find the least-squares estimate of B.

CASE 20.1   FINAGLING THE FORECASTS

Mark Lawrence—the man with two first names—has been pursuing a vision for more than two years. This pursuit began when he became frustrated in his role as director of human resources at Cutting Edge, a large company manufacturing computers and computer peripherals. At that time, the human resources department under his direction provided records and benefits administration to the 60,000 Cutting Edge employees throughout the United States, and 35 separate records and benefits administration centers existed across the country. Employees contacted these records and benefits centers to obtain information about dental plans and stock options, to change tax forms and personal information, and to process leaves of absence and retirements. The decentralization of these administration centers caused numerous headaches for Mark. He had to deal with employee complaints often since each center interpreted company policies differently—communicating inconsistent and sometimes inaccurate answers to employees. His department also suffered high operating costs, since operating 35 separate centers created inefficiency.

His vision? To centralize records and benefits administration by establishing one administration center. This centralized records and benefits administration center would perform two distinct functions: data management and customer service. The data management function would include updating employee records after performance reviews and maintaining the human resource management system. The customer service function would include establishing a call center to answer employee questions concerning records and benefits and to process records and benefits changes over the phone.

One year after proposing his vision to management, Mark received the go-ahead from Cutting Edge corporate headquarters. He prepared his "to do" list—specifying computer and phone systems requirements, installing hardware and software, integrating data from the 35 separate administration centers, standardizing record-keeping and response procedures, and staffing the administration center. Mark delegated the systems requirements, installation, and integration jobs to a competent group of technology specialists. He took on the responsibility of standardizing procedures and staffing the administration center.

Mark had spent many years in human resources and therefore had little problem with standardizing record-keeping and response procedures. He encountered trouble in determining the number of representatives needed to staff the center, however. He was particularly worried about staffing the call center since the representatives answering phones interact directly with customers—the 60,000 Cutting Edge employees. The customer service representatives would receive extensive training so that they would know the records and benefits policies backward and forward—enabling them to answer questions accurately and process changes efficiently. Overstaffing would cause Mark to suffer the high costs of training unneeded representatives and paying the surplus representatives the high salaries that go along with such an intense job. Understaffing would cause Mark to continue to suffer the headaches from customer complaints—something he definitely wanted to avoid.

The number of customer service representatives Mark needed to hire depends on the number of calls that the records and benefits call center would receive. Mark therefore needed to forecast the number of calls that the new centralized center would receive. He approached the forecasting problem by using judgmental forecasting. He studied data from one of the 35 decentralized administration centers and learned that the decentralized center had serviced 15,000 customers and had received 2,000 calls per month. He concluded that since the new centralized center would service four times the number of customers—60,000 customers—it would receive four times the number of calls—8,000 calls per month.

Mark slowly checked off the items on his "to do" list, and the centralized records and benefits administration center opened one year after Mark had received the go-ahead from corporate headquarters.

Now, after operating the new center for 13 weeks, Mark's call center forecasts are proving to be terribly inaccurate. The number of calls the center receives is roughly three times as large as the 8,000 calls per month that Mark had forecasted. Because of demand overload, the call center is slowly going to hell in a handbasket. Customers calling the center must wait an average of 5 minutes before speaking to a representative, and Mark is receiving numerous complaints. At the same time, the customer service representatives are unhappy and on the verge of quitting because of the stress created by the demand overload. Even corporate headquarters has become aware of the staff and service inadequacies, and executives have been breathing down Mark's neck demanding improvements.

Mark needs help, and he approaches you to forecast demand for the call center more accurately.

Luckily, when Mark first established the call center, he realized the importance of keeping operational data, and he provides you with the number of calls received on each day of the week over the last 13 weeks. The data (shown below) begins in week

44 of the last year and continues to week 5 of the current year. Mark indicates that the days where no calls were received were holidays.

	Monday	Tuesday	Wednesday	Thursday	Friday
Week 44	1,130	851	859	828	726
Week 45	1,085	1,042	892	840	799
Week 46	1,303	1,121	1,003	1,113	1,005
Week 47	2,652	2,825	1,841	0	0
Week 48	1,949	1,507	989	990	1,084
Week 49	1,260	1,134	941	847	714
Week 50	1,002	847	922	842	784
Week 51	823	0	0	401	429
Week 52/1	1,209	830	0	1,082	841
Week 2	1,362	1,174	967	930	853
Week 3	924	954	1,346	904	758
Week 4	886	878	802	945	610
Week 5	910	754	705	729	772

(a) Mark first asks you to forecast daily demand for the next week using the data from the past 13 weeks. You should make the forecasts for all the days of the next week now (at the end of week 5), but you should provide a different forecast for each day of the week by treating the forecast for a single day as being the actual call volume on that day.

(1) From working at the records and benefits administration center, you know that demand follows "seasonal" patterns within the week. For example, more employees call at the beginning of the week when they are fresh and productive than at the end of the week when they are planning for the weekend. You therefore realize that you must account for the seasonal patterns and adjust the data that Mark gave you accordingly. What is the seasonally adjusted call volume for the past 13 weeks?

(2) Using the seasonally adjusted call volume, forecast the daily demand for the next week using the last-value forecasting method.

(3) Using the seasonally adjusted call volume, forecast the daily demand for the next week using the averaging forecasting method.

(4) Using the seasonally adjusted call volume, forecast the daily demand for the next week using the moving-average forecasting method. You decide to use the five most recent days in this analysis.

(5) Using the seasonally adjusted call volume, forecast the daily demand for the next week using the exponential smoothing forecasting method. You decide to use a smoothing constant of 0.1 because you believe that demand without seasonal effects remains relatively stable. Use the daily call volume average over the past 13 weeks for the initial estimate.

(b) After 1 week, the period you have forecasted passes. You realize that you are able to determine the accuracy of your forecasts because you now have the actual call volumes from the week you had forecasted. The actual call volumes are shown next.

	Monday	Tuesday	Wednesday	Thursday	Friday
Week 6	723	677	521	571	498

For each of the forecasting methods, calculate the mean absolute deviation for the method and evaluate the performance of the method. When calculating the mean absolute deviation, you should use the actual forecasts you found in part (a) above. You should not recalculate the forecasts based on the actual values. In your evaluation, provide an explanation for the effectiveness or ineffectiveness of the method.

(c) You realize that the forecasting methods that you have investigated do not provide a great degree of accuracy, and you decide to use a creative approach to forecasting that combines the statistical and judgmental approaches. You know that Mark had used data from one of the 35 decentralized records and benefits administration centers to perform his original forecasting. You therefore suspect that call volume data exist for this decentralized center. Because the decentralized centers performed the same functions as the new centralized center currently performs, you decide that the call volumes from the decentralized center will help you forecast the call volumes for the new centralized center. You simply need to understand how the decentralized volumes relate to the new centralized volumes. Once you understand this relationship, you can use the call volumes from the decentralized center to forecast the call volumes for the centralized center.

You approach Mark and ask him whether call center data exist for the decentralized center. He tells you that data exist, but they do not exist in the format that you need. Case volume data—not call volume data—exist. You do not understand the distinction, so Mark continues his explanation. There are two types of demand data—case volume data and call volume data. Case volume data count the actions taken by the representatives at the call center. Call volume data count the number of calls answered by the representatives at the call center. A case may require one call or multiple calls to resolve it. Thus, the number of cases is always less than or equal to the number of calls.

You know you only have case volume data for the decentralized center, and you certainly do not want to compare apples and oranges. You therefore ask if case volume data exist for the new centralized center. Mark gives you a wicked grin and nods his head. He sees where you are going with your forecasts, and he tells you that he will have the data for you within the hour.

At the end of the hour, Mark arrives at your desk with two data sets: weekly case volumes for the decentralized center and weekly case volumes for the centralized center. You ask Mark if he has data for daily case volumes, and he tells you that he does not. You therefore first have to forecast the weekly demand for the next week and then break this weekly demand into daily demand.

The decentralized center was shut down last year when the new centralized center opened, so you have the decentralized case data spanning from week 44 of two years ago to week 5 of last year. You compare this decentralized data to the centralized data spanning from week 44 of last year to week 5 of this year. The weekly case volumes are shown in the table below.

	Decentralized Case Volume	Centralized Case Volume
Week 44	612	2,052
Week 45	721	2,170
Week 46	693	2,779
Week 47	540	2,334
Week 48	1,386	2,514
Week 49	577	1,713

	Decentralized Case Volume	Centralized Case Volume
Week 50	405	1,927
Week 51	441	1,167
Week 52/1	655	1,549
Week 2	572	2,126
Week 3	475	2,337
Week 4	530	1,916
Week 5	595	2,098

(1) Find a mathematical relationship between the decentralized case volume data and the centralized case volume data.

(2) Now that you have a relationship between the weekly decentralized case volume and the weekly centralized case volume, you are able to forecast the weekly case volume for the new center. Unfortunately, you do not need the weekly case volume; you need the daily call volume. To calculate call volume from case volume, you perform further analysis and determine that each case generates an average of 1.5 calls. To calculate daily call volume from weekly call volume, you decide to use the seasonal factors as conversion factors. Given the following case volume data from the decentralized center for week 6 of last year, forecast the daily call volume for the new center for week 6 of this year.

	Week 6
Decentralized case volume	613

(3) Using the actual call volumes given in part (b), calculate the mean absolute deviation and evaluate the effectiveness of this forecasting method.

(d) Which forecasting method would you recommend Mark use and why? As the call center continues its operation, how would you recommend improving the forecasting procedure?

21

Markov Decision Processes

Chapter 16 introduced *Markov chains* and their analysis. Most of the chapter was devoted to *discrete time* Markov chains, i.e., Markov chains that are observed only at discrete points in time (e.g., the end of each day) rather than continuously. Each time it is observed, the Markov chain can be in any one of a number of *states*. Given the current state, a (one-step) *transition matrix* gives the probabilities for what the state will be next time. Given this transition matrix, Chap. 16 focused on *describing the behavior* of a Markov chain, e.g., finding the steady-state probabilities for what state it is in.

Many important systems (e.g., many queueing systems) can be modeled as either a discrete time or continuous time Markov chain. It is useful to describe the behavior of such a system (as we did in Chap. 17 for queueing systems) in order to evaluate its performance. However, it may be even more useful to *design the operation* of the system so as to *optimize its performance* (as we did in Chap. 18 for queueing systems).

This chapter focuses on how to design the operation of a discrete time Markov chain so as to optimize its performance. Therefore, rather than passively accepting the design of the Markov chain and the corresponding fixed transition matrix, we now are being proactive. For each possible state of the Markov chain, we make a decision about which one of several alternative actions should be taken in that state. The action chosen affects the *transition probabilities* as well as both the *immediate costs* (or rewards) and *subsequent costs* (or rewards) from operating the system. We want to choose the optimal actions for the respective states when considering both immediate and subsequent costs. The decision process for doing this is referred to as a *Markov decision process*.

The first section gives a prototype example of an application of a Markov decision process. Section 21.2 formulates the basic model for these processes. The next three sections describe how to solve them.

21.1 A PROTOTYPE EXAMPLE

A manufacturer has one key machine at the core of one of its production processes. Because of heavy use, the machine deteriorates rapidly in both quality and output. Therefore, at the end of each week, a thorough inspection is done that results in classifying the condition of the machine into one of four possible states:

State	Condition
0	Good as new
1	Operable—minor deterioration
2	Operable—major deterioration
3	Inoperable—output of unacceptable quality

After historical data on these inspection results are gathered, statistical analysis is done on how the state of the machine evolves from month to month. The following matrix shows the relative frequency (probability) of each possible transition from the state in one month (a row of the matrix) to the state in the following month (a column of the matrix).

State	0	1	2	3
0	0	$\frac{7}{8}$	$\frac{1}{16}$	$\frac{1}{16}$
1	0	$\frac{3}{4}$	$\frac{1}{8}$	$\frac{1}{8}$
2	0	0	$\frac{1}{2}$	$\frac{1}{2}$
3	0	0	0	1

In addition, statistical analysis has found that these transition probabilities are unaffected by also considering what the states were in prior months. This "lack-of-memory property" is the *Markovian property* described in Sec. 16.2. Therefore, for the random variable X_t, which is the state of the machine at the end of month t, it has been concluded that the stochastic process $\{X_t, t = 0, 1, 2, \ldots\}$ is a *discrete time Markov chain* whose (one-step) *transition matrix* is just the above matrix.

As the last entry in this transition matrix indicates, once the machine becomes inoperable (enters state 3), it remains inoperable. In other words, state 3 is an *absorbing state*. Leaving the machine in this state would be intolerable, since this would shut down the production process, so the machine must be replaced. (Repair is not feasible in this state.) The new machine then will start off in state 0.

The replacement process takes 1 week to complete so that production is lost for this period. The cost of the lost production (lost profit) is $2,000, and the cost of replacing the machine is $4,000, so the total cost incurred whenever the current machine enters state 3 is $6,000.

Even before the machine reaches state 3, costs may be incurred from the production of defective items. The expected costs per week from this source are as follows:

State	Expected Cost Due to Defective Items, $
0	0
1	1,000
2	3,000

We now have mentioned all the relevant costs associated with one particular *maintenance policy* (replace the machine when it becomes inoperable but do no maintenance otherwise). Under this policy, the evolution of the state of the *system* (the succession of machines) still is a Markov chain, but now with the following transition matrix:

State	0	1	2	3
0	0	$\frac{7}{8}$	$\frac{1}{16}$	$\frac{1}{16}$
1	0	$\frac{3}{4}$	$\frac{1}{8}$	$\frac{1}{8}$
2	0	0	$\frac{1}{2}$	$\frac{1}{2}$
3	1	0	0	0

To evaluate this maintenance policy, we should consider both the immediate costs incurred over the coming week (just described) and the subsequent costs that result from having the system evolve in this way. As introduced in Sec. 16.5, one such widely used measure of performance for Markov chains is the (long-run) **expected average cost per unit time**.[1]

To calculate this measure, we first derive the *steady-state probabilities* π_0, π_1, π_2, and π_3 for this Markov chain by solving the following steady-state equations:

$$\pi_0 = \pi_3,$$

$$\pi_1 = \frac{7}{8}\pi_0 + \frac{3}{4}\pi_1,$$

$$\pi_2 = \frac{1}{16}\pi_0 + \frac{1}{8}\pi_1 + \frac{1}{2}\pi_2,$$

$$\pi_3 = \frac{1}{16}\pi_0 + \frac{1}{8}\pi_1 + \frac{1}{2}\pi_2,$$

$$1 = \pi_0 + \pi_1 + \pi_2 + \pi_3.$$

The simultaneous solution is

$$\pi_0 = \frac{2}{13}, \qquad \pi_1 = \frac{7}{13}, \qquad \pi_2 = \frac{2}{13}, \qquad \pi_3 = \frac{2}{13}.$$

Hence, the (long-run) expected average cost per week for this maintenance policy is

$$0\pi_0 + 1{,}000\pi_1 + 3{,}000\pi_2 + 6{,}000\pi_3 = \frac{25{,}000}{13} = \$1{,}923.08.$$

However, there also are other maintenance policies that should be considered and compared with this one. For example, perhaps the machine should be replaced before it reaches

---

[1]The term *long-run* indicates that the average should be interpreted as being taken over an *extremely* long time so that the effect of the initial state disappears. As time goes to infinity, Sec. 16.5 discusses the fact that the *actual* average cost per unit time essentially always converges to the *expected* average cost per unit time.

TABLE 21.1 Cost data for the prototype example

Decision	State	Expected Cost Due to Producing Defective Items, $	Maintenance Cost, $	Cost (Lost Profit) of Lost Production, $	Total Cost per Week, $
1. Do nothing	0	0	0	0	0
	1	1,000	0	0	1,000
	2	3,000	0	0	3,000
2. Overhaul	2	0	2,000	2,000	4,000
3. Replace	1, 2, 3	0	4,000	2,000	6,000

state 3. Another alternative is to *overhaul* the machine at a cost of $2,000. This option is not feasible in state 3 and does not improve the machine while in state 0 or 1, so it is of interest only in state 2. In this state, an overhaul would return the machine to state 1. A week is required, so another consequence is $2,000 in lost profit from lost production.

In summary, the possible decisions after each inspection are as follows:

Decision	Action	Relevant States
1	Do nothing	0, 1, 2
2	Overhaul (return system to state 1)	2
3	Replace (return system to state 0)	1, 2, 3

For easy reference, Table 21.1 also summarizes the relevant costs for each decision for each state where that decision could be of interest.

What is the optimal maintenance policy? We will be addressing this question to illustrate the material in the next four sections.

21.2   A MODEL FOR MARKOV DECISION PROCESSES

The model for the Markov decision processes considered in this chapter can be summarized as follows.

1. The state i of a discrete time Markov chain is observed after each transition ($i = 0$, $1, \ldots, M$).
2. After each observation, a *decision* (action) k is chosen from a set of K possible decisions ($k = 1, 2, \ldots, K$). (Some of the K decisions may not be relevant for some of the states.)
3. If decision $d_i = k$ is made in state i, an immediate *cost* is incurred that has an expected value C_{ik}.
4. The decision $d_i = k$ in state i determines what the *transition probabilities*[1] will be for the next transition from state i. Denote these transition probabilities by $p_{ij}(k)$, for $j = 0$, $1, \ldots, M$.

---

[1]The solution procedures given in the next two sections also assume that the resulting transition matrix is *irreducible*.

5. A specification of the decisions for the respective states $(d_0, d_1, \ldots, d_M)$ prescribes a *policy* for the Markov decision process.

6. The objective is to find an *optimal policy* according to some cost criterion which considers both immediate costs and subsequent costs that result from the future evolution of the process. One common criterion is to minimize the (long-run) *expected average cost per unit time.* (An alternative criterion is considered in Sec. 21.5.)

To relate this general description to the prototype example presented in Sec. 21.1, recall that the Markov chain being observed there represents the state (condition) of a particular machine. After each inspection of the machine, a choice is made between three possible decisions (do nothing, overhaul, or replace). The resulting immediate expected cost is shown in the rightmost column of Table 21.1 for each relevant combination of state and decision. Section 21.1 analyzed one particular policy $(d_0, d_1, d_2, d_3) = (1, 1, 1, 3)$, where decision 1 (do nothing) is made in states 0, 1, and 2 and decision 3 (replace) is made in state 3. The resulting transition probabilities are shown in the last transition matrix given in Sec. 21.1.

Our general model qualifies to be a Markov decision process because it possesses the Markovian property that characterizes any Markov process. In particular, given the current state and decision, any probabilistic statement about the future of the process is completely unaffected by providing any information about the history of the process. This property holds here since (1) we are dealing with a Markov chain, (2) the new transition probabilities depend on only the current state and decision, and (3) the immediate expected cost also depends on only the current state and decision.

Our description of a policy implies two convenient (but unnecessary) properties that we will assume throughout the chapter (with one exception). One property is that a policy is **stationary;** i.e., whenever the system is in state i, the rule for making the decision always is the same regardless of the value of the current time t. The second property is that a policy is **deterministic;** i.e., whenever the system is in state i, the rule for making the decision definitely chooses one particular decision. (Because of the nature of the algorithm involved, the next section considers *randomized* policies instead, where a probability distribution is used for the decision to be made.)

Using this general framework, we now return to the prototype example and find the optimal policy by enumerating and comparing all the relevant policies. In doing this, we will let R denote a specific policy and $d_i(R)$ denote the corresponding decision to be made in state i.

Solving the Prototype Example by Exhaustive Enumeration

The relevant policies for the prototype example are these:

Policy	Verbal Description	$d_0(R)$	$d_1(R)$	$d_2(R)$	$d_3(R)$
R_a	Replace in state 3	1	1	1	3
R_b	Replace in state 3, overhaul in state 2	1	1	2	3
R_c	Replace in states 2 and 3	1	1	3	3
R_d	Replace in states 1, 2, and 3	1	3	3	3

Each policy results in a different transition matrix, as shown below.

	R_a			
State	**0**	**1**	**2**	**3**
0	0	$\frac{7}{8}$	$\frac{1}{16}$	$\frac{1}{16}$
1	0	$\frac{3}{4}$	$\frac{1}{8}$	$\frac{1}{8}$
2	0	0	$\frac{1}{2}$	$\frac{1}{2}$
3	1	0	0	0

	R_b			
State	**0**	**1**	**2**	**3**
0	0	$\frac{7}{8}$	$\frac{1}{16}$	$\frac{1}{16}$
1	0	$\frac{3}{4}$	$\frac{1}{8}$	$\frac{1}{8}$
2	0	1	0	0
3	1	0	0	0

	R_c			
State	**0**	**1**	**2**	**3**
0	0	$\frac{7}{8}$	$\frac{1}{16}$	$\frac{1}{16}$
1	0	$\frac{3}{4}$	$\frac{1}{8}$	$\frac{1}{8}$
2	1	0	0	0
3	1	0	0	0

	R_d			
State	**0**	**1**	**2**	**3**
0	0	$\frac{7}{8}$	$\frac{1}{16}$	$\frac{1}{16}$
1	1	0	0	0
2	1	0	0	0
3	1	0	0	0

From the rightmost column of Table 21.1, the values of C_{ik} are as follows:

Decision / State	C_{ik} (in Thousands of Dollars)		
	1	**2**	**3**
0	0	—	—
1	1	—	6
2	3	4	6
3	—	—	6

As indicated in Sec. 16.5, the (long-run) expected average cost per unit time $E(C)$ then can be calculated from the expression

$$E(C) = \sum_{i=0}^{M} C_{ik}\pi_i,$$

where $k = d_i(R)$ for each i and $(\pi_0, \pi_1, \ldots, \pi_M)$ represents the steady-state distribution of the state of the system under the policy R being evaluated. After $(\pi_0, \pi_1, \ldots, \pi_M)$ are solved for under each of the four policies (as can be done with your OR Courseware), the calculation of $E(C)$ is as summarized here:

Policy	$(\pi_0, \pi_1, \pi_2, \pi_3)$	$E(C)$, in Thousands of Dollars
R_a	$\left(\dfrac{2}{13}, \dfrac{7}{13}, \dfrac{2}{13}, \dfrac{2}{13}\right)$	$\dfrac{1}{13}[2(0) + 7(1) + 2(3) + 2(6)] = \dfrac{25}{13} = \$1{,}923$
R_b	$\left(\dfrac{2}{21}, \dfrac{5}{7}, \dfrac{2}{21}, \dfrac{2}{21}\right)$	$\dfrac{1}{21}[2(0) + 15(1) + 2(4) + 2(6)] = \dfrac{35}{21} = \$1{,}667 \leftarrow$ Minimum
R_c	$\left(\dfrac{2}{11}, \dfrac{7}{11}, \dfrac{1}{11}, \dfrac{1}{11}\right)$	$\dfrac{1}{11}[2(0) + 7(1) + 1(6) + 1(6)] = \dfrac{19}{11} = \$1{,}727$
R_d	$\left(\dfrac{1}{2}, \dfrac{7}{16}, \dfrac{1}{32}, \dfrac{1}{32}\right)$	$\dfrac{1}{32}[16(0) + 14(6) + 1(6) + 1(6)] = \dfrac{96}{32} = \$3{,}000$

Thus, the optimal policy is R_b; that is, replace the machine when it is found to be in state 3, and overhaul the machine when it is found to be in state 2. The resulting (long-run) expected average cost per week is $1,667.

Using exhaustive enumeration to find the optimal policy is appropriate for this tiny example, where there are only four relevant policies. However, many applications have so many policies that this approach would be completely infeasible. For such cases, algorithms that can efficiently find an optimal policy are needed. The next three sections consider such algorithms.

21.3 LINEAR PROGRAMMING AND OPTIMAL POLICIES

Section 21.2 described the main kind of policy (called a *stationary, deterministic* policy) that is used by Markov decision processes. We saw that any such policy R can be viewed as a rule that prescribes decision $d_i(R)$ whenever the system is in state i, for each $i = 0$, $1, \ldots, M$. Thus, R is characterized by the values

$$\{d_0(R), d_1(R), \ldots, d_M(R)\}.$$

Equivalently, R can be characterized by assigning values $D_{ik} = 0$ or 1 in the matrix

$$\text{State} \quad \begin{array}{c} 0 \\ 1 \\ \vdots \\ M \end{array} \begin{array}{ccccc} & \overset{\text{Decision } k}{} & & \\ 1 & 2 & \cdots & K \\ \begin{bmatrix} D_{01} & D_{02} & \cdots & D_{0K} \\ D_{11} & D_{12} & \cdots & D_{1K} \\ \multicolumn{4}{c}{\dotfill} \\ D_{M1} & D_{M2} & \cdots & D_{MK} \end{bmatrix} \end{array},$$

where each D_{ik} ($i = 0, 1, \ldots, M$ and $k = 1, 2, \ldots, K$) is defined as

$$D_{ik} = \begin{cases} 1 & \text{if decision } k \text{ is to be made in state } i \\ 0 & \text{otherwise.} \end{cases}$$

Therefore, each row in the matrix must contain a single 1 with the rest of the elements 0s. For example, the optimal policy R_b for the prototype example is characterized by the matrix

$$
\text{State}
\begin{array}{c}
\\
0 \\
1 \\
2 \\
3
\end{array}
\begin{array}{c}
\text{Decision } k \\
\begin{array}{ccc}
1 & 2 & 3
\end{array} \\
\left[
\begin{array}{ccc}
1 & 0 & 0 \\
1 & 0 & 0 \\
0 & 1 & 0 \\
0 & 0 & 1
\end{array}
\right];
\end{array}
$$

i.e., do nothing (decision 1) when the machine is in state 0 or 1, overhaul (decision 2) in state 2, and replace the machine (decision 3) when it is in state 3.

Randomized Policies

Introducing D_{ik} provides motivation for a *linear programming formulation.* It is hoped that the expected cost of a policy can be expressed as a linear function of D_{ik} or a related variable, subject to linear constraints. Unfortunately, the D_{ik} values are integers (0 or 1), and continuous variables are required for a linear programming formulation. This requirement can be handled by expanding the interpretation of a policy. The previous definition calls for making the same decision every time the system is in state i. The new interpretation of a policy will call for determining a probability distribution for the decision to be made when the system is in state i.

With this new interpretation, the D_{ik} now need to be redefined as

$$D_{ik} = P\{\text{decision} = k \,|\, \text{state} = i\}.$$

In other words, given that the system is in state i, variable D_{ik} is the *probability* of choosing decision k as the decision to be made. Therefore, $(D_{i1}, D_{i2}, \ldots, D_{iK})$ is the *probability distribution* for the decision to be made in state i.

This kind of policy using probability distributions is called a **randomized policy,** whereas the policy calling for $D_{ik} = 0$ or 1 is a *deterministic policy.* Randomized policies can again be characterized by the matrix

$$
\text{State}
\begin{array}{c}
\\
0 \\
1 \\
\vdots \\
M
\end{array}
\begin{array}{c}
\text{Decision } k \\
\begin{array}{cccc}
1 & 2 & \cdots & K
\end{array} \\
\left[
\begin{array}{cccc}
D_{01} & D_{02} & \cdots & D_{0K} \\
D_{11} & D_{12} & \cdots & D_{1K} \\
\multicolumn{4}{c}{\dotfill} \\
D_{M1} & D_{M2} & \cdots & D_{MK}
\end{array}
\right],
\end{array}
$$

where each row sums to 1, and now

$$0 \le D_{ik} \le 1.$$

To illustrate, consider a randomized policy for the prototype example given by the matrix

$$
\begin{array}{c}
\text{Decision } k \\
\begin{array}{cccc}
 & 1 & 2 & 3 \\
\end{array} \\
\text{State}
\begin{array}{c}
0 \\
1 \\
2 \\
3
\end{array}
\begin{bmatrix}
1 & 0 & 0 \\
\frac{1}{2} & 0 & \frac{1}{2} \\
\frac{1}{4} & \frac{1}{4} & \frac{1}{2} \\
0 & 0 & 1
\end{bmatrix}.
\end{array}
$$

This policy calls for *always* making decision 1 (do nothing) when the machine is in state 0. If it is found to be in state 1, it is left as is with probability $\frac{1}{2}$ and replaced with probability $\frac{1}{2}$, so a coin can be flipped to make the choice. If it is found to be in state 2, it is left as is with probability $\frac{1}{4}$, overhauled with probability $\frac{1}{4}$, and replaced with probability $\frac{1}{2}$. Presumably, a random device with these probabilities (possibly a table of random numbers) can be used to make the actual decision. Finally, if the machine is found to be in state 3, it always is overhauled.

By allowing randomized policies, so that the D_{ik} are continuous variables instead of integer variables, it now is possible to formulate a linear programming model for finding an optimal policy.

A Linear Programming Formulation

The convenient decision variables (denoted here by y_{ik}) for a linear programming model are defined as follows. For each $i = 0, 1, \ldots, M$ and $k = 1, 2, \ldots, K$, let y_{ik} be the steady-state unconditional probability that the system is in state i *and* decision k is made; i.e.,

$$y_{ik} = P\{\text{state} = i \text{ and decision} = k\}.$$

Each y_{ik} is closely related to the corresponding D_{ik} since, from the rules of conditional probability,

$$y_{ik} = \pi_i D_{ik},$$

where π_i is the steady-state probability that the Markov chain is in state i. Furthermore,

$$\pi_i = \sum_{k=1}^{K} y_{ik},$$

so that

$$D_{ik} = \frac{y_{ik}}{\pi_i} = \frac{y_{ik}}{\displaystyle\sum_{k=1}^{K} y_{ik}}.$$

There exist several constraints on y_{ik}:

1. $\sum_{i=1}^{M} \pi_i = 1$ so that $\sum_{i=0}^{M} \sum_{k=1}^{K} y_{ik} = 1$.

2. From results on steady-state probabilities (see Sec. 16.5),[1]

$$\pi_j = \sum_{i=0}^{M} \pi_i p_{ij}$$

so that

$$\sum_{k=1}^{K} y_{jk} = \sum_{i=0}^{M} \sum_{k=1}^{K} y_{ik} p_{ij}(k), \qquad \text{for } j = 0, 1, \ldots, M.$$

3. $y_{ik} \geq 0$,   for $i = 0, 1, \ldots, M$ and $k = 1, 2, \ldots, K$.

The long-run expected average cost per unit time is given by

$$E(C) = \sum_{i=0}^{M} \sum_{k=1}^{K} \pi_i C_{ik} D_{ik} = \sum_{i=0}^{M} \sum_{k=1}^{K} C_{ik} y_{ik}.$$

Hence, the linear programming model is to choose the y_{ik} so as to

Minimize $Z = \sum_{i=0}^{M} \sum_{k=1}^{K} C_{ik} y_{ik}$,

subject to the constraints

(1) $\sum_{i=0}^{M} \sum_{k=1}^{K} y_{ik} = 1$.

(2) $\sum_{k=1}^{K} y_{jk} - \sum_{i=0}^{M} \sum_{k=1}^{K} y_{ik} p_{ij}(k) = 0$,   for $j = 0, 1, \ldots, M$.

(3) $y_{ik} \geq 0$,   for $i = 0, 1, \ldots, M$; $k = 1, 2, \ldots, K$.

Thus, this model has $M + 2$ functional constraints and $K(M + 1)$ decision variables. [Actually, (2) provides one *redundant* constraint, so any one of these $M + 1$ constraints can be deleted.]

Assuming that the model is not too huge, it can be solved by the *simplex method*. Once the y_{ik} values are obtained, each D_{ik} is found from

$$D_{ik} = \frac{y_{ik}}{\sum_{k=1}^{K} y_{ik}}.$$

The optimal solution obtained by the simplex method has some interesting properties. It will contain $M + 1$ basic variables $y_{ik} \geq 0$. It can be shown that $y_{ik} > 0$ for at least

---

[1]The argument k is introduced in $p_{ij}(k)$ to indicate that the appropriate transition probability depends upon the decision k.

one $k = 1, 2, \ldots, K$, for each $i = 0, 1, \ldots, M$. Therefore, it follows that $y_{ik} > 0$ for only *one k* for each $i = 0, 1, \ldots, M$. Consequently, each $D_{ik} = 0$ or 1.

The key conclusion is that the optimal policy found by the simplex method is *deterministic* rather than randomized. Thus, allowing policies to be randomized does not help at all in improving the final policy. However, it serves an extremely useful role in this formulation by converting integer variables (the D_{ik}) to continuous variables so that linear programming (LP) can be used. (The analogy in *integer programming* is to use the *LP relaxation* so that the simplex method can be applied and then to have the *integer solutions property* hold so that the optimal solution for the LP relaxation turns out to be integer anyway.)

Solving the Prototype Example by Linear Programming

Refer to the prototype example of Sec. 21.1. The first two columns of Table 21.1 give the relevant combinations of states and decisions. Therefore, the decision variables that need to be included in the model are $y_{01}, y_{11}, y_{13}, y_{21}, y_{22}, y_{23}$, and y_{33}. (The general expressions given above for the model include y_{ik} for *irrelevant* combinations of states and decisions here, so these $y_{ik} = 0$ in an optimal solution, and they might as well be deleted at the outset.) The rightmost column of Table 21.1 provides the coefficients of these variables in the objective function. The transition probabilities $p_{ij}(k)$ for each relevant combination of state i and decision k also are spelled out in Sec. 21.1.

The resulting linear programming model is

Minimize $\quad Z = 1{,}000y_{11} + 6{,}000y_{13} + 3{,}000y_{21} + 4{,}000y_{22} + 6{,}000y_{23}$
$$+ 6{,}000y_{33},$$

subject to

$$y_{01} + y_{11} + y_{13} + y_{21} + y_{22} + y_{23} + y_{33} = 1$$
$$y_{01} - (y_{13} + y_{23} + y_{33}) = 0$$
$$y_{11} + y_{13} - \left(\frac{7}{8}y_{01} + \frac{3}{4}y_{11} + y_{22}\right) = 0$$
$$y_{21} + y_{22} + y_{23} - \left(\frac{1}{16}y_{01} + \frac{1}{8}y_{11} + \frac{1}{2}y_{21}\right) = 0$$
$$y_{33} - \left(\frac{1}{16}y_{01} + \frac{1}{8}y_{11} + \frac{1}{2}y_{21}\right) = 0$$

and

$$\text{all } y_{ik} \geq 0.$$

Applying the simplex method, we obtain the optimal solution

$$y_{01} = \frac{2}{21}, \qquad (y_{11}, y_{13}) = \left(\frac{5}{7}, 0\right), \qquad (y_{21}, y_{22}, y_{23}) = \left(0, \frac{2}{21}, 0\right), \qquad y_{33} = \frac{2}{21},$$

so

$$D_{01} = 1, \qquad (D_{11}, D_{13}) = (1, 0), \qquad (D_{21}, D_{22}, D_{23}) = (0, 1, 0), \qquad D_{33} = 1.$$

This policy calls for leaving the machine as is (decision 1) when it is in state 0 or 1, overhauling it (decision 2) when it is in state 2, and replacing it (decision 3) when it is in state 3. This is the same optimal policy found by exhaustive enumeration at the end of Sec. 21.2.

21.4   POLICY IMPROVEMENT ALGORITHM FOR FINDING OPTIMAL POLICIES

You now have seen two methods for deriving an optimal policy for a Markov decision process: *exhaustive enumeration* and *linear programming*. Exhaustive enumeration is useful because it is both quick and straightforward for very small problems. Linear programming can be used to solve vastly larger problems, and software packages for the simplex method are very widely available.

We now present a third popular method, namely, a *policy improvement algorithm*. The key advantage of this method is that it tends to be very efficient, because it usually reaches an optimal policy in a relatively small number of iterations (far fewer than for the simplex method with a linear programming formulation).

By following the model of Sec. 21.2 and as a joint result of the current state i of the system and the decision $d_i(R) = k$ when operating under policy R, two things occur. An (expected) cost C_{ik} is incurred that depends upon only the observed state of the system and the decision made. The system moves to state j at the next observed time period, with transition probability given by $p_{ij}(k)$. If, in fact, state j influences the cost that has been incurred, then C_{ik} is calculated as follows. Denote by $q_{ij}(k)$ the (expected) cost incurred when the system is in state i and decision k is made and then it evolves to state j at the next observed time period. Then

$$C_{ik} = \sum_{j=0}^{M} q_{ij}(k)p_{ij}(k).$$

Preliminaries

Referring to the description and notation for Markov decision processes given at the beginning of Sec. 21.2, we can show that, for any given policy R, there exist values $g(R)$, $v_0(R), v_1(R), \ldots, v_M(R)$ that satisfy

$$g(R) + v_i(R) = C_{ik} + \sum_{j=0}^{M} p_{ij}(k)\, v_j(R), \qquad \text{for } i = 0, 1, 2, \ldots, M.$$

We now shall give a heuristic justification of these relationships and an interpretation for these values.

Denote by $v_i^n(R)$ the total expected cost of a system starting in state i (beginning the first observed time period) and evolving for n time periods. Then $v_i^n(R)$ has two components: C_{ik}, the cost incurred during the first observed time period, and $\sum_{j=0}^{M} p_{ij}(k)\, v_j^{n-1}(R)$, the total expected cost of the system evolving over the remaining $n - 1$ time periods. This gives the *recursive equation*

$$v_i^n(R) = C_{ik} + \sum_{j=0}^{M} p_{ij}(k)\, v_j^{n-1}(R), \qquad \text{for } i = 0, 1, 2, \ldots, M,$$

where $v_i^1(R) = C_{ik}$ for all i.

It will be useful to explore the behavior of $v_i^n(R)$ as n grows large. Recall that the (long-run) expected average cost per unit time following any policy R can be expressed as

$$g(R) = \sum_{i=0}^{M} \pi_i C_{ik},$$

which is independent of the starting state i. Hence, $v_i^n(R)$ behaves approximately as $n\, g(R)$ for large n. In fact, if we neglect small fluctuations, $v_i^n(R)$ can be expressed as the sum of two components

$$v_i^n(R) \approx n\, g(R) + v_i(R),$$

where the first component is independent of the initial state and the second is dependent upon the initial state. Thus, $v_i(R)$ can be interpreted as the effect on the total expected cost due to starting in state i. Consequently,

$$v_i^n(R) - v_j^n(R) \approx v_i(R) - v_j(R),$$

so that $v_i(R) - v_j(R)$ is a measure of the effect of starting in state i rather than state j.

Letting n grow large, we now can substitute $v_i^n(R) = n\, g(R) + v_i(R)$ and $v_j^{n-1}(R) = (n-1)g(R) + v_j(R)$ into the *recursive equation*. This leads to the system of equations given in the opening paragraph of this subsection.

Note that this system has $M + 1$ equations with $M + 2$ unknowns, so that one of these variables may be chosen arbitrarily. By convention, $v_M(R)$ will be chosen equal to zero. Therefore, by solving the system of linear equations, we can obtain $g(R)$, the (long-run) expected average cost per unit time when policy R is followed. In principle, all policies can be enumerated and that policy which minimizes $g(R)$ can be found. However, even for a moderate number of states and decisions, this technique is cumbersome. Fortunately, there exists an algorithm that can be used to evaluate policies and find the optimal one without complete enumeration, as described next.

The Policy Improvement Algorithm

The algorithm begins by choosing an arbitrary policy R_1. It then solves the system of equations to find the values of $g(R_1)$, $v_0(R)$, $v_1(R)$, . . . , $v_{M-1}(R)$ [with $v_M(R) = 0$]. This step is called *value determination*. A better policy, denoted by R_2, is then constructed. This step is called *policy improvement*. These two steps constitute an iteration of the algorithm. Using the new policy R_2, we perform another iteration. These iterations continue until two successive iterations lead to identical policies, which signifies that the optimal policy has been obtained. The details are outlined below.

Summary of the Policy Improvement Algorithm

Initialization: Choose an arbitrary initial trial policy R_1. Set $n = 1$.
Iteration n:
Step 1: Value determination: For policy R_n, use $p_{ij}(k)$, C_{ik}, and $v_M(R_n) = 0$ to solve the system of $M + 1$ equations

$$g(R_n) = C_{ik} + \sum_{j=0}^{M} p_{ij}(k)\, v_j(R_n) - v_i(R_n), \qquad \text{for } i = 0, 1, \ldots, M,$$

for all $M + 1$ unknown values of $g(R_n)$, $v_0(R_n)$, $v_1(R_n)$, ..., $v_{M-1}(R_n)$.

Step 2: Policy improvement: Using the current values of $v_i(R_n)$ computed for policy R_n, find the alternative policy R_{n+1} such that, for each state i, $d_i(R_{n+1}) = k$ is the decision that minimizes

$$C_{ik} + \sum_{j=0}^{M} p_{ij}(k) \, v_j(R_n) - v_i(R_n)$$

i.e., for *each* state i,

$$\underset{k=1, 2, \ldots, k}{\text{Minimize}} \quad [C_{ik} + \sum_{j=0}^{M} p_{ij}(k) \, v_j(R_n) - v_i(R_n)],$$

and then set $d_i(R_{n+1})$ equal to the minimizing value of k. This procedure defines a new policy R_{n+1}.

Optimality test: The current policy R_{n+1} is optimal if this policy is identical to policy R_n. If it is, stop. Otherwise, reset $n = n + 1$ and perform another iteration.

Two key properties of this algorithm are

1. $g(R_{n+1}) \leq g(R_n)$,   for $n = 1, 2, \ldots$.
2. The algorithm terminates with an optimal policy in a finite number of iterations.[1]

Solving the Prototype Example by the Policy Improvement Algorithm

Referring to the prototype example presented in Sec. 21.1, we outline the application of the algorithm next.

Initialization. For the initial trial policy R_1, we arbitrarily choose the policy that calls for replacement of the machine (decision 3) when it is found to be in state 3, but doing nothing (decision 1) in other states. This policy, its transition matrix, and its costs are summarized below.

Policy R_1			Transition matrix					Costs	
State	Decision	State	0	1	2	3		State	C_{ik}
0	1	0	0	$\frac{7}{8}$	$\frac{1}{16}$	$\frac{1}{16}$		0	0
1	1							1	1,000
2	1	1	0	$\frac{3}{4}$	$\frac{1}{8}$	$\frac{1}{8}$		2	3,000
3	3	2	0	0	$\frac{1}{2}$	$\frac{1}{2}$		3	6,000
		3	1	0	0	0			

---

[1]This termination is guaranteed under the assumptions of the model given in Sec. 21.2, including particularly the (implicit) assumptions of a finite number of states ($M + 1$) and a finite number of decisions (K), but not necessarily for more general models. See R. Howard, *Dynamic Programming and Markov Processes*, M.I.T. Press, Cambridge, MA, 1960. Also see pp. 1291–1293 in A. F. Veinott, Jr., "On Finding Optimal Policies in Discrete Dynamic Programming with No Discounting," *Annals of Mathematical Statistics*, **37**: 1284–1294, 1966.

Iteration 1.   With this policy, the value determination step requires solving the following four equations simultaneously for $g(R_1)$, $v_0(R_1)$, $v_1(R_1)$, and $v_2(R_1)$ [with $v_3(R_1) = 0$].

$$g(R_1) = \quad\quad\quad\quad + \frac{7}{8}v_1(R_1) + \frac{1}{16}v_2(R_1) - v_0(R_1).$$

$$g(R_1) = 1,000 \quad\quad\quad + \frac{3}{4}v_1(R_1) + \frac{1}{8}v_2(R_1) \quad - v_1(R_1).$$

$$g(R_1) = 3,000 \quad\quad\quad\quad\quad\quad\quad + \frac{1}{2}v_2(R_1) \quad - v_2(R_1).$$

$$g(R_1) = 6,000 + v_0(R_1).$$

The simultaneous solution is

$$g(R_1) = \frac{25,000}{13} = 1,923$$

$$v_0(R_1) = -\frac{53,000}{13} = -4,077$$

$$v_1(R_1) = -\frac{34,000}{13} = -2,615$$

$$v_2(R_1) = \frac{28,000}{13} = 2,154.$$

Step 2 (policy improvement) can now be applied. We want to find an improved policy R_2 such that decision k in state i minimizes the corresponding expression below.

State 0: $C_{0k} - p_{00}(k)(4,077) - p_{01}(k)(2,615) + p_{02}(k)(2,154) + 4,077$
State 1: $C_{1k} - p_{10}(k)(4,077) - p_{11}(k)(2,615) + p_{12}(k)(2,154) + 2,615$
State 2: $C_{2k} - p_{20}(k)(4,077) - p_{21}(k)(2,615) + p_{22}(k)(2,154) - 2,154$
State 3: $C_{3k} - p_{30}(k)(4,077) - p_{31}(k)(2,615) + p_{32}(k)(2,154).$

Actually, in state 0, the only decision allowed is decision 1 (do nothing), so no calculations are needed. Similarly, we know that decision 3 (replace) must be made in state 3. Thus, only states 1 and 2 require calculation of the values of these expressions for alternative decisions.

For state 1, the possible decisions are 1 and 3. For each one, we show below the corresponding C_{1k}, the $p_{1j}(k)$, and the resulting value of the expression.

	State 1					
Decision	C_{1k}	$p_{10}(k)$	$p_{11}(k)$	$p_{12}(k)$	$p_{13}(k)$	**Value of Expression**
1	1,000	0	$\frac{3}{4}$	$\frac{1}{8}$	$\frac{1}{8}$	1,923 ← Minimum
3	6,000	1	0	0	0	4,538

Since decision 1 minimizes the expression, it is chosen as the decision to be made in state 1 for policy R_2 (just as for policy R_1).

The corresponding results for state 2 are shown below for its three possible decisions.

	State 2					
Decision	C_{2k}	$p_{20}(k)$	$p_{21}(k)$	$p_{22}(k)$	$p_{23}(k)$	**Value of Expression**
1	3,000	0	0	$\frac{1}{2}$	$\frac{1}{2}$	1,923
2	4,000	0	1	0	0	−769 ← Minimum
3	6,000	1	0	0	0	−231

Therefore, decision 2 is chosen as the decision to be made in state 2 for policy R_2. Note that this is a change from policy R_1.

We summarize our new policy, its transition matrix, and its costs below.

Policy R_2

State	Decision
0	1
1	1
2	2
3	3

Transition matrix

State	0	1	2	3
0	0	$\frac{7}{8}$	$\frac{1}{16}$	$\frac{1}{16}$
1	0	$\frac{3}{4}$	$\frac{1}{8}$	$\frac{1}{8}$
2	0	1	0	0
3	1	0	0	0

Costs

State	C_{ik}
0	0
1	1,000
2	4,000
3	6,000

Since this policy is not identical to policy R_1, the optimality test says to perform another iteration.

Iteration 2. For step 1 (value determination), the equations to be solved for this policy are shown below.

$$g(R_2) = \qquad\qquad + \frac{7}{8}v_1(R_2) + \frac{1}{16}v_2(R_2) - v_0(R_2).$$

$$g(R_2) = 1,000 \qquad + \frac{3}{4}v_1(R_2) + \frac{1}{8}v_2(R_2) - v_1(R_2).$$

$$g(R_2) = 4,000 \qquad + \quad v_1(R_2) \qquad\quad - v_2(R_2).$$

$$g(R_2) = 6,000 + v_0(R_2).$$

The simultaneous solution is

$$g(R_2) = \frac{5,000}{3} = 1,667$$

$$v_0(R_2) = -\frac{13,000}{3} = -4,333$$

$$v_1(R_2) = -3,000$$

$$v_2(R_2) = -\frac{2,000}{3} = -667.$$

Step 2 (policy improvement) can now be applied. For the two states with more than one possible decision, the expressions to be minimized are

State 1: $C_{1k} - p_{10}(k)(4,333) - p_{11}(k)(3,000) - p_{12}(k)(667) + 3,000$

State 2: $C_{2k} - p_{20}(k)(4,333) - p_{21}(k)(3,000) - p_{22}(k)(667) + 667.$

The first iteration provides the necessary data (the transition probabilities and C_{ik}) required for determining the new policy, except for the values of each of these expressions for each of the possible decisions. These values are

Decision	Value for State 1	Value for State 2
1	1,667	3,333
2	—	1,667
3	4,667	2,334

Since decision 1 minimizes the expression for state 1 and decision 2 minimizes the expression for state 2, our next trial policy R_3 is

Policy R_3

State	Decision
0	1
1	1
2	2
3	3

Note that policy R_3 is identical to policy R_2. Therefore, the optimality test indicates that this policy is optimal, so the algorithm is finished.

Another example illustrating the application of this algorithm is included in your OR Tutor. The OR Courseware also includes an *interactive* routine for efficiently learning and applying the algorithm.

21.5 DISCOUNTED COST CRITERION

Throughout this chapter, we have measured policies on the basis of their (long-run) expected average cost per unit time. We now turn to an alternative measure of performance, namely, the **expected total discounted cost.**

As first introduced in Sec. 19.2, this measure uses a *discount factor* α, where $0 < \alpha < 1$. The discount factor α can be interpreted as equal to $1/(1 + i)$, where i is the current interest rate per period. Thus, α is the *present value* of one unit of cost one period in the future. Similarly, α^m is the *present value* of one unit of cost m periods in the future.

This *discounted cost criterion* becomes preferable to the *average cost criterion* when the time periods for the Markov chain are sufficiently long that the *time value of money* should be taken into account in adding costs in future periods to the cost in the current period. Another advantage is that the discounted cost criterion can readily be adapted to dealing with a *finite-period* Markov decision process where the Markov chain will terminate after a certain number of periods.

Both the policy improvement technique and the linear programming approach still can be applied here with relatively minor adjustments from the average cost case, as we describe next. Then we will present another technique, called the *method of successive approximations,* for quickly approximating an optimal policy.

A Policy Improvement Algorithm

To derive the expressions needed for the value determination and policy improvement steps of the algorithm, we now adopt the viewpoint of *probabilistic dynamic programming* (as described in Sec. 11.4). In particular, for each state i ($i = 0, 1, \ldots, M$) of a Markov decision process operating under policy R, let $V_i^n(R)$ be the *expected total discounted cost* when the process starts in state i (beginning the first observed time period) and evolves for n time periods. Then $V_i^n(R)$ has two components: C_{ik}, the cost incurred during the first observed time period, and $\alpha \sum_{j=0}^{M} p_{ij}(k)V_j^{n-1}(R)$, the expected total discounted cost of the process evolving over the remaining $n - 1$ time periods. For each $i = 0, 1, \ldots, M$, this yields the recursive equation

$$V_i^n(R) = C_{ik} + \alpha \sum_{j=0}^{M} p_{ij}(k)V_j^{n-1}(R),$$

with $V_i^1(R) = C_{ik}$, which closely resembles the recursive relationships of probabilistic dynamic programming found in Sec. 11.4.

As n approaches infinity, this recursive equation converges to

$$V_i(R) = C_{ik} + \alpha \sum_{j=0}^{M} p_{ij}(k)V_j(R), \qquad \text{for } i = 0, 1, \ldots, M,$$

where $V_i(R)$ can now be interpreted as the expected total discounted cost when the process starts in state i and continues indefinitely. There are $M + 1$ equations and $M + 1$ unknowns, so the simultaneous solution of this system of equations yields the $V_i(R)$.

To illustrate, consider again the prototype example of Sec. 21.1. Under the average cost criterion, we found in Secs. 21.2, 21.3, and 21.4 that the optimal policy is to do nothing in states 0 and 1, overhaul in state 2, and replace in state 3. Under the discounted cost criterion, with $\alpha = 0.9$, this same policy gives the following system of equations:

$$V_0(R) = \qquad\quad + 0.9\left[\frac{7}{8}V_1(R) + \frac{1}{16}V_2(R) + \frac{1}{16}V_3(R)\right]$$

$$V_1(R) = 1,000 + 0.9\left[\frac{3}{4}V_1(R) + \frac{1}{8}V_2(R) + \frac{1}{8}V_3(R)\right]$$

$$V_2(R) = 4,000 + 0.9[\qquad V_1(R)]$$

$$V_3(R) = 6,000 + 0.9[V_0(R)].$$

The simultaneous solution is

$$V_0(R) = 14,949$$
$$V_1(R) = 16,262$$
$$V_2(R) = 18,636$$
$$V_3(R) = 19,454.$$

Thus, assuming that the system starts in state 0, the expected total discounted cost is $14,949.

This system of equations provides the expressions needed for a policy improvement algorithm. After summarizing this algorithm in general terms, we shall use it to check whether this particular policy still is optimal under the discounted cost criterion.

Summary of the Policy Improvement Algorithm (Discounted Cost Criterion).

Initialization: Choose an arbitrary initial trial policy R_1. Set $n = 1$.
Iteration n:
Step 1: Value determination: For policy R_n, use $p_{ij}(k)$ and C_{ik} to solve the system of $M + 1$ equations

$$V_i(R_n) = C_{ik} + \alpha \sum_{j=0}^{M} p_{ij}(k)V_j(R_n), \qquad \text{for } i = 0, 1, \ldots, M,$$

for all $M + 1$ unknown values of $V_0(R_n), V_1(R_n), \ldots, V_M(R_n)$.
Step 2: Policy improvement: Using the current values of the $V_i(R_n)$, find the alternative policy R_{n+1} such that, for each state i, $d_i(R_{n+1}) = k$ is the decision that minimizes

$$C_{ik} + \alpha \sum_{j=0}^{M} p_{ij}(k)V_j(R_n)$$

i.e., for *each* state i,

$$\underset{k=1, 2, \ldots, K}{\text{Minimize}} \quad \left[C_{ik} + \alpha \sum_{j=0}^{M} p_{ij}(k)V_j(R_n) \right],$$

and then set $d_i(R_{n+1})$ equal to the minimizing value of k. This procedure defines a new policy R_{n+1}.
Optimality test: The current policy R_{n+1} is optimal if this policy is identical to policy R_n. If it is, stop. Otherwise, reset $n = n + 1$ and perform another iteration.

Three key properties of this algorithm are as follows:

1. $V_i(R_{n+1}) \leq V_i(R_n)$, for $i = 0, 1, \ldots, M$ and $n = 1, 2, \ldots$.
2. The algorithm terminates with an optimal policy in a finite number of iterations.
3. The algorithm is valid without the assumption (used for the average cost case) that the Markov chain associated with every transition matrix is irreducible.

Your OR Courseware includes an *interactive* routine for applying this algorithm.

Solving the Prototype Example by This Policy Improvement Algorithm. We now pick up the prototype example where we left it before summarizing the algorithm. We already have selected the optimal policy under the average cost criterion to be our initial trial policy R_1. This policy, its transition matrix, and its costs are summarized below.

Policy R_1	
State	**Decision**
0	1
1	1
2	2
3	3

Transition matrix

State	0	1	2	3
0	0	$\frac{7}{8}$	$\frac{1}{16}$	$\frac{1}{16}$
1	0	$\frac{3}{4}$	$\frac{1}{8}$	$\frac{1}{8}$
2	0	1	0	0
3	1	0	0	0

Costs

State	C_{ik}
0	0
1	1,000
2	4,000
3	6,000

We also have already done step 1 (value determination) of iteration 1. This transition matrix and these costs led to the system of equations used to find $V_0(R_1) = 14{,}949$, $V_1(R_1) = 16{,}262$, $V_2(R_1) = 18{,}636$, and $V_3(R_1) = 19{,}454$.

To start step 2 (policy improvement), we only need to construct the expression to be minimized for the two states (1 and 2) with a choice of decisions.

State 1: $C_{1k} + 0.9[p_{10}(k)(14{,}949) + p_{11}(k)(16{,}262) + p_{12}(k)(18{,}636)$
$+ p_{13}(k)(19{,}454)]$

State 2: $C_{2k} + 0.9[p_{20}(k)(14{,}949) + p_{21}(k)(16{,}262) + p_{22}(k)(18{,}636)$
$+ p_{23}(k)(19{,}454)].$

For each of these states and their possible decisions, we show below the corresponding C_{ik}, the $p_{ij}(k)$, and the resulting value of the expression.

			State 1				
Decision	C_{1k}	$p_{10}(k)$	$p_{11}(k)$	$p_{12}(k)$	$p_{13}(k)$	**Value of Expression**	
1	1,000	0	$\frac{3}{4}$	$\frac{1}{8}$	$\frac{1}{8}$	16,262	← Minimum
3	6,000	1	0	0	0	19,454	

			State 2				
Decision	C_{2k}	$p_{20}(k)$	$p_{21}(k)$	$p_{22}(k)$	$p_{23}(k)$	**Value of Expression**	
1	3,000	0	0	$\frac{1}{2}$	$\frac{1}{2}$	20,140	
2	4,000	0	1	0	0	18,636	← Minimum
3	6,000	1	0	0	0	19,454	

Since decision 1 minimizes the expression for state 1 and decision 2 minimizes the expression for state 2, our next trial policy (R_2) is as follows:

Policy R_2

State	Decision
0	1
1	1
2	2
3	3

Since this policy is identical to policy R_1, the optimality test indicates that this policy is optimal. Thus, the optimal policy under the average cost criterion also is optimal under the discounted cost criterion in this case. (This often occurs, but not always.)

Linear Programming Formulation

The linear programming formulation for the discounted cost case is similar to that for the average cost case given in Sec. 21.3. However, we no longer need the first constraint given in Sec. 21.3; but the other functional constraints do need to include the discount factor α. The other difference is that the model now contains constants β_j for $j = 0, 1, \ldots, M$. These constants must satisfy the conditions

$$\sum_{j=0}^{M} \beta_j = 1, \qquad \beta_j > 0 \qquad \text{for } j = 0, 1, \ldots, M,$$

but otherwise they can be chosen arbitrarily without affecting the optimal policy obtained from the model.

The resulting model is to choose the values of the *continuous* decision variables y_{ik} so as to

$$\text{Minimize} \qquad Z = \sum_{i=0}^{M} \sum_{k=1}^{K} C_{ik} y_{ik},$$

subject to the constraints

$$(1) \qquad \sum_{k=1}^{K} y_{jk} - \alpha \sum_{i=0}^{M} \sum_{k=1}^{K} y_{ik} p_{ij}(k) = \beta_j, \qquad \text{for } j = 0, 1, \ldots, M,$$

$$(2) \qquad y_{ik} \geq 0, \qquad \text{for } i = 0, 1, \ldots, M; k = 1, 2, \ldots, K.$$

Once the simplex method is used to obtain an optimal solution for this model, the corresponding optimal policy then is defined by

$$D_{ik} = P\{\text{decision} = k \text{ and state} = i\} = \frac{y_{ik}}{\displaystyle\sum_{k=1}^{K} y_{ik}}.$$

The y_{ik} now can be interpreted as the *discounted* expected time of being in state i and making decision k, when the probability distribution of the *initial state* (when observations begin) is $P\{X_0 = j\} = \beta_j$ for $j = 0, 1, \ldots, M$. In other words, if

$$z_{ik}^n = P\{\text{at time } n, \text{ state} = i \text{ and decision} = k\},$$

then

$$y_{ik} = z_{ik}^0 + \alpha z_{ik}^1 + \alpha^2 z_{ik}^2 + \alpha^3 z_{ik}^3 + \cdots.$$

With the interpretation of the β_j as *initial state probabilities* (with each probability greater than zero), Z can be interpreted as the corresponding expected total discounted cost. Thus, the choice of β_j affects the optimal value of Z (but not the resulting optimal policy).

It again can be shown that the optimal policy obtained from solving the linear programming model is deterministic; that is, $D_{ik} = 0$ or 1. Furthermore, this technique is valid without the assumption (used for the average cost case) that the Markov chain associated with every transition matrix is irreducible.

Solving the Prototype Example by Linear Programming.

The linear programming model for the prototype example (with $\alpha = 0.9$) is

Minimize $Z = 1{,}000y_{11} + 6{,}000y_{13} + 3{,}000y_{21} + 4{,}000y_{22} + 6{,}000y_{23}$
$$+ 6{,}000y_{33},$$

subject to

$$y_{01} - 0.9(y_{13} + y_{23} + y_{33}) = \frac{1}{4}$$

$$y_{11} + y_{13} - 0.9\left(\frac{7}{8}y_{01} + \frac{3}{4}y_{11} + y_{22}\right) = \frac{1}{4}$$

$$y_{21} + y_{22} + y_{23} - 0.9\left(\frac{1}{16}y_{01} + \frac{1}{8}y_{11} + \frac{1}{2}y_{21}\right) = \frac{1}{4}$$

$$y_{33} - 0.9\left(\frac{1}{16}y_{01} + \frac{1}{8}y_{11} + \frac{1}{2}y_{21}\right) = \frac{1}{4}$$

and

$$\text{all } y_{ik} \geq 0,$$

where β_0, β_1, β_2, and β_3 are arbitrarily chosen to be $\frac{1}{4}$. By the simplex method, the optimal solution is

$$y_{01} = 1.210, \qquad (y_{11}, y_{13}) = (6.656, 0), \qquad (y_{21}, y_{22}, y_{23}) = (0, 1.067, 0),$$
$$y_{33} = 1.067,$$

so

$$D_{01} = 1, \qquad (D_{11}, D_{13}) = (1, 0), \qquad (D_{21}, D_{22}, D_{23}) = (0, 1, 0), \qquad D_{33} = 1.$$

This optimal policy is the same as that obtained earlier in this section by the policy improvement algorithm.

The value of the objective function for the optimal solution is $Z = 17{,}325$. This value is closely related to the values of the $V_i(R)$ for this optimal policy that were obtained by the policy improvement algorithm. Recall that $V_i(R)$ is interpreted as the expected total discounted cost given that the system starts in state i, and we are interpreting β_i as the probability of starting in state i. Because each β_i was chosen to equal $\frac{1}{4}$,

$$17,325 = \frac{1}{4}[V_0(R) + V_1(R) + V_2(R) + V_3(R)]$$

$$= \frac{1}{4}(14,949 + 16,262 + 18,636 + 19,454).$$

Finite-Period Markov Decision Processes and the Method of Successive Approximations

We now turn our attention to an approach, called the *method of successive approxima-tions,* for *quickly* finding at least an *approximation* to an optimal policy.

We have assumed that the Markov decision process will be operating indefinitely, and we have sought an optimal policy for such a process. The basic idea of the method of suc-cessive approximations is to instead find an optimal policy for the decisions to make in the first period when the process has only n time periods to go before termination, start-ing with $n = 1$, then $n = 2$, then $n = 3$, and so on. As n grows large, the corresponding optimal policies will converge to an optimal policy for the infinite-period problem of in-terest. Thus, the policies obtained for $n = 1, 2, 3, \ldots$ provide *successive approximations* that lead to the desired optimal policy.

The reason that this approach is attractive is that we already have a quick method of finding an optimal policy when the process has only n periods to go, namely, probabilis-tic dynamic programming as described in Sec. 11.4.

In particular, for $i = 0, 1, \ldots, M$, let

V_i^n = expected total discounted cost of following an optimal policy, given that process starts in state i and has only n periods to go.[1]

By the *principle of optimality* for dynamic programming (see Sec. 11.2), the V_i^n are ob-tained from the recursive relationship

$$V_i^n = \min_k \left\{ C_{ik} + \alpha \sum_{j=0}^{M} p_{ij}(k)V_j^{n-1} \right\}, \quad \text{for } i = 0, 1, \ldots, M.$$

The minimizing value of k provides the optimal decision to make in the first period when the process starts in state i.

To get started, with $n = 1$, all the $V_i^0 = 0$ so that

$$V_i^1 = \min_k \{C_{ik}\}, \quad \text{for } i = 0, 1, \ldots, M.$$

Although the method of successive approximations may not lead to an optimal pol-icy for the infinite-period problem after only a few iterations, it has one distinct advan-tage over the policy improvement and linear programming techniques. It never requires

---

[1]Since we want to allow n to grow indefinitely, we are letting n be the *number of periods to go,* instead of the *number of periods from the beginning* (as in Chap. 11).

solving a system of simultaneous equations, so each iteration can be performed simply and quickly.

Furthermore, if the Markov decision process actually does have just n periods to go, n iterations of this method definitely will lead to an optimal policy. (For an n-period problem, it is permissible to set $\alpha = 1$, that is, no discounting, in which case the objective is to minimize the expected total cost over n periods.)

Your OR Courseware includes an interactive routine to help guide you to use this method efficiently.

Solving the Prototype Example by the Method of Successive Approximations.

We again use $\alpha = 0.9$. Refer to the rightmost column of Table 21.1 at the end of Sec. 21.1 for the values of C_{ik}. Also note in the first two columns of this table that the only feasible decisions k for each state i are $k = 1$ for $i = 0$, $k = 1$ or 3 for $i = 1$, $k = 1, 2,$ or 3 for $i = 2$, and $k = 3$ for $i = 3$.

For the first iteration ($n = 1$), the value obtained for each V_i^1 is shown below, along with the minimizing value of k (given in parentheses).

$$V_0^1 = \min_{k=1} \{C_{0k}\} = 0 \qquad\qquad (k = 1)$$

$$V_1^1 = \min_{k=1,3} \{C_{1k}\} = 1{,}000 \qquad (k = 1)$$

$$V_2^1 = \min_{k=1,2,3} \{C_{2k}\} = 3{,}000 \qquad (k = 1)$$

$$V_3^1 = \min_{k=3} \{C_{3k}\} = 6{,}000 \qquad (k = 3)$$

Thus, the first approximation calls for making decision 1 (do nothing) when the system is in state 0, 1, or 2. When the system is in state 3, decision 3 (replace the machine) is made.

The second iteration leads to

$$V_0^2 = 0 + 0.9\left[\frac{7}{8}(1{,}000) + \frac{1}{16}(3{,}000) + \frac{1}{16}(6{,}000)\right] \qquad\qquad = 1{,}294 \qquad (k = 1)$$

$$V_1^2 = \min\left\{1{,}000 + 0.9\left[\frac{3}{4}(1{,}000) + \frac{1}{8}(3{,}000) + \frac{1}{8}(6{,}000)\right],\right.$$
$$\left. 6{,}000 + 0.9[1(0)]\right\} = 2{,}688 \qquad (k = 1)$$

$$V_2^2 = \min\left\{3{,}000 + 0.9\left[\frac{1}{2}(3{,}000) + \frac{1}{2}(6{,}000)\right],\right.$$
$$\left. 4{,}000 + 0.9[1(1{,}000)],\ 6{,}000 + 0.9[1(0)]\right\} = 4{,}900 \qquad (k = 2)$$

$$V_3^2 = \qquad\qquad\qquad\qquad\qquad 6{,}000 + 0.9[1(0)] = 6{,}000 \qquad (k = 3).$$

where the *min* operator has been deleted from the first and fourth expressions because only one alternative for the decision is available. Thus, the second approximation calls for leaving the machine as is when it is in state 0 or 1, overhauling when it is in state 2, and replacing the machine when it is in state 3. Note that this policy is the optimal one for the infinite-period problem, as found earlier in this section by both the policy improvement algorithm and linear programming. However, the V_i^2 (the expected total discounted cost when starting in state i for the two-period problem) are not yet close to the V_i (the corresponding cost for the infinite-period problem).

The third iteration leads to

$$V_0^3 = 0 + 0.9\left[\frac{7}{8}(2,688) + \frac{1}{16}(4,900) + \frac{1}{16}(6,000)\right] \qquad = 2,730 \qquad (k = 1)$$

$$V_1^3 = \min\left\{1,000 + 0.9\left[\frac{3}{4}(2,688) + \frac{1}{8}(4,900) + \frac{1}{8}(6,000)\right],\right.$$

$$\left. 6,000 + 0.9[1(1,294)]\right\} = 4,041 \qquad (k = 1)$$

$$V_2^3 = \min\left\{3,000 + 0.9\left[\frac{1}{2}(4,900) + \frac{1}{2}(6,000)\right],\right.$$

$$\left. 4,000 + 0.9[1(2,688)], \ 6,000 + 0.9[1(1,294)]\right\} = 6,419 \qquad (k = 2)$$

$$V_3^3 = \qquad\qquad\qquad\qquad 6,000 + 0.9[1(1,294)] \ = 7,165 \qquad (k = 3).$$

Again the optimal policy for the infinite-period problem is obtained, and the costs are getting closer to those for that problem. This procedure can be continued, and V_0^n, V_1^n, V_2^n, and V_3^n will converge to 14,949, 16,262, 18,636, and 19,454, respectively.

Note that termination of the method of successive approximations after the second iteration would have resulted in an optimal policy for the infinite-period problem, although there is no way to know this fact without solving the problem by other methods.

As indicated earlier, the method of successive approximations definitely obtains an optimal policy for an n-period problem after n iterations. For this example, the first, second, and third iterations have identified the optimal immediate decision for each state if the remaining number of periods is one, two, and three, respectively.

21.6 CONCLUSIONS

Markov decision processes provide a powerful tool for optimizing the performance of stochastic processes that can be modeled as a discrete time Markov chain. Applications arise in a variety of areas. Selected Reference 6 provides an interesting survey of these applications, and Selected Reference 5 gives an update on one that won a prestigious prize.

The two primary measures of performance used are the (long-run) *expected average cost per unit time* and the *expected total discounted cost*. The latter measure requires determination of the appropriate value of a discount factor, but this measure is useful when it is important to take into account the time value of money.

The two most important methods for deriving optimal policies for Markov decision processes are *policy improvement algorithms* and *linear programming*. Under the discounted cost criterion, the *method of successive approximations* provides a quick way of approximating an optimal policy.

SELECTED REFERENCES

1. Bertsekas, D. P.: *Dynamic Programming: Deterministic and Stochastic Models,* Prentice-Hall, Englewood Cliffs, NJ, 1987.
2. Denardo, E.: *Dynamic Programming Theory and Applications,* Prentice-Hall, Englewood Cliffs, NJ, 1982.

3. Feinberg, E. A., and A. Shwartz: *Markov Decision Processes: Research Directions and Applications,* Kluwer Academic Publishers, Boston, 2001.

4. Puterman, M. L.: *Markov Decision Processes: Discrete Stochastic Dynamic Programming,* Wiley, New York, 1994.

5. Wang, K. C. P., and J. P. Zaniewski: "20/30 Hindsight: The New Pavement Optimization in the Arizona State Highway Network," *Interfaces,* **26**(3): 77–89, May–June 1996.

6. White, D. J.: "Real Applications of Markov Decision Processes," *Interfaces,* **15**(6): 73–83, November–December 1985.

7. Whittle, P.: *Optimization over Time: Dynamic Programming and Stochastic Control,* Wiley, New York, vol. 1, 1982; vol. 2, 1983.

LEARNING AIDS FOR THIS CHAPTER IN YOUR OR COURSEWARE

A Demonstration Example in OR Tutor:

Policy Improvement Algorithm—Average Cost Case

Interactive Routines:

Enter Markov Decision Model
Interactive Policy Improvement Algorithm—Average Cost
Interactive Policy Improvement Algorithm—Discounted Cost
Interactive Method of Successive Approximations

Automatic Routines:

Enter Transition Matrix
Steady-State Probabilities

"Ch. 21—Markov Decision Proc" Files for Solving the Linear Programming Formulations:

Excel File
LINGO/LINDO File
MPL/CPLEX File

See Appendix 1 for documentation of the software.

PROBLEMS

The symbols to the left of some of the problems (or their parts) have the following meaning:

D: The demonstration example listed above may be helpful.

I: We suggest that you use the corresponding interactive routine listed above (the printout records your work).

A: The automatic routines listed above can be helpful.

C: Use the computer with any of the software options available to you (or as instructed by your instructor) to solve your linear programming formulation.

An asterisk on the problem number indicates that at least a partial answer is given in the back of the book.

21.2-1.* During any period, a potential customer arrives at a certain facility with probability $\frac{1}{2}$. If there are already two people at the facility (including the one being served), the potential customer leaves the facility immediately and never returns. However, if there is one person or less, he enters the facility and becomes an actual customer. The manager of the facility has two types of service configurations available. At the beginning of each period, a decision must be made on which configuration to use. If she uses her "slow" configuration at a cost of \$3 and any customers are present during the period, one customer will be served and leave the facility with probability $\frac{3}{5}$. If she uses her "fast" configuration at a cost of \$9 and any customers are present during the period, one customer will be served and leave the facility with probability $\frac{4}{5}$. The probability of more than one customer arriving or more than one customer being served in a period is zero. A profit of \$50 is earned when a customer is served.

(a) Formulate the problem of choosing the service configuration period by period as a Markov decision process. Identify the states and decisions. For each combination of state and decision, find the *expected net immediate cost* (subtracting any profit from serving a customer) incurred during that period.
(b) Identify all the (stationary deterministic) policies. For each one, find the transition matrix and write an expression for the (long-run) expected average net cost per period in terms of the unknown steady-state probabilities ($\pi_0, \pi_1, \ldots, \pi_M$).
A **(c)** Use your OR Courseware to find these steady-state probabilities for each policy. Then evaluate the expression obtained in part (*b*) to find the optimal policy by exhaustive enumeration.

21.2-2.* A student is concerned about her car and does not like dents. When she drives to school, she has a choice of parking it on the street in one space, parking it on the street and taking up two spaces, or parking in the lot. If she parks on the street in one space, her car gets dented with probability $\frac{1}{10}$. If she parks on the street and takes two spaces, the probability of a dent is $\frac{1}{50}$ and the probability of a \$15 ticket is $\frac{3}{10}$. Parking in a lot costs \$5, but the car will not get dented. If her car gets dented, she can have it repaired, in which case it is out of commission for 1 day and costs her \$50 in fees and cab fares. She can also drive her car dented, but she feels that the resulting loss of value and pride is equivalent to a cost of \$9 per school day. She wishes to determine the optimal policy for where to park and whether to repair the car when dented in order to minimize her (long-run) expected average cost per school day.

(a) Formulate this problem as a Markov decision process by identifying the states and decisions and then finding the C_{ik}.
(b) Identify all the (stationary deterministic) policies. For each one, find the transition matrix and write an expression for the (long-run) expected average cost per period in terms of the unknown steady-state probabilities ($\pi_0, \pi_1, \ldots, \pi_M$).

A **(c)** Use your OR Courseware to find these steady-state probabilities for each policy. Then evaluate the expression obtained in part (*b*) to find the optimal policy by exhaustive enumeration.

21.2-3. A soap company specializes in a luxury type of bath soap. The sales of this soap fluctuate between two levels—low and high—depending upon two factors: (1) whether they advertise and (2) the advertising and marketing of new products by competitors. The second factor is out of the company's control, but it is trying to determine what its own advertising policy should be. For example, the *marketing manager's proposal* is to advertise when sales are low but not to advertise when sales are high (a particular policy). Advertising in any quarter of a year has primary impact on sales in the *following* quarter. At the beginning of each quarter, the needed information is available to forecast accurately whether sales will be low or high that quarter and to decide whether to advertise that quarter.

The cost of advertising is \$1 million for each quarter of a year in which it is done. When advertising is done during a quarter, the probability of having high sales the next quarter is $\frac{1}{2}$ or $\frac{3}{4}$ depending upon whether the current quarter's sales are low or high. These probabilities go down to $\frac{1}{4}$ or $\frac{1}{2}$ when advertising is not done during the current quarter. The company's quarterly profits (excluding advertising costs) are \$4 million when sales are high but only \$2 million when sales are low. Management now wants to determine the advertising policy that will maximize the company's (long-run) expected average *net profit* (profit minus advertising costs) per quarter.

(a) Formulate this problem as a Markov decision process by identifying the states and decisions and then finding the C_{ik}.
(b) Identify all the (stationary deterministic) policies. For each one, find the transition matrix and write an expression for the (long-run) expected average net profit per period in terms of the unknown steady-state probabilities ($\pi_0, \pi_1, \ldots, \pi_M$).
A **(c)** Use your OR Courseware to find these steady-state probabilities for each policy. Then evaluate the expression obtained in part (*b*) to find the optimal policy by exhaustive enumeration.

21.2-4. Every Saturday night a man plays poker at his home with the same group of friends. If he provides refreshments for the group (at an expected cost of \$14) on any given Saturday night, the group will begin the following Saturday night in a good mood with probability $\frac{7}{8}$ and in a bad mood with probability $\frac{1}{8}$. However, if he fails to provide refreshments, the group will begin the following Saturday night in a good mood with probability $\frac{1}{8}$ and in a bad mood with probability $\frac{7}{8}$, regardless of their mood this Saturday. Furthermore, if the group begins the night in a bad mood and then he fails to provide refreshments, the group will gang up on him so that he incurs expected poker losses of \$75. Under other circumstances, he averages no gain or loss on his poker play. The man wishes to find the policy regarding when to provide refreshments that will minimize his (long-run) expected average cost per week.

(a) Formulate this problem as a Markov decision process by identifying the states and decisions and then finding the C_{ik}.

(b) Identify all the (stationary deterministic) policies. For each one, find the transition matrix and write an expression for the (long-run) expected average cost per period in terms of the unknown steady-state probabilities ($\pi_0, \pi_1, \ldots, \pi_M$).

A (c) Use your OR Courseware to find these steady-state probabilities for each policy. Then evaluate the expression obtained in part (b) to find the optimal policy by exhaustive enumeration.

21.2-5.* When a tennis player serves, he gets two chances to serve in bounds. If he fails to do so twice, he loses the point. If he attempts to serve an ace, he serves in bounds with probability $\frac{3}{8}$. If he serves a lob, he serves in bounds with probability $\frac{7}{8}$. If he serves an ace in bounds, he wins the point with probability $\frac{2}{3}$. With an in-bounds lob, he wins the point with probability $\frac{1}{3}$. If the cost is $+1$ for each point lost and -1 for each point won, the problem is to determine the optimal serving strategy to minimize the (long-run) expected average cost per point. (*Hint:* Let state 0 denote point over, two serves to go on next point; and let state 1 denote one serve left.)

(a) Formulate this problem as a Markov decision process by identifying the states and decisions and then finding the C_{ik}.

(b) Identify all the (stationary deterministic) policies. For each one, find the transition matrix and write an expression for the (long-run) expected average cost per point in terms of the unknown steady-state probabilities ($\pi_0, \pi_1, \ldots, \pi_M$).

A (c) Use your OR Courseware to find these steady-state probabilities for each policy. Then evaluate the expression obtained in part (b) to find the optimal policy by exhaustive enumeration.

21.2-6. Each year Ms. Fontanez has the chance to invest in two different no-load mutual funds: the Go-Go Fund or the Go-Slow Mutual Fund. At the end of each year, Ms. Fontanez liquidates her holdings, takes her profits, and then reinvests. The yearly profits of the mutual funds are dependent upon how the market reacts each year. Recently the market has been oscillating around the 12,000 mark from one year end to the next, according to the probabilities given in the following transition matrix:

	11,000	12,000	13,000
11,000	0.3	0.5	0.2
12,000	0.1	0.5	0.4
13,000	0.2	0.4	0.4

Each year that the market moves up (down) 1,000 points, the Go-Go Fund has profits (losses) of $20,000, while the Go-Slow Fund

has profits (losses) of $10,000. If the market moves up (down) 2,000 points in a year, the Go-Go Fund has profits (losses) of $50,000, while the Go-Slow Fund has profits (losses) of only $20,000. If the market does not change, there is no profit or loss for either fund. Ms. Fontanez wishes to determine her optimal investment policy in order to minimize her (long-run) expected average cost (loss minus profit) per year.

(a) Formulate this problem as a Markov decision process by identifying the states and decisions and then finding the C_{ik}.

(b) Identify all the (stationary deterministic) policies. For each one, find the transition matrix and write an expression for the (long-run) expected average cost per period in terms of the unknown steady-state probabilities ($\pi_0, \pi_1, \ldots, \pi_M$).

A (c) Use your OR Courseware to find these steady-state probabilities for each policy. Then evaluate the expression obtained in part (b) to find the optimal policy by exhaustive enumeration.

21.2-7. Buck and Bill Bogus are twin brothers who work at a gas station and have a counterfeiting business on the side. Each day a decision is made as to which brother will go to work at the gas station, and then the other will stay home and run the printing press in the basement. Each day that the machine works properly, it is estimated that 60 usable $20 bills can be produced. However, the machine is somewhat unreliable and breaks down frequently. If the machine is not working at the beginning of the day, Buck can have it in working order by the beginning of the next day with probability 0.6. If Bill works on the machine, the probability decreases to 0.5. If Bill operates the machine when it is working, the probability is 0.6 that it will still be working at the beginning of the next day. If Buck operates the machine, it breaks down with probability 0.6. (Assume for simplicity that all breakdowns occur at the end of the day.) The brothers now wish to determine the optimal policy for when each should stay home in order to maximize their (long-run) expected average *profit* (amount of usable counterfeit money produced) per day.

(a) Formulate this problem as a Markov decision process by identifying the states and decisions and then finding the C_{ik}.

(b) Identify all the (stationary deterministic) policies. For each one, find the transition matrix and write an expression for the (long-run) expected average net profit per period in terms of the unknown steady-state probabilities ($\pi_0, \pi_1, \ldots, \pi_M$).

A (c) Use your OR Courseware to find these steady-state probabilities for each policy. Then evaluate the expression obtained in part (b) to find the optimal policy by exhaustive enumeration.

21.2-8. A person often finds that she is up to 1 hour late for work. If she is from 1 to 30 minutes late, $4 is deducted from her paycheck; if she is from 31 to 60 minutes late for work, $8 is deducted from her paycheck. If she drives to work at her normal speed (which is well under the speed limit), she can arrive in 20 minutes. However, if she exceeds the speed limit a little here and there on her way to work, she can get there in 10 minutes, but she runs the risk of getting a speeding ticket. With probability $\frac{1}{8}$ she will get caught speeding and will be fined \$20 and delayed 10 minutes, so that it takes 20 minutes to reach work.

As she leaves home, let s be the time she has to reach work before being late; that is, $s = 10$ means she has 10 minutes to get to work, and $s = -10$ means she is already 10 minutes late for work. For simplicity, she considers s to be in one of four intervals: $(20, \infty)$, $(10, 19)$, $(-10, 9)$, and $(-20, -11)$.

The transition probabilities for s tomorrow if she does not speed today are given by

	(20, ∞)	**(10, 19)**	**(−10, 9)**	**(−20, −11)**
(20, ∞)	$\frac{3}{8}$	$\frac{1}{4}$	$\frac{1}{4}$	$\frac{1}{8}$
(10, 19)	$\frac{1}{2}$	$\frac{1}{4}$	$\frac{1}{8}$	$\frac{1}{8}$
(−10, 9)	$\frac{5}{8}$	$\frac{1}{4}$	$\frac{1}{8}$	0
(−20, −11)	$\frac{3}{4}$	$\frac{1}{4}$	0	0

The transition probabilities for s tomorrow if she speeds to work today are given by

	(20, ∞)	**(10, 19)**	**(−10, 9)**	**(−20, −11)**
(20, ∞)				
(10, 19)	$\frac{3}{8}$	$\frac{1}{4}$	$\frac{1}{4}$	$\frac{1}{8}$
(−10, 9)				
(−20, −11)	$\frac{5}{8}$	$\frac{1}{4}$	$\frac{1}{8}$	0

Note that there are no transition probabilities for $(20, \infty)$ and $(-10, 9)$, because she will get to work on time and from 1 to 30 minutes late, respectively, regardless of whether she speeds. Hence, speeding when in these states would not be a logical choice.

Also note that the transition probabilities imply that the later she is for work and the more she has to rush to get there, the more likely she is to leave for work earlier the next day.

She wishes to determine when she should speed and when she should take her time getting to work in order to minimize her (long-run) expected average cost per day.

(a) Formulate this problem as a Markov decision process by identifying the states and decisions and then finding the C_{ik}.

(b) Identify all the (stationary deterministic) policies. For each one, find the transition matrix and write an expression for the (long-run) expected average cost per period in terms of the unknown steady-state probabilities ($\pi_0, \pi_1, \ldots, \pi_M$).

A (c) Use your OR Courseware to find these steady-state probabilities for each policy. Then evaluate the expression obtained in part (b) to find the optimal policy by exhaustive enumeration.

21.2-9. Consider an infinite-period inventory problem involving a single product where, at the beginning of each period, a decision must be made about how many items to produce during that period. The setup cost is \$10, and the unit production cost is \$5. The holding cost for each item not sold during the period is \$4 (a *maximum* of 2 items can be stored). The demand during each period has a known probability distribution, namely, a probability of $\frac{1}{3}$ of 0, 1, and 2 items, respectively. If the demand exceeds the supply available during the period, then those sales are lost and a shortage cost (including lost revenue) is incurred, namely, \$8 and \$32 for a shortage of 1 and 2 items, respectively.

(a) Consider the policy where 2 items are produced if there are no items in inventory at the beginning of a period whereas no items are produced if there are any items in inventory. Determine the (long-run) expected average cost per period for this policy. In finding the transition matrix for the Markov chain for this policy, let the states represent the inventory levels at the beginning of the period.

(b) Identify all the *feasible* (stationary deterministic) inventory policies, i.e., the policies that never lead to exceeding the storage capacity.

21.3-1. Reconsider Prob. 21.2-1.

(a) Formulate a linear programming model for finding an optimal policy.

C (b) Use the simplex method to solve this model. Use the resulting optimal solution to identify an optimal policy.

21.3-2.* Reconsider Prob. 21.2-2.

(a) Formulate a linear programming model for finding an optimal policy.

C (b) Use the simplex method to solve this model. Use the resulting optimal solution to identify an optimal policy.

21.3-3. Reconsider Prob. 21.2-3.

(a) Formulate a linear programming model for finding an optimal policy.

c **(b)** Use the simplex method to solve this model. Use the resulting optimal solution to identify an optimal policy.

21.3-4. Reconsider Prob. 21.2-4.
(a) Formulate a linear programming model for finding an optimal policy.
c **(b)** Use the simplex method to solve this model. Use the resulting optimal solution to identify an optimal policy.

21.3-5.* Reconsider Prob. 21.2-5.
(a) Formulate a linear programming model for finding an optimal policy.
c **(b)** Use the simplex method to solve this model. Use the resulting optimal solution to identify an optimal policy.

21.3-6. Reconsider Prob. 21.2-6.
(a) Formulate a linear programming model for finding an optimal policy.
c **(b)** Use the simplex method to solve this model. Use the resulting optimal solution to identify an optimal policy.

21.3-7. Reconsider Prob. 21.2-7.
(a) Formulate a linear programming model for finding an optimal policy.
c **(b)** Use the simplex method to solve this model. Use the resulting optimal solution to identify an optimal policy.

21.3-8. Reconsider Prob. 21.2-8.
(a) Formulate a linear programming model for finding an optimal policy.
c **(b)** Use the simplex method to solve this model. Use the resulting optimal solution to identify an optimal policy.

21.3-9. Reconsider Prob. 21.2-9.
(a) Formulate a linear programming model for finding an optimal policy.
c **(b)** Use the simplex method to solve this model. Use the resulting optimal solution to identify an optimal policy.

D,I **21.4-1.** Use the policy improvement algorithm to find an optimal policy for Prob. 21.2-1.

D,I **21.4-2.*** Use the policy improvement algorithm to find an optimal policy for Prob. 21.2-2.

D,I **21.4-3.** Use the policy improvement algorithm to find an optimal policy for Prob. 21.2-3.

D,I **21.4-4.** Use the policy improvement algorithm to find an optimal policy for Prob. 21.2-4.

D,I **21.4-5.*** Use the policy improvement algorithm to find an optimal policy for Prob. 21.2-5.

D,I **21.4-6.** Use the policy improvement algorithm to find an optimal policy for Prob. 21.2-6.

D,I **21.4-7.** Use the policy improvement algorithm to find an optimal policy for Prob. 21.2-7.

D,I **21.4-8.** Use the policy improvement algorithm to find an optimal policy for Prob. 21.2-8.

D,I **21.4-9.** Use the policy improvement algorithm to find an optimal policy for Prob. 21.2-9.

D,I **21.4-10.** Consider the blood-inventory problem presented in Prob. 16.6-5. Suppose now that the number of pints of blood delivered (on a regular delivery) can be specified at the time of delivery (instead of using the old policy of receiving 1 pint at each delivery). Thus, the number of pints delivered can be 0, 1, 2, or 3 (more than 3 pints can never be used). The cost of regular delivery is $50 per pint, while the cost of an emergency delivery is $100 per pint. Starting with the proposed policy given in Prob. 16.6-5, perform two iterations of the policy improvement algorithm.

I **21.5-1.*** Joe wants to sell his car. He receives one offer each month and must decide immediately whether to accept the offer. Once rejected, the offer is lost. The possible offers are $600, $800, and $1,000, made with probabilities $\frac{5}{8}$, $\frac{1}{4}$, and $\frac{1}{8}$, respectively (where successive offers are independent of each other). There is a maintenance cost of $60 per month for the car. Joe is anxious to sell the car and so has chosen a discount factor of $\alpha = 0.95$.

Using the policy improvement algorithm, find a policy that minimizes the expected total discounted cost. (*Hint:* There are two actions: Accept or reject the offer. Let the state for month t be the offer in that month. Also include a state ∞, where the process goes to state ∞ whenever an offer is accepted and it remains there at a monthly cost of 0.)

21.5-2.* Reconsider Prob. 21.5-1.
(a) Formulate a linear programming model for finding an optimal policy.
c **(b)** Use the simplex method to solve this model. Use the resulting optimal solution to identify an optimal policy.

I **21.5-3.*** For Prob. 21.5-1, use three iterations of the method of successive approximations to approximate an optimal policy.

I **21.5-4.** The price of a certain stock is fluctuating between $10, $20, and $30 from month to month. Market analysts have predicted that if the stock is at $10 during any month, it will be at $10 or $20 the next month, with probabilities $\frac{4}{5}$ and $\frac{1}{5}$, respectively; if the stock is at $20, it will be at $10, $20, or $30 the next month, with probabilities $\frac{1}{4}$, $\frac{1}{4}$, and $\frac{1}{2}$, respectively; and if the stock is at $30, it will be at $20 or $30 the next month, with probabilities $\frac{3}{4}$ and $\frac{1}{4}$, respectively. Given a discount factor of 0.9, use the policy improvement algorithm to determine when to sell and when to hold the stock to maximize the expected total discounted profit. (*Hint:* Include a state that is reached with probability 1 when the stock is sold and with probability 0 when the stock is held.)

21.5-5. Reconsider Prob. 21.5-4.
(a) Formulate a linear programming model for finding an optimal policy.
C **(b)** Use the simplex method to solve this model. Use the resulting optimal solution to identify an optimal policy.

I **21.5-6.** For Prob. 21.5-4, use three iterations of the method of successive approximations to approximate an optimal policy.

21.5-7. A chemical company produces two chemicals, denoted by 0 and 1, and only one can be produced at a time. Each month a decision is made as to which chemical to produce that month. Because the demand for each chemical is predictable, it is known that if 1 is produced this month, there is a 70 percent chance that it will also be produced again next month. Similarly, if 0 is produced this month, there is only a 20 percent chance that it will be produced again next month.

To combat the emissions of pollutants, the chemical company has two processes, process *A*, which is efficient in combating the pollution from the production of 1 but not from 0, and process *B*, which is efficient in combating the pollution from the production of 0 but not from 1. Only one process can be used at a time. The amount of pollution from the production of each chemical under each process is

	0	1
A	100	10
B	10	30

Unfortunately, there is a time delay in setting up the pollution control processes, so that a decision as to which process to use must be made in the month prior to the production decision. Management wants to determine a policy for when to use each pollution control process that will minimize the expected total discounted amount of all future pollution with a discount factor of $\alpha = 0.5$.
(a) Formulate this problem as a Markov decision process by identifying the states, the decisions, and the C_{ik}. Identify all the (stationary deterministic) policies.
I **(b)** Use the policy improvement algorithm to find an optimal policy.

21.5-8. Reconsider Prob. 21.5-7.
(a) Formulate a linear programming model for finding an optimal policy.
C **(b)** Use the simplex method to solve this model. Use the resulting optimal solution to identify an optimal policy.

I **21.5-9.** For Prob. 21.5-7, use two iterations of the method of successive approximations to approximate an optimal policy.

I **21.5-10.** Reconsider Prob. 21.5-7. Suppose now that the company will be producing either of these chemicals for only 4 more months, so a decision on which pollution control process to use 1 month hence only needs to be made three more times. Find an optimal policy for this three-period problem.

I **21.5-11.*** Reconsider the prototype example of Sec. 21.1. Suppose now that the production process using the machine under consideration will be used for only 4 more weeks. Using the discounted cost criterion with a discount factor of $\alpha = 0.9$, find the optimal policy for this four-period problem.

22

Simulation

In this final chapter, we now are ready to focus on the last of the key techniques of operations research. *Simulation* ranks very high among the most widely used of these techniques. Furthermore, because it is such a flexible, powerful, and intuitive tool, it is continuing to rapidly grow in popularity.

This technique involves using a computer to *imitate* (simulate) the operation of an entire process or system. For example, simulation is frequently used to perform risk analysis on financial processes by repeatedly imitating the evolution of the transactions involved to generate a profile of the possible outcomes. Simulation also is widely used to analyze stochastic systems that will continue operating indefinitely. For such systems, the computer randomly generates and records the occurrences of the various events that drive the system just as if it were physically operating. Because of its speed, the computer can simulate even years of operation in a matter of seconds. Recording the performance of the simulated operation of the system for a number of alternative designs or operating procedures then enables evaluating and comparing these alternatives before choosing one.

The first section describes and illustrates the essence of simulation. The following section then presents a variety of common applications of simulation. Sections 22.3 and 22.4 focus on two key tools of simulation, the generation of random numbers and the generation of random observations from probability distributions. Section 22.5 outlines the overall procedure for applying simulation. The next section describes how some simulations now can be performed efficiently on spreadsheets. Section 22.7 introduces some special techniques for improving the precision of the estimates of the measures of performance of the system being simulated. The chapter concludes by presenting an innovative statistical method for analyzing the output of a simulation.

22.1 ESSENCE OF SIMULATION

The technique of *simulation* has long been an important tool of the designer. For example, simulating airplane flight in a wind tunnel is standard practice when a new airplane is designed. Theoretically, the laws of physics could be used to obtain the same information about how the performance of the airplane changes as design parameters are altered, but, as a practical matter, the analysis would be too complicated to do it all. Another alternative would be to build real airplanes with alternative designs and test them in actual flight to choose the final design, but this would be far too expensive (as well as unsafe). Therefore, after some preliminary theoretical analysis is performed to develop a *rough* design, simulating flight in a wind tunnel is a vital tool for experimenting with *specific* designs. This simulation amounts to *imitating* the performance of a real airplane in a controlled environment in order to *estimate* what its actual performance will be. After a detailed design is developed in this way, a prototype model can be built and tested in actual flight to fine-tune the final design.

The Role of Simulation in Operations Research Studies

Simulation plays essentially this same role in many OR studies. However, rather than designing an airplane, the OR team is concerned with developing a design or operating procedure for some *stochastic system* (a system that evolves *probabilistically* over time). Some of these stochastic systems resemble the examples of Markov chains and queueing systems described in Chaps. 16 to 18, and others are more complicated. Rather than use a wind tunnel, the performance of the real system is *imitated* by using probability distributions to *randomly generate* various events that occur in the system. Therefore, a simulation model *synthesizes* the system by building it up component by component and event by event. Then the model *runs* the simulated system to obtain *statistical observations* of the performance of the system that result from various randomly generated events. Because the *simulation runs* typically require generating and processing a vast amount of data, these simulated statistical experiments are inevitably performed on a computer.

When simulation is used as part of an OR study, commonly it is preceded and followed by the same steps described earlier for the design of an airplane. In particular, some preliminary analysis is done first (perhaps with approximate mathematical models) to develop a rough design of the system (including its operating procedures). Then simulation is used to experiment with specific designs to estimate how well each will perform. After a detailed design is developed and selected in this way, the system probably is tested in actual use to fine-tune the final design.

To prepare for simulating a complex system, a detailed **simulation model** needs to be formulated to describe the operation of the system and how it is to be simulated. A simulation model has several basic building blocks:

1. A definition of the *state of the system* (e.g., the number of customers in a queueing system).
2. Identify the *possible states* of the system that can occur.
3. Identify the *possible events* (e.g., arrivals and service completions in a queueing system) that would change the state of the system.
4. A provision for a *simulation clock,* located at some address in the simulation program, that will record the passage of (simulated) time.
5. A method for *randomly generating the events* of the various kinds.
6. A formula for identifying *state transitions* that are generated by the various kinds of events.

Great progress is being made in developing special software (described in Sec. 22.5) for efficiently integrating the simulation model into a computer program and then performing the simulations. Nevertheless, when dealing with relatively complex systems, simulation tends to be a relatively expensive procedure. After formulating a detailed simulation model, considerable time often is required to develop and debug the computer programs needed to run the simulation. Next, many long computer runs may be needed to obtain good estimates of how well all the alternative designs of the system would perform. Finally, all these data should be carefully analyzed before drawing any final conclusions. This entire process typically takes a lot of time and effort. Therefore, simulation should not be used when a less expensive procedure is available that can provide the same information.

Simulation typically is used when the stochastic system involved is too complex to be analyzed satisfactorily by the kinds of mathematical models (e.g., queueing models) described in the preceding chapters. One of the main strengths of a mathematical model is that it abstracts the essence of the problem and reveals its underlying structure, thereby providing insight into the cause-and-effect relationships within the system. Therefore, if the modeler is able to construct a mathematical model that is both a reasonable idealization of the problem and amenable to solution, this approach usually is superior to simulation. However, many problems are too complex to permit this approach. Thus, simulation often provides the only practical approach to a problem.

Discrete-Event versus Continuous Simulation

Two broad categories of simulations are discrete-event and continuous simulations.

A **discrete-event simulation** is one where changes in the state of the system occur instantaneously at random points in time as a result of the occurrence of *discrete events*. For example, in a queueing system where the state of the system is the number of customers in the system, the discrete events that change this state are the arrival of a customer and the departure of a customer due to the completion of its service. Most applications of simulation in practice are discrete-event simulations.

A **continuous simulation** is one where changes in the state of the system occur *continuously* over time. For example, if the system of interest is an airplane in flight and its state is defined as the current position of the airplane, then the state is changing continuously over time. Some applications of continuous simulations occur in design studies of such engineering systems.

Continuous simulations typically require using differential equations to describe the rate of change of the state variables. Thus, the analysis tends to be relatively complex.

By approximating continuous changes in the state of the system by occasional discrete changes, it often is possible to use a discrete-event simulation to approximate the behavior of a continuous system. This tends to greatly simplify the analysis.

This chapter focuses hereafter on discrete-event simulations. We assume this type in all subsequent references to simulation.

Now let us look at two examples to illustrate the basic ideas of simulation. These examples have been kept considerably simpler than the usual application of this technique in order to highlight the main ideas more readily. The first system is so simple, in fact, that the simulation does not even need to be performed on a computer. The second system incorporates more of the normal features of a simulation, although it, too, is simple enough to be solved analytically.

EXAMPLE 1   **A Coin Flipping Game**

You are the lucky winner of a sweepstakes contest. Your prize is an all-expense-paid vacation at a major hotel in Las Vegas, including some chips for gambling in the hotel casino.

Upon entering the casino, you find that, in addition to the usual games (blackjack, roulette, etc.), they are offering an interesting new game with the following rules.

Rules of the Game.

1. Each play of the game involves repeatedly flipping an unbiased coin until the *difference* between the number of heads tossed and the number of tails is 3.
2. If you decide to play the game, you are required to pay $1 for each flip of the coin. You are not allowed to quit during a play of the game.
3. You receive $8 at the end of each play of the game.

Thus, you win money if the number of flips required is fewer than 8, but you lose money if more than 8 flips are required. Here are some examples (where H denotes a head and T a tail).

HHH	3 flips.	You win $5
THTTT	5 flips.	You win $3
THHTHTHTTTT	11 flips.	You lose $3

How would you decide whether to play this game?

Many people would base this decision on *simulation,* although they probably would not call it by that name. In this case, simulation amounts to nothing more than playing the game alone many times until it becomes clear whether it is worthwhile to play for money. Half an hour spent in repeatedly flipping a coin and recording the earnings or losses that would have resulted might be sufficient. This is a true simulation because you are *imitating* the actual play of the game *without* actually winning or losing any money.

Now let us see how a computer can be used to perform this same *simulated experiment.* Although a computer cannot flip coins, it can *simulate* doing so. It accomplishes this by generating a sequence of *random observations* from a uniform distribution between 0 and 1, where these random observations are referred to as *uniform random numbers* over the interval [0, 1]. One easy way to generate these uniform random numbers is to use the **RAND()** function in Excel. For example, the lower left-hand corner of Fig. 22.1 indicates that = RAND() has been entered into cell C10 and then copied into the range C11:C59 with the Copy command. (The parentheses need to be included with this function, but nothing is inserted between them.) This causes Excel to generate the random numbers shown in cells C10:C59 of the spreadsheet. (Rows 24–53 have been hidden to save space in the figure.)

The probabilities for the outcome of flipping a coin are

$$P(\text{heads}) = \frac{1}{2}, \qquad P(\text{tails}) = \frac{1}{2}.$$

	A	B	C	D	E	F	G
1	Coin Flipping Game						
2							
3		**Summary of Game**					
4		Number of Flips =		11			
5		Winnings =		-$3			
6							
7				Result			
8			Random	(0=Tails,	Total	Total	
9		Flip	Number	1=Heads)	Heads	Tails	Stop?
10		1	0.7520	0	0	1	
11		2	0.4184	1	1	1	
12		3	0.4189	1	2	1	
13		4	0.5982	0	2	2	
14		5	0.9559	0	2	3	
15		6	0.1403	1	3	3	
16		7	0.9345	0	3	4	
17		8	0.0801	1	4	4	
18		9	0.6892	0	4	5	
19		10	0.5146	0	4	6	
20		11	0.6290	0	4	7	Stop
21		12	0.1612	1	5	7	NA
22		13	0.0989	1	6	7	NA
23		14	0.1155	1	7	7	NA
54		45	0.1898	1	25	20	NA
55		46	0.3814	1	26	20	NA
56		47	0.7810	0	26	21	NA
57		48	0.5110	0	26	22	NA
58		49	0.9735	0	26	23	NA
59		50	0.0881	1	27	23	NA

	D
4	=COUNTBLANK(G10:G59)+1
5	=8-D4

	C	D	E	F	G
10	=RAND()	=IF(C10<0.5,1,0)	=D10	=B10-E10	
11	=RAND()	=IF(C11<0.5,1,0)	=E10+D11	=B11-E11	
12	=RAND()	=IF(C12<0.5,1,0)	=E11+D12	=B12-E12	=IF(ABS(E12-F12)>=3,"Stop","")
13	=RAND()	=IF(C13<0.5,1,0)	=E12+D13	=B13-E13	=IF(G12="",IF(ABS(E13-F13)>=3,"Stop",""),"NA")
14	=RAND()	=IF(C14<0.5,1,0)	=E13+D14	=B14-E14	=IF(G13="",IF(ABS(E14-F14)>=3,"Stop",""),"NA")
15	=RAND()	=IF(C15<0.5,1,0)	=E14+D15	=B15-E15	=IF(G14="",IF(ABS(E15-F15)>=3,"Stop",""),"NA")
16	:	:	:	:	:
17	:	:	:	:	:

FIGURE 22.1
A spreadsheet model for a simulation of the coin flipping game (Example 1).

Therefore, to simulate the flipping of a coin, the computer can just let *any half* of the possible random numbers correspond to *heads* and the *other half* correspond to *tails*. To be specific, we will use the following correspondence.

　　　0.0000 to 0.4999　　correspond to　　*heads.*
　　　0.5000 to 0.9999　　correspond to　　*tails.*

By using the formula,

　　$= \text{IF(RAND()} < 0.5, 1, 0)$,

in each of the column D cells in Fig. 22.1, Excel inserts a 1 (to indicate heads) if the random number is less than 0.5 and inserts a 0 (to indicate tails) otherwise. Consequently, the first 11 random numbers generated in column C yield the following sequence of heads (H) and tails (T):

　　THHTTHTHTTT,

at which point the game stops because the number of tails (7) exceeds the number of heads (4) by 3. Cells D4 and D5 record the total number of flips (11) and resulting winnings ($8 − $11 = −$3).

The equations at the bottom of Fig. 22.1 show the formulas that have been entered into the various cells by entering them at the top and then using the Copy command to copy them down the columns. Using these equations, the spreadsheet then records the simulation of one complete play of the game. To virtually ensure that the game will be completed, 50 flips of the coin have been simulated. Columns E and F record the cumulative number of heads and tails after each flip. The equations entered into the column G cells leave each cell blank until the difference in the numbers of heads and tails reaches 3, at which point STOP is inserted into the cell. Thereafter, NA (for Not Applicable) is inserted instead. Using the equations shown in the upper right-hand side of Fig. 22.1, cells D4 and D5 record the outcome of the simulated play of the game.

Such simulations of plays of the game can be repeated as often as desired with this spreadsheet. Each time, Excel will generate a new sequence of random numbers, and so a new sequence of heads and tails. (Excel will repeat a sequence of random numbers only if you select the range of numbers you want to repeat, copy this range with the Copy command, select Paste Special from the Edit menu, choose the Values option, and click on OK.)

Simulations normally are repeated many times to obtain a more reliable estimate of an average outcome. Therefore, this same spreadsheet has been used to generate the data table in Fig. 22.2 for 14 plays of the game. As indicated in the upper right-hand side of Fig. 22.2, this is done by entering equations into the first row of the data table that refer to the output cells of interest in Fig. 22.1, so =D4 is entered into cell J6 and =D5 is entered into cell K6. The next step is to select the entire contents of the table (cells I6:K20) and choose Table from the Data menu. Finally, choose *any* blank cell (e.g., cell E4) for the column input cell and click OK. Excel then recalculates the output cells in columns J and K for each row where *any* number is entered in row I. Entering the equations, =AVERAGE(J7:J20) or (K7:K20), into cells J22 and K22 provides the averages given in these cells.

Although this particular simulation run required using two spreadsheets—one to perform each replication of the simulation and the other to record the outcomes of the replications on a data table—we should point out that the replications of some other simula-

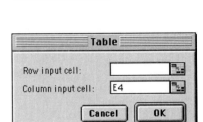

	Play	Number of Flips	Winnings
		7	$1
	1	11	-$3
	2	5	$3
	3	5	$3
	4	9	-$1
	5	7	$1
	6	7	$1
	7	5	$3
	8	3	$5
	9	17	-$9
	10	5	$3
	11	5	$3
	12	3	$5
	13	9	-$1
	14	7	$1
	Average	7	$1.00

Data Table for Coin Flipping Game (14 Replications)

	J	K
6	=D4	=D5

Table

Row input cell:

Column input cell: E4

Cancel   OK

FIGURE 22.2
A data table that records the results of performing 14 replications of a simulation with the spreadsheet in Fig. 22.1.

tions can be performed on a single spreadsheet. This is the case whenever each replication can be performed and recorded on a single row of the spreadsheet. For example, if only a single uniform random number is needed to perform a replication, then the entire simulation run can be done and recorded by using a spreadsheet similar to Fig. 22.1.

Returning to Fig. 22.2, cell J22 shows that this sample of 14 plays of the game gives a sample average of 7 flips. The sample average provides an *estimate* of the true *mean* of the underlying probability distribution of the number of flips required for a play of the game. Hence, this sample average of 7 would seem to indicate that, on the average, you should win about $1 (cell K22) each time you play the game. Therefore, if you do not have a relatively high aversion to risk, it appears that you should choose to play this game, preferably a large number of times.

However, *beware*! One common error in the use of simulation is that conclusions are based on overly small samples, because statistical analysis was inadequate or totally lacking. In this case, the *sample standard deviation* is 3.67, so that the estimated *standard deviation* of the *sample average* is $3.67/\sqrt{14} \approx 0.98$. Therefore, even if it is assumed that the probability distribution of the number of flips required for a play of the game is a *normal distribution* (which is a gross assumption because the true distribution is *skewed*), any reasonable *confidence interval* for the true *mean* of this distribution would extend far above 8. Hence, a much larger sample size is required before we can draw a valid conclusion at a reasonable level of statistical significance. Unfortunately, because the standard deviation of a sample average is inversely proportional to the *square root* of the sample size, a large increase in the sample size is required to yield a relatively small increase in the precision of the estimate of the true mean. In this case, it appears that 100 simulated plays (replications) of the game *might* be adequate, depending on how close the sample average then is to 8, but 1,000 replications would be much safer.

It so happens that the true *mean* of the number of flips required for a play of this game is 9. (This mean can be found analytically, but not easily.) Thus, in the long run, you actually would average losing about $1 each time you played the game. Part of the reason that the above simulated experiment failed to draw this conclusion is that you have a small chance of a very large loss on any play of the game, but you can never win more than $5 each time. However, 14 simulated plays of the game were not enough to obtain any observations far out in the tail of the probability distribution of the amount won or lost on one play of the game. Only one simulated play gave a loss of more than $3, and that was only $9.

Figure 22.3 gives the results of running the simulation for 1,000 plays of the games (with rows 17–1000 not shown). Cell J1008 records the average number of flips as 8.98, very close to the true mean of 9. With this number of replications, the average winnings of −$0.98 in cell K1008 now provides a reliable basis for concluding that this game will not win you money in the long run. (You can bet that the casino already has used simulation to verify this fact in advance.)

Although formally constructing a full-fledged *simulation model* was not needed to perform this simple simulation, we do so now for illustrative purposes. The *stochastic system* being simulated is the successive flipping of the coin for a play of the game. The *sim-*

FIGURE 22.3
This data table improves the reliability of the simulation recorded in Fig. 22.2 by performing 1,000 replications instead of only 14.

	H	I	J	K
1		Data Table for Coin Flipping Game		
2		(1000 Replications)		
3				
4			Number	
5		Play	of Flips	Winnings
6			3	$5
7		1	15	-$7
8		2	9	-$1
9		3	11	-$3
10		4	9	-$1
11		5	3	$5
12		6	7	$1
13		7	11	-$3
14		8	9	-$1
15		9	11	-$3
16		10	7	$1
1001		995	3	$5
1002		996	15	-$7
1003		997	7	$1
1004		998	11	-$3
1005		999	7	$1
1006		1000	3	$5
1007				
1008		Average	8.98	-$0.98

ulation clock records the number of (simulated) flips t that have occurred so far. The information about the system that defines its current status, i.e., the *state of the system,* is

$N(t)$ = number of heads minus number of tails after t flips.

The *events* that change the state of the system are the flipping of a head or the flipping of a tail. The *event generation method* is the generation of a *uniform random number* over the interval [0, 1], where

0.0000 to 0.4999 $\Rightarrow$ a head,
0.5000 to 0.9999 $\Rightarrow$ a tail.

The *state transition formula* is

$$\text{Reset } N(t) = \begin{cases} N(t-1) + 1 & \text{if flip } t \text{ is a head} \\ N(t-1) - 1 & \text{if flip } t \text{ is a tail.} \end{cases}$$

The simulated game then ends at the first value of t where $N(t) = \pm 3$, where the resulting sampling *observation* for the simulated experiment is $8 - t$, the amount won (positive or negative) for that play of the game.

The next example will illustrate these building blocks of a simulation model for a prominent stochastic system from queueing theory.

EXAMPLE 2   **An *M/M/*1 Queueing System**

Consider the *M/M/*1 queueing theory model (Poisson input, exponential service times, and single server) that was discussed at the beginning of Sec. 17.6. Although this model already has been solved analytically, it will be instructive to consider how to study it by using simulation. To be specific, suppose that the values of the *arrival rate* λ and *service rate* μ are

$\lambda = 3$ per hour, $\mu = 5$ per hour.

To summarize the physical operation of the system, arriving customers enter the queue, eventually are served, and then leave. Thus, it is necessary for the simulation model to describe and synchronize the arrival of customers and the serving of customers.

Starting at time 0, the simulation clock records the amount of (simulated) time t that has transpired so far during the simulation run. The information about the queueing system that defines its current status, i.e., the state of the system, is

$N(t)$ = number of customers in system at time t.

The events that change the state of the system are the *arrival* of a customer or a *service completion* for the customer currently in service (if any). We shall describe the event generation method a little later. The state transition formula is

$$\text{Reset } N(t) = \begin{cases} N(t) + 1 & \text{if arrival occurs at time } t \\ N(t) - 1 & \text{if service completion occurs at time } t. \end{cases}$$

There are two basic methods used for advancing the simulation clock and recording the operation of the system. We did not distinguish between these methods for Example

1 because they actually coincide for that simple situation. However, we now describe and illustrate these two **time advance methods** (fixed-time incrementing and next-event incrementing) in turn.

With the **fixed-time incrementing** time advance method, the following two-step procedure is used repeatedly.

Summary of Fixed-Time Incrementing.

1. *Advance time* by a small *fixed amount.*
2. *Update the system* by determining what events occurred during the elapsed time interval and what the resulting state of the system is. Also record desired information about the performance of the system.

For the queueing theory model under consideration, only two types of events can occur during each of these elapsed time intervals, namely, one or more *arrivals* and one or more *service completions.* Furthermore, the probability of two or more arrivals or of two or more service completions during an interval is negligible for this model if the interval is relatively short. Thus, the only two possible events during such an interval that need to be investigated are the arrival of one customer and the service completion for one customer. Each of these events has a known probability.

To illustrate, let us use 0.1 hour (6 minutes) as the small fixed amount by which the clock is advanced each time. (Normally, a considerably smaller time interval would be used to render negligible the probability of multiple arrivals or multiple service completions, but this choice will create more action for illustrative purposes.) Because both interarrival times and service times have an exponential distribution, the probability P_A that a time interval of 0.1 hour will include an *arrival* is

$$P_A = 1 - e^{-3/10} = 0.259,$$

and the probability P_D that it will include a *departure* (service completion), given that a customer was being served at the beginning of the interval, is

$$P_D = 1 - e^{-5/10} = 0.393.$$

To randomly generate either kind of event according to these probabilities, the approach is similar to that in Example 1. The computer again is used to generate a *uniform random number* over the interval [0, 1], that is, a random observation from the *uniform distribution* between 0 and 1. If we denote this uniform random number by r_A,

$$r_A < 0.259 \Rightarrow \text{arrival occurred,}$$
$$r_A \geq 0.259 \Rightarrow \text{arrival did not occur.}$$

Similarly, with *another* uniform random number r_D,

$$r_D < 0.393 \Rightarrow \text{departure occurred,}$$
$$r_D \geq 0.393 \Rightarrow \text{departure did not occur,}$$

given that a customer was being served at the beginning of the time interval. With no customer in service then (i.e., no customers in the system), it is assumed that no departure can occur during the interval even if an arrival does occur.

TABLE 22.1 Fixed-time incrementing applied to Example 2

t, time (min)	N(t)	r_A	Arrival in Interval?	r_D	Departure in Interval?
0	0				
6	1	0.096	Yes	—	
12	1	0.569	No	0.665	No
18	1	0.764	No	0.842	No
24	0	0.492	No	0.224	Yes
30	0	0.950	No	—	
36	0	0.610	No	—	
42	1	0.145	Yes	—	
48	1	0.484	No	0.552	No
54	1	0.350	No	0.590	No
60	0	0.430	No	0.041	Yes

Table 22.1 shows the result of using this approach for 10 iterations of the *fixed-time incrementing* procedure, starting with no customers in the system and using time units of minutes.

Step 2 of the procedure (updating the system) includes recording the desired measures of performance about the aggregate behavior of the system during this time interval. For example, it could record the *number of customers* in the queueing system and the *waiting time* of any customer who just completed his or her wait. If it is sufficient to estimate only the mean rather than the probability distribution of each of these random variables, the computer will merely add the value (if any) at the end of the current time interval to a cumulative sum. The sample averages will be obtained after the simulation run is completed by dividing these sums by the sample sizes involved, namely, the total number of time intervals and the total number of customers, respectively.

To illustrate this estimating procedure, suppose that the simulation run in Table 22.1 were being used to estimate W, the steady-state expected waiting time of a customer in the queueing system (including service). Two customers arrived during this simulation run, one during the first time interval and the other during the seventh one, and each remained in the system for three time intervals. Therefore, since the duration of each time interval is 0.1 hour, the estimate of W is

$$\text{Est}\{W\} = \frac{3 + 3}{2} (0.1 \text{ hour}) = 0.3 \text{ hour.}$$

This is, of course, only an extremely rough estimate, based on a sample size of only two. (Using the formula for W given in Sec. 17.6, its true value is $W = 1/(\mu - \lambda) = 0.5$ hour.) A much, much larger sample size normally would be used.

Another deficiency with using only Table 22.1 is that this simulation run started with no customers in the system, which causes the initial observations of waiting times to tend to be somewhat smaller than the expected value when the system is in a steady-state condition. Since the goal is to estimate the *steady-state* expected waiting time, it is important to run the simulation for some time without collecting data until it is believed that the simulated system has essentially reached a steady-state condition. (Section 22.8 describes a special method for circumventing this problem.) This initial period waiting to essentially reach a steady-state condition before collecting data is called the **warm-up period.**

Next-event incrementing differs from fixed-time incrementing in that the simulation clock is incremented by a *variable* amount rather than by a fixed amount each time. This variable amount is the time from the event that has just occurred until the *next event* of any kind occurs; i.e., the clock jumps from event to event. A summary follows.

Summary of Next-Event Incrementing.

→**1.** *Advance time* to the time of the *next event* of any kind.
└**2.** *Update the system* by determining its new state that results from this event and by randomly generating the time until the next occurrence of any event type that can occur from this state (if not previously generated). Also record desired information about the performance of the system.

For this example the computer needs to keep track of two future events, namely, the next arrival and the next service completion (if a customer currently is being served). These times are obtained by taking a random observation from the probability distribution of interarrival and service times, respectively. As before, the computer takes such a random observation by generating and using a random number. (This technique will be discussed in Sec. 22.4.) Thus, each time an arrival or service completion occurs, the computer determines how long it will be until the next time this event will occur, adds this time to the current clock time, and then stores this sum in a computer file. (If the service completion leaves no customers in the system, then the generation of the time until the next service completion is postponed until the next arrival occurs.) To determine which event will occur next, the computer finds the minimum of the clock times stored in the file. To expedite the bookkeeping involved, simulation programming languages provide a "timing routine" that determines the occurrence time and type of the next event, advances time, and transfers control to the appropriate subprogram for the event type.

Table 22.2 shows the result of applying this approach through five iterations of the next-event incrementing procedure, starting with no customers in the system and using time units of minutes. For later reference, we include the *uniform random numbers* r_A and r_D used to generate the interarrival times and service times, respectively, by the method to be described in Sec. 22.4. These r_A and r_D are the same as those used in Table 22.1 in order to provide a truer comparison between the two time advance mechanisms.

TABLE 22.2 Next-event incrementing applied to Example 2

t, time (min)	N(t)	r_A	Next Interarrival Time	r_D	Next Service Time	Next Arrival	Next Departure	Next Event
0	0	0.096	2.019	—	—	2.019	—	Arrival
2.019	1	0.569	16.833	0.665	13.123	18.852	15.142	Departure
15.142	0	—	—	—	—	18.852	—	Arrival
18.852	1	0.764	28.878	0.842	22.142	47.730	40.994	Departure
40.994	0	—	—	—	—	47.730	—	Arrival
47.730	1							

FIGURE 22.4
The output obtained by using the Queueing Simulator in this chapter's Excel file to perform a simulation of Example 2 over a period of 10,000 customer arrivals.

	A	B	C	D	E	F	G	H
1	Template for Queueing Simulation							
2							Results	
3			Data			Point	95% Confidence Interval	
4		Number of Servers =	1			Estimate	Low	High
5					L =	1.418286281	1.320246685	1.516325877
6		Interarrival Times			L_q =	0.820371314	0.734901398	0.905841229
7		Distribution =	Exponential		W =	0.475627484	0.447222041	0.504032927
8		Mean =	0.333333333		W_q =	0.275114516	0.248998719	0.301230313
9								
10					P_0 =	0.402085033	0.386200645	0.417969421
11		Service Times			P_1 =	0.244395195	0.236088826	0.252701564
12		Distribution =	Exponential		P_2 =	0.145351997	0.138638859	0.152065136
13		Mean =	0.2		P_3 =	0.09046104	0.084038151	0.096883929
14					P_4 =	0.052988644	0.047272227	0.05870506
15					P_5 =	0.030234667	0.025540066	0.034929268
16		Length of Simulation Run			P_6 =	0.015582175	0.012223063	0.018941288
17		Number of Arrivals =	10,000		P_7 =	0.008315125	0.005760629	0.010869622
18					P_8 =	0.004584301	0.002657593	0.006511009
19					P_9 =	0.00271883	0.001266236	0.004171425
20		Run Simulation			P_{10} =	0.001392827	0.000427267	0.002358388
21								

The Excel file for this chapter in your OR Courseware includes an automatic routine, called **Queueing Simulator,** for applying the next-event incrementing procedure to various kinds of queueing systems. The system can have either a single server or multiple servers. Several options (exponential, Erlang, degenerate, uniform, or translated exponential) are available for the probability distributions of interarrival times and service times. Figure 22.4 shows the input and output (in units of hours) from applying Queueing Simulator to the current example for a simulation run with 10,000 customer arrivals. Using the notation for various measures of performance for queueing systems introduced in Sec. 17.2, column F gives the estimate of each of these measures provided by the simulation run. [Using the formulas given in Sec. 17.6 for an $M/M/1$ queueing system, the true values of these measures are $L = 1.5$, $L_q = 0.9$, $W = 0.5$, $W_q = 0.3$, $P_0 = 0.4$, and $P_n = 0.4(0.6)^n$.] Columns G and H show the corresponding 95 percent confidence interval for each of these measures. Note that these confidence intervals are somewhat wider than might have been expected after such a long simulation run. In general, surprisingly long simulation runs are required to obtain relatively precise estimates (narrow confidence intervals) for the measures of performance for a queueing system (or for most stochastic systems).

The next-event incrementing procedure is considerably better suited for this example and similar stochastic systems than the fixed-time incrementing procedure. Next-event incrementing requires fewer iterations to cover the same amount of simulated time, and it generates a precise schedule for the evolution of the system rather than a rough approximation.

The next-event incrementing procedure will be illustrated again in Sec. 22.8 (see Table 22.12) in the context of a full statistical experiment for estimating certain measures of performance for another queueing system. That section also will describe the statistical method that is used by Queueing Simulator to obtain its point estimates and confidence intervals.

Several pertinent questions about how to conduct a simulation study of this type still remain to be answered. These answers are presented in a broader context in subsequent sections.

More Examples in Your OR Courseware

Simulation examples are easier to understand when they can be *observed in action,* rather than just talked about on a printed page. Therefore, the simulation area of your OR Tutor includes two *demonstration examples* that should be viewed at this time.

Both examples involve a bank that plans to open up a new branch office. The questions address how many teller windows to provide and then how many tellers to have on duty at the outset. Therefore, the system being studied is a *queueing system.* However, in contrast to the *M/M/*1 queueing system just considered in Example 2, this queueing system is too complicated to be solved analytically. This system has multiple servers (tellers), and the probability distributions of interarrival times and service times do not fit the standard models of queueing theory. Furthermore, in the second demonstration, it has been decided that one class of customers (merchants) needs to be given nonpreemptive priority over other customers, but the probability distributions for this class are different from those for other customers. These complications are typical of those that can be readily incorporated into a simulation study.

In both demonstrations, you will be able to see customers arrive and served customers leave as well as the next-event incrementing procedure being applied simultaneously to the simulation run.

The demonstrations also introduce you to an *interactive routine* that you should find very helpful in dealing with some of the problems at the end of this chapter.

22.2 SOME COMMON TYPES OF APPLICATIONS OF SIMULATION

Simulation is an exceptionally versatile technique. It can be used (with varying degrees of difficulty) to investigate virtually any kind of stochastic system. This versatility has made simulation the most widely used OR technique for studies dealing with such systems, and its popularity is continuing to increase.

Because of the tremendous diversity of its applications, it is impossible to enumerate all the specific areas in which simulation has been used. However, we will briefly describe here some particularly important categories of applications.

The first three categories concern types of stochastic systems considered in some preceding chapters. It is common to use the kinds of mathematical models described in those chapters to analyze simplified versions of the system and then to apply simulation to refine the results.

Design and Operation of Queueing Systems

Section 17.3 gives many examples of commonly encountered queueing systems that illustrate how such systems pervade many areas of society. Many mathematical models are available (including those presented in Chap. 17) for analyzing relatively simple types of queueing systems. Unfortunately, these models can only provide rough approximations at best of more complicated queueing systems. However, simulation is well suited for dealing with even very complicated queueing systems, so many of its applications fall into this category.

The two demonstration examples of simulation in your OR Tutor (both dealing with how much teller service to provide a bank's customers) are of this type. Because queueing applications of simulation are so pervasive, the automatic routine in the simulation area of your OR Courseware (called the Queueing Simulator) is for simulating queueing systems.

Among the six award-winning applications of queueing models presented in Sec. 18.6, two of these also made heavy use of simulation. One was the study of New York City's arrest-to-arraignment system that led to great improvements in the efficiency of this system plus annual savings of $9.5 million. The other was AT&T developing a PC-based system to help its business customers design or redesign their call centers, resulting in more than $750 million in annual profit for these customers.

Managing Inventory Systems

Sections 19.5 to 19.7 present models for the management of inventory systems when the products involved have uncertain demand. Section 19.8 then describes the kinds of larger inventory systems that commonly arise in practice. Although mathematical models sometimes can help analyze these more complicated systems, simulation often plays a key role as well.

As one example, an article in the April 1996 issue of *OR/MS Today* describes an OR study of this kind that was done for the *IBM PC Company* in Europe. Facing unrelenting pressure from increasingly agile and aggressive competitors, the company had to find a way to greatly improve its performance in quickly filling customer orders. The OR team analyzed how to do this by simulating various redesigns of the company's entire *supply chain* (the network of facilities that spans procurement, manufacturing, and distribution, including all the inventories accumulated along the way). This led to major changes in the design and operation of the supply chain (including its inventory systems) that greatly improved the company's competitive position. Direct cost savings of $40 million per year also were achieved.

Section 22.6 will illustrate the application of simulation to a relatively simple kind of inventory system.

Estimating the Probability of Completing a Project by the Deadline

One of the key concerns of a project manager is whether his or her team will be able to complete the project by the deadline. Section 10.4 describes how the PERT three-estimate approach can be used to obtain a rough estimate of the probability of meeting the deadline with the current project plan. That section also describes three simplifying approximations made by this approach to be able to estimate this probability. Unfortunately, because of these approximations, the resulting estimate always is overly optimistic, and sometimes by a considerable amount.

Consequently, it is becoming increasingly common now to use simulation to obtain a better estimate of this probability. This involves generating random observations from the probability distributions of the duration of the various activities in the projects. By using the project network, it then is straightforward to simulate when each activity begins and ends, and so when the project finishes. By repeating this simulation thousands of times (in one computer run), a very good estimate can be obtained of the probability of meeting the deadline.

We shall illustrate this particular kind of application in Sec. 22.6.

Design and Operation of Manufacturing Systems

Surveys consistently show that a large proportion of the applications of simulation involve manufacturing systems. Many of these systems can be viewed as a queueing system of some kind (e.g., a queueing system where the machines are the servers and the jobs to be processed are the customers). However, various complications inherent in these systems (e.g., occasional machine breakdowns, defective items needing to be reworked, and multiple types of jobs) go beyond the scope of the usual queueing models. Such complications are no problem for simulation.

Here are a few examples of the kinds of questions that might be addressed.

1. How many machines of each type should be provided?
2. How many materials-handling units of each type should be provided?
3. Considering their due dates for completion of the entire production process, what rule should be used to choose the order in which the jobs currently at a machine should be processed?
4. What are realistic due dates for jobs?
5. What will be the bottleneck operations in a new production process as currently designed?
6. What will be the throughput (production rate) of a new production process?

Design and Operation of Distribution Systems

Any major manufacturing corporation needs an efficient *distribution system* for distributing its goods from its factories and warehouses to its customers. There are many uncertainties involved in the operation of such a system. When will vehicles become available for shipping the goods? How long will a shipment take? What will be the demands of the various customers? By generating random observations from the relevant probability distributions, simulation can readily deal with these kinds of uncertainties. Thus, it is used quite often to test various possibilities for improving the design and operation of these systems.

One award-winning application of this kind is described in the January–February 1991 issue of *Interfaces. Reynolds Metal Company* spends over $250 million annually to deliver its products and receive raw materials. Shipments are made by truck, rail, ship, and air across a network of well over a hundred shipping locations including plants, warehouses, and suppliers. A combination of mixed binary integer programming (Chap. 12) and simulation was used to design a new distribution system with central dispatching. The new system both improved on-time delivery of shipments and reduced annual freight costs by over $7 million.

Financial Risk Analysis

Financial risk analysis was one of the earliest application areas of simulation, and it continues to be a very active area. For example, consider the evaluation of a proposed capital investment with uncertain future cash flows. By generating random observations from the probability distributions for the cash flow in each of the respective time periods (and considering relationships between time periods), simulation can generate thousands of scenarios for how the investment will turn out. This provides a *probability distribution* of the return (e.g., net present value) from the investment. This distribution (sometimes called the *risk profile*) enables management to assess the risk involved in making the investment.

A similar approach enables analyzing the risk associated with investing in various securities, including the more exotic financial instruments such as puts, calls, futures, stock options, etc.

Section 22.6 includes an example of using simulation for financial risk analysis.

Health Care Applications

Health care is another area where, like the evaluation of risky investments, analyzing future uncertainties is central to current decision making. However, rather than dealing with uncertain future cash flows, the uncertainties now involve such things as the evolution of human diseases.

Here are a few examples of the kinds of computer simulations that have been performed to guide the design of health care systems.

1. Simulating the use of hospital resources when treating patients with coronary heart disease.
2. Simulating health expenditures under alternative insurance plans.
3. Simulating the cost and effectiveness of screening for the early detection of a disease.
4. Simulating the use of the complex of surgical services at a medical center.
5. Simulating the timing and location of calls for ambulance services.
6. Simulating the matching of donated kidneys with transplant recipients.
7. Simulating the operation of an emergency room.

Applications to Other Service Industries

Like health care, other service industries also have proved to be fertile fields for the application of simulation. These industries include government services, banking, hotel management, restaurants, educational institutions, disaster planning, the military, amusement parks, and many others. In many cases, the systems being simulated are, in fact, queueing systems of some type.

The January–February 1992 issue of *Interfaces* describes an award-winning application in this category. The *United States Postal Service* had identified *automation technology* as the only way it would be able to handle its increasing mail volume while remaining price competitive and satisfying service goals. Extensive planning over several years was required to convert to a largely automated system that would meet these goals. The backbone of the analysis leading to the adopted plan was performed with a comprehensive simulation model called META (model for evaluating technology alternatives). This model was first applied extensively at the national level, and then it was moved down to the local level for detailed planning. The resulting plan required a cumulative capital investment of $12 billion, but also was projected to achieve labor savings of over $4 billion per year. Another consequence of this highly successful application of simulation was that the value of OR tools now is recognized at the highest levels of the Postal Service. Operations research techniques continue to be used by the planning staff both at headquarters and in the field divisions.

New Applications

More new innovative applications of simulation are being made each year. Many of these applications are first announced publicly at the annual Winter Simulation Conference, held each December in some U.S. city. Since its beginning in 1967, this conference has been an institution in the simulation field. It now is attended by nearly a thousand participants, divided roughly equally between academics and practitioners. Hundreds of papers are presented to announce both methodological advances and new innovative applications.

22.3 GENERATION OF RANDOM NUMBERS

As the examples in Sec. 22.1 demonstrated, implementing a simulation model requires random numbers to obtain random observations from probability distributions. One method for generating such random numbers is to use a physical device such as a spinning disk or an electronic randomizer. Several tables of random numbers have been generated in this way, including one containing 1 million random digits, published by the Rand Corporation. An excerpt from the Rand table is given in Table 22.3.

Physical devices now have been replaced by the computer as the primary source for generating random numbers. For example, we pointed out in Sec. 22.1 that Excel uses the RAND() function for this purpose. Many other software packages also have the capability of generating random numbers whenever needed during a simulation run.

TABLE 22.3 Table of random digits

09656	96657	64842	49222	49506	10145	48455	23505	90430	04180
24712	55799	60857	73479	33581	17360	30406	05842	72044	90764
07202	96341	23699	76171	79126	04512	15426	15980	88898	06358
84575	46820	54083	43918	46989	05379	70682	43081	66171	38942
38144	87037	46626	70529	27918	34191	98668	33482	43998	75733
48048	56349	01986	29814	69800	91609	65374	22928	09704	59343
41936	58566	31276	19952	01352	18834	99596	09302	20087	19063
73391	94006	03822	81845	76158	41352	40596	14325	27020	17546
57580	08954	73554	28698	29022	11568	35668	59906	39557	27217
92646	41113	91411	56215	69302	86419	61224	41936	56939	27816
07118	12707	35622	81485	73354	49800	60805	05648	28898	60933
57842	57831	24130	75408	83784	64307	91620	40810	06539	70387
65078	44981	81009	33697	98324	46928	34198	96032	98426	77488
04294	96120	67629	55265	26248	40602	25566	12520	89785	93932
48381	06807	43775	09708	73199	53406	02910	83292	59249	18597
00459	62045	19249	67095	22752	24636	16965	91836	00582	46721
38824	81681	33323	64086	55970	04849	24819	20749	51711	86173
91465	22232	02907	01050	07121	53536	71070	26916	47620	01619
50874	00807	77751	73952	03073	69063	16894	85570	81746	07568
26644	75871	15618	50310	72610	66205	82640	86205	73453	90232

Source: Reproduced with permission from The Rand Corporation, *A Million Random Digits with 100,000 Normal Deviates.* Copyright, The Free Press, Glencoe, IL, 1955, top of p. 182.

Characteristics of Random Numbers

The procedure used by a computer to obtain random numbers is called a *random number generator.*

> A **random number generator** is an algorithm that produces sequences of numbers that follow a specified probability distribution and possess the appearance of randomness.

The reference to *sequences of numbers* means that the algorithm produces many random numbers in a serial manner. Although an individual user may need only a few of the numbers, generally the algorithm must be capable of producing many numbers. *Probability distribution* implies that a probability statement can be associated with the occurrence of each number produced by the algorithm.

We shall reserve the term **random number** to mean a random observation from some form of a *uniform distribution,* so that all possible numbers are *equally likely.* When we are interested in some other probability distribution (as in the next section), we shall refer to *random observations* from that distribution.

Random numbers can be divided into two main categories, random integer numbers and uniform random numbers, defined as follows:

> A **random integer number** is a random observation from a *discretized uniform distribution* over some range $\underline{n}, \underline{n} + 1, \ldots, \overline{n}$. The probabilities for this distribution are
>
> $$P(\underline{n}) = P(\underline{n} + 1) = \cdots = P(\overline{n}) = \frac{1}{\overline{n} - \underline{n} + 1}.$$

Usually, $\underline{n} = 0$ or 1, and these are convenient values for most applications. (If $\underline{n}$ has another value, then subtracting either $\underline{n}$ or $\underline{n} - 1$ from the random integer number changes the lower end of the range to either 0 or 1.)

> A **uniform random number** is a random observation from a (continuous) *uniform distribution* over some interval $[a, b]$. The probability density function of this uniform distribution is
>
> $$f(x) = \begin{cases} \dfrac{1}{b - a} & \text{if } a \leq x \leq b \\ 0 & \text{otherwise.} \end{cases}$$

When a and b are not specified, they are assumed to be $a = 0$ and $b = 1$.

The random numbers initially generated by a computer usually are random integer numbers. However, if desired, these numbers can immediately be converted to a uniform random number as follows:

> For a given *random integer number* in the range 0 to $\overline{n}$, dividing this number by $\overline{n}$ yields (approximately) a *uniform random number.* (If $\overline{n}$ is small, this approximation should be improved by adding $\frac{1}{2}$ to the random integer number and then dividing by $\overline{n} + 1$ instead.)

This is the usual method used for generating uniform random numbers. With the huge values of $\overline{n}$ commonly used, it is an essentially exact method.

Strictly speaking, the numbers generated by the computer should not be called random numbers because they are predictable and reproducible (which sometimes is advantageous), given the random number generator being used. Therefore, they are sometimes given the name **pseudo-random numbers.** However, the important point is that they satisfactorily play the role of random numbers in the simulation if the method used to generate them is valid.

Various relatively sophisticated statistical procedures have been proposed for testing whether a generated sequence of numbers has an acceptable appearance of randomness. Basically the requirements are that each successive number in the sequence have an equal probability of taking on any one of the possible values and that it be statistically independent of the other numbers in the sequence.

Congruential Methods for Random Number Generation

There are a number of random number generators available, of which the most popular are the *congruential methods* (additive, multiplicative, and mixed). The mixed congruential method includes features of the other two, so we shall discuss it first.

The **mixed congruential method** generates a *sequence* of random integer numbers over the range from 0 to $m - 1$. The method always calculates the next random number from the last one obtained, given an initial random number x_0, called the **seed,** which may be obtained from some published source such as the Rand table. In particular, it calculates the $(n + 1)$st random number x_{n+1} from the nth random number x_n by using the recurrence relation

$$x_{n+1} \equiv (ax_n + c)(\text{modulo } m),$$

where a, c, and m are positive integers ($a < m$, $c < m$). This mathematical notation signifies that x_{n+1} is the *remainder* when $ax_n + c$ is divided by m. Thus, the *possible* values of x_{n+1} are 0, 1, . . . , $m - 1$, so that m represents the desired number of *different* values that could be generated for the random numbers.

To illustrate, suppose that $m = 8$, $a = 5$, $c = 7$, and $x_0 = 4$. The resulting sequence of random numbers is calculated in Table 22.4. (The sequence cannot be continued fur-

TABLE 22.4 Illustration of the mixed congruential method

n	x_n	$5x_n + 7$	$(5x_n + 7)/8$	x_{n+1}
0	4	27	$3 + \frac{3}{8}$	3
1	3	22	$2 + \frac{6}{8}$	6
2	6	37	$4 + \frac{5}{8}$	5
3	5	32	$4 + \frac{0}{8}$	0
4	0	7	$0 + \frac{7}{8}$	7
5	7	42	$5 + \frac{2}{8}$	2
6	2	17	$2 + \frac{1}{8}$	1
7	1	12	$1 + \frac{4}{8}$	4

ther because it would just begin repeating the numbers in the same order.) Note that this sequence includes each of the eight possible numbers exactly once. This property is a necessary one for a sequence of *random* integer numbers, but it does not occur with some choices of a and c. (Try $a = 4$, $c = 7$, and $x_0 = 3$.) Fortunately, there are rules available for choosing values of a and c that will guarantee this property. (There are no restrictions on the seed x_0 because it affects only where the sequence begins and not the progression of numbers.)

The number of consecutive numbers in a sequence before it begins repeating itself is referred to as the **cycle length.** Thus, the cycle length in the example is 8. The *maximum* cycle length is m, so the only values of a and c considered are those that yield this maximum cycle length.

Table 22.5 illustrates the conversion of random integer numbers to uniform random numbers. The left column gives the random integer numbers obtained in the rightmost column of Table 22.4. The right column gives the corresponding uniform random numbers from the formula

$$\text{Uniform random number} = \frac{\text{random integer number} + \dfrac{1}{2}}{m}.$$

Note that each of these uniform random numbers lies at the midpoint of one of the eight equal-sized intervals 0 to 0.125, 0.125 to 0.25, . . . , 0.875 to 1. The small value of $m = 8$ does not enable us to obtain other values over the interval [0, 1], so we are obtaining fairly rough approximations of real uniform random numbers. In practice, *far* larger values of m generally are used.

For a binary computer with a word size of b bits, the usual choice for m is $m = 2^b$; this is the total number of nonnegative integers that can be expressed within the capacity of the word size. (Any undesired integers that arise in the sequence of random numbers are just not used.) With this choice of m, we can ensure that each possible number occurs exactly once before any number is repeated by selecting any of the values $a = 1, 5, 9, 13, \ldots$ and $c = 1, 3, 5, 7, \ldots$. For a decimal computer with a word size of d digits, the usual choice for m is $m = 10^d$, and the same property is ensured by selecting any of the values $a = 1, 21, 41, 61, \ldots$ and $c = 1, 3, 7, 9, 11, 13, 17, 19, \ldots$ (that is, all positive *odd* integers *except* those ending with the digit 5). The specific selection can be made on

TABLE 22.5 Converting random integer numbers to uniform random numbers

Random Integer Number	Uniform Random Number
3	0.4375
6	0.8125
5	0.6875
0	0.0625
7	0.9375
2	0.3125
1	0.1875
4	0.5625

the basis of the *serial correlation* between successively generated numbers, which differs considerably among these alternatives.[1]

Occasionally, random integer numbers with only a relatively small number of digits are desired. For example, suppose that only three digits are desired, so that the possible values can be expressed as 000, 001, . . . , 999. In such a case, the usual procedure still is to use $m = 2^b$ or $m = 10^d$, so that an extremely large number of random integer numbers can be generated before the sequence starts repeating itself. However, except for purposes of calculating the next random integer number in this sequence, all but three digits of each number generated would be discarded to obtain the desired three-digit random integer number. One convention is to take the *last* three digits (i.e., the three trailing digits).

The **multiplicative congruential method** is just the special case of the mixed congruential method where $c = 0$. The **additive congruential method** also is similar, but it sets $a = 1$ and replaces c by some random number preceding x_n in the sequence, for example, x_{n-1} (so that more than one seed is required to start calculating the sequence).

Among the possible random number generators (choices of a and m) based on the multiplicative congruential method, perhaps the most widely used is the *Learmouth-Lewis generator*

$$x_{n+1} \equiv 7^5 x_n (\text{modulo } 2^{31} - 1).$$

This generator has been tested extensively, and the results of the statistical tests indicate that it is very satisfactory. Versions of this generator are used, e.g., in IBM versions of APL, in the International Mathematics and Statistics Library (IMSL) package, and in the random number generator package LLRANDOM. Tables of suitable seeds also are available.

22.4 GENERATION OF RANDOM OBSERVATIONS FROM A PROBABILITY DISTRIBUTION

Given a sequence of random numbers, how can one generate a sequence of random observations from a given probability distribution? Several different approaches are available, depending on the nature of the distribution.

Simple Discrete Distributions

For some simple discrete distributions, a sequence of random *integer* numbers can be used to generate random observations in a straightforward way. Merely allocate the possible values of a random number to the various outcomes in the probability distribution in direct proportion to the respective probabilities of those outcomes.

For Example 1 in Sec. 22.1, where flips of a coin are being simulated, the possible outcomes of one flip are a head or a tail, where each outcome has a probability of $\frac{1}{2}$. Therefore, rather than using uniform random numbers (as was done in Sec. 22.1), it would have been sufficient to use *random digits* to generate the outcomes. Five of the ten possible values of a random digit (say, 0, 1, 2, 3, 4) would be assigned an association with a head and the other five (say, 5, 6, 7, 8, 9) a tail.

As another example, consider the probability distribution of the outcome of a throw of two dice. It is known that the probability of throwing a 2 is $\frac{1}{36}$ (as is the probability of throw-

[1]See R. R. Coveyou, "Serial Correlation in the Generation of Pseudo-Random Numbers," *Journal of the Association of Computing Machinery,* **7:** 72–74, 1960.

ing a 12), the probability of throwing a 3 is $\frac{2}{36}$, and so on. Therefore, $\frac{1}{36}$ of the possible values of a random integer number should be associated with throwing a 2, $\frac{2}{36}$ of the values with throwing a 3, and so forth. Thus, if two-digit random integer numbers are being used, 72 of the 100 values will be selected for consideration, so that a random integer number will be rejected if it takes on any one of the other 28 values. Then 2 of the 72 possible values (say, 00 and 01) will be assigned an association with throwing a 2, four of them (say 02, 03, 04, and 05) will be assigned an association with throwing a 3, and so on.

Using random *integer* numbers in this kind of way is convenient when they either are being drawn from a table of random numbers or are being generated directly by a congruential method. However, when performing the simulation on a computer, it usually is more convenient to have the computer generate *uniform* random numbers and then use them in the corresponding way. All the subsequent methods for generating random observations use uniform random numbers.

The Inverse Transformation Method

For more complicated distributions, whether discrete or continuous, the *inverse transformation method* can sometimes be used to generate random observations. Letting X be the random variable involved, we denote the cumulative distribution function by

$$F(x) = P\{X \leq x\}.$$

Generating each observation then requires the following two steps.

Summary of Inverse Transformation Method.

1. Generate a *uniform random number r* between 0 and 1.
2. Set $F(x) = r$ and solve for x, which then is the desired random observation from the probability distribution.

This procedure is illustrated in Fig. 22.5 for the case where $F(x)$ is plotted graphically and the uniform random number r happens to be 0.5269.

FIGURE 22.5
Illustration of the inverse transformation method for obtaining a random observation from a given probability distribution.

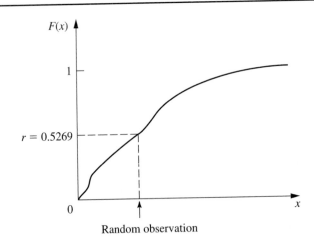

Although the graphical procedure illustrated by Fig. 22.5 is convenient if the simulation is done manually, the computer must revert to some alternative approach. For *discrete* distributions, a *table lookup approach* can be taken by constructing a table that gives a "range" (jump) in the value of $F(x)$ for each possible value of $X = x$. Excel provides a convenient VLOOKUP function to implement this approach when performing a simulation on a spreadsheet.

To illustrate how this function works, suppose that a company is simulating the *maintenance program* for its machines. The time between breakdowns of one of these machines always is 4, 5, or 6 days, where these times occur with probabilities 0.25, 0.5, and 0.25, respectively. The first step in simulating these breakdowns is to create the table shown in Fig. 22.6 somewhere in the spreadsheet. Note that each number in the second column gives the cumulative probability *prior* to the number of days in the third column. The second and third columns (below the column headings) constitute the "lookup table." The VLOOKUP function has three arguments. The first argument gives the address of the cell that is providing the uniform random number being used. The second argument identifies the range of cell addresses for the lookup table. The third argument indicates which column of the lookup table provides the random observation, so this argument equals 2 in this case. The VLOOKUP function with these three arguments is entered as the equation for each cell in the spreadsheet where a random observation from the distribution is to be entered.

For certain *continuous* distributions, the inverse transformation method can be implemented on a computer by first solving the equation $F(x) = r$ *analytically* for x. We illustrate this approach next with the exponential distribution.

Exponential and Erlang Distributions

As indicated in Sec. 17.4, the cumulative distribution function for the **exponential distribution** is

$$F(x) = 1 - e^{-\alpha x}, \quad \text{for } x \geq 0,$$

where $1/\alpha$ is the mean of the distribution. Setting $F(x) = r$ thereby yields

$$1 - e^{-\alpha x} = r,$$

FIGURE 22.6
The table that would be constructed in a spreadsheet for using Excel's VLOOKUP function to implement the inverse transformation method for the maintenance program example.

Distribution of time between breakdowns

Probability	Cumulative	Number of Days
0.25	0	4
0.5	0.25	5
0.25	0.75	6

so that

$$e^{-\alpha x} = 1 - r.$$

Therefore, taking the natural logarithm of both sides gives

$$\ln e^{-\alpha x} = \ln (1 - r),$$

so that

$$-\alpha x = \ln (1 - r),$$

which yields

$$x = \frac{\ln (1 - r)}{-\alpha}$$

as the desired random observation from the exponential distribution.

This direct application of the inverse transformation method provides the most straightforward way of generating random observations from an exponential distribution. (More complicated techniques also have been developed for this distribution[1] that are faster for a computer than calculating a logarithm.)

Note that $1 - r$ is itself a uniform random number. Therefore, to save a subtraction, it is common in practice simply to use the *original* uniform random number r directly in place of $1 - r$.

A natural extension of this procedure for the exponential distribution also can be used to generate a random observation from an **Erlang** (gamma) **distribution** (see Sec. 17.7). The sum of k independent exponential random variables, each with mean $1/(k\alpha)$, has the Erlang distribution with shape parameter k and mean $1/\alpha$. Therefore, given a sequence of k uniform random numbers between 0 and 1, say, $r_1, r_2, \ldots, r_k$, the desired random observation from the Erlang distribution is

$$x = \sum_{i=1}^{k} \frac{\ln (1 - r_i)}{-k\alpha},$$

which reduces to

$$x = -\frac{1}{k\alpha} \ln \left[\prod_{i=1}^{k} (1 - r_i) \right],$$

where Π denotes multiplication. Once again, the subtractions may be eliminated simply by using r_i directly in place of $1 - r_i$.

Normal and Chi-Square Distributions

A particularly simple (but inefficient) technique for generating a random observation from a **normal distribution** is obtained by applying the central limit theorem. Because a uniform random number has a *uniform distribution* from 0 to 1, it has mean $\frac{1}{2}$ and standard

---

[1]For example, see J. H. Ahrens and V. Dieter, "Efficient Table-Free Sampling Methods for Exponential, Cauchy, and Normal Distributions," *Communications of the ACM,* **31:** 1330–1337, 1988.

deviation $1/\sqrt{12}$. Therefore, this theorem implies that the sum of n uniform random numbers has approximately a normal distribution with mean $n/2$ and standard deviation $\sqrt{n/12}$. Thus, if $r_1, r_2, \ldots, r_n$ are a sample of uniform random numbers, then

$$x = \frac{\sigma}{\sqrt{n/12}} \sum_{i=1}^{n} r_i + \mu - \frac{n}{2} \frac{\sigma}{\sqrt{n/12}}$$

is a random observation from an approximately normal distribution with mean μ and standard deviation σ. This approximation is an excellent one (except in the tails of the distribution), even with small values of n. Thus, values of n from 5 to 10 may be adequate; $n = 12$ also is a convenient value, because it eliminates the square root terms from the preceding expression.

Since tables of the normal distribution are widely available (e.g., see Appendix 5), another simple method to generate a close approximation of a random observation is to use such a table to implement the inverse transformation method directly. This is fairly convenient when you are generating a few random observations by hand, but less so for computer implementation since it requires storing a large table and then using a table lookup.

Various *exact* techniques for generating random observations from a normal distribution have also been developed.[1] These exact techniques are sufficiently fast that, in practice, they generally are used instead of the approximate methods described above. A routine for one of these techniques usually is already incorporated into a software package with simulation capabilities. For example, Excel uses the function, NORMINV(RAND(), μ, σ), to generate a random observation from a normal distribution with mean μ and standard deviation σ.

A simple method for handling the **chi-square distribution** is to use the fact that it is obtained by summing squares of standardized normal random variables. Thus, if y_1, $y_2, \ldots, y_n$ are n random observations from a normal distribution with mean 0 and standard deviation 1, then

$$x = \sum_{i=1}^{n} y_i^2$$

is a random observation from a chi-square distribution with n degrees of freedom.

The Acceptance-Rejection Method

For many continuous distributions, it is not feasible to apply the inverse transformation method because $x = F^{-1}(r)$ cannot be computed (or at least computed efficiently). Therefore, several other types of methods have been developed to generate random observations from such distributions. Frequently, these methods are considerably faster than the inverse transformation method even when the latter method can be used. To provide some notion of the approach for these alternative methods, we now illustrate one called the **acceptance-rejection method** on a simple example.

---

[1]Ibid.

Consider the *triangular distribution* having the probability density function

$$f(x) = \begin{cases} x & \text{if } 0 \le x \le 1 \\ 1 - (x - 1) & \text{if } 1 \le x \le 2 \\ 0 & \text{otherwise.} \end{cases}$$

The acceptance-rejection method uses the following two steps (perhaps repeatedly) to generate a random observation.

1. Generate a uniform random number r_1 between 0 and 1, and set $x = 2r_1$ (so that the range of possible values of x is 0 to 2).
2. Accept x with

$$\text{Probability} = \begin{cases} x & \text{if } 0 \le x \le 1 \\ 1 - (x - 1) & \text{if } 1 \le x \le 2, \end{cases}$$

to be the desired random observation [since this probability equals $f(x)$]. *Otherwise, reject x and repeat the two steps.*

To randomly generate the event of accepting (or rejecting) x according to this probability, the method implements step 2 as follows:

2. Generate a uniform random number r_2 between 0 and 1.

Accept x if $r_2 \le f(x)$.
Reject x if $r_2 > f(x)$.

If x is rejected, repeat the two steps.

Because $x = 2r_1$ is being accepted with a probability $= f(x)$, the probability distribution of *accepted values* has $f(x)$ as its density function, so accepted values are valid *random observations* from $f(x)$.

We were fortunate in this example that the *largest* value of $f(x)$ for any x was exactly 1. If this largest value were $L \ne 1$ instead, then r_2 would be multiplied by L in step 2. With this adjustment, the method is easily extended to other probability density functions over a finite interval, and similar concepts can be used over an infinite interval as well.

22.5   OUTLINE OF A MAJOR SIMULATION STUDY

Thus far, this chapter has focused mainly on the *process* of performing a simulation and some applications from doing so. We now place this material into broader perspective by briefly outlining all the typical steps involved in a major operations research study that is based on applying simulation. (Nearly the same steps also apply when the study is applying other operations research techniques instead.)

We should emphasize that some applications of simulation do not require all the effort described in the following steps. The advent of Excel and Excel add-ins for efficiently performing basic simulations on a spreadsheet (as described in the next section) now often enables conducting the study with far less time and expense than previously. However, major applications of simulation still require the extended effort described in this section.

Step 1: Formulate the Problem and Plan the Study

The operations research team needs to begin by meeting with management to address the following kinds of questions.

1. What is the problem that management wants studied?
2. What are the overall objectives for the study?
3. What specific issues should be addressed?
4. What kinds of alternative system configurations should be considered?
5. What measures of performance of the system are of interest to management?
6. What are the time constraints for performing the study?

In addition, the team also will meet with engineers and operational personnel to learn the details of just how the system would operate. (The team generally will also include one or more members with a first-hand knowledge of the system.) If a current version of the system is in operation, the team will observe the system to identify its components and the linkages between them.

Before concluding this step, the head of the OR team also needs to plan the overall study in terms of the number of people, their responsibilities, the schedule, and a budget for the study.

Step 2: Collect the Data and Formulate the Simulation Model

The types of data needed depend on the nature of the system to be simulated. For a queueing system, key pieces of data would be the distribution of *interarrival times* and the distribution of *service times*. For a single-product inventory system, the team would need the distribution of *demand* for the product and the distribution of the *lead time* between placing an order to replenish inventory and receiving the amount ordered. For a PERT project network where the activity durations are uncertain, distributions of the *durations of the activities* are needed. For a manufacturing system involving machines that occasionally break down, the team needs to determine the distribution of the *time until a machine breaks down* and the distribution of *repair times*.

In each of these examples, note that it is the *probability distributions* of the relevant quantities that are needed. In order to generate representative scenarios of how a system would perform, it is essential that a simulation generate *random observations* from these distributions rather than simply using averages.

Generally, it will only be possible to *estimate* these distributions. This is done after taking direct observations from an existing version of the system under study, or from a similar system. After examining these data for a particular quantity, if the *form* of the distribution is unclear but resembles the form of a standard type of distribution, a statistical test called the *chi-square goodness of fit test* can be used to test whether the data fit this standard form. The sample mean and sample variance of the data also provide an estimate of the mean and variance of the distribution. If no relevant data can be obtained because no similar system exists, other possible sources of information for estimating a distribution include industrial engineering time studies, engineering records, operating manuals, machine specifications, and interviews with individuals who have experience with similar kinds of operations.

A simulation model often is formulated in terms of a *flow diagram* that links together the various components of the system. Operating rules are given for each component, including the probability distributions that control when events will occur there. The model only needs to contain enough detail to capture the essence of the system. For a large study, it is a good idea to begin by formulating and debugging a relatively simple version of the model before adding important details.

Step 3: Check the Accuracy of the Simulation Model

Before constructing a computer program, the OR team should engage the people most intimately familiar with how the system will operate in checking the accuracy of the simulation model. This often is done by performing a structured walk-through of the conceptual model, using an overhead projector, before an audience of all the key people. At a typical such meeting, several erroneous model assumptions will be discovered and corrected, a few new assumptions will be added, and some issues will be resolved about how much detail is needed in the various parts of the model.

In addition to helping to ensure the accuracy of the simulation model, this process tends to provide the key people with some sense of ownership of the model and the study.

Step 4: Select the Software and Construct a Computer Program[1]

There are four major classes of software used for computer simulations. One is *spreadsheet software.* Example 1 in Sec. 22.1 illustrated how Excel is able to perform some basic simulations on a spreadsheet. In addition, some excellent Excel add-ins now are available to enhance this kind of spreadsheet modeling. The next section focuses on the use of these add-ins.

The other three classes of software for simulations are intended for more extensive applications where it is no longer convenient to use spreadsheet software. One such class is a *general-purpose programming language,* such as C, FORTRAN, PASCAL, BASIC, etc. Such languages (and their predecessors) often were used in the early history of the field because of their great flexibility for programming any sort of simulation. However, because of the considerable programming time required, they are not used nearly as much now.

The third class is a **general-purpose simulation language.** These languages provide many of the features needed to program a simulation model, and so may reduce the required programming time substantially. They also provide a natural framework for simulation modeling. Although less flexible than a general-purpose programming language, they are capable of programming almost any kind of simulation model. However, some degree of expertise in the language is needed.

Prominent general-purpose simulation languages include the current version of GPSS, SIMSCRIPT, SLAM, and SIMAN. The initial versions of these languages date back to 1961, 1963, 1979, and 1983, respectively, but all have stood the test of time.

A key development in the 1980s and 1990s has been the emergence of the fourth class of software, called **applications-oriented simulators** (or just *simulators* for short). Each of these simulators is designed for simulating fairly specific types of systems, such as certain types of manufacturing, computer, and communications systems. Some are very

---

[1]This subsection does not attempt to enumerate or describe the individual simulation software packages that currently are available. For details about 54 such packages, see the 1999 Simulation Software Survey on pp. 38–51 of the February 1999 issue of *OR/MS Today.*

specific (e.g., for oil and gas production engineering, or nuclear power plant analysis, or cardiovascular physiology). Their *goal* is to be able to construct a simulation "program" by the use of menus and graphics, without the need for programming. They are relatively easy to learn and have modeling constructs closely related to the system of interest.

A simulator can be wonderful if the system you wish to simulate fits right into the prescribed category for the simulator. However, the prescription of allowable system features tends to be fairly narrow. Therefore, the major drawback of many simulators is that they are limited to modeling only those system configurations that are allowed by their standard features. Some simulators do allow the option of incorporating routines written in a general-purpose programming language to handle nonstandard features. This option is frequently needed when simulating relatively complex systems.

Another key development in recent years has been the development of **animation** capabilities for displaying computer simulations in action. In an animation, key elements of a system are represented in a computer display by icons that change shape, color, or position when there is a change in the state of the simulation system. Most simulation software vendors now offer a version of their software with animation capabilities. Furthermore, the animation is becoming increasingly elaborate, including even three-dimensional capabilities in some cases.

The major reason for the popularity of animation is its ability to communicate the essence of a simulation model (or of a simulation run) to managers and other key personnel. This greatly increases the credibility of the simulation approach. In addition, animation can be helpful in debugging the computer program for a simulation program.

Step 5: Test the Validity of the Simulation Model

After the computer program has been constructed and debugged, the next key step is to test whether the simulation model incorporated into the program is providing valid results for the system it is representing. Specifically, will the measures of performance for the real system be closely approximated by the values of these measures generated by the simulation model?

This question usually is difficult to answer because most versions of the "real" system do not currently exist. Typically, the purpose of simulation is to investigate and compare various proposed system configurations to help choose the best one.

However, some version of the real system may currently be in operation. If so, its performance data should be compared with the corresponding output measures generated by pilot runs of the simulation model.

In some cases, a mathematical model may be available to provide results for a simple version of the system. If so, these results also should be compared with the simulation results.

When no real data are available to compare with simulation results, one possibility is to conduct a *field test* to collect such data. This would involve constructing a small prototype of some version of the proposed system and placing it into operation. This prototype might also be used after the simulation study has been completed to fine-tune the design of the system before the real system is installed.

Another useful validation test is to have knowledgeable operational personnel check the creditability of how the simulation results change as the configuration of the simulated system is changed. Even when no basis exists for checking the reasonableness of the measures of performance obtained for a particular version of the system, some conclusions often can be drawn about how the *relative* performance of the system should change as its parameters are changed.

Watching animations of simulation runs is another way of checking the validity of the simulation model. Once the model is operating properly, animations also generate interest and credibility in the simulation study for both management and operational personnel.

Step 6: Plan the Simulations to Be Performed

At this point, you need to begin making decisions on which system configurations to simulate. This often is an evolutionary process, where the initial results for a range of configurations help you to hone in on which specific configurations warrant detailed investigation.

Decisions also need to be made now on some statistical issues. One such issue (unless using the special technique described in Sec. 22.8) is the *length of the warm-up period* while waiting for the system to essentially reach a steady-state condition before starting to collect data. Preliminary simulation runs often are used to analyze this issue. Since systems frequently require a surprisingly long time to essentially reach a steady-state condition, it is helpful to select *starting conditions* for a simulated system that appear to be roughly representative of steady-state conditions in order to reduce this required time as much as possible.

Another key statistical issue is the *length of the simulation run* following the warm-up period for each system configuration being simulated. Keep in mind that simulation does not produce *exact* values for the measures of performance of a system. Instead, each simulation run can be viewed as a *statistical experiment* that is generating *statistical observations* of the performance of the simulated system. These observations are used to produce *statistical estimates* of the measures of performance. Increasing the length of a run increases the precision of these estimates.

The statistical theory for designing statistical experiments conducted through simulation is little different than for experiments conducted by directly observing the performance of a physical system.[1] Therefore, the inclusion of a professional statistician (or at least an experienced simulation analyst with a strong statistical background) on the OR team can be invaluable at this step.

Step 7: Conduct the Simulation Runs and Analyze the Results

The output from the simulation runs now provides statistical estimates of the desired measures of performance for each system configuration of interest. In addition to a *point estimate* of each measure, a *confidence interval* normally should be obtained to indicate the range of likely values of the measure (just as was done for Example 2 in Sec. 22.1). Section 22.8 will describe one method for doing this.[2]

---

[1] For details about the relevant statistical theory for applying simulation, see Chaps. 9–12 in A. M. Law and W. D. Kelton, *Simulation Modeling and Analysis,* McGraw-Hill, New York, 2d ed., 1991.

[2] See pp. 556–557 in the reference cited in the preceding footnote for alternative methods.

These results might immediately indicate that one system configuration is clearly superior to the others. More often, they will identify the few strong candidates to be the best one. In the latter case, some longer simulation runs would be conducted to better compare these candidates. Additional runs also might be used to fine-tune the details of what appears to be the best configuration.

Step 8: Present Recommendations to Management

After completing its analysis, the OR team needs to present its recommendations to management. This usually would be done through both a written report and a formal oral presentation to the managers responsible for making the decisions regarding the system under study.

The report and presentation should summarize how the study was conducted, including documentation of the validation of the simulation model. A demonstration of the *animation* of a simulation run might be included to better convey the simulation process and add credibility. Numerical results that provide the rationale for the recommendations need to be included.

Management usually involves the OR team further in the initial implementation of the new system, including the indoctrination of the affected personnel.

22.6 PERFORMING SIMULATIONS ON SPREADSHEETS

Section 22.5 outlines the typical steps involved in major simulation studies of complex systems. However, not all simulation studies are nearly that involved. In fact, when studying relatively simple systems, it is sometimes possible to run the needed simulations quickly and easily on spreadsheets.

Basically, whenever a spreadsheet model would be used to analyze a problem without taking uncertainties into account (except through sensitivity analysis), the tools now are available to use simulation to consider the effect of the uncertainties. As illustrated by Example 1 in Sec. 22.1, the standard Excel package has some basic simulation capabilities, including the ability to generate uniform random numbers and to generate random observations from some probability distributions. Furthermore, some simulation add-ins for Excel have been developed that greatly enhance the ability to use simulation to analyze spreadsheet models. Two prominent simulation add-ins with similar capabilities are @RISK, developed by Palisade Corporation, and Crystal Ball, developed by Decisioneering. Other simulation add-ins also are available as shareware. One is RiskSim, developed by Professor Michael Middleton.

We have provided the academic version of RiskSim for you in your OR Courseware. (If you want to continue to use it after this course, you should register and pay the shareware fee.) In addition, the full version of @RISK can be obtained from the Palisade Corp. for a free trial period of 10 days in either of two ways. It can be downloaded directly from the Palisade website, www.Palisade.com. Alternatively, it can be ordered on a CD-ROM from this website. Like any Excel add-ins, these add-ins need to be installed before they will show up in Excel.

This section focuses on the use of @RISK to illustrate what can be done with these simulation add-ins. However, if you decide to use RiskSim (which has many of the capabilities of @RISK), its documentation is included in the CD-ROM.

Business spreadsheets typically include some *input cells* that display key data (e.g., the various costs associated with producing or marketing a product) and one or more *output cells* that show measures of performance (e.g., the profit from producing or marketing the product). The user writes Excel equations to link the inputs to the outputs so that the output cells will show the values that correspond to the values that are entered into the input cells. In some cases, there will be uncertainty about what the correct values for the input cells will turn out to be. Sensitivity analysis can be used to check how the outputs change as the values for the input cells change. However, if there is considerable uncertainty about the values of some input cells, a more systematic approach to analyzing the effect of the uncertainty would be helpful. This is where simulation enters the picture.

With a simulation, instead of entering a single number in an input cell where there is uncertainty, a *probability distribution* that describes the uncertainty is entered instead. By generating a *random observation* from the probability distribution for each such input cell, the spreadsheet can calculate the output values in the usual way. Each time this is done is referred to as an **iteration** by @RISK. By running the number of iterations specified by the user (typically hundreds or thousands), the simulation thereby generates the same number of random observations of the output values. The @RISK program records all this information and then gives you the choice of printing out detailed statistics in tabular or graphical form (or both) that roughly shows the underlying *probability distribution* of the output values. A summary of the results also includes estimates of the mean and standard deviation of this distribution.

Now let us look at three examples that illustrate this process.

Inventory Management—Freddie the Newsboy's Problem

Consider the following problem being faced by a newsboy named Freddie. One of the daily newspapers that Freddie sells from his newsstand is the *Financial Journal.* He pays $1.50 per copy delivered to him at the beginning of the day, sells it at $2.50 per copy, and then receives a refund of $0.50 per copy unsold at the end of the day. He has 9 requests to purchase a copy on 30 percent of the days, 10 requests on 40 percent of the days, and 11 requests on 30 percent of the days. The decision Freddie needs to make is how many copies (9, 10, or 11) per day to order from the distributor.

You may recognize this problem as an example of the *newsboy problem* discussed in Sec. 19.5. Thus, the *stochastic one-period inventory model for perishable products* (with no setup cost) presented there can be used to solve this problem. However, for illustrative purposes, we now will show how simulation can be used to analyze this simple inventory system in the same way that it analyzes more complex inventory systems that are beyond the reach of available inventory models.

Figure 22.7 shows the @RISK spreadsheet for this problem. Since the only uncertain input quantity is the day's demand for this newspaper, its probability distribution is entered in the range E4:F6. Because this is a *discrete* probability distribution, the RISKDISCRETE function is used to generate random observations from this distribution. This involves entering the formula, =RISKDISCRETE(E4:E6, F4:F6), in cell C12 (which shows a typical random observation in Fig. 22.7). The simulation eventually needs to be run three times, once for each of the three order quantities under consideration, so we start with one of these order quantities (9) in cell C9. The regular Excel functions are used to cal-

	A	B	C	D	E	F
1	Simulating Freddie the Newsboy's Problem					
2						
3			Data		Demand Distribution	
4		Unit sale price =	$2.50		9	0.3
5		Unit purchase cost =	$1.50		10	0.4
6		Unit salvage value =	$0.50		11	0.3
7						
8		Decision Variable				
9		Order Quantity =	9			
10						
11		Simulated Quantities				
12		Demand =	10			
13						
14		Sales Revenue =	$22.50			
15		Purchasing Cost =	$13.50			
16		Salvage Value =	$0.00			
17						
18		Total Profit =	$9.00			

	C
12	=RiskDiscrete(E4:E6,F4:F6)
13	
14	=C4*MIN(C9,C12)
15	=C5*C9
16	=C6*MAX(C9-C12,0)
17	
18	=C14-C15+C16

FIGURE 22.7
The @RISK spreadsheet for Freddie the newsboy's problem.

culate the simulated quantities in cells C14, C15, and C16 as C14 = C4*MIN (C9,C12), C15 = C5*C9, and C16 = C6*MAX(C9−C12,0). Similarly, the profit in cell C18 (the one output cell) is calculated as C18 = C14 − C15 + C16.

Given this spreadsheet, the @RISK toolbar buttons are used to run the simulation. To indicate that profit is the only output of interest, select cell C18 and click on the Add Output button. Next, click on the Sim Set button to select the quantity of iterations (we chose 250) and the number of simulations (1 for this first order quantity). Finally, click on the Simulate button to run the simulation.

Once the iterations have been completed for all three simulations, you see an @RISK screen with a new menu bar, an expanded toolbar, a Results window, and a Summary Statistics window. The Results window is a good place to start to see a summary of the simulation results, and then the Summary Statistics window can be used if you want to see more detailed statistics. Figure 22.8 shows the summary of the results obtained for all three simulations with the respective order quantities. This figure shows that an order quantity of 10 gave the largest mean profit per day. An order quantity of 11 gave a larger maximum profit on the best days, but also gave a lower minimum and a lower overall mean. Therefore, these results indicate that an order quantity of 10 is the best choice for Freddie.

Summary of Results

Cell	Name	Minimum	Mean	Maximum
C18	Total Profit = / $ 9		9	9
C12	(Input) Demand	9	10	11

Order Quantity = 9

Summary of Results

Cell	Name	Minimum	Mean	Maximum
C18	Total Profit = / $ 8		9.4	10
C12	(Input) Demand	9	10	11

Order Quantity = 10

FIGURE 22.8
The summary of results obtained by @RISK after running the simulations in Fig. 22.7 for all three order quantities under consideration.

Summary of Results

Cell	Name	Minimum	Mean	Maximum
C18	Total Profit = / $ 7		9	11
C12	(Input) Demand	9	10	11

Order Quantity = 11

You normally can obtain a *histogram* that graphically depicts the frequency with which various daily profits are generated by each simulation by selecting the corresponding output cell in the Results window and clicking on the Graph button. (We will show you a similar histogram in the next example.) However, an exception occurs here for an order quantity of 9. The reason is that @RISK will not produce a histogram if the output value never changes during the simulation. This is what happens with an order quantity of 9, since this order quantity always gives Freddie a daily profit of $9 regardless of whether the demand turns out to be 9, 10, or 11.

Because an inventory model is available that yields an exact analytical solution for Freddie's problem, simulation is not the only feasible way of studying this problem. However, the situation will be somewhat different in the next example, which deals with finding the probability of completing a project by its deadline. In this case, there is again an analytical method available (through the PERT three-estimate approach), but this method only provides a rough, overly optimistic *approximation* of the true probability. Therefore, simulation frequently is used to obtain a much more precise estimate of this probability. This illustrates a common role for simulation—refining the results from a preliminary analysis conducted with approximate mathematical models.

Improving PERT—Revisiting the Reliable Construction Co. Problem

We now consider the prototype example that is introduced in Sec. 10.1 and then continued through most of Chap. 10. Here are the essential facts needed for the example. The Reliable Construction Company has just made the winning bid to construct a new plant for a major manufacturer. However, the contract includes a large penalty if construction is not completed by the deadline 47 weeks from now. Therefore, a key element in evaluating alternative construction plans is the *probability of meeting this deadline* under each plan. There are 14 major activities involved in carrying out this construction project, as

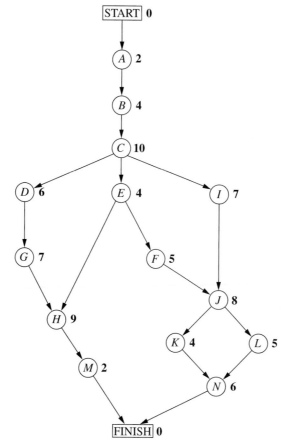

Activity Code

A. Excavate
B. Foundation
C. Rough wall
D. Roof
E. Exterior plumbing
F. Interior plumbing
G. Exterior siding
H. Exterior painting
I. Electrical work
J. Wallboard
K. Flooring
L. Interior painting
M. Exterior fixtures
N. Interior fixtures

FIGURE 22.9
The project network for the
Reliable Construction Co.
project.

listed on the right-hand side of Fig. 22.9 (which repeats Fig. 10.1 for your convenience). The project network in this figure depicts the precedence relationships between the activities. Thus, there are six sequences of activities (*paths* through the network), all of which must be completed to finish the project. These six sequences are listed below.

Path 1: START $\rightarrow A \rightarrow B \rightarrow C \rightarrow D \rightarrow G \rightarrow H \rightarrow M \rightarrow$ FINISH.
Path 2: START $\rightarrow A \rightarrow B \rightarrow C \rightarrow E \rightarrow H \rightarrow M \rightarrow$ FINISH.
Path 3: START $\rightarrow A \rightarrow B \rightarrow C \rightarrow E \rightarrow F \rightarrow J \rightarrow K \rightarrow N \rightarrow$ FINISH.
Path 4: START $\rightarrow A \rightarrow B \rightarrow C \rightarrow E \rightarrow F \rightarrow J \rightarrow L \rightarrow N \rightarrow$ FINISH.
Path 5: START $\rightarrow A \rightarrow B \rightarrow C \rightarrow I \rightarrow J \rightarrow K \rightarrow N \rightarrow$ FINISH.
Path 6: START $\rightarrow A \rightarrow B \rightarrow C \rightarrow I \rightarrow J \rightarrow L \rightarrow N \rightarrow$ FINISH.

The numbers next to the activities in the project network represent the *estimates* of the number of weeks the activities will take if they are carried out in the normal manner with the usual crew sizes, etc. Adding these times over each of the paths (as was done in Table 10.2) reveals that Path 4 is the *longest path,* requiring a total of 44 weeks. Since the project is finished as soon as its longest path is completed, this indicates that the project can be completed in 44 weeks, 3 weeks before the deadline.

Now we come to the crux of the problem. The times for the activities in Fig. 22.9 are only estimates, and there actually is considerable uncertainty about what the duration of each activity will be. Therefore, the duration of the entire project could well differ substantially from the estimate of 44 weeks, so there is a distinct possibility of missing the deadline of 47 weeks. What is the *probability* of missing this deadline? To estimate this probability, we need to learn more about the *probability distribution* of the duration of the project.

This is the reason for the PERT three-estimate approach described in Sec. 10.4. This approach involves obtaining three estimates—a *most likely estimate,* an *optimistic estimate,* and a *pessimistic estimate*—of the duration of each activity. (Table 10.4 lists these estimates for all 14 activities for the project under consideration.) These three quantities are intended to estimate the *most likely* duration, the *minimum* duration, and the *maximum* duration, respectively. Using these three quantities, PERT assumes (somewhat arbitrarily) that the form of the probability distribution of the duration of an activity is a *beta distribution.* By also making three simplifying approximations (described in Sec. 10.4), this leads to an analytical method for roughly approximating the probability of meeting the project deadline.

One key advantage of simulation is that it does not need to make most of the simplifying approximations that may be required by analytical methods. Another is that there is great flexibility about which probability distribution to use. It is not necessary to choose an analytically convenient one.

When dealing with the duration of an activity, simulations commonly use a *triangular distribution* as the distribution of this duration. A triangular distribution has the shape shown in Fig. 22.10, where *o, m,* and *p* are the labels for the optimistic estimate, the most

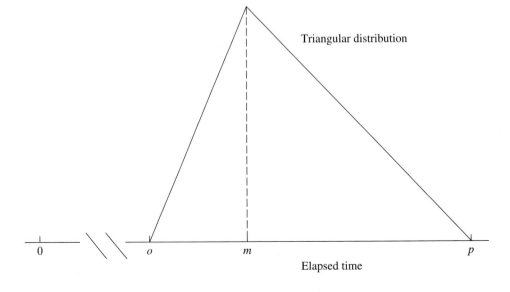

FIGURE 22.10
The shape of a triangular distribution for the duration of an activity, where the minimum lies at the optimistic estimate *o,* the most likely value lies at the most likely estimate *m,* and the maximum lies at the pessimistic estimate *p.*

likely estimate, and the pessimistic estimate, respectively. The @RISK formula for this distribution is $= \text{RISKTRIANG}(o,m,p)$. [Other popular distributions are the *normal distribution* with mean μ and standard deviation σ, which has the @RISK formula $= \text{RISKNORMAL}(\mu,\sigma)$, and the *uniform distribution* from a to b, which has the @RISK formula $= \text{RISKUNIFORM}(a,b)$.]

Figure 22.11 shows the @RISK spreadsheet for simulating the duration of the Reliable Construction Company's project. The formula, $= \text{RISKTRIANG}(o,m,p)$, is inserted into each input cell representing the duration of an activity, where the values of o, m, and p are obtained from Table 10.4. Each path length is obtained by adding the durations of the activities (in weeks) on that path. For each iteration of the simulation, the maximum of the six path lengths gives the duration of the project (in weeks). One output cell gives this duration and the other indicates whether this duration meets the deadline by not exceeding 47 weeks (where 1 indicates yes and 0 indicates no).

To run this simulation, we chose 1,000 as the number of iterations and 1 as the number of simulations (since only one construction plan is being simulated here). The upper right-hand side of Fig. 22.12 shows the resulting summary of the results. The most crucial piece of information here is the mean for the output cell that indicates whether the deadline has been met, because this mean gives the proportion of the 1,000 iterations where the deadline was met. Therefore, the estimate of the probability of meeting the deadline is 0.591. Note how much smaller this relatively precise estimate is than the rough estimate of 0.84 obtained by the PERT three-estimate approach in Sec. 10.4. Thus, the simulation estimate provides much better guidance to management in deciding whether the construction plan should be changed to improve the chances of meeting the deadline.

FIGURE 22.11
A spreadsheet model for a simulation of the Reliable Construction Co. project.

	A	B	C	D	E	F	G	H	I
1	**Simulation of Reliable Construction Co. Project**								
2									
3			Immediate	Time Estimates			Start	Activity	Finish
4		Activity	Predecessor	o	m	p	Time	Time	Time
5		A	-	1	2	3	0	2	2
6		B	A	2	3.5	8	2	4.5	6.5
7		C	B	6	9	18	6.5	11	17.5
8		D	C	4	5.5	10	17.5	6.5	24
9		E	C	1	4.5	5	17.5	3.5	21
10		F	E	4	4	10	21	6	27
11		G	D	5	6.5	11	24	7.5	31.5
12		H	E,G	5	8	17	31.5	10	41.5
13		I	C	3	7.5	9	17.5	6.5	24
14		J	F,I	3	9	9	27	7	34
15		K	J	4	4	4	34	4	38
16		L	J	1	5.5	7	34	4.5	38.5
17		M	H	1	2	3	41.5	2	43.5
18		N	K,L	5	5.5	9	38.5	6.5	45
19									
20							Project Completion =		45
21							Project Deadline =		47
22							Deadline Met (1=yes, 0 = no)?		1

	G	H	I
5	0	=RiskTriang(D5,E5,F5)	=G5+H5
6	=I5	=RiskTriang(D6,E6,F6)	=G6+H6
7	=I6	=RiskTriang(D7,E7,F7)	=G7+H7
8	=I7	=RiskTriang(D8,E8,F8)	=G8+H8
9	=I7	=RiskTriang(D9,E9,F9)	=G9+H9
10	=I9	=RiskTriang(D10,E10,F10)	=G10+H10
11	=I8	=RiskTriang(D11,E11,F11)	=G11+H11
12	=MAX(I9,I11)	=RiskTriang(D12,E12,F12)	=G12+H12
13	=I7	=RiskTriang(D13,E13,F13)	=G13+H13
14	=MAX(I10,I13)	=RiskTriang(D14,E14,F14)	=G14+H14
15	=I14	=RiskTriang(D15,E15,F15)	=G15+H15
16	=I14	=RiskTriang(D16,E16,F16)	=G16+H16
17	=I12	=RiskTriang(D17,E17,F17)	=G17+H17
18	=MAX(I15,I16)	=RiskTriang(D18,E18,F18)	=G18+H18
19			
20		Project Completion =	=MAX(I17,I18)
21		Project Deadline =	47
22		Deadline Met (1=yes, 0 = no)?	=IF(I20<=I21,1,0)

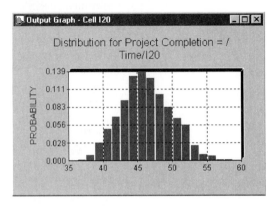

Simulation Statistics

Name	Project Completion	Deadline Met
Description	Output	Output
Cell	'[Reliable.xls]Reliab	'[Reliable.xls]R
Minimum =	36.98942	0
Maximum =	58.48365	1
Mean =	46.24534	0.591
Std Deviation =	3.63146	0.4916493
Variance =	13.1875	0.241719
Skewness =	0.1696594	-0.3701826
Kurtosis =	2.707775	1.137035
Errors Calculated =	0	0
Mode =	47.2127	1
5% Perc =	40.31811	0
10% Perc =	41.5235	0
15% Perc =	42.4042	0
20% Perc =	43.09111	0
25% Perc =	43.75802	0
30% Perc =	44.31891	0
35% Perc =	44.79782	0
40% Perc =	45.15918	0
45% Perc =	45.56504	1
50% Perc =	45.96362	1
55% Perc =	46.60467	1
60% Perc =	47.05931	1
65% Perc =	47.50695	1
70% Perc =	48.17402	1
75% Perc =	48.7167	1
80% Perc =	49.44214	1
85% Perc =	50.19196	1
90% Perc =	51.19381	1
95% Perc =	52.36878	1

Summary of Results

Cell	Name	Minimum	Mean	Maximum
I20	Project Completion = / Time i	36.98942	46.24534	58.48365
I22	Deadline Met (1=yes, 0 = no)	0	0.591	1

FIGURE 22.12
The various outputs generated by @RISK after running the Reliable Construction Co. simulation in Fig. 22.11 for 1,000 iterations.

This illustrates how useful simulation can be in refining the results obtained by approximate analytical methods.

In addition to the probability of meeting the deadline, management also will be interested in the overall probability distribution of the duration of the project. What simulation has provided is 1,000 random observations from this distribution, so the *frequency distribution* from these random observations provides a close approximation to the true probability distribution. Among other information, the Summary Statistics window gives the various *percentiles* of the frequency distribution shown on the left-hand side of Fig. 22.12. The percentile for each percentage gives the project duration such that this percentage of the random observations was less than this duration. For example, the value for the 5 percent percentile means that the project durations from 5 percent of the iterations of the simulation were less than this value (so 95 percent were larger).

A histogram of this frequency distribution of project durations can be obtained by showing the Results window, highlighting the project duration cell, and clicking on the Graph button on the toolbar. The lower right-hand side of Fig. 22.12 shows this histogram.

Financial Risk Analysis—The Think-Big Development Co. Problem

The THINK-BIG DEVELOPMENT CO. is a major investor in commercial real-estate development projects. It has been considering taking a share in three large construction projects—a high-rise office building, a hotel, and a shopping center. In each case, the partners in the project would spend three years with the construction, then retain ownership for three years while establishing the property, and then sell the property in the seventh year. By using estimates of expected cash flows, as well as constraints on the amounts of investment capital available both now and over the next three years, linear programming has been applied to obtain the following proposal for how many 1 percent shares Think-Big should take in each of these projects.

Proposal.

Do not take any shares of the high-rise building project.
Take 16.5 shares of the hotel project.
Take 13.1 shares of the shopping center project.

This proposal is estimated to return a *net present value* (NPV) of $18.1 million to Think-Big.

However, Think-Big management understands very well that such decisions should not be made without taking risk into account. These are very risky projects, since it is unclear how well these properties will compete in the marketplace when they go into operation in a few years. Although the construction costs during the first three years can be estimated fairly closely, the net incomes during the following three years of operation are very uncertain. Consequently, there is an extremely wide range of possible values for each sale price in year 7. Therefore, management wants *risk analysis* to be performed in the usual way (with simulation) to obtain a *risk profile* of what the total NPV might actually turn out to be with this proposal.

To perform this risk analysis, Think-Big staff now has devoted considerable time to estimating the amount of uncertainty in the cash flows for each project over the next 7 years. These data are summarized in Table 22.6 (in units of thousands of dollars per share taken in each project). In years 1 through 6 for each project, the probability distribution of cash flow is assumed to be a *normal distribution,* where the first number shown is the estimated *mean* and the second number is the estimated *standard deviation* of the distribution. In year 7, the income from the sale of the property is assumed to have a *uniform distribution* over the range from the first number shown to the second number shown.

TABLE 22.6 Think-Big's estimated cash flows per share taken in the hotel and shopping center projects

Hotel Project		Shopping Center Project	
Year	**Cash Flow ($1,000's)**	**Year**	**Cash Flow ($1,000's)**
0	−800	0	−900
1	Normal (−800, 50)	1	Normal (−600, 50)
2	Normal (−800, 100)	2	Normal (−200, 50)
3	Normal (−700, 150)	3	Normal (−600, 100)
4	Normal (+300, 200)	4	Normal (+250, 150)
5	Normal (+400, 200)	5	Normal (+350, 150)
6	Normal (+500, 200)	6	Normal (+400, 150)
7	Uniform (+2,000, 8,440)	7	Uniform (+1,600, 6,000)

A	B	C	D	E	F	G	H	I	J	K	L	M	N
1	**Simulation of Think-Big Development Co. Problem**												
2													
3	Hotel Project:												
4													
5	Construction Costs per Share ($1,000's)						Revenue per Share ($1,000's)					Selling Price per Share ($1,000's)	
6	(Normal Distribution)						(Normal Distribution)					(Uniform Distribution)	
7		Year 0	Year 1	Year 2	Year 3			Year 4	Year 5	Year 6			Year 7
8	Mean	-800	-800	-800	-700		Mean	300	400	500		Minimum	2000
9	St. Dev.	0	50	100	150		St. Dev.	200	200	200		Maximum	8440
10													
11													
12	Shopping Center Project:												
13													
14	Construction Costs per Share ($1,000's)						Revenue per Share ($1,000's)					Selling Price per Share ($1,000's)	
15	(Normal Distribution)						(Normal Distribution)					(Uniform Distribution)	
16		Year 0	Year 1	Year 2	Year 3			Year 4	Year 5	Year 6			Year 7
17	Mean	-900	-600	-200	-600		Mean	250	350	400		Minimum	1600
18	St. Dev.	0	50	50	100		St. Dev.	150	150	150		Maximum	6000
19													
20													
21	Number of Shares:					Cash Flow ($1,000's):			Net Present Value ($1,000's):				
22		Hotel =	16.5			Year 0	-24,990			18,128			
23	Shopping Center =		13.1			Year 1	-21,060						
24						Year 2	-15,820						
25	Cost of Capital:		10%			Year 3	-19,410						
26						Year 4	8,225						
27						Year 5	11,185						
28						Year 6	13,490						
29						Year 7	135,910						

	G
22	=D22*RiskNormal(C8,C9)+D23*RiskNormal(C17,C18)
23	=D22*RiskNormal(D8,D9)+D23*RiskNormal(D17,D18)
24	=D22*RiskNormal(E8,E9)+D23*RiskNormal(E17,E18)
25	=D22*RiskNormal(F8,F9)+D23*RiskNormal(F17,F18)
26	=D22*RiskNormal(I8,I9)+D23*RiskNormal(I17,I18)
27	=D22*RiskNormal(J8,J9)+D23*RiskNormal(J17,J18)
28	=D22*RiskNormal(K8,K9)+D23*RiskNormal(K17,K18)
29	=D22*RiskUniform(N8,N9)+D23*RiskUniform(N17,N18)

	J
22	=G22+NPV(D25,G23:G29)

FIGURE 22.13
A spreadsheet model for using simulation to perform risk analysis on the proposed real estate investments by the Think-Big Development Co.

To compute NPV, a cost of capital of 10 percent per annum is being used. Thus, the cash flow in year n is divided by 1.1^n before adding these discounted cash flows to obtain NPV.

Figure 22.13 shows the @RISK spreadsheet for using simulation to perform risk analysis on the proposal. (The numbers currently in cells J22 and G22:G29 are expected values computed by @RISK.) For each iteration of the simulation, @RISK uses its functions, RISKNORMAL(μ, σ) and RISKUNIFORM(a, b), to generate a random observation from each of the normal distributions and uniform distributions specified in Table

22.6. (@RISK provides numerous such functions for a wide variety of probability distributions.) These simulated cash flows then are used to calculate the total NPV for both projects in cell J22. By repeating this process for 1,000 iterations, we thereby obtain 1,000 random observations from the underlying probability distribution of the total NPV. These 1,000 observations constitute a *frequency distribution* of the total NPV that is virtually identical to the underlying probability distribution.

Figure 22.14 provides information about this frequency distribution in the usual variety of forms. The first row of *Summary of Results* in the upper-right hand corner of the figure indicates that the values of NPV over the 1,000 iterations ranged from about −$35 million to over $65 million, with a mean of $18.13 million. (The subsequent rows in this table show the corresponding statistics for the cash flows per share in each year for each

---

FIGURE 22.14

The various risk analysis outputs generated by @RISK after running the Think-Big Development Co. computer simulation in Fig. 22.13 for 1,000 iterations.

Simulation Statistics

Name	Year 0 / Net Present Value ($1,000's):
Description	Output
Cell	'[Think-Big.xls]Think-Big'!J22
Minimum =	-35081.42
Maximum =	65575.85
Mean =	18130.33
Std Deviation =	18454.18
Variance =	3.405569E+08
Skewness =	6.662419E-02
Kurtosis =	2.416611
Errors Calculated =	0
Mode =	30378.72
5% Perc =	-12015.1
10% Perc =	-6042.757
15% Perc =	-1854.977
20% Perc =	1074.422
25% Perc =	4529.095
30% Perc =	6973.988
35% Perc =	9016.386
40% Perc =	12694.53
45% Perc =	15508.2
50% Perc =	18096.57
55% Perc =	20573.64
60% Perc =	22957.77
65% Perc =	25336.25
70% Perc =	28073.93
75% Perc =	31178.28
80% Perc =	34770.37
85% Perc =	39226.43
90% Perc =	42792.96
95% Perc =	48366.65

Summary of Results

Cell	Name	Minimum	Mean	Maximum
J22	Year 0 / Net Present Value ($1,000's): in ([Think-Big.xls]Think-Big')	-35081.42	18130.33	65575.85
G22	(Input) Year 0 in ([Think-Big.xls]Think-Big)	-800	-800	-800
G22	(Input) Year 0 in ([Think-Big.xls]Think-Big)	-900	-900	-900
G23	(Input) Year 1 / Year 1 in ([Think-Big.xls]Think-Big)	-991.5456	-800.0345	-639.1625
G23	(Input) Year 1 / Year 1 in ([Think-Big.xls]Think-Big)	-770.6567	-600.0127	-440.2328
G24	(Input) Year 2 / Year 2 in ([Think-Big.xls]Think-Big)	-1132.84	-799.9891	-457.1893
G24	(Input) Year 2 / Year 2 in ([Think-Big.xls]Think-Big)	-360.6227	-199.9776	-23.98881
G25	(Input) Year 3 / Year 3 in ([Think-Big.xls]Think-Big)	-1163.719	-699.9891	-189.6448
G25	(Input) Year 3 / Year 3 in ([Think-Big.xls]Think-Big)	-923.2188	-599.9961	-289.8651
G26	(Input) Year 4 / Year 4 in ([Think-Big.xls]Think-Big)	-322.4218	300.1159	1017.854
G26	(Input) Year 4 / Year 4 in ([Think-Big.xls]Think-Big)	-284.7605	250.0473	826.9261
G27	(Input) Year 5 / Year 5 in ([Think-Big.xls]Think-Big)	-227.1319	400.0233	1043.294
G27	(Input) Year 5 / Year 5 in ([Think-Big.xls]Think-Big)	-130.6366	350.0098	840.8525
G28	(Input) Year 6 / Year 6 in ([Think-Big.xls]Think-Big)	-127.4213	500.0163	1162.403
G28	(Input) Year 6 / Year 6 in ([Think-Big.xls]Think-Big)	-144.3892	400.022	925.3484
G29	(Input) Year 7 / Year 7 in ([Think-Big.xls]Think-Big)	2004.445	5219.979	8436.119
G29	(Input) Year 7 / Year 7 in ([Think-Big.xls]Think-Big)	1600.293	3800.036	5999.864

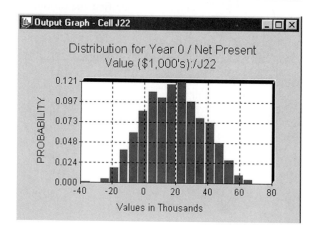

Output Graph - Cell J22

Distribution for Year 0 / Net Present Value ($1,000's):/J22

project.) The *Simulation Statistics* on the left side gives detailed information about the frequency distribution. For example, the fact that the 15 percent percentile has a negative NPV while it is positive at the 20 percent percentile reveals that the probability of incurring a loss by adopting the proposal is between 0.15 and 0.20. The *histogram* in the lower right-hand corner displays the frequency distribution graphically. This histogram provides management with the *risk profile* for the proposal. With this information, a managerial decision now needs to be made about whether the likelihood of a sizable profit justifies the significant risk of incurring a loss and perhaps even a very substantial loss.

Thus, as when using other OR techniques, management makes the decision but simulation provides the information needed for making a sound decision.

22.7 VARIANCE-REDUCING TECHNIQUES

Because considerable computer time usually is required for simulation runs, it is important to obtain as much and as precise information as possible from the amount of simulation that can be done. Unfortunately, there has been a tendency in practice to apply simulation uncritically without giving adequate thought to the efficiency of the experimental design. This tendency has occurred despite the fact that considerable progress has been made in developing special techniques for increasing the precision (i.e., decreasing the variance) of sample estimators.

These variance-reducing techniques often are called **Monte Carlo techniques** (a term sometimes applied to simulation in general). Because they tend to be rather sophisticated, it is not possible to explore them deeply here. However, we shall attempt to impart the flavor of these techniques and the great increase in precision they sometimes provide by presenting two when applied to the following example.

Consider the exponential distribution whose parameter has a value of 1. Thus, its probability density function is $f(x) = e^{-x}$, as shown in Fig. 22.15, and its cumulative distribution function is $F(x) = 1 - e^{-x}$. It is known that the mean of this distribution is 1. However, suppose that this mean is not known and that we want to estimate this mean by using simulation.

To provide a standard of comparison of the two variance-reducing techniques, we consider first the straightforward simulation approach, sometimes called the **crude Monte Carlo technique.** This approach involves generating some *random observations* from the

FIGURE 22.15
Probability density function for the example for variance-reducing techniques, where the objective is to estimate the mean of this distribution.

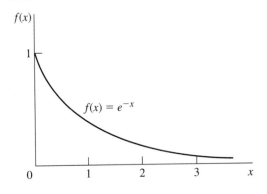

TABLE 22.7 Application of the crude Monte Carlo
technique to the example

i	Random Number* r_i	Random Observation $x_i = -\ln(1 - r_i)$
1	0.495	0.684
2	0.335	0.408
3	0.791	1.568
4	0.469	0.633
5	0.279	0.328
6	0.698	1.199
7	0.013	0.014
8	0.761	1.433
9	0.290	0.343
10	0.693	1.183

Total = 7.793
Estimate of mean = 0.779

*Actually, 0.0005 was added to the indicated value for each of the r_i
so that the range of their possible values would be from 0.0005 to
0.9995 rather than from 0.000 to 0.999.

exponential distribution under consideration and then using the *average* of these observations to estimate the mean. As described in Sec. 22.4, these random observations would be

$$x_i = -\ln(1 - r_i), \quad \text{for } i = 1, 2, \ldots, n,$$

where $r_1, r_2, \ldots, r_n$ are uniform random numbers between 0 and 1. We use the first three digits in the fifth column of Table 22.3 to obtain 10 such uniform random numbers; the resulting random observations are shown in Table 22.7. (These same random numbers also are used to illustrate the variance-reducing techniques to sharpen the comparison.)

Notice that the sample average in Table 22.7 is 0.779, as opposed to the true mean of 1.000. However, because the standard deviation of the sample average happens to be $1/\sqrt{n}$, or $1/\sqrt{10}$ in this case (as could be estimated from the sample), an error of this amount or larger would occur approximately one-half of the time. Furthermore, because the standard deviation of a sample average is always inversely proportional to $\sqrt{n}$, this sample size would need to be quadrupled to reduce this standard deviation by one-half. These somewhat disheartening facts suggest the need for other techniques that would obtain such estimates more precisely and more efficiently.

Stratified Sampling

Stratified sampling is a relatively simple Monte Carlo technique for obtaining better estimates. There are two shortcomings of the crude Monte Carlo approach that are rectified by stratified sampling. First, by the very nature of randomness, a random sample may not provide a particularly uniform cross section of the distribution. For example, the random sample given in Table 22.7 has no observations between 0.014 and 0.328, even though the probability that a random observation will fall inside this interval is greater than $\frac{1}{4}$.

TABLE 22.8 Formulation of the stratified sampling approach to the example

Stratum	Portion of Distribution	Stratum Random No.	Sample Size	Sampling Weight
1	$0 \leq F(x) \leq 0.64$	$r_i' = 0 + 0.64r_i$	4	$w_i = \dfrac{4/10}{0.64} = \dfrac{5}{8}$
2	$0.64 \leq F(x) \leq 0.96$	$r_i' = 0.64 + 0.32r_i$	4	$w_i = \dfrac{4/10}{0.32} = \dfrac{5}{4}$
3	$0.96 \leq F(x) \leq 1$	$r_i' = 0.96 + 0.04r_i$	2	$w_i = \dfrac{2/10}{0.04} = 5$

Second, certain portions of a distribution may be more critical than others for obtaining a precise estimate, but random sampling gives no special priority to obtaining observations from these portions. For example, the tail of an exponential distribution is especially critical in determining its mean. However, the random sample in Table 22.7 includes no observations larger than 1.568, even though there is at least a small probability of *much* larger values. This explanation is the basic one for why this particular sample average is far below the true mean. Stratified sampling circumvents these difficulties by dividing the distribution into portions called *strata,* where each stratum would be sampled individually with disproportionately heavy sampling of the more critical strata.

To illustrate, suppose that the distribution is divided into three strata in the manner shown in Table 22.8. These strata were chosen to correspond to observations approximately from 0 to 1, from 1 to 3, and from 3 to ∞, respectively. To ensure that the random observations generated for each stratum actually lie in that portion of the distribution, the uniform random numbers must be converted to the indicated range for $F(x)$, as shown in the third column of Table 22.8. The number of observations to be generated from each stratum is given in the fourth column.[1] The rightmost column then shows the resulting *sampling weight* for each stratum, i.e., the *ratio* of the *sampling proportion* (the fraction of the total sample to be drawn from the stratum) to the *distribution proportion* (the probability of a random observation falling inside the stratum). These sampling weights roughly reflect the relative importance of the respective strata in determining the mean.

Given the formulation of the stratified sampling approach shown in Table 22.8, the same uniform random numbers used in Table 22.7 yield the observations given in the fifth column in Table 22.9. However, it would not be correct to use the unweighted average of these observations to estimate the mean, because certain portions of the distribution have been sampled more than others. Therefore, before we take the average, we divide the observations from each stratum by the sampling weight for that stratum to give proportionate weightings to the different portions of the distribution, as shown in the rightmost column of Table 22.9. The resulting *weighted* average of 0.948 provides the desired estimate of the mean.

---

[1] These sample sizes are roughly based on a recommended guideline that they be proportional to the *product* of the *probability* of a random observation's falling inside the corresponding stratum *times* the *standard deviation* within this stratum.

TABLE 22.9 Application of stratified sampling to the example

Stratum	i	Random Number r_i	Stratum Random No. r_i'	Stratum Random Observation $x_i' = -\ln(1 - r_i')$	Sampling Weight w_i	x_i'/w_i
1	1	0.495	0.317	0.381	$\frac{5}{8}$	0.610
	2	0.335	0.215	0.242	$\frac{5}{8}$	0.387
	3	0.791	0.507	0.707	$\frac{5}{8}$	1.131
	4	0.469	0.300	0.357	$\frac{5}{8}$	0.571
2	5	0.279	0.729	1.306	$\frac{5}{4}$	1.045
	6	0.698	0.864	1.995	$\frac{5}{4}$	1.596
	7	0.013	0.644	1.033	$\frac{5}{4}$	0.826
	8	0.761	0.884	2.154	$\frac{5}{4}$	1.723
3	9	0.290	0.9716	3.561	5	0.712
	10	0.693	0.9877	4.398	5	0.880

Total = 9.481
Estimate of mean = 0.948

Method of Complementary Random Numbers

The second variance-reducing technique we shall mention is the method of *complementary random numbers*.[1] The motivation for this method is that the "luck of the draw" on the uniform random numbers generated may cause the average of the resulting random observations to be substantially on one side of the true mean, whereas the *complements* of those uniform random numbers (which are themselves uniform random numbers) would have tended to yield a nearly opposite result. (For example, the uniform random numbers in Table 22.7 average less than 0.5, and none are as large as 0.8, which led to an estimate substantially below the true mean.) Therefore, using *both* the original uniform random numbers *and* their complements to generate random observations and then calculating the *combined* sample average should provide a more precise estimator of the mean. This approach is illustrated in Table 22.10,[2] where the first three columns come from Table 22.7 and the two rightmost columns use the complementary uniform random numbers, which results in a combined sample average of 0.920.

---

[1]This method is a special case of the method of *antithetic variates,* which attempts to generate *pairs* of random observations having a high *negative* correlation, so that the combined average will tend to be closer to the mean.

[2]Note that 20 calculations of a logarithm were required in this case, in contrast to the 10 that were required by each of the preceding techniques.

TABLE 22.10 Application of the method of complementary random numbers to the example

i	Random Number r_i	Random Observation $x_i = -\ln(1 - r_i)$	Complementary Random Number $r_i' = 1 - r_i$	Random Observation $x_i' = -\ln(1 - r_i')$
1	0.495	0.684	0.505	0.702
2	0.335	0.408	0.665	1.092
3	0.791	1.568	0.209	0.234
4	0.469	0.633	0.531	0.756
5	0.279	0.328	0.721	1.275
6	0.698	1.199	0.302	0.359
7	0.013	0.014	0.987	4.305
8	0.761	1.433	0.239	0.272
9	0.290	0.343	0.710	1.236
10	0.693	1.183	0.307	0.366

Total = 7.793   Total = 10.597

Estimate of mean = $\frac{1}{2}(0.779 + 1.060) = 0.920$

Conclusions

This example has suggested that the variance-reducing techniques provide a much more precise estimator of the mean than does straightforward simulation (the crude Monte Carlo technique). These results definitely were not a coincidence, as a derivation of the variance of the estimators would show. In comparison with straightforward simulation, these techniques (including several more complicated ones not presented here) do indeed provide a much more precise estimator with the same amount of computer time, or they provide an equally precise estimator with much less computer time. Despite the fact that additional analysis may be required to incorporate one or more of these techniques into the simulation study, the rewards should not be forgone readily.

Although this example was particularly simple, it is often possible, though more difficult, to apply these techniques to much more complex problems. For example, suppose that the objective of the simulation study is to estimate the expected waiting time of customers in a queueing system (such as those described in Sec. 18.1). Because both the probability distribution of interarrival times and the probability distribution of service times are involved, and because consecutive waiting times are not statistically independent, this problem may appear to be beyond the capabilities of the variance-reducing techniques. However, as has been described in detail elsewhere,[1] these techniques and others can indeed be applied to this type of problem very advantageously. For example, the method of *complementary random numbers* can be applied simply by repeating the original simulation run, substituting the complements of the original uniform random numbers to generate the corresponding random observations.

---

[1]S. Ehrenfeld and S. Ben-Tuvia, "The Efficiency of Statistical Simulation Procedures," *Technometrics,* **4**(2): 257–275, 1962. Also see Chap. 11 of Selected Reference 11. For additional information on variance-reducing techniques, see the November 1989 issue of *Management Science* for a special issue on this topic.

22.8 REGENERATIVE METHOD OF STATISTICAL ANALYSIS

The statistical analysis of a simulation run involves using the output to obtain both a point estimate and confidence interval of some steady-state measure (or measures) of performance of the system. (For example, one such measure for a queueing system would be the mean of the steady-state distribution of waiting times for the customers.) To do this analysis, the simulation run can be viewed as a statistical experiment that is generating a series of sample observations of the measure. The question is how to use these sample observations to compute the point estimate and confidence interval.

Traditional Methods and Their Shortcomings

The most straightforward approach would be to use standard statistical procedures to compute these quantities from the observations. However, there are two special characteristics of the observations from a simulation run that require some modification of this approach.

One characteristic is that the system is not in a steady-state condition when the simulation run begins, so the initial observations are not random observations from the underlying probability distribution for the steady-state measure of performance. The traditional approach to circumventing this difficulty is to not start collecting data until it is believed that the simulated system has essentially reached a steady-state condition. Unfortunately, it is difficult to estimate just how long this *warm-up period* needs to be. Furthermore, available analytical results suggest that a surprisingly long period is required, so that a great deal of unproductive computer time must be expended.

The second special characteristic of a simulated experiment is that its observations are likely to be highly correlated. This is the case, for example, for the waiting times of successive customers in a queueing system. On the other hand, standard statistical procedures for computing the confidence interval for some measure of performance assume that the sample observations are *statistically independent* random observations from the underlying probability distribution for the measure.

One traditional method of circumventing this difficulty is to execute a series of completely separate and independent simulation runs of equal length and to use the average measure of performance for each run (excluding the initial warm-up period) as an individual observation. The main disadvantage is that each run requires an initial warm-up period for approaching a steady-state condition, so that much of the simulation time is unproductive. The second traditional method eliminates this disadvantage by making the runs consecutively, using the ending condition of one run as the steady-state starting condition for the next run. In other words, one continuous overall simulation run (except for the one initial warm-up period) is divided for bookkeeping purposes into a series of equal portions (referred to as *batches*). The average measure of performance for each batch is then treated as an individual observation. The disadvantage of this method is that it does not eliminate the correlation between observations entirely, even though it may reduce it considerably by making the portions sufficiently long.

The Regenerative Method Approach

We now turn to an innovative statistical approach that is specially designed to eliminate the shortcomings of the traditional methods described above. (This is the approach used by *Queueing Simulator* to obtain its point estimates and confidence intervals.)

The basic concept underlying this approach is that for many systems a simulation run can be divided into a series of **cycles** such that the evolution of the system in a cycle is a probabilistic replica of the evolution in any other cycle. Thus, if we calculate an appropriate measure of the length of the cycle along with some *statistic* to summarize the behavior of interest within each cycle, these statistics for the respective cycles constitute a series of independent and identically distributed observations that can be analyzed by standard statistical procedures. Because the system keeps going through these independent and identically distributed cycles regardless of whether it is in a steady-state condition, these observations are directly applicable from the outset for estimating the steady-state behavior of the system.

For cycles to possess these properties, they must each *begin* at the same **regeneration point,** i.e., at the point where the system probabilistically restarts and can proceed without any knowledge of its past history. The system can be viewed as *regenerating* itself at this point in the sense that the probabilistic structure of the future behavior of the system depends upon being at this point and not on anything that happened previously. (This property is the *Markovian property* described in Sec. 16.2 for Markov chains.) A cycle *ends* when the system again reaches the regeneration point (when the next cycle begins). Thus, the **length of a cycle** is the elapsed time between consecutive occurrences of the regeneration point. This elapsed time is a random variable that depends upon the evolution of the system.

When *next-event incrementing* is used, a typical regeneration point is a point at which an event has just occurred but no future events have yet been scheduled. Thus, nothing needs to be known about the history of previous schedulings, and the simulation can start from scratch in scheduling future events. When *fixed-time incrementing* is used, a regeneration point is a point at which the probabilities of possible events occurring during the next unit of time do not depend upon when any past events occurred, only on the current state of the system.

Not every system possesses regeneration points, so this **regenerative method** of collecting data cannot always be used. Furthermore, even when there are regeneration points, the one chosen to define the beginning and ending points of the cycles must recur frequently enough that a substantial number of cycles will be obtained with a reasonable amount of computer time.[1] Thus, some care must be taken to choose a suitable regeneration point.

Perhaps the most important application of the regenerative method to date has been the simulation of queueing systems, including queueing networks (see Sec. 17.9) such as the ones that arise in computer modeling.[2]

---

[1] The basic theoretical requirements for the method are that the expected cycle length be *finite* and that the number of cycles would go to infinity if the system continued operating indefinitely. For details, see P. W. Glynn and D. L. Iglehart, "Conditions for the Applicability of the Regenerative Method," *Management Science,* **39:** 1108–1111, 1993.

[2] See, e.g., D. L. Iglehart and G. S. Shedler, *Regenerative Simulation of Passage Times in Networks of Queues,* Lecture Notes in Control and Information Sciences, vol. 4, Springer-Verlag, New York, 1980. For another exposition that emphasizes applications to computer system modeling, see G. S. Shedler, *Regeneration and Networks of Queues,* Springer-Verlag, New York, 1987.

Example. Suppose that information needs to be obtained about the steady-state behavior of a system that can be formulated as a *single-server queueing system* (see Sec. 17.2). However, both the interarrival and service times have a *discrete uniform distribution* with a probability of $\frac{1}{10}$ of the values of 6, 8, . . . , 24 and the values of 1, 3, . . . , 19, respectively. Because analytical results are not available, simulation with *next-event incrementing* is to be used to obtain the desired results.

Except for the distributions involved, the general approach is the same as that described in Sec. 22.1 for Example 2. In particular, the building blocks of the simulation model are the same as specified there, including defining the state of the system as the number of customers in the system. Suppose that one-digit random integer numbers are used to generate the random observations from the distributions, as shown in Table 22.11. Beginning the simulation run with no customers in the system then yields the results summarized in Table 22.12 and Fig. 22.16, where the random numbers are obtained sequentially as needed from the tenth row of Table 22.3.[1] (Note in Table 22.12 that, at time 98, the arrival of one customer and the service completion for another customer occur simultaneously, so these canceling events are not visible in Fig. 22.16.)

---

[1]When both an interarrival time and a service time need to be generated at the same time, the interarrival time is obtained first.

TABLE 22.11 Correspondence between random numbers and random observations for the queueing system example

Random Number	Interarrival Time	Service Time
0	6	1
1	8	3
⋮	⋮	⋮
9	24	19

FIGURE 22.16
Outcome of the simulation run for the queueing system example.

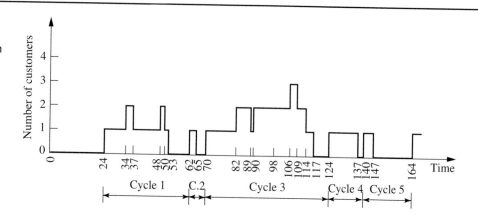

TABLE 22.12 Simulation run for the queueing system example

Time	Number of Customers	Random Number	Next Arrival	Next Service Completion
0	0	9	24	—
24	1	2, 6	34	37
34	2	4	48	37
37	1	6	48	50
48	2	4	62	50
50	1	1	62	53
53	0	—	62	—
62	1	1, 1	70	65
65	0	—	70	—
70	1	3, 9	82	89
82	2	1	90	89
89	1	4	90	98
90	2	1	98	98
98	2	1, 5	106	109
106	3	6	124	109
109	2	2	124	114
114	1	1	124	117
117	0	—	124	—
124	1	5, 6	140	137
137	0	—	140	—
140	1	9, 3	164	147
147	0	—	164	—
164	1			

For this system, one *regeneration point* is where an *arrival* occurs with *no* previous customers left. At this point, the process probabilistically restarts, so the probabilistic structure of when future arrivals and service completions will occur is completely independent of any previous history. The only relevant information is that the system has just entered the special state of having had no customers *and* having the time until the next arrival reach zero. The simulation run would not previously have scheduled any future events but would now generate *both* the next interarrival time and the service time for the customer that just arrived.

The only other regeneration points for this system are where an arrival and a service completion occur simultaneously, with a prespecified number of customers in the system. However, the regeneration point described in the preceding paragraph occurs much more frequently and thus is a better choice for defining a cycle. With this selection, the first five complete cycles of the simulation run are those shown in Fig. 22.16. (In most cases, you should have a considerably larger number of cycles in the entire simulation run in order to have sufficient precision in the statistical analysis.)

Various types of information about the steady-state behavior of the system can be obtained from this simulation run, including *point estimates* and *confidence intervals* for the expected number of customers in the system, the expected waiting time, and so on. In each case, it is necessary to use only the corresponding statistics from the respective cycles and the lengths of the cycles. We shall first present the general statistical expressions for the regenerative method and then apply them to this example.

Statistical Formulas

Formally speaking, the statistical problem for the regenerative method is to obtain estimates of the expected value of some random variable X of interest. This estimate is to be obtained by calculating a statistic Y for each cycle and an appropriate measure Z of the *size* of the cycle such that

$$E(X) = \frac{E(Y)}{E(Z)}.$$

(The regenerative property ensures that such a *ratio formula* holds for many steady-state random variables X.) Thus, if n complete cycles are generated during the simulation run, the data gathered are $Y_1, Y_2, \ldots, Y_n$ and $Z_1, Z_2, \ldots, Z_n$ for the respective cycles.

By letting $\overline{Y}$ and $\overline{Z}$, respectively, denote the sample averages for these two sets of data, the corresponding *point estimate* of $E(X)$ would be obtained from the formula

$$\text{Est }\{E(X)\} = \frac{\overline{Y}}{\overline{Z}}.$$

To obtain a *confidence interval* for $E(X)$, we must first calculate several quantities from the data. These quantities include the *sample variances*

$$s_{11}^2 = \frac{1}{n-1} \sum_{i=1}^{n} (Y_i - \overline{Y})^2 = \frac{1}{n-1} \sum_{i=1}^{n} Y_i^2 - \frac{1}{n(n-1)} \left(\sum_{i=1}^{n} Y_i \right)^2,$$

$$s_{22}^2 = \frac{1}{n-1} \sum_{i=1}^{n} (Z_i - \overline{Z})^2 = \frac{1}{n-1} \sum_{i=1}^{n} Z_i^2 - \frac{1}{n(n-1)} \left(\sum_{i=1}^{n} Z_i \right)^2,$$

and the combined *sample covariance*

$$s_{12}^2 = \frac{1}{n-1} \sum_{i=1}^{n} (Y_i - \overline{Y})(Z_i - \overline{Z})$$

$$= \frac{1}{n-1} \sum_{i=1}^{n} Y_i Z_i - \frac{1}{n(n-1)} \left(\sum_{i=1}^{n} Y_i \right)\left(\sum_{i=1}^{n} Z_i \right).$$

Also let

$$s^2 = s_{11}^2 - 2\frac{\overline{Y}}{\overline{Z}} s_{12}^2 + \left(\frac{\overline{Y}}{\overline{Z}} \right)^2 s_{22}^2.$$

Finally, let α be the constant such that $1 - 2\alpha$ is the desired *confidence coefficient* for the confidence interval, and look up K_α in Table A5.1 (see App. 5) for the normal distribution. If n is not too small, an *asymptotic confidence interval* for $E(X)$ is then given by

$$\frac{\overline{Y}}{\overline{Z}} - \frac{K_\alpha s}{\overline{Z}\sqrt{n}} \leq E(X) \leq \frac{\overline{Y}}{\overline{Z}} + \frac{K_\alpha s}{\overline{Z}\sqrt{n}};$$

i.e., the probability is approximately $1 - 2\alpha$ that the endpoints of an interval generated in this way will surround the actual value of $E(X)$.

Application of the Statistical Formulas to the Example

Consider first how to estimate the *expected waiting time* for a customer *before* beginning service (denoted by W_q in Chap. 17). Thus, the random variable X now represents a customer's waiting time excluding service, so that

$W_q = E(X)$.

The corresponding information gathered during the simulation run is the *actual* waiting time (excluding service) incurred by the respective customers. Therefore, for each cycle, the summary statistic Y is the *sum of the waiting times,* and the size of the cycle Z is the *number of customers,* so that

$$W_q = \frac{E(Y)}{E(Z)}.$$

Refer to Fig. 22.16 and Table 22.12; for cycle 1, a total of three customers are processed, so $Z_1 = 3$. The first customer incurs no waiting before beginning service, the second waits 3 units of time (from 34 to 37), and the third waits 2 units of time (from 48 to 50), so $Y_1 = 5$. We proceed similarly for the other cycles. The data for the problem are

$$
\begin{aligned}
Y_1 &= 5, & Z_1 &= 3 \\
Y_2 &= 0, & Z_2 &= 1 \\
Y_3 &= 34, & Z_3 &= 5 \\
Y_4 &= 0, & Z_4 &= 1 \\
Y_5 &= 0, & Z_5 &= 1 \\
\overline{Y} &= 7.8, & \overline{Z} &= 2.2.
\end{aligned}
$$

Therefore, the *point estimate* of W_q is

$$\text{Est } \{W_q\} = \frac{\overline{Y}}{\overline{Z}} = \frac{7.8}{2.2} = 3\frac{6}{11}.$$

To obtain a 95 percent confidence interval for W_q, the preceding formulas are first used to calculate

$$s_{11}^2 = 219.20, \qquad s_{22}^2 = 3.20, \qquad s_{12}^2 = 24.80, \qquad s = 9.14.$$

Because $1 - 2\alpha = 0.95$, then $\alpha = 0.025$, so that $K_\alpha = 1.96$ from Table A5.1. The resulting confidence interval is

$$-0.09 \leq W_q \leq 7.19;$$

or

$$W_q \leq 7.19.$$

The reason that this confidence interval is so wide (even including impossible negative values) is that the number of sample observations (cycles), $n = 5$, is so small. Note in the general formula that the width of the confidence interval is *inversely pro-*

portional to the *square root* of *n*, so that, e.g., quadrupling *n* reduces the width by half (assuming no change in *s* or $\bar{Z}$). Given preliminary values of *s* and $\bar{Z}$ from a short preliminary simulation run (such as the run in Table 22.12), this relationship makes it possible to estimate in advance the width of the confidence interval that would result from any given choice of *n* for the full simulation run. The final choice of *n* can then be made based on the trade-off between computer time and the precision of the statistical analysis.

Now suppose that this simulation run is to be used to estimate P_0, the probability of having no customers in the system. (Because λ/μ is the utilization factor for the server in a single-server queueing system, the theoretical value is known to be $P_0 = 1 - \lambda/\mu = 1 - \frac{1}{15}/\frac{1}{10} = \frac{1}{3}$.) The corresponding information obtained during the simulation run is the fraction of time during which the system is empty. Therefore, the summary statistic *Y* for each cycle is the *total time* during which no customers are present, and the size *Z* is the *length* of the cycle, so that

$$P_0 = \frac{E(Y)}{E(Z)}.$$

The length of cycle 1 is 38 (from 24 to 62), so that $Z_1 = 38$. During this time, the system is empty from 53 to 62, so that $Y_1 = 9$. Proceeding in this manner for the other cycles, we obtain the following data for the problem:

$$
\begin{aligned}
Y_1 &= 9, & Z_1 &= 38 \\
Y_2 &= 5, & Z_2 &= 8 \\
Y_3 &= 7, & Z_3 &= 54 \\
Y_4 &= 3, & Z_4 &= 16 \\
Y_5 &= 17, & Z_5 &= 24 \\
\bar{Y} &= 8.2, & \bar{Z} &= 28.
\end{aligned}
$$

Thus, the *point estimate* of P_0 is

$$\text{Est } \{P_0\} = \frac{8.2}{28} = 0.293.$$

By calculating

$$s_{11}^2 = 29.20, \qquad s_{22}^2 = 334, \qquad s_{12}^2 = 17, \qquad s = 6.92,$$

a 95 percent confidence interval for P_0 is found to be

$$0.076 \leq P_0 \leq 0.510.$$

(The wide range of this interval indicates that a much longer simulation run would be needed to obtain a relatively precise estimate of P_0.)

If we redefine *Y* appropriately, the same approach also can be used to estimate other probabilities involving the number of customers in the system. However, because this number never exceeded 3 during this simulation run, a much longer run will be needed if the probability involves larger numbers.

The other basic expected values of queueing theory defined in Sec. 17.2 (W, L_q, and L) can be estimated from the estimate of W_q by using the relationships among these four expected values given near the end of Sec. 17.2. However, the other expected values can also be estimated directly from the results of the simulation run. For example, because the expected number of customers waiting to be served is

$$L_q = \sum_{n=2}^{\infty} (n-1)P_n,$$

it can be estimated by defining

$$Y = \sum_{n=2}^{\infty} (n-1)T_n,$$

where T_n is the *total time* that exactly n customers are in the system during the cycle. (This definition of Y actually is equivalent to the definition used for estimating W_q.) In this case, Z is defined as it would be for estimating any P_n, namely, the *length* of the cycle. The resulting *point estimate* of L_q then turns out to be simply the *point estimate* of W_q *multiplied by* the actual *average arrival rate* for the complete cycles observed.

It is also possible to estimate *higher moments* of these probability distributions by redefining Y accordingly. For example, the *second moment* about the origin of the number of customers waiting to be served N_q

$$E(N_q^2) = \sum_{n=2}^{\infty} (n-1)^2 P_n$$

can be estimated by redefining

$$Y = \sum_{n=2}^{\infty} (n-1)^2 T_n.$$

This point estimate, along with the point estimate of L_q (the first moment of N_q) just described, can then be used to estimate the *variance* of N_q. Specifically, because of the general relationship between variance and moments, this variance is

$$\text{Var } (N_q) = E(N_q^2) - L_q^2.$$

Therefore, its point estimate is obtained by substituting in the point estimates of the quantities on the right-hand side of this relationship.

Finally, we should mention that it was unnecessary to generate the first *interarrival* time (24) for the simulation run summarized in Table 22.12 and Fig. 22.16, because this time played no role in the statistical analysis. It is more efficient with the regenerative method just to start the run at the regeneration point.

Selected Reference 5 provides considerably more information about the regenerative method, including how it can be applied to more complicated kinds of problems than those considered here. (Also see the references given in the second footnote at the beginning of this section.)

22.9   CONCLUSIONS

Simulation is a widely used tool for estimating the performance of complex stochastic systems if contemplated designs or operating policies are to be used.

We have focused in this chapter on the use of simulation for predicting the *steady-state* behavior of systems whose states change only at discrete points in time. However, by having a series of runs begin with the prescribed *starting conditions,* we can also use simulation to describe the *transient* behavior of a proposed system. Furthermore, if we use differential equations, simulation can be applied to systems whose states change *continuously* with time.

Simulation is one of the most popular techniques of operations research because it is such a flexible, powerful, and intuitive tool. In a matter of seconds or minutes, it can simulate even years of operation of a typical system while generating a series of statistical observations about the performance of the system over this period. Because of its exceptional versatility, simulation has been applied to a wide variety of areas. Furthermore, its horizons continue to broaden because of the great progress being made in simulation software, including software for performing simulations on spreadsheets.

On the other hand, simulation should not be viewed as a panacea when studying stochastic systems. When applicable, analytical methods (such as those presented in Chaps. 15 to 21) have some significant advantages. Simulation is inherently an imprecise technique. It provides only *statistical estimates* rather than exact results, and it *compares alternatives* rather than generating an optimal one. Furthermore, despite impressive advances in software, simulation still can be a relatively *slow and costly* way to study complex stochastic systems. For such systems, it usually requires a large amount of time and expense for analysis and programming, in addition to considerable computer running time. Simulation models tend to become unwieldy, so that the number of cases that can be run and the accuracy of the results obtained often turn out to be inadequate. Finally, simulation yields only *numerical data* about the performance of the system, so that it provides no additional insight into the cause-and-effect relationships within the system except for the clues that can be gleaned from these numbers (and from the analysis required to construct the simulation model). Therefore, it is very expensive to conduct a sensitivity analysis of the parameter values assumed by the model. The only possible way would be to conduct new series of simulation runs with different parameter values, which would tend to provide relatively little information at a relatively high cost.

For all these reasons, analytical methods (when available) and simulation have important complementary roles for studying stochastic systems. An analytical method is well suited for doing at least preliminary analysis, for examining cause-and-effect relationships, for doing some rough optimization, and for conducting sensitivity analysis. When the mathematical model for the analytical method does not capture all the important features of the stochastic system, simulation is well suited for incorporating all these features and then obtaining detailed information about the measures of performance of the few leading candidates for the final system configuration.

Simulation provides a way of *experimenting* with proposed systems or policies without actually implementing them. Sound statistical theory should be used in designing these experiments. Surprisingly long simulation runs often are needed to obtain *statistically significant* results. However, *variance-reducing techniques* can be very helpful in reducing the length of the runs needed.

Several tactical problems arise when we apply traditional statistical estimation procedures to simulated experiments. These problems include prescribing appropriate *starting conditions,* determining how long a *warm-up period* is needed to essentially reach a steady-state condition, and dealing with *statistically dependent* observations. These problems can be eliminated by using the *regenerative method* of statistical analysis. However, there are some restrictions on when this method can be applied.

Simulation unquestionably has a very important place in the theory and practice of OR. It is an invaluable tool for use on those problems where analytical techniques are inadequate, and its usage is continuing to grow.

SELECTED REFERENCES

1. Andradóttir, S.: "Optimization of the Transient and Steady-State Behavior of Discrete Event Simulations," *Management Science,* **42:** 717–737, 1996.
2. Banks, J. (ed.): *Handbook of Simulation: Principles, Methodology, Advances, Applications, and Practice,* Wiley, New York, and Industrial Engineering & Management Press, Norcross, GA, 1998.
3. Banks, J., J. S. Carson, II, and B. L. Nelson: *Discrete-Event System Simulation,* 2d ed., Prentice-Hall, Upper Saddle River, NJ, 1995.
4. Cochran, J. K, G. T. Mackulak, and P. A. Savory: "Simulation Project Characteristics in Industrial Settings," *Interfaces,* **25**(4): 104–113, July–August 1995.
5. Crane, M. A., and A. J. Lemoine: *An Introduction to the Regenerative Method for Simulation Analysis,* Springer-Verlag, Berlin, 1977.
6. Fishman, G. S.: *Monte Carlo: Concepts, Algorithms and Applications,* Springer-Verlag, New York, 1996.
7. Harrell, C., and K. Tumay: *Simulation Made Easy: A Manager's Guide,* Industrial Engineering and Management Press, Norcross, GA, 1995.
8. Hillier, F. S., M. S. Hillier, and G. J. Lieberman: *Introduction to Management Science: A Modeling and Case Studies Approach with Spreadsheets,* Irwin/McGraw-Hill, Burr Ridge, IL, 2000, chap. 15.
9. Kleijnen, J. P. C.: *Statistical Tools for Simulation Practitioners,* Marcel Dekker, New York, 1987.
10. Law, A. M.: "Introduction to Simulation: A Powerful Tool for Complex Manufacturing Systems," *Industrial Engineering,* **18**(5): 46–63, May 1986.
11. Law, A. M., and W. D. Kelton: *Simulation Modeling and Analysis,* 2d ed., McGraw-Hill, New York, 1991.
12. Nelson, B. L.: *Stochastic Modeling: Analysis and Simulation,* McGraw-Hill, New York, 1995.
13. Pegden, C. D., R. P. Sadowski, and R. E. Shannon: *Introduction to Simulation Using SIMAN,* 2d ed., McGraw-Hill, New York, 1995.
14. Pooch, U. W., and J. A. Wall: *Discrete Event Simulation: A Practical Approach,* CRC Press, Boca Raton, FL, 1992.
15. Pritsker, A. A. B., C. E. Sigal, and R. D. J. Hammesfahr: *SLAM II: Network Models for Decision Support,* The Scientific Press, South San Francisco, 1994.
16. Schriber, T. J.: *An Introduction to Simulation,* Wiley, New York, 1991.
17. Whitt, W.: "Planning Queueing Simulations," *Management Science,* **35:** 1341–1366, 1989.

LEARNING AIDS FOR THIS CHAPTER IN YOUR OR COURSEWARE

Demonstration Examples in OR Tutor:

Simulating a Basic Queueing System
Simulating a Queueing System with Priorities

Interactive Routines:

Enter Queueing Problem
Interactively Simulate Queueing Problem

"Ch. 22—Simulation" Excel File:

Spreadsheet Examples
Queueing Simulator

Excel Add-Ins:

RiskSim (academic version)
(*@RISK* is on the website, www.Palisade.com)

PROBLEMS

The symbols to the left of some of the problems (or their parts) have the following meaning:

D: The demonstration examples for this chapter may be helpful.
I: We suggest that you use the interactive routines listed above (the printout records your work).
E: Use Excel.
A: Use one of the Excel add-ins listed above.
Q: Use the Queueing Simulator.
R: Use *three-digit* uniform random numbers (0.096, 0.569, etc.) that are obtained from the consecutive random digits in Table 22.3, starting from the front of the top row, to do each problem part.

22.1-1.* Use the uniform random numbers in cells C10:C15 of Fig. 22.1 to generate six random observations for each of the following situations.
(a) Throwing an unbiased coin.
(b) A baseball pitcher who throws a strike 60 percent of the time and a ball 40 percent of the time.
(c) The color of a traffic light found by a randomly arriving car when it is green 40 percent of the time, yellow 10 percent of the time, and red 50 percent of the time.

22.1-2. The weather can be considered a stochastic system, because it evolves in a probabilistic manner from one day to the next. Suppose for a certain location that this probabilistic evolution satisfies the following description:

The probability of rain tomorrow is 0.6 if it is raining today. The probability of its being clear (no rain) tomorrow is 0.8 if it is clear today.
(a) Use the uniform random numbers in cells C14:C23 of Fig. 22.1 to simulate the evolution of the weather for 10 days, beginning the day after a clear day.

E **(b)** Now use a computer with the uniform random numbers generated by Excel to perform the simulation requested in part (*a*) on a spreadsheet.

22.1-3. Jessica Williams, manager of Kitchen Appliances for the Midtown Department Store, feels that her inventory levels of stoves have been running higher than necessary. Before revising the inventory policy for stoves, she records the number sold each day over a period of 25 days, as summarized below.

Number sold	2	3	4	5	6
Number of days	4	7	8	5	1

(a) Use these data to estimate the probability distribution of daily sales.
(b) Calculate the mean of the distribution obtained in part (*a*).
(c) Describe how uniform random numbers can be used to simulate daily sales.
(d) Use the uniform random numbers 0.4476, 0.9713, and 0.0629 to simulate daily sales over 3 days. Compare the average with the mean obtained in part (*b*).
E **(e)** Formulate a spreadsheet model for performing a simulation of the daily sales. Perform 300 replications and obtain the average of the sales over the 300 simulated days.

22.1-4. The William Graham Entertainment Company will be opening a new box office where customers can come to make ticket purchases in advance for the many entertainment events being held in the area. Simulation is being used to analyze whether to have one or two clerks on duty at the box office.

While simulating the beginning of a day at the box office, the first customer arrives 5 minutes after it opens and then the inter-arrival times for the next four customers (in order) are 3 minutes, 9 minutes, 1 minute, and 4 minutes, after which there is a long delay until the next customer arrives. The service times for these first five customers (in order) are 8 minutes, 6 minutes, 2 minutes, 4 minutes, and 7 minutes.

(a) For the alternative of a single clerk, plot a graph that shows the evolution of the number of customers at the box office over this period.

(b) Use this figure to estimate the usual measures of performance—L, L_q, W, W_q, and the P_n (as defined in Sec. 17.2)—for this queueing system.

(c) Repeat part (a) for the alternative of two clerks.

(d) Repeat part (b) for the alternative of two clerks.

22.1-5. Consider the $M/M/1$ queueing theory model that was discussed in Sec. 17.6 and Example 2, Sec. 22.1. Suppose that the mean arrival rate is 5 per hour, the mean service rate is 10 per hour, and you are required to estimate the expected waiting time before service begins by using simulation.

R **(a)** Starting with the system empty, use next-event incrementing to perform the simulation by hand until two service completions have occurred.

R **(b)** Starting with the system empty, use fixed-time incrementing (with 2 minutes as the time unit) to perform the simulation by hand until two service completions have occurred.

D,I **(c)** Use the interactive routine for simulation in your OR Courseware (which incorporates next-event incrementing) to interactively execute a simulation run until 20 service completions have occurred.

Q **(d)** Use the Queueing Simulator to execute a simulation run with 10,000 customer arrivals.

E **(e)** Use the Excel template for this model in the Excel file for Chap. 17 to obtain the usual measures of performance for this queueing system. Then compare these exact results with the corresponding point estimates and 95 percent confidence intervals obtained from the simulation run in part (d). Identify any measure whose exact result falls outside the 95 percent confidence interval.

22.1-6. The Rustbelt Manufacturing Company employs a maintenance crew to repair its machines as needed. Management now wants a simulation study done to analyze what the size of the crew should be, where the crew sizes under consideration are 2, 3, and 4. The time required by the crew to repair a machine has a uniform distribution over the interval from 0 to twice the mean, where the mean depends on the crew size. The mean is 4 hours with two crew members, 3 hours with three crew members, and 2 hours with four crew members. The time between breakdowns of some machine has an exponential distribution with a mean of 5 hours. When

a machine breaks down and so requires repair, management wants its average waiting time before repair begins to be no more than 3 hours. Management also wants the crew size to be no larger than necessary to achieve this.

(a) Develop a simulation model for this problem by describing its basic building blocks listed in Sec. 22.1 as they would be applied to this situation.

R **(b)** Consider the case of a crew size of 2. Starting with no machines needing repair, use next-event incrementing to perform the simulation by hand for 20 hours of simulated time.

R **(c)** Repeat part (b), but this time with fixed-time incrementing (with 1 hour as the time unit).

D,I **(d)** Use the interactive routine for simulation in your OR Courseware (which incorporates next-event incrementing) to interactively execute a simulation run over a period of 10 breakdowns for each of the three crew sizes under consideration.

Q **(e)** Use the Queueing Simulator to simulate this system over a period of 10,000 breakdowns for each of the three crew sizes.

(f) Use the $M/G/1$ queueing model presented in Sec. 17.7 to obtain the expected waiting time W_q analytically for each of the three crew sizes. (You can either calculate W_q by hand or use the template for this model in the Excel file for Chap. 17.) Which crew size should be used?

22.1-7. While performing a simulation of a single-server queueing system, the number of customers in the system is 0 for the first 10 minutes, 1 for the next 17 minutes, 2 for the next 24 minutes, 1 for the next 15 minutes, 2 for the next 16 minutes, and 1 for the next 18 minutes. After this total of 100 minutes, the number becomes 0 again. Based on these results for the first 100 minutes, perform the following analysis (using the notation for queueing models introduced in Sec. 17.2).

(a) Plot a graph showing the evolution of the number of customers in the system over these 100 minutes.

(b) Develop estimates of P_0, P_1, P_2, P_3.

(c) Develop estimates of L and L_q.

(d) Develop estimates of W and W_q.

22.1-8. View the first demonstration example (*Simulating a Basic Queueing System*) in the simulation area of your OR Tutor.

D,I **(a)** Enter this *same problem* into the interactive routine for simulation in your OR Courseware. Interactively execute a simulation run for 20 minutes of simulated time.

Q **(b)** Use the Queueing Simulator with 5,000 customer arrivals to estimate the usual measures of performance for this queueing system under the current plan to provide two tellers.

Q **(c)** Repeat part (b) if three tellers were to be provided.

Q **(d)** Now perform some sensitivity analysis by checking the effect if the level of business turns out to be even higher than projected. In particular, assume that the average time between customer arrivals turns out to be only 0.9 minute instead of 1.0 minute. Evaluate the alternatives of two tellers and three tellers under this assumption.

(e) Suppose *you* were the manager of this bank. Use your simulation results as the basis for a managerial decision on how many tellers to provide. Justify your answer.

D,I **22.1-9.** View the second demonstration example (*Simulating a Queueing System with Priorities*) in the simulation area of your OR Tutor. Then enter this *same problem* into the interactive routine for simulation in your OR Courseware. Interactively execute a simulation run for 20 minutes of simulated time.

22.1-10.* Hugh's Repair Shop specializes in repairing German and Japanese cars. The shop has two mechanics. One mechanic works on only German cars and the other mechanic works on only Japanese cars. In either case, the time required to repair a car has an exponential distribution with a mean of 0.2 day. The shop's business has been steadily increasing, especially for German cars. Hugh projects that, by next year, German cars will arrive randomly to be repaired at a mean rate of 4 per day, so the time between arrivals will have an exponential distribution with a mean of 0.25 day. The mean arrival rate for Japanese cars is projected to be 2 per day, so the distribution of interarrival times will be exponential with a mean of 0.5 day.

For either kind of car, Hugh would like the expected waiting time in the shop before the repair is completed to be no more than 0.5 day.

(a) Formulate a simulation model for performing a simulation to estimate what the expected waiting time until repair is completed will be next year for either kind of car.

D,I **(b)** Considering only German cars, use the interactive routine for simulation in your OR Courseware to interactively perform this simulation over a period of 10 arrivals of German cars.

Q **(c)** Use the Queueing Simulator to perform this simulation for German cars over a period of 10,000 car arrivals.

Q **(d)** Repeat part (*c*) for Japanese cars.

D,I **(e)** Hugh is considering hiring a second mechanic who specializes in German cars so that two such cars can be repaired simultaneously. (Only one mechanic works on any one car.) Repeat part (*b*) for this option.

Q **(f)** Use the Queueing Simulator with 10,000 arrivals of German cars to evaluate the option described in part (*e*).

Q **(g)** Another option is to train the two current mechanics to work on either kind of car. This would increase the expected repair time by 10 percent, from 0.2 day to 0.22 day. Use the Queueing Simulator with 20,000 arrivals of cars of either kind to evaluate this option.

(h) Because both the interarrival-time and service-time distributions are exponential, the *M/M/*1 and *M/M/s* queueing models

introduced in Sec. 17.6 can be used to evaluate all the above options analytically. Use these models to determine *W*, the expected waiting time until repair is completed, for each of the cases considered in parts (*c*), (*d*), (*f*), and (*g*). (You can either calculate *W* by hand or use the template for the *M/M/s* model in the Excel file for Chap. 17.) For each case, compare the estimate of *W* obtained by computer simulation with the analytical value. What does this say about the number of car arrivals that should be included in the simulation?

(i) Based on the above results, which option would you select if you were Hugh? Why?

22.1-11. Vistaprint produces monitors and printers for computers. In the past, only some of them were inspected on a sampling basis. However, the new plan is that they all will be inspected before they are released. Under this plan, the monitors and printers will be brought to the inspection station one at a time as they are completed. For monitors, the interarrival time will have a uniform distribution between 10 and 20 minutes. For printers, the interarrival time will be a constant 15 minutes.

The inspection station has two inspectors. One inspector works on only monitors and the other one only inspects printers. In either case, the inspection time has an exponential distribution with a mean of 10 minutes.

Before beginning the new plan, management wants an evaluation made of how long the monitors and printers will be held up waiting at the inspection station.

(a) Formulate a simulation model for performing a simulation to estimate the expected waiting times (both before beginning inspection and after completing inspection) for either the monitors or the printers.

D,I **(b)** Considering only the monitors, use the interactive routine for simulation in your OR Courseware to interactively perform this simulation over a period of 10 arrivals of monitors.

D,I **(c)** Repeat part (*b*) for the printers.

Q **(d)** Use the Queueing Simulator to repeat parts (*b*) and (*c*) with 10,000 arrivals in each case.

Q **(e)** Management is considering the option of providing new inspection equipment to the inspectors. This equipment would not change the expected time to perform an inspection but it would decrease the variability of the times. In particular, for either product, the inspection time would have an Erlang distribution with a mean of 10 minutes and shape parameter $k = 4$. Use the Queueing Simulator to repeat part (*d*) under this option. Compare the results with those obtained in part (*d*).

22.2-1. Section 22.2 introduced four actual applications of simulation that are described in articles in *Interfaces*. (The citations for the two that also use queueing models are given in Sec. 18.6.) Select one of these applications and read the corresponding article.

Write a two-page summary of the application and the benefits it provided.

22.2-2. Read the articles about all four applications of simulation mentioned in Prob. 22.2-1. For each one, write a one-page summary of the application and the benefits it provided.

22.3-1.* Use the mixed congruential method to generate the following sequences of random numbers.
(a) A sequence of 10 *one-digit* random integer numbers such that $x_{n+1} \equiv (x_n + 3)$ (modulo 10) and $x_0 = 2$
(b) A sequence of eight random integer numbers between 0 and 7 such that $x_{n+1} \equiv (5x_n + 1)$ (modulo 8) and $x_0 = 1$
(c) A sequence of five *two-digit* random integer numbers such that $x_{n+1} \equiv (61x_n + 27)$ (modulo 100) and $x_0 = 10$

22.3-2. Reconsider Prob. 22.3-1. Suppose now that you want to convert these random integer numbers to (approximate) uniform random numbers. For each of the three parts, give a formula for this conversion that makes the approximation as close as possible.

22.3-3. Use the mixed congruential method to generate a sequence of five *two-digit* random integer numbers such that $x_{n+1} \equiv (41x_n + 33)$ (modulo 100) and $x_0 = 48$.

22.3-4. Use the mixed congruential method to generate a sequence of three *three-digit* random integer numbers such that $x_{n+1} \equiv (201x_n + 503)$ (modulo 1,000) and $x_0 = 485$.

22.3-5. You need to generate five uniform random numbers.
(a) Prepare to do this by using the mixed congruential method to generate a sequence of five random integer numbers between 0 and 31 such that $x_{n+1} \equiv (13x_n + 15)$ (modulo 32) and $x_0 = 14$.
(b) Convert these random integer numbers to uniform random numbers as closely as possible.

22.3-6. You are given the *multiplicative congruential generator* $x_0 = 1$ and $x_{n+1} \equiv 7x_n$ (modulo 13) for $n = 0, 1, 2, \ldots$.
(a) Calculate x_n for $n = 1, 2, \ldots, 12$.
(b) How often does each integer between 1 and 12 appear in the sequence generated in part (*a*)?
(c) Without performing additional calculations, indicate how x_{13}, $x_{14}, \ldots$ will compare with $x_1, x_2, \ldots$.

22.4-1. Reconsider the coin flipping game introduced in Sec. 22.1 and analyzed with simulation in Figs. 22.1, 22.2, and 22.3.
(a) Simulate one play of this game by repeatedly flipping your own coin until the game ends. Record your results in the format shown in columns *B*, *D*, *E*, *F*, and *G* of Fig. 22.1. How much would you have won or lost if this had been a real play of the game?
E **(b)** Revise the spreadsheet model in Fig. 22.1 by using Excel's VLOOKUP function instead of the IF function to generate

each simulated flip of the coin. Then perform a simulation of one play of the game.
E **(c)** Use this revised spreadsheet model to generate a data table with 14 replications like Fig. 22.2.
E **(d)** Repeat part (*c*) with 1,000 replications (like Fig. 22.3).

22.4-2.* Apply the inverse transformation method as indicated below to generate three random observations from the uniform distribution between -10 and 40 by using the following uniform random numbers: 0.0965, 0.5692, 0.6658.
(a) Apply this method graphically.
(b) Apply this method algebraically.
(c) Write the equation that Excel would use to generate each such random observation.

R **22.4-3.** Obtaining uniform random numbers as instructed at the beginning of the Problems section, generate three random observations from each of the following probability distributions.
(a) The uniform distribution from 25 to 75.
(b) The distribution whose probability density function is

$$f(x) = \begin{cases} \dfrac{1}{4}(x + 1)^3 & \text{if } -1 \le x \le 1 \\ 0 & \text{otherwise.} \end{cases}$$

(c) The distribution whose probability density function is

$$f(x) = \begin{cases} \dfrac{1}{200}(x - 40) & \text{if } 40 \le x \le 60 \\ 0 & \text{otherwise.} \end{cases}$$

R **22.4-4.** Obtaining uniform random numbers as instructed at the beginning of the Problems section, generate three random observations from each of the following probability distributions.
(a) The random variable X has $P\{X = 0\} = \frac{1}{2}$. Given $X \ne 0$, it has a uniform distribution between -5 and 15.
(b) The distribution whose probability density function is

$$f(x) = \begin{cases} x - 1 & \text{if } 1 \le x \le 2 \\ 3 - x & \text{if } 2 \le x \le 3. \end{cases}$$

(c) The geometric distribution with parameter $p = \frac{1}{3}$, so that

$$P\{X = k\} = \begin{cases} \dfrac{1}{3}\left(\dfrac{2}{3}\right)^{k-1} & \text{if } k = 1, 2, \ldots \\ 0 & \text{otherwise.} \end{cases}$$

22.4-5.* Suppose that random observations are needed from the triangular distribution whose probability density function is

$$f(x) = \begin{cases} 2x & \text{if } 0 \le x \le 1 \\ 0 & \text{otherwise.} \end{cases}$$

(a) Derive an expression for each random observation as a function of the uniform random number r.

(b) Generate five random observations for this distribution by using the following uniform random numbers: 0.0956, 0.5629, 0.6695, 0.7634, 0.8426.

(c) The inverse transformation method was applied to generate the following three random observations from this distribution: 0.09, 0.64, 0.49. Identify the three uniform random numbers that were used.

(d) Write an equation that Excel can use to generate each random observation from this distribution.

22.4-6. Each time an unbiased coin is flipped three times, the probability of getting 0, 1, 2, and 3 heads is $\frac{1}{8}$, $\frac{3}{8}$, $\frac{3}{8}$, and $\frac{1}{8}$, respectively. Therefore, with eight groups of three flips each, *on the average,* one group will yield 0 heads, three groups will yield 1 head, three groups will yield 2 heads, and one group will yield 3 heads.

(a) Using your own coin, flip it 24 times divided into eight groups of three flips each, and record the number of groups with 0 head, with 1 head, with 2 heads, and with 3 heads.

(b) Obtaining uniform random numbers as instructed at the beginning of the Problems section, simulate the flips specified in part (*a*) and record the information indicated in part (*a*).

E **(c)** Formulate a spreadsheet model for performing a simulation of three flips of the coin and recording the number of heads. Perform one replication of this simulation.

E **(d)** Use this spreadsheet to generate a data table with 8 replications of the simulation. Compare this frequency distribution of the number of heads with the probability distribution of the number of heads with three flips.

E **(e)** Repeat part (*d*) with 800 replications.

22.4-7. Eddie's Bicycle Shop has a thriving business repairing bicycles. Trisha runs the reception area where customers check in their bicycles to be repaired and then later pick up their bicycles and pay their bills. She estimates that the time required to serve a customer on each visit has a uniform distribution between 3 minutes and 8 minutes.

Apply the inverse transformation method as indicated below to simulate the service times for five customers by using the following five uniform random numbers: 0.6505, 0.0740, 0.8443, 0.4975, 0.8178.

(a) Apply this method graphically.

(b) Apply this method algebraically.

(c) Calculate the average of the five service times and compare it to the mean of the service-time distribution.

E **(d)** Use Excel to generate 500 random observations and calculate the average. Compare this average to the mean of the service-time distribution.

22.4-8.* The game of craps requires the player to throw two dice one or more times until a decision has been reached as to whether he (or she) wins or loses. He wins if the first throw results in a

sum of 7 or 11 or, alternatively, if the first sum is 4, 5, 6, 8, 9, or 10 and the same sum reappears before a sum of 7 has appeared. Conversely, he loses if the first throw results in a sum of 2, 3, or 12 or, alternatively, if the first sum is 4, 5, 6, 8, 9, or 10 and a sum of 7 appears before the first sum reappears.

E **(a)** Formulate a spreadsheet model for performing a simulation of the throw of two dice. Perform one replication.

E **(b)** Perform 25 replications of this simulation.

(c) Trace through these 25 replications to determine both the number of times the simulated player would have won the game of craps and the number of losses when each play starts with the next throw after the previous play ends. Use this information to calculate a preliminary estimate of the probability of winning a single play of the game.

(d) For a large number of plays of the game, the proportion of wins has *approximately* a normal distribution with mean = 0.493 and standard deviation = $0.5\sqrt{n}$. Use this information to calculate the number of simulated plays that would be required to have a probability of at least 0.95 that the proportion of wins will be less than 0.5.

22.4-9. The random variable X has the cumulative distribution function $F(x)$ whose value or derivative $F'(x)$ is shown below for various values of x.

$$F(0) = 0.$$

$$F'(x) = \frac{1}{8}, \quad \text{for } 0 < x < 2.$$

$$P\{X = 2\} = \frac{1}{2}, \quad \text{so} \quad F(2) = \frac{3}{4}.$$

$$F'(x) = \frac{1}{4}, \quad \text{for } 2 < x < 3.$$

$$F(3) = 1.$$

Generate four random observations from this probability distribution by using the following uniform random numbers: $\frac{3}{4}$, $\frac{1}{2}$, $\frac{1}{4}$, $\frac{7}{8}$. Also calculate the sample average and compare it with the true mean $\left(\frac{15}{8}\right)$ for this probability distribution.

R **22.4-10.** Obtaining uniform random numbers as instructed at the beginning of the Problems section, use the inverse transformation method and the table of the normal distribution given in Appendix 5 (with linear interpolation between values in the table) to generate 10 random observations (to three decimal places) from a normal distribution with mean = 1 and variance = 4. Then calculate the sample average of these random observations.

R **22.4-11.** Obtaining uniform random numbers as instructed at the beginning of the Problems section, generate three random observations (approximately) from a normal distribution with main = 0 and standard deviation = 1.

(a) Do this by applying the central limit theorem, using three uniform random numbers to generate each random observation.

(b) Now do this by using the table for the normal distribution given in Appendix 5 and applying the inverse transformation method.

R **22.4-12.** Obtaining uniform random numbers as instructed at the beginning of the Problems section, generate four random observations (approximately) from a normal distribution with mean $= 0$ and standard deviation $= 1$.

(a) Do this by applying the central limit theorem, using three uniform random numbers to generate each random observation.

(b) Now do this by using the table for the normal distribution given in Appendix 5 and applying the inverse transformation method.

(c) Use your random observations from parts (a) and (b) to generate random observations from a chi-square distribution with 2 degrees of freedom.

R **22.4-13.*** Obtaining uniform random numbers as instructed at the beginning of the Problems section, generate two random observations from each of the following probability distributions.

(a) The exponential distribution with mean $= 4$

(b) The Erlang distribution with mean $= 4$ and shape parameter $k = 2$ (that is, standard deviation $= 2\sqrt{2}$)

(c) The normal distribution with mean $= 4$ and standard deviation $= 2\sqrt{2}$. (Use the central limit theorem and $n = 6$ for each observation.)

22.4-14. Richard Collins, manager and owner of Richard's Tire Service, wishes to use simulation to analyze the operation of his shop. One of the activities to be included in the simulation is the installation of automobile tires (including balancing the tires). Richard estimates that the cumulative distribution function (CDF) of the probability distribution of the time (in minutes) required to install a tire has the graph shown below.

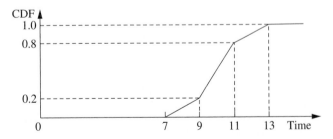

(a) Use the inverse transformation method to generate five random observations from this distribution when using the following five uniform random numbers: 0.2655, 0.3472, 0.0248, 0.9205, 0.6130.

(b) Use a nested IF function to write an equation that Excel can use to generate each random observation from this distribution.

R **22.4-15.** Obtaining uniform random numbers as instructed at the beginning of the Problems section, generate four random observations from an exponential distribution with mean $= 1$. Then use these four observations to generate one random observation from an Erlang distribution with mean $= 4$ and shape parameter $k = 4$.

22.4-16. You need to generate 10 random observations from the probability distribution

$$P\{X = n\} = \begin{cases} \dfrac{1}{10} & \text{if } n = 0, 1, 2, \ldots, 9 \\ 0 & \text{otherwise.} \end{cases}$$

(a) Prepare to do this by generating 16 random integer numbers from the mixed congruential generator, $x_{n+1} \equiv (5x_n + 3) \pmod{16}$ and $x_0 = 1$.

(b) Use the single-digit random integer numbers from part (a) to generate the desired random observations.

(c) Note that once a particular value of X is generated in part (b), it can never be repeated because each of the 16 possible random integer numbers is generated exactly once in part (a). In which ways does this violate the desirable properties of random observations? What change would you make in what was done in parts (a) and (b) to alleviate this problem?

(d) Now convert the first 10 random integer numbers from part (a) to (approximate) uniform random numbers, and then apply the inverse transformation method to obtain the desired random observations.

(e) Does the procedure prescribed in part (d) actually give a probability of $\frac{1}{10}$ of generating each of the 10 possible values of X each time? Explain. What change would you make in what was done in parts (a) and (d) to alleviate this problem?

22.4-17. Let $r_1, r_2, \ldots, r_n$ be uniform random numbers. Define $x_i = -\ln r_i$ and $y_i = -\ln (1 - r_i)$, for $i = 1, 2, \ldots, n$, and $z = \sum_{i=1}^{n} x_i$. Label each of the following statements as true or false, and then justify your answer.

(a) The numbers $x_1, x_2, \ldots, x_n$ and $y_1, y_2, \ldots, y_n$ are random observations from the same exponential distribution.

(b) The average of $x_1, x_2, \ldots, x_n$ is equal to the average of $y_1, y_2, \ldots, y_n$.

(c) z is a random observation from an Erlang (gamma) distribution.

22.4-18. Consider the discrete random variable X that is uniformly distributed (equal probabilities) on the set $\{1, 2, \ldots, 9\}$. You wish to generate a series of random observations x_i ($i = 1, 2, \ldots$) of X. The following three proposals have been made for doing this. For each one, analyze whether it is a valid method and, if not, how it can be adjusted to become a valid method.

(a) Proposal 1: Generate uniform random numbers r_i ($i = 1$, 2, . . .), and then set $x_i = n$, where n is the integer satisfying $n/8 \leq r_i < (n + 1)/8$.

(b) Proposal 2: Generate uniform random numbers r_i ($i = 1$, 2, . . .), and then set x_i equal to the greatest integer less than or equal to $1 + 8r_i$.

(c) Proposal 3: Generate x_i from the mixed congruential generator $x_{n+1} \equiv (5x_n + 7)$ (modulo 8), with starting value $x_0 = 4$.

R **22.4-19.** Obtaining uniform random numbers as instructed at the beginning of the Problems section, use the acceptance-rejection method to generate three random observations from the triangular distribution used to illustrate this method in Sec. 22.4.

R **22.4-20.** Obtaining uniform random numbers as instructed at the beginning of the Problems section, use the acceptance-rejection method to generate three random observations from the probability density function

$$f(x) = \begin{cases} \dfrac{1}{50}(x - 10) & \text{if } 10 \leq x \leq 20 \\ 0 & \text{otherwise.} \end{cases}$$

R **22.4-21.** An insurance company insures four large risks. The number of losses for each risk is independent and identically distributed on the points $\{0, 1, 2\}$ with probabilities 0.7, 0.2, and 0.1, respectively. The size of an individual loss has the following cumulative distribution function:

$$F(x) = \begin{cases} \dfrac{\sqrt{x}}{20} & \text{if } 0 \leq x \leq 100 \\ \dfrac{x}{200} & \text{if } 100 < x \leq 200 \\ 1 & \text{if } x > 200. \end{cases}$$

Obtaining uniform random numbers as instructed at the beginning of the Problems section, perform a simulation experiment twice of the total loss generated by the four large risks.

22.4-22. A company provides its three employees with health insurance under a group plan. For each employee, the probability of incurring medical expenses during a year is 0.9, so the number of employees incurring medical expenses during a year has a binomial distribution with $p = 0.9$ and $n = 3$. Given that an employee incurs medical expenses during a year, the total amount for the year has the distribution $100 with probability 0.9 or $10,000 with probability 0.1. The company has a $5,000 deductible clause with the insurance company so that each year the insurance company pays the total medical expenses for the group in excess of $5,000. Use the uniform random numbers 0.01 and 0.20, in the order given, to generate the number of claims based on a binomial distribution for each of 2 years. Use the following uniform random numbers,

in the order given, to generate the amount of each claim: 0.80, 0.95, 0.70, 0.96, 0.54, 0.01. Calculate the total amount that the insurance company pays for 2 years.

A **22.6-1.** Reconsider Prob. 10.4-3, which involves trying to find the probability that a project will be completed by the deadline. Assume now that the duration of each activity has a triangular distribution that is based on the three estimates in the manner depicted in Fig. 22.10. Obtain a close estimate of the probability of meeting the deadline by performing 1,000 iterations of a simulation of the project on a spreadsheet. Generate the various available kinds of outputs similar to Fig. 22.12.

A **22.6-2.** Look ahead at the scenario described in Prob. 22.7-5. Obtain a close estimate of the expected cost of insurance coverage for the corporation's employees by performing 500 iterations of a simulation of an employee's health insurance experience on a spreadsheet. Also generate the frequency distribution of the cost of insurance coverage.

A **22.6-3.** The Avery Co. factory has been having a maintenance problem with the control panel for one of its production processes. This control panel contains four identical electromechanical relays that have been the cause of the trouble. The problem is that the relays fail fairly frequently, thereby forcing the control panel (and the production process it controls) to be shut down while a replacement is made. The current practice is to replace the relays only when they fail. However, a proposal has been made to replace all four relays whenever any one of them fails to reduce the frequency with which the control panel must be shut down. The objective is to compare these two alternatives on a cost basis.

The pertinent data are the following. For each relay, the operating time until failure has approximately a uniform distribution from 1,000 to 2,000 hours. The control panel must be shut down for 1 hour to replace one relay or for 2 hours to replace all four relays. The total cost associated with shutting down the control panel and replacing relays is $1,000 per hour plus $200 for each new relay.

Use simulation on a spreadsheet to evaluate and compare the two alternatives on a cost basis. In each case, perform 1,000 iterations (where the end of each iteration coincides with the end of a shutdown of the control panel) and generate the various available results.

A **22.6-4.** For one new product to be produced by the Aplus Company, bushings will need to be drilled into a metal block and cylindrical shafts inserted into the bushings. The shafts are required to have a radius of at least 1.0000 inch, but the radius should be as little larger than this as possible. With the proposed production process for producing the shafts, the probability distribution of the radius of a shaft has a triangular distribution with a minimum of

1.0000 inch, a most likely value of 1.0010 inches, and a maximum value of 1.0020 inches. With the proposed method of drilling the bushings, the probability distribution of the radius of a bushing has a normal distribution with a mean of 1.0020 inches and a standard deviation of 0.0010 inch. The clearance between a bushing and a shaft is the difference in their radii. Because they are selected at random, there occasionally is interference (i.e., negative clearance) between a bushing and a shaft to be mated.

Management is concerned about the disruption in the production of the new product that would be caused by this occasional interference. Perhaps the production processes for the shafts and bushings should be improved (at considerable cost) to lessen the chance of interference. To evaluate the need for such improvements, management has asked you to determine how frequently interference would occur with the currently proposed production processes.

Estimate the probability of interference by performing 500 iterations of a simulation on a spreadsheet. Also generate other available results regarding the frequency distribution of the clearance (positive or negative).

A **22.6-5.** Refer to the financial risk analysis example presented at the end of Sec. 22.6, including its results shown in Fig. 22.14. Think-Big management is quite concerned about the risk profile for the proposal. Two statistics are causing particular concern. One is that there is nearly a 20 percent chance of losing money (a negative NPV). Second, there is a 10 percent chance of losing at least a full third ($6 million) as much as the mean gain ($18 million). Therefore, management is wondering whether it would be more prudent to go ahead with just one of the two projects. Thus, in addition to option 1 (the proposal), option 2 is to take 16.5 shares of the hotel project only (so no shares of the shopping center project) and option 3 is to take 13.1 shares of the shopping center option only (so no shares of the hotel project). Management wants to choose one of the three options. Risk profiles now are needed to evaluate the latter two.

A **(a)** Generate risk analysis outputs similar to those in Fig. 22.14 for option 2 after performing a simulation with 1,000 iterations for this option.

A **(b)** Repeat part (a) for option 3.

(c) Suppose *you* were the CEO of the Think-Big Development Co. Use the results in Fig. 22.14 for option 1 along with the corresponding results obtained for the other two options as the basis for a managerial decision on which of the three options to choose. Justify your answer.

A **22.6-6.** Reconsider Prob. 22.4-8 involving the game of craps. Now the objective is to estimate the probability of winning a play of this game. If the probability is greater than 0.5, you will want to go to Las Vegas to play the game numerous times until you eventually win a considerable amount of money. However, if the probability is less than 0.5, you will stay home.

You have decided to perform simulation on a spreadsheet to estimate this probability. Perform the number of iterations (plays of the game) indicated below *twice.*
(a) 100 iterations.
(b) 1,000 iterations.
(c) 10,000 iterations.
(d) The true probability is 0.493. What conclusion do you draw from the above simulation runs about the number of iterations that appears to be needed to give reasonable assurance of obtaining an estimate that is within 0.007 of the true probability?

R **22.7-1.*** Consider the probability distribution whose probability density function is

$$f(x) = \begin{cases} \dfrac{1}{x^2} & \text{if } x \geq 1 \\ 0 & \text{otherwise.} \end{cases}$$

The problem is to perform a simulated experiment, with the help of variance-reducing techniques, for estimating the mean of this distribution. To provide a standard of comparison, also derive the mean analytically.

For each of the following cases, use the same 10 uniform random numbers (obtained as instructed at the beginning of the Problems section) to generate random observations, and calculate the resulting estimate of the mean.
(a) Use the crude Monte Carlo technique.
(b) Use stratified sampling with three strata—$0 \leq F(x) \leq 0.6$, $0.6 < F(x) \leq 0.9$, and $0.9 < F(x) \leq 1$—with 3, 3, and 4 observations, respectively.
(c) Use the method of complementary random numbers.

22.7-2. Simulation is being used to study a system whose measure of performance X will be partially determined by the outcome of a certain external factor. This factor has three possible outcomes (unfavorable, neutral, and favorable) that will occur with equal probability ($\frac{1}{3}$). Because the favorable outcome would greatly increase the spread of possible values of X, this outcome is more critical than the others for estimating the mean and variance of X. Therefore, a stratified sampling approach has been adopted, with six random observations of the value of X generated under the favorable outcome, three generated under the neutral outcome, and one generated under the unfavorable outcome, as follows:

Outcome of External Factor	Simulated Values of X
Favorable	8, 5, 1, 6, 3, 7
Neutral	3, 5, 2
Unfavorable	2

(a) Develop the resulting estimate of $E(X)$.

(b) Develop the resulting estimate of $E(X^2)$.

R **22.7-3.** A random variable X has $P\{X = 0\} = 0.9$. Given $X \neq 0$, it has a uniform distribution between 5 and 15. Thus, $E(X) = 1$. Obtaining uniform random numbers as instructed at the beginning of the Problems section, use simulation to estimate $E(X)$.

(a) Estimate $E(X)$ by generating five random observations from the distribution of X and then calculating the sample average. (This is the crude Monte Carlo technique.)

(b) Estimate $E(X)$ by using stratified sampling with two strata— $0 \leq F(x) \leq 0.9$ and $0.9 < F(x) \leq 1$—with 1 and 4 observations, respectively.

22.7-4.* Reconsider Eddie's Bicycle Shop described in Prob. 22.4-7. Forty percent of the bicycles require only a minor repair. The repair time for these bicycles has a uniform distribution between 0 and 1 hour. Sixty percent of the bicycles require a major repair. The repair time for these bicycles has a uniform distribution between 1 hour and 2 hours. You now need to estimate the mean of the overall probability distribution of the repair times for all bicycles by using the following alternative methods.

(a) Use the uniform random numbers—0.7256, 0.0817, and 0.4392—to simulate whether each of three bicycles requires minor repair or major repair. Then use the uniform random numbers—0.2243, 0.9503, and 0.6104—to simulate the repair times of these bicycles. Calculate the average of these repair times to estimate the mean of the overall distribution of repair times.

(b) Draw the cumulative distribution function (CDF) for the overall probability distribution of the repair times for all bicycles.

(c) Use the inverse transformation method with the latter three uniform random numbers given in part (a) to generate three random observations from the overall distribution considered in part (b). Calculate the average of these observations to estimate the mean of this distribution.

(d) Repeat part (c) with the *complements* of the uniform random numbers used there, so the new uniform random numbers are 0.7757, 0.0497, and 0.3896.

(e) Use the method of complementary random numbers to estimate the mean of the overall distribution of repair times by combining the random observations from parts (c) and (d).

(f) The true mean of the overall probability distribution of repair times is 1.1. Compare the estimates of this mean obtained in parts (a), (c), (d), and (e). For the method that provides the closest estimate, give an intuitive explanation for why it performed so well.

E **(g)** Formulate a spreadsheet model to apply the method of complementary random numbers. Use 300 uniform random numbers to generate 600 random observations from the distribution considered in part (b) and calculate the average of

these random observations. Compare this average with the true mean of the distribution.

(h) The drawbacks of the approach described in part (a) are that (1) it does not ensure that the repair times for both minor repairs and major repairs are adequately sampled and (2) it requires two uniform random numbers to generate each random observation of a repair time. To overcome these drawbacks, combine stratified sampling and the method of complementary random numbers by using the first three uniform random numbers given in part (a) to generate six random *minor repair* times and the other three uniform random numbers to generate six random *major repair* times. Calculate the resulting estimate of the mean of the overall distribution of repair times.

22.7-5. The employees of General Manufacturing Corp. receive health insurance through a group plan issued by Wellnet. During the past year, 40 percent of the employees did not file any health insurance claims, 40 percent filed only a small claim, and 20 percent filed a large claim. The small claims were spread uniformly between 0 and $2,000, whereas the large claims were spread uniformly between $2,000 and $20,000.

Based on this experience, Wellnet now is negotiating the corporation's premium payment per employee for the upcoming year. You are an OR analyst for the insurance carrier, and you have been assigned the task of estimating the average cost of insurance coverage for the corporation's employees.

Follow the instructions of Prob. 22.7-4, where the size of an employee's health insurance claim (including 0 if no claim was filed) now plays the role that the repair time for a bicycle did in Prob. 22.7-4. [For part (f), the true mean of the overall probability distribution of the size of an employee's health insurance claim is $2,600.]

22.7-6. Consider the probability distribution whose probability density function is

$$f(x) = \begin{cases} 1 - |x| & \text{if } -1 \leq x \leq 1 \\ 0 & \text{otherwise.} \end{cases}$$

Use the method of complementary random numbers with two uniform random numbers, 0.096 and 0.569, to estimate the mean of this distribution.

22.7-7. Consider the probability distribution whose probability density function is

$$f(x) = \begin{cases} \dfrac{3}{2}x^2 & \text{if } -1 \leq x \leq 1 \\ 0 & \text{otherwise.} \end{cases}$$

Use the method of complementary random numbers with two uniform random numbers, 0.096 and 0.569, to estimate the mean of this distribution.

22.7-8. The probability distribution of the number of heads in 3 flips of a fair coin is the binomial distribution with $n = 3$ and $p = \frac{1}{2}$, so that

$$P\{X = k\} = \binom{3}{k}\left(\frac{1}{2}\right)^k\left(\frac{1}{2}\right)^{3-k} = \frac{3!}{k!(3-k)!}\left(\frac{1}{2}\right)^3$$

$$\text{for } k = 0, 1, 2, 3.$$

The mean is 1.5.

R **(a)** Obtaining uniform random numbers as instructed at the beginning of the Problems section, use the inverse transformation method to generate three random observations from this distribution, and then calculate the sample average to estimate the mean.

(b) Use the method of complementary random numbers [with the same uniform random numbers as in part (a)] to estimate the mean.

R **(c)** Obtaining uniform random numbers as instructed at the beginning of the Problems section, simulate repeatedly flipping a coin in order to generate three random observations from this distribution, and then calculate the sample average to estimate the mean.

(d) Repeat part (c) with the method of complementary random numbers [with the same uniform random numbers as in part (c)] to estimate the mean.

R **22.7-9.** Reconsider Prob. 22.6-4. Suppose now that more careful statistical analysis has provided new estimates of the probability distributions of the radii of the shafts and bushings. In actuality, the probability distribution of the radius of a shaft (in inches) has the probability density function

$$f_s(x) = \begin{cases} 400e^{-400(x-1.0000)} & \text{if } x \geq 1.0000 \\ 0 & \text{otherwise.} \end{cases}$$

Similarly, the probability distribution of the radius of a bushing (in inches) has the probability density function

$$f_B(x) = \begin{cases} 100 & \text{if } 1.0000 \leq x \leq 1.0100 \\ 0 & \text{otherwise.} \end{cases}$$

Obtaining uniform random numbers as instructed at the beginning of the Problems section, perform a simulated experiment for estimating the probability of interference. Notice that almost all cases of interference will occur when the radius of the bushing is much closer to 1.0000 inch than to 1.0100 inches. Therefore, it appears that an efficient experiment would generate most of the simulated bushings from this critical portion of the distribution. Take this observation into account in part (b). For each of the following cases, use the same 10 pairs of uniform random numbers to generate random observations, and calculate the resulting estimate of the probability of interference.

(a) Use the crude Monte Carlo technique.

(b) Develop and apply a stratified sampling approach to this problem.

(c) Use the method of complementary random numbers.

22.8-1.* A certain single-server system has been simulated, with the following sequence of waiting times before service for the respective customers. Use the regenerative method to obtain a point estimate and 90 percent confidence interval for the steady-state expected waiting time before service.

(a) 0, 5, 4, 0, 2, 0, 3, 1, 6, 0
(b) 0, 3, 2, 0, 3, 1, 5, 0, 0, 2, 4, 0, 3, 5, 2, 0

22.8-2. Consider the queueing system example presented in Sec. 22.8 for the regenerative method. Explain why the point where a *service completion* occurs with *no* other customers left is *not* a regeneration point.

22.8-3. Reconsider Prob. 22.6-3. You now wish to begin the analysis by performing a short simulation by hand and then applying the regenerative method of statistical analysis when possible.

R **(a)** Starting with four new tubes, simulate the operation of the two alternative policies for 5,000 hours of simulated time. Obtain the needed uniform random numbers as instructed at the beginning of the Problems section.

(b) Use the data from part (a) to make a preliminary comparison of the two alternatives on a cost basis.

(c) For the *proposed* policy, describe an appropriate regeneration point for defining cycles that will permit applying the regenerative method of statistical analysis. Explain why the regenerative method cannot be applied to the *current* policy.

(d) For the proposed policy, use the regenerative method to obtain a point estimate and 95 percent confidence interval for the steady-state expected cost per hour from the data obtained in part (a).

(e) Write a computer simulation program for the two alternative policies. Then repeat parts (a), (b), and (d) on the computer, with 100 cycles for the proposed policy and 55,000 hours of simulated time (including a warm-up period of 5,000 hours) for the current policy.

22.8-4. One of the main lessons of queueing theory (Chaps. 17 and 18) is that the amount of variability in the service times and interarrival times has a substantial impact on the measures of performance of the queueing system. Significantly decreasing variability helps considerably.

This phenomenon is well illustrated by the $M/G/1$ queueing model presented at the beginning of Sec. 17.7. For this model, the four fundamental measures of performance (L, L_q, W, and W_q) are expressed directly in terms of the *variance* of service times (σ^2), so we can see immediately what the impact of decreasing σ^2 would be.

Consider an $M/G/1$ queueing system with mean arrival rate $\lambda = 0.8$ and mean service rate $\mu = 1$, so the utilization factor is $\rho = \lambda/\mu = 0.8$.

Q **(a)** Use the Queueing Simulator to execute a simulation run with 10,000 customer arrivals for each of the following cases: (i) $\sigma = 1$ (corresponds to an exponential distribution of service times), (ii) $\sigma = 0.5$ (corresponds to an Erlang distribution of service times with shape parameter $k = 4$), and (iii) $\sigma = 0$ (constant service times). Using the point estimates of L_q obtained, calculate the ratio of L_q for case (ii) to L_q for case (i). Also calculate the ratio of L_q for case (iii) to L_q for case (i).

(b) For each of the three cases considered in part (a), use the formulas given in Sec. 15.7 to compute the exact values of L, L_q, W, and W_q. Compare these exact values to the point estimates and 95 percent confidence intervals obtained in part (a). Identify any exact values that fall outside the 95 percent confidence interval. Also calculate the exact values of the ratios requested in part (a).

Q **22.8-5.** Follow the instructions of part (a) of Prob. 22.8-4 for an $M/G/2$ queueing system (two servers), with $\lambda = 1.6$ and $\mu = 1$ [so $\rho = \lambda/(2\mu) = 0.8$] and with σ^2 still being the variance of service times.

22.8-6. Reconsider Prob. 22.8-4. For the single-server queueing system under consideration, suppose now that service times definitely have an exponential distribution. However, it now is possible to reduce the variability of *interarrival times,* so we want to explore the impact of doing so.

Assume now that $\lambda = 1$ and $\mu = 1.25$, so $\rho = 0.8$. Let σ^2 now denote the variance of interarrival times.

Follow the instructions of Prob. 22.8-4a, where the distributions for the three cases now are for interarrival times instead of service times.

CASE 22.1 PLANNING PLANERS

This was the first time that Carl Schilling had been summoned to meet with the bigwigs in the fancy executive offices upstairs. And he hopes it will be the last time. Carl doesn't like the pressure. He has had enough pressure just dealing with all the problems he has been encountering as the foreman of the planer department on the factory floor. What a nightmare this last month has been!

Fortunately, the meeting had gone better than Carl had feared. The bigwigs actually had been quite nice. They explained that they needed to get Carl's advice on how to deal with a problem that was affecting the entire factory. The origin of the problem is that the planer department has had a difficult time keeping up with its workload. Frequently there are a number of workpieces waiting for a free planer. This waiting has seriously disrupted the production schedule for subsequent operations, thereby greatly increasing the cost of in-process inventory as well as the cost of idle equipment and resulting lost production. They understood that this problem was not Carl's fault. However, they needed to get his ideas on what changes were needed in the planer department to relieve this bottleneck. Imagine that! All these bigwigs with graduate degrees from the fanciest business schools in the country asking advice from a poor working slob like him who had barely made it through high school. He could hardly wait to tell his wife that night.

The meeting had given Carl an opportunity to get two pet peeves off his chest. One peeve is that he has been telling his boss for months that he really needs another planer, but nothing ever gets done about this. His boss just keeps telling him that the planers he already has aren't being used 100 percent of the time, so how can adding even more capacity be justified. Doesn't his boss understand about the big backlogs that build up during busy times?

Then there is the other peeve—all those peaks and valleys of work coming to his department. At times, the work just pours in and a big backlog builds up. Then there might be a long pause when not much comes in so the planers stand idle part of the time.

If only those departments that are feeding castings to his department could get their act together and even out the work flow, many of his backlog problems would disappear.

Carl was pleased that the bigwigs were nodding their heads in seeming agreement as he described these problems. They really appeared to understand. And they seemed very sincere in thanking him for his good advice. Maybe something is actually going to get done this time.

Here are the details of the situation that Carl and his "bigwigs" are addressing. The company has two planers for cutting flat smooth surfaces in large castings. The planers currently are being used for two purposes. One is to form the top surface of the *platen* for large hydraulic lifts. The other is to form the mating surface of the final drive *housing* for a large piece of earth-moving equipment. The time required to perform each type of job varies somewhat, depending largely upon the number of passes that must be made. In particular, for each platen, the time required by a planer has an Erlang distribution with a mean of 25 minutes and shape parameter $k = 4$. For each housing, the time required has a translated exponential distribution, where the minimum time is 10 minutes and the additional time beyond 10 minutes has an exponential distribution with a mean of 10 minutes. (Recall that a distribution of this type is one of the options in the Queueing Simulator in this chapter's Excel file.)

Castings of both types arrive one at a time to the planer department. For the castings for forming platens, the arrivals occur randomly with a mean rate of 2 per hour. For the castings for forming housings, the interarrival times have a uniform distribution over the interval from 20 to 40 minutes.

Based on Carl Schilling's advice, management has asked an OR analyst (you) to analyze the following three proposals for relieving the bottleneck in the planer department:

Proposal 1: Obtain one additional planer. The total incremental cost (including capital recovery cost) is estimated to be $30 per hour. (This estimate takes into account the fact that, even with an additional planer, the total running time for all the planers will remain the same.)

Proposal 2: Eliminate the variability in the interarrival times of the platen castings, so that the castings would arrive regularly, one every 30 minutes. This would require making some changes in the preceding production processes, with an incremental cost of $40 per hour.

Proposal 3: This is the same as proposal 2, but now for the housing castings. The incremental cost in this case would be $20 per hour.

These proposals are not mutually exclusive, so any combination can be adopted.

It is estimated that the total cost associated with castings having to wait to be processed (including processing time) is $200 per hour for each platen casting and $100 per hour for each housing casting, provided the waits are not excessive. To avoid excessive waits for either kind of casting, all the castings are processed as soon as possible on a first-come, first-served basis.

Management's objective is to minimize the expected total cost per hour.

Use simulation to evaluate and compare all the alternatives, including the status quo and the various combinations of proposals. Then make your recommendation to management.

CASE 22.2   PRICING UNDER PRESSURE

Elise Sullivan moved to New York City in September to begin her first job as an analyst working in the Client Services Division of FirstBank, a large investment bank providing brokerage services to clients across the United States. The moment she arrived in the Big Apple after graduating with an undergraduate degree in industrial engineering that included a concentration in finance, she hit the ground running—or more appropriately—working. She spent her first six weeks in training, where she met new FirstBank analysts like herself and learned the basics of FirstBank's approach to accounting, cash flow analysis, customer service, and federal regulations.

After completing training, Elise moved into her bullpen on the fortieth floor of the Manhattan FirstBank building to begin work. Her first few assignments have allowed her to learn the ropes by placing her under the direction of senior staff members who delegate specific tasks to her.

Today, she has an opportunity to distinguish herself in her career, however. Her boss, Michael Steadman, has given her an assignment that is under her complete direction and control. A very eccentric, wealthy client and avid investor by the name of Emery Bowlander is interested in purchasing a European call option that provides him with the right to purchase shares of Fellare stock for $44.00 on the first of February— 12 weeks from today. Fellare is an aerospace manufacturing company operating in France, and Mr. Bowlander has a strong feeling that the European Space Agency will award Fellare with a contract to build a portion of the International Space Station some time in January. In the event that the European Space Agency awards the contract to Fellare, Mr. Bowlander believes the stock will skyrocket, reflecting investor confidence in the capabilities and growth of the company. If Fellare does not win the contract, however, Mr. Bowlander believes the stock will continue its current slow downward trend. To guard against this latter outcome, Mr. Bowlander does not want to make an outright purchase of Fellare stock now.

Michael has asked Elise to price the option. He expects a figure before the stock market closes so that if Mr. Bowlander decides to purchase the option, the transaction can take place today.

Unfortunately, the investment science course Elise took to complete her undergraduate degree did not cover options theory; it only covered valuation, risk, capital budgeting, and market efficiency. She remembers from her valuation studies that she should discount the value of the option on February 1 by the appropriate interest rate to obtain the value of the option today. Because she is discounting over a 12-week period, the formula she should use to discount the option is [(Value of the option)/(1 + Weekly interest rate)^{12}]. As a starting point for her calculations, she decides to use an annual interest rate of 8 percent. But she now needs to decide how to calculate the value of the option on February 1.

(a) Elise knows that on February 1, Mr. Bowlander will take one of two actions: either he will exercise the option to purchase shares of Fellare stock or he will not exercise the option. Mr. Bowlander will exercise the option if the price of Fellare stock on February 1 is above his exercise price of $44.00. In this case, he purchases Fellare stock for $44.00 and then immediately sells it for the market price on February 1. Under this scenario, the value of the option would be the difference between the stock price and the exercise price. Mr. Bowlander will not exercise the option if the price of Fellare stock is below his exercise price of $44.00. In this case, he does nothing, and the value of the option would be $0.

The value of the option is therefore determined by the value of Fellare stock on February 1. Elise knows that the value of the stock on February 1 is uncertain and is therefore represented by a probability distribution of values. Elise recalls from an operations research course in college that she can use simulation to estimate the mean of this distribution of stock values. Before she builds the simulation model, however, she needs to know the price movement of the stock. Elise recalls from a probability and statistics course that the price of a stock can be modeled as following a random walk and either growing or decaying according to a lognormal distribution. Therefore, according to this model, the stock price at the end of the next week is the stock price at the end of the current week multiplied by a growth factor. This growth factor is expressed as the number e raised to a power that is equal to a normally distributed random variable. In other words:

$$s_n = e^N s_c,$$

where s_n = the stock price at the end of next week,

$\qquad s_c$ = the stock price at the end of the current week,

$\qquad N$ = a random variable that has a normal distribution.

To begin her analysis, Elise looks in the newspaper to find that the Fellare stock price for the current week is $42.00. She decides to use this price to begin her 12-week analysis. Thus, the price of the stock at the end of the first week is this current price multiplied by the growth factor. She next estimates the mean and standard deviation of the normally distributed random variable used in the calculation of the growth factor. This random variable determines the degree of change (volatility) of the stock, so Elise decides to use the current annual interest rate and the historical annual volatility of the stock as a basis for estimating the mean and standard deviation.

The current annual interest rate is $r = 8$ percent, and the historical annual volatility of the aerospace stock is 30 percent. But Elise remembers that she is calculating the *weekly* change in stock—*not* the *annual* change. She therefore needs to calculate the weekly interest rate and weekly historical stock volatility to obtain estimates for the mean and standard deviation of the weekly growth factor. To obtain the weekly interest rate w, Elise must make the following calculation:

$$w = (1 + r)^{(1/52)} - 1.$$

The historical weekly stock volatility equals the historical annual volatility divided by the square root of 52. She calculates the mean of the normally distributed random variable by subtracting one half of the square of the weekly stock volatility from the weekly interest rate w. In other words:

Mean $= w - 0.5(\text{weekly stock volatility})^2$.

The standard deviation of the normally distributed random variable is simply equal to the weekly stock volatility.

Elise is now ready to build her simulation model.

(1) Describe the components of the system, including how they are assumed to interrelate.

(2) Define the state of the system.

(3) Describe a method for randomly generating the simulated events that occur over time.

(4) Describe a method for changing the state of the system when an event occurs.

(5) Define a procedure for advancing the time on the simulation clock.

(6) Build the simulation model to calculate the value of the option in today's dollars.

(b) Run three separate simulations to estimate the value of the call option and hence the price of the option in today's dollars. For the first simulation, run 100 iterations of the simulation. For the second simulation, run 500 iterations of the simulation. For the third simulation, run 1,000 iterations of the simulation. For each simulation, record the price of the option in to-day's dollars.

(c) Elise takes her calculations and recommended price to Michael. He is very impressed, but he chuckles and indicates that a simple, closed-form approach exists for calculating the value of an option: the Black-Scholes formula. Michael grabs an investment science book from the shelf above his desk and reveals the very powerful and very complicated Black-Scholes formula:

$$V = N[d_1]P - N[d_2]PV[K]$$

where $d_1 = \dfrac{\ln[P/PV[K]]}{\sigma\sqrt{t}} + \dfrac{\sigma\sqrt{t}}{2}$,

$d_2 = d_1 - \sigma\sqrt{t}$,

$N[x]$ = the Excel function NORMSDIST(x) where $x = d_1$ or $x = d_2$,

P = current price of the stock,

K = exercise price,

$PV[K]$ = present value of exercise price = $\dfrac{K}{(1 + w)^t}$,

t = number of weeks to exercise date,

σ = weekly volatility of stock.

Use the Black-Scholes formula to calculate the value of the call option and hence the price of the option. Compare this value to the value obtained in part (b).

(d) In the specific case of Fellare stock, do you think that a random walk as described above completely describes the price movement of the stock? Why or why not?

APPENDIX 1

DOCUMENTATION FOR THE OR COURSEWARE

You will find a wealth of software resources on the CD-ROM packaged in the back of the book. The entire software package is called *OR Courseware*.

The installation instructions and system requirements are specified on the front of the CD-ROM. Although the CD-ROM is designed for use on a Windows-based IBM-compatible PC, much of the software also can be run on a Macintosh (as specified later for the individual cases).

To get started, and to see an overview of the available software resources, refer to the introductory screens on the CD-ROM. The individual software packages also are discussed briefly below.

OR TUTOR

OR Tutor is a Web document consisting of a set of HTML pages that often contain JavaScript. Any browser that supports JavaScript can be used, including Netscape Navigator 4.0 (or higher) or Internet Explorer 4.5 (or higher). It can be viewed with either an IBM-compatible PC or a Macintosh.

This resource has been designed to be your personal tutor by illustrating and illuminating key concepts in an interactive manner. It contains 16 *demonstration examples* that supplement the examples in the book in ways that cannot be duplicated on the printed page. Each one vividly demonstrates one of the algorithms or concepts of OR in action. Most combine an *algebraic description* of each step with a *geometric display* of what is happening. Some of these geometric displays become quite dynamic, with moving points or moving lines, to demonstrate the evolution of the algorithm. The demonstration examples also are integrated with

the book, using the same notation and terminology, with references to material in the book, etc. Students find them an enjoyable and effective learning aid.

INTERACTIVE ROUTINES

Another key tutorial feature of the OR Courseware is a set of interactive routines implemented in Excel spreadsheets and/or Visual Basic. These routines can be viewed with recent versions of Microsoft Excel such as Excel 97, 98 (for Macintosh), or 2000. Each one is a self-contained routine that uses prompts or help files to provide the necessary information for execution. Either Excel spreadsheets or graphic interfaces are supplied to allow easy entry of problem data.

Each of these routines enables you to *interactively execute* one of the algorithms of OR. While viewing all relevant information on the computer screen, you make the decision on how the next step of the algorithm should be performed, and then the computer does all the necessary number crunching to execute that step. When a previous mistake is discovered, the routine allows you to quickly backtrack to correct the mistake. To get you started properly, the computer points out any mistake made on the first iteration (where possible). When done, you can print out all the work performed to turn in for homework.

In our judgment, these interactive routines provide the "right" way in this computer age for students to do homework designed to help them learn the algorithms of OR. The routines enable you to focus on concepts rather than mindless number crunching, thereby making the learning process far more efficient and effective as well as stimulating. They also point you in the right direction, including organizing the work to be done. However, the routines do not do the thinking for you. As in any good homework assignment, you are allowed to make mistakes (and to learn from those mistakes), so that hard thinking will need to be done to try to stay on the right path. We have been careful in designing the division of labor between the computer and the student to provide an efficient, complete learning process.

SPECIAL AUTOMATIC ROUTINES

Once you have learned the logic of a particular algorithm with the help of an interactive routine, you will want to be able to apply the algorithm quickly with an automatic routine thereafter. Such a routine is provided by one or more of the software packages discussed below for most of the algorithms described in this book. However, for a few algorithms that are not included in these commercial packages, we have provided special automatic routines in the OR Courseware. Like the interactive routines, these automatic routines are implemented in Excel spreadsheets and/or Visual Basic for viewing with a recent version of Excel.

EXCEL FILES

The OR Courseware includes a separate Excel file for nearly every chapter in this book. Each file typically includes several spreadsheets that will help you formulate and solve the various kinds of models described in the chapter. Two types of spreadsheets are included. First, each time an example is presented that can be solved using Excel, the complete spreadsheet formulation and solution is given in that chapter's Excel file. This provides a convenient reference, or even useful templates, when you set up spreadsheets to solve similar problems with the Excel Solver (or the Premium Solver discussed in the next subsection). Second, for many of the models in the book, template files are provided that already include all the equations necessary to solve the model. You simply enter the data for the model and the solution is immediately calculated.

EXCEL ADD-INS

Four Excel add-ins are included in OR Courseware. One is *Premium Solver* for Education (Version 3.5), which is a more powerful version of the standard Solver in Excel. It works with Excel 5, 95, 97, and 2000 on Windows systems (but not

with Excel 98 for Macintosh). Premium Solver offers four times the capacity (800 decision variables) of the standard Solver for linear programming problems, and twice the capacity (400 decision variables) for nonlinear programming problems, plus solution speeds 3 to 10 times faster than the standard Solver. A product of the same organization that developed the standard Solver in Excel (Frontline Systems Inc.), Premium Solver is fully upward compatible with the standard Solver. The organization's website is www.frontsys.com. Technical support currently is provided at (775) 831-0300 or by e-mail at ‹info@frontsys.com›.

The other three Excel add-ins are academic versions of *SensIt* (introduced in Sec. 15.2), *TreePlan* (introduced in Sec. 15.4), and *RiskSim* (introduced in Sec. 22.6). All are shareware developed by Professor Michael R. Middleton for Excel 5, 95, 97, 98, and 2000 for Windows and Macintosh. Documentation is included on the CD-ROM for all three add-ins. The accompanying website is www.usfca.edu/fac-staff/middleton. This software is shareware, so those desiring to use it after the course should register and pay the shareware fee.

As with any Excel add-in, each of these add-ins needs to be installed in Excel before it is operational. (The same is true for the standard Excel Solver.) Installation instructions are included in the OR Courseware for each one.

Another Excel add-in discussed extensively in Sec. 22.6 is *@RISK* for simulation, from Palisade Corporation. Although Palisade declined to make this add-in available on our CD-ROM, it can be downloaded from the website, www.palisade.com, for a 10-day trial period.

MPL/CPLEX

As discussed at length in Secs. 3.7 and 4.8, MPL is a state-of-the-art modeling language and its prime solver CPLEX is a particularly prominent and powerful solver. The student version of MPL and CPLEX is included in the OR Courseware. Although this student version is limited to *much* smaller problems than the massive linear, integer, and quadratic programming problems commonly solved in practice by the full version, it still can handle up to 300 functional constraints and 300 decision variables (including any integer variables). The system requirements for the student version are an IBM-compatible PC with a 486 or Pentium processor, 16 Mb of memory, 4 Mb of free hard-disk space, and Microsoft Windows 95/98, NT (3.51 or higher), or 2000.

The CD-ROM provides an extensive MPL tutorial and documentation, as well as MPL/CPLEX formulations and solutions for virtually every example in the book to which they can be applied. Also included in the OR Courseware is the student version of OptiMax 2000, which enables fully integrating MPL models into Excel and solving with CPLEX. In addition, the powerful nonlinear programming solver CONOPT is included in MPL for solving such problems.

The website for further exploring MPL and its solvers, or for downloading updated student versions of MPL/CPLEX is, www.maximal-usa.com.

LINGO/LINDO FILES

This book also features the popular modeling language LINGO (see especially Appendix 3.1 and the end of Sec. 3.7) and the companion solver LINDO (see Sec. 4.8 and Appendix 4.1). Although they were not available for inclusion in the OR Courseware, student versions of both LINGO and LINDO (as well as the companion spreadsheet solver *What's Best*) can be downloaded from the website, www.lindo.com. Designed for use on a Windows platform, each of these downloads currently can handle up to 150 functional constraints and 300 decision variables. In the case of integer programming or nonlinear programming, they are restricted to 30 integer variables or 30 nonlinear variables. (Extended versions of this software can solve vastly larger problems.)

The OR Courseware includes extensive LINGO/LINDO files or (when LINDO is not relevant) LINGO files for many of the chapters. Each file provides the LINGO and LINDO models and solutions for the various examples in the chapter to which they can be applied. The solutions often are displayed in a What's Best spreadsheet. The CD-ROM also provides LINGO and LINDO tutorials.

MICROSOFT PROJECT

Chapter 10 (especially Sec. 10.2) describes how Microsoft Project can be used to help construct and evaluate a project network while using PERT/CPM. The version included in the OR Courseware is Microsoft Project 98, which is designed for use on a Windows platform. (Microsoft also markets an earlier version, Project 4, for Macintosh). The CD-ROM includes a document READTH~1.HTM in the Project folder with various links that provide extensive documentation of the software. The OR Courseware also includes an MS Project folder that has the main kinds of worksheets that Microsoft Project would generate for the prototype example of Chapter 10.

UPDATES

The software world evolves very rapidly during the lifetime of one edition of a textbook. We believe that the documentation provided in this appendix is accurate at the time of this writing, but changes inevitably will occur as time passes.

With each new printing of this edition, we plan to provide updated versions of the software in the OR Courseware whenever feasible. You can also visit the book's website, www.mhhe.com/hillier, for information about software updates.

APPENDIX 2

CONVEXITY

As introduced in Chap. 13, the concept of *convexity* is frequently used in OR work, especially in the area of nonlinear programming. Therefore, we further introduce the properties of convex or concave functions and convex sets here.

CONVEX OR CONCAVE FUNCTIONS OF A SINGLE VARIABLE

We begin with definitions.

> **Definitions:** A *function* of a single variable $f(x)$ is a **convex function** if, for *each* pair of values of x, say, x' and x'' ($x' < x''$),
>
> $$f[\lambda x'' + (1 - \lambda)x'] \leq \lambda f(x'') + (1 - \lambda) f(x')$$
>
> for all values of λ such that $0 < \lambda < 1$. It is a **strictly convex function** if $\leq$ can be replaced by $<$. It is a **concave function** (or a **strictly concave function**) if this statement holds when $\leq$ is replaced by $\geq$ (or by $>$).

This definition of a convex function has an enlightening geometric interpretation. Consider the graph of the function $f(x)$ drawn as a function of x, as illustrated in Fig. A2.1 for a function $f(x)$ that decreases for $x < 1$, is constant for $1 \leq x \leq 2$, and increases for $x > 2$. Then $[x', f(x')]$ and $[x'', f(x'')]$ are two points on the graph of $f(x)$, and $[\lambda x'' + (1 - \lambda)x', \lambda f(x'') + (1 - \lambda) f(x')]$ represents the various points on the line segment between these two points (but excluding these endpoints) when $0 < \lambda < 1$. Thus, the $\leq$ inequality in the definition indicates that this line segment lies entirely above or on the graph of the function, as in Fig. A2.1. Therefore, $f(x)$ is *convex* if, for *each* pair of points on the graph of $f(x)$, the line segment joining these two points lies entirely above or on the graph of $f(x)$.

For example, the particular choice of x' and x'' shown in Fig. A2.1 results in the entire line segment (except the two endpoints) lying *above* the graph of $f(x)$. This also occurs for other choices of x' and x'' where either $x' < 1$ or $x'' > 2$ (or both). If $1 \leq x' < x'' \leq 2$, then the entire line segment lies *on* the graph of $f(x)$. Therefore, this $f(x)$ is convex.

This geometric interpretation indicates that $f(x)$ is convex if it only "bends upward" whenever it bends at all. (This condition is sometimes referred to as *concave upward,* as opposed to *concave downward* for a concave function.) To be more precise, if $f(x)$ possesses a second derivative everywhere, then $f(x)$ is convex if and only if $d^2f(x)/dx^2 \geq 0$ for all possible values of x.

The definitions of a *strictly convex function,* a *concave function,* and a *strictly concave function* also have analogous geometric interpretations. These interpretations are summarized below in terms of the second derivative of the function, which provides a convenient test of the status of the function.

> **Convexity test for a function of a single variable:** Consider any function of a single variable $f(x)$ that possesses a second derivative at all possible values of x. Then $f(x)$ is
>
> 1. *Convex* if and only if $\dfrac{d^2f(x)}{dx^2} \geq 0$ for all possible values of x
>
> 2. *Strictly convex* if and only if $\dfrac{d^2f(x)}{dx^2} > 0$ for all possible values of x

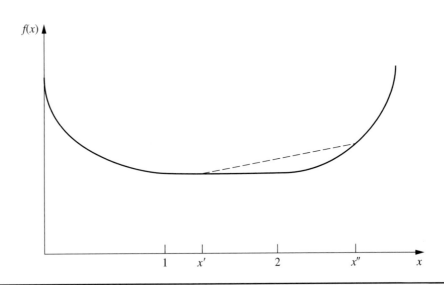

FIGURE A2.1
A convex function.

3. *Concave* if and only if $\dfrac{d^2f(x)}{dx^2} \leq 0$ for all possible values of x

4. *Strictly concave* if and only if $\dfrac{d^2f(x)}{dx^2} < 0$ for all possible values of x

Note that a strictly convex function also is convex, but a convex function is *not* strictly convex if the second derivative equals zero for some values of x. Similarly, a strictly concave function is concave, but the reverse need not be true.

Figures A2.1 to A2.6 show examples that illustrate these definitions and this convexity test.

Applying this test to the function in Fig. A2.1, we see that as x is increased, the slope (first derivative) either increases (for $0 \leq x < 1$ and $x > 2$) or remains constant (for $1 \leq x_1 \leq 2$). Therefore, the second derivative always is nonnegative, which verifies that the function is convex. However, it is *not* strictly convex because the second derivative equals zero for $1 \leq x \leq 2$.

However, the function in Fig. A2.2 is strictly convex because its slope always is increasing so its second derivative always is greater than zero.

The piecewise linear function shown in Fig. A2.3 changes its slope at $x = 1$. Consequently, it does not possess a first or second derivative at this point, so the convexity test cannot be fully applied. (The fact that the second derivative equals zero for $0 \leq x < 1$ and $x > 1$ makes the function eligible to be either convex or concave, depending upon its be-

havior at $x = 1$.) Applying the definition of a concave function, we see that if $0 < x' < 1$ and $x'' > 1$ (as shown in Fig. A2.3), then the entire line segment joining $[x', f(x')]$ and $[x'', f(x'')]$ lies *below* the graph of $f(x)$, except for the two endpoints of the line segment. If either $0 \leq x' < x'' \leq 1$ or $1 \leq x' < x''$, then the entire line segment lies *on* the graph of $f(x)$. Therefore, $f(x)$ is concave (but *not* strictly concave).

The function in Fig. A2.4 is strictly concave because its second derivative always is less than zero.

As illustrated in Fig. A2.5, any linear function has its second derivative equal to zero everywhere and so is both convex and concave.

The function in Fig. A2.6 is *neither* convex nor concave because as x increases, the slope fluctuates between de-

FIGURE A2.2
A strictly convex function.

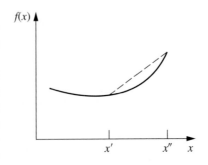

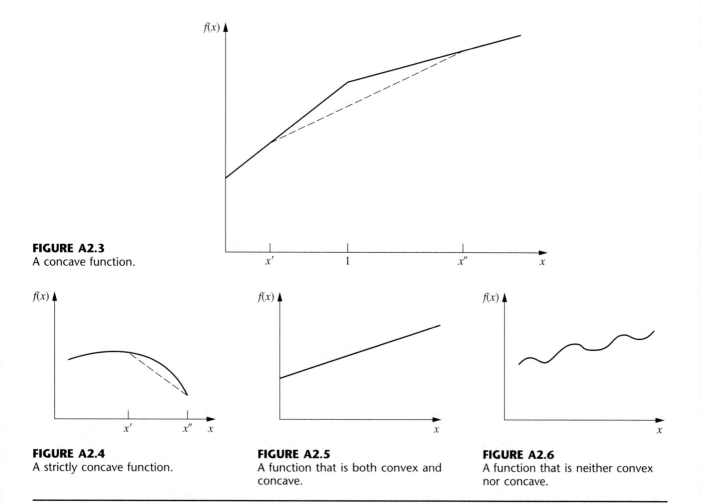

FIGURE A2.3
A concave function.

FIGURE A2.4
A strictly concave function.

FIGURE A2.5
A function that is both convex and
concave.

FIGURE A2.6
A function that is neither convex
nor concave.

creasing and increasing so the second derivative fluctuates between being negative and positive.

CONVEX OR CONCAVE FUNCTIONS OF SEVERAL VARIABLES

The concept of a convex or concave function of a single variable also generalizes to functions of more than one variable. Thus, if $f(x)$ is replaced by $f(x_1, x_2, \ldots, x_n)$, the definition still applies if x is replaced everywhere by $(x_1, x_2, \ldots, x_n)$. Similarly, the corresponding geometric interpretation is still valid after generalization of the concepts of *points* and *line segments*. Thus, just as a particular value of (x, y) is interpreted as a point in two-dimensional space, each possible value of $(x_1, x_2, \ldots, x_m)$ may be thought of as a point in

m-dimensional (Euclidean) space. By letting $m = n + 1$, the points on the graph of $f(x_1, x_2, \ldots, x_n)$ become the possible values of $[x_1, x_2, \ldots, x_n, f(x_1, x_2, \ldots, x_n)]$. Another point, $(x_1, x_2, \ldots, x_n, x_{n+1})$, is said to lie above, on, or below the graph of $f(x_1, x_2, \ldots, x_n)$, according to whether x_{n+1} is larger, equal to, or smaller than $f(x_1, x_2, \ldots, x_n)$, respectively.

Definition: The **line segment** joining any two points $(x_1', x_2', \ldots, x_m')$ and $(x_1'', x_2'', \ldots, x_m'')$ is the collection of points

$$(x_1, x_2, \ldots, x_m) = [\lambda x_1'' + (1 - \lambda)x_1', \lambda x_2'' + (1 - \lambda)x_2', \ldots, \lambda x_m'' + (1 - \lambda)x_m']$$

such that $0 \le \lambda \le 1$.

Thus, a line segment in m-dimensional space is a direct generalization of a line segment in two-dimensional space. For example, if

$$(x_1', x_2') = (2, 6), \qquad (x_1'', x_2'') = (3, 4),$$

then the line segment joining them is the collection of points

$$(x_1, x_2) = [3\lambda + 2(1 - \lambda), 4\lambda + 6(1 - \lambda)],$$

where $0 \leq \lambda \leq 1$.

Definition: $f(x_1, x_2, \ldots, x_n)$ is a **convex function** if, for each pair of points on the graph of $f(x_1, x_2, \ldots, x_n)$, the line segment joining these two points lies entirely above or on the graph of $f(x_1, x_2, \ldots, x_n)$. It is a **strictly convex function** if this line segment actually lies entirely above this graph except at the endpoints of the line segment. **Concave functions** and **strictly concave functions** are defined in exactly the same way, except that *above* is replaced by *below*.

Just as the second derivative can be used (when it exists everywhere) to check whether a function of a single variable is convex, so second partial derivatives can be used to check functions of several variables, although in a more complicated way. For example, if there are two variables and all partial derivatives exist everywhere, then the convexity test assesses whether *all three quantities* in the first column of Table A2.1 satisfy the inequalities shown in the appropriate column for *all possible values* of (x_1, x_2).

When there are more than two variables, the convexity test is a generalization of the one shown in Table A2.1. For example, in mathematical terminology, $f(x_1, x_2, \ldots, x_n)$ is

convex if and only if its $n \times n$ Hessian matrix is positive semidefinite for all possible values of $(x_1, x_2, \ldots, x_n)$.

To illustrate the convexity test for two variables, consider the function

$$f(x_1, x_2) = (x_1 - x_2)^2 = x_1^2 - 2x_1x_2 + x_2^2.$$

Therefore,

$$(1) \quad \frac{\partial^2 f(x_1, x_2)}{\partial x_1^2} \frac{\partial^2 f(x_1, x_2)}{\partial x_2^2} - \left[\frac{\partial^2 f(x_1, x_2)}{\partial x_1 \partial x_2} \right]^2 = 2(2) - (-2)^2 = 0,$$

$$(2) \quad \frac{\partial^2 f(x_1, x_2)}{\partial x_1^2} = 2 > 0,$$

$$(3) \quad \frac{\partial^2 f(x_1, x_2)}{\partial x_2^2} = 2 > 0.$$

Since ≥ 0 holds for all three conditions, $f(x_1, x_2)$ is convex. However, it is *not* strictly convex because the first condition only gives $= 0$ rather than > 0.

Now consider the negative of this function

$$g(x_1, x_2) = -f(x_1, x_2) = -(x_1 - x_2)^2 = -x_1^2 + 2x_1x_2 - x_2^2.$$

In this case,

$$(4) \quad \frac{\partial^2 g(x_1, x_2)}{\partial x_1^2} \frac{\partial^2 g(x_1, x_2)}{\partial x_2^2} - \left[\frac{\partial^2 g(x_1, x_2)}{\partial x_1 \partial x_2} \right]^2 = -2(-2) - 2^2 = 0,$$

$$(5) \quad \frac{\partial^2 g(x_1, x_2)}{\partial x_1^2} = -2 < 0,$$

$$(6) \quad \frac{\partial^2 g(x_1, x_2)}{\partial x_2^2} = -2 < 0.$$

TABLE A2.1 Convexity test for a function of two variables

Quantity	Convex	Strictly Convex	Concave	Strictly Concave
$\frac{\partial^2 f(x_1, x_2)}{\partial x_1^2} \frac{\partial^2 f(x_1, x_2)}{\partial x_2^2} - \left[\frac{\partial^2 f(x_1, x_2)}{\partial x_1 \partial x_2} \right]^2$	≥ 0	> 0	≥ 0	> 0
$\frac{\partial^2 f(x_1, x_2)}{\partial x_1^2}$	≥ 0	> 0	≤ 0	< 0
$\frac{\partial^2 f(x_1, x_2)}{\partial x_2^2}$	≥ 0	> 0	≤ 0	< 0
Values of (x_1, x_2)	All possible values			

Because ≥ 0 holds for the first condition and ≤ 0 holds for the other two, $g(x_1, x_2)$ is a concave function. However, it is *not* strictly concave since the first condition gives $= 0$.

Thus far, convexity has been treated as a general property of a function. However, many nonconvex functions do satisfy the conditions for convexity over certain intervals for the respective variables. Therefore, it is meaningful to talk about a function being convex over a certain region. For example, a function is said to be convex within a neighborhood of a specified point if its second derivative or partial derivatives satisfy the conditions for convexity at that point. This concept is useful in Appendix 3.

Finally, two particularly important properties of convex or concave functions should be mentioned. First, if $f(x_1, x_2, \ldots, x_n)$ is a convex function, then $g(x_1, x_2, \ldots, x_n) = -f(x_1, x_2, \ldots, x_n)$ is a concave function, and vice versa, as illustrated by the above example where $f(x_1, x_2) = (x_1 - x_2)^2$. Second, the sum of convex functions is a convex function, and the sum of concave functions is a concave function. To illustrate,

$$f_1(x_1) = x_1^4 + 2x_1^2 - 5x_1$$

and

$$f_2(x_1, x_2) = x_1^2 + 2x_1x_2 + x_2^2$$

are both convex functions, as you can verify by calculating their second derivatives. Therefore, the sum of these functions

$$f(x_1, x_2) = x_1^4 + 3x_1^2 - 5x_1 + 2x_1x_2 + x_2^2$$

is a convex function, whereas its negative

$$g(x_1, x_2) = -x_1^4 - 3x_1^2 + 5x_1 - 2x_1x_2 - x_2^2,$$

is a concave function.

CONVEX SETS

The concept of a convex function leads quite naturally to the related concept of a **convex set.** Thus, if $f(x_1, x_2, \ldots, x_n)$ is a convex function, then the collection of points that lie above or on the graph of $f(x_1, x_2, \ldots, x_n)$ forms a convex set. Similarly, the collection of points that lie below or on the graph of a concave function is a convex set. These cases are illustrated in Figs. A2.7 and A2.8 for the case of a single independent variable. Furthermore, convex sets have the important property that, for any given group of convex sets, the collection of points that lie in all of them (i.e., the intersection of these convex sets) is also a convex set. Therefore, the collection of points that lie both above or on a convex function and below or on a concave function is a convex set, as illustrated in Fig. A2.9. Thus, convex sets may be viewed intuitively as a collection of points whose bottom boundary is a convex function and whose top boundary is a concave function.

Although describing convex sets in terms of convex and concave functions may be helpful for developing intuition about their nature, their actual definition has nothing to do (directly) with such functions.

> **Definition:** A **convex set** is a collection of points such that, for each pair of points in the collection, the entire line segment joining these two points is also in the collection.

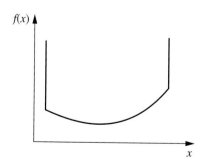

FIGURE A2.7
Example of a convex set determined by a convex function.

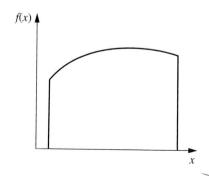

FIGURE A2.8
Example of a convex set determined by a concave function.

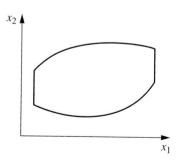

FIGURE A2.9
Example of a convex set determined by both convex and concave functions.

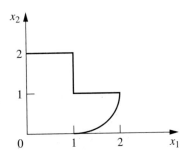

FIGURE A2.10
Example of a set that is not convex.

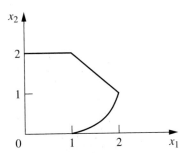

FIGURE A2.11
Example of a convex set.

The distinction between nonconvex sets and convex sets is illustrated in Figs. A2.10 and A2.11. Thus, the set of points shown in Fig. A2.10 is not a convex set because there exist many pairs of these points, for example, $(1, 2)$ and $(2, 1)$, such that the line segment between them does not lie entirely within the set. This is not the case for the set in Fig. A2.11, which is convex.

In conclusion, we introduce the useful concept of an extreme point of a convex set.

Definition: An **extreme point** of a convex set is a point in the set that does not lie on any line segment that joins two other points in the set.

Thus, the extreme points of the convex set in Fig. A2.11 are $(0, 0)$, $(0, 2)$, $(1, 2)$, $(2, 1)$, $(1, 0)$, and all the infinite number of points on the boundary between $(2, 1)$ and $(1, 0)$. If this particular boundary were a line segment instead, then the set would have only the five listed extreme points.

APPENDIX 3

CLASSICAL OPTIMIZATION METHODS

This appendix reviews the classical methods of calculus for finding a solution that maximizes or minimizes (1) a function of a single variable, (2) a function of several variables, and (3) a function of several variables subject to equality constraints on the values of these variables. It is assumed that the functions considered possess continuous first and second derivatives and partial derivatives everywhere. Some of the concepts discussed next have been introduced briefly in Secs. 13.2 and 13.3.

UNCONSTRAINED OPTIMIZATION OF A FUNCTION OF A SINGLE VARIABLE

Consider a function of a single variable, such as that shown in Fig. A3.1. A necessary condition for a particular solution $x = x^*$ to be either a minimum or a maximum is that

$$\frac{df(x)}{dx} = 0 \qquad \text{at } x = x^*.$$

Thus, in Fig. A3.1 there are five solutions satisfying these conditions. To obtain more information about these five **critical points,** it is necessary to examine the second derivative. Thus, if

$$\frac{d^2f(x)}{dx^2} > 0 \qquad \text{at } x = x^*,$$

then x^* must be at least a **local minimum** [that is, $f(x^*) \leq f(x)$ for all x sufficiently close to x^*]. Using the language in-

troduced in Appendix 2, we can say that x^* must be a local minimum if $f(x)$ is *strictly convex* within a neighborhood of x^*. Similarly, a sufficient condition for x^* to be a **local maximum** (given that it satisfies the necessary condition) is that $f(x)$ be *strictly concave* within a neighborhood of x^* (that is, the second derivative is *negative* at x^*). If the second derivative is zero, the issue is not resolved (the point may even be an *inflection point*), and it is necessary to examine higher derivatives.

To find a **global minimum** [i.e., a solution x^* such that $f(x^*) \leq f(x)$ for all x], it is necessary to compare the local minima and identify the one that yields the smallest value of $f(x)$. If this value is less than $f(x)$ as $x \rightarrow -\infty$ and as $x \rightarrow +\infty$ (or at the endpoints of the function, if it is defined only over a finite interval), then this point is a global minimum. Such a point is shown in Fig. A3.1, along with the **global maximum,** which is identified in an analogous way.

However, if $f(x)$ is known to be either a convex or a concave function (see Appendix 2 for a description of such functions), the analysis becomes much simpler. In particular, if $f(x)$ is a *convex* function, such as the one shown in Fig. A2.1, then any solution x^* such that

$$\frac{df(x)}{dx} = 0 \qquad \text{at } x = x^*$$

is known automatically to be a *global minimum*. In other words, this condition is not only a *necessary* but also a *sufficient* condition for a global minimum of a convex func-

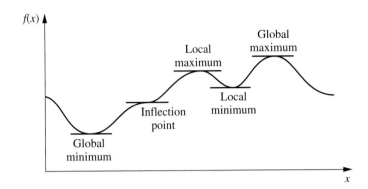

FIGURE A3.1
A function having several
maxima and minima.

tion. This solution need not be unique, since there could be a tie for the global minimum over a single interval where the derivative is zero. On the other hand, if $f(x)$ actually is *strictly convex,* then this solution must be the only global minimum. (However, if the function is either always decreasing or always increasing, so the derivative is nonzero for all values of x, then there will be no global minimum at a finite value of x.)

Similarly, if $f(x)$ is a *concave* function, then having

$$\frac{df(x)}{dx} = 0 \qquad \text{at } x = x^*$$

becomes both a *necessary* and *sufficient* condition for x^* to be a *global maximum.*

UNCONSTRAINED OPTIMIZATION OF A FUNCTION OF SEVERAL VARIABLES

The analysis for an unconstrained function of several variables $f(\mathbf{x})$, where $\mathbf{x} = (x_1, x_2, \ldots, x_n)$, is similar. Thus, a *necessary* condition for a solution $\mathbf{x} = \mathbf{x}^*$ to be either a minimum or a maximum is that

$$\frac{\partial f(\mathbf{x})}{\partial x_j} = 0 \qquad \text{at } \mathbf{x} = \mathbf{x}^*, \text{ for } j = 1, 2, \ldots, n.$$

After the critical points that satisfy this condition are identified, each such point is then classified as a local minimum or maximum if the function is *strictly convex* or *strictly concave,* respectively, within a neighborhood of the point. (Additional analysis is required if the function is neither.) The

global minimum and *maximum* would be found by comparing the local minima and maxima and then checking the value of the function as some of the variables approach $-\infty$ or $+\infty$. However, if the function is known to be *convex* or *concave,* then a critical point must be a *global minimum* or a *global maximum,* respectively.

CONSTRAINED OPTIMIZATION WITH EQUALITY CONSTRAINTS

Now consider the problem of finding the *minimum* or *maximum* of the function $f(\mathbf{x})$, subject to the restriction that $\mathbf{x}$ must satisfy all the equations

$$g_1(\mathbf{x}) = b_1$$
$$g_2(\mathbf{x}) = b_2$$
$$\vdots$$
$$g_m(\mathbf{x}) = b_m,$$

where $m < n$. For example, if $n = 2$ and $m = 1$, the problem might be

$$\text{Maximize} \qquad f(x_1, x_2) = x_1^2 + 2x_2,$$

subject to

$$g(x_1, x_2) = x_1^2 + x_2^2 = 1.$$

In this case, (x_1, x_2) is restricted to be on the circle of radius 1, whose center is at the origin, so that the goal is to find the point on this circle that yields the largest value of $f(x_1, x_2)$. This example will be solved after a general approach to the problem is outlined.

A classical method of dealing with this problem is the **method of Lagrange multipliers.** This procedure begins by formulating the **Lagrangian function**

$$h(\mathbf{x}, \boldsymbol{\lambda}) = f(\mathbf{x}) - \sum_{i=1}^{m} \lambda_i[g_i(\mathbf{x}) - b_i],$$

where the new variables $\boldsymbol{\lambda} = (\lambda_1, \lambda_2, \ldots, \lambda_m)$ are called *Lagrange multipliers.* Notice the key fact that for the *feasible* values of $\mathbf{x}$,

$$g_i(\mathbf{x}) - b_i = 0, \qquad \text{for all } i,$$

so $h(\mathbf{x}, \boldsymbol{\lambda}) = f(\mathbf{x})$. Therefore, it can be shown that if $(\mathbf{x}, \boldsymbol{\lambda}) = (\mathbf{x}^*, \boldsymbol{\lambda}^*)$ is a *local* or *global minimum* or *maximum* for the unconstrained function $h(\mathbf{x}, \boldsymbol{\lambda})$, then $\mathbf{x}^*$ is a corresponding *critical point* for the original problem. As a result, the method now reduces to analyzing $h(\mathbf{x}, \boldsymbol{\lambda})$ by the procedure just described for unconstrained optimization. Thus, the $n + m$ partial derivatives would be set equal to zero

$$\frac{\partial h}{\partial x_j} = \frac{\partial f}{\partial x_j} - \sum_{i=1}^{m} \lambda_i \frac{\partial g_i}{\partial x_j} = 0, \qquad \text{for } j = 1, 2, \ldots, n,$$

$$\frac{\partial h}{\partial \lambda_i} = -g_i(\mathbf{x}) + b_i = 0, \qquad \text{for } i = 1, 2, \ldots, m,$$

and then the critical points would be obtained by solving these equations for $(\mathbf{x}, \boldsymbol{\lambda})$. Notice that the last m equations are equivalent to the constraints in the original problem, so only feasible solutions are considered. After further analysis to identify the *global minimum* or *maximum* of $h(\cdot)$, the resulting value of $\mathbf{x}$ is then the desired solution to the original problem.

From a practical computational viewpoint, the method of Lagrange multipliers is not a particularly powerful procedure. It is often essentially impossible to solve the equations to obtain the critical points. Furthermore, even when the points can be obtained, the number of critical points may be so large (often infinite) that it is impractical to attempt to identify a global minimum or maximum. However, for certain types of small problems, this method can sometimes be used successfully.

To illustrate, consider the example introduced earlier. In this case,

$$h(x_1, x_2) = x_1^2 + 2x_2 - \lambda(x_1^2 + x_2^2 - 1),$$

so that

$$\frac{\partial h}{\partial x_1} = 2x_1 - 2\lambda x_1 = 0,$$

$$\frac{\partial h}{\partial x_2} = 2 - 2\lambda x_2 = 0,$$

$$\frac{\partial h}{\partial \lambda} = -(x_1^2 + x_2^2 - 1) = 0.$$

The first equation implies that either $\lambda = 1$ or $x_1 = 0$. If $\lambda = 1$, then the other two equations imply that $x_2 = 1$ and $x_1 = 0$. If $x_1 = 0$, then the third equation implies that $x_2 = \pm 1$. Therefore, the two critical points for the original problem are $(x_1, x_2) = (0, 1)$ *and* $(0, -1)$. Thus, it is apparent that these points are the global maximum and minimum, respectively.

THE DERIVATIVE OF A DEFINITE INTEGRAL

In presenting the classical optimization methods just described, we have assumed that you are already familiar with derivatives and how to obtain them. However, there is a special case of importance in OR work that warrants additional explanation, namely, the derivative of a definite integral. In particular, consider how to find the derivative of the function

$$F(y) = \int_{g(y)}^{h(y)} f(x, y) \, dx,$$

where $g(y)$ and $h(y)$ are the limits of integration expressed as functions of y.

To begin, suppose that these limits of integration are constants, so that $g(y) = a$ and $h(y) = b$, respectively. For this special case, it can be shown that, given the regularity conditions assumed at the beginning of this appendix, the derivative is

$$\frac{d}{dy} \int_a^b f(x, y) \, dx = \int_a^b \frac{\partial f(x, y)}{\partial y} \, dx.$$

For example, if $f(x, y) = e^{-xy}$, $a = 0$, and $b = \infty$, then

$$\frac{d}{dy} \int_0^\infty e^{-xy} \, dx = \int_0^\infty (-x)e^{-xy} \, dx = -\frac{1}{y^2}$$

at any positive value of y. Thus, the intuitive procedure of interchanging the order of differentiation and integration is valid for this case.

However, finding the derivative becomes a little more complicated than this when the limits of integration are functions. In particular,

$$\frac{d}{dy}\int_{g(y)}^{h(y)} f(x,\,y)\ dx = \int_{g(y)}^{h(y)} \frac{\partial f(x,\,y)}{\partial y}\ dx +$$

$$f(h(y),\,y)\,\frac{dh(y)}{dy} - f(g(y),\,y)\,\frac{dg(y)}{dy},$$

where $f(h(y),\,y)$ is obtained by writing out $f(x,\,y)$ and then replacing x by $h(y)$ wherever it appears, and similarly for $f(g(y),\,y)$. To illustrate, if $f(x,\,y) = x^2y^3$, $g(y) = y$, and $h(y) = 2y$, then

$$\frac{d}{dy}\int_{y}^{2y} x^2y^3\ dx = \int_{y}^{2y} 3x^2y^2\ dx + (2y)^2y^3(2) - y^2y^3(1)$$

$$= 14y^5$$

at any positive value of y.

APPENDIX 4

MATRICES AND MATRIX OPERATIONS

A **matrix** is a rectangular array of numbers. For example,

$$\mathbf{A} = \begin{bmatrix} 2 & 5 \\ 3 & 0 \\ 1 & 1 \end{bmatrix}$$

is a 3×2 matrix (where 3×2 is said "3 by 2") because it is a rectangular array of numbers with three rows and two columns. (Matrices are denoted in this book by **boldface capital letters**.) The numbers in the rectangular array are called the **elements** of the matrix. For example,

$$\mathbf{B} = \begin{bmatrix} 1 & 2.4 & 0 & \sqrt{3} \\ -4 & 2 & -1 & 15 \end{bmatrix}$$

is a 2×4 matrix whose elements are 1, 2.4, 0, $\sqrt{3}$, -4, 2, -1, and 15. Thus, in more general terms,

$$\mathbf{A} = \begin{bmatrix} a_{11} & a_{12} & \cdots & a_{1n} \\ a_{21} & a_{22} & \cdots & a_{2n} \\ \cdots\cdots\cdots\cdots\cdots\cdots \\ a_{m1} & a_{m2} & \cdots & a_{mn} \end{bmatrix} = \| a_{ij} \|$$

is an $m \times n$ matrix, where $a_{11}, \ldots, a_{mn}$ represent the numbers that are the elements of this matrix; $\| a_{ij} \|$ is shorthand notation for identifying the matrix whose element in row i and column j is a_{ij} for every $i = 1, 2, \ldots, m$ and $j = 1, 2, \ldots, n$.

MATRIX OPERATIONS

Because matrices do not possess a numerical value, they cannot be added, multiplied, and so on as if they were individual numbers. However, it is sometimes desirable to perform certain manipulations on arrays of numbers. There-

fore, rules have been developed for performing operations on matrices that are analogous to arithmetic operations. To describe these, let $\mathbf{A} = \| a_{ij} \|$ and $\mathbf{B} = \| b_{ij} \|$ be two matrices having the same number of rows and the same number of columns. (We shall change this restriction on the size of $\mathbf{A}$ and $\mathbf{B}$ later when discussing matrix multiplication.)

Matrices $\mathbf{A}$ and $\mathbf{B}$ are said to be *equal* ($\mathbf{A} = \mathbf{B}$) if and only if *all* the corresponding elements are equal ($a_{ij} = b_{ij}$ for all i and j).

The operation of *multiplying a matrix by a number* (denote this number by k) is performed by multiplying each element of the matrix by k, so that

$$k\mathbf{A} = \| ka_{ij} \|.$$

For example,

$$3\begin{bmatrix} 1 & \frac{1}{3} & 2 \\ 5 & 0 & -3 \end{bmatrix} = \begin{bmatrix} 3 & 1 & 6 \\ 15 & 0 & -9 \end{bmatrix}.$$

To add two matrices $\mathbf{A}$ and $\mathbf{B}$, simply add the corresponding elements, so that

$$\mathbf{A} + \mathbf{B} = \| a_{ij} + b_{ij} \|.$$

To illustrate,

$$\begin{bmatrix} 5 & 3 \\ 1 & 6 \end{bmatrix} + \begin{bmatrix} 2 & 0 \\ 3 & 1 \end{bmatrix} = \begin{bmatrix} 7 & 3 \\ 4 & 7 \end{bmatrix}.$$

Similarly, *subtraction* is done as follows:

$$\mathbf{A} - \mathbf{B} = \mathbf{A} + (-1)\mathbf{B},$$

so that

$$\mathbf{A} - \mathbf{B} = \| a_{ij} - b_{ij} \|.$$

For example,

$$\begin{bmatrix} 5 & 3 \\ 1 & 6 \end{bmatrix} - \begin{bmatrix} 2 & 0 \\ 3 & 1 \end{bmatrix} = \begin{bmatrix} 3 & 3 \\ -2 & 5 \end{bmatrix}.$$

Note that, with the exception of multiplication by a number, all the preceding operations are defined only when the two matrices involved are the same size. However, all of these operations are straightforward because they involve performing only the same comparison or arithmetic operation on the corresponding elements of the matrices.

There exists one additional elementary operation that has not been defined—**matrix multiplication**—but it is considerably more complicated. To find the element in row i, column j of the matrix resulting from multiplying matrix $\mathbf{A}$ times matrix $\mathbf{B}$, it is necessary to multiply each element in row i of $\mathbf{A}$ by the corresponding element in column j of $\mathbf{B}$ and then to add these products. To do this element-by-element multiplication, we need the following restriction on the sizes of $\mathbf{A}$ and $\mathbf{B}$:

Matrix multiplication $\mathbf{AB}$ is defined if and only if the *number of columns* of $\mathbf{A}$ equals the *number of rows* of $\mathbf{B}$.

Thus, if $\mathbf{A}$ is an $m \times n$ matrix and $\mathbf{B}$ is an $n \times s$ matrix, then their product is

$$\mathbf{AB} = \left\| \sum_{k=1}^{n} a_{ik} b_{kj} \right\|,$$

where this product is an $m \times s$ matrix. However, if $\mathbf{A}$ is an $m \times n$ matrix and $\mathbf{B}$ is an $r \times s$ matrix, where $n \neq r$, then $\mathbf{AB}$ is not defined.

To illustrate matrix multiplication,

$$\begin{bmatrix} 1 & 2 \\ 4 & 0 \\ 2 & 3 \end{bmatrix} \begin{bmatrix} 3 & 1 \\ 2 & 5 \end{bmatrix} = \begin{bmatrix} 1(3)+2(2) & 1(1)+2(5) \\ 4(3)+0(2) & 4(1)+0(5) \\ 2(3)+3(2) & 2(1)+3(5) \end{bmatrix}$$

$$= \begin{bmatrix} 7 & 11 \\ 12 & 4 \\ 12 & 17 \end{bmatrix}.$$

On the other hand, if one attempts to multiply these matrices in the reverse order, the resulting product

$$\begin{bmatrix} 3 & 1 \\ 2 & 5 \end{bmatrix} \begin{bmatrix} 1 & 2 \\ 4 & 0 \\ 2 & 3 \end{bmatrix}$$

is not even defined.

Even when both $\mathbf{AB}$ and $\mathbf{BA}$ are defined,

$$\mathbf{AB} \neq \mathbf{BA}$$

in general. Thus, *matrix multiplication* should be viewed as a specially designed operation whose properties are quite different from those of *arithmetic multiplication*. To understand why this special definition was adopted, consider the following system of equations:

$$\begin{aligned} 2x_1 - x_2 + 5x_3 + x_4 &= 20 \\ x_1 + 5x_2 + 4x_3 + 5x_4 &= 30 \\ 3x_1 + x_2 - 6x_3 + 2x_4 &= 20. \end{aligned}$$

Rather than write out these equations as shown here, they can be written much more concisely in matrix form as

$$\mathbf{Ax} = \mathbf{b},$$

where

$$\mathbf{A} = \begin{bmatrix} 2 & -1 & 5 & 1 \\ 1 & 5 & 4 & 5 \\ 3 & 1 & -6 & 2 \end{bmatrix}, \quad \mathbf{x} = \begin{bmatrix} x_1 \\ x_2 \\ x_3 \\ x_4 \end{bmatrix}, \quad \mathbf{b} = \begin{bmatrix} 20 \\ 30 \\ 20 \end{bmatrix}.$$

It is this kind of multiplication for which matrix multiplication is designed.

Carefully note that *matrix division* is *not* defined.

Although the matrix operations described here do not possess certain of the properties of arithmetic operations, they do satisfy these laws

$$\begin{aligned} \mathbf{A} + \mathbf{B} &= \mathbf{B} + \mathbf{A}, \\ (\mathbf{A} + \mathbf{B}) + \mathbf{C} &= \mathbf{A} + (\mathbf{B} + \mathbf{C}), \\ \mathbf{A}(\mathbf{B} + \mathbf{C}) &= \mathbf{AB} + \mathbf{AC}, \\ \mathbf{A}(\mathbf{BC}) &= (\mathbf{AB})\mathbf{C}, \end{aligned}$$

when the relative sizes of these matrices are such that the indicated operations are defined.

Another type of matrix operation, which has no arithmetic analog, is the **transpose operation**. This operation involves nothing more than interchanging the rows and columns of the matrix, which is frequently useful for performing the multiplication operation in the desired way. Thus, for any matrix $\mathbf{A} = \|a_{ij}\|$, its transpose $\mathbf{A}^T$ is

$$\mathbf{A}^T = \|a_{ji}\|.$$

For example, if

$$\mathbf{A} = \begin{bmatrix} 2 & 5 \\ 1 & 3 \\ 4 & 0 \end{bmatrix},$$

then

$$\mathbf{A}^T = \begin{bmatrix} 2 & 1 & 4 \\ 5 & 3 & 0 \end{bmatrix}.$$

SPECIAL KINDS OF MATRICES

In arithmetic, 0 and 1 play a special role. There also exist special matrices that play a similar role in matrix theory. In particular, the matrix that is analogous to 1 is the **identity matrix I,** which is a *square* matrix whose elements are 0s except for 1s along the main diagonal. Thus,

$$\mathbf{I} = \begin{bmatrix} 1 & 0 & 0 & \cdots & 0 \\ 0 & 1 & 0 & \cdots & 0 \\ 0 & 0 & 1 & \cdots & 0 \\ \hdotsfor{5} \\ 0 & 0 & 0 & \cdots & 1 \end{bmatrix}$$

The number of rows or columns of **I** can be specified as desired. The analogy of **I** to 1 follows from the fact that for any matrix **A**,

$$\mathbf{IA} = \mathbf{A} = \mathbf{AI},$$

where **I** is assigned the appropriate number of rows and columns in each case for the multiplication operation to be defined.

Similarly, the matrix that is analogous to 0 is the **null matrix 0,** which is a matrix of any size whose elements are *all* 0s. Thus,

$$\mathbf{0} = \begin{bmatrix} 0 & 0 & \cdots & 0 \\ 0 & 0 & \cdots & 0 \\ \hdotsfor{4} \\ 0 & 0 & \cdots & 0 \end{bmatrix}$$

Therefore, for any matrix **A**,

$$\mathbf{A} + \mathbf{0} = \mathbf{A}, \quad \mathbf{A} - \mathbf{A} = \mathbf{0}, \quad \text{and}$$
$$\mathbf{0A} = \mathbf{0} = \mathbf{A0},$$

where **0** is the appropriate size in each case for the operations to be defined.

On certain occasions, it is useful to partition a matrix into several smaller matrices, called **submatrices.** For example, one possible way of partitioning a 3×4 matrix would be

$$\mathbf{A} = \left[\begin{array}{c|ccc} a_{11} & a_{12} & a_{13} & a_{14} \\ a_{21} & a_{22} & a_{23} & a_{24} \\ a_{31} & a_{32} & a_{33} & a_{34} \end{array} \right] = \begin{bmatrix} a_{11} & \mathbf{A}_{12} \\ \mathbf{A}_{21} & \mathbf{A}_{22} \end{bmatrix},$$

where

$$\mathbf{A}_{12} = [a_{12}, \quad a_{13}, \quad a_{14}], \qquad \mathbf{A}_{21} = \begin{bmatrix} a_{21} \\ a_{31} \end{bmatrix},$$

$$\mathbf{A}_{22} = \begin{bmatrix} a_{22} & a_{23} & a_{24} \\ a_{32} & a_{33} & a_{34} \end{bmatrix}$$

all are submatrices. Rather than perform operations element by element on such partitioned matrices, we can do them in terms of the submatrices, provided the partitionings are such that the operations are defined. For example, if **B** is a partitioned 4×1 matrix such that

$$\mathbf{B} = \begin{bmatrix} b_1 \\ b_2 \\ b_3 \\ b_4 \end{bmatrix} = \begin{bmatrix} b_1 \\ \mathbf{B}_2 \end{bmatrix},$$

then

$$\mathbf{AB} = \begin{bmatrix} a_{11}b_1 + \mathbf{A}_{12}\mathbf{B}_2 \\ \mathbf{A}_{21}b_1 + \mathbf{A}_{22}\mathbf{B}_2 \end{bmatrix}.$$

VECTORS

A special kind of matrix that plays an important role in matrix theory is the kind that has either a *single row* or a *single column*. Such matrices are often referred to as **vectors.** Thus,

$$\mathbf{x} = [x_1, x_2, \ldots, x_n]$$

is a **row vector,** and

$$\mathbf{x} = \begin{bmatrix} x_1 \\ x_2 \\ \vdots \\ x_n \end{bmatrix}$$

is a **column vector.** (Vectors are denoted in this book by **boldface lowercase letters.**) These vectors also are sometimes called *n-vectors* to indicate that they have *n* elements. For example,

$$\mathbf{x} = [1, 4, -2, \tfrac{1}{3}, 7]$$

is a 5-vector.

A **null vector 0** is either a row vector or a column vector whose elements are *all* 0s, that is,

$$\mathbf{0} = [0, 0, \ldots, 0] \quad \text{or} \quad \mathbf{0} = \begin{bmatrix} 0 \\ 0 \\ \vdots \\ 0 \end{bmatrix}.$$

(Although the same symbol **0** is used for either kind of *null vector,* as well as for a *null matrix,* the context normally will identify which it is.)

One reason vectors play an important role in matrix theory is that any $m \times n$ matrix can be partitioned into either m row vectors or n column vectors, and important properties of the matrix can be analyzed in terms of these vectors. To amplify, consider a set of *n-vectors* $\mathbf{x}_1, \mathbf{x}_2, \ldots, \mathbf{x}_m$ of the same type (i.e., they are either all row vectors or all column vectors).

Definition: A set of vectors $\mathbf{x}_1, \mathbf{x}_2, \ldots, \mathbf{x}_m$ is said to be **linearly dependent** if there exist m numbers (denoted by $c_1, c_2, \ldots, c_m$), some of which are not zero, such that

$$c_1\mathbf{x}_1 + c_2\mathbf{x}_2 + \cdots + c_m\mathbf{x}_m = \mathbf{0}.$$

Otherwise, the set is said to be **linearly independent.**

To illustrate, if $m = 3$ and

$$\mathbf{x}_1 = [1, 1, 1], \qquad \mathbf{x}_2 = [0, 1, 1], \qquad \mathbf{x}_3 = [2, 5, 5],$$

then there exist three numbers, namely, $c_1 = 2$, $c_2 = 3$, and $c_3 = -1$, such that

$$2\mathbf{x}_1 + 3\mathbf{x}_2 - \mathbf{x}_3 = [2, 2, 2] + [0, 3, 3] - [2, 5, 5]$$
$$= [0, 0, 0],$$

so, $\mathbf{x}_1, \mathbf{x}_2, \mathbf{x}_3$ are linearly dependent. Note that showing they are linearly dependent required finding three particular numbers (c_1, c_2, c_3) that make $c_1\mathbf{x}_1 + c_2\mathbf{x}_2 + c_3\mathbf{x}_3 = \mathbf{0}$, which is not always easy. Also note that this equation implies that

$$\mathbf{x}_3 = 2\mathbf{x}_1 + 3\mathbf{x}_2.$$

Thus, $\mathbf{x}_1, \mathbf{x}_2, \mathbf{x}_3$ can be interpreted as being linearly dependent because one of them is a linear combination of the others. However, if $\mathbf{x}_3$ were changed to

$$\mathbf{x}_3 = [2, 5, 6]$$

instead, then $\mathbf{x}_1, \mathbf{x}_2, \mathbf{x}_3$ would be linearly independent because it is impossible to express one of these vectors (say, $\mathbf{x}_3$) as a linear combination of the other two.

Definition: The **rank** of a *set* of vectors is the largest number of *linearly independent vectors* that can be chosen from the set.

Continuing the preceding example, we see that the rank of the set of vectors $\mathbf{x}_1, \mathbf{x}_2, \mathbf{x}_3$ was 2 (any pair of the vectors is linearly independent), but it became 3 after $\mathbf{x}_3$ was changed.

Definition: A **basis** for a *set* of vectors is a collection of linearly independent vectors taken from the set such that every vector in the set is a linear combination of the vectors in the collection (i.e., every vector in the set equals the sum of certain multiples of the vectors in the collection).

To illustrate, any pair of the vectors (say, $\mathbf{x}_1$ and $\mathbf{x}_2$) constituted a basis for $\mathbf{x}_1, \mathbf{x}_2, \mathbf{x}_3$ in the preceding example before $\mathbf{x}_3$ was changed. After $\mathbf{x}_3$ is changed, the basis becomes all three vectors.

The following theorem relates the last two definitions.

Theorem A4.1: A collection of r linearly independent vectors chosen from a set of vectors is a basis for the set if and only if the set has rank r.

SOME PROPERTIES OF MATRICES

Given the preceding results regarding vectors, it is now possible to present certain important concepts regarding matrices.

Definition: The **row rank** of a matrix is the rank of its set of row vectors. The **column rank** of a matrix is the rank of its column vectors.

For example, if matrix $\mathbf{A}$ is

$$\mathbf{A} = \begin{bmatrix} 1 & 1 & 1 \\ 0 & 1 & 1 \\ 2 & 5 & 5 \end{bmatrix},$$

then the preceding example of linearly dependent vectors shows that the row rank of $\mathbf{A}$ is 2. The column rank of $\mathbf{A}$ is also 2. (The first two column vectors are linearly independent but the second column vector minus the third equals $\mathbf{0}$.) Having the same column rank and row rank is no coincidence, as the following general theorem indicates.

Theorem A4.2: The row rank and column rank of a matrix are equal.

Thus, it is only necessary to speak of the rank of a matrix.

The final concept to be discussed is the **inverse of a matrix.** For any nonzero number k, there exists a reciprocal or inverse $k^{-1} = 1/k$ such that

$$kk^{-1} = 1 = k^{-1}k.$$

Is there an analogous concept that is valid in matrix theory? In other words, for a given matrix $\mathbf{A}$ other than the null matrix, does there exist a matrix $\mathbf{A}^{-1}$ such that

$$\mathbf{A}\mathbf{A}^{-1} = \mathbf{I} = \mathbf{A}^{-1}\mathbf{A}?$$

If $\mathbf{A}$ is not a square matrix (i.e., if the number of rows and the number of columns of $\mathbf{A}$ differ), the answer is *never,* because these matrix products would necessarily have a different number of rows for the multiplication to be defined (so that the equality operation would not be defined). However, if $\mathbf{A}$ is square, then the answer is *under certain circumstances,* as described by the following definition and Theorem A4.3.

Definition: A matrix is **nonsingular** if its rank equals both the number of rows and the number of columns. Otherwise, it is **singular.**

Thus, only square matrices can be *nonsingular.* A useful way of testing for nonsingularity is provided by the fact that a square matrix is nonsingular if and only if *its determinant is nonzero.*

Theorem A4.3: (*a*) If $\mathbf{A}$ is nonsingular, there is a unique nonsingular matrix $\mathbf{A}^{-1}$, called the **inverse of A,** such that $\mathbf{A}\mathbf{A}^{-1} = \mathbf{I} = \mathbf{A}^{-1}\mathbf{A}$.
(*b*) If $\mathbf{A}$ is nonsingular and $\mathbf{B}$ is a matrix for which either $\mathbf{A}\mathbf{B} = \mathbf{I}$ or $\mathbf{B}\mathbf{A} = \mathbf{I}$, then $\mathbf{B} = \mathbf{A}^{-1}$.
(*c*) Only nonsingular matrices have inverses.

To illustrate matrix inverses, consider the matrix

$$\mathbf{A} = \begin{bmatrix} 5 & -4 \\ 1 & -1 \end{bmatrix}.$$

Notice that $\mathbf{A}$ is nonsingular since its determinant, $5(-1) - 1(-4) = -1$, is nonzero. Therefore, $\mathbf{A}$ must have an inverse, which happens to be

$$\mathbf{A}^{-1} = \begin{bmatrix} 1 & -4 \\ 1 & -5 \end{bmatrix}.$$

Hence,

$$\mathbf{A}\mathbf{A}^{-1} = \begin{bmatrix} 5 & -4 \\ 1 & -1 \end{bmatrix}\begin{bmatrix} 1 & -4 \\ 1 & -5 \end{bmatrix} = \begin{bmatrix} 1 & 0 \\ 0 & 1 \end{bmatrix},$$

and

$$\mathbf{A}^{-1}\mathbf{A} = \begin{bmatrix} 1 & -4 \\ 1 & -5 \end{bmatrix}\begin{bmatrix} 5 & -4 \\ 1 & -1 \end{bmatrix} = \begin{bmatrix} 1 & 0 \\ 0 & 1 \end{bmatrix}.$$

APPENDIX 5

TABLES

TABLE A5.1 Areas under the normal curve from K_α to ∞

$$P\{\text{standard normal} > K_\alpha\} = \int_{K_\alpha}^{\infty} \frac{1}{\sqrt{2\pi}}\ e^{-x^2/2}\ dx = \alpha$$

K_α	.00	.01	.02	.03	.04	.05	.06	.07	.08	.09
0.0	.5000	.4960	.4920	.4880	.4840	.4801	.4761	.4721	.4681	.4641
0.1	.4602	.4562	.4522	.4483	.4443	.4404	.4364	.4325	.4286	.4247
0.2	.4207	.4168	.4129	.4090	.4052	.4013	.3974	.3936	.3897	.3859
0.3	.3821	.3783	.3745	.3707	.3669	.3632	.3594	.3557	.3520	.3483
0.4	.3446	.3409	.3372	.3336	.3300	.3264	.3228	.3192	.3156	.3121
0.5	.3085	.3050	.3015	.2981	.2946	.2912	.2877	.2843	.2810	.2776
0.6	.2743	.2709	.2676	.2643	.2611	.2578	.2546	.2514	.2483	.2451
0.7	.2420	.2389	.2358	.2327	.2296	.2266	.2236	.2206	.2177	.2148
0.8	.2119	.2090	.2061	.2033	.2005	.1977	.1949	.1922	.1894	.1867
0.9	.1841	.1814	.1788	.1762	.1736	.1711	.1685	.1660	.1635	.1611
1.0	.1587	.1562	.1539	.1515	.1492	.1469	.1446	.1423	.1401	.1379
1.1	.1357	.1335	.1314	.1292	.1271	.1251	.1230	.1210	.1190	.1170
1.2	.1151	.1131	.1112	.1093	.1075	.1056	.1038	.1020	.1003	.0985
1.3	.0968	.0951	.0934	.0918	.0901	.0885	.0869	.0853	.0838	.0823
1.4	.0808	.0793	.0778	.0764	.0749	.0735	.0721	.0708	.0694	.0681
1.5	.0668	.0655	.0643	.0630	.0618	.0606	.0594	.0582	.0571	.0559
1.6	.0548	.0537	.0526	.0516	.0505	.0495	.0485	.0475	.0465	.0455
1.7	.0446	.0436	.0427	.0418	.0409	.0401	.0392	.0384	.0375	.0367
1.8	.0359	.0351	.0344	.0336	.0329	.0322	.0314	.0307	.0301	.0294
1.9	.0287	.0281	.0274	.0268	.0262	.0256	.0250	.0244	.0239	.0233
2.0	.0228	.0222	.0217	.0212	.0207	.0202	.0197	.0192	.0188	.0183
2.1	.0179	.0174	.0170	.0166	.0162	.0158	.0154	.0150	.0146	.0143
2.2	.0139	.0136	.0132	.0129	.0125	.0122	.0119	.0116	.0113	.0110
2.3	.0107	.0104	.0102	.00990	.00964	.00939	.00914	.00889	.00866	.00842
2.4	.00820	.00798	.00776	.00755	.00734	.00714	.00695	.00676	.00657	.00639
2.5	.00621	.00604	.00587	.00570	.00554	.00539	.00523	.00508	.00494	.00480
2.6	.00466	.00453	.00440	.00427	.00415	.00402	.00391	.00379	.00368	.00357
2.7	.00347	.00336	.00326	.00317	.00307	.00298	.00289	.00280	.00272	.00264
2.8	.00256	.00248	.00240	.00233	.00226	.00219	.00212	.00205	.00199	.00193
2.9	.00187	.00181	.00175	.00169	.00164	.00159	.00154	.00149	.00144	.00139

K_α	.0	.1	.2	.3	.4	.5	.6	.7	.8	.9
3	.00135	$.0^3968$	$.0^3687$	$.0^3483$	$.0^3337$	$.0^3233$	$.0^3159$	$.0^3108$	$.0^4723$	$.0^4481$
4	$.0^4317$	$.0^4207$	$.0^4133$	$.0^5854$	$.0^5541$	$.0^5340$	$.0^5211$	$.0^5130$	$.0^6793$	$.0^6479$
5	$.0^6287$	$.0^6170$	$.0^7996$	$.0^7579$	$.0^7333$	$.0^7190$	$.0^7107$	$.0^8599$	$.0^8332$	$.0^8182$
6	$.0^9987$	$.0^9530$	$.0^9282$	$.0^9149$	$.0^{10}777$	$.0^{10}402$	$.0^{10}206$	$.0^{10}104$	$.0^{11}523$	$.0^{11}260$

Source: F. E. Croxton, *Tables of Areas in Two Tails and in One Tail of the Normal Curve.* Copyright 1949 by Prentice-Hall, Inc., Englewood Cliffs, NJ.

TABLE A5.2 100 α percentage points of Student's t distribution

$P\{$Student's t with v Degrees of Freedom $\geq$ Tabled Value$\} = \alpha$

v \ α	0.40	0.25	0.10	0.05	0.025	0.01	0.005	0.0025	0.001	0.0005
1	0.325	1.000	3.078	6.314	12.706	31.821	63.657	127.32	318.31	636.62
2	0.289	0.816	1.886	2.920	4.303	6.965	9.925	14.089	22.327	31.598
3	0.277	0.765	1.638	2.353	3.182	4.541	5.841	7.453	10.214	12.924
4	0.271	0.741	1.533	2.132	2.776	3.747	4.604	5.598	7.173	8.610
5	0.267	0.727	1.476	2.015	2.571	3.365	4.032	4.773	5.893	6.869
6	0.265	0.718	1.440	1.943	2.447	3.143	3.707	4.317	5.208	5.959
7	0.263	0.711	1.415	1.895	2.365	2.998	3.499	4.029	4.785	5.408
8	0.262	0.706	1.397	1.860	2.306	2.896	3.355	3.833	4.501	5.041
9	0.261	0.703	1.383	1.833	2.262	2.821	3.250	3.690	4.297	4.781
10	0.260	0.700	1.372	1.812	2.228	2.764	3.169	3.581	4.144	4.587
11	0.260	0.697	1.363	1.796	2.201	2.718	3.106	3.497	4.025	4.437
12	0.259	0.695	1.356	1.782	2.179	2.681	3.055	3.428	3.930	4.318
13	0.259	0.694	1.350	1.771	2.160	2.650	3.012	3.372	3.852	4.221
14	0.258	0.692	1.345	1.761	2.145	2.624	2.977	3.326	3.787	4.140
15	0.258	0.691	1.341	1.753	2.131	2.602	2.947	3.286	3.733	4.073
16	0.258	0.690	1.337	1.746	2.120	2.583	2.921	3.252	3.686	4.015
17	0.257	0.689	1.333	1.740	2.110	2.567	2.898	3.222	3.646	3.965
18	0.257	0.688	1.330	1.734	2.101	2.552	2.878	3.197	3.610	3.922
19	0.257	0.688	1.328	1.729	2.093	2.539	2.861	3.174	3.579	3.883
20	0.257	0.687	1.325	1.725	2.086	2.528	2.845	3.153	3.552	3.850
21	0.257	0.686	1.323	1.721	2.080	2.518	2.831	3.135	3.527	3.819
22	0.256	0.686	1.321	1.717	2.074	2.508	2.819	3.119	3.505	3.792
23	0.256	0.685	1.319	1.714	2.069	2.500	2.807	3.104	3.485	3.767
24	0.256	0.685	1.318	1.711	2.064	2.492	2.797	3.091	3.467	3.745
25	0.256	0.684	1.316	1.708	2.060	2.485	2.787	3.078	3.450	3.725
26	0.256	0.684	1.315	1.706	2.056	2.479	2.779	3.067	3.435	3.707
27	0.256	0.684	1.314	1.703	2.052	2.473	2.771	3.057	3.421	3.690
28	0.256	0.683	1.313	1.701	2.048	2.467	2.763	3.047	3.408	3.674
29	0.256	0.683	1.311	1.699	2.045	2.462	2.756	3.038	3.396	3.659
30	0.256	0.683	1.310	1.697	2.042	2.457	2.750	3.030	3.385	3.646
40	0.255	0.681	1.303	1.684	2.021	2.423	2.704	2.971	3.307	3.551
60	0.254	0.679	1.296	1.671	2.000	2.390	2.660	2.915	3.232	3.460
120	0.254	0.677	1.289	1.658	1.980	2.358	2.617	2.860	3.160	3.373
∞	0.253	0.674	1.282	1.645	1.960	2.326	2.576	2.807	3.090	3.291

Source: Table 12 of *Biometrika Tables for Statisticians*, vol. I, 3d ed., 1966, by permission of the Biometrika Trustees.

PARTIAL ANSWERS TO SELECTED PROBLEMS

CHAPTER 3

3.1-1. (a)

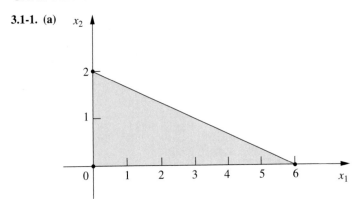

3.1-4. $(x_1, x_2) = (13, 5); Z = 31.$

3.1-11. (b) $(x_1, x_2, x_3) = (26.19, 54.76, 20); Z = 2,904.76.$

3.2-3. (b) Maximize $\quad Z = 4{,}500x_1 + 4{,}500x_2,$

subject to

$$
\begin{aligned}
x_1 && \leq && 1 \\
x_2 &\leq& 1 \\
5{,}000x_1 + 4{,}000x_2 &\leq& 6{,}000 \\
400x_1 + 500x_2 &\leq& 600
\end{aligned}
$$

and

$$x_1 \geq 0, \quad x_2 \geq 0.$$

3.4-1. (a) *Proportionality*: OK since it is implied that a fixed fraction of the radiation dosage at a given entry point is absorbed by a given area.

Additivity: OK since it is stated that the radiation absorption from multiple beams is additive.

Divisibility: OK since beam strength can be any fractional level.

Certainty: Due to the complicated analysis required to estimate the data on radiation absorption in different tissue types, there is considerable uncertainty about the data, so sensitivity analysis should be used.

3.4-11. (b) From Factory 1, ship 200 units to Customer 2 and 200 units to Customer 3.
From Factory 2, ship 300 units to Customer 1 and 200 units to Customer 3.

3.4-13. (c) $Z = \$152,880$; $A_1 = 60,000$; $A_3 = 84,000$; $D_5 = 117,600$. All other decision variables are 0.

3.4-16. (b) Each optimal solution has $Z = \$13,330$.

3.6-1. (c, e)

Resource	Resource Usage per Unit of Each Activity		Totals		Resource Available
	Activity 1	Activity 2			
1	2	1	10	$\leq$	10
2	3	3	20	$\leq$	20
3	2	4	20	$\leq$	20
Unit Profit	20	30	$166.67		
Solution	3.333	3.333			

3.6-4. (a) Minimize $\quad Z = 84C + 72T + 60A,$

subject to

$$90C + 20T + 40A \geq 200$$
$$30C + 80T + 60A \geq 180$$
$$10C + 20T + 60A \geq 150$$

and

$$C \geq 0, \quad T \geq 0, \quad A \geq 0.$$

CHAPTER 4

4.1-1. (a) The corner-point solutions that are *feasible* are $(0, 0)$, $(0, 1)$, $(\frac{1}{4}, 1)$, $(\frac{2}{3}, \frac{2}{3})$, $(1, \frac{1}{4})$, and $(1, 0)$.

4.3-4. $(x_1, x_2, x_3) = (0, 10, 6\frac{2}{3})$; $Z = 70$.

4.6-1. (a, c) $(x_1, x_2) = (2, 1)$; $Z = 7$.

4.6-4. (a, c, e) $(x_1, x_2, x_3) = (\frac{4}{5}, \frac{9}{5}, 0)$; $Z = 7$.

4.6-10. (a, b, d) $(x_1, x_2, x_3) = (0, 15, 15)$; $Z = 90$.
(c) For both the Big M method and the two-phase method, only the final tableau represents a feasible solution for the real problem.

4.6-15. (a, c) $(x_1, x_2) = (-\frac{8}{7}, \frac{18}{7})$; $Z = \frac{80}{7}$.

4.7-6. (a) $(x_1, x_2, x_3) = (0, 1, 3)$; $Z = 7$.
(b) $y_1^* = \frac{1}{2}$, $y_2^* = \frac{5}{2}$, $y_3^* = 0$. These are the marginal values of resources 1, 2, and 3, respectively.

CHAPTER 5

5.1-1. (a) $(x_1, x_2) = (2, 2)$ is optimal. Other CPF solutions are $(0, 0)$, $(3, 0)$, and $(0, 3)$.

5.1-14. $(x_1, x_2, x_3) = (0, 15, 15)$ is optimal.

5.2-2. $(x_1, x_2, x_3, x_4, x_5) = (0, 5, 0, \frac{5}{2}, 0)$; $Z = 50$.

5.3-1. (a) Right side is $Z = 8$, $x_2 = 14$, $x_6 = 5$, $x_3 = 11$.
(b) $x_1 = 0$, $2x_1 - 2x_2 + 3x_3 = 5$, $x_1 + x_2 - x_3 = 3$.

CHAPTER 6

6.1-2. (a) Minimize $W = 15y_1 + 12y_2 + 45y_3$,

subject to

$$-y_1 + y_2 + 5y_3 \geq 10$$
$$2y_1 + y_2 + 3y_3 \geq 20$$

and

$$y_1 \geq 0, \qquad y_2 \geq 0, \qquad y_3 \geq 0.$$

6.3-1. (c)

Complementary Basic Solutions

Primal Problem			Dual Problem	
Basic Solution	**Feasible?**	**Z = W**	**Feasible?**	**Basic Solution**
$(0, 0, 20, 10)$	Yes	0	No	$(0, 0, -6, -8)$
$(4, 0, 0, 6)$	Yes	24	No	$\left(1\frac{1}{5}, 0, 0, -5\frac{3}{5}\right)$
$(0, 5, 10, 0)$	Yes	40	No	$(0, 4, -2, 0)$
$\left(2\frac{1}{2}, 3\frac{3}{4}, 0, 0\right)$	Yes and optimal	45	Yes and optimal	$\left(\frac{1}{2}, 3\frac{1}{2}, 0, 0\right)$
$(10, 0, -30, 0)$	No	60	Yes	$(0, 6, 0, 4)$
$(0, 10, 0, -10)$	No	80	Yes	$(4, 0, 14, 0)$

6.3-7. (c) Basic variables are x_1 and x_2. The other variables are nonbasic.
(e) $x_1 + 3x_2 + 2x_3 + 3x_4 + x_5 = 6$, $4x_1 + 6x_2 + 5x_3 + 7x_4 + x_5 = 15$, $x_3 = 0$, $x_4 = 0$, $x_5 = 0$. Optimal CPF solution is $(x_1, x_2, x_3, x_4, x_5) = (\frac{3}{2}, \frac{3}{2}, 0, 0, 0)$.

6.4-3. Maximize $W = 8y_1 + 6y_2$,

subject to

$$y_1 + 3y_2 \leq 2$$
$$4y_1 + 2y_2 \leq 3$$
$$2y_1 \qquad \leq 1$$

and

$$y_1 \geq 0, \qquad y_2 \geq 0.$$

6.4-8. (a) Minimize $\quad W = 120y_1 + 80y_2 + 100y_3,$

subject to

$$y_2 - 3y_3 = -1$$
$$3y_1 - y_2 + y_3 = 2$$
$$y_1 - 4y_2 + 2y_3 = 1$$

and

$$y_1 \geq 0, \quad y_2 \geq 0, \quad y_3 \geq 0.$$

6.6-1. (d) Not optimal, since $2y_1 + 3y_2 \geq 3$ is violated for $y_1^* = \frac{1}{5}, y_2^* = \frac{3}{5}.$
(f) Not optimal, since $3y_1 + 2y_2 \geq 2$ is violated for $y_1^* = \frac{1}{5}, y_2^* = \frac{3}{5}.$

6.7-1.

Part	New Basic Solution $(x_1, x_2, x_3, x_4, x_5)$	Feasible?	Optimal?
(a)	(0, 30, 0, 0, −30)	No	No
(b)	(0, 20, 0, 0, −10)	No	No
(c)	(0, 10, 0, 0, 60)	Yes	Yes
(d)	(0, 20, 0, 0, 10)	Yes	Yes
(e)	(0, 20, 0, 0, 10)	Yes	Yes
(f)	(0, 10, 0, 0, 40)	Yes	No
(g)	(0, 20, 0, 0, 10)	Yes	Yes
(h)	(0, 20, 0, 0, 10, $x_6 = -10$)	No	No
(i)	(0, 20, 0, 0, 0)	Yes	Yes

6.7-2. $-10 \leq \theta \leq \frac{10}{9}$

6.7-16. (a) $b_1 \geq 2, 6 \leq b_2 \leq 18, 12 \leq b_3 \leq 24$
(b) $0 \leq c_1 \leq \frac{15}{2}, c_2 \geq 2$

CHAPTER 7

7.1-2. $(x_1, x_2, x_3) = (\frac{2}{3}, 2, 0)$ with $Z = \frac{22}{3}$ is optimal.

7.1-6.

Part	New Optimal Solution	Value of Z
(a)	$(x_1, x_2, x_3, x_4, x_5) = (0, 0, 9, 3, 0)$	117
(b)	$(x_1, x_2, x_3, x_4, x_5) = (0, 5, 5, 0, 0)$	90

7.2-1. (a, b)

Range of θ	Optimal Solution	$Z(\theta)$
$0 \leq \theta \leq 2$	$(x_1, x_2) = (0, 5)$	$120 - 10\theta$
$2 \leq \theta \leq 8$	$(x_1, x_2) = \left(\frac{10}{3}, \frac{10}{3}\right)$	$\dfrac{320 - 10\theta}{3}$
$8 \leq \theta$	$(x_1, x_2) = (5, 0)$	$40 + 5\theta$

7.2-4.

Range of θ	Optimal Solution		$Z(\theta)$
	x_1	x_2	
$0 \leq \theta \leq 1$	$10 + 2\theta$	$10 + 2\theta$	$30 + 6\theta$
$1 \leq \theta \leq 5$	$10 + 2\theta$	$15 - 3\theta$	$35 + \theta$
$5 \leq \theta \leq 25$	$25 - \theta$	0	$50 - 2\theta$

7.3-3. $(x_1, x_2, x_3) = (1, 3, 1)$ with $Z = 8$ is optimal.

7.5-6. $(x_1, x_2) = (15, 0)$ is optimal.

CHAPTER 8

8.1-2. (b)

		Destination			Supply
		Today	Tomorrow	Dummy	
Source	Dick	3.0	2.7	0	5
	Harry	2.9	2.8	0	4
	Demand	3	4	2	

8.2-2. (a) Basic variables: $x_{11} = 4$, $x_{12} = 0$, $x_{22} = 4$, $x_{23} = 2$, $x_{24} = 0$, $x_{34} = 5$, $x_{35} = 1$, $x_{45} = 0$;
$Z = 53$.
(b) Basic variables: $x_{11} = 4$, $x_{23} = 2$, $x_{25} = 4$, $x_{31} = 0$, $x_{32} = 0$, $x_{34} = 5$, $x_{35} = 1$, $x_{42} = 4$; $Z = 45$.
(c) Basic variables: $x_{11} = 4$, $x_{23} = 2$, $x_{25} = 4$, $x_{32} = 0$, $x_{34} = 5$, $x_{35} = 1$, $x_{41} = 0$, $x_{42} = 4$; $Z = 45$.

8.2-8. (a) $x_{11} = 3$, $x_{12} = 2$, $x_{22} = 1$, $x_{23} = 1$, $x_{33} = 1$, $x_{34} = 2$; three iterations to reach optimality.
(b, c) $x_{11} = 3$, $x_{12} = 0$, $x_{13} = 0$, $x_{14} = 2$, $x_{23} = 2$, $x_{32} = 3$; already optimal.

8.2-11. $x_{11} = 10$, $x_{12} = 15$, $x_{22} = 0$, $x_{23} = 5$, $x_{25} = 30$, $x_{33} = 20$, $x_{34} = 10$, $x_{44} = 10$; cost =
$77.30. Also have other tied optimal solutions.

8.2-12. (b) Let x_{ij} be the shipment from plant i to distribution center j. Then $x_{13} = 2$, $x_{14} = 10$,
$x_{22} = 9$, $x_{23} = 8$, $x_{31} = 10$, $x_{32} = 1$; cost = $20,200.

8.3-4. (a)

		Task				
		Backstroke	Breaststroke	Butterfly	Freestyle	Dummy
	Carl	37.7	43.4	33.3	29.2	0
	Chris	32.9	33.1	28.5	26.4	0
Assignee	David	33.8	42.2	38.9	29.6	0
	Tony	37.0	34.7	30.4	28.5	0
	Ken	35.4	41.8	33.6	31.1	0

CHAPTER 9

9.3-3. (a) $O \to A \to B \to D \to T$ or $O \to A \to B \to E \to D \to T$, with length = 16.

9.4-1. (a) $\{(O, A); (A, B); (B, C); (B, E); (E, D); (D, T)\}$, with length = 18.

9.5-1. (a)

Arc	(1, 2)	(1, 3)	(1, 4)	(2, 5)	(3, 4)	(3, 5)	(3, 6)	(4, 6)	(5, 7)	(6, 7)
Flow	4	4	1	4	1	0	3	2	4	5

CHAPTER 10

10.2-2. Since activities D, E, J, and K are not immediate predecessors of any other activities, the corresponding nodes have arcs leading directly to the Finish node.

10.3-4. (b) Ken will be able to meet his deadline if no delays occur.
(c) Critical paths: Start $\to B \to E \to J \to M \to$ Finish
                     Start $\to C \to G \to L \to N \to$ Finish
Focus attention on activities with 0 slack.
(d) If activity I takes 2 extra weeks, there will be no delay because its slack is 3.

10.3-7. Critical path: Start $\to A \to B \to C \to E \to F \to J \to K \to N \to$ Finish
          Total duration = 26 weeks

10.4-1. $\mu = 37$, $\sigma^2 = 9$

10.4-5. (a)

Activity	μ	σ^2
A	12	0
B	23	16
C	15	1
D	27	9
E	18	4
F	6	4

(b) Start $\to A \to C \to E \to F \to$ Finish   Length = 51 days   Mean critical path
      Start $\to B \to D \to$ Finish   Length = 50 days

(d) $\dfrac{d - \mu_p}{\sqrt{\sigma_p^2}} = \dfrac{57 - 50}{\sqrt{25}} = 1.4 \Rightarrow P(T \le 57) = 0.9192$ (from the Normal table)

10.5-4. (a) Critical path: Start $\to A \to C \to E \to$ Finish
          Total duration = 12 weeks
(b) New plan:

Activity	Duration	Cost
A	3 weeks	$54,000
B	3 weeks	$65,000
C	3 weeks	$68,666
D	2 weeks	$41,500
E	2 weeks	$80,000

$7,834 is saved by this crashing schedule.

10.5-5. (b)

Activity	Time Normal	Time Crash	Cost Normal	Cost Crash	Maximum Time Reduction	Crash Cost per Week Saved	Start Time	Time Reduction	Finish Time
A	5	3	$20	$30	2	$ 5	0	2	3
B	3	2	$10	$20	1	$10	0	1	2
C	4	2	$16	$24	2	$ 4	3	0	7
D	6	3	$25	$43	3	$ 6	3	0	9
E	5	4	$22	$30	1	$ 8	2	0	7
F	7	4	$30	$48	3	$ 6	2	0	9
G	9	5	$25	$45	4	$ 5	7	1	15
H	8	6	$30	$44	2	$ 7	9	2	15

Finish Time = 15
Total Cost = $217

10.6-2. (d)

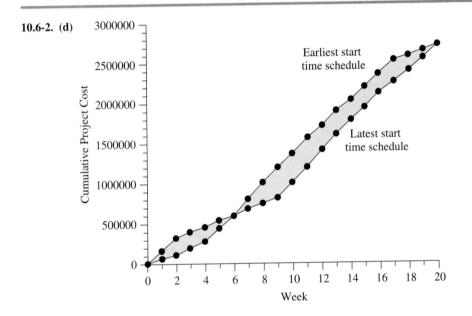

CHAPTER 11

11.3-1.

	Store		
	1	**2**	**3**
Allocations	1	2	2
	3	2	0

11.3-8. (a)

Phase	(*a*)	(*b*)
1	2M	2.945M
2	1M	1.055M
3	1M	0
Market share	6%	6.302%

11.3-14. $x_1 = -2 + \sqrt{13} \approx 1.6056$, $x_2 = 5 - \sqrt{13} \approx 1.3944$; $Z = 98.233$.

11.4-3. Produce 2 on first production run; if none acceptable, produce 2 on second run. Expected cost = \$575.

CHAPTER 12

12.1-2. (a) Minimize $Z = 4.5x_{em} + 7.8x_{ec} + 3.6x_{ed} + 2.9x_{el} + 4.9x_{sm} + 7.2x_{sc} + 4.3x_{sd} + 3.1x_{sl}$,

subject to

$$x_{em} + x_{ec} + x_{ed} + x_{el} = 2$$
$$x_{sm} + x_{sc} + x_{sd} + x_{sl} = 2$$
$$x_{em} + x_{sm} = 1$$
$$x_{ec} + x_{sc} = 1$$
$$x_{ed} + x_{sd} = 1$$
$$x_{el} + x_{sl} = 1$$

and

all x_{ij} are binary.

12.3-1. (b)

Constraint	Product 1	Product 2	Product 3	Product 4	Totals	Modified Right-Hand Side	Original Right-Hand Side
First	5	3	6	4	6000 ≤	6000	6000
Second	4	6	3	5	12000 ≤	105999	6000
Marginal revenue	\$70	\$60	\$90	\$80	\$80000		
Solution	0	2000	0	0			
	≤	≤	≤	≤			
	0	9999	0	0			
Set Up?	0	1	0	0	1 ≤	2	
Start-up Cost	\$50,000	\$40,000	\$70,000	\$60,000			

Contingency Constraints:

Product 3:	0	≤	1	:Product 1 or 2
Product 4:	0	≤	1	:Product 1 or 2

Which Constraint (0 = First, 1 = Second):	0

12.3-5. (b, d) (long, medium, short) = (14, 0, 16), with profit of $95.6 million.

12.4-3. (b)

Constraint	Product 1	Product 2	Product 3	Total		Right-Hand Side
Milling	9	3	5	498	≤	500
Lathe	5	4	0	349	≤	350
Grinder	3	0	2	135	≤	150
Sales Potential	0	0	1	0	≤	20
Unit Profit	50	20	25	$2870		
Solution	45	31	0			
	≤	≤	≤			
	999	999	0			
Produce?	1	1	0	2	≤	2

12.4-6. (a) Let $x_{ij} = \begin{cases} 1 & \text{if arc } i \to j \text{ is included in shortest path} \\ 0 & \text{otherwise.} \end{cases}$

Mutually exclusive alternatives: For each column of arcs, exactly one arc is included in the shortest path. Contingent decisions: The shortest path leaves node i only if it enters node i.

12.5-1. (a) $(x_1, x_2) = (2, 3)$ is optimal.
(b) None of the feasible rounded solutions are optimal for the integer programming problem.

12.6-1. $(x_1, x_2, x_3, x_4, x_5) = (0, 0, 1, 1, 1)$, with $Z = 6$.

12.6-7. (b)

Task	1	2	3	4	5
Assignee	1	3	2	4	5

12.6-9. $(x_1, x_2, x_3, x_4) = (0, 1, 1, 0)$, with $Z = 36$.

12.7-1. (a, b) $(x_1, x_2) = (2, 1)$ is optimal.

12.8-1. (a) $x_1 = 0$, $x_3 = 0$

CHAPTER 13

13.2-7. (a) Concave.

13.4-1. Approximate solution = 1.0125.

13.5-4. Exact solution is $(x_1, x_2) = (2, -2)$.

13.5-8. (a) Approximate solution is $(x_1, x_2) = (0.75, 1.5)$.

13.6-3.
$$-4x_1^3 - 4x_1 - 2x_2 + 2u_1 + u_2 = 0 \quad (\text{or} \leq 0 \text{ if } x_1 = 0).$$
$$-2x_1 - 8x_2 + u_1 + 2u_2 = 0 \quad (\text{or} \leq 0 \text{ if } x_2 = 0).$$
$$-2x_1 - x_2 + 10 = 0 \quad (\text{or} \leq 0 \text{ if } u_1 = 0).$$
$$-x_1 - 2x_2 + 10 = 0 \quad (\text{or} \leq 0 \text{ if } u_2 = 0).$$
$$x_1 \geq 0, \quad x_2 \geq 0, \quad u_1 \geq 0, \quad u_2 \geq 0.$$

13.6-8. $(x_1, x_2) = (1, 2)$ cannot be optimal.

13.6-10. (a) $(x_1, x_2) = (1 - 3^{-1/2}, 3^{-1/2})$.

13.7-2. (a) $(x_1, x_2) = (2, 0)$ is optimal.
(b) Minimize $\quad Z = z_1 + z_2,$

subject to

$$
\begin{array}{rl}
2x_1 \qquad + u_1 - y_1 \qquad\qquad + z_1 \qquad & = 8 \\
2x_2 + u_1 \qquad - y_2 \qquad\quad + z_2 & = 4 \\
x_1 + \; x_2 \qquad\qquad\quad + v_1 \qquad & = 2
\end{array}
$$

$x_1 \geq 0, \qquad x_2 \geq 0, \qquad u_1 \geq 0, \qquad y_1 \geq 0, \qquad y_2 \geq 0, \qquad v_1 \geq 0, \qquad z_1 \geq 0,$
$z_2 \geq 0.$

13.8-3. (b) Maximize $\quad Z = 3x_{11} - 3x_{12} - 15x_{13} + 4x_{21} - 4x_{23},$

subject to

$$
\begin{array}{l}
x_{11} + \; x_{12} + \; x_{13} + 3x_{21} + 3x_{22} + 3x_{23} \leq \; 8 \\
5x_{11} + 5x_{12} + 5x_{13} + 2x_{21} + 2x_{22} + 2x_{23} \leq 14
\end{array}
$$

and

$$0 \leq x_{ij} \leq 1, \qquad \text{for } i = 1, 2, 3; j = 1, 2, 3.$$

13.9-1. $(x_1, x_2) = (5, 0)$ is optimal.

13.9-10. (a) $(x_1, x_2) = \left(\dfrac{1}{3}, \dfrac{2}{3} \right).$

13.10-5. (a) $P(x; r) = -2x_1 - (x_2 - 3)^2 - r \left(\dfrac{1}{x_1 - 3} + \dfrac{1}{x_2 - 3} \right).$

(b) $(x_1, x_2) = \left[3 + \left(\dfrac{r}{2} \right)^{1/2}, 3 + \left(\dfrac{r}{2} \right)^{1/3} \right].$

CHAPTER 14

14.2-2. (a) Player 1: strategy 2; player 2: strategy 1.

14.2-7. (a) Politician 1: issue 2; politician 2: issue 2.
(b) Politician 1: issue 1; politician 2: issue 2.

14.4-3. (a) $(x_1, x_2) = (\frac{2}{5}, \frac{3}{5}); (y_1, y_2, y_3) = (\frac{1}{5}, 0, \frac{4}{5}); v = \frac{8}{5}.$

14.5-2. (a) Maximize $\quad x_4,$

subject to

$$
\begin{array}{rl}
5x_1 + 2x_2 + 3x_3 - x_4 & \geq 0 \\
4x_2 + 2x_3 - x_4 & \geq 0 \\
3x_1 + 3x_2 \qquad\quad - x_4 & \geq 0 \\
x_1 + 2x_2 + 4x_3 - x_4 & \geq 0 \\
x_1 + \; x_2 + \; x_3 \qquad & = 1
\end{array}
$$

and

$$x_1 \geq 0, \qquad x_2 \geq 0, \qquad x_3 \geq 0, \qquad x_4 \geq 0.$$

CHAPTER 15

15.2-1. (a)

	State of Nature	
Alternative	Sell 10,000	Sell 100,000
Build Computers	0	54
Sell Rights	15	15

(c) Let p = prior probability of selling 10,000. They should build when $p \le 0.722$, and sell when $p > 0.722$.

15.2-3. (c) Warren should make the countercyclical investment.

15.2-5. (d)

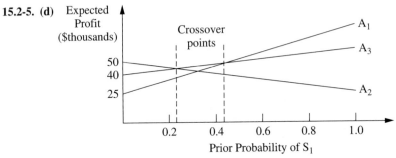

A_2 and A_3 cross at approximately $p = 0.25$. A_1 and A_3 cross at approximately $p = 0.43$.

15.2-8. Order 25.

15.3-1. (a) EVPI = EP (with perfect info) − EP (without more info) = 34.5 − 27 = $7.5 million.
(d)

Data:		P (Finding | State)	
		Finding	
State of Nature	Prior Probability	Sell 10,000	Sell 100,000
Sell 10,000	0.5	0.666666667	0.333333333
Sell 100,000	0.5	0.333333333	0.666666667

Posterior Probabilities:		P (State | Finding)	
		State of Nature	
Finding	P (Finding)	Sell 10,000	Sell 100,000
Sell 10,000	0.5	0.666666667	0.333333333
Sell 100,000	0.5	0.333333333	0.666666667

15.3-3. (b) EVPI = EP (with perfect info) − EP (without more info) = 53 − 35 = $18
(c) Betsy should consider spending up to $18 to obtain more information.

15.3-8. (a) Up to $230,000
(b) Order 25.

15.3-9. (a)

	State of Nature		
Alternative	Poor Risk	Average Risk	Good Risk
Extend Credit	−15,000	10,000	20,000
Don't Extend Credit	0	0	0
Prior Probabilities	0.2	0.5	0.3

(c) EVPI = EP (with perfect info) − EP (without more info) = 11,000 − 8,000 = $3,000. This indicates that the credit-rating organization should not be used.

15.3-13. (a) Guess coin 1.
(b) Heads: coin 2; tails: coin 1.

15.4-1. (b) The optimal policy is to do no market research and build the computers.

15.4-4. (c) EVPI = EP (with perfect info) − EP (without more info) = 1.8 − 1 = $800,000
(d)

Prior Probabilities P (state)	Conditional Probabilities P (finding|state)	Joint Probabilities P (state and finding)	Posterior Probabilities P (state|finding)

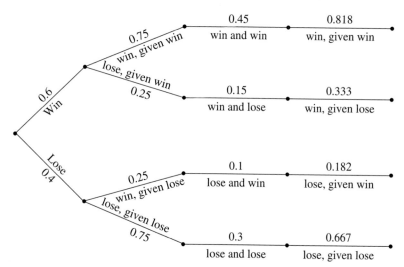

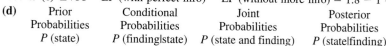

(f, g) Leland University should hire William. If he predicts a winning season then they should hold the campaign. If he predicts a losing season then they should not hold the campaign.

15.4-10. (a) Choose to introduce the new product (expected payoff is $12.5 million).
(b) EVPI = EP (with perfect info) − EP (without more info) = 20 − 12.5 = $7.5 million
(c) The optimal policy is not to test but to introduce the new product.

15.5-2. (a) Choose not to buy insurance (expected payoff is $249,840).
(b) u(insurance) = 499.82
u(no insurance) = 499.8
Optimal policy is to buy insurance.

15.5-4. $u(10) = 9$

CHAPTER 16

16.3-3. (c) $\pi_0 = \pi_1 = \pi_2 = \pi_3 = \pi_4 = \frac{1}{5}$.

16.4-1. (a) All states belong to the same recurrent class.

16.5-8. (a) $\pi_0 = 0.182$, $\pi_1 = 0.285$, $\pi_2 = 0.368$, $\pi_3 = 0.165$.
(b) 6.50

CHAPTER 17

17.2-1. Input source: population having hair; customers: customers needing haircuts; and so forth for the queue, queue discipline, and service mechanism.

17.2-2. (b) $L_q = 0.375$
(d) $W - W_q = 24.375$ minutes

17.4-2. (c) 0.0527

17.5-5. (a) State:

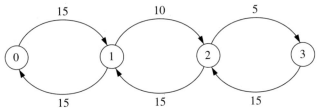

(c) $P_0 = \frac{9}{26}$, $P_1 = \frac{9}{26}$, $P_2 = \frac{3}{13}$, $P_3 = \frac{1}{13}$.
(d) $W = 0.11$ hour.

17.5-9. (b) $P_0 = \frac{2}{5}$, $P_n = (\frac{3}{5})(\frac{1}{2})^n$
(c) $L = \frac{6}{5}$, $L_q = \frac{3}{5}$, $W = \frac{1}{25}$, $W_q = \frac{1}{50}$

17.6-1. (a) $P_0 + P_1 + P_2 + P_3 + P_4 = 0.96875$ or 97 percent of the time.

17.6-21. (a) Combined expected waiting time = 0.211
(c) An expected process time of 3.43 minutes would cause the expected waiting times to be the same for the two procedures.

17.6-29. (a) 0.429

17.6-33. (a) three machines
(b) three operators

17.7-1. (a) W_q (exponential) = $2W_q$ (constant) = $\frac{8}{5}W_q$ (Erlang).
(b) W_q (new) = $\frac{1}{2}W_q$ (old) and L_q (new) = L_q (old) for all distributions.

17.7-6. (a, b) Under the current policy an airplane loses 1 day of flying time as opposed to 3.25 days under the proposed policy.
Under the current policy 1 airplane is losing flying time per day as opposed to 0.8125 airplane.

17.7-10.

Service Distribution	P_0	P_1	P_2	L
Erlang	0.561	0.316	0.123	0.561
Exponential	0.571	0.286	0.143	0.571

17.8-1. (a) This system is an example of a nonpreemptive priority queueing system.

(c) $\dfrac{W_q \text{ for first-class passengers}}{W_q \text{ for coach-class passengers}} = \dfrac{0.033}{0.083} = 0.4$

17.8-4. (a) $W = \frac{1}{2}$
(b) $W_1 = 0.20$, $W_2 = 0.35$, $W_3 = 1.10$
(c) $W_1 = 0.125$, $W_2 = 0.3125$, $W_3 = 1.250$

CHAPTER 18

18.3-1. (a) $E(WC) = 16$
(b) $E(WC) = 26.5$

18.4-2. 4 cash registers

18.4-5. (a) Model 2 with s fixed at 1
(b) Adopt the proposal.

18.4-10. (d) $E(TC)$ for status quo $= \$85$ per hour
$E(TC)$ for proposal $= \$83$ per hour

18.4-13. (a) The customers are trucks to be loaded or unloaded and the servers are crews. The system currently has 1 server.
(e) A one-person team should not be considered since that would lead to a utilization factor of $\rho = 1$, which is not permitted in this model.
(f, g) $E(TC)$ for 4 members $= \$82.50$ per hour
$E(TC)$ for 3 members $= \$65$ per hour
$E(TC)$ for 2 members $= \$55$ per hour
A crew of 2 people will minimize the expected total cost per hour.

18.4-25. One doctor: $E(TC) = \$624.80$, two doctors: $\$92.50$; have two doctors.

CHAPTER 19

19.3-1. (a) $t = 1.83$, $Q = 54.77$
(b) $t = 1.91$, $Q = 57.45$, $S = 52.22$

19.3-3. (a) Data

$D =$	676	(demand/year)
$K =$	\$75	(setup cost)
$h =$	\$600.00	(unit holding cost)
$L =$	3.5	(lead time in days)
$WD =$	365	(working days/year)

Results

Reorder point =	6.5
Annual setup cost =	\$10,140
Annual holding cost =	\$ 1,500
Total variable cost =	\$11,640

Decision

$Q =$	5	(order quantity)

(d) Data

$D =$	676	(demand/year)
$K =$	$75	(setup cost)
$h =$	$600	(unit holding cost)
$L =$	3.5	(lead time in days)
$WD =$	365	(working days/year)

Results

Reorder point =	6.48
Annual setup cost =	$3,900
Annual holding cost =	$3,900
Total variable cost =	$7,800

Decision

$Q =$	13	(order quantity)

The results are the same as those obtained in part (c).

(f) Number of orders per year = 52
$ROP = 6.5 -$ inventory level when each order is placed

(g) The optimal policy reduces the total variable inventory cost by $3,840 per year, which is a 33 percent reduction.

19.3-7. (a) $h = 3 per month which is 15 percent of the acquisition cost.
(c) Reorder point is 10.
(d) $ROP = 5$ hammers, which adds $20 to his TVC (5 hammers × $4 holding cost).

19.3-9. $t = 3.26$, $Q = 26,046$, $S = 24,572$

19.3-15. (a) Optimal $Q = 500$

19.4-4. Produce 3 units in period 1 and 4 units in period 3.

19.5-6. (b) Ground Chuck: $R = 145$.
Chuck Wagon: $R = 829$.
(c) Ground Chuck: safety stock = 45.
Chuck Wagon: safety stock = 329.
(f) Ground Chuck: $39,378.71.
Chuck Wagon: $41,958.61.
Jed should choose Ground Chuck as their supplier.
(g) If Jed would like to use the beef within a month of receiving it, then Ground Chuck is the better choice. The order quantity with Ground Chuck is roughly 1 month's supply, whereas with Chuck Wagon the optimal order quantity is roughly 3 month's supply.

19.6-4. (a) Optimal service level = 0.667
(c) $Q^* = 500$
(d) The probability of running short is 0.333.
(e) Optimal service level = 0.833

19.6-8. (a) This problem can be interpreted as an inventory problem with uncertain demand for a perishable product with euro-traveler's checks as the product. Once Stan gets back from his trip the checks are not good anymore, so they are a perishable product. He can redeposit the amount into his savings account but will incur a fee of lost interest. Stan must decide how many checks to buy without knowing how many he will need.

C_{under} = value of 1 day − cost of 1 day − cost of 1 check = $49.
C_{over} = cost of check + lost interest = $3

(b) Purchase 4 additional checks.

(c) Optimal service level = 0.94
Buy 4 additional checks.

19.7-3. If $x \leq 46$, order $46 - x$ units; otherwise, do not order.

19.7-10. (a) $G(y) = \frac{3}{10}y + 70e^{-y/25} - \frac{15}{2}$
(b) $(k, Q) = (21, 100)$ policy

CHAPTER 20

20.4-1. (c) Forecast = 36

20.4-3. Forecast = 2,091

20.4-7. Forecast (0.1) = 2,072

20.6-2. Forecast = 552

20.6-4. Forecast for next production yield = 62 percent

20.7-1. (a) MAD = 15

20.7-4. (a) Since sales are relatively stable, the averaging method would be appropriate for forecasting future sales. This method uses a larger sample size than the last-value method, which should make it more accurate. Since the older data are still relevant, they should not be excluded, as would be the case in the moving-average method.
(e) Considering the MAD values, the averaging method is the best one to use.
(f) Unless there is reason to believe that sales will not continue to be relatively stable, the averaging method is likely to be the most accurate in the future as well. However, 12 data points generally are inadequate for drawing definitive conclusions.

20.9-1. (b) $y = 410 + 17.6x$
(d) $y = 604$

CHAPTER 21

21.2-1. (c) Use slow service when no customers or one customer is present and fast service when two customers are present.

21.2-2. (a) The possible states of the car are dented and not dented.
(c) When the car is not dented, park it on the street in one space. When the car is dented, get it repaired.

21.2-5. (c) State 0: attempt ace; state 1: attempt lob.

21.3-2. (a) Minimize $\quad Z = 4.5y_{02} + 5y_{03} + 50y_{14} + 9y_{15}$,

subject to

$$y_{01} + y_{02} + y_{03} + y_{14} + y_{15} = 1$$

$$y_{01} + y_{02} + y_{03} - \left(\frac{9}{10}y_{01} + \frac{49}{50}y_{02} + y_{03} + y_{14}\right) = 0$$

$$y_{14} + y_{15} - \left(\frac{1}{10}y_{01} + \frac{1}{50}y_{02} + y_{15}\right) = 0$$

and

all $y_{ik} \geq 0$.

21.3-5. (a) Minimize $\quad Z = -\frac{1}{8}y_{01} + \frac{7}{24}y_{02} + \frac{1}{2}y_{11} + \frac{5}{12}y_{12}$,

subject to

$$y_{01} + y_{02} - \left(\frac{3}{8}y_{01} + y_{11} + \frac{7}{8}y_{02} + y_{12}\right) = 0$$

$$y_{11} + y_{12} - \left(\frac{5}{8}y_{01} \qquad + \frac{1}{8}y_{02}\right) \qquad = 0$$

$$y_{01} + y_{02} + \quad y_{11} + y_{12} = 1$$

and

$$y_{ik} \geq 0 \qquad \text{for } i = 0, 1; \, k = 1, 2.$$

21.4-2. Car not dented: park it on the street in one space. Car dented: repair it.

21.4-5. State 0: attempt ace. State 1: attempt lob.

21.5-1. Reject $600 offer, accept any of the other two.

21.5-2. (a) Minimize $\quad Z = 60(y_{01} + y_{11} + y_{21}) - 600y_{02} - 800y_{12} - 1{,}000y_{22}$,

subject to

$$y_{01} + y_{02} - (0.95)\left(\frac{5}{8}\right)(y_{01} + y_{11} + y_{21}) = \frac{5}{8}$$

$$y_{11} + y_{12} - (0.95)\left(\frac{1}{4}\right)(y_{01} + y_{11} + y_{21}) = \frac{1}{4}$$

$$y_{21} + y_{22} - (0.95)\left(\frac{1}{8}\right)(y_{01} + y_{11} + y_{21}) = \frac{1}{8}$$

and

$$y_{ik} \geq 0 \qquad \text{for } i = 0, 1, 2; \, k = 1, 2.$$

21.5-3. After three iterations, approximation is, in fact, the optimal policy given for Prob. 21.5-1.

21.5-11. In periods 1 to 3: Do nothing when the machine is in state 0 or 1; overhaul when machine is in state 2; and replace when machine is in state 3. In period 4: Do nothing when machine is in state 0, 1, or 2; replace when machine is in state 3.

CHAPTER 22

22.1-1. (b) Let the numbers 0.0000 to 0.5999 correspond to strikes and the numbers 0.6000 to 0.9999 correspond to balls. The random observations for pitches are 0.7520 = ball, 0.4184 = strike, 0.4189 = strike, 0.5982 = strike, 0.9559 = ball, and 0.1403 = strike.

22.1-10. (b) Use $\lambda = 4$ and $\mu = 5$.
(i) Answers will vary. The option of training the two current mechanics significantly decreases the waiting time for German cars, without a significant impact on the wait for Japanese cars, and does so without the added cost of a third mechanic. Adding a third mechanic lowers the average wait for German cars even more, but comes at an added cost for the third mechanic.

22.3-1. (a) 5, 8, 1, 4, 7, 0, 3, 6, 9, 2

22.4-2. (b) $F(x) = 0.0965$ when $x = -5.18$
$F(x) = 0.5692$ when $x = 18.46$
$F(x) = 0.6658$ when $x = 23.29$

22.4-5. (a) $x = \sqrt{r}$

22.4-8. (a) Here is a sample replication.

Summary of Results:

Win? (1 = Yes, 0 = No)	0
Number of Tosses =	3

Simulated Tosses

Toss	Die 1	Die 2	Sum
1	4	2	6
2	3	2	5
3	6	1	7
4	5	2	7
5	4	4	8
6	1	4	5
7	2	6	8

Results

Win?	Lose?	Continue?
0	0	Yes
0	0	Yes
0	1	No
NA	NA	No
NA	NA	No
NA	NA	No
NA	NA	No

22.4-13. (a) $x = -4 \ln (1 - r)$
(b) $x = -2 \ln [(1 - r_1)(1 - r_2)]$

(c) $x = 4 \sum_{i=1}^{6} r_i - 8$

22.7-1. Use the first 10 three-digit decimals from Table 22.3 and generate observations from

$$x_i = \frac{1}{1 - r_i}.$$

Method:	Analytic	Monte Carlo	Stratified sampling	Complementary random numbers
Mean:	∞	4.3969	8.7661	3.812

22.7-4. (a) Let the numbers 0.0000 to 0.3999 correspond to a minor repair and 0.4000 to 0.9999 correspond to a major repair. The average repair time is then $(1.224 + 0.950 + 1.610)/3 = 1.26$ hours.
(c) The average repair time is 1.28 hours.
(e) The average repair time is 1.09 hours.
(f) The method of complementary random numbers in part (e) gave the closest estimate. It performs well because using complements helps counteract the more extreme random numbers (such as 0.9503).

22.8-1. (a) Est. $\{W_q\} = \frac{7}{3}$ and $P\{1.572 \le W_q \le 3.094\} = 0.90$

AUTHOR INDEX

SUBJECT INDEX

We would like to express our appreciation to the following companies for providing complimentary copies of the indicated software on the CD-ROM:

ARKI Corporation for providing the CONOPT nonlinear programming solver used with the MPL Student Edition.

Frontline Systems for providing Premium Solver.

ILOG for providing the CPLEX solver used with the MPL Student Edition.

Maximal Software for providing the MPL Student Edition and the OptiMax 2000 Component Library Student Edition.

Microsoft Corporation for providing MS Project.

(All these software names are registered trademarks of these companies, and all rights are reserved by the companies.)

We also thank Maximal Software for providing extensive tutorial material on the CD-ROM (including formulations and solutions for the relevant examples in the book) and LINDO Systems for doing the same for the student versions of LINDO and LINGO (available through downloading from the website, www.lindo.com).

Finally, we would like to thank Professor Michael Middleton for providing three Excel add-ins—RiskSim, SensIt, and TreePlan—on the CD-ROM. This shareware is available to you throughout this course. However, if you want to continue to use it after the course, you should register and pay the shareware fee.